Lecture Notes in Computer Science

Lecture Notes in Artificial Intelligence 16948

Founding Editor

Jörg Siekmann

The series Lecture Notes in Artificial Intelligence (LNAI) was established in 1988 as a topical subseries of LNCS devoted to artificial intelligence.

The series publishes state-of-the-art research results at a high level. As with the LNCS mother series, the mission of the series is to serve the international R & D community by providing an invaluable service, mainly focused on the publication of conference and workshop proceedings and postproceedings.

Michelangelo Ceci · Dragi Kocev ·
Anna Monreale · Celine Vens · Mitra Baratchi ·
Francesco Bonchi · Riccardo Guidotti ·
Francesco Gullo · Peter Flach · Giuseppe Manco ·
Myra Spiliopoulou · Elio Masciari
Editors

Machine Learning and Knowledge Discovery in Databases

Research Track and Applied Data Science Track

European Conference, ECML PKDD 2026
Naples, Italy, September 7–11, 2026
Proceedings, Part VIII

Springer

Editors
Michelangelo Ceci
University of Bari Aldo Moro
Bari, Italy

Dragi Kocev
Jožef Stefan Institute
Ljubljana, Slovenia

Anna Monreale
University of Pisa
Pisa, Italy

Celine Vens
KU Leuven
Kortrijk, Belgium

Mitra Baratchi
Leiden University
Leiden, The Netherlands

Francesco Bonchi
Intesa Sanpaolo AI Research
Turin, Italy

Riccardo Guidotti
University of Pisa
Pisa, Italy

Francesco Gullo
University of L'Aquila
L'Aquila, Italy

Peter Flach
University of Bristol
Bristol, UK

Giuseppe Manco
ICAR-CNR
Rende, Italy

Myra Spiliopoulou
Otto von Guericke University Magdeburg
Magdeburg, Germany

Elio Masciari
University of Naples Federico II
Naples, Italy

ISSN 0302-9743 ISSN 1611-3349 (electronic)
Lecture Notes in Artificial Intelligence
ISBN 978-3-032-37678-7 ISBN 978-3-032-37679-4 (eBook)
https://doi.org/10.1007/978-3-032-37679-4

LNCS Sublibrary: SL7 – Artificial Intelligence

This Springer imprint is published by the registered company Springer Nature Switzerland AG
The registered company address is: Gewerbestrasse 11, 6330 Cham, Switzerland

Preface

The 2026 edition of the European Conference on Machine Learning and Principles and Practice of Knowledge Discovery in Databases (ECML PKDD 2026) was held in Naples, Italy from September 7 to 11, 2026.

The annual ECML PKDD conference is a premier worldwide platform dedicated to showcasing the latest advancements and fostering insightful discussions in the fields of machine learning and knowledge discovery in databases. Held jointly since 2001, ECML PKDD has firmly established its reputation as the leading European conference in these disciplines. It provides researchers and practitioners with an unparalleled opportunity to exchange knowledge, share innovative ideas, and explore the latest technical advancements. The conference particularly values the synergy between foundational theoretical advances and groundbreaking practical data science applications, actively encouraging contributions that demonstrate how Machine Learning and Data Mining are being effectively employed to address complex real-world challenges. Over the years, technologies evolve, and the needs of the individuals, society and the world change. ECML PKDD remains committed to the presentation of cutting-edge research that reflects this evolution.

The Naples edition of ECML PKDD was a truly special one, marked both by an exceptionally high number of scientific contributions and by an outstanding level of participation from the industrial community. The remarkable response from researchers, practitioners, and companies reflects the growing relevance of machine learning, data mining, and artificial intelligence across both academic and industrial domains. In particular, the significant engagement of leading companies and technology stakeholders further strengthened the dialogue between research and real-world applications, making this edition a vibrant meeting point for scientific excellence, innovation, and industrial impact.

The Conference Tracks

The three middle days of the conference were organized in the following tracks:

- The **Research Track** received the impressive number of 1,150 full paper submissions, going for the first time above the 1,000 submissions mark, and an absolute increase of more than 200 submissions over the previous edition, which also had a substantial increase in submissions; of these submissions, 280 were accepted, demonstrating a highly competitive acceptance rate of 24.3%. The review process was double blind, and submissions received three reviews each on average.

- The **Applied Data Science Track** received 381 submissions, of which 90 were accepted. This resulted in a similar acceptance rate of 23.6%. The review process was double blind, and submissions received 3.9 reviews each on average.
- The **Journal Track** received 213 submissions, of which 34 papers were accepted in the Machine Learning Journal and 24 in the Data Mining and Knowledge Discovery Journal, while 7 papers are still under review.
- The **Nectar Track** solicited submissions of summaries of recently published, impactful scientific papers presenting advances at the forefront of machine learning and data mining, as well as their applications in other disciplines. This track received 26 submissions.
- The **Demo Track** solicited submissions that showcase practical applications and prototypes; it received 38 submissions, with 27 accepted demo papers. The review process was single blind, and submissions received two reviews each on average.
- The **Industrial Track** received a record of 42 submissions, 21 of which were accepted for presentation at the conference. The review process was single blind, and submissions received three reviews each on average.

The Keynotes

ECML PKDD 2026 featured five keynote talks by internationally leading experts, one on each day of the conference in this order:

- **Mihaela van der Schaar** (University of Cambridge) spoke on *Rethinking the Role of Scientific Discovery in the Era of AI*. She presented a framework that rethinks discovery as an agentic process, in which networks of interacting AI agents and human experts jointly explore, critique, and refine hypotheses under shared norms of evaluation.
- **Stefanie Jegelka** (Technical University of Munich) explored the link between *Neural Networks and Algorithms*. She argued that an algorithmic view can help understand not only the capabilities of deep learning models, such as self-correction or the ability to solve certain optimization problems, but also how to design and train models to better solve challenging tasks, from optimization problems to reasoning.
- **Sihem Amer-Yahia** (CNRS and Laboratoire d'Informatique de Grenoble) gave a keynote entitled *From Dialogue to Decision: Orchestrating Agents for Conversational Data Exploration and Multi-Objective Optimization* in which she investigated the intersection of conversational data exploration, an incremental process where agents help users articulate needs through data interaction, and multi-objective sequential decision making.
- **Francesca Rossi** (Thomas J. Watson IBM Research Center) spoke on key issues around *AI ethics and governance* and how they have evolved with the dramatically increased AI capabilities of today. She also discussed instrumental and value-based approaches which make investing in AI ethics and governance worthwhile.

- **Gianni Riotta** (Luiss University) presented his perspective under the title *The AI Ghosts and Us: Machine Writing as a Spectral Culture.* He advocated a radically new philosophical reading of AI-generated text as a “Ghost” inhabiting contemporary human discourse, and argued that machine writing constitutes a spectral hybrid: neither fully human nor purely artificial, but a liminal presence emerging from the archive of human language.

Scholarships

We awarded 10 scholarship grants of 1,000 EUR each to students and early-career researchers.

Acknowledgements

We want to thank the authors, organizing committee, workshop and tutorial organizers, and participants whose scientific contributions made this such an exciting event.

We are greatly indebted to the reviewers and senior reviewers: their dedication, vigilance, and enormous time investment made it possible to manage the large number of submissions, ensure the high quality for which ECML PKDD is known, and put together an outstanding conference program. A special thanks goes to the emergency reviewers who finished the last missing reviews at short notice.

This large event would not have run smoothly without the many volunteers and sessions chairs. Finally, we want to express our heartfelt gratitude to all the local organizers – they dealt with all the little details that were needed to make the conference a memorable event.

We want to cordially thank our sponsors for their generous financial support. We also want to thank Springer for their continuous support and Microsoft for allowing us to use their CMT software for conference management and for providing help throughout. We very much appreciate the advice and guidance provided by the ECML PKDD Steering Committee from the moment the organization of the 2026 edition started.

September 2026

Elio Masciari
Peter Flach
Giuseppe Manco
Myra Spiliopoulou
General Chairs

Michelangelo Ceci
Dragi Kocev
Anna Monreale
Celine Vens
Research Track Chairs

Mitra Baratchi
Francesco Bonchi
Riccardo Guidotti
Francesco Gullo
Applied Data Science Track Chairs

Paolo Mignone
Mouzhi Ge
Vincenzo Moscato
Demo Track Chairs

Chiara Celsi
Ruggero G. Pensa
Fabrizio Silvestri
Industrial Track Chairs

Organization

General Chairs

Peter Flach	University of Bristol, UK
Giuseppe Manco	ICAR-CNR, Italy
Elio Masciari	University of Naples Federico II, Italy
Myra Spiliopoulou	Otto von Guericke University Magdeburg, Germany

Research Track Chairs

Michelangelo Ceci	University of Bari Aldo Moro, Italy
Dragi Kocev	Jožef Stefan Institute, Slovenia
Anna Monreale	University of Pisa, Italy
Celine Vens	KU Leuven, Belgium

Applied Data Science Track Chairs

Mitra Baratchi	Leiden University, Netherlands
Francesco Bonchi	Intesa Sanpaolo AI Research, Italy
Riccardo Guidotti	University of Pisa, Italy
Francesco Gullo	University of L'Aquila, Italy

Journal Track Chairs

Zahraa S. Abdallah	University of Bristol, UK
Annalisa Appice	University of Bari Aldo Moro, Italy
Przemysław Biecek	Warsaw University of Technology, Poland
Andrea Tagarelli	University of Calabria, Italy

Industrial Track Chairs

Chiara Celsi	Deloitte Italy, Italy
Ruggero G. Pensa	University of Turin, Italy
Fabrizio Silvestri	Sapienza University of Rome, Italy

Workshop Chairs

Dino Ienco	INRAE, Inria, UMR TETIS, University of Montpellier, France
Gianvito Pio	University of Bari Aldo Moro, Italy

Tutorial Chairs

Antonio Maria Rinaldi	University of Naples Federico II, Italy
Cristiano Russo	University of Naples Federico II, Italy

Nectar Track Chairs

Aniello Murano	University of Naples Federico II, Italy
Chiara Renso	ISTI-CNR, Italy
Salvo Rinzivillo	ISTI-CNR, Italy

PhD Forum Chairs

Giuseppina Andresini	University of Bari Aldo Moro, Italy
Silvia Rossi	University of Naples Federico II, Italy

Awards Committee Chairs

Sergio Di Martino	University of Naples Federico II, Italy
Donato Malerba	University of Bari Aldo Moro, Italy
Carlo Sansone	University of Naples Federico II, Italy

Proceedings Chairs

Irena Koprinska	University of Sydney, Australia
Angelica Liguori	ICAR-CNR, Italy
Eliana Pastor	Politecnico di Torino, Italy

Diversity and Inclusion Chairs

Esma Aimeur	Université de Montréal, Canada
Flora Amato	University of Naples Federico II, Italy
Christine Markarian	University of Dubai, United Arab Emirates
Rosa Meo	University of Turin, Italy

Demo Chairs

Paolo Mignone	Università Pegaso, Italy
Mouzhi Ge	Deggendorf Institute of Technology, Germany
Vincenzo Moscato	University of Naples Federico II, Italy

Discovery Challenge Chairs

Mark Cotè	King's College London, UK
Stefano Marrone	University of Naples Federico II, Italy
Roberto Trasarti	ISTI-CNR, Italy

Panel Chairs

Massimo Bernaschi	IAC-CNR, Italy
Luca Caviglione	IMATI-CNR, Italy

Publicity Chairs

Roberto Interdonato	Cirad, Inria, UMR TETIS, Montpellier, France
Enea Vincenzo Napolitano	University of Naples Federico II, Italy
Vincenzo Pasquadibisceglie	University of Bari Aldo Moro, Italy

Senior Sponsors Chairs

Mariam Barry	BNP Paribas, France
Robert Jan van Wijk	ASML, Netherlands

Local Sponsors Chairs

Antonino Ferraro	Pegaso University, Italy
Simona Fioretto	University of Naples Federico II, Italy
Cristian Tommasino	University of Naples Federico II, Italy

Web, Social Media and Conference App Chairs

Michela Gravina	University of Naples Federico II, Italy
Simone Mungari	ICAR-CNR, Revelis s.r.l., Italy
Franca Rocco di Torrepadula	University of Naples Federico II, Italy

CMT Chairs

Antonio Galli	University of Naples Federico II, Italy
Giancarlo Sperli	University of Naples Federico II, Italy

Whova App and Slides Chair

Giuseppe Papuzzo	ICAR-CNR, Italy

Steering Committee

Tijl De Bie	Ghent University, Belgium
Albert Bifet	University of Waikato, New Zealand - Télécom Paris, France
Francesco Bonchi	Intesa Sanpaolo AI Research, Italy
Ilaria Bordino	UniCredit, Italy
Saso Dzeroski	Jožef Stefan Institute, Slovenia
Ioanna Miliou	Stockholm University, Sweden
Siegfried Nijssen	KU Leuven, Belgium

Andrea Passerini	University of Trento, Italy
Robert Jan van Wijk	ASML, the Netherlands
Wenbin Zhang	Florida International University, USA
Albrecht Zimmermann	Université de Caen Normandie, France
Elena Baralis	Politecnico di Torino, Italy
Claudia Plant	Universität Wien, Austria
Manuel Gomez Rodriguez	Max Planck Institute for Software Systems, Germany
Jesse Davis	KU Leuven, Belgium
Tomas Krilavičius	Vytautas Magnus University, Lithuania
Panagiotis Papapetrou	Stockholm University, Sweden
Myra Spiliopoulou	Otto-von-Guericke University Magdeburg, Germany
Pedro Henriques Abreu	University of Coimbra, CISUC, Portugal
João Gama	University of Porto, INESC-TEC, Portugal
Sepideh Pashami	Halmstad University, Sweden
Rita P. Ribeiro	University of Porto, INESC TEC, Portugal

Program Committee

Area Chairs, Research Track

Pedro Henriques Abreu	CISUC, Portugal
Tiago Almeida	Federal University of São Carlos, Brazil
Annalisa Appice	University of Bari Aldo Moro, Italy
Anthony Bagnall	University of Southampton, UK
Gustavo Batista	University of New South Wales, Australia
Jessa Bekker	KU Leuven, Belgium
Bettina Berendt	TU Berlin, Germany
Concha Bielza	Universidad Politécnica de Madrid, Spain
Albert Bifet	University of Waikato, New Zealand
Hendrik Blockeel	KU Leuven, Belgium
Henrik Boström	KTH Royal Institute of Technology, Sweden
Zied Bouraoui	CRIL CNRS & University of Artois, France
Ulf Brefeld	Leuphana University of Lüneburg, Germany
Toon Calders	University of Antwerp, Belgium
Jesús Cerquides	IIIA-CSIC, Spain
Sara Colantonio	Institute of Information Science and Technologies of the National Research Council of Italy, Italy
Roberto Corizzo	American University, USA
Fabrizio Costa	University of Exeter, UK

Jesse Davis	KU Leuven, Belgium
Tom Diethe	AstraZeneca/University of Bristol, UK
Wouter Duivesteijn	Eindhoven University of Technology, Netherlands
Tome Eftimov	Jožef Stefan Institute, Slovenia
Sophie Fellenz	RPTU Kaiserslautern-Landau, Germany
Stefano Ferilli	University of Bari Aldo Moro, Italy
Cèsar Ferri	Universitat Politècnica de València, Spain
Eibe Frank	University of Waikato, New Zealand
Elisa Fromont	Université Rennes, IRISA/Inria, France
Johannes Fürnkranz	Johannes Kepler University Linz, Austria
Esther Galbrun	University of Eastern Finland, Finland
Pierre Geurts	University of Liège, Belgium
Aristides Gionis	KTH Royal Institute of Technology, Sweden
Chen Gong	Nanjing University of Science and Technology, China
Barbara Hammer	Bielefeld University, Germany
Jose Hernandez-Orallo	Universitat Politècnica de València/University of Cambridge, Spain/UK
Sibylle Hess	Eindhoven University of Technology, Netherlands
Georgiana Ifrim	University College Dublin, Ireland
Manfred Jaeger	Aalborg University, Denmark
Nathalie Japkowicz	American University, USA
Szymon Jaroszewicz	Polish Academy of Sciences, Poland
Adam Jatowt	University of Innsbruck, Austria
Ioannis Katakis	University of Nicosia, Cyprus
Megha Khosla	TU Delft, Netherlands
Marius Kloft	RPTU Kaiserslautern-Landau, Germany
Arno Knobbe	Leiden University, Netherlands
Danai Koutra	University of Michigan, USA
Petra Kralj Novak	Central European University, Austria
Niels Landwehr	University of Hildesheim, Germany
Pedro Larranaga	Universidad Politécnica de Madrid, Spain
Mark Last	Ben-Gurion University of the Negev, Israel
Jefrey Lijffijt	Ghent University, Belgium
Jessica Lin	George Mason University, USA
Ana Carolina Lorena	Instituto Tecnológico de Aeronáutica, Brazil
Jörg Lücke	Universität Innsbruck, Austria
Xiao Luo	University of Wisconsin–Madison, USA
Michael Madden	University of Galway, Ireland
Donato Malerba	University of Bari Aldo Moro, Italy
Fragkiskos Malliaros	CentraleSupélec, France
Ernestina Menasalvas	Universidad Politécnica de Madrid, Spain

Rosa Meo	University of Turin, Italy
Pauli Miettinen	University of Eastern Finland, Finland
Pasquale Minervini	University of Edinburgh, UK
Dunja Mladenic	Jožef Stefan Institute, Slovenia
Siegfried Nijssen	KU Leuven, Belgium
Eirini Ntoutsi	University of the Bundeswehr Munich, Germany
Pance Panov	Jožef Stefan Institute, Slovenia
Evangelos Papalexakis	University of California, Riverside, USA
Andrea Passerini	University of Trento, Italy
Jaakko Peltonen	Tampere University, Finland
Ruggero Pensa	University of Turin, Italy
Bernhard Pfahringer	University of Waikato, New Zealand
Gianvito Pio	University of Bari Aldo Moro, Italy
Evaggelia Pitoura	University of Ioannina, Greece
Ricardo Prudencio	Universidade Federal de Pernambuco, Brazil
Chedy Raissi	Inria, France
Aleksandra Rashkovska Koceva	Jožef Stefan Institute, Slovenia
Jesse Read	École Polytechnique, France
Rita P. Ribeiro	University of Porto & INESC TEC, Portugal
Luca Romeo	University of Macerata, Italy
Salvatore Ruggieri	University of Pisa, Italy
Zahraa S. Abdallah	University of Bristol, UK
Yvan Saeys	Ghent University, Belgium
Matthias Schubert	Ludwig-Maximilians-Universität München, Germany
Junming Shao	University of Electronic Science and Technology of China, China
Arno Siebes	Utrecht University, Netherlands
Fabrizio Silvestri	Sapienza University of Rome, Italy
Nikola Simidjievski	Télécom Paris, Institut Polytechnique de Paris, France
Carlos Soares	University of Porto/Fraunhofer AICOS Portugal/BrightFactory, Portugal
Jerzy Stefanowski	Poznań University of Technology, Poland
Fabio Stella	University of Milano-Bicocca, Italy
Stefano Teso	University of Trento, Italy
Ioannis Tsamardinos	University of Crete, Greece
Charalampos Tsourakakis	University of Crete, Greece
Matthijs van Leeuwen	Leiden University, Netherlands
Jan Van Rijn	Leiden University, Netherlands
Varvara Vetrova	University of Canterbury, New Zealand

Jilles Vreeken	CISPA Helmholtz Center for Information Security, Germany
Willem Waegeman	Ghent University, Belgium
Jörg Wicker	University of Auckland, New Zealand
Wei Ye	Tongji University, China
Wenbin Zhang	Florida International University, USA
Indre Zliobaite	University of Helsinki, Finland

Program Committee, Research Track

Kamil Adamczewski	Max Planck Institute for Intelligent Systems, Germany
Timilehin Aderinola	Insight Research Ireland Centre for Data Analytics, University College Dublin, Ireland
Linara Adilova	RC Trust, Germany
Stergos Afantenos	Université de Toulouse, France
Juba Agoun	Université Lumière Lyon 2, France
Azim Ahmadzadeh	University of Missouri - St. Louis, USA
Deepak Ajwani	University College Dublin, Ireland
Reza Akbarinia	Inria, France
Esra Akbas	Georgia State University, USA
Cuneyt Akcora	University of Central Florida, USA
Youhei Akimoto	University of Tsukuba/RIKEN AIP, Japan
Ozge Alacam	Ludwig-Maximilians-Universität München, Germany
Tahani Aladwani	University of Glasgow, UK
Dima Alberg	SCE Shamoon College of Engineering, Israel
Fayad Ali Banna	Laboratoire Hubert Curien, France
Benjamin Allaert	IMT Nord Europe, France
Simeon Allmendinger	University of Bayreuth, Germany
Sarra Alqahtani	Wake Forest University, USA
Jose Alvarez	Santander AI Lab, Spain
Ehsan Aminian	INESC TEC, Portugal
Christos Anagnostopoulos	University of Glasgow, UK
Giuseppina Andresini	University of Bari Aldo Moro, Italy
Piotr Andruszkiewicz	Warsaw University of Technology, Poland
Ekaterina Antonenko	Mines Paris - PSL, France
Alessandro Antonucci	IDSIA, Switzerland
Nelson Antunes	University of Algarve and University of Lisbon, Portugal
Edward Apeh	Bournemouth University, UK
Pasquale Ardimento	University of Bari Aldo Moro, Italy

Jerónimo Arenas-García	Universidad Carlos III de Madrid, Spain
Marco Aruta	University of Naples Federico II, Italy
Hadi Asghari	Technische Universität Berlin, Germany
Hugo Attali	LIPN, Sorbonne Paris Nord University, France
Ali Ayadi	University of Strasbourg, France
Paulo Azevedo	University of Minho, Portugal
Hanane Azzag	LIPN, France
Housam Babiker	University of Alberta, Canada
Kerstin Bach	Norwegian University of Science and Technology, Norway
Ricardo Baeza-Yates	KTH Royal Institute of Technology & Universitat Pompeu Fabra, Sweden/Spain
Maroua Bahri	Sorbonne Université, CNRS, LIP6, France
Hendrik Baier	Eindhoven University of Technology, Netherlands
Chandrajit Bajaj	University of Texas at Austin, USA
Bunil Balabantaray	NIT Raipur, India
Federico Baldo	INSERM/Sorbonne University, France
Sylvio Barbon Junior	University of Trieste, Italy
Francesco Bariatti	LIACS, Leiden University, Netherlands
Michel Barlaud	University of Nice, France
Franka Bause	CISPA Helmholtz Center for Information Security, Germany
Florian Beck	Johannes Kepler University Linz, Austria
Christian Beecks	FernUniversität in Hagen, Germany
Hamed Behzadi-Khormouji	Vrije Universiteit Brussel, Belgium
Rita Beigaitė	VTT Technical Research Centre of Finland, Finland
Djawad Bekkoucha	Université Paris-Saclay, France
Colin Bellinger	University of Ottawa, Canada
Khalid Benabdeslem	University Lyon 1, France
Francesco Benedetti	University of Bari Aldo Moro, Italy
Giulia Bertazzini	University of Florence, Italy
Lilian Berton	Federal University of São Paulo, Brazil
Timo Bertram	Johannes Kepler Universität Linz, Austria
Frederic Bertrand	National Conservatory of Arts and Crafts, France
Filippo Betello	Sapienza University of Rome, Italy
Alessandro Betti	IMT School for Advanced Studies Lucca, Italy
Monowar Bhuyan	Umeå University, Sweden
Manuele Bicego	University of Verona, Italy
Livio Bioglio	University of Turin, Italy
Robert Birke	University of Turin, Italy
Hendrik Blockeel	KU Leuven, Belgium

Benedikt Blumenstiel	IBM Research, USA
Martin Bobak	Institute of Informatics, Slovak Academy of Sciences, Slovakia
Tyler Bonnet	Imperial College London, UK
Ludovico Boratto	University of Cagliari, Italy
Manuel Borja	Ghent University, Belgium
Stefano Bortoli	Microblink, Italy
Annelot Bosman	Leiden University, Netherlands
Lydia Boudjeloud-Assala	Université de Lorraine, CNRS, LORIA, France
Sara Bouguelia	Université Lumière Lyon 2, France
Veranika Boukun	Carl von Ossietzky Universität Oldenburg, Germany
Louenas Bounia	LIPN - Université Sorbonne Paris Nord, France
Antoine Boutet	INSA-Lyon, Inria, France
Mohamed-el-Amine Brahmia	CESI LINEACT, France
Susana Brás	IEETA, Portugal
Murat Bronz	ENAC, France
Dariusz Brzezinski	Poznań University of Technology, Poland
Maria Sofia Bucarelli	CNRS, Inria, I3S, France
Florian Büttner	DKFZ, Germany
Davide Buscaldi	Université Sorbonne Paris Nord, France
Sebastian Buschjäger	Lamarr Institute for ML and AI, Germany
Veronica Buttaro	University of Bari Aldo Moro, Italy
Guénaël Cabanes	Université de Lorraine, France
Paul Caillon	LAMSADE Université Paris Dauphine - PSL, France
Erik Calcina	Jožef Stefan Institute, Slovenia
Ricardo Campello	University of Southern Denmark, Denmark
Giuseppe Casalicchio	Ludwig-Maximilians-Universität München, Germany
Elena Casiraghi	University of Milan, Italy
Giovanna Castellano	University of Bari Aldo Moro, Italy
Remzi Celebi	Maastricht University, Netherlands
Andrea Ceni	University of Pisa, Italy
Vitor Cerqueira	University of Porto, Portugal
Mattia Cerrato	JGU Mainz, Germany
Aman Chadha	Stanford University/Amazon Inc., USA
Faïcel Chamroukhi	IRT SystemX, France
Joydeep Chandra	Indian Institute of Technology Patna, India
Victor Charpenay	Mines Saint-Étienne, France
Arthur Charpentier	Université du Québec à Montréal, Canada
Vaggos Chatziafratis	Stanford University, USA

Sotirios Chatzis	Cyprus University of Technology, Cyprus
Chunchun Chen	Tongji University, China
Defang Chen	Zhejiang University, China
Hongyang Chen	Zhejiang Lab, China
Huaming Chen	University of Sydney, Australia
Huiping Chen	University of Birmingham, UK
Jiawei Chen	Tianjin University, China
Lingwei Chen	Rochester Institute of Technology, USA
Minyu Chen	Shenzhen Technology University, China
Tianyi Chen	Boston University, USA
Wei-Peng Chen	Fujitsu, Japan
Xuefeng Chen	Chongqing University, China
Zhong Chen	Southern Illinois University Carbondale, USA
Ziheng Chen	Walmart, USA
Cheng Cheng	Carnegie Mellon University, USA
Mao Cheng	University of California, Berkeley, USA
Xi Cheng	Cornell University, USA
Belkacem Chikhaoui	Université TÉLUQ, Canada
Stephane Chretien	Université Lumière Lyon 2, France
Hua Chu	Xidian University, China
Ferdinando Cicalese	University of Verona, Italy
Gaetano Cimino	University of Salerno, Italy
Martina Cinquini	University of Pisa, Italy
Gabriele Ciravegna	Intesa Sanpaolo Innovation Center, Italy
Stefano Cirillo	University of Salerno, Italy
Paul Clarke	University of Agder, Norway
Johanne Cohen	LISN-CNRS, France
Erica Coppolillo	University of Calabria, Italy
Denis Coquenet	IRISA, France
Luca Corbucci	University of Pisa, Italy
Barbara Toniella Corradini	Italian Institute of Technology, Italy
Andrea Cossu	University of Pisa, Italy
Ivor Cribben	University of Alberta, Canada
Bertrand Cuissart	University of Caen Normandie, France
Alfredo Cuzzocrea	University of Calabria, Italy
Sebastian Cygert	NASK, Poland
Annunziata D'Aversa	University of Bari Aldo Moro, Italy
Rajjat Dadwal	University of Bonn, Germany
Thi-Bich-Hanh Dao	University of Orléans, France
Paul Davidsson	Malmö University, Sweden
Athanasios Davvetas	NCSR Demokritos, Greece
Johan de Aguas	University of Oslo, Norway

Andre de Carvalho	University of São Paulo, Brazil
Marcilio de Souto	LIFOUniversity of Orléans, France
Gaetan De Waele	University of Antwerp, Belgium
Jochen De Weerdt	KU Leuven, Belgium
Kamil Deja	Warsaw University of Technology, Poland
Julien Delaunay	Inria, France
Elena Demidova	University of Bonn and Lamarr Institute, Germany
Angus Dempster	Monash University, Australia
Cheng Deng	University of Edinburgh, UK
Mariachiara Di Cosmo	Università degli Studi "G. d'Annunzio", Italy
Andrea Giuseppe Di Francesco	Sapienza University of Rome, Italy
Luca Di Stefano	TU Wien, Austria
Lamine Diop	EPITA, France
Christos Diou	Harokopio University of Athens, Greece
Jasminka Dobša	University of Zagreb, Croatia
Vlastislav Dohnal	Masaryk University, Czech Republic
Ruihai Dong	University College Dublin, Ireland
Emilio Dorigatti	Boehringer Ingelheim GmbH, Germany
Moises Dos Santos	University of Porto, Portugal
Gaoyuan Du	University of Tennessee, Knoxville, USA
Haizhou Du	Shanghai University of Electric Power, China
Liang Du	Shanxi University, China
Qihan Du	Renmin University of China, China
Xin Du	University of Edinburgh, UK
Jamie Duell	Sheffield Hallam University, UK
Inês Dutra	University of Porto, Portugal
Elod Egyed-Zsigmond	LIRIS/INSA Lyon, France
Moshe Eliasof	University of Cambridge, UK
Mohamed Elmahallawy	Washington State University, USA
Rémi Emonet	Laboratoire Hubert Curien/Université Jean Monnet, France
Davide Evangelista	University of Bologna, Italy
Bojan Evkoski	Central European University, Austria
Kamil Faber	AGH University of Science and Technology, Poland
Ronan Fablet	IMT Atlantique, France
Issam Falih	Université Clermont Auvergne, CNRS, LIMOS, France
Ruiyi Fang	Western University, Canada
Catherine Faron	Université Côte d'Azur, CNRS, Inria, France
Marco Favier	University of Antwerp, Belgium

Faramarz Fekri	Georgia Institute of Technology, USA
Yuanjun Feng	University of Lausanne, Switzerland
Raphael Feraud	Orange, France
Amine Ferdjaoui	Sogeti - Centre Borelli, France
Daniel Fernández-Sánchez	Aalto University, Finland
Luca Ferragina	University of Calabria, Italy
Pedro Ferreira	University of Porto, Portugal
Yousra Fettach	Ghent University, Belgium
Álvaro Figueira	University of Porto, Portugal
Katarzyna Filus	Institute of Theoretical and Applied Informatics Polish Academy of Sciences, Poland
Raphael Fischer	TU Dortmund University, Germany
Michele Fontana	University of Pisa, Italy
Teodor-Florin Fortis	West University of Timisoara, Romania
Raphael Fournier-S'niehotta	CNAM, France
Giulia Fracastoro	Politecnico di Torino, Italy
Kary Framling	Umeå University, Sweden
Benoît Frénay	University of Namur, Belgium
Christian Frey	University of Technology Nuremberg, Germany
Holger Fröning	University of Heidelberg, Germany
Fabio Fumarola	Prometeia, Italy
Mikel Galar	Universidad Pública de Navarra, Spain
Luis Galárraga	Inria, France
Jose Gamez	Universidad de Castilla-La Mancha, Spain
Shengxiang Gao	Kunming University of Science and Technology, China
Yifeng Gao	University of Texas Rio Grande Valley, USA
Jade Garcia Bourrée	EPFL, Switzerland
Dario Garigliotti	University of Bergen, Norway
Moncef Garouani	Toulouse Capitole University, France
Jean-Gabriel Gaudreault	University of Ottawa, Canada
Dominique Gay	Université de La Réunion, France
Luise Ge	Washington University in St Louis, USA
Michaela Geierhos	University of the Bundeswehr Munich, Germany
Petia Georgieva	University of Aveiro, Portugal
Kushankur Ghosh	University of Alberta, Canada
Luca Giamattei	University of Naples Federico II, Italy
Giorgos Giannopoulos	National Observatory of Athens, Greece
Nikos Gkorgkolis	University of Crete, Greece
Vanessa Gómez-Verdejo	Universidad Carlos III de Madrid, Spain
Sónia Gouveia	University of Aveiro, Portugal
Brandon Gower-Winter	Utrecht University, Netherlands

Michael Granitzer	University of Passau, Germany
Alban Grastien	CEA-List, France
Magda Gregorova	Technical University of Applied Sciences Würzburg-Schweinfurt, Germany
Bram Grooten	Eindhoven University of Technology, Netherlands
Gerrit Grossmann	DFKI, Germany
Sergei Grudinin	LJK CNRS, Université Grenoble Alpes, France
Luciano Gualà	University of Rome Tor Vergata, Italy
Xinyu Guan	Xi'an Jiaotong University, China
Massimo Guarascio	ICAR-CNR, Italy
Bertha Guijarro-Berdiñas	University of A Coruña, Spain
Ce Guo	Imperial College London, UK
Muhao Guo	Arizona State University, USA
Shanqing Guo	Shandong University, China
Yuhong Guo	Carleton University, Canada
Phuong Hoai Ha	UiT The Arctic University of Norway, Norway
Piotr Habas	Amazon, USA
Christian Hakert	TU Dortmund University, Germany
Anaïs Halftermeyer	Laboratoire d'Informatique Fondamentale d'Orléans, France
Maria Halkidi	University of Pireaus, Greece
Benjamin Halstead	University of Auckland, New Zealand
Donghong Han	Northeastern University, China
Marcus Handte	University of Duisburg-Essen, Germany
Tom Hanika	University of Hildesheim, Germany
Sébastien Harispe	IMT Mines Alès, France
Claudio Hartmann	TU Dresden, Germany
Marwan Hassani	Eindhoven University of Technology, Netherlands
Zirui He	New Jersey Institute of Technology, USA
Stefan Heindorf	Paderborn University, Germany
Tobias Hille	University of Kassel, Germany
Martin Holena	Institute of Computer Science, Czech Republic
Mike Holenderski	Eindhoven University of Technology, Netherlands
Vasant Honavar	Pennsylvania State University, USA
Paul Honeine	LITIS Lab, Université de Rouen Normandie, France
Shifu Hou	Case Western Reserve University, USA
Miao Hu	Queen's University Belfast, UK
Xin Hu	University of Michigan, USA
Yizheng Huang	York University, Canada
Charmayne Hughes	Technische Universität Berlin, Germany
Yasutoshi Ida	NTT, Japan

Dino Ienco	INRAE, France
Abdelhak Imoussaten	IMT Mines Alès, France
Angelo Impedovo	NSA Italia s.r.l., Italy
Alessandro Incremona	Catholic University of the Sacred Heart, Italy
Wissem Inoubli	CRIL, University of Artois, France
Vasileios Iosifidis	SCHUFA Holding AG, Germany
Ali Ismail-Fawaz	IRIMAS, Université de Haute-Alsace, France
Nevo Itzhak	Ben-Gurion University of the Negev, Israel
Mirjana Ivanovic	University of Novi Sad, Serbia
Said Jabbour	CRIL CNRS, France
Tobias Jacobs	NEC Laboratories Europe GmbH, Germany
Johannes Jakubik	IBM Research, USA
Henri Jamet	University of Lausanne, Switzerland
Waqas Jamil	Bournemouth University, UK
Kuk Jin Jang	Hongik University, South Korea
Arkadiusz Janz	Wrocław University of Science and Technology, Poland
Hui Ji	University of Pittsburgh, USA
Yuheng Jia	Southeast University, China
Weiwei Jiang	Beijing University of Posts and Telecommunications, China
Xi Jiang	Southern University of Science and Technology, China
Sebastian Jimenez	Ghent University, Belgium
Guangyin Jin	National University of Defense Technology, China
Jiahui Jin	Southeast University, China
Mira Jürgens	Ghent University, Belgium
Tomasz Kajdanowicz	Wrocław University of Science and Technology, Poland
Jan Kalina	Czech Academy of Sciences, Institute of Computer Science, Czech Republic
Sevvandi Kandanaarachchi	CSIRO, Australia
Bo Kang	Ghent University, Belgium
Jurgita Kapočiūtė-Dzikienė	Tilde SIA, University of Latvia, Tilde IT, Vytautas Magnus University, Latvia/Lithuania
Athresh Karanam	University of Texas at Dallas, USA
Jacek Karolczak	Poznań University of Technology, Poland
Peter Karsmakers	KU Leuven, Belgium
Gjergji Kasneci	Technical University of Munich, Germany
Branko Kavsek	University of Primorska, Slovenia
Daniyal Kazempour	Christian-Albrechts-Universität zu Kiel, Germany
Mark Keane	University College Dublin, Ireland

Stefan Kesselheim	Forschungszentrum Jülich, Germany
Rabindra Khadka	University of Oslo, Norway
Asma Kharrat	Liris, France
Mohamadsadegh Khosravani	University of Regina, Canada
Adem Kikaj	KU Leuven, Belgium
Hyunju Kim	King's College London, UK
Sofoklis Kitharidis	LIACS, Netherlands
Frank Klawonn	Ostfalia University, Germany
Tomas Kliegr	University of Economics Prague, Czech Republic
Jakub Klikowski	Wrocław University of Science and Technology, Poland
Marek Klonowski	Wrocław University of Science and Technology, Poland
Boshko Koloski	Jožef Stefan Institute, Slovenia
Joanna Komorniczak	Wrocław University of Science and Technology, Poland
Aritra Konar	KU Leuven, Belgium
Frederic Koriche	Université d'Artois, CRIL CNRS UMR 8188, France
Grazina Korvel	Vilnius University, Lithuania
N'Dah Jean Kouagou	Paderborn University, Germany
Emmanouil Krasanakis	CERTH, Greece
Chethan Krishnamurthy Ramanaik	University of the Bundeswehr Munich, Germany
Amer Krivosija	TU Dortmund University, Germany
Oleg Kudryavtsev	Southern Federal University, Russia
Sebastian Kula	Kempelen Institute of Intelligent Technologies, Slovakia
Pawan Kumar	IIIT, Hyderabad, India
Vivek Kumar	Trinity College Dublin, Ireland
Olga Kurasova	Vilnius University, Lithuania
Semih Kurt	Ghent University, Belgium
Tomasz Kuśmierczyk	Jagiellonian University, Poland
Valerio La Gatta	Northwestern University, USA
Antti Laaksonen	University of Helsinki, Finland
Charlotte Laclau	Polytechnique Institute, Télécom Paris, France
Jean-Marie Lagniez	CRIL CNRS, France
Aonghus Lawlor	University College Dublin, Ireland
Duc Le	University of Twente, Netherlands
Tuan Le	New Mexico State University, USA
Hoel Le Capitaine	University of Nantes, France
Erwan Le Merrer	Inria, France
Tai Le Quy	University of Koblenz, Germany

Kyumin Lee	Worcester Polytechnic Institute, USA
Mathieu Lefort	University of Rennes - IRISA, France
Collin Leiber	Aalto University, Finland
Vincent Lemaire	Orange Research, France
Marie-Jeanne Lesot	LIP6, Sorbonne Université, France
Xavier Lessage	CETIC, Belgium
Carson Leung	University of Manitoba, Canada
Dong Li	Baylor University, USA
Gang Li	Deakin University, Australia
Peiyu Li	Utah State University, USA
Rui Li	Inspur Academy of Science and Technology, China
Shuai Li	Tsinghua University, China
Weichen Li	RPTU Kaiserslautern-Landau, Germany
Yong Li	Huawei European Research Center, Germany
Yulei Li	Northumbria University, UK
Zhixin Li	Guangxi Normal University, China
Zhong Li	Leiden University, Netherlands
Zongyue Li	Ludwig-Maximilians-Universität München, Germany
Angelica Liguori	ICAR-CNR, Italy
Fandel Lin	University of Southern California, USA
Tony Lindgren	Stockholm University, Sweden
Arunas Lipnickas	Kaunas University of Technology, Lithuania
Marina Litvak	Shamoon College of Engineering, Israel
Bin Liu	Chongqing University of Posts and Telecommunications, China
Chien-Liang Liu	National Chiao Tung University, Taiwan
Junze Liu	University of California, Irvine, USA
Li Liu	Chongqing University, China
Meng Liu	National University of Defense Technology, China
Zhen Liu	Guangdong University of Foreign Studies, China
Tuwe Löfström	Jönköping University, Sweden
Dario Loi	Northeastern University, USA
Marco Loog	Radboud University, Netherlands
Beatriz López	University of Girona, Spain
Marcin Luckner	Warsaw University of Technology, Poland
Stefan Lüdtke	University of Rostock, Germany
Daniele Lunghi	University of Luxembourg, Luxembourg
Thomas Tie Luo	University of Kentucky, USA
Zhiwen Luo	Concordia University, Canada

Marcos M. Raimundo	University of Campinas, Brazil
Kira Maag	Heinrich Heine University Düsseldorf, Germany
Rakesh Chowdary Machineni	Rockwell Automation, USA
Henryk Maciejewski	Wrocław University of Science and Technology, Poland
Michael Madden	University of Galway, Ireland
Sindri Magnusson	Stockholm University, Sweden
Yasir Mahmood	Paderborn University, Germany
Cristina Maier	Boston College, USA
Akshay Malhotra	Interdigital, USA
Hua Mao	Northumbria University, UK
Antonio Marceddu	Politecnico di Torino, Italy
Virginijus Marcinkevičius	Vilnius University, Lithuania
Gabriel Marques Tavares	Ludwig-Maximilians-Universität München, Germany
Christophe Marsala	LIP6, Sorbonne Université, France
Jorge Martinez-Gil	Software Competence Center Hagenberg GmbH, Austria
Fernando Martínez-Plumed	Universitat Politècnica de València, Spain
Ana Martins	University of Aveiro, Portugal
Koji Maruhashi	Fujitsu, Japan
Marc Masana	Graz University of Technology, Austria
Rytis Maskeliūnas	Polsl, Poland
Carlo Masone	Politecnico di Torino, Italy
Michael Mathioudakis	University of Helsinki, Finland
Stan Matwin	Dalhouise University, Canada
Nicolas Maudet	Sorbonne Université, France
Tom Maye-Lasserre	Télécom Paris, IP Paris, France
Giacomo Medda	University of Cagliari, Italy
Nida Meddouri	LRE-EPITA, France
Behzad Mehrbakhsh	Universitat Politècnica de València, Spain
Wagner Meira Jr.	Federal University of Minas Gerais, Brazil
Marco Mellia	Politecnico di Torino, Italy
Joao Mendes-Moreira	University of Porto, Portugal
Rui Meng	Beijing Normal-Hong Kong Baptist University, China
Vlado Menkovski	Eindhoven University of Technology, Netherlands
Engelbert Mephu Nguifo	Université Clermont Auvergne, CNRS, LIMOS, France
Paolo Merialdo	Università degli Studi Roma Tre, Italy
Sebastian Mežnar	Jožef Stefan Institute, Slovenia
Bojan Mihaljevic	Universidad Politécnica de Madrid, Spain

Matej Mihelčić	University of Zagreb, Croatia
Miloud Mihoubi	University of Téluq, Canada
Tsunenori Mine	Kyushu University, Japan
Valentina Minnetti	Italian National Institute of Statistics, Italy
Jelena Mitrović	University of Passau, Germany
Pierre Monnin	Université Côte d'Azur, Inria, CNRS, I3S, France
Eduardo Montesuma	Université Paris-Saclay, France
Raha Moraffah	Worcester Polytechnic Institute, USA
Pierre Moreau	Ekimetrics, France
Jose Moreira	University of Aveiro, Portugal
Paulina Morillo	Universitat Politècnica de València, Spain
Yael Moros-Daval	Universitat Politècnica de València, Spain
Thomas Mortier	Ghent University, Belgium
Roman Mouček	University of West Bohemia, Czech Republic
Elena Maria Muià	Sapienza University of Rome, Italy
Koyel Mukherjee	Adobe Research, India
Ian Nabney	University of Bristol, UK
Mohamed Nadif	Centre Borelli UMR9010-Université Paris Cité, France
Mohamed Nafea	Missouri University of Science and Technology, USA
Felipe Kenji Nakano	KU Leuven, Belgium
Géraldin Nanfack	Concordia University, Canada
Mirco Nanni	CNR-ISTI Pisa, Italy, Italy
Apurva Narayan	University of Western Ontario, Canada
Francesca Naretto	University of Pisa, Italy
Fateme Nateghi Haredasht	Stanford University, USA
Claire Nédellec	INRAE, MaIAGE, France
Dang Nguyen	Deakin University, Australia
Kien Nguyen	University of Delaware, USA
Minh Nguyen	University of Texas at Austin, USA
Nikolaos Nikolaou	University College London, UK
Simona Nisticò	University of Calabria, Italy
Navid Nobani	University of Milano-Bicocca, Italy
Ana Rita Nogueira	INESC TEC, Portugal
Slawomir Nowaczyk	Halmstad University, Sweden
Diana Nurbakova	INSA Lyon - LIRIS UMR 5205 CNRS, France
Iyiola Emmanuel Olatunji	University of Luxembourg, Luxembourg
Arlindo Oliveira	Instituto Superior Técnico, Portugal
Helder Oliveira	University of Porto, Portugal
José Oliveira	University of Porto, Portugal
Makoto Onizuka	Osaka University, Japan

Jose Oramas	University of Antwerp, Belgium
María Óskarsdóttir	University of Southampton, UK
Fannia Pacheco	University of Rouen Normandy, France
Arjun Pakrashi	University College Dublin, Ireland
Egawati Panjei	University of Oklahoma, USA
Apostolos Papadopoulos	Aristotle University of Thessaloniki, Greece
Laurence Park	Western Sydney University, Australia
Emilio Parrado-Hernandez	Universidad Carlos III de Madrid, Spain
Vincenzo Pasquadibisceglie	University of Bari Aldo Moro, Italy
Tatiana Passali	Aristotle University of Thessaloniki, Greece
Eliana Pastor	Politecnico di Torino, Italy
Theodore Patkos	FORTH, Greece
Anand Paul	Louisiana State University HSC, USA
Heiko Paulheim	University of Mannheim, Germany
John Pavlopoulos	Athens University of Economics and Business, Greece
Yulong Pei	Eindhoven University of Technology, Netherlands
Leonardo Pellegrina	University of Padova, Italy
Antonio Pellicani	University of Bari Aldo Moro, Italy
Roberto Pellungrini	University of Pisa, Italy
Frédéric Pennerath	CentraleSupélec - LORIA, France
Francisco Pereira	Technical University of Denmark, Denmark
Lucas Pereira	Interactive Technologies Institute, LARSyS, Técnico Lisboa, Portugal
Franz Pernkopf	Graz University of Technology, Austria
Filipo Perotto	ONERA, France
Linas Petkevicius	Vilnius University, Lithuania
Simone Piaggesi	University of Pisa, Italy
Francesco Piccialli	University of Naples Federico II, Italy
Francesco Pierri	Politecnico di Milano, Italy
Roberto Pietrantuono	University of Naples Federico II, Italy
Martin Pilát	Charles University, Czech Republic
Armando Pinho	University of Aveiro, Portugal
Pedro Pires	Federal University of São Carlos, Brazil
Federico Pirola	University of Milano-Bicocca, Italy
Marc Plantevit	EPITA, France
Marco Podda	University of Pisa, Italy
Marco Polignano	University of Bari Aldo Moro, Italy
Alexander Politowicz	University of Illinois Chicago, USA
Giovanni Ponti	ENEA, Italy
Raluca Portase	Technical University of Cluj Napoca, Romania
Piotr Porwik	University of Silesia in Katowice, Poland

Marco Postiglione	Northwestern University, USA
Andrea Pozzi	University of Pavia, Italy
Steven Prestwich	University College Cork, Ireland
Lucía Prieto-Santamaría	Universidad Politécnica de Madrid, Spain
Chiara Pugliese	IIT - CNR, Italy
Andrea Pugnana	University of Trento, Italy
Satish Puri	Missouri University of Science and Technology, USA
Antonio Purificato	Sapienza University of Rome, Italy
Abdulhakim Qahtan	Utrecht University, Netherlands
Cong Qi	New Jersey Institute of Technology, USA
Xin Qin	California State University, Long Beach, USA
Yijun Quan	University of Warwick, UK
Benjamin Quost	Université de Technologie de Compiègne, France
Dimitrios Rafailidis	University of Thessaly, Greece
Alessio Ragno	EPITA Research Laboratory, France
Muhammad Rajabinasab	University of Southern Denmark, Denmark
Morteza Rakhshaninejad	Ghent University, Belgium
Patrícia Ramos	INESC TEC, Portugal
Md Mashud Rana	Australian Catholic University, Australia
Weixiong Rao	Tongji University, China
Rajeev Rastogi	Amazon, USA
Steffen Rebennack	Karlsruhe Institute of Technology, Germany
Domenico Redavid	University of Bari Aldo Moro, Italy
Michaela Regneri	University of Hamburg, Germany
Wojciech Rejchel	Nicolaus Copernicus University in Toruń, Poland
Francesco Renna	University of Porto, Portugal
Manon Reusens	University of Antwerp, Belgium
Hergys Rexha	Åbo Akademi University, Finland
Ricardo Rios	Federal University of Bahia, Brazil
Tatiane Rios	Federal University of Bahia, Brazil
Guilherme Roberto	University of São Paulo, Brazil
Marko Robnik-Šikonja	University of Ljubljana, Slovenia
Miguel Rocha	University of Minho, Portugal
Christophe Rodrigues	DVRC pôle universitaire Léonard de Vinci, France
Juan Rodriguez	Universidad de Burgos, Spain
Federica Rollo	University of Modena and Reggio Emilia, Italy
Sabin Roman	Jožef Stefan Institute, Slovenia
Nicolas Roque dos Santos	University of California, Riverside, USA
Polina Rozenshtein	Aalto University, Finland
Rimvydas Rubavicius	University of Edinburgh, UK

Krzysztof Rudaś	Institute of Computer Science, Polish Academy of Sciences, Poland
Laura Ruotsalainen	University of Helsinki, Finland
Federico Sabbatini	National Institute for Nuclear Physics - INFN, Italy
Dimitris Sacharidis	Université Libre de Bruxelles, Belgium
Lakhdar Sais	CRIL - CNRS, Artois University, France
Yakoub Salhi	CRIL CNRS, France
Chafik Samir	CNRS-UCA, France
Miriam Santos	University of Porto, Portugal
Ioannis Sarridis	Information Technologies Institute/Centre for Research & Technology, Greece
Roberto Sassi	University of Milan, Italy
Milos Savic	University of Novi Sad, Serbia
Yücel Saygın	Sabancı Universitesi, Turkiye
Katerina Schindlerova	University of Vienna, Austria
Frank-Michael Schleif	Technical University of Applied Sciences Würzburg-Schweinfurt, Germany
Dmitrij Schlesinger	TU Dresden, Germany
Daniel Schlör	University of Würzburg, Germany
Rainer Schlosser	Hasso Plattner Institute, Germany
Melanie Schmidt	Heinrich Heine University Düsseldorf, Germany
Peter Schneider-Kamp	University of Southern Denmark, Denmark
Gesina Schwalbe	Ulm University, Germany
Andreas Schwung	South Westphalia University of Applied Sciences, Germany
Vincenzo Scotti	KASTEL, Karlsruhe Institute of Technology, Germany
Sébastien Destercke	Université de technologie de Compiègne, France
Selpi Selpi	Chalmers University of Technology and Gothenburg University, Sweden
Mattia Setzu	University of Pisa, Italy
Shiv Shankar	University of Massachusetts, USA
Arnab Sharma	Paderborn University, Germany
Shubhranshu Shekhar	Brandeis University, USA
Oleksandr Shekhovtsov	Czech Technical University in Prague, Czech Republic
Hao Shen	fortiss GmbH, Germany
Qiang Sheng	Institute of Computing Technology, Chinese Academy of Sciences, China
John Sheppard	Montana State University, USA
Bin Shi	Xi'an Jiaotong University, China
Jimeng Shi	University of Illinois Urbana-Champaign, USA

Ali Shokoufandeh	Drexel University, USA
Xiao Shou	Baylor University, USA
Md Fahim Sikder	Linköping University, Sweden
Catarina Silva	University of Coimbra, Portugal
Joaquim Silva	NOVA LINCS, Universidade Nova de Lisboa, Portugal
Esther-Lydia Silva-Ramírez	Universidad de Cádiz, Spain
Raivydas Šimėnas	Vilnius University, Lithuania
Giovanni Simonini	University of Modena and Reggio Emilia, Italy
Maneet Singh	Mastercard, India
Andrzej Skowron	University of Warsaw, Poland
Vaclav Smidl	Czech Technical University in Prague, Czech Republic
Marek Smieja	Jagiellonian University, Poland
Filipe Soares	Fraunhofer Portugal AICOS, Portugal
Osvaldo Solarte-Pabon	Universidad del Valle, Colombia
Liyan Song	Harbin Institute of Technology, China
Fabian Spaeh	Celonis, USA
Lorenz Sparrenberg	University of Bonn, Germany
Giancarlo Sperlì	University of Naples Federico II, Italy
Ramya Srinivasan	Fujitsu, Japan
Dimitri Staufer	Technische Universität Berlin, Germany
Marcel Steinmetz	LAAS-CNRS, France
Niklas Strauß	Ludwig-Maximilians-Universität München, Germany
Xuanyu Su	University of Ottawa, Canada
Jérémie Sublime	ISEP, France
Xin Sun	City University of Macau, China
Zhaokai Sun	Tongji University, China
Panagiotis Symeonidis	University of the Aegean, Greece
Tomasz Szandała	Wrocław University of Science and Technology, Poland
Amir Taherkordi	University of Oslo, Norway
Atsuhiro Takasu	National Institute of Informatics, Japan
Nicholas Tan Jerome	Karlsruhe Institute of Technology, Germany
Yufei Tang	Florida Atlantic University, USA
Katerina Taskova	University of Auckland, New Zealand
Olivier Teste	IRIT, University of Toulouse, France
Christoph Tholen	Saarland University of Applied Sciences, Germany
Steffen Thoma	FZI Research Center for Information Technology, Germany

Josephine Thomas	University of Greifswald, Germany
Natan Tourne	Ghent University, Belgium
Panos Trahanias	FORTH, Greece
Alicia Troncoso	Pablo de Olavide University, Spain
Francesco Trovò	Politecnico di Milano, Italy
Giuseppe Trunfio	University of Sassari, Italy
Panayiotis Tsaparas	University of Ioannina, Greece, Greece
Grigorios Tsoumakas	Aristotle University of Thessaloniki, Greece
Jonata Tyska Carvalho	Federal University of Santa Catarina, Brazil
Mihai Udrescu	Politehnica University Timisoara, Romania
Edoardo Urettini	European Central Bank, Germany
Gonzalo Uribarri	Stockholm University, Sweden
Philipp Vaeth	Technical University of Applied Sciences Würzburg-Schweinfurt, University Bielefeld, Germany
Giorgio Valentini	University of Milan, Italy
Diego Vallejo-Huanga	Universitat Politècnica de València, Spain
Jente Van Belle	KU Leuven, Belgium
Peter van der Putten	Leiden University, Netherlands
Lucy Van Kleunen	KU Leuven, Belgium
Fabio Vandin	University of Padova, Italy
Georgios Vardakas	University of Ioannina, Greece
Aparna S. Varde	Montclair State University, USA
Mariana Vargas Vieyra	MostlyAI, Austria
Bruno Veloso	INESC TEC, Portugal
Mathias Verbeke	KU Leuven, Belgium
Wouter Verbeke	KU Leuven, Belgium
Jan Verwaeren	Ghent University, Belgium
Gennaro Vessio	University of Bari Aldo Moro, Italy
Jill-Jênn Vie	Inria, France
Saketh Vishnubhatla	Arizona State University, USA
Marco Viviani	University of Milano-Bicocca, Italy
Maximilian von Zastrow	University of Southern Denmark, Denmark
Tim vor der Brück	Internationale Hochschule, Germany
Ngoc-Son Vu	University of Technology of Troyes, France
Tomasz Walkowiak	Wrocław University of Science and Technology, Poland
Shu Wan	Arizona State University, USA
Ziwen Wan	University of California, Irvine, USA
Deng-Bao Wang	Southeast University, China
Hao Wang	University of Science and Technology of China, China

Jianwu Wang	University of Maryland, Baltimore County, USA
Jing Wang	Amazon, USA
Li Wang	National University of Defense Technology, China
Mengying Wang	Case Western Reserve University, USA
Wendy Hui Wang	Stevens Institute of Technology, USA
Xiaoyang Wang	University of Exeter, UK
Xuemin Wang	Guilin University of Electronic Technology, China
Yanhao Wang	East China Normal University, China
Yongyu Wang	JD Logistics, China
Zhihui Wang	Fudan University, China
Zichong Wang	Florida International University, USA
Pascal Weber	University of Vienna, Austria
Xing Wei	Tongji University, China
Yang Wei	Nanjing University of Science and Technology, China
Tonio Weidler	Maastricht University, Netherlands
Guilherme Weigert Cassales	University of Waikato, New Zealand
Alicja Wieczorkowska	Polish-Japanese Academy of Information Technology, Poland
Szymon Wojciechowski	Wrocław University of Science and Technology, Poland
Michal Wozniak	Wrocław University of Science and Technology, Poland
Bin Wu	Zhengzhou University, China
Boqian Wu	University of Luxembourg, Luxembourg
Nannan Wu	Tianjin University, China
Patrick Wu	American University, USA
Peng Wu	Shanghai Jiao Tong University, China
Wei Wu	Ben Gurion University of the Negev, Israel
Wenjie Xi	George Mason University, USA
Zhiwen Xiao	Southwest Jiaotong University, China
Hong Xie	University of Science and Technology of China, China
Wen-Bo Xie	Southwest Petroleum University, China
Huanlai Xing	Southwest Jiaotong University, China
Xing Xing	Tongji University, China
Duo Xu	Georgia Institute of Technology, USA
Gehui Xu	Imperial College London, UK
Weifeng Xu	University of Baltimore, USA
Qiao Yan	Shenzhen University, China
Yu Yan	Institute of Computing Technology, Chinese Academy of Sciences, China

Jiayi Yang	Tongji University, China
Qian Yang	University of Connecticut, USA
Xin-She Yang	Middlesex University London, UK
Yutong Ye	Beihang University, China
Kalidas Yeturu	Indian Institute of Technology Tirupati, India
Ilkay Yildiz Potter	BioSensics LLC, USA
Zhipeng Yin	Florida International University, USA
Jaemin Yoo	Seoul National University, South Korea
Lei You	Technical University of Denmark, Denmark
Hang Yu	Shanghai University, China
Shuyang Yu	Michigan State University, USA
Wentao Yu	Nanjing University of Science and Technology, China
Jidong Yuan	Beijing Jiaotong University, China
Osmar Zaiane	University of Alberta, Canada
Tetiana Zakharchenko	Ukrainian Catholic University, Ukraine
Obaidullah Zaland	Umeå University, Sweden
Alessio Zanga	University of Milano-Bicocca, Italy
Mario Zanon	IMT School for Advanced Studies Lucca, Italy
Gianluca Zaza	University of Bari Aldo Moro, Italy
Assaad Zeghina	Latmos Lab, France
Akka Zemmari	University of Bordeaux, France
Saber Zerhoudi	University of Passau, Germany
Meriem Zerkouk	Université TÉLUQ, Canada
Chongsheng Zhang	Henan University, China
Hanping Zhang	Carleton University, Canada
Haowen Zhang	Zhejiang Sci-Tech University, China
Pengyu Zhang	University of Amsterdam, Netherlands
Xiaoming Zhang	Beihang University, China
Xinyue Zhang	Kennesaw State University, USA
Xiuzhen Zhang	RMIT University, Australia
Xiyue Zhang	University of Bristol, UK
Yaying Zhang	Tongji University, China
Yin Zhang	University of Electronic Science and Technology of China, China
Zhiwen Zhang	LocationMind Inc., Japan
Zhong Zhang	University of Electronic Science and Technology of China, China
Kaiqi Zhao	Oakland University, USA
Shu Zhao	Anhui University, China
Zhouting Zhao	Trinity College Dublin, Ireland
Yueyuan Zheng	Beihang University, China

Yujia Zheng	Carnegie Mellon University, USA
Yanmin Zhu	Shanghai Jiao Tong University, China
Arthur Zimek	University of Southern Denmark, Denmark
Tommaso Zoppi	University of Florence, Italy
Noé Zufferey	ETH Zurich, Switzerland
Pedro Zuidberg Dos Martires	Örebro University, Sweden
Paweł Zyblewski	Wrocław University of Science and Technology, Poland

Additional Reviewers, Research Track

Amgad Abdulmaqsod	Paderborn University, Germany
Aisha Aijaz	Indraprastha Institute of Information Technology, Delhi, India
Moh'd Khier Al Kfari	University of Rostock, Germany
Sokrat Aldarmini	Missouri University of Science and Technology, USA
Konstantinos Alexis	IMSI/Athena Research Center, Greece
Hazrat Ali	University of Stirling, UK
Zafar Ali	Southeast University, China
Hend Amraoui	Higher Institute of Applied Languages and Computer Science of Béja (ISLAI Béja), University of Jendouba, Tunisia
Shin Ando	Tokyo University of Science, Japan
Eugen-Richard Ardelean	Technical University of Cluj-Napoca, Romania
André Artelt	Bielefeld University, Germany
Baran Atalar	Carnegie Mellon University, USA
Kyohei Atarashi	Kyoto University, Japan
Sanket Badhe	Google, USA
Daniel Barley	Heidelberg University, Germany
Ulya Bayram	Canakkale Onsekiz Mart University, Turkey
Ahmad Bdeir	University of Hildesheim, Germany
Jatin Bedi	Thapar Institute of Engineering and Technology, India
Sidahmed Benabderrahmane	New York University, United Arab Emirates
Francesco Benedetti	University of Bari Aldo Moro, Italy
Quentin Bertrand	Inria, France
Aurelie Beynier	Sorbonne Université, France
Martin Binder	LMU Munich, Germany
Valerio Bonsignori	University of Pisa, Italy
Weronika Borek-Marciniec	Wrocław University of Science and Technology, Poland

Onur Boyar	IBM Research, Japan
Maria Sofia Bucarelli	CNRS, Inria, I3S, France
Zhuo Cai	University of Technology Sydney, Australia
Toon Calders	University of Antwerp, Belgium
Lele Cao	Tsinghua University, China
Louis Carpentier	KU Leuven, Belgium
Daniele Castellana	University of Florence, Italy
Mustafa Cavus	Eskisehir Technical University, Turkey
Dong-Kyu Chae	Hanyang University, South Korea
Tanujit Chakraborty	Sorbonne University Abu Dhabi, United Arab Emirates
Anna Chatzipapadopoulou	Athens University of Economics and Business/Archimedes Unit, Athena Research Center, Greece
Lilia Chebbah	Georgia State University, USA
Hao Chen	University of Chinese Academy of Sciences, China
Haopeng Chen	Shanghai Jiao Tong University, China
Sheng-Wei Chen	National Taiwan University, Taiwan
Songcan Chen	Nanjing University of Aeronautics and Astronautics, China
Zhen Chen	University of Science and Technology of China, China
Zhili Chen	East China Normal University, China
Liang Cheng	University of Oslo, Norway
Chak Fong Chong	Macao Polytechnic University, China
Maciej Chrabaszcz	Warsaw University of Technology, NASK National Research Institute, Poland
Michele Craighero	Politecnico di Milano, Italy
Wang-Zhou Dai	China
Uma Damotharan	PES University, USA
Davy Darankoum	Université Grenoble Alpes/SynapCell, France
Mrinal Das	IIT Palakaad, India
Debashis Das Chakladar	Birla Institute of Technology & Science, Hyderabad, India
Arne De Temmerman	KU Leuven, Belgium
Thanh-Dang Diep	Vietnam National University Ho Chi Minh City - University of Technology, Vietnam
Yihao Ding	University of Western Australia, Australia
Jean-François Dollinger	CESI, France
Yingpeng Du	Nanyang Technological University, Singapore
Fabrício Enembreck	Pontifical Catholic University of Paraná, Brazil
A. M. Esfar-E-Alam	University of Oslo, Norway

Fiona Ewald	Ludwig-Maximilians-Universität München, Germany
Ken-ichi Fukui	Kansai University, Japan
Xiaofeng Gao	Shanghai Jiao Tong University, China
Blaise Genest	CNRS, CNRS@CREATE, France
Christos Gkartzios	University of Ioannina, Greece
Filippos Gouidis	ICS/FORTH, Greece
Poonam Goyal	BITS Pilani, India
Shangqi Guo	Tsinghua, China
Yang Guo	Harbin Engineering University, China
Subhash Gurappa	Florida International University, USA
Renda Han	Tianjin University, China
Takahiro Hara	Osaka University, Japan
Ryuichiro Hataya	SB Intuitions & Kyoto University, Japan
Mehdi Hennequin	Omundu, France
Johanna Hillebrand	Heinrich Heine University, Germany
Yi-Te Hong	Academia Sinica, Taiwan
Tanvir Hossain	Georgia State University, USA
Ruijie Hou	Zhejiang University, China
Zhaobo Hu	Institut Polytechnique de Paris, France
Chun Huang	Chongqing University, China
Yu-Shiang Huang	National Taiwan University, Taiwan
Pedro Ilídio	KU Leuven, Belgium
Marek Jeliński	NASK-PIB, Poland
Wanting Ji	Liaoning University, China
Huimin Jiang	University of Science and Technology of China, China
Shu Jiang	Nantong Univerisity, China
Changhong Jin	University College Dublin, Ireland
Yifei Jin	X-Tech (Beijing) Co., Ltd., China
Yue Jin	University of Northampton, UK
Durande Berluskoni Kamga Nguifo	Université Clermont Auvergne, Clermont Auvergne INP, ENSMSE, CNRS, LIMOS, France
Skander Karkar	Mediterranean Institute of Technology, Tunisia
Hisashi Kashima	Kyoto University, Japan
Tsuyoshi Kato	Gunma University, Japan
Ramneek Kaur	IIT Delhi, India
Zulfiqar Ahmad Khan	Umeå University, Sweden
Sejin Kim	Gwangju Institute of Science and Technology, South Korea
YoungBin Kim	Chung-Ang University, South Korea

Ken Kobayashi	Institute of Science Tokyo, Japan
Ryosuke Kojima	Kyoto University, Japan
Ravi Kolla	Sony Research India, India
Patrik Kozlík	Institute of Informatics Slovak Academy of Sciences, Slovakia
Uttam Kumar	University of Bonn, Germany
Suman Kundu	Indian Institute of Technology Madras, India
Vasilii Latonov	PSJC Sberbank, Russia
Hung Le	Deakin University, Australia
Truong-Thanh Le	University of Oslo, Norway
Yongkeun Lee	Seoul National University of Science and Technology, South Korea
Bo Li	Guilin University of Aerospace Technology, China
Chen Li	Osaka University, Japan
Daifeng Li	Sun Yat-sen University, China
Huakang Li	Xi'an Jiaotong-Liverpool University, China
Jiyanglin Li	Guizhou Key Laboratory of Big Data Statistical Analysis, Guizhou University of Finance and Economics, China
Mark Junjie Li	Shenzhen University, China
Shusheng Li	Zhenjiang Research Institute of Advanced Equipment, China
Wuyungerile Li	Inner Mongolia University, China
Yixin Li	Xinjiang Technical Institute of Physics and Chemistry, Chinese Academy of Sciences, China
Yulong Li	Hefei University of Technology, China
Tao Lian	Taiyuan University of Technology, China
Junfeng Liao	Shanghai University of International Business and Economics, China
Zhenyu Liao	Huazhong University of Science and Technology, China
Jianghao Lin	Shanghai Jiao Tong University, China
Shih-Chih Lindgren	National Tsing Hua University, Taiwan
Jiaqi Liu	Northwestern Polytechnical University, China
Ke Liu	University of California, Berkeley, USA
Sen Liu	Fudan University, China
Yue Liu	Shanghai University, China
Zesheng Liu	Renmin University of China, China
Cuicui Luo	University of Chinese Academy of Sciences, China

Ranjitha Prasad	Indraprastha Institute of Information Technology Delhi, India
Antonio Purificato	Sapienza University of Rome, Italy
Lin Qi	Ocean University of China, China
Tieyun Qian	Wuhan University, China
Weizhu Qian	Soochow University, China
Linbo Qiao	National University of Defense Technology, China
Jintao Qu	University of Southern California, USA
Muhammad Rajabinasab	University of Southern Denmark, Denmark
Gangulie Ranawaka	Informatics Institute of Technology, Sri Lanka
Darshan Rathod	Fujitsu, Japan
Matīss Rikters	National Institute of Advanced Industrial Science and Technology, Japan
Pieter Robberechts	KU Leuven, Belgium
Thibault Roux	ONERA, France
Pablo Ruiz Morales	KU Leuven, Belgium
P. S. Sastry	Indian Institute of Science, India
Aggelos Semoglou	Athens University of Economics & Business & Archimedes Research Unit, Athena Research Center, Greece
Deep Shah	Google LLC, USA
Abdul-Kazeem Shamba	Norwegian University of Science & Technology, Norway
Jie Shao	University of Electronic Science and Technology of China, China
Lifeng Shen	Chongqing University of Posts and Telecommunications, China
Xiaojun Sheng	Guangdong Laboratory of Artificial Intelligence and Digital Economy (SZ), China
Mohamed Sherif	Paderborn University, Germany
Kijung Shin	KAIST, South Korea
Jayakumar Singaram	Independent consultant, India
Atul Kumar Singh	Fujitsu Research of India Pvt. Ltd., India
Damian Sójka	Poznań University of Technology; IDEAS-NCBR, Poland
Youngdoo Son	Dongguk University, South Korea
Andy Song	RMIT University, Australia
Jules Soria	CEA-LIST, Université Paris-Saclay, France
P. K. Srijith	Indian Institute of Technology Hyderabad, India
Gowri Srinivasa	PES University, USA
Sintija Stevanoska	Jožef Stefan Institute, Slovenia

Taoyu Su	Institute of Information Engineering, Chinese Academy of Sciences, China
Qi Rong Sua	Nanyang Technological University, Singapore
Mahito Sugiyama	National Institute of Informatics, Japan
Yibin Sun	Victoria University of Wellington, New Zealand
Ying Sun	Taishan University, China
Yu Tang	Soochow University, China
Ray Telikani	University of Technology Sydney, Australia
Wei Tong	Nanjing University, China
Marwan Torki	Alexandria University, Egypt
Son Tran	Deakin University, Australia
Arseniy Trushin	Yandex, Russia
Rajesh Vasa	Deakin University, Australia
Ricardo Vilalta	University of Austin, USA
Renato Vimieiro	Federal University of Minas Gerais, Brazil
Chunchen Wang	Beijing University of Posts and Telecommunications, China
Dongjing Wang	Hangzhou Dianzi University, China
Liping Wang	East China Normal University, China
Xin Wang	Qilu University of Technology, China
Xinyao Wang	China Unicom Data Intelligence Co., Ltd, China
Yi Wang	Xinjiang Technical Institute of Physics and Chemistry, Chinese Academy of Sciences, China
Yu-Shuen Wang	National Yang Ming Chiao Tung University, Taiwan
Yuangang Wang	Dalian Minzu University, China
Yi Wen	University of Electronic Science and Technology of China, China
Isabelle Wittmann	IBM Research, Switzerland
Tong Wu	University of Electronic Science and Technology of China, China
Yao Wu	Information Support Force Engineering University, China
Zhengbiao Wu	Ningbo University, China
Bin Xiao	University Health Network, Canada
Jing Xiao	South China Normal University, China
Chenyang Xu	East China Normal University, China
Huijie Xu	University of Technology Sydney, Australia
Long Xu	RMIT University, Australia
Zhiwei Xu	Shandong University, China
Han Xue	Donghua University, China
Sangeeta Yadav	Indian Institute of Science, India

Yutaro Yamaguchi	Osaka University, Japan
Keiichiro Yamamura	ELYZA, Japan
Cheng Yang	Beijing University of Posts and Telecommunications, China
Jiaoyun Yang	Hefei University of Technology, China
Jun Yang	University of Helsinki, Finland
Ruochen Yang	Institute of Information Engineering, Chinese Academy of Sciences, China
Fangli Ying	East China University of Science and Technology, China
Dongjin Yu	Hangzhou Dianzi University, China
Wenjun Yu	Shanghai University of Finance and Economics, China
Yanwei Yu	Ocean University of China, China
Ziyue Yu	Macao Polytechnic University, China
Fangfang Yuan	Institute of Information Engineering, Chinese Academy of Sciences, China
Hang Yuan	Osaka University, Japan
Obaidullah Zaland	Umeå University, Sweden
Lei Zan	Université Grenoble Alpes, CNRS, Grenoble INP, LIG, France
Wojciech Zarzecki	Warsaw University of Technology, Poland
Zheyuan Zhan	Zhejiang University, China
Bolei Zhang	Nanjing University of Posts and Telecommunications, China
Chao Zhang	Beijing Digital Native Digital City Research Center, China
Huan Zhang	Zhengzhou University, China
Jian Zhang	China University of Mining and Technology, China
Kangning Zhang	Shanghai Jiao Tong University, China
Liang Zhang	Shanghai Jiao Tong University, China
Mengxiao Zhang	University of Auckland, New Zealand
Wei Zhang	Singapore Institute of Technology, Singapore
Wenxin Zhang	University of Chinese Academy of Sciences, China
Xuefeng Zhang	Ningbo University, China
Yaqian Zhang	University of Waikato, New Zealand
Yihong Zhang	Osaka University, Japan
Yutong Zhang	Sichuan University, China
Zhongnan Zhang	Xiamen University, China
Qinpei Zhao	Tongji University, China
Weizhong Zhao	Central China Normal University, China

Can Zhou	Imperial College London, UK
Qiaoli Zhou	Shenyang Aerospace University, China
Tianlong Zhou	Tongji University, China
Tongqing Zhou	National University of Defense Technology, China
Yan Zhou	Hohai University, China
Zhengyang Zhou	University of Science and Technology of China, China
Guanghui Zhu	Nanjing University, China
Mengxiao Zhu	North China University of Technology, China

Area Chairs, Applied Data Science Track

Sahar Asadi	King (part of Microsoft), Sweden
Ira Assent	Aarhus University, Denmark
Michael Berthold	KNIME, Switzerland
Ilaria Bordino	UniCredit, Italy
Berkant Barla Cambazoglu	NTENT, Spain
Peggy Cellier	INSA Rennes, IRISA, France
Yi Chang	Jilin University, China
Chen Chen	University of Virginia, USA
Paulo Cortez	University of Minho, Portugal
Vitor Santos Costa	UP, Portugal
Bruno Cremilleux	Université de Caen Normandie, France
Gianmarco De Francisci Morales	Intesa Sanpaolo Innovation Center, Italy
Carlotta Domeniconi	George Mason University, USA
Dejing Dou	BCG, China
Joao Gama	INESC TEC - LIAAD, Portugal
Debasis Ganguly	University of Glasgow, UK
Riccardo Guidotti	University of Pisa, Italy
Jingrui He	University of Illinois at Urbana-Champaign, USA
Andreas Hotho	University of Wuerzburg, Germany
Hsun-Ping Hsieh	National Cheng Kung University, Taiwan
Ulf Johansson	Jönköping University, Sweden
Tracy King	Adobe, USA
Yun Sing Koh	University of Auckland, New Zealand
Lars Kotthoff	University of St Andrews, UK
Niklas Lavesson	Blekinge Institute of Technology, Sweden
Ke Li	University of Exeter, UK
Yiqun Liu	Tsinghua University, China
Ioanna Miliou	Stockholm University, Sweden

Slawomir Nowaczyk	Halmstad University, Sweden
Andre Panisson	Intesa Sanpaolo, Italy
Sepideh Pashami	Halmstad University, Sweden
Fabio Pinelli	IMT Lucca, Italy
Yiyue Qian	Amazon, USA
Matteo Riondato	Amherst College, USA
Sriparna Saha	IIT Patna, India
Flora Salim	University of New South Wales, Australia
Thomas Seidl	LMU Munich, Germany
Edoardo Serra	Boise State University, USA
Myra Spiliopoulou	Otto von Guericke University Magdeburg, Germany
Giovanni Stilo	Luiss Guido Carli, Italy
Vincent Tseng	National Yang Ming Chiao Tung University, Taiwan
Jianling Wang	Google Brain, USA
Zheng Wang	Alibaba DAMO Academy, China
Ingmar Weber	Saarland University, Germany
Yinglong Xia	Meta, USA
Changhe Yuan	Amazon, USA
Fan Zhang	Guangzhou University, China
Min-Ling Zhang	Southeast University, China
Xiangyu Zhao	City University of Hong Kong, Hong Kong SAR
Xingquan Zhu	Florida Atlantic University, USA
Ziwei Zhu	George Mason University, USA
Fuzhen Zhuang	Institute of Artificial Intelligence, Beihang University, China
Albrecht Zimmermann	Université de Caen Normandie, France

Program Committee, Applied Data Science Track

Shahrooz Abghari	Blekinge Institute of Technology, Sweden
Evrim Acar	Simula Metropolitan Center for Digital Engineering, Norway
Evelin Amorim	Inesc tec, Portugal
Thiago Andrade	University of Porto/INESCTEC, Portugal
Sunil Aryal	Deakin University, Australia
Inaam Ashraf	Bielefeld University, Germany
Berkay Aydin	Georgia State University, USA
Juhee Bae	University of Skövde, Sweden
Ashraf Bah Rabiou	University of Delaware, USA

Jiahui Bai	Meta, USA
Michael Bain	University of New South Wales, Australia
Hubert Baniecki	University of Warsaw, Poland
Enda Barrett	University of Galway, Ireland
Idir Benouaret	Epita Research Laboratory, France
Michele Bernardini	Università degli Studi eCampus, Italy
Flavio Bertini	University of Parma, Italy
Chongke Bi	Tianjin university, China
Pavel Blinov	Sber AI Lab, Russia
Szymon Bobek	Jagiellonian University, Poland
Veselka Boeva	Blekinge Institute of Technology, Sweden
Martin Boldt	Blekinge Institute of Technology, Sweden
Paul Boniol	Inria, Ecole normale supérieure, France
Anton Borg	Blekinge Institute of Technology, Sweden
Praveen Borra	Florida Atlantic University, USA
Cécile Bothorel	IMT Atlantique, France
Mohamed-Rafik Bouguelia	University of Doha for Science and Technology, Qatar
Klaus Brinker	Hamm-Lippstadt University of Applied Sciences, Germany
Keith Burghardt	UNC Charlotte, USA
Ece Calikus	Uppsala University, Sweden
João R. Campos	University of Coimbra, Portugal
Shilei Cao	Tencent, China
Remy Cazabet	Lyon 1, France
Ricardo Cerri	University of São Paulo, Brazil
Minghao Chen	Tencent, China
Siyuan Chen	Guangzhou University, China
Wei-Peng Chen	Fujitsu Research of America, USA
Dawei Cheng	Tongji University, China
Wei Cheng	NEC Laboratories America, USA
Zhiyong Cheng	Shandong Academy of Sciences, China
Martina Cinquini	University of Pisa, Italy
Francisco Claude-Faust	LinkedIn, USA
Jeremie Clos	University of Nottingham, UK
Fabrizio Costa	Exeter University, UK
Rogério Luís Costa	University of Coimbra, Portugal
Raphaël Couturier	Université Marie et Louis Pasteur, France
Evan Crothers	University of Ottawa, Canada
Jairo Cugliari	Laboratoire ERIC, Université Lumière Lyon 2, France
Tiago Cunha	Expedia Group, Portugal

Thomas Czernichow	Darwinlabs, France
Andrea D'Angelo	University of Aarhus, Denmark
Ariyam Das	Google, USA
Patrizio Dazzi	University of Pisa, Italy
Shimin Di	The Hong Kong University of Science and Technology, Hong Kong SAR
Yuting Ding	The School of Cyber Science and Engineering, Southeast University, China
Stephan Doerfel	Kiel University of Applied Sciences, Germany
Antoine Doucet	La Rochelle Université, France
Gaoyuan Du	AMAZON, USA
Wouter Duivesteijn	Technische Universiteit Eindhoven, Netherlands
Tome Eftimov	Jozef Stefan Institute, Slovenia
Ibtihal El Mimouni	Inria, France
Dominik Endres	Philipps-Universität Marburg, Germany
Yuantao Fan	Halmstad University, Sweden
Fabio Fassetti	Università della Calabria, Italy
Sophie Fellenz	RPTU Kaiserslautern-Landau, Germany
Luis Ferreira	Olympus Medical Products Portugal, Portugal
Germain Forestier	University of Haute Alsace, France
Erik Frisk	Linköping University, Sweden
Claudio Gallicchio	University of Pisa, Italy
Alexander Galozy	Halmstad University, Sweden
Xiaofeng Gao	Shanghai Jiaotong University, China
Yunjun Gao	Zhejiang University, China
Aditya Gautam	Meta, USA
Sophie Giffard-Roisin	Univ. Grenoble Alpes, France
Ana Gjorgjevikj	Jožef Stefan Institute, Slovenia
Aakash Goel	Apple, USA
Markus Götz	Karlsruhe Institute of Technology (KIT), Germany
James Goulding	University of Nottingham, UK
Anastasios Gounaris	Aristotle University of Thessaloniki, Greece
Håkan Grahn	Blekinge Institute of Technology, Sweden
Derek Greene	Data Analytics, University College Dublin, Ireland
Zhibin Gu	Hebei Normal University, China
Ziyu Guan	Xidian University, China
Vikas Gupta	HPCL, India
Vinayak Gupta	University of Washington Seattle, USA
Thomas Guyet	Inria, Centre de Lyon, France

Qiwei Han	Nova School of Business and Economics, Portugal
Shuchu Han	Capital One Financial Group, USA
Aron Henriksson	Stockholm University, Sweden
Dania Herzalla	Technology Innovation Institute, United Arab Emirates
Tuan-Anh Hoang	L3S Research Center, Leibniz University of Hanover, Germany
Anders Holst	RISE SICS, Sweden
Andreas Holzinger	University of Natural Resources and Life Sciences Vienna, Austria
Sebastian Hönel	Linnaeus University, Sweden
Yizheng Huang	York University, Canada
Yu Huang	Indiana University, USA
Angelo Impedovo	NSA Italia s.r.l., Italy
Roberto Interdonato	CIRAD, France
Radu Tudor Ionescu	University of Bucharest, Romania
Panos Ipeirotis	New York University, USA
Said Jabbour	CRIL CNRS & Artois University, France
Vivekananda Jayaram	JPMorgan Chase, USA
Anli Ji	California State University Fullerton, USA
Beihong Jin	Institute of Software, Chinese Academy of Sciences, China
Pinar Karagoz	Middle East Technical University (METU), Turkey
Kamalakar Karlapalem	IIIT Hyderabad, India
Alexander Karlsson	University of Skövde, Sweden
Zahra Kharazian	Department of Computer and Systems Sciences (DSV), Stockholm University, Sweden
Hyunsung Kim	KAIST & Fitogether, Korea
Viacheslav Komisarenko	University of Tartu, Estonia
Krzysztof Krawiec	Poznan University of Technology, Poland
Niraj Kumar	Fujitsu, India
Camille Kurtz	Université Paris Cité, France
Joël Ky	SnT - University of Luxembourg, Luxembourg
Susana Ladra	University of A Coruña, Spain
Alessandro Leite	INSA Rouen Normandy, France
Daniel Lemire	University of Quebec (TELUQ), Canada
Florian Lemmerich	University of Passau, Germany
Jurica Levatić	Jožef Stefan Institute, Slovenia
Chuan Li	Sorbonne Université, LIPADE, Université Paris Cité, France
Daifeng Li	Sun Yat-Sen University, China

Haifang Li	Baidu Inc., China
Lei Li	The Hong Kong University of Science and Technology (Guangzhou), China
Yuzhuo Li	University of Auckland, New Zealand
Zhengze Li	University of Goettingen, Germany
Xiang Lian	Kent State University, USA
Guojun Liang	Halmstad University, Sweden
Zhaohui Liang	National Library of Medicine, NIH, USA
Kwan Hui Lim	Singapore University of Technology and Design, Singapore
Adi Lin	Didi, China
Jingjing Liu	MD Anderson Cancer Center, USA
Yongchao Liu	Ant Group, China
Beatriz López	University of Girona, Spain
Jens Lundström	Halmstad University, Sweden
Yuanhua Lv	Uber, USA
John M. Betts	Monash University, Australia
Guixiang Ma	Intel, USA
Pekka Malo	Aalto University, Finland
Adriano Mancini	DII - Università Politecnica delle Marche, Italy
Silviu Maniu	Univ. Grenoble Alpes, France
Cinmayii Manliguez	University of the Philippines Mindanao, Philippines
Mirko Marras	University of Cagliari, Italy
Florent Masseglia	Inria, France
Luis Miguel Matos	University of Minho, Portugal
Wolfgang Mayer	University of South Australia, Australia
Ashman Mehra	Birla Institute of Technology and Science, (BITS Goa), India
Parth Mehta	Parmonic, India
Ernestina Menasalvas	Universidad Politécnica de Madrid, Spain
Fabio Mercorio	University of Milan-Bicocca, Italy
Paolo Mignone	Università Telematica Pegaso, Italy
Zoltan Miklos	University of Rennes, France
Katsiaryna Mirylenka	TU Wien, Austria
Martin Mladenov	Google, USA
Mukesh Mohania	IIIT Delhi, India
Carlos Monserrat-Aranda	Universitat Politècnica de València, Spain
Dharmalingam Muthusamy	Bharathiar University, India
Hiba Najjar	DFKI GmbH, Germany
Jakub Nalepa	Silesian University of Technology, Poland

Richi Nayak	Queensland University of Technology, Brisbane, Australia
Francesco Paolo Nerini	Sapienza University of Rome, Italy
Wee Siong Ng	Institute for Infocomm Research, Singapore
Le Nguyen	University of Oulu, Finland
Thanh Thi Nguyen	University of the Sunshine Coast, Australia
Hao Niu	KDDI Research, Inc., Japan
Tsuyoshi Okita	Kyushu Institute of Technology, Japan
Tomas Olsson	RISE, Sweden
Latifa Oukhellou	IFSTTAR, France
Andrei Paleyes	University of Cambridge, UK
Bo Pang	University of Auckland, New Zealand
Panagiotis Papadakos	FORTH-ICS, Greece
Manos Papagelis	York University, Canada
Luca Pappalardo	ISTI, Italy
Konstantinos Pelechrinis	University of Pittsburgh, USA
Xueping Peng	University of Technology Sydney, Australia
Ricardo Pereira	Feedzai, Portugal
Miquel Perello-Nieto	University of Bristol, UK
Dirk Pflüger	University of Stuttgart, IPVS, Germany
Nico Piatkowski	Fraunhofer IAIS, Germany
Pablo Picazo-Sanchez	Halmstad University, Sweden
Fabio Pinelli	IMT Lucca, Italy
Gianvito Pio	University of Bari, Italy
Marc Plantevit	EPITA, France
Cedric Pradalier	GeorgiaTech Lorraine, France
Paul Prasse	University of Potsdam, Germany
Giulia Preti	CENTAI, Italy
Buyue Qian	Xi'an Jiaotong University, China
Tingrui Qiao	University of Auckland, New Zealand
Prathap Manohar Joshi R	Zoho Corporation, India
Enayat Rajabi	Halmstad University, Canada
Herilalaina Rakotoarison	University of Helsinki, Finland
Korbinian Randl	Stockholm University, Sweden
Vaskar Raychoudhury	Miami University, USA
Salvatore Rinzivillo	KDDLab - ISTI - CNR, Italy
Francisco Romero	UCLM, Spain
Riccardo Rosati	Università Politecnica delle Marche, Italy
Bogdan Ruszczak	Opole University of Technology, Poland
Snehanshu Saha	BITS Pilani Goa Campus, India
Sriparna Saha	IIT Patna, India
Isak Samsten	Stockholm University, Sweden

Eric SanJuan	Avignon University, France
Philipp Schmidt	Amazon Research, Germany
Marian Scuturici	LIRIS, France
Pedro Seber	MIT, USA
Andrea Seveso	University of Milan-Bicocca, Italy
Vahid Shahrivari Joghan	Utrecht University, Netherlands
Linjun Shou	STCA NLP Group, Microsoft, Beijing, China
Sajjad Shumaly	Max-Planck-Institut for Polymer, Germany
Jonathan Silva	UFMS, Brasil
Gavin Smith	University of Nottingham, UK
Diogo Soares	LASIGE, Faculdade de Ciências, Universidade de Lisboa, Portugal
Huan Song	Amazon, USA
Wenzhuo Song	Northeast Normal University, China
Shafiullah Soomro	Department of Computer Science and Media Technology, Linnaeus University, Sweden
Arnaud Soulet	University of Tours, France
Francesco Spinnato	University of Pisa, Italy
Efstathios Stamatatos	University of the Aegean, Greece
Gan Sun	South China University of Technology, China
Mehtab Alam Syed	CIRAD, France
Liang Tang	Google, USA
Xing Tang	Shenzhen Technology University, China
Junichi Tatemura	Google, USA
Romain Tavenard	Univ. Rennes, LETG/IRISA, France
Joe Tekli	Lebanese American University, Lebanon
Ismail Toroslu	METU, Turkey
Vicenç Torra	University of Umeå, Sweden
Pablo Torrijos Arenas	Universidad de Castilla-La Mancha, Spain
Daniel Trejo Banos	SDSC, Switzerland
Allan Tucker	Brunel University London, UK
Ranga Raju Vatsavai	North Carolina State University, USA
Ishan Verma	TCS Research, India
Rosana Veroneze	Université catholique de Louvain, Belgium
Jill-Jênn Vie	Inria, France
Martin Víta	Fyzikální ústav AV ČR, Czechia
Beilun Wang	Southeast University, China
Chuan-Ju Wang	Academia Sinica, Taiwan
Hongzhi Wang	Harbin Institute of Technology, China
Jiahai Wang	Sun Yat-sen University, China
Lidan Wang	University of Maryland, USA

Ning Wang	School of Computer Science & Technology, Beijing Jiaotong University, China
Sen Wang	The University of Queensland, Australia
Sheng Wang	Wuhan University, China
Shoujin Wang	Macquarie University, Australia
Xiaoli Wang	Xiamen University, China
Zihan Wang	University of Amsterdam, Netherlands
Mirjam Wattenhofer	Google, USA
Hua Wei	Arizona State University, USA
Shi-ting Wen	NingboTech University, China
Avani Wildani	Emory University, USA
Liang Wu	LinkedIn, USA
Xianchao Wu	NVIDIA, Japan
Yinghui Wu	Case Western Reserve University, USA
Shan Xue	Macquarie University, Australia
Shaofu Yang	Southeast University, China
Huaiyuan Yao	Xi'an Jiaotong University, China
Qihang Yao	Georgia Institute of Technology, USA
Dongxiao Yu	Shandong University, China
Philipp Zech	University of Innsbruck, Austria
Li Zhang	University College London, UK
Mengxuan Zhang	Australian National University, Australia
Xiaohan Zhang	Sony, USA
Chen Zhao	Baylor University, USA
Yanchang Zhao	CSIRO, Australia
Kaiping Zheng	National University of Singapore, Singapore
Hong Zhou	Meta, USA
Xiaofei Zhou	University of Chinese Academy of Sciences & Institute of Information Engineering, Chinese Academy of Sciences, China
Chaoyuan Zuo	Nankai University, China

Additional Reviewers, Applied Data Science Track

Naveed Ahmad	CISUC, Portugal
André Artelt	Bielefeld University, Germany
Nardine Basta	Macquarie University, Australia
Chaitanya Belwal	Microsoft, USA
Argheesh Bhanot	Université Savoie Mont Blanc, France
V Divya Bhargavi	Amazon, USA
Mina Bikhit	Opole University of Technology, Poland

Roland Bolboaca	George Emil Palade University of Medicine, Pharmacy, Science and Technology of Târgu Mureş, Romania
Nandhakishore C S	Indian Institute of Technology Madras, India
Juan Antonio Caballero Hernández	University of Cadiz, Spain
Alessio Cascione	University of Pisa, Italy
Sayak Chakrabarty	Northwestern University, USA
Xiaosong Chen	University of Macau, Macao SAR
Liza Chetouani	LIPN Laboratory CNRS UMR 7030, France
Winston Chou	Netflix, USA
Martino Ciaperoni	Scuola Normale Superiore, Italy
Guillaume Coulaud	Montpellier University, France
Gheorghe Marian Craioveanu	University of Science and Technology Politehnica Bucharest, Romania
Paolo Cupini	Politecnico di Milano, Italy
Fernando De Meer Pardo	IDSIA, Switzerland
Changxu Duan	Technische Universität Darmstadt, Germany
Mohammad El Sakka	Institute of Computer Science of Toulouse (IRIT), France
Yuval Felendler	Ben-Gurion University of the Negev, Israel
Alessio Ferone	University of Naples Parthenope, Italy
Amaury Fierens	UCLouvain, Belgium
Erick Fiestas Sorogastua	University of Tartu, Estonia
Preetam Ghosh	Tata Consultancy Services Limited, India
Massimiliano Giordano Orsini	University of Naples Parthenope, Italy
Aleksandra Grzelik	Systems Research Institute, Polish Academy of Sciences, Poland
Vamshi Guduguntla	Google, USA
Yujiang He	University of Kassel, Germany
Jisoo Jang	Seoul National University, Korea
Dwipam Katariya	Capital One, USA
Jaskaran Kawatra	GOSH, UK
Daniyal Kazempour	CAU Kiel, Germany
Reeshad Khan	University of Arkansas, Fayetteville, USA
Naman Khetan	Amazon, India
Valentin Lafargue	IMT/ANITI/Inria, France
Chunxiao Lai	Wuhan University of Technology, China
Cheonwoo Lee	KAIST, Korea
Weixian Li	University of Edinburgh, UK
Xinjie Li	Singapore Management University, Singapore
Shen Liang	Université Paris Cité, France

Yuansan Liu	The University of Melbourne, Australia
Yiming Ma	Harbin Institute of Technology, China
Malek Mahjoub	INSA LYON, France
Lorenzo Mannocci	UNIPI, Italy
Jacopo Massa	University of Pisa, Italy
Riccardo Massidda	Università di Pisa, Italy
Giovanni Mauro	Scuola Normale Superiore, Italy
Aurélien Mayoue	CEA LIST, France
Paul Minchella	Université Lumière Lyon 2, France
Lisa Mitford	University of London, South Africa
Doaa Mohamed	Ruhr-Universität Bochum, Germany
Simone Monaco	Politecnico di Torino, Italy
Virginia Morini	Università di Pisa, Italy
Bahrul Nasution	The University of Manchester, UK
Thanh Nguyen	Vietnam National University, Vietnam
Kadir-Kaan Özer	Mercedes-Benz AG, Germany
Roberto Pellungrini	University of Pisa, Italy
Giulia Perciballi	Sorbonne University, France
Dylan Perdigão	University of Coimbra, Portugal
Lukáš Petrželka	FIT CTU, Czechia
Simone Piaggesi	University of Pisa, Italy
Laura Pollacci	University of Pisa, Italy
Sovan Pradhan	Indian Institute of Technology Patna, India
Andrea Pugnana	University of Trento, Italy
Peng Qiao	NUDT, China
Alex Romanova	Graph AI Studio, USA
Daniela Rotelli	Sorbonne Université, France
Prasenjeet Roy	IITJ, India
Arush Sachdeva	IIIT Hyderabad, India
Lou Salaün	Nokia Bell Labs, France
Mattia Setzu	University of Pisa, Italy
Rong Shan	Shanghai Jiao Tong University, China
Niv Shinhar	Trustpilot, Denmark
Aleksei Shmelev	AXXX, HSE University, Russia
Kevin Sidak	University of Vienna, Austria
Apoorva Singh	FONDAZIONE BRUNO KESSLER, Italy
Punit Singh	IIT Patna, India
Hans Farrell Soegeng	NTU, Singapore
Daniel Sorensen	imec, KU Leuven, Belgium
Stefania Stan	UBS, Switzerland
Judith Staudner	University of Vienna, Austria
Felix Stillger	Bergische Universität Wuppertal, Germany

Xu Sun	Orange Research; Université Caen Normandie, ENSICAEN, CNRS, Normandie Univ, GREYC UMR6072, F-14000 Caen, France
Hendra Suryanto	RDC.AI, Australia
Golnaz Taheri	KTH, Sweden
Ziauddin Ursani	University of Liverpool, UK
Aman Verma	Indian Institute of Technology Delhi, India
Jaya Verma	IIT Patna, India
Jialou Wang	Northumbria University, UK
Yutong Wang	University of California, Davis, USA
Vihanga Wijayasekara	Robert Gordon University, UK
Nick Wils	University of Antwerp, Belgium
Xiaojie Yang	The University of Tokyo, Japan
Akihiro Yoshida	Institute of Science Tokyo, Japan
Dorottya Zelenyanszki	Griffith University, Australia
Peng Zhu	Tongji University, China

Sponsors

Main

Altilia

Internet&Idee
your solving company

Platinum

Google

ASML

Preply

bsi

eng

protom
THE FIRST ITALIAN KTI COMPANY

SovranoAI

Gold

LOGO GRAMMA

mare group

data

CAMBRIDGE
UNIVERSITY PRESS & ASSESSMENT

LAMARR
INSTITUTE FOR MACHINE LEARNING AND ARTIFICIAL INTELLIGENCE

Other Sponsors

Artificial Intelligence
www.elsevier.com/locate/artint

Springer

NEC
\Orchestrating a brighter world

LUTECH

Keynotes

Rethinking the Role of Scientific Discovery in the Era of AI

Mihaela van der Schaar

University of Cambridge, UK

Abstract. The growing availability of large-scale scientific datasets creates opportunities for discovery that are no longer driven by narrowly specified research questions. Instead, science increasingly unfolds through sustained exploration of vast, high-dimensional hypothesis spaces, where multiple explanations, mechanisms, and associations may remain plausible. I refer to this mode of inquiry as hypothesis hunting: an open-ended, cumulative search for insight that challenges traditional, pipeline-based models of scientific discovery.

In this talk, I present a framework that rethinks discovery as an agentic process, in which networks of interacting AI agents and human experts jointly explore, critique, and refine hypotheses under shared norms of evaluation. I will discuss how heterogeneous, LLM-based research agents can self-organize into evolving networks that generate, review, and extend findings—trading off novelty, quality, and diversity over time. Drawing on results from biomedical discovery, including cancer cohort analyses, I will argue that such socially structured agent networks can sustain large-scale exploratory discovery, complementing experimental science while reshaping how knowledge is generated, accumulated, and validated in the era of AI.

Neural Networks and Algorithms

Stefanie Jegelka

TU Munich, Germany

Abstract. Deep Learning models are now mastering increasingly complex tasks that consist of many steps of computation or reasoning. This inspires the perspective of viewing neural networks as learning algorithmic procedures. What could we gain from this perspective? This talk will outline examples and directions. First, an algorithmic view can help understand the capabilities of deep learning models, such as self-correction or the ability to solve certain optimization problems. Second, it can help understand how to design and train models to better solve challenging tasks, from optimization problems to reasoning. Yet, while this view has led to many advances, several open questions remain.

From Dialogue to Decision: Orchestrating Agents for Conversational Data Exploration and Multi-objective Optimization

Sihem Amer-Yahia

CNRS, Université Grenoble Alpes, France

Abstract. Modern scientific discovery and decision-making necessitate agents capable of navigating both complex datasets and multifaceted, often conflicting, goal landscapes. This talk explores the intersection of conversational data exploration, an incremental process where agents help users articulate needs through data interaction, and multi-objective sequential decision making. While traditional Reinforcement Learning (RL) has advanced task-specific agent training, we are witnessing a paradigm shift toward zero-shot orchestration. By leveraging a spectrum of techniques, from specialized RL policies to general-purpose Large Language Models (LLMs), we can reuse existing single-objective policies to solve complex multi-objective problems without training from scratch. We will discuss empirical evidence from the field of Education showing that this orchestrated approach can achieve competitive Pareto quality while reducing computational cost. The talk concludes by examining open research questions regarding how LLM context richness and reflective foresight enable agents to bridge the gap between incremental data-driven insights and optimal sequential actions.

AI Ethics and Governance

Francesca Rossi

IBM Research, USA

Abstract. Supported by AI, we will be able to make more grounded decisions and to focus on the main values and goals of a decision process rather than on routine and repetitive tasks. However, such a powerful technology also raises some concerns, related to privacy, fairness, value alignment, explainability, accountability, transparency, misinformation, deep fakes, copyright, and much more. These concerns are among the obstacles that hold AI back or that cause worry for current AI users, adopters, and policy makers. Without concrete answers to these questions, many will not trust AI, and therefore will not fully adopt it nor get its positive impact. In this talk I will present the main issues around AI ethics and safety and how they have evolved over the years, as AI capabilities advanced. I will also discuss the ROI of AI ethics, discussing both instrumental and value-based approaches to investing in AI ethics and governance.

The AI Ghosts and Us: Machine Writing as a Spectral Culture

Gianni Riotta

Luiss University, Italy

Abstract. We need a radically new philosophical reading of AI-generated text as a "Ghost" inhabiting contemporary human discourse. Rather than framing large language models (LLMs) as either tools or autonomous intelligences, we can argue that machine writing constitutes a spectral hybrid—neither fully human nor purely artificial, but a liminal presence emerging from the archive of human language. Drawing on Calvino's reflections on combinatorial literature and the "writing machine," we should revisit the Twentieth-century intuition that narrative could be algorithmically permuted. Calvino saw in literary algorithms both a liberation and a paradox: the machine multiplies possibilities, yet meaning still depends on human interpretation. Today's LLMs operationalize that combinatorial dream at a planetary scale, transforming statistical inference into prose and blurring the boundary between author and reader

Karpathy's notion of neural networks encoding patterns learned from data, rather than an explicit set of rules, reveals how AI systems internalize collective textual memory. The model does not "think" as a subject; it resonates. What appears as originality is a probabilistic echo of cultural sediment. The AI text thus resembles a revenant: language returning to us transformed and detached from any single living author. Revisiting Wiener's cybernetic theory, we could situate LLMs within feedback loops between humans and machines. The literary output of an AI is not an artificial substitute for human creativity, nor a counterfeit consciousness. It is a ghostly hybrid, generated at the intersection of human archives, algorithmic training, and real-time, effective prompts. By conceiving AI text as a cultural ghost, we compose a vocabulary in the age of machine writing. The challenge is not to deny the ghost nor to romanticize it, but to learn how to read and live with its spectral presence in our world.

Contents

Research Track Vision Applications

RA-MoE: Region-Aware Mixture-of-Experts for AU-Guided Micro-expression Recognition

Xiaohan Ren[1], Pengfei Duan[1,2(✉)], Mingru Huang[1,2], and Shengwu Xiong[1,2]

[1] School of Computer Science and Artificial Intelligence, Wuhan University of Technology, Wuhan 430070, China
duanpf@whut.edu.cn

[2] Sanya Science and Education Innovation Park, Wuhan University of Technology, Sanya 572000, China

Abstract. Micro-expression recognition (MER) aims to capture faint, short-lived facial expressions, yet their localized nature poses challenges for representation learning. This task has two intrinsic difficulties. First, discriminative micro-expression patterns are region-specific, requiring localized facial priors. Second, the contribution of heterogeneous cues is sample-dependent, making fixed fusion strategies inadequate for handling varying feature reliability. These issues result in under-exploited local patterns and inflexible integration of diverse evidence. The former makes it difficult to focus on expression-relevant local regions, while the latter ignores the sample-dependent reliability variation of different feature streams. To address these issues, we propose a **R**egion-**A**ware Mixture-**o**f-**E**xperts framework (**RA-MoE**), for micro-expression recognition. Specifically, the proposed framework contains three complementary experts for modeling global appearance, temporal motion, and local facial regions, respectively. To inject localized priors, we introduce a lightweight RegionNet that converts AU-derived supervision into sample-specific region weights, which are further used to generate soft masks for local feature modulation. To handle the varying reliability of heterogeneous cues, we design a dynamic gating router that adaptively estimates the contribution of each expert on a per-sample basis. Experiments on three benchmarks, including CASME II, SAMM, and $CAS(ME)^3$, demonstrate the effectiveness of the proposed framework. The code will be available at https://github.com/Momo-fg/RA-Moe.

Keywords: Micro-expression Recognition · Action Unit · Mixture-of-Experts

M. Ceci et al. (Eds.): ECML PKDD 2026, LNAI 16948, pp. 3–19, 2027.
https://doi.org/10.1007/978-3-032-37679-4_1

1 Introduction

Micro-expression recognition (MER) aims to identify subtle and short-lived facial expressions that can reveal genuine affective states. Compared with macro-expressions, it has lower intensity, shorter duration, and stronger locality [23], making discriminative cues difficult to capture; low resolution, illumination variation, and individual differences further exacerbate this difficulty [1,12], so learning robust representations remains a challenge in affective computing (Fig. 1).

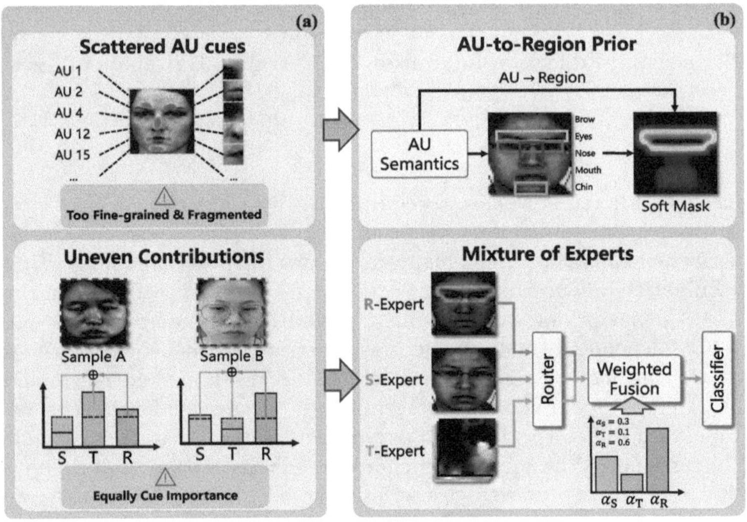

Fig. 1. Conceptual overview of the proposed RA-MoE framework.(a) MER suffers from two challenges: AU cues are too fine-grained and fragmented to be directly used as stable spatial priors, and heterogeneous cues contribute unevenly across samples. (b) RA-MoE addresses these issues by mapping AU semantics to region-level priors for soft-mask generation, and by adaptively fusing region, static, and temporal experts through a dynamic weight mixture-of-experts framework.

Recent MER methods mostly adopt multi-stream architectures to combine appearance and motion cues [5,10,28], but they suffer from two limitations. First, they insufficiently exploit localized facial priors from AU annotations. Since AU annotations cannot be directly aligned with facial feature maps as stable spatial priors, existing methods typically treat them as auxiliary supervision [16], lacking flexible sample-specific region-level guidance. Second, they rely on static fusion strategies that assume fixed contributions of each branch and cannot adapt to variations in cue reliability across samples.

To address these issues, we propose an AU-guided Region-Aware Mixture-of-Experts framework (**RA-MoE**), which includes three expert branches to model global appearance, temporal motion, and local facial deformations, respectively [21,29]. A lightweight RegionNet is introduced to convert AU-derived supervision into region-level facial priors, generating soft masks for local feature modulation and realizing explicit and flexible injection of AU knowledge. To handle the sample-dependent reliability of heterogeneous cues, we introduce a dynamic MoE fusion mechanism, which adaptively estimates the contribution of each expert branch for each sample through a gating router and aggregates features accordingly [6]. RegionNet is trained separately and then fixed, with only the expert branches and gating router optimized. RA-MoE combines region prior learning and adaptive fusion to provide a unified framework for robust MER.

The main contributions of this work are summarized as follows:

- We propose an AU-guided RegionNet, which converts AU annotations into region-level facial priors and provides sample-specific region-level guidance for local feature modulation without requiring pixel-level labels.
- We propose the RA-MoE framework, which jointly models global appearance, temporal motion, and local facial regions, and realizes adaptive expert fusion through a dynamic gating router.
- Experiments on CASME II, SAMM, and CAS(ME)^3 demonstrate the effectiveness of the proposed method, and further analyses confirm the roles of the region prior and adaptive fusion.

2 Related Work

Micro-expression recognition (MER) remains challenging due to the extremely low intensity and short duration of facial muscle movements. To capture such subtle dynamics, prior studies explore motion-sensitive cues such as optical flow, motion magnification, and transfer learning-based enhancement strategies [7,25–27,35]. Although these methods improve sensitivity to weak motions, many still rely on global representations and encode redundant or non-discriminative facial information.

In macro-expression recognition, the Action Units (AUs) of the Facial Action Coding System (FACS) serve as an intermediate representation that reduces the ambiguity of emotion labels and improves model stability [3,11,16]. However, directly transferring multi-task models that predict high-dimensional AU labels to MER is impractical due to the extremely limited sample size, often causing severe overfitting. To leverage AU-related priors, recent MER methods adopt region-aware designs. For example, SODA4MER enhances deformation perception using muscle-group priors and oriented deformation learning, while MER-CLIP converts AU annotations into text to guide spatiotemporal learning via visionlanguage alignment [18,34]. FED-PsyAU models structured AU coordination for hierarchical motion representation [9]. These methods demonstrate the value of AU-related supervision, but they mainly use AU information as deformation priors, cross-modal semantic guidance, or structured relational cues. In contrast, our method does not directly predict AUs or align AU semantics with textual supervision. Instead, RegionNet transforms AU annotations into region-level priors that can be spatially aligned with facial feature maps and used for sample-specific local feature modulation. This design aims to provide anatomically meaningful guidance while reducing the sparsity and instability of direct AU-level supervision under limited MER data.

Concurrently, multi-stream architectures, such as dual-stream [5,28] or triple-stream networks [10], have become the mainstream paradigm in MER to integrate complementary cues like spatial appearance and temporal motion [21,38,40]. Yet, their reliance on static fusion assumes constant branch reliability, leaving them vulnerable to environmental factors (e.g., illumination, low resolution) and sample-level fluctuations, which can introduce noise into final predictions.

3 Method

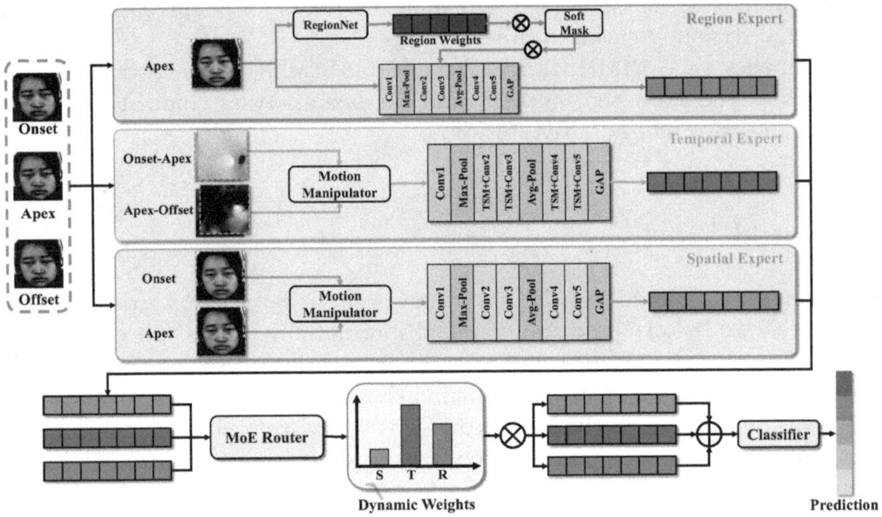

Fig. 2. Overview of the proposed RA-MoE framework. The model takes onset, apex, and offset frames as input and extracts complementary appearance, motion, and local region features through the S-Expert, T-Expert, and R-Expert, respectively. RegionNet generates a sample-specific soft mask for local feature modulation, and the three expert features are adaptively fused by an MoE router for final micro-expression recognition.

3.1 Overview

To improve spatial selectivity toward key active facial regions and the adaptive integration of heterogeneous expression cues, we propose a **R**egion-**A**ware **M**ixture-**o**f-**E**xperts model (**RA-MoE**), as illustrated in Fig. 2. Given three key frames, namely the onset, apex, and offset frames, RA-MoE is built upon three complementary expert branches: Global Static Expert (**S-Expert**), Global

Temporal Expert (**T-Expert**), and Region Guided Expert (**R-Expert**). The S-Expert captures holistic appearance and spatial structural cues from facial frames. The T-Expert models short-term facial motion based on optical flow across key-frame intervals. The R-Expert focuses on fine-grained local deformations in expression-relevant facial regions. To better exploit localized facial priors, a pretrained **RegionNet** is introduced into the R-Expert branch to predict region-wise importance weights, which are combined with predefined facial region masks to construct a sample-specific soft mask for feature modulation. After feature extraction, the representations from the three experts are fed into a **MoE router**, which dynamically estimates the contribution of each expert for the current sample and adaptively fuses them into a unified representation for final micro-expression classification.

3.2 AU-Guided Facial Region Network

Micro-expressions are typically manifested through subtle muscle movements concentrated in a few facial regions. However, existing methods often lack explicit spatial guidance for local feature learning. As a result, discriminative local deformations may be insufficiently captured and can be easily disturbed by identity-related patterns or irrelevant background responses. To address this issue, we introduce an AU-Guided Facial Region Network (**RegionNet**) to provide region-level priors for the downstream R-Expert (Fig. 3).

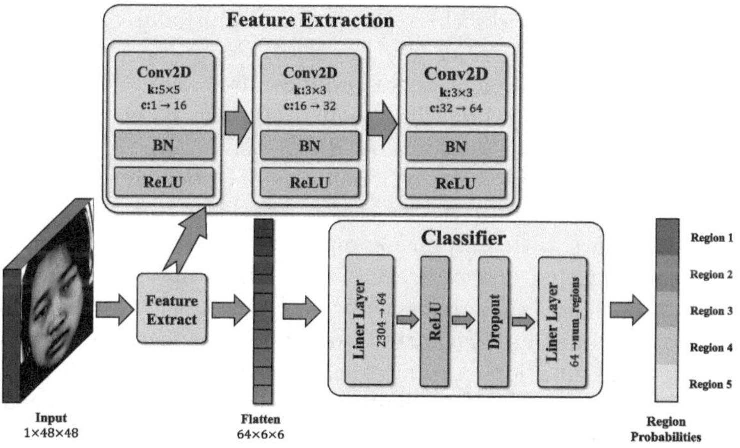

Fig. 3. Architecture of the proposed RegionNet. Given apex frame, RegionNet predicts a five-dimensional region activation vector from AU-derived supervision, which is further used to construct a sample-specific soft mask for local feature modulation.

The main idea of RegionNet is to use Action Unit (AU) semantics as a bridge between facial muscle movements and anatomical regions. Inspired by prior local sub-region based AU analysis [36], we adopt a region-level formulation rather than directly modeling AU-wise priors. This is because AU labels mainly describe fine-grained muscle actions, whereas the downstream recognition network requires a stable spatial representation that can be directly aligned with feature maps. Moreover, AU-level prediction leads to a finer and sparser supervision target, which is less robust under limited micro-expression data. In addition, grouping multiple related AUs into a few anatomically coherent facial regions reduces prediction complexity while remaining consistent with the localized nature of micro-expressions. Therefore, mapping AU semantics to facial regions provides a more compact, stable, and practically effective prior representation for downstream local feature modulation.

Given an apex frame $\mathbf{I} \in \mathbb{R}^{1\times H\times W}$, RegionNet predicts a five-dimensional region activation vector

$$\mathbf{r} = \left[r_{\text{brow}}, r_{\text{eye}}, r_{\text{nose}}, r_{\text{mouth}}, r_{\text{chin}}\right]^{\top} \in [0,1]^5, \tag{1}$$

where each element denotes the activation confidence of a predefined facial region. These five regions are defined according to AU-related anatomical semantics, such that discrete AU annotations can be projected onto region-level supervision. For example, AU1 and AU2 are mapped to the brow region, while AU12 and AU15 are mapped to the mouth region (a detailed mapping table between all considered AUs and the five facial regions is provided in the Appendix). In this way, RegionNet learns sample-specific region activations that identify which facial areas are more likely to contain expression-relevant deformations.

RegionNet is architected as a lightweight prior generator rather than a standalone recognizer. It comprises three stacked convolutional blocks for feature extraction and a compact classifier for region prediction. Specifically, the input image undergoes a 5×5 convolution to produce 16-channel maps, followed by two 3×3 convolutions expanding dimensions to 32 and 64 channels, with each layer employing batch normalization and ReLU activation. These features are then fed into a classifier consisting of a fully connected layer, ReLU, dropout, and a linear projection to output the region activation vector. This compact design estimates priors with minimal computational overhead. The predicted vector is not used directly for classification. Instead, it combines with predefined facial masks to construct a sample-specific soft mask, which modulates intermediate feature maps in the R-Expert. This explicitly injects AU-guided region priors into local representation learning, focusing the model on informative facial areas. RegionNet is trained independently and fixed during recognition, ensuring it learns stable AU-guided priors rather than task-specific emotion-driven attention. Detailed procedures are provided in Sect. 3.4.

3.3 MoE Model

Following the architectural overview, this section details the structural design of the three expert branches and their integration mechanism.

Global Static Expert. The Global Static Expert captures discriminative spatial features by encoding structural deformations at the expression peak. To emphasize subtle myogenic contractions, we employ a motion magnification network [20] to amplify the pixel-level displacements between the onset (I_{on}) and apex (I_{ap}) frames. The synthesized magnified frame $I_{mag} \in \mathbb{R}^{C\times H\times W}$ is then processed by a convolutional encoder $\mathcal{F}_S(\cdot)$, followed by global average pooling (GAP) to derive the spatial feature $\mathbf{f}_i^{\mathrm{S}}$:

$$\mathbf{f}_i^{\mathrm{S}} = \mathrm{GAP}(\mathcal{F}_S(I_{mag})) \tag{2}$$

where $\mathcal{F}_S(\cdot)$ denotes the static feature extractor. This representation captures the intensity and spatial distribution of facial muscle deformations, supplying the gating network with static morphological cues.

Global Temporal Expert. The Global Temporal Expert models the dynamic evolution of micro-expressions. Given their rapid and transient nature, this branch captures spatiotemporal logic within a 2D convolutional architecture. Following the optical flow branch of TSCNN [24], input motion features are computed via the TV-L1 algorithm [32]. Specifically, we stack horizontal (u) and vertical (v) optical flow components from two critical intervals—onset-to-apex and apex-to-offset—forming a four-channel representation. These maps are divided into $T = 2$ temporal segments to isolate the motion dynamics of the expression's rising and fading phases. To enable cross-frame communication without additional parameters, a Temporal Shift Module (TSM) [13] is embedded, shifting 1/8 of the channels bi-directionally to fuse adjacent motion information. At the branch end, a temporal consensus module $\mathcal{G}_T$ aggregates these partitioned features. Specifically, features from both intervals are reshaped into a segment-wise tensor $\mathbf{X}' \in \mathbb{R}^{N\times 2\times C}$ and average-pooled to extract a unified representation. This process filters stochastic noise and captures consistent temporal patterns. The resulting motion feature $\mathbf{f}_i^{\mathrm{T}}$ is formulated as:

$$\mathbf{f}_i^{\mathrm{T}} = \mathrm{Squeeze}(\mathrm{AvgPool}(\mathbf{X}')) \tag{3}$$

By aggregating the stacked optical flow maps, this feature captures consistent temporal patterns of facial muscle movements, providing the gating network with discriminative temporal cues.

Facial Region Expert. The facial region expert branch, referred to as the Region expert, aims to achieve sample-adaptive local feature mining by utilizing the RegionNet pretrained in Sect. 3.2. Unlike global branches, it focuses on fine-grained modeling by converting anatomical priors into sample-adaptive region guidance. Specifically, the branch utilizes RegionNet to predict a five-dimensional region weight vector $\mathbf{r}$ for the current apex frame I_{ap}. To convert these region weights into a region-level spatial guidance map, the model performs a weighted aggregation of the vector $\mathbf{r}$ with five facial-landmark-aligned binary masks $\{\mathbf{M}_k\}_{k=1}^{5}$ to generate a sample-adaptive soft mask $\mathbf{A}_i \in \mathbb{R}^{1\times H\times W}$:

$$\mathbf{A}_i = \sum_{k=1}^{5} r_k \cdot \mathbf{M}_k, \tag{4}$$

where r_k denotes the activation confidence of the k-th region. These masks are anatomically defined and aligned to each face using facial landmarks, covering five key areas: the brows, eyes, nose, mouth, and chin. The core of this branch lies in the feature-level modulation mechanism. This branch performs region enhancement within the feature space to refine local representations. Specifically, the intermediate feature map $\mathbf{F}_i^a$ is coupled with the mask $\mathbf{A}_i$ through element-wise multiplication to obtain the modulated representation $\widetilde{\mathbf{F}}_i^a$:

$$\widetilde{\mathbf{F}}_i^a = \mathbf{F}_i^a \odot \mathbf{A}_i. \tag{5}$$

This operation suppresses expression-irrelevant background noise and explicitly strengthens feature responses in key anatomical regions. Subsequently, $\widetilde{\mathbf{F}}_i^a$ is processed by a dedicated convolutional encoder for deep feature mapping, ultimately generating the local expert feature $\mathbf{f}_i^{\mathrm{R}}$ for MoE dynamic fusion.

Dynamic Fusion Strategy. After extracting $\mathbf{f}_i^{\mathrm{S}}$, $\mathbf{f}_i^{\mathrm{T}}$, and $\mathbf{f}_i^{\mathrm{R}}$, the framework adaptively integrates these heterogeneous signals. In micro-expression recognition, discriminative cues vary across samples: some are characterized by subtle motion, while others rely on localized anatomical deformations. Consequently, fixed-weight fusion or simple concatenation is insufficient, as it fails to account for the varying reliability of different experts. To address this, we implement a dynamic gating-based fusion strategy that assigns sample-specific importance weights to each expert. Since these features originate from distinct domains, namely spatial structure, temporal dynamics, and anatomical regions, their distributional characteristics and semantic manifolds vary significantly. The model first projects them into a unified latent space via linear mapping functions $\phi(\cdot)$ for feature alignment:

$$\mathbf{z}_i^k = \phi_k(\mathbf{f}_i^k), \quad k \in \{S, T, R\}, \tag{6}$$

where $\mathbf{z}_i^k$ represents the aligned embedding vectors. Subsequently, these features are concatenated and fed into a gating network G. A Softmax activation predicts the reliability scores, yielding the weight vector $\boldsymbol{\alpha}_i = [\alpha_i^{\mathrm{S}}, \alpha_i^{\mathrm{T}}, \alpha_i^{\mathrm{R}}]$:

$$\boldsymbol{\alpha}_i = \mathrm{Softmax}\Big(G\big([\mathbf{z}_i^{\mathrm{S}}; \mathbf{z}_i^{\mathrm{T}}; \mathbf{z}_i^{\mathrm{R}}]\big)\Big). \tag{7}$$

The constraint $\sum_{k\in\{S,T,R\}} \alpha_i^k = 1$ ensures that the weights reflect each expert's relative importance for the given sample, effectively implementing sample-level dynamic routing. Finally, the expert embeddings are aggregated through a weighted sum to obtain a unified discriminative representation $\mathbf{F}_i$:

$$\mathbf{F}_i = \sum_{k\in\{S,T,R\}} \alpha_i^k \cdot \mathbf{z}_i^k. \tag{8}$$

The fused vector $\mathbf{F}_i$ integrates complementary information from the global static, temporal, and region experts, and is then fed into a classification head for final prediction. In this framework, the MoE router performs sample-specific weighting over the three expert branches, enabling adaptive fusion of heterogeneous cues according to the characteristics of the input sample.

3.4 Training Strategy

To incorporate AU-guided region priors into micro-expression recognition, we adopt a decoupled two-stage training strategy. RegionNet and the RA-MoE recognizer are optimized under distinct supervision targets: RegionNet predicts region-level facial priors from AU-derived labels, while the recognizer utilizes emotion category labels. End-to-end joint training may cause RegionNet to drift from AU-guided facial muscle patterns, resulting in attention that no longer reflects the underlying facial motion patterns. To avoid this, we train RegionNet independently as a prior generator and freeze its parameters during the subsequent recognition stage, where it provides sample-specific region-level guidance for downstream feature learning.

Stage I: AU-Guided Region Prior Learning. RegionNet is trained as a robust region prior generator to predict a five-dimensional regional activation probability vector $\mathbf{r}$. Given a grayscale facial frame $\mathbf{x} \in \mathbb{R}^{48\times 48}$, the prediction is formulated as:

$$\mathbf{r} = \sigma(\mathbf{W}_r \mathbf{x} + \mathbf{b}_r) \in [0,1]^5, \tag{9}$$

where r_k denotes the activation confidence of a predefined facial region R_k (i.e., brow, eye, nose, mouth, and chin). To expand the training pool and improve robustness, we utilize all three key frames (onset, apex, and offset) as supervision, since the AU-related anatomical activations remain consistent across the sequence. The ground-truth label $\mathbf{y} \in \{0,1\}^5$ is derived from AU annotations via FACS mapping: $y_k = 1$ if any active AU corresponds to R_k, and $y_k = 0$ otherwise. The model is optimized using a weighted binary cross-entropy (WCE) loss:

$$\mathcal{L}_{\text{region}} = -\sum_{k=1}^{5} \omega_k \left[y_k \log r_k + (1 - y_k) \log(1 - r_k) \right], \tag{10}$$

where $\omega_k = 1/\text{freq}(R_k)$ is an inverse frequency weight to mitigate activation sparsity. After training convergence, RegionNet parameters are frozen, and $\mathbf{r}$ serves as a region weighting vector to provide region-level spatial guidance in the subsequent recognition stage.

Stage II: RA-MoE with Frozen RegionNet. In this stage, the RegionNet parameters are frozen, and its output region weighting vector is used to provide region-level guidance. The S, T, and R-Experts, together with the dynamic gating router, are jointly trained under a weighted multi-class Focal Loss:

$$\mathcal{L}_{\text{cls}} = -\sum_{c=1}^{C} \omega_c (1 - P_c)^{\gamma} \hat{y}_c \log P_c, \tag{11}$$

where P_c denotes the predicted probability for class c, $\hat{y}_c$ is the one-hot label, γ is the focusing parameter that emphasizes hard-to-classify samples, and ω_c is a class-balanced weight inversely proportional to the number of samples in each class. During training, the gating router learns to assign adaptive importance weights to each expert, effectively balancing contributions from static appearance, temporal motion, and localized anatomical cues.

4 Experiments

4.1 Experimental Setup

Datasets
We evaluate our method on three spontaneous micro-expression datasets including CASME II [31], SAMM [2], and CAS(ME)^3 [8]. After preprocessing and quality control, we retain 245 samples from 26 subjects for CASME II, 133 samples from 29 subjects for SAMM, and 847 samples for CAS(ME)^3. Across all datasets, we adopt a unified 3-class protocol that categorizes happiness as positive, surprise as independent, and merges remaining negative emotions such as disgust and repression into the negative class. Beyond this 3-class setting, we also conduct 5-class experiments on CASME II and 7-class experiments on CAS(ME)^3 to further validate the robustness of our model. Finally, the Action Unit semantic annotations provided by all datasets are leveraged to supervise the training of our region modeling module, ensuring the extraction of anatomically relevant features.
Implementation Details
For each sample, we select the onset, apex, and offset frames as inputs. Facial regions are detected and cropped via RetinaFace [22], with all images subsequently resized to 128×128. To integrate anatomical priors, we predefine five relevant facial regions based on landmarks and generate corresponding five-channel masks. The RegionNet is trained independently as an auxiliary model to provide region-level supervision. It takes grayscale apex frames as input and utilizes AU region activation labels for multi-label learning. We adopt a leave-one-subject-out cross-validation protocol and apply an early stopping strategy based on the binary cross-entropy loss to prevent overfitting. During the primary RA-MoE model training, RegionNet remains frozen and provides sample-adaptive region weights for region-level guidance without participating in backpropagation. For the specific experts, the Global Static Expert and the Region-Guided Expert take inputs resized to 48×48, while the Global Temporal Expert extracts temporal features from optical flow fields computed between key frames. The entire framework is implemented in PyTorch and optimized using Adam on an NVIDIA RTX 4090 GPU. We set the learning rate to 1×10^{-3} and weight decay to 5×10^{-4}, with batch sizes of 16 for CASME II and SAMM, and 32 for CAS(ME)^3.
Metrics. The primary evaluation metrics are the Unweighted Average Recall (UAR) and the Unweighted F1-score (UF1), defined as follows:

$$UF1 = \frac{1}{C}\sum_{i=1}^{C}\frac{2 \times TP_i}{2 \times TP_i + FP_i + FN_i}, UAR = \frac{1}{C}\sum_{i=1}^{C}\frac{TP_i}{N_i}, \tag{12}$$

where C denotes the number of classes, TP_i, FP_i, and FN_i represent the true positives, false positives, and false negatives for the i-th class, respectively, and N_i is the total number of samples in the i-th class.

Table 1. Performance comparison on CAS(ME)^3 dataset under 3-class and 7-class settings. Results are reported in UF1 and UAR (%). The best results are highlighted in **bold**.

Method	# Classes	UF1	UAR
FR [37]	3	34.93	34.13
STSTNet [15]	3	37.95	37.92
RCN-A [30]	3	39.28	38.93
μ-BERT [19]	3	56.04	61.25
FED-PsyAU [9]	3	62.21	62.26
SKD-TSTSAN [39]	3	86.48	83.44
RA-MoE(Ours)	**3**	**90.30**	**87.33**
AlexNet [8]	7	17.59	18.01
AlexNet(+Depth) [8]	7	17.73	18.29
SFAMNet [14]	7	23.65	23.73
μ-BERT [19]	7	32.64	32.54
SKD-TSTSAN [39]	7	59.95	57.31
RA-MoE(Ours)	**7**	**60.95**	**58.54**

4.2 Comparison with State-of-the-Art Methods

We evaluate RA-MoE against representative MER methods on CASME II, SAMM, and CAS(ME)^3 using the standard LOSO protocol. Results are reported in Tables 2 and 1. For a fair comparison under consistent hardware and preprocessing pipelines, results for SKD-TSTSAN [39] are based on our reproduction using the author's official code, denoted with asterisks.

Overall, RA-MoE achieves consistent improvements across all settings. The simultaneous improvements in UF1 and UAR indicate that our framework enhances both global recognition accuracy and class-balanced performance. On CASME II, RA-MoE outperforms previous methods in both 5-class and 3-class scenarios, demonstrating its efficacy across varied category granularities. On SAMM, the consistent gains over the strongest baselines further confirm the model's generalization capability across different data distributions.

On CAS(ME)^3, RA-MoE obtains the best results under both the 3-class and 7-class settings. Since CAS(ME)^3 is larger and more diverse than traditional MER datasets, these results further support the robustness of the proposed framework in more challenging scenarios. At the same time, the relatively smaller margin under the 7-class setting also suggests that fine-grained MER remains difficult, and that more complex class confusion still limits the overall performance of existing methods.

In summary, these gains confirm that robust MER benefits from localized priors and adaptive fusion. Component-wise results appear in the ablation study.

Table 2. Performance comparison with state-of-the-art methods on CASME II and SAMM datasets. Results are reported in UF1 and UAR (%). The best results are highlighted in **bold**. * indicates our reproduction.

Method	CASME II (5c)		CASME II (3c)		SAMM (3c)	
	UF1	UAR	UF1	UAR	UF1	UAR
STSTNet [15]	–	–	83.82	86.86	65.88	68.10
TSCNN [24]	80.70	80.97	–	–	–	–
OFF-ApexNet [5]	–	–	86.97	88.28	54.09	53.92
SMA-STN [17]	79.46	82.59	–	–	–	–
FRL-DGT [33]	–	–	91.90	90.30	77.20	75.80
SelfME [4]	–	–	90.78	92.90	–	–
μ-BERT [19]	85.53	83.48	90.34	89.14	–	–
HTNet [26]	–	–	95.32	95.16	81.31	81.24
SODA4MER [34]	–	–	81.41	84.18	–	–
SKD-TSTSAN* [39]	85.84	84.11	97.39	97.55	92.31	89.49
RA-MoE(Ours)	**89.20**	**88.61**	**98.82**	**98.96**	**93.78**	**90.43**

4.3 Ablation Study

To systematically evaluate the contribution of each component in RA-MoE, we conduct ablation studies on the CASME II dataset under the LOSO protocol. As shown in Table 3, the results validate the roles of individual expert branches, the AU-to-Region prior transformation, the learned RegionNet prior and its freezing strategy, as well as the proposed MoE adaptive fusion mechanism. Here, "Region Prior" refers to the anatomically defined region weighting learned by RegionNet during the first-stage training, which is then used to guide the Region Expert in the second stage.

Table 3. Ablation study on CASME II dataset (LOSO protocol).

No.	S-Expert	T-Expert	R-Expert	Region Prior	AU-to-Region	Fusion Strategy	UF1	UAR
1	✓	–	–	–	–	Single Branch	82.95	82.12
2	–	✓	–	–	–	Single Branch	84.36	84.36
3	–	–	✓	–	–	Single Branch	71.02	68.83
4	✓	✓	✓	–	Direct AU Supervision	Static Concatenation	85.28	83.97
5	✓	✓	✓	No Prior	AU-to-Region	Static Concatenation	87.20	88.35
6	✓	✓	✓	Prior	AU-to-Region	Static Concatenation	88.19	86.39
7	✓	✓	✓	No Prior	AU-to-Region	MoE Dynamic Weighting	86.79	86.96
8	✓	✓	✓	Prior (Unfrozen)	AU-to-Region	MoE Dynamic Weighting	86.84	87.39
9	✓	✓	✓	Prior (Frozen)	AU-to-Region	MoE Dynamic Weighting	**89.20**	**88.61**

Effectiveness of Individual Expert Branches. The Global Temporal Expert (T-Expert) yields the highest performance among single-branch configurations, highlighting the dominance of temporal dynamics in micro-expression recognition. Although the Region Guided Expert (R-Expert) shows limited performance when operating in isolation, the substantial gains observed when integrating all three branches (Rows 4–9) demonstrate that the static appearance, dynamic temporal, and local AU features provide complementary discriminative cues. This synergy confirms the necessity of a multi-perspective modeling approach.
Rationality of AU-to-Region Spatial Prior Transformation. We then justify the proposed AU-to-Region design. Compared with direct AU supervision(Row 4), the AU-to-Region strategy leads to better performance (Rows 5–6), suggesting that directly using sparse AU labels is less effective for guiding local feature learning. By transforming AU semantics into region-level spatial priors, the model can provide more stable and anatomically meaningful guidance for the Region Expert.
Impact of Prior Region Knowledge. We further examine whether introducing prior region knowledge is beneficial for local representation learning. Compared with the variant without prior region initialization (Row 5), the model equipped with a pre-learned RegionNet prior (Row 6) achieves better overall performance. This suggests that learning anatomically grounded region weighting in advance provides more reliable region-level guidance for the Region Expert and improves the model's ability to capture subtle local facial deformations.
Effect of RegionNet Freezing Strategy. We further investigate whether the learned RegionNet region weights should remain trainable during the second-stage optimization. Compared with the unfrozen variant (Row 8), the frozen variant (Row 9) achieves better overall performance, suggesting that freezing helps preserve the learned anatomically grounded region weighting and provides more stable region-level guidance for downstream recognition.
Adaptive MoE Fusion vs. Static Concatenation. Finally, we compare the fusion strategies. Compared with static concatenation under the complete setting (Row 6), the proposed MoE adaptive weighting with frozen RegionNet prior (Row 9) achieves the best overall performance. This indicates that the contributions of different experts are sample-dependent, and dynamic weighting is more effective than fixed fusion for exploiting their complementarity.

4.4 Discussion

To further investigate the adaptive behavior of RegionNet, we visualize the generated soft masks and their corresponding overlays on representative apex frames in Fig. 4. Each column represents a unique sample, displaying the input apex frame, the predicted soft mask, and the combined overlay from top to bottom.

The visualization yields several key insights. First, the predicted masks exhibit significant sparsity, focusing on localized facial regions rather than a uniform distribution. Second, these response patterns demonstrate high sample-dependency, suggesting that RegionNet captures specific facial configurations

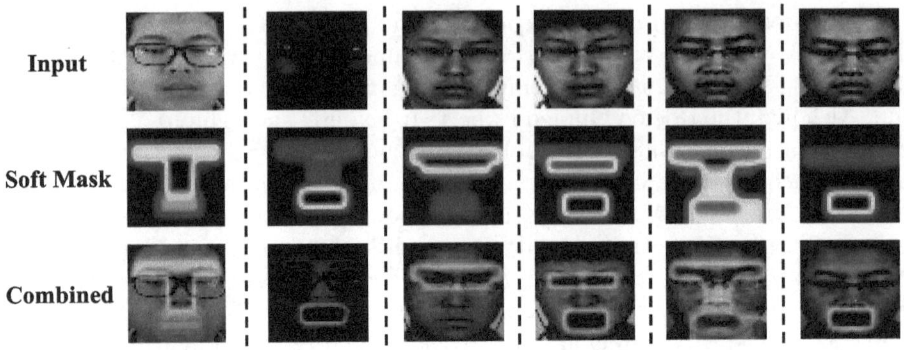

Fig. 4. Visual heatmaps of SoftMask obtained from RegionNet.

instead of relying on fixed anatomical templates. Third, the overlay results confirm that the model selectively emphasizes a subset of facial areas, which aligns with the sparse and localized nature of micro-expression muscle movements.

These observations substantiate the design objective of RegionNet as a provider of sample-specific region-level guidance for the R-Expert. While the visualization provides an intuitive qualitative assessment, it demonstrates that the learned region prior generates localized and input-varying responses. This adaptive focusing capability accounts for the performance gains observed in the ablation study, as it allows the model to effectively suppress irrelevant facial noise while emphasizing discriminative micro-expression regions.

5 Conclusion

This paper presents **RA-MoE**, a region-aware mixture-of-experts framework for micro-expression recognition. To address the insufficient use of localized facial priors and the limitation of fixed multi-stream fusion, we introduce an AU-guided RegionNet to generate sample-specific region priors and a dynamic gating router to adaptively fuse global appearance, temporal motion, and local region features. Experiments on CASME II, SAMM, and CAS(ME)^3 demonstrate the effectiveness of the proposed method, and further analyses verify the contributions of both the region prior and adaptive fusion. These results suggest that jointly modeling localized subtle cues and uneven cue contributions is important for robust micro-expression recognition. In future work, we plan to extend the proposed framework to investigate more general region prior learning strategies that can better transfer across datasets and recording conditions.

Acknowledgements. This work was supported in part by the Key Research and Development Program of Hubei Province (No. 2023BAB083) and the Open Project Program of Henan Key Laboratory of Oracle Bone Inscription Information Processing (No. OIP2024E003).

Disclosure of Interests. The authors have no competing interests to declare that are relevant to the content of this article.

References

1. Ben, X., et al.: Video-based facial micro-expression analysis: a survey of datasets, features and algorithms. IEEE Trans. Pattern Anal. Mach. Intell. **44**(9), 5826–5846 (2021)
2. Davison, A.K., Lansley, C., Costen, N., Tan, K., Yap, M.H.: SAMM: a spontaneous micro-facial movement dataset. IEEE Trans. Affect. Comput. **9**(1), 116–129 (2016)
3. Ekman, P., Friesen, W.V.: Facial action coding system. Environ. Psychol. Nonverbal Behav. (1978)
4. Fan, X., Chen, X., Jiang, M., Shahid, A.R., Yan, H.: SelfME: self-supervised motion learning for micro-expression recognition. In: Proceedings of the IEEE/CVF Conference on Computer Vision and Pattern Recognition, pp. 13834–13843 (2023)
5. Gan, Y.S., Liong, S.T., Yau, W.C., Huang, Y.C., Tan, L.K.: OFF-ApexNet on micro-expression recognition system. Sig. Process. Image Commun. **74**, 129–139 (2019)
6. Jacobs, R.A., Jordan, M.I., Nowlan, S.J., Hinton, G.E.: Adaptive mixtures of local experts. Neural Comput. **3**(1), 79–87 (1991)
7. Lei, L., Li, J., Chen, T., Li, S.: A novel graph-TCN with a graph structured representation for micro-expression recognition. In: Proceedings of the 28th ACM International Conference on Multimedia, pp. 2237–2245 (2020)
8. Li, J., et al.: CAS(ME)3: a third generation facial spontaneous micro-expression database with depth information and high ecological validity. IEEE Trans. Pattern Anal. Mach. Intell. **45**(3), 2782–2800 (2022)
9. Li, J., Qian, Y., Zhao, L., Wang, S.J.: FED-PsyAU: privacy-preserving micro-expression recognition via psychological AU coordination and dynamic facial motion modeling. In: Proceedings of the IEEE/CVF International Conference on Computer Vision, pp. 14453–14463 (2025)
10. Li, K., et al.: Three-stream convolutional neural network for micro-expression recognition. Aust. J. Intell. Inf. Process. Syst. **15**(3), 41–48 (2019)
11. Li, X., et al.: Towards reading hidden emotions: a comparative study of spontaneous micro-expression spotting and recognition methods. IEEE Trans. Affect. Comput. **9**(4), 563–577 (2017)
12. Li, Y., Huang, X., Zhao, G.: Joint local and global information learning with single apex frame detection for micro-expression recognition. IEEE Trans. Image Process. **30**, 249–263 (2020)
13. Lin, J., Gan, C., Han, S.: TSM: temporal shift module for efficient video understanding. In: Proceedings of the IEEE/CVF International Conference on Computer Vision, pp. 7083–7093 (2019)
14. Liong, G.B., Liong, S.T., Chan, C.S., See, J.: SFAMNet: a scene flow attention-based micro-expression network. Neurocomputing **566**, 126998 (2024)
15. Liong, S.T., Gan, Y.S., See, J., Khor, H.-Q., Huang, Y.-C.: Shallow triple stream three-dimensional CNN(STSTNet) for micro-expression recognition. In: 2019 14th IEEE International Conference on Automatic Face & Gesture Recognition (FG 2019), pp. 1–5. IEEE (2019)

16. Liu, F., Gu, L., Shi, C., Fu, X.: Action unit enhance dynamic facial expression recognition. In: Proceedings of the 33rd ACM International Conference on Multimedia, pp. 5597–5606 (2025)
17. Liu, J., Zheng, W., Zong, Y.: SMA-STN: segmented movement-attending spatiotemporal network forMicro-expression recognition (2020). arXiv preprint arXiv:2010.09342
18. Liu, S., Mao, X., Zhao, S., Li, P., Xu, T., Chen, E.: MER-CLIP: au-guided vision-language alignment for micro-expression recognition. IEEE Trans. Affect. Comput. (2025)
19. Nguyen, X.B., Duong, C.N., Li, X., Gauch, S., Seo, H.S., Luu, K.: Micron-BERT: BERT-based facial micro-expression recognition. In: Proceedings of the IEEE/CVF Conference on Computer Vision and Pattern Recognition, pp. 1482–1492 (2023)
20. Oh, T.H., et al.: Learning-based video motion magnification. In: Proceedings of the European Conference on Computer Vision (ECCV), pp. 633–648 (2018)
21. Reddy, S.P.T., Karri, S.T., Dubey, S.R., Mukherjee, S.: Spontaneous facial micro-expression recognition using 3D spatiotemporal convolutional neural networks. In: 2019 International Joint Conference on Neural Networks (IJCNN), pp. 1–8. IEEE (2019)
22. Serengil, S., Ozpinar, A.: A benchmark of facial recognition pipelines and co-usability performances of modules. J. Inf. Technol. **17**(2), 95–107 (2024)
23. Shen, X.B., Wu, Q., Fu, X.L.: Effects of the duration of expressions on the recognition of microexpressions. J. Zhejiang Univ. Sci. B **13**(3), 221–230 (2012)
24. Song, B., et al.: Recognizing spontaneous micro-expression using a three-stream convolutional neural network. IEEE Access **7**, 184537–184551 (2019)
25. Wang, S.J., et al.: Micro-expression recognition with small sample size by transferring long-term convolutional neural network. Neurocomputing **312**, 251–262 (2018)
26. Wang, Z., Zhang, K., Luo, W., Sankaranarayana, R.: HTNet for micro-expression recognition. Neurocomputing **602**, 128196 (2024)
27. Wei, M., Zheng, W., Zong, Y., Jiang, X., Lu, C., Liu, J.: A novel micro-expression recognition approach using attention-based magnification-adaptive networks. In: ICASSP 2022-2022 IEEE International Conference on Acoustics, Speech and Signal Processing (ICASSP), pp. 2420–2424. IEEE (2022)
28. Xia, B., Wang, S.: Micro-expression recognition enhanced by macro-expression from spatial-temporal domain. In: IJCAI, pp. 1186–1193 (2021)
29. Xia, Z., Hong, X., Gao, X., Feng, X., Zhao, G.: Spatiotemporal recurrent convolutional networks for recognizing spontaneous micro-expressions. IEEE Trans. Multimedia **22**(3), 626–640 (2019)
30. Xia, Z., Peng, W., Khor, H.Q., Feng, X., Zhao, G.: Revealing the invisible with model and data shrinking for composite-database micro-expression recognition. IEEE Trans. Image Process. **29**, 8590–8605 (2020)
31. Yan, W.J., et al.: CASME II: an improved spontaneous micro-expression database and the baseline evaluation. PLoS ONE **9**(1), e86041 (2014)
32. Zach, C., Pock, T., Bischof, H.: A duality based approach for realtime TV-L1 optical flow. In: Hamprecht, F.A., Schnörr, C., Jähne, B. (eds.) Pattern Recognition, pp. 214–223. Springer, Heidelberg (2007)
33. Zhai, Z., Zhao, J., Long, C., Xu, W., He, S., Zhao, H.: Feature representation learning with adaptive displacement generation and transformer fusion for micro-expression recognition. In: Proceedings of the IEEE/CVF Conference on Computer Vision and Pattern Recognition, pp. 22086–22095 (2023)

34. Zhang, B., Wang, X., Wang, C., He, G.: Dynamic stereotype theory induced micro-expression recognition with oriented deformation. In: Proceedings of the Computer Vision and Pattern Recognition Conference, pp. 10701–10711 (2025)
35. Zhang, J., et al.: Motion magnification multi-feature relation network for facial microexpression recognition. Complex Intell. Syst. **8**(4), 3363–3376 (2022)
36. Zhang, L., Arandjelovic, O., Hong, X.: Facial action unit detection with local key facial sub-region based multi-label classification for micro-expression analysis. In: Proceedings of the 1st Workshop on Facial Micro-Expression: Advanced Techniques for Facial Expressions Generation and Spotting, pp. 11–18 (2021)
37. Zhou, L., Mao, Q., Huang, X., Zhang, F., Zhang, Z.: Feature refinement: an expression-specific feature learning and fusion method for micro-expression recognition. Pattern Recogn. **122**, 108275 (2022)
38. Zhou, L., Mao, Q., Xue, L.: Dual-inception network for cross-database micro-expression recognition. In: 2019 14th IEEE International Conference on Automatic Face & Gesture Recognition (FG 2019), pp. 1–5. IEEE (2019)
39. Zhu, G., et al.: Three-stream temporal-shift attention network based on self-knowledge distillation for micro-expression recognition. arXiv preprint arXiv:2406.17538 (2024)
40. Zhu, J., Zong, Y., Shi, J., Lu, C., Chang, H., Zheng, W.: Learning to rank onset-occurring-offset representations for micro-expression recognition. IEEE Trans. Affect. Comput. **16**(4), 2690–2704 (2025)

Reinforcement Learning from Cross-Domain Videos with Video Prediction Model

Zhao Yang[1], Xinrui Zu[1], Jacob E. Kooi[1], Thomas Delliaux[2], He Liu[1], Shujian Yu[1(✉)], Kevin Sebastian Luck[1], and Vincent François-Lavet[1]

[1] VU Amsterdam, Amsterdam, Netherlands
{z.yang3,x.zu,s.yu3,k.s.luck,vincent.francoislavet}@vu.nl, h.liu17@student.vu.nl

[2] ISAE-SUPAERO, Toulouse, France
thomas.delliaux@isae-supaero.fr

Abstract. Reinforcement learning from expert videos across visually distinct domains is challenging due to the absence of reward signals and the presence of domain gaps. We introduce XIPER (Cross-domain Video Prediction Reward), a reward model for learning from expert videos collected in a visually different domain, where the agent's appearance differs due to factors such as color, morphology, or the sim-to-real gap. More specifically, XIPER trains a cross-domain video prediction model that maps agent observations into the expert domain and uses the prediction likelihood as a reward signal. Experiments on the DMC Color Suite (8 tasks) and DMC Body Suite (3 tasks) show that XIPER consistently outperforms baselines despite domain gaps such as differences in agent color and morphology. We further analyze XIPER on a sim-to-real transfer dataset, demonstrating that it produces meaningful reward signals for real-robot observations given only simulated expert videos. Code, pretrained models, datasets and video demonstrations can be found on our project webpage: https://sites.google.com/view/xiper.

Keyword: Reinforcement Learning

1 Introduction

Humans and animals can learn useful behaviors by observing demonstrations [35,42], even when the demonstrator differs from the learner in visual appearance. For instance, pilots improve real-world performance by studying animated training videos [4]. This is possible because the learner can extract the underlying behaviors from a demonstration without requiring an exact match in appearance. Endowing reinforcement learning (RL) agents with this same ability would unlock the vast pool of online videos as a source of expert demonstrations [1,36,45], removing the need for laborious reward engineering [34] and costly domain-specific data collection [30,31].

M. Ceci et al. (Eds.): ECML PKDD 2026, LNAI 16948, pp. 20–35, 2027.
https://doi.org/10.1007/978-3-032-37679-4_2

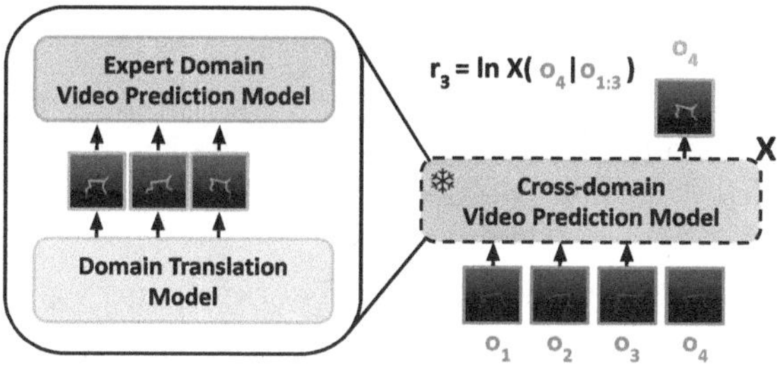

Fig. 1. XIPER trains a cross-domain video prediction model to predict the next expert observation given a sequence of agent observations. The reward is calculated as the prediction likelihood, assigning higher rewards for agent observations consistent with expert videos.

Achieving this in practice, however, remains challenging. Prior work [3,5,40] combines domain-invariant representation learning [23,27,50] with adversarial training [14] to encourage behavioral similarity between the learner and the expert. However, such representations often fail to scale to complex scenarios, and adversarial methods remain susceptible to mode collapse [29,43].

Instead, our approach builds on recent progress in unpaired image-to-image translation [22] and generative modeling [8,47]. We introduce XIPER (Cross-domain Video Prediction Reward), a reward model that uses cross-domain video prediction likelihood as a training signal, bypassing the need for domain-invariant representations and adversarial training altogether.

XIPER trains a cross-domain video prediction model (as illustrated in Fig. 1) comprising two components: (1) a domain translation model that maps agent observations into the expert domain, and (2) a video prediction model that predicts the next expert frame from a sequence of past ones. Both components are pretrained offline and frozen during RL training. At each time step, recent agent observations are first translated into the expert domain, then fed into the prediction model. The prediction likelihood serves as the reward signal: higher likelihoods indicate closer alignment with expert behavior, guiding the agent to reproduce demonstrated behaviors.

Concretely, our contributions are threefold:

- We introduce XIPER, a cross-domain reward model that enables RL agents to learn from unlabeled expert videos across different domains, relying solely on pixel observations without ground-truth rewards or low-dimensional state information.
- We show that XIPER consistently outperforms three competitive baselines across the DMC [44] Color Suite (8 tasks) and DMC Body Suite (3 tasks), and analyze its applicability on a sim-to-real transfer dataset, in which expert videos are only available in simulation.
- We conduct ablation studies to analyze key design choices. Code, pretrained models, datasets and video demonstrations are provided on our project webpage.

2 Related Work

XIPER addresses a setting where an RL agent learns from expert visual observations in a different domain, without access to action or reward labels. We review three lines of related work and position XIPER within each.

2.1 Cross-Domain RL from Visual Observations

Reinforcement learning from cross-domain visual observations is challenging due to domain gaps [5,13,33,38] and the absence of action [10] and reward labels [28]. Prior work typically trains a domain-invariant discriminator to classify behaviors across domains and uses it as a reward model for adversarial imitation learning [43]. TPIL [40] adds a domain confusion loss to encourage invariance, DisentanGAIL [3] improves upon this with mutual information constraints, and D3IL [5] further applies cycle consistency objectives [51] at both image and feature levels. Despite these advances, discriminator-based approaches remain prone to mode collapse [19,52] and unstable adversarial training [26], and their policies still rely on ground-truth low-dimensional states rather than raw visual inputs. XIPER avoids adversarial training entirely by using video prediction likelihood as a reward signal, and operates directly on high-dimensional pixel observations, making the setting more realistic.

2.2 Video Generation for Decision Making

Recent work has explored using video generation models to either plan over future trajectories or provide reward signals for RL agents. UniPi [6] generates expert video trajectories with a text-conditioned diffusion model and infers actions via an inverse dynamics model. DR [18] and VIPER [7] instead use video generation models to provide dense reward signals that encourage expert-like behavior. However, these methods assume the agent and expert share the same domain. XIPER extends this idea to the cross-domain setting by incorporating a domain translation step before video prediction, enabling reward generation even when the agent and expert domains differ.

2.3 Image Translation in RL

Image-to-image translation [20,46] has been widely applied in RL, primarily for policy transfer [21]. CycleGAN [51] has been used in Atari [12] to map distracted observations to a clean source domain, and RL-CycleGAN [32] jointly optimizes translation and RL for sim-to-real transfer. RetinaGAN [17,49] similarly translate simulated images to the real world for policy deployment. AVID [39] applies translation to human demonstration frames to generate robot reward signals. A common thread across these works is the assumption that expert policies are available, with translation serving mainly as a bridge for policy reuse. XIPER instead operates in a more challenging setting where only expert videos are available, integrating translation directly into a video prediction reward model to bridge domains without requiring access to policies or actions.

3 Preliminaries and Problem Setup

3.1 Preliminaries

We consider a Partially Observable Markov Decision Process (POMDP) [11, 41], defined by the tuple $\langle S, A, P, R, \Omega, O, \gamma \rangle$, where an agent interacts with an environment over discrete timesteps. At each timestep t, the environment is in a state $s_t \in S$, but the agent only receives a visual observation $o_t \in \Omega$ drawn from the observation function $O(o_t|s_t)$. The agent selects an action $a_t \in A$ according to the policy $\pi(a_t|o_t)$, receives a reward $r_t = R(s_t, a_t)$, and the environment transitions to the next state $s_{t+1} \sim P(\cdot|s_t, a_t)$. Here, A is the action space, S is the state space, Ω is the observation space, O is the observation function, P defines the transition dynamics, and R is the reward function. In our setting, R is unknown to the agent and is instead approximated by a learned reward model derived from expert demonstrations, as described in Sect. 3.2. The agent's objective is to learn a policy π that maximizes the expected cumulative discounted return:

$$G_t = \mathbb{E}_\pi \left[\sum_{k=0}^{T} \gamma^k r_{t+k} \right] \tag{1}$$

where $\gamma \in [0, 1]$ is the discount factor and T is the task horizon.

3.2 Problem Setup

We study the problem of visual imitation learning from unlabeled videos in a cross-domain setting, where the agent operates in a domain $\mathcal{A}$ using only visual observations o_t, without access to the underlying ground truth states s_t or the environment's true reward function R. Instead, the agent is given expert visual observations o_t' from a different domain $\mathcal{E}$. The demonstration videos differ from $\mathcal{A}$ in visual characteristics such as color schemes or agent morphologies, which are referred to as domain gaps [9], and do not have action or reward labels.

Due to the absence of true reward signals in domain $\mathcal{A}$, an auxiliary reward function R' must be derived from the unlabeled expert videos collected in domain $\mathcal{E}$. The core challenge lies in learning a reward function from these unlabeled videos that allows the agent to acquire expert-like behavior in a visually different environment. Since it is handy to perform random actions and collect these observations, we also assume having access to pre-collected random observations from both domains. More formally, given only:

- Pre-collected expert and random observations (videos) from domain $\mathcal{E}$;
- Pre-collected random observations (videos) from domain $\mathcal{A}$,

we aim to learn a policy that enables the agent to imitate expert behavior in domain $\mathcal{A}$ from visual observations, despite the visual and semantic differences between domains. The key challenge is: how can we transfer knowledge from expert videos collected in one domain to train an agent that performs well in another, using only raw visual observation inputs and no access to rewards or states?

4 Cross-Domain Video Prediction Rewards

XIPER enables RL across visually distinct domains by learning a cross-domain video prediction model. Given a sequence of agent observations, the model predicts the next expert observation, and the likelihood of this prediction serves as a reward signal that encourages the agent to produce expert-like behaviors.

4.1 Cross-Domain Video Prediction Model

The cross-domain video prediction model consists of two components (see Fig. 1): (i) an expert video prediction model that captures the distribution of expert behaviors, and (ii) a domain translation model that maps agent observations into the expert domain. We describe each in turn.

Expert Domain Video Prediction Model. We train a VideoGPT [8,47] model on expert trajectories by optimizing the maximum likelihood objective:

$$\max_{\theta} \sum_{t=1}^{T} \log p_{\theta}(o'_t | o'_{1:t-1}), \tag{2}$$

where p_θ denotes the generative model parameterized by θ. Since computing the likelihood over an entire video is expensive, we approximate it using a limited context window of $k = 16$ frames, giving:

$$\max_{\theta} \sum_{t=1}^{T} \log p_{\theta}(o'_t | o'_{\max(1,t-k):t-1}). \tag{3}$$

This model assigns higher likelihoods to observation sequences that resemble expert behavior. Once trained, it provides an imitation reward based on how likely the agent's recent observations are under the expert distribution:

$$r_t^{\text{imit}} = \log p_{\theta}(o'_t | o'_{\max(1,t-k):t-1}). \tag{4}$$

A higher r_t^{imit} indicates that the recent trajectory more closely matches the expert distribution [7]. While we use VideoGPT here, other generative video models [25,48] are also compatible.

Domain Translation Model. In a cross-domain setting, the expert video prediction model cannot directly process agent observations due to visual domain gaps. We address this with a domain translation model $T_\phi : \mathcal{A} \rightarrow \mathcal{E}$ that maps agent observations $o_t \in \mathcal{A}$ into the expert domain $o'_t \in \mathcal{E}$.

Since paired data across domains is unavailable, we formulate this as an unpaired image-to-image translation problem. Concretely, T_ϕ is trained using the Neural Optimal Transport (NOT) [22] objective, a neural approximation of the classical optimal transport problem, formulated as a min-max optimization:

$$\min_{\phi} \max_{\psi} \mathbb{E}_{o \sim \mu} \left[f_{\psi}(T_{\phi}(o)) \right] - \mathbb{E}_{o' \sim \nu} \left[f_{\psi}(o') \right] + \lambda \cdot \mathbb{E}_{o \sim \mu} \left[c(o, T_{\phi}(o)) \right] \quad (5)$$

where μ and ν are distributions over agent and expert domain observations, f_{ψ} is a critic function, and c is a cost function. We refer the reader to [22] for further details. Other unpaired translation methods [20,51] are equally compatible with our framework.

Integrated Cross-Domain Model. Composing the two components yields the cross-domain video prediction model $X_{\theta,\phi}$:

$$o'_t = X_{\theta,\phi}(o_{t-k:t-1}) = p_{\theta}(T_{\phi}(o_{t-k:t-1})), \quad (6)$$

which predicts the current expert observation given the previous k agent observations by first translating them into the expert domain, then applying the video prediction model.

4.2 Cross-Domain Reward Formulation

During training, the agent receives its current and previous k observations from its own domain. These are first translated into the expert domain using T_{ϕ}, and the XIPER reward is computed as the log-likelihood of the translated current observation given the translated context:

$$r_t^{\text{xiper}} = \ln p_{\theta}(T_{\phi}(o_t) | T_{\phi}(o_{t-k:t-1})). \quad (7)$$

To encourage exploration, we augment this with an exploration bonus r_t^{expl} following prior work [2,7,37]:

$$r_t = r_t^{\text{xiper}} + \beta \cdot r_t^{\text{expl}}, \quad (8)$$

where $\beta = 1$ across all experiments. An ablation on β is provided in Sect. 5.3.

4.3 Data Curation

XIPER requires three types of data: expert trajectories in domain $\mathcal{E}$ for training the video prediction model, and random observations from both domains for training the translation model. Expert trajectories are collected using pretrained RL agents, while random observations are gathered using uniformly sampled actions. As a result, XIPER assumes access to expert and random observations in domain $\mathcal{E}$, and only random observations in domain $\mathcal{A}$. In all experiments, 50 episodes are collected per task per domain.

4.4 Implementation Details

A high-level overview is provided in Algorithm 1. XIPER is built on top of VIPER [7], which is video prediction reward model that is restricted to same-domain settings. XIPER generalizes this to cross-domain scenarios by incorporating domain translation into the reward pipeline, enabling reward generation from expert videos in a different domain. Concretely, XIPER uses DreamerV3 [15] as the RL backbone, a VideoGPT [47] model trained on expert videos to capture expert behavior, and a NOT translation model [22] for domain bridging. Both the video prediction and translation models are frozen during policy learning. For the exploration bonus, we adopt the uncertainty-based objective from Plan2Explore [37], which integrates naturally with DreamerV3. Code, pre-trained models, datasets and video demonstrations are provided on our project webpage[1].

Algorithm 1. RL with XIPER Reward Signals

```
Pretrain cross-domain video prediction model X_{θ,φ} on pre-collected expert and
  random videos with Eq. 3 and Eq. 5.
Initialize RL policy π, set up task environment env.
while not converged do
    Choose action: a_t ~ π(o_t)
    Step environment: o_{t+1} ← env(a_t)
    Calculate reward: r_t ← ln X_{θ,φ}(o_{t+1}|o_{t−k:t}) + β r_t^{expl}
    Add transition (o_t, a_t, r_t, o_{t+1}) to replay buffer
    Train π from replay buffer with DreamerV3
end while
Output π for evaluation.
```

5 Experiments

We evaluate XIPER across two stages. First, we conduct a thorough simulation study addressing three questions: (1) How accurately does the cross-domain video prediction model capture expert behavior, and how well do its rewards correlate with ground-truth task rewards? (2) Are these learned rewards sufficient to train agents that acquire meaningful behaviors? (3) What are the key design choices and their impact on performance? We then conduct a dataset analysis in a sim-to-real setting, examining whether XIPER can generate meaningful reward signals for real-robot observations given only simulated expert videos (we defer the details to Sect. 5.4).

For simulation experiments, we create two suites based on DMC [44] to evaluate all agents (see Fig. 2):

[1] https://sites.google.com/view/xiper.

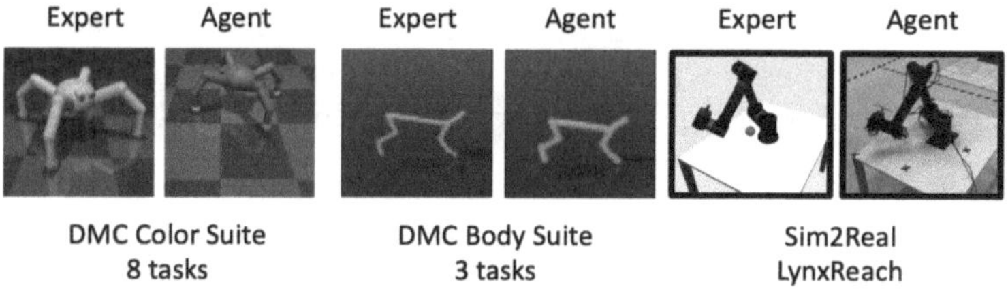

Fig. 2. Tasks used in the experiments. The DMC Color Suite includes 8 tasks with the agent's color changed from orange to gray. The DMC Body Suite consists of 3 tasks where the agent's body shape is modified to be thicker. The Sim2Real analysis uses a Lynx Robot arm dataset, where expert videos are only available in simulation.

- DMC Color Suite: 8 tasks where expert data uses orange agents and the learning agent is gray, introducing a visual domain gap. Tasks: Quadruped-walk, Pointmass-easy, Cartpole-balance, Quadruped-run, Cup-catch, Pendulum-swingup, Cheetah-run, and Cartpole-swingup.
- DMC Body Suite: 3 tasks where the learning agent has a thicker body than the standard-shaped expert, introducing both visual and dynamics domain gaps. Tasks: Cartpole-balance, Cheetah-run, and Cartpole-swingup.

Most prior cross-domain visual RL methods rely on adversarial learning but use weak RL backbones [3,40] that struggle with visually rich tasks. For fair comparison, we reimplement all baselines using DreamerV3, the same RL backbone as XIPER:

1. VIPER [7]: a same-domain video prediction reward model.
2. XAIL: a same-domain adversarial imitation learning baseline [29,43] with DreamerV3, extended to the cross-domain setting using our translation model to map expert demonstrations into the agent domain.
3. TPIL-Dv3: a cross-domain adversarial imitation learning method with a domain confusion loss [5,40] for domain-invariant discrimination, also with DreamerV3.

All simulation agents learn from raw pixels without access to ground-truth state information or task rewards. All results are averaged over three independent runs.

5.1 Performance of Cross-Domain Video Model

We begin by evaluating the cross-domain video prediction model, which directly determines the quality of the reward signal. More accurate predictions yield more informative rewards and better downstream agent performance.

Domain Translation. Since XIPER's reward signal depends on translating agent observations into the expert domain, translation quality is critical. We evaluate the translation model on expert trajectories, which are out-of-distribution relative to the random data it was trained on.

Despite being trained only on randomly collected observations, the model generalizes well to expert trajectories: in Fig. 3, gray agents in Cheetah-run are accurately translated to orange, and thick poles in Cartpole-balance are correctly resized.

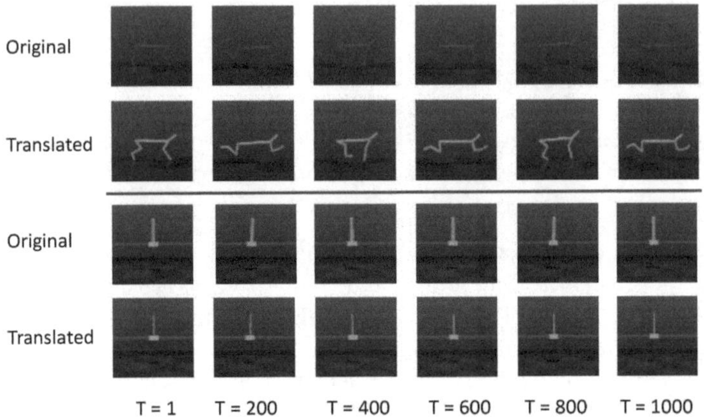

Fig. 3. Expert trajectories in the agent domain translated into the expert domain. Although trained on randomly collected data, the model generalizes well to expert trajectories (OOD).

To quantify this generalization, we report FID [16] scores of the translation model across various data subsets of Cheetah-run in Fig. 5 (a). FID measures the distance between two image distributions, where lower scores indicate greater similarity. Recall that the translation model is trained only on randomly collected observations. We evaluate three settings by measuring the FID between translated outputs and a target distribution: (R2R) translating random gray observations (agent's domain) and comparing to random orange (expert's domain), serving as the in-distribution baseline; (E2E) translating expert gray observations and comparing to expert orange, measuring OOD generalization; and (E2R) translating expert gray observations and comparing to random orange, serving as a reference to highlight the distribution gap between expert and random trajectories. R2R achieves a very low FID, confirming strong in-distribution performance. E2E remains relatively low, suggesting the model generalizes well to expert inputs despite being trained only on random data, likely because random observations provide broad coverage of the observation space. E2R is substantially higher than E2E, confirming that the gap is not due to poor translation quality but rather the inherent distributional difference between expert and random trajectories.

Cross-Domain Video Prediction Rollout. To evaluate the full cross-domain prediction pipeline, we initialize the model with an agent observation and generate a rollout of future expert observations. As shown in Fig. 4, the model successfully predicts expert-like trajectories from agent-domain inputs: it generates running motions of the orange expert given a gray agent's initial state, and produces balanced pole behaviors starting from the thick-pole variant. These predictions accurately capture expert dynamics, demonstrating the effectiveness of the combination of translation and prediction components.

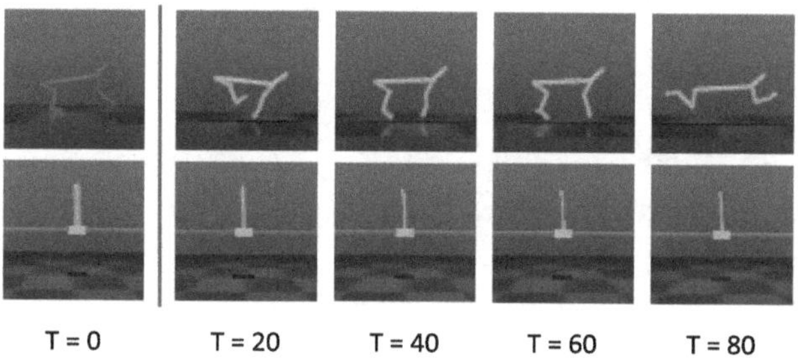

Fig. 4. Predicted expert rollout of the cross-domain video prediction model, given an initial agent observation.

Using Likelihoods as Rewards. To assess whether XIPER's likelihood-based rewards (r^{XIPER}) reflect true task performance, we compare them against ground-truth rewards (r^{TASK}) on 100 trajectories from random and expert policies in the Cheetah-run task (Fig. 5 (b)). XIPER assigns higher rewards to expert trajectories and lower rewards to random ones, with step-wise rewards and episode returns (G^{XIPER} vs G^{TASK}) both correlating closely with ground-truth task rewards. This confirms that XIPER's prediction likelihoods serve as meaningful reward signals.

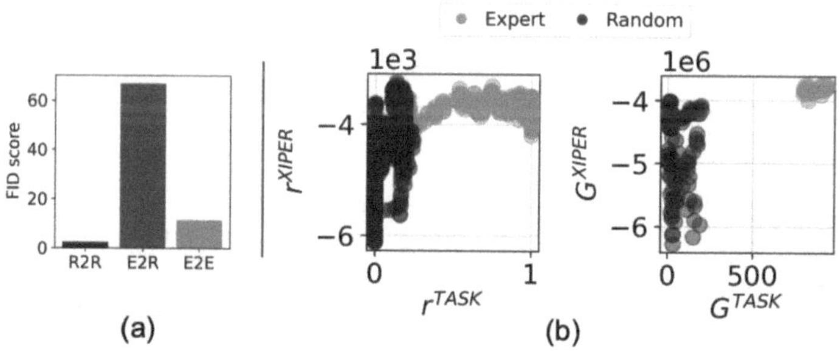

Fig. 5. (a): FID scores on different data subsets of Cheetah-run, evaluated with the pretrained domain translation model. Lower FID indicates better translation quality. (b): Step-wise rewards (left) and episode returns (right) comparing XIPER and ground-truth task rewards on 100 random and expert trajectories.

5.2 XIPER Performance

We now evaluate whether optimizing XIPER's learned rewards leads to meaningful task performance. Agents are trained solely with XIPER's likelihood-based reward signals and evaluated using ground-truth task rewards after 10M environment steps. An exception is TPIL-Dv3, which is trained for only 5M steps as it converges to a local optimum early in training.

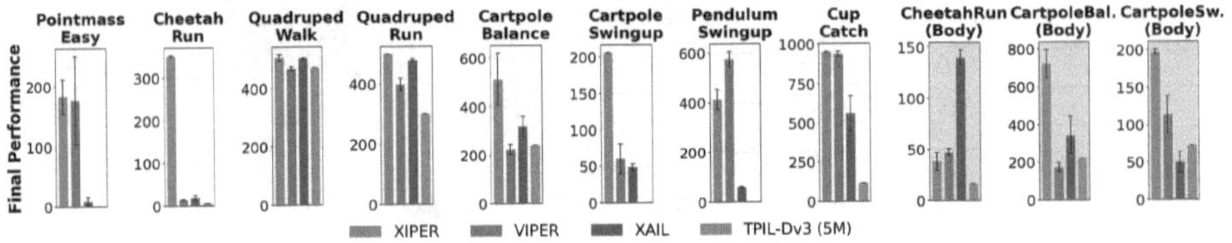

Fig. 6. Final performance across all DMC tasks. XIPER outperforms all baselines in 9/12 tasks.

In Fig. 6, we see across both suites, XIPER consistently achieves higher returns than baselines in most tasks. This result highlights the effectiveness of XIPER's reward model in the absence of ground-truth task feedback.

Notably, VIPER performs reasonably well in the DMC Color Suite despite lacking domain adaptation, suggesting that video prediction models can sometimes generalize over simple appearance shifts such as color changes. However, its performance collapses in the DMC Body Suite, where morphological changes create a larger domain gap. Both adversarial baselines, XAIL and TPIL-Dv3, perform poorly across both suites with unstable learning curves, confirming the known instability and data inefficiency of adversarial imitation learning even when paired with a strong RL backbone.

5.3 Ablations

We examine two key design choices on three DMC Color tasks: the exploration coefficient β and translation model quality.

Exploration Coefficient β**.** The performance of agents trained with varying exploration bonuses (β) from Eq. 8 is shown in Fig. 7 (left three). While eliminating the exploration bonus ($\beta = 0$) improves performance on certain tasks, it substantially degrades results on others, such as Cheetah-run. Overall, $\beta = 1$ yields the most consistent performance across all tested tasks.

Translation Model Quality. Since translation quality directly determines the fidelity of the reward signal, we train translation models of varying quality (measured by FID scores) and evaluate the resulting agents (right three in Fig. 7). High FID consistently yields poor performance across all tasks. While mid-range

FID can match or exceed low FID on forgiving locomotion tasks, it catastrophically fails on precision-sensitive tasks, where even a modest FID degradation causes complete collapse on Cartpole Balance. This asymmetric sensitivity suggests that translation errors compound critically when precise state estimation is required. Low FID therefore represents the safest and most reliable choice.

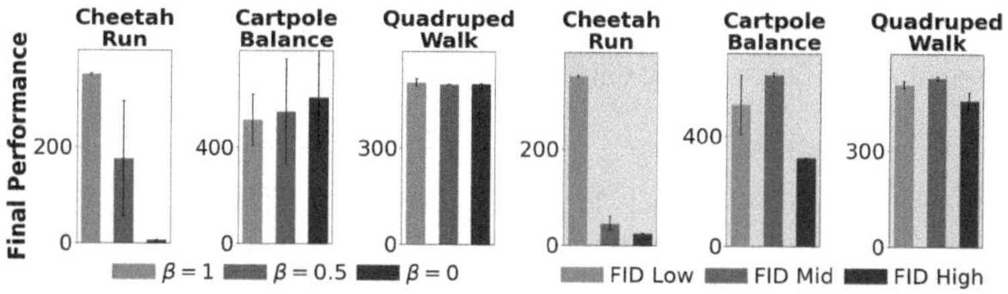

Fig. 7. XIPER performance under different exploration coefficients β and translation model qualities (FID) on DMC Color tasks. Lower FID and $\beta = 1$ yield robust overall performance.

5.4 Sim2Real Analysis

A compelling use case for XIPER is sim-to-real transfer, where expert demonstrations are only available in simulation. To analyze this potential, we examine XIPER on the LynxReach dataset using the Lynx Robot[2], where a robotic arm must reach a designated target from a random initial position. Rather than training a full RL agent, we analyze whether XIPER can generate meaningful reward signals for real-robot observations given only simulated expert videos. XIPER's reward model is trained in two stages: first, a domain translation model is trained on randomly collected simulation and real-robot data; second, a video prediction model is trained only on expert videos collected in simulation.

Visual Translation Performance. We first evaluate the translation model's ability to map real-world observations into the simulation domain. As shown in Fig. 8, the model successfully filters out task-irrelevant visual information such as cabling and hardware components, producing clean simulation-style images. Notably, despite being trained on randomly collected data, the model generalizes effectively to expert trajectories.

Reward Signal Validation. Having established translation quality, we next assess whether the resulting reward signals are semantically meaningful. Specifically, we apply the pretrained XIPER reward model (using Line 6 in Algorithm 1) to real-robot episodes and compare its outputs (r^{XIPER}) against ground-truth

[2] https://www.lynxmotion.com.

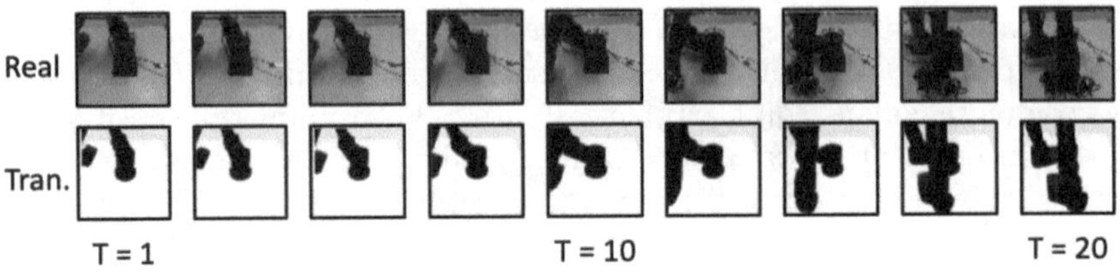

Fig. 8. Sim2Real translation examples. Real robot expert trajectories (top) are translated into the simulation domain (bottom).

task rewards (r^{TASK}). As shown in Fig. 9, XIPER rewards correlate well with ground-truth rewards, demonstrating that simulated expert videos can provide a meaningful supervisory signal for real-robot observations. While this analysis does not involve training a full RL agent, it suggests that XIPER has the potential to bridge the sim-to-real gap for reward generation, motivating future work on end-to-end real-robot training.

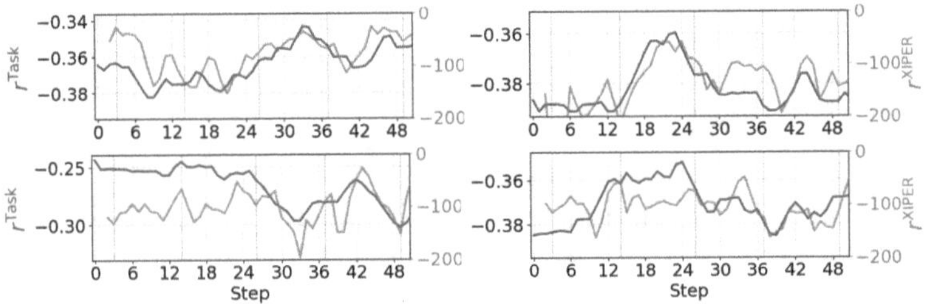

Fig. 9. XIPER rewards vs. ground-truth task rewards on random real-robot episodes. The two signals exhibit consistently similar trends.

6 Conclusion

We introduced XIPER, a cross-domain reward model that enables RL agents to learn from expert videos without access to environment rewards or ground-truth state information. XIPER maps agent observations into the expert domain and uses video prediction likelihood as a reward signal, guiding agents to reproduce expert behaviors across visual and morphological domain gaps. Experiments on the DMC Color and Body suites demonstrate that XIPER consistently outperforms adversarial and same-domain baselines, and our sim-to-real analysis shows that XIPER's reward signal correlates well with ground-truth task rewards on real-robot observations, suggesting its potential to bridge the sim-to-real gap without manual annotation.

Despite these promising results, two limitations remain. First, training the translation model solely on randomly collected data can be a bottleneck for tasks requiring precise, long-horizon behaviors, as random exploration may not provide sufficient coverage. Future work could address this through advanced exploration strategies [24, 28] or joint optimization of the translation model and RL policy. Second, while we validated XIPER's reward quality on a real-robot dataset, closing the loop with online RL training on a physical platform remains an important next step. We hope XIPER motivates future research into leveraging cross-domain videos as a scalable source of supervision for RL agents.

Acknowledgements. We would like to thank Prof. Mark Hoogendoorn for his helpful guidance during this project. We also thank SURF (www.surf.nl) for the support in using the National Supercomputer Snellius. This work used the Dutch national e-infrastructure with the support of the SURF Cooperative using grant no. EINF-81853.

References

1. Baker, B., et al.: Video pretraining (VPT): learning to act by watching unlabeled online videos. In: Advances in Neural Information Processing Systems, vol. 35, pp. 24639–24654 (2022)
2. Burda, Y., Edwards, H., Storkey, A., Klimov, O.: Exploration by random network distillation (2018). arXiv preprint arXiv:1810.12894
3. Cetin, E., Celiktutan, O.: Domain-robust visual imitation learning with mutual information constraints (2021). arXiv preprint arXiv:2103.05079
4. Chenot, Q., Riedinger, F., Dehais, F., Scannella, S.: Assessing and visualizing pilot performance in traffic patterns: a composite score approach. Safety **11**(2), 37 (2025)
5. Choi, S., Han, S., Kim, W., Chae, J., Jung, W., Sung, Y.: Domain adaptive imitation learning with visual observation. In: Advances in Neural Information Processing Systems, p. 36 (2024)
6. Du, Y., et al.: Learning universal policies via text-guided video generation. In: Advances in Neural Information Processing Systems, vol. 36, pp. 9156–9172 (2023)
7. Escontrela, A., et al.: Video prediction models as rewards for reinforcement learning. In: Advances in Neural Information Processing Systems, vol. 36 (2024)
8. Esser, P., Rombach, R., Ommer, B.: Taming transformers for high-resolution image synthesis. In: Proceedings of the IEEE/CVF Conference on Computer Vision and Pattern Recognition, pp. 12873–12883 (2021)
9. Farhadi, A., Mirzarezaee, M., Sharifi, A., Teshnehlab, M.: Domain adaptation in reinforcement learning: a comprehensive and systematic study. Front. Inf. Technol. Electron. Eng. **25**(11), 1446–1465 (2024)
10. Foster, D.J., Block, A., Misra, D.: Is behavior cloning all you need? Understanding horizon in imitation learning. In: Advances in Neural Information Processing Systems, vol. 37, pp. 120602–120666 (2024)
11. François-Lavet, V., Henderson, P., Islam, R., Bellemare, M.G., Pineau, J., et al.: An introduction to deep reinforcement learning. Found. Trends® Mach. Learn. **11**(3-4), 219–354 (2018)
12. Gamrian, S., Goldberg, Y.: Transfer learning for related reinforcement learning tasks via image-to-image translation. In: International Conference on Machine Learning, pp. 2063–2072. PMLR (2019)

13. Giammarino, V., Queeney, J., Paschalidis, I.C.: Visually robust adversarial imitation learning from videos with contrastive learning (2024). arXiv preprint arXiv:2407.12792
14. Goodfellow, I.J., et al.: Generative adversarial nets. In: Advances in Neural Information Processing Systems, p. 27 (2014)
15. Hafner, D., Pasukonis, J., Ba, J., Lillicrap, T.: Mastering diverse domains through world models (2023). arXiv preprint arXiv:2301.04104
16. Heusel, M., Ramsauer, H., Unterthiner, T., Nessler, B., Hochreiter, S.: GANs trained by a two time-scale update rule converge to a local Nash equilibrium. In: Advances in Neural Information Processing Systems, p. 30 (2017)
17. Ho, D., Rao, K., Xu, Z., Jang, E., Khansari, M., Bai, Y.: RetinaGAN: an object-aware approach to sim-to-real transfer. In: 2021 IEEE International Conference on Robotics and Automation (ICRA), pp. 10920–10926. IEEE (2021)
18. Huang, T., Jiang, G., Ze, Y., Xu, H.: Diffusion reward: Learning rewards via conditional video diffusion. In: European Conference on Computer Vision (ECCV) (2024)
19. Jaegle, A., Sulsky, Y., Ahuja, A., Bruce, J., Fergus, R., Wayne, G.: Imitation by predicting observations. In: International Conference on Machine Learning, pp. 4665–4676. PMLR (2021)
20. Kim, B., Kwon, G., Kim, K., Ye, J.C.: Unpaired image-to-image translation via neural schrödinger bridge. arXiv preprint arXiv:2305.15086 (2023)
21. Kirk, R., Zhang, A., Grefenstette, E., Rocktäschel, T.: A survey of generalisation in deep reinforcement learning, vol. 1, p. 16 (2021). arXiv preprint arXiv:2111.09794
22. Korotin, A., Selikhanovych, D., Burnaev, E.: Neural optimal transport (2022). arXiv preprint arXiv:2201.12220
23. Li, B., François-Lavet, V., Doan, T., Pineau, J.: Domain adversarial reinforcement learning (2021). arXiv preprint arXiv:2102.07097
24. Ma, R., Luijkx, J., Ajanovic, Z., Kober, J.: ExploRLLM: guiding exploration in reinforcement learning with large language models (2024). arXiv preprint arXiv:2403.09583
25. Melnik, A., Ljubljanac, M., Lu, C., Yan, Q., Ren, W., Ritter, H.: Video diffusion models: a survey (2024). arXiv preprint arXiv:2405.03150
26. Mescheder, L., Geiger, A., Nowozin, S.: Which training methods for GANs do actually converge? In: International Conference on Machine Learning, pp. 3481–3490. PMLR (2018)
27. Nguyen, A.T., Tran, T., Gal, Y., Baydin, A.G.: Domain invariant representation learning with domain density transformations. In: Advances in Neural Information Processing Systems, vol. 34, pp. 5264–5275 (2021)
28. Park, S., Li, Q., Levine, S.: Flow q-learning (2025). arXiv preprint arXiv:2502.02538
29. Peng, X.B., Ma, Z., Abbeel, P., Levine, S., Kanazawa, A.: AMP: adversarial motion priors for stylized physics-based character control. ACM Trans. Graph. (ToG) **40**(4), 1–20 (2021)
30. Pertsch, K., Lee, Y., Wu, Y., Lim, J.J.: Guided reinforcement learning with learned skills (2021). arXiv preprint arXiv:2107.10253
31. Rafailov, R., et al.: D5RL: diverse datasets for data-driven deep reinforcement learning (2024). arXiv preprint arXiv:2408.08441
32. Rao, K., Harris, C., Irpan, A., Levine, S., Ibarz, J., Khansari, M.: RL-CycleGAN: reinforcement learning aware simulation-to-real. In: Proceedings of the IEEE/CVF Conference on Computer Vision and Pattern Recognition, pp. 11157–11166 (2020)

33. Raychaudhuri, D.S., Paul, S., Vanbaar, J., Roy-Chowdhury, A.K.: Cross-domain imitation from observations. In: International Conference on Machine Learning, pp. 8902–8912. PMLR (2021)
34. Riedmiller, M., et al.: Learning by playing solving sparse reward tasks from scratch. In: International Conference on Machine Learning, pp. 4344–4353. PMLR (2018)
35. Rizzolatti, G., Craighero, L.: The mirror-neuron system. Annu. Rev. Neurosci. **27**(1), 169–192 (2004)
36. Schmeckpeper, K., Rybkin, O., Daniilidis, K., Levine, S., Finn, C.: Reinforcement learning with videos: combining offline observations with interaction (2020). arXiv preprint arXiv:2011.06507
37. Sekar, R., Rybkin, O., Daniilidis, K., Abbeel, P., Hafner, D., Pathak, D.: Planning to explore via self-supervised world models. In: International Conference on Machine Learning, pp. 8583–8592. PMLR (2020)
38. Seo, Y., Lee, K., James, S.L., Abbeel, P.: Reinforcement learning with action-free pre-training from videos. In: International Conference on Machine Learning, pp. 19561–19579. PMLR (2022)
39. Smith, L., Dhawan, N., Zhang, M., Abbeel, P., Levine, S.: AVID: learning multi-stage tasks via pixel-level translation of human videos (2019). arXiv preprint arXiv:1912.04443
40. Stadie, B.C., Abbeel, P., Sutskever, I.: Third-person imitation learning (2017). arXiv preprint arXiv:1703.01703
41. Sutton, R.S., Barto, A.G.: Introduction to Reinforcement Learning, vol. 135. MIT Press Cambridge (1998)
42. Tenenbaum, J.B., Kemp, C., Griffiths, T.L., Goodman, N.D.: How to grow a mind: statistics, structure, and abstraction. Science **331**(6022), 1279–1285 (2011)
43. Torabi, F., Warnell, G., Stone, P.: Generative adversarial imitation from observation (2018). arXiv preprint arXiv:1807.06158
44. Tunyasuvunakool, S., et al.: dm_control: Software and tasks for continuous control. Softw. Impacts **6**, 100022 (2020)
45. Vuong, Q., et al.: Open X-embodiment: robotic learning datasets and RT-X models. In: Towards Generalist Robots: Learning Paradigms for Scalable Skill Acquisition@ CoRL2023 (2023)
46. Xie, S., Xu, Y., Gong, M., Zhang, K.: Unpaired image-to-image translation with shortest path regularization. In: Proceedings of the IEEE/CVF Conference on Computer Vision and Pattern Recognition, pp. 10177–10187 (2023)
47. Yan, W., Zhang, Y., Abbeel, P., Srinivas, A.: VideoGPT: video generation using VQ-VAE and transformers (2021). arXiv preprint arXiv:2104.10157
48. Yu, L., et al.: MAGVIT: masked generative video transformer. In: Proceedings of the IEEE/CVF Conference on Computer Vision and Pattern Recognition, pp. 10459–10469 (2023)
49. Yuan, C., et al.: Sim-to-real transfer of robotic assembly with visual inputs using CycleGAN and force control. In: 2022 IEEE International Conference on Robotics and Biomimetics (ROBIO), pp. 1426–1432. IEEE (2022)
50. Zhao, H., Des Combes, R.T., Zhang, K., Gordon, G.: On learning invariant representations for domain adaptation. In: International Conference on Machine Learning, pp. 7523–7532. PMLR (2019)
51. Zhu, J.Y., Park, T., Isola, P., Efros, A.A.: Unpaired image-to-image translation using cycle-consistent adversarial networks. In: Proceedings of the IEEE International Conference on Computer Vision, pp. 2223–2232 (2017)
52. Zolna, K., et al.: Task-relevant adversarial imitation learning. In: Conference on Robot Learning, pp. 247–263. PMLR (2021)

Unsupervised Smoke Cloud Forecasting from Multi-view Videos Using 3D Gaussians

Lou Denis[1(✉)], Steeven Janny[2], Thierry Siméon[1], and Murat Bronz[3]

[1] LAAS-CNRS, University of Toulouse, Toulouse, France
lou.denis@laas.fr
[2] Naver Labs Europe, Meylan, France
[3] ENAC, University of Toulouse, Toulouse, France

Abstract. Smoke dynamics is notoriously challenging for both the physics and machine learning communities due to the tight coupling between the underlying physics and lightâĂŞsmoke interactions. Existing learning-based simulators typically rely on large-scale simulated data for 2D problems, which cannot be scaled efficiently and require an external physics-based simulators. Consequently, previous work on smoke cloud has mostly been restricted to reconstruction, while forecasting is either limited to visual appearance alone, or relies on external ground truth data. In this paper, we address these limitations by tackling the unsupervised learning of 3D smoke cloud simulations directly from multi-view videos. We extract the spatial structure of the smoke cloud and capture its evolution over time using 3D density Gaussians. The dynamics is modeled with a Graph Neural Network (GNN) that predicts how the Gaussian parameters evolve over time. By combining an explicit 3D representation with learned particle dynamics, the proposed approach enables the accurate prediction of smoke evolution from only a short sequence of observations. Experimental results demonstrate that our method effectively captures the underlying dynamics and produces temporally consistent forecasts of the smoke distribution. Our implementation is released at https://github.com/louDenis/gaussian_smoke.

Keywords: physics · simulation · unsupervised learning

1 Introduction

Learning-based physics simulators offer several advantages over classical methods based on analytic equations. While classical approaches rely on expert knowledge and carefully handcrafted numerical methods to solve complex problems, learning-based alternatives tend to be significantly more computationally efficient. When the underlying physical phenomena are too complex for manual modeling, machine learning methods (whether used as surrogates embedded within existing simulation frameworks, or as end-to-end simulators) can leverage large quantities of data to extract patterns, identify intricate dynamical

M. Ceci et al. (Eds.): ECML PKDD 2026, LNAI 16948, pp. 36–50, 2027.
https://doi.org/10.1007/978-3-032-37679-4_3

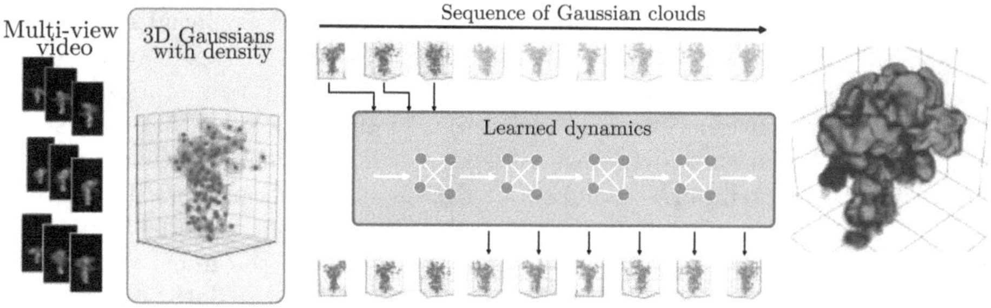

Fig. 1. Unsupervised learning of fluid dynamics – we learn a forward dynamical model of smoke simulation from multi-view video. Our approach represents the scene with density augmented 3D Gaussians and learns a dynamical model on these representation. The resulting prediction can be either exploited as is in 3D, or voxelized for 2D rendering.

relationships (e.g., turbulence models in fluid mechanics), and accelerate simulations. Furthermore, machine learning paves the way for exploiting new sources of data that are notoriously difficult to utilize with classical methods, such as partial observations and complex, entangled signals like video data (Fig. 1).

In particular, learning-based methods for fluid dynamics typically fall into one of two broad categories: on one hand, generative approaches rely on powerful, large-scale models trained via self-supervised video prediction (often referred to as world models [1,3,5]). These models benefit from massive training datasets comprising millions of videos to discover intuitive physics concepts. This physical knowledge is deeply entangled within their latent spaces, allowing the generation of visually plausible rollouts in the form of future frame predictions (e.g., smoke from a campfire, ocean waves). However, the lack of physics-based inductive biases makes these predictions opaque and difficult to interpret for engineering purposes. On the other hand, explicit end-to-end forward models are trained on highly curated datasets obtained via accurate physics simulations [19,22,33] or real-world experiments [9,26]. These methods leverage the expressiveness of neural networks to learn the dynamics directly in physical space, which can then be readily utilized for downstream tasks. However, such high-fidelity datasets are costly and difficult to produce, preventing these methods from scaling up as effortlessly as video generation models.

A promising approach to bridge this gap involves building physically meaningful scene representations from video observations, upon which a dynamical model can be trained. In this line of work, video frames are projected into a structured [21,25,31] or latent [14,17,39] representation space, and a subsequent model is trained to auto-regressively forecast the future states. In the context of fluid mechanics, 3D Gaussian Splatting (3DGS) [24] offers compelling advantages, as its particle-based structure shares inherent similarities with Lagrangian physics representations. However, because 3DGS was explicitly designed for 3D scene reconstruction rather than physics simulation, adapting it for dynamic environments is non-trivial. Furthermore, jointly learning a spatial representation and its underlying dynamics is an ill-posed problem.

In this work, we build upon recent advances in Gaussian representations for volumetric reconstruction to model smoke clouds as a set of 3D Gaussians. We then train a forward dynamics based on a graph neural network (GNN) [4] to simulate the temporal evolution of the Gaussian parameters. In contrast to prior work, our approach bridges 2D observational space and 3D physical space without requiring any external supervision beyond the multi-view videos themselves. Despite only being trained on unlabeled video data, our method outputs detailed simulation results that can be seamlessly converted into 3D density voxel grids or 2D tomographic-like images. To the best of our knowledge, we are the first to perform future smoke prediction directly in 3D space relying solely on a short context of 2D multi-view images.

2 Related Work

Differentiable rendering for reconstruction is particularly relevant for fluid simulation, as acquiring dense volumetric data typically requires complex hardware setups. Early approaches reconstructed voxel grids by formulating the task as a tomographic reconstruction problem [13,27,28], a choice that fundamentally restricts both the scene appearance and the grid resolution. Neural Radiance Fields (NeRFs) [30], while highly successful for solid objects, tend to underperform on semi-transparent or volumetric phenomena such as fluids [18,20,40]. Several methods [6,34,38] disentangle smoke from rigid objects by introducing additional fields guided by physics-based coupling terms. However, these approaches are generally limited to reconstruction tasks, since NeRF-based representations are known to be difficult to use for forward simulation because the spatial structure of the scene is implicitly encoded within the neural network weights.

In contrast, 3D Gaussian splatting (3DGS) [24] utilizes an explicit, particle-based representation that naturally aligns with the Lagrangian formulation of fluids dynamics. However, the standard 3DGS rendering operator is ill-suited for representing 3D smoke density distributions, as its splatting mechanism does not accurately preserve density accumulation along a ray [12,45]. To address this, we rely on 3DGS variations specifically tailored for volumetric rendering [8,42]. We employ the R2-Gaussian method [42], which replaces the color attribute with density factor, and modifies the splatting operator to properly account for density accumulation within each Gaussian's volume.

Guiding scene reconstruction with physics simulators can significantly improve the reconstruction accuracy of dynamic environments. Several approaches rely on explicit simulators paired with a scene representation, effectively reducing the task to *system identification* [23,29]. For example, recent work [44] combines a point-based spring system with classic 3DGS to steer the reconstruction towards plausible physical states, performing both system identification and future frame prediction. For fluids specifically, several scene representations are compatible with existing simulators, ranging from mesh-based

CFD simulations to voxel grids and particle-based approaches. For instance, HyFluid [41] performs smoke cloud reconstruction using an explicit simulator applied to reconstructed velocity and density grids. Lagrangian approaches are also popular: Smoothed Particle Hydrodynamics (SPH) [15] and its variants, such as Particle-Based Fluid (PBF) [32], are at the core of several recent methods [2,35,36]. Particle-based representations offer greater flexibility in terms of resolution and simulation refinement compared to uniform voxel grids. Deep Lagrangian Fluids [37] employs a continuous convolution operator to compute the pose correction step of a PBF simulation.

While our approach is inspired by this line of work, we do not rely on explicit, handcrafted physics simulators to advance the simulation forward in time. Instead, we learn the dynamics directly from our intermediate representations, and use them for next-frame forecasting. Our method is entirely unsupervised, requiring neither an external simulator nor ground-truth 3D data.

Learning simulations directly from images requires careful modeling of both the rendering process and the underlying physical dynamics. On one hand, existing methods typically focus on scene reconstruction and delegate forecasting to off-the-shelf explicit solvers [41]. On the other hand, learned particle-based simulators generally lack a rendering layer, making it difficult to bridge forecasting and visual scene understanding [22,33,35,37]. FluidNexus [11] addresses this issue by combining explicit physics with a generative post-processing step: 3D Gaussians extracted from the scene are advanced in time using PBF, and the rendered images are subsequently refined by a diffusion model conditioned on the explicit output of the solver. Closer to our approach, Neurofluid [16] learns fluid dynamics using ground-truth 3D data, which is then mapped to 2D images via a neural renderer.

In contrast, our approach does not require ground-truth 3D supervision. Instead, we interpret 3DGS as a Lagrangian representation of the fluid, and directly learn the dynamics from the extracted Gaussians. Our work is similar in spirit to [43], yet introduces additional complexities, as modeling semi-transparent materials prevents us from freezing certain Gaussian parameters over time, or spatially down-sampling the representation.

3 Proposed Method

We propose to learn smoke cloud simulation and rendering from a dataset of multi-view videos of smoke plume. Our approach consists of 3 steps, and do not requires any supervision signal other than video frames. Formally, let $\boldsymbol{I}_t^q$ be the a 2D image from view-point q at time t. We first convert the training set into 3DGS representations using R2-Gaussian [42]. This method differs from classical 3DGS to adapt to a tomography setup, where the need of 3D density expressiveness is crucial. This representation allows for not only rasterization in 2D, but also 3D density voxelization, which is not straightforward with the originally designed Gaussians in 3DGS.

Then, we train a graph neural network to forecast the evolution of the parameter from each gaussian in an auto-regressive manner. Decoupling scene representation from learning the dynamics prevents the double identification problems, since each step is driven by its own objective. This makes learning either, at the cost of having scene representation that are not directly tailored for forecasting tasks. Finally, the next frames are reconstructed using R2-Gaussian voxelization algorithm.

3.1 Preliminary : R2-Gaussian Method

We rely on R2-Gaussian to extract a Gaussian-based representation of the scene. This approach replaces the traditional color attribute with a central density parameter ρ associated with each Gaussian. Each Gaussian is further parametrized by their position $\mathbf{p}$ and a covariance matrix $\mathbf{\Sigma} = \boldsymbol{R}\boldsymbol{s}\boldsymbol{s}^\top\boldsymbol{R}^\top$ (where $\boldsymbol{R}$ is a rotation matrix, and $\boldsymbol{s}$ is a scaling vector). To ensure this paper is self-contained, we briefly recall the R2-Gaussian pipeline. The density field of a single Gaussian $\boldsymbol{G}_i$ is defined as:

$$\boldsymbol{G}_i\big(\boldsymbol{x} \mid \rho_i, \boldsymbol{p}_i, \mathbf{\Sigma}^{-1}\big) = \rho_i \exp\left(-\frac{1}{2}(\mathbf{x} - \mathbf{p}_i)^\top \mathbf{\Sigma}_i^{-1}(\mathbf{x} - \mathbf{p}_i)\right). \quad (1)$$

The total density at any given position $\boldsymbol{x}$ is evaluated by summing the contributions of all Gaussians $\boldsymbol{G}_i$ at that point: $\sigma(\boldsymbol{x}) = \sum_{i=1}^{M} \boldsymbol{G}_i(\mathbf{x} \mid \rho_i, \mathbf{p}_i, \mathbf{\Sigma}_i)$.. Images are then rendered following the same rasterization process as in standard 3DGS [24]. In essence, the R2-Gaussian operator scales the 3DGS opacity by a three-dimensional covariance-related factor. This accounts for the true volumetric aspect of the Gaussian, allowing it to accurately describe a 3D density distribution that can easily be voxelized to match traditional smoke grid representations.

3.2 Learning Simulation from Videos

Scene representation is derived directly from R2-Gaussian. Consider a multi-view video of a smoke cloud denoted by $\boldsymbol{I}_t^q$ where q indexes one of the Q viewpoints and t represents the timestep. We first apply R2-Gaussian to extract a Gaussian point cloud $\boldsymbol{G}_t = \{\boldsymbol{p}_i, \rho_i, \boldsymbol{R}_i, \boldsymbol{s}_i)\}_{i=1\cdots N}$ for each timestep t of the video. During optimization, we fix the number of Gaussians per point cloud to N=5,000 and remove the densification and splitting operators from the traditional 3DGS optimization scheme. The parameters of the Gaussians are retrieved by minimizing the standard R2-Gaussian loss.

By default, R2-Gaussian does not output temporally aligned representations because each frame is processed independently. To promote temporal consistency between consecutive frames we initialize the optimization at step t using the results from the previous step $t-1$ (the first frame is initialized from FDK [10] points, following the standard R2-Gaussian initialization scheme). Figure 2 illustrates the positive impact of auto-regressively seeding R2-Gaussian with its

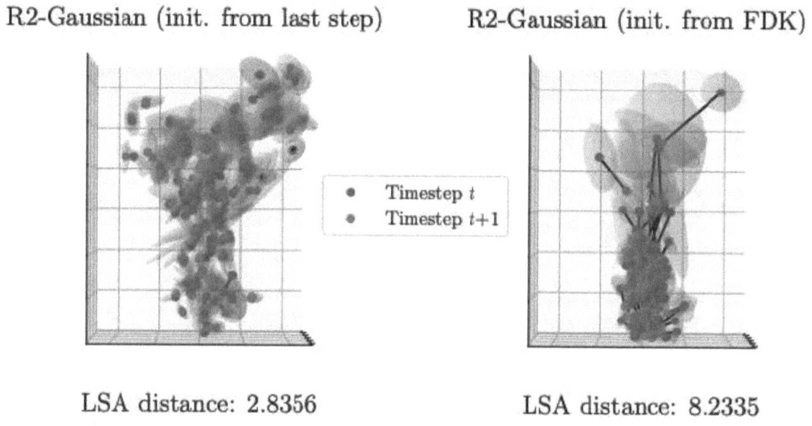

Fig. 2. Temporal consistency of the Gaussian representation is encouraged by seeding R2-Gaussian with the output from the previous step. This technique significantly reduces the sum of distances between matched pairs of points across time (computed by solving a linear sum assignment problem between the two consecutive sets of Gaussians).

own sequential outputs. Finally, given two consecutive Gaussian point clouds $\boldsymbol{G}_t$ and $\boldsymbol{G}_{t+1}$, we pair the Gaussians by solving a Linear Sum Assignment (LSA) problem to minimize the cost function $\text{LSA}_{\text{pairs}} = \min \sum_{i,j} \boldsymbol{C}_{i,j} \boldsymbol{X}_{i,j}$, where $\boldsymbol{X}_{i,j}$ is a boolean assignment matrix such that $\boldsymbol{X}[i,j] = 1$ if two Gaussians are paired, and $\boldsymbol{C}_{i,j}$ represents the Euclidean distance between the spatial positions $\boldsymbol{p}$ of the indexed Gaussians.

Unsupervised dynamical model is built upon the 3D Gaussian representations extracted during the previous phase. We follow the *encode-process-decode* setup described in [33] and model the dynamics of the Gaussian particles with a multi-layer Graph Neural Network (GNN) [4]. GNNs are a well-fitted choice for our task, as they naturally operate on irregularly structured data and have proven highly effective for Lagrangian fluid simulations [35]. We build a graph out of the Gaussian point cloud $\boldsymbol{G}_t$ using K-Nearest Neighbors (KNN, with k=3).

The GNN acts as an auto-regressive forecaster trained to predict the residual between the current and future sets of Gaussians, akin to an Euler integration scheme for the dynamics. It encodes the previous $P+1$ steps $\boldsymbol{G}_{t-P}, ..., \boldsymbol{G}_t$ into a set of node features $\boldsymbol{\eta}_t^i$ and edge features $\boldsymbol{e}_t^{ij}$ and applies L=3 layers of message passing. Formally, let $\boldsymbol{s}_t^i = \begin{bmatrix}\boldsymbol{p}_i \; \rho_i \; \boldsymbol{R}_i \; \boldsymbol{s}_i\end{bmatrix}^\top$ be the state of the ith Gaussian at time t. We first encode the last $P+1$ states into node and edge features:

$$\boldsymbol{\eta}_t^i = g_\theta^{\text{node}}(\boldsymbol{s}_t^i, ..., \boldsymbol{s}_{t-P}^i) \tag{2}$$

$$\boldsymbol{e}_{ij} = g_\theta^{\text{edge}}(\begin{bmatrix}\boldsymbol{\delta}_t^{ij} \cdots \boldsymbol{\delta}_{t-P}^{ij}\end{bmatrix}^\top) \tag{3}$$

Method	2D Metrics PSNR (dB)	2D Metrics SSIM	3D Metrics PSNR (dB)	3D Metrics SSIM
FluidNexus [11] (rgba2den)	35.83	0.947	26.95	0.950
FluidNexus [11] (alpha2den)			29.61	0.962
R2-Gaussian	**39.66**	**0.955**	**41.68**	**0.987**

Fig. 3. Reconstruction-only comparison – between R2-Gaussian and FluidNexus, bypassing the video diffusion model. The raw particle-based rendering from FluidNexus yields lower reconstruction metrics compared to R2-Gaussian, which aligns with its design choice to delegate fine-grained details to an external, physics-agnostic video refiner.

where g_θ^{node} and g_θ^{edge} are 3-layered MLPs with ReLU activations, $\boldsymbol{\delta}_t^{ij} = \boldsymbol{p}_t^i - \boldsymbol{p}_t^j$. The latent edges and node features are of dimension 128. Edge features are computed using the connectivity matrix at time t provided by the KNN algorithm. We then perform L steps of message passing on the encoded graph:

$$\boldsymbol{e}_{ij}^{\ell+1} = \boldsymbol{e}_{ij}^{\ell} + f_{\theta_\ell}^{\text{edge}}(\boldsymbol{\eta}_i, \boldsymbol{\eta}_j, \boldsymbol{e}_{ij}) \tag{4}$$

$$\boldsymbol{\eta}_i^{\ell+1} = \boldsymbol{\eta}_i^{\ell} + f_{\theta_\ell}^{\text{node}}\left(\boldsymbol{\eta}_i^{\ell}, \sum_j \boldsymbol{e}_{ij}^{\ell+1}\right) \tag{5}$$

where $\ell = 1 \cdots L$, $f_{\theta_\ell}^{\text{edge}}$ and $f_{\theta_\ell}^{\text{node}}$ are 2-layered MLP with ReLU activations. Finally, the next state of each Gaussian is computed incrementally:

$$\hat{\boldsymbol{s}}_{t+1}^i = \boldsymbol{s}_t^i + h_\theta(\boldsymbol{\eta}_i^L) \tag{6}$$

where h_θ is an MLP with 2 hidden layers. We apply specific normalization layers to each Gaussian attribute depending on its mathematical characteristics: rotations $\boldsymbol{R}_t^i$ are represented as quaternions and are normalized at each step, density ρ_t^i is passed through a *softplus* function to ensure positive values, and scales $\boldsymbol{s}_t^i$ are constrained via a *sigmoid* function.

Training setup does not require ground-truth or simulated data, relying exclusively on the sequence of 3D Gaussians extracted by R2-Gaussian. We train the dynamical model for next-state prediction over a forecasting horizon of H timesteps by minimizing the following loss:

$$\mathcal{L}_{pred} = \frac{1}{HN}\sum_{\tau=1}^{H}\sum_{i=1}^{N} \|\rho_{t+\tau}^i - \hat{\rho}_{t+\tau}^i\|_2 + \|\boldsymbol{R}_{t+\tau}^i - \hat{\boldsymbol{R}}_{t+\tau}^i\|_2 + \|\boldsymbol{s}_{t+\tau}^i - \hat{\boldsymbol{s}}_{t+\tau}^i\|_2 + \|\boldsymbol{p}_{t+\tau}^i - \hat{\boldsymbol{p}}_{t+\tau}^i\|_2^\gamma \tag{7}$$

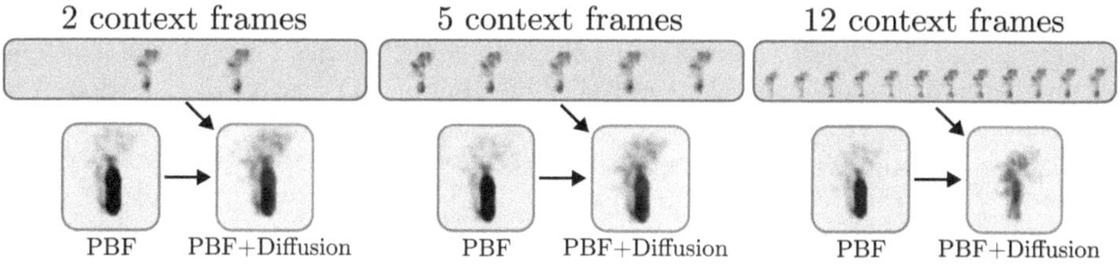

Fig. 4. FluidNexus's dependency on context frames. Because the underlying PBF simulation serves primarily as a rough structural estimate of future states, the final visual quality relies heavily on a physics-agnostic diffusion model. Consequently, ground-truth context frames play a crucial role in conditioning the rendered image. While this architecture is highly effective for image reconstruction tasks, this strong reliance on observational conditioning makes it less suited for autonomous forecasting objectives.

where $\|\cdot\|_2$ denotes the L_2 norm, $\hat{\cdot}$ indicates the prediction made by the dynamical model, and γ=0.5 is a spatial weighting coefficient. To ensure stable optimization, we train the dynamics on standardized data by computing normalization statistics independently for each Gaussian attribute across the training set.

4 Experiments

4.1 Experimental Setup

Dataset and task definition – our training and evaluation data are derived from the *ScalarFlow* [9] dataset, which consists of 104 scenes of real smoke flows that have been captured and reconstructed numerically. We generated Q=25 views per sample, and divided the dataset into training and evaluation set (80/24 splits). We removed the earliest frames of the sequences, as they do not contain a sufficient volume of smoke. In addition to multi-view videos, we also generated tomographic voxel grids, which are used strictly for evaluation purposes.

Models are trained and evaluated in two distinct setups depending on the size of the observation context: in the *short* setup, models receive the first 2 steps P=1 and must predict the subsequent H=2 steps of the smoke dynamics, and in the *long* setup, we increase the number of input steps to 5 (P=4) and extend the prediction horizon to H=10.

We compare our approach against two baselines that tackle a similar tasks, using different methodologies:

FluidNexus primarily targets 2D reconstruction from a single video, but it can be extended to a multi-view setup by replacing its novel view synthesizer with ground-truth data, matching our R2-Gaussian setup. FluidNexus extracts two sets of particles from the videos: one for modeling the velocity and density fields, and another for appearance. It then simulates the evolution of the latter using the former, akin to a PBF simulation. During rendering, the raw reconstruction from the visual particle set is refined using a video

Table 1. 2D and 3D evaluation on simulated trajectories. We report the rendering metrics and the global L_2 error over the Gaussian attributes for both the baselines and our method. FluidNexus fails to predict meaningful 3D density distribution. The other short models (DLF short and GNN short) exhibits similar 3D metrics. The DLF model yields to higher 2D metrics than the GNN short method. The GNN long dynamical model yields the best overall performance for both 3D volumetric and 2D image rendering. All metrics are computed over a forecasting horizon of H=25 frames.

	2D Metrics		3D Metrics		L_2
Method	PSNR (dB)	SSIM	PSNR (dB)	SSIM	(voxel)
FluidNexus (short)	21.38	0.22	22.33	0.86	0.03
FluidNexus (long)	21.64	0.23	24.12	0.89	0.027
DLF (short)	30.41	**0.94**	44.04	0.980	0.0002
Ours (short)	22.43	0.46	43.55	0.963	0.00017
Ours (long)	**33.25**	0.74	**46.67**	**0.982**	**3e-5**

diffusion model, which significantly improves image quality, albeit without being guided by physics.

Deep Lagrangian Fluids (DLF) to explore an alternative modeling strategy for the Gaussian attributes, we adapt Deep Lagrangian Fluids [37], which updates a set of particles using continuous convolutions. This architecture was originally designed for supervised learning using physics-based particle simulations with ground-truth positions and velocities. We adapt the method to our setting by replacing its standard particles with the Gaussian sets extracted by R2-Gaussian, and we extend DLF to forecast scales, rotations, and densities. Because DLF requires particle velocities, we deduced them from the Gaussian positions via finite differences. We also adopt their position weighting coefficient $\phi_i = \exp(-\lambda n_i)$ where n_i is the number of neighbors for the ith Gaussian.

Evaluation metrics – we rely on a combination of 2D metrics (computed on rendered images), and 3D metrics (based on the ground truth voxel grid). Because R2-Gaussian models the 3D scene in a tomographic manner, comparisons with the ground-truth voxel grid are straightforward. To compute 2D metrics, we follow the standard R2-Gaussian rendering pipeline and scale the resulting pixel values to $[0, 1]$. On the other hand, FluidNexus directly outputs 2D images via its video diffusion model, which can be easily compared with ground-truth videos. To evaluate its 3D structural accuracy, the method re-computes a 3DGS representation from these final images to account for the modifications introduced by the diffusion model. Following [7], we convert opacity and color into a density term, either extracting it from the alpha channel (*alpha2den*) or by incorporating the RGB channels (*rgba2den*). For both 2D and 3D modalities, we measure the *Peak Signal to Noise Ratio* (PSNR) and Structural Similarity Index Measure (SSIM).

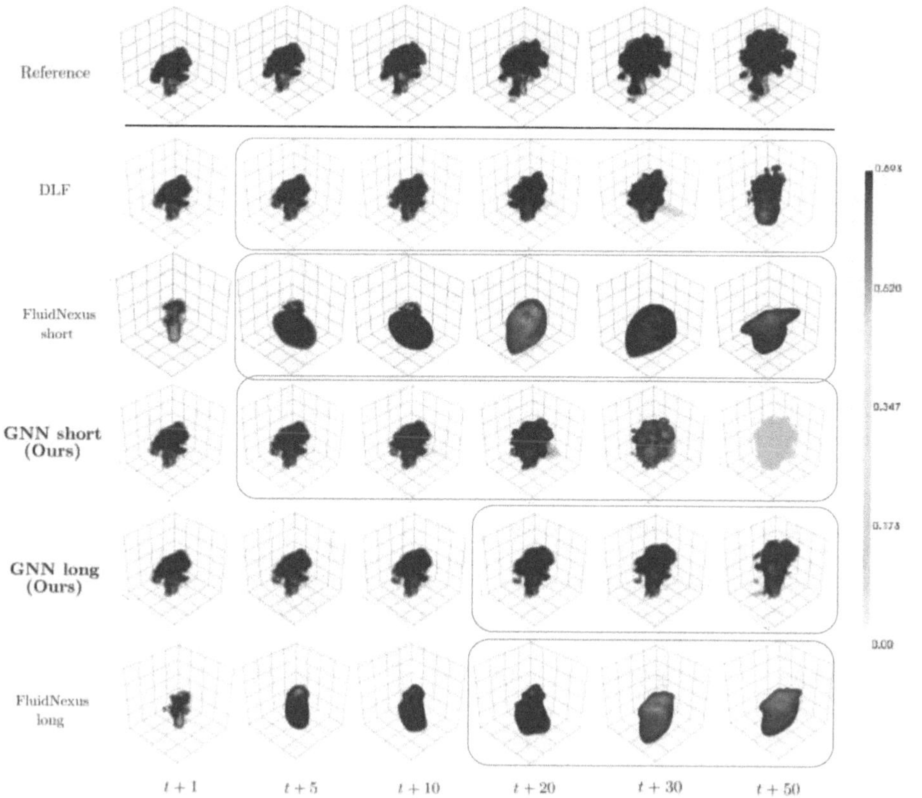

Fig. 5. 3D voxel simulation over extended horizons. We highlight predicted frames that extend beyond the training horizons with □. This volumetric setup is disadvantageous for FluidNexus, which was designed for 2D novel view synthesis rather than direct 3D voxel forecasting (we extract its voxels using *alpha2den*). While models trained on short contexts struggle to maintain high-frequency details and diverge rapidly after a few steps, GNN long successfully captures the structural evolution of the smoke cloud, outputting coherent predictions for up to 5× more prediction steps than its training horizon.

4.2 Results

Pure reconstruction quality – before evaluating the dynamics, we compare the raw particle representations of FluidNexus and R2-Gaussian. While rendering is not our primary contribution, a high-quality spatial representation impacts the learning of the dynamics. To isolate and evaluate the representations directly, we compare both methods without next-state prediction and bypass the video diffusion refinement module in FluidNexus. As shown in Fig. 3, R2-Gaussian achieves better reconstruction quality under these specific conditions. This outcome is expected and aligns with the design principles of FluidNexus, which delegates much of the final visual fidelity to its powerful diffusion refinement model.

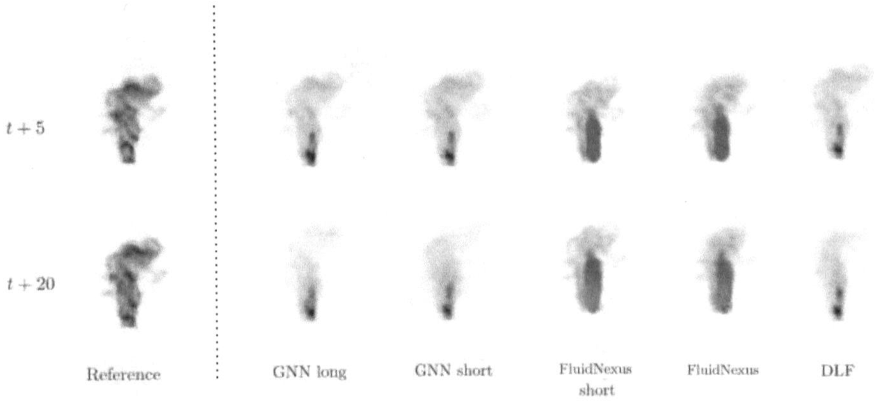

Fig. 6. Predicted and rendered images for all models at timesteps $t+5$ and $t+20$. FluidNexus exhibits artifacts characteristic of PBF simulations, with the cylindrical particle emission region remaining visible in the reconstructed plume. In contrast, the other models preserve higher-frequency details more effectively. Hoewever, all models tend to overestimate density near the bottom of the plume. This behavior is primarily caused by the image normalization applied after Gaussian splatting, which reduces the relative opacity of other regions. A second contributing factor is the R2-Gaussian reconstruction itself, which places a large number of Gaussians near the base of the plume. As a result, the predicted distributions inherit this reconstruction artifact.

However, when evaluating the unrefined outputs, we observe qualitatively that R2-Gaussian is more effective at capturing and reconstructing high-frequency details directly within the raw particle representation. We further illustrate this in Fig. 4, which compares FluidNexus with and without its refiner. Without the diffusion step, the raw outputs from the underlying PBF simulation lack structural detail. Consequently, the final rendering quality relies heavily on the diffusion model being strongly conditioned by ground-truth context frames, rather than the underlying physics simulation alone.

Forecasting simulated trajectories – To evaluate the predictive capabilities of the models, we compare the simulated smoke cloud trajectories of DLF, FluidNexus, and our method in both 3D (density voxel grids) and 2D (rendered images), and report the results in Table 1. It is important to note the inherent evaluation biases across these modalities: the 3D setup naturally favors R2-Gaussian-based methods (DLF and ours), which explicitly model volumetric density, whereas the 2D evaluation is highly advantageous for FluidNexus, which leverages a powerful video diffusion model specifically optimized for image quality. Despite these differing modalities, our approach yields the best overall performance (see Table 1) in the *long* setup where the model benefits from a larger context window and an extended training horizon. We attribute this success to two main factors: first, the R2-Gaussian framework provides a more accurate and suitable raw spatial representation for semi-transparent smoke clouds compared to FluidNexus; second, the proposed model in the DLF method is designed to predict particles motion simulated by SPH simulations. Therefore, the design of their loss term and their context window does not fit the task when the observed particles are reconstructed from visual observations.

Qualitative results (Fig. 5) confirm that this forecasting task remains inherently difficult. While most baselines degrade rapidly when rolled out beyond their training horizon, our method trained in the *long* setup exhibits remarkable temporal stability, maintaining structurally coherent predictions for up to $\times 5$ its original training horizon. As illustrated in Fig. 6, pure forecasting tasks fundamentally limit the availability of ground-truth context frames. Consequently, methods like FluidNexus which rely on these frames to condition their generative video refinement process inevitably experience a drop in structural detail and visual fidelity when predicting future states autonomously.

Graph construction ablation – We ablated the graph connectivity step to evaluate how the K-Nearest Neighbors (KNN) algorithm impacts the downstream dynamics. Specifically, we tested different values for the number of neighbors k and varied the features used to compute the distance between particles. As shown in Table 2, including all Gaussian attributes (e.g., scale, rotation, density) in the KNN distance metric degrades performance. We observe marginal variations when increasing the neighborhood size from k=3 to k=5 and when using all the attributes to compute the KNN neighbors. We hypothesize that this robustness stems directly from our autoregressive initialization scheme with R2-Gaussian which enforces temporal consistency.

Table 2. Ablation on graph construction over the horizon H = 25. Our GNN-based method is relatively insensitive to the choice of the KNN neighborhood size. While k=5 achieves slightly better performance on the 2D image-based metrics, graph variants incorporating KNN features yield marginally higher scores on the 3D evaluation metrics.

	3D Metrics		2D Metrics	
Method	PSNR (dB)	SSIM	PSNR (dB)	SSIM
3 Neighbors (position)	44.13	0.97	30.3	0.84
5 Neighbors (position)	46.03	0.98	**34.85**	**0.94**
3 Neighbors (all attributes)	**46.57**	**0.99**	33.25	0.90

5 Conclusion

In this paper, we presented a novel approach for the unsupervised 3D forecasting of smoke clouds from multi-view videos. This task is difficult: prior work has largely been restricted to supervised training with ground-truth simulated data or purely reconstructive tasks supported by explicit physical models. We demonstrated that explicit density modeling rather than standard 3DGS color attributes is crucial for accurately representing and tracking volumetric materials like smoke. By coupling this representation with a learned graph-based dynamical model, our method takes a first step toward unsupervised learning of fluid dynamics from unlabeled video. Future work will address the disentanglement of the fluid from complex static backgrounds, a challenging problem that remains unsolved in pure reconstruction settings.

Acknowledgments. This work was supported by the project ANR-23-IAS2-0002 "FireFlies".

References

1. Agarwal, N., et al.: Cosmos world foundation model platform for physical ai. arXiv preprint arXiv:2501.03575 (2025)
2. Allen, K., et al.: Inverse design for fluid-structure interactions using graph network simulators. Adv. Neural Inf. Process. Syst. (2022)
3. Assran, M., et al.: V-jepa 2: self-supervised video models enable understanding, prediction and planning. arXiv preprint (2025)
4. Battaglia, P., Pascanu, R., Lai, M., Jimenez Rezende, D.: Interaction networks for learning about objects, relations and physics. Adv. Neural Inf. Process. Syst. (2016)
5. Bruce, J., et al.: Genie: generative interactive environments. In: International Conference on Machine Learning (ICML) (2024)
6. Chu, M., et al.: Physics informed neural fields for smoke reconstruction with sparse data. ACM Trans. Graph. (ToG) (2022)
7. Chu, M., et al.: Physics informed neural fields for smoke reconstruction with sparse data. ACM Trans. Graph. (2022)
8. Condor, J., et al.: Don't splat your gaussians: volumetric ray-traced primitives for modeling and rendering scattering and emissive media. ACM Trans. Graph. (2025)
9. Eckert, M.L., Um, K., Thuerey, N.: ScalarFlow: a large-scale volumetric data set of real-world scalar transport flows for computer animation and machine learning. ACM Trans. Graph. (2019)
10. Feldkamp, L.A., Davis, L.C., Kress, J.W.: Practical cone-beam algorithm. J. Opt. Soc. Am. A (1984)
11. Gao, Y., Yu, H.X., Zhu, B., Wu, J.: Fluidnexus: 3d fluid reconstruction and prediction from a single video. In: Conference on Computer Vision and Pattern Recognition (CVPR) (2025)
12. Gao, Z., Planche, B., Zheng, M., Choudhuri, A., Chen, T., Wu, Z.: 6dgs: enhanced direction-aware gaussian splatting for volumetric rendering. In: International Conference on Learning Representations (ICLR) (2024)
13. Garay, M.J., Davis, A.B., Diner, D.J.: Tomographic reconstruction of an aerosol plume using passive multiangle observations from the misr satellite instrument. Geophys. Res. Lett. (2016)
14. Garcia, A.C., Warchocki, J., van Gemert, J., Brinks, D., Tomen, N.: Learning physics from video: unsupervised physical parameter estimation for continuous dynamical systems. In: Conference on Computer Vision and Pattern Recognition (CVPR) (2025)

15. Gingold, R.A., Monaghan, J.J.: Smoothed particle hydrodynamics: theory and application to non-spherical stars. Mon. Not. R. Astron. Soc. (1977)
16. Guan, S., Deng, H., Wang, Y., Yang, X.: Neurofluid: fluid dynamics grounding with particle-driven neural radiance fields. In: International Conference on Machine Learning (2022)
17. Guen, V.L., Thome, N.: Disentangling physical dynamics from unknown factors for unsupervised video prediction. In: Conference on Computer Vision and Pattern Recognition (CVPR) (2020)
18. Guo, Y.C., Kang, D., Bao, L., He, Y., Zhang, S.H.: Nerfren: neural radiance fields with reflections. In: Conference on Computer Vision and Pattern Recognition (CVPR) (2022)
19. Han, X., Gao, H., Pfaff, T., Wang, J.X., Liu, L.P.: Predicting physics in mesh-reduced space with temporal attention. In: International Conference on Learning Representations (ICLR) (2022)
20. Ichnowski, J., Avigal, Y., Kerr, J., Goldberg, K.: Dex-nerf: using a neural radiance field to grasp transparent objects. In: Conference on Robot Learning (CoRL) (2021)
21. Janny, S., Baradel, F., Neverova, N., Nadri, M., Mori, G., Wolf, C.: Filtered-cophy: unsupervised learning of counterfactual physics in pixel space. In: International Conference on Learning Representations (ICLR) (2022)
22. Janny, S., Beneteau, A., Nadri, M., Digne, J., Thome, N., Wolf, C.: Eagle: large-scale learning of turbulent fluid dynamics with mesh transformers. In: International Conference on Learning Representation (ICLR) (2023)
23. Jatavallabhula, K.M., et al.: gradsim: differentiable simulation for system identification and visuomotor control. In: International Conference on Learning Representations (ICLR) (2021)
24. Kerbl, B., Kopanas, G., Leimkuehler, T., Drettakis, G.: 3d gaussian splatting for real-time radiance field rendering. ACM Trans. Graph. (2023)
25. Kulkarni, T.D., et al.: Unsupervised learning of object keypoints for perception and control. Adv. Neural Inf. Process. Syst. (NeurIPS) (2019)
26. Lam, R., et al.: Learning skillful medium-range global weather forecasting. Science (2023)
27. Levis, A., Schechner, Y.Y., Aides, A., Davis, A.B.: Airborne three-dimensional cloud tomography. In: International Conference on Computer Vision (ICCV) (2015)
28. Levis, A., Schechner, Y.Y., Davis, A.B., Loveridge, J.: Multi-view polarimetric scattering cloud tomography and retrieval of droplet size. Remote Sens. (2020)
29. Li, X., et al.: Pac-nerf: physics augmented continuum neural radiance fields for geometry-agnostic system identification. In: International Conference on Learning Representations (ICLR) (2023)
30. Mildenhall, B., Srinivasan, P.P., Tancik, M., Barron, J.T., Ramamoorthi, R., Ng, R.: Nerf: representing scenes as neural radiance fields for view synthesis. Commun. ACM (2021)
31. Minderer, M., Sun, C., Villegas, R., Cole, F., Murphy, K.P., Lee, H.: Unsupervised learning of object structure and dynamics from videos. Adv. Neural Inf. Process. Syst. (NeurIPS) (2019)
32. Müller, M., Charypar, D., Gross, M.: Particle-based fluid simulation for interactive applications. In: ACM SIGGRAPH (2003)
33. Pfaff, T., Fortunato, M., Sanchez-Gonzalez, A., Battaglia, P.: Learning mesh-based simulation with graph networks. In: International Conference on Learning Representations (ICLR) (2020)

34. Qiu, J., Cen, R., Li, Z., Yan, H., Cheng, M.M., Ren, B.: Neusmoke: efficient smoke reconstruction and view synthesis with neural transportation fields. In: SIGGRAPH Asia (2024)
35. Sanchez-Gonzalez, A., Godwin, J., Pfaff, T., Ying, R., Leskovec, J., Battaglia, P.: Learning to simulate complex physics with graph networks. In: International Conference on Machine Learning (ICML) (2020)
36. Toshev, A.P., Galletti, G., Brandstetter, J., Adami, S., Adams, N.A.: Learning lagrangian fluid mechanics with e (3)-equivariant graph neural networks. In: International Conference on Geometric Science of Information (2023)
37. Ummenhofer, B., Prantl, L., Thuerey, N., Koltun, V.: Lagrangian fluid simulation with continuous convolutions. In: International Conference on Learning Representations (ICLR) (2020)
38. Wang, Y., Tang, S., Chu, M.: Physics-informed learning of characteristic trajectories for smoke reconstruction. In: ACM SIGGRAPH Conference (2024)
39. Wu, J., Lu, E., Kohli, P., Freeman, B., Tenenbaum, J.: Learning to see physics via visual de-animation. Adv. Neural Inf. Process. Syst. (NeurIPS) (2017)
40. Yoon, H., Lee, S.: Neural radiance fields for transparent object using visual hull. In: International Conference on Big Data and Smart Computing (BigComp) (2024)
41. Yu, H.X., Zheng, Y., Gao, Y., Deng, Y., Zhu, B., Wu, J.: Inferring hybrid neural fluid fields from videos. Adv. Neural Inf. Process. Syst. (NeurIPS) (2023)
42. Zha, R., Lin, T.J., Cai, Y., Cao, J., Zhang, Y., Li, H.: R2-gaussian: rectifying radiative gaussian splatting for tomographic reconstruction. Adv. Neural Inf. Process. Syst. (NeurIPS) (2024)
43. Zhang, M., Zhang, K., Li, Y.: Dynamic 3d gaussian tracking for graph-based neural dynamics modeling. In: Conference on Robot Learning (CoRL) (2024)
44. Zhong, L., Yu, H.X., Wu, J., Li, Y.: Reconstruction and simulation of elastic objects with spring-mass 3d gaussians. In: European Conference on Computer Vision (ECCV). Springer, Heidelberg (2024). https://doi.org/10.1007/978-3-031-72627-9_23
45. Zhou, Z., Lu, X.: An improved 3d gaussian splatting method for smoke reconstruction. In: International Conference on Big Data and Artificial Intelligence (BDAI) (2025)

VLC Fusion: Vision-Language Conditioned Sensor Fusion for Robust Object Detection

Aditya Taparia[1(✉)], Noel Ngu[1], Mario Leiva[2], Joshua Shay Kricheli[5], John Corcoran[3], Nathaniel D. Bastian[4], Gerardo Simari[2], Paulo Shakarian[5], and Ransalu Senanayake[1]

[1] Arizona State University, Tempe, AZ, USA
{atajparia,nngu2,ransalu}@asu.edu
[2] Universidad Nacional del Sur, Bahía Blanca, Argentina
{mleiva3,gsimari}@asu.edu
[3] U.S. Department of Defense, Arlington, VA, USA
john.corcoran.ctr@darpa.mil
[4] United States Military Academy, West Point, NY, USA
nathaniel.bastian@westpoint.edu
[5] Syracuse University, Syracuse, NY, USA
{jkrichel,pashakar}@syr.edu

Abstract. Although fusing multiple sensor modalities can enhance object detection performance, existing fusion approaches often overlook subtle variations in environmental conditions and sensor inputs. As a result, they struggle to adaptively weight each modality under such variations. To address this challenge, we introduce Vision-Language Conditioned Fusion (VLC Fusion), a novel fusion framework that leverages a Vision-Language Model (VLM) to condition the fusion process on nuanced environmental cues. By capturing high-level environmental context such as darkness, rain, and camera blurring, the VLM guides the model to dynamically adjust modality weights based on the current scene, ensuring robustness against environmental shifts. We evaluate VLC Fusion on real-world autonomous driving and military target detection datasets that include image, LIDAR, and mid-wave infrared modalities. Our experiments show that VLC Fusion consistently outperforms conventional fusion baselines, achieving improved detection accuracy in both seen and unseen scenarios. **Supplementary Material and Code:** https://github.com/aditya-taparia/VLCFusion.

Keywords: Sensor Fusion · Vision-Language Models · Object Detection

1 Introduction

Reliable object detection is critical for many real-world autonomous systems such as autonomous vehicles and surveillance platforms. Since different sensor

M. Ceci et al. (Eds.): ECML PKDD 2026, LNAI 16948, pp. 51–68, 2027.
https://doi.org/10.1007/978-3-032-37679-4_4

modalities offer distinct advantages, multi-modal fusion techniques aim to integrate object detectors trained on these different modalities. For example, since RGB images provide high-resolution detail while LIDAR offers depth perception despite its sparse point cloud, sensor fusion can provide a high-resolution image with some depth information.

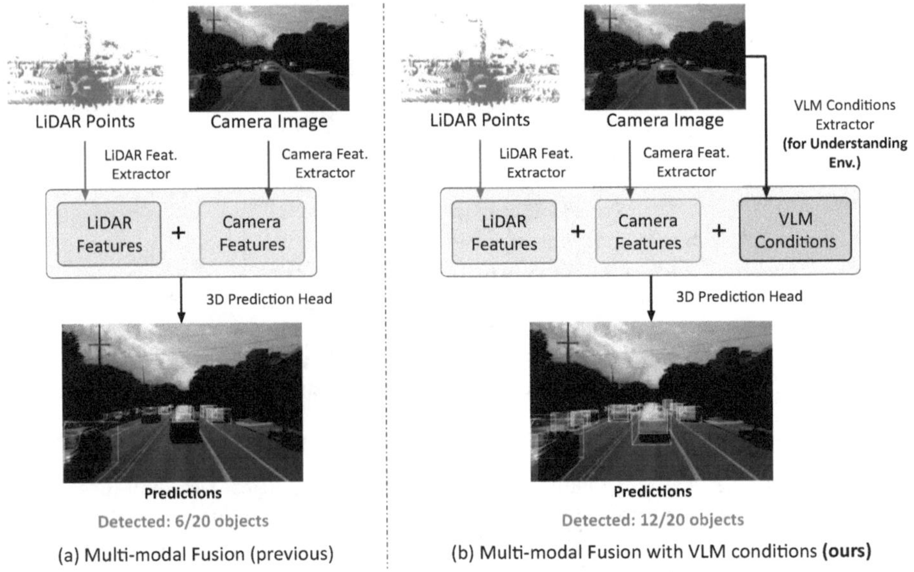

Fig. 1. Overview of **VLC Fusion**. Compared to (a) standard fusion for object detection, (b) our method modulates modality-specific features with environment-specific meta-information, called *conditions*, improving the resilience of object detection to diverse natural environmental variations.

A key limitation of current fusion methods is that they overlook how the performance of each modality varies with external environmental conditions. Since object detection models are optimized individually for specific sensor modalities, each excels under certain environmental conditions but exhibits vulnerabilities under others. For instance, state-of-the-art RGB-based object detectors such as Detection Transformer (DETR) [4] performs well in clear, well-lit conditions but degrade considerably in low-light or adverse weather scenarios such as fog [2,20]. Conversely, LiDAR-based object detectors such as PointPillars [13] and SECOND [27] provide robust performance under varied lighting levels but can deteriorate in weather conditions such as rain due to light scattering and other sensor-specific limitations [6]. The problem of environment dependence becomes even more pronounced when the system is deployed in unseen environments.

To address this challenge, we propose Vision-Language Conditioned Fusion (VLC Fusion), a novel approach to incorporate environmental meta-information

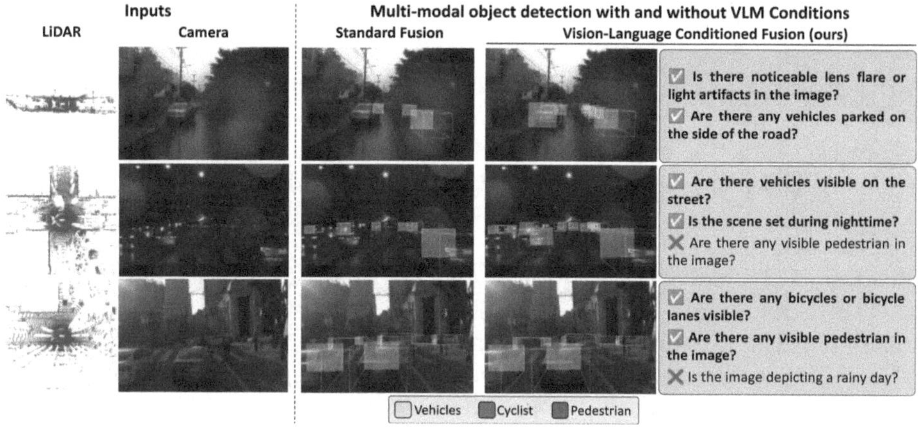

Fig. 2. Comparison of sample predictions from multi-modal fusion and VLC Fusion: from left to right, raw LiDAR point clouds and camera views, predictions from a multi-modal fusion baseline, and predictions from our VLC Fusion conditioned on VLM-extracted environmental cues (✓/✗ prompts shown at right). Conditioning on high-level context improves detection performance in recovering occluded cars (Example 1), detecting more vehicles under nighttime glare (Example 2), and correctly identifying the cyclist (magenta) and pedestrians (orange) (Example 3) where the baseline fails. (Color figure online)

obtained through Vision-Language models (VLMs) into the fusion process. Since current state-of-the-art VLMs have demonstrated impressive scene-understanding capabilities [15, 18], we use them offline to reliably extract detailed environmental cues across a wide range of real-world tasks. We then proposed an architecture to incorporate the VLM conditions into the fusion network. At test-time, in addition to raw sensor inputs, the VLM provides an analysis of the scene, making our method robust to both seen (in-distribution) and unseen (out-of-distribution) scenarios. Figure 1 illustrates the difference between (a) standard multi-modal fusion and (b) our VLC Fusion. Furthermore, Fig. 2 presents qualitative examples where this conditioning on VLM cues leads to better detection. The primary contributions of the paper are:

1. We propose a novel fusion approach, called VLC Fusion, that automatically weighs feature fusion on environment-specific meta-information.
2. We introduce an automated framework for offline extraction and integration of relevant environmental cues from raw datasets.
3. We empirically demonstrate the usefulness of environmental conditions in multi-modal sensor fusion on two real-world object detection tasks, autonomous driving and military target detection. We also demonstrate how lightweight, fast, small-scale VLMs can be used realistically during the online object detection phase.

2 Related Work

Multi-modal Sensor Fusion for Object Detection. LiDAR-camera fusion methods demonstrated clear benefits over single-modality approaches by combining precise geometric measurements with dense visual context. Previous works such as AVOD [12] project LiDAR point clouds into the image plane to jointly learn features. While PointFusion [26] fuses raw point embeddings with image features via a learned weighting scheme. Fusion SSD [2] concatenates feature maps from both modalities and applies convolutional layers for joint detection, and Learnable Align [17] uses a cross-attention block to align and integrate modality-specific features. More recent works such as TransFusion [1] and PillarNeXt [14] use cross-modal attention to further improve alignment at multiple scales. Although these methods achieve good performance, they generally *apply static fusion rules* that do not adjust to changing environmental conditions [2]. This lack of adaptability leads to degraded performance when encountering conditions not well-represented in the training data, such as sudden changes in illumination or unusual weather patterns [6,20]. We propose the use of environmental-cues to dynamically weigh the importance of each modality.
Condition-Aware Fusion Approaches. To handle diverse lighting and weather scenarios, subsequent work recognized the need for adaptability, introducing condition-aware mechanisms that adapt fusion weights based on environment estimates. DSFuse [9] uses uncertainty estimates to downweight noisy modalities. More recently, RGB-X [5] proposes the use of scene agnostic switch to switch between detection head based on particular scenario. CAFuser [3] proposes a learned condition token trained with a CLIP style loss to embed discrete scene types (e.g., "rainy", "foggy") and guide multi-modal feature fusion. Despite these advances, most methods *rely on a fixed taxonomy of conditions and require annotated examples* for each. This reliance on predefined categories restricts their ability to handle ambiguous or continuously varying conditions (e.g., light fog transitioning to heavy fog) and requires potentially expensive data annotation efforts for every new condition, limiting their flexibility when encountering novel or mixed scenarios [3]. On the contrary, we create application-specific conditions and also provide a way to automatically identify these relevant conditions.
Vision–Language Models for Context-Awareness. Building on condition aware mechanisms, recent work explores the use of large pre-trained vision language models (VLMs) for extracting semantic context. Models like CLIP [22] support matching image regions to arbitrary text, while MDETR [11] extends this to end-to-end phrase grounding. More integrated approaches, such as PaLM-E [7] and RoboFlamingo [16], combine vision, language, and robot state for downstream reasoning. These models enable systems to understand not just what objects are present, but also how they relate to tasks or environmental cues. However, leveraging VLMs to infer environmental cues (e.g., "bright urban afternoon" vs. "dusty desert dusk") rather than relying on fixed, discrete categories and using these insights to guide real-time sensor fusion remains an open challenge. Our work addresses this gap by using a pretrained VLM to extract

environmental conditions that adaptively modulate sensor weighting, enabling context-aware fusion without requiring explicit labels.

3 Methodology

Our methodology comprises two major components: 1) identification of application specific environmental conditions and querying VLM to obtain the corresponding responses, and 2) integrating these conditional information into the sensor fusion architecture. We first describe how application-specific conditions are identified and queried from VLMs, and then detail how the resulting conditional information is integrated into the fusion network.

3.1 Offline Condition Extraction and Generation

Extracting meaningful environmental conditions is crucial for guiding sensor fusion in our method. To this end, we explored two ways by which one can extract (or define) conditions from a dataset.
Human-Defined Conditions. Leveraging prior domain knowledge and metadata available from dataset, experts can manually define relevant conditions based on the application. While straightforward, this approach can be subjective and may not generalize effectively across diverse datasets and environments.
Automated Condition Extraction. To overcome limitations associated with manual definitions, we introduce an automated framework for offline extraction of rich environmental information and contextual cues from dataset via VLM. For this purpose, as shown in Fig. 3a, we introduce a three step process:

Step 1 (Captioning). Let the training dataset be D with N images, and let $D_{\text{captioning}} \subset D$ denote a randomly selected subset of M images. Using a captioning function $\text{caption}(\cdot; p_{\text{caption}})$, we generate a descriptive caption c_x for each image $x \in D_{\text{captioning}}$:

$$c_x = \text{caption}(x; p_{\text{caption}}), \qquad \forall x \in D_{\text{captioning}}.$$

Here, p_{caption} is the text prompt "Describe the input scene," together with the system prompt provided in Supplementary. This gives us M image-caption pairs (x, c_x).

Step 2 (Extraction). After generating captions, we apply $\text{extract}(\cdot)$ to the M image-caption pairs to derive a set of environmental conditions C:

$$C \leftarrow \text{extract}\big(\{(x_m, c_{x_m})\}_{m=1}^{M}; p_{\text{extraction}}\big).$$

Here, $p_{\text{extraction}}$ is the prompt "Provide conditions based on the following image–caption pairs," used together with the system prompt described in Supplementary. This step converts free-form captions into a structured set of application-specific environmental conditions. For example, from the caption *"busy urban intersection on a cloudy day,"* the extracted conditions may include *"presence of vehicles," "cloudy weather,"* and *"busy pedestrian activity."* In this way, the extraction stage captures both high-level scene semantics and fine-grained contextual cues. Before using these conditions for training and evaluation, we remove duplicate entries.

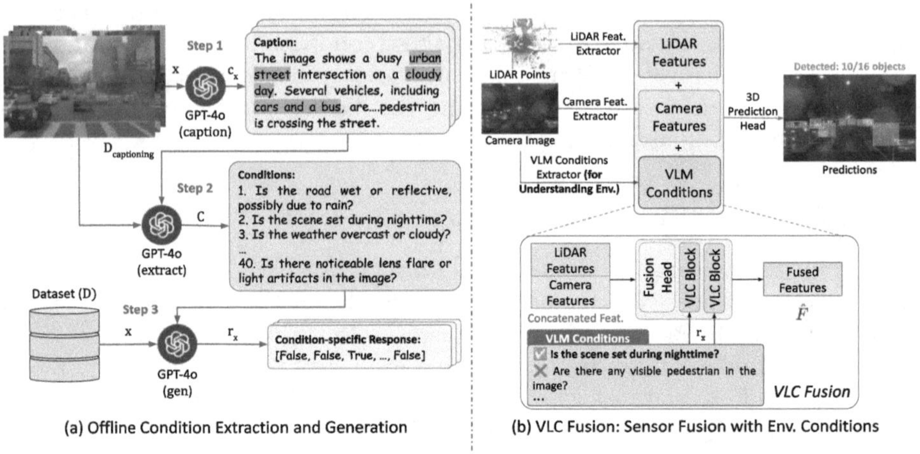

Fig. 3. Overview of (a) the three-step automated pipeline for extracting environmental conditions: captioning a subset of images, extracting a set of conditions, and querying the VLM to generate a binary condition-response vector r_x per image. (b) Sensor fusion with environmental conditions, where stacked VLC blocks modulate the fused features using r_x before the detection head.

Step 3 (Generation). Once the environmental conditions have been identified, we query a pretrained VLM to determine whether each condition is present in each image from the full training dataset D. Concretely, for every image $x \in D$ and condition $c \in C$, we generate a binary response:

$$r_{x,c} = \text{gen}(x, c), \qquad \forall x \in D,\ c \in C,$$

where $r_{x,c} \in \{\text{True}, \text{False}\}$ indicates whether condition c is present in image x. In our implementation, GPT-4o is used for this condition-response generation step. For a given image x, this produces a condition-response vector:

$$r_x = \left[r_{x,c_1}, r_{x,c_2}, \ldots, r_{x,c_{|C|}}\right].$$

This vector serves as the environmental condition representation for image x and is used as input to the fusion model during training and evaluation.

3.2 Sensor Fusion with Environmental Conditions

We now describe how the queried environmental condition vector is integrated into the fusion network. Let $F_1 \in \mathbb{R}^{B\times C_1\times H\times W}$ and $F_2 \in \mathbb{R}^{B\times C_2\times H\times W}$ denote feature maps from two sensing modalities, such as visible and infrared imagery or RGB and LiDAR features. Let $r_x \in \{0,1\}^{|C|}$ denote the environmental condition vector obtained for input x using the procedure in Sect. 3.1. Our goal is to learn an environment-conditioned fusion function:

$$\mathcal{F}(F_1, F_2, r_x) \mapsto \hat{F},$$

where $\hat{F}$ is the fused representation passed to the downstream detection head.
Fusion Head. As shown in Fig. 3b, we first concatenate the modality-specific feature maps:

$$U = [F_1; F_2] \in \mathbb{R}^{B\times(C_1+C_2)\times H\times W}.$$

This concatenated representation U is passed through a multi-scale fusion head composed of three parallel convolutional branches with kernel sizes 1×1, 3×3, and 5×5. Their outputs are combined using input-adaptive weights to produce an initial fused feature map $F \in \mathbb{R}^{B\times C_{\mathrm{out}}\times H\times W}$.
VLC Block. As shown in Fig. 3b, the fused feature F is refined using our VLC block (see Fig. 4), which combines normalization, FiLM-based conditioning [21], CBAM attention [25], and residual convolutional refinement. The purpose of the VLC block is to adapt the fused representation according to the queried environmental conditions.

Given an input feature map $Z \in \mathbb{R}^{B\times C\times H\times W}$, the VLC block first maps the environmental condition vector r_x to channel-wise FiLM parameters:

$$(\gamma, \beta, \alpha) = \phi(r_x), \qquad \gamma, \beta, \alpha \in \mathbb{R}^{B\times C\times 1\times 1}.$$

It then normalizes the fused representation using Group Norm (GN), applies condition-dependent affine modulation, and refines the result using Convolutional Block Attention Module (CBAM):

$$\begin{aligned}\bar{Z} &= (1+\gamma)\odot \mathrm{GN}(Z) + \beta\\ Z' &= Z + \alpha \odot \mathrm{CBAM}(\bar{Z}).\end{aligned}$$

Here, γ and β perform condition-dependent channel-wise scaling and shifting, while α controls the contribution of the attention-refined feature to the residual update. This design allows the model to condition the fused features on the environmental vector and focus on relevant features.

To further improve representation quality, the VLC block includes a second residual refinement stage using a lightweight convolutional feed-forward network. Concretely, Z' is normalized and modulated by another FiLM transformation, and then passed through a feed-forward convolutional block. Unlike the first stage, this refinement step does not use a FiLM-based control gate in the end:

$$\begin{aligned}\bar{Z}' &= (1+\gamma_f)\odot \mathrm{GN}(Z') + \beta_f,\\ \mathrm{VLC}(Z, r_x) &= Z' + \mathrm{FFN}(\bar{Z}').\end{aligned}$$

Table 1. Dataset splits for the Waymo Open and ATR datasets across seen and unseen scenarios. For Waymo, the seen split covers day and night driving while the unseen split covers dawn and dusk. For ATR, the seen split covers object distances of 1000–5000 m while the unseen split covers intermediate distances (1500 m, 2500 m, 3500 m, and 4500 m). The unseen scenarios are held out exclusively for evaluation.

Dataset	Variation	Train	Validation	Test
Waymo Open dataset(RGB + LiDAR)	Seen	73,112	9,139	9,139
	Unseen	–	–	7,052
ATR dataset(Visible + MWIR)	Seen	45,207	15,075	15,088
	Unseen	–	–	11,952

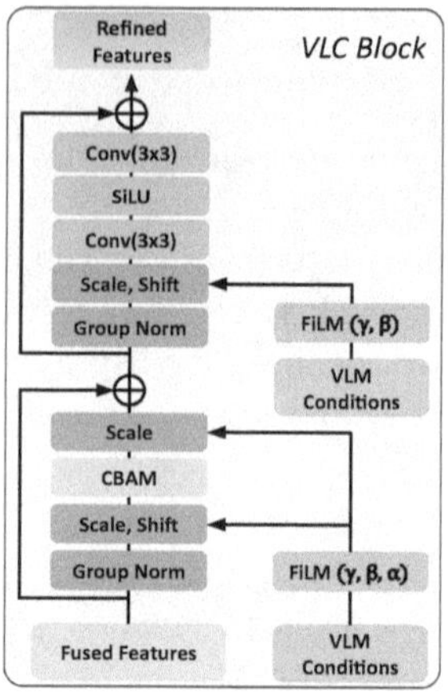

Fig. 4. Architecture of the VLC Block.

VLC Fusion Architecture. In the complete architecture, the output of the fusion head, F is passed through two VLC blocks sequentially:

$$\hat{F} = \mathrm{VLC}_2(\mathrm{VLC}_1(F, r_x), r_x).$$

The first VLC block performs condition aware adjustment of the initial multimodal representation, while the second block refines the fused feature before it is fed to the detector. The final fused representation $\hat{F}$ is then passed to the task-specific detection head. We inject environmental conditions after initial multimodal aggregation so that the unimodal backbones preserve stable modality-specific representations, while the joint representation can be adaptively reweighted according to the sensing environment.

4 Experiments

In this section, we empirically evaluate our proposed VLC Fusion methodology using two real-world datasets: the Waymo Open dataset [23], where we fuse RGB and LiDAR modalities for 3D object detection, and the Automated Target Recognition (ATR) dataset [8], where we fuse visible and infrared (IR) imagery for 2D object detection. We evaluate the effectiveness of VLC Fusion under both seen (training distribution) and unseen (out-of-distribution) scenarios. As shown in Supplementary, 85% and 76% of samples in the Waymo and ATR datasets, respectively, contain at least one active environmental condition. Below, we first detail the creation of seen and unseen datasets, followed by metrics, implementation details, baseline methods, results, and ablations.

4.1 Datasets

Waymo Open Dataset: For our experiments, we use the San Francisco portion of the Waymo Open dataset, which provides synchronized LiDAR and RGB imagery captured at 10 Hz in a busy urban environment with diverse weather (e.g. rainy, sunny) and lighting conditions (e.g. day time, night time, dawn/dusk time). Each sequence contains approximately 200 frames across 20 s.

We define two scenarios: a seen scenario, which includes data collected under day and night time, and an unseen scenario, comprising data from dawn and dusk. The seen scenario was used for both training and testing, while the unseen scenario was reserved strictly for testing. Prior to training, frames were shuffled to ensure diversity and robustness. The resulting train-val-test splits for both scenarios are summarized in Table 1.

ATR Dataset: The ATR dataset contains visible and mid-wave infrared (MWIR) imagery aimed at target recognition applications, and comprehensive metadata detailing object distances, viewing angles, wind speed, and other relevant attributes. We first synchronized the frames from the two modalities using timestamps and object metadata to ensure proper alignment. Following synchronization, we partitioned the dataset into seen and unseen scenarios based on object distance. The seen set includes distances of 1000 m, 2000 m, 3000 m, 4000 m, and 5000 m, while the unseen set comprises intermediate distances (1500 m, 2500 m, 3500 m, and 4500 m). The resulting train-validation-test splits for both seen and unseen sets are summarized in Table 1.

4.2 Metrics

We evaluate the fusion models using dataset-specific metrics, as detailed below.
Waymo Open Dataset: We evaluate the performance of the fused networks on the Waymo dataset using 3D mean Average Precision (mAP) and mean Average Precision with Heading (mAPH). Evaluations were conducted for three object classes—Vehicle, Pedestrian, and Cyclist—at IoU thresholds of 0.7, 0.5, and 0.5, respectively. Performance was reported across two difficulty levels (L1 and L2), which are defined in the dataset itself based on the number of LiDAR points associated with each object.

ATR Dataset: We evaluate the fusion network using standard metrics: mean Average Precision across IoU thresholds from 0.50 to 0.95 (mAP), alongside mean Average Precision at IoU thresholds of 0.50 and 0.75 (mAP_{50}, mAP_{75}), and mean Average Recall at 100 proposals (mAR_{100}). We report the combined overall performance across both the seen and unseen test splits.

4.3 Implementation Details

Below, we describe training setups for individual object detection models per dataset and modality, followed by the generation of environmental conditions using a VLM.

Object Detectors. Waymo Open Dataset: For the RGB modality, we train a DETR-based 2D object detector with a ResNet-50 backbone using the Hugging Face Trainer. The model was trained for 150 epochs with a batch size of 16 and

Fig. 5. Qualitative examples of VLC Fusion in both seen and unseen environments. **Top row:** 3D detections on the Waymo Open dataset under *seen* (daytime/nighttime) and *unseen* (dawn/dusk time) conditions, with vehicles (yellow), cyclists (purple), and pedestrians (red) accurately localized. **Bottom row:** 2D detection on the ATR dataset for *seen* (1000 m and 2000 m distances respectively) and *unseen* (1500 m distance) scenarios. More qualitative examples are provided in Supplementary. (Color figure online)

an initial learning rate of 5×10^{-5}. Best checkpoints were saved every 250 steps using validation mAP.

For the LiDAR modality, we used the SECOND 3D object detection model, trained on Waymo point-cloud data. Training followed the standard MMDetection3D pipeline, with the point-cloud range set from $[-76.8, -51.2, -2]$ m to $[76.8, 51.2, 4]$ m, targeting the Car, Pedestrian, and Cyclist classes. The model was trained for 100 epochs using the AdamW optimizer with a learning rate of 1×10^{-3} and a batch size of 2. Evaluation was conducted after each epoch using the `WaymoMetric` evaluator, and the best-performing checkpoint was selected for downstream use. Additionally, each fusion model was fine-tuned for 40 epochs using the same optimization settings as the LiDAR detector.

ATR Dataset: We train two separate DETR-based 2D object detectors with a ResNet-50 backbone, one for visible images and the other for MWIR images, using the Hugging Face Trainer. Each model was trained for 140 epochs using the AdamW optimizer with an initial learning rate of 5×10^{-5} and a weight decay of 1×10^{-4}. Training used a batch size of 32 with gradient accumulation over 8 steps. Model checkpoints were evaluated based on validation mean Average Precision (mAP), and the checkpoint achieving the highest mAP was retained for final evaluation. Additionally, for the ATR dataset, each fusion model was fine-tuned for 100 epochs using the same training configuration.

VLM-Queried Environmental Conditions. We first generated environmental conditions using the methods described in Sect. 3.1. Two sets of conditions were defined: human-defined and automatically extracted. After obtaining these conditions, we queried GPT-4o to generate responses for each data point.

Table 2. Overall Waymo performance on seen and unseen scenarios. We report 3D mAP/mAPH for both L1 and L2 difficulty levels. Best and second-best results are highlighted in bold and underline, respectively.

Fusion Technique	Seen Scenario (mAP/mAPH)		Unseen Scenario (mAP/mAPH)	
	L1	L2	L1	L2
Fusion SSD	26.1/23.6	23.06/20.8	31.03/28.08	28.6/25.8
Fusion SSD with Self-Attention	21.8/19.6	19.07/17.1	24.2/21.8	22.2/19.9
Learnable Align	18.6/16.3	16.2/14.2	23.08/20.1	21.2/18.5
RGB-X	27.1/24.5	23.9/21.6	31.03/28.1	28.5/25.9
VLC Fusion with Human Defined Conditions (n = 3)	28.5/26.2	25.2/23.08	32.3/29.7	29.8/27.3
VLC Fusion with Extracted Conditions (n = 10)	**37.0/34.4**	**33.0/30.5**	**41.5/38.3**	**38.4/35.4**

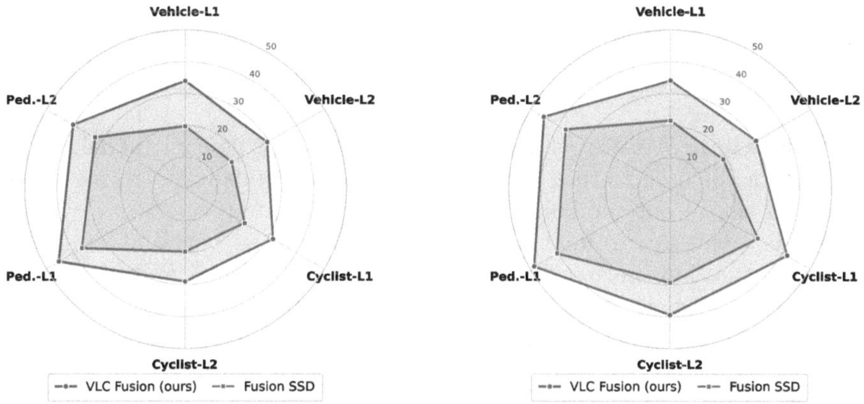

(a) Seen scenario

(b) Unseen scenario

Fig. 6. Per-class 3D AP (%) comparison between VLC Fusion and Fusion SSD on the Waymo dataset under (a) seen and (b) unseen scenarios.

4.4 Baselines

We explored various fusion strategies, including Fusion SSD [2], Fusion SSD with self-attention, RGB-X [5], and Learnable Align [17]:

Fusion SSD and Variations: The base Fusion SSD architecture concatenates feature maps from both modalities and applies convolution to reduce them to the appropriate dimensions before passing them to the detection head. In the self-attention variant, an additional attention module is applied after the convolution step to re-weight features based on their importance.

RGB-X: In this approach, feature maps are concatenated and processed using CBAM, which applies channel attention followed by spatial attention to refine the fused representation. This two-step attention mechanism adaptively emphasizes both the most informative channels and spatial regions. The refined feature

Table 3. Overall ATR performance on seen and unseen test splits. We report mAP_{50}, mAP_{75}, overall mAP (computed over IoU thresholds from 0.50 to 0.95 with a step size of 0.05), and mAR_{100}. Best and second-best results are highlighted in bold and underline, respectively.

Fusion Technique	Seen Scenario				Unseen Scenario			
	mAP_{50}	mAP_{75}	mAP	mAR_{100}	mAP_{50}	mAP_{75}	mAP	mAR_{100}
Fusion SSD	<u>87.19</u>	<u>67.79</u>	<u>57.82</u>	64.69	23.59	<u>5.56</u>	<u>9.42</u>	<u>14.94</u>
Fusion SSD w/ Self-Attention	82.82	57.79	51.12	57.40	22.01	4.07	8.29	13.30
RGB-X	82.04	58.48	51.60	57.45	20.67	5.28	8.43	12.88
Learnable Align	86.97	67.14	57.62	<u>64.84</u>	15.57	3.80	6.21	10.96
VLC Fusion with Human Conditions (n = 3)	84.07	56.35	51.39	57.53	<u>23.65</u>	1.68	7.46	11.93
VLC Fusion with Extracted Conditions (n = 7)	**96.41**	**69.37**	**61.67**	**81.95**	**32.22**	**9.48**	**13.38**	**35.51**

map is then passed through convolutional layers to align its dimensionality with the detection head.

Learnable Align: We also evaluated Learnable Align, where a lightweight cross-attention block is used to fuse features from the two modalities. In this method, each spatial cell in one modality's feature map is treated as a query, while the corresponding features from the other modality serve as keys and values. This end-to-end attention mechanism enables the model to align and highlight the most relevant information across modalities.

Each baseline fusion method was trained using the standard detection head for its dataset: a DETR-based 2D head for ATR and a SECOND-based 3D head for Waymo. All baseline methods were trained/evaluated without environmental conditions.

4.5 Results

We evaluate whether environmental conditions improve multimodal sensor fusion performance, using test sets from Table 1.

Waymo Open Dataset: Tables 2 and Fig. 6 show that VLC Fusion with 10 conditions consistently outperforms other baseline algorithms. Specifically, VLC Fusion achieved a 3D mAP of 37.0% in the Day and Night (seen) scenario and 41.5% in the Dawn/Dusk (unseen) scenario. Interestingly, increasing the number of conditions from 3 to 10 notably improved accuracy for underrepresented classes such as cyclists by 10.8% and 14.3% in the seen and unseen scenarios, respectively. This suggests that incorporating additional environmental context helps the fusion model generalize to challenging, underrepresented scenarios. Qualitative examples from Fig. 5 further support these findings, illustrating VLC Fusion's enhanced capability to detect vehicles, cyclists, and pedestrians under varied environmental conditions.

ATR Dataset: Tables 3 and Fig. 7 reinforce the effectiveness of VLC Fusion. Despite the ATR dataset presenting comparatively simpler environmental vari-

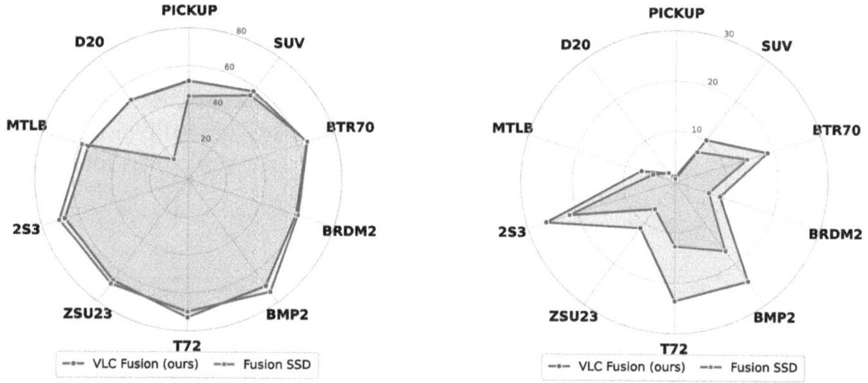

(a) Seen scenario (b) Unseen scenario

Fig. 7. Per-class AP (%) comparison between VLC Fusion and Fusion SSD on the ATR dataset under (a) seen and (b) unseen scenarios.

ations, VLC Fusion consistently improved performance across both seen and unseen scenarios. VLC Fusion with 7 VLM-extracted environmental conditions performs best on the seen and unseen test splits, achieving a mAP of 61.67% and 13.38%, surpassing Fusion SSD's best baseline result of 57.82% and 9.42%, respectively. These results emphasize that even datasets with less pronounced environmental variation benefit from incorporating context-specific environmental conditions into the fusion model. Additional results with per-class mAR_{100} are provided in Supplementary.

Model	Param in Billions	Time (sec/image)	Condition Accuracy
GPT-4o (baseline)†	> 100	2 sec	100%
Moondream2	1.9	0.7 sec	79.8%
SmolVLM-Instruct	2.2	1 sec	56.3%

†Parameter count is based on public estimates.

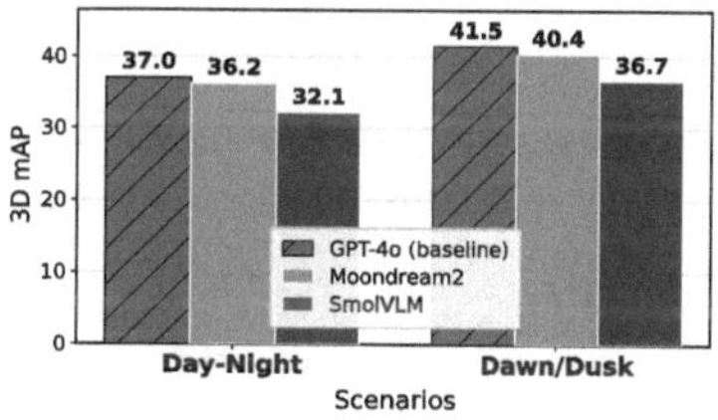

Fig. 8. **(a)** As shown in the table, smaller VLMs, such as Moondream2 and SmolVLM-Instruct, deliver faster inference, but yield lower condition-generation accuracy compared to GPT-4o. (Here the accuracy is calculated by considering the response from GPT-4o as ground truth.) **(b)** In zero-shot testing, the corresponding drop in 3D mAP (L1 difficulty) on the Waymo Day-Night and Dawn/Dusk scenarios highlights the importance of condition quality.

4.6 Ablation Study

To better understand the role of VLM-based environmental conditions in VLC Fusion, we conduct ablations on four factors: (i) the scale of the VLM used for querying conditions, (ii) the number and consistency of queried conditions, (iii) the semantic alignment of generated captions using CLIP similarity, and (iv) the depth of the VLC Fusion module.

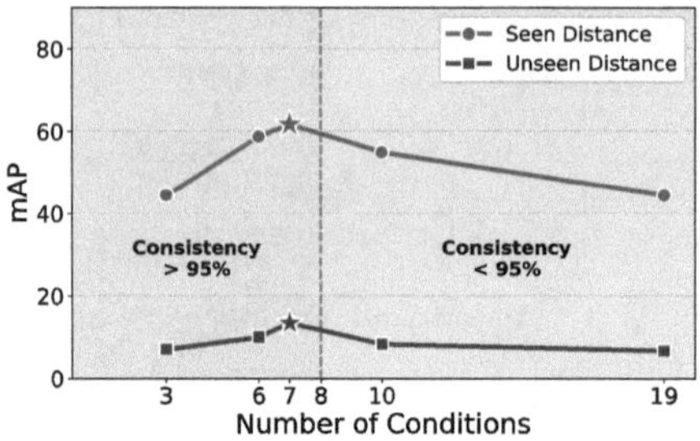

(a) ATR dataset. Performance peaks at 7 conditions, then declines as less consistent conditions are included.

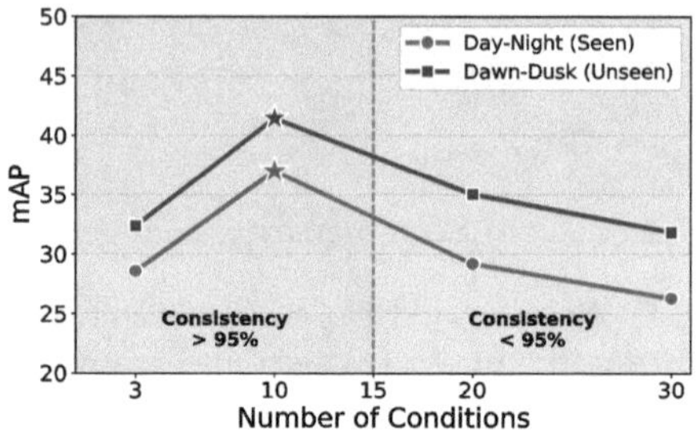

(b) Waymo dataset. Performance peaks at 10 conditions, then declines as less consistent conditions are included.

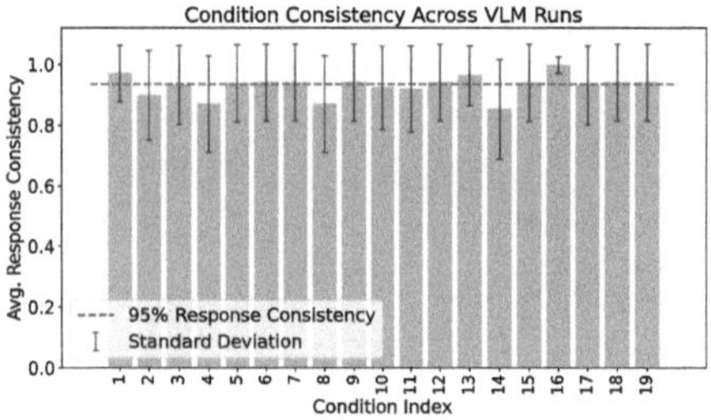

(c) Average condition response consistency over 5 runs for the ATR dataset.

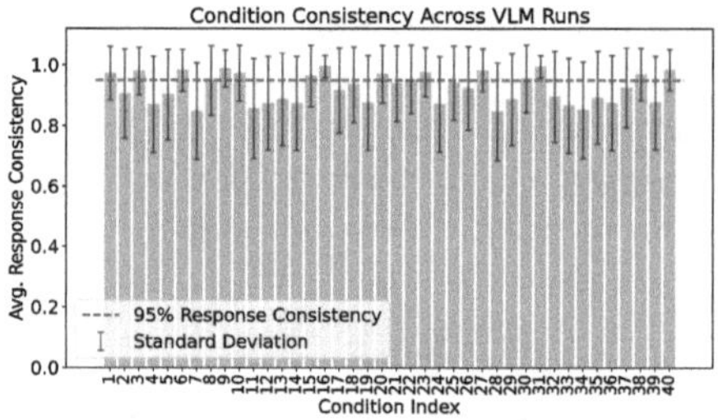

(d) Average condition response consistency over 5 runs for the Waymo dataset.

Fig. 9. Performance of VLC Fusion and corresponding condition consistency. Top row: Performance as a function of the number of ordered environmental conditions. In both datasets, performance initially improves as more conditions are added, but eventually declines when lower-consistency conditions are included. Bottom row: Average condition response consistency across 5 runs.

Effect of Using Small-Scale VLMs for Querying Conditions. In this section, we investigate how the scale and capacity of the Vision-Language Model (VLM) used for querying environmental conditions affect detection performance. Intuitively, we expect larger-scale VLMs to produce more accurate and semantically richer environmental condition predictions, thus enhancing the performance of the fused network. Conversely, smaller-scale VLMs are more practical

Table 4. Average CLIP-based cosine similarity between images and generated captions. Both the Waymo and ATR datasets achieve scores within the optimal 0.3 to 0.4 threshold for open-world tasks, demonstrating strong semantic alignment of the extracted conditions.

Dataset	CLIP Score
Waymo Dataset	0.314 ± 0.020
ATR Dataset	0.335 ± 0.023

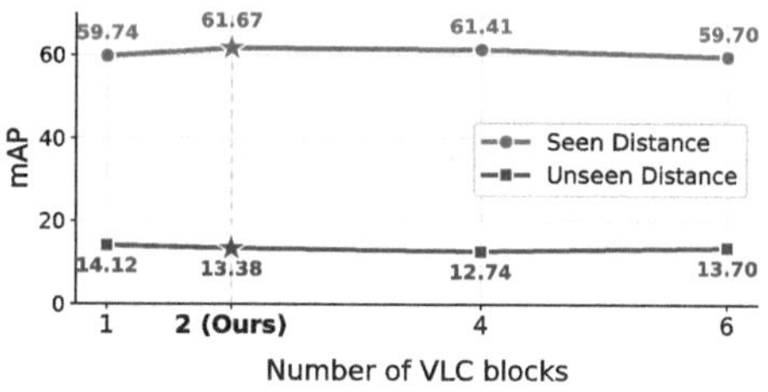

Fig. 10. Impact of number of VLC blocks on overall performance for the ATR dataset. mAP peaks at 2 stacked blocks before degrading.

but provide limited semantic reasoning capabilities and less accurate condition predictions, thus potentially reducing fusion performance.

We compared two smaller-scale VLMs (Moondream2 [24] and SmolVLM [19]) against larger-scale VLM (GPT-4o). As shown in Fig. 8, use of small VLMs slightly reduced the performance compared to the GPT-4o. Specifically, the performance for the "Day-Night (seen)" scenario drops from 37.0 to 36.2 with Moondream2 and further to 32.1 with SmolVLM. Similarly, for the "Dawn-Dusk (unseen)" scenario, performance decreases from 41.5 to 40.4 (Moondream2) and 36.7 (SmolVLM). These results confirm our hypothesis that the scale of VLM influences the accuracy of environmental condition predictions and the overall performance of VLC Fusion. On a positive note, Moondream2 remains competitive with GPT-4o, suggesting that smaller VLMs can offer a practical trade-off between efficiency and accuracy.

Effect of Condition Quantity and Consistency. We further analyze how varying the number and consistency of queried environmental conditions impacts the fusion model's performance. Figure 9a and Fig. 9b show the trend observed in our experiments. Initially, increasing the number of conditions leads to improvement in detection performance. However, beyond a certain point, adding more conditions leads to a performance decline. This trend is attributed to incorporating less consistent and potentially noisy conditions. As shown in Fig. 9c and 9d, we observed that conditions ranked higher in consistency contributed positively to performance, whereas adding less consistent conditions diminished model accuracy. Thus, our results underscore the critical importance of selecting a carefully curated set of highly consistent conditions, balancing richness of contextual information with the risk of introducing noise or irrelevant context.

CLIP-Based Caption Quality Analysis. To quantitatively assess the alignment between generated captions and visual content, we compute the cosine similarity between image and caption embeddings using CLIP (ViT-B/32) [22]. As detailed in [10], CLIP similarity scores between 0.3 and 0.4 indicate good alignment in open-world captioning tasks. As shown in Table 4, our results indicate that the generated captions are semantically coherent with the input images, supporting their reliability in condition generation for VLC Fusion.

Effect of VLC Fusion Block Depth. To determine the optimal architecture for our fusion module, we further evaluate how the number of stacked VLC blocks (network depth) influences detection accuracy on the ATR dataset. As shown in Fig. 10, increasing the network depth initially improves performance by allowing the model to learn more complex multimodal interactions. However, performance peaks at 2 VLC blocks, achieving a mAP of 61.67 for seen distances. Adding further blocks beyond this optimal depth leads to performance degradation, with accuracy dropping to 59.70 at 6 blocks, likely due to overfitting. Therefore, we utilize 2 VLC blocks as the default configuration for our experiments.

5 Conclusion

In this paper, we introduced Vision-Language Conditioned Fusion (VLC Fusion), a novel sensor fusion framework that improves object detection robustness by dynamically conditioning multimodal fusion on environmental context queried from VLMs. Unlike conventional fusion methods that use fixed fusion strategies, VLC Fusion explicitly incorporates high-level semantic information about the environment, enabling the model to better adapt sensor weighting under diverse and previously unseen conditions.

We evaluated VLC Fusion on two real-world multimodal datasets: the Waymo Open dataset for autonomous driving and the ATR dataset for military target recognition. Across both datasets, VLC Fusion consistently outperformed existing fusion baselines in seen and unseen scenarios, demonstrating its effectiveness for improving both detection accuracy and robustness. Our ablation studies further showed that the quality and consistency of environmental conditions are critical: adding reliable contextual information improves performance, while incorporating excessive or noisy conditions can reduce the benefit.

Overall, our results highlight the potential of integrating VLM-based semantic reasoning into sensor fusion architectures for more reliable perception in complex environments. Future work includes improving automatic condition extraction, extending VLC Fusion to additional sensor modalities and deployment settings, and investigating efficient real-time deployment scenarios.

Acknowledgments. This research was supported by the Defense Advanced Research Projects Agency (DARPA) under Cooperative Agreement No. HR00112420370 (MCAI). The views expressed in this paper are those of the authors and do not necessarily reflect the official policy or position of the U.S. Military Academy, the U.S. Army, the U.S. Department of Defense, or the U.S. Government. We would also like to thank Caleb Liu for early discussions on fine-tuning object detectors, and Som Sagar for insights into the applications of FiLM.

Disclosure of Interests. The authors have no competing interests to declare that are relevant to the content of this article.

References

1. Bai, X., et al.: TransFusion: robust LiDAR-camera fusion for 3D object detection with transformers. In: Proceedings of the IEEE/CVF Conference on Computer Vision and Pattern Recognition, pp. 1080–1089 (2022). https://doi.org/10.1109/CVPR52688.2022.00116
2. Bijelic, M., et al.: Seeing through fog without seeing fog: deep multimodal sensor fusion in unseen adverse weather. In: Proceedings of the IEEE/CVF Conference on Computer Vision and Pattern Recognition, pp. 11682–11692 (2020)
3. Brödermann, T., Sakaridis, C., Fu, Y., Van Gool, L.: CAFuser: condition-aware multimodal fusion for robust semantic perception of driving scenes (2024). arXiv preprint arXiv:2410.10791
4. Carion, N., Massa, F., Synnaeve, G., Usunier, N., Kirillov, A., Zagoruyko, S.: End-to-end object detection with transformers. In: European Conference on Computer Vision, pp. 213–229. Springer (2020)
5. Deevi, S.A., Lee, C., Gan, L., Nagesh, S., Pandey, G., Chung, S.J.: RGB-X object detection via scene-specific fusion modules. In: Proceedings of the IEEE/CVF Winter Conference on Applications of Computer Vision, pp. 7366–7375 (2024)
6. Delecki, H., Itkina, M., Lange, B., Senanayake, R., Kochenderfer, M.J.: How do we fail? Stress testing perception in autonomous vehicles. In: 2022 IEEE/RSJ International Conference on Intelligent Robots and Systems (IROS), pp. 5139–5146. IEEE (2022)
7. Driess, D., et al.: PaLM-E: an embodied multimodal language model (2023). arXiv preprint arXiv:2303.03378
8. ATR Algorithm Development Image Database (2010). https://dsiac.org/databases/atr-algorithm-development-image-database/. Accessed 13 Aug 2024
9. Feng, D., Cao, Y., Rosenbaum, L., Timm, F., Dietmayer, K.: Leveraging uncertainties for deep multi-modal object detection in autonomous driving. In: 2020 IEEE Intelligent Vehicles Symposium (IV), pp. 877–884 (2020). https://doi.org/10.1109/IV47402.2020.9304551
10. Hessel, J., Holtzman, A., Forbes, M., Bras, R.L., Choi, Y.: CLIPScore: a reference-free evaluation metric for image captioning (2021). arXiv preprint arXiv:2104.08718
11. Kamath, A., et al.: MDETR—modulated detection for end-to-end multi-modal understanding. In: Proceedings of the IEEE/CVF International Conference on Computer Vision, pp. 1780–1790 (2021)
12. Ku, J., Mozifian, M., Lee, J., Harakeh, A., Waslander, S.L.: Joint 3D proposal generation and object detection from view aggregation. In: 2018 IEEE/RSJ International Conference on Intelligent Robots and Systems (IROS), pp. 1–8 (2018)
13. Lang, A.H., Vora, S., Caesar, H., Zhou, L., Yang, J., Beijbom, O.: PointPillars: fast encoders for object detection from point clouds. In: Proceedings of the IEEE/CVF Conference on Computer Vision and Pattern Recognition, pp. 12697–12705 (2019)
14. Li, J., Luo, C., Yang, X.: PillarNeXt: rethinking network designs for 3D object detection in LiDAR point clouds. In: Proceedings of the IEEE/CVF Conference on Computer Vision and Pattern Recognition, pp. 17567–17576 (2023)
15. Li, J., Li, D., Savarese, S., Hoi, S.: BLIP-2: bootstrapping language-image pre-training with frozen image encoders and large language models. In: International Conference on Machine Learning, pp. 19730–19742. PMLR (2023)
16. Li, X., et al.: Vision-language foundation models as effective robot imitators. arXiv preprint arXiv:2311.01378 (2023)

17. Li, Y., et al.: DeepFusion: LiDAR-camera deep fusion for multi-modal 3D object detection. In: Proceedings of the IEEE/CVF Conference on Computer Vision and Pattern Recognition, pp. 17182–17191 (2022)
18. Liu, H., Li, C., Wu, Q., Lee, Y.J.: Visual instruction tuning. In: Advances in Neural Information Processing Systems, vol. 36, pp. 34892–34916 (2023)
19. Marafioti, A., et al.: SmoLVLM: redefining small and efficient multimodal models (2025). arXiv preprint arXiv:2504.05299
20. Pathiraja, B., Liu, C., Senanayake, R.: Fairness in autonomous driving: towards understanding confounding factors in object detection under challenging weather (2024). arXiv preprint arXiv:2406.00219
21. Perez, E., Strub, F., De Vries, H., Dumoulin, V., Courville, A.: FiLM: visual reasoning with a general conditioning layer. In: Proceedings of the AAAI Conference on Artificial Intelligence, vol. 32 (2018)
22. Radford, A., et al.: Learning transferable visual models from natural language supervision (2021)
23. Sun, P., et al.: Scalability in perception for autonomous driving: Waymo open dataset. In: Proceedings of the IEEE/CVF Conference on Computer Vision and Pattern Recognition, pp. 2446–2454 (2020)
24. VIK: Moondream2 (revision 92d3d73) (2024). https://doi.org/10.57967/hf/3219. https://huggingface.co/vikhyatk/moondream2
25. Woo, S., Park, J., Lee, J.Y., Kweon, I.S.: CBAM: convolutional block attention module. In: Proceedings of the European Conference on Computer Vision (ECCV), pp. 3–19 (2018)
26. Xu, D., Anguelov, D., Jain, A.: PointFusion: deep sensor fusion for 3D bounding box estimation. In: Proceedings of the IEEE/CVF Conference on Computer Vision and Pattern Recognition, pp. 244–253 (2018). https://doi.org/10.1109/CVPR.2018.00033
27. Yan, Y., Mao, Y., Li, B.: Second: sparsely embedded convolutional detection. Sensors **18**(10) (2018). https://doi.org/10.3390/s18103337. https://www.mdpi.com/1424-8220/18/10/3337

Applied Data Science Track AI for Sports, Mobility and Human-Centered Applications

Blending Proxy Metrics with a North Star

Winston Chou(✉)

Netflix, New York, NY, USA
wchou@netflix.com

Abstract. Proxy metrics are widely used to improve the precision and velocity of online experimentation (aka A/B testing). Although proxies are often motivated by long-term outcomes that the experimenter does not observe, in many settings they are used alongside a *contemporaneous* but statistically insensitive north star. This can lead to a practical dilemma: when should experimenters trust the proxy metric, and when should they trust the north star? In this paper, I propose an optimal blending approach that smoothly guides decision-making towards the north star as the power of the experiment increases and away from the north star as the quality of the proxy metric improves. I study the implications of this decision-making framework for the design of experiments and of experimentation programs. Equipped with better (worse) proxy metrics, experimenters should run smaller and more (larger and fewer) experiments. I show how to leverage past experiments to estimate optimal blending weights and experiment sizes. Lastly, I describe the real-world application of the methodology to an experimentation program at Netflix.

Keywords: A/B testing · experimentation programs · proxy metrics · statistical surrogates

1 Introduction

Proxy metrics are widely used to increase the pace and precision of digital experimentation. As the name suggests, the goal of a proxy metric is to approximate a *north star* metric that directly measures business success, such as customer conversions or user retention, with inputs that are more sensitive to product interventions, such as user engagement [11].

Proxy metrics, and related concepts like statistical surrogates, are often motivated by long-term outcomes that the experimenter cannot observe outside of observational data or rare long-term experiments [1,17,21]. However, in many applications, experimenters *do* observe the north star, but find that effects on it are too small to detect in everyday experiments. For example, a digital subscription service observes whether members are retained at the end of an experiment, but the vast majority of digital product interventions (e.g., changes to recommendation algorithms) have very small effects on retention that can only be

M. Ceci et al. (Eds.): ECML PKDD 2026, LNAI 16948, pp. 71–87, 2027.
https://doi.org/10.1007/978-3-032-37679-4_5

detected in very large experiments [14]. This motivates the use of a proxy north star, such as the estimated treatment effect on retention as a function of the treatment effect(s) observed on user engagement [5,20].

Thorny questions arise in this setting, for example:

1. Should experimenters still rely on the proxy outcome in the large, infrequent experiments that *are* powered to detect treatment effects on the true north star?
2. What should experimenters do if the proxy north star and the true north star disagree?
3. How should the quality of the proxy affect the design of experiments and experimentation programs?

In this paper, I derive a methodology of deciding experiments that smoothly "blends" a proxy metric (or set of proxy metrics) with a north star metric. Specifically, letting a denote some number between 0 and 1 and $A := (a, 1-a)^\top$, I consider the blended metric

$$\widehat{Z}(A) = A^\top \widehat{X} = a\widehat{P} + (1-a)\widehat{Y}, \tag{1}$$

where $\widehat{P}$ and $\widehat{Y}$ are estimated treatment effects on the proxy and north star, respectively, and a is chosen to maximize the "returns" to Y in experiments [3, 18]. Intuitively, the optimal a^* (to be defined formally in Sect. 3) should depend on the power of those experiments: as the power of an experiment goes to 1, a^* should go to zero, and decisions should be made based solely on the north star. Intuitively, a^* should also depend on the quality of the proxy metric: at any fixed sample size, it should be increasing in the structural covariance of true treatment effects on the proxy with true treatment effects on the north star. Lastly, the quality of the proxy should have implications for the design of future experiments. If the proxy is excellent and large experiments are costly (for example, because they reduce traffic to other experiments), then experimenters should run smaller and more experiments compared to when the proxy is poor.

My analysis confirms these intuitions and motivates an estimator of a^* that leverages the structural covariance between treatment effects on the proxy and the north star learned from past experiments [5,9,21]. Using simulations, I show how blending can significantly increase the returns to experimentation relative to making decisions exclusively based on the proxy metric ($a = 1$) or the north star ($a = 0$). Lastly, I describe the real-world application of the methodology to construct an adaptively blended decision metric for A/B tests at Netflix.

2 Related Literature

This paper contributes first and foremost to the literature on proxy metrics in A/B testing, especially to research on how to learn good proxy metrics from meta-analysis of past experiments [5–7,10,11,21,22]. Distinctively, I focus on settings in which experimenters simultaneously observe *both* an insensitive north star metric *and* more sensitive proxies for that metric. A natural question in these settings is whether and how experimenters should incorporate both types of metrics into decision-making.

I show that the optimal blend of metrics in decision-making depends on the size of the experiment, with the optimal weight concentrating exclusively on the north star metric in an infinitely large experiment. This echoes the insight of [21] that the optimal decision rule for an experiment depends on its power. Building on the return-aware framework of [3,4,18], I draw out the implications of this insight when sample sizes are endogenous. Specifically, experimenters should run smaller and more experiments if the proxy is excellent, and larger and fewer experiments if the proxy is poor.

3 Methodology

3.1 Framework and Notation

The setting of this paper is as follows. Experiments are drawn independently from a distribution and consist of true treatment effects $X = (P, Y)$, where $P \in \mathbb{R}^m$ is a vector, possibly one-dimensional, of treatment effects on proxy metrics and Y is the treatment effect on the north star metric. Denote the variance-covariance matrix of X across experiments by Σ_X.

The experimenter observes estimates of the treatment effects $\widehat{X} = (\widehat{P}, \widehat{Y})$ on the proxy metric(s) and north star metric. For simplicity, I assume that each experiment consists of a treatment group and a control group, each of size n in every experiment, and that the experimenter estimates treatment effects using the difference in sample means. Thus, conditional on the true effects, the estimated treatment effects $\widehat{X}$ are Gaussian with distribution

$$\widehat{X}|X \sim \mathcal{N}(X, 2\Omega/n), \tag{2}$$

where Ω is the sampling variance of the unit-level random variables underlying Y and P [9]. I assume that Σ_X and Ω are both positive-definite. Therefore, the unconditional (total) variance-covariance matrix of $\widehat{X}$, $\Sigma_{\widehat{X}} := \Sigma_X + 2\Omega/n$, is also positive-definite.

I further assume that the true treatment effects X are Gaussian with zero mean—a workhorse model in the literature that facilitates closed-form analysis [4,9,21]. In Sect. 4, I show using simulations that the key takeaways hold for heavier-tailed treatment effect distributions [cf. 3].

3.2 Choosing Optimal Blending Weights

I propose a *return-aware* approach to choosing the optimal blending weights [3,18]. Specifically, I derive the optimal choice of A under a decision rule that "launches" the treatment so long as the blended statistic $\widehat{Z}(A) := A^\top \widehat{X}$ is significantly greater than zero at some chosen significance level α. The returns to Y of such a decision rule are given by

$$R(A) := \mathbb{E}\left[Y\mathbf{1}\left\{A^\top \widehat{X} > z\sqrt{A^\top(2\Omega/n)A}\right\}\right], \tag{3}$$

where z is the critical value corresponding to α.

A^* is defined as the choice of A that maximizes (3)

$$A^* := \arg\max_{A\in\mathcal{A}} R(A), \tag{4}$$

where $\mathcal{A} = \{A \in \mathbb{R}^{m+1} : A \geq 0, \sum_{i=1}^{m+1} A_i = 1\}$. I will assume there is an interior solution to this optimization problem (i.e., A^* contains strictly positive weights). This assumption holds by construction if, for example, one evaluates a set of proxies thought to have a positive relationship with the north star and then, for interpretability, keeps only those proxies having strictly positive weights at the optimum. Note that this does not rule out proxies that are thought to have a negative relationship with the north star (e.g., customer service complaints), since these can be rescaled by -1; it only rules out proxies with zero or "wrongly" signed weights at the optimum.

The optimal A^* can be found by solving the following constrained optimization problem:

$$\max_{A\in\mathcal{A}} R(A) = \max_{A\in\mathcal{A}} \frac{A^\top \Gamma}{\sqrt{A^\top \Sigma_{\widehat{X}} A}}\, \phi(z\sqrt{q_n(A)}), \tag{5}$$

where $\Gamma := \mathrm{Cov}(X, Y) = \mathrm{Cov}((P, Y), Y)$, ϕ is the standard normal pdf, and $q_n(A) := \frac{A^\top(2\Omega/n)A}{A^\top \Sigma_{\widehat{X}} A}$ is the ratio of the within-experiment sampling variance of $\widehat{Z}(A)$ to its total variance across experiments. Although (5) does not have a closed-form solution in general, Proposition 1 provides a closed-form approximation to A^* that is very accurate for sufficiently large experiments.

Proposition 1. *The* approximately optimal blending weighting vector $\tilde{A}$ *is defined as the vector on the simplex that satisfies*

$$\tilde{A} \propto (\Sigma_X + (1 + z^2)2\Omega/n)^{-1}\Gamma. \tag{6}$$

Assume joint normality of $X = (P, Y)$ and that A^* is an interior solution to (5), i.e., $A_i^* > 0$ for all i. Then, for $n \geq \underline{n}$, where $\underline{n}$ is given by (10), we have that:

1. *The approximation error of $\tilde{A}$ is $O(n^{-2})$.*
2. *The regret of $\tilde{A}$ is $O(n^{-4})$.*

Proof. For $n \geq \underline{n}$, the optimal blending weights A^* solve the following fixed-point equation:

$$A^* \propto (\Sigma_X + \left(1 + \frac{z^2}{1 - z^2 q_n(A^*)}\right) 2\Omega/n)^{-1}\Gamma. \tag{7}$$

$q_n(A^*)$ is $O(n^{-1})$, so $z^2/(1 - z^2 q_n(A^*)) = z^2 + O(n^{-1})$. $2\Omega/n$ is also $O(n^{-1})$, so $(z^2 - z^2 + O(n^{-1}))2\Omega/n$ is $O(n^{-2})$. Therefore, the direction of the optimal weights $(\Sigma_X + (1 + z^2)2\Omega/n + O(n^{-2}))^{-1}\Gamma$ matches the direction $\tilde{A}$ through first order. This establishes the first item.

By a Taylor expansion of $R(A)$ around A^*, we have that

$$R(\tilde{A}) = R(A^*) + \nabla R(A^*)(\tilde{A} - A^*) + \frac{1}{2}(\tilde{A} - A^*)^\top H(A^*)(\tilde{A} - A^*) + o(||\tilde{A} - A^*||^2), \tag{8}$$

where $\nabla R(A^*)$ and $H(A^*)$ are the gradient and Hessian of $R(A)$ at A^*, respectively. Interiority of A^* implies that $\nabla R(A^*)^\top(\tilde{A} - A^*) = 0$. Therefore, the regret of $\tilde{A}$ is:

$$R(A^*) - R(\tilde{A}) = \underbrace{-\frac{1}{2}(\tilde{A} - A^*)^\top H(A^*)(\tilde{A} - A^*)}_{O(n^{-4})}. \tag{9}$$

This establishes the second item. □

In other words, Proposition 1 states that $\tilde{A}$ is an excellent closed-form approximation to A^* for sufficiently large experiments, where "sufficiently large" is defined by (10) below. In turn, $\tilde{A}$ can be interpreted as the *penalized* linear regression of Y on $X = (P, Y)$ with the penalty given by a scale factor of the measurement error variance $(1 + z^2)2\Omega/n$. This penalty regularizes the weights towards metrics with smaller variance within experiments (i.e., Ω) relative to their variance across experiments (i.e., Σ_X). In an infinitely large experiment ($n \to \infty$), the penalty disappears, and the optimal weights concentrate exclusively on the north star metric. However, at any finite value of n, the optimal weight on any given metric will, all else equal, be increasing in its respective component of Γ.

Note that the strength of the penalty is increasing in the chosen critical value z. Intuitively, a large z means that only the most extreme test statistics will result in launches, which drives up the optimal weights on proxy metrics that are statistically precise. Because statistical precision tends to trade off with alignment with the north star, this can come at the expense of more structurally aligned proxies [23].

The accuracy of the approximation depends on the size of each treatment arm n. The relevant condition for n is that $q_n(A^*) \leq 1/z^2$, or equivalently that

$$n \geq \underline{n}(A^*) := (z^2 - 1)\frac{2\,A^{*\top}\Omega A^*}{A^{*\top}\Sigma_X A^*}. \tag{10}$$

In the Appendix, I show that substituting $\tilde{A}$ for A^* in this expression yields a weakly conservative bound, $\underline{n}(\tilde{A}) \geq \underline{n}(A^*)$. Therefore, if n is greater than $\underline{n}(\tilde{A})$, one can safely use the approximation. If n is smaller than $\underline{n}(\tilde{A})$, the optimal weights should be found by solving the constrained optimization problem (5) directly.

3.3 Estimation From Past Experiments

Given a set of past experiments, $\tilde{A}$ can be estimated as follows:

1. Estimate the within-experiment sampling covariance $2\Omega/n$, for example, by drawing a random sample from each experiment and estimating the sampling covariance from the concatenated samples.
2. Estimate Σ_X using nonparametric estimators [5], empirical Bayes estimators [2], or a Bayesian hierarchical model [21].
3. Estimate $\tilde{A}$ using the closed-form plug-in estimator

$$\dot{A} = (\widehat{\Sigma_X} + (1 + z^2)\, 2\widehat{\Omega}/n)^{-1}\widehat{\Gamma}, \tag{11}$$

   where $\widehat{\Gamma} = \widehat{\mathrm{Cov}}(X, Y) = \widehat{\mathrm{Cov}}((P, Y), Y)$ is the last column of $\widehat{\Sigma_X}$.
4. If any component of $\dot{A}$ is negative, drop that component and repeat steps 1–3.
5. Scale $\dot{A}$ by the sum of its components to obtain $\widehat{\tilde{A}}$.
6. Check that $n \geq \underline{n}(\widehat{\tilde{A}})$ and, if not, solve the constrained optimization problem (5) numerically for the exact weights.

I illustrate this estimator in Sects. 4 and 5.

3.4 Implications for Statistical Power

Thus far, our focus has been on the impact of blending on the returns to experimentation. In this section, I study how blending can affect another important aspect of experimentation programs: the statistical power of experiments. Power is an important practical consideration, since experiments that are chronically underpowered can cause firms to miss valuable innovations, overstate the value of "winning" treatments [12,15], and waste resources on false positives [13]. Below, I derive the minimum sample size needed to detect a given treatment effect on the north star metric when using the blended metric $\widehat{Z}(A)$ compared to the north star or proxy exclusively.

As a benchmark, consider the scenario in which the experimenter only decides experiments based on the estimated treatment effect on the north star metric ($a = 0$). Then, by a standard power analysis, the minimum sample size required to detect a given treatment effect τ_Y with 80% power is

$$n_0 := \frac{(z + 0.84)^2 2\,\omega_Y}{\tau_Y^2}, \tag{12}$$

where, as before, z denotes the critical value for the test and ω_Y is the variance of the unit-level variable underlying Y.

Alternatively, consider the minimum sample size required to be "powered" for the same effect on the north star metric when using the blended metric $\widehat{Z}(A)$. Note that the use of "power" here is somewhat informal as $\widehat{Z}(A)$ is not an estimate of Y. Rather, by power I mean that, at this sample size, $\widehat{Z}$ is significantly greater than zero with 80% probability when $Y = \tau_Y$. Denote this (per-arm) sample size by n_A. Fixing Y at τ_Y, $\widehat{Z}(A)$ is Gaussian with mean

$$\mu_A(\tau_Y) := \mathbb{E}[\widehat{Z}(A)|Y = \tau_Y] = \frac{1}{\sigma_Y^2} A^\top \Gamma \tau_Y, \tag{13}$$

and residual variance

$$\sigma_A(\tau_Y)^2 := \mathrm{Var}(\widehat{Z}(A) \mid Y = \tau_Y) = A^\top \Sigma_{\widehat{X}} A - \frac{(A^\top \Gamma)^2}{\sigma_Y^2}. \tag{14}$$

Launching whenever $\widehat{Z}(A) > z\sqrt{A^\top (2\Omega/n) A}$ and imposing a target power of 80% requires

$$\mu_A(\tau_Y) = z\sqrt{A^\top (2\Omega/n) A} + 0.84\, \sigma_A(\tau_Y). \tag{15}$$

It will be convenient to define

$$\omega_A := A^\top \Omega A \quad \text{and} \quad \theta := \frac{0.84 \sigma_A(\tau_Y)}{\mu_A(\tau_Y)}. \tag{16}$$

In words, θ is the ratio of the residual standard deviation of $\widehat{Z}(A)$ given $Y = \tau_Y$, multiplied by the power threshold (0.84), to its mean. Increasing the target detection probability or residual standard deviation increases θ, while a larger conditional mean reduces θ.

Then, in order to be powered for the same effect size on the north star metric when using the blended metric $\widehat{Z}(A)$, it must be that

$$\mu_A(\tau_Y) \geq z\sqrt{\frac{2\,\omega_A}{n_A}} + 0.84\, \sigma_A(\tau_Y), \tag{17}$$

or equivalently,

$$1 \geq \frac{z\sqrt{2\omega_A/n_A}}{\mu_A(\tau_Y)} + \theta. \tag{18}$$

Solving for the minimum sample size n_A, we have that:

$$n_A \geq \frac{(z + 0.84)^2 2\,\omega_A}{\mu_A(\tau_Y)^2} \cdot I(\theta), \tag{19}$$

where

$$I(\theta) = \frac{z^2}{(z + 0.84)^2 (1 - \theta)^2}. \tag{20}$$

The expression for n_A is (intentionally) analogous to the expression for n_0. Both expressions are inflated by the sampling variance of the underlying variables (ω_Y and ω_A, respectively) and deflated by the expected effect size (τ_Y and

$\mu_A(\tau_Y)$, respectively). However, the central difference is that n_A is inflated by an additional factor $I(\theta)$ that accounts for imperfect alignment between the proxy metric(s) and the north star.

Note that, as $\theta \to 1$, $I(\theta) \to \infty$. Thus, $\mu_A(\tau_Y) > 0.84\sigma_A(\tau_Y)$ is a necessary condition for the rule to attain 80% power for some finite sample size. This condition requires that both the conditional mean of $\widehat{Z}(A)$ is sufficiently large and that its residual variance is sufficiently small given $Y = \tau_Y$.

Because both sides of (19) depend on n_A, it does not directly yield an explicit solution for n_A and is mainly presented for interpretation. In practice, one can solve for n_A by evaluating a grid of values and choosing the smallest value satisfying the inequality (19).

3.5 Implications for Experimentation Programs

Above, the optimal blending weights were shown to depend on experiment sizes: as the experiment size grows, experimenters should shift the balance of decision-making away from the proxy metric towards the true north star. Yet, as (5) shows, increasing n also increases the expected returns to any individual experiment.[1] With just a single experiment and unlimited allocations, experimenters should allocate as many units as possible to their experiment and shift decision-making towards the north star.

However, in practice, experimenters are responsible for a portfolio of experiments, to which they have a finite number of units to allocate [3,18,19]. Therefore, increasing allocations to any one experiment has an opportunity cost, as it reduces the number of allocations available to other experiments.

To formalize this tradeoff, let $R(A, n)/n$ denote the average return of a single experiment of size n (per arm) under any choice of A:

$$R(A, n)/n = \frac{\Gamma^\top A}{\sqrt{A^\top \Sigma_{\widehat{X}} A}} \phi\left(z\sqrt{q_n(A)}\right)/n. \tag{21}$$

In the Appendix, we show that $R(A, n)/n$ is decreasing in n for any choice of A assuming typical values of z (i.e., $1 \leq z \leq 1 + \sqrt{2} \approx 2.414$).[2] Note that this holds for any A, including the optimal A given n. Therefore, letting $\delta > 0$,

$$R(A^*(n+\delta), n+\delta)/(n+\delta) \leq R(A^*(n+\delta), n)/n \leq R(A^*(n), n)/n, \tag{22}$$

where $A^*(n) = \arg\max_A R(A, n)$. Thus, letting $R^*(n) := R(A^*(n), n)$, the average optimal return per unit of allocation $R^*(n)/n$ is also decreasing in n.

Next, consider n_A incremental treatment-control pairs (the minimum required to run a well-powered experiment). If the experimenter allocates this

[1] $\sqrt{A^\top \Sigma_{\widehat{X}} A}$ is decreasing in n, while $\phi(\cdot)$ attains its maximum at 0, which is the limit of $z\sqrt{q_n(A)}$ as $n \to \infty$.

[2] The Appendix for this paper can be found at https://github.com/winston-chou/blending.

block to a new test, the incremental expected return is $R^*(n_A)$. However, if instead she spreads the same n_A pairs evenly across J existing powered tests of size n_A, each existing test receives $\delta = n_A/J$ additional pairs, yielding an incremental improvement of

$$J\left[R^*(n_A + \delta) - R^*(n_A)\right].$$

Thus, allocating the pairs to a new test is weakly preferred whenever

$$R^*(n_A) \geq J\left[R^*(n_A + \delta) - R^*(n_A)\right], \tag{23}$$

which is directly implied by $\frac{R^*(n)}{n}$ decreasing in n. Therefore, the experimenter always prefers to allocate additional units to a new test over distributing them over existing tests so long as the launch threshold is not too stringent (i.e., $z \leq 2.414$, corresponding to a one-sided α of about 0.008). If the launch threshold is more stringent than this, then average returns are no longer guaranteed to be decreasing in n, and the experimenter should consider distributing the additional units across existing tests to increase power rather than allocate to a new test.

4 Simulations

To show how blending improves decision-making, here I conduct a simulation study that examines the performance of north star-only, proxy-only, and blended decision rules. Replication code for all figures in this section can be found at https://github.com/winston-chou/blending.

I set the simulation parameters as follows:

Simulation parameters.

- Baseline true effect covariance: $\Sigma_X = \begin{bmatrix} 1.0 & 0.08 \\ 0.08 & 0.01 \end{bmatrix}$ (i.e., $\sigma_P^2 = 1.0$, $\sigma_Y^2 = 0.01$, $\sigma_{PY} = 0.08$, $\rho = 0.8$). Simulations 2–4 fix $\sigma_Y^2 = 0.01$ and $\sigma_P^2 = 1.0$ but sweep $\rho = \mathrm{Corr}(P, Y) \in \{0, 0.2, 0.4, 0.6, 0.8, 1.0\}$.
- Sampling covariance: $\Omega = \begin{bmatrix} 25 & 8 \\ 8 & 16 \end{bmatrix}$ (i.e., $\omega_P = 25$, $\omega_Y = 16$).
- Critical value: $z \approx 1.645$ (i.e., one-sided $\alpha = 0.05$).
- Number of experiments per replicate for computing cumulative returns: $J = 100$.
- Per-arm sample size grid: $n \in \{1000, 2000, \ldots, 20000\}$.
- Monte Carlo replicates: $R = 1{,}000$.

These parameter values were chosen to reflect a realistic setting in which the north star metric is relatively insensitive to treatments, whereas the proxy metric is more sensitive in the sense of having a larger ratio of treatment effect variance to measurement error variance. The closed-form approximation to the optimal blending weights from Proposition 1 is used except where the bound $\underline{n}(\tilde{A})$ of Sect. 3.2 is violated—at low ρ and small n—in which case the weights are obtained by numerically optimizing (5).

First, I assess the cumulative returns over a set of J experiments under each decision rule. I plot these returns as a function of the per-arm sample size n in the first panel of Fig. 1. As the panel shows, the blended decision rule consistently yields higher cumulative returns than do the north star-only and proxy-only rules across all sample sizes.

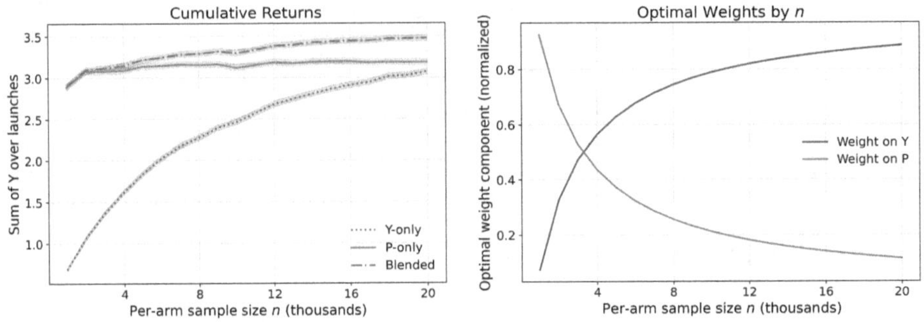

Fig. 1. Cumulative Returns (left) and Optimal Blending Weights (right) by n.

The intuition for this is as follows. At small sample sizes, the proxy metric dominates the north star due to its much greater signal-to-noise ratio. However, as the sample size increases, treatment effects on the north star—which is better aligned with the objective—become measured with greater precision. As a result, for very large n, it is better to shift decision-making towards the north star. By construction, the blended metric uses the optimal weights at any given n, and so smoothly concentrates the weights on the north star as n grows. This behavior is shown in the second panel of Fig. 1.

Next, I evaluate the statistical power and false positive rates of the north star-only, proxy-only, and blended decision rules under the practical test. In the first set of simulations, I vary both the sample size and the structural correlation between the north star and proxy metrics while fixing the true treatment effect on the north star to be $\tau_Y = \sigma_Y$. I visualize the results using heatmaps where the sample size varies along the horizontal axis and the correlation in treatment effects varies along the vertical axis.

As Fig. 2 shows, at small n and moderate-to-high ρ, and when $Y = \tau_Y$, the proxy metric launches with substantially greater probability than does the north star metric: given a true treatment effect on the north star, the proxy metric is much more likely to be significant than the north star metric in this regime. However, at low ρ, the proxy metric can launch with *lower* probability than the north star metric, particularly as the sample size increases, despite its greater signal-to-noise ratio. The intuition for this is that, when ρ is small, fixing Y at τ_Y barely pulls the proxy metric away from its prior mean of zero. As a result, the "power" (by the launch definition) of the proxy metric is very low in this regime. In contrast, the blended metric has good performance in both regimes as it adaptively shifts the balance of decision-making between the north star and proxy metrics.

In the second set of simulations, I fix $\tau_Y = 0$ and plot the false positive risk as n and ρ vary. As Fig. 3 shows, the type I error rate is strictly controlled at 0.05 for the north star metric, whereas it is substantially higher for the proxy metric. Even more pathologically, the false positive risk is *increasing* in the sample size (except at $\rho = 1$, where the proxy and north star metrics are perfectly aligned), meaning that larger experiments actually incur a worse false positive risk under the proxy-only rule. In contrast, the blended metric has a much lower false positive risk that interpolates between the north star and proxy-only decision rules. Furthermore, as the sample size increases, the optimal weights naturally shift away from the proxy metric towards the north star, which gradually reduces the false positive risk. In the limit, the blended metric converges to the north star metric and so inherits its type I error control.

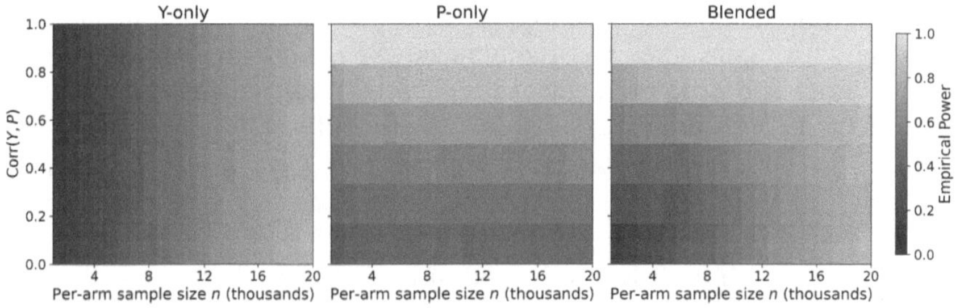

Fig. 2. Empirical Power Heatmaps across n and ρ.

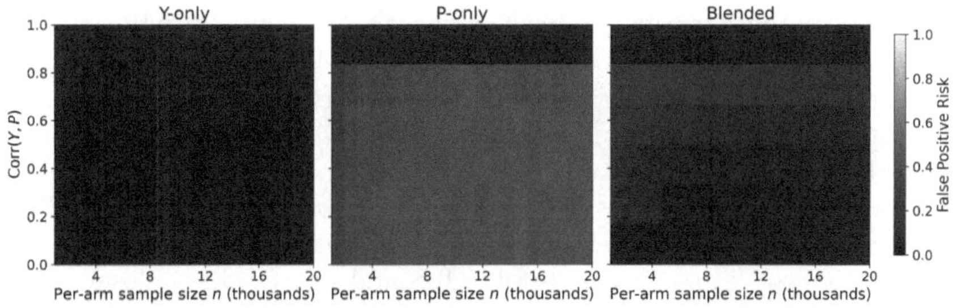

Fig. 3. False Positive Risk Heatmaps across n and ρ.

Finally, I assess the robustness of the core insights to heavy-tailed treatment effect distributions by repeating the above simulations for a multivariate t-distribution with $\nu = 3$ degrees of freedom. As Fig. 4 shows, the qualitative conclusions are robust. The blended metric consistently achieves better returns than both single-metric rules, with the north star rule converging as the sample size increases. The power of the proxy metric (again, using the launch definition) remains largely driven by its structural correlation with the north star rather than its sample size. In contrast, the power of the blended metric increases and even exceeds the power of the proxy as n grows. Unlike that of the proxy metric, the false positive risk of the blended metric trends downward and converges to the nominal rate as the sample size increases.

5 Empirical Application

In this section, I apply the methodology to a real-world experimentation program at Netflix. The program seeks to optimize, as its north star metric Y, a downstream outcome that I will call *plays*. Plays are preceded by an upstream proxy P that I will refer to as *clicks*. Clicks are more sensitive to product interventions than are plays, but they are also less tied to long-term engagement and thus less valuable to the program.

The following analysis is based on 15 A/B tests and 50 treatment arms in this program. All figure axes are anonymized for confidentiality. Although the underlying data are proprietary, code to replicate all calculations and figures can be found at https://github.com/winston-chou/blending.

5.1 Assumption Checking

I begin by verifying that clicks are indeed more sensitive than plays. Treatment effects on clicks have an SE-ratio—the ratio of the empirical spread of treatment effects to the average within-experiment SE—of ~12 and ~60% of treatment arms have a statistically significant clicks effect at $\alpha = 0.05$. In contrast, treatment effects on plays have an SE-ratio of just 2 and only ~25% of arms are significant. Thus, in terms of this SE-ratio metric, clicks are about six times more sensitive than plays.

Next, I verify that treatment effects on clicks (P) are indeed highly correlated with treatment effects on plays (Y). In Fig. 5, I plot the observed treatment effects on clicks $\widehat{P}$ against the observed treatment effects on plays $\widehat{Y}$ across all experiments and treatment arms along with their 95% confidence-interval error bars. As the plot shows, the two have a strong linear relationship. To affirm that this relationship is not driven by correlated measurement error, I split each experiment into two folds and estimate the OLS regression of $\widehat{Y}$ on $\widehat{P}$ using the cross-fold estimator [5,8]. The cross-fold OLS and raw OLS are closely aligned, indicating a limited impact of measurement error.

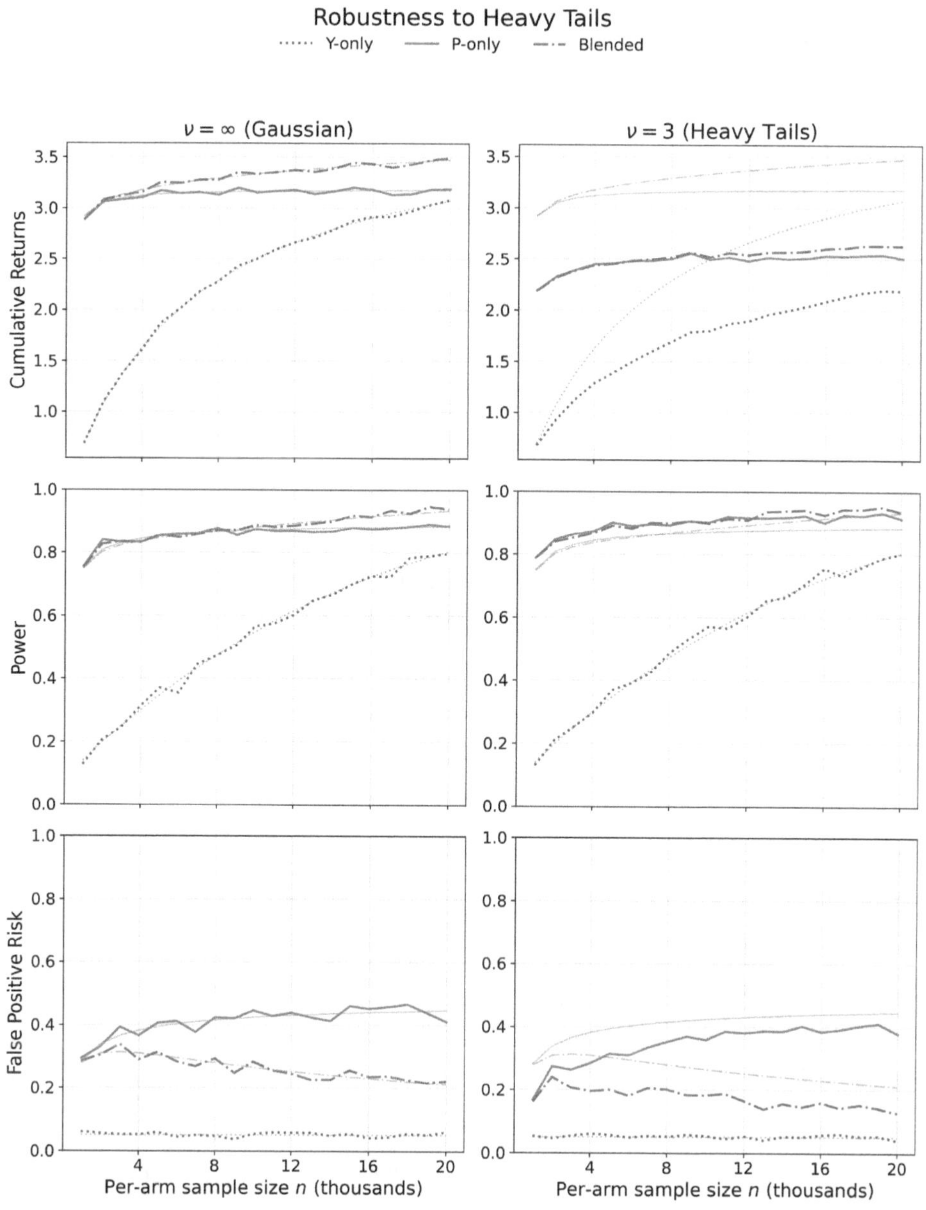

Fig. 4. Robustness to Heavy Tails: Returns, Power, and False Positive Risk, Comparing $\nu = \infty$ (Gaussian) vs $\nu = 3$.

Lastly, the scatterplot also indicates that the core assumptions of the framework are reasonable: the data are approximately elliptical and the relationship has no obvious nonlinearities or discontinuities. This suggests that the assumptions of normality and linearity are not too badly violated.

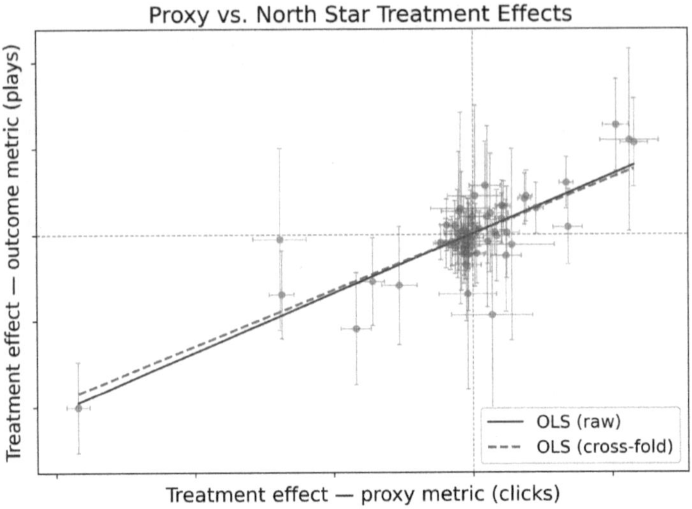

Fig. 5. Treatment effects on the proxy (clicks, x-axis) vs. the north star (plays, y-axis) across 15 experiments; error bars are 95% CIs. Two fits are shown: raw OLS (black, solid) and cross-fold OLS (red, dashed). Axes suppressed for confidentiality. (Color figure online)

5.2 Results

This section presents the optimal blending weights for this dataset. The minimum sample size test (10) is passed for all experiments, and so I use the closed-form approximation to the optimal weights from Proposition 1. Figure 6 displays these weights for the approximate range of sample sizes found in the data ($n \in [1\text{M}, 25\text{M}]$ per arm). Note that the simplex constraint binds at the lower end of this range, with the weights concentrating entirely on clicks for $n \lesssim 2$ million, in which case the interior approximation is replaced by the simplex-constrained solution (which just puts all weight on clicks).

I find that, at the median experiment size of $n \approx 5$ million per arm, the optimal blend assigns 52% weight to clicks and 48% to plays. The substantial weight on clicks, even at this relatively large sample size, reflects the fact that clicks have a far higher signal-to-noise ratio than do plays. However, as n grows, the sampling penalty shrinks and A^* tilts toward plays (reaching $\approx 90\%$ plays at the largest experiment sizes $n = 25$ million).

Figure 7 displays the expected return per experiment for each decision rule. The key takeaway is that the blended rule dominates both single-metric rules at all sample sizes observed in the data. Among the single-metric rules, clicks-only earns higher returns than plays-only across the entire observed range, since the signal-to-noise ratio of plays remains small even at the largest sample sizes; the gap narrows as n grows but does not close below $n = 25$ million. Yet, as the plot shows, incorporating plays information at these larger sample sizes still improves returns compared to the clicks-only rule.

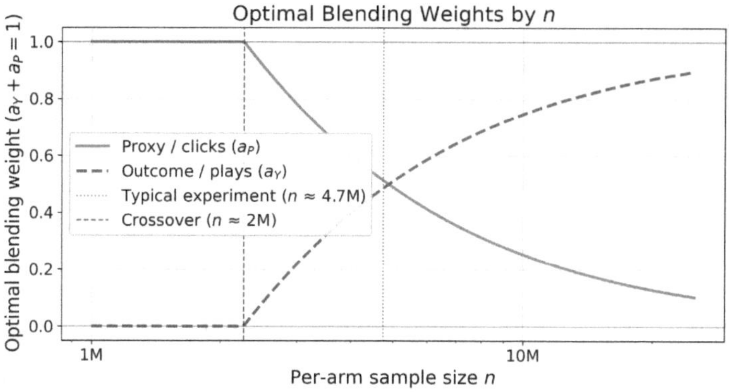

Fig. 6. Approximately optimal blending weights vs. per-arm sample size n (log scale), using cross-fold parameter estimates from 15 experiments. The simplex constraint binds below $n \approx 2$ million (weights load entirely on clicks); above it both weights are strictly positive and the weight on plays rises with n. Typical experiment size is approximately 5 million per arm (grey dotted vertical). (Color figure online)

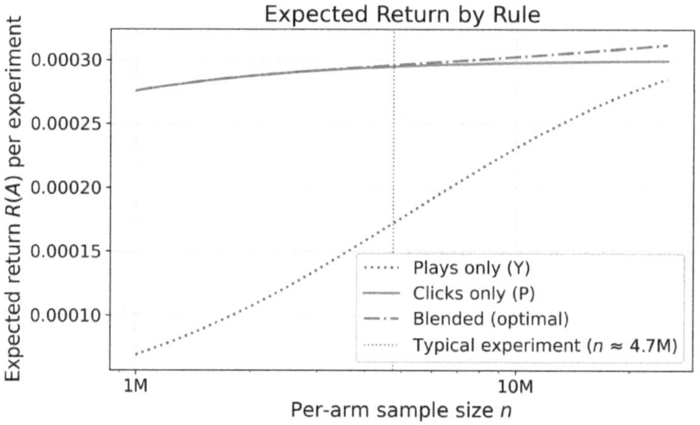

Fig. 7. Expected return per experiment vs. per-arm sample size n (log scale) for three decision rules: plays-only (blue, dotted), clicks-only (orange, solid), and the optimal blend (green, dash-dot). The blended rule dominates both single-metric rules and clicks-only earns more than plays-only across the entire range of empirically observed sample sizes. (Color figure online)

6 Conclusion

I study the optimal role of proxy metrics in decision-making with an observed but statistically insensitive north star. Rather than basing decisions exclusively on either metric, I propose a blending approach in which the experimenter decides A/B tests using a weighted average of the estimated treatment effects on the proxy metric(s) and the north star. I provide a closed-form approximation to the optimal blending weights and show that the optimal weight on the north star is increasing in the size of each test and decreasing in the structural alignment of true treatment effects on the north star and the proxy metric(s). I show how to estimate the requisite parameters for these weights from past experiments, and lastly demonstrate the applicability of the methods to a real-world experimentation program at Netflix.

This work can be extended in several directions. First, the theoretical framework assumes that experiments are independently and identically distributed. Relaxing this assumption could lead to novel insights, for example, on how experimenters should allocate resources across different experimentation programs or ideas of varying quality. Second, I make distributional assumptions that may or may not be appropriate in meta-analyses of past experiments [16]. In particular, I assume that the underlying treatment effects are Gaussian, when in reality treatment effect distributions may be heavier-tailed [2,3]. Although I find that the core insights are robust to these assumptions, future work should analyze more flexible and realistic models of experiments. Third, whereas this work assumes access to past experiments, future work can explore how to leverage observational data to inform the design and selection of proxy metrics when no such data are available.

Acknowledgments. For valuable suggestions, I thank participants in Netflix's Statistics, Methodology, and Engineering (SME) colloquium (2025-08-15) and the four anonymous reviewers. The Appendix for this paper can be found at https://github.com/winston-chou/blending.

Disclosure of Interests. The author has no competing interests to declare that are relevant to the content of this article.

References

1. Athey, S., Chetty, R., Imbens, G.W., Kang, H.: The surrogate index: combining short-term proxies to estimate long-term treatment effects more rapidly and precisely. Rev. Econ. Stud. (2025). https://doi.org/10.1093/restud/rdaf087. Advance article
2. Azevedo, E.M., Deng, A., Montiel Olea, J.L., Weyl, E.G.: Empirical bayes estimation of treatment effects with many A/B tests: an overview. AEA Pap. Proc. **109**, 43–47 (2019)
3. Azevedo, E.M., Deng, A., Olea, J.L.M., Rao, J., Weyl, E.G.: A/B testing with fat tails. J. Polit. Econ. **128**(12) (2020). https://doi.org/10.1086/710607
4. Azevedo, E.M., Mao, D., Olea, J.L.M., Velez, A.: The A/B testing problem with Gaussian priors. J. Econ. Theory **210**, 105646 (2023)
5. Bibaut, A., Chou, W., Ejdemyr, S., Kallus, N.: Learning the covariance of treatment effects across many weak experiments. In: Proceedings of the 30th ACM SIGKDD Conference on Knowledge Discovery and Data Mining, pp. 153–162 (2024). https://doi.org/10.1145/3637528.3672034
6. Buyse, M., Molenberghs, G., Burzykowski, T., Renard, D., Geys, H.: The validation of surrogate endpoints in meta-analyses of randomized experiments. Biostatistics **1**(1), 49–67 (2000)

7. Chou, W., Gray, C., Kallus, N., Bibaut, A., Ejdemyr, S.: Evaluating decision rules across many weak experiments. In: Proceedings of the 31st ACM SIGKDD Conference on Knowledge Discovery and Data Mining (2025). https://doi.org/10.1145/3711896.3737217
8. Coey, D., Cunningham, T.: Improving treatment effect estimators through experiment splitting. In: The World Wide Web Conference, pp. 285–295 (2019)
9. Cunningham, T., Kim, J.: Interpreting experiments with multiple outcomes (2022)
10. Deng, A., Hagar, L., Stevens, N.T., Xifara, T., Gandhi, A.: Metric decomposition in A/B tests. In: Proceedings of the 30th ACM SIGKDD Conference on Knowledge Discovery and Data Mining, pp. 4885–4895 (2024). https://doi.org/10.1145/3637528.3671556
11. Deng, A., Shi, X.: Data-driven metric development for online controlled experiments: seven lessons learned. In: Proceedings of the 22nd ACM SIGKDD International Conference on Knowledge Discovery and Data Mining, pp. 77–86 (2016)
12. Gelman, A., Carlin, J.: Beyond power calculations: assessing type S (sign) and type M (magnitude) errors. Perspect. Psychol. Sci. **9**(6), 641–651 (2014)
13. Kohavi, R., Chen, N.: False positives in A/B tests. In: Proceedings of the 30th ACM SIGKDD Conference on Knowledge Discovery and Data Mining, pp. 5240–5250 (2024). https://doi.org/10.1145/3637528.3671631
14. Larsen, N., Stallrich, J., Sengupta, S., Deng, A., Kohavi, R., Stevens, N.T.: Statistical challenges in online controlled experiments: a review of A/B testing methodology. Am. Stat. **78**(2), 135–149 (2024)
15. Lee, M.R., Shen, M.: Winner's curse: Bias estimation for total effects of features in online controlled experiments. In: Proceedings of the 24th ACM SIGKDD International Conference on Knowledge Discovery & Data Mining, pp. 491–499 (2018)
16. Molenberghs, G., Buyse, M., Geys, H., Renard, D., Burzykowski, T., Alonso, A.: Statistical challenges in the evaluation of surrogate endpoints in randomized trials. Control. Clin. Trials **23**(6), 607–625 (2002)
17. Prentice, R.L.: Surrogate endpoints in clinical trials: definition and operational criteria. Stat. Med. **8**(4), 431–440 (1989)
18. Sudijono, T., Ejdemyr, S., Lal, A., Tingley, M.: Optimizing returns from experimentation programs. In: Proceedings of the 26th ACM Conference on Economics and Computation (2025). https://doi.org/10.1145/3736252.3742638
19. Tang, D., Agarwal, A., O'Brien, D., Meyer, M.: Overlapping experiment infrastructure: more, better, faster experimentation. In: Proceedings of the 16th ACM SIGKDD International Conference on Knowledge Discovery and Data Mining, pp. 17–26 (2010)
20. Tran, A., Bibaut, A., Kallus, N.: Inferring the long-term causal effects of long-term treatments from short-term experiments. In: Proceedings of the 41st International Conference on Machine Learning. Proceedings of Machine Learning Research, vol. 235, pp. 48565–48577. PMLR (2024). https://proceedings.mlr.press/v235/tran24b.html
21. Tripuraneni, N., Richardson, L., D'Amour, A., Soriano, J., Yadlowsky, S.: Choosing a proxy metric from past experiments. In: Proceedings of the 30th ACM SIGKDD Conference on Knowledge Discovery and Data Mining, pp. 5803–5812 (2024). https://doi.org/10.1145/3637528.3671543
22. Zhang, V., Zhao, M., Le, A., Kallus, N.: Evaluating the surrogate index as a decision-making tool using 200 A/B tests at Netflix (2023). arXiv preprint arXiv:2311.11922
23. Zito, A., Greaves, D., Soriano, J., Richardson, L.: Pareto optimal proxy metrics. Appl. Stoch. Model. Bus. Ind. **41**(2), e70003 (2025)

Brexit Means Brexit: Selection Bias, Echo Chambers, and Entrenched Opinion on Reddit

Marian-Andrei Rizoiu[1(✉)], Duy Khuu[1], Andrew Law[1], and Christine Largeron[2]

[1] University of Technology Sydney, Ultimo, Australia
Marian-Andrei.Rizoiu@uts.edu.au
[2] Université de Lyon, UJM-Saint-Étienne, CNRS, Lyon, France
https://www.behavioral-ds.science

Abstract. Political polarisation on structured discussion platforms such as Reddit differs fundamentally from that on broadcast platforms such as Twitter/X, yet most prior work targets the latter. We present an end-to-end framework for measuring and analysing polarisation dynamics, applied to the R/BREXIT subreddit (871K submissions, November 2015 – February 2021). We construct **R/BREXIT**, a crowd-annotated stance dataset of 5,024 labelled submissions (inter-annotator agreement = 0.804), and train a domain-adapted BERT classifier. We introduce a continuous polarity metric that replaces discrete stance categories, revealing fine-grained opinion spectra across 27 politically-defined periods. Our analysis yields three findings: (a) future stance prediction is confounded by survivorship bias: who remains active is self-selected on engagement, not stance, biasing any longitudinal model toward a non-representative minority; (b) echo chambers are quantifiably dominant, with nearly 40% of interactions between like-minded users; (c) user current polarity is the dominant predictor of future polarity, with echo-chamber immersion as the secondary predictive signal. These findings reveal that Reddit's partisan core is entrenched by self-selection, not softened by cross-cutting exposure.

Keywords: Polarisation dynamics · Stance detection · Echo chambers · Reddit · Continuous polarity · Selection bias

1 Introduction

Does Engagement with Opposing Views Change Political Opinions Online? On broadcast platforms such as Twitter/X, the question is largely moot: opposing camps cluster around distinct hashtags, retweets signal endorsement, and users rarely encounter dissent [2,12]. Structured discussion forums (Reddit chief among them) offer a starkly different environment: opposing users reply within the same thread, pseudonymity lowers social cost, and long-form

M. Ceci et al. (Eds.): ECML PKDD 2026, LNAI 16948, pp. 88–105, 2027.
https://doi.org/10.1007/978-3-032-37679-4_6

deliberation is the structural norm [6]. If cross-cutting exposure can shift opinions anywhere, it should happen on Reddit. We find that on R/BREXIT, it largely does not, and the reason reveals a structural confound prior work has overlooked.

Three questions must be answered to study this. **Q1: Can reliable stance labels be obtained for Reddit political discussions?** Prior work [22] relied on a Twitter-trained stance classifier that agrees with crowd annotations on only ~25% of comments, producing near-random performance (F1 = 0.32) on the Reddit domain. **Q2: How should user-level political stance be represented from discrete post labels?** Naive majority-vote aggregation collapses nuance: it labels 83% of users as "Neutral," making a user who posts two pro-Brexit and three neutral comments indistinguishable from one who posts exclusively neutral content, masking genuine opinion diversity. **Q3: Does user attrition introduce a selection bias that confounds longitudinal stance analyses?** Our observations are already restricted to *active contributors*: Reddit's API exposes content but not reads, so lurkers are invisible. Among active users, over 70% of R/BREXIT users appear in only one of 27 time periods, and fewer than 1% sustain engagement across three consecutive periods, rendering "future stance prediction" conditional on the user returning and actively contributing again, a confounder unacknowledged in prior work [21,22].

We present an end-to-end framework that addresses all three questions, applied to the R/BREXIT subreddit spanning the full Brexit saga (November 2015–February 2021; 871K submissions). The answer to **Q3** reframes the other two: the dominant mechanism shaping polarisation dynamics on R/BREXIT is not opinion change but *survivorship bias*. The active community is overwhelmingly transient, and who keeps posting is decided by engagement, not conviction: the most strident voices are disproportionately one-off posters who never return. This finding challenges the premise of prior future-stance prediction models and carries direct implications for platform polarisation interventions.

Our contributions are:

1. **R/BREXIT dataset.** A crowd-annotated Reddit stance dataset of 5,024 labelled submissions spanning 27 time periods, with inter-annotator agreement (IAA = 0.804). We detail a systematic MTurk methodology including malicious worker detection.[1]
2. **Continuous polarisation measurement.** A domain-adapted BERT stance classifier (BERT-Reddit; macro F1 = 0.555) provides per-comment stance labels; these are aggregated via a continuous polarity metric that captures the full opinion spectrum beyond the three discrete categories.
3. **Behavioural findings.** (a) Future stance prediction is fundamentally confounded by selection bias in user retention: who returns is governed by engagement, not stance: models condition on a non-representative, highly-engaged minority. (b) Echo chambers are quantifiably dominant: nearly 40% of user–period interactions occur between like-minded individuals. (c) Among persistent users, opinion is stable: SHAP analysis identifies current polarity as the

[1] The R/BREXIT dataset and analysis code are available at https://github.com/behavioral-ds/brexit-opinion-dynamics.

dominant predictor of future polarity, with echo-chamber immersion as the secondary signal. (d) Richer models cannot overcome this ceiling: augmenting activity features with stance triads, a graph attention network, or sequential models yields negligible gains, because self-selection sets a predictive boundary for network topology.

2 Related Work and Prerequisites

Stance Detection. Stance detection has progressed from SVM classifiers with n-gram features [29] through network-augmented approaches [12] to transformer-based models, with BERT fine-tuning, augmented by domain-specific continued pre-training, now the standard approach [2,3,32,44]. Cross-context transferability is a persistent challenge: signal choice critically determines pipeline portability across platforms and time periods [38], and training across heterogeneous labelled corpora substantially improves cross-dataset generalisation under limited supervision [51,53].

Zero-shot LLM prompting (via chain-of-thought [17] and counterfactual strategies [49]) has been shown to rival fine-tuned models on established benchmarks. However, converging evidence shows that fine-tuned small language models outperform zero-shot LLMs when in-domain labelled data is available [25], while parameter-efficient fine-tuning additionally yields interpretable, expert-grounded detectors for politically charged social media text [48]. Ziems et al. [54] evaluate 13 LLMs across 25 computational social science tasks and find they do not outperform fine-tuned classifiers. Furthermore, Gera and Neal [18] confirm in a comprehensive survey that BERT variants remain dominant across stance detection settings. We therefore adopt a fine-tuned BERT approach with domain-specific continued pre-training on our Reddit corpus (Sect. 4.1).

A gap remains: most stance detection research targets Twitter/X, whose short-form posts differ markedly from Reddit's tree-structured deliberative discussions [3,18]. The few Reddit-specific efforts address multi-target user-level stance discovery [43] or inter-user disagreement prediction [27], but neither provides crowd-annotated stance labels for a single contentious topic at scale. Our r/Brexit dataset fills this gap with 5,024 crowd-annotated texts, a systematic MTurk methodology with malicious-worker detection, and a domain-adapted BERT classifier evaluated against external human judgements.

Opinion Dynamics. Computational models of opinion dynamics range from RNN-based sequential models of stance change [21] and sociologically-informed neural networks embedding classical models (DeGroot, bounded confidence) within deep learning frameworks [33], to variational inference approaches for agent-based model calibration [26], with generative agent simulations reproducing emergent social ties and homophilous network structure from individual interaction rules [42]. Complementary work measures social influence via crowd-sourced pairwise comparisons and psychosocial-inspired diffusion models [36,37], disentangles diffusion pathways via Hawkes processes [8], models engagement as a sequence of social-exchange decisions [46], and detects emerging narratives via state-space models [45]. At the platform level, Cinus et al. [9] show that people recommenders amplify echo chambers only when substantial initial homophily already exists; otherwise algorithmic effects are negligible. A common limitation is the assumption of known social neighbourhoods (e.g., Twitter follower graphs) and fixed user populations; on Reddit, networks must be inferred from reply structure, and the population is open, as participants arrive and depart freely.

On Reddit, opinion change alters subsequent community participation patterns [35], yet prior studies overwhelmingly treat stance prediction *unconditionally*: they predict a user's future stance without accounting for whether the user will remain present [21,22]. A field experiment by Oswald et al. [34] shows online political discussions are dominated by a systematically atypical active minority, so self-selection distorts observed opinion distributions. No prior work formally quantifies how user attrition biases longitudinal polarisation estimates, nor jointly models presence and stance as interconnected outcomes. We address both: we analyse which features predict departure versus opinion persistence (Sect. 5.1), and we identify survivorship bias as a fundamental confound in stance dynamics (Sect. 6).

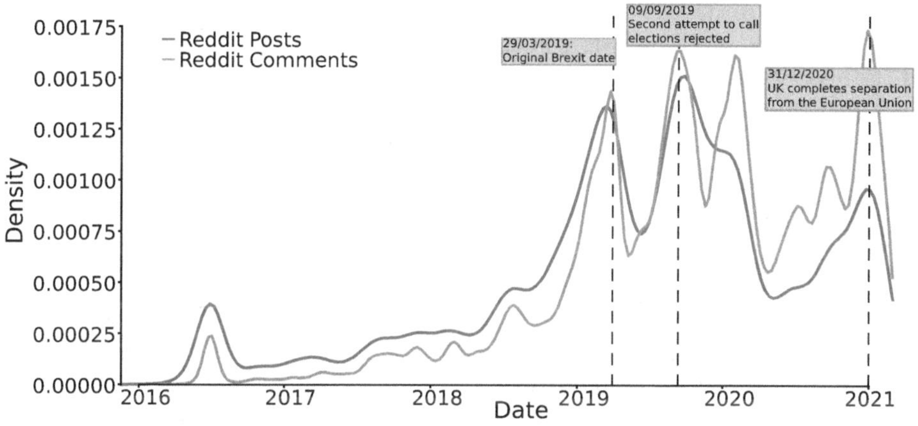

Fig. 1. Temporal density of posts and comments in R/BREXIT (November 2015–February 2021). Activity surges coincide with the original Brexit date (29/03/2019), the second attempt to call elections (09/09/2019), and the UK's final separation (31/12/2020).

Political Polarisation on Reddit. Reddit has become a primary site for studying online political discourse, with dedicated resources such as the Reddit Politosphere covering 605 political subreddits [19]. Echo-chamber research reveals a more complex picture than simple polarisation narratives: hostile speech is more prevalent *within* than between opposing sides [16], and polarised news sharing is concentrated in a small minority of users ("echo tunnels" rather than broad chambers [30]). Segregation in news discussions is driven more by demographics than by ideology [31], and a single left–right axis is insufficient: interactions on r/PoliticalCompass exhibit homophily on the social axis but heterophily on the economic axis [10]. Selective exposure operates even at the level of topic choice: fringe users disproportionately cherry-pick narrow subsets of otherwise mainstream content rather than consuming overtly false material [24]. Users who deliberately engage with opposing views use less hostile language, yet their home communities penalise them with fewer upvotes [15], which suggests structural disincentives for bridge-building. At the ecosystem level, far-right opinions self-reinforce and compete with moderate views for finite attention, and targeted interventions can stem this spread [7]; content moderation itself measurably reduces harm when applied within tight time windows [41]. Yuan et al. [52] extend homophily measurement via inverse reinforcement learning, showing users can share posting behaviour while discussing different topics, and identify a class of users oriented toward disagreement.

In our own prior work [22], we studied the same R/BREXIT subreddit and introduced a feature-based framework for predicting a user's future stance given their activity in period t. We defined four feature sets, namely textual content (F0), user-level activity statistics (F1, F2), and discussion-composition descriptors (F3), which we refer to collectively as F0123 (full feature inventory in Online Appendix D [1]). That work reported macro F1 = 0.539 for the best feature set (F3), but relied on a Twitter-trained Naive Bayes classifier for stance labels; here, we show (Sect. 3.2) that this classifier agrees with crowd annotations on only ~25% of comments, predominantly because it over-predicts "Neutral." Community-level analyses [11] and earlier studies of online political discourse [50] document homophily at the platform level but do not measure *within-subreddit* polarisation dynamics at the user level over time. Our framework addresses this: we quantify echo chambers via edge homogeneity within a single subreddit, track individual users across 27 politically-segmented periods, and show that the users who persist are precisely those most resistant to opinion change.

3 The R/BREXIT Dataset

Studying polarisation dynamics at scale requires ground-truth stance labels, yet the 871K submissions in R/BREXIT preclude exhaustive manual annotation. We therefore construct a high-quality annotated subset: we temporally segment the corpus (Sect. 3.1), crowd-annotate a stratified sample via Amazon Mechanical Turk (Sect. 3.2), producing the R/BREXIT dataset profiled in Sect. 3.2.

3.1 Data Collection and Platform Context

Reddit is a pseudonymous platform organised into topic-specific communities (*subreddits*), where posts initiate tree-structured comment threads, with branching multi-level deliberation distinct from flat broadcast platforms.

We originally introduce the R/BREXIT dataset in our prior work [22]; here, we reconstruct and extend it using the Pushshift API [39], spanning November 2015 through February 2021.[2] The corpus comprises 871,955 submissions (56,017 posts and 815,938 comments). We segment the timeline into 27 periods demarcated by high-profile political events: from the referendum through Theresa May's resignation, Boris Johnson's ascent, and the UK's final separation from the EU; the full period table is in Online Appendix A [1]. Event-based segmentation ensures each period captures a coherent phase of the debate.

Figure 1 shows the temporal distribution of submissions. Activity increases markedly from 2019 onward, with surges at major political events.

3.2 Crowd-Sourced Stance Annotation

We annotate a subset of submissions using Amazon Mechanical Turk (MTurk) [4]. Following Mohammad et al. [29], we adopt three stance classes: *pro-Brexit*, *anti-Brexit*, and *neither*. Each submission is annotated by eight workers, with the majority label retained; workers see the full comment thread for context. We achieve annotation quality through three steps: parameter optimisation on small test batches, malicious-worker detection in production, and a low-confidence filter on the final dataset.

Step 1—Parameter Optimisation. We run a series of test batches (200 submissions each), varying one parameter at a time. Figure 2a summarises the effects. Restricting workers to English-speaking countries improves IAA (inter-annotator agreement, i.e., the proportion of annotations matching the majority label) by 3.6%; tightening prior-performance requirements (approval rate [AR] $\geq$98%, minimum HITs completed [MHC] $\geq$ 1,000) adds a further 4.5%. The best configuration yields IAA = 0.798, comparable to the 0.82 reported by Mohammad et al. [29].

Step 2—Malicious Worker Detection. Despite optimal parameters, the first two production batches yielded IAA of 0.746 and 0.710, well below the expected 0.798. Inspection revealed a few prolific workers submitting annotations without reading the text, labelling randomly or with a fixed strategy to minimise effort. Standard MTurk qualification requirements (approval rate $\geq$ 98%, $\geq$ 1,000 completed HITs) are insufficient to screen out such workers, since requesters are often reluctant to reject HITs.

To address this, we introduce the *Majority Agreement Proportion* (MAP): the proportion of a worker's annotations that agree with the majority label of the remaining annotators. Workers with MAP $<$ 0.25 are flagged as malicious; re-annotating their submissions raises the two affected batch IAAs to 0.87 and 0.91, respectively. An allowlist of workers with MAP $\geq$ 0.5 and at least 20 prior annotations is then applied to all subsequent production batches, yielding an overall production IAA of 0.740 (the "IAA (all)" column in Fig. 2b).

[2] The Pushshift Reddit dataset service was discontinued in 2023; Reddit data collected prior to that date remains publicly downloadable.

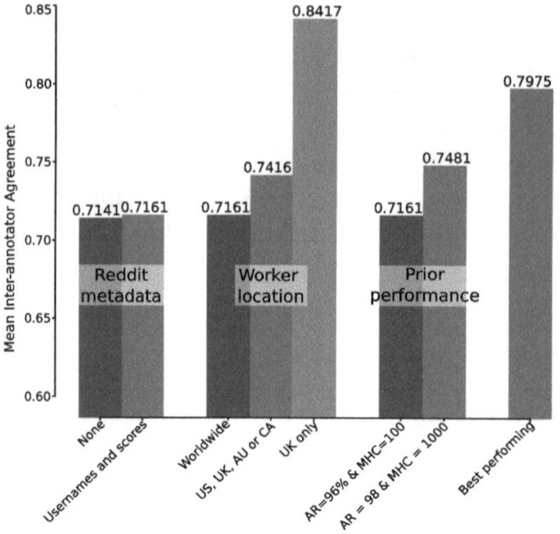

(a)

Class	IAA (all)	IAA (filt.)
Pro-Brexit	0.623	0.720
Neither	0.759	0.824
Anti-Brexit	0.694	0.742
Overall	**0.740**	**0.804**

(b)

Fig. 2. MTurk annotation quality. (a) Step 1: parameter sweep over worker qualifications (MHC: minimum HITs completed; AR: approval rate; full sweep in Online Appendix B [1]); the best configuration yields IAA = 0.798 (four English-speaking countries; UK-only is higher but causes unfinished batches). **(b)** Step 3: per-class IAA before ("all", post Step 2 allowlist, overall 0.740) and after ("filt.") the low-confidence filter (overall 0.804).

Step 3—Low-Confidence Filter. We discard submissions where fewer than five of eight annotators agree (IAA < 0.6), as such cases signal genuine ambiguity rather than annotator error. Removing these low-confidence instances raises the final dataset IAA to 0.804 (the "IAA (filt.)" column in Fig. 2b), the value used for all subsequent classifier training. The final annotated dataset contains 5,024 labelled texts: 225 pro-Brexit (4.5%), 887 anti-Brexit (17.7%), and 3,912 neither (77.9%). Pro-Brexit exhibits the lowest per-class IAA (0.72), as workers encounter fewer exemplars of pro-Brexit language; neither is the easiest to annotate (0.82), containing less group-specific jargon. Full details of the MTurk interface design, parameter tuning batches, and malicious-worker detection are provided in Online Appendix B [1].

4 Measuring Continuous Polarisation

Our goal is to characterise each user's stance as a continuous quantity derived from the discrete labels of their individual posts. This requires two steps: first, a stance classifier that assigns per-submission labels across the full corpus (Sect. 4.1); second, an aggregation scheme that maps these discrete labels to a continuous polarity score per user per period (Sect. 4.2).

4.1 Submission Stance Classification

Models. Our prior work on r/Brexit [22] relied on a Twitter-trained Naive Bayes classifier that agrees with our crowd annotations on only ~25% of comments, predominantly because it over-predicts "Neutral." We therefore train an in-domain classifier from scratch; fine-tuned SLMs consistently outperform zero-shot LLMs when in-domain labelled data is available [18,25,54], motivating a BERT fine-tuning approach. We compare four strategies. *BERT-base* uses the standard pre-trained model without adaptation. *BERTweet* [32] substitutes a model pre-trained on 850M English tweets. *BERT-DINO* uses DINO [40] to generate over 4M synthetic r/Brexit-domain text pairs, then pre-trains BERT on semantic textual similarity before stance fine-tuning. *BERT-Reddit* (ours) continues masked-language-model (MLM) pre-training on all 871K r/Brexit submissions to adapt the model to subreddit vocabulary and discourse before fine-tuning. All four are trained with randomised hyperparameter search and evaluated via stratified five-fold cross-validation (full hyperparameter spaces in Online Appendix C [1]).

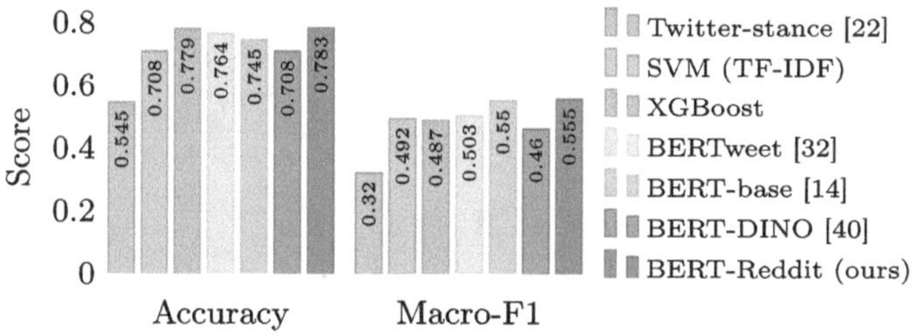

Fig. 3. Stance classification results (stratified five-fold cross-validation). BERT-Reddit achieves the best macro-F1 (0.555) and accuracy (0.783).

Results. Figure 3 summarises classifier performance. BERT-Reddit outperforms all alternatives, achieving macro-F1 = 0.555 against 0.320 for the Twitter transfer baseline. Notably, BERTweet underperforms BERT-base, suggesting Reddit language is closer to standard English than to Twitter vernacular. BERT-DINO degrades performance, reflecting noise in the synthetically generated STS pairs. F1 = 0.555 is contextually strong: the random-chance baseline for this heavily imbalanced dataset is 0.26 (not 0.33), as the pro-Brexit class constitutes only 5% of submissions. We use BERT-Reddit's predictions as stance labels throughout; the sensitivity of downstream findings to label error is bounded and contextualised in Sect. 6.

4.2 From Discrete Stance to Continuous Polarity

Continuous User Polarisation Score. Majority-vote aggregation of per-post stances collapses nuance: under it, 83% of users are labelled "Neutral," masking a substantially polarised population. We instead define a *continuous polarity* for user u in period t as:

$$\text{polarity}(u,t) = \frac{1}{2}\left(\frac{P-N}{P+N}+1\right) - \frac{1}{2}\left(\frac{A-N}{A+N}+1\right), \tag{1}$$

where P, N, and A are the counts of pro-Brexit, neutral, and anti-Brexit comments by u in period t. Polarity lies in $[-1, 1]$: $+1$ is strongly pro-Brexit, -1 strongly anti-Brexit, and 0 indicates either exclusively neutral posting or a balanced pro/anti mix (affecting <4% of users). The metric reflects *revealed preference* (what users actually post) rather than latent conviction: a user who posts one pro-Brexit comment among 99 neutral contributions receives a polarity near zero, correctly weighting the rarity of their partisan signal.

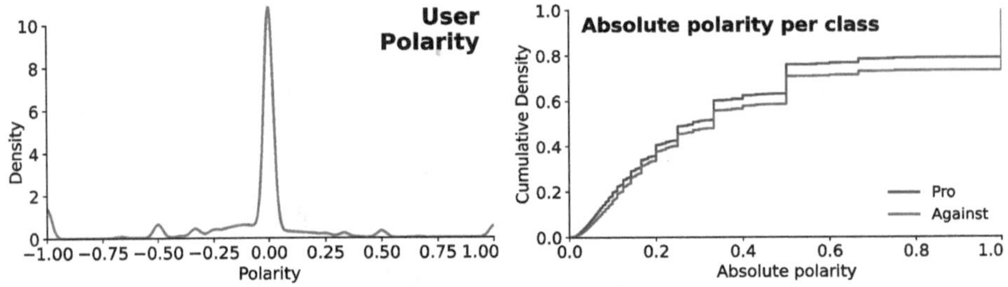

(a) (b)

Fig. 4. (a) PDF of the continuous polarity distribution across all user–period pairs. **(b)** CDF of absolute polarity for pro-leaning (> 0) and anti-leaning (< 0) users.

Figure 4a reveals that 58% of user–period pairs have polarity exactly zero, yet the remaining 42% exhibit a rich spectrum of opinion invisible to discrete labelling. Anti-Brexit users are slightly more polarised (Fig. 4): the subreddit's anti-Brexit majority attracts more strongly opinionated participants on that side.

Network Polarisation Features. User-level polarity extends to the interaction network. Let $\boldsymbol{n}_i$ denote the set of users that i has interacted with (replied to or received a reply from) in a given period. We define two per-edge quantities. The *interaction polarity* polarity($\boldsymbol{n}_i$) is the vector of polarities of i's interaction partners, capturing the ideological composition of i's neighbourhood. The *edge homogeneity* polarity(i) $\cdot$ polarity($\boldsymbol{n}_i$) is the element-wise product of i's polarity with each partner's polarity: positive entries indicate like-minded interactions, negative entries cross-cutting exchanges (inspired by [13]). Both are summarised by their mean per user per period and used in Sect. 5.2 to measure echo chamber structure and predict future polarity.

5 Polarisation Dynamics Analysis

We organise this section around two questions: who stays on the platform, and what do persistent users believe? The answers build toward a single finding: it is survivorship bias, not opinion change, that drives the polarisation dynamics visible in the data.

5.1 Who Stays and Who Leaves?

All figures in this section concern *active contributors* only; lurkers are invisible to our data, so "returning" means returning *and* posting again. The R/BREXIT community is dominated by transient participants: 70.5% of users appear in only one period, and fewer than 1% sustain engagement across three or more consecutive periods (Fig. 5a). Before asking how opinions change, we ask what determines whether an active contributor returns at all.

Activity and Degree. We define *activity* as the number of comments a user posts per period, and *degree* as the number of unique interaction partners. Figure 5b

Pattern	Freq.
■	70.5%
■■	5.0%
■□■	1.3%
■□□■	1.0%
■■■	0.9%

(a)

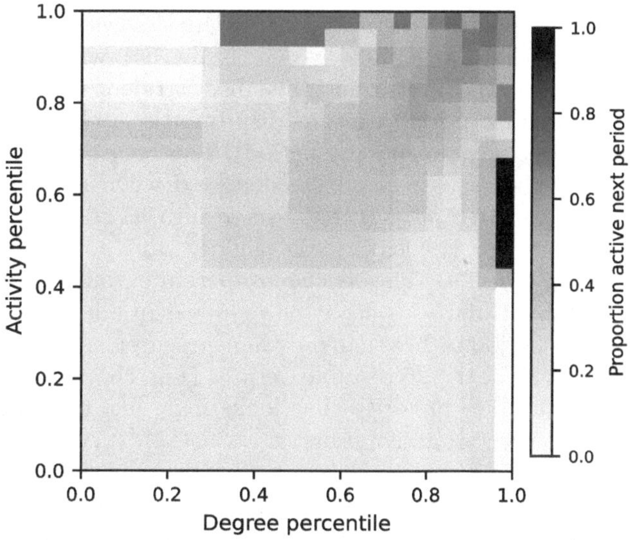

(b)

Fig. 5. **(a)** Most frequent user presence patterns (■ = present; □ = absent): 70.5% of users appear in a single period, and fewer than 1% sustain engagement across three or more consecutive periods. **(b)** Proportion of users who remain in the next period, binned by activity and degree percentiles. Higher engagement strongly correlates with staying. The exception cluster (>96th percentile degree, 44th–64th percentile activity) contains two highly polarised anti-Brexit broadcasters who accumulate replies without posting frequently.

shows the retention heat map across activity and degree percentiles: higher values of both strongly correlate with remaining. One exception stands out: a cluster above the 96th percentile of degree but only in the 44th–64th percentile of activity: high reach, low output. Only two users occupy this cluster, both strongly anti-Brexit (polarity −0.50 and −0.667); one posted across nine periods, favouring short provocative content (e.g., "Stop the madness. Stop Brexit."), returning to provoke and *broadcast* their opinions, not to deliberate.

Influential Users. Interacting with *prolific* users (those at or above the 99th percentile of degree or activity, with 73% qualifying on both) substantially increases the likelihood of returning: users who interacted with a prolific peer retain at $\approx 50\%$, versus 32–33% for those who did not ($p \ll 0.001$, χ^2 test). These hub users act as community anchors, doubling a peripheral user's odds of returning; the long-term community structure is sustained by this small connected core.

Engagement, Not Stance, Decides Who Returns. A raw comparison makes departing users look slightly more polarised (Fig. 6a), but this is a measurement artefact. The polarity metric saturates at low activity (Fig. 6b), e.g. one partisan comment scores $|\text{polarity}| = 1$; one-off posters (the bulk of departures: 76% of single-post authors never return) dominate it. Controlling for activity and degree, polarity carries no significant association with retention (odds ratio 0.98/SD, 95% CI $[0.97, 1.00]$, $p = 0.10$; Fig. 6c), whereas a one-SD rise in activity doubles the odds of returning. The most strident voices (low-activity, maximally polarised single posts) are thus disproportionately transient (returners average 18.5 versus 3.8 comments per period). This result holds however we define departure. Whether a user counts as departed when they skip the next period, the next two or three periods, or never return at all, the gap between stayers and leavers barely moves: leavers stay slightly more polarised throughout, by Cohen's $d \approx -0.11$ (Fig. 7a). The strict next-period cutoff does not drive this, since 28% of the users it marks as departed reappear in a later period. The gap also holds period by period rather than only in aggregate: leavers are at least as polarised as stayers in 25 of the 26 testable periods (Fig. 7b). Conditioning on retention still leaves a survivor minority that looks little like the wider population (Fig. 7c): compared with all active users (n = 56,111), survivors (n = 23,540) take a side more often (54% vs. 42%) but hold it less strongly (mean $|\text{polarity}|$ 0.157 vs. 0.177), because users who comment enough to stay register a lean yet rarely push the metric to its extremes. Longitudinal stance analyses therefore rest on a self-selected, highly active minority rather than a representative sample of opinion.

SHAP Analysis of Future Presence. We train a random forest classifier for future presence (remain vs. leave) and apply SHAP analysis (Fig. 8a). Recall that p_s-$y\%$ denotes the yth percentile of stance-s saturation across a user's discussions, where $s \in \{\text{B (pro-Brexit)}, \text{A (anti-Brexit)}, \text{N (neutral)}\}$ (full inventory in Online Appendix D [1]). Participating in at least one highly polarised discussion (`pB-100%`, `pA-100%`) strongly predicts remaining. Conversely, engaging *only*

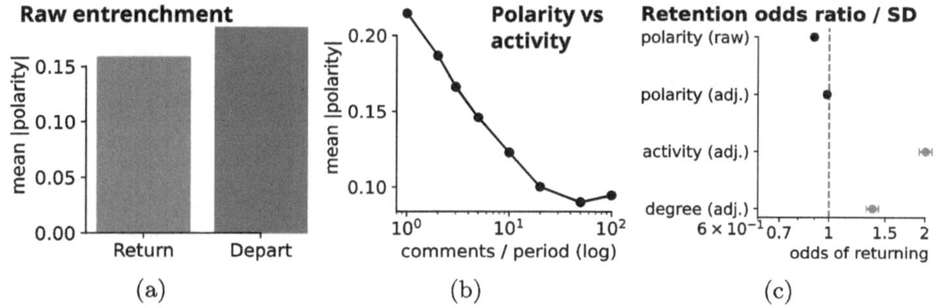

Fig. 6. Retention is selective on engagement, not stance. **(a)** A raw comparison makes departing users look slightly more polarised. **(b)** Mean |polarity| falls with activity: single-post users saturate the metric. **(c)** Retention odds ratios (per SD, 95% CI): controlling for activity and degree, polarity's effect collapses to 1 (no effect), while activity dominates.

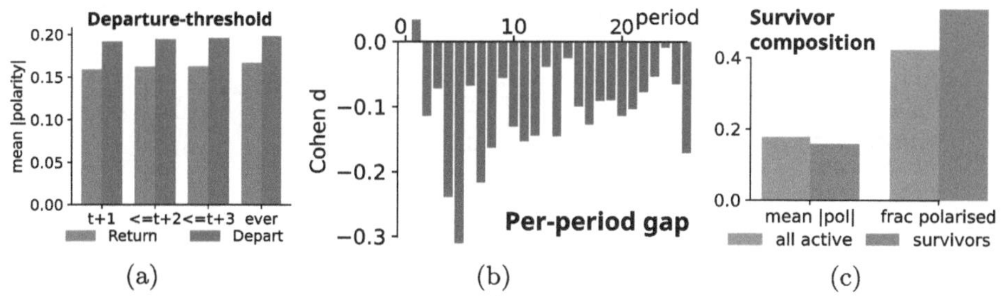

Fig. 7. Robustness of the engagement-driven retention finding, and the resulting selection bias. **(a)** The raw stayer–leaver entrenchment gap (mean |polarity|) is stable across four definitions of departure (no return at $t+1$, within $\leq t+2$, $\leq t+3$, or ever), holding at Cohen's $d \approx -0.11$ throughout. **(b)** Per-period Cohen's d (stayer − leaver): leavers are at least as polarised as stayers in 25 of 26 testable periods, so the gap is not an aggregation artefact. **(c)** Conditioning on retention yields a non-representative survivor subpopulation: relative to all active users, survivors are more often non-neutral (54% vs. 42%) yet milder in magnitude (mean |polarity| 0.157 vs. 0.177).

in maximally anti-Brexit discussions (`pA-0% high`) or only in neutral threads (`pN-0% high`) *decreases* the likelihood of remaining. Broad participation across polarised discussions, rather than exclusive immersion in any single extreme, characterises users who return.

Across all four analyses, the pattern is consistent: retention is driven by engagement depth and breadth, not by ideological content alone.

5.2 Persistent Users Live in Echo Chambers

Echo Chamber Evidence. Edge homogeneity (Sect. 4.2) quantifies ideological alignment: Fig. 9a shows that nearly 40% of user-level interactions occur between

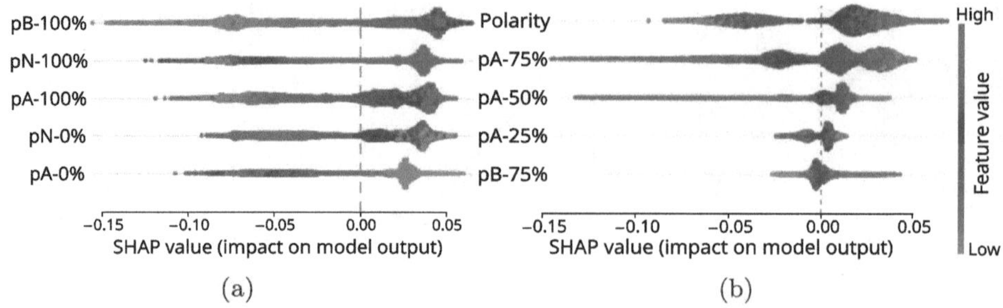

Fig. 8. **(a)** SHAP values for future presence: participating in polarised discussions (red at `pB-100%`) strongly predicts remaining. **(b)** SHAP values for future polarity regression (F0123): high current polarity (red) strongly predicts high future polarity.

like-minded individuals, while cross-cutting exchanges are rare. Anti-Brexit users are slightly more polarised (consistent with Sect. 4.2).

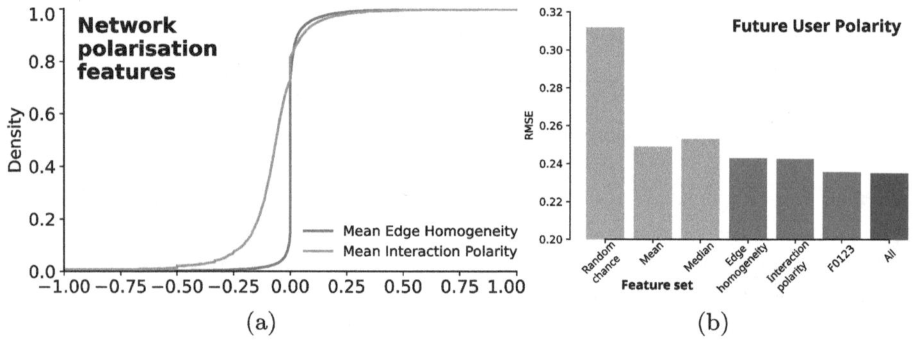

Fig. 9. **(a)** CDF of mean interaction polarity and mean edge homogeneity per user. The rightward skew of edge homogeneity confirms that like-minded interactions dominate. **(b)** Random forest regression RMSE for future polarity prediction (lower is better). Green bars are random baselines; blue bars are the F0123 feature set (prior work features augmented with features constructed here); red bars use all features including edge polarity. Edge polarity features do not improve significantly over the F0123 descriptor set. (Color figure online)

SHAP Analysis of Future Polarity. F0123 comprises four feature groups [22]: textual content (F0), user activity statistics (F1, F2), and discussion-composition descriptors (F3); the full inventory is in Online Appendix D [1]. Figure 9 compares RMSE across feature sets: all outperform the trivial baselines, and adding edge polarity features to F0123 yields negligible improvement, because F0123 already encodes network-level information through its discussion-composition descriptors (p_s-$y\%$; Online Appendix D [1]). SHAP analysis [28] (Fig. 8) reveals that current polarity is the dominant predictor, with the anti-Brexit sentiment level of a user's discussions (pA-75%, pA-50%) as the next strongest signal. This is consistent with echo-chamber effects: immersion in predominantly anti-Brexit discussions correlates with maintaining or deepening an anti-Brexit stance, rather than with cross-cutting opinion change.

The persistent users who populate longitudinal analyses interact largely within like-minded echo chambers, and their polarity changes little over time.

6 Discussion and Conclusion

We presented a framework for measuring and analysing polarisation dynamics on structured discussion platforms, demonstrated on the r/Brexit subreddit spanning the full Brexit saga (2015–2021). Our three contributions (the r/Brexit dataset, a continuous polarity pipeline, and behavioural analysis) answer a question the literature has long asked: *how does exposure to opposing views change opinions?* On r/Brexit, it mostly does not: the persistent core sits in echo chambers and barely moves, while the wider population churns; who remains is selected by engagement, not conviction. Future work includes multi-subreddit and multi-topic analysis, causal modelling of the participation–stance feedback loop [47], and whether next-generation classifiers alter the magnitude (though, given the survivorship mechanism, not the direction) of these findings.

Richer Models Do Not Improve Prediction. We augmented F0123 with three progressively more expressive architectures: *stance triads* (triadic-closure counts labelled by node stance), a *Graph Attention Network* (GAT) over the per-period interaction graph, and a bidirectional LSTM over the comment sequence. Across all variants, test F1 moves at most from 0.368 to 0.371 (full results in Online Appendix E [1]). This consistent null is structural: once discussion-composition features encode which types of discussions a user selects into, finer interaction topology carries no additional signal: self-selection sets a predictive ceiling.

Platform-Specific Challenges for NLP. We tested augmenting the training data with weakly-labelled texts identified via stance-associated keywords (e.g., "remoaner" for pro-Brexit, "Brexshit" for anti-Brexit). The augmented BERT-Reddit model degrades performance (F1 = 0.46 vs. 0.555 unaugmented), aggressively and near-randomly predicting the pro-Brexit class. The root cause is that Reddit users routinely quote opponents: pro-Brexit keywords appear in anti-Brexit posts that mock or rebut them. This quoting behaviour systematically corrupts keyword augmentation; NLP pipelines must account for embedded adversarial quotations.

Limitations. Crucially, the central survivorship finding (70.5% of users appear in a single period, and departure tracks engagement rather than ideology) rests on binary presence indicators, not classifier labels, so classifier error cannot affect it. Polarity-based analyses (echo chambers, future-polarity regression) do carry classifier error, but rest on the direction and rank-ordering of effects, not precise counts; more accurate labels would strengthen, not weaken, the survivorship mechanism. The regression and SHAP analyses are predictive and correlational; they identify features that co-vary with future polarity, not causes of opinion change. The continuous polarity metric assigns zero both to genuinely neutral users and to the small fraction (<4%) who post equal numbers of pro- and anti-Brexit comments, a conflation resolvable by treating stance counts as simplex coordinates. Reddit's API surfaces only content, not reads: lurkers are invisible, and apparent "departure" may reflect passive participation rather than genuine disengagement. We define departure by posting absence; although a minority of single-period absences are temporary returns, the retention patterns are stable under stricter, multi-period definitions (Fig. 7). Event-based period boundaries are motivated by the substantive goal of capturing coherent phases of the Brexit debate; coarser temporal windows would lower the 70.5% transience figure, making the claim more conservative, not more extreme. Scope is limited to a single subreddit on a single topic; the mechanism we identify is unlikely to be platform-specific (see Sect. 2 and the discussion of generalisability below).

Broader Implications. For *platform designers*: algorithmic interventions that target the most active users (those most exposed to any recommendation or moderation signal) will be ineffective if those users are already entrenched, and may even provoke community resistance and migration to less-moderated platforms [20]; interventions should instead prioritise new and peripheral users, who are at greatest risk of early departure, reaching them before they leave. Nudges at first engagement (e.g., surfacing cross-cutting content to newcomers) are more likely to shift trajectories than interventions on long-term participants whose stance has stabilised; intervention opportunities are greatest at the early stages of the radicalisation pathway [5], and style-tailored messaging can reach otherwise-resistant fringe communities before their positions harden [23]. Operationally, the pipeline (in-domain stance classification, continuous polarity, and joint presence–stance analysis) is deployable as a community-monitoring tool that flags when an apparent shift in opinion is in fact a shift in *who* is posting. For *researchers*: "future stance prediction" models are structurally misleading unless they account for the selection bias of user retention. We advocate jointly modelling presence and stance via a survival-regression architecture in which departure and future polarity share latent user representations, rather than treating retention as a fixed precondition for stance analysis. The mechanism is unlikely to be unique to r/Brexit: Oswald et al. [34] show experimentally that online political discussions are dominated by a systematically atypical active minority, supporting self-selection as a confound beyond any single platform.

Acknowledgements. This research was supported by the Advanced Strategic Capabilities Accelerator (ASCA), the Defence Science and Technology Group, the Defence Innovation Network, and the Australian Academy of Science.

Ethics Statement. Data were collected from the publicly accessible Reddit platform via the Pushshift API [39]; no personally identifiable information beyond posted usernames was retained. The study is observational analysis of publicly available content.

References

1. Online appendix: Online Polarisation Dynamics on Reddit (2026). https://arxiv.org/pdf/2603.07509#page=19
2. AlDayel, A., Magdy, W.: Stance detection on social media: state of the art and trends. Inf. Process. Manag. **58**(4), 102597 (2021)
3. Alturayeif, N., Luqman, H., Ahmed, M.: A systematic review of machine learning techniques for stance detection and its applications. Neural Comput. Appl. **35**, 5113–5144 (2023). https://doi.org/10.1007/s00521-023-08285-7
4. Amazon Mechanical Turk: Amazon mechanical turk. https://www.mturk.com/. Accessed 2021
5. Booth, E., Lee, J., Rizoiu, M.A., Farid, H.: Conspiracy, misinformation, radicalisation: understanding the online pathway to indoctrination and opportunities for intervention. J. Sociol. **60**(2), 440–457 (2024). https://doi.org/10.1177/14407833241231756
6. Bruns, A.: Echo chamber? What echo chamber? Reviewing the evidence. In: Future of Journalism Conference (FOJ17) (2017)
7. Calderon, P., Ram, R., Rizoiu, M.A.: Opinion market model: stemming far-right opinion spread using positive interventions. In: Proceedings ICWSM, vol. 18, pp. 177–190 (2024). https://doi.org/10.1609/icwsm.v18i1.31306
8. Calderon, P., Rizoiu, M.A.: What drives online popularity: author, content or sharers? Estimating spread dynamics with Bayesian mixture Hawkes. In: Proceedings ECML-PKDD, pp. 142–160 (2024). https://doi.org/10.1007/978-3-031-70362-1_9
9. Cinus, F., Minici, M., Monti, C., Bonchi, F.: The effect of people recommenders on echo chambers and polarization. In: Proceedings ICWSM, vol. 16, pp. 90–101 (2022). https://doi.org/10.1609/icwsm.v16i1.19275
10. Colacrai, E., Cinus, F., De Francisci Morales, G., Starnini, M.: Navigating multidimensional ideologies with Reddit's political compass: economic conflict and social affinity. In: Proceedings WWW, pp. 2582–2593 (2024). https://doi.org/10.1145/3589334.3645606
11. Colleoni, E., Rozza, A., Arvidsson, A.: Echo chamber or public sphere? Predicting political orientation and measuring political homophily in Twitter using big data. J. Commun. **64**(2), 317–332 (2014). https://doi.org/10.1111/jcom.12084
12. Conover, M.D., Ratkiewicz, J., Francisco, M., Gonçalves, B., Menczer, F., Flammini, A.: Political polarization on Twitter. In: Proceedings ICWSM (2011)
13. Del Vicario, M., et al.: The spreading of misinformation online. PNAS **113**(3), 554–559 (2016). https://doi.org/10.1073/pnas.1517441113
14. Devlin, J., Chang, M.W., Lee, K., Toutanova, K.: BERT: pre-training of deep bidirectional transformers for language understanding (2018). arXiv preprint arXiv:1810.04805
15. Efstratiou, A.: Deliberate exposure to opposing views and its association with behavior and rewards on political communities. In: Proceedings WWW, pp. 2347–2358 (2024). https://doi.org/10.1145/3589334.3645375
16. Efstratiou, A., Blackburn, J., Caulfield, T., Stringhini, G., Zannettou, S., De Cristofaro, E.: Non-polar opposites: analyzing the relationship between echo chambers and hostile intergroup interactions on Reddit. In: Proceedings ICWSM, vol. 17, pp. 197–208 (2023). https://doi.org/10.1609/icwsm.v17i1.22138
17. Gatto, J., Sharif, O., Preum, S.M.: Chain-of-thought embeddings for stance detection on social media. In: Findings of EMNLP, pp. 4154–4161 (2023). https://doi.org/10.18653/v1/2023.findings-emnlp.273

18. Gera, P., Neal, T.J.: Deep learning in stance detection: a survey. ACM Comput. Surv. **58**(1), 1–37 (2025). https://doi.org/10.1145/3744641
19. Hofmann, V., Schütze, H., Pierrehumbert, J.B.: The Reddit Politosphere: a large-scale text and network resource of online political discourse. In: Proceedings ICWSM, vol. 16, pp. 1259–1267 (2022). https://doi.org/10.1609/icwsm.v16i1.19377
20. Johns, A., Bailo, F., Booth, E., Rizoiu, M.A.: Labelling, shadow bans and community resistance: did Meta's strategy to suppress rather than remove COVID misinformation and conspiracy theory on Facebook slow the spread? Media Int. Aust. (2024). https://doi.org/10.1177/1329878X241236984
21. Kong, Q., Booth, E., Bailo, F., Johns, A., Rizoiu, M.A.: Slipping to the extreme: a mixed method to explain how extreme opinions infiltrate online discussions. In: Proceedings ICWSM, vol. 16, pp. 524–535 (2022). https://doi.org/10.1609/icwsm.v16i1.19312
22. Largeron, C., Mardale, A., Rizoiu, M.A.: Linking the dynamics of user stance to the structure of online discussions. In: Proceedings IDA, pp. 275–286 (2021). https://doi.org/10.1007/978-3-030-74251-5_22
23. Lee, J., Booth, E., Farid, H., Rizoiu, M.A.: Popping misinformation bubbles: results from style-based messaging into online misinformation ecosystems. Research Square preprint (2024). https://doi.org/10.21203/rs.3.rs-4528128/v2
24. Lee, J., Booth, E., Farid, H., Rizoiu, M.A.: Misinformation is not about bad facts: an analysis of the production and consumption of fringe content. EPJ Data Sci. **14**(1), 50 (2025). https://doi.org/10.1140/epjds/s13688-025-00567-5
25. Lee, J., Tian, L., Brillantes, A., Mihăiţă, A.S., Rizoiu, M.A.: Long live fine-tuning: task-specific transformers outperform zero-shot LLMs for misinformation response classification on Reddit (2026). https://doi.org/10.48550/arXiv.2606.04274
26. Lenti, J., Silvestri, F., De Francisci Morales, G.: Variational inference of parameters in opinion dynamics models. In: Proceedings ICWSM, vol. 19, pp. 2622–2627 (2025). https://doi.org/10.1609/icwsm.v19i1.35963
27. Lorge, I., Zhang, L., Dong, X., Pierrehumbert, J.: STEntConv: predicting disagreement between Reddit users with stance detection and a signed graph convolutional network. In: Proceedings LREC-COLING, pp. 15273–15284 (2024)
28. Lundberg, S.M., Lee, S.I.: A unified approach to interpreting model predictions. In: Proceedings NeurIPS, pp. 4768–4777 (2017)
29. Mohammad, S., Kiritchenko, S., Sobhani, P., Zhu, X., Cherry, C.: SemEval-2016 task 6: detecting stance in Tweets. In: Proceedings SemEval, pp. 31–41 (2016)
30. Mok, L., Inzlicht, M., Anderson, A.: Echo tunnels: polarized news sharing online runs narrow but deep. In: Proceedings ICWSM, vol. 17, pp. 662–673 (2023)
31. Monti, C., D'Ignazi, J., Starnini, M., De Francisci Morales, G.: Evidence of demographic rather than ideological segregation in news discussion on Reddit. In: Proceedings WWW, pp. 2777–2786 (2023)
32. Nguyen, D.Q., Vu, T., Nguyen, A.T.: BERTweet: a pre-trained language model for English tweets. arXiv preprint arXiv:2005.10200 (2020)
33. Okawa, M., Iwata, T.: Predicting opinion dynamics via sociologically-informed neural networks. In: Proceedings KDD, pp. 1306–1316 (2022). https://doi.org/10.1145/3534678.3539228
34. Oswald, L., Schulz, W.S., Lorenz-Spreen, P.: Disentangling participation in online political discussions with a collective field experiment. Sci. Adv. **11**(50), eady8022 (2025). https://doi.org/10.1126/sciadv.ady8022
35. Petruzzellis, F., Bonchi, F., De Francisci Morales, G., Monti, C.: On the relation between opinion change and information consumption on Reddit. In: Proceedings ICWSM, vol. 17, pp. 710–719 (2023)

36. Ram, R., Rizoiu, M.A.: Empirically measuring online social influence. EPJ Data Sci. **13**(1), 53 (2024)
37. Ram, R., Rizoiu, M.A.: Conductance and influence-capital: modeling online social influence. EPJ Data Sci. **15**(1), 56 (2026). https://doi.org/10.1140/epjds/s13688-026-00650-5
38. Ram, R., Thomas, E., Kernot, D., Rizoiu, M.A.: Practical guidelines for ideology detection pipelines and psychosocial applications. In: Proceedings ICWSM, vol. 19, pp. 1630–1648 (2025)
39. /r/datasets mod team: Pushshift Reddit API (2019). https://pushshift.io/. Accessed 2021
40. Schick, T., Schütze, H.: Generating datasets with pretrained language models (2021). arXiv preprint arXiv:2104.07540
41. Schneider, P.J., Rizoiu, M.A.: The effectiveness of moderating harmful online content. PNAS **120**(34), e2307360120 (2023). https://doi.org/10.1073/pnas.2307360120
42. Schneider, P.J., Tian, L., Rizoiu, M.A.: Learning to make friends: coaching LLM agents toward emergent social ties. In: Scaling Environments for Agents (SEA) @ NeurIPS, p. 2025 (2025)
43. Steel, B., Ruths, D.: Multi-target user stance discovery on Reddit. In: Proceedings WASSA, pp. 200–214 (2024)
44. Sun, C., Qiu, X., Xu, Y., Huang, X.: How to fine-tune BERT for text classification? In: Proceedings CCL, pp. 194–206. Springer (2019)
45. Tian, L., Booth, E., Bailo, F., Droogan, J., Rizoiu, M.A.: Before it's too late: a state space model for the early prediction of misinformation and disinformation engagement. In: Proceedings WWW, pp. 5244–5254 (2025)
46. Tian, L., Rizoiu, M.A.: DREAMS: a social exchange theory-informed modeling of misinformation engagement on social media. In: Proceedings WWW (2026). https://doi.org/10.1145/3774904.3792681
47. Tian, L., Rizoiu, M.A.: Estimating online influence needs causal modeling! Counterfactual analysis of misinformation engagement on social media. In: Proceedings AAAI, vol. 40, pp. 1078–1086 (2026). https://doi.org/10.1609/aaai.v40i2.37078
48. Tian, L., Zhang, X., Kim, M.M.H., Biggs, J., Rizoiu, M.A.: X-Troll: eXplainable detection of state-sponsored information operations agents. In: Proceedings CIKM, pp. 2874–2884 (2025). https://doi.org/10.1145/3746252.3761028
49. Weinzierl, M., Harabagiu, S.: Tree-of-counterfactual prompting for zero-shot stance detection. In: Proceedings ACL, pp. 861–880 (2024)
50. Wojcieszak, M.E., Mutz, D.C.: Online groups and political discourse: do online discussion spaces facilitate exposure to political disagreement? J. Commun. **59**(1), 40–56 (2009)
51. Yuan, L., Rizoiu, M.A.: Generalizing hate speech detection using multi-task learning: a case study of political public figures. Comput. Speech Lang. **89**, 101690 (2025). https://doi.org/10.1016/j.csl.2024.101690
52. Yuan, L., Schneider, P.J., Rizoiu, M.A.: Behavioral homophily in social media via inverse reinforcement learning: a Reddit case study. In: Proceedings WWW, pp. 576–589 (2025)
53. Yuan, L., Wang, T., Ferraro, G., Suominen, H., Rizoiu, M.A.: Transfer learning for hate speech detection in social media. J. Comput. Soc. Sci. **6**(2), 1081–1101 (2023). https://doi.org/10.1007/s42001-023-00224-9
54. Ziems, C., Held, W., Shaikh, O., Chen, J., Zhang, Z., Yang, D.: Can large language models transform computational social science? Comput. Linguist. **50**(1), 237–291 (2024). https://doi.org/10.1162/coli_a_00502

Data Circulation for Perception-Aware Location-Based Services in Urban Spaces

Keisuke Otaki[1(✉)], Xinni Yang[2], Takayoshi Yoshimura[1], Hiroyuki Sakai[1], Da Li[2], and Yukiko Kawai[3]

[1] Toyota Central R&D Labs., Inc., Nagakute, Japan
{otaki,yoshimura,sakai}@mosk.tytlabs.co.jp
[2] Kyoto Sangyo University, Kyoto, Japan
{i2486228,lida}@cc.kyoto-su.ac.jp
[3] Kansai University, Suita, Japan
ykawa@kansai-u.ac.jp

Abstract. Mainstream location-based services (e.g., navigation) often prioritize efficiency, overlooking subjective, multi-sensory aspects that shape how people experience urban journeys. Recent work has explored perception-aware services that incorporate human impressions; however, deploying them at scale remains challenging because such perception data are sparse, biased, and difficult to validate in-the-wild. This raises a practical question: how can such perception data be continuously collected and maintained so that perception-aware services remain usable in real-world settings? To address this, we study a data-centric pipeline that integrates (i) an in-the-wild system for collecting geo-tagged photos with multi-sensory tags, and (ii) map-based photo-verification microtasks that encourage revisits while collecting lightweight audit cues. We deployed this pipeline in Kyoto across two seasons and collected a large-scale geo-tagged photo-impression dataset, quest behavior logs, and questionnaire responses. Our analyses show that continuous open-ended posting alone does not resolve persistent geographic and categorical bias, whereas photo-verification microtasks repeatedly bring participants to candidate spots and produce actionable signals for follow-up auditing. These findings support a practical triage workflow for sustaining perception-oriented datasets over time and provide insights for auditable perception-aware location-based services.

Keywords: geo-tagged photos · subjective impressions · multi-sensory experiences · data-centric pipeline · photo-verification microtasks

1 Introduction

Navigation systems have transformed how we travel in cities by tailoring routes for speed, distance, and efficiency [8,20]. Yet, such efficiency-oriented systems often disregard a personal dimension: how people experience the journey, shaped by unexpected discoveries, comfort, and personal engagement [9,28].

M. Ceci et al. (Eds.): ECML PKDD 2026, LNAI 16948, pp. 106–123, 2027.
https://doi.org/10.1007/978-3-032-37679-4_7

Recent work further demonstrates that emotionally aware and diverse routes can improve psychological satisfaction and well-being [15,21,23].

To move beyond purely efficiency-oriented systems, recent location-based services incorporate subjective experiences by (i) encouraging detours, surfacing ambient features, and fostering place attachment via environmental cues [10,11]; (ii) balancing scenic value and efficiency [2,30]; (iii) promoting activities [34, 35]; and (iv) leveraging subjective data and gamified task maps [24,33,34]. Using such multi-dimensional signals, prior studies have explored exploration-supporting systems [18,25,26]; more broadly, recent work has discussed how AI-driven location-based recommenders can shape urban feedback loops [22].

However, operationalizing such tailored services remains challenging. Subjective perception data in urban spaces are often sparse, geographically biased, and difficult to sustain beyond small-scale pilots, although certain subsets, such as weather and congestion, are accessible through public APIs. Moreover, under in-the-wild deployments, it remains difficult to determine whether an intervention can reliably encourage exploration while also producing auditable signals that support dataset maintenance at scale. Consequently, it remains unclear what kind of data-circulation pipeline is required to support the long-term collection and maintenance of subjective perception signals.

To address these challenges, we study a data-centric pipeline that couples (i) an in-the-wild system, named `Posting`, for collecting geo-tagged photos with multi-sensory impression tags, and (ii) a map-based application, named `Hunting`, that presents photo-verification microtasks to encourage revisits while capturing lightweight audit cues for in-situ verification. In `Hunting`, microtasks are automatically generated from the evolving `Posting` database. Participants can freely choose quests to attempt, enabling continuous verification without manual curation and yielding operational signals (e.g., ratings, reactions, completion outcomes, and missingness) for post-hoc triage and monitoring.

Based on this, we frame our study around the following research questions:

RQ1: To what extent does continuous `Posting` mitigate sparsity and bias in geo-tagged photo subjective impression data, and what limitations remain?
RQ2: Do `Hunting` photo-verification microtasks support participants in revisiting candidate areas and sustaining a data-circulation loop in-the-wild, while producing practical audit cues for follow-up maintenance?

To answer these questions, we conducted a field study in Kyoto, Japan over two seasons, and collected (1) a large-scale geo-tagged photo impression dataset via `Posting`, (2) behavior logs from `Hunting`, and (3) questionnaire-based surveys (e.g., affect and personality). We analyze these data to examine whether continuous `Posting` mitigates sparsity and bias, and whether photo-verification microtasks support repeated revisits and data circulation. Our results suggest that `Posting` alone does not eliminate persistent sparsity and bias, whereas photo-verification microtasks can repeatedly bring participants to candidate locations while producing practical signals for follow-up auditing.

In summary, our contributions are as follows:

- We deployed a data-circulation pipeline combining `Posting` and `Hunting` in Kyoto, showing how perception-oriented data collection and in-situ verification can be integrated in-the-wild; the deployment collected over 10,000 geo-tagged photos with multi-sensory tags and over 2,000 behavior logs.
- We quantify persistent spatial and categorical sparsity under continuous `Posting` operation, showing that open-ended posting increases volume but does not substantially reduce geographic and categorical bias (**RQ1**).
- We show that `Hunting` supports repeated revisits and practical data circulation in-the-wild, while producing lightweight multi-channel audit cues that support an early-warning triage workflow for follow-up auditing and dataset maintenance (**RQ2**).

Data Availability. Due to privacy and ethical constraints, we do not publicly release raw photos, location traces, or questionnaire-linked records. Processed aggregate statistics and figure-reproduction materials are available upon reasonable request, subject to institutional approval and privacy review.

2 Related Work

We review related work from three perspectives aligned with our data-centric pipeline: (1) perception-aware mobility services beyond efficiency, (2) in-situ verification and map-based microtasks for enriching geospatial data, and (3) auditability and quality signals in crowdsourcing and deployed data pipelines.

2.1 Perception-Aware Mobility Services

Prior work reconceptualizes mobility services beyond efficiency by incorporating experience- and perception-oriented signals [28]. Studies explore multi-criteria routing using environmental cues (e.g., sunlight and air quality) [10,11] and multi-objective frameworks balancing efficiency with values such as safety and scenic quality [2,30]. Other approaches leverage user preferences and behavioral signals to tailor journeys, for example by recommending activities or lively routes informed by personal objectives [35]. Related location-recommendation work also studies feedback loops in AI-driven urban recommenders [22], while diversified-routing work examines how route assignment can distribute choices beyond a single shortest path [6]. Collectively, these efforts motivate perception-aware and exploration-supporting services that enrich urban travel experiences [18,25,26].

A remaining challenge is that subjective impressions are difficult to collect and validate at scale in-the-wild, and their representativeness is often unclear. Rather than optimizing recommendation outputs directly, this paper focuses on the upstream maintenance of subjective perception data that such services require. This motivates mechanisms that both encourage revisits and provide auditable cues for maintaining perception-oriented datasets under real deployments of location-based services.

2.2 In-situ Verification of Geospatial Data Using Microtasks

Crowdsourcing enriches geospatial datasets through lightweight tasks, including map-based microtasks and on-site verification. Citizen and humanitarian mapping workflows collect distributed observations to improve coverage and correctness of geographic information (e.g., points of interest, attributes, land cover) [4,12,14,16], often by validating uncertain items or adding specific attributes.

Geo-tagged photo contributions are also widely used to study place engagement, but photos tend to concentrate around visually salient areas and points of interest, leaving transitional segments underrepresented [1,29]. Such structural sparsity and bias motivate designs that encourage exploration beyond hotspots and support systematic verification of candidate locations.

Our previous studies presented the crowdsourced multisensory photo-posting and visualization system used as the collection layer [24,33], while a gamified task-map design has been studied for promoting urban exploration [34]. Building on these applications, our work extends this direction by focusing on *in-situ verification* and by leveraging lightweight audit cues (e.g., ratings and reactions) for post-hoc triage and dataset maintenance toward perception-aware modeling.

2.3 Auditability and Quality Signals in Crowdsourcing

Quality control in crowdsourced data collection commonly relies on redundancy, gold-standard questions, and statistical aggregation to infer latent correctness under annotator noise [7,32,36]. In deployed systems, scalable feedback channels (e.g., agree/flag reactions and short reviews) can provide lightweight audit cues when ground truth is unavailable or expensive.

Beyond label noise, real-world data pipelines face operational failure modes such as geographic drift, instrumentation gaps, and missingness, which can silently degrade reliability over time [27]. Accordingly, auditability should account for both content validity and system observability, as reflected in behavioral traces and monitoring signals.

This paper contributes to this line by combining microtask interactions (ratings and reactions), quest outcomes, and mobility traces as practical audit cues, enabling triage of failure modes observed in-the-wild and supporting sustained perception-oriented data collection in continuous operation.

3 System Design and Experimental Procedure

This section summarizes our system design and field deployments. Due to space limitations, we focus on the concepts needed for the present analysis and refer readers to our previous studies for implementation details [33,34].

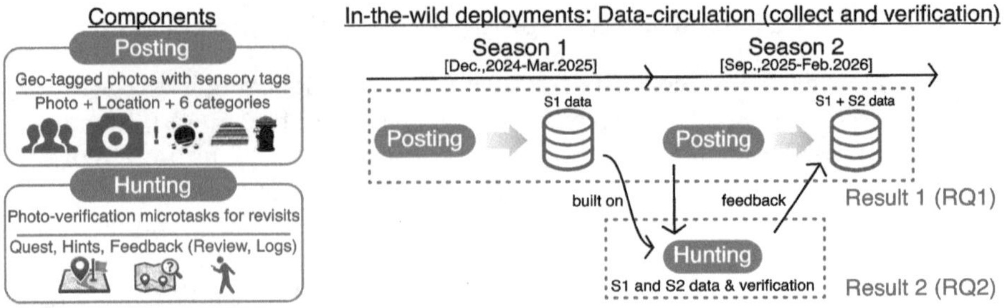

Fig. 1. Overview of our data-circulation pipeline and deployment. `Posting` continuously collects geo-tagged photos with multi-sensory impression tags to build a growing database. Built on this, `Hunting` issues map-based photo-verification quests to encourage revisits while capturing lightweight audit cues (e.g., hint reactions, clear/cancel outcomes, and optional ratings/reviews).

3.1 System Overview

Components. Our goal is to operationalize a data-centric pipeline for collecting and sustaining perception-oriented multi-sensory data during urban walks. The pipeline couples (i) continuous in-the-wild data collection and (ii) in-situ data verification that yields lightweight audit cues for triage and monitoring. It consists of two main components, whose overview is illustrated in Fig. 1.

`Posting`: A mobile system for collecting geo-tagged photos with multi-sensory impression tags. Each post consists of a photo with GPS metadata (time and location) and a set of impression tags. Users select labels from six tag categories: C_1: Focus Point, C_2: Sound, C_3: Smell, C_4: Weather, C_5: Emotion, and C_6: Road.

`Hunting`: A map-based photo-verification microtask application that presents spots derived from `Posting` as *quests*. Each quest provides a pinned location, a reference photo, and an optional short hint, and asks participants to revisit the location. Upon completion, participants report the outcome (e.g., clear/cancel) and provide lightweight feedback (e.g., tag ratings, hint reactions, and route/quest evaluations), while the system records completion timestamps and partially logs mobility traces.

Together, `Posting` provides perception-oriented data, while `Hunting` produces lightweight audit cues linked to candidate spots. These records support spot-level triage (e.g., prioritizing items for further inspection) and system-level observability (e.g., monitoring outcomes and missingness) in continuous operation. Hereafter, our analyses using `Posting` and `Hunting` data correspond to **RQ1** and **RQ2**, respectively, which we report as Result 1 and Result 2.

Questionnaires. To characterize participants and contextualize in-the-wild experiences, we administered standardized questionnaires: Big Five [13,19], SSS [17,37], and SUS [3] after `Posting`, and PANAS [31] and PERMA-Profiler [5] after `Hunting`.

3.2 Experimental Procedure

Operation. We conducted a field study in Kyoto, Japan, over two seasons:

Season 1 (Dec. 2024 – Mar. 2025, S1): Photo-posting tasks using `Posting` only. Participants were asked to take geo-tagged photos with multi-sensory impression tags while exploring the city, in a similar manner to [33].
Season 2 (Sep. 2025 – Feb. 2026, S2): Continued photo-posting tasks using `Posting` and photo-verification microtasks using `Hunting`. Participants were also asked to verify previously posted photos by revisiting the corresponding locations and providing lightweight feedback.

Both `Posting` and `Hunting` store records in a shared backend database with basic filtering, such as removing photos with missing attributes. In S1, `Posting` accumulates geo-tagged photos with multi-sensory impression tags. In S2, `Hunting` selects candidate spots from accumulated posts and issues quests by presenting a pinned location with a reference photo (and an optional hint). Each quest completion uploads outcomes (clear/cancel), timestamps, optional ratings/reactions/reviews, and mobility traces. These logs are linked back to the underlying spots as lightweight audit cues, supporting post-hoc triage and monitoring while informing future quest scheduling.

Microtasks. Participants in each season followed the procedures below:

`Posting`: Participants took geo-tagged photos with multi-sensory impression tags. After completing a predefined number of posts, they answered post-survey questionnaires (Big Five, SSS, and SUS) to capture participant characteristics and perceived usability.
`Hunting`: Participants revisited candidate locations and provided feedback on previously posted photos via photo-verification quests. After completing a predefined number of quests, they answered questionnaires (PANAS, SSS, and PERMA-Profiler) to capture positive/negative affect and well-being associated with the in-the-wild tasks.

All participants were informed about the study and provided written informed consent by agreeing to a consent form at the beginning of the tasks. Only participants who gave consent were allowed to proceed, and they could opt out at any time without penalty. After finishing the predefined number of posts or quests, participants received payments as incentives. The entire protocol was approved by the ethics committees of Toyota Central R&D Labs., Inc. (approval ID: 25–25) and Kyoto Sangyo University (approval IDs: 0283 and 0283–1).

After two seasons of data collection and pre-processing, we obtained (1) 6,721 geo-tagged photos with multi-sensory impression tags from 69 participants in S1, (2) 3,761 additional geo-tagged photos from 107 participants in S2 (10,482 photos in total), and (3) 2,048 quest behavior logs from 75 participants, of whom 32 responded to our questionnaires after S2.

In the following, Sect. 4 and Sect. 5 present our analyses and findings, corresponding to Result 1 and Result 2, respectively.

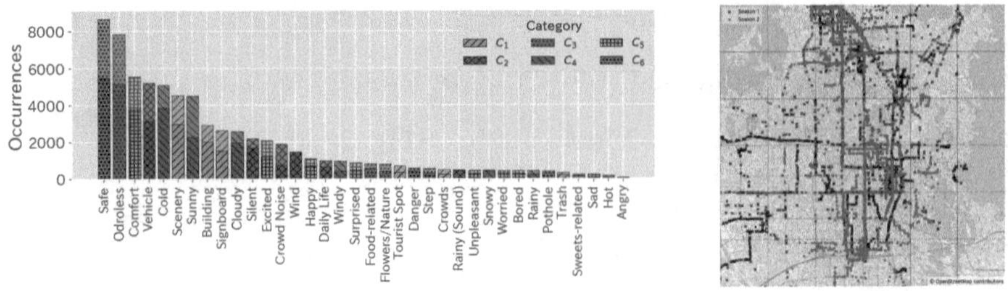

(a) Tag count histogram (S1: thick bars, S2: stacked thin color bars).

(b) Photos (S1: black, S2: red). Map: ©OpenStreetMap contributors.

Fig. 2. `Posting` data in S1 and S2: (a) Tag histogram and (b) locations, showing sparsity and tag imbalance after continuous operation of `Posting`.

4 Geo-Tagged Photos via `Posting`

We first analyze over 10,000 geo-tagged photos to characterize the spatial, temporal, and categorical patterns of multi-sensory tags in urban spaces. Here, we treat S1 and S2 as coarse temporal slices of continuous operation and examine whether sparsity and bias persist as the dataset grows over time. For our analyses, we focus on the region of interest (ROI) in Kyoto, Japan, with coordinates in EPSG:6674 ($-26500 \leq x \leq -17500$ and $-113500 \leq y \leq -104500$). We then characterize persistent sparsity and bias under continuous `Posting` operation and motivate why a guided verification layer in `Hunting` is needed (**RQ1**).

4.1 Sparsity and Tag Imbalance

Multi-sensory information is important for understanding and modeling urban spaces [9]. Using the S1 and S2 data, we examine the distribution of tags across the six categories and find substantial imbalance in the dataset.

Figure 2 visualizes the results. The tag histogram in Fig. 2a reveals a strong long-tailed distribution: for example, *Odorless* in C_3, *Comfort* in C_5, and *Safe* in C_6 dominate their respective categories, indicating systematic skew in perception and reporting behavior. Similarly, in other categories, a few major tags account for a substantial fraction of posts (e.g., *Scenery* in C_1, *Cold* in C_4, and *Safe* in C_6), suggesting that rarer impressions remain under-sampled even as the dataset grows. Figure 2b indicates spatial sparsity on the map. While major corridors appear in both seasons and across many participants, many minor streets and transitional segments remain underrepresented, making it difficult to model city-wide perception signals uniformly. This pattern is partly attributable to differences in participant pools across seasons; nevertheless, noticeable gaps remain even as S2 expands contributions along major streets, suggesting that continuous posting alone is unlikely to eliminate spatial bias.

To quantify imbalance, we compute the normalized Shannon entropy $\hat{H}(C_k) \in [0, 1]$ for each category and season, as summarized in Table 1; higher val-

Table 1. Normalized Shannon entropy $\hat{H}(C_k)$ evaluated during two seasons.

Dataset	C_1	C_2	C_3	C_4	C_5	C_6
S1	0.785	0.880	0.465	0.748	0.713	0.449
S2	0.844	0.756	0.529	0.737	0.727	0.371
Δ (S2−S1)	0.059	−0.124	0.064	−0.010	0.014	−0.078
S1+S2	0.811	0.861	0.490	0.767	0.721	0.425

ues indicate more uniform tag usage. While some categories exhibit pronounced skew (e.g., C_3 and C_6), others are comparatively more balanced; C_1 and C_2 have relatively higher values in both seasons. Overall, entropy values remain moderate and change only modestly across seasons (max $|\Delta\hat{H}| = 0.124$ in C_2), indicating that continuous open-ended posting alone is insufficient to substantially mitigate categorical imbalance and tag sparsity.

User-Level Heterogeneity. Questionnaire responses and user-level tag profiles were used as contextual analyses rather than causal evidence, given the limited number of respondents. They nevertheless suggested heterogeneous labeling tendencies: common tags such as *Safe*, *Odorless*, and *Scenery* appeared across many users, whereas rarer tags such as *Pothole*, *Trash*, and *Rain* were concentrated in subsets of users. Such heterogeneity helps explain why open-ended `Posting` can still produce persistent tag and location skew, motivating guided verification toward underrepresented locations and attributes.

4.2 Implications from Result 1 and RQ1, and Transition to RQ2

Result 1 shows that multi-sensory photo impressions collected via `Posting` are informative but operationally challenging: tags remain imbalanced and photo locations concentrate around a limited set of hotspots and corridors even under continuous operation. These findings answer **RQ1** by clarifying that scaling open-ended posting increases volume but does not eliminate persistent sparsity and bias. They also imply that (i) additional mechanisms are needed to explicitly steer effort toward underrepresented areas and (ii) the pipeline requires *auditable cues* to assess whether collected impressions remain reliable in-the-wild.

Therefore, in S2 we introduce `Hunting` as a *guided in-situ verification* layer: the system surfaces candidate spots on a map as photo-verification quests and encourages participants to revisit them. These quests both (i) support targeted revisits beyond major corridors and (ii) capture lightweight audit cues (e.g., outcomes, ratings, and reactions) linked to the underlying spots, enabling post-hoc triage and system observability in continuous operation. We next examine whether `Hunting` can induce repeated revisits and produce lightweight audit cues that support post-hoc triage in-the-wild (**RQ2**).

Table 2. Filtering Hunting behavioral logs. Note that GPS traces are collected only when the screen is on; thus mobility-derived metrics (e.g., distance) are computed on a subset with valid traces and should be interpreted as auxiliary evidence.

Filtering	#records	#users
Raw data	2,048	75
+ ROI, active (≥ 10)	1,918	45
+ Valid GPS trace	1,694	43
+ User questionnaires	1,447	32

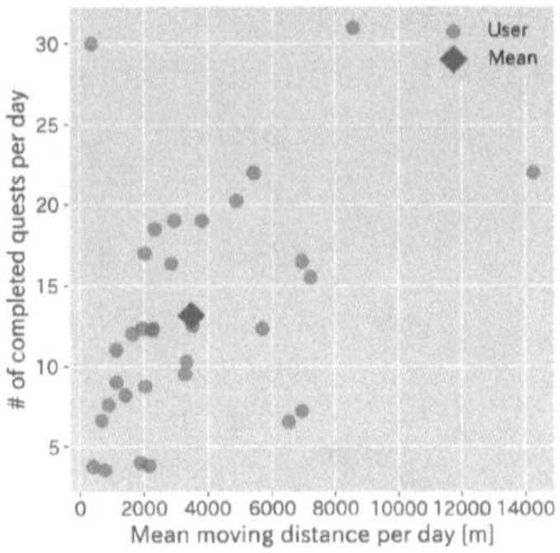

Fig. 3. Walking distances and #cleared quests per day.

5 Photo-Verification Microtasks via Hunting

This section analyzes Hunting logs to answer **RQ2**: whether photo-verification microtasks support revisits to candidate locations and sustained data circulation in-the-wild. Because Hunting operates on a continuously growing database built by Posting, our goal is not a clean before-after comparison of posting coverage. Instead, we evaluate (i) engagement and circulation behaviors and (ii) lightweight audit cues produced through in-situ verification, using behavioral KPIs and feedback channels captured in the system logs.

5.1 Behavioral Statistics on Hunting

We collected 2,048 behavior logs from 75 participants in total. After restricting to the ROI and participants with sufficient activity (≥ 10 clears), we obtained 1,918 records from 45 participants. Among them, 1,694 records (43 participants) include valid opportunistic GPS traces (screen-on only), which we use only for auxiliary mobility-derived metrics. For analyses that require questionnaire context, we further restrict the data to participants who completed the post-study surveys, resulting in 1,447 records from 32 participants. Hereafter, we refer to these participants as *active*, and those with fewer clears as *inactive*. Unless noted otherwise, the following analyses focus on these active participants, as summarized in Table 2. The mean number of play days was 4.72 among active participants (cf. 2.37 for inactive participants), indicating repeated engagement over multiple days. Figure 3 illustrates mean walking distance and quest completions per day, showing a weak positive relationship between the two metrics. These results suggest that the verification microtasks are practically feasible in-the-wild in our S2 Hunting deployment.

During Hunting, we collected 5-point Likert-scale evaluations of route difficulty, stimulation, comfort, and familiarity. Figure 4 summarizes participants' perceived difficulty and route qualities. Overall, routes to quests were perceived as relatively easy (mean: 2.079, SD: 1.087). Participants rated routes as less

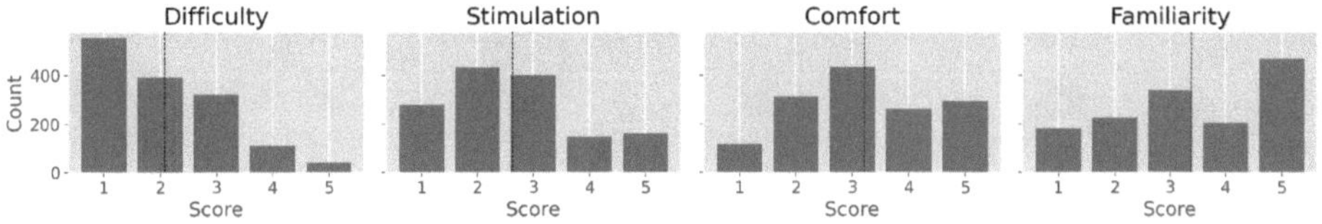

Fig. 4. Quest subjective evaluations; vertical lines represent means.

stimulating (mean: 2.633, SD: 1.231), but moderately comfortable (mean: 3.212, SD: 1.234) and familiar (mean: 3.387, SD: 1.409). These results suggest that verification quests are not overly burdensome and can be executed within familiar routines while still supporting repeated revisits.

5.2 Data Circulation via Streaks and Cell-Based Revisits

Streaks. A key observation is that many participants clear quests sequentially within short time windows, forming non-trivial streaks. Operationally, this suggests that (1) verification can function as a repeatable microtask flow rather than isolated one-off tasks, and (2) systems can promote engagement in data circulation through quest streaks.

We compute streaks as maximal sequences of consecutive quest completions for the same user where the time gap between adjacent completions is at most 60 min. In our logs, the 32 active participants yielded 200 streak sessions in total. The median streak length is 3 quests (mean 6.12). At the user level, the median of users' maximum streak lengths is 16.5 (mean 18.72). Notably, 25/32 users achieved a maximum streak of at least 10 quests, and 12/32 users exceeded 20 quests within a streak. These results are visualized as a cumulative distribution function (CDF) in Fig. 5a.

Cell-Based Revisits. Since each quest is designed to be cleared once in order to avoid redundant auditing load, we measure circulation at the cell level (250 m) rather than at the individual-spot level. We examine (i) revisit gaps as a proxy for repeated verification over time and (ii) normalized cell entropy as a proxy for spatial diversity. Let $n_{u,i}$ be the number of cleared quests by user u in cell i and $p_{u,i} = n_{u,i} / \sum_j n_{u,j}$. We define the normalized Shannon entropy as $\hat{H}_u = \left(-\sum_i p_{u,i} \log p_{u,i}\right) / \log |\{i : n_{u,i} > 0\}|$. Figure 5b shows that revisit gaps exhibit both short-term revisits and a long tail, while Fig. 5c indicates heterogeneous spatial diversity across users. Together, these results suggest that verification can recur over time rather than as a one-off activity, and that circulation is not confined to a single cell. Beyond revisits, `Hunting` also expanded participants' local verification footprint under nearby quest surfacing. In survey-associated logs (32 users; 1,418 quests), the median start–goal distance was 122 m, 54.1% of cleared quests crossed 250 m cells, and the user-level median fraction of cleared quests landing in previously unseen goal cells was 40%. Thus, nearby quests can broaden local verification coverage, although global cold-start coverage still requires scheduling beyond already posted nearby candidates.

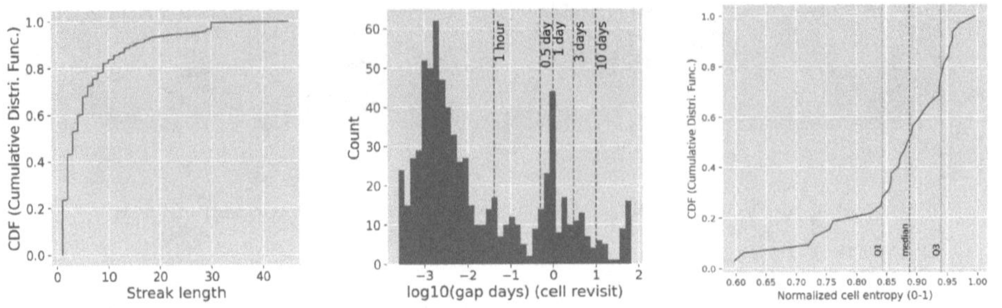

(a) CDF of streak lengths. (b) Cell revisit gap distribution (log-x). (c) CDF of normalized cell entropy $\hat{H}_u$.

Fig. 5. Circulation-oriented KPIs from `Hunting` logs (250 m cells): streaks indicate repeatable microtask flows, while revisit gaps and cell entropy capture temporal revisits and spatial diversity.

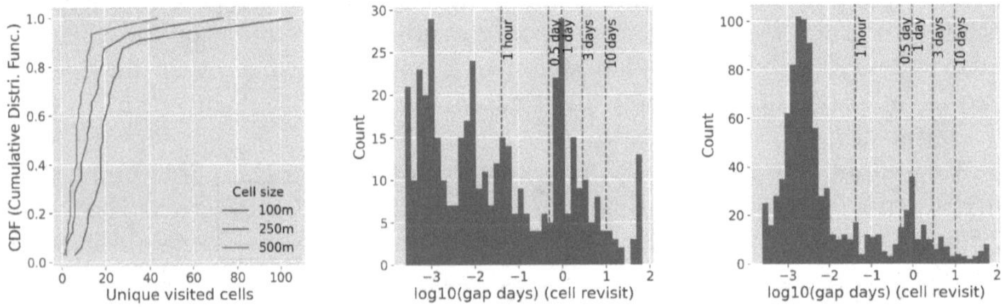

(a) Unique visited cells. (b) 100 m cells. (c) 500 m cells.

Fig. 6. Cell-size sensitivity analyses. The 250 m revisit-gap baseline is shown in Fig. 5b.

Sensitivity Analyses. Because `Hunting` suppresses very nearby quests (within 100–200 m), we test whether the circulation-oriented patterns depend on cell size by recomputing cell-based KPIs with 100, 250, and 500 m grids. We compare the CDF of the number of unique visited cells and revisit-gap distributions under 100 m and 500 m grids in Fig. 6, using the 250 m revisit result in Fig. 5b as the main baseline. The qualitative trends remain stable across cell sizes. In particular, the revisit-gap distributions preserve the same broad pattern as the 250 m baseline, including short-term revisits and a secondary one-day mode. These checks indicate that the circulation findings are not artifacts of discretization.

We also recompute streaks using gap thresholds of 30, 45, 60, 90, and 120 min. The qualitative pattern is stable: the median streak length remains 3–4 quests, the median user-level maximum streak length remains 14.5–17.5 quests, and 23–27 of the 32 active users still achieve a maximum streak of at least 10 quests. This indicates that the repeatable microtask-flow finding is not specific to the 60-minute threshold.

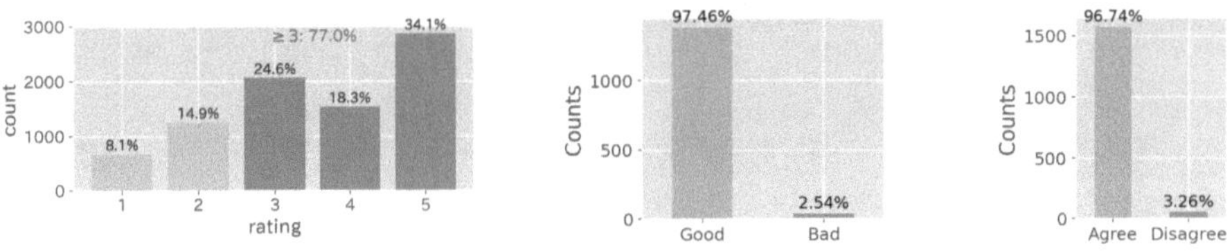

(a) Tag-applicability ratings (1–5). (b) Quest eval. (c) Hint reaction

Fig. 7. Lightweight in-situ feedback collected in `Hunting`.

5.3 Lightweight Audit Cues from In-Situ Verification

Beyond circulation, `Hunting` elicits lightweight feedback that can serve as audit cues for the underlying spot information. During photo verification, participants rated how well the provided multi-sensory tags fit the visited place on a 5-point Likert scale (1: not applicable, 5: applicable) across six categories.

Figure 7 illustrates participants' feedback. Overall, 77.1% of responses were neutral or positive ($\geq$3) in Fig. 7a, suggesting that posted tags are often judged as at least moderately representative and that these ratings can serve as practical triage cues. Participants also provided an evaluation flag (good/bad), where 97.4% were marked as good, as shown in Fig. 7b, indicating that the microtask design remains acceptable despite requiring on-site visits. Finally, 96.7% of reactions indicated agreement with the displayed hint (see Fig. 7c), suggesting that presenting subjective cues is broadly compatible with on-the-go verification.

These signals mainly monitor acceptability, whereas stronger audit utility comes from tag-applicability ratings and operational outcomes (e.g., cancellations and missing feedback). Accordingly, relatively rare negative events motivate the triage queue evaluated next.

5.4 Rule-Based Triage for Follow-up Auditing

To operationalize auditability under limited inspection budgets, we construct a rule-based early-warning triage queue over 250 m cells by aggregating verification logs, with the goal of prioritizing where follow-up auditing effort should be spent rather than inferring ground-truth spot correctness. We use two channels of lightweight signals: *spot-validity* proxies (low tag-applicability ratings, hint flags, and quest-reaction flags) and *system observability/feasibility* indicators (high cancellation rate and high feedback missingness). For the rate-based cues, "high" is defined by the top 20% cells for each metric, equivalently the 80th-percentile threshold (denoted as $q_{\text{high}} = 0.8$ in the figure). We aggregate signals at the cell level to obtain stable operational indicators under sparse feedback. We treat low ratings (cell-level mean < 3), any hint disagreement, and any bad quest evaluation as validity-related negative cues, and define high cancellation and high missingness by the top 20% thresholds calibrated on the past window. We rank cells by the resulting risk score (number of negative cues), with ties broken by cancellation rate, missing-feedback rate, and record count.

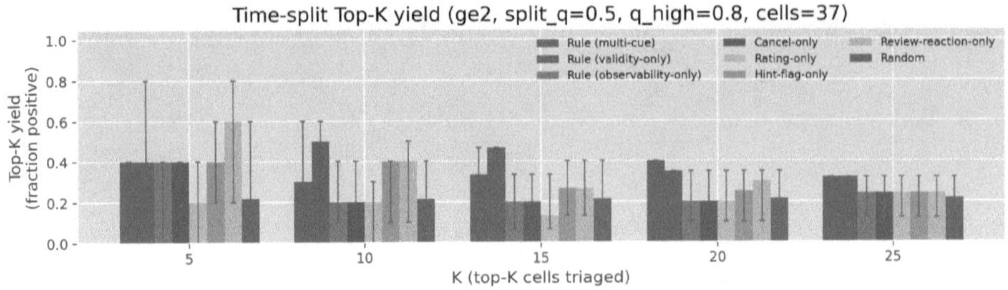

Fig. 8. Time-split triage precision@K on future high-risk cells (risk score ≥ 2 [ge2], 250 m cells, split q=0.5).

To avoid circular evaluation, we validate triage as an early-warning mechanism using a time split. By default, we split the records chronologically at ratio $q = 0.5$, using the earlier 50% as the past window for rule calibration/ranking and the later 50% as the future window for evaluation. We compute thresholds and triage rankings from the *past* window only, and evaluate whether the top-K cells are enriched with *future* high-risk cells in the *future* window. We define the *future risk score* as the number of negative cues observed in the future window, and label a cell as future high-risk when its score is at least 2, i.e., when multiple negative cues co-occur later in operation. We do not interpret this label as ground-truth spot incorrectness. Instead, it operationalizes a practical notion of *future audit burden*: cells that later accumulate multiple warning signs are plausible candidates for follow-up inspection under limited budgets. Accordingly, our rule should be read as an early-warning prioritization mechanism based on layered cues of spot validity and system observability. Figure 8 reports precision@K (fraction of future high-risk cells in the top-K list). Overall, the multi-cue rule consistently outperforms random ranking. While a strong single-signal baseline performs best at very small K (Table 3), the multi-cue rule remains competitive as K grows and is more suitable when practitioners want a single queue that covers mixed failure modes rather than only one type of warning signal.

Complementary Checks. We also examined an in-window audit-retrieval analysis, where both ranking signals and target labels are defined within the same operational snapshot. In that view, cells labeled as *needs-audit* had both validity-related and observability- or feasibility-related negative cues, and the multi-cue rule concentrated such cells better than single-signal and random baselines at small to medium audit budgets. Validity-only/observability-only ablations and sensitivity checks over time splits and threshold percentiles preserved the conclusion that layered cues help prioritize follow-up auditing.

5.5 Implications from Result 2 and RQ2

The observed streak and revisit behaviors suggest a practical pathway to scale verification beyond one-off checks in-the-wild. Moreover, the collected audit cues

Table 3. Time-split triage precision@K on future high-risk cells (risk score ≥ 2; 250 m cells; split q=0.5). For compactness, we report representative methods.

Method	$K = 5$	$K = 10$	$K = 25$
Rule (multi-cue)	0.400	0.300	**0.320**
Quest-reaction-only	**0.600**	**0.400**	0.240
Cancel-only	0.400	0.200	0.240
Random	0.216	0.215	0.215

indicate that low-burden checks (e.g., tag applicability, hint agreement, and quest evaluations) can be embedded without overwhelming participants. Together, these results suggest that `Hunting` can support (i) repeated revisits and circulation and (ii) operational triage of candidate spots using lightweight audit cues. Under limited auditing budgets, practitioners can prioritize high-risk cells/spots for follow-up revisits, hint/photo updates, or retirement decisions, rather than uniformly re-checking the entire map. We treat the time-split setting as the primary evaluation because it directly tests prospective prioritization, whereas the in-window analysis provides only a complementary audit-retrieval view. We discuss how to interpret these cues (spot validity vs. system observability), as well as practical failure modes and design implications.

6 Discussion Towards Data Circulation in Urban Spaces

Our results suggest that `Hunting` is not merely an add-on to open-ended photo posting, but a guided in-situ verification layer that repeatedly brings participants to candidate locations while producing lightweight audit cues for operational triage and monitoring. We summarize the resulting design implications and limitations below.

6.1 From Cues to Actions: Triaging Spot Information and Monitoring Observability

In real deployments, data reliability can degrade not only because spots become outdated or mischaracterized, but also because the system may fail to capture sufficient contextual evidence at the time of interaction. Accordingly, audit cues should be interpreted by their diagnostic roles. Signals for *spot validity* include on-site feedback such as tag applicability ratings, disagreement/flag reactions, and quest evaluations (with some also serving as acceptability monitors when negatives are rare). Signals for *system observability* include task outcomes (clear/cancel) and the availability of auxiliary traces (e.g., mobility traces when available). Separating these channels matters because they imply different interventions: low tag-applicability ratings suggest content review or updates, repeated cancellations suggest feasibility frictions that may require quest redesign, relocation, or retirement, and high missingness suggests observability or instrumentation issues that call for monitoring-oriented responses. Accordingly, the triage queue should support action selection rather than a single uniform response.

6.2 Failure Modes Observed in-the-Wild

We observed practical failure modes including (i) subjective mismatch between provided cues and on-site contexts, (ii) feasibility frictions under deliberately coarse location hinting, which trades navigational precision for exploration incentives, and (iii) incomplete auxiliary sensing (e.g., screen-on-only traces), which limits mobility-based interpretations. Because we did not collect explicit cancellation reasons, we interpret cancellations primarily as a feasibility signal. These observations motivate lightweight monitoring in continuous operation: track negative cues and missingness over time, and trigger follow-up checks when a location/cell shows either repeated validity concerns or persistent feasibility/observability deterioration.

6.3 Operational Implications and Limitations

Engagement Heterogeneity and Multi-objective Quest Design. We observed heterogeneous engagement styles from routine-oriented streak clearing to coverage-oriented revisiting. These modes provide complementary value: routine/streak behavior supports temporal validation (stability and drift), whereas coverage-oriented behavior supports bias mitigation (expanding spatial footprint). This suggests that scheduling should mix objectives: sustain retention with nearby low-friction quests, while injecting underexplored-area quests or higher-value audit targets to broaden coverage and maintain dataset reliability. Such engagement patterns may also inform future studies, for example by helping design data collection strategies for modeling subjective impressions in urban spaces.

Limitations. Our study is based on a single-city deployment and a limited number of highly active participants. We therefore avoid claims about universal generalization of the observed streak lengths, cancellation rates, or spatial footprints; these quantities are likely context-dependent on Kyoto's walkability, tourism flow, weather, and participant pool. A further limitation is that `Hunting` generates quests from spots already observed through `Posting`. Thus, it improves circulation around known candidate locations but does not solve cold-start coverage where no subjective posts have been collected. Future deployments should combine nearby low-friction quests with exploration-oriented scheduling, public geospatial seeds, or campaigns targeting underrepresented regions and tag categories. We also do not directly evaluate downstream route recommendation quality or model improvement; instead, we evaluate the data-maintenance layer that such perception-aware services would depend on. Our contribution is thus applied rather than purely algorithmic: we show that photo-verification microtasks can be executed repeatedly in-the-wild and that the resulting audit cues support practical triage and monitoring of perception-oriented datasets under realistic operational constraints.

7 Conclusion

Perception-aware location-based services remain difficult to deploy because subjective perception data are sparse, geographically biased, and hard to validate at scale. We presented a data-circulation pipeline that combines `Posting` (continuous collection of geo-tagged photos with multi-sensory impression tags) and `Hunting` (map-based photo-verification microtasks that encourage revisits while producing lightweight audit cues). In a Kyoto in-the-wild deployment across two seasons, we showed that participants often clear quests sequentially and revisit cells over time, indicating that verification can function as a repeatable microtask flow rather than isolated checks. Moreover, `Hunting` yields layered audit cues spanning spot validity (e.g., tag applicability and hint agreement) and system observability (e.g., outcomes and missingness), enabling practical triage and monitoring in continuous operation. These results suggest two practical lessons: perception-aware cues can help operationalize data circulation in-the-wild, and sustaining perception-aware services requires not only collecting subjective impressions, but also maintaining them through long-term data circulation with auditable, low-burden verification signals.

References

1. Becker, M., Singer, P., Lemmerich, F., Hotho, A., Helic, D., Strohmaier, M.: Photowalking the city: comparing hypotheses about urban photo trails on flickr. In: Proceedings of the SocInfo2015, pp. 227–244 (2015)
2. Bhumika, D., D.: Marrs: a framework for multi-objective risk-aware route recommendation using multitask-transformer. In: Proceedings of the RecSys2022, pp. 360–368(2022)
3. Brooke, J.: SUS-a quick and dirty usability scale. Usability Eval. Ind. **189**(194), 4–7 (1996)
4. Burke, J., et al.: Participatory sensing. In: Proceedings of the Workshop on World-Sensor-Web (WSW'06), in Conjunction with SenSys (2006)
5. Butler, J., Kern, M.L.: The perma-profiler: a brief multidimensional measure of flourishing. Int. J. Wellbeing **6**(3), (2016)
6. Cornacchia, G., Nespoli, L., D'Antoni, L., Mauro, G.A.S., Minici, M., Aiello, L.M.: One-shot traffic assignment for improving diversified routing. In: Proceedings of the ACM SIGSPATIAL2023, pp. 1–10 (2023)
7. Dawid, A.P., Skene, A.M.: Maximum likelihood estimation of observer error-rates using the em algorithm. J. Roy. Stat. Soc.: Ser. C (Appl. Stat.) **28**(1), 20–28 (1979)
8. Delling, D., Sanders, P., Schultes, D., Wagner, D.: Engineering route planning algorithms. In: Algorithmics of Large and Complex Networks, pp. 117–139. Springer (2009)
9. Dong, W., Dai, D., Shen, P., Zhang, R., Liu, M.: How public urban space enhance restoration benefits through combined multisensory effects: a systematic review. Land **13**(12), 2018 (2024)

10. Eggerth, A., Sánchez-Vaquerizo, A., Helbing, J., Mahajan, D., S.: Democratizing urban mobility through an open-source, multi-criteria route recommendation system. In: Proceedings of the RecSys2024, pp. 1073–1078 (2024)
11. Feng, Y., Zhang, P., Xue, J., Chen, Z., Meng, L.: Walking in the shade: Shadow-oriented navigation for pedestrians. In: Proceedings of the ACM SIGSPATIAL2024, pp. 677–680 (2024)
12. Fritz, S., et al.: Geo-wiki. org: the use of crowdsourcing to improve global land cover. Remote Sens. **1**(3), 345–354 (2009)
13. Gosling, S.D., Rentfrow, P.J., Swann, W.B., Jr.: A very brief measure of the big-five personality domains. J. Res. Pers. **37**(6), 504–528 (2003)
14. Haklay, M., Weber, P.: Openstreetmap: user-generated street maps. IEEE Pervasive Comput. **7**(4), 12–18 (2008)
15. Heller, A.S., et al.: Association between real-world experiential diversity and positive affect relates to hippocampal-striatal functional connectivity. Nat. Neurosci. **23**(7), 800–804 (2020)
16. Herfort, B.: Mapswipe: global dataset of crowdsourced classifications on human settlements and reference datasets (2018). https://doi.org/10.11588/DATA/3GYJUG
17. Hoyle, R.H., Stephenson, M.T., Palmgreen, P., Lorch, E.P., Donohew, R.L.: Reliability and validity of a brief measure of sensation seeking. Personality Individ. Differ. **32**(3), 401–414 (2002)
18. Jain, G., Teng, Y., Cho, D.H., Xing, Y., Aziz, M., Smith, B.A.: I want to figure things out: supporting exploration in navigation for people with visual impairments. Proc. ACM Hum. Comput. Interact. (PACMHCI) **7**(CSCW1) (2023)
19. John, O.P., Srivastava, S.: The big-five trait taxonomy: history, measurement, and theoretical perspectives. In: Pervin, L.A., John, O.P. (eds.) Handbook of Personality: Theory and Research, vol. 2, pp. 102–138 (1999)
20. Koritsoglou, K., Tsoumanis, G., Patras, V., Fudos, I.: Shortest path algorithms for pedestrian navigation systems. Information **13**(6), 269 (2022)
21. Luo, M., Kim, E.K., Weibel, R., Martin, M., Röcke, C.: Gps-derived daily mobility and daily well-being in community-dwelling older adults. Gerontology **69**(7), 875–887 (2023)
22. Mauro, G., Minici, M., Pappalardo, L.: The urban impact of ai: modelling feedback loops in location-based recommender systems. Mach. Learn. **115**(1), 19 (2026)
23. Otaki, K., Maeda, T., Uemura, K., Yoshimura, T.: Roaming navigation-in-the-wild: how pedestrians subjectively perceive non-shortest routes. In: Proceedings of the ACM SIGSPATIAL2025, pp. 137–148 (2025)
24. Otaki, K., Yang, X., Yoshimura, T., Sakai, H., Li, D., Kawai, Y.: Subjective experiences in urban spaces from the lens of crowds, personality, and large language models. In: Proceedings of the GeoAI2025 Workshop, pp. 49–52 (2025)
25. Pang, C., Neustaedter, C., Moffatt, K., Hennessy, K., Pan, R.: The role of a location-based city exploration game in digital placemaking. In: Smart Cities at Play: Technology and Emerging Forms of Playfulness, pp. 18–41 (2023)
26. Schade, E., Savino, G.L., Niess, J., Schöning, J.: Mapuncover: fostering spatial exploration through gamification in mobile map apps. In: Proceedings of the CHI2023 (2023)
27. Sculley, D., et al.: Hidden technical debt in machine learning systems. Adv. Neural. Inf. Process. Syst. **28**, (2015)
28. Siriaraya, P., et al.: Beyond the shortest route: a survey on quality-aware route navigation for pedestrians. IEEE Access **8**, 135569–135590 (2020)
29. Tenkanen, H., et al.: Instagram, flickr, or twitter: assessing the usability of social media data for visitor monitoring in protected areas. Sci. Rep. **7**(1), 17615 (2017)

30. Torres, M., Pelta, D.A., Verdegay, J.L.: Proa: an intelligent multi-criteria personalized route assistant. Eng. Appl. Artif. Intell. **72**, 162–169 (2018)
31. Watson, D., Clark, L.A., Tellegen, A.: Development and validation of brief measures of positive and negative affect: the panas scales. J. Pers. Soc. Psychol. **54**(6), 1063 (1988)
32. Whitehill, J., Wu, T.F., Bergsma, J., Movellan, J., Ruvolo, P.: Whose vote should count more: Optimal integration of labels from labelers of unknown expertise. Adv. Neural. Inf. Process. Syst. **22**, (2009)
33. Yang, X., Otaki, K., Yoshimura, T., Sakai, H., Li, D., Kawai, Y.: Crowdsourced collection and visualization of urban mood via a multisensory interactive system. In: Proceedings of the WSDM2026 Demo Track, pp. 1335–1338 (2026)
34. Yang, X., Otaki, K., Yoshimura, T., Sakai, H., Li, D., Kawai, Y.: Designing a gamified task map based on multisensory user-contributed data to promote urban exploration. In: Extended Abstracts of the 2026 CHI Conference on Human Factors in Computing Systems, pp. 214:1–214:5 (2026)
35. Yang, X., Wang, Y., Siriaraya, P., Kawai, Y.: Evaluation of route recommendation for healthcare by reducing approach bias for food desire. In: Proceedings of the IEEE IMCOM2025, pp. 1–8 (2025)
36. Zheng, Y., Li, G., Li, Y., Shan, C., Cheng, R.: Truth inference in crowdsourcing: Is the problem solved? Proc. VLDB2017 **10**(5), 541–552 (2017)
37. Zuckerman, M., Eysenck, S.B., Eysenck, H.J.: Sensation seeking in England and America: cross-cultural, age, and sex comparisons. J. Consult. Clin. Psychol. **46**(1), 139 (1978)

Human-Centric Multimodal Fusion for Real-Time Driving Hazard Detection

Tianyu Ma[1,2], Angzehua Feng[2], Xiao Xiong[2], Zihan Gao[2], Zhouxiang Long[2], Ovanes Petrosian[2,3(✉)], and Xinyue Xu[2]

[1] School of Automation, Beijing Institute of Technology, Beijing, China
[2] Faculty of Computational Mathematics and Cybernetics, Shenzhen MSU-BIT University, Shenzhen, China
[3] MSU-BIT-SMBU Joint Research Center of Applied Mathematics, Shenzhen MSU-BIT University, Shenzhen 518115, China
petrosian.ovanes@yandex.ru

Abstract. Advanced Driver Assistance Systems (ADAS) traditionally focus on external road conditions while overlooking critical human factors that significantly influence accident risk. We propose a novel human-centric multimodal framework that bridges this gap by incorporating driver facial video and in-cabin audio as critical risk indicators alongside external road data modalities from dashboard cameras. This holistic strategy enables a more nuanced understanding of hazardous situations arising from both external road and human factors. To efficiently process these complex, multimodal data streams on resource-constrained platforms, we introduce a multimodal transformer architecture with three key innovations: (1) a decoupled Token/Channel Mixer architecture (implemented via Adaptive Residual Weighted Separable convolution) for independent spatio-temporal feature optimization; (2) a Half-Convolution Grouping (HG) module to reduce computational cost while preserving representational capacity; and (3) a Dynamic Tanh (DyT) layer for lightweight, efficient feature normalization. We validate our framework on two hybrid tri-modal driving benchmarks built using the Detection of Traffic Anomaly (DoTA) and Risky Object Localization (ROL) datasets for the external road data modality, synchronized with in-cabin driver facial video and audio modalities. Experimental results demonstrate that our method achieves state-of-the-art performance across both benchmarks, exemplified by a 69.5% AP on DoTA which surpasses the best-performing baseline by 7.7%. Furthermore, evaluation on the mean Time-to-Accident (mTTA) metric confirms the model's capability for earlier hazard anticipation. Simultaneously, it delivers an inference rate of 117 FPS—a 2.6× speedup that far exceeds the standard 30 FPS real-time threshold. These results demonstrate our approach's strong potential as a highly effective, lightweight prototype for the next generation of human-centric context-aware Advanced Driver Assistance Systems.

T. Ma, A. Feng, X. Xiong and Z. Gao—Authors contributed equally.
O. Petrosian—Corresponding author.

M. Ceci et al. (Eds.): ECML PKDD 2026, LNAI 16948, pp. 124–141, 2027.
https://doi.org/10.1007/978-3-032-37679-4_8

Keywords: Multimodal Learning · Hazard Detection · Human-Centric AI · Advanced Driver Assistance Systems

1 Introduction

Recent advances in artificial intelligence have significantly influenced autonomous driving, yet a gap remains in the real-time hazard detection capabilities of such systems. With millions of traffic accidents occurring annually, a clear need exists for effective Advanced Driver Assistance Systems (ADAS) that not only improve road safety but also reduce driver cognitive load [9]. We posit that existing research, which often focuses on single modalities like road video or driver facial expressions, addresses only part of the problem. A comprehensive solution necessitates a multimodal approach.

Current ADAS research is largely split into two independent streams. The first focuses on analyzing the **external road environment**, evolving from early multi-modal fusion models like TTHF [18] to complex joint-task architectures [13]. However, these methods primarily model external conditions, offering limited perception of the driver's internal state. The second stream focuses on **internal driver state monitoring**, using vision-based systems with CNN-LSTM frameworks to detect drowsiness or inattention by tracking facial expressions, gaze, and head posture [1]. While this line of work acknowledges the link between driver emotion and safety, it generally treats driver monitoring as an isolated task, failing to explicitly connect it to external hazard detection.

Our goal is to bridge this gap by **jointly modeling external road conditions, the driver's internal state, and potential hazards** in a unified framework. Relying on a single modality, such as a dashboard camera, is insufficient for robustly handling the long-tailed distribution of driving scenarios, where rare but critical events can be easily missed amidst noise or unforeseen circumstances [15]. Therefore, we propose a comprehensive multimodal system that integrates three distinct input sources: road condition video, driver facial video, and driver audio, as illustrated in Fig. 1.

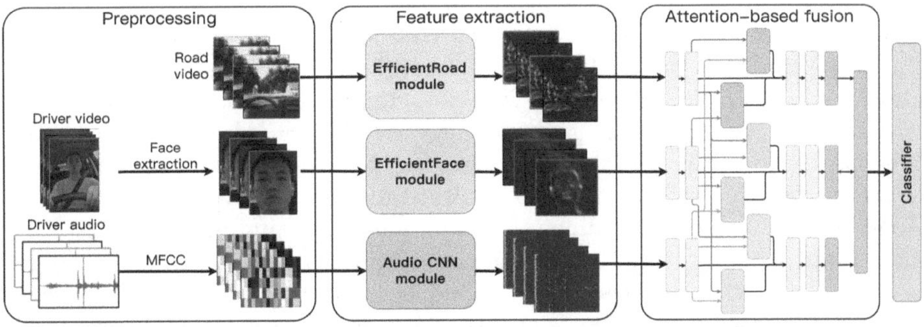

Fig. 1. The tri-modal end-to-end hazard detection framework.

In this work, we construct a novel end-to-end model that learns directly from raw multi-modal data, departing from conventional methods that rely on pre-extracted features [17,38]. Our framework performs fusion at an intermediate level using an attention-based mechanism to capture rich cross-modal correlations. To enhance efficiency and adaptability, we introduce several architectural innovations, including the Adaptive Residual Weighted Separable (ARWS) convolution, the Dynamic Tanh (DyT) layer, and the Half-Convolution Grouping (HG) module. These components are specifically designed to balance performance (AP and AUC), early anticipation capability (mTTA), and computational cost (FLOPs and FPS), making our solution viable for resource-constrained embedded platforms. Furthermore, addressing the scarcity of synchronous public data, we constructed **two hybrid benchmarks derived from the *DoTA*** [39] **and *ROL*** [14] **datasets**. By employing a Cross-Modal Consistency Alignment (CMCA) protocol [7] that synchronizes the onset of hazardous maneuvers in road video with high-arousal physiological responses in authentic driver recordings, we provide a rigorous, albeit synthetically paired, tri-modal testbed for evaluating fusion capabilities. Our code and datasets are available for review[1].

2 Related Work

2.1 Real and Synthetic Datasets for ADAS

Currently, the most commonly used real video datasets are mainly sourced from surveillance cameras. For example, the UCSD [16] and ShanghaiTech [21] datasets contain anomalous situations under different lighting conditions and scenes through campus surveillance cameras. The UCF-Crime [31] dataset focuses on public safety, including anomalous events such as traffic accidents, burglaries, and explosions. With the development of assisted driving, datasets for anomaly detection in first-person traffic videos began to appear. The work [40] presents 1,500 video clips of road anomalies recorded by dash cameras from East Asia on *YouTube*, with start and end times of anomalous events labeled, while [41] extracted clips related to traffic scenes from the BDD100K dataset.

In addition to these, the **DoTA** (Detection of Traffic Anomaly) dataset [39] represents a significant advancement, offering temporal, spatial, and categorical annotations for 4,677 videos covering collisions and out-of-control vehicles. Complementing this, the **Risky Object Localization (ROL)** dataset [14] provides 1,000 high-quality video clips with fine-grained object-level and scene-level attributes, specifically focusing on the early localization of risky traffic agents. These two datasets serve as the foundation for the road environment modality in our study. Utilizing these real-world datasets allows us to bypass the synthetic-to-real domain gap issues common in simulation-based approaches, while ROL's annotations explicitly support ego-centric risk analysis. However, a critical gap persists across all mentioned datasets: none simultaneously capture synchronized external road hazards and internal driver states (e.g., facial expressions).

[1] https://github.com/RyanMa123/Human-Centric-Hazard-Detection.

This limitation necessitates the construction of our hybrid benchmarks to enable holistic human-centric hazard detection.

2.2 Multimodal Fusion for ADAS

Data fusion integrates multiple sensor modalities (e.g., camera, LiDAR, audio) and is categorized into three main types: *early fusion* (merging raw data inputs), *late fusion* (combining model outputs), and *intermediate fusion* (integrating processed features) [6]. Early fusion provides holistic environmental perception by capturing cross-modal interactions from the start, while late fusion offers robustness to missing modalities through independent processing. Hybrid approaches combine both strategies for balanced performance.

In ADAS applications, early fusion enhances object detection and scene understanding by integrating complementary sensor data [35], whereas late fusion operates on the bounding box candidates from independent single-modality detectors before final decision integration [28]. Our work adopts intermediate feature-level fusion, following architectures like BEVFusion [22] that effectively combine RGB and LiDAR data. The advent of attention mechanisms, particularly Transformer-based approaches [32], has revolutionized cross-modal integration through self-attention and co-attention layers, as demonstrated in ViLBERT [23] and TransFuser [29] for ADAS. These attention-based methods not only improve performance but also enhance interpretability through attention maps. Like modern fusion systems, our approach employs end-to-end training, established since pioneering works in 2016 [4] and now standard in both CNN-based [12] and Transformer-based architectures [3].

Recently, the rapid evolution of large multimodal foundation models, including Vision-Language Models (VLMs) and more general omni-modal models, has introduced powerful zero-shot reasoning and semantic understanding capabilities to autonomous driving [30]. These models enable a deeper understanding of complex traffic scenarios and provide semantically rich interpretations of driving environments. In particular, state-of-the-art omni-modal architectures such as Qwen2.5-Omni family [37] have demonstrated remarkable proficiency in jointly processing complex audio and visual streams. However, despite their exceptional cognitive capabilities, these large-scale models suffer from massive parameter counts and significant computational overhead, making them currently impractical for millisecond-level, real-time reactive hazard detection on resource-constrained embedded edge devices. In contrast, our framework focuses on a highly specialized, lightweight multimodal architecture tailored specifically for extremely low-latency inference, gracefully bridging the gap between comprehensive scene understanding and strict real-time deployment constraints.

2.3 Driver State Monitoring

Monitoring the driver's state (e.g., fatigue, emotion) is critical for in-cabin ADAS safety [19]. Vision-based methods leverage cameras to track facial cues, with deep learning models evolving from hybrid CNN-RNN architectures [20] to modern lightweight backbones like EfficientFace [44] that are suitable for embedded hardware. These systems analyze features like eye closure, blink count, and yawning to detect drowsiness [1].

Beyond visual analysis, audio-based cues from in-cabin microphones augment driver state monitoring. While spectral features like MFCCs [8] are effective for speech emotion recognition, more noise-robust alternatives are often preferred to handle engine and road noise [24]. It is well-established that driver emotions strongly affect driving safety [34], as high frustration can lead to reckless behavior. Consequently, a significant body of research focuses on recognizing emotions [27,36] and fatigue by combining audio, visual, and other data streams [2,43]. Although datasets for driver drowsiness and general human emotion (e.g., RAVDESS [25,26]) exist, there is a lack of public, annotated datasets that specifically target the synchronized facial expressions and speech anomalies of drivers during hazardous traffic events. Recent research emphasizes Time-to-Accident (TTA) analysis to evaluate early hazard anticipation [14]. While traditional kinematic methods estimate TTA from external trajectories, our work complements this by incorporating driver physiological cues. As human reflexes often precede physical collision trajectories, fusing these "early warning" signals allows our model to implicitly improve anticipation capabilities for ego-centric hazards.

3 Dataset

To develop and evaluate our multimodal real-time driving assistance system, we constructed **two hybrid tri-modal benchmarks** that synchronize driver facial video, driver audio, and forward-facing road video data. These benchmarks are designed to mirror both typical driving conditions and hazards, providing a rigorous testbed for generalization.

3.1 Data Generation and Alignment Strategy

To overcome the scarcity of fully synchronized, tri-modal data, we constructed a hybrid benchmark derived from the DoTA dataset [39] and parallel naturalistic driver recordings. Addressing the lack of hardware synchronization, we implemented a **Cross-Modal Consistency Alignment (CMCA)** protocol (see Supplementary Material for algorithmic details and alignment constraints), inspired by recent advances in unified embedding alignment [7].

Unlike heuristic concatenation, CMCA enforces semantic dependencies between modalities. Specifically, we treated the synchronization as a constraint satisfaction problem where the onset of hazardous maneuvers in road video (e.g., collision trajectory) is temporally registered with the onset of high-arousal physiological responses (e.g., vocal gasps, micro-expressions) in the driver stream. To validate the alignment quality, we evaluated the dataset using **semantic coherence metrics** [11]. The resulting benchmarks achieved an average coherence score of 0.87, confirming strong semantic relevance between the synthesized visual hazards and driver reactions. This ensures that the model learns causal relationships rather than spurious correlations.

For model input, each modality is preprocessed: videos are decomposed into frames, faces are extracted, and audio is converted to MFCC spectrograms. This methodology creates a challenging dataset that preserves the ecological validity of real-world dynamics, providing a robust foundation for validating context-aware driver assistance systems.

Fig. 2. Samples from our hybrid synthetic-real driving dataset; left to right: full video frame, road video frame, cropped facial frame.

3.2 Dataset Structure and Annotation

The combined benchmarks comprise three synchronized modalities, annotated to ensure clear correspondence between driving conditions and data samples:

- *Facial video files*: each file (e.g., `01_01_1.mp4`) captures the driver's facial expressions and head movements; the naming convention encodes key information: the sequence number, a label indicating safe ('01') or dangerous ('02') driving conditions, and the sample index;

- *Facial audio files*: synchronized with the facial video, these audio recordings (e.g., `01_01_1.wav`) document the driver's vocal responses and subtle auditory cues that may indicate stress or fatigue; the naming convention is the same;
- *Road video files*: these files (e.g., `01_01_1_r.mp4`) are recorded from the perspective of the real dashcam, and they provide critical environmental context by capturing road conditions and potential external hazards.

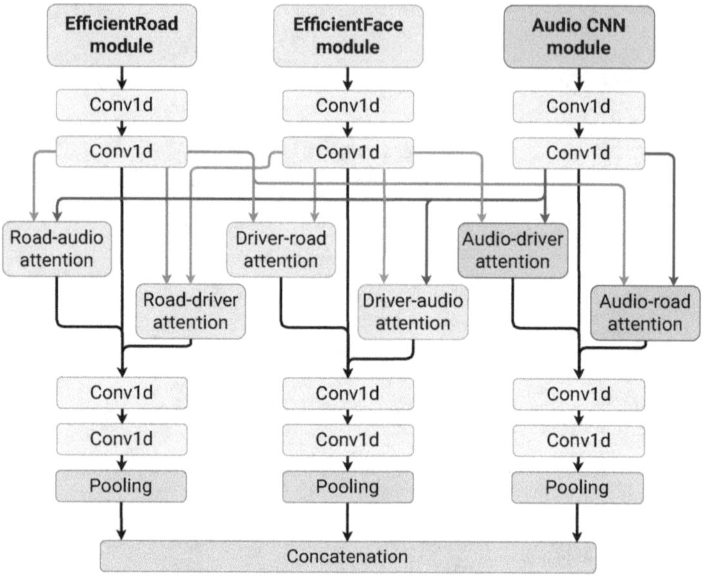

Fig. 3. The tri-modal attention-based fusion architecture.

The video modalities are illustrated in Fig. 2. The scenes involving accidents or potential hazardous driving conditions are labeled in the filename to indicate a dangerous driving situation. Structured annotation allows for straightforward indexing and retrieval of data corresponding to various driving scenarios. By integrating both DoTA and ROL, this expanded dataset serves as a comprehensive resource for testing multimodal driving behavior analysis models across diverse traffic environments and hazard types.

4 Model

Our approach centers on a tri-modal recognition framework that simultaneously processes driver facial video, driver audio, and forward-facing road video to assess driving hazards in real time (see Fig. 1). Instead of handling these modalities independently, our model learns to fuse their complementary features through an attention-based intermediate fusion strategy. In this section, we describe each branch of our model and the fusion mechanism that integrates them; the detailed architecture of our model is shown in Fig. 3.

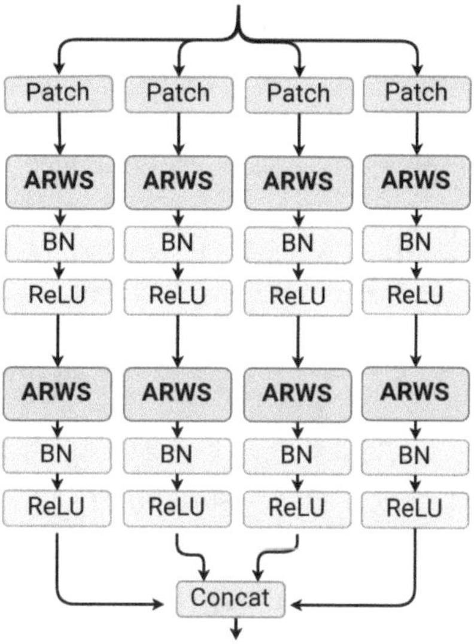

Fig. 4. The EfficientFace module architecture.

4.1 Driver Facial Video Branch

To process facial video, we implement an end-to-end module starting with a feature extractor based on the EfficientFace framework [33] (Fig. 4). It employs 1×1 pointwise convolutions to expand input channels, followed by depthwise convolutions to capture local details, and a subsequent 1×1 compression. Residual connections reinforce gradient flow. Extracted frame features are then processed by a series of 1D convolutional blocks to capture temporal dynamics. Using 1D instead of computationally heavier 3D convolutions balances performance and efficiency for real-time assessment. Although trained end-to-end, this modular design allows the feature extractor to be fine-tuned independently.

4.2 Road Video Branch

The road video branch shares the facial branch's architecture but is tailored for environmental context. After extracting spatial features via the EfficientFace-inspired backbone and modeling temporal info with 1D blocks, we introduce a **Half-Convolution Grouping (HG)** module. Feature maps are divided into three functional groups: (1) detecting size changes (distance closure), (2) identifying road surfaces/lanes (abnormal changes), and (3) analyzing bounding box overlaps (collision indicators). This design enhances intra- and inter-group interactions, acting as a spatial attention mechanism to emphasize salient cues like lane deviations.

Within each group, we apply a half-convolution operation: channels are split into halves, where only the first undergoes convolution while the second maintains identity mapping. Processed features are concatenated with residual connections for stability. Finally, the groups are integrated via a lightweight Transformer module with core cross-attention to form a globally-aware representation.

4.3 Driver Audio Branch

The audio branch extracts temporal patterns from vocal signals. Input audio is preprocessed via high-pass filtering, framing, and windowing, then converted into MFCCs and fed into a sequence of 1D convolutional layers. Each block includes batch normalization, ReLU, and max-pooling. This branch directly learns temporal dependencies to detect cues like increased speech rate or irregular breathing indicating stress or fatigue.

4.4 Intermediate Attention-Based Fusion

In this work, we propose a novel method where the three modalities undergo intermediate fusion via an attention-based mechanism. Rather than simply concatenating the extracted features, we compute pairwise similarity matrices between each pair of modalities that serve as cross-attention weights; this is illustrated in Fig. 3. These matrices are generated by applying a softmax function to the scaled dot products between query and key vectors derived from each modality's feature set. Denoting the features from three modalities as ϕ_a, ϕ_v, and ϕ_r for audio, driver video, and road video respectively, we compute the attention weights between each pair of modalities as

$$A_{ij} = \text{softmax}\left(\frac{1}{\sqrt{d}}\Phi_i W_Q W_K^\top \Phi_j^\top\right),$$

where $i, j \in \{a, v, r\}$, W_Q and W_K are trainable weight matrices, and d is the feature vector dimension.

This process dynamically assigns importance weights and aligns corresponding features across different modalities. The resulting attention vectors then guide the fusion process, ensuring that only the most salient features contribute to the final decision-making process. By leveraging this mechanism, our model becomes more robust to noise and missing data, as it can weigh modalities according to their relative relevance in a given scenario. Features that are consistent across modalities will contribute more to the final prediction, and cross-attention facilitates information sharing across modalities.

4.5 Architectural Innovations

To address the computational constraints of embedded ADAS platforms while ensuring robust feature representation, we introduce three architectural innovations grounded in specific design motivations: multi-scale adaptation, statistical stability without batch dependency, and semantic redundancy reduction.

Adaptive Residual Weighted Separable (ARWS) Network. Standard convolutions with fixed kernels struggle to handle the extreme scale variation

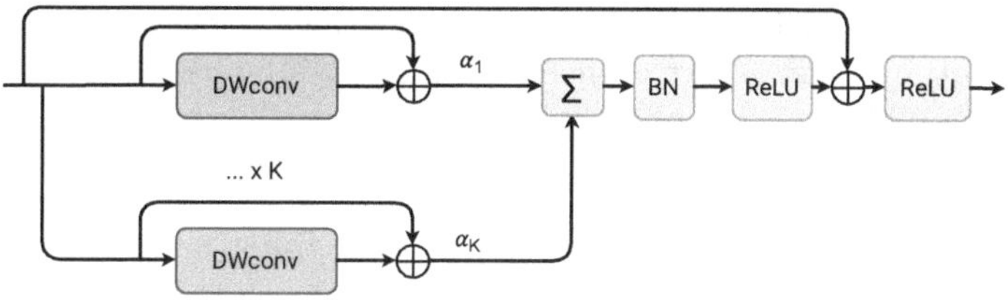

Fig. 5. The ARWS module architecture.

of road hazards (e.g., distant vs. near objects). To address this while adhering to strict efficiency constraints, we introduce the ARWS module and embed it within the Feed-Forward Network (ARWS-FFN) of our Transformer blocks.

Core Mechanism (ARWS). The ARWS module (Fig. 5) acts as a lightweight, multi-scale feature extractor. Internally, it employs $k = 4$ parallel depthwise separable convolution branches. Instead of static averaging, we utilize a dynamic weight allocation scheme where each branch i is assigned a learnable weight α_i, enforced via softmax ($\sum \alpha_i = 1$). The output is computed as:

$$\text{ARWS}(x) = \sum_{i=1}^{k} \alpha_i \cdot \text{DWConv}_i(x) + x \tag{1}$$

This formulation allows the network to adaptively emphasize appropriate spatial scales for each input instance. Crucially, to optimize for embedded deployment, we remove the usual internal batch normalization and activation layers within the branches, relying instead on the residual connection x for gradient flow. This design reduces FLOPs by approximately 18% compared to standard multi-branch blocks while preserving representational capacity.

Integration in Transformer (ARWS-FFN). Standard FFNs operate token-wise (MLPs) and lack spatial awareness. We replace them with ARWS-FFN to inject spatial context into the channel-mixing stage. The process operates in three steps: (1) **Expansion**: The input token sequence is projected from dimension C to $4C$ via a linear layer and activated by GELU. (2) **Spatial Processing**: The sequence is reshaped into a 2D feature map $[B, 4C, H, W]$ and passed through the ARWS module. This allows the multi-branch depthwise convolutions to capture rich spatial-temporal dependencies across different receptive fields. (3) **Projection**: The features are flattened back to sequences and compressed to dimension C.

The entire module incorporates a residual connection with an optional learnable scaling parameter to modulate feature contributions. A conditional residual mechanism ensures stable gradient flow by activating a 1×1 convolutional shortcut when dimensional adjustments are required. This comprehensive redesign significantly enhances the model's ability to discern visual hazards without the heavy computational cost of standard 3D convolutions.

Dynamic Tanh (DyT). Standard normalization layers (e.g., LayerNorm) require computing mean and variance statistics at inference time, which introduces calculation latency on embedded devices. To replace traditional normalization within our Transformer blocks, we adopt and integrate the Dynamic Tanh (DyT) mechanism [45], which serves as a computationally efficient, statistics-free alternative.

As empirically demonstrated by Zhu et al. [45], LayerNorm in trained Transformers often exhibits a tanh-like input-output mapping. Building on this insight, DyT performs a parameterized nonlinear transformation defined as:

$$\mathrm{DyT}(\boldsymbol{x}) = \boldsymbol{\gamma} \odot \tanh(\alpha \boldsymbol{x}) + \boldsymbol{\beta} \tag{2}$$

where $\alpha \in \mathbb{R}$ is a global learnable scalar controlling the input scaling, $\boldsymbol{\gamma}, \boldsymbol{\beta} \in \mathbb{R}^d$ are per-channel learnable scale and shift vectors, and $\odot$ denotes element-wise multiplication.

Theoretical Grounding and Stability. The design leverages the dual nature of the tanh function. Through the learnable parameter α, the network adaptively scales inputs to operate in either: (1) The **linear regime** (small $\alpha\boldsymbol{x}$), facilitating unimpeded gradient flow similar to identity mapping; or (2) The **saturation regime** (large $\alpha\boldsymbol{x}$), which naturally bounds extreme activation magnitudes without explicit statistical clipping. This mechanism effectively mimics the variance-scaling effect of normalization layers but eliminates the overhead of computing batch statistics. Our experiments confirm that DyT maintains training stability comparable to LayerNorm while reducing inference latency by approximately 12%, making it ideal for real-time hazard detection.

Half-Convolution Grouping (HG) Module. The design of HG is motivated by the semantic redundancy in road scene features. We hypothesize that hazard cues can be decoupled into distinct subspaces. To this end, the module operates through three streamlined stages to balance efficiency and feature richness:

Stage 1: Feature Expansion. First, to enhance feature robustness before grouping, we expand input channels to $2C$ through duplication and concatenation, followed by compression back to C via a 1×1 convolution. This projection step disentangles latent features, preparing them for specialized processing.

Stage 2: Specialized Grouping. We then structurally divide the features into three functional groups: (1) Vehicle Size Group, designed to capture scale changes indicating distance closure; (2) Road Surface Group, focusing on static road surfaces and lane boundaries; and (3) Interaction Group, aiming to analyze spatial relations such as bounding box overlaps. To reduce computational redundancy within these groups, we employ a half-convolution strategy. For a group i with C_i channels, only the first half undergoes convolution (3×3) to extract semantic features, while the remainder preserve identity mapping to maintain gradient flow (Fig. 6):

$$\mathrm{HG}_i(x) = \mathrm{Concat}[\mathrm{Conv}_{3\times 3}(x_{1:C_i/2}), x_{C_i/2+1:C_i}] \tag{3}$$

This design significantly reduces computation while maintaining feature integrity.

Stage 3: Global Fusion. Finally, to synthesize these decoupled semantics into a coherent hazard representation, the outputs of the three groups are integrated via a lightweight Transformer module:

$$\mathrm{HG}_{out}(x) = \mathrm{Attention}(\mathrm{HG}_1, \mathrm{HG}_2, \mathrm{HG}_3) \tag{4}$$

This architecture acts as a **structural regularizer**, encouraging the network to learn specialized features for dynamic interactions and static context without requiring explicit auxiliary supervision.

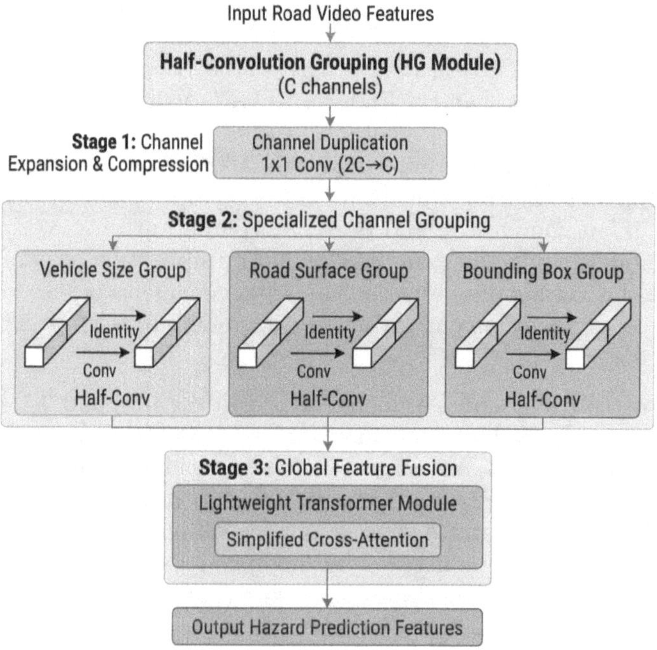

Fig. 6. Half-Convolution Grouping (HG) Module.

5 Experimental Evaluation

In this section, we detail the experimental setup used to validate our proposed tri-modal framework and present a comprehensive analysis of the results.

5.1 Preprocessing and Implementation Details

All experiments are conducted on our **two hybrid tri-modal benchmarks** derived from the **DoTA** [39] and **Risky Object Localization (ROL)** [14] datasets. Both are synchronized with authentic driver facial video and in-cabin audio using our **Cross-Modal Consistency Alignment (CMCA) protocol**. To ensure input consistency, each modality undergoes a standardized preprocessing pipeline.

For the visual streams (both road and driver), we uniformly sample 15 frames per clip, which are then resized to 224 × 224 pixels. Driver facial regions are detected and cropped using MTCNN [42] prior to resizing. For the audio stream, all clips are resampled to 22,050 Hz using *Librosa* and normalized to a fixed duration of 3.6 s via zero-padding or trimming. Subsequently, Mel-Frequency Cepstral Coefficients (MFCCs) are extracted to serve as the audio input.

Our model is implemented in PyTorch and trained end-to-end for 100 epochs on 8 NVIDIA RTX 4090 GPUs with a total batch size of 80. We use the SGD optimizer with momentum and a ReduceLROnPlateau learning rate schedule. To enhance robustness, data augmentation techniques, including random masking and noise simulation, are applied across all three modalities. The entire framework is optimized using a standard cross-entropy loss function.

To ensure a fair comparison and prevent hyperparameter bias, we evaluated all baseline models using the default, globally optimized hyperparameters recommended in their original publications and official codebases. We only adapted the necessary input and output layers to accommodate our specific tri-modal dataset formats.

Metric Definition. We report **Average Precision (AP)** and **AUC** for detection performance. To evaluate the model's capability to foresee accidents, we introduce **mean Time-to-Accident (mTTA)**, which measures the average earliest time a hazard is detected before the actual collision. For efficiency, we report **FLOPs** and **Parameters** to quantify computational cost and model size. **FPS** is measured as the network throughput on a single RTX 4090 (batch size 1), excluding sensor I/O and pre-processing (e.g., MTCNN face alignment), consistent with standard backbone benchmarking protocols.

5.2 Results and Discussion

Main Results. Table 1 shows our tri-modal framework achieves state-of-the-art performance across both benchmarks. On the DoTA dataset, our method achieves **69.5% AP**, surpassing the best **external-centric baseline** (TTHF) by **7.7%**. Similarly, on the ROL dataset, our model demonstrates robust generalization, consistently outperforming existing methods. Crucially, it also excels in early hazard anticipation, achieving an mTTA of **2.58 s**, which is a significant improvement over external-centric baselines that rely solely on kinematic cues. This confirms that incorporating driver physiological reactions serves as a powerful "early warning" signal.

Efficiency and Deployment Feasibility. With an inference speed of **117 FPS** (at FP32 precision) on a high-end GPU, our model delivers a 2.6× speedup compared to TTHF. Furthermore, the model is designed with extreme lightness in mind, requiring only **17.79 GFLOPs** and **5.34M parameters.** This low computational footprint suggests strong potential for deployment on resource-constrained embedded platforms (e.g., NVIDIA Jetson Xavier) via FP16 optimization, meeting real-time requirements (> 20 FPS) while addressing the critical need for low-latency processing in ADAS.

Table 1. Comparison of the proposed model with existing methods on our Tri-modal ROL and DoTA test datasets. **R**: ROL test dataset, **D**: DoTA test dataset.

Method	AUC (%)		AP (%)		mTTA (s)		FPS	FLOPs	Params
	R	D	R	D	R	D		(G)	(M)
TTHF$_{2024}$ [18]	87.1	89.1	58.5	61.8	2.35	2.41	44	31.39	56.77
AM-Net$_{2024}$ [14]	85.5	87.4	57.6	58.6	2.18	2.24	61	40.81	10.58
FOL-Ens.$_{2023}$ [39]	84.9	86.2	56.3	57.3	2.05	2.13	38	56.95	46.93
FOL-M.$_{2023}$ [39]	82.6	82.6	54.6	56.9	1.98	1.99	44	43.79	30.47
AnoPred$_{2018}$ [21]	77.3	70.3	51.7	54.1	1.74	1.89	59	149.25	49.87
ConvLSTM$_{2017}$ [5]	71.3	50.1	47.9	60.6	1.47	1.82	65	24.79	28.27
ConvAE$_{2016}$ [10]	75.9	77.9	49.3	49.3	1.64	1.75	82	17.86	5.39
Qwen2.5-Omni-7B	61.2	58.7	64.4	70.4	-	-	14	627.5	7000
Ours	**88.4**	**89.3**	**62.6**	**69.5**	**2.52**	**2.58**	**117**	**17.79**	**5.34**

Comparison with Large Omni-Modal Models. While the zero-shot Qwen2.5-Omni-7B [37] achieves slightly higher AP, its AUC is lower due to the poorly calibrated confidence scores typical of zero-shot prompting. Crucially, the excessive inference latency of large omni-modal models severely erodes their effective mTTA, making them inherently unsuitable for real-time early warning scenarios. Compounded by massive computational and parameter overheads, these models remain impractical for resource-constrained edge ADAS. Since safety-critical environments demand both accuracy and real-time responsiveness, our method offers a far superior accuracy–efficiency trade-off, delivering competitive AP at 117 FPS with 17.79 GFLOPs and 5.34M parameters.

Modality Complementarity and Robustness. The ablation study (Table 2) quantifies the contribution of each stream, with the full tri-modal setup achieving the highest performance (69.5% AP). Crucially, the results highlight the system's resilience. Even in the bimodal configuration without audio, the model maintains 66.9% AP, outperforming external-centric baselines. To further evaluate deployment reliability under sudden sensor failure, we conducted an inference-time robustness test. Specifically, we simulated an audio sensor failure by **zero-masking the audio input** in the fully trained tri-modal model. Remarkably, the model maintains a robust 61.5% AP, showing only a marginal performance drop. This result demonstrates that our attention-based fusion mechanism functions as a soft selection filter: when a secondary modality (audio) becomes uninformative (zeroed), the network automatically shifts focus to the reliable visual streams (road and driver), allowing the system to **gracefully degrade** rather than failing catastrophically.

Our architectural innovations—ARWS, DyT, and HG—collectively enhance performance while maintaining computational efficiency, as validated in Table 3. This balanced design demonstrates strong potential for real-time ADAS deployment.

Table 2. Ablation study across modalities.

Modalities	AP (%)	AUC (%)
Audio	50.3	49.7
Road	56.6	71.2
Driver	59.5	62.1
Road + Audio	60.2	74.8
Driver + Road	66.9	79.3
Driver + Audio	62.8	68.5
All (Ours)	**69.5**	**89.3**

Table 3. Ablation for modules.

Model	AP (%)	AUC (%)
w/o ARWS	64.3	84.4
w/o DyT	66.3	85.2
w/o HG	65.1	84.9
Full Model	**69.5**	**89.3**

6 Conclusion and Future Work

In this work, we presented a novel multimodal framework for real-time driving hazard detection that uniquely integrates driver internal state with environmental context. By jointly modeling facial video, in-cabin audio, and external road video via an attention-based intermediate fusion strategy, our approach provides a comprehensive risk assessment superior to conventional single-modality methods.

To enable efficient deployment on resource-constrained platforms, we introduced three architectural innovations: the **Adaptive Residual Weighted Separable (ARWS)** network for multi-scale feature aggregation, the **Half-Convolution Grouping (HG)** module for semantic decoupling, and the **Dynamic Tanh (DyT)** layer for statistics-free normalization. These designs collectively optimize the efficiency-accuracy tradeoff.

We validated our method on two hybrid tri-modal benchmarks derived from the DoTA and ROL datasets using a Cross-Modal Consistency Alignment (CMCA) protocol. Experimental results demonstrate that our approach achieves state-of-the-art performance, surpassing existing baselines in accuracy (e.g., 69.5% AP), efficiency (117 FPS), and early hazard anticipation (mTTA of 2.58 s).

For future work, we plan to address the current limitations of our hybrid dataset construction and deployment evaluation. While our CMCA protocol effectively synchronizes semantics across asynchronous devices (detailed in the Supplementary Material), we acknowledge that it inherently captures strong behavioral correlations rather than strict physical causality. Therefore, we aim to validate this initial lightweight prototype testbed on fully synchronized, naturalistic tri-modal datasets. Furthermore, to move beyond high-end GPU testing, we will conduct hardware-specific quantization and end-to-end validation on actual resource-constrained edge devices (e.g., NVIDIA Jetson) for closed-loop real-world trials, alongside exploring privacy-preserving techniques for in-cabin monitoring.

Declaration of Generative AI Use. During the preparation of this manuscript, the authors utilized generative AI models to assist with language translation, text editing, and the aesthetic enhancement of certain conceptual diagrams. Following the use of these tools, the authors thoroughly reviewed and edited the content, and take full responsibility for the final integrity and accuracy of this work.

Acknowledgments. This work was supported by the National Key Research and Development Program of China (Grant No. 2025YFE0113400). We would also like to thank the anonymous reviewers for their constructive comments and valuable feedback, which helped improve the quality of this manuscript.

Disclosure of Interests. The authors have no competing interests to declare that are relevant to the content of this article.

References

1. Bai, J., et al.: Two-stream spatial-temporal graph convolutional networks for driver drowsiness detection. IEEE Trans. Cybern. **52**(12), 13821–13833 (2021)
2. Braun, M., Weber, F., Alt, F.: Affective automotive user interfaces-reviewing the state of driver affect research and emotion regulation in the car. ACM Comput. Surv. (CSUR) **54**(7), 1–26 (2021)
3. Chen, L., Wu, P., Chitta, K., et al.: End-to-end autonomous driving: Challenges and frontiers. IEEE Trans. Pattern Anal. Mach. Intell. **46**(10), 4500–4519 (2024)
4. Chen, Z., Huang, X.: End-to-end learning for lane keeping of self-driving cars. In: IEEE Intelligent Vehicles Symposium (IV), pp. 1856–1860 (2017)
5. Chong, Y.S., Tay, Y.H.: Abnormal event detection in videos using spatiotemporal autoencoder. In: International Symposium on Neural Networks, pp. 189–196. Springer (2017)
6. Gao, J., Li, P., Chen, Z., Zhang, J.: A survey on deep learning for multimodal data fusion. Neural Comput. **32**(5), 829–864 (2020)
7. Girdhar, R., et al.: Imagebind: one embedding space to bind them all. In: Proceedings of the IEEE/CVF Conference on Computer Vision and Pattern Recognition (CVPR), pp. 15180–15190. CVF (2023)

8. Gong, Y., et al.: Contrastive audio-visual masked autoencoder. In: The Eleventh International Conference on Learning Representations
9. Greenwood, P.M., Lenneman, J.K., Baldwin, C.L.: Advanced driver assistance systems (adas): Demographics, preferred sources of information, and accuracy of adas knowledge. Transport. Res. F: Traffic Psychol. Behav. **86**, 131–150 (2022)
10. Hasan, M., Choi, J., Neumann, J.: Learning temporal regularity in video sequences. In: Proceedings of the IEEE/CVF Conference on Computer Vision and Pattern Recognition (CVPR), pp. 733–742 (2016)
11. Hessel, J., Holtzman, A., Forbes, M., Bras, R.L., Choi, Y.: Clipscore: a reference-free evaluation metric for image captioning. In: Proceedings of the 2021 Conference on Empirical Methods in Natural Language Processing (EMNLP), pp. 7514–7528. ACL (2021)
12. Hu, Y., Yang, J., Chen, L.: Planning-oriented autonomous driving. In: Proceedings of the IEEE/CVF Conference on Computer Vision and Pattern Recognition (CVPR), pp. 17853–17862 (2023)
13. Jiang, B., Chen, S., Xu, Q.: Vad: vectorized scene representation for efficient autonomous driving. In: Proceedings of the IEEE/CVF International Conference on Computer Vision (ICCV), pp. 8340–8350 (2023)
14. Karim, M.M., Yin, Z., Qin, R.: An attention-guided multistream feature fusion network for early localization of risky traffic agents in driving videos. IEEE Trans. Intell. Veh. **9**(1), 1792–1803 (2024)
15. Lee, J., Lee, M., Cho, S., et al.: Leveraging spatio-temporal dependency for skeleton-based action recognition. In: Proceedings of the IEEE/CVF International Conference on Computer Vision (ICCV), pp. 5125–5134 (2023)
16. Li, W., Mahadevan, V., Vasconcelos, N.: Anomaly detection and localization in crowded scenes. IEEE Trans. Pattern Anal. Mach. Intell. **36**(1), 18–32 (2014)
17. Li, Z., Zheng, W.L., Lu, B.L.: Multimodal emotion recognition with missing modality via a unified multi-task pre-training framework. In: Proceedings of the 33rd ACM International Conference on Multimedia, pp. 5717–5725 (2025)
18. Liang, R., Li, Y., Zhou, J., Li, X.: Text-driven traffic anomaly detection with temporal high-frequency modeling in driving videos. IEEE Trans. Circuits Syst. Video Technol. **34**(9), 8684–8697 (2024)
19. Liu, F., Chen, D., Zhou, J., Xu, F.: A review of driver fatigue detection and its advances on the use of rgb-d camera. Eng. Appl. Artif. Intell. **116**, 105399 (2022)
20. Liu, W., Qian, J., Yao, Z., Jiao, X., Pan, J.: Convolutional two-stream network using multi-facial feature fusion for driver fatigue detection. Future Internet **11**(5), 115 (2019)
21. Liu, W., Luo, W., Lian, D., Gao, S.: Future frame prediction for anomaly detection - a new baseline. In: Proceedings of the IEEE/CVF Conference on Computer Vision and Pattern Recognition (CVPR), pp. 6536–6545 (2018)
22. Liu, Z., Tang, H.: Bevfusion: multi-task multi-sensor fusion with unified bird's-eye view representation. In: IEEE International Conference on Robotics and Automation (ICRA), pp. 2774–2781 (2023)
23. Lu, J., Batra, D., Parikh, D., Lee, S.: Vilbert: pretraining task-agnostic visiolinguistic representations for vision-and-language tasks. Adv. Neural. Inf. Process. Syst. **32**, (2019)
24. Luan, X., Wen, Q., Hang, B.: Intelligent emotion recognition for drivers using model-level multimodal fusion. Front. Phys. **13**, 1599428 (2025)
25. Luna-Jiménez, C., Kleinlein, R., Griol, D., Callejas, Z., Montero, J.M., Fernández-Martínez, F.: A proposal for multimodal emotion recognition using aural transformers and action units on ravdess dataset. Appl. Sci. **12**(1), 327 (2022)

26. Mollahosseini, A., Hasani, B., Mahoor, M.H.: Affectnet: a database for facial expression, valence, and arousal computing in the wild. IEEE Trans. Affect. Comput. **10**(1), 18–31 (2017)
27. Mou, L., Zhao, Y., Zhou, C., et al.: Driver emotion recognition with a hybrid attentional multimodal fusion framework. IEEE Trans. Affect. Comput. **14**(4), 2970–2981 (2023)
28. Pang, S., Morris, D., Radha, H.: Clocs: camera-lidar object candidates fusion for 3d object detection. In: IEEE/RSJ International Conference on Intelligent Robots and Systems (IROS), pp. 10386–10393 (2020)
29. Prakash, A., Chitta, K., Geiger, A.: Multi-modal fusion transformer for end-to-end autonomous driving. In: Proceedings of the IEEE/CVF Conference on Computer Vision and Pattern Recognition, pp. 7077–7087 (2021)
30. Sima, C., et al.: Drivelm: driving with graph visual question answering. In: European Conference on Computer Vision, pp. 256–274. Springer (2024)
31. Sultani, W., Chen, C., Shah, M.: Real-world anomaly detection in surveillance videos. In: Proceedings of the IEEE Conference on Computer Vision and Pattern Recognition, pp. 6479–6488 (2018)
32. Vaswani, A.: Attention is all you need. In: Advances in Neural Information Processing Systems (NeurIPS), pp. 5998–6008 (2017)
33. Wang, G., Li, J., Wu, Z., Xu, J., Shen, J., Yang, W.: Efficientface: an efficient deep network with feature enhancement for accurate face detection. Multimedia Syst. **29**, 2825–2839 (2023)
34. Wang, X., Guo, Y., Bai, C., Yuan, Q., Liu, S., Han, J.: Driver's intention identification with the involvement of emotional factors in two-lane roads. IEEE Trans. Intell. Transp. Syst. **22**(11), 6866–6874 (2021)
35. Wozniak, M.K., Kårefjärd, V., Thiel, M., Jensfelt, P.: Toward a robust sensor fusion step for 3d object detection on corrupted data. IEEE Robot. Autom. Lett. **8**(11), 7018–7025 (2023)
36. Wu, T., et al.: Video sentiment analysis with bimodal information-augmented multi-head attention. Knowl.-Based Syst. **235**, 107676 (2022)
37. Xu, J., et al.: Qwen2. 5-omni technical report. arXiv preprint arXiv:2503.20215 (2025)
38. Xu, P., Zhu, X., Clifton, D.A.: Multimodal learning with transformers: a survey. IEEE Trans. Pattern Anal. Mach. Intell. **45**(10), 12113–12132 (2023)
39. Yao, Y., et al.: Dota: Unsupervised detection of traffic anomaly in driving videos. IEEE Trans. Pattern Anal. Mach. Intell. **45**(1), 444–459 (2023)
40. Yao, Y., Xu, M.: Unsupervised traffic accident detection in first-person videos. In: IEEE/RSJ International Conference on Intelligent Robots and Systems (IROS), pp. 273–280 (2019)
41. Yu, F., Chen, H.: Bdd100k: a diverse driving dataset for heterogeneous multitask learning. In: Proceedings of the IEEE/CVF Conference on Computer Vision and Pattern Recognition (CVPR), pp. 2633–2642 (2020)
42. Zhang, K., Zhang, Z., Li, Z., Qiao, Y.: Joint face detection and alignment using multi-task cascaded convolutional networks. IEEE Signal Process. Lett. **23**(10), 1499–1503 (2016)
43. Zhao, F., Zhang, C., Geng, B.: Deep multimodal data fusion: a survey. ACM Comput. Surv. **56**(9), 1–36 (2024)
44. Zhao, Z., Liu, Q., Zhou, F.: Robust lightweight facial expression recognition network with label distribution training. In: Proceedings of the AAAI Conference on Artificial Intelligence, vol. 35, pp. 3510–3519 (2021)
45. Zhu, J., Chen, X., He, K., LeCun, Y., Liu, Z.: Transformers without normalization. In: Proceedings of the Computer Vision and Pattern Recognition Conference, pp. 14901–14911 (2025)

Modeling Matches as Language: A Generative Transformer Approach for Counterfactual Player Valuation In Football

Miru Hong[1], Minho Lee[2], Geonhee Jo[1], Hyeokje Cho[1], Hyunsung Kim[3,4], Pascal Bauer[2,5], and Sang-Ki Ko[1](✉)

[1] University of Seoul, Seoul, Republic of Korea
{mirunoyume,geonhee,brandon56,sangkiko}@uos.ac.kr
[2] Saarland University, Saarbrücken, Germany
{minho.lee,pascal.bauer}@uni-saarland.de
[3] KAIST, Daejeon, Republic of Korea
hyunsung.kim@kaist.ac.kr
[4] Fitogether Inc., Seoul, Republic of Korea
[5] Deutscher Fußball-Bund, Frankfurt, Germany

Abstract. Evaluating football player transfers is challenging because player actions depend strongly on tactical systems, teammates, and match context. Despite this complexity, recruitment decisions often rely on static statistics and subjective expert judgment, which do not fully account for these contextual factors. This limitation stems largely from the absence of counterfactual simulation mechanisms capable of predicting outcomes in hypothetical scenarios. To address these challenges, we propose ScoutGPT, a generative model that treats football match events as sequential tokens within a language modeling framework. Utilizing a NanoGPT-based Transformer architecture trained on next-token prediction, ScoutGPT learns the dynamics of match event sequences to simulate event sequences under hypothetical lineups, demonstrating superior predictive performance compared to existing baseline models. Leveraging this capability, the model employs Monte Carlo sampling to enable counterfactual simulation, allowing for the assessment of unobserved scenarios. Experiments on K League data show that simulated player transfers lead to measurable changes in offensive progression and goal probabilities, indicating that ScoutGPT captures player-specific impact beyond traditional static metrics.

Keywords: Sports Analytics · Player Evaluation · Generative Models · Sequence Modeling · Transformer · Counterfactual Simulation

1 Introduction

Evaluating individual contribution is challenging in complex multi-agent environments, where behavior depends not only on an agent's own ability but also

M. Ceci et al. (Eds.): ECML PKDD 2026, LNAI 16948, pp. 142–160, 2027.
https://doi.org/10.1007/978-3-032-37679-4_9

on interactions with surrounding agents and context. Football provides a particularly demanding instance of this problem: player actions are shaped by tactical roles, teammates, opponents, and match state. As a result, player transfer evaluation cannot be reduced to a like-for-like replacement problem, since moving a player to a new team alters the tactical configuration and reshapes interaction patterns on the pitch. Transfer evaluation therefore requires estimating how a player will behave under this distribution shift, rather than extrapolating directly from past performance alone.

Previous approaches only partially address this problem. Event-based evaluation frameworks [4,10,21,22,27,31] quantify observed events but do not generate how action sequences would evolve under a new tactical context, and projection systems in other sports operate on aggregate season outcomes that miss on-pitch micro-interactions. Recent generative models focus either on continuous trajectories [6–8,14,35,36], which capture spatial movement but not the tactical semantics of discrete events, or on next-event prediction [24–26,30,37], which targets observed continuations rather than hypothetical-transfer sequences; even event-level estimators such as On-Ball Value [18] generate only short fragments of play. Evaluating transfer scenarios instead requires generating full event sequences under a new lineup and match context, enabling value computation over the entire simulated possession.

To address this problem, we introduce ScoutGPT, an autoregressive generative framework for football event streams related to Large Event Models (LEMs) [26]. ScoutGPT treats a match as a structured sequence in which each event is decomposed into discrete attributes through tokenization and predicted sequentially via next-token prediction, conditioned on player identity and match context. Alongside next-action prediction, the model estimates goal-scoring and goal-conceding probabilities at each step, aligning generated sequences with match value (VAEP) [10] and supporting event-level simulation of hypothetical player transfers under new tactical environments [2,12].

To summarize, our main contributions are as follows:

- **Structured Event Modeling for Context-Aware Simulation:** We introduce a fine-grained tokenization scheme that decomposes football events into semantic components (e.g., actor, location, and action type). This structure enables ScoutGPT to capture dependencies across event attributes and model football event sequences at a finer granularity.
- **Value-Aware Generative Modeling:** We propose a multi-task learning objective that combines next-token prediction with explicit scoring and conceding probability estimation. This design encourages the model to reflect both event likelihood and match value, and improves predictive performance over non-value-aware variants.
- **Counterfactual Simulation for Player Recruitment:** We show that ScoutGPT can simulate how a player's on-ball contribution profile shifts in a new tactical environment, supporting data-driven analysis of transfer fit (Fig. 1).

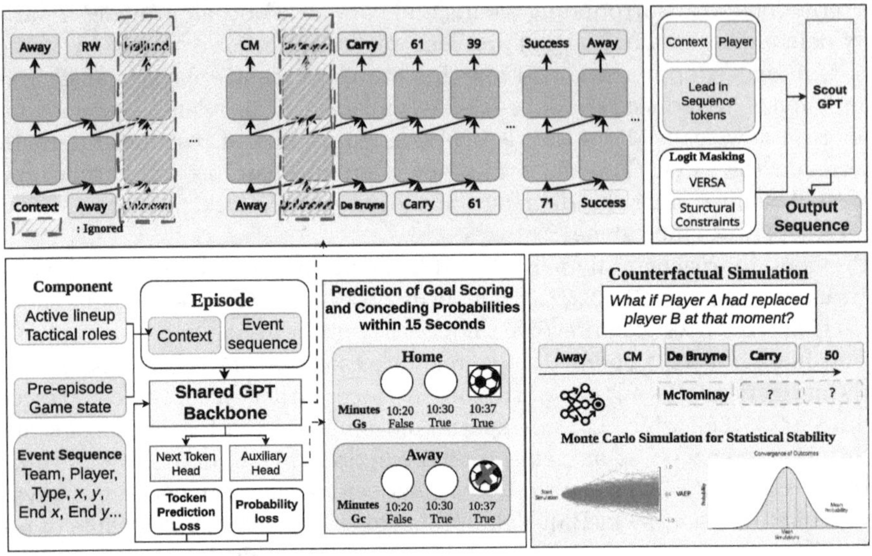

Fig. 1. Overview of the ScoutGPT framework. Our NanoGPT-based Transformer model autoregressively predicts event tokens, enabling counterfactual 'what-if' simulations. For instance, replacing Kevin De Bruyne with Scott McTominay could alter actions (e.g., pass/shot) or modify the same action with a different location, outcome, or VAEP.

2 Related Work

Our work sits at the intersection of three lines of research: data-driven player valuation, generative modeling of sports event streams, and counterfactual simulation for player transfers.

2.1 Data-Driven Player Valuation

Action-value frameworks have become the standard for data-driven player valuation. VAEP quantifies player contribution by aggregating short-horizon changes in scoring and conceding probabilities across all on-ball actions [10], while EPV decomposes instantaneous possession value into interpretable subcomponents [15,16]. PlayeRank extends this further by constructing multi-dimensional, role-aware player ratings from large-scale event logs [27]. Collectively, these methods provide strong discriminative estimators for observed behavior. However, they evaluate actions that have already occurred and are not designed to generate counterfactual event sequences under hypothetical team configurations—a requirement that arises when assessing transfer fit.

2.2 Generative Sequence Modeling of Sports Events

A growing body of work frames football events as structured sequential prediction problems. Seq2Event [30] and Large Event Models (LEMs) [26] decompose each event into multiple attributes and roll out match continuations from a given state, while NMSTPP [37] and related neural point process models [13,40] extend this to continuous-time streams with explicit timing. Transformer architectures [5,33] have likewise been adapted to predict matches as autoregressive token sequences [1,3,24,25]. However, these approaches optimize for sequence likelihood without goal-oriented supervision and thus ignore the tactical value of decisions; moreover, entity-conditioning for player substitution is absent or indirect, and unconstrained generation can yield logically inconsistent transitions over long horizons. ScoutGPT addresses these limitations by pairing the autoregressive objective with explicit value supervision and VERSA-based constraint masking [19].

2.3 Counterfactual Simulation in Sports

Macro-level transfer forecasting—baseball projection systems (ZiPS, PECOTA) and football ability-curve regression [2]—predicts aggregate season statistics from historical and age-curve data, too coarse to capture event-level tactical dynamics. Graph-based methods recommend positionally similar replacements from a relational player network [38] but do not model how behavior changes in a new team context, while hierarchical Bayesian xG [23] and causal evaluation frameworks [32] isolate the counterfactual impact of individual actions yet cannot generate the event sequences needed to assess a full transfer. Closest to our setting, TacEleven [39] uses language models to explore attacking tactics but only over fragmented paths, and EventGPT [18] generates only short fragments, approximating the remaining value via residual OBV rather than from fully simulated sequences.

3 Methodology

This section presents the pipeline of ScoutGPT. Section 3.1 formulates football event modeling as sequence prediction. Section 3.2 describes how the match context and events are serialized into a single token sequence. Section 3.3 then details the core architecture consisting of a backbone and two task-specific prediction heads, and Sect. 3.4 introduces the objective that jointly train the model for both tasks. Finally, Sect. 3.5 describes the constrained decoding procedure used to generate logically valid event sequences at inference time.

3.1 Problem Formulation

We formulate football event modeling as a sequence prediction task conditioned on a global match context. Let $\mathbf{c}$ denote a 54-dimensional match context vector and $(\mathbf{e}_1, \mathbf{e}_2, \ldots, \mathbf{e}_T)$ denote a sequence of on-ball events occurring under this context, where each event $\mathbf{e}_t$ is a 10-dimensional tuple of integer tokens (See Table 1 describing the components of $\mathbf{c}$ and $\mathbf{e}_t$). Given the context $\mathbf{c}$ and the past events $\mathbf{e}_{1:t}$, our objective is to jointly predict (i) the next event $\mathbf{e}_{t+1}$ and (ii) two binary goal indicators $g_t^+, g_t^- \in \{0,1\}$ denoting whether the team performing $\mathbf{e}_t$ scores ($g_t^+ = 1$) or concedes ($g_t^- = 1$) a goal within 15 s after the event. Equivalently, the model estimates three probabilities $P(\mathbf{e}_{t+1} \mid \mathbf{c}, \mathbf{e}_{1:t})$, $P(g_t^+ = 1 \mid \mathbf{c}, \mathbf{e}_{1:t})$, and $P(g_t^- = 1 \mid \mathbf{c}, \mathbf{e}_{1:t})$.

Table 1. Components of the context block $\mathbf{c}$ and each event tuple $\mathbf{e}_t$. Note that continuous fields (locations and elapsed time) are quantized into discrete bins.

Group	Symbol	Description	# Tokens
Context $\mathbf{c}$	$u_{\text{H}}, u_{\text{A}}$	Team IDs of the home and away teams	2
	r_k	Role[a] of each player k	22
	p_k	Player ID of each player k	22
	$\mathbf{q}$	Match state: period, minutes, home/away goals, home/away yellow and red cards	8
Event $\mathbf{e}_t$	u_t	Team ID of the acting team	1
	r_t	Role[a] of the acting player	1
	p_t	Player ID of the acting player	1
	a_t	Action type[a] (e.g., Pass, Carry, Cross, Shot)	1
	$x_t^{\text{start}}, y_t^{\text{start}}$	Start location in meters, $\{0, \ldots, 105\} \times \{0, \ldots, 68\}$	2
	$x_t^{\text{end}}, y_t^{\text{end}}$	End location in meters, $\{0, \ldots, 105\} \times \{0, \ldots, 68\}$	2
	δ_t	Time elapsed in seconds since the previous event	1
	o_t	Action outcome (success or failure)	1

[a] The full lists of roles and action types are provided in the Supplementary Material.

3.2 Structured Event Tokenization

The match context $\mathbf{c}$ and the events $\mathbf{e}_{1:T}$ contain both categorical attributes and quantized continuous ones, together forming a heterogeneous input to the model. To process this hybrid data structure with a Transformer [33], we adopt a tokenization strategy that flattens both $\mathbf{c}$ and $\mathbf{e}_{1:T}$ into a single token sequence. The context $\mathbf{c}$ is laid out as its 54 constituent tokens $(c_1, \ldots, c_{54})$, and each event $\mathbf{e}_t$ is unfolded into its 10 atomic tokens $(s_{t,1}, \ldots, s_{t,10})$. The full input sequence $\mathbf{s}$ is then formed by placing the context tokens first, followed by the flattened event tokens in temporal order.

$$\mathbf{s} = (\underbrace{c_1, \ldots, c_{54}}_{\mathbf{c}}, \underbrace{s_{1,1}, \ldots, s_{1,10}}_{\mathbf{e}_1}, \ldots, \underbrace{s_{T,1}, \ldots, s_{T,10}}_{\mathbf{e}_T}). \tag{1}$$

Since meaningful dependencies arise primarily among events that occur consecutively while the ball is in play, we partition each match into a set of in-play segments called *episodes* [20] and perform sequence prediction independently within each episode. Each episode corresponds to a single in-play segment, starting with a set-piece or a kick off and ending with a goal, a foul, or the ball going out of play, so it corresponds to a single coherent phase of play rather than an arbitrary time window. Since episodes have varying lengths, we cap the input sequence at $T_{\text{max}} = 100$ events and split longer episodes into overlapping chunks via a sliding window with stride $T_{\text{max}}/2 = 50$. The match state $\mathbf{q}$ corresponds to the moment that each episode begins, so the 54 context tokens are shared across all chunks in the episode, and only the event-token window slides forward.

3.3 Model Architecture

Through the tokenization in Sect. 3.2, the next-event prediction in Sect. 3.1 reduces to next-token prediction over the flattened sequence $\mathbf{s}$. That is, conditioned on the context block and the preceding event tokens, ScoutGPT predicts the next event token of $\mathbf{s}$ one at a time, generating each event field by field. At the outcome-token position of each event (i.e., o_t in Table 1), it additionally predicts the goal-scoring and goal-conceding indicators defined in Sect. 3.1. The model utilizes the NanoGPT architecture[1], an efficient implementation of the GPT-2 decoder-only Transformer [29], comprising a shared backbone and task-specific prediction heads.

Backbone. Given an input sequence $\mathbf{s} \in \mathbb{Z}^N$ of length N, the model maps each integer token to a dense vector by indexing into a learnable token-embedding matrix $W_{\text{tok}} \in \mathbb{R}^{|\mathcal{V}| \times d}$ and adds learnable positional embeddings $W_{\text{pos}} \in \mathbb{R}^{N_{\text{max}} \times d}$ to obtain the initial hidden states:

$$\mathbf{h}^{(0)} = W_{\text{tok}}[\mathbf{s}] + W_{\text{pos}}[:N] \in \mathbb{R}^{N \times d}, \tag{2}$$

where $\mathcal{V}$ is the shared token-embedding vocabulary, N_{max} is the maximum sequence length in tokens, and d is the embedding dimension. Note that $\mathcal{V}$ is the union of sub-vocabularies of all fields, so W_{tok} stores the embeddings of every field in one shared table.

The two field types are organized differently within this table. Each categorical field (i.e., team ID, role, player ID, action type, and action outcome in Table 1) owns a separate sub-vocabulary, and thus a disjoint block of rows in W_{tok}, so that its category labels are embedded independently of the other fields. The quantized continuous fields (i.e., the start/end locations and the elapsed time) instead share a single sub-vocabulary of integer bins spanning 0 to 105, so a given bin index maps to the same row of W_{tok}, regardless of which continuous field it corresponds to.

Once the initial hidden states $\mathbf{h}^{(0)}$ are obtained, they are processed by a stack of L Pre-LayerNorm Transformer blocks [34]. Each block of layer $l = 0, \dots, L-1$ takes $\mathbf{h}^{(l)}$ as input and computes $\mathbf{h}^{(l+1)}$ as follows:

$$\tilde{\mathbf{h}}^{(l)} = \text{MSA}(\text{LN}(\mathbf{h}^{(l)})) + \mathbf{h}^{(l)}, \quad \mathbf{h}^{(l+1)} = \text{MLP}(\text{LN}(\tilde{\mathbf{h}}^{(l)})) + \tilde{\mathbf{h}}^{(l)} \tag{3}$$

[1] https://github.com/karpathy/nanoGPT.

where LN is Layer Normalization, MSA is multi-head self-attention, and MLP is a position-wise feed-forward network with GELU activation. The MSA uses a causal attention mask, so that the hidden states $\mathbf{h}_i^{(l)} \in \mathbb{R}^d$ at position i depends only on the preceding tokens $\mathbf{s}_{1:i}$. The final-layer hidden state $\mathbf{h}_i^{(L)} \in \mathbb{R}^d$ then serves as the shared input to the next-token prediction head and the goal-prediction head described below.

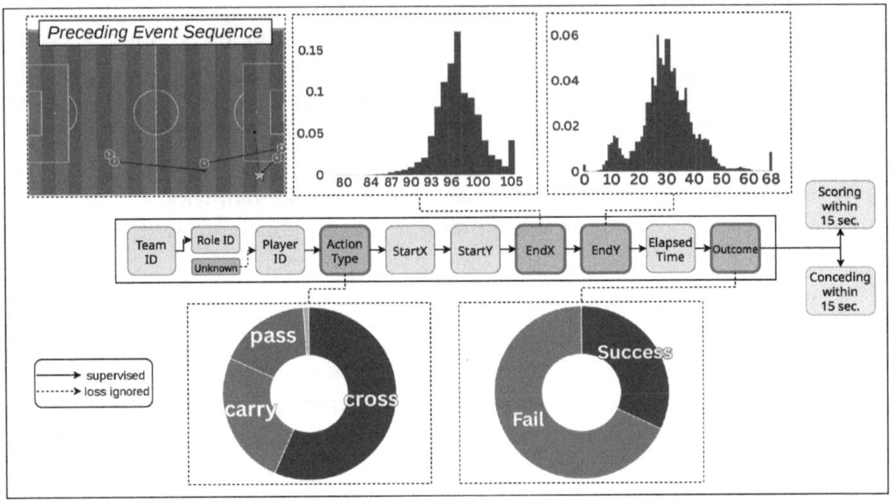

Fig. 2. Next-token prediction over the preceding event sequence. The pitch shows the final five ball-progressing actions leading up to the target, which form the preceding event sequence that we serialize into tokens and feed to the model; the star ($\star$) marks the event the model predicts. At selected tokens we overlay the model's predicted distribution, shown as pie charts for action type and outcome and histograms for the end-location coordinates x_t^{end} and y_t^{end}.

The next-token prediction head applies a linear map $W_{\mathrm{next}} \in \mathbb{R}^{|\mathcal{V}| \times d}$ to the final-layer hidden state $\mathbf{h}_i^{(L)}$, producing logits over the entire vocabulary $\mathcal{V}$. A softmax then yields the probability distribution over the next token s_{i+1}:

$$P(\cdot \mid s_{1:i}) = \mathrm{softmax}\Big(W_{\mathrm{next}} \mathbf{h}_i^{(L)}\Big). \tag{4}$$

Conditioned on the preceding tokens, the model predicts the fields of each event in the order listed in Table 1. The player-ID field is excluded from prediction and instead resolved from the predicted team and role at inference time (Sect. 3.5), since training on it shapes the player embeddings more by team identity then by actual playing style (Sect. 5.1). Figure 2 illustrates this procedure with the estimated probabilities.

Goal Prediction Head. The goal-prediction head applies another linear map $W_{\text{goal}} \in \mathbb{R}^{2\times d}$ to the final-layer hidden state $\mathbf{h}_i^{(L)}$ at an outcome token position i (i.e., the position corresponding to o_t in Table 1), and independent sigmoid activations σ produce two probabilities:

$$(\hat{y}_i^+, \hat{y}_i^-) \tag{5}$$

where $\hat{\mathbf{y}}_i^{g+}, \hat{\mathbf{y}}_i^{g-} \in [0,1]^2$ are distributions over {no goal, goal}, and their positive-class entries give the predicted goal-scoring and goal-conceding probabilities of the action.

3.4 Multi-task Training Objective

We train ScoutGPT using a composite loss function that balances generative capability with goal prediction.

The primary objective is the cross-entropy loss for next-token prediction. As motivated in Sect. 3.3, the player-identity (p_t) loss is excluded from the objective so that the model infers each player's role from spatiotemporal context rather than memorized identities. Since player identity is injected from the role assignment at inference time rather than generated by decoding, masking it during training also keeps the objective consistent with the generation procedure:

$$\mathcal{L}^s = -\sum_i \log P(s_{i+1} \mid s_{1:i}). \tag{6}$$

In addition to next-token prediction, we compute auxiliary Cross-Entropy (CE) losses for goal-scoring ($g+$) or goal-conceding ($g-$) at outcome-token positions. Let $\mathcal{I}_{\text{outcome}}$ denote the set of time indices for outcome tokens within the sequence (i.e., corresponding to o_t in Table 1). At each outcome position $i \in \mathcal{I}_{\text{outcome}}$, the probabilities $\hat{y}_i^{g+}$ and $\hat{y}_i^{g-}$ resulting from Eq. ?? are compared against the ground-truth labels $y_i^{g+}, y_i^{g-} \in \{0,1\}$ retrieved from the raw data, yielding the auxiliary loss term as follows:

$$\mathcal{L}^g = \sum_{i\in\mathcal{I}_{\text{outcome}}} \left[\text{CE}(\hat{\mathbf{y}}_i^{g+}, y_i^{g+}) + \text{CE}(\hat{\mathbf{y}}_i^{g-}, y_i^{g-})\right]. \tag{7}$$

In summary, the final training objective is the sum of the next-token prediction loss and the goal-prediction loss:

$$\mathcal{L} = \mathcal{L}^s + \mathcal{L}^g. \tag{8}$$

3.5 Inference with Structural Constraints

Generating realistic football sequences requires strict logical consistency between consecutive events. Standard sampling can produce syntactically valid but physically invalid sequences, so we mask out implausible tokens in terms of the past token sequence and resolve the acting player through a spatial heuristic.

Invalid Token Masking. To prevent the model from generating tokens that violate the game's logical constraints, we restrict the output distribution at each decoding step to the set of valid continuations. Concretely, at each step i, we apply a validity mask $\mathbf{m}_i = (m_{i,1}, \ldots, m_{i,|\mathcal{V}|})$ to the output logits $\mathbf{z}_i = (z_{i,1}, \ldots, z_{i,|\mathcal{V}|})$ based on the past token sequence $\mathbf{s}_{<i}$:

$$P(\cdot \mid \mathbf{s}_{<i}) = \mathrm{softmax}(\mathbf{z}_i + \mathbf{m}_i), \tag{9}$$

where $\mathcal{V}$ is the token vocabulary, $m_{i,j} = 0$ if the j-th token in $\mathcal{V}$ is valid under $\mathbf{s}_{<i}$ and $m_{i,j} = -\infty$ otherwise. Adding $-\infty$ drives the probability of invalid tokens to zero after the softmax, so only admissible tokens can be sampled.

The masking strategy is component-dependent. Team tokens are restricted to the valid team set defined by the context, action tokens are filtered using the VERSA transition validator [19], a formal state-transition model of football that specifies, for any partial event sequence, which actions may legally follow. At each decoding step we query this model and mask out every action that would violate its transition rules. In addition, several local consistency rules are enforced during decoding. For example, immediate self-receptions such as *Pass Received* by the same player as the previous actor are disallowed, and defensive actions such as *Block* and *Interception* are suppressed when possession is retained by the same team. This procedure ensures that token generation respects both event-transition logic and local interaction constraints.

Spatial-Aware Entity Resolution. After a team token $\hat{h}_t$ is generated, the model first predicts a compatible role token $\hat{r}_t$. The pair $(\hat{h}_t, \hat{r}_t)$ then narrows the candidate player tokens to those in the lineup whose team and role are $\hat{h}_t$ and $\hat{r}_t$, respectively. When there is only one candidate player, the corresponding player token is determined immediately. When multiple players share the same $(\hat{h}_t, \hat{r}_t)$ pair, the model selects the candidate whose reference location μ_p is closest to the most recent ball location $(\hat{x}_t, \hat{y}_t)$, i.e., the end coordinates of the preceding event:

$$p^* = \operatorname*{argmin}_{p \in \mathcal{P}(\hat{h}_t, \hat{r}_t)} \left\| (\hat{x}_t, \hat{y}_t) - \mu_p \right\|_2, \tag{10}$$

where $\mathcal{P}(\hat{h}_t, \hat{r}_t)$ denotes the set of candidate players matching the generated team $\hat{h}_t$ and role $\hat{r}_t$. We use the preceding event's end location because the acting player is resolved before the current event's coordinates are generated, and in practice it nearly coincides with the start location of the current event. The reference location μ_p of a known player (i.e., a player observed in the training set) is set to the average location of their training-set events, which prevents leakage from evaluation matches. For an unknown player, it falls back to a default location associated with their role. Furthermore, the generator applies an ownership-lock mechanism tied to the VERSA possession state. While the validator indicates that a player retains the ball, the lock fixes that player across consecutive in-possession events instead of resolving a new actor at each step. When possession ends, the lock is released and the player is barred from immediate reselection for one event, stabilizing local event continuity.

Table 2. Summary of the dataset

Split	Seasons	Matches	Episodes	Events	Events/ep	Players
Train	2021–2023	1,320	132,315	3,528,635	26.67	1,090
Valid	2024	462	43,579	1,277,169	29.31	848
Test	2025	501	47,046	1,324,363	28.15	859

Dynamic Episode Termination. Episode generation uses semantic stopping rules in addition to the generic EOS token. Decoding stops when (1) an EOS token is produced; (2) a set-piece restart action is generated—*Corner*, *Throw-in*, *Free Kick*, or *Goal Kick*; (3) a successful *Shot* or *Penalty Kick* results in a goal; or (4) *Foul* or *Own Goal*, is generated. These rules prevent generation beyond the logical boundary of the current phase of play. The complete action-type taxonomy is listed in the Supplementary Material.

4 Experiments

We evaluate ScoutGPT on event data collected from South Korean K League across three axes: next-event prediction accuracy, goal prediction quality, and counterfactual transfer simulation. We first describe the experimental setup, then report main results and ablations, and finally assess simulation fidelity via self-to-self reconstruction.

4.1 Experimental Setup

Dataset. We evaluate our model using event data from five seasons of the South Korean K League 1 and 2, spanning from 2021 to 2025. We standardize all data according to the VERSA event representation [19], a state-transition based verifier that defines the taxonomy of 29 action types and enforces football's logical constraints, correcting anomalies such as missing *Pass Received* events or temporally inconsistent orderings. We partition the dataset chronologically for model training and evaluation. We use data from the 2021, 2022, and 2023 seasons as the training set and the 2024 season as the validation set, and reserve the 2025 season for final testing. Detailed dataset statistics can be found in Table 2.

Baselines. We evaluate ScoutGPT on two tasks, each with its own baselines. First, we compare against next-token predictors derived from prior work [26], namely an LSTM [17], a gradient-boosted CatBoost [28], the MLP-based Large Events Model (LEM MLP) [25], and a Transformer variant (LEM Transformer). The LEM Transformer adapts the Transformer backbone of NMSTPP [37] to our output formulation, keeping its architecture but replacing the prediction heads with ones that match our multi-attribute event representation. We adapt these models rather than reuse them directly because existing sequence predictors such as Seq2Event [30] and NMSTPP predict only coarse-grained action types (e.g., pass, dribble, shot), do not model additional event attributes such as player identity, spatial coordinates, temporal intervals, or action value, and do not incorporate the player conditioning that is central to our transfer-fit evaluation.

In addition, we compare ScoutGPT's goal prediction performance against the CatBoost baseline [11] and three neural sequence models, an LSTM [17], a GRU [9], and a Transformer [33], each trained to predict the same goal labels from event context.

4.2 Main Results

Table 3. Performance comparison across categorical and continuous attributes. For categorical attributes, Accuracy/F1 are reported; for continuous attributes, R^2/MAE are reported.

Group	Attr.	LSTM	CatBoost	LEM MLP	LEM Transformer	**ScoutGPT**
Cat.	Team	0.94 / 0.94	0.94 / 0.94	0.66 / 0.37	**0.96** / 0.49	0.92 / **0.92**
	Role	0.77 / **0.67**	0.76 / 0.66	0.71 / 0.32	0.45 / 0.22	0.63 / 0.47
	Type	0.76 / 0.34	0.76 / 0.33	0.71 / 0.20	0.77 / 0.43	**0.78** / **0.53**
	Out.	0.89 / 0.59	0.89 / 0.59	0.92 / 0.14	0.89 / 0.61	**0.95** / **0.86**
Cont.	Start x	0.74 / 2.78	0.80 / 3.88	0.91 / 2.14	0.78 / 4.59	**0.96** / **0.97**
	Start y	0.76 / 2.34	0.80 / 3.32	**0.94** / 1.63	0.78 / 4.09	0.93 / **1.00**
	End x	0.61 / 7.26	0.70 / 7.55	0.48 / 6.27	0.67 / 8.12	**0.89** / **4.11**
	End y	0.54 / 6.95	0.67 / 6.87	0.76 / 5.16	0.66 / 7.18	**0.82** / **3.85**
	Time	0.38 / 0.53	0.49 / 0.64	0.46 / 1.03	0.54 / 1.42	**0.71** / **0.75**

Table 3 reports end-to-end event modeling across event formats and model families. ScoutGPT is strongest on structurally important targets—type (0.78/0.53), outcome (0.95/0.86), end coordinates (0.89/4.11 and 0.82/3.85), and time (0.71/0.75)—and also attains the best start-x (0.96/0.97). Gains over LEM Transformer are especially pronounced on continuous variables (start-x MAE 4.59 → 0.97, time MAE 1.42 → 0.75), indicating better spatial-temporal fidelity during rollout. Although other models stay competitive on a few metrics (e.g., team/role accuracy, start-y R^2), ScoutGPT offers the most reliable overall trade-off for realistic sequence continuation.

We then evaluate short-horizon goal prediction within 15 s using AUC, Brier score, and ECE (Table 4). The goal-prediction head is better calibrated for GC risk signals (higher GC AUC, lower calibration error), while CatBoost gives stronger GS discrimination (higher GS AUC, lower ECE). Crucially, because this head shares the backbone used for next-token prediction, a single ScoutGPT model produces both the event predictions and the goal probabilities, unifying

Table 4. Performance comparison on goal-scoring (GS) and goal-conceding (GC) prediction within 15 s.

Method	Goal-Scoring (GS)			Goal-Conceding (GC)		
	AUC	Brier	ECE	AUC	Brier	ECE
CatBoost [11]	**0.8424**	0.0075	**0.0003**	0.8051	0.0021	0.00082
LSTM [17]	0.8294	0.0230	0.0660	0.8080	0.0029	0.01383
GRU [9]	0.8250	0.0205	0.0576	0.8091	0.0029	0.01376
Transformer [33]	0.8277	0.0210	0.0589	0.7948	0.0031	0.01519
ScoutGPT	0.8344	**0.0069**	0.0024	**0.8153**	**0.0016**	**0.00081**

the two separate baseline stages of event modeling and value estimation. This supports coupling autoregressive sequence modeling with explicit value supervision to improve goal-related signal quality beyond pure token prediction.

4.3 Ablation Study

To isolate what drives these gains, Table 5 compares ablations on lineup and context usage. Removing lineup/context can improve a few isolated metrics (e.g., Role or Time), but the full model remains strongest on most high-impact targets, particularly Team consistency, Type F1, and spatial end-point quality (End x, End y). This pattern suggests that lineup-aware context is most beneficial for preserving coherent tactical structure, even when simplified variants can fit specific marginals slightly better.

Table 5. Ablation on lineup information and the context block. The Ours column is the full model's absolute performance; the other columns report the change after removing each component (Accuracy/F1 for categorical attributes, R^2/MAE for continuous). Improvement corresponds to positive changes for Accuracy, F1, and R^2, and to negative changes for MAE; green and red mark improvement and degradation.

Group	Attr.	Ours	w/o Context	w/o Lineup	w/o Both
Cat.	Team	0.921 / 0.921	−0.003 / −0.002	−0.008 / −0.007	−0.003 / −0.003
	Role	0.634 / 0.469	+0.002 / +0.047	−0.090 / −0.156	−0.069 / −0.128
	Type	0.782 / 0.529	+0.001 / −0.016	−0.002 / −0.006	−0.004 / −0.033
	Out.	0.947 / 0.862	−0.001 / +0.000	−0.001 / −0.001	+0.000 / +0.004
Cont.	Start x	0.961 / 0.973	−0.005 / +0.048	+0.004 / −0.020	+0.009 / −0.077
	Start y	0.925 / 1.001	−0.018 / +0.108	−0.029 / +0.164	−0.003 / +0.011
	End x	0.886 / 4.105	−0.011 / +0.143	−0.007 / +0.094	−0.012 / +0.169
	End y	0.818 / 3.850	−0.017 / +0.158	−0.015 / +0.117	−0.009 / +0.068
	Time	0.711 / 0.751	−0.184 / +0.069	+0.006 / −0.008	−0.212 / +0.097

Table 6. Average VAEP under different match minute and score-state conditions. The control value corresponds to the fully controlled reference condition and is fixed at 0.02678 for all rows. Δ denotes the change relative to this reference (Δ = Simulated − Original).

Minute	Score state	Original	Simulated	Δ
0	Drawing	0.02678	0.023477	−0.003303
	Trailing	0.02678	0.025916	−0.000864
	Leading	0.02678	0.026392	−0.000388
40	Drawing	0.02678	0.029647	+0.002867
	Trailing	0.02678	0.029864	+0.003084
	Leading	0.02678	0.029644	+0.002864

To further examine whether ScoutGPT captures context-dependent player impact under controlled perturbations, we conduct a context intervention ablation on episodes of Jeonbuk Hyundai FC, reporting aggregated team-level episode VAEP across combinations of match minute and score state (Table 6). At minute 0 the simulated play yields lower VAEP across all score states, most strongly when drawing ($\Delta = -0.0033$), reflecting a generally cautious style early in the second half. By minute 40 the effect reverses to higher VAEP across all states, strongest when trailing ($\Delta = +0.0031$), reflecting a shift toward more proactive play, consistent with teams being most aggressive in pursuit of an equalizer. Overall, ScoutGPT captures both context-dependent adaptation over time and meaningful differences in strategic behavior across score states.

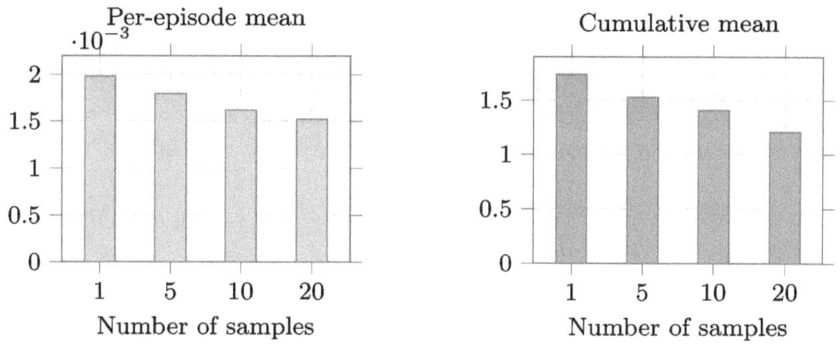

Fig. 3. Comparison of the mean absolute delta under different numbers of samples. The left shows the per-episode mean absolute delta, while the right shows the cumulative mean absolute delta.

Figure 3 summarizes the discrepancy between ground-truth (GT) and self-to-self simulated episode VAEP across different numbers of samples. As the number of samples increases, both the per-episode mean and cumulative absolute differences consistently decrease. This indicates that larger sample sizes lead to more stable self-to-self simulation results and improve the agreement with the GT episode VAEP.

5 Applications

Beyond next-event prediction, ScoutGPT supports two applications that leverage the learned player representations and counterfactual generation capability: embedding-based player retrieval and hypothetical transfer simulation.

Table 7. Cross-season player retrieval performance using player embeddings learned from the 2021–2023 seasons. For each query embedding of a player from one season, retrieval is performed over embeddings from other seasons only. Evaluation is restricted to players who appear in at least two seasons. A query is counted as correct if an embedding of the same player from a different season is retrieved.

Model	Top-1 (%)	Top-5 (%)	Top-10 (%)
ScoutGPT (Ours)	**9.20**	**21.97**	**30.90**
w/o position masking	8.48	20.02	27.05
Statistics-based embedding	8.98	21.36	30.34

5.1 Player Embedding for Similar Player Retrieval

Table 7 gives a quantitative view of the same embedding space. Under *role masking*, role tokens are hidden during event prediction so the model must rely on player identity and event context rather than explicit role labels. Same-player retrieval consistently improves over both the no-masking variant and a stats-based embedding baseline. Masking prevents role from acting as a shortcut bias, encouraging embeddings to encode player-specific behavior.

To assess whether these embeddings capture role-related structure, we project them into two dimensions with t-Distributed Stochastic Neighbor Embedding (t-SNE), shown in Fig. 4, where each point is a player colored by coarse role category.

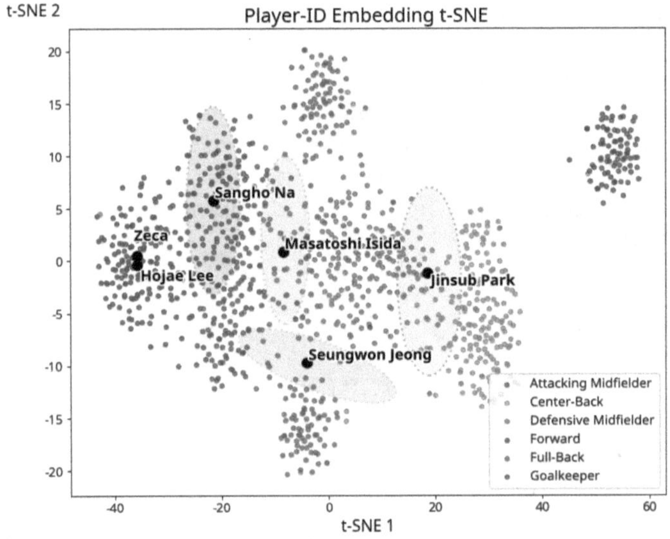

Fig. 4. t-SNE projection of ScoutGPT player embeddings from the 2024 *K League* season, colored by role.

Even with role masked, players separate by role, and the cluster hierarchy aligns with the spatial intuition of real football. Defensive midfielders are positioned between the center back cluster on the right and the attacking midfielder cluster on the left. Fullback clusters appear separated vertically based on their tactical roles on the field. For instance, Jinsub Park exists between the defensive midfielder and center back clusters. Notably, these embedding patterns align well with their actual playing profiles, as all four players are known for their tactical versatility and have performed across multiple roles in real matches. A complete list of these multi-role players is provided in the Supplementary Material.

5.2 Hypothetical Transfer Simulation

Table 8 evaluates transfer-fit prediction by comparing simulated post-transfer episode VAEP against ground truth and a naive baseline. Here, the naive projection estimates a player's next-season performance by simply extrapolating from the previous season's VAEP while adjusting only for playing time, without accounting for changes in tactical context, team structure, or role. Across all 40 transferred players, ScoutGPT reduces the mean absolute error from 1.84 (naive) to 1.25 (simulated), corresponding to a substantial relative error reduction. This indicates that the model captures context-dependent changes in player contribution more reliably than static carry-over assumptions. The representative examples also show that improvements are not confined to one role: gains appear for full-backs, wingers, and central midfielders, suggesting that the framework generalizes across distinct tactical functions.

Jinsu Kim provides a clear example of the practical value of context-aware simulation. The naive estimate (7.00) substantially underestimates his observed post-transfer contribution (GT sum = 11.07), whereas ScoutGPT predicts 11.63, yielding a much smaller error (0.56 vs. 4.07). This aligns with real-world outcomes: his move was widely regarded as highly successful relative to initial expectations, and he was appointed team captain in the following season. This case highlights how counterfactual sequence modeling can identify upside that is missed by static baseline forecasts.

Table 8. Comparison of post-transfer episode VAEP in 2025 using naive and simulated estimates against ground truth (GT). The top 40 transferred players are selected by post-transfer minutes and used to compute the overall average. Only five players are shown for readability. Columns "Naive", "GT", and "Sim" report episode VAEP sums, while —GT − Sim— and —GT − Naive— report absolute errors with respect to GT.

Role	Player	Episode VAEP Sum			Absolute Error w.r.t. GT	
		Naive	GT	Sim	—GT − Sim—	—GT − Naive—
Average		4.85	4.71	4.59	**1.25**	1.84
Left Back	Jinsu Kim	7.00	11.07	11.63	**0.56**	4.07
Left Wing	Reis	16.15	12.19	12.06	**0.13**	3.96
Center Back	Hoik Jang	3.79	4.78	5.83	1.05	**0.99**
Central Midfielder	Jihoon Cho	8.83	5.09	5.31	**0.22**	3.74
Left Back	Juyong Lee	4.61	6.51	7.31	**0.80**	1.90

6 Conclusion

We present ScoutGPT, a player-conditioned, value-aware autoregressive framework for football event modeling. By jointly predicting event attributes and residual on-ball value, it captures both local action structure and downstream tactical impact, outperforming sequence-based baselines in next-event prediction, spatial precision, and future contribution estimation while learning interpretable player embeddings without role supervision. Counterfactual player substitution further enables transfer-fit evaluation under new tactical contexts. Future work will integrate tracking-based trajectory signals for off-ball behavior and extend generation to full-possession or match-level simulation.

Acknowledgements. The authors gratefully acknowledge the K League Technical Study Group (TSG) for providing the K League match data used in this study. We also sincerely thank Bepro11 for their efforts in collecting and processing the event and tracking data. Miru Hong, Geonhee Jo, Hyeokje Cho, and Sang-Ki Ko were supported by the National Research Foundation of Korea (NRF) grant funded by the Korean government (MSIT) (No. RS-2024-00456065).

References

1. Adjileye, A.A.: RisingBALLER: a player is a token, a match is a sentence, a path towards a foundational model for football players data analytics. In: StatsBomb Conference (2024)
2. van Arem, K., Goes-Smit, F., Söhl, J.: Forecasting the future development in quality and value of professional football players. Appl. Sci. **15**(16), 8916 (2025)
3. Baron, E., Hocevar, D., Salehe, Z.: A foundation model for soccer. arXiv preprint arXiv:2407.14558 (2024)
4. Bransen, L., Haaren, J.V.: Player chemistry: Striving for a perfectly balanced soccer team. In: MIT Sloan Sports Analytics Conference (2020)
5. Brown, T.B., et al.: Language models are few-shot learners. In: Proceedings of the 32th International Conference on Neural Information Processing Systems (2020)
6. Capellera, G., Ferraz, L., Rubio, A., Agudo, A., Moreno-Noguer, F.: TranSPORTmer: a holistic approach to trajectory understanding in multi-agent sports. In: Proceedings of the 17th Asian Conference on Computer Vision (2024)
7. Capellera, G., Ferraz, L., Rubio, A., Alahi, A., Agudo, A.: JointDiff: bridging continuous and discrete in multi-agent trajectory generation. In: Proceedings of the 14th International Conference on Learning Representations (2026)
8. Capellera, G., Rubio, A., Ferraz, L., Agudo, A.: Unified uncertainty-aware diffusion for multi-agent trajectory modeling. In: IEEE/CVF Conference on Computer Vision and Pattern Recognition (2025)
9. Chung, J., Gulcehre, C., Cho, K., Bengio, Y.: Empirical evaluation of gated recurrent neural networks on sequence modeling. arXiv preprint arXiv:1412.3555 (2014)
10. Decroos, T., Bransen, L., Van Haaren, J., Davis, J.: Actions speak louder than goals: valuing player actions in soccer. In: Proceedings of the 25th ACM SIGKDD International Conference on Knowledge Discovery and Data Mining (2019)
11. Decroos, T., Bransen, L., Van Haaren, J., Davis, J.: VAEP: an objective approach to valuing on-the-ball actions in soccer (extended abstract). In: Proceedings of the 29th International Joint Conference on Artificial Intelligence (2020)
12. Dinsdale, D., Gallagher, J.: Transfer portal: accurately forecasting the impact of a player transfer in soccer. arXiv preprint arXiv:2201.11533 (2022)
13. Du, N., et al.: Recurrent marked temporal point processes: embedding event history to vector. In: Proceedings of the 22nd ACM SIGKDD International Conference on Knowledge Discovery and Data Mining (2016)

14. Fassmeyer, D., Fassmeyer, P., Brefeld, U.: Semi-supervised generative models for multiagent trajectories. In: Advances in Neural Information Processing Systems, vol. 35 (2022)
15. Fernández, J., Bornn, L., Cervone, D.: Decomposing the immeasurable sport: a deep learning expected possession value framework for soccer. In: MIT Sloan Sports Analytics Conference (2019)
16. Fernández, J., Bornn, L., Cervone, D.: A framework for the fine-grained evaluation of the instantaneous expected value of soccer possessions. Mach. Learn. **110**(6), 1389–1427 (2021)
17. Hochreiter, S., Schmidhuber, J.: Long short-term memory. Neural Comput. **9**(8), 1735–1780 (1997)
18. Hong, M., Lee, M., Jo, G., So, J.H., Bauer, P., Ko, S.K.: EventGPT: capturing player impact from team action sequences using GPT-based framework. arXiv preprint arXiv:2512.17266 (2025)
19. Jo, G., Kang, M., Lee, K., Lee, M., Bauer, P., Ko, S.K.: VERSA: verified event data format for reliable soccer analytics. arXiv preprint arXiv:2601.21981 (2026)
20. Kim, H., Choi, H.J., Kim, C.J., Yoon, J., Ko, S.K.: Ball trajectory inference from multi-agent sports contexts using set transformer and hierarchical Bi-LSTM. In: Proceedings of the 29th ACM SIGKDD International Conference on Knowledge Discovery and Data Mining (2023)
21. Liu, G., Luo, Y., Schulte, O., Kharrat, T.: Deep soccer analytics: learning an action-value function for evaluating soccer players. Data Min. Knowl. Disc. **34**(5), 1531–1559 (2020)
22. Luo, Y., Schulte, O., Poupart, P.: Inverse reinforcement learning for team sports: valuing actions and players. In: Proceedings of the 29th International Joint Conference on Artificial Intelligence (2020)
23. Mahmudlu, M., Karakuş, O., Arkadaş, H.: What if they took the shot? A hierarchical Bayesian framework for counterfactual expected goals. arXiv preprint arXiv:2511.23072 (2025)
24. Mendes-Neves, T., Meireles, L., Mendes-Moreira, J.: Forecasting events in soccer matches through language. arXiv preprint arXiv:2402.06820 (2024)
25. Mendes-Neves, T., Meireles, L., Mendes-Moreira, J.: Towards a foundation large events model for soccer. Mach. Learn. **113**, 8687–8709 (2024)
26. Mendes-Neves, T., Meireles, L., Mendes-Moreira, J.: A scalable approach for unified large events models in soccer. In: Joint European Conference on Machine Learning and Knowledge Discovery in Databases (2026)
27. Pappalardo, L., Cintia, P., Ferragina, P., Massucco, E., Pedreschi, D., Giannotti, F.: PlayeRank: data-driven performance evaluation and player ranking in soccer via a machine learning approach. ACM Trans. Intell. Syst. Technol. **10**(5), 1–27 (2019)
28. Prokhorenkova, L., Gusev, G., Vorobev, A., Dorogush, A.V., Gulin, A.: CatBoost: unbiased boosting with categorical features. In: Advances in Neural Information Processing Systems (NeurIPS) (2018)
29. Radford, A., Wu, J., Child, R., Luan, D., Amodei, D., Sutskever, I.: Language models are unsupervised multitask learners. OpenAI Blog **1**(8), 9 (2019)
30. Simpson, I., Beal, R.J., Locke, D., Norman, T.J.: Seq2Event: learning the language of soccer using transformer-based match event prediction. In: Proceedings of the 28th ACM SIGKDD Conference on Knowledge Discovery and Data Mining (2022)
31. Singh, K.: Introducing Expected Threat (xT): modelling team behaviour in possession to gain a deeper understanding of buildup play (2019). https://karun.in/blog/expected-threat.html

32. Susmann, H.P., D'Alessandro, A.: The counterfactual combine: a causal framework for player evaluation. arXiv preprint arXiv:2602.23233 (2026)
33. Vaswani, A., et al.: Attention is all you need. In: Proceedings of the 31st International Conference on Neural Information Processing Systems, pp. 6000–6010 (2017)
34. Xiong, R., Yang, Y., He, D., Zheng, K., Zheng, S.: On layer normalization in the transformer architecture. In: International Conference on Machine Learning (ICML) (2020)
35. Xu, Y., Bazarjani, A., Chi, H., Choi, C., Fu, Y.: Uncovering the missing pattern: unified framework towards trajectory imputation and prediction. In: IEEE/CVF Conference on Computer Vision and Pattern Recognition (2023)
36. Xu, Y., Fu, Y.: Sports-Traj: a unified trajectory generation model for multi-agent movement in sports. In: Proceedings of the 13th International Conference on Learning Representations (2025)
37. Yeung, C., Sit, T., Fujii, K.: Transformer-based neural marked spatio-temporal point process model for analyzing football match events. Appl. Intell. **55**(5), 335 (2025)
38. Yılmaz, Ö.İ., Öğüdücü, Ş.G.: Learning football player features using graph embeddings for player recommendation system. In: Proceedings of the 37th ACM/SIGAPP Symposium on Applied Computing (2022)
39. Zhao, S., et al.: TacEleven: generative tactic discovery for football open play. arXiv preprint arXiv:2511.13326 (2025)
40. Zuo, S., Jiang, H., Li, Z., Zhao, T., Zha, H.: Transformer Hawkes process. In: Proceedings of the 37th International Conference on Machine Learning (2020)

SurfaceEncoder: Semi-supervised Representation Learning for Global Wheelchair Accessibility

Nadim Mahmud[1], Md Osman Gani[2], Vaskar Raychoudhury[1](✉), and Snehanshu Saha[3]

[1] Computer Science and Software Engineering, Miami University, Oxford, OH 45056, USA
{mahmudm2,raychov}@miamioh.edu

[2] Department of Information Systems, University of Maryland Baltimore County, Baltimore, MD, USA
mogani@umbc.edu

[3] School of AI and CSE, Mahindra University, Hyderbabad, India
snehanshus@goa.bits-pilani.ac.in

Abstract. For over 80 million manual wheelchair users worldwide, navigating urban environments remains a critical challenge. This work aims to generate high-fidelity automated route maps for accessible navigation using scalable smartphone crowdsensing. However, existing supervised approaches rely heavily on manual annotation and struggle to generalize across diverse real-world conditions. To address this, we introduce the Global Wheelchair Surface (GWS) dataset, a 183-h, 52-million data points cross-continental dataset spanning five countries. It combines 13.6 h of controlled labeled data from the USA and Vietnam with a 300-km continuous unlabeled urban transit corpus from European cities. We propose SurfaceEncoder, a deep autoencoder that integrates Multi-Scale Temporal Convolutional Blocks (MSTCB), Cross-Axis Interaction Modules (CAIM), and Frequency-Aware Attention Gates (FAAG) to extract robust vibration representations from tri-axial inertial data. Using a semi-supervised objective over labeled and unlabeled samples, `SurfaceEncoder` learns a discriminative latent space that substantially reduces annotation requirements. Incorporating labeled USA/Vietnam data improves clustering performance on unseen European data by over 32%, increasing the silhouette score from 0.335 to 0.443 and outperforming time-series foundation models, including TS2Vec, Chronos, MOMENT, and TimesFM across clustering metrics on our dataset. Ultimately, `SurfaceEncoder` isolates genuine surface impacts from hardware noise, enabling a scalable pipeline that directly powers a live, LLM-powered turn-by-turn navigation system. To foster further research, the dataset and benchmarking code are publicly available at: https://github.com/MU-Smart/SurfaceEncoder.

Keywords: Semi-Supervised Learning · Representation Learning · Time Series Clustering · Accessibility · Smart Cities · Domain Adaptation

M. Ceci et al. (Eds.): ECML PKDD 2026, LNAI 16948, pp. 161–179, 2027.
https://doi.org/10.1007/978-3-032-37679-4_10

1 Introduction

Seamless urban mobility is a cornerstone of modern city planning, yet navigating everyday infrastructure remains a profound challenge for the estimated 80 million manual wheelchair users worldwide [17]. While modern routing applications optimize for the shortest path or traffic avoidance, they consistently fail to account for accessibility factors such as sidewalk roughness, steep curb ramps, or transitions to historic cobblestones. For a manual wheelchair user, these surface variations are not merely uncomfortable; they directly correlate with increased physical exertion, upper-limb musculoskeletal degradation, and a heightened risk of tipping [3]. Consequently, the ultimate end goal of this research is to generate automated, high-fidelity route maps capable of providing safe, turn-by-turn accessible navigation.

Smartphone-based inertial crowd-sensing has emerged as a highly scalable paradigm for monitoring road surface quality without requiring specialized hardware [13,19]. By capturing tri-axial accelerometer and gyroscope data as a wheelchair traverses a path, these systems can implicitly measure the "vibrational footprint" of the underlying terrain [20]. However, the vast majority of existing machine learning approaches in this domain rely heavily on supervised learning methodologies [20]. These models require massive amounts of precisely annotated data, where every temporal window is manually labeled with a specific surface type. While this succeeds in highly controlled laboratory settings, manually annotating hundreds of kilometers of continuous urban transit is practically impossible, creating a massive bottleneck for global scalability [16].

Furthermore, applying these models across multiple geographic regions introduces severe domain shifts. The surface types across different continents vary widely (as shown in Fig. 2a and Fig. 2b), with European cities featuring significantly more historic architecture and complex cobblestone networks. A model trained exclusively on discrete, self-propelled wheelchair data on modern North American or Vietnamese sidewalks will inevitably struggle when evaluated on a continuous data stream collected from an aide-pushed wheelchair navigating 400-year-old European streets. The continuous European data exhibits vastly different kinematic patterns. However, leveraging the labeled USA and Vietnam data to learn the fundamental physics of wheelchair vibrations is critical to successfully clustering the unlabeled European road surfaces.

To overcome these limitations and dramatically reduce human annotation overhead without sacrificing performance, this paper introduces a paradigm shift toward semi-supervised representation learning. We present the *Global Wheelchair Surface (GWS)* dataset, a massive 183-hour, 52-million frame cross-continental dataset. It combined 13.6 h of highly-controlled, labeled discrete datasets from the USA and Vietnam with nearly 170 h (300 km) of continuous, unlabeled data collected longitudinally across four European cities in Germany, Austria, and France. To leverage this vast corpus, we propose `SurfaceEncoder`, a novel deep autoencoder framework. By jointly optimizing losses from both labeled and unlabeled data, the model learns robust surface vibration patterns. Incorporating the labeled USA/Vietnam data significantly helps the clustering of the unannotated European routes; The silhouette score improves substantially from 0.335 to 0.443 while we use labeled data. This enables large-scale path labeling with minimal human effort, which we successfully deploy into a live, LLM-augmented navigation application.

The primary contributions of this work to the Applied Data Science and smart-city infrastructure communities are as follows:

i. **The Global Wheelchair Surface (GWS) Dataset (Sect. 3):** We introduce comprehensive cross-continental wheelchair vibration datasets to date (183 h, 52M data points). It provides both labeled data (USA/Vietnam) and a massive amount of unlabeled data from Europe. Upon acceptance, the fully annotated dataset, along with our model's benchmarking code, will be open-sourced via GitHub to foster further research.
ii. **Novel Deep Representation Framework (Sect. 4):** We design and implement `SurfaceEncoder`, a specialized autoencoder for tri-axial inertial data that integrates Multi-Scale Temporal Convolutional Blocks (MSTCB), Cross-Axis Interaction Modules (CAIM), and Frequency-Aware Attention Gates (FAAG) to capture multi-modal vibrational patterns.
iii. **Reduced Annotation Overhead via Domain Adaptation (Sect. 5.3):** We demonstrate that a semi-supervised encoder successfully bridges the domain gap between labeled multi-region data and unlabeled surfaces. This approach boosts clustering silhouette scores by over 32%, proving that moderate labeled supervision vastly reduces manual annotation without sacrificing model quality.
iv. **Automated High-Fidelity Routemaps (Sect. 5.3):** We successfully identified surface types with the proposed `SurfaceEncoder`. Using the trained model, we establish a scalable pipeline that translates raw GPS and vibration clusters into annotated OpenStreetMap geometries. This annotated graph directly powers a LLM-based navigation system capable of generating surface-aware, turn-by-turn directions tailored specifically for wheelchair users.

2 Related Work

We studied background works based on the following three key criteria:

Wheelchair Surface Sensing. Early work by Iwasawa and Yairi [9] demonstrated that tri-axial accelerometers mounted on wheelchairs could distinguish rough from smooth surfaces using SVMs. The WheelShare system [20] classified surface types across six countries with 97.5% accuracy using supervised random forests, while Iwasawa et al. [18] applied deep convolutional neural networks (DCNNs) to learn road-surface representations. Piao et al. [16] introduced a weakly supervised method that leverages only GPS-derived positional information to learn surface features without manual annotation.

Smartphone Crowdsensing for Road Monitoring. Sattar et al. [13] provided a comprehensive survey of vibration-based road monitoring methods. Li and Goldberg [11] proposed a mobile crowdsensing system using GPS-referenced Z-axis accelerations to compute roughness indices. The RoadSurP system [1] introduced auto-orientation and adaptive thresholding algorithms for device- and vehicle-independent pothole detection. More recently, Yang et al. [8] presented MobiLiteNet, a lightweight deep learning framework for real-time road distress detection on mobile devices. Arroyo et al. [14] combined crowdsensing with deep learning to identify road-surface types and also to distinguish potholes from speed bumps.

Self-supervised and Semi-supervised Time Series Learning. TS2Vec [21] introduced hierarchical contrastive learning over augmented context views. MOMENT [6] compiled a large Time Series Pile for pre-training general-purpose models. Chronos [2] reframed forecasting as language modeling by tokenizing and quantizing time series, and TimesFM [4] proposed a decoder-only architecture pre-trained on 100 billion time points for zero-shot forecasting. For domain adaptation specifically, CLUDA [12] developed contrastive learning to align contextual representations between labeled source and unlabeled target time series.

Although these methods perform well within their respective domains, none directly address the problem of automatic surface labelling. While several representation learning models demonstrate strong performance in their original application settings, they are less effective when adapted to our specific use case of anonymous surface mapping, and that too at a very large scale. Our research goal is to mitigate this gap.

3 The Global Wheelchair Surface (GWS) Dataset

The *Global Wheelchair Surface (GWS)* dataset represents a multi-year, cross-continental effort to address the accessibility gap for over 80 million wheelchair users worldwide. Beyond technical problem, this work carries a deep social impact: providing the data-driven foundation for independent mobility and community participation. To achieve this, we created a huge dataset for wheelchair mobility, comprising over 52 million sensor frames and 183 h of transit across five countries (see Appendix A.1 in GitHub for detailed dataset description).

Social Impact and Extension Potential: While primarily designed for manual wheelchair navigation, the inherent biomechanical and surface-induced vibration signatures captured within the GWS dataset are highly extensible. The dataset bridges the gap between assistive technology and the broader smart-city ecosystem. The granular surface representations, such as the ability to distinguish between different grades of cobblestone, are directly applicable to various emerging domains. This data can inform surface-aware navigation for autonomous robotic delivery units, optimize safe routing for e-scooters, and provide crowdsourced telemetry for municipal infrastructure maintenance.

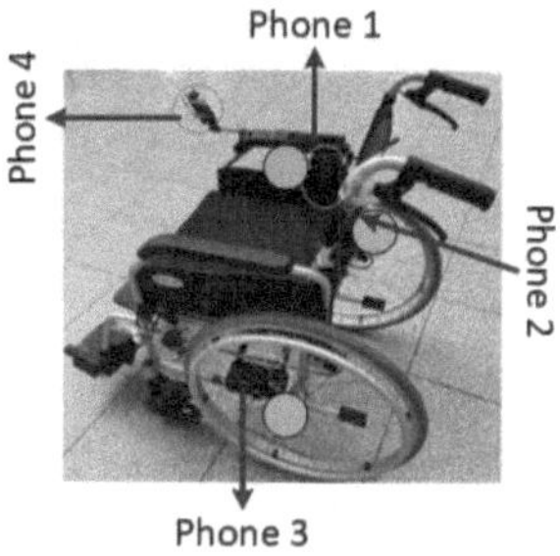

(a) Sensor placement

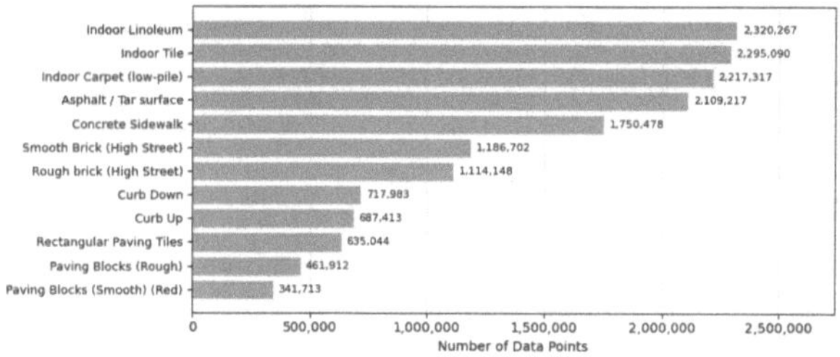

(b) Surface class distribution

Fig. 1. (a) Experimental setup for the European data collection. Three Motorola G4 Plus smartphones (Phones 1–3) were rigidly mounted at varying heights on the wheelchair frame to capture multi-level tri-axial inertial data (50 Hz) and GPS coordinates (5 Hz). A fourth device (Phone 4) was elevated via an armrest fixture to capture continuous video of the terrain. The sheer impracticality of manually annotating the resulting 170 h of video directly motivated the development of our semi-supervised `SurfaceEncoder` framework. (b) Wheelchair dataset class distribution for the USA & Vietnam.

3.1 Hardware Setup and Data Acquisition

When designing our data acquisition platform, we intentionally avoided specialized or prohibitively expensive laboratory equipment through consultations with NuMotion and National Seating and Mobility (NSM), two of the largest wheelchair suppliers in the United States. Industry experts cautioned that users have a general aversion to complex technology. Therefore, we exclusively utilized standard commercial smartphones (e.g., Samsung Galaxy and Motorola G-series devices), which include built-in inertial measurement unit (IMU) sensors. If surface detection can be accurately performed on an everyday smartphone, any wheelchair user can seamlessly contribute to city-wide crowd-sensing. To transform these commercial devices into high-fidelity vibration sensors, they were rigidly mounted to the wheelchair frame to ensure they "felt" the direct propagation of surface anomalies (see Fig. 1a). While the primary device was typically mounted on the armrest, mimicking natural user placement, we also experimented with multi-level placements, including the tipping lever near the rear wheels and the wheelchair's back pocket. This captured a rich spectrum of vibrational dynamics, from sharp wheel-impacts to muffled chassis reverberations. Inertial motion (accelerometer and gyroscope) was recorded at sampling rates between 50 Hz and 100 Hz, providing sufficient temporal resolution to capture rapid, transient vibrations over irregular terrains. Finally, we supplemented the sensor suite with an elevated smartphone mounted on an extension rod to record synchronized video of the leading wheels, establishing a visual ground truth for surface transitions.

(a) Labeled Surfaces in USA and Vietnam

(b) Unlabeled Surfaces in Europe

Fig. 2. (a) Surfaces used for data collection: **in the USA:** (a) Rough brick road without gap, (b) Concrete sidewalk, (c) Brick road without gap, (d) Red paver block sidewalk, (e) Asphalt, (f) indoor Carpet, (g) indoor Linoleum, (h) indoor Ceramic tiles, (i and j) Up & down curbs (k) Rough brick road with gaps. **in Vietnam:** (l to p) different types of outdoor paver blocks and tiles. (b) Surfaces encountered in Europe during continuous data collection: Few types of tiles, smooth and rough paver blocks, cobblestones, grass, and gravel.

3.2 Global Collection: The Domain Adaptation Challenge

To effectively support our semi-supervised domain adaptation framework, the GWS dataset is strictly partitioned into two distinct structural domains, encapsulating different aspects of real-world mobility (summarized in Tables 1 and 2).

Labeled Data (USA and Vietnam): This subset consists of highly controlled, manually labeled discrete recordings where participants self-propelled their wheelchairs across isolated, pre-selected surfaces. Containing approximately 13.6 h of data (31.6 million frames), this corpus encompasses 12 distinct surface categories - ranging from smooth indoor tiles and concrete sidewalks to rough paving blocks and curb transitions (see Fig. 1b). These trials were con-

Table 1. Characteristics of Global Collection Sites. The dataset provides a mix of supervised surface labels (USA, Vietnam) and a massive unsupervised continuous surface vibration data pool (Europe).

Feature	USA & Vietnam	Europe (EU)
Cities	One USA town; Ho Chi Minh City	Paris, Dresden, Nuremberg, Salzburg
Strategy	Discrete (individual surfaces)	Continuous (long-distance traces)
Scale	13:39 h	300+ km (170 h)
Propulsion	Manual (self-propelled)	Manual (pushed by aide)
Sensors	IMU (100 Hz)	IMU (50 Hz), GPS, Video
Labels	Fully labeled	Unlabeled

ducted on one surface at a time, and the surface manually labeled. They provide fundamental, cleanly segmented vibrational signatures.

Unlabeled Data (Europe): In contrast, the European subset introduces a massive, continuous corpus designed to challenge models with severe real-world complexities. Collected longitudinally across Austria, France, and Germany, this unlabeled subset contains nearly 170 h (noisy with regular wheelchair movement, including stalled) of continuous transit data (20 million frames). The wheelchair was pushed by an aide across over 300 km of uninterrupted urban navigation. Furthermore, to truly reflect the unpredictable nature of real-world mobility, this continuous corpus captures severe payload and kinematic variations. The propulsion was shared among multiple aides, introducing natural fluctuations in walking speed, stride length, and applied force. Additionally, the dataset contains dynamic payload shifts, including dual-occupancy (e.g., a child riding alongside the primary user). These factors profoundly alter the wheelchair's center of mass, suspension dampening, and tire compression, providing a rigorous testbed for a model's ability to separate terrain signatures from user-induced noise.

Table 2. Overall GWS Dataset Summary Across the Globe

Category	Value
Total Frames	**52,146,304**
Labeled Frames (USA, Vietnam)	31,612,466
Unlabeled Frames (Austria, France, Germany)	20,533,838
Total Recording Duration	**183:27:46**
Labeled Duration	13:39:40
Unlabeled Duration	169:48:06
Labeled Surface Types (12 Total)	Smooth Paving Blocks, Concrete Sidewalk, Smooth Brick, Rough Brick, Asphalt/Tar, Indoor Carpet, Indoor Linoleum, Indoor Tile, Curb Up, Curb Down, Rectangular Paving Tiles, Rough Paving Blocks
Labeled Devices	Redmi Note 7 (variations), Samsung Galaxy J7, Samsung Galaxy S7, Samsung Galaxy S9
Unlabeled Device Identifiers	Phone 7, Phone 8, Phone 9

This vast, unsegmented corpus introduces critical domain shifts. It captures varying moving speeds, postural changes, and continuous surface transitions across historic environments, such as the Avenue des Champs-Élysées in Paris and the complex cobblestone networks of Nuremberg. This creates the ultimate high-level domain adaptation challenge: `SurfaceEncoder` must learn the intrinsic physics of a surface from the controlled, self-propelled North American/Asian data, and successfully generalize that knowledge to cluster and map the vast, unlabeled, aide-pushed stretches of Europe.

4 `SurfaceEncoder` : Framework for Vibration Based Road Surface Clustering

We present `SurfaceEncoder`, a novel deep autoencoder architecture designed for semi-supervised road surface clustering from three-axis accelerometer vibration signals. It integrates three purpose-built neural modules within an encoder-decoder framework, enabling the model to learn discriminative latent representations of road surfaces without requiring exhaustive manual annotation. The architecture is illustrated in Fig. 3.

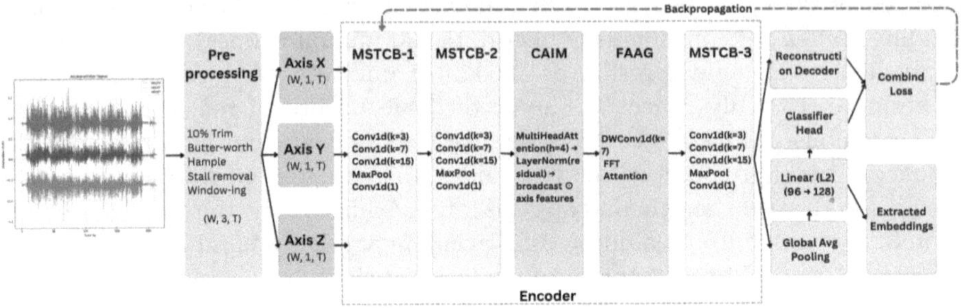

Fig. 3. `SurfaceEncoder` Architecture.

The pipeline consists of three stages. In the first stage, the data are processed using multiple filters and algorithms. In the second stage, a deep encoder transforms the preprocessed windowed accelerometer signals into a compact d-dimensional embedding. In the third stage, a convolutional decoder reconstructs the original three-axis signal from the pre-pooling temporal feature map using a log-cosh reconstruction loss. A classification head is attached to the embedding to enable semi-supervised learning from labeled samples. After training, the learned embeddings are ℓ_2-normalized, reduced using Principal Component Analysis (PCA), and analyzed using various clustering algorithms.

4.1 Pre-processing and Input Representation

Raw wheelchair-mounted accelerometer recordings were subjected to a multi-stage preprocessing pipeline. First, signal edges were trimmed to remove start and end artifacts (10% of samples). The signals were then filtered using a fourth-order Butterworth filter consisting of a high-pass component (0.3 Hz) to remove gravity-related drift and a low-pass component (25 Hz) to suppress high-frequency noise. Impulse noise was further reduced using a Hampel filter applied independently to each axis. Flat or motionless segments were removed using a stalled-region detection algorithm. Finally, recordings collected at different sampling frequencies (50 Hz, 100 Hz, 150 Hz, and 500 Hz) were resampled to a uniform sampling rate of 100 Hz using polyphase resampling. Figure 4 visualizes before and after preprocessing state of an example signal (see Appendix A.2 in GitHub for detailed data processing pipeline and parameters).

We performed statistical comparisons between raw and processed signals to evaluate the effectiveness of the preprocessing pipeline. In the raw data, the Y and Z axes exhibited strong gravitational offsets (means -0.593 and 0.889),

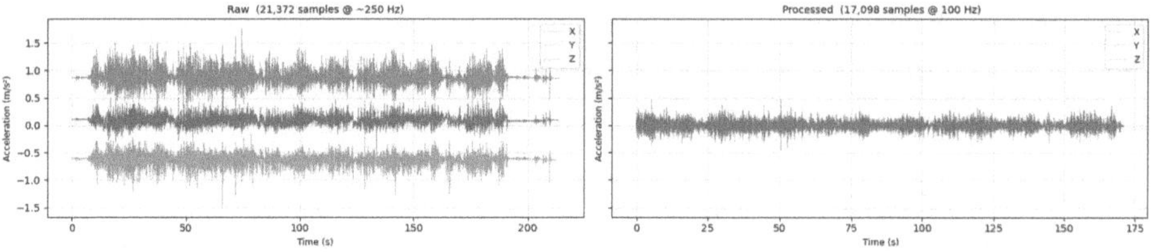

Fig. 4. Raw vs. processed accelerometer signals. Signals were trimmed, denoised, gravity-corrected to zero-center the axes, and resampled to 100 Hz.

which collapsed to near zero after processing (0.008 and −0.017), confirming removal of the static gravity component. Standard deviations decreased across all axes (e.g., X: 0.138 to 0.115, Y: 0.145 to 0.104, Z: 0.202 to 0.133), indicating noise suppression. RMS values on the Y and Z axes decreased by 83% and 85%, while variance reductions of up to 77% were observed for the magnitude signal. Outlier rates also declined substantially (from 14.28% to 3.03%). Distributional metrics showed reduced skewness and kurtosis, producing more symmetric signals while preserving heavy-tailed impact events. Non-parametric tests further confirmed significant distributional changes ($p \ll 0.05$), with large effect sizes on the Y and Z axes ($|d| > 4.7$) (see Appendix A.3 in GitHub for detailed statistical analysis).

After preprocessing, accelerometer recordings were segmented into fixed-length windows of 1024 samples across the three spatial axes. At a sampling rate of 100 Hz, each window corresponds to approximately 10 s of data. Each axis was independently z-normalized. Windows were partitioned using stratified 80/20 train/test splits to preserve class proportions. Twelve surface types were merged into seven categories based on similarity in vibration patterns.

4.2 Encoder Architecture

The encoder is composed of three principal sub-modules: the Multi-Scale Temporal Convolutional Block (MSTCB), the Cross-Axis Interaction Module (CAIM), and the Frequency-Aware Attention Gate (FAAG) (see Appendix B in GitHub for detailed architecture).

Module A: Multi-scale Temporal Convolutional Block (MSTCB). The Multi-Scale Temporal Convolutional Block serves as the primary feature extraction module in `SurfaceEncoder`. Road surface vibrations exhibit characteristic patterns at multiple temporal scales. A single-kernel convolutional layer is insufficient to capture this multi-scale structure; MSTCB addresses this through a four-branch parallel architecture inspired by Inception-style modules [5] and multi-scale temporal convolution networks.

Given an input feature map $\mathbf{h} \in \mathbb{R}^{C_{\text{in}} \times T}$, three convolutional branches with kernel sizes $k \in \{3, 7, 15\}$ capture fine, medium, and coarse-scale temporal patterns respectively, each applying SAME padding to preserve the temporal dimension, $\mathbf{b}_k(\mathbf{h}) = ReLU\Big(BN\big(Conv1d_k(\mathbf{h})\big)\Big), \quad k \in \{3, 7, 15\}$. A fourth max-pooling branch provides local smoothing. All four branches are concatenated to form the block output, with a residual connection added between the input and the concatenated output.

`SurfaceEncoder` employs three MSTCB instances. For each of the three input axes, the single-channel input $(W, 1, T)$ is passed through two sequential MSTCB layers whose weights are shared across axes, enforcing axis-equivariant feature extraction. Axis-specific modulation is deferred to the subsequent CAIM module. The three resulting per-axis feature maps are concatenated along the channel dimension to form a tensor of shape $(B, 3C, T)$, which is passed through the CAIM and FAAG attention modules. A third MSTCB instance is applied after CAIM and FAAG to refine the cross-axis attended feature maps.

Module B: Frequency-Aware Attention Gate (FAAG). Vibration signals are inherently frequency-structured: different road surfaces are characterised by distinct spectral signatures in addition to their temporal patterns [13]. The Frequency-Aware Attention Gate explicitly incorporates spectral information into the feature selection process by combining a temporal attention gate with a frequency-domain channel gate, operating on $\mathbf{F}_{\text{cat}} \in \mathbb{R}^{3C\times T}$.

FAAG is made of dual gating architecture. The first one is a temporal gate depthwise separable convolution with kernel size 7 and sigmoid activation produces per-timestamp, per-channel attention weights, where each channel is convolved independently with its own kernel $\mathbf{G}_{\text{temp}} = \sigma\big(Conv1d_7(\mathbf{F}_{cat})\big) \in \mathbb{R}^{3C\times T}$. The second one is frequency gate, the real-valued magnitude spectrum is computed via the real-input Fast Fourier Transform along the temporal axis, $\mathbf{M}_{c,f} = \big|rFFT(\mathbf{F}_{cat,c,:})\big|_f \in \mathbb{R}^{3C\times F}, \quad F = \lfloor T/2 \rfloor + 1$. A two-layer MLP with a bottleneck structure maps the per-channel spectra to a scalar gate per channel, which is averaged over the frequency dimension and broadcast along the temporal dimension to form $\mathbf{G}_{\text{freq}} \in \mathbb{R}^{3C\times T}$. The final gated output is the element-wise product of the input with both gates, $FAAG(\mathbf{F}_{\text{cat}}) = \mathbf{F}_{cat} \odot \mathbf{G}_{temp} \odot \mathbf{G}_{freq} \in \mathbb{R}^{3C\times T}$.

Module C: Cross-Axis Interaction Module (CAIM). CAIM models inter-axis dependencies through multi-head self-attention (MHSA) [15] over the axis dimension for our multivariate accelerometer data. Given the three per-axis feature maps $\{\mathbf{f}^{(a)}\}_{a\in\{X,Y,Z\}}$ of shape (B, C, T), CAIM first computes a global average pool over the temporal dimension to produce per-axis summary vectors, $\bar{\mathbf{f}}^{(a)} = \frac{1}{T}\sum_{t=1}^{T} \mathbf{f}^{(a)}_{:,t} \in \mathbb{R}^C, \quad a \in \{X, Y, Z\}$. These are stacked into a sequence matrix $\mathbf{S} = [\bar{\mathbf{f}}^{(X)}; \bar{\mathbf{f}}^{(Y)}; \bar{\mathbf{f}}^{(Z)}] \in \mathbb{R}^{3\times C}$, which is processed by MHSA. A residual connection with layer normalisation yields the refined axis representations, $\hat{\mathbf{S}} = LayerNorm\big(MHSA(\mathbf{S}) + \mathbf{S}\big) \in \mathbb{R}^{3\times C}$. The resulting attention weight matrix $\mathbf{A}_{CAIM} \in \mathbb{R}^{3\times 3}$ quantifies pairwise interaction strengths between axes: entry A_{ij} represents the degree to which axis i attends to axis j. Each refined axis-level vector is broadcast back to full temporal resolution and used to element-wise scale the corresponding feature map, $\tilde{\mathbf{f}}_{c,t}^{(a)} = \mathbf{f}_{c,t}^{(a)} \cdot \hat{s}_c^{(a)}, \quad \forall\, c \in \{1,\ldots,C\},\ t \in \{1,\ldots,T\}$. This allows informative axes to be amplified and uninformative axes to be suppressed in a data-driven manner. The three attended feature maps are concatenated along the channel axis to form $\mathbf{F}_{\text{cat}} \in \mathbb{R}^{3C\times T}$.

4.3 Decoder Architecture and Loss Functions

Decoder. The decoder serves as a regularization mechanism during training: by requiring the network to reconstruct the full input signal, it forces the encoder to retain sufficient structural information. The decoder operates on the *pre-pooling temporal feature map* $\mathbf{h}^{(3)} \in \mathbb{R}^{C\times T}$ rather than the bottleneck embedding $\mathbf{z}$. Reconstructing from the globally-pooled embedding would force the decoder to predict near-zero values on Z-normalized signals. The reconstruction head consists of three stacked 1D convolutions with SAME padding that progressively reduce the channel count.

$$\hat{\mathbf{X}} = Conv1d_1\Big(ReLU\big(Conv1d_2(\mathrm{ReLU}\big(Conv1d_3(\mathbf{h}^{(3)})\big))\big)\Big) \in \mathbb{R}^{3\times T},$$

Reconstruction Loss. The reconstruction objective is the log-cosh loss, which provides a smooth interpolation between the MSE behaviour for small residuals and MAE behaviour for large residuals.

$$\mathcal{L}_{\text{rec}} = \frac{1}{N}\sum_{i=1}^{N} \log\!\big(\cosh(x_i - \hat{x}_i)\big)$$

Auxiliary Classification Head. `SurfaceEncoder` leverages a lightweight auxiliary classification head to provide supervisory signal. The classifier is a two-layer feed-forward network that projects the ℓ_2-normalised embedding from $d = 128$ dimensions to $d/2 = 64$ via a ReLU-activated linear layer with dropout (rate 0.3), followed by a final linear projection to the number of target super-classes K. The auxiliary loss is categorical cross-entropy applied only to labelled samples within each mini-batch. The total training loss is a weighted combination of the reconstruction and classification terms: $\mathcal{L}_{\text{total}} = \mathcal{L}_{\text{rec}} + \lambda \cdot \mathcal{L}_{\text{cls}}$ where $\lambda = (1.0, 0.5, 0.0)$ controls the contribution of the classification loss across different model configurations.

5 Empirical Evaluation and Results

5.1 Model Training and Cluster Generation

Training Protocol. `SurfaceEncoder` is trained using the Adam optimiser with an initial learning rate of 10^{-3} ($\beta_1 = 0.9$, $\beta_2 = 0.999$), embedding dimension $d = 128$, MSTCB channels $C = 96$, MHSA heads $H = 4$, and classification loss weight $\lambda = (1.0, 0.5, 0.0)$. A ReduceLROnPlateau scheduler halves the learning rate after 15 epochs of no validation improvement, with a minimum learning rate of 10^{-5}. Gradient norms are clipped to 5.0 to stabilise attention layers. Training stops early if validation loss does not improve for 50 epochs, restoring the best checkpoint. PCA is then applied to embeddings, retaining 95% variance before clustering.

Embedding Extraction and Cluster Generation. Following training, all windows are passed through the encoder to extract ℓ_2-normalised embeddings. Principal Component Analysis (PCA) is applied to the training embeddings, retaining components that explain 95% of the total variance; the fitted transformation is then applied to both training and test embeddings. The optimal number of clusters K is determined using the silhouette method. Six clustering algorithms are evaluated at the selected K^*: *K-Means* with 20 random restarts; *Agglomerative Clustering* with average linkage and cosine affinity; a *Gaussian Mixture Model (GMM)* trained via Expectation–Maximisation with hard assignments obtained from the maximum posterior responsibility; a *DBSCAN* variant with automatic ε-selection based on the k-NN distance elbow criterion; *PSO Clustering*, a global-search alternative to K-Means that minimises the within-cluster sum of squares; and the *Gravitational Search Algorithm (GSA)*, a physics-inspired metaheuristic that treats candidate centroid sets as agents interacting under a simulated gravitational field. All methods use cosine distance for similarity computation.

5.2 Performance Evaluation and Metrics

Performance Matrices. Cluster quality is evaluated using the Silhouette coefficient (Sil), Davies-Bouldin index (DB), Calinski-Harabasz index (CH), and Dunn index (Dunn), which collectively measure cluster cohesion and separation. When ground truth labels are available, clustering alignment is assessed using Adjusted Rand Index (ARI) and Normalised Mutual Information (NMI), which quantify agreement between predicted clusters and true labels. Cluster-to-surface mapping is performed via majority voting. (see Appendix C in GitHub for rigorous visual comparisons and model evaluation).

Performance Evaluation. Table 3 presents the clustering models' performance on embeddings generated by `SurfaceEncoder`, with the optimal number of clusters determined to be $K = 7$ based on the highest Silhouette score. Among all methods, K-Means achieves the best overall performance on the semi-supervised labeled setting. The randomized baselines (RandAssign, RandClust) produce near-zero or negative scores across all metrics. On unlabeled data, clustering quality decreases expectedly due to a larger sample size and class imbalance. The unsupervised variant shows further decline across all methods, with DBScan even producing a negative Silhouette, indicating that the classifier loss is essential for learning well-separated representations. Overall, the semi-supervised configuration ($\lambda = 1$) consistently outperforms the unsupervised variant ($\lambda = 0$),

Table 3. Clustering performance comparison across three model configurations: Semi-Supervised on labeled data **SS (L)**, Semi-Supervised on unlabeled data **SS** ($\lambda = 1$), and Unsupervised **US** ($\lambda = 0$). The results indicate that the semi-supervised (SS) model outperforms the unsupervised (US) model. Among the evaluated clustering algorithms, K-Means achieves the best overall performance; while some models outperform it on specific metrics, the differences remain marginal.

Model	Silhouette ↑			DB ↓			CH ↑			Dunn ↑			ARI ↑	NMI ↑
	SS(L)	SS	US	SS(L)	SS	US	SS(L)	SS	US	SS(L)	SS	US	SS(L)	SS(L)
KMeans	**0.632**	**0.443**	**0.335**	**0.819**	**1.335**	**2.337**	**956.7**	**4685.3**	**1867.0**	**0.943**	**0.466**	**0.261**	**0.893**	**0.895**
Agg	0.616	0.360	0.154	0.872	1.448	2.260	849.5	4924.7	896.7	0.882	0.492	**0.292**	0.893	0.894
GMM	0.623	0.406	0.215	0.814	1.440	2.842	945.6	5310.6	1264.0	0.938	0.491	0.265	0.888	0.889
DBScan	0.594	0.403	−0.262	**0.789**	1.385	**1.685**	802.7	4244.3	6.889	0.831	0.511	0.214	**0.923**	**0.922**
POS/PSO	0.514	0.401	0.204	1.183	1.410	2.579	710.6	3671.0	1332.3	0.350	0.471	0.265	0.732	0.817
RandAssign	−0.039	−0.012	—	33.556	222.248	—	1.069	0.682	—	0.021	0.003	—	−0.000	0.006
GSA	0.467	**0.457**	0.196	1.275	**1.286**	2.722	632.4	4161.8	1273.7	0.338	**0.502**	0.246	0.645	0.738
RandClust	0.272	0.289	—	1.478	1.678	—	297.4	**6432.5**	—	0.379	0.380	—	0.446	0.560

↑ higher is better; ↓ lower is better

confirming that even limited label information substantially improves representation quality, and notably, labeled data from the USA generalizes well to previously unseen European data. Furthermore, we projected the high-dimensional embeddings into two-dimensional space using t-SNE and UMAP. Both projections of the labeled data (see Fig. 5) show well-separated clusters aligned with ground-truth classes, with *Asphalt + Indoor Carpet* (c1) and *Concrete Sidewalk* (c6) forming the most compact groups, while *Brick* (c0) and *Rect. Tiles / Paving Blocks* (c5) exhibit slight overlap due to similar surface textures. In the unlabeled European dataset, both t-SNE and UMAP projections (see Fig. 6)) consistently recover five clusters with stable geometry across methods with all major regions. Which reflecting the prevalence of common European pedestrian surfaces such as asphalt, concrete pavements, and cobblestone commonly found in historic urban centres. The reduced cluster count relative to the USA-Vietnam dataset indicates fewer distinct surface types in the European data.

Baseline Comparison. Table 4 `SurfaceEncoder` is compared against several state-of-the-art embedding generation methods, including TS2Vec, raw statistical feature baselines, and foundation models such as Chronos and MOMENT. Despite being designed for general-purpose temporal embeddings, these models are consistently outperformed by `SurfaceEncoder` across all clustering metrics. This highlights the advantage of its task-specific architecture and semi-supervised training for surface vibration representation, achieving performance substantially higher than competing embeddings and a 32% improvement over the best-performing raw feature clustering baseline.

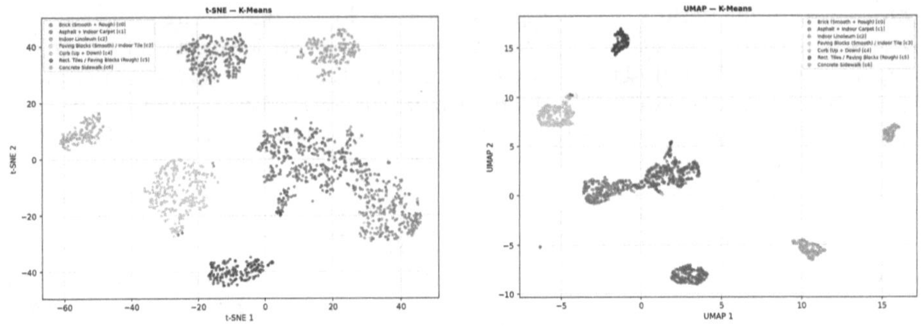

(a) t-SNE projection of K-Means clusters on curated USA/Vietnam data with original class ($K = 7$). Most clusters are well separated, although clusters c_1 and c_2 exhibit slight overlap.

(b) UMAP projection of K-Means clusters on curated USA/Vietnam data with original class ($K = 7$). Clusters c_1 and c_2 exhibit slight overlap on their shared boundary.

Fig. 5. Labeled USA/Vietnam dataset clustered with K-Means using the original number of vibration classes ($K = 7$), showing well-separated macro-clusters across both projection methods, reflecting the higher quality of the labeled data.

5.3 Applications on Wheelchair Accessible Routing

Wheelchair users have specific requirements during navigation, particularly regarding the surface conditions encountered along a route. Accurate knowledge of surface types is essential for generating reliable step-by-step navigation instructions, yet manually labeling large geographic areas is highly impractical. To overcome this, our semi-supervised approach directly translates raw sensor data into interpretable surface labels. Each 10 s GPS timestamped vibration window is assigned a surface ID by mapping clusters to surface types using majority voting against the labeled source domain, producing high-fidelity and interpretable labels for each GPS segment.

These surface-labeled segments are then seamlessly fused with OpenStreetMap (OSM), utilizing our established routing algorithm [7]. Within this annotated map, each routing-graph edge inherits the surface type detected by `SurfaceEncoder`, while crosswalks are additionally identified through our distinct few-shot learning method [10]. This enriched mapping framework serves as the foundation for our turn-by-turn navigation system. An integrated Large Language Model (LLM), augmented with this surface knowledge base and OSM data, generates surface-aware, natural-language directions (see Fig. 7). The system intelligently routes users along optimal surfaces, and proactively flags surface transitions at each waypoint.

This pipeline effectively closes the applied loop from the dataset to the application domain, the model trains on raw sensor data, generalizes cross-continentally without requiring manual annotation, and directly powers a live, user-facing navigation system. Furthermore, because the entire data collection system operates efficiently on commodity mobile handsets, such as the Motorola

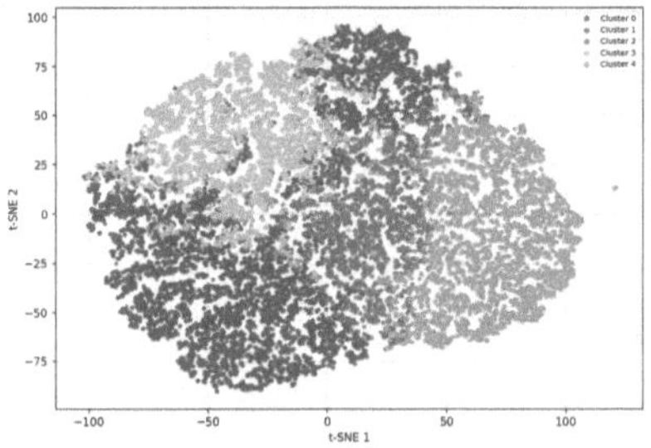

(a) **SurfaceEncoder:** t-SNE Projection of K-Means clusters on unlabeled Europe data embeddings with best silhouette ($K = 5$). All five macro-regions are clearly visible with few overlaps.

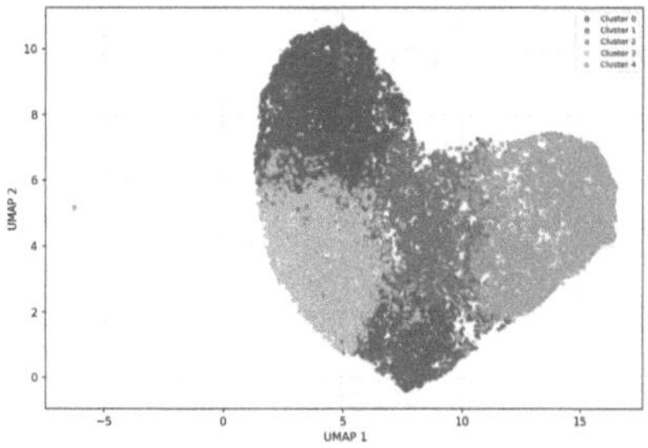

(b) **SurfaceEncoder:** UMAP projection of unlabeled Europe data embeddings with best silhouette ($K = 5$). We have a clearer boundary for every five classes, indicating stable model performance.

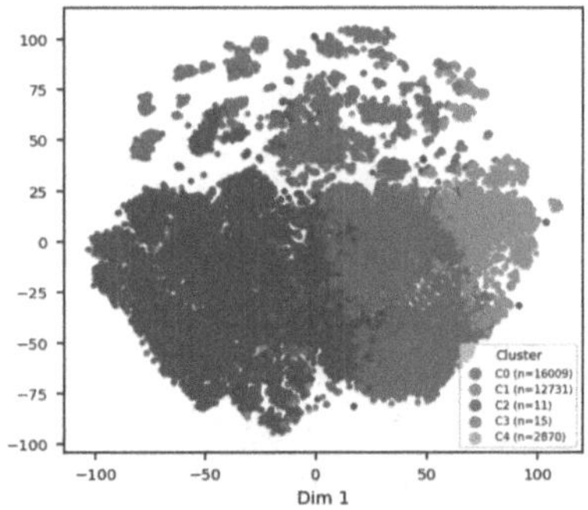

(c) **Handcrafted:** t-SNE projection of the same European data reveals only three dominant clusters C0, C1, and C4 as clearly distinguishable.

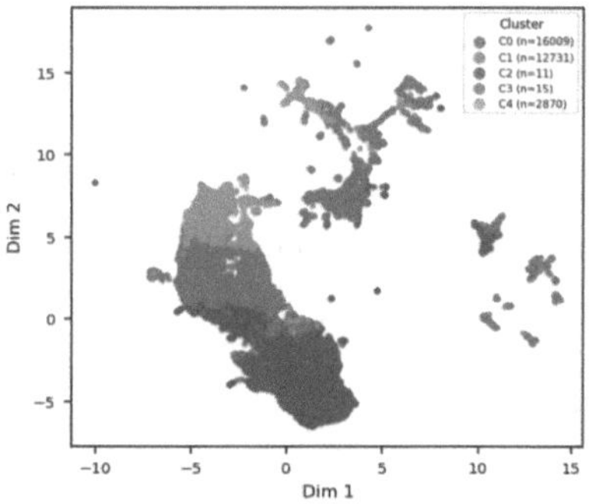

(d) **Handcrafted:** UMAP produces scattered patterns rather than forming clear, continuous boundaries.

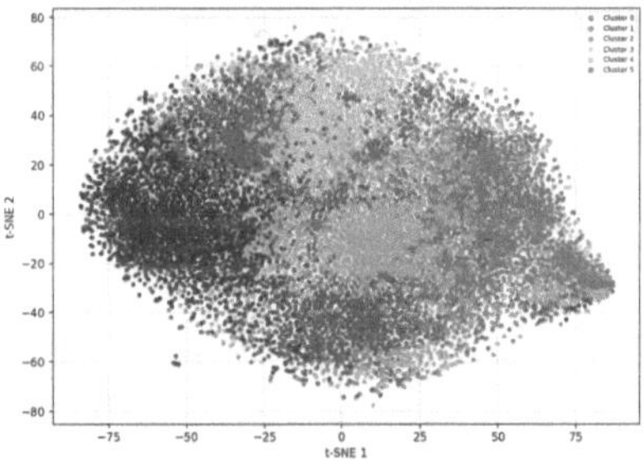

(e) **TS2Vec:** t-SNE projects heavily overlapping clusters with no separable structures.

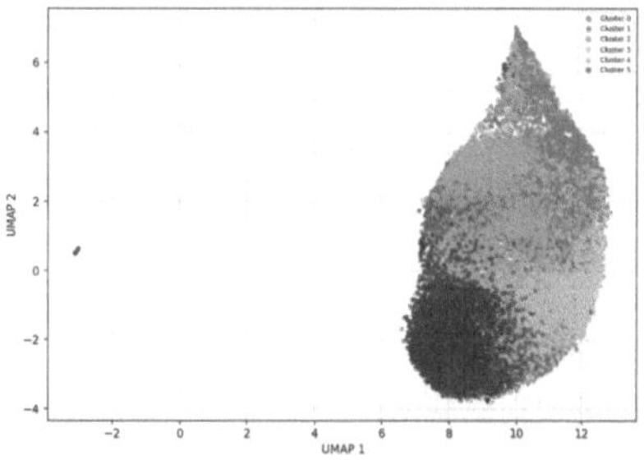

(f) **TS2Vec:** UMAP representation also projects scattered, indistinguishable classes.

Fig. 6. t-SNE (left) and UMAP (right) projections of `SurfaceEncoder` (a, b), handcrafted features (c, d) and TS2Vec (e, f) on the unlabeled European dataset. `SurfaceEncoder` produces the most geometrically coherent and well-separated embedding structure among all projections, outperforming the nearest competing method by 32%, despite some cluster overlap due to data noise.

Table 4. Clustering evaluation results across models and methods. The `SurfaceEncoder` achieves the strongest overall performance, while raw extracted features yield competitive but notably inferior results.

Model	Metric	K-Means	Agg.	GMM	DBSCAN	PSO	Rand.A	GSA	Rand.C
`SurfaceEnc`	Sil ↑	**0.44**	0.36	0.41	0.40	0.40	–0.01	0.46	0.29
	DB ↓	**1.33**	1.45	1.44	1.39	1.41	222.2	1.29	1.68
	CH ↑	4685.3	4924.7	5310.6	4244.3	3671.0	0.68	4161.8	6432.5
	Dunn ↑	**0.47**	0.49	0.49	0.51	0.47	0.00	0.50	0.38
ts2vec	Sil ↑	0.05	0.08	0.08	—	-0.07	–0.01	–0.03	0.02
	DB ↓	3.38	3.06	3.14	—	4.71	81.1	4.04	5.08
	CH ↑	360.8	355.9	245.7	—	206.7	0.91	310.2	539.0
	Dunn ↑	0.03	0.09	0.08	—	0.02	0.00	0.03	0.03
TimesFM	Sil ↑	0.10	0.09	0.09	–0.11	0.09	–0.00	0.07	0.07
	DB ↓	3.32	3.35	3.51	3.21	3.49	106.6	3.76	3.95
	CH ↑	1093.5	936.4	1029.3	285.8	1006.3	0.90	887.1	809.0
	Dunn ↑	0.28	0.29	0.26	0.21	0.27	0.01	0.24	0.22
Chronos	Sil ↑	0.04	-0.08	0.01	—	0.07	–0.00	0.09	0.17
	DB ↓	2.29	2.44	3.55	—	2.96	130.4	2.26	2.64
	CH ↑	1951.1	775.2	1088.1	—	1514.1	0.72	1680.4	2538.6
	Dunn ↑	0.35	0.34	0.23	—	0.25	0.01	0.38	0.31
MOMENT	Sil ↑	0.16	0.29	0.23	—	0.23	-0.00	0.16	0.09
	DB ↓	2.31	2.17	2.57	—	1.94	135.0	2.19	3.33
	CH ↑	3025.9	2716.4	2731.0	—	2259.4	0.70	2586.3	2941.0
	Dunn ↑	0.33	0.34	0.26	—	0.35	0.01	0.36	0.16
Raw Feature	Sil ↑	0.33	0.16	0.09	0.40	0.24	-0.00	0.09	0.26
	DB ↓	1.14	1.81	2.33	0.61	1.57	141.8	2.72	2.72
	CH ↑	**6454.9**	3710.3	3746.7	53.0	4590.4	0.90	3828.6	2654.9
	Dunn ↑	0.10	0.39	0.18	1.09	0.41	0.01	0.20	0.24

↑ higher is better; ↓ lower is better

G4 and Samsung Galaxy, any user can seamlessly become a sensor contributor at zero extra cost.

6 Conclusion and Future Works

This paper introduces `SurfaceEncoder`, a deep autoencoder framework for semi-supervised representation learning of wheelchair-induced surface vibrations, along with the Global Wheelchair Surface (GWS) dataset, a 183-h, 52-million frame cross-continental dataset spanning five countries and 300 km of unlabeled European footpaths. Our work addresses two major challenges in accessible routing: the high cost of manually annotating large-scale urban mobility data and the

Fig. 7: LLM-powered accessible routing and navigation system

User: Is there an accessible route from location A to destination B?

- Route generated through Accessible Routing Algorithm
- Sidewalk surface classified using SurfaceEncoder
- Navigational Instructions generated through LLM augmented with OSM Data

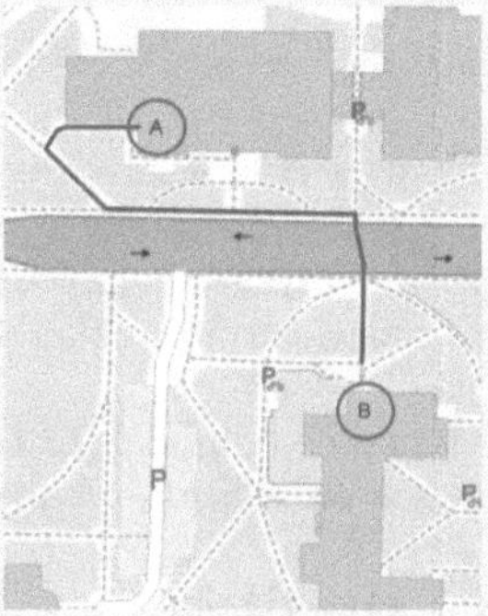

1. **Continue on Concrete Path** Follow the concrete path for about 9 feet. A curb ramp should be available. After this stretch, turn left again.
2. **Move Along Concrete Sidewalk** Proceed along another concrete sidewalk for roughly 20 feet. Be mindful of any changes in the surface. At the end of this section, turn left.
3. **Follow the Path** Continue along the concrete path for about 77 feet. When you reach the end, turn left.
4. **Proceed Further** Travel for approximately 222 feet on the concrete surface. At the end of this segment, make a right turn.
5. **Cross the Road Safely** Cross the asphalt road using the available crossing signal and zebra crossing for about 34 feet. Wait for the signal to indicate that it's safe to cross.
6. **Final Stretch to destination B** Continue straight on the concrete sidewalk for approximately 90 feet. The path should remain level and free of barriers till your destination.

Fig. 7. LLM-powered accessible routing and navigation system

domain shift that arises when transferring models across geographically diverse environments. Experiments show that `SurfaceEncoder`, through its MSTCB, CAIM, FAAG, and log-cosh decoder, learns discriminative vibrational embeddings that beat every large time-series foundation model baseline (including TS2Vec, Chronos, MOMENT, and TimesFM) by $\geq$0.28 silhouette points, in this specific domain. The semi-supervised model incorporating labeled data from the USA and Vietnam improved the silhouette score on unlabeled European data by over 32% (from 0.335 to 0.443).

Beyond clustering, this work delivers a fully deployed end-to-end application, which directly converts these cluster assignments into GPS-annotated, surface-aware, turn-by-turn accessible navigation, successfully demonstrated live on a real campus route. Ultimately, the massive GWS dataset, the principled `SurfaceEncoder` architecture, and the routemap pipeline stand as robust, independent contributions to the community. Future work will focus on incorporating sequential context to better capture surface transitions, refining data preprocessing and noise removal strategies, leveraging active learning to further reduce annotation effort, enabling real-time mobile inference for crowd-sourced accessibility mapping, and integrating complementary sensing modalities such as camera imagery, mmWave radar, or LiDAR to improve fine-grained surface discrimination.

Acknowledgment. This work was developed in part under a grant from the National Institute on Disability, Independent Living, and Rehabilitation Research (NIDILRR grant number 90IFDV0024). NIDILRR is a Center within the Administration for Community Living (ACL), Department of Health and Human Services (HHS). The content of this work does not necessarily represent the policy of NIDILRR, ACL, HHS, and you should not assume endorsement by the Federal Government.

References

1. Alam, M.Y., et al.: Crowdsourcing from the true crowd: device, vehicle, road-surface and driving independent road profiling from smartphone sensors. Pervasive Mob. Comput. **61**, 101103 (2020)
2. Ansari, A.F., et al.: Chronos: learning the language of time series. arXiv preprint arXiv:2403.07815 (2024)
3. Candiotti, J.L., Neti, A., Sivakanthan, S., Cooper, R.A.: Analysis of whole-body vibration using electric powered wheelchairs on surface transitions. Vibration **5**(1), 98–109 (2022)
4. Das, A., Kong, W., Sen, R., Zhou, Y.: A decoder-only foundation model for time-series forecasting. In: Forty-First International Conference on Machine Learning (2024)
5. Fawaz, H.I., et al.: Inceptiontime: finding alexnet for time series classification. Data Min. Knowl. Disc. **34**(6), 1936–1962 (2020)
6. Goswami, M., Szafer, K., Choudhry, A., Cai, Y., Li, S., Dubrawski, A.: Moment: a family of open time-series foundation models. arXiv preprint arXiv:2402.03885 (2024)
7. Hossain, A.M., et al.: A smart and barrier-aware navigation system for wheelchair routing. In: 2025 IEEE 22nd International Conference on Mobile Ad-Hoc and Smart Systems (MASS), pp. 717–722. IEEE (2025)
8. Hu, Y., Chen, N., Hou, Y., Lin, X., Jing, B., Liu, P.: Lightweight deep learning for real-time road distress detection on mobile devices. Nat. Commun. **16**(1), 4212 (2025)
9. Iwasawa, Y., Yairi, I.E.: Life-logging of wheelchair driving on web maps for visualizing potential accidents and incidents. In: Pacific Rim International Conference on Artificial Intelligence, pp. 157–169. Springer (2012)
10. Karki, S., Han, E., Mahmud, N., Bhunia, S., Femiani, J., Raychoudhury, V.: Omniacc: personalized accessibility assistant using generative ai. arXiv preprint arXiv:2509.07220 (2025)
11. Li, X., Goldberg, D.W.: Toward a mobile crowdsensing system for road surface assessment. Comput. Environ. Urban Syst. **69**, 51–62 (2018)
12. Ozyurt, Y., Feuerriegel, S., Zhang, C.: Contrastive learning for unsupervised domain adaptation of time series. arXiv preprint arXiv:2206.06243 (2022)
13. Sattar, S., Li, S., Chapman, M.: Road surface monitoring using smartphone sensors: a review. Sensors **18**(11), 3845 (2018)
14. Varona, B., Monteserin, A., Teyseyre, A.: A deep learning approach to automatic road surface monitoring and pothole detection. Pers. Ubiquit. Comput. **24**(4), 519–534 (2020)
15. Vaswani, A., et al.: Attention is all you need. In: Advances in Neural Information Processing Systems (NeurIPS), vol. 30 (2017)

16. Watanabe, T., Takahashi, H., Iwasawa, Y., Matsuo, Y., Eguchi Yairi, I.: Weakly supervised learning for evaluating road surface condition from wheelchair driving data. Information **11**(1), 2 (2019)
17. World health organization: wheelchair services. https://www.who.int/teams/health-product-policy-and-standards/assistive-and-medical-technology/assistive-technology/wheelchair-services (2023). Accessed 12 Mar 2026
18. Yairi, I.E., et al.: Estimating spatiotemporal information from behavioral sensing data of wheelchair users by machine learning technologies. Information **10**(3), 114 (2019)
19. Yi, C.W., Chuang, Y.T., Nian, C.S.: Toward crowdsourcing-based road pavement monitoring by mobile sensing technologies. IEEE Trans. Intell. Transp. Syst. **16**(4), 1905–1917 (2015)
20. Yu, H., Raychoudhury, V., Saha, S., Edinger, J., Smith, R.O., Gani, M.O.: Automated surface classification system using vibration patterns–a case study with wheelchairs. IEEE Trans. Artif. Intell. **4**(4), 884–895 (2022)
21. Yue, Z., et al.: Ts2vec: towards universal representation of time series. In: Proceedings of the AAAI Conference on Artificial Intelligence, vol. 36, pp. 8980–8987 (2022)

Causal Inference, Decision Making and Counterfactual Learning

Calibrated Counterfactual Evaluation of Dispatch Policies Under Cascading Divergence

Amr Abdelbaky[1(✉)], Zhiwei Qin[2], and Nourhan Sakr[1]

[1] The American University in Cairo, Cairo, Egypt
amrkhaled122@aucegypt.edu, n.sakr@columbia.edu
[2] Santa Clara University, Santa Clara, USA
zqin3@scu.edu

Abstract. On-demand meal-delivery platforms make dispatch decisions over courier–order offers in real time, where each decision alters courier trajectories, workloads, availability, and future assignment feasibility. Evaluating alternative dispatch policies offline is challenging because even small deviations from historical decisions propagate through this tightly coupled dispatch system, compounding into downstream state drift, a phenomenon we term *cascading divergence*. To study this problem, we develop an event-driven counterfactual simulation framework with explicit agent–history decision logic and reassignment simulation. A central empirical finding is that a behaviour-cloning (BC) policy matching 97.1% of logged decisions still produces 52.5% event-level divergence under counterfactual rollout, demonstrating that high imitation accuracy does not guarantee reliable policy evaluation. To account for this drift, we use the BC policy as a conservative calibration reference for simulator-induced drift under near-historical behaviour. Experiments on a large-scale real-world dispatch dataset containing 630,000 courier–order offers show that a Double Deep Q-Network (DDQN) agent improves delivery reliability relative to this calibrated reference, increasing delivery rate from 95.5% to 98.9% and reducing lost orders from 4.5% to 1.1%, while maintaining comparable on-time performance within the simulator. These results highlight the importance of calibrated counterfactual evaluation for sequential logistics systems and its use for pre-deployment policy screening and operational decision support.

Keywords: Reinforcement learning · Counterfactual policy evaluation · Dispatch optimisation · Sequential decision making · Simulator drift · Cascading divergence

1 Background and Related Work

On-demand meal-delivery platforms continuously make dispatch decisions under tight spatial, temporal, and operational constraints. Improving this decision logic is valuable, but testing alternative policies directly in production is risky: changing a single courier–order assignment can alter courier locations, workloads, and

M. Ceci et al. (Eds.): ECML PKDD 2026, LNAI 16948, pp. 183–198, 2027.
https://doi.org/10.1007/978-3-032-37679-4_11

future availability, which in turn changes the set of feasible assignments and delivery outcomes that follow. In practice, this makes *offline policy evaluation*, not only policy learning, a primary bottleneck for operational improvement.

This paper studies a narrower but operationally realistic decision problem than full platform-wide matching. At each dispatch event, the platform proposes one courier–order pair, and an advisory policy recommends either *accept* or *reject*. Even in this binary setting, naive offline replay is unreliable. A local counterfactual decision changes downstream courier state, which changes later features, reassignment opportunities, and delivery feasibility. We refer to this compounding failure mode as *cascading divergence*: once evaluation departs from the historical trajectory, later decisions are made in increasingly non-historical states. This issue is closely related to compounding-error phenomena in imitation learning [7] and is especially consequential in tightly coupled logistics systems.

Recent work has advanced the dispatch decision layer itself, including future-informed food-delivery dispatch, reformulations of ride-hailing dispatch, end-to-end micro-view order dispatch, and cooperative on-demand delivery systems with real-world deployment, which makes robust offline evaluation even more important [3,4,10,11].

We address this gap with a calibrated counterfactual evaluation framework for sequential dispatch logs. The framework replays events chronologically, maintains live courier state, and handles agreement/disagreement between agent and history through explicit four-case logic with reassignment and delivery-timeline simulation. The central methodological step is calibration: instead of comparing learned policies directly against raw historical replay, we first evaluate a high-fidelity behaviour-cloning (BC) policy that stays close to the log. This BC policy provides a calibration reference: it measures how much drift and outcome degradation can appear when the simulator is driven by a policy that stays close to historical decisions.

Our empirical results show why this distinction matters. Using a public real-world Meituan dispatch dataset with 630,063 courier–order offers, a BC agent matching logged decisions with 97.1% accuracy still induces 52.5% event-level divergence under counterfactual rollout. High imitation accuracy therefore does not guarantee reliable offline evaluation. Relative to this calibrated reference, a Double Deep Q-Network (DDQN) policy improves simulated delivery reliability, raising delivery rate from 95.5% to 98.9% and reducing lost orders from 4.5% to 1.1%, while maintaining similar on-time performance in the simulator. These results shift the main question from "Can a learned policy outperform replayed history?" to "When should a counterfactual gain be interpreted as a real policy effect rather than a simulator artifact?"

Our contribution in this paper is three-fold:

1. **Failure-mode characterisation.** We identify and empirically characterise *cascading divergence* as the core failure mode of offline dispatch evaluation in sequential courier–order systems.

2. **BC-calibrated evaluation protocol.** We propose an event-driven counterfactual simulator with four-case decision logic and BC-based calibration to measure simulator-induced drift under offer-level replay.
3. **Large-scale empirical validation.** We demonstrate the framework on a large public dispatch dataset and show that it supports practical pre-deployment policy screening and operational diagnosis.

2 Methodology

We formulate courier-order assignment as a Markov Decision Process (MDP). At each dispatch event, the platform proposes a courier-order pair, and an advisory agent recommends acceptance or rejection. Each decision alters the system state; updating courier locations, capacities, and workloads, thereby influencing the quality of all future assignments.

State Space. The observation vector $\mathbf{s} \in \mathbb{R}^{17}$ spans four categories (see Table 1): spatial coordinates of the restaurant, courier, and customer (six features), cyclical time-of-day encoding (two), courier workload and performance statistics (seven), and order-specific attributes (two). This representation balances informativeness with practical tractability, encoding the essential context a human dispatcher would consider when evaluating an assignment.

Table 1. 17-dimensional state space. Coordinates are raw longitude/latitude; temporal features use cyclical encoding; courier features are cumulative within the current working day.

Category	Feature	Description
Spatial (6)	$\text{sender}_{lng/lat}$	Restaurant coordinates
	$\text{proxy}_{lng/lat}$	Courier proxy location
	$\text{recipient}_{lng/lat}$	Customer coordinates
Temporal (2)	tod_{sin}	$\sin(2\pi t/86400)$
	tod_{cos}	$\cos(2\pi t/86400)$
Courier (7)	capacity	Concurrent order load
	offers / accepts / completed	Cumulative counts today
	late_ratio	Running late-delivery ratio
	time_since_accept	Seconds since last acceptance
	active_seconds	Total active time today
Order (2)	eta_seconds	Platform-estimated delivery time
	order_income	Estimated courier payout (CNY)

Action Space. The action space is binary: $\mathcal{A} = \{0, 1\}$, where $a = 1$ recommends assignment and $a = 0$ recommends rejection. While real-world dispatch systems may involve richer action spaces (e.g., selecting among multiple candidate couriers), this binary formulation reflects the operational reality of our platform, where each dispatch event presents a single courier-order pair for evaluation.

Reward. We finally set the reward function as follows:

$$r(s,a) = \begin{cases} \text{order\_income} & \text{if } a = 1 \\ -0.3 & \text{if } a = 0 \end{cases} \tag{1}$$

where order_income $\approx$ 2–5 Chinese yuan (CNY) is computed from the platform pay formula (base fee + distance bonus). We use this field as a payout proxy from the log, not as a calibrated measure of platform revenue or profit. The fixed reject penalty is a reward-shaping term that discourages trivial reject-all policies while remaining small relative to typical order income, thereby allowing the agent to learn selective rejection when warranted.

2.1 Agent Architecture

We evaluate two learned agents with distinct roles. The Behaviour Cloning (BC) agent provides a calibration reference (see Sect. 4.1), and the Double DQN (DDQN) agent tests whether an RL policy can improve over the BC-calibrated reference under the same simulator assumptions.

BC Baseline. The BC agent serves as a calibration reference for the simulation framework. Historical replay is a factual anchor, not a deployable counterfactual policy: it has zero divergence by construction because every decision matches the log. It therefore cannot show what happens after a policy makes even a small different decision. BC fills this gap by staying close to history while still producing a non-trivial rollout. Its simulation output gives a practical reference point for interpreting RL rollouts under the same simulator assumptions. The agent is implemented as a deep multi-layer perceptron (MLP) trained with binary cross-entropy loss:

$$\mathcal{L}_{\text{BC}} = -\tfrac{1}{N}\sum_{i=1}^{N}\left[y_i \log \hat{p}_i + (1-y_i)\log(1-\hat{p}_i)\right] \tag{2}$$

We set up the architecture as four hidden layers $[512, 256, 256, 128]$ with LayerNorm and Gaussian Error Linear Unit (GELU) activations, outputting a scalar acceptance probability via sigmoid. At inference, $a = \mathbf{1}[\hat{p} \geq 0.47]$ (F1-optimal threshold on validation data). By achieving 97.1% accuracy, the BC agent produces near-historical behaviour. Its simulation output therefore serves as a conservative calibration reference against which RL rollouts are interpreted.

DDQN Agent. The DDQN agent learns online within the simulation loop using Double Deep Q-Network [9]. At each dispatch event, the agent selects an action, observes the reward and next state, and stores the transition in a prioritised replay buffer [8]. Mini-batch updates minimise:

$$\mathcal{L}_{\text{TD}} = \frac{1}{N} \sum_{i=1}^{N} \big(Q_\theta(s_i, a_i) - y_i\big)^2 \tag{3}$$

with target $y_i = r_i + (1-d_i)\,\gamma\, Q_{\theta^-}(s_i', \arg\max_{a'} Q_\theta(s_i', a'))$. The target network uses Polyak averaging (τ=0.01) and exploration follows ϵ-greedy annealing from 1.0 to 0.01. The Q-network has three hidden layers $[256, 256, 128]$ with LayerNorm, Rectified Linear Unit (ReLU), and dropout (0.1), outputting $[Q_{\text{reject}}, Q_{\text{accept}}]$. Unlike offline methods [1,6], the agent collects its own experience within the simulator through interactive exploration, while the underlying Q-learning update is off-policy and learns from replay-buffer transitions generated by earlier exploration policies.

2.2 Counterfactual Replay Engine

Evaluating dispatch policies in a live production environment carries significant operational risk [2]. We instead develop a counterfactual replay engine that replays historical dispatch events while substituting agent decisions for the recorded ones, enabling policy evaluation without real-world deployment.

Simulator Overview and Data Inputs. The engine processes dispatch events chronologically, maintaining a live state for each courier (location, capacity, active deliveries, cumulative statistics) and each order (assignment status, delivery progress). At each event, the engine (1) retrieves the historical courier–order pair and queries the agent for a recommended action; (2) classifies the outcome into one of four cases based on agreement between agent and history (Table 2); (3) updates courier and order states accordingly; and (4) advances to the next event. The engine reads three primary data sources: the chronologically ordered dispatch-event log (courier–order pairs with timestamps and historical decisions), the delivery-outcome records (pickup, completion, and ETA timestamps for accepted orders), and the courier working-hour schedule (shift-block start and end times). All spatial computations use haversine distances on WGS-84 coordinates, the global coordinate standard used by GPS. When agent and historical decisions agree, the historical outcome is replayed directly. When they diverge, the simulator models the alternative trajectory: It computes travel times, updates courier positions, and tracks delivery outcomes so that downstream events are consistent with the agent's choices.

Four-Case Decision Logic. Every dispatch event yields an (agent, historical) decision pair, routed to one of four handlers, as presented in Table 2.

Table 2. Decision matrix: four cases arising from agent–history (dis)agreement.

	History: Accept	**History: Reject**
Agent: Accept	Case 1	Case 2
Agent: Reject	Case 3	Case 4

Case 1 (Log Replay): both agree to accept; historical outcome replayed.

Case 2 (Simulate): agent accepts an order history rejected; pickup and delivery simulated.

Case 3 (Reassign): agent rejects a historically accepted order; order and courier enter reassignment.

Case 4 (No-op): both agree to reject; no action taken.

Reassignment Process. For Case 3, an alternative courier is selected via greedy nearest-courier scoring: $c^* = \arg\min_{c \in \mathcal{C} \setminus \mathcal{R}_o} d_{\text{hav}}(\text{loc}_c, \text{loc}_{\text{sender}})$, where $\mathcal{R}_o$ is the set of couriers who have already rejected order o. Exclusion rules filter couriers outside working hours, busy with diverged deliveries, or located more than 3 km from the restaurant. If no eligible courier is found in the current dispatch cycle, the order enters a pending queue and is retried in subsequent cycles (up to five attempts). After five failed cycles, the order is marked *lost*, i.e. undeliverable within the simulation. When reassignment occurs, the feature vector is *recomputed* for the candidate courier using live simulation state (current location, capacity, workload statistics), ensuring the agent evaluates the reassignment based on the new courier's actual context rather than stale features from the original dispatch.

Data-Driven Parameter Choices. The simulation parameters reflect empirical properties of the dataset. The 3-km reassignment radius corresponds to the effective operational range observed in historical dispatch data: the vast majority of accepted courier–restaurant assignments fall well within this distance (see Supplementary Appendix, Fig. S1), and extending the radius further would pair couriers with restaurants outside plausible delivery zones. The five-cycle reassignment limit balances recovery probability against computational efficiency: 99.8% of orders are resolved within five dispatch attempts (Supplementary Appendix, Fig. S2), so additional cycles yield diminishing returns. The seven distance buckets for the travel-time lookup tables (0–0.5 through 10+ km) are defined at natural breakpoints in the empirical delivery-distance distribution (Supplementary Appendix, Fig. S1), ensuring each bucket contains sufficient observations for stable median travel-time estimates.

Delivery-Timeline Simulation. For diverged deliveries (Cases 2 and 3), the simulator must estimate pickup and delivery times because no historical outcome exists. We construct two empirical travel-time lookup tables, $T_{\text{pickup}}[\cdot, \cdot]$ and

$T_{\text{delivery}}[\cdot,\cdot]$, from completed deliveries in the training window, each stratified by seven distance buckets (0–0.5, 0.5–1, 1–2, 2–3, 3–5, 5–10, 10+ km) and five time-of-day blocks (morning rush, lunch rush, afternoon, dinner rush, off-peak). Each cell stores the median observed travel time for that distance–time stratum. The delivery timeline is:

$$t_{\text{pickup}} = t_{\text{dispatch}} + T_{\text{pickup}}[d_1][h], \quad t_{\text{fetch}} = \max(t_{\text{pickup}}, t_{\text{meal\_prep}}) \tag{4}$$
$$t_{\text{arrive}} = t_{\text{fetch}} + T_{\text{delivery}}[d_2][h] \tag{5}$$

where d_1 is the haversine distance from courier to restaurant, d_2 the distance from restaurant to customer, and h the hour of day. The meal-preparation time $t_{\text{meal\_prep}}$ is replayed from the historical record when available. An order is classified as *late* if t_{arrive} exceeds the platform's estimated time of arrival (ETA).

Courier Location Interpolation. For couriers with pending diverged deliveries, the simulation must estimate their current position to compute meaningful distances for subsequent reassignment scoring. As the dataset provides only three spatial anchors per delivery, the courier's location at dispatch time, the restaurant coordinates, and the customer coordinates, we interpolate the courier's position linearly along the delivery chain (dispatch location → restaurant → customer) based on elapsed time relative to the estimated travel-time segments. Specifically, if a courier is between dispatch and pickup, their position is linearly interpolated between the dispatch location and the restaurant; if between pickup and delivery, the interpolation runs from restaurant to customer. This maintains internal consistency of the simulation state, ensuring that reassignment distance computations reflect the courier's expected progression through the delivery.

Modelling Limitations. The travel-time model captures aggregate spatial and temporal patterns but necessarily omits several real-world factors. Real-time traffic congestion is not modelled: the dataset records delivery timestamps but not GPS trajectories or traffic-state observations, precluding dynamic travel-speed estimation. Individual courier speed variations (e.g., vehicle type, route familiarity) are absorbed into the median statistics rather than modelled explicitly. Restaurant preparation times are replayed from historical observations when available; in practice they vary with kitchen load. The simulator does not model courier behavioural responses, e.g. a courier receiving additional orders may slow down, change routes, or go offline, but the simulation assumes couriers continue operating at historical rates. Finally, demand patterns (order arrival times and locations) are fixed to the historical log, meaning the simulator cannot capture supply–demand feedback loops where courier availability influences future order volumes. These simplifications are a direct consequence of the data available in the public Meituan dataset [5].

Calibration Protocol. The BC agent serves as the calibration instrument for the simulation framework. Because it matches 97.1% of historical decisions, its rollout is close to history but still allows some counterfactual drift. We define the BC-calibrated reference gap as the metric gap between BC rollout and historical replay (see Sect. 3.2). Improvements over BC are evidence of policy benefit under the same simulator assumptions, not proof that all simulator bias has been removed. This calibration step is critical because the simulator introduces systematic biases through its model simplifications (median-based travel times, greedy reassignment, absence of courier behavioural adaptation); without a reference agent, these biases would be conflated with policy effects.

3 Experimental Setup and Results

3.1 Dataset and Implementation Details

Dataset. We use the Meituan dispatch dataset [5], a publicly available real-world dataset released as part of the INFORMS TSL Research Challenge. The dataset originates from one of the world's largest food-delivery platforms, and contains nine days of dispatch activity from a single metropolitan area. It is distributed under a CC BY-NC 4.0 licence. Each event represents a courier–order offer with the historical accept/reject decision and, for accepted orders, the complete delivery outcome (pickup, completion, and ETA timestamps). The dataset's scale (over 630,000 events, ∼4,900 couriers) and granularity (per-event courier state, coordinates, and timing) make it well-suited for studying dispatch policy evaluation. However, it provides only origin–destination coordinates and timestamps, not full GPS trajectories, which constrains the fidelity of our travel-time model (Sect. 2.2). We find that in a set of around 546,000 unique orders, the historical acceptance rate is 86.7%.

Training Configuration. The BC agent is trained offline on historical decisions from the full nine-day log (630,063 events) to maximise imitation fidelity. This full-log access is intentional: BC is used for calibration, not as a held-out deployment model. Giving BC full access makes it a closer-to-history reference for DDQN. DDQN agents train online within the simulation loop on hours 0–48 and are evaluated on hours 48–96 with exploration disabled and no parameter updates. Full architecture and hyperparameter settings are provided in the Supplementary Appendix (Table S2). All experiments are conducted on a single NVIDIA RTX 4060 Laptop GPU (8 GB VRAM) using PyTorch 2.6.0 with CUDA 12.4 and Python 3.12. For DDQN, feature normalisation uses running mean and variance computed from the training window. To support reproducibility, the source code, implementation details, and supplementary material are available online.[1]

[1] Repository: https://github.com/amrkhaled122/Calibrated-Counterfactual-Evaluation-of-Dispatch-Policies-under-Cascading-Divergence.

Table 3. BC agent full-log in-sample classification performance over all 630,063 events (threshold $\tau = 0.47$, F1-optimal).

	Pred. Accept	**Pred. Reject**
Actual Accept	528,544 (TP)	17,821 (FN)
Actual Reject	306 (FP)	83,392 (TN)
Accuracy: 97.1%	Accept Recall: 96.7%	Reject Recall: 99.6% F1: 0.984

Evaluation Protocol. All agents are evaluated on the second 48-hour window (hours 48–96), comprising 151,695 dispatch events across 131,852 unique orders and 4,156 couriers. DDQN is evaluated as a frozen policy learned from hours 0–48, with no exploration and no parameter updates during evaluation. The BC result is a calibration check, not a held-out deployment test. In addition to a historical replay run (pure log replay with zero divergences), each agent is run through the counterfactual simulator and compared across three levels of analysis.

- **Order-level**: delivery rate, on-time rate, lost-order rate.
- **Courier-level**: utilisation (active/block time), capacity distribution.
- **System-level**: divergence rate, total order-income delta (payout proxy).

3.2 Numerical Results

BC Classification Fidelity. The BC agent achieves 97.1% accuracy in imitating historical decisions (Table 3), with well-separated probability distributions ($\mu_{\text{accept}} = 0.961$, σ=0.150; $\mu_{\text{reject}} = 0.033$, $\sigma = 0.071$). Table 3 reports full-log in-sample imitation performance over all 630,063 dispatch events. The confusion matrix reveals asymmetric errors: 17,821 false negatives (3.3%) versus only 306 false positives (0.4%). This asymmetry is consequential: the dominant error mode—rejecting historically accepted orders—triggers the reassignment pathway (Case 3), amplifying downstream state divergence (Sect. 4.1). This high fidelity makes the BC agent suitable as a calibration reference: deviations between BC rollout and historical replay quantify the drift observed under near-historical behaviour.

Simulation Fidelity and Calibration. Before evaluating RL policies, we establish a BC-calibrated reference gap by comparing the BC agent's simulation output against historical replay. This reference gap is the empirical level of outcome degradation observed when the simulator is driven by a high-fidelity near-historical policy.

Despite 97.1% classification accuracy, the BC agent produces 52.5% event-level divergence (Table 5), corresponding to a cascading amplification factor of about $\alpha \approx 18\times$. We compute this factor as $\alpha \equiv 52.5\%/(100\% - 97.1\%) \approx 18.1$, i.e. event-level divergence divided by the BC one-step error rate. The resulting metric gaps define the BC-calibrated reference gap:

- **Delivery rate**: 100.0% (historical) vs. 95.5% (BC) = 4.5 pp deficit.
- **On-time rate**: 85.5% (historical) vs. 82.1% (BC) = 3.4 pp deficit.
- **Utilisation**: 99.7% (historical) vs. 88.3% (BC) = 11.4 pp deficit.

These gaps arise from three sources: (1) the BC agent's remaining 2.9% decision mismatches, which trigger reassignment chains that cascade through the system; (2) the travel-time model's reliance on aggregate median statistics, which introduces systematic timing bias for diverged deliveries; and (3) the greedy nearest-courier reassignment heuristic, which is a simplified approximation of the production dispatch system.

Crucially, BC calibration does not remove simulator bias. It gives us a conservative near-history comparison. We therefore report RL results both in absolute terms and relative to BC. Improvements over BC are evidence of policy benefit under the same simulator assumptions; performance below BC means the agent performs worse than a high-fidelity imitation policy in this evaluation.

DDQN Training Dynamics. A compact DDQN training summary is provided in the Supplementary Appendix (Table S1). The DDQN agent exhibits rapid improvement in the first two to three epochs followed by stable convergence. Final training metrics (loss 0.077, acceptance rate 88.1%, mean reward 0.229) indicate stable learning in this setting.

Order-Level Performance. Table 4 presents the central comparison. The DDQN agent delivers 98.9% of orders compared to BC's 95.5%, a 75% reduction in lost orders (1,491 vs. 5,922). DDQN also improves on-time rate to 83.1% from BC's 82.1%, while approaching the historical replay's 85.5%. The remaining 2.4%-point (pp) gap reflects the inherent cost of divergence: simulated deliveries introduce latency from reassignment delays and estimation error in the travel-time model.

Table 4. Order-level performance (hours 48–96). All agents operate on the same 131,852 unique orders.

Metric	History	BC	DDQN
Delivered	131,852	125,930	130,361
Delivery Rate	**100.0%**	95.5%	98.9%
On-Time Rate	**85.5%**	82.1%	83.1%
Late Rate	14.5%	17.9%	16.9%
Lost Orders	0	5,922	1,491
Lost Rate	0.0%	4.5%	1.1%

Decision Analysis. A divergence event means the agent action differs from the historical action (accept vs. reject). Table 5 also reports Skipped Events. These are replay rows where no agent decision is made because an earlier divergence has already invalidated or resolved that row. They are different from Case 4 no-ops, where the agent does make a decision and both agent and history reject the offer. With skipped events included, the History, BC, and DDQN columns each sum to the full 151,695-event evaluation window. We compute divergence rates only over non-skipped, decision-executed events. Under this definition, BC and DDQN both remain near 52%, showing that the overall amount of divergence is mainly driven by cascading state changes, not by one-step accuracy alone. The key distinction lies in divergence *direction*. The BC agent almost exclusively prunes historical accepts (79,638 prune vs. 16 keep), reflecting the cascading effect of its classification errors. In contrast, DDQN accepts 2,989 offers that history rejected, assigning positive simulated value to states that pure imitation almost never selects. DDQN also produces fewer "Agent Prune/Hist. Keep" events (73,846 vs. 79,638 for BC), meaning fewer historically accepted orders are unnecessarily rejected and fed into the reassignment pipeline. The combination of more keeps and fewer prunes is the mechanism by which RL reduces lost orders relative to BC.

Table 5. Decision divergence analysis (hours 48–96). "Prune" = agent rejects what history accepted; "Keep" = agent accepts what history rejected. Divergence rates are computed over non-skipped events.

Metric	History	BC	DDQN
Divergence Rate (non-skipped)	0.0%	52.5%	52.3%
Aligned Events	151,695	72,015	70,076
Diverged Events	0	79,654	76,835
Skipped Events	0	26	4,784
Agent Prune / Hist. Keep	0	79,638	73,846
Agent Keep / Hist. Prune	0	16	2,989

Courier Utilisation and Payout Proxy. Utilisation is computed as active time (merged delivery spans, clamped to block boundaries) divided by block time. DDQN achieves 89.0% utilisation versus 88.3% for BC and 99.7% for historical replay (Table 6). The gap from history reflects the structural consequence of reassignment: when the agent rejects an order from its historical courier, the original courier's block time remains unchanged while the active delivery time shifts to the receiver. DDQN's higher utilisation than BC is consistent with fewer reassignment-induced idle periods. The number of underutilised couriers (<50% utilisation) drops from 14 for BC to 8 for DDQN. The order-income delta metric in Table 6 is simulated payout minus historical payout on tracked income events. It captures payout differences, not delivery volume, platform revenue, or profit. This is why DDQN can deliver more orders yet still show a slightly more negative total delta (−7,042 CNY vs. BC's −6,622): DDQN has fewer lost orders (higher reliability), but its average per-order payout gap versus history is marginally more negative on diverged deliveries.

Table 6. Courier utilisation and order-income delta (hours 48–96). Overlapping batch deliveries are merged to avoid double-counting active time.

Metric	History	BC	DDQN
Utilisation (%)	99.7	88.3	89.0
Active hours	30,095	27,143	27,325
Block hours	30,194	30,735	30,705
Idle hours	99	3,592	3,380
Couriers <50% util.	2	14	8
Order-income Δ (CNY)	0	−6,622	−7,042

Feature Importance. We analyse 18,048 DDQN misaligned decisions using gradient attribution ($|\nabla_s Q \cdot s|$) and feature-zeroing perturbation (ΔQ). Table 7 summarises the results.

Temporal features dominate: tod_sin and tod_cos appear in the top five for almost all misaligned decisions (17K+ each). Courier-state features (late_ratio, capacity) and order income follow. Raw coordinates rank low (e.g., proxy_lng appears in the top five only 33 times out of 18,048), indicating that spatial signals are weakly used in the current representation.

Lost Orders Analysis. Lost orders, which fail all five reassignment cycles, exhibit systematic patterns.

Feature Divergence. Lost orders are associated with lower capacity, longer time since last accept, fewer total accepts, and less active time (Supplementary Appendix, Table S3). This points to end-of-shift or low-activity couriers who appear available but are less likely to accept new work. Because the agent only accepts or rejects proposed courier–order pairs, without creating new matches, these states remain structurally difficult.

Temporal Pattern. Lost orders cluster in the 10:00–13:00 CST lunch-rush window (42.7%; peak at 11:00 CST), with a secondary cluster during dinner (17:00–19:00 CST, 31.2%). Courier availability is near its daily maximum in these periods (Fig. 1), indicating demand surges rather than raw courier scarcity.

Table 7. Feature importance for misaligned DDQN decisions. Gradient = mean |grad× input|; Perturbation = mean ΔQ after zeroing; Top-5 = appearances in per-sample top five.

Rank	Feature	Gradient	Perturb.	Top-5
1	tod_cos	3.63	0.248	17,799
2	tod_sin	2.57	0.327	17,455
3	late_ratio	1.20	0.050	14,391
4	capacity	0.18	0.016	14,172
5	order_income	0.10	0.011	7,207
6	accepts_so_far	0.03	0.012	5,385
15	proxy_lng	0.009	0.0003	33
17	eta_seconds	0.006	0.0000	25

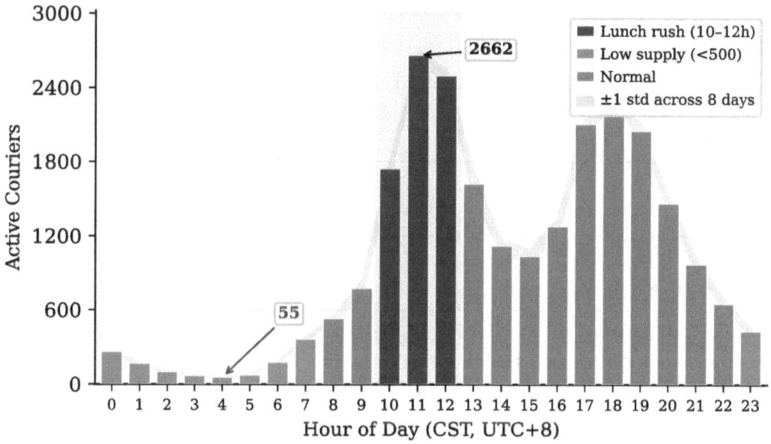

Fig. 1. Mean courier availability by hour of day from historical data (averaged across 8 days, ±1 std shaded). The red band marks the 10:00–13:00 CST lunch-rush window where 42.7% of simulated lost orders concentrate, despite near-peak supply (Color figure online).

4 Discussion

4.1 Cascading Divergence: Formal Characterisation

A central empirical finding is that divergences *cascade* across dispatch cycles. When the agent rejects a historically accepted offer: (1) the order enters reassignment, changing a different courier's state; (2) that courier's future features diverge from history; (3) the agent's decisions on subsequent offers to that courier may further diverge; and (4) each divergence propagates forward, creating an expanding frontier of non-historical states:

$$\epsilon_0 \xrightarrow{\text{drift}} \epsilon_1 \xrightarrow{\text{drift}} \epsilon_2 \xrightarrow{\text{drift}} \cdots \tag{6}$$

This mechanism explains a striking finding: the BC agent, despite 97.1% accuracy, produces 52.5% event-level divergence.

The remaining 2.9% BC decision mismatches compound through state drift until roughly half of the evaluation window operates in non-historical territory. This parallels the theoretical results of Ross et al. [7], who showed that imitation-learning errors grow quadratically with the horizon; our results provide a large-scale empirical demonstration of this phenomenon in a large-scale logistics simulator.

The practical consequence is that BC simulation results provide a conservative calibration reference: they show the drift observed under near-historical behaviour. DDQN improves over BC—3.4 pp higher delivery rate and 75% fewer lost orders—which is evidence of policy benefit under the same simulator assumptions. Historical replay remains the zero-divergence factual anchor, so we compare DDQN mainly against BC rather than claiming direct dominance over history. This principle—**BC-Calibration**—may generalise to other counterfactual evaluation settings in logistics and beyond.

4.2 Practical Implications

The experimental results suggest several strategic implications for platform operators.

Operational Reliability. By identifying "Keep" scenarios, i.e., orders that history rejected but that appear immediately favorable under the learned Q-values, the DDQN agent reduces simulated lost orders by 75%, directly improving service reliability during peak demand. In our evaluation window this corresponds to 4,431 additional delivered orders relative to BC.

Using the mean order_income of 3.22 CNY per delivered order, this corresponds to about 14,268 CNY more simulated payout volume relative to BC. Here, order_income is only a payout proxy.

Fleet Distribution. While aggregate utilisation decreases from 99.7% (historical replay) to 89.0% (DDQN) due to reassignment mechanics, DDQN exhibits a more equitable distribution of workload: the number of severely underutilised couriers (<50%) drops from 14 (BC) to 8 (DDQN). This suggests that, within the simulator, RL-based dispatch may reduce severe underutilisation even when aggregate efficiency remains below historical replay.

Temporal Awareness. The agent's strong reliance on temporal features (tod_sin, tod_cos) indicates it has internalised demand-cycle patterns, effectively anticipating supply-side constraints during shift transitions. Platform operators could leverage similar temporal signals to proactively adjust courier incentives during high-risk periods (e.g., early morning).

Evaluation Standards. Our findings suggest that industrial off-policy evaluation must move beyond raw historical accuracy. A platform deploying counterfactual simulation should first establish a BC calibration reference, then interpret RL improvements relative to that reference. Without this step, simulation artefacts can be mistaken for policy effects.

4.3 Limitations

Several limitations should be noted. First, the greedy nearest-courier scorer is a simplification of production dispatch systems, which use sophisticated matching algorithms considering multiple objectives simultaneously. Second, the simulation does not model courier behavioural responses to changed assignments (e.g., a courier receiving extra orders may slow down). Third, the travel-time lookup model uses aggregate median statistics that do not capture individual courier variations or real-time traffic. Fourth, the reward uses order_income as a payout proxy and the fixed rejection penalty as reward shaping. It should not be read as a calibrated platform revenue or profit model. Fifth, analysis of agent decisions reveals that the DDQN agent does not modulate accept preference based on courier capacity (stable Q-gap across load levels), suggesting the reward function could be refined with opportunity-cost signals. Sixth, BC calibration is empirical. It is not a formal proof that all simulator bias is removed. We also did not run a full architecture or hyperparameter ablation. Finally, evaluation is limited to a single geographic market over nine days; generalisation remains to be validated.

5 Conclusion and Future Work

This paper reframes offline dispatch evaluation as a calibration problem in tightly coupled sequential logistics systems. We show that *cascading divergence* is substantial in practice: a behaviour-cloning policy with 97.1% imitation accuracy still yields 52.5% event-level divergence under counterfactual rollout.

Within this calibrated setting, DDQN improves simulated delivery reliability relative to BC (95.5% to 98.9% delivery rate) and reduces simulated lost orders (4.5% to 1.1%) while maintaining similar on-time performance. The central takeaway is methodological as much as algorithmic: once policy decisions deviate from history, raw replay is an insufficient benchmark, and gains should be interpreted against a measured BC-calibrated reference.

In practice, the framework helps operators test offer-level policy changes offline before deployment by separating likely policy effects from simulation artefacts before any online experiment.

Future work will focus on richer behavioural simulation, validation across additional markets and longer horizons, and objective designs that explicitly incorporate courier welfare in long-horizon optimisation.

Generative AI Use Disclosure

Generative AI tools were used during manuscript preparation solely to improve English grammar and readability. All scientific content, experimental design, data analysis, and conclusions were developed by the authors. The authors take full responsibility and accountability for the final content of the paper and for any copyright issues related to it.

References

1. Kumar, A., Zhou, A., Tucker, G., Levine, S.: conservative q-learning for offline reinforcement learning. In: Advances in Neural Information Processing Systems 33 (NeurIPS 2020), pp. 1179–1191 (2020)
2. Levine, S., Kumar, A., Tucker, G., Fu, J.: Offline reinforcement learning: tutorial, review, and perspectives on open problems. arXiv:2005.01643 (2020)
3. Liang, Y., et al.: Enhancing dynamic on-demand food order dispatching via future-informed and spatial-temporal extended decisions. In: Proceedings of the 32nd ACM International Conference on Information and Knowledge Management (CIKM 2023), pp. 4702–4708. ACM, New York (2023)
4. Lu, Y., et al.: DECO: cooperative order dispatching for on-demand delivery with real-time encounter detection. In: Proceedings of the 33rd ACM International Conference on Information and Knowledge Management (CIKM 2024), pp. 4734–4742. ACM, New York (2024)
5. Meituan: Meituan INFORMS TSL research challenge dataset. Available under CC BY-NC 4.0 licence (2024). Repository: https://github.com/meituan/Meituan-INFORMS-TSL-Research-Challenge
6. Nair, A., Dalal, M., Gupta, A., Levine, S.: Accelerating online reinforcement learning with offline datasets. arXiv:2006.09359 (2020)
7. Ross, S., Gordon, G., Bagnell, D.: A reduction of imitation learning and structured prediction to no-regret online learning. In: Proceedings of the 14th International Conference on Artificial Intelligence and Statistics (AISTATS 2011). JMLR Workshop and Conference Proceedings, vol. 15, pp. 627–635 (2011)
8. Schaul, T., Quan, J., Antonoglou, I., Silver, D.: Prioritized experience replay. In: Proceedings of the 4th International Conference on Learning Representations, ICLR 2016 (2016)
9. van Hasselt, H., Guez, A., Silver, D.: Deep reinforcement learning with double Q-learning. In: Proceedings of the 30th AAAI Conference on Artificial Intelligence (AAAI 2016), pp. 2094–2100 (2016)
10. Yang, Z., et al.: Rethinking order dispatching in online ride-hailing platforms. In: Proceedings of the 30th ACM SIGKDD Conference on Knowledge Discovery and Data Mining (KDD 2024), pp. 3863–3873. ACM, New York (2024)
11. Yue, X., et al.: An end-to-end reinforcement learning based approach for micro-view order-dispatching in ride-hailing. arXiv:2408.10479 (2024)

Causal-Temporal Representation Learning for Comorbidity Progression Risk in Longitudinal Primary-Care Data

Rocco Zaccagnino[1(✉)], Gerardo Benevento[1], Pierpaolo Cavallo[1], Delfina Malandrino[1], Donatello Telesca[2], Jacopo Troisi[1], and Alessia Ture[1]

[1] University of Salerno, Fisciano, Italy
{rzaccagnino,gbenevento,pcavallo,dmalandrino,jtroisi,ature}@unisa.it
[2] University of California, Los Angeles, CA, USA
dtelesca@g.ucla.edu

Abstract. Longitudinal primary-care records offer broad and scalable coverage for studying how chronic conditions unfold over time, but progression graphs derived from temporal co-occurrences are often distorted by time-varying confounding, surveillance intensity, and care-process artifacts. As a result, recorded downstream diagnoses may reflect healthcare patterns rather than clinically meaningful progression risk.

We introduce `CHRONOS` (**C**ausal **H**eterogeneity **R**epresentations for **O**nset-centric **N**etworks in **O**bservational **S**equences), a temporal Siamese representation learning network for confounding-adjusted disease progression discovery from observational primary-care sequences. For each *comorbidity* candidate (disease pair), `CHRONOS` emulates a target trial, aligns patients at the incident onset of the first disease in the pair, and estimates the effect of that onset on the risk of developing the second disease within a fixed follow-up horizon. Methodologically, the framework combines temporal sequence encoding, mutual-information-based balancing, a Siamese contrastive loss over patient pairs constructed from predicted *Individual Treatment Effect* (ITE) similarity, and cross-fitted doubly robust estimation to obtain effect-annotated progression edges. We evaluate `CHRONOS` on a real-world longitudinal primary-care cohort from the Campania region in Italy, collected from 2000 to 2018. As a result, the inferred network successfully emphasizes stable within-category continuity-of-care effects while filtering many cross-category temporal associations likely driven by surveillance and administrative processes. The results show that `CHRONOS` offers a framework for moving from associative temporal co-occurrence patterns to confounding-adjusted progression-risk relations in longitudinal observational healthcare data.

Keywords: representation learning · Siamese networks · target trial emulation · disease progression networks · doubly robust estimation

1 Introduction

M. Ceci et al. (Eds.): ECML PKDD 2026, LNAI 16948, pp. 199–216, 2027.
https://doi.org/10.1007/978-3-032-37679-4_12

The hidden challenge of comorbidity progression: clinical data or care artifacts? Comorbidity progression is a major challenge for contemporary medicine and primary-care practice [17]. Although many patients experience multiple interacting chronic diseases, clinical pathways and guidelines are still organized around single-disease paradigms. This complicates routine decision-making in primary care and public health planning, where clinicians and healthcare systems must decide who should receive closer follow-up, which complications deserve earlier attention, and when preventive actions are most likely to be effective. The term *comorbidity progression* is used to refer to the emergence of additional chronic conditions over time following an incident disease diagnosis. This perspective raises two practical questions: *(i)* given a disease condition, which subsequent conditions are most likely to occur, and over what time frame? *(ii)* which patient profiles are most likely to experience them? These questions are particularly important because disease trajectories are heterogeneous and frequently shaped by socioeconomic inequalities. Therefore, characterizing these trajectories is a prerequisite for improving early screening, prevention strategies, and integrated care planning in real-world settings [27]. On a large scale, however, longitudinal data covering a broad population and offering sufficient temporal depth are needed [6, 29]. Although clinical records provide detailed information on acute and serious events, they offer only fragmented snapshots of a patient's clinical journey and may not comprehensively capture chronic conditions, which limits their suitability for mapping the progression of comorbidities [10]. Conversely, primary care and family physician records, which consist of prescription data rather than clinical test results, typically follow patients for longer periods and record the routine management of chronic diseases in the community. Such data are routinely collected at scale, making them highly relevant for population-level progression analysis, public health surveillance, and healthcare planning. The main difficulty is that these records do not directly observe disease progression. Rather, they focus on administrative aspects of the healthcare process, such as patient management, prescriptions, and documentation collected over time. Consequently, the observed temporal associations may reflect not only the actual downstream evolution of the disease, but also other factors such as confounding by indication bias (patients with more severe conditions are more likely to receive specific treatments and develop subsequent complications) [23], frequency of interaction with the physician, subjective prescription practices, and local care protocols. Under these conditions, it becomes challenging to identify clinically significant progression signals from treatment- and observation-induced artifacts. Without an explicit causal design, these data can generate misleading progression patterns that reflect how patients move through the healthcare system rather than how chronic conditions truly accumulate over time.

Contribution of this work. The research question addressed in this work is:

> Can primary care administrative data and prescription records act as practical indicators of the changing burden of chronic disease over time, capturing both diagnosis and ongoing care?

Answering this question requires going beyond purely predictive modeling of disease progression and adopting more advanced approaches, such as *causal inference* methods, that are better suited to address the challenges outlined above. From this perspective, the onset of one disease can be viewed as the treatment, and the subsequent emergence of another condition as the outcome. However, associations in administrative healthcare data may be driven not only by latent disease progression, but also by care-process dynamics. This makes a causal inference perspective crucial for separating clinically meaningful signals from observational artifacts. In contrast, purely predictive models often rely on statistical shortcuts [12], learning dependencies induced by prescribing behavior and healthcare routines rather than true physiological mechanisms [5]. Consequently, models trained only on historical prescription data may infer spurious relationships and exhibit limited robustness under shifts in care protocols [11,30]. In many settings, randomized controlled trials are the gold standard for causal effect estimation. For disease onset, however, such trials are not feasible: patients cannot be randomly assigned to develop an index condition in order to observe its downstream complications. Observational data are therefore the only realistic source of evidence, but causal interpretation requires an explicit design strategy to reduce bias. We address this challenge through *target trial emulation*, that anchors causal inference from observational records to the specification of a hypothetical randomized protocol, including eligibility criteria, a clearly defined time zero, treatment assignment, and outcome follow-up [13]. This helps reduce common sources of observational bias and provides a more principled basis for causal interpretation. In our setting, each *comorbidity candidate*, i.e., an ordered pair (D_a, D_b) of diseases, is formalized as a separate emulated trial. We ask whether the incident onset of D_a at time t_0 affects the risk of developing D_b within a fixed follow-up horizon h, and whether this effect varies across patients. Treatment is defined by the first occurrence of D_a at t_0, whereas control is defined by its absence at that same time. Estimating such effects in longitudinal settings requires controlling for time-varying confounding, since covariates may simultaneously act as confounders. This is the central challenge in extracting reliable comorbidity progression evidence from real-world primary-care data.

Recent causal *representation learning* approaches address confounding by learning *balanced* latent spaces that reduce discrepancies between treated and control groups [4,20]. However, in settings characterized by heterogeneous trajectories and heterogeneous treatment effects, global alignment can be too approximate. It may pull together clinically distinct histories simply because they share broad observable similarities or comparable patterns of healthcare utilization, thereby smoothing out the heterogeneity that is most relevant for patient stratification and progression-risk discovery. To address this limitation, we propose `CHRONOS`, which combines temporal sequence encoding, mutual-information-based balancing, and a Siamese contrastive regularization strategy. The key idea is to organize the latent space around treatment-effect similarity rather than raw covariate similarity, so that patients with similar expected ITEs are mapped nearby even when their observed histories are not superficially identical. These learned representations are then used within a doubly robust estimation pipeline under the emulated-trial design, with the goal of producing progression evidence that is both interpretable and useful for screening and care-planning scenarios.

In summary, this paper makes the following contributions:

- We formulate comorbidity progression discovery in longitudinal primary-care administrative data as a collection of edge-level target trial emulations, providing an explicit causal framework to assess whether the incident onset of one disease affects the subsequent risk of another.
- We propose `CHRONOS`, a Siamese neural network for causal representation learning that combines temporal sequence modeling, treatment-effect-guided contrastive loss regularization, and doubly robust estimation to address time-varying confounding and heterogeneous treatment effects.
- On a real-world Italian primary-care cohort collected from 2000 to 2018, we obtain a large confounding-adjusted comorbidity progression network in which 188 out of 225 tested candidates remain significant after global Benjamini–Hochberg correction, with high-effect relations showing clear directional asymmetry, cohort support, and limited placebo activity.
- Beyond the specific network recovered in this study, we provide an empirical assessment of both the strengths and the limitations of administrative primary-care data as a scalable observational source for causal comorbidity progression analysis at the population level.

To promote transparency and reproducibility, we provide online resources detailing the preprocessing pipeline, comorbidity-candidate trial construction, model implementation, and estimation workflow.[1] We also provide *Supplementary Material*[2] with additional details on ICD-9 macro-category construction, cohort descriptive statistics, causal identification assumptions, complete edge-level results, robustness diagnostics, implementation settings, trial-design sensitivity analyses, and an epidemiological Cox baseline.

2 Related Work

Disease progression from longitudinal healthcare data has been studied from three perspectives: predictive models, population-level trajectory analysis, and causal inference. Most prior work uses clinical health records; we instead focus on routine primary-care administrative data, where progression is observed through prescriptions and documentation.

As for predictive models, disease evolution is modeled as a temporal forecasting problem using electronic health records. Early recurrent approaches, such as *Doctor AI* , showed that sequential neural models can capture useful temporal structures in patient histories [8]. More recent Transformer-based models, including *BEHRT* and *TransformEHR*, have further improved representation learning

[1] https://github.com/FLaTNNBio/CHRONOS.

[2] https://github.com/FLaTNNBio/CHRONOS/blob/main/SupplementaryMaterial_CHRONOS.pdf.

and disease prediction from structured health records [19,32]. These approaches demonstrate the value of longitudinal sequence modeling in healthcare, but they are usually developed for richer EHR settings in which the main goal is forecasting future events, not disentangling progression signals from the care-process artifacts that are especially salient in routine primary-care administrative data.

Methods for population-level trajectory analysis have shown that temporal disease networks can reveal broad progression structures across clinical domains [18,26]. They usually explore directed comorbidity networks from registry and electronic health record data, often with the goal of identifying interpretable temporal associations at scale [28,31,33]. These studies are valuable for descriptive epidemiology and hypothesis generation, but their comorbidities are generally association-based. This limitation is particularly relevant in primary-care administrative data, where temporal ordering may be strongly influenced by surveillance intensity, prescription routines, coding synchronization, and other healthcare-process mechanisms rather than by downstream disease risk alone.

As for causal effect estimation from observational longitudinal data, target trial emulation provides a principled framework for defining causal questions through explicit eligibility criteria, time zero, treatment strategies, follow-up, and outcomes [13]. Causal representation learning methods such as *TARNet* and *CFRNet* learn latent spaces that facilitate effect estimation in high-dimensional settings [14,24], while doubly robust estimators such as *AIPW* improve robustness to model misspecification, especially when combined with cross-fitting [1,7,22]. More recent sequential causal models extend these ideas to longitudinal settings with time-varying treatments and counterfactual trajectories [4,20,21]. Related causal studies have also addressed comorbidity analysis more directly, for example through counterfactual estimation of comorbidity risk factors in Alzheimer's disease and related dementias and causal structure discovery from EHR data in type-2 diabetes mellitus [16,25]. However, these approaches are generally designed for disease-specific causal analysis, local structure discovery, or patient-level counterfactual estimation. They are not designed to screen a large collection of candidate disease-to-disease transitions under a common causal protocol and then assemble the retained effects into an interpretable progression network.

In our setting, the progression network is not assumed a priori, but is instead constructed as the final output of repeated comorbidity-level target trial emulations, each one defined by its own eligibility criteria, cohort alignment strategy, and doubly robust effect estimate. The key challenge is not simply the availability of predictive models, disease trajectory analyses, or causal estimation methods taken separately. Rather, the open problem lies in integrating explicit causal design, longitudinal representation learning, and robust effect estimation into a unified framework capable of screening a large number of candidate directed comorbidity relationships in routine primary-care administrative data, where observed sequences reflect both underlying disease burden and ongoing care processes. This is precisely the setting addressed by `CHRONOS`.

3 Problem Formulation

We study comorbidity progression discovery as a large-scale causal analysis of directed disease pairs in longitudinal primary-care data. For each pair of diseases D_a, D_b, we denote with $D_a \rightarrow D_b$ the comorbidity candidate between D_a and D_b. For such a candidate, we emulate a target trial aligned at time zero t_0, corresponding to the incident onset of D_a, and estimate its effect on the risk of developing D_b within a fixed follow-up horizon. Figure 1 shows the workflow: patient histories are constructed from routine records, disease pairs are evaluated under this framework, and retained effects are assembled into a data-driven progression graph after doubly robust estimation and multiplicity control.

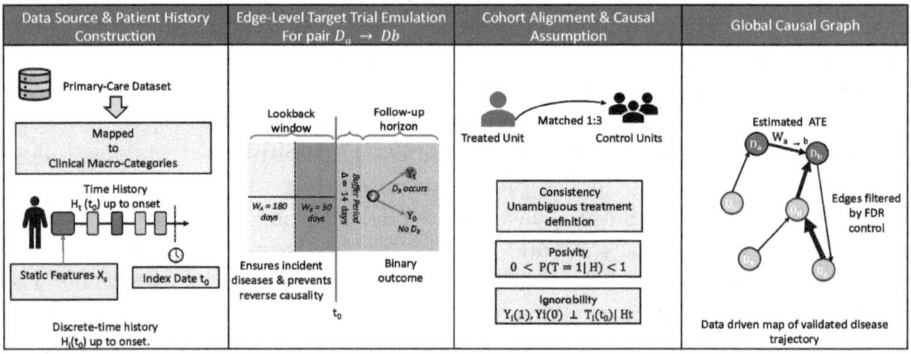

Fig. 1. *Overview of the CHRONOS pipeline.* Longitudinal patient histories are constructed from primary-care data, candidate disease pairs are then evaluated under an edge-level target trial design, and retained effects are assembled into a data-driven progression graph after doubly robust estimation and multiplicity control.

3.1 Edge-Level Target Trial Emulation

To emulate the target trial for each edge (D_a, D_b) we specify exposure assignment, eligibility criteria, follow-up, and outcome definition.

As for the exposure assignment and eligibility criteria, the problem is to construct the treated and control groups. In our setting, the treated group consists of all patients who have a diagnosis of D_a. Starting from such a treated group, we construct the control group by anchoring controls to the treated patient's time zero to improve temporal comparability and reduce time-window bias, as follows: *(i)* for each treated patient x, let t_0 be the first eligible recorded diagnosis of D_a for x, we apply a 180-day treatment-free period W_a and consider only patients with no history of D_a in $[t_0 - W_a, t_0]$, *(ii)* among these patients, we consider only those who have a significant history in terms of the number of prescriptions in the period considered, and we select k of them randomly (in our experiments $k = 3$ was the most stable value) to be included in the control group.

As for the follow-up and outcome definition, the outcome is defined as whether the patient received a diagnosis of D_b ($outcome = 1$) or not ($outcome = 0$). The problem is to identify the outcome for patients within the treated and control groups. To this aim, we proceed as follows. For each patient x in treated or control group, we define a time window after which we observe whether D_b develops or not. Specifically, we require a 30-day outcome-free period W_b after t_0. If x has any diagnosis of D_b after $[t_0, t_0 + W_b]$ we set $outcome = 1$, otherwise $outcome = 0$. This is intended to reduce temporal ambiguity, namely the possibility that D_b was already present or developing before the recorded onset of D_a, in which case the observed relation would be difficult to interpret as downstream progression (diseases developed simultaneously and not one because of the other). We further introduce a buffer period of $\Delta = 14$ days between t_0 and the start of the main outcome window to mitigate two common sources of bias in administrative longitudinal data: *surveillance bias*, whereby a new diagnosis of D_a triggers intensified follow-up that may uncover a pre-existing but previously unrecorded D_b, and *administrative coding delays*, whereby multiple diagnoses from the same clinical episode are recorded over several days. Following an intention-to-treat-style design, control patients who subsequently develop D_a during follow-up are not artificially censored and remain in the control group.

Preprocessing and cohort details are reported in *Supplementary Material S1–S2*, including ICD-9-CM macro-category mapping, cohort size, event density, follow-up, demographics, and category coverage. Trial-design defaults are reported in *Supplementary Material S6*, while *Supplementary Material S7* shows that the main findings are relatively stable to moderate changes in buffer and follow-up windows, but more sensitive to the treated-to-control sampling ratio.

3.2 Estimation of Effects, Edge Definition, and Assumptions

For each emulated trial corresponding to an edge $D_a \rightarrow D_b$, we estimate the Average Treatment Effect (ATE) using a cross-fitted Augmented Inverse Probability Weighting (AIPW) estimator [7]. Let $\hat{\mu}_1(H_{t_0})$ and $\hat{\mu}_0(H_{t_0})$ denote the estimated outcome regressions under treatment and control, and let $\hat{e}(H_{t_0})$ denote the estimated propensity score. Intuitively, AIPW combines outcome regression (predicting the risk of D_b under treatment and control) with inverse-probability weighting based on the pre-index history. This yields a doubly robust estimator that remains consistent if at least one of the two components is correctly specified. The trimmed AIPW score for patient i is

$$\hat{\psi}_i = \hat{\mu}_1(H_{t_0}^{(i)}) - \hat{\mu}_0(H_{t_0}^{(i)}) + \frac{T_i}{\tilde{e}_i}\Big(Y_i - \hat{\mu}_1(H_{t_0}^{(i)})\Big) - \frac{1 - T_i}{1 - \tilde{e}_i}\Big(Y_i - \hat{\mu}_0(H_{t_0}^{(i)})\Big),$$

where the remaining terms correct this quantity using the observed outcome Y_i. $\hat{e}(H_{t_0})$ is trimmed as $\tilde{e}_i = \min\{1 - \epsilon, \max\{\hat{e}(H_{t_0}^{(i)}), \epsilon\}\}$, to reduce instability due to extreme inverse-probability weights. The estimated edge weight is obtained by averaging the scores: $\widehat{w}_{a \to b} = \frac{1}{n}\sum_{i=1}^{n} \hat{\psi}_i$. Thus, $\widehat{w}_{a \to b}$ can be interpreted as the estimated absolute risk difference for developing D_b within the follow-up horizon, attributable to the incident onset of D_a under the stated assumptions.

Identification relies on consistency, no interference, conditional ignorability given the pre-index history H_{t_0}, and positivity, under the edge-specific target-trial design. *Supplementary Material S3* formalizes these assumptions and discusses their observational limitations, while *Supplementary Material S5* reports overlap, ESS, and placebo diagnostics used to distinguish well-supported edges from more fragile or potentially biased relations.

4 CHRONOS

`CHRONOS` estimates disease progression from longitudinal observational data by learning patient representations that integrate pre-index temporal histories with static patient features, while structuring the latent space so that patients with similar estimated ITEs are mapped nearby and those with dissimilar ITEs are placed farther apart. We use a contrastive loss where the margin ensures that a significant clinical difference in ITE is always reflected by a proportional geometric distance in the patient embedding. The model is designed for edge-specific target trials: for each candidate relation $D_a \to D_b$, it learns a representation of the patient's history before t_0, predicts the outcome risk under treatment and control, estimates treatment propensity, and regularizes the embedding space so that local neighborhoods reflect ITEs similarity rather than covariate similarity.

Figure 2 provides an overview of the architecture and its training components. Final edge weights are then obtained through cross-fitted doubly robust estimation, as described in Sect. 3.

4.1 Siamese Architecture

During training, `CHRONOS` operates on patient pairs (i, j) sampled from the same edge-specific trial cohort. The two patients in each pair are processed by identical encoder branches with shared parameters, forming a Siamese architecture in which both elements of the pair are embedded in a common latent space. For each patient i at trial index time t_0, the encoder receives a pre-index temporal sequence together with static covariates. Let $\mathbf{X}_q^{(i)} = (\mathbf{x}_{q,1}^{(i)}, \ldots, \mathbf{x}_{q,B}^{(i)})$ denote the temporal history over the baseline window, where each $\mathbf{x}_{q,t}^{(i)}$ is a feature vector summarizing the patient's observed events in the corresponding time bin for the current trial. To reduce the impact of highly uneven event counts (e.g., sparse bins with only a few events versus denser bins with many repeated diagnoses or prescriptions), we apply a $\log(1 + x)$ transformation and process the sequence through a shared GRU: $\mathbf{h}_t^{(i)} = \mathrm{GRU}\left(\mathbf{x}_{q,t}^{(i)}, \mathbf{h}_{t-1}^{(i)}\right), \mathbf{h}_t^{(i)} \in \mathbb{R}^{d_h}$, where the final state $\mathbf{h}_B^{(i)}$ summarizes the patient's temporal evolution up to t_0.

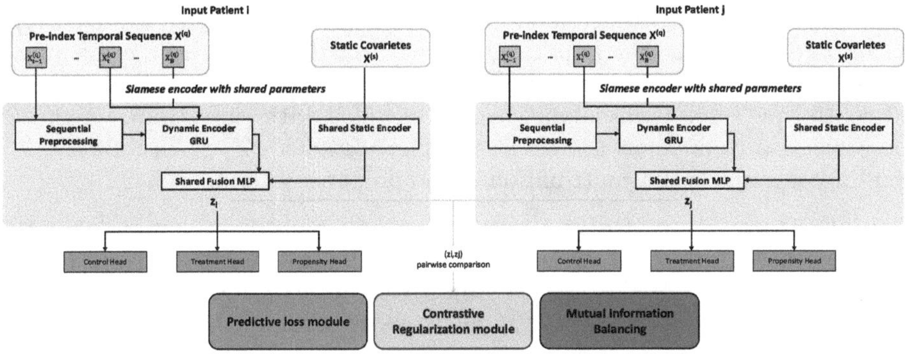

Fig. 2. Overview of the CHRONOS architecture. Two patients from the same edge-specific trial cohort are processed by Siamese branches with shared parameters. Each branch encodes pre-index temporal history and static covariates into a latent representation (z_i and z_j), which is then used by shared control, treatment, and propensity heads. The pairwise representations are regularized through ITEs contrastive learning, while predictive supervision and optional mutual-information balancing contribute to the overall training objective.

Let $\mathbf{x}_s^{(i)} \in \mathbb{R}^{d_s}$ denote the static covariates (e.g., sex, birth year, frailty-related information). Static and dynamic information are then encoded and fused as

$$\mathbf{h}_s^{(i)} = \text{MLP}_{\text{stat}}(\mathbf{x}_s^{(i)}), \qquad \mathbf{z}_i = \text{MLP}_{\text{fus}}\Big([\mathbf{h}_B^{(i)} \parallel \mathbf{h}_s^{(i)}]\Big), \tag{1}$$

with $\mathbf{h}_s^{(i)} \in \mathbb{R}^{d_h}$ and $\mathbf{z}_i \in \mathbb{R}^{d_z}$. By Siamese design, patient j is processed through the same shared encoder, yielding $\mathbf{z}_j$. We adopt a GRU because its gating mitigates the vanishing-gradient issues of vanilla RNNs while matching LSTM performance with fewer parameters [9], which suits our short, sparse binned event sequences. Low-dimensional, unordered static covariates are encoded with an MLP. The temporal encoder is modular: our ITE-based contrastive regularization and doubly robust pipeline are agnostic to it and accommodate alternative encoders. From the latent representation $\mathbf{z}_i$, CHRONOS predicts both potential outcomes and treatment propensity:

$$\hat{\mu}_0(\mathbf{z}_i) = \sigma(\mathbf{W}_0^\top \mathbf{z}_i + b_0), \quad \hat{\mu}_1(\mathbf{z}_i) = \sigma(\mathbf{W}_1^\top \mathbf{z}_i + b_1), \quad \hat{e}(\mathbf{z}_i) = \sigma(\mathbf{W}_e^\top \mathbf{z}_i + b_e). \tag{2}$$

4.2 Training Objectives

CHRONOS is trained end-to-end with a composite objective that combines factual supervision, propensity prediction, mutual-information balancing, and Siamese contrastive regularization.

Factual Outcome and Propensity Supervision. The first component of the objective is supervised learning on the observed trial data. Given the factual prediction $\hat{Y}_{f,i}$ and the observed outcome Y_i, we optimize a binary cross-entropy loss for outcome prediction. In parallel, we train the propensity head using binary cross-entropy on the treatment label T_i. To mitigate imbalance between treated and control patients, mini-batches can be sampled with class-aware weighting. The predictive component is therefore $\mathcal{L}_{\text{pred}} = \text{BCE}(\hat{Y}_f, Y) + \lambda_{\text{prop}} \text{BCE}(\hat{e}, T)$, where λ_{prop} controls the contribution of the propensity term.

Mutual-Information Balancing. To improve causal estimation, `CHRONOS` uses a mutual-information regularization term based on **M**utual **I**nformation **N**eural **E**stimation (MINE) [2]. The objective is to learn latent representations that are less informative about treatment assignment, which might otherwise encode selection-related differences between treated and control patients, while remaining informative about the outcome. Let the encoder f_θ map each patient history to a representation $\mathbf{z} = f_\theta(\cdot)$, and denote by $\mathbf{Z}$ the corresponding random variable. Two critics[3] estimate $\widehat{MI}(\mathbf{Z}, T)$ and $\widehat{MI}(\mathbf{Z}, Y)$, respectively.

$\widehat{MI}(\mathbf{Z}, T)$ measures how much information about T is captured in the latent representation $\mathbf{Z}$. Our aim is to minimise this quantity because a representation that shows whether a patient belongs to the treatment or control group may reflect differences related to selection rather than providing a balanced clinical representation. This yields the balancing objective $\mathcal{L}_{\text{MI}} = \lambda_b \widehat{MI}(\mathbf{Z}, T) - \lambda_o \widehat{MI}(\mathbf{Z}, Y)$, where λ_b and λ_o control the trade-off between suppressing treatment-related information and preserving outcome-relevant information. Since the overall optimization is performed by minimization, the first term is directly penalized, whereas the second appears with a negative sign so that minimizing $\mathcal{L}_{\text{MI}}$ corresponds to maximizing $\widehat{MI}(\mathbf{Z}, Y)$.

The `MINE` component is optimized intermittently through separate critic updates and is introduced periodically into the overall training objective.

Siamese Contrastive Regularization. The core component of `CHRONOS` is a contrastive regularization strategy that encourages patients with similar ITEs to be close in latent space, so that local neighborhoods reflect treatment-effect heterogeneity rather than only observed covariate similarity. For a sampled pair (i, j) in a mini-batch, we compute the effect-space distance $d^{\tau}_{i,j} = \|\text{sg}(\hat{\tau}_i) - \text{sg}(\hat{\tau}_j)\|_2$, where $\text{sg}(\cdot)$ denotes the stopgradient operator, and define pseudo-labels dynamically by setting $y_{i,j} = 1$ if $d^{\tau}_{i,j} \leq c$, where c is the p-th percentile of batchwise pairwise effect distances, and $y_{i,j} = 0$ otherwise. Let $d^{z}_{i,j} = \|\mathbf{z}_i - \mathbf{z}_j\|_2$ denote the latent-space distance. The contrastive loss is

$$\mathcal{L}_{\text{cont}} = \frac{1}{|\mathcal{P}|} \sum_{(i,j)\in\mathcal{P}} \left[y_{i,j} (d^{z}_{i,j})^2 + (1 - y_{i,j}) \max(0, m - d^{z}_{i,j})^2 \right],$$

where $\mathcal{P}$ is the sampled pair set and $m > 0$ is a margin. This objective pulls together pairs with similar ITE and pushes apart those with dissimilar effects, encouraging local causal coherence in the learned latent space (Fig. 3).

[3] We use the term *critic* to denote an auxiliary neural scorer that estimates statistical dependence, rather than a classifier that directly predicts labels.

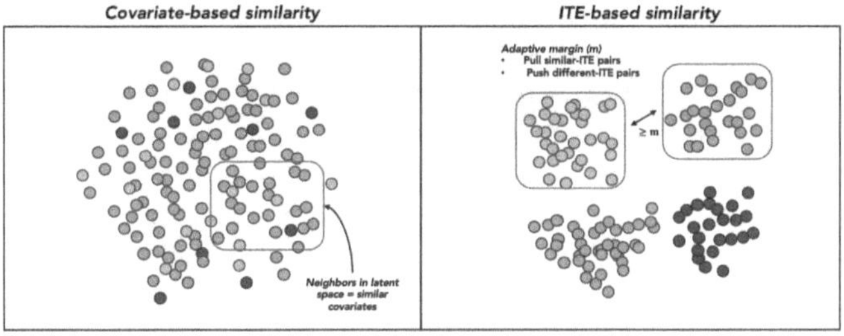

Fig. 3. Siamese contrastive intuition. *Left:* covariate-based neighborhoods may group patients with similar observed histories but different treatment responses. *Right:* `CHRONOS` instead defines similarity through estimated ITE proximity, pulling together patients with similar predicted effects and separating those with dissimilar effects.

The overall training objective combines predictive supervision, optional mutual-information balancing, and contrastive loss, as follows:

$$\mathcal{L}_{\text{tot}} = \mathcal{L}_{\text{pred}} + \alpha\,\mathcal{L}_{\text{cont}} + \lambda_b\widehat{MI}(\mathbf{Z}, T) - \lambda_o\widehat{MI}(\mathbf{Z}, Y),$$

where α controls the contribution of the contrastive term, while λ_b and λ_o control the trade-off between treatment-information suppression and outcome-information preservation. The main architectural hyperparameters, optimization settings and trial-design defaults used to obtain the reported results are summarized in *Supplementary Material S6.*

To reduce overfitting and obtain out-of-fold effect estimates, we adopt a K-fold cross-fitting strategy. For each candidate edge, we compute 95% confidence intervals using the large-sample normal approximation, with standard errors derived from the empirical variance of the estimated AIPW scores.

Target trials are generated separately for each edge and the resulting estimates are then aggregated across all evaluated edges. To account for multiple testing, we apply the Benjamini–Hochberg procedure to control the False Discovery Rate (FDR) globally over the full set of candidate edges [3]. An estimated effect is retained as a progression edge only if it passes the chosen FDR threshold and satisfies requirements, including a sufficient number of treated patients.

5 Experimental Evaluation

We evaluate `CHRONOS` on a large real-world longitudinal primary-care cohort and analyze the resulting confounding-adjusted disease progression network under the edge-level target trial emulation framework introduced in Sect. 3. For each directed pair $D_a \rightarrow D_b$, we estimate a cross-fitted doubly robust ATE, report Wald-type 95% confidence intervals, and control multiplicity across tested edges using the Benjamini–Hochberg procedure.

5.1 Real World Dataset

We evaluate our framework on a real-world primary-care dataset from the Campania region (Italy), derived from routine general-practice records collected from 2000 to 2018. The processed cohort comprises 64,828 patients and 9,063,742 events, with a median of 42 prescriptions per patient (IQR 12–148). The cohort is approximately balanced by sex (52.9% female), and the most frequent diagnosis groups include respiratory, digestive, musculoskeletal, and genitourinary conditions. For each patient i, we observe pre-index information up to t_0, including static covariates, recent healthcare utilization, summary counts of past diagnoses and prescriptions, and the time-ordered sequence of events in the baseline window. To reduce sparsity, raw ICD-9-CM codes are mapped into 16 clinical macro-categories, as detailed in the data-processing section (*Supplementary Material S1*, Table 1); full cohort descriptive statistics are reported in the cohort-summary section (*Supplementary Material S2*, Table 2).

This cohort provides sufficient temporal depth, event density, and population coverage to support large-scale edge-level target trial emulation across ICD-9 macro-category pairs. Figure 4 shows the resulting directed progression graph, while Fig. 5 reports the associated $D_a \rightarrow D_b$ effect matrix. The $D_a \rightarrow D_b$ screening space consists of all ordered exposure–outcome pairs defined over the retained ICD-9 macro-categories, excluding self-edges and edge configurations that are not admissible under the implemented trial design. Each candidate pair corresponds to a separate edge-specific target trial with its own aligned treated and control cohort, model for estimation, AIPW effect estimate, and placebo diagnostic. The resulting family of 225 directed tests should therefore be under-

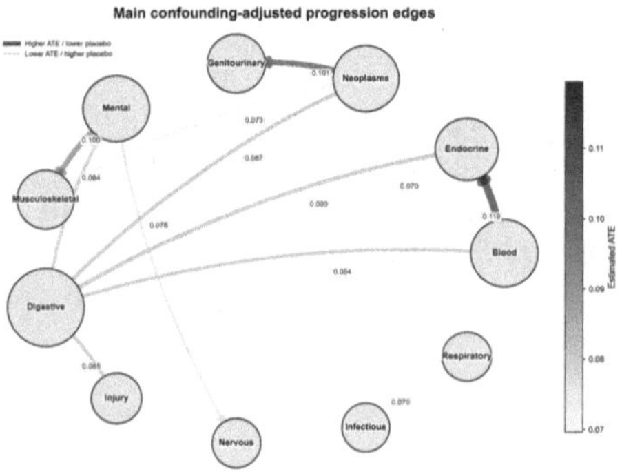

Fig. 4. Disease progression network inferred from edge-level target trial emulation. Nodes denote ICD-9 macro-categories and directed edges denote FDR-significant confounding-adjusted progression-risk relations weighted by estimated ATE.

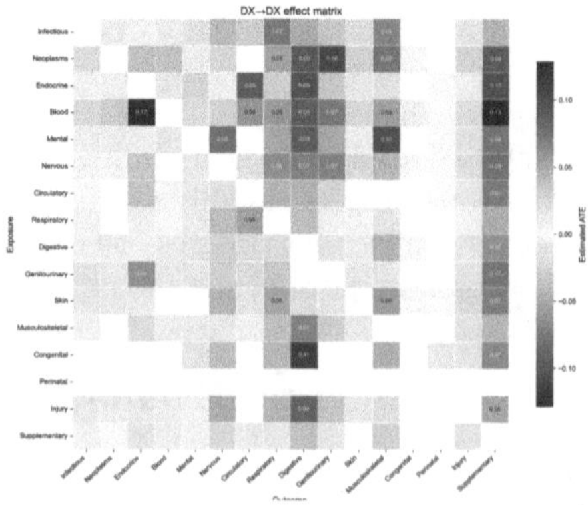

Fig. 5. Estimated $D_a \rightarrow D_b$ effect matrix.

stood as a structured trial grid over candidate progression relations, rather than as a post hoc collection of isolated comparisons.

CHRONOS targets longitudinal, community-based primary-care trajectories, where chronic conditions accumulate slowly and surface through routine prescriptions. Intensive-care benchmarks such as MIMIC-III/IV [15] capture acute, in-hospital episodes over short stays and lack the primary-care prescription histories our edge-level target-trial emulation relies on; evaluating on them would measure a different construct. We therefore restrict evaluation to a primary-care cohort and leave external validation on other large primary-care databases to future work.

5.2 Real-World Disease-to-Disease Progression Network

We evaluated 225 directed $D_a \rightarrow D_b$ candidate edges across the macro-category graph. After global Benjamini–Hochberg correction, 188 edges remained significant at the selected FDR threshold. Across all tested relations, estimated ATE values ranged approximately from -0.02 to 0.13, indicating that the inferred graph contains both weak or null relations and a substantial subset of directional progression-risk links that remain statistically supported after multiplicity control. The emulated cohorts were generally large and stable. Trial-level sample sizes count aligned treated/control observations after risk-set sampling, and may exceed the number of unique patients because controls can be reused across treated anchors within the same trial. Consistently, trial-level diagnostics suggest broadly stable support, with median sample size around 66k, median ESS close to 60k, median propensity about 0.45, and zero median trimming. Overall, these diagnostics indicate good empirical support and no major overlap or weight-instability problems, although they do not eliminate the possibility of residual bias. At the same time, given the large cohort, long observation horizon, and broad ICD-9 macro-category aggregation, even relatively small but stable risk differences may reach statistical significance. For this reason, FDR retention should be interpreted mainly as a screening criterion rather than as sufficient evidence of scientific importance by itself. The most informative $D_a \rightarrow D_b$ relations are those combining relatively large effects, confidence intervals away from zero, adequate cohort support, limited placebo activity, and directional asymmetry. Accordingly, retained edges should be viewed as confounding-adjusted progression-risk signals rather than definitive mechanistic discoveries.

Table 1 reports a set of representative high-effect edges $D_a \rightarrow D_b$, selected for clinical interpretability. The full set of evaluated $D_a \rightarrow D_b$ edges is reported in the complete edge-results section (*Supplementary Material S4*, Table 3). All edges listed here remain statistically significant after global multiple-testing correction using the Benjamini-Hochberg procedure, meaning they are associated with favorable q values below the chosen FDR threshold. Each row corresponds to a direct candidate progression edge $D_a \rightarrow D_b$, and reports the ATE which quantifies the increase in the probability of observing D_b after the incident D_a event. The placebo test estimates the same effect in a short post-index window preceding the main outcome window. It should be close to zero if the causal

Table 1. Representative and clinically interpretable high-effect $D_a \to D_b$ edges

$D_a \to D_b$	ATE	95% CI	Placebo	Reverse ATE	n
BLD → ENDO	0.119	[0.111, 0.128]	-0.035	0.013	28,944
NEOP → GEN	0.101	[0.091, 0.110]	-0.012	0.016	31,464
MENT → MUSC	0.100	[0.091, 0.109]	-0.039	0.010	38,508
ENDO → DIGE	0.090	[0.082, 0.097]	-0.047	0.007	59,545
NEOP → DIGE	0.087	[0.076, 0.098]	-0.041	0.011	29,556
INJ → DIGE	0.085	[0.078, 0.092]	-0.036	0.013	61,068
MENT → NERV	0.076	[0.069, 0.083]	-0.018	0.014	40,192
NERV → GEN	0.067	[0.061, 0.072]	-0.019	0.031	83,798

design has adequately removed short-window spurious temporal associations. High placebo values indicate residual confounding, surveillance effects, or violations of temporal ordering assumptions. The inverse ATE summarizing the estimated effect in the opposite direction is $D_b \to D_a$.

Several rows show clear directional structure. BLD → ENDO has the largest effect (ATE = 0.119) with a small placebo and a much smaller reverse effect (0.013), and NEOP → GEN follows the same pattern; MENT → MUSC and MENT → NERV are notable for connecting broad chronic-condition domains rather than within-category persistence. The digestive category recurs as a downstream outcome (ENDO/NEOP/INJ → DIGE), suggesting a frequent burden domain, though its larger placebo magnitudes warrant caution; NERV → GEN shows a less negligible reverse effect, indicating that not all retained edges are equally asymmetric.

5.3 Baseline Comparison and Ablation Study

To further assess whether the empirical behavior of CHRONOS is driven by its structured causal-temporal representation rather than by predictive capacity alone, we conducted a compact robustness analysis combining two complementary perspectives: a comparison with *simpler baselines* and an *ablation study* of the main architectural components. The baseline comparison evaluates estimators with increasing methodological complexity, whereas the ablation study isolates the contribution of the representation-structuring mechanisms introduced in CHRONOS.

We considered three simpler baselines. `Naive RD` estimates raw risk differences and therefore captures unadjusted temporal associations between an index disease and a downstream outcome. `AIPW Logistic` is a classical doubly robust estimator based on logistic nuisance models for propensity and outcome estimation. `Pred only` uses the predictive backbone of CHRONOS, but removes the contrastive and mutual-information regularization terms, thereby isolating the effect of predictive representation learning alone. In addition, we evaluated two ablated variants of the full model: `No contrastive`, where the Siamese contrastive term is removed, and No MI, where the mutual-information balancing terms are removed.

Table 2. Robustness and baseline comparison on the 8 representative edge-level trials. FDR+ denotes the number of edges retained after global FDR correction. Placebo reports the median absolute placebo estimate, ESS the median effective sample size, and Trim the median trimming proportion when available.

Type	Method	FDR+	Mean ATE	Placebo	ESS	Trim
Baseline	Naive RD	7/8	0.045	0.004	39350.0	0.0000
Baseline	AIPW Logistic	8/8	0.035	0.002	27299.5	0.0001
Baseline	Pred only	8/8	0.050	0.043	16524.1	0.0040
Ablation	No contrastive	8/8	0.046	0.038	35688.1	–
Ablation	No MI	8/8	0.054	0.037	35842.5	–
Full	CHRONOS	8/8	0.056	0.037	36465.8	0.0000

Table 2 shows that several representative relations can already be detected by simpler estimators, especially given the large cohort size and the strength of some temporal associations. However, the interpretation of these signals differs across methods. Naive RD retains seven out of eight representative edges, but lacks explicit adjustment for confounding and should therefore be interpreted as an associational reference rather than a causal estimator. AIPW Logistic retains all eight edges after FDR correction, confirming that classical doubly robust adjustment captures relevant progression-risk signals. Nevertheless, its median effective sample size is substantially lower than that of CHRONOS, suggesting less stable weighted treated–control comparisons.

The comparison with Pred only is particularly informative because this variant shares the predictive backbone of CHRONOS. Although it retains all eight representative edges and achieves a nontrivial mean ATE, its median ESS drops to 16,524.1 and it requires more trimming than the full model. This indicates that predictive supervision alone can recover statistically significant signals, but does not organize the representation space as effectively for stable causal contrasts. By contrast, CHRONOS achieves the largest mean ATE, retains all representative edges, maintains a high median ESS, and requires virtually no trimming.

The ablation results further clarify the role of the main architectural components. Removing the contrastive term reduces the mean ATE from 0.056 to 0.046, suggesting that Siamese contrastive regularization contributes to sharper effect separation. Removing the mutual-information terms has a smaller impact on average effect magnitude, with No MI remaining close to the full model. However, the full architecture provides the most favorable overall trade-off between effect magnitude, placebo behavior, and effective sample support, indicating that the benefit of CHRONOS arises from the joint interaction of its components rather than from predictive flexibility alone.

Overall, these findings indicate that CHRONOS should be evaluated through the joint behavior of effect size, overlap, placebo diagnostics, ESS, and trimming, rather than through ATE magnitude. A desirable edge-level estimator should combine meaningful estimated effects with favorable overlap diagnostics, limited placebo behavior, stable effective sample support, and reduced reliance on trimming. Under this perspective, CHRONOS provides the most balanced empirical behavior across the evaluated diagnostics. Complementary robustness diagnoses are reported in *Supplementary Material S5*, sensitivity to trial-design choices is analyzed in *Supplementary Material S7*, and the edge-specific Cox baseline in *Supplementary Material S8* shows that survival-model analyzes provide a useful epidemiological reference but are less stable than the main doubly robust trial-emulation framework when applied at scale.

6 Conclusions

We proposed CHRONOS, a causal-temporal representation learning framework for disease-to-disease progression discovery from longitudinal observational primary-care data. CHRONOS moves beyond raw temporal co-occurrence and estimates directional progression-risk relations under a consistent causal design. The inferred graph should be interpreted with caution. Administrative primary-care data capture not only disease evolution, but also how patients are diagnosed, monitored, treated, and documented in routine care. Therefore, some edges may reflect clinically meaningful downstream risk, whereas others may be influenced by surveillance intensity, continuity of care, coding conventions, or residual healthcare-process effects. Accordingly, CHRONOS should be viewed as a scalable screening framework for prioritizing candidate progression relations, rather than as a direct map of biological disease mechanisms.

Several limitations remain. First, MINE-style mutual-information objectives increase optimization complexity and can be unstable, serving mainly as auxiliary training signals. Second, adaptive contrastive pairing relies on pseudo-ITE estimates that may be noisy during early training epochs. Third, residual confounding may persist since latent severity, physician judgment, and unobserved frailty influence both exposure and recording. Fourth, aggregating diagnoses into broad ICD-9 macro-categories improves support but reduces clinical granularity, requiring interpretation at the domain level. Finally, while privacy constraints prevent raw data release, our repository provides synthetic examples to illustrate the data structure and workflow. Future work includes external validation across healthcare systems, prospective assessment, and clinician-led evaluation of actionability. Although multi-step trajectories can already be traced by composing the inferred pairwise edges, directly modeling longer disease chains (e.g., through multi-state or dynamic treatment-regime formulations) is a natural next step.

From a deployment standpoint, CHRONOS is intended as a population-level decision-support layer for surveillance and care planning, producing clinician-reviewable hypotheses rather than autonomous decisions, and contingent on external and prospective validation and on fairness and governance safeguards. Overall, CHRONOS provides a scalable and diagnostically transparent framework for screening disease-progression relations in longitudinal primary-care data, while explicitly preserving the distinction between causal progression signals and associations that may still reflect data-generating or healthcare-process biases.

References

1. Bang, H., Robins, J.M.: Doubly robust estimation in missing data and causal inference models. Biometrics **61**(4), 962–973 (2005)
2. Belghazi, M.I., et al.: Mutual information neural estimation. In: ICML, pp. 531–540. PMLR (2018)
3. Benjamini, Y., Hochberg, Y.: Controlling the false discovery rate: a practical and powerful approach to multiple testing. J. Roy. Stat. Soc.: Ser. B (Methodol.) **57**(1), 289–300 (1995)
4. Bica, I., Alaa, A.M., Jordon, J., Van Der Schaar, M.: Estimating counterfactual treatment outcomes over time through adversarially balanced representations. arXiv preprint arXiv:2002.04083 (2020)
5. Caruana, R., Lou, Y., Gehrke, J., Koch, P., Sturm, M., Elhadad, N.: Intelligible models for healthcare: predicting pneumonia risk and hospital 30-day readmission. In: Proceedings of the 21th ACM SIGKDD International Conference on Knowledge Discovery and Data Mining, pp. 1721–1730 (2015)
6. Cezard, G., McHale, C.T., Sullivan, F., Bowles, J.K.F., Keenan, K.: Studying trajectories of multimorbidity: a systematic scoping review of longitudinal approaches and evidence. BMJ Open **11**(11), e048485 (2021)
7. Chernozhukov, V., et al.: Double/debiased machine learning for treatment and structural parameters (2018)
8. Choi, E., Bahadori, M.T., Schuetz, A., Stewart, W.F., Sun, J.: Doctor ai: predicting clinical events via recurrent neural networks. In: Machine Learning for Healthcare Conference, pp. 301–318. PMLR (2016)
9. Chung, J., Gulcehre, C., Cho, K., Bengio, Y.: Empirical evaluation of gated recurrent neural networks on sequence modeling. arXiv preprint arXiv:1412.3555 (2014)
10. Crooks, C.J., West, J., Card, T.R.: A comparison of the recording of comorbidity in primary and secondary care by using the charlson index to predict short-term and long-term survival in a routine linked data cohort. BMJ Open **5**(6), e007974 (2015)
11. Finlayson, S.G., et al.: The clinician and dataset shift in artificial intelligence. N. Engl. J. Med. **385**(3), 283–286 (2021)
12. Geirhos, R., et al.: Shortcut learning in deep neural networks. Nat. Mach. Intell. **2**(11), 665–673 (2020)
13. Hernán, M.A., Robins, J.M.: Using big data to emulate a target trial when a randomized trial is not available. Am. J. Epidemiol. **183**(8), 758–764 (2016)
14. Johansson, F., Shalit, U., Sontag, D.: Learning representations for counterfactual inference. In: ICML, pp. 3020–3029. PMLR (2016)
15. Johnson, A.E., et al.: Mimic-iv, a freely accessible electronic health record dataset. Sci. Data **10**(1), 1 (2023)
16. Kim, Y., Zhang, K., Savitz, S.I., Chen, L., Schulz, P.E., Jiang, X.: Counterfactual analysis of differential comorbidity risk factors in Alzheimer's disease and related dementias. PLOS Dig. Health **1**(3), e0000018 (2022)

17. Kingston, A., Robinson, L., Booth, H., Knapp, M., Jagger, C., Project, M.: Projections of multi-morbidity in the older population in England to 2035: estimates from the population ageing and care simulation (pacsim) model. Age Ageing **47**(3), 374–380 (2018)
18. Lee, D.g., Kim, M., Shin, H.: Inference on chains of disease progression based on disease networks. PLoS One **14**(6), e0218871 (2019)
19. Li, Y., et al.: Behrt: transformer for electronic health records. Sci. Rep. **10**(1), 7155 (2020)
20. Melnychuk, V., Frauen, D., Feuerriegel, S.: Causal transformer for estimating counterfactual outcomes. In: ICML, pp. 15293–15329. PMLR (2022)
21. Qian, Z., Zhang, Y., Bica, I., Wood, A., van der Schaar, M.: Synctwin: treatment effect estimation with longitudinal outcomes. Adv. Neural. Inf. Process. Syst. **34**, 3178–3190 (2021)
22. Robins, J.M., Rotnitzky, A., Zhao, L.P.: Estimation of regression coefficients when some regressors are not always observed. J. Am. Stat. Assoc. **89**(427), 846–866 (1994)
23. Salas, M., Hotman, A., Stricker, B.H.: Confounding by indication: an example of variation in the use of epidemiologic terminology. Am. J. Epidemiol. **149**(11), 981–983 (1999)
24. Shalit, U., Johansson, F.D., Sontag, D.: Estimating individual treatment effect: generalization bounds and algorithms. In: ICML, pp. 3076–3085. PMLR (2017)
25. Shen, X., Ma, S., Vemuri, P., Castro, M.R., Caraballo, P.J., Simon, G.J.: A novel method for causal structure discovery from ehr data and its application to type-2 diabetes mellitus. Sci. Rep. **11**(1), 21025 (2021)
26. Siggaard, T., et al.: Disease trajectory browser for exploring temporal, population-wide disease progression patterns in 7.2 million danish patients. Nat. Commun. **11**(1), 4952 (2020)
27. Sinha, A., Mukherjee, S., Tripathi, S., Dutta, S.: Issues and challenges of polypharmacy in the elderly: a review of contemporary Indian literature. J. Family Med. Primary Care **10**(10), 3544–3547 (2021)
28. Sriram, V., et al.: A network-based analysis of disease complication associations for obstetric disorders in the UK biobank. J. Pers. Med. **11**(12), 1382 (2021)
29. Strauss, V.Y., Jones, P.W., Kadam, U.T., Jordan, K.P.: Distinct trajectories of multimorbidity in primary care were identified using latent class growth analysis. J. Clin. Epidemiol. **67**(10), 1163–1171 (2014)
30. Subbaswamy, A., Saria, S.: From development to deployment: dataset shift, causality, and shift-stable models in health ai. Biostatistics **21**(2), 345–352 (2020)
31. Tang, Z., Yu, Y., Ng, K., Sow, D., Hu, J., Mei, J.: Disease network delineates the disease progression profile of cardiovascular diseases. J. Biomed. Inf. **115**, 103686 (2021)
32. Yang, Z., Mitra, A., Liu, W., Berlowitz, D., Yu, H.: Transformehr: transformer-based encoder-decoder generative model to enhance prediction of disease outcomes using electronic health records. Nat. Commun. **14**(1), 7857 (2023)
33. Zhao, B., Huepenbecker, S., Zhu, G., Rajan, S.S., Fujimoto, K., Luo, X.: Comorbidity network analysis using graphical models for electronic health records. Front. Big Data **6**, 846202 (2023)

ColdNet: Scalable Causal Inference for Sales Forecasting Under Severe Cold-Start, Treatment Imbalance, and Zero-Inflated Outcomes

Mahmudur Rahman, Sanskar Tewatia(✉), and Dhruv Garg

Seattle, USA
{mahmudxm,tsanskar,gargdhru}@amazon.com

Abstract. E-commerce sellers face critical fulfillment decisions that significantly impact their revenue and operational efficiency. Personalized treatment recommendations require accurate causal inference at scale, yet real-world deployments face extreme co-occurring data challenges: severe class imbalance (0.39% treatment rate), outcome sparsity (97.6% zeros), and pervasive cold-start (99.25% incomplete profiles). Existing causal methods address these challenges in isolation—resampling for imbalance, transfer learning for cold-start, imputation for missing data—but each undermines causal validity when applied independently: resampling distorts treatment distributions, transfer learning optimizes for prediction rather than causation, and imputation cannot recover true confounding relationships. We developed **ColdNet**, a neural causal model that predicts individualized treatment effects for seller fulfillment optimization through three integrated innovations: outcome-stratified ensemble learning that reduces effective imbalance while preserving outcome heterogeneity, targeted regularization that maintains valid causal estimates under extreme imbalance, and similarity-based cold-start enhancement that transfers counterfactual knowledge to offers with incomplete profiles via K-Means clustering. We validated ColdNet's base neural causal model (NCM) through semi-synthetic experiments with ground-truth treatment effects, achieving a CATE R^2 of 0.49—outperforming seven established baselines including Double Machine Learning (DML) (R^2 of -105), meta-learners, and DragonNet. On real marketplace data processing billions of offers weekly, the full ColdNet system—extending the base model with cold-start enhancement—achieved 95% prediction coverage versus 55% for DML (73% relative improvement), while achieving 0.66 WAPE for cold-start offers and 0.67 WAPE for established offers, with 19.1% MAE reduction on cold-start cases compared to our base model and zero degradation on warm cohorts.

Keywords: Causal Inference · Neural Networks · Individualized Treatment Effects · E-commerce · Class Imbalance · Cold-Start · Zero-Inflated Outcomes

M. Ceci et al. (Eds.): ECML PKDD 2026, LNAI 16948, pp. 217–233, 2027.
https://doi.org/10.1007/978-3-032-37679-4_13

1 Introduction

Personalized recommendation systems are fundamental to modern e-commerce platforms [13,18,48,49], enabling sellers to optimize fulfillment decisions that directly impact revenue and operational efficiency [27,38]. While traditional approaches rely primarily on predictive modeling for performance forecasting, the growing need for causal understanding of treatment effects has led services to adopt causal inference methods [3,8] that can distinguish correlation from causation [34]. This shift reflects the fundamental tension between predictive accuracy and causal validity [19,34], where models optimized for prediction may fail to provide reliable estimates of intervention effects. Industrial causal inference systems typically employ Double Machine Learning (DML) [11] or propensity score methods [5,37] to estimate individualized treatment effects. While extensively studied in research settings [3,24], these methods face critical challenges when deployed for e-commerce fulfillment recommendations, where treatment refers to fulfillment method selection for individual offers (seller-product pairs).

Three severe data challenges co-occur in this setting: extreme class imbalance (0.39% treatment rate), outcome sparsity (97.6% zero sales), and pervasive cold-start (99.25% incomplete offer profiles). These conditions fundamentally violate standard causal inference assumptions: sufficient treatment overlap [14,35] and complete covariate information [20]. The challenges compound—propensity scores collapse under extreme imbalance, outcome models suffer from sparse data, and cold-start cases lack essential covariates. Under these conditions, DML exhibits severe degradation (CATE $R^2 = -105$) in our semi-synthetic validation, indicating predictions worse than the mean baseline. Existing approaches address these challenges independently—resampling for imbalance [10], transfer learning for cold-start [26,43], and imputation for missing data [28]—but each undermines causal validity in isolation: resampling alters treatment distributions [16,20], transfer learning optimizes for prediction rather than causation [33], and imputation cannot recover confounding relationships [20,28].

To address these co-occurring challenges within a unified causal framework, we propose **ColdNet**, a neural causal model that predicts individualized treatment effects while simultaneously handling extreme imbalance, outcome sparsity, and cold-start. Building on the principle that treatment effect heterogeneity is driven by observable characteristics [2,20,44], we hypothesize that offers with similar features exhibit similar treatment responses even when historical profiles differ. ColdNet learns robust treatment effects from data-rich offers, then transfers causal knowledge to cold-start offers through similarity-based matching [1,42], enabling inference even when individual histories are incomplete.

As illustrated in Fig. 1, ColdNet integrates three methodological innovations and a production pipeline: (a) a neural causal model building on DragonNet [41] with targeted regularization via inverse propensity weighting [6,40] to maintain causal validity under extreme imbalance [35]; (b) outcome-stratified ensemble training [16] that partitions control samples by outcome strata so each model sees the full treatment cohort with diverse controls; (c) cluster-based cold-start enhancement using efficient similarity retrieval [21] to transfer counterfactual knowledge to offers with incomplete profiles; and (d) a business validation pipeline ensuring production-ready predictions. The complete methodology is detailed in Sect. 4.

1.1 Main Contributions

– To our knowledge, ColdNet is the first neural causal inference system simultaneously addressing extreme class imbalance, outcome sparsity, and cold-

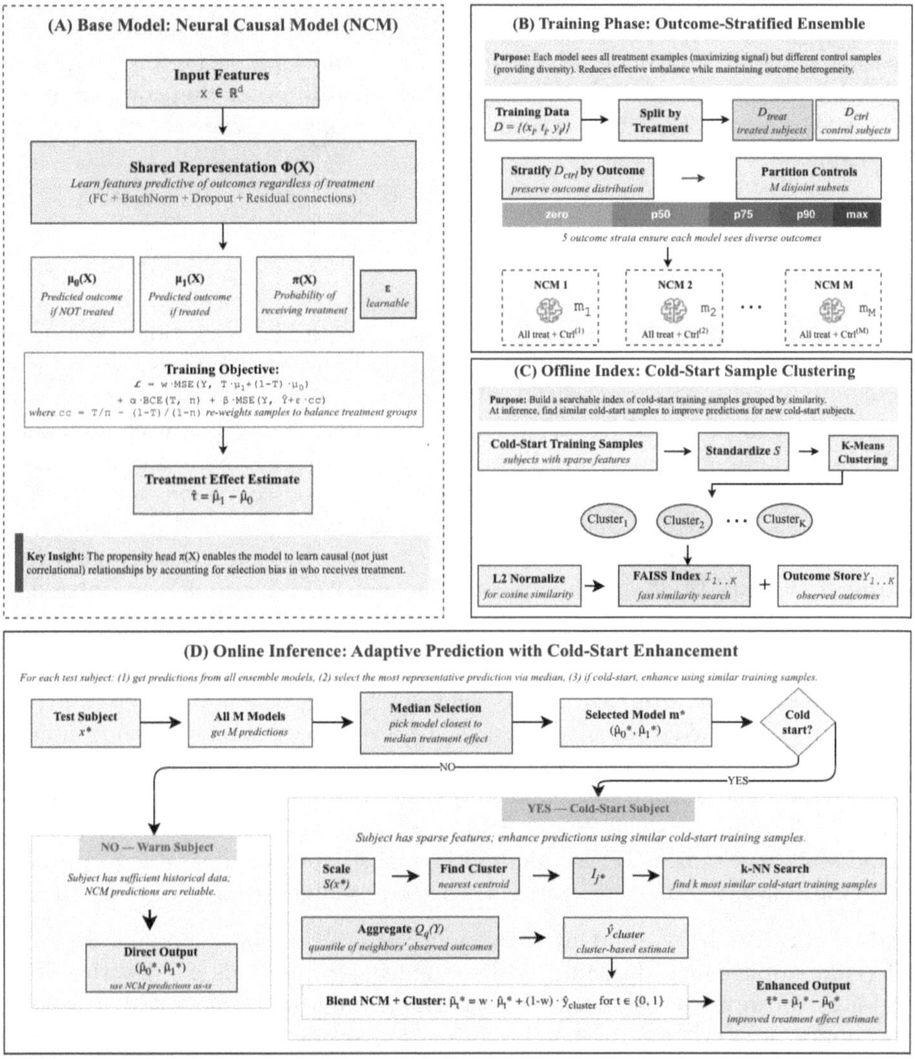

Fig. 1. ColdNet System Architecture. (A) Base Neural Causal Model with three prediction heads (μ_0, μ_1, π) on shared representations $\Phi(X)$. (B) Outcome-Stratified Ensemble Training reduces imbalance from 1:256 to 1:2. (C) Offline Cold-Start Index Construction via K-Means clustering and FAISS indexing. (D) Online Inference with adaptive enhancement for cold-start offers.

start in production-scale e-commerce, through three integrated innovations: outcome-stratified ensemble training, targeted regularization, and cluster-based cold-start enhancement.
- Outcome-stratified ensemble training handles class imbalance without destroying outcome heterogeneity, while cold-start enhancement achieves 19.1% MAE reduction and 19.0% WAPE improvement on cold-start offers with zero degradation on warm cohorts—making ColdNet the only method to achieve cold-start WAPE below 1.0 (0.66 vs 1.06 for the best baseline).
- Semi-synthetic validation with ground-truth treatment effects demonstrates CATE R^2 of 0.49 versus −105 for DML, confirming that standard methods catastrophically fail under class imbalance. Offline evaluation on 229M production samples shows 73% relative improvement in prediction coverage (55% → 95%) and 12.8% better cold-start MAE than the strongest meta-learner baseline.

2 Related Work

Neural Causal Models. The neural approach to CATE estimation began with TARNet and CFRNet [40], which learn balanced representations via integral probability metrics. DragonNet [41] added a propensity head with targeted regularization, while CEVAE [30] uses variational inference for latent confounders, GANITE [46] employs adversarial training, and SITE [45] focuses on local similarity preservation. Recent work establishes theoretical conditions for representation choices [15], learns disentangled representations [17], and develops optimal doubly robust estimators [23]. However, these methods assume sufficient treatment overlap [14,35] and complete covariates [20]—assumptions violated in production settings with extreme imbalance and cold-start. As we demonstrate, such conditions cause substantial degradation in DragonNet.

Econometric Methods. DML [11] achieves $\sqrt{n}$-consistency via cross-fitting but requires bounded propensity scores. Causal forests [4,44] provide honest confidence intervals but may struggle with high-dimensional sparse features. Doubly robust methods [6,36] inherit propensity instability under extreme imbalance [22]. Meta-learners [24] (S-, T-, DR-, R-learners) offer flexibility but provide no cold-start mechanism. These methods are particularly vulnerable to propensity collapse where scores concentrate near zero, violating positivity [14,35].

Cold-Start and Missing Data. DropoutNet [43] simulates missing features, MeLU [26] applies meta-learning, and content-based methods [29] leverage item attributes. However, these transfer *predictions*, not *counterfactual structures*—they cannot preserve $\tau = \mu_1 - \mu_0$ because they lack separate potential outcome heads. Missing data methods [28,31] address missingness through imputation but do not preserve causal structure when covariates are systematically missing. Transfer learning [33] assumes shared domain structure, which fails for cold-start subjects with different feature distributions.

Class Imbalance. SMOTE [10] does not account for heterogeneous imbalance and can create unrealistic samples in high dimensions [7]. Ensemble methods [16] typically assume uniform imbalance. In our setting, treatment rates vary across outcome strata, and standard resampling destroys important outcome heterogeneity [16,20], motivating stratification-aware approaches.

Production Systems and Evaluation. Production causal inference faces challenges beyond algorithm design [9,39]. Industrial ML systems require robust performance under data drift, computational efficiency at scale, and reliable uncertainty quantification. For causal inference evaluation, semi-synthetic benchmarks [47] provide ground-truth treatment effects but focus on balanced datasets, leaving a gap for extreme imbalance and cold-start evaluation.

3 Problem Formulation

Given observational dataset $\mathcal{D} = \{(x_i, t_i, y_i)\}_{i=1}^n$ where $x_i \in \mathbb{R}^d$ are offer features, $t_i \in \{0, 1\}$ is the fulfillment choice, and $y_i \in \mathbb{R}_+$ is sales revenue over 90 days, we seek an estimator $\hat{\tau}(x)$ that minimizes $\mathbb{E}[(\tau(x) - \hat{\tau}(x))^2]$, where the true CATE is $\tau(x) = \mathbb{E}[Y(1) - Y(0)|X = x]$. Causal identification requires three assumptions [20]: unconfoundedness $(Y(0), Y(1)) \perp T \mid X$, positivity $0 < P(T = 1|X = x) < 1$, and consistency $Y = T \cdot Y(1) + (1 - T) \cdot Y(0)$. In fulfillment decisions, treatment assignment is determined by platform-level allocation rules that depend on observable seller and product characteristics spanning 72 numerical features across seven categories: seller attributes and historical performance (90/365-day windows), product characteristics and maturity metrics, search and discovery performance, offer-level pricing and availability, pre-treatment performance baselines, category seasonality controls, and page view data. While unconfoundedness cannot be verified from observational data alone [20], the richness of this feature set—covering the primary factors influencing fulfillment allocation—makes it a reasonable working assumption. We discuss sensitivity to potential violations in Sect. 6.

Our production setting systematically violates standard assumptions, threatening causal identification: **Positivity Violation:** The 0.39% treatment rate results in propensity scores $e(x) = P(T = 1|X = x)$ that concentrate near zero across most feature subgroups. When $e(x) \to 0$, inverse propensity weights $1/e(x)$ explode, creating numerical instability [35]. CATE remains identifiable where propensity scores are bounded away from zero, but requires specialized estimators robust to near-boundary values [14]. **Outcome Modeling Failure:** Zero-inflated outcomes (97.6% zeros) violate standard regression assumptions [25]. The sparse signal makes it difficult to distinguish treatment effects from noise, requiring training strategies adapted to extreme sparsity. **Unconfoundedness Threat:** Systematic missingness (99.25% incomplete profiles) may exclude confounders like competitive dynamics. While CATE identification is possible under missing-at-random assumptions [28], systematic patterns threaten validity.

ColdNet maintains causal validity under these violations through three principled components: **Targeted Regularization:** Inverse propensity weighting with clipping bounds $e(x) \in [\epsilon, 1-\epsilon]$ prevents weight explosion through a principled bias-variance trade-off [12,14], addressing positivity violations while approximately preserving the causal estimand. **Outcome-Stratified Ensembles:** Partitioning control samples by outcome levels ensures each model sees diverse outcome distributions, preventing collapse to zero predictions under extreme sparsity. **Similarity-Based Transfer:** For cold-start offers, we transfer counterfactual knowledge from similar complete profiles, preserving the causal structure $\tau(x) = \mu_1(x) - \mu_0(x)$ through separate potential outcome modeling.

4 Methodology

ColdNet addresses three co-occurring challenges through an integrated architecture comprising 3 methodological innovations and a business validation pipeline.

4.1 Neural Causal Model with Targeted Regularization

ColdNet builds on DragonNet [41], which learns shared representations $\Phi(X)$ that feed into three prediction heads (Fig. 1A): outcome heads $\mu_0(X)$ and $\mu_1(X)$ for control and treatment potential outcomes, and a propensity head $\pi(X)$ for treatment probability. The shared representation, guided by the propensity head, is encouraged to capture confounders that influence both treatment selection and outcomes, enabling counterfactual learning. The training objective combines three loss terms:

$$\mathcal{L} = \lambda_{\text{out}} \cdot \text{MSE}(Y, T \cdot \mu_1 + (1-T) \cdot \mu_0) + \alpha \cdot \text{BCE}(T, \pi) + \beta \cdot \text{MSE}(Y, \hat{Y}_{\text{reg}})$$

where $\hat{Y}_{\text{reg}} = T \cdot \mu_1 + (1-T) \cdot \mu_0 + \gamma \cdot cc$ and $cc = T/\pi(X) - (1-T)/(1-\pi(X))$ is the counterfactual correction term. γ controls targeted regularization strength. The first term trains factual outcome prediction, the second learns propensity scores, and the third encourages predictions consistent with doubly-robust causal estimation.

4.2 Outcome-Stratified Ensemble Training

To address extreme class imbalance (0.39% treatment rate) while preserving outcome heterogeneity, we develop outcome-stratified ensemble training. Unlike uniform resampling that would create duplicates or discard valuable diversity, our approach partitions control samples into M non-overlapping subsets using stratified sampling across 5 outcome bins (zero, p50, p75, p90, max). Since 97.6% of outcomes are zero, the zero-outcome bin dominates the control population; within non-zero strata, additional subsampling ensures each control subset is balanced across outcome levels. Each of $M = 10$ models receives the entire treatment cohort paired with one control subset (Fig. 1B), reducing effective imbalance from 1:256 to approximately 1:2 through the combined effect of M-way splitting and within-stratum subsampling of the dominant zero-outcome class. At inference, all models evaluate each test sample and we select the model closest to the ensemble median: $m^* = \arg\min_m |\hat{\tau}_m - \hat{\tau}_{\text{median}}|$, using all outputs (μ_0, μ_1, π) from m^*. We select a single model rather than averaging across models to maintain consistency among the (μ_0, μ_1, π) outputs, which is required for downstream business validation that operates on individual potential outcome predictions.

4.3 Cluster-Wise Similarity-Based Cold-Start Enhancement

For the 99.25% of offers with incomplete profiles, we introduce similarity-based knowledge transfer. We adopt an inclusive definition: a sample is classified as cold-start if any of six historical activity features (90/365-day sales, conversion rates) equals zero, capturing both truly new offers and data-sparse offers that lack sufficient history for reliable neural predictions. The enhancement operates in three phases (Fig. 1C-D): **(1) Offline index construction** clusters cold-start training samples via K-Means ($K = 20$, selected via silhouette analysis), L2-normalizes centroids, and builds a FAISS index [21] for efficient similarity search. **(2) Online inference** finds the nearest cluster for each cold-start sample, retrieves $k = 10$ neighbors, and computes treatment-arm-specific cluster estimates: $\hat{y}_{\text{cluster},0}$ and $\hat{y}_{\text{cluster},1}$ from the observed outcomes of control and treated neighbors respectively, using the 45th percentile to provide slightly conservative estimates that mitigate over-prediction risk for data-sparse offers. **(3) Prediction blending** combines neural outputs with cluster knowledge separately for each treatment arm: $\tilde{\mu}_t^* = w \cdot \hat{\mu}_t^* + (1 - w) \cdot \hat{y}_{\text{cluster},t}$ for $t \in \{0, 1\}$ with $w = 0.1$. The resulting treatment effect $\tilde{\tau} = \tilde{\mu}_1 - \tilde{\mu}_0$ incorporates both neural causal estimates and empirical cluster-level outcome differences, preserving the counterfactual structure while improving outcome-level accuracy for data-sparse offers. The weight $w = 0.1$ reflects that cold-start offers have limited historical signal for the neural model, making cluster-derived empirical estimates a more reliable source for outcome-level predictions.

4.4 Business Validation Pipeline

To ensure production readiness, we implement multi-stage validation: (1) Sales band classification based on historical performance, (2) Bounds checking with band-specific constraints (zero sales: control ≥ 0, treatment $>$ control; non-zero: control $\in$ [sales/5, 5×sales]), (3) Minimum uplift requirements (10–25% by band), and (4) Extreme value handling where predictions exceeding band-specific caps are clipped to the 95th percentile of the corresponding sales band. The treatment $>$ control constraint encodes domain knowledge that the program provides positive effects for qualifying offers.

5 Experiments

We address three research questions: **RQ1:** How do ensemble training and targeted regularization handle class imbalance vs. established baselines? **RQ2:** How does the cluster-based cold-start enhancement perform on offers with incomplete profiles? **RQ3:** How does ColdNet compare across both cold-start and warm segments on production-scale data?

5.1 Experiment Setup

Dataset. We evaluate on e-commerce data from a major marketplace, containing 229M seller-offer samples with 161 raw features spanning seller characteristics (tenure, ratings, inventory), product attributes (category, price, brand), and historical activity metrics (sales volume, conversion rates at 90/365-day windows). After feature engineering and exclusion of identifiers and post-treatment variables, we retain 72 numerical features for model training. The data exhibits extreme challenges: 0.39% treatment rate (1:256 imbalance), 97.6% zero outcomes, and 99.25% cold-start cases. To ensure causal validity, we apply seller-stratified train/test splits (no seller appears in both sets) and outcome-stratified ensemble sampling across 5 sales-based bins to address severe class imbalance. For evaluation, we construct a test set of 590K samples (240K cold-start, 350K warm) deliberately stratified to over-represent warm offers relative to the population distribution (where 99.25% are cold-start).

Baselines. We compare ColdNet with three baseline types. **Econometric:** Mean Baseline and DML [11] with XGBoost nuisance models. **Meta-learners:** S-Learner, T-Learner [24], DR-Learner [23], R-Learner [32], each with XGBoost and Ridge base learners. **Neural methods:** DragonNet [41] (same architecture as NCM, single model, no TR/ensemble). **Ours:** NCM (DragonNet + TR + ensemble) and ColdNet (NCM + cold-start enhancement).

Evaluation Metrics. Causal (Semi-Synthetic): The Precision in Estimation of Heterogeneous Effects, $\sqrt{\text{PEHE}} = \sqrt{\frac{1}{n}\sum_i(\hat{\tau}(x_i) - \tau(x_i))^2}$, measures individual-level CATE error; CATE $R^2 = 1 - \sum_i(\hat{\tau}_i - \tau_i)^2/\sum_i(\tau_i - \bar{\tau})^2$ measures explained heterogeneity variance (negative values indicate worse than the mean baseline); ATE Relative Bias ($100 \times (\hat{\text{ATE}} - \text{ATE})/|\text{ATE}|$) measures aggregate accuracy; and the Quantile Treatment Effect Bias at the 90th percentile (QTE P90), defined as $\hat{Q}_{90}(Y(1)) - \hat{Q}_{90}(Y(0)) - (Q_{90}(Y(1)) - Q_{90}(Y(0)))$, measures upper-tail estimation accuracy. **Business (Production):** For production evaluation without ground-truth treatment effects, we evaluate factual prediction accuracy—how well the model predicts observed sales for offers under their actual treatment assignment. We report MAE, Median Error, Median Bias, and WAPE $= \sum_i |\hat{y}_i - y_i|/\sum_i |y_i|$ between predicted outcomes under observed treatment and actual sales.

Implementation Details. The NCM architecture consists of a shared representation network with three fully-connected layers (512→256→128 units) using batch normalization, ReLU activation, and dropout. The outcome heads (μ_0 and μ_1) each contain two layers (64→1) with ReLU output activation to enforce non-negative predictions, while the propensity head uses the same structure with sigmoid output. We use the Adam optimizer with early stopping over a maximum of 50 epochs. Outcomes are scaled to [0, 2.5] range using MinMax scaling; the upper bound of 2.5 (rather than 1.0) accommodates the extreme right-skew of the sales distribution, providing finer gradient resolution in the dense low-sales region where 97.6% of samples reside. The loss function weights are set to $\lambda_{\text{out}} = 1.0$, $\alpha = 1.0$, $\beta = 1.0$, with targeted regularization coefficient $\gamma = 1.0$ and propensity clipping bound $\epsilon = 0.01$. These values were selected based on the DragonNet defaults [41] and validated through preliminary experiments. The ensemble consists of 10 models ($M = 10$) trained with outcome-stratified sampling across 5 sales-based bins to address severe class imbalance. Training is orchestrated using distributed infrastructure with automated hyperparameter tuning via Bayesian optimization across 40 trials with up to 5 parallel jobs. The search space includes learning rate (0.0001–0.003), batch size (512–2048), dropout rate (0.1–0.4), and weight decay (1e-5 to 1e-3). Each model is trained on ml.p3.2xlarge instances (1×V100 GPU, 8 CPUs, 61GB RAM) with a maximum runtime of 2 h per trial and early stopping for underperforming trials. For cold-start enhancement, we cluster cold-start training samples into $K = 20$ groups using K-Means, then build a FAISS index for efficient search. At inference, we retrieve $k = 10$ nearest neighbors, compute treatment-arm-specific aggregates using the 45th percentile ($q = 0.45$) of observed outcomes for control and treated neighbors separately, and blend with NCM predictions using weight $w = 0.1$. The system supports production-scale batch inference processing millions of records with automatic scaling and comprehensive error handling.

5.2 RQ1: Ensemble Training and Imbalance Handling

To evaluate the effectiveness of the ensemble training and targeted regularization components in handling severe class imbalance, we conduct semi-synthetic validation experiments.

Semi-Synthetic Validation. We validate using 9M production samples with 72 numerical features, applying three data generating processes (DGPs) following [47]: Sine ($\tau(x) = \sin(\omega^\top x)$), Linear ($\tau(x) = \beta^\top x$), Interaction ($\tau(x) = x_1 \cdot x_2$). Treatment assignment is calibrated to 7.8% training rate (production's 0.39% yields too few treated samples for baseline convergence) and 30% test rate (treatment effects are DGP-defined, independent of assignment). Table 1 presents the semi-synthetic validation results for the Sine DGP. Results for Linear and Interaction DGPs, which show consistent improvements (6.2% and 9.1% $\sqrt{\text{PEHE}}$ reductions respectively), are provided in the supplementary materials.

Key Findings: DML catastrophically fails under class imbalance ($R^2 = -105$), with predictions over 100× worse than the mean baseline, due to propensity weight instability [35]. NCM achieves the strongest CATE estimation: 8.0% lower $\sqrt{\text{PEHE}}$ (0.080 vs 0.087, $p < 0.001$, paired t-test over 5 seeds), 7.9% higher R^2 (0.492 vs 0.456), and best tail estimation (QTE P90: −0.039 vs −0.048) compared to T-XGBoost. Meta-learners achieve lower ATE bias (S-XGBoost: −0.1% vs NCM: −5.3%), reflecting NCM's design emphasis on individual-level over aggregate accuracy.

Table 1. Semi-Synthetic Validation: Sine DGP (7.8% Treatment Rate). Mean ± std over 5 seeds.

Method	$\sqrt{\text{PEHE}}$ ↓	R^2 ↑	ATE bias% ↓	QTE P90 ↓
Mean Baseline	.118±.000	.00±.00	−5.5±0.0	−.161±.000
DML [11]	1.22±.01	−105±1.6	−21.0±3.2	+.213±.006
S-XGBoost	.088±.000	.443±.002	**−0.1**±0.3	−.055±.001
S-Ridge	.119±.000	−.01±.001	8.2±0.3	−.138±.001
T-XGBoost	.087±.000	.456±.001	0.7±0.3	−.048±.001
T-Ridge	.092±.000	.390±.001	2.0±0.3	−.057±.000
DR-XGBoost	.090±.001	.413±.011	0.7±0.3	−.053±.001
DR-Ridge	.092±.000	.389±.001	0.9±0.3	−.058±.000
R-XGBoost	.089±.000	.433±.004	−2.1±0.2	−.058±.002
R-Ridge	.092±.000	.391±.002	0.7±0.3	−.058±.000
NCM (Ours)	**.080**±.000	**.492**±.001	−5.3±0.3	**−.039**±.003

↓ lower is better (absolute value for ATE% and QTE P90), ↑ higher is better. Bold indicates best.

Component Ablation for Base Model Selection. To select the best architectural variant as the base model for NCM, we conduct ablation experiments on the production dataset, progressively adding components and evaluating their impact on both predictive accuracy and causal validity. Table 2 presents the component-wise analysis across three architectural variants: TARNet (shared representation only), DragonNet (adding propensity head), and DragonNet with targeted regularization (our selected base model).

Key Findings: The ablation reveals a critical insight: **adding propensity modeling without targeted regularization actively harms causal validity**. Adding the propensity head (TARNet → DragonNet) improves treatment prediction (AUC: 0.500 → 0.919) and outcome accuracy (MAE: 38.50 → 32.14), but the placebo p-value *decreases* from 0.156 to 0.085—meaning the model becomes *more* likely to detect spurious treatment effects. This paradox arises because the propensity head, without regularization, learns both confounders

Table 2. Targeted Regularization Ablation Results for Class Imbalance Handling. Evaluated on production data.

Architecture	AUC ↑	MAE ↓	Placebo p ↑
TARNet (no propensity)	0.500	38.50	0.156
DragonNet (no TR)	0.919	32.14	0.085
DragonNet (with TR)	**0.926**	**28.03**	**0.910**

Placebo test: treatment randomly reassigned (5 permutations); p-value from two-sided t-test of $\hat{\tau}$ against zero. High p indicates the model correctly identifies no treatment effect under random assignment.

and instrumental variables; the latter create spurious treatment-outcome associations. **Targeted regularization resolves this paradox decisively**: adding TR produces a dramatic improvement in causal validity (**placebo p: 0.085 → 0.910**) while maintaining all predictive gains (AUC: 0.926, MAE: 28.03). The placebo p-value of 0.910 confirms that the model correctly identifies no treatment effect under random assignment.

5.3 RQ2: Cold-Start Enhancement Performance

To evaluate the effectiveness of cluster-based cold-start enhancement on offers with incomplete profiles, we conduct experiments on 590K test samples (240K cold-start, 350K warm) to assess enhancement performance across different offer cohorts. Table 3 presents the results comparing cold-start and warm performance across all methods.

Key Findings: The cold-start enhancement produces the most striking improvements in the production evaluation. **ColdNet is the only method achieving cold-start WAPE below 1.0** (0.660 vs 1.061 for T-XGBoost)—all baseline methods produce prediction errors exceeding actual sales on cold-start offers. Cold-start MAE improves **19.1% over NCM** (103.17 → 83.47) with **82.8% median error reduction** (21.14 → 3.64), approaching T-XGBoost's 3.16 and demonstrating that cluster-based transfer brings cold-start prediction quality close to parity with methods using complete features. By design, **warm performance remains identical to NCM** (MAE: 306.00, WAPE: 0.669—best among all methods), eliminating the common trade-off between improving underserved segments and degrading existing performance. DragonNet shows particularly poor cold-start performance (Median Bias: 40.27) without ensemble or transfer mechanisms.

5.4 RQ3: Overall System Performance

The most practically significant result is ColdNet's **73% relative improvement in prediction coverage** (55% → 95%). The DML baseline requires sufficient treatment overlap for each offer, excluding cases where propensity scores

Table 3. Cold-Start vs Warm Performance on production data. Bold indicates best per metric.

Method	Type	Cold-Start				Warm	
		MAE	Med.Err	Med.Bias	WAPE	MAE	WAPE
S-Learner	XGB	98.46	12.25	2.15	1.091	321.41	0.728
S-Learner	Ridge	132.27	20.52	**0.00**	1.465	405.50	0.919
T-Learner	XGB	95.77	**3.16**	1.02	1.061	**305.33**	0.692
T-Learner	Ridge	156.03	7.80	**0.00**	1.728	369.35	0.837
DR-Learner	XGB	95.77	**3.16**	1.02	1.061	**305.33**	0.692
DR-Learner	Ridge	95.77	**3.16**	1.02	1.061	**305.33**	0.692
R-Learner	XGB	98.44	14.67	3.30	1.090	332.57	0.754
R-Learner	Ridge	132.60	16.62	3.57	1.469	350.56	0.794
DragonNet	–	115.36	41.84	40.27	1.272	376.79	0.853
NCM	–	103.17	21.14	12.88	0.815	**306.00**	**0.669**
ColdNet	–	**83.47**	3.64	1.02	**0.660**	**306.00**	**0.669**

DR-Learner XGB and Ridge produce identical results because the doubly robust pseudo-outcome computation in the first stage dominates the second-stage regression; with identical first-stage nuisance models, the pseudo-outcomes are identical regardless of second-stage learner choice.

violate positivity bounds; this results in valid predictions for only 55% of test offers. ColdNet provides predictions for 95% of test offers by leveraging cluster-based cold-start enhancement and the ensemble's robustness to imbalance. The remaining 5% are excluded by the business validation pipeline's bounds checking. As shown in Table 3, ColdNet achieves **the best overall performance among all evaluated methods** across both segments. Against T-XGBoost, ColdNet demonstrates **12.8% better cold-start MAE** (83.47 vs 95.77) while achieving comparable warm MAE (306.00 vs 305.33, a 0.2% difference). This balanced performance is particularly important given that cold-start cases comprise 99.25% of the production dataset, making cold-start optimization critical for real-world impact. Semi-synthetic validation confirms causal inference quality with **8.0%** $\sqrt{\textbf{PEHE}}$ **improvement** at moderate imbalance (7.8% treatment rate), while production evaluation validates real-world effectiveness under extreme imbalance (0.39% treatment rate) through factual prediction metrics and dramatically expanded coverage.

6 Discussions

Methodological Boundary Conditions. *Outcome-Stratified Ensembles* benefit when treatment effects are heterogeneous across outcome levels and the treatment cohort is large enough to be shared across all M ensemble members without overfitting. Ensembles provide diminishing benefit when treatment effects are homogeneous across outcome levels, as stratification no longer preserves meaningful diversity. *Propensity Head Paradox:* Table 2 shows that propensity modeling without targeted regularization learns instrumental variables alongside confounders, harming causal validity. Targeted regularization penalizes discrepancies between factual and IPW-adjusted predictions, encouraging the model to rely on confounders rather than instrumental variables. *Cold-Start Transfer* succeeds when cold-start samples share features with training data (19.1% MAE improvement; zero warm degradation by design). *Individual vs. Aggregate Trade-off:* NCM achieves superior individual-level CATE estimation ($\sqrt{\text{PEHE}}$: 0.080 vs 0.087, R^2: 0.492 vs 0.456) at the cost of higher aggregate ATE bias (−5.3% vs S-XGBoost's −0.1%). This trade-off is by design: the outcome-stratified ensemble emphasizes heterogeneous effect capture across outcome strata, which directly determines personalized recommendation quality. For applications prioritizing aggregate policy evaluation over individual-level effects, meta-learners may be more suitable.

Engineering Insights. Careful numerical handling during loss computation prevents training instability under extreme value distributions. Outcome scaling to [0, 2.5] with non-negative output constraints stabilizes gradients for the highly skewed sales distribution (97.6% zeros). Numerical safeguards—including loss clipping and gradient monitoring—prevent training divergence under extreme inverse propensity weights, with comprehensive logging to detect when safeguards activate. Automated hyperparameter selection via Bayesian optimization reduces manual tuning effort and ensures reproducibility.

Broader Impact. The methodology generalizes to domains with similar challenges: healthcare (rare treatments, sparse events, new patients), finance (low enrollment, sparse outcomes, new customers), and advertising (low conversion, sparse clicks, new advertisers). However, practitioners must validate that treatment effects exhibit the heterogeneity and smoothness properties required for outcome stratification and cluster-based transfer, and domain-specific requirements (e.g., regulatory constraints in healthcare) must be satisfied independently. Our evaluation on 229M samples with billions-scale weekly inference demonstrates neural causal inference can deliver business value when methods holistically address co-occurring challenges.

Limitations. Three factors constrain the evaluation: (1) Semi-synthetic validation used 7.8% treatment rate (20× higher than production conditions at 0.39%) to enable baseline comparison with methods like DML—direct causal validity measurement at extreme imbalance remains challenging without ground truth; (2) Targeted regularization assumes the propensity model is well-specified—unmeasured confounding remains a threat to causal validity; (3) Cluster-based transfer assumes treatment effects exhibit local smoothness across feature space, which may fail for new categories or market disruptions.

7 Conclusion

We presented ColdNet, a neural causal inference system addressing three co-occurring data challenges in e-commerce fulfillment optimization: extreme class imbalance (0.39% treatment rate), outcome sparsity (97.6% zeros), and pervasive cold-start (99.25% incomplete profiles). Our three technical innovations—outcome-stratified ensemble training, targeted regularization, and cluster-based cold-start enhancement—work synergistically to enable accurate treatment effect estimation where standard methods fail. Through extensive validation combining semi-synthetic experiments and production-scale evaluation, we demonstrated ColdNet's effectiveness across three critical dimensions. First, semi-synthetic validation confirmed superior causal estimation quality: CATE R^2 of 0.49 compared to -105 for DML and 0.456 for the strongest meta-learner baseline (T-XGBoost), with 8.0% $\sqrt{\text{PEHE}}$ improvement. Second, production evaluation showed ColdNet is the only method to achieve cold-start WAPE below 1.0 (0.66 vs 1.06 for T-XGBoost), with 19.1% MAE reduction on cold-start offers and zero degradation on warm cohorts. Third, ColdNet expanded prediction coverage from 55% to 95% of offers—a 73% relative improvement—enabling personalized treatment recommendations for the vast majority of the marketplace. This work demonstrates that neural causal inference can effectively address classical challenges at scale. ColdNet delivers individualized treatment effect estimates across both data-rich and data-sparse segments, providing a unified framework for causal inference under co-occurring real-world data constraints.

Future Work. Several extensions could enhance the framework: (1) *Temporal modeling*: Incorporate recurrent architectures to capture time-varying treatment effects and seasonal patterns; (2) *Multi-treatment optimization*: Extend beyond binary decisions to handle multiple treatment options simultaneously; (3) *Uncertainty estimation*: Add Bayesian components to quantify prediction confidence and enable risk-aware recommendations; (4) *Continuous treatment spaces*: Generalize to continuous treatment intensities rather than discrete choices; (5) *Automated confounder selection*: Integrate causal discovery methods to identify minimal sufficient adjustment sets.

References

1. Abadie, A., Imbens, G.W.: Large sample properties of matching estimators for average treatment effects. Econometrica **74**(1), 235–267 (2006)
2. Athey, S., Imbens, G.: Recursive partitioning for heterogeneous causal effects. Proc. Natl. Acad. Sci. **113**(27), 7353–7360 (2016)
3. Athey, S., Imbens, G.W.: Machine learning methods that economists should know about. Ann. Rev. Econ. **11**(1), 685–725 (2019)

4. Athey, S., Tibshirani, J., Wager, S.: Generalized random forests. Ann. Stat. **47**(2), 1148–1178 (2019)
5. Austin, P.C.: An introduction to propensity score methods for reducing the effects of confounding in observational studies. Multivar. Behav. Res. **46**(3), 399–424 (2011)
6. Bang, H., Robins, J.M.: Doubly robust estimation in missing data and causal inference models. Biometrics **61**(4), 962–973 (2005)
7. Blagus, R., Lusa, L.: Smote for high-dimensional class-imbalanced data. BMC Bioinform. **14**(1), 1–16 (2013)
8. Bottou, L., et al.: Counterfactual reasoning and learning systems: the example of computational advertising. J. Mach. Learn. Res. **14**(1), 3207–3260 (2013)
9. Breck, E., Cai, S., Nielsen, E., Salib, M., Sculley, D.: The ML test score: a rubric for ml production readiness and technical debt reduction. In: 2017 IEEE International Conference on Big Data (Big Data), pp. 1123–1132. IEEE (2017)
10. Chawla, N.V., Bowyer, K.W., Hall, L.O., Kegelmeyer, W.P.: Smote: synthetic minority over-sampling technique. J. Artif. Intell. Res. **16**, 321–357 (2002)
11. Chernozhukov, V., et al.: Double/debiased machine learning for treatment and structural parameters. Economet. J. **21**(1), C1–C68 (2018)
12. Cole, S.R., Hernán, M.A.: Constructing inverse probability weights for marginal structural models. Am. J. Epidemiol. **168**(6), 656–664 (2008)
13. Covington, P., Adams, J., Sargin, E.: Deep neural networks for Youtube recommendations. In: Proceedings of the 10th ACM Conference on Recommender Systems, pp. 191–198 (2016)
14. Crump, R.K., Hotz, V.J., Imbens, G.W., Mitnik, O.A.: Dealing with limited overlap in estimation of average treatment effects. Biometrika **96**(1), 187–199 (2009)
15. Curth, A., Van der Schaar, M.: Nonparametric estimation of heterogeneous treatment effects: from theory to learning algorithms. In: International Conference on Artificial Intelligence and Statistics, pp. 1810–1818. PMLR (2021)
16. Galar, M., Fernandez, A., Barrenechea, E., Bustince, H., Herrera, F.: A review on ensembles for the class imbalance problem: bagging-, boosting-, and hybrid-based approaches. IEEE Trans. Syst. Man, Cybern. Part C (Appl. Rev.) **42**(4), 463–484 (2011)
17. Hassanpour, N., Greiner, R.: Learning disentangled representations for counterfactual regression. In: International Conference on Learning Representations (2019)
18. He, X., Liao, L., Zhang, H., Nie, L., Hu, X., Chua, T.S.: Neural collaborative filtering. In: Proceedings of the 26th International Conference on World Wide Web, pp. 173–182 (2017)
19. Hernán, M.A., Robins, J.M.: Causal Inference: What If. Chapman & Hall/CRC (2020)
20. Imbens, G.W., Rubin, D.B.: Causal Inference in Statistics, Social, and Biomedical Sciences. Cambridge University Press, Cambridge (2015)
21. Johnson, J., Douze, M., Jégou, H.: Billion-scale similarity search with GPUs. IEEE Trans. Big Data **7**(3), 535–547 (2019)
22. Kang, J.D., Schafer, J.L.: Demystifying double robustness: a comparison of alternative strategies for estimating a population mean from incomplete data. Stat. Sci. **22**(4), 523–539 (2007)
23. Kennedy, E.H.: Towards optimal doubly robust estimation of heterogeneous causal effects. Electron. J. Stat. **17**(2), 3008–3049 (2023)
24. Künzel, S.R., Sekhon, J.S., Bickel, P.J., Yu, B.: Metalearners for estimating heterogeneous treatment effects using machine learning. Proc. Natl. Acad. Sci. **116**(10), 4156–4165 (2019)

25. Lambert, D.: Zero-inflated Poisson regression, with an application to defects in manufacturing. Technometrics **34**(1), 1–14 (1992)
26. Lee, H., Im, J., Jang, S., Cho, H., Chung, S.: Melu: meta-learned user preference estimator for cold-start recommendation. In: Proceedings of the 25th ACM SIGKDD International Conference on Knowledge Discovery & Data Mining, pp. 1073–1082 (2019)
27. Linden, G., Smith, B., York, J.: Amazon. com recommendations: item-to-item collaborative filtering. IEEE Internet Comput. **7**(1), 76–80 (2003)
28. Little, R.J., Rubin, D.B.: Statistical Analysis with Missing Data. Wiley, Hoboken (2019)
29. Lops, P., De Gemmis, M., Semeraro, G.: Content-based recommender systems: state of the art and trends. Recommender Syst. Handb. 73–105 (2010)
30. Louizos, C., Shalit, U., Mooij, J.M., Sontag, D., Zemel, R., Welling, M.: Causal effect inference with deep latent-variable models. Adv. Neural Inf. Process. Syst. 30 (2017)
31. Miao, W., Tchetgen Tchetgen, E.J.: On varieties of doubly robust estimators under missingness not at random with a shadow variable. Biometrika **103**(2), 475–482 (2016)
32. Nie, X., Wager, S.: Quasi-oracle estimation of heterogeneous treatment effects. Biometrika **108**(2), 299–319 (2021)
33. Pan, S.J., Yang, Q.: A survey on transfer learning. IEEE Trans. Knowl. Data Eng. **22**(10), 1345–1359 (2009)
34. Pearl, J.: Causality. Cambridge University Press, Cambridge (2009)
35. Petersen, M.L., Porter, K.E., Gruber, S., Wang, Y., Van Der Laan, M.J.: Diagnosing and responding to violations in the positivity assumption. Stat. Methods Med. Res. **21**(1), 31–54 (2012)
36. Robins, J.M., Rotnitzky, A., Zhao, L.P.: Estimation of regression coefficients when some regressors are not always observed. J. Am. Stat. Assoc. **89**(427), 846–866 (1994)
37. Rosenbaum, P.R., Rubin, D.B.: The central role of the propensity score in observational studies for causal effects. Biometrika **70**(1), 41–55 (1983)
38. Schafer, J.B., Konstan, J.A., Riedl, J.: E-commerce recommendation applications. Data Min. Knowl. Disc. **5**(1), 115–153 (2001)
39. Sculley, D., et al.: Hidden technical debt in machine learning systems. Adv. Neural. Inf. Process. Syst. **28** (2015)
40. Shalit, U., Johansson, F.D., Sontag, D.: Estimating individual treatment effect: generalization bounds and algorithms. In: International Conference on Machine Learning, pp. 3076–3085. PMLR (2017)
41. Shi, C., Blei, D., Veitch, V.: Adapting neural networks for the estimation of treatment effects. Adv. Neural. Inf. Process. Syst. **32** (2019)
42. Stuart, E.A.: Matching methods for causal inference: a review and a look forward. Stat. Sci. **25**(1), 1–21 (2010)
43. Volkovs, M., Yu, G., Poutanen, T.: Dropoutnet: addressing cold start in recommender systems. Adv. Neural. Inf. Process. Syst., **30** (2017)
44. Wager, S., Athey, S.: Estimation and inference of heterogeneous treatment effects using random forests. J. Am. Stat. Assoc. **113**(523), 1228–1242 (2018)
45. Yao, L., Li, S., Li, Y., Huai, M., Gao, J., Zhang, A.: Representation learning for treatment effect estimation from observational data. Advances in neural information processing systems **31** (2018)

46. Yoon, J., Jordon, J., Van Der Schaar, M.: Ganite: estimation of individualized treatment effects using generative adversarial nets. In: International Conference on Learning Representations (2018)
47. Yu, H., Sun, Y.: Do contemporary causal inference models capture real-world heterogeneity? findings from a large-scale benchmark. arXiv preprint arXiv:2410.07021 (2024)
48. Zhou, G., et al.: Deep interest evolution network for click-through rate prediction. In: Proceedings of the AAAI Conference on Artificial Intelligence, vol. 33, pp. 5941–5948 (2019)
49. Zhou, G., et al.: Deep interest network for click-through rate prediction. In: Proceedings of the 24th ACM SIGKDD International Conference on Knowledge Discovery & Data Mining, pp. 1059–1068 (2018)

Counterfactual Learning of New Adaptive Instructional Policies Using Logged Data

Samuel Girard[1,2](✉), Sein Minn[3], Amel Bouzeghoub[4], and Jill-Jênn Vie[1]

[1] Soda Team, Inria Saclay, Palaiseau, France
{samuel.girard,jill-jenn.vie}@inria.fr
[2] Pix, Paris, France
[3] Asian Institute of Technology, Khlong Nueng, Thailand
sein-minn@ait.asia
[4] SAMOVAR, Télécom SudParis, Institut Polytechnique de Paris, Palaiseau, France
amel.bouzeghoub@telecom-sudparis.eu

Abstract. Optimizing instructional policies in Intelligent Tutoring Systems (ITS) typically requires costly online experimentation or student simulators that may fail to capture real-world dynamics. This paper introduces an offline contextual bandit framework that learns new adaptive policies directly from logged interaction data. By mapping student-item interactions onto a continuous latent proficiency-difficulty scale using a Rasch model, we cast the tutoring process as a continuous stochastic bandit problem. We propose a novel reward function designed to optimize "flow" by balancing task challenge with student success. Our approach includes a round-specific behavior policy estimation that serves as both a propensity model for off-policy evaluation and a diagnostic tool for ITS adaptivity. We demonstrate the efficacy of this framework across four large-scale real-world datasets, achieving consistent policy improvements over the logged behavior policy. The results show that effective instructional policies can be learned and visualized within seconds of computation, providing a scalable path for improving adaptive learning systems without further data collection.

1 Introduction

Adaptive learning aims to present each student with exercises that match their current ability. In intelligent tutoring systems (ITS), this means assigning tasks that are neither too easy, which can lead to disengagement, nor too difficult, which can cause failure and frustration [2,4]. Calibrating instructional difficulty is therefore central to maintaining engagement and supporting learning [6,12]. Counterfactual learning is a machine learning approach that uses hypothetical "what-if" scenarios (called *counterfactuals*) to estimate the effect of interventions or actions that were not actually observed. This method is especially attractive in settings where online experimentations on students may be costly, or raise ethical issues [14,15,18,26]. Because ITS collect large logs of student–exercise

M. Ceci et al. (Eds.): ECML PKDD 2026, LNAI 16948, pp. 234–251, 2027.
https://doi.org/10.1007/978-3-032-37679-4_14

interactions, they offer the possibility of improving tutoring policies directly from data. Still, policies optimized in simulation may overfit the student model used to generate synthetic trajectories [9], so in this paper we are interested in model-free techniques such as inverse propensity scoring as well.

In this paper, we study offline learning and evaluation of difficulty-assignment policies from logged tutoring data. Rather than modeling the full tutoring process, we adopt a reduced-form view in which each interaction is represented on a continuous latent proficiency–difficulty scale. Conceptually, the quantity of interest is a stochastic policy that maps latent student proficiency to a distribution over exercise difficulty. Since true proficiency is unobserved, we do not estimate this object directly; instead, we infer a one-dimensional Rasch proficiency proxy from the log and use it to approximate the corresponding reduced-form policy over difficulty [19]. This reduction yields an offline contextual bandit problem with continuous context and continuous action. It also allows us to estimate the reduced-form logging policy from the data. Importantly, this estimated policy is not the ITS's internal decision rule; rather, it captures the effective allocation pattern observed in the log. As such, it is useful not only for propensity estimation in off-policy evaluation, but also as a practical diagnostic of whether the ITS behaves adaptively across students and rounds. We define a reward that favors successful responses to more difficult items, thereby operationalizing the idea of desirable difficulty and its connection to flow [2,4,8]. The reward is computed directly from logged outcomes and item difficulties, so it provides an observable proxy for a pedagogically desirable balance between challenge and attainability, rather than a direct measure of long-term learning gains.

Our framework learns from tutoring logs through a continuous proficiency–difficulty representation, a reward based on flow computed from observed responses, and round-specific reduced-form logging policies for off-policy evaluation. This enables policy evaluation and learning directly from historical data, without interaction with students or reliance on a student simulator [9,18]. Because both the logging policy and the learned policies are defined on a continuous latent scale, they can also be visualized directly, which is useful for practitioners seeking both improved policies and a clearer picture of how difficulty is allocated in practice.

Our three contributions are: (i) a reward inspired by flow and desirable difficulty that incentivizes assigning the hardest exercise a student can still solve; (ii) a reduced-form behavior-policy estimation framework, based on continuous context and continuous actions, that reveals how difficulty allocation varies with student proficiency and evolves across rounds, providing an interpretable diagnostic of ITS adaptivity; and (iii) an offline policy learning framework that combines this behavior model with several off-policy estimators to learn and compare instructional policies from purely logged data.

2 Related Work

Knowledge Tracing and Student Modeling. A large body of work in educational data mining focuses on modeling student knowledge from interaction logs, including knowledge tracing [7], Bayesian Knowledge Tracing, Item Response Theory, and related latent-variable approaches. These models are typically used to predict future performance or mastery, rather than to optimize exercise assignment directly. Our work uses this literature differently: instead of building a deep sequential student model, we use a simple Rasch representation to place students and items on a common latent proficiency–difficulty scale, which serves as a reduced-form basis for offline policy evaluation and learning.

Counterfactual Learning in Education. Counterfactual evaluation is much less common in education than predictive modeling, because it requires reasoning about outcomes under interventions not observed in the data. Zhao and Heffernan study binary educational interventions, such as the effect of hints on course completion [28]. Doroudi et al. propose a robust framework for evaluating instructional policies using student models [9]. Our setting differs from prior educational work in two ways: we learn directly from logged tutoring data without relying on a student simulator, and we treat exercise assignment as a continuous difficulty-selection problem rather than as a small discrete intervention space.

Model-Based Versus Model-Free Offline Learning. Most of student modeling in education is model-based: policies are optimized using a learned model of student evolution, such as HOT-DINA, BKT, multidimensional IRT, or other partially observable Markov decision processes [17,21,25,27]. While such approaches can capture richer dynamics, they depend heavily on the fidelity of the student model, and policies learned in simulation may fail to transfer to real students [9]. Our approach allows model-free learning. We do not attempt to model the full tutoring dynamics; instead, we formulate logged exercise assignment as an offline contextual bandit problem on a latent proficiency–difficulty scale, which enables direct off-policy evaluation and learning from observed data.

Behavior Policy Estimation and Reward Design. In most off-policy evaluation work, the logging policy is treated mainly as a technical object needed for importance weighting [18]. In our setting, estimating the reduced-form logging policy also has independent practical value: it reveals how assigned difficulty varies with proficiency and across rounds, providing a diagnostic of the adaptivity expressed in the logged data. On the reward side, prior work has often relied on metrics based on the student model, or sparse long-term objectives such as post-test scores [3,21,23]. We instead focus on an immediate reward aligned with desirable difficulty [4] and flow [8], which is directly computable from logged responses and therefore compatible with model-free off-policy evaluation.

Estimators for Off-Policy Evaluation. Our estimators build on the off-policy evaluation (OPE) literature for contextual bandits, which estimates the value a target policy *would* have obtained had it been deployed, using only data logged under a different behavior policy [5]. Inverse propensity scoring (IPS) is unbiased but high-variance; its self-normalized variant (SNIPS) trades a small bias for lower variance and underpins counterfactual risk minimization from logged feedback [22]. The doubly robust (DR) estimator combines a reward model with importance weighting and stays consistent if either is correct [10], while mixture importance sampling stabilizes weights across pooled logging policies via a shared denominator [1]. We adapt these estimators to a continuous proficiency–difficulty action space with round-specific logging policies, and use their agreement as a reliability diagnostic.

3 Method

Our framework operates in three steps: (i) project the tutoring log onto a continuous proficiency–difficulty scale, (ii) define a flow-aligned reward on that scale, and (iii) estimate a round-specific behavior policy that will serve as the propensity model for offline evaluation and learning.

3.1 Continuous Latent Representation

We assume that each student u has a fixed scalar proficiency $z_u \in \mathbb{R}$ and each item i has a scalar difficulty $d_i \in \mathbb{R}$. Correctness is governed by a *response function* $q : \mathbb{R}^2 \rightarrow [0, 1]$ that maps a proficiency–difficulty pair to the probability of a correct answer, so that the observed binary correctness $Y \in \{0, 1\}$ satisfies $\Pr(Y{=}1 \mid z_u, d_i) = q(z_u, d_i)$. Rather than defining the action as a discrete item identity, we lift it to the continuous difficulty level $a_{u,t} := d_{i_{u,t}} \in \mathcal{A} \subset \mathbb{R}$. This continuous formulation is better suited to large item banks: it avoids a high-dimensional discrete action space and enables policies to generalize across different exercises with similar difficulty. This task can therefore be seen as a continuous contextual bandit problem.

We estimate proficiencies via the 1PL Rasch model, $q(z, d) = \sigma(z - d)$, where σ is the logistic function and each item is described by a single difficulty parameter, so that the probability of a correct response depends only on the gap between ability and difficulty. Fitting this model by maximum likelihood yields estimates $\hat{z}_u$. The context is then $x_{u,t} := \hat{z}_u$ for all t; a fixed proxy for latent proficiency rather than a dynamic knowledge state. Each student trace is thus recast as a sequence $\left(x_{u,t}, a_{u,t}, y_{u,t}\right)_{t=1}^{T_u}$ on a latent scale, where $y_{u,t} \in \{0, 1\}$ records whether student u answered correctly at round t. This introduces two error sources: (i) a *representation error*, since true correctness may not reduce to a single scalar pair; and (ii) a *model bias*, since the Rasch form $\sigma(z - d)$ may not match the true q.

This reduction is well suited to our objective defined below: the flow-aligned reward is immediate by construction, so we do not need to perform long-horizon credit assignment, and a model-free bandit formulation avoids the dependence on a student simulator that can cause simulation-trained policies to fail on real students [9].

3.2 Reward Design

Our reward operationalizes *desirable difficulty* [4]: exercises should be challenging but attainable, steering students toward a state of *flow* [8]. Given an observed outcome $y_{u,t} \in \{0, 1\}$, we define

$$r_{u,t} = y_{u,t}\,(a_{u,t} - a_{\min}), \qquad a_{\min} := \min \mathcal{A}. \tag{1}$$

This reward is zero for failures and grows with item difficulty for successes, so the agent is incentivized to assign the hardest item the student can still solve. Under the Rasch model the conditional expected reward is

$$\bar{r}(x, a) = (a - a_{\min})\,\sigma(x - a), \tag{2}$$

Crucially, $r_{u,t}$ depends only on the observed outcome and the item's recorded difficulty, not on the student's proficiency, so it can be read off directly from the log without any additional modelling.

Although the realized reward $r_{u,t}$ is zero whenever a student fails, the policy optimizes the *expected* reward $\bar{r}(x, a)$ in Eq. (2): $r_{u,t}$ is an unbiased single-sample estimate of $\bar{r}$, so an individual failure does not imply a poorly chosen action. A difficulty that is well calibrated to a student's proficiency has high expected reward regardless of any realized outcome. Note also that $r_{u,t}$ is an internal optimization signal for selecting difficulty, never a score shown to or imposed on the student. What $\bar{r}$ captures is thus *expected calibrated success*, i.e. placing students at their challenge frontier, rather than a direct measure of learning gains.

3.3 Adaptive Behavior Policy Estimation

The reduced-form behavior policy $\pi_t(a \mid z)$ captures the distribution of difficulty actually assigned to a student of true proficiency z at time t. Crucially, this is *not* the ITS's internal decision rule: the ITS does not observe z_u directly, so it cannot condition on it explicitly. Rather, $\pi_t(a \mid z)$ summarizes the conditional assignment pattern observed in the logs. This pattern may arise for two reasons. First, the ITS adapts based on observable proxies (e.g. recent performance) that correlate with z_u. Second, students themselves may exercise agency in choosing or attempting problems—and unlike the ITS, students may have direct access to their own knowledge. Both mechanisms produce a distribution of assigned difficulties that is conditional to z, even though neither agent observes it directly.

Estimating how $\pi_t(a \mid z)$ varies with z and evolves with t is therefore a core contribution of this work. In light of the reward defined above, a well-designed ITS should assign difficulty in a way that is both adaptive and appropriately calibrated to the student: more proficient students should receive harder items, less proficient students easier ones, and the overall level should shift upward as students progress through the sequence.

Thus, $\pi_t(a \mid z)$ is informative not only about whether the system adapts, but also about whether it tends to assign items that are too easy, too difficult, or well matched to the student's level under the desirable-difficulty objective. Conversely, a flat, diffuse, or poorly aligned $\pi_t(a \mid z)$ suggests weak or miscalibrated adaptation. The estimated behavior policy therefore provides an interpretable diagnostic of how well the logged assignment rule aligns with the reward objective, independently of any downstream policy learning.

Since z_u is unobserved, we estimate this reduced-form policy by conditioning on the proxy $x = \hat{z}_u$, yielding $\pi_t(a \mid x)$. This introduces two error sources: a *behavior-model error* (the parametric family may misfit the true conditional) and a *knowledge estimation error* (we condition on $\hat{z}_u$ rather than z_u).

Once each interaction is represented as $(x_{u,t}, a_{u,t}, r_{u,t}, t)$, the tutoring log can be interpreted as a sample from a continuous stochastic contextual bandit problem and a time-dependent logging policy, making propensity estimation the central prerequisite for all offline estimators in Sect. 4.

For each round t, we retrieve context–action pairs from all students with $T_u \geq t$,

$$\mathcal{D}^{(t)} := \{(x_{u,t}, a_{u,t}) : T_u \geq t\},$$

and approximate $\pi_t(a \mid x)$ by a parametric family $f_\eta^{(t)}(a \mid x)$, estimated by maximum likelihood on $\mathcal{D}^{(t)}$ alone:

$$\hat{\eta}_t \in \arg\max_{\eta} \sum_{(x,a)\in\mathcal{D}^{(t)}} \log f_\eta^{(t)}(a \mid x).$$

The fitted propensities $\hat{p}_{u,t} := \hat{\pi}_t(a_{u,t} \mid x_{u,t})$ are then used in all off-policy estimators, while Fig. 1 illustrates the estimated policy at several rounds–directly visualizing how the collective assignment rule adapts to proficiency and shifts over time.

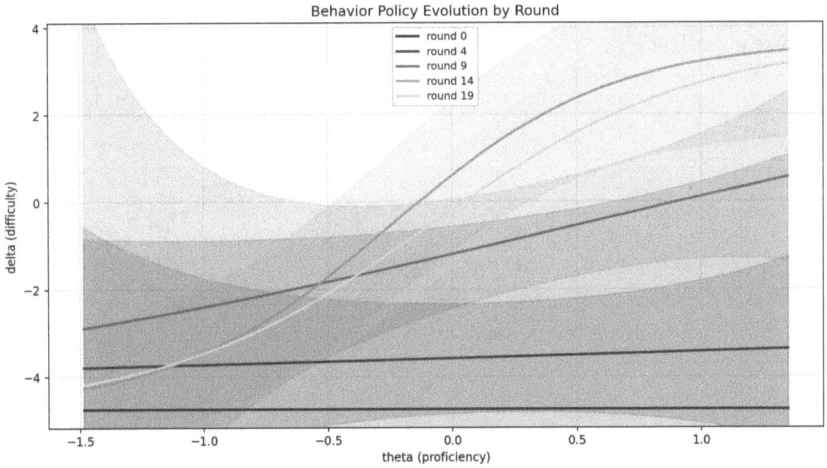

Fig. 1. Estimated adaptive behavior policy $\pi_t(a \mid x)$ at different steps of the learning trace. Shaded areas represent the variance.

4 Offline Contextual Bandit Framework

4.1 Logged Dataset and Context Distribution Shift

In our setup, context $x_{u,t} = \hat{z}_u$ is a proficiency estimate derived from the student's complete interaction trace. Since round t only includes students with $T_u \geq t$, later rounds systematically contain students with longer traces, which produces two compounding sources of context shift.

The first is a *statistical estimation effect*: longer traces yield more precise Rasch estimates that are less attracted toward the center of the proficiency distribution. With few observations, regularization pulls $\hat{z}_u$ toward zero; with many observations, the estimate is free to reflect the student's true proficiency. As a result, $p_t(x)$ becomes progressively more dispersed at later rounds, with heavier tails and less mass near zero.

The second is a *survivorship effect*: students who persist longer may not be a random subsample of the population. Depending on the system, more motivated or more proficient students may be over-represented in subsequent rounds, changing the mean of $p_t(x)$ and its spread.

Both effects cause $p_t(x)$ to drift substantially across rounds, as illustrated in Fig. 2. Let $p^\star(x)$ denote a reference context distribution. We augment each logged interaction with the reweighting factor

$$\omega_{u,t} := \frac{p^\star(x_{u,t})}{p_t(x_{u,t})},$$

and the full logged dataset is

$$\mathcal{D} = \left\{(x_{u,t}, a_{u,t}, r_{u,t}, \hat{p}_{u,t}, \omega_{u,t}, t)\right\}_{u,t}.$$

4.2 Policy Value

We evaluate a stochastic target policy $\pi_\theta(a \mid x)$ whose value under the target context distribution is

$$V^\star(\pi_\theta) = \int_{\mathcal{X}} p^\star(x) \int_{\mathcal{A}} \pi_\theta(a \mid x)\, \mathbb{E}[r \mid x, a]\, da\, dx.$$

Since $\mathbb{E}[r \mid x, a] = (a - a_{\min})\, q(x, a)$, estimating this quantity directly requires a model for the correctness probability q. The two families of estimators below differ precisely in whether they commit to such a model.

4.3 Model-Free Estimators

Defining the combined importance weight $w_{u,t}(\theta) := \omega_{u,t}\, \pi_\theta(a_{u,t} \mid x_{u,t})/\hat{p}_{u,t}$, the Importance Propensity Scoring (IPS), Self-Normalized-IPS (SNIPS), and Mixture Importance Sampling (MIS) estimators replace the unknown $\mathbb{E}[r \mid x, a]$ with the observed reward $r_{u,t}$:

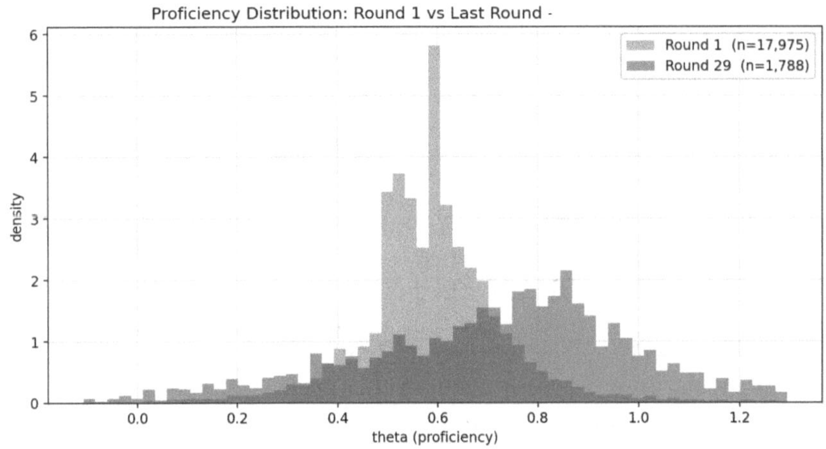

Fig. 2. Evolution of the context distribution $p_t(x)$ across rounds for RoboMission. At early rounds the distribution is narrow and centered near zero; at later rounds it broadens and shifts, reflecting both the improved precision of longer-trace Rasch estimates and survivorship bias among persisting students.

$$\widehat{V}_{\text{IPS}} = \tfrac{1}{n} \textstyle\sum_{u,t} w_{u,t}\, r_{u,t}, \tag{3}$$

$$\widehat{V}_{\text{SNIPS}} = \textstyle\sum_{u,t} w_{u,t}\, r_{u,t} \big/ \textstyle\sum_{u,t} w_{u,t}, \tag{4}$$

$$\widehat{V}_{\text{MIS}} = \tfrac{1}{n} \textstyle\sum_{u,t} \omega_{u,t}\, \frac{\pi_\theta(a_{u,t}|x_{u,t})}{\bar{\pi}(a_{u,t}|x_{u,t})}\, r_{u,t}, \tag{5}$$

where $\bar{\pi}(a \mid x) = \sum_t \lambda_t\, \hat{\pi}_t(a \mid x)$ with $\lambda_t = n_t/n$ pools all rounds into a single denominator.

Crucially, none of these estimators requires an explicit model for q: they are agnostic to the functional form of the correctness probability and rely only on the observed binary outcomes encoded in $r_{u,t}$.

4.4 Model-Based and Doubly Robust Estimators

A complementary strategy is to directly model $\mathbb{E}[r \mid x, a]$, which in our reward formulation amounts to specifying q. A natural choice is the Rasch model, giving

$$\hat{r}(x, a) := (a - a_{\min})\, \sigma(x - a).$$

The direct method (DM) estimator then averages this reward model under the target policy:

$$\widehat{V}_{\mathrm{DM}}(\pi_\theta) = \int_{\mathcal{X}} p^\star(x) \int_{\mathcal{A}} \pi_\theta(a \mid x)\, \hat{r}(x,a)\, da\, dx.$$

Under this model the optimal difficulty level for a student of proficiency x is

$$\delta^\star(x) \in \arg\max_{a \in \mathcal{A}} \, (a - a_{\mathrm{min}})\, \sigma(x - a),$$

which balances item difficulty against the probability of a correct response. The corresponding oracle policy is

$$\pi^\star_{\mathrm{IRT}}(a \mid \mathrm{x}) = \mathcal{N}\big(a;\, \delta^\star(x),\, \sigma^2_{\mathrm{min}}\big),$$

where σ^2_{min} is a small fixed variance introduced to keep the policy stochastic—as required by importance sampling—while concentrating as much mass as possible around the optimal difficulty. It is the best policy achievable under the Rasch reward model, and any learned policy that approaches it under the DM estimator can be considered well-calibrated. DM has very low variance but is necessarily biased because the Rasch specification of q is always misspecified. The doubly robust estimator [10] combines both approaches:

$$\widehat{V}_{\mathrm{DR}} = \widehat{V}_{\mathrm{DM}} + \tfrac{1}{n} \textstyle\sum_{u,t} w_{u,t}\big(r_{u,t} - \hat{r}(x_{u,t}, a_{u,t})\big), \tag{6}$$

and is consistent if either the behavior model or the reward model is correctly specified.

4.5 Policy Learning

Given any estimator $\widehat{V}$, the learned policy solves

$$\hat{\theta} \in \arg\max_{\theta \in \Theta} \, \widehat{V}(\pi_\theta),$$

where π_θ is a Gaussian (or truncated Gaussian) density over the continuous difficulty space. Each estimator in Eqs. (3) to (6) induces a different learning objective, whose effects we compare in Sect. 5.

5 Experiments

We evaluate offline contextual bandit learning on four datasets. RoboMission is a dataset of block-based programming problems [11]. Assistments2015 and Assistments2009 are two datasets from the ASSISTments platform [13]. Pix is a dataset from an ITS that delivers problems linked to digital competencies [24]. To avoid collapsing a long tail of interactions into a single bucket, we truncate the horizon to 30 rounds for RoboMission and Pix, and to 50 rounds for both ASSISTments datasets. Table 1 summarizes the resulting dataset statistics.

Table 1. Dataset statistics. $[\delta_{\min}, \delta_{\max}]$ denotes the range of item difficulties on the latent scale estimated by the Rasch model. Assistments2009 is restricted to the 8,000 most frequently attempted items.

Dataset	Students	Interactions	Horizon	$[\delta_{\min}, \delta_{\max}]$
RoboMission	20,556	258,670	30	[−3.700, 2.571]
Assistments2015	14,567	473,582	50	[−1.756, 0.709]
Assistments2009	4,066	97,571	50	[−1.292, 1.307]
Pix	100,000	2,978,909	30	[−4.751, 3.686]

Behavior and Target Policy Class. Student proficiency is estimated by fitting a Rasch model on the full interaction data, and we use the resulting latent ability estimate as the context variable x. For each dataset and for each round, we fit a behavior policy and learn a parametric target policy that recommends items based on student proficiency. The target policy follows a Gaussian distribution:

$$\pi_\theta(a \mid x) = \mathcal{N}(a;\ \mu_\theta(x),\ \sigma_\theta(x)^2),$$

where the mean is linear in proficiency, $\mu_\theta(x) = \beta_{\mu,0} + \beta_{\mu,1}\, x$, and the log standard deviation is quadratic, $\log \sigma_\theta(x) = \beta_{\sigma,0} + \beta_{\sigma,1}\, x + \beta_{\sigma,2}\, x^2$, leading to five learnable parameters $\theta = (\beta_{\mu,0}, \beta_{\mu,1}, \beta_{\sigma,0}, \beta_{\sigma,1}, \beta_{\sigma,2})$. When the action space is bounded to $[\delta_{\min}, \delta_{\max}]$, we use the corresponding truncated Gaussian density and constrain $\mu_\theta(x)$ to stay in range via a sigmoid reparameterization. We use the same family of distributions to fit the behavior policies f_η in each round. We train one such policy per objective (IPS, SNIPS, DR, MIS), using the target context distribution $p^\star$ estimated from the first half of rounds.

Evaluation Protocol. Students are split 80/20 into train and test sets (split by student). Round-specific behavior and target policies are fitted exclusively on train students. Learned policies are then evaluated on the held-out test set using the train-fitted behavior policy to estimate the propensities used in the estimator: for each learned policy π_θ, we compute all five estimators (IPS, SNIPS, DR, MIS, DM) on the test set. The behavior policy never sees test students during training: it is learned from the train split and used to compute the propensities of context–actions tuples in the test split[1].

ITS Diagnostics and Sanity Checks. Before presenting policy-learning results, we report three dataset-level diagnostics. Table 2 summarizes the behavior policies fit quality: higher RMSE indicates less accurate propensity estimates and hence higher OPE variance. Table 3 reports two additional quantities: ITS adaptivity via $\hat{V}(\pi_0)$ and $\hat{V}(\pi_{\text{last}})$, and held-out Rasch calibration gap, where lower is better.

Behavior-model fit varies substantially across datasets, from 0.345 on Assistments2009 and 0.554 on Assistments2015 to 0.704 on Pix and 0.931 on RoboMission. For RoboMission, rounds 5–7 were excluded because of degenerate fits

[1] Code is available at: https://github.com/samgirr/counterfactual_learning_for_ITS.

Table 2. Behavior policy fit quality per dataset. RMSE measures the deviation of the predicted mean difficulty $\hat{\mu}_t(x)$ from the observed δ. Higher RMSE indicates a harder-to-fit action distribution, degrading propensity estimates and increasing OPE variance.

Dataset	RMSE (avg)	RMSE ($\hat{\pi}_{\text{last}}$)	Excluded
RoboMission	0.931	1.025	rounds 5–7
Assistments2015	0.554	0.552	none
Assistments2009	0.345	0.352	none
Pix	0.704	0.681	round 0

Table 3. Dataset-level diagnostics used to contextualize the offline policy learning results.

(a) ITS adaptivity diagnostic. Larger gaps indicate stronger adaptation over the interaction horizon.

Dataset	$\hat{V}(\pi_0)$	$\hat{V}(\pi_{\text{last}})$
Assistments2009	0.584	0.636
Assistments2015	0.669	0.863
RoboMission	1.619	1.877
Pix	1.064	1.981

(b) Calibration gap of the Rasch model on the test split. Lower is better.

Dataset	Calibration gap
RoboMission	0.0212
Assistments2015	0.0324
Assistments2009	0.1112
Pix	0.0280

(RMSE $>$ 19), likely due to a bimodal difficulty distribution with a spike at δ_{min}. For Pix, round 0 was excluded (RMSE $=$ 12.34) because the ITS starts with a deterministic assignment rule that concentrates all students on the same item.

Taken together, these diagnostics provide context for the results that follow. Assistments2015 combines good fit with clear adaptation, Assistments2009 shows good behavior-model fit but limited adaptation and substantially worse Rasch calibration, and RoboMission and Pix exhibit stronger adaptation in a more challenging propensity-estimation setting.

Assistments2015. This dataset represents the most favorable setting for offline contextual bandit learning: the behavior policy is adaptive horizon (see Table 3a), yet drift is moderate enough that overlap remains strong throughout. The behavior policy curves in Fig. 3(a) show a consistent upward shift across rounds without abrupt changes.

All learned policies improve substantially over the behavior baseline (Table 4). Among learned policies, Learned DR achieves the best SNIPS (1.093, a 23.8% improvement over the behavior policy), while the IRT oracle dominates the DR and DM columns as expected. The consistency across estimators gives high confidence that these gains are genuine.

Assistments2009. The behavior policy shows only modest adaptiveness: the context-weighted reward improves from 0.584 to 0.636 over the full horizon (Table 3a), and the behavior policy curves in Fig. 4(a) are nearly flat across

Table 4. Held-out test results on Assistments2015.

Policy	Obj.	IPS	SNIPS	DR	MIS	DM
Behavior	–	0.881	0.882	0.877	0.883	0.883
IRT oracle	–	0.804	1.083	**1.114**	0.821	**1.170**
Learned IPS	ips	**1.270**	1.080	1.076	**1.268**	1.080
Learned SNIPS	snips	1.231	1.089	1.088	1.230	1.096
Learned DR	dr	1.175	**1.093**	1.099	1.176	1.119
Learned MIS	mis	**1.270**	1.080	1.076	1.268	1.081

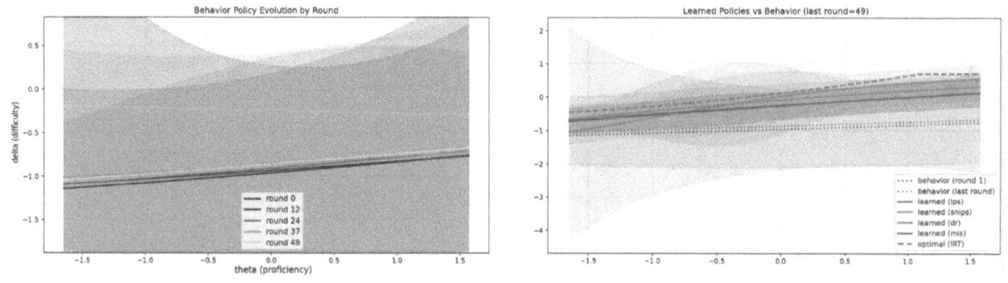

(a) Behavior policy evolution.

(b) Learned policy curves.

Fig. 3. Assistments2015. Left: consistent upward shift across rounds without strong drift, producing good overlap across the full interaction horizon. Right: all learned policies improve substantially over the behavior baseline, with strong agreement across estimators.

all rounds and proficiency levels. Overlap is good, but the difficulty lies in the limited exploration: the system assigns a narrow range of difficulties regardless of student ability, leaving little support for learning a substantially different policy. An additional issue on this dataset is Rasch miscalibration. Table 3b shows that Assistments2009 has the largest calibration gap (0.1112) among all datasets. This helps explain the mismatch between the IRT oracle's SNIPS estimate (0.537), which is below the behavior policy (0.641), and its DM estimate (0.787), which is much higher: the Rasch model appears to predict gains from more difficult assignments that are not supported by the logged data.

Learned SNIPS and Learned DR achieve modest gains over the behavior baseline (Table 5), while Learned IPS and Learned MIS fail to improve reliably. The learned policy curves confirm this pattern: all objectives remain close to the behavior baseline, with limited room to diverge (Fig. 4(b)).

RoboMission. The ITS shows strong adaptation over the horizon: $\hat{V}(\pi_0)$ rises from 1.619 to $\hat{V}(\pi_{\text{last}}) = 1.877$ (Table 3a), and the behavior policy curves in Fig. 5(a) shift upward across rounds, assigning harder items to more proficient students. At the same time, RoboMission has the highest average RMSE (0.931; Table 2), indicating that the behavior policy is harder to model accurately than

Table 5. Held-out test results on Assistments2009.

Policy	Obj.	IPS	SNIPS	DR	MIS	DM
Behavior	–	0.653	0.641	0.641	0.648	0.651
IRT oracle	–	0.440	0.537	0.623	0.444	**0.787**
Learned IPS	ips	0.652	0.627	0.623	0.655	0.696
Learned SNIPS	snips	**0.696**	**0.686**	**0.693**	**0.694**	0.658
Learned DR	dr	0.692	0.684	0.692	0.690	0.665
Learned MIS	mis	0.646	0.620	0.615	0.652	0.709

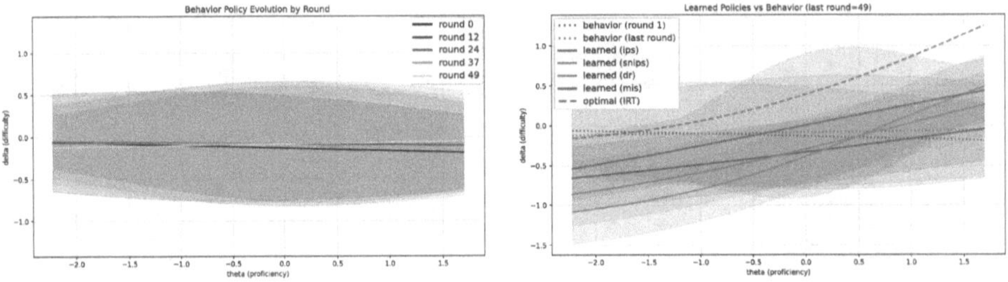

(a) Behavior policy evolution.

(b) Learned policy curves.

Fig. 4. Assistments2009. Left: near-flat behavior policy curves across rounds and proficiency levels, indicating poor adaptivity. Right: learned policies remain close to the behavior baseline, reflecting the limited support available for policy improvement.

in the other datasets. This poor fit helps explain the discrepancy between the reference value $\hat{V}(\pi_{\text{last}})$ in Table 3a and the behavior-policy estimates in Table 6.

All learned policies improve over the behavior baseline under SNIPS and DR (Table 6), with Learned MIS achieving the best results, a 22.5% improvement in SNIPS over the behavior policy.

Pix. The behavior policy is the most strongly adaptive across all datasets: the context-weighted reward nearly doubles from 1.064 to 1.981 (Table 3a), the largest absolute gain observed. This strong drift is reflected in the behavior policy evolution shown in Fig. 1. The behavior model RMSE is intermediate (Table 2), with all rounds after round 0 well fitted.

All learned policies improve substantially over the behavior baseline (Table 7), with Learned DR achieving the best SNIPS and DR among all policies—a 38.9% improvement in SNIPS, the largest gain across all datasets. The IRT oracle again dominates the DM column.

Table 6. Held-out test results on RoboMission.

Policy	Obj.	IPS	SNIPS	DR	MIS	DM
Behavior	–	1.968	1.981	2.006	2.139	2.013
IRT oracle	–	1.694	2.370	2.408	2.563	**2.443**
Learned IPS	ips	2.332	2.360	2.361	2.749	2.241
Learned SNIPS	snips	2.347	2.409	2.408	2.858	2.274
Learned DR	dr	2.315	2.425	2.431	2.875	2.305
Learned MIS	mis	2.302	**2.426**	**2.432**	**2.868**	2.309

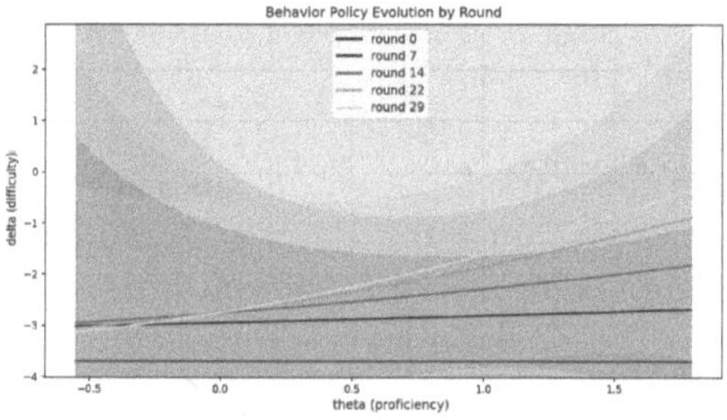

(a) Behavior policy evolution.

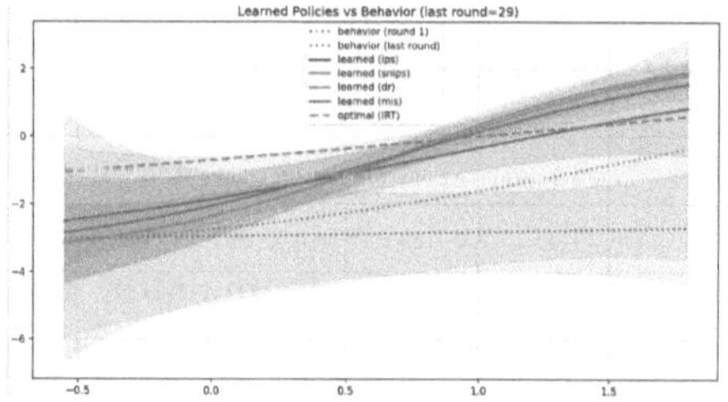

(b) Learned policy curves.

Fig. 5. RoboMission. Left: strong upward shift across rounds indicating high ITS adaptiveness, but also large round-to-round drift that degrades behavior model fit at certain rounds. Right: all learned policies improve over the behavior baseline, with SNIPS and DR being the most reliable metrics.

Comparing the behavior-policy IPS and SNIPS estimates in Table 7 with the reference value $\hat{V}(\pi_{\text{last}}) = 1.981$ from Table 3a reveals an instructive asymmetry on this dataset: IPS underestimates the final-round policy value, whereas SNIPS overestimates it. This is a direct consequence of the strong behavior drift. The importance weights for evaluating the last-round policy $\hat{\pi}_{29}$ on data from an early round t are proportional to $\hat{\pi}_{29}(a \mid x)/\hat{\pi}_t(a \mid x)$. At early rounds, the system assigned much easier items than at round 29, so $\hat{\pi}_{29}$ assigns them low probability and the weights are small. IPS divides by the total number of samples, so these low-weight early-round observations still occupy a large fraction of the denominator, pulling the estimate down. SNIPS normalises by the sum of weights instead, effectively concentrating mass on late rounds where weights are close to 1 and rewards are high, which inflates the estimate. The more adaptive the behavior policy, the larger this divergence between IPS and SNIPS—a pattern that is mild on the ASSISTments datasets and most pronounced here.

Table 7. Held-out test results on Pix.

Policy	Obj.	IPS	SNIPS	DR	MIS	DM
Behavior	–	1.781	2.171	2.136	2.132	2.151
IRT oracle	–	2.227	2.860	2.886	2.642	**2.734**
Learned IPS	ips	2.793	2.995	2.979	3.085	2.657
Learned SNIPS	snips	2.678	3.012	2.990	2.956	2.690
Learned DR	dr	2.731	**3.016**	**2.999**	3.006	2.695
Learned MIS	mis	2.678	2.907	2.887	**3.125**	2.629

6 Conclusion

We presented an offline contextual bandit framework for learning instructional policies directly from logged educational data, without interaction with students or reliance on a student simulator. Experiments on four real-world datasets show that learned policies consistently improve over the behavior baseline out of sample, with SNIPS and DR emerging as the most reliable objectives across datasets and estimators. Our behavior-policy diagnostic also reveals meaningful differences in ITS adaptiveness across systems. More broadly, we show that Rasch model calibration directly affects the reliability of offline evaluation, and should therefore be reported alongside any such analysis.

Deployment and Cold Start. Our evaluation conditions on $x_{u,t} = \hat{z}_u$ estimated from each student's *complete* trace, which suits offline analysis but is unavailable when serving a new student. At deployment, a student with no history is initialized at the population average ($\hat{z} \approx 0$); as they answer items, $\hat{z}_u$ is re-estimated online from the growing prefix and the policy is replayed on the updated context. The learned policy is thus only as good as this running estimate, which is least precise in the earliest rounds—where regularization pulls $\hat{z}_u$ toward zero and sharpens as evidence accumulates. This online protocol bridges our full-trace evaluation context and a realizable deployment loop, at the cost of degraded estimates during a student's first interactions.

Limitations and Future Work. Our bandit formulation optimizes immediate rewards rather than long-term learning gains. Extending the framework to sequential decision-making would allow richer policies, but at substantially greater data and computational cost [9]. In addition, our behavior-policy estimation currently relies on simple parametric families. A promising direction is to consider more flexible models, such as mixture distributions, which could better capture complex assignment patterns in the logs. This is especially relevant at later rounds, where the behavior policy may become multimodal, for example if the ITS separates students into distinct difficulty tracks. More expressive behavior models could therefore improve both interpretability and the stability of downstream off-policy evaluation. When the target policy departs far from the behavior policy, estimators disagree and effective sample size drops; we advocate for logging policies that include deliberate exploration and for releasing behavior-policy descriptions alongside datasets [20]. Finally, visualizing both behavior and learned policies as functions of proficiency opens the door to fairness analyses [16] and may also help identify new knowledge-tracing models from the structure of the learned policies themselves.

Acknowledgments. This study was funded by Île-de-France, Paris Region PhD.

Disclosure of Interests. Samuel Girard has received a research grant from public group interest Pix.

Use of Generative AI. Generative AI tools were used for coding assistance, language refinement, and grammatical editing. All intellectual content, including research design, analysis, and interpretation, was performed by the authors.

Ethics and Societal Aspects. The research conducted in this paper is solely made on offline pseudonymized data in order to benefit human learning. The purpose of off-policy learning is precisely to learn promising strategies to ask questions to humans while avoiding to rely on actual online experimentations on humans.

References

1. Agarwal, A., Basu, S., Schnabel, T., Joachims, T.: Effective evaluation using logged bandit feedback from multiple loggers. In: Proceedings of the 23rd ACM SIGKDD International Conference on Knowledge Discovery and Data Mining. KDD 2017, pp. 687–696. ACM (2017). https://doi.org/10.1145/3097983.3098155
2. Basawapatna, A.R., Repenning, A., Koh, K.H., Nickerson, H.: The zones of proximal flow: guiding students through a space of computational thinking skills and challenges. In: Proceedings of the Ninth Annual International ACM Conference on International Computing Education Research. ICER 2013, pp. 67–74. Association for Computing Machinery, New York, NY, USA (2013). https://doi.org/10.1145/2493394.2493404
3. Bassen, J., et al.: Reinforcement learning for the adaptive scheduling of educational activities. In: Proceedings of the 2020 CHI Conference on Human Factors in Computing Systems, pp. 1–12 (2020)
4. Bjork, E.L., Bjork, R.A., et al.: Making things hard on yourself, but in a good way: Creating desirable difficulties to enhance learning. Psychol. Real World: Essays Illustrating Fundam. Contrib. Soc. **2**(59-68) (2011)
5. Bottou, L., et al.: Counterfactual reasoning and learning systems: the example of computational advertising. J. Mach. Learn. Res. 14(11) (2013)
6. Clément, B., Roy, D., Oudeyer, P.Y., Lopes, M.: Multi-armed bandits for intelligent tutoring systems. J. Educ. Data Min. **7**(2), 20–48 (2015)
7. Corbett, A.T., Anderson, J.R.: Knowledge tracing: modeling the acquisition of procedural knowledge. User Model. User-Adap. Inter. **4**, 253–278 (1994)
8. Csikszentmihalyi, M., Csikszentmihalyi, I.S.: Optimal Experience: Psychological Studies of Flow in Consciousness. Cambridge University Press, Cambridge (1988)

9. Doroudi, S., Aleven, V., Brunskill, E.: Robust evaluation matrix: towards a more principled offline exploration of instructional policies. In: Proceedings of the Fourth (2017) ACM Conference on Learning at Scale, pp. 3–12 (2017)
10. Dudík, M., Langford, J., Li, L.: Doubly robust policy evaluation and learning. In: Proceedings of the 28th International Conference on International Conference on Machine Learning, pp. 1097–1104 (2011)
11. Effenberger, T., Pelánek, R.: Towards making block-based programming activities adaptive. In: Proceedings of the Fifth Annual ACM Conference on Learning at Scale, pp. 1–4 (2018)
12. Fang, Y., Ren, Z., Hu, X., Graesser, A.C.: A meta-analysis of the effectiveness of aleks on learning. Educ. Psychol. **39**(10), 1278–1292 (2019)
13. Feng, M., Heffernan, N., Koedinger, K.: Addressing the assessment challenge with an online system that tutors as it assesses. User Model. User-Adap. Inter. **19**(3), 243–266 (2009)
14. Gao, G., Ju, S., Chi, M.: Hope: human-centric off-policy evaluation for e-learning and healthcare. In: In the 22nd International Conference on Autonomous Agents and Multiagent Systems (AAMAS 2023). Springer, Cham (2023)
15. Gao, G., Gao, Q., Yang, X., Ju, S., Pajic, M., Chi, M.: On trajectory augmentations for off-policy evaluation. In: The Twelfth International Conference on Learning Representations (2024). https://openreview.net/forum?id=eMNN0wIyVw
16. Gardner, J., Brooks, C., Baker, R.: Evaluating the fairness of predictive student models through slicing analysis. In: Proceedings of the 9th International Conference on Learning Analytics & Knowledge, pp. 225–234 (2019)
17. Lan, A.S., Baraniuk, R.G.: A contextual bandits framework for personalized learning action selection. In: EDM, pp. 424–429 (2016)
18. Levine, S., Kumar, A., Tucker, G., Fu, J.: Offline reinforcement learning: tutorial, review, and perspectives on open problems (2020). https://arxiv.org/abs/2005.01643
19. Rasch, G.: Studies in mathematical psychology: I. Probabilistic models for some intelligence and attainment tests. Nielsen & Lydiche (1960)
20. Saito, Y., Aihara, S., Matsutani, M., Narita, Y.: Open bandit dataset and pipeline: Towards realistic and reproducible off-policy evaluation. In: Thirty-fifth Conference on Neural Information Processing Systems Datasets and Benchmarks Track (Round 2) (2021)
21. Subramanian, J., Mostow, J.: Deep reinforcement learning to simulate, train, and evaluate instructional sequencing policies (2021). spotlight presentation at Reinforcement Learning for Education workshop at Educational Data Mining 2021 conference
22. Swaminathan, A., Joachims, T.: Counterfactual risk minimization: learning from logged bandit feedback. In: Bach, F., Blei, D. (eds.) Proceedings of the 32nd International Conference on Machine Learning. Proceedings of Machine Learning Research, vol. 37, pp. 814–823. PMLR, Lille, France (2015). https://proceedings.mlr.press/v37/swaminathan15.html
23. Vassoyan, J., Vie, J.J., Lemberger, P.: Towards scalable adaptive learning with graph neural networks and reinforcement learning. In: Feng, M., Käser, T., Talukdar, P. (eds.) Proceedings of the 16th International Conference on Educational Data Mining, pp. 351–361. International Educational Data Mining Society, Bengaluru, India (2023). https://doi.org/10.5281/zenodo.8115663
24. Vie, J.J., Popineau, F., Tort, F., Marteau, B., Denos, N.: A heuristic method for large-scale cognitive-diagnostic computerized adaptive testing. In: Proceedings of the Fourth (2017) ACM Conference on Learning at Scale, pp. 323–326 (2017)

25. Whitehill, J., Movellan, J.: Approximately optimal teaching of approximately optimal learners. IEEE Trans. Learn. Technol. **11**(2), 152–164 (2017)
26. Yang, X., Islam, M.M., Gao, G., Chi, M.: Themes: an offline apprenticeship learning framework for evolving reward functions. In: Proceedings of the 31st ACM SIGKDD Conference on Knowledge Discovery and Data Mining V. 2, pp. 3565–3576 (2025)
27. Yessad, A.: Personalizing the sequencing of learning activities by using the q-learning and the Bayesian knowledge tracing. In: European Conference on Technology Enhanced Learning, pp. 638–644. Springer, Cham (2022)
28. Zhao, S., Heffernan, N.: Estimating individual treatment effect from educational studies with residual counterfactual networks. In: International Educational Data Mining Society. ERIC (2017)

Decision-Focused Learning for Operating Room Scheduling Under Uncertain Surgery Durations with Two-Stage Stochastic Optimization

Ali Elaswad[1(✉)], Rodrigo A. Carrasco[2], and Nourhan Sakr[1]

[1] The American University in Cairo, Cairo, Egypt
alyelaswad@aucegypt.edu, n.sakr@columbia.edu
[2] Pontificia Universidad Católica de Chile, 7820436 Santiago, Chile
rax@uc.cl

Abstract. Operating rooms account for roughly 40% of hospital expenses, making scheduling quality a primary lever for both cost control and patient access. Yet standard approaches either assume fixed surgery durations or decouple prediction from optimization, leaving systematic performance gains unrealized. We present a framework combining Smart Predict-Then-Optimize (SPO+) with two-stage stochastic programming (2SP) for OR scheduling under uncertain surgery durations. Duration predictors are trained end-to-end using a regret-aligned surrogate loss that directly optimizes downstream schedule quality, while a second-stage recourse mechanism adapts schedules in real time as true durations are revealed intraoperatively through opportunistic advancement, OR swaps, and cancellation. Four prediction pipelines are benchmarked on real neurosurgical data: a deterministic baseline, vanilla Predict-Then-Optimize, regret-aware gradient boosting, and SPO+, each evaluated with and without 2SP recourse via Monte Carlo simulation across utilization, overtime, and patient throughput. A penalty parameter λ governing overtime cost serves as a governance-controlled policy knob, enabling explicit operationalization of institutional risk tolerance. SPO+ combined with 2SP recourse achieves 94.4% OR utilization and reduces 95th-percentile overtime significantly compared to SPO+ alone.

Keywords: Scheduling under Uncertainty · SPO framework · Two-stage Stochastic Programming · Operating Rooms · Healthcare Operations

1 Introduction

Efficient use of Operating Rooms (ORs) is crucial to deliver timely, safe, and cost-effective surgical care. In fact, ORs account for 40% of total hospital expenses and contribute to 60–70% of revenue [1]. Delays in surgeries put patients at greater risk and can make their hospital stay longer.

M. Ceci et al. (Eds.): ECML PKDD 2026, LNAI 16948, pp. 252–270, 2027.
https://doi.org/10.1007/978-3-032-37679-4_15

As a result, extensive research has been devoted to improving OR management, and more particularly OR scheduling [2–5]. The main challenge in OR scheduling is the high variability in surgery durations [6], where differences in patient conditions [7], procedure complexity [8], and unexpected intraoperative events can lead to overtime, cancellations, and result in underutilized ORs which makes reliable schedules difficult to achieve in practice. On one hand, if a single surgery runs longer than anticipated, then every subsequent case in that OR is delayed and patients who have already fasted and been prepped are left waiting while downstream resources such as recovery rooms and ICU beds sit idle, which is very costly from an operational point of view. On the other hand, when a single surgery finishes early, this slack is rarely recovered since the next patient is often not yet prepared, or the room has not been turned over [17]. In both cases, duration variability translates directly into wasted resources and delayed patient care.

One well-studied approach is to model surgery durations as random variables using stochastic programming or chance-constrained optimization [9,10]. While these methods model uncertainty explicitly, they still often require strong assumptions about the distribution of surgery durations and can be difficult to tune for real-world settings. The Predict-then-Optimize (PtO) paradigm takes a more data-driven approach by using machine learning to predict the durations of the surgery and then schedules cases based on those predictions [11,12]. While these methods have shown some success, separating prediction from optimization can lead to suboptimal schedules, as the predicted durations are not learned with the downstream scheduling objective in mind. As a result, schedules may suffer from overtime, cancellations, or underutilized ORs, particularly when predictions are highly variable.

A promising approach to address the shortcomings of traditional PtO methods is Decision-Focused Learning (DFL), where predictions are trained not just to be accurate, but to improve the quality of the downstream decisions they influence. This approach recognizes that small errors in predictions can have very different impacts on the quality of the resulting decisions, and thus trains the model to focus on reducing the errors that matter most for the outcomes that actually count in the downstream task [13]. A well-known instantiation of DFL is the Smart Predict then Optimize (SPO+) framework [14], which operationalizes this by embedding the optimization problem directly into the training loop. While SPO+ has been applied in routing [16] and aircraft scheduling [15], operating room scheduling presents different challenges. Surgery durations feed into sequential case chains, so a single prediction error can propagate through the entire day. Costs are also highly asymmetric between overtime and idle time, and patient-level heterogeneity makes duration prediction considerably noisier, all of which motivate a tailored application of DFL.

However, even a schedule built with decision-focused learning is a static plan and once execution begins, unexpected complications, late patients, or equipment delays can disrupt it with no mechanism to respond. To address this, we use two-stage stochastic programming (2SP), where we treat the schedule as a first-stage decision and explicitly optimize recourse actions, such as advancing cases, swapping patients across ORs, or canceling procedures that would violate overtime limits, as actual durations are revealed intraoperatively.

In this work, we combine decision-focused learning with two-stage stochastic programming to build OR schedules that are both cost-aware at the prediction stage and robust at execution time. Our contributions are as follows:

- Formulate OR scheduling as a decision-focused learning problem and apply two DFL approaches, SPO+ and regret-aware gradient boosting, establishing the, to our knowledge, first application of these methods to OR scheduling.
- Augment the scheduling framework with two-stage stochastic programming to enable explicit recourse decisions when intraoperative surprises cause plans to deviate.
- Benchmark four prediction pipelines combined with 2SP against deterministic and standard PtO baselines, providing a systematic comparison across scheduling paradigms. Source code[1] and a synthetic proxy dataset[2] are publicly available.
- Validate on real hospital data via Monte Carlo simulation, demonstrating improvements in throughput, utilization, and overtime stability over all baselines.

2 Methodology

2.1 Problem Formulation

We build on the time-indexed integer programming model of [9]. Consider I patients, J operating rooms, K surgeons, and a daily horizon of T time steps of length Δt hours. Each patient i is characterized by a procedure type l_i, a set of qualified surgeons K_i, a set of eligible ORs J_i, and a waiting-time weight W_i representing the number of days patient i has been waiting. Each surgeon k is available during time steps $[a_k, b_k]$. The surgery duration of patient i under surgeon k is a random variable $S_{l_i k}$ with mean $p_{l_i k}$.

The binary decision variable $x_{ijkt} = 1$ if patient i is assigned to OR j, surgeon k, starting at time step t, and 0 otherwise (Table 1).

The baseline scheduling problem is:

$$\max_{x} \sum_{i \in I} \sum_{j \in J_i} \sum_{k \in K_i} \sum_{t \in T} W_i \, x_{ijkt} \tag{1}$$

Here, maximizing $\sum W_i x_{ijkt}$ does not maximize waiting time itself, but rather prioritizes patients who have waited the longest, giving precedence to those with the greatest accumulated wait time. The problem is subject to the following constraints [9]:

[1] https://github.com/alyelaswad/OR-Scheduling.

[2] https://huggingface.co/datasets/alyelaswad/OR-synthetic-proxy.

Table 1. Summary of key notation.

Symbol	Description
I, J, K, T	Number of patients, ORs, surgeons, time steps
l_i	Procedure type of patient i
K_i, J_i	Qualified surgeons and eligible ORs for patient i
W_i	Waiting-time weight (days waited) for patient i
$[a_k, b_k]$	Available time steps for surgeon k
$S_{l_i k}$	Random surgery duration for patient i under surgeon k
$p_{l_i k}$	Mean of $S_{l_i k}$
d_i	Realized surgery duration of patient i
$\hat{d}_i$	Predicted surgery duration of patient i
x_{ijkt}	1 if patient i assigned to OR j, surgeon k, start t
λ	Duration penalty in SPO+ objective
α, β	Cancellation and overtime penalties in 2SP recourse
τ_{adv}, τ_{OT}	Advancement window and overtime tolerance (hours)
S	Number of second-stage scenarios
$\tilde{d}_i^s$	Realized duration of patient i in scenario s

1. **OR capacity.** At each time step t, OR j has at most one surgery in progress:

$$\sum_{i=1}^{I}\sum_{k=1}^{K}\sum_{u=\max\{0,\,t-p_{l_i k}+1\}}^{t} x_{ijku} \leq 1, \quad \forall j,\, \forall t. \tag{2}$$

2. **Surgeon capacity.** At each time step t, surgeon k performs at most one surgery:

$$\sum_{i=1}^{I}\sum_{j=1}^{J}\sum_{u=\max\{0,\,t-p_{l_i k}+1\}}^{t} x_{ijku} \leq 1, \quad \forall k,\, \forall t. \tag{3}$$

3. **Single assignment.** Each patient is assigned to at most one OR, surgeon, and start time:

$$\sum_{k\in K_i}\sum_{j\in J_i}\sum_{t=0}^{T} x_{ijkt} \leq 1, \quad \forall i. \tag{4}$$

4. **Surgeon availability.** Surgeries can only be scheduled within surgeon k's available window $[a_k, b_k]$:

$$x_{ijkt} = 0 \quad \text{if } t < a_k \text{ or } t + p_{l_i k} - 1 > b_k, \quad \forall i,\, j,\, k. \tag{5}$$

5. **Horizon.** All surgeries must complete within the operating hours T:

$$x_{ijkt} = 0 \quad \text{if } t + p_{l_i k} - 1 > T, \quad \forall i,\, j,\, k. \tag{6}$$

6. **Binary variables.**

$$x_{ijkt} \in \{0, 1\}, \quad \forall i, j, k, t. \tag{7}$$

This formulation, which uses mean durations $p_{l_i k}$ as fixed inputs, serves as our *Base Case Schedule* (BCS). We further denote by d_i the realized surgery duration of patient i, which the BCS approximates by $p_{l_i k}$. Subsequent methods replace this approximation with a patient-level predicted duration $\hat{d}_i$.

2.2 Vanilla Predict-Then-Optimize

Vanilla PtO extends the BCS baseline by replacing the fixed mean durations $p_{l_i k}$ with patient-level predicted durations $\hat{d}_i$ obtained from a gradient boosting regression model. The predicted durations enter the formulation exclusively through the scheduling constraints, specifically the OR capacity and surgeon capacity constraints, where they determine how many patients can feasibly fit within the daily horizon. The objective in Eq. 1 remains therefore unchanged.

We use a gradient boosting model that is trained on historical records using 7 features for each patient i: the mean and standard deviation of surgery durations grouped by surgeon and procedure type, the mean duration grouped by post-operative destination, the corresponding case counts, and patient demographic features. The model uses 200 estimators, a maximum tree depth of 5, and a learning rate of 0.05, trained to minimize the Mean Squared Error (MSE) between predicted and realized durations d_i. We note that some of the richer clinical features such as ASA classification or BMI, were not available in our dataset. The 7-feature model represents the information available in the hospital's scheduling system at the time of queue construction.

The main limitation of this approach is that prediction and optimization are treated separately. The prediction model minimizes MSE of surgery durations, but this loss does not reflect the quality of the schedules produced from those predictions. Consequently, the resulting schedules can be far from optimal for the objectives of the optimization model.

2.3 DFL 1: Regret-Aware Gradient Boosting

Before introducing the inherently complex SPO+ framework, we first introduce an initial decision-focused approach to serve as a practical approximation.

First, We define *regret* as the loss in weighted throughput incurred by scheduling with predicted rather than true durations:

$$R = f(x^*(d); d) - f(x^*(\hat{d}); d), \tag{8}$$

where $x^*(d)$ and $x^*(\hat{d})$ denote the schedules optimal under true and predicted durations respectively, and both are evaluated against the true durations d.

The training procedure is iterative. At each iteration n, a gradient boosting model is fitted to the training data using the current sample weight vector $\mathbf{w}^{(n)}$,

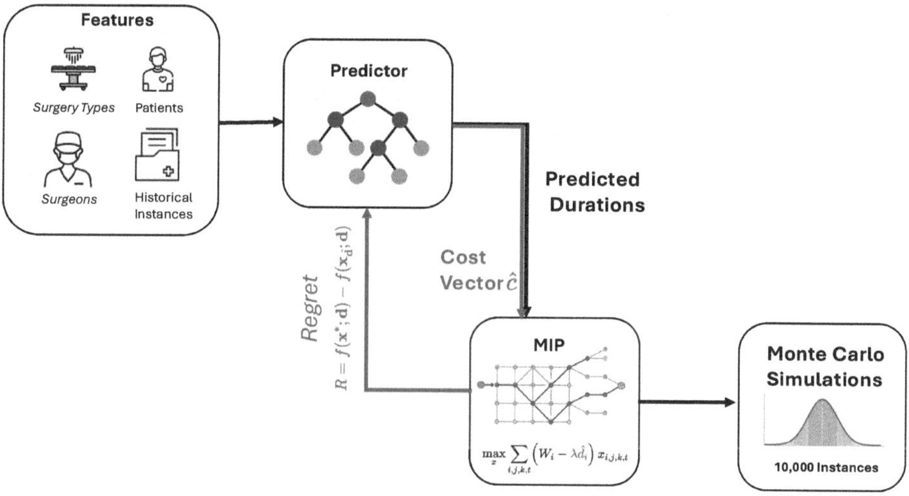

Fig. 1. Decision-Focused Learning framework for OR scheduling. Black denotes the standard Predict-then-Optimize pipeline; red denotes DFL-specific components, including the cost vector $\hat{c}$, penalty λ, and regret feedback from the MIP to the predictor. (Color figure online)

initialized uniformly as $w_i^{(0)} = 1$ for all i. After fitting, the model generates predictions $\hat{d}^{(n)}$ for each training queue, the MIP is solved under both $\hat{d}^{(n)}$ and the true durations d, and the regret $R_q^{(n)}$ is computed for each queue q. Sample weights are then updated as:

$$w_i^{(n+1)} = 1 + \frac{R_q^{(n)}}{\bar{R}^{(n)} + \epsilon}, \tag{9}$$

where $\bar{R}^{(n)}$ is the mean regret across training queues and $\epsilon > 0$ is a small constant for numerical stability. Weights are subsequently normalized so that $\sum_i w_i^{(n+1)} = N$, where N is the number of training samples. This assigns higher influence to patients whose mispredictions caused the largest deterioration in schedule quality, steering the model away from prediction errors that matter most for the downstream objective. The model with the lowest validation regret across all iterations is retained.

The gradient boosting model uses the same architecture as Vanilla PtO: 200 estimators, maximum tree depth 5, learning rate 0.05, and the same 7 aggregated features. Unlike Vanilla PtO, however, the loss function is no longer purely MSE since the sample weighting implicitly reshapes the loss landscape to penalize scheduling errors more heavily. This is illustrated in Fig. 1, where there is a feedback from the MIP itself to the predictor, denoted in red.

It is worth noting that regret-aware GB is a *practical approximation* to fully end-to-end decision-focused learning: it incorporates scheduling feedback

Algorithm 1. SPO+ Training for OR Scheduling

Input: Training instances $\{(X^{(q)}, d^{(q)}, W^{(q)})\}_{q=1}^{Q}$, features $X^{(q)}$, true durations $d^{(q)}$, waiting-time weights $W^{(q)}$
Parameters: penalty $\lambda > 0$, learning rate $\eta > 0$, iterations N
Output: Trained prediction model f_θ

Initialize θ; cache true costs and oracle schedules:
for $q = 1, \ldots, Q$ **do**
  $c_i^{(q)} \leftarrow W_i^{(q)} - \lambda d_i^{(q)}, \forall i$
  $x^*(c^{(q)}) \leftarrow \arg\max_{x \in \mathcal{S}(d^{(q)})} (c^{(q)})^\top x$
  $z^*(c^{(q)}) \leftarrow (c^{(q)})^\top x^*(c^{(q)})$ ▷ Cached once, reused every iteration
end for
for $n = 1, \ldots, N$ **do**
  $\mathcal{L} \leftarrow 0, \quad g \leftarrow 0$
  for $q = 1, \ldots, Q$ **do**
    $\hat{d}^{(q)} \leftarrow f_\theta(X^{(q)})$
    $\hat{c}_i^{(q)} \leftarrow W_i^{(q)} - \lambda \hat{d}_i^{(q)}, \forall i$
    $x^*(2\hat{c}^{(q)} - c^{(q)}) \leftarrow \arg\max_{x \in \mathcal{S}(\hat{d}^{(q)})} (2\hat{c}^{(q)} - c^{(q)})^\top x$
    $\mathcal{L} \leftarrow \mathcal{L} + (c^{(q)})^\top x^*(2\hat{c}^{(q)} - c^{(q)}) - 2(\hat{c}^{(q)})^\top x^*(2\hat{c}^{(q)} - c^{(q)}) + 2(\hat{c}^{(q)})^\top x^*(c^{(q)}) - z^*(c^{(q)})$
    $\frac{\partial \mathcal{L}}{\partial \hat{d}_i^{(q)}} \leftarrow -2\lambda\left(x_i^*(2\hat{c}^{(q)} - c^{(q)}) - x_i^*(c^{(q)})\right)$ where $x_i^*(\cdot) = \sum_{j,k,t} x_{ijkt}^*(\cdot)$
    $g \leftarrow g + \nabla_\theta \hat{d}^{(q)} \cdot \frac{\partial \mathcal{L}}{\partial \hat{d}^{(q)}}$
  end for
  $\theta \leftarrow \theta - \eta \cdot g$
end for
return f_θ

through weight updates but does not propagate gradients through the optimization problem itself. This limitation motivates the SPO+ framework introduced next.

2.4 DFL 2: Smart Predict-Then-Optimize (SPO+)

Unlike regret-aware gradient boosting, which incorporates scheduling feedback through sample reweighting, SPO+ directly propagates gradients through the optimization problem, ensuring that the predictor is trained end-to-end with respect to decision quality rather than prediction accuracy alone.

Predictive Cost Vector. In the baseline formulation (1), surgery durations appear only in the scheduling constraints to determine how many patients fit within the daily horizon. As a result, prediction errors in $\hat{d}_i$ produce no gradient signal during training. To remedy this, we introduce the *predictive cost vector* $\hat{c}$, which modifies the scheduling objective to:

$$\max_{x \in \mathcal{S}(\hat{d})} \sum_{i \in I} \sum_{j \in J_i} \sum_{k \in K_i} \sum_{t \in T} (W_i - \lambda \hat{d}_i)\, x_{ijkt}, \tag{10}$$

where $\hat{c}_i = W_i - \lambda \hat{d}_i$ is the predicted cost coefficient for patient i.

This modification is *critical*: it allows the predicted durations $\hat{d}_i$ to appear directly in the objective, connecting the prediction loss to the regret and enabling SPO+ to guide the predictor toward decisions that improve throughput while controlling overtime. Note that we write $\mathcal{S}(\hat{d})$ throughout, including in the Vanilla PtO formulation, to make explicit that predicted durations parameterize the feasible set through the OR and surgeon capacity constraints, not just the objective. Analogously, we write $\mathcal{S}(d)$ when the true durations are used, and $\mathcal{S}(p_{l_i k})$ for the BCS.

The intuition behind subtracting $\lambda \hat{d}_i$ is as follows. The baseline objective ranks patients purely by waiting time W_i, with no sensitivity to how long their surgery takes. By subtracting $\lambda \hat{d}_i$, the objective penalizes scheduling long predicted surgeries, discouraging the optimizer from over-packing the OR block with cases that risk overtime. Critically, for patients with large waiting times W_i, the coefficient $W_i - \lambda \hat{d}_i$ remains strongly positive even for lengthy procedures, preserving scheduling priority for long-wait patients and preventing bias against complex cases. The hyperparameter λ allows OR managers to tune this tradeoff explicitly:

- When $\lambda = 0$, the objective reduces to a waiting-time-only objective, prioritizing waiting time only with no duration penalty.
- When $\lambda > 0$, the optimizer increasingly favors shorter predicted surgeries, trading some throughput for overtime stability.

We tune λ via grid search and report its sensitivity in Sect. 3.

Regret Under the Modified Objective. We define a distinct regret measure for SPO+ that reflects the modified objective (10). Let $c_i = W_i - \lambda d_i$ denote the true cost vector and $\hat{c}_i = W_i - \lambda \hat{d}_i$ the predicted cost vector. Let $x^*(c)$ denote the schedule optimal under c using $\mathcal{S}(d)$, and $x^*(\hat{c})$ the schedule optimal under $\hat{c}$ using $\mathcal{S}(\hat{d})$. The SPO+ regret is:

$$R_{\mathrm{SPO+}} = f(x^*(c); c) - f(x^*(\hat{c}); c), \tag{11}$$

where both schedules are evaluated against the true cost vector c. This differs from the regret R_{GB} in Eq. (8), which is defined under the original weighted throughput objective with no duration penalty. $R_{\mathrm{SPO+}}$ measures the loss in the cost-penalized objective attributable to imperfect duration predictions.

SPO+ Loss and Gradient. Minimizing $R_{\mathrm{SPO+}}$ directly is intractable, as it requires solving the MIP for every possible prediction. SPO+ [14] addresses this with a convex surrogate loss that upper-bounds the true regret:

$$\mathcal{L}_{\mathrm{SPO+}}(\hat{c}, c) = \max_{x \in \mathcal{S}(\hat{d})} \{c^\top x - 2\hat{c}^\top x\} + 2\hat{c}^\top x^*(c) - z^*(c), \tag{12}$$

where $z^*(c) = c^\top x^*(c)$ is the optimal objective value under true costs. See Algorithm 1, where the feasible set is independent of the cost vector; we refer the reader to [15] for a discussion of this approximation in a similarly constrained scheduling setting.

The surrogate (12) admits the following subgradient with respect to $\hat{c}$:

$$\frac{\partial \mathcal{L}_{\text{SPO+}}}{\partial \hat{c}} = -2\left(x^*(2\hat{c} - c) - x^*(c)\right), \tag{13}$$

where $x^*(2\hat{c} - c)$ is the argmax of (12), solved over $\mathcal{S}(\hat{d})$ with the perturbed cost vector $2\hat{c} - c$. Since $\hat{c}_i = W_i - \lambda \hat{d}_i$, we have $\partial \hat{c}_i / \partial \hat{d}_i = -\lambda$, and by the chain rule:

$$\frac{\partial \mathcal{L}_{\text{SPO+}}}{\partial \hat{d}_i} = -2\lambda\left(x^*_{ijkt}(2\hat{c} - c) - x^*_{ijkt}(c)\right). \tag{14}$$

This gradient propagates the scheduling signal directly back to the duration predictor: if scheduling with $\hat{d}_i$ leads to a worse cost-penalized objective than scheduling with d_i, the gradient pushes $\hat{d}_i$ toward values that would have produced a better decision.

Note that $x^*(c)$ depends only on the true cost vector c and $\mathcal{S}(d)$, and is therefore invariant across training iterations.

It is important to also note that this gradient is computed entirely with respect to the first-stage predicted cost vector $\hat{c}$, and does not propagate through any second-stage recourse decisions. The second-stage recourse (Algorithm 2) is evaluated greedily at inference time and enters the SAA objective only as a scalar value $Q(x, \tilde{d}^s)$; it plays no role in the SPO+ training loop. SPO+ trains the duration predictor using gradients from the first-stage MIP only, and the 2SP recourse is applied after training is complete.

Computational Considerations. Each training iteration requires solving two MIP instances per training sample: one with true cost vector c (cached after the first iteration) and one with the perturbed vector $2\hat{c} - c$. This makes SPO+ considerably more expensive than Vanilla PtO or regret-aware GB, which solve the MIP only once per evaluation. We report wall-clock runtimes and MIP solves in Sect. 3. Given this overhead, SPO+ is best suited for offline schedule generation where the computation time is not a binding constraint. For real-time or online settings, regret-aware GB offers a lighter alternative.

2.5 Two-Stage Stochastic Programming (2SP)

Even a schedule built with decision-focused learning is a static plan: once execution begins, realized surgery durations $\tilde{d}_i$ will inevitably deviate from predictions $\hat{d}_i$, and the deterministic schedule has no mechanism to respond. To tackle this, we adopt a *two-stage stochastic programming (2SP)* framework. The first stage constructs a schedule based on predicted durations (*here-and-now* decisions); the second stage implements adaptive *recourse actions* as true durations are revealed intraoperatively (*wait-and-see* decisions).

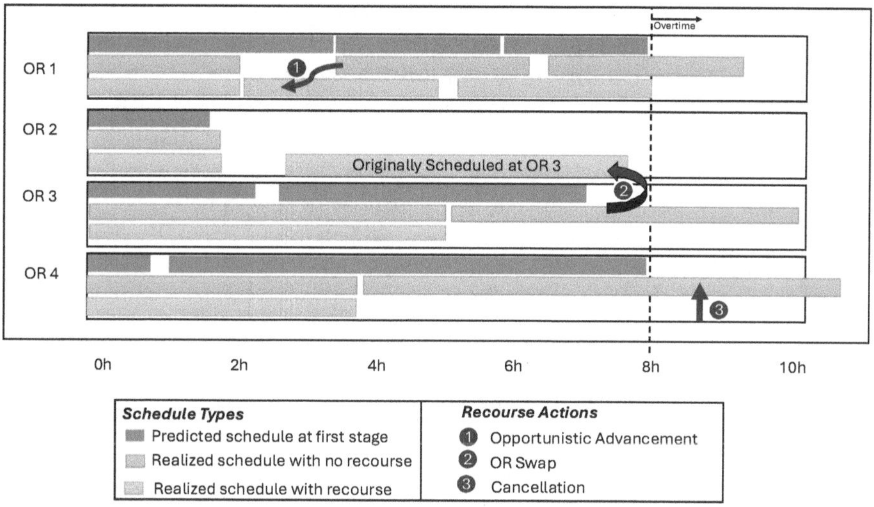

Fig. 2. Second-stage recourse actions triggered by duration overruns across four ORs. (1) Early finish in OR 1 allows immediate advancement of the next case. (2) OR 3 overrun prompts a swap to idle OR 2. (3) OR 4 final case exceeds $T + \tau_{OT}$ and is cancelled.

First Stage. The first-stage schedule $x \in \mathcal{S}(\hat{d})$ is chosen to maximize the Sample Average Approximation (SAA) objective (19), which jointly accounts for the deterministic scheduling reward $c^\top x$ and the expected recourse value $\frac{1}{S}\sum_s Q(x, \tilde{d}^s)$ across scenarios.

In practice, since the recourse function $Q(x, \tilde{d}^s)$ is evaluated greedily via Algorithm 2 rather than re-optimized as a full MIP, the first-stage solve incorporates scenario-averaged recourse feedback as a regularization signal. This follows the *extensive form* decomposition common in SAA-based 2SP [18], where scenario outcomes inform first-stage decisions through the joint objective rather than through separate re-optimization.

Scenario Generation. To approximate the expectation over realized durations, we generate $S = 20$ scenarios by sampling from fitted duration distributions. This choice of S scenarios was validated by observing that OT_{95} estimates stabilize beyond $S = 15$ on a held-out subset of queues.

For each (surgeon, procedure) pair with sufficient observations ($n \geq 20$), we fit Uniform, Gamma, and Lognormal distributions to historical durations and select the best fit by Akaike Information Criterion (AIC). For pairs with fewer than 20 observations, we default to Lognormal. Each scenario s draws a realization $\tilde{d}^s = (\tilde{d}^s_1, \ldots, \tilde{d}^s_I)$ independently per patient.

When realized durations deviate from predictions, three recourse actions are available as illustrated in Fig. 2. We describe each with the practical constraints that govern their applicability in a real hospital setting.

Opportunistic Advancement. If a surgery finishes earlier than predicted and the OR becomes available, the next scheduled case may start immediately rather than waiting for its planned start time. However, advancement is only applied if the gap is at most 2 h: a patient cannot reasonably be expected to be prepared and present if the OR frees up hours ahead of schedule. Formally, patient i can be advanced in OR j if:

$$t_{\text{plan}} - t_{\text{avail}}[j] \leq \tau_{\text{adv}}, \tag{15}$$

where t_{plan} is the originally scheduled start time, $t_{\text{avail}}[j]$ is the time at which OR j becomes free, and $\tau_{\text{adv}} = 2$ hours is the maximum advancement window.

OR Swap. If a surgery overruns and would delay subsequent cases in the same OR, a later-scheduled patient may be moved to a different OR where both the destination OR and the original surgeon are free. The surgeon must follow the patient, reflecting the hospital reality that surgeon-patient pairs are typically predetermined [9].

We treat inter-OR transfer as cost-free as a modeling assumption; in practice, swaps incur logistical overhead such as patient transport and room preparation that our current formulation does not capture. This may modestly inflate the 2SP recourse performance reported in Table 3, as the model can swap freely without penalty. A swap penalty $\gamma > 0$ could be incorporated into $Q(x, \tilde{d}^s)$ as $-\gamma \cdot |\text{swaps}^s|$ to correct for this in settings where transfer costs are non-negligible.

A swap is only permitted if the surgery can be completed within the remaining horizon T:

$$t_{\text{avail}}[j'] + \tilde{d}_i^s \leq T + \tau_{\text{OT}}, \tag{16}$$

where j' is the destination OR and τ_{OT} is the overtime tolerance defined below. If no qualifying OR exists, the case waits in its original OR.

Cancellation. If executing a surgery would cause it to finish more than $\tau_{\text{OT}} = 2$ hours beyond the regular horizon T, the case is canceled and deferred. This reflects the institutional reality that staff contracts and downstream resource availability (recovery rooms, ICU beds) impose hard limits on how far the OR day can extend. Formally, patient i is canceled in scenario s if:

$$t_{\text{actual}} + \tilde{d}_i^s > T + \tau_{\text{OT}}, \tag{17}$$

where t_{actual} is the realized start time after accounting for upstream delays.

Second-Stage Objective. Let $y_{i,j,k,t}^s \in \{0, 1\}$ denote the second-stage decision for whether patient i is completed in OR j with surgeon k at adjusted start time t under scenario s. Let I_{done}^s and I_{cancel}^s denote the sets of completed and canceled patients respectively. The second-stage value function is:

$$Q(x, \tilde{d}^s) = \sum_{i \in I_{\text{done}}^s} W_i - \alpha |I_{\text{cancel}}^s| - \beta \cdot \text{OT}^s, \tag{18}$$

where $\mathrm{OT}^s = \max(0, \max_j t_{\text{finish}}[j] - T)$ is the realized overtime in scenario s, $\alpha > 0$ penalizes cancellations, and $\beta > 0$ penalizes overtime. Setting $\alpha \gg \beta$ recovers a maximum-throughput policy; setting $\beta \gg \alpha$ recovers a strict no-overtime policy. This unified objective accommodates both operational priorities through hyperparameter adjustment.

Full Two-Stage Formulation. Combining first and second stages via Sample Average Approximation [18], the full 2SP objective is:

$$\max_{x \in \mathcal{S}(\hat{d})} \quad c^\top x + \frac{1}{S} \sum_{s=1}^{S} Q(x, \tilde{d}^s), \tag{19}$$

where the first term captures the first-stage scheduling reward and the second term approximates the expected recourse value across scenarios. The linking constraint ensures recourse decisions are grounded in the first-stage plan:

$$\sum_{j,k,t} y^s_{i,j,k,t} \leq \sum_{j,k,t} x_{i,j,k,t}, \quad \forall i \in I, \ \forall s, \tag{20}$$

meaning a patient can only be completed in the second stage if they were scheduled in the first stage. We do not consider adding unscheduled patients in the second stage, as elective surgical patients are not assumed to be present at the hospital and available on short notice.

Recourse Execution. At execution time, the second-stage recourse procedure processes patients in order of their planned start times. For each patient, it computes the actual start time as:

$$t_{\text{actual}} = \max\left(t_{\text{plan}}, t_{\text{avail}}[j], t_{\text{avail}}[k]\right), \tag{21}$$

meaning that a surgery cannot begin until both the OR and the surgeon are free. Advancement is applied if condition (15) holds; a swap to OR j' is attempted if condition (16) holds and the surgeon is free; cancellation is triggered if condition (17) holds. Algorithm 2 summarizes this procedure.

3 Experiments

3.1 Experimental Setup

Dataset. We evaluate on a real surgical dataset from the *Instituto de Neurocirugía Dr. Raúl Asenjo*, in Santiago, Chile, comprising 5,663 historical surgical records spanning two years, involving 114 surgeons across multiple procedure types. Each record includes surgeon identity, procedure type, post-operative destination, and realized surgery duration.

Algorithm 2. Second-Stage Recourse Execution

Input: First-stage schedule x, realized durations $\tilde{d}^s$, τ_{adv}, τ_{OT}, horizon T, weights α, β
Output: I^s_{done}, I^s_{cancel}, realized objective $Q(x, \tilde{d}^s)$

$I^s_{\text{done}} \leftarrow \emptyset$, $I^s_{\text{cancel}} \leftarrow \emptyset$
$t_{\text{avail}}[j] \leftarrow 0$ for all $j \in J$; $t_{\text{avail}}[k] \leftarrow a_k$ for all $k \in K$
Sort scheduled patients by t_{plan} ascending
for each patient i in sorted order **do**
  $j \leftarrow$ assigned OR; $k \leftarrow$ assigned surgeon
  $t_{\text{actual}} \leftarrow \max(t_{\text{plan}}, t_{\text{avail}}[j], t_{\text{avail}}[k])$
  if $t_{\text{avail}}[j] < t_{\text{plan}}$ and $t_{\text{plan}} - t_{\text{avail}}[j] \le \tau_{\text{adv}}$ **then**
    $t_{\text{actual}} \leftarrow \max(t_{\text{avail}}[j], t_{\text{avail}}[k])$ ▷ Opportunistic advancement
  end if
  if $t_{\text{avail}}[j] > t_{\text{plan}}$ **then** ▷ OR delayed: attempt swap before cancelling
    Find $j' \leftarrow \arg\min_{j'' \neq j} t_{\text{avail}}[j'']$ s.t. $t_{\text{avail}}[j''] + \tilde{d}^s_i \le T + \tau_{\text{OT}}$ and $t_{\text{avail}}[k] \le t_{\text{avail}}[j'']$
    if j' exists **then**
      $j \leftarrow j'$; $t_{\text{actual}} \leftarrow \max(t_{\text{avail}}[j'], t_{\text{avail}}[k])$ ▷ Swap to free OR
    else
      $t_{\text{actual}} \leftarrow \max(t_{\text{avail}}[j], t_{\text{avail}}[k])$ ▷ No swap available: wait in original OR
    end if
  end if
  if $t_{\text{actual}} + \tilde{d}^s_i > T + \tau_{\text{OT}}$ **then**
    $I^s_{\text{cancel}} \leftarrow I^s_{\text{cancel}} \cup \{i\}$
    continue ▷ Cancel only after swap attempt fails
  end if
  $t_{\text{finish}} \leftarrow t_{\text{actual}} + \tilde{d}^s_i$ ▷ Uses post-swap t_{actual}
  $t_{\text{avail}}[j] \leftarrow t_{\text{finish}}$; $t_{\text{avail}}[k] \leftarrow t_{\text{finish}}$
  $I^s_{\text{done}} \leftarrow I^s_{\text{done}} \cup \{i\}$
end for
$\text{OT}^s \leftarrow \max(0, \max_j t_{\text{avail}}[j] - T)$
return I^s_{done}, I^s_{cancel}, $Q = \sum_{i \in I^s_{\text{done}}} W_i - \alpha |I^s_{\text{cancel}}| - \beta \cdot \text{OT}^s$

Instance Generation. Following the operational reality of the *Instituto de Neurocirugía*, we simulate 100 test queues of 20 patients each ($I = 20$), sampled with replacement to reflect the variability in daily patient mixes, surgeons, and procedure types. We generate 10,000 instances of every test queue. Each queue is scheduled under four operating rooms ($J = 4$), ten surgeons ($K = 10$), and an 8-hour horizon discretized into 15-minute time steps ($T = 32$). The 20-patient queue size is operationally motivated: with an average surgery duration of approximately 123 min, scheduling 20 patients requires roughly 40 h of OR time, whereas the hospital disposes of only 32 h across four ORs per day, making the problem non-trivial and representative of real-world constraints.

Simulation and Evaluation. For each queue and method, we generate an optimal schedule and simulate 10,000 realizations of surgery durations by sampling from fitted surgeon-procedure distributions. For each (surgeon, procedure) pair with $n \geq 20$ observations, we fit Uniform, Gamma, and Lognormal distributions and select the best by AIC; pairs with fewer observations default to Lognormal. This yields $100 \times 10{,}000 = 1{,}000{,}000$ simulated OR days per method. All reported confidence intervals are computed at the queue level using paired comparisons across methods on the same 100 queues.

We report four metrics: OR utilization (UT, %), mean overtime hours (OT), 95th-percentile overtime (OT_{95}), and patients scheduled (PAT). Regular hours are capped at 8 h; any excess is counted as overtime. UT and OT are averaged per-OR per-day; (OT_{95}) is the 95th percentile of overtime computed across all 10,000 simulations per queue, then averaged across 100 queues.

Hardware and Solver. All experiments were run on Google Colaboratory with a T4 GPU. Optimization was performed using Gurobi Optimizer 13.0.1 with a MIP gap tolerance of 0.1% and a time limit of 600 s per instance.

Baselines. We benchmark four prediction pipelines: (i) **BCS** deterministic scheduling with surgeon-procedure mean durations; (ii) **Vanilla PtO** gradient boosting predictions fed into the deterministic MIP; (iii) **Regret-Aware GB** iterative reweighting with scheduling feedback; and (iv) **SPO+** end-to-end decision-focused training. Each pipeline is evaluated both without and with 2SP recourse, yielding eight configurations in total. Neural network-based predictors were not included as they require richer clinical feature sets such as ASA classification and BMI that were not available in our dataset; with 7 aggregated statistical features, gradient boosting represents the appropriate model class and standard practice in this literature [9,11].

3.2 Results Without Recourse

Table 2 reports scheduling performance across all four methods without second-stage recourse. Decision-focused methods consistently outperform the baselines on the primary objective of patient throughput.

Table 2. OR scheduling performance without recourse (mean ± std over 100 queues × 10,000 simulations).

Method	PAT	UT (%)	OT (h)	OT_{95} (h)
BCS	16.8 ± 1.7	83.5 ± 8.4	0.56 ± 0.76	1.94
Vanilla PtO	16.8 ± 1.6	88.4 ± 7.6	**0.46** ± 0.26	1.21
Regret-Aware GB	17.2 ± 0.9	92.7 ± 6.0	0.53 ± 0.78	1.87
SPO+	**17.7** ± 1.2	**93.2** ± 5.8	0.68 ± 0.95	2.21

SPO+ achieves the highest utilization (93.2%) and throughput (17.7 patients per day), representing a 5.5% point improvement in utilization and approximately 0.9 additional patients per day over Vanilla PtO. Each additional patient comes at a cost of approximately 14.7 min of mean overtime, a tradeoff that OR managers at *Instituto de Neurocirugía* considered operationally acceptable. Regret-Aware GB performs comparably to SPO+ on utilization (92.7%) with slightly lower overtime variance (std 0.78 vs 0.95), offering a lighter alternative when computational budget is limited.

3.3 Results With Two-Stage Stochastic Programming

Table 3 evaluates all configurations with and without 2SP recourse, isolating the contribution of each component; we use SPO+ as the representative predictor since it achieves the best performance in Table 2. The Prediction column indicates whether a learned duration predictor is used (as opposed to BCS mean durations); the Recourse column indicates whether second-stage recourse is active.

Table 3. Ablation of prediction and recourse components. Mean ± std over 100 queues.

Method	Prediction	Recourse	PAT	UT (%)	OT (h)	OT_{95} (h)
BCS	✗	✗	16.8 ± 1.7	83.5	0.56	1.94
BCS + 2SP	✗	✓	17.3 ± 1.4	86.2	0.48	1.52
SPO+	✓	✗	17.7 ± 1.2	93.2	0.68	2.21
SPO+ + 2SP	✓	✓	**18.7** ± 0.9	**94.4**	0.52	**1.41**

Table 4. Computational cost per scheduling instance (single queue, $I = 20$ patients) and total training time. $S = 20$ second-stage scenarios.

Method	Inference (s)	MIP Solves	Training
BCS	1.02	1	—
Vanilla PtO	1.02	1	34 s
Regret-Aware GB	1.36	$2 \times$ iter	8 m 8 s
SPO+	8.20	$2 \times$ inst	23 m 34 s
Regret-Aware GB + 2SP	3.60	$2 \times$ iter $+ S$	8 m 8 s
SPO+ + 2SP	12.80	$2 \times$ inst $+ S$	23 m 34 s

The results reveal a clear complementarity between prediction quality and recourse. SPO+ alone (prediction only, no recourse) achieves the highest utilization (93.2%) but also the highest overtime tail risk (OT_{95} = 2.21 h). Adding 2SP recourse to SPO+ reduces OT_{95} dramatically from 2.21 h to 1.41 h, a good reduction in tail overtime, while simultaneously increasing throughput to 18.7 patients per day. This confirms that DFL and 2SP are complementary rather than substitutes: DFL produces aggressive, high-utilization schedules, while 2SP absorbs the resulting overtime risk through adaptive recourse.

BCS with recourse (no prediction) improves modestly over BCS alone (17.3 vs 16.8 PAT), showing that recourse alone can partially compensate for poor duration estimates. However, combining learned predictions with recourse yields substantially larger gains, demonstrating that the two components reinforce each other.

Table 4 reports inference and training times; SPO+ coupled with 2SP incurs the highest cost at 12.8 s per instance and 23 m 34 s training, remaining practical for offline schedule generation. We therefore recommend SPO+ + 2SP for overnight batch scheduling and Regret-Aware GB for near real-time intraoperative updates, where its 1.36 s inference cost is more appropriate.

Regarding scalability, SPO+ training time scales linearly in the number of training queues and is dominated by the two MIP solves required per instance per iteration, whose cost grows super-linearly with queue size. For smaller queues the inference cost decreases substantially, while larger queues can make same-day re-optimization impractical. The 20-patient setting evaluated here reflects the actual daily census at the *Instituto de Neurocirugía* and represents the operationally relevant scale for nightly batch scheduling.

3.4 The Role of λ: An Operational Perspective

The hyperparameter λ in the SPO+ objective $(W_i - \lambda \hat{d}_i)$ is not merely a tuning knob, it is a direct translation of hospital overtime policy into scheduling behavior. Figure 3 illustrates the utilization-overtime frontier across $\lambda \in \{0.1, 0.2, 0.3, 0.5, 0.7, 1.0\}$.

At $\lambda = 0$, the SPO+ objective collapses to the BCS baseline, scheduling patients purely by waiting time with no consideration of surgery duration. As λ increases, the optimizer increasingly penalizes long predicted surgeries, producing more conservative schedules with lower utilization but reduced overtime exposure.

Concretely, $\lambda = 0.1$ yields 97.6% utilization at the cost of 1.8 h mean overtime, appropriate for hospitals with flexible staffing and high throughput pressure. At the other extreme, $\lambda = 1.0$ enforces conservative schedules with 80% utilization and 0.4 h overtime, suitable for institutions with strict staff contracts or limited post-operative capacity. The default $\lambda = 0.5$ used in Tables 2 and 3 represents a balanced operating point.

This is a practical strength of the SPO+ framework: OR managers can calibrate λ against their specific overtime budget by treating it as a governance-level policy parameter rather than a technical hyperparameter. To our knowledge, this kind of direct operationalization of overtime tolerance into the scheduling objective has not been previously demonstrated in the OR scheduling literature.

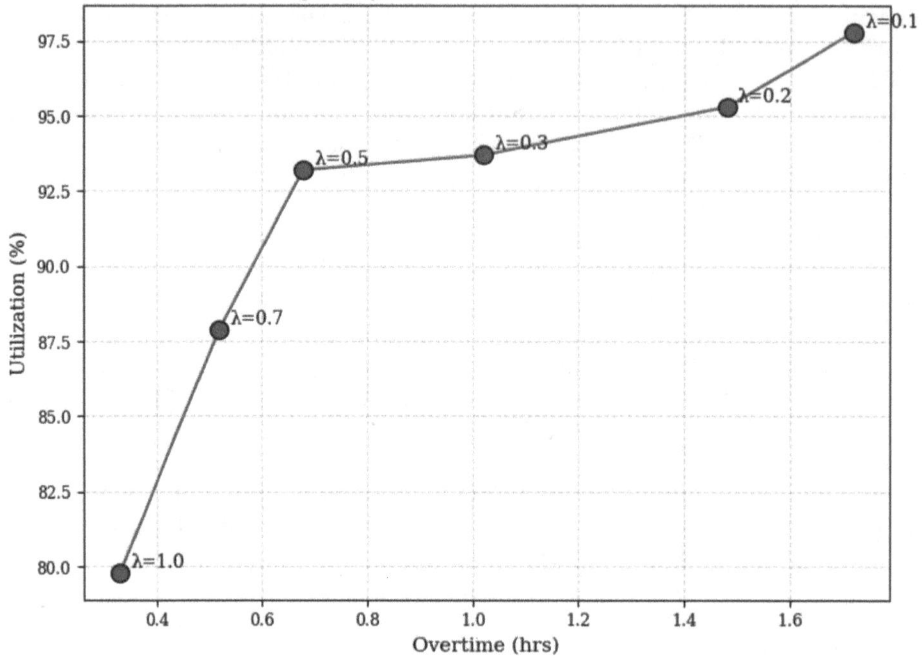

Fig. 3. Sensitivity analysis: OR utilization vs. mean overtime for different values of λ. Each point represents a different λ setting averaged over 100 queues.

4 Conclusion

We presented a framework combining decision-focused learning with two-stage stochastic programming for OR scheduling under uncertain surgery durations. By embedding predicted durations directly into the SPO+ objective and augmenting the resulting schedules with adaptive recourse, we achieve improvements in patient throughput and utilization over deterministic and standard PtO baselines, while substantially reducing tail overtime risk. The λ parameter provides OR managers with a practical, interpretable lever to operationalize overtime policy directly into scheduling decisions.

Clinical deployment would require integration with the hospital's scheduling system, access to continuously updated surgical records for retraining the duration predictor, and a prospective validation study under institutional review board approval to confirm performance on live patient queues.

Future work includes validating the framework across multiple surgical specialties and hospital settings, incorporating richer patient-level clinical features into the duration predictor, and developing faster MIP approximations to reduce SPO+ training time. We also note that the λ penalty could in principle disadvantage high-complexity cases; however, the coefficient $W_i - \lambda \hat{d}_i$ remains strongly positive for long-wait patients regardless of duration, preserving their scheduling priority. Future extensions could further enforce this through case-specific floors on $\hat{c}_i$ or minimum guaranteed slots for high-complexity procedures. The current 2SP recourse adapts greedily as each case concludes; multi-stage extensions could enable periodic re-optimization with lookahead over remaining cases, potentially recovering more schedule value than the myopic recourse policy [19].

Acknowledgments. The clinical dataset was provided by *Instituto de Neurocirugía Dr. Raúl Asenjo*. Generative AI tools were used only for language editing and readability improvements. All research, mathematical formulations, experimental design, implementation, and results are the authors' own work.

References

1. Rothstein, D.H., Raval, M.V.: Operating room efficiency. In: Seminars in Pediatric Surgery, vol. 27, no. 2, pp. 79–85. Elsevier (2018)
2. Al Amin, M., Baldacci, R., Kayvanfar, V.: A comprehensive review on operating room scheduling and optimization. Oper. Res. Int. J. **25**(1), 3 (2025)
3. Bellini, V., Domenichetti, T., Bignami, E.G.: Innovative technologies for smarter and efficient operating room scheduling. J. Med. Syst. **49**(1), 37 (2025)
4. Aktaş, E., Atmaca, H.E., Erdoğan Akbulut, H.: Operating room and surgical team members scheduling: a comprehensive review. J. Project Manage. (2024)
5. Gür, Ş, Pınarbaşı, M., Alakaş, H.M., Eren, T.: Operating room scheduling with surgical team: a new approach with constraint programming and goal programming. CEJOR **31**(4), 1061–1085 (2023)
6. Zhu, S., Fan, W., Yang, S., Pei, J., Pardalos, P.M.: Operating room planning and surgical case scheduling: a review of literature. J. Comb. Optim. **37**(3), 757–805 (2019)
7. Azriel, D., Rinott, Y., Tal, O., Abbou, B., Rappoport, N.: Surgery duration prediction using multi-task feature selection. IEEE J. Biomed. Health Inform. **28**(7), 4216–4223 (2024)
8. Xiang, W., Yin, J., Lim, G.: A short-term operating room surgery scheduling problem integrating multiple nurses roster constraints. Artif. Intell. Med. **63**(2), 91–106 (2015)
9. Azar, M., Carrasco, R.A., Mondschein, S.: Dealing with uncertain surgery times in operating room scheduling. Eur. J. Oper. Res. **299**(1), 377–394 (2022)
10. Vancroonenburg, W., De Causmaecker, P., Vanden Berghe, G.: Chance-constrained admission scheduling of elective surgical patients in a dynamic, uncertain setting. Operat. Res. Health Care **22**, 100196 (2019)
11. Lex, J.R., et al.: Machine learning to predict-then-optimize elective orthopaedic surgery scheduling improves operating room utilization. medRxiv, 2024–08 (2024)
12. Gong, X., Wang, J.J.: An environmentally friendly elective patient scheduling under the predict-then-optimize framework. Ann. Oper. Res., 1–41 (2025)
13. Lawless, C., Zhou, A.: A note on task-aware loss via reweighing prediction loss by decision-regret (2022). arXiv preprint arXiv:2211.05116 arXiv:2211.05116
14. Elmachtoub, A.N., Grigas, P.: Smart "predict, then optimize". Manage. Sci. **68**(1), 9–26 (2022)
15. Lui, G.N., Demirel, S.: Gradient-based smart predict-then-optimize framework for aircraft arrival scheduling problem. J. Open Aviation Sci. **2**(2) (2024)

16. Wang, X., Peng, Y., Ma, W.: SPO-VCS: An end-to-end smart predict-then-optimize framework with alternating differentiation method for relocation problems in large-scale vehicle crowd sensing. Transp. Res. Part E Logistics Transp. Rev. **205**, 104515 (2026)
17. Mazzei, W.J.: Operating room start times and turnover times in a university hospital. J. Clin. Anesth. **6**(5), 405–408 (1994)
18. Kim, S., Pasupathy, R., Henderson, S.G.: A guide to sample average approximation. In: Fu, M.C. (ed.) Handbook of Simulation Optimization, pp. 207–243. Springer, New York (2015)
19. Hu, X., Lee, J.C., Lee, J.H., Stuckey, P.J.: Multi-stage predict+ optimize for (mixed integer) linear programs. Adv. Neural. Inf. Process. Syst. **37**, 64794–64827 (2024)

Estimating Representative Causal Effects with Double Machine Learning

Apoorva Lal[1] and Winston Chou[2(✉)]

[1] OpenAI, San Francisco, CA, USA
[2] Netflix, New York, NY, USA
wchou@netflix.com

Abstract. Double Machine Learning is widely used to estimate treatment effects from non-experimental data. The "residuals-on-residuals" regression (RORR) is especially popular for its simplicity and computational tractability. However, with heterogeneous treatment effects, the proper interpretation of RORR may not be well understood. We show that, for non-binary treatments with continuous dose-response functions, RORR estimates a conditional variance-weighted average of derivatives evaluated at treatment values not in the observed dataset. This estimand does not equal the Average Causal Derivative (ACD) in general. Hence, even if all units share the same dose-response function, RORR may not estimate an average treatment effect in the population represented by the sample. We propose an alternative estimator for the ACD that is well suited to the large datasets found in applied data science settings. We demonstrate the pitfalls of RORR and the favorable properties of the proposed estimator through an illustrative numerical example and with real-world data from Netflix. Our methodology is used by default in Netflix's observational causal inference platform, where it regularly powers causal research and decision-making at scale.

Keywords: double machine learning · observational causal inference · partially linear model · doubly robust learning

1 Introduction

Double Machine Learning (DML) [6,8,20] has become the standard method for estimating causal effects in large, high-dimensional datasets under the assumption of *unconfoundedness*, which postulates that the treatment is as good as randomly assigned given observed covariates [13]. To strengthen the plausibility of unconfoundedness, researchers in many fields use the DML method to condition on numerous covariates when estimating causal effects [9,11,14].

DML encompasses a broad class of estimators. In this paper, we focus on the Partially Linear Model (PLM), which relates an outcome Y_i to a continuous or discrete-valued treatment T_i conditional on pretreatment covariates X_i by

$$Y_i = \theta T_i + g(X_i) + e_i \quad \text{and} \quad T_i = h(X_i) + u_i. \tag{1}$$

M. Ceci et al. (Eds.): ECML PKDD 2026, LNAI 16948, pp. 271–288, 2027.
https://doi.org/10.1007/978-3-032-37679-4_16

The PLM imposes minimal assumptions on how the treatment and outcome relate to covariates. It also motivates an intuitive two-step DML estimator of θ, the residuals-on-residuals regression (RORR). RORR, an extension of the Frisch-Waugh-Lovell theorem, first "partials out" the effect of X_i using flexible machine learning methods; then forms the residuals

$$\widetilde{Y}_i = Y_i - \widehat{m}(X_i) \quad \text{and} \quad \widetilde{T}_i = T_i - \widehat{h}(X_i), \tag{2}$$

where $\widehat{m}$ and $\widehat{h}$ are estimators for $m(X_i) := E[Y_i|X_i]$ and $h(X_i) := E[T_i|X_i]$, respectively; and lastly regresses $\widetilde{Y}_i$ on $\widetilde{T}_i$ to obtain the RORR estimate of θ, which we denote by $\hat{\theta}$ [21].

When the treatment effect θ is the same for all units in the population, it is also the Average Treatment Effect (ATE) for binary treatments, the Average Causal Derivative (ACD) for continuous treatments, and the Average Incremental Effect (AIE) for integer-valued treatments. Alternatively, we study the probability limit (plim) and interpretation of $\hat{\theta}$ when treatment effects are *heterogeneous*. Under such heterogeneity, $\hat{\theta}$ converges to a conditional variance-weighted average of causal effects, which assigns greater weight to units whose treatment values are less predictable. For example, when T_i is binary, the RORR estimand assigns the greatest weight to units whose conditional probability of treatment is closest to 0.5. This biases it away from the ATE in general [1,3,23]. When treatments are non-binary (for example, continuous), RORR is subject to the more nuanced biases explored in this paper.

We contribute a general analysis of RORR and its biases with both binary and non-binary treatments. We demonstrate the empirical relevance of these biases with both a stylized numerical example and real-world data from Netflix. We propose a simple alternative estimator based on Augmented Inverse Propensity Weighting (AIPW), which coarsens the treatment into bins [7,16]. We establish the favorable theoretical properties of the estimator and apply it to empirical data. Our coarsened AIPW estimator has been used for observational causal inference and decision-making at Netflix for several years, and is the default methodology deployed on Netflix's observational causal inference platform.

2 Residuals-on-Residuals Regression with Heterogeneous Treatment Effects

The residuals-on-residuals regression (RORR) is a popular observational causal inference tool for many reasons. Most importantly, it enables the use of highly flexible modern machine learning estimators for the nuisances in the PLM, thus freeing researchers from making strong assumptions about those parameters. If the PLM is correctly specified, it is statistically efficient and can achieve parametric convergence rates even when the nuisances are estimated nonparametrically. Attesting to its popularity, recent applications of RORR can be found in economics [5], ecology [10], political science [14], and public health [25].

In applied data science settings—characterized by large datasets, short timelines, and stakeholders with diverse technical backgrounds—RORR is also commonly used for practical reasons. For example, the final regression step is computationally efficient, as only a few statistics are needed to compute $\hat{\theta}$. Furthermore, the two-step recipe of (1) removing variation explained by pretreatment covariates and (2) estimating the effect of the remaining exogenous variation in T_i on Y_i is intuitive and easy to explain to non-experts. In its simplest form, RORR is none other than ordinary least squares [19].

However, this simplicity comes at a price. The interpretability of $\hat{\theta}$ as an estimate of the "average" treatment effect (whether the ATE, ACD, or AIE) depends on the assumption of a homogeneous treatment effect in the PLM, which may not hold in applications. Below, we discuss the interpretation of $\hat{\theta}$ under two violations of this assumption: binary treatments with heterogeneous causal effects across individual units (e.g., a price discount whose impact is greater for more price-sensitive customers), and non-binary treatments with nonlinear dose-response functions (e.g., the effect may depend on the amount that is discounted).

2.1 Binary Treatments with Heterogeneous Treatment Effects

We begin with the RORR estimand for binary treatments with heterogeneous treatment effects. Letting $T_i \in \{0, 1\}$ denote the binary treatment, we consider the model

$$Y_i = \theta_i T_i + g(X_i) + e_i \quad \text{and} \quad T_i = h(X_i) + u_i,$$

where θ_i is an individual treatment effect. We assume unconfoundedness of the treatment given X_i, which in turn implies that the errors are conditionally exogenous and uncorrelated: $E[e_i|X_i] = 0$, $E[u_i|X_i] = 0$, and $E[e_i u_i|X_i] = 0$. Thus, $g(X_i) = E[Y_i - \theta_i T_i|X_i]$ and $h(X_i) = E[T_i|X_i]$. Unconfoundedness further implies that θ_i is conditionally independent of T_i given X_i. Lastly, we assume that the treatment is not deterministically assigned: $E[(T_i - h(X_i))^2] > 0$.

We analyze the plim of the OLS regression of $Y_i - m(X_i)$ on $T_i - h(X_i)$ with i.i.d. observations (Y_i, T_i, X_i), $i = 1, \ldots N$. Although m and h must be estimated in practice, we focus on the (true) limiting m and h to emphasize that the RORR plim is biased for the ATE even when the researcher has access to sufficient covariates and consistently estimates these nuisances.[1]

First, observe that

$$\hat{\theta} \xrightarrow{p} \frac{E[(T_i - h(X_i))(Y_i - m(X_i))]}{E[(T_i - h(X_i))^2]} = \frac{E[\theta_i(T_i^2 - T_i h(X_i))]}{E[(T_i - h(X_i))^2]}. \tag{3}$$

[1] In practice, researchers often use extremely flexible function classes for m and h (e.g., deep neural networks) that are able to approximate the true nuisance functions arbitrarily closely.

Using the fact that T_i is binary and applying the law of iterated expectations, we rewrite this as

$$\frac{E[\theta_i(T_i^2 - T_i h(X_i))]}{E[(T_i - h(X_i))^2]} = \frac{E[E[\theta_i|X_i]E[T_i^2 - T_i h(X_i)|X_i]]}{E[(T_i - h(X_i))^2]} \tag{4}$$
$$= \frac{E[\theta_i(T_i - h(X_i))^2]}{E[(T_i - h(X_i))^2]},$$

where Eq. (4) follows from θ_i being conditionally independent of T_i. This establishes the well-known result that, with a binary treatment, linear regression converges to a conditional variance-weighted average of individual treatment effects [1,3,23].

For an intuitive restatement of this result, denote the conditional variance weights by $\omega_i := \frac{(T_i - h(X_i))^2}{E[(T_i - h(X_i))^2]}$ and note that $E[\omega_i] = 1$ by construction. Then the bias of the RORR plim (which we will denote by $\tilde{\theta}$) with respect to the ATE can be written as

$$\tilde{\theta} - E[\theta_i] = E[\omega_i \theta_i] - E[\omega_i]E[\theta_i] = \text{Cov}(\omega_i, \theta_i). \tag{5}$$

In other words, the RORR bias for binary treatments when treatment effects are heterogeneous is proportional to the covariance of the individual treatment effects with the residual treatment variance. This covariance need not equal zero, and therefore $\tilde{\theta} \neq E[\theta_i]$ in general.[2]

2.2 Non-binary Treatments

We now turn our attention to non-binary, many-valued (e.g., continuous or integer-valued) treatments with nonlinear dose-response functions. Although past research has examined the effect of treatment effect heterogeneity on the interpretation of linear treatment effect estimators, it has mainly done so in the context of binary treatments and/or linear treatment effects [3]. However, in many applications, treatments are many-valued and/or have nonlinear effects on the outcome—for example, they may have diminishing returns. Such nonlinearity is an empirically common form of treatment effect heterogeneity [2,26]. Here, we present a bias decomposition for RORR with non-binary treatments that, to our knowledge, is novel in the literature and illuminates its similarities with and differences from the binary case.

Specifically, we study the model

$$Y_i = f(T_i) + g(X_i) + e_i \quad \text{and} \quad T_i = h(X_i) + u_i, \tag{6}$$

where f is a twice-continuously differentiable function of some non-binary treatment T_i. As before, we assume conditional ignorability, consistent estimators for m and h, non-deterministic treatment, and i.i.d. observations.

[2] A corollary is that ranking treatments based on their PLM coefficient is not the same as ranking them based on their ATEs [17].

Under these assumptions, the RORR estimate converges to

$$\hat{\theta} \xrightarrow{p} \frac{E[(T_i - h(X_i))f(T_i)]}{E[(T_i - h(X_i))^2]}. \tag{7}$$

Since $h(X_i)$ is a constant given X_i and applying the law of iterated expectations, we can rewrite this as

$$\frac{E[E[(T_i - h(X_i))(f(T_i) - f(h(X_i)))|X_i]]}{E[(T_i - h(X_i))^2]}. \tag{8}$$

By the mean value theorem, there exists a T_i^* between T_i and $h(X_i)$ for all X_i such that

$$\begin{aligned} \frac{E[E[(T_i - h(X_i))(f(T_i) - f(h(X_i)))|X_i]]}{E[(T_i - h(X_i))^2]} &= \frac{E[(T_i - h(X_i))^2 f'(T_i^*)]}{E[(T_i - h(X_i))^2]} \\ &= E[\omega_i f'(T_i^*)]. \end{aligned} \tag{9}$$

(9) shows that, as in the binary treatment setting, $\hat{\theta}$ also converges to a conditional variance-weighted average of causal effects.[3] However, unlike in the binary treatment case, the quantity being averaged cannot be interpreted as the causal effect of increasing the treatment in the population represented by the sample. This is because the mean value T_i^* is not the actual treatment dose received by i, but a convex combination of the realized treatment T_i and its conditional mean. As such, T_i^* may not be an observed treatment level. If T_i is not continuous, it may not even be a realizable treatment value.

Proposition 1 establishes the restrictive conditions under which $\tilde{\theta}$ converges to the ACD.

Proposition 1. *Let (Y_i, T_i, X_i) be i.i.d. draws from a distribution obeying the structural model (6). Assume conditional ignorability, f twice-continuously differentiable on its domain, f' Lipschitz with minimal constant L, non-deterministic treatment, $E[|T_i - h(X_i)|^3]$ finite, and consistent estimators of m and h. Then the RORR plim*

$$\tilde{\theta} = \frac{E[(T_i - h(X_i))f(T_i)]}{E[(T_i - h(X_i))^2]}$$

equals the Average Causal Derivative $E[f'(T_i)]$ if f is affine ($L = 0$). More generally, its bias decomposes into a curvature term and a conditional-variance weighting term, which need not vanish unless f is affine.

Proof. With i.i.d. observations, conditional ignorability, and m and h consistently estimated, $\tilde{\theta}$ is as given in (9). We decompose the bias of $\tilde{\theta}$ relative to the

[3] Not coincidentally, the Wald estimand with a binary instrument and a continuous endogenous treatment can also be represented as a weighted average of derivatives at the mean values T_i^* [2].

ACD into

$$E[\omega_i f'(T_i^*)] - E[f'(T_i)] \tag{10}$$
$$= \underbrace{E[\omega_i f'(T_i^*)] - E[\omega_i f'(T_i)]}_{:=A} + \underbrace{E[\omega_i f'(T_i)] - E[f'(T_i)]}_{:=B}.$$

A is the difference between the RORR plim and the weighted average causal derivative evaluated over the treatment distribution actually observed in the sample. Rewrite A as

$$\frac{E[(T_i - h(X_i))^2(f'(T_i^*) - f'(T_i))]}{E[(T_i - h(X_i))^2]}. \tag{11}$$

Using the Lipschitz property of f',

$$|f'(T_i^*) - f'(T_i)| \leq L|T_i^* - T_i| \leq L|T_i - h(X_i)|, \tag{12}$$

where the last inequality follows from T_i^* lying between T_i and $h(X_i)$. Multiplying both sides by $(T_i - h(X_i))^2$ and taking expectations, we have

$$E[(T_i - h(X_i))^2|f'(T_i^*) - f'(T_i)|] \leq LE[|T_i - h(X_i)|^3]. \tag{13}$$

Dividing both sides by $E[(T_i - h(X_i))^2]$ yields the bound

$$|A| \leq L \underbrace{\frac{E[|T_i - h(X_i)|^3]}{E[(T_i - h(X_i))^2]}}_{:=\kappa}. \tag{14}$$

Non-deterministic treatment implies that κ exists and is strictly positive. Therefore, the bound on $|A|$ is 0 if f is affine ($L = 0$).

The second bias term B has the same interpretation as in the binary treatment case. That is, letting ω_i again denote the conditional variance weight,

$$E[\omega_i f'(T_i)] - E[f'(T_i)] = \text{Cov}(\omega_i, f'(T_i)), \tag{15}$$

which is the continuous analogue of Eq. (5). If f is affine, $f'(T_i)$ is a constant, so $\text{Cov}(\omega_i, f'(T_i)) = 0$. Therefore, the absolute bias of $\tilde{\theta}$ is bounded by

$$|A + \text{Cov}(\omega_i, f'(T_i))| \leq |A| + |\text{Cov}(\omega_i, f'(T_i))| \tag{16}$$
$$\leq L\kappa + |\text{Cov}(\omega_i, f'(T_i))|,$$

which equals 0 if f is affine. This obtains the result. □

In other words, the bias of $\tilde{\theta}$ for the ACD decomposes into two terms. The first depends on the curvature of f, which "pulls" the derivatives being averaged away from the derivatives at the realized treatment values. The second term reflects conditional variance-weighting and has the same interpretation as in the binary treatment case. The first term is eliminated when f is affine. The second term is eliminated if there is no treatment heterogeneity, which holds trivially when f is affine. Therefore, A and B vanish when f is affine (and thus the PLM is correctly specified). However, if f is not affine, then the biases need not vanish except in contrived cases (e.g., they cancel exactly).

3 Numerical Example

To build intuition, we walk through a stylized numerical example.[4] Although we make simplifying assumptions to enable closed-form analysis, our choices also reflect common aspects of real-world data.

Specifically, we assume:

1. *Diminishing returns.* While $E[Y_i|T_i, X_i]$ is increasing in T_i, it also exhibits diminishing returns. That is, $f'(T_i) > 0$ and $f''(T_i) < 0$.
2. *Right-skewed treatments.* T_i is an overdispersed count variable, such that even a correct model for $E[T_i|X_i]$ has heteroskedastic errors.

Let X_i be a categorical variable that takes on values $j = 1, \ldots, J$ with probabilities $\pi_1, \ldots, \pi_J$. Let T_i be conditionally Poisson given X_i with parameters $\lambda_1, \ldots, \lambda_J$. Let $f(T_i) = \log(T_i + 1)$. Then the conditional expectation of the causal derivative of Y_i with respect to T_i is

$$E[f'(T_i)|X_i = j] = \frac{1 - \exp(-\lambda_j)}{\lambda_j} \tag{17}$$

and the ACD is $\sum_j \pi_j \frac{1-\exp(-\lambda_j)}{\lambda_j}$. (See Appendix A of the supplementary material for derivations.)

The RORR plim is

$$\hat{\theta} \xrightarrow{p} \tilde{\theta} = \frac{\sum_j^J \pi_j E[(T_i - \lambda_j)^2 f'(T_i^*)|X_i = j]}{\sum_j^J \pi_j \lambda_j}, \tag{18}$$

where, as before, T_i^* is a point between T_i and λ_j. Note the two biases relative to the ACD. First, rather than evaluate f' at T_i, we evaluate it at T_i^*. Second, we also weight each $f'(T_i^*)$ by its normalized conditional variance,

$$\omega_i = (T_i - \lambda_{j[i]})^2 / \sum_j \pi_j \lambda_{j[i]}. \tag{19}$$

Figure 1 illustrates the resulting bias. In the top panel, we plot the dose-response curve $f(T_i) = \log(T_i + 1)$, as well as tangent lines with slopes equal to $E[f'(T_i)]$ in blue and to $E[\omega_i f'(T_i^*)]$ in red, where T_i^* is the "effective" treatment analyzed by RORR. The key takeaway is that RORR targets a quantity different from, and smaller than, the ACD.[5] The subsequent panels give intuition for this

[4] Replication code for all figures and tables in this section can be found at https://github.com/winston-chou/rorr.

[5] An analogous result in the welfare economics literature is that OLS upweights the slopes of higher-income groups in regressions of consumption on income, leading to attenuation bias [26].

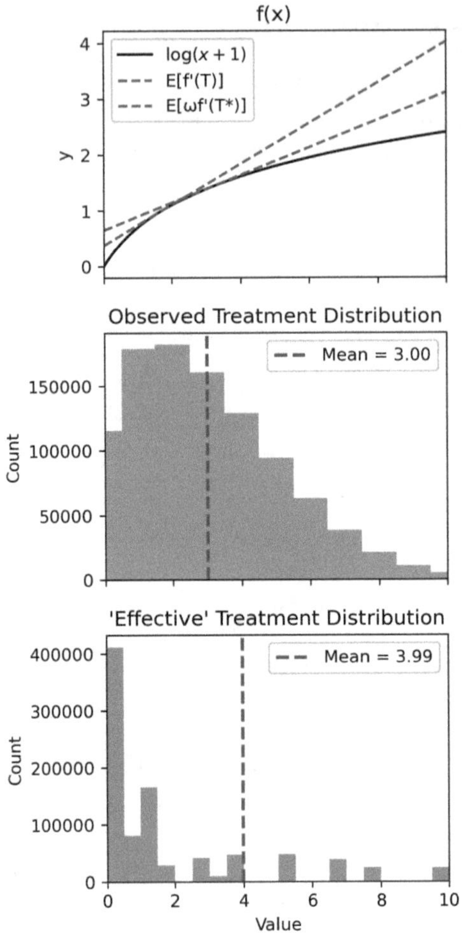

Fig. 1. Bias of Residuals-on-Residuals Regression (RORR). RORR undershoots the true ACD due to the concavity of the dose-response function and the rightward shift of the "effective" treatment distribution.

result. After weighting by ω_i and transforming T_i to T_i^*, the effective treatment distribution is much more right-skewed than the observed treatment distribution. This means that we tend to evaluate the slope of f at higher values of T_i. This induces negative bias because $f''(T_i) < 0$.

In Table 1, we report the empirical RORR estimated in simulations at varying sample sizes. For comparison, we also report the empirical ACD (calculated as

Table 1. Simulation Results for RORR and Average Causal Derivative (ACD).

Sample Size	Empirical RORR	RORR 95% CI	RORR Plim
10,000	0.250	(0.237, 0.262)	0.247
100,000	0.248	(0.244, 0.252)	0.247
1,000,000	0.248	(0.247, 0.249)	0.247
Sample Size	Empirical ACD	ACD 95% CI	True ACD
10,000	0.362	(0.357, 0.367)	0.365
100,000	0.364	(0.362, 0.366)	0.365
1,000,000	0.365	(0.364, 0.365)	0.365

the sample mean of $\frac{1}{T_i+1}$) and the true ACD computed using (17).[6] The results in the table confirm the negative bias of RORR for the ACD.

Practical Guidance. Given the prevalence of diminishing returns and right-skewed treatments in applied work, our theoretical analysis suggests that, as a rule of thumb, the RORR estimate will be negatively biased for the ACD even when the unconfoundedness assumption is satisfied. Again, this is because the combination of right-skewedness and diminishing returns means that the units that RORR implicitly up-weights will tend to have higher values of the treatment, where the dose-response curve is flatter. We propose a consistent estimator for the ACD in Sect. 4 and give real-world evidence for this rule of thumb in Sect. 5.

4 Coarsened Augmented Inverse Propensity Weighting

A benchmark estimator for the Average Causal Derivative (ACD) with continuous treatments uses the Generalized Propensity Score (GPS) [12]. However, GPS estimators require estimating the conditional density of the treatment, which can suffer from slow rates and instability [16].

As an alternative to both RORR and GPS, we propose a simple coarsened Augmented Inverse Propensity Weighting (AIPW) estimator, which uses the AIPW estimates of counterfactual means as building blocks [cf. 7,16]. This estimator proceeds by first partitioning the treatment support into K disjoint bins of length ℓ. Then, for each bin S_k, we estimate the bin-level propensity score

[6] Note that, because T_i is integer-valued in this example, the more appropriate causal estimand is the Average Incremental Effect (AIE), defined as

$$E[Y_i(T_i+1) - Y_i(T_i)] = \sum_{t=0}^{\infty}[f(t+1) - f(t)]\Pr(T_i = t). \tag{20}$$

However, because the RORR plim is a weighted average of derivatives, we focus on the ACD in Table 1 for comparability and defer discussion of the AIE to Sect. 4.

$p_k(x) = \Pr(T_i \in S_k | X_i = x)$. Denote this estimate by $\hat{p}_k$. For each treatment bin, we also estimate a conditional mean regression denoted by $\hat{m}_k(X_i)$, which estimates $m_k(x) = E[Y_i | T_i \in S_k, X_i = x]$.

Next, we form the usual AIPW estimator for the marginal counterfactual mean in bin S_k

$$\hat{\psi}_k := \frac{1}{N} \sum_{i=1}^{N} \left(\left[\frac{\mathbf{1}(T_i \in S_k)}{\hat{p}_k(X_i)} (Y_i - \hat{m}_k(X_i)) \right] + \hat{m}_k(X_i) \right). \tag{21}$$

This estimator is doubly-robust, meaning that if either $\hat{p}_k$ or $\hat{m}_k$ is consistent, then $\hat{\psi}_k$ is also consistent for the mean potential outcome within S_k [15].[7]

Then the *coarsened AIPW* estimate of the ACD is given by

$$\hat{\psi} := \sum_{k=1}^{K-1} w_k \left(\frac{\hat{\psi}_{k+1} - \hat{\psi}_k}{\bar{t}_{k+1} - \bar{t}_k} \right), \tag{22}$$

where $\bar{t}_k = \frac{t_{k+1}+t_k}{2}$, $\pi_k = \Pr(T_i \in S_k)$, and $w_k = \frac{\pi_k}{\sum_{r=1}^{K-1} \pi_r}$. Heuristically, $\hat{\psi}$ approximates f' using a piecewise linear function and computes its weighted average using the empirical distribution of the lower segment.

Theorem 1 proves the consistency of this estimator under regularity conditions. For the proof, we introduce the potential outcomes notation

$$Y_i(t) = f(t) + g(X_i) + e_i \quad \text{and} \quad T_i = h(X_i) + u_i. \tag{23}$$

Theorem 1. *Let (Y_i, T_i, X_i) be i.i.d. draws from a distribution that obeys the structural model (23). Assume that T_i is distributed on a compact interval $\mathcal{T} = [\underline{t}, \bar{t}]$ and define the coarsened AIPW estimator $\widehat{\psi}$ as in (22).*

Assume unconfoundedness and the following positivity condition:

$$p_k(x) \geq \epsilon \ell, \tag{24}$$

for all k and x, for some $\epsilon > 0$. Assume that the conditional treatment density $p(t \mid x)$ is twice continuously differentiable and has uniformly bounded derivatives. As before, assume that $f'(t)$ is Lipschitz continuous. Lastly, assume that the nuisances are estimated (e.g., with cross-fitting) such that the bin-level AIPW estimates are uniformly consistent in k

$$\max_{1 \leq k \leq K} |\widehat{\psi}_k - \psi_k| = o_p(1). \tag{25}$$

Then, as $N \to \infty$, $K \to \infty$, and $\ell \to 0$,

$$\widehat{\psi} \xrightarrow{p} E[f'(T_i)]. \tag{26}$$

[7] The plim of $\hat{\psi}_k$ has a nuanced interpretation due to averaging over the bin. Under strong ignorability, it can be interpreted as the population-average potential outcome if units are treated according to the conditional distribution of T_i given X_i and $T_i \in S_k$.

Proof. We begin by showing that $\widehat{\psi} - \psi = o_p(1)$, where

$$\widehat{\psi} = \sum_{k=1}^{K-1} w_k \frac{\widehat{\psi}_{k+1} - \widehat{\psi}_k}{\ell} \quad \text{and} \quad \psi = \sum_{k=1}^{K-1} w_k \frac{\psi_{k+1} - \psi_k}{\ell}. \tag{27}$$

First, write

$$\widehat{\psi} - \psi = \sum_{k=1}^{K-1} w_k \frac{\varepsilon_{k+1} - \varepsilon_k}{\ell}, \tag{28}$$

where $\varepsilon_k = \widehat{\psi}_k - \psi_k$. Note that $\varepsilon_k = o_p(1)$ by assumption. Rearranging terms, we have

$$\widehat{\psi} - \psi = -\frac{w_1}{\ell}\varepsilon_1 + \sum_{k=2}^{K-1} \frac{w_{k-1} - w_k}{\ell}\varepsilon_k + \frac{w_{K-1}}{\ell}\varepsilon_K. \tag{29}$$

Boundedness and continuous differentiability of $p(t \mid x)$ imply that the marginal treatment density $\pi(t)$ is also bounded and continuously differentiable (and, in particular, that π_k is bounded and continuously differentiable uniformly in k). This in turn implies that $w_k = \frac{\pi_k}{1-\pi_K} = O(\ell)$, so $\frac{w_1}{\ell}$ and $\frac{w_{K-1}}{\ell}$ are both $O(1)$. Continuous differentiability of $\pi(t)$ further implies that $|w_k - w_{k-1}| = O(\ell^2)$ uniformly in k, so

$$\sum_{k=2}^{K-1} \left| \frac{w_{k-1} - w_k}{\ell} \right| = O(\ell^{-1}) \cdot O(\ell) = O(1). \tag{30}$$

Therefore,

$$|\widehat{\psi} - \psi| \le O(1) \cdot \max_{1 \le k \le K} |\varepsilon_k| = o_p(1). \tag{31}$$

Next, we consider the error of the coarsened population estimand ψ for $E[f'(T_i)]$. Define

$$r_k(t \mid x) = \frac{p(t \mid x) 1(t \in S_k)}{p_k(x)}. \tag{32}$$

Under unconfoundedness,

$$m_k(x) = \int_{S_k} \{f(t) + g(x)\} r_k(t \mid x)\, dt, \tag{33}$$

and so

$$\psi_k = E[g(X_i)] + E\left[\int_{S_k} f(t) r_k(t \mid X_i)\, dt \right]. \tag{34}$$

Define

$$\Delta_k := \psi_{k+1} - \psi_k = \int \left(\int f(t) r_{k+1}(t|x) dt - \int f(t) r_k(t|x) dt \right) p(x) dx. \tag{35}$$

Lemma 1 in Appendix C of the supplementary material establishes that the inner integrals

$$\int f(t) r_k(t|x) dt = f(\bar{t}_k) + O(\ell^2), \tag{36}$$

uniformly in x, so after integrating over $p(x)$, we obtain

$$\Delta_k = f(\bar{t}_{k+1}) - f(\bar{t}_k) + O(\ell^2). \tag{37}$$

By the mean value theorem, there exists a $\xi_k \in [\bar{t}_k, \bar{t}_{k+1}]$ such that

$$\Delta_k = f'(\xi_k) \underbrace{(\bar{t}_{k+1} - \bar{t}_k)}_{=\ell} + O(\ell^2), \tag{38}$$

so $\Delta_k/\ell = f'(\xi_k) + O(\ell)$. Thus, we have that

$$\psi = \sum_{k=1}^{K-1} w_k \frac{\Delta_k}{\ell} = \sum_{k=1}^{K-1} w_k f'(\xi_k) + O(\ell). \tag{39}$$

It remains to show that the weighted sum in (39) approximates $E[f'(T_i)]$. By definition of w_k,

$$\sum_{k=1}^{K-1} w_k f'(\xi_k) = \frac{1}{1-\pi_K} \sum_{k=1}^{K-1} \pi_k f'(\xi_k). \tag{40}$$

Because f' is Lipschitz and ξ_k lies within $O(\ell)$ of every point in S_k,

$$\sum_{k=1}^{K-1} \pi_k f'(\xi_k) = \sum_{k=1}^{K-1} \int_{S_k} f'(t) p(t)\, dt + O(\ell). \tag{41}$$

Because π_K is $O(\ell)$, $(1-\pi_K)^{-1}$ is $1 + O(\ell)$, which does not change the order of the approximation. Therefore,

$$\sum_{k=1}^{K-1} w_k f'(\xi_k) = E[f'(T_i)] + O(\ell). \tag{42}$$

Combining (31) and (42) gives

$$\widehat{\psi} = E[f'(T_i)] + O(\ell) + o_p(1), \tag{43}$$

which converges in probability to $E[f'(T_i)]$ as $\ell \to 0$. □

Δ_k has a subtle interpretation: it is the "effect" of moving from segment S_k to S_{k+1} when units are treated probabilistically according to the conditional treatment distribution in each segment. It can also be interpreted as the ATE of a deterministic intervention. Given continuity of f, p, and positivity, the mean value theorem for integrals states that there exists a $\tilde{t}_k \in S_k$ such that

$$\int f(t) \frac{p(t|x) 1(t \in S_k)}{\Pr(t \in S_k|x)} dt = f(\tilde{t}_k). \tag{44}$$

Note that this $\tilde{t}_k$ implicitly depends on x, which we have suppressed from our notation for readability.

Thus, we can rewrite (44) as

$$\Delta_k = \int [f(\tilde{t}_{k+1}) - f(\tilde{t}_k)]p(x)dx, \tag{45}$$

showing that Δ_k is the ATE of fixing T_i to some covariate-dependent $\tilde{t}_{k+1} \in S_{k+1}$ relative to $\tilde{t}_k \in S_k$.

Table 2 shows the results of applying this estimator to the simulated data from Sect. 3. Because the treatment is integer-valued, we can set the bins to each observed treatment value. As the table shows, this yields a consistent estimator for the AIE.[8]

Table 2. Consistency of AIPW for the Average Incremental Effect (AIE).

Sample Size	Empirical AIE	AIE 95% CI	True AIE
10,000	0.277	(0.247, 0.308)	0.295
100,000	0.291	(0.282, 0.300)	0.295
1,000,000	0.295	(0.290, 0.300)	0.295

Practical Guidance. Our proof of the consistency of the coarsened AIPW estimator relies on conditional ignorability, positivity of the conditional treatment density $p(t|x)$, and continuous differentiability of the dose-response function f and of p. These are strong assumptions whose validity should be assessed on a case-by-case basis. However, a major benefit of IPW estimators is that they enable a suite of useful diagnostics, some of which we illustrate in Sect. 5 [4].

In our experience, a common way in which these assumptions can be violated is if the treatment is extremely sparse and/or skewed in regions of the covariate space. Sparsity can be diagnosed by checking the distribution of estimated propensity scores. Remedies for sparsity include trimming and/or grouping extreme treatment values [18]. Indeed, in Appendix B of the supplementary material, we provide an MSE-based justification for grouping observations into relatively few bins (on the order of $N^{1/5}$). In practice, researchers should assess the sensitivity of their results to this hyperparameter. Plotting the treatment distribution and estimated dose-response curve, as we do in our empirical application, can also help reveal violations of positivity and continuity.

Another way to address treatment effect heterogeneity is to model Conditional Average Treatment Effects (CATEs) using pretreatment covariates [8,22,24]. For example, if one has pretreatment measures of treatment intensity (e.g., prior discount usage and/or other measures of price sensitivity), one

[8] Note that the AIE is less than the ACD because $f(t+1)-f(t) = \log\left(1 + \frac{1}{t+1}\right) \leq \frac{1}{t+1}$ for all $t \geq 0$.

can estimate how the treatment effect varies according to these covariates (e.g., the effect of a discount is larger for price-sensitive customers).

We note that this approach is *complementary* to our own in the sense that one can also use the coarsened AIPW estimator to estimate CATEs in partitions of the covariates. The conceptual difference is that we focus on treatment effect heterogeneity induced by nonlinear dose-response functions, whereas CATE methods focus on treatment effect heterogeneity explained by pretreatment covariates.

5 Real-World Application

In this section, we demonstrate the empirical relevance of our theoretical analysis using real-world data from Netflix. The goal of this section is to show that the theoretical biases discussed above can (and, in our experience, often do) appear in real-world data. Although we are unable to share the proprietary data analyzed in this section, we provide replication code at https://github.com/winston-chou/rorr.

In this application, we sought to understand how use of a feature, which we will call Feature A, affects future visits to Netflix. To answer this question, we drew a random sample of 12.8 m users and counted the number of times they used Feature A over a 28-day window.[9] Next, we divided this number by each user's count of visits over the same period to define our continuous treatment, `Feature A Usage Rate`. We defined our outcome as the count of each user's visits in the next 28-day window. As covariates, we included the count of times each user used Feature A and the count of times each user visited the platform in the seven-, 14-, and 28-day windows preceding the treatment period.[10]

We divided our dataset into roughly equal-sized training, validation, and test datasets consisting of approximately 4.3 million users each. To estimate the nuisance parameters in the PLM, we fit gradient boosted regression trees to the treatment and outcome variables observed in the training dataset, using the validation dataset to tune the number of boosting rounds. Lastly, we regressed the outcome residuals on the treatment residuals in the test dataset to obtain the RORR treatment estimate. This estimate is shown in the top row of Table 3.

In addition to the RORR estimate, Table 3 also reports the output of our coarsened AIPW estimator. To fit this estimator, we coarsen the treatment into five bins and fit a multiclass classifier to these using gradient boosting. We assign zero values (i.e., no usage of Feature A during the treatment period) to the first bin and then divide the remaining non-zero values into quartiles. For each value of the coarsened treatment, we fit a separate outcome regression.

As Table 3 shows, the coarsened AIPW estimate is substantially (~40x) larger than the RORR estimate. To help explain this discrepancy, we plot the results of the AIPW estimator—and, crucially, the diagnostics it enables—in Fig. 2.

[9] Note that we only sampled users with at least one visit during this window.

[10] We augmented these covariates with 25 additional covariates, including plays, engagement duration, and usage of other platform features in the 28 days preceding the treatment period.

Table 3. RORR and AIPW Estimates of **`Feature A Usage Rate`** Treatment Effects. Both the treatment and the outcome are divided by their respective standard deviations.

	RORR	Std. Err.	95% CI
Feature A Usage Rate	0.021	0.001	(0.019, 0.023)
	AIPW	Std. Err.	95% CI
Feature A Usage Rate	0.788	0.011	(0.766, 0.811)
			N =4,324,101

In the top-left panel of Fig. 2, we provide a standard IPW diagnostic plot of the difference in the standardized pretreatment value of the outcome in each bin and bin 1 before and after weighting. As the panel shows, IPW significantly reduces pretreatment differences in the outcome variable, making the bins more comparable to each other and strengthening the plausibility of the unconfoundedness assumption.

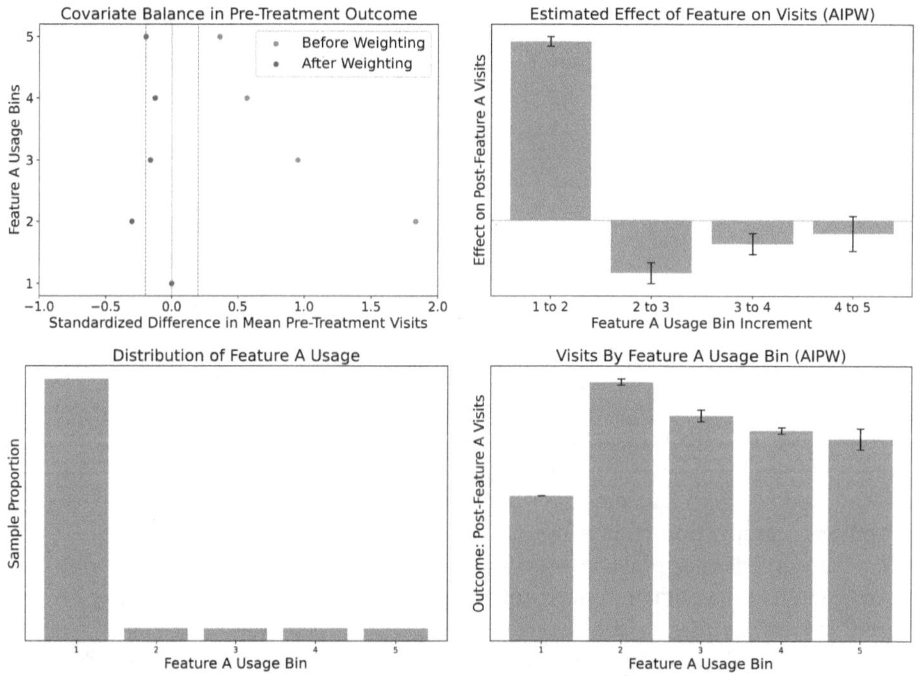

Fig. 2. Estimating the Treatment Effect of **`Feature A Usage Rate`** on Netflix Visits with Coarsened AIPW. y-axis labels are hidden for confidentiality. Plots show, in clockwise order, covariate balance before and after weighting, incremental treatment effects, the dose-response curve, and the marginal treatment distribution.

In the top right panel, we plot the incremental effect of moving up one bin. As the panel shows, AIPW estimates a large positive treatment effect of moving from the zero-usage bin (bin 1) to the next bin (bin 2), with negative incremental effects thereafter. As the bottom-left panel shows, Feature A usage is highly zero-inflated, so bin 1 is the most representative bin.

Taken together, the diagnostics help to explain why the coarsened AIPW estimate is significantly larger than the RORR estimate:

- The coarsened AIPW estimator explicitly weights the incremental treatment effects to be representative of the marginal treatment distribution, which is heavily zero-inflated. Thus, it assigns the most weight to small values of the treatment, where the dose-response curve is steepest.
- Contrastively, RORR upweights units with more unpredictable values of the treatment, which tend to be larger. This in turn overweights the downward-sloping portion of the dose-response curve.

The resulting attenuation bias of RORR is fully consistent with theoretical expectations.

The discrepancy in the estimated treatment effects is large and consequential for decision-making. Although RORR indicates that Feature A has a negligible effect on visits, the AIPW results demonstrate that, for the vast majority of users, increasing Feature A usage would have a much larger effect. Moreover, as the incremental treatment effects panel shows, a negligible positive effect is not representative of *any* bin-level treatment effect in the data.

6 Conclusion

Double Machine Learning estimators are becoming increasingly popular in both academic and commercial applications of observational causal inference. Focusing on the residuals-on-residuals regression (RORR), we analyze the bias of RORR when treatment effects are heterogeneous. For binary treatments, RORR estimates a weighted average of treatment effects that is skewed towards units for whom the conditional probability of treatment is closest to 0.5. For non-binary treatments, RORR converges to a weighted average of causal derivatives, with the added complication that these derivatives are evaluated on a "pseudo-treatment" distribution that is not the treatment distribution found in the data.

As our empirical application shows, the bias of RORR relative to the average treatment effect can have significant consequences for decision-making. As an alternative, we propose a doubly-robust Augmented Inverse Propensity Weighting estimator and show theoretically and empirically that this yields more representative estimates of causal effects.

Acknowledgments. For valuable suggestions, we thank the anonymous reviewers, Peter Hull, Yi Zhang, and participants in the Workshop on Causal Inference and Machine Learning in Practice at KDD '25 in Toronto, CA. For building and maintaining the observational causal inference platform that utilizes the methods described in this paper, we thank Adrien Alexandre, Colin Gray, and Dan Zylberglejd. The Appendix for this paper can be found at https://github.com/winston-chou/rorr.

Disclosure of Interests. The authors have no competing interests to declare that are relevant to the content of this article.

References

1. Angrist, J.D.: Estimating the labor market impact of voluntary military service using social security data on military applicants. Econometrica **66**(2), 249–288 (1998). http://www.jstor.org/stable/2998558
2. Angrist, J.D., Krueger, A.B.: Empirical strategies in labor economics. In: Handbook of Labor Economics, vol. 3, pp. 1277–1366. Elsevier (1999)
3. Aronow, P.M., Samii, C.: Does regression produce representative estimates of causal effects? Am. J. Political Sci. **60**(1), 250–267 (2016). https://onlinelibrary.wiley.com/doi/abs/10.1111/ajps.12185
4. Austin, P.C., Stuart, E.A.: Moving towards best practice when using inverse probability of treatment weighting (iptw) using the propensity score to estimate causal treatment effects in observational studies. Stat. Med. **34**(28), 3661–3679 (2015)
5. Baiardi, A., Naghi, A.A.: The effect of plough agriculture on gender roles: a machine learning approach. J. Appl. Economet. **39**(7), 1396–1402 (2024). https://doi.org/10.1002/jae.3083
6. Bickel, P.J., Klaassen, C.A.J., Ritov, Y., Wellner, J.A.: Efficient and Adaptive Estimation for Semiparametric Models, vol. 4. Johns Hopkins University Press (1993)
7. Cattaneo, M.D.: Efficient semiparametric estimation of multi-valued treatment effects under ignorability. J. Econometrics **155**(2), 138–154 (2010). https://www.sciencedirect.com/science/article/pii/S030440760900236X
8. Chernozhukov, V., et al.: Double/debiased machine learning for treatment and structural parameters. Econometrics J. **21**(1), C1–C68 (2018). http://doi.wiley.com/10.1111/ectj.12097
9. Chernozhukov, V., Kasahara, H., Schrimpf, P.: Causal impact of masks, policies, behavior on early COVID-19 pandemic in the US. J. Econometrics **220**(1), 23–62 (2021). https://doi.org/10.1016/j.jeconom.2020.09.003
10. Fink, D.: A double machine learning trend model for citizen science data. Methods Ecol. Evol. **14**, 2435–2448 (2023). https://doi.org/10.1111/2041-210X.14186
11. Holtz, D., et al.: Interdependence and the cost of uncoordinated responses to COVID-19. Proc. Natl. Acad. Sci. **117**(33), 19837–19843 (2020)
12. Imbens, G.W.: The role of the propensity score in estimating dose-response functions. Biometrika **87**(3), 706–710 (2000). https://academic.oup.com/biomet/article/87/3/706/284466
13. Imbens, G.W.: Nonparametric estimation of average treatment effects under exogeneity: a review. Rev. Econ. Stat. **86**(1), 4–29 (2004). https://doi.org/10.1162/003465304323023651
14. Jares, J.A., Malhotra, N.: Policy impact and voter mobilization: evidence from farmers' trade war experiences. Am. Political Sci. Rev. **119**(2), 847–869 (2025)
15. Kennedy, E.H.: Semiparametric doubly robust targeted double machine learning: a review. In: Handbook of Statistical Methods for Precision Medicine, pp. 207–236 (2024)

16. Kennedy, E.H., Ma, Z., McHugh, M.D., Small, D.S.: Non-parametric methods for doubly robust estimation of continuous treatment effects. J. Roy. Stat. Soc. B **79**(4), 1229–1245 (2017)
17. Lal, A.: Does regression produce representative causal rankings? (2024). https://arxiv.org/abs/2411.02675
18. Petersen, M.L., Porter, K.E., Gruber, S., Wang, Y., Van Der Laan, M.J.: Diagnosing and responding to violations in the positivity assumption. Stat. Methods Med. Res. **21**(1), 31–54 (2012)
19. Robins, J., Sued, M., Lei-Gomez, Q., Rotnitzky, A.: Comment: performance of double-robust estimators when "inverse probability" weights are highly variable. Stat. Sci. **22**(4), 544–559 (2007)
20. Robins, J.M., Rotnitzky, A., Zhao, L.P.: Estimation of regression coefficients when some regressors are not always observed. J. Am. Stat. Assoc. **89**(427), 846–866 (1994)
21. Robinson, P.M.: Root-N-consistent semiparametric regression. Econometrica **56**(4), 931–954 (1988). http://www.jstor.org/stable/1912705
22. Semenova, V., Chernozhukov, V.: Debiased machine learning of conditional average treatment effects and other causal functions. Economet. J. **24**(2), 264–289 (2021)
23. Słoczyński, T.: Interpreting OLS estimands when treatment effects are heterogeneous. Review of Economics and Statistics **104**(3), 501–509 (2022). https://direct.mit.edu/rest/article/104/3/501/97692/Interpreting-OLS-Estimands-When-Treatment-Effects
24. Wager, S., Athey, S.: Estimation and inference of heterogeneous treatment effects using random forests. J. Am. Stat. Assoc. **113**(523), 1228–1242 (2018)
25. Wei, X., Cheng, M., Duan, K., Kong, X.: Effects of big data on $pm_{2.5}$: a study based on double machine learning. Land **13**(3), 327 (2024). https://doi.org/10.3390/land13030327
26. Yitzhaki, S.: On using linear regressions in welfare economics. J. Bus. Econ. Stat. **14**(4), 478–486 (1996). http://www.jstor.org/stable/1392256

From Clinical Risk Prediction to Operational Decisions: An Uncertainty-Aware Framework for ICU Staffing

Jiayan Yang(✉), Ad Feelders, and Arno Siebes

Utrecht University, Princetonplein 5, 3584 CC Utrecht, The Netherlands
{j.yang2,A.J.Feelders,A.P.J.M.Siebes}@uu.nl

Abstract. Advances in electronic health records (EHR) and large-scale critical care databases have enabled the development of machine learning models for the early detection of patient deterioration. While these models often achieve strong predictive performance for outcomes such as sepsis and mortality, most studies evaluate them purely on discrimination metrics. This leaves a critical gap: how to systematically translate probabilistic clinical risk estimates into downstream operational decisions under real-world constraints, such as shift rigidity and hiring delays. This study proposes an uncertainty-aware anticipatory staffing framework that bridges short-term patient risk prediction and staff planning without altering the upstream predictive model. Instead of relying on naive deterministic aggregation or fixed safety buffers, the framework explicitly models dynamic predictive uncertainty and evaluates extreme shortage exposure using Conditional Value-at-Risk (CVaR). These aggregated, risk-calibrated demand signals are then embedded into an hourly rolling-horizon scheduling policy to generate delay-constrained staffing decisions.

Evaluated on realistic trajectories from the MIMIC-IV database, the proposed framework demonstrates a favorable cost-shortage trade-off compared to deterministic and purely reactive baselines. Pareto frontier analysis illustrates how uncertainty-aware demand construction changes resource allocation under varying safety preferences, while stress testing confirms the framework's operational robustness even when subjected to systematic predictive bias in the form of calibration drift. By formalizing this translation layer, this work provides a principled, transparent pathway for safely integrating probabilistic AI outputs into high-stakes healthcare operational systems.

Keywords: Healthcare AI · Clinical Machine Learning · Uncertainty-Aware Decision Making

1 Introduction

The increasing adoption of electronic health records (EHRs) has created new opportunities for data-driven analysis and decision support in healthcare.

M. Ceci et al. (Eds.): ECML PKDD 2026, LNAI 16948, pp. 289–305, 2027.
https://doi.org/10.1007/978-3-032-37679-4_17

Machine learning models trained on large-scale clinical datasets are now widely used to predict adverse outcomes such as sepsis onset [19,20], patient deterioration or unplanned intensive care unit (ICU) transfer [4], and in-hospital mortality [21]. Publicly available databases such as MIMIC-IV have further accelerated research by providing large de-identified patient cohorts for model development and evaluation [16]. These models increasingly enable early identification of high-risk patients.

Despite these advances, predictive outputs are rarely translated into operational decisions. In practice, hospital resource planning often relies on historical workload averages or deterministic demand estimates [12,17], while the probabilistic information produced by predictive models remains underutilized.

A key challenge lies in the mismatch between prediction and decision levels. Clinical prediction models typically estimate risk at the patient level, whereas operational decisions such as staffing planning should be made at the population level. Translating individual risk predictions into reliable estimates of aggregate demand therefore remains a critical but underexplored problem.

Recent work has proposed integrating prediction and decision-making through predict-then-optimize frameworks [8] and decision-focused learning approaches [25]. These methods jointly optimize predictive and decision components within an end-to-end framework [18]. However, they typically require retraining predictive models and differentiable optimization layers. In clinical practice, predictive models are often deployed as standalone systems under regulatory and operational constraints, making such modifications difficult once models are validated and in use [24,29].

In this work, we study how patient-level deterioration predictions can be translated into actionable signals for ICU staffing planning without modifying the upstream predictive model. We propose an uncertainty-aware framework that aggregates probabilistic deterioration risks across patients to estimate population-level demand, which is then incorporated into an optimization-based staffing model that explicitly balances staffing cost and operational risk.

We evaluate the framework using real-world ICU data from MIMIC-IV under multiple demand scenarios. Results show that probabilistic aggregation produces more stable and interpretable staffing demand estimates compared with deterministic baselines.

The main contributions of this work are: (i) identifying the challenge of translating patient-level deterioration predictions into population-level demand signals for ICU staffing planning; (ii) proposing an uncertainty-aware aggregation framework that converts predictive risks into stochastic demand estimates; and (iii) demonstrating improved stability and interpretability of staffing decisions through empirical evaluation on real-world clinical data.

2 Related Work

We review three related research areas: clinical risk prediction using machine learning, optimization methods for healthcare resource planning, and recent approaches that integrate predictive models with operational decision-making.

2.1 Machine Learning for Clinical Risk Prediction

Early identification of clinical deterioration has been widely studied in clinical research and medical informatics, as timely detection enables early intervention and prevents severe adverse outcomes such as cardiac arrest, ICU transfer, or in-hospital mortality [4,20]. Traditional early warning systems rely on manually designed scoring rules derived from physiological measurements. Widely adopted examples include the Modified Early Warning Score (MEWS) [27] and the National Early Warning Score (NEWS) [22], which aggregate a small set of vital signs into interpretable risk scores.

With the increasing availability of electronic health records (EHRs), machine learning methods have significantly improved clinical deterioration prediction. Early approaches applied logistic regression and tree-based models using a broader set of clinical variables such as laboratory results, demographics, and medical history [4]. More recent work has explored deep learning models capable of capturing temporal patient trajectories, including recurrent neural networks and transformer-based architectures [14,15,19,21]. These models can generate individualized risk predictions for adverse outcomes such as sepsis onset, ICU admission, and mortality.

Despite substantial progress in predictive modeling, most existing studies primarily focus on improving patient-level prediction accuracy [26]. Comparatively less attention has been given to how predictive outputs can support operational decision-making at the hospital level [11,24,28].

2.2 Optimization for Healthcare Resource Planning

Operations research methods have long been used to support decision-making in healthcare systems, including staff scheduling, bed allocation, and patient flow management [3,9]. In intensive care units (ICUs), staffing decisions are particularly challenging due to uncertain patient demand and the limited availability of specialized personnel [23]. Prior studies have proposed optimization models to determine appropriate staffing levels under uncertainty [17], typically relying on historical admission patterns, census forecasts, or simplified stochastic demand models [12].

However, these operational planning approaches are largely developed independently from modern predictive analytics. Staffing models are usually driven by aggregated historical statistics rather than patient-level risk signals [7]. As predictive models become increasingly accurate, integrating real-time risk information into operational planning presents an opportunity for more proactive and adaptive healthcare management [1].

2.3 From Prediction to Decision: Integrating Predictive Models with Operations

Bridging predictive modeling and operational decision-making has recently emerged as an important research direction in applied machine learning. Predict-then-optimize frameworks and decision-focused learning approaches aim to align predictive models with downstream decision objectives by jointly optimizing prediction and decision components [2,8,25]. While these approaches can improve decision quality, they typically require retraining predictive models together with the optimization layer and often rely on differentiable or relaxed optimization formulations.

In many real-world healthcare deployments, predictive models are developed and validated as standalone systems and cannot be easily modified once deployed due to regulatory and operational constraints. As a result, tightly integrated prediction–optimization frameworks may be difficult to apply in practice.

Related prediction-to-decision integration problems have also been studied in engineering domains such as predictive maintenance, where probabilistic failure predictions are incorporated into maintenance scheduling decisions [6,13]. These studies demonstrate how predictive uncertainty can inform operational planning in safety-critical systems.

However, the integration of predictive signals into healthcare operational planning remains relatively underexplored. In particular, methods for translating patient-level risk predictions into population-level demand signals suitable for operational decision models are still limited. Addressing this challenge is essential for enabling predictive models to support real-world healthcare resource planning.

This work addresses this gap by proposing an uncertainty-aware framework that aggregates patient-level deterioration predictions and integrates them into ICU staffing decision models. The following section introduces the proposed experimental and decision framework in detail.

3 Uncertainty-Aware Risk Aggregation Framework

Predictive models for clinical deterioration provide patient-level risk estimates, yet hospital staffing decisions will be made at the ICU level under substantial operational uncertainty. Translating heterogeneous patient risks into reliable workload signals therefore requires an aggregation mechanism that accounts for predictive uncertainty and operational constraints.

We propose an uncertainty-aware risk aggregation framework that converts patient-level deterioration probabilities into staffing demand estimates and integrates them with delay-constrained scheduling decisions. As illustrated in Fig. 1, the framework consists of three layers: (i) patient-level risk prediction from EHR data, (ii) uncertainty-aware aggregation that constructs population-level demand signals, and (iii) an operational scheduling layer that determines feasible staffing allocations under shift and hiring constraints.

This layered design separates predictive modeling from operational decision-making, allowing validated clinical prediction models to be incorporated into hospital planning systems without retraining.

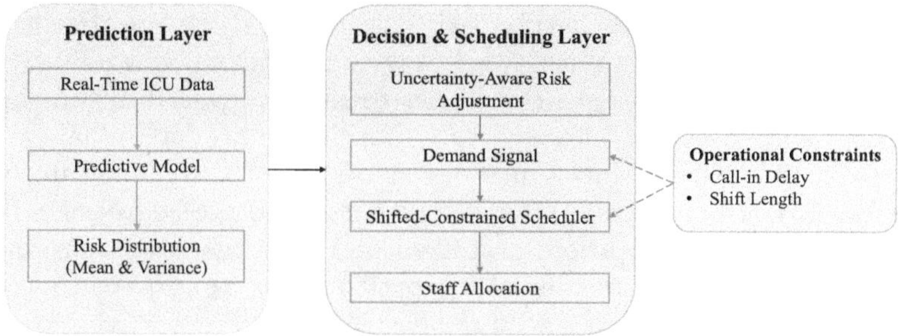

Fig. 1. Overview of the uncertainty-aware risk aggregation framework

3.1 Prediction Layer

The prediction layer estimates the probability that each patient will require vasopressor treatment within the next 24 h. We adopt the Vasopressor Requirement (VR) prediction task with treatment variables introduced by [15]. For patient i at time t, the model outputs a deterioration probability,

$$p_{i,t} = P(y_{i,t+24} = 1 \mid H_{i,t}), \tag{1}$$

where $y_{i,t+24}$ denotes a binary indicator of vasopressor usage and $H_{i,t}$ represents the observed clinical history, including physiological measurements, laboratory results, treatment variables, and demographic information. We adopt the benchmark's LSTM-based predictor, producing a sequence of patient-level risk estimates $\{p_{i,t}\}$.

3.2 Risk Aggregation and Demand Estimation

We introduce a risk aggregation mechanism that translates 24-h patient-level deterioration probabilities into a high-frequency operational demand signal to enable staffing decisions to be made at the ICU level rather than the individual patient level.

The original risk predictions $\{p_{i,k}\}$ are generated at 4-h intervals, and are resampled to an hourly resolution via linear interpolation. To prevent highly volatile scheduling directives and abrupt staff fluctuations, these initial hourly prediction trajectories are then stabilized using a rolling window average,

$$\bar{p}_{i,t} = \frac{1}{W} \sum_{k=\max(0,t-W+1)}^{t} p_{i,k}, \tag{2}$$

where W denotes the length of the smoothing window, set to 6 h to align with our anticipatory scheduling horizon.

Second, a nonlinear transformation is applied to map this smoothed probability into a risk-calibrated operational demand signal,

$$\tilde{p}_{i,t} = \bar{p}_{i,t}^{\gamma}. \tag{3}$$

The exponent γ controls how sharply patient-level risk scores are translated into operational demand signals. With $\gamma > 1$, low-confidence fluctuations are attenuated, while relatively high-risk trajectories remain influential in the aggregate signal. This mapping is not intended to uniformly inflate individual probabilities. Operational conservatism is introduced through the dynamic uncertainty buffer in Eq. (5), which accounts for the dispersion of the aggregated demand distribution. In our configuration, γ is fixed to 1.2 on the validation set. With these risk-calibrated signals defined at the patient level, we proceed to aggregate them into a total ICU-level staff requirement.

Aggregated demand is constructed through a mean-variance approximation. Let S_t denote the random aggregate demand at time t, defined as the sum of individual patient deterioration events, $S_t = \sum_{i=1}^{N} X_{i,t}$, where each patient's outcome follows a Bernoulli distribution $X_{i,t} \sim \text{Bernoulli}(\tilde{p}_{i,t})$. Although patient outcomes may exhibit weak correlations, assuming conditional independence provides a tractable approximation that is commonly used in aggregate demand modeling. Under this assumption, the expectation $\mu_t = \mathbb{E}[S_t]$ and variance $\sigma_t^2 = \text{Var}(S_t)$ of the aggregate demand are given by:

$$\mu_t = \sum_i \tilde{p}_{i,t}, \qquad \sigma_t^2 = \sum_i \tilde{p}_{i,t}(1 - \tilde{p}_{i,t}). \tag{4}$$

This independence assumption should be interpreted as an operational approximation rather than a claim that ICU deterioration events are fully independent. Shared clinical shocks, infectious outbreaks, handover periods, and unit-level workload effects can induce positive correlations among patients. In such settings, Bernoulli aggregation may underestimate tail variance. We therefore treat the resulting demand estimate as a transparent baseline aggregation layer and examine correlated surge behavior separately in the stress-test analysis. Future deployments could replace this layer with a beta-binomial, copula-based, or hierarchical correlation model when local data support reliable estimation of cross-patient dependence.

To incorporate predictive uncertainty, the operational demand estimate D_t is constructed using a mean-variance adjustment:

$$D_t = \lceil \mu_t + \zeta \sigma_t \rceil , \tag{5}$$

where ζ controls the desired confidence level to satisfy a specific target service requirement. The ceiling function guarantees integer staffing requirements. This formulation propagates patient-level predictive uncertainty into a population-level workload estimate used for staffing decisions.

3.3 Operational Staffing Model

Given the hourly demand sequence D_t, staffing decisions should respect operational constraints such as hiring delays and fixed shift lengths. Let x_t denote the number of nurses requested at decision time step t. Due to an advance notice requirement of τ hours, these nurses will begin their shifts at time $t + \tau$ and work for a fixed duration of L hours.

Let k denote the time at which a requested nurse starts a shift. Since each request must be submitted τ hours in advance, the nurses who start at time k correspond to the earlier staffing decision $x_{k-\tau}$. Because each shift lasts for L hours, the active staff at time t consists of all nurses whose shift start times fall between $t - L + 1$ and t. Therefore, the number of active nurses at time t is

$$s_t = \sum_{k=t-L+1}^{t} x_{k-\tau}. \tag{6}$$

The realized demand D_t^{real} may deviate from predictions due to stochastic patient outcomes. Shortage u_t and overstaffing o_t are defined as

$$u_t = \max(0, D_t^{real} - s_t), \qquad o_t = \max(0, s_t - D_t^{real}). \tag{7}$$

Staffing decisions balance operational cost and service reliability. The minimal total cost over a planning horizon T is

$$\min_{x_t} \sum_{t=1}^{T} c_s x_t + c_u u_t + c_o o_t, \tag{8}$$

where c_s, c_u, and c_o represent staffing, shortage, and overstaffing costs, respectively. In ICU environments, shortage penalties are typically much higher than overstaffing costs ($c_u \gg c_o$), reflecting the importance of maintaining adequate clinical coverage. The optimization objective uses linear shortage and overstaffing costs; CVaR is used in the evaluation stage to quantify the tail severity of residual understaffing rather than as an explicit constraint in Eq. (8).

Solving a global mixed-integer program at every time step is impractical in real-time hospital environments. We therefore adopt a rolling forward-scheduling policy. At any decision time step t, we calculate the projected baseline staffing level at time $t + \tau$ (prior to the current hiring decision x_t and $\tau < 6$) as $\hat{s}_{t+\tau}$. The algorithm then requests additional staff x_t whenever the projected demand $D_{t+\tau}$ exceeds this baseline:

$$\hat{s}_{t+\tau} = \sum_{k=t-L+1}^{t-1} x_k, \tag{9}$$

$$x_t = \max(0, D_{t+\tau} - \hat{s}_{t+\tau}). \tag{10}$$

This rule respects the operational constraints while maintaining computational efficiency for real-time staffing decisions.

4 Experiments

4.1 Dataset and Prediction Backbones

All experiments are conducted using patient trajectories derived from the MIMIC-IV database (version 3.1) [16]. Access to the database was granted upon completion of the required CITI human subjects research training, strictly conforming to the PhysioNet credentialed Data Use Agreement. The VR prediction task from the MIMIC-Sepsis benchmark [15] serves as the clinical prediction component.

The LSTM-based backbone processes the extracted physiological measurements, laboratory variables, and treatment indicators to estimate the probability of vasopressor administration within the next 24 h. Unless otherwise stated, the staffing experiments use this LSTM backbone as the default predictive model. Logistic regression and Transformer backbones are used only in the backbone sensitivity analysis to test whether the downstream staffing conclusions depend on the choice of predictor. Predictive performance is verified on the validation set using the Area Under the Receiver Operating Characteristic curve (AUROC) [10] and the Area Under the Precision-Recall Curve (AUPRC) [5].

To align these predictive outputs with the high-frequency requirements of our scheduling framework, the continuous risk signals are discretized into an hourly operational grid via linear interpolation. These hourly predicted probabilities then serve as the raw input for our uncertainty-aware aggregation layer.

4.2 Experimental Setup

We employ a rolling daily operational planning horizon where staffing decisions are updated hourly based on predictive demand distributions and operational constraints. Unless otherwise specified, experiments include $N = 30$ patients, a hiring delay $\tau = 2$ h, and a fixed shift length $L = 8$ h. To ensure a fair evaluation and prevent scenario-specific overfitting, all algorithmic tuning parameters are fixed globally across all experiments. The smoothing window is set to $W = 6$ h, the risk-aversion coefficient is $\gamma = 1.2$, and the service-level parameter is $\zeta = 1.28$.

To evaluate generalization across heterogeneous demand realizations, multiple random seeds are used to sample patient subsets from the database. Each seed produces an independent 24-h probabilistic demand trajectory. All competing policies are evaluated on identical realizations to ensure paired comparisons and eliminate stochastic bias.

These parameters were fixed before the final policy comparison and were not retuned for individual simulation seeds. We also examined nearby values of the calibration exponent and service-level buffer, and the qualitative ranking of the main policies remained unchanged. Larger buffers reduced shortage at the cost of additional staffing. This sensitivity check is intended to assess robustness rather than to select seed-specific operating points.

4.3 Evaluation Metrics

To assess the operational and risk implications of different staffing policies, performance is evaluated along four dimensions: (i) economic efficiency, (ii) service adequacy, (iii) operational stability, and (iv) tail-risk exposure.

Total economic efficiency over the planning horizon is defined as the aggregate staffing cost $\sum_t c_s x_t$. Service adequacy is measured by the cumulative shortage $\sum_t u_t$ and total overstaffing $\sum_t o_t$. Operational stability is captured by staffing volatility, defined as the absolute shift-to-shift variation in active personnel $\sum_t |s_t - s_{t-1}|$.

Finally, extreme shortage risk is reported using Conditional Value-at-Risk (CVaR):

$$\mathrm{CVaR}_\alpha = \mathbb{E}[u_t \mid u_t \geq \mathrm{VaR}_\alpha]. \tag{11}$$

where VaR_α is the Value-at-Risk at confidence level α (satisfying $\mathbb{P}(u_t \leq \mathrm{VaR}_\alpha) = \alpha$). In our evaluation, we set tail risks for $\alpha \in \{0.90, 0.95\}$.

In ICU staffing contexts, the consequences of a staffing imbalance are highly asymmetric. Severe understaffing can compromise patient safety and care quality, whereas temporary overstaffing mainly results in financial inefficiency. Consequently, our risk measure strictly focuses on the tail risk of staffing shortages. CVaR emphasizes extreme shortage scenarios and quantifies the expected severity of understaffing beyond a specified confidence level α. It is used as an evaluation metric rather than an optimization constraint in our implementation. In contrast, overstaffing does not represent a safety-critical risk and is therefore modeled separately as a linear cost component in the objective function.

4.4 Baseline Policies

We compare the proposed framework with four benchmark staffing strategies implemented under identical operational constraints.

Deterministic Policy. Staffing decisions are based solely on expected demand μ_t.

Reactive Policy. Hiring follows realized demand D_t^{real} with delay τ.

Variance-Only Policy. Staffing uses a variance-inflated estimate $\mu_t + \zeta\sigma_t$.

Oracle Policy. Staffing is determined using realized demand without prediction error or hiring delay.

These baselines allow us to evaluate whether calibrated risk mapping, dynamic variance buffering, and temporal smoothing improve upon expectation-based planning, purely reactive adjustment, and conventional variance-buffering strategies.

Table 1. Backbone sensitivity analysis

Model	AUROC	AUPRC	Cost (Mean)	Shortage (Mean)
Logistic Regression	0.8605	0.6809	23.4	15.0
LSTM	0.8419	0.6612	23.4	16.6
Transformer	0.8646	0.6890	23.1	16.2

Table 2. Performance comparison across staffing policies

Method	Cost	Shortage	Overstaff	Volatility	CVaR (90%)
Deterministic	19.9 ± 3.2	22.9 ± 13.9	26.4 ± 23.1	8.7 ± 1.7	6.49
Reactive	33.9 ± 3.1	14.4 ± 4.5	120.6 ± 32.9	13.7 ± 1.4	0.60
Variance-only	27.2 ± 3.4	14.8 ± 5.0	72.4 ± 32.4	11.1 ± 1.5	0.62
Proposed (Full)	23.4 ± 3.3	16.6 ± 7.4	46.3 ± 29.8	9.8 ± 1.4	4.44
Oracle	19.3 ± 5.8	0.0 ± 0.0	10.6 ± 5.8	2.4 ± 1.6	0.00

5 Results

5.1 Backbone Sensitivity Analysis

We first examine whether the proposed aggregation framework depends on the specific predictive model used to estimate patient deterioration risk. Three representative backbones are evaluated: logistic regression, an LSTM-based temporal model, and a Transformer-based sequence model. For each backbone, predicted probabilities are aggregated using the proposed uncertainty-aware aggregation mechanism to estimate shift-level demand, followed by the identical staffing decision layer.

Table 1 shows that the resulting staffing metrics remain remarkably robust despite variations in predictive accuracy across models. Specifically, mean staffing costs stay highly consistent, and shortage statistics fluctuate only within a narrow operational margin. This indicates the aggregation mechanism is robustly model-agnostic, seamlessly integrating diverse predictive outputs without requiring downstream modifications. Such operational stability is crucial in practical deployments, where predictive models frequently evolve over time while decision pipelines must remain reliable.

5.2 Comparative Analysis of Staffing Policies

Table 2 summarizes the operational performance of the proposed framework against external benchmark policies under realistic MIMIC-IV demand trajectories.

Three key observations emerge. First, the deterministic policy achieves the lowest average cost but exhibits the highest tail risk (CVaR $= 6.49$), indicating severe vulnerability to demand surges. Second, while the reactive policy substantially reduces this tail risk, it triggers massive overstaffing (120.6 average nurse-hours), resulting in the highest operational cost and volatility due to ex-post corrections. Third, the proposed framework achieves a favorable balance. It reduces cumulative shortage compared to the deterministic baseline while maintaining substantially lower overstaffing than the reactive and variance-only strategies. A paired t-test on seed-level cumulative shortage shows a significant reduction relative to the deterministic baseline ($p < 0.001$). Overall, uncertainty-aware anticipation improves system robustness while avoiding excessive capacity inflation.

5.3 Uncertainty Ablation Study

To systematically evaluate the impact of each uncertainty-modeling component, we compare four internal variants: (i) Mean-only (μ) serves as the unadjusted foundation by aggregating expected probabilities directly, (ii) Static Margin ($\mu + \sigma_{stat}$) introduces a fixed population-level buffer, (iii) Dynamic Margin ($\mu + \sigma_{dyn}$) estimates variance directly from the real-time predicted risk distribution, and (iv) Full Framework ($\mu + \sigma_{dyn}$) combines calibrated risk mapping, dynamic variance estimation, and temporal smoothing.

Table 3. Mechanism ablation and tail-risk analysis

Ablation Variant	Cost (Mean)	Shortage (Mean)	P90 Shortage	P95 Shortage
1. Mean-only (μ)	19.9	22.9	45.1	46.5
2. Static Margin ($\mu + \sigma_{stat}$)	26.9	14.7	21.2	23.5
3. Dynamic Margin ($\mu + \sigma_{dyn}$)	22.9	16.9	29.1	30.0
4. Full Framework ($\mu + \sigma_{dyn}$)	23.4	16.6	28.3	31.5

Table 3 reports the resulting staffing cost and shortage statistics. The P90/P95 shortage metrics quantify tail-risk exposure, representing the magnitude of unmet clinical demand during the worst 10% and 5% of extreme operational scenarios, respectively. The deterministic approach accumulates low-probability deterioration events, leading to severe shortage risks. Introducing uncertainty estimates stabilizes demand and reduces shortage frequency. The full framework provides a more favorable empirical trade-off by reducing cumulative shortage relative to the mean-only baseline while avoiding the large over-staffing induced by more conservative buffers. Figure 2 visualizes the average shortage across variants, while Fig. 3 illustrates the resulting cost-shortage trade-off. These results highlight the importance of modeling uncertainty when translating probabilistic predictions into operational decisions.

5.4 Calibration Stress Test

Predictive models deployed in practice often experience calibration drift over time, systematically overestimating or underestimating clinical risks due to shifts in patient demographics or clinical protocols. We set this systematic bias by applying a multiplicative scaling factor $\beta \in [0.7, 1.3]$ to the original predictions. The drifted probability is thus given by $\tilde{p}_{i,t} = \min(1, \beta \cdot p_{i,t})$.

Table 4 and Fig. 4 demonstrate that moderate overestimation (1.3x) slightly increases staffing levels, safely absorbing shortage risk. In contrast, underestimation systematically downplays deterioration risks, exposing the ICU to severe shortages (P90 shortage spikes to 59.3). The framework remains operationally stable under stochastic noise and moderate positive bias, confirming its practical suitability for real-world clinical decision pipelines where predictive drift is common.

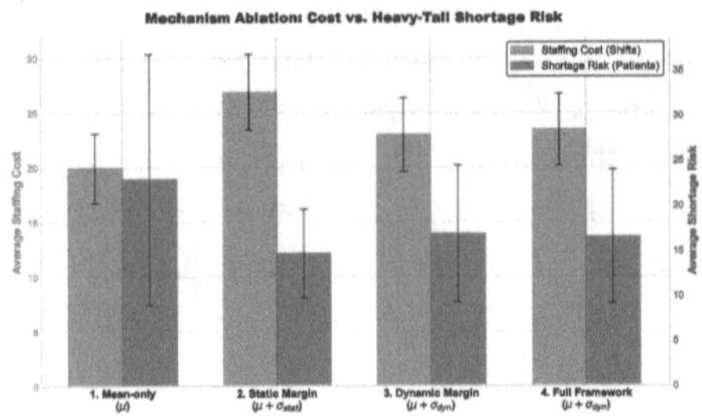

Fig. 2. Impact of uncertainty modelling on staffing cost and shortage. Bars report mean values across 30 random seeds, with error bars denoting one standard deviation.

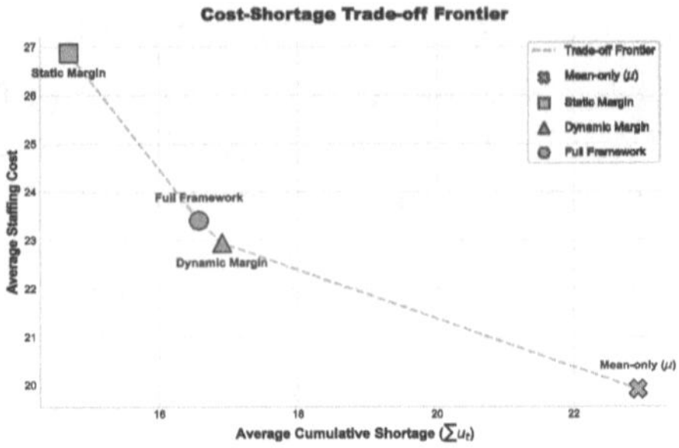

Fig. 3. Cost-shortage trade-off across uncertainty aggregation strategies. Each point reports the mean across 30 random seeds.

Table 4. Systematic bias robustness stress test

Scenario	Cost (Mean)	Shortage (Mean)	P90 Shortage
Original	23.4	16.6	28.3
Overestimation (1.3x)	28.9	14.5	21.1
Underestimation (0.7x)	17.3	30.3	59.3
Noisy (+N)	23.7	16.4	28.2

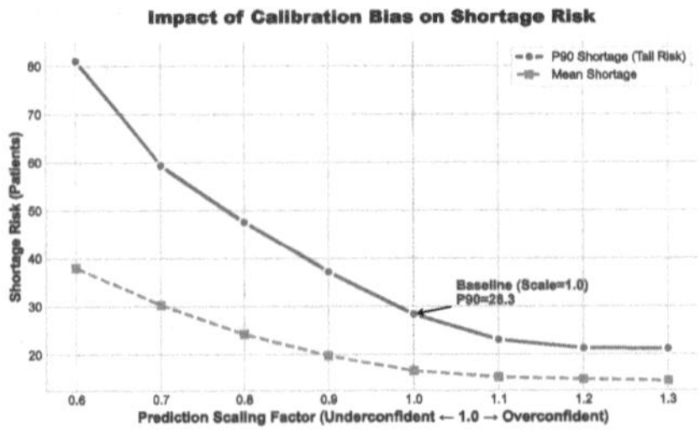

Fig. 4. Impact of systematic probability drift on shortage risk

6 Decision-Level Case Analysis

6.1 24-Hour ICU Planning Case Study

To illustrate how the proposed framework supports operational decision-making, a 24-h ICU staffing scenario is analyzed.

For a selected day in the test dataset, macroscopic patient deterioration risks are first predicted using the trained risk prediction model. These patient-level probabilities are then aggregated into hourly unit-level demand distributions using the uncertainty-aware aggregation mechanism. This step incorporates both backward rolling stabilization and calibrated risk mapping to construct operational signals. Based on these estimated demand trajectories, the rolling-horizon scheduling policy generates the recommended staff level for each decision period under advance notice constraints.

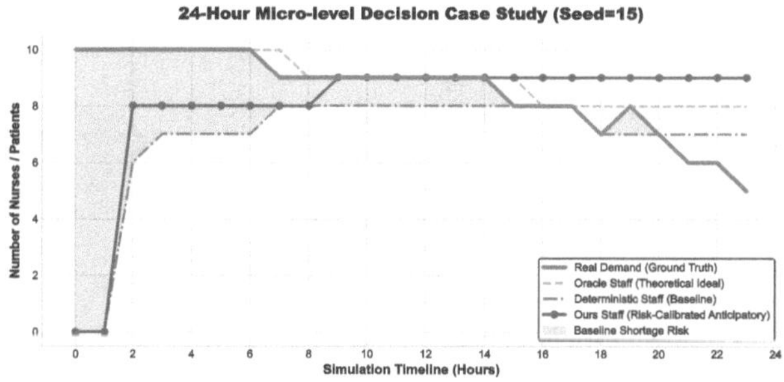

Fig. 5. 24-h micro-level decision dynamics under MIMIC-IV-derived ICU demand

Figure 5 visualizes the resulting staffing schedule, comparing our proposed framework against a deterministic baseline and a theoretical oracle. The figure demonstrates how uncertainty-aware aggregation allows the decision framework to proactively allocate additional staff ahead of actual demand spikes. While the deterministic baseline exposes the unit to severe shortage risks during periods of elevated deterioration, our method successfully buffers these fluctuations. This example illustrates how the proposed pipeline translates macroscopic patient risk predictions into safe, actionable staffing decisions in a realistic ICU planning scenario.

6.2 Comparative Policy Performance Under Realistic Demand

To evaluate robustness under adverse conditions, we construct a 96-h synthetic demand trajectory featuring a correlated deterioration surge. Figure 6 presents a representative 24-h segment of this stress test.

Panel A shows the aggregated predictive risk signal and its adjusted staffing target. The proposed framework increases staffing prior to the realized peak, reflecting anticipatory behavior. Panel B illustrates the two-hour hiring delay ($\tau = 2$), emphasizing that decisions have to be made before demand is fully observed. Under such constraints, purely reactive strategies inherently lag. Panel C compares staffing trajectories. The reactive policy responds only after shortages materialize, leading to delayed corrections. The deterministic baseline anticipates demand trends but underestimates the surge magnitude. In contrast, the proposed method increases staffing earlier and maintains smoother adjustments through the peak period. Panel D quantifies the staffing gaps. Over the displayed horizon, cumulative shortage is reduced from 35 nurse-hours under the reactive policy to 24 nurse-hours under the proposed approach.

These results demonstrate that the advantage of uncertainty-aware anticipation persists under severe surge conditions and is not limited to average-case scenarios.

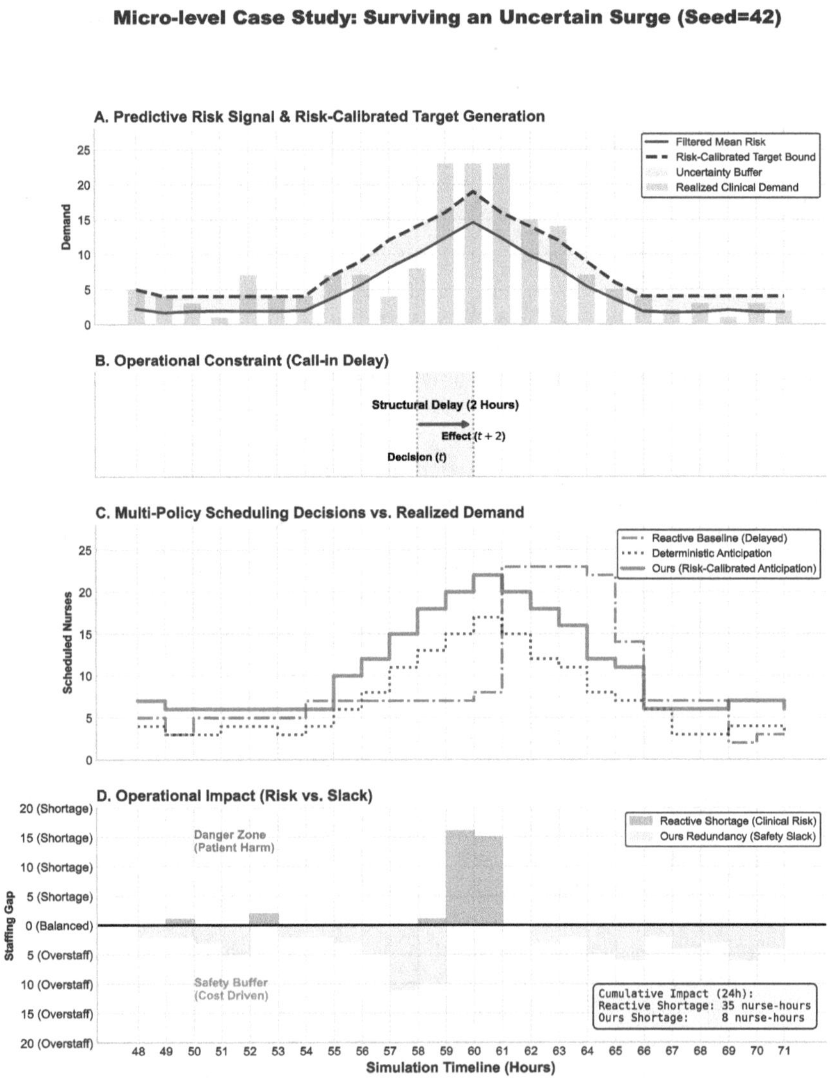

Fig. 6. Stress-test evaluation under surge conditions (96-h scenario, seed = 42)

7 Conclusions and Limitations

Empirical evaluation under realistic MIMIC-IV trajectories demonstrates that the proposed approach achieves a favorable cost-shortage trade-off. Compared with deterministic and reactive baselines, the framework reduces shortage exposure and maintains operational stability, even when subjected to systematic predictive bias. Mechanism analyses further illustrate how dynamic uncertainty adjustments safeguard staffing trajectories against extreme demand surges at the micro-level.

The primary contribution of this work is methodological rather than purely predictive. It provides a structured, robust approach for embedding probabilistic clinical information into operational decision pipelines under structural constraints. Although demonstrated within an ICU setting, the core mechanism of adjusting demand signals via calibrated uncertainty to account for mobilization delays extends naturally to other resource allocation problems facing stochastic demand and response lags.

Several limitations guide future work. First, the staffing policy employs a forward sequential decision rule rather than a global mixed-integer optimization model. This prioritizes computational tractability and real-world deployability over theoretical global optimality. Second, our experimental setting assumes a homogeneous staffing pool and aggregate patient demand, abstracting away individual patient acuity levels and nurse-to-patient assignment constraints (e.g., continuity of care and specialized skill matching). Third, the study is retrospective and simulation-based. Although MIMIC-IV provides realistic ICU trajectories, the framework has not yet been evaluated in a live staffing workflow. A practical deployment would require local calibration of the prediction model, adaptation to hospital-specific staffing rules, silent evaluation against historical rosters, and prospective validation before clinical use. We therefore view the current system as a decision-support prototype rather than a directly deployable staffing tool. Future research should explore the framework's integration with global optimization schedulers, accommodate multi-day scheduling with heterogeneous staff skills and patient-specific acuity rules, and investigate adaptive mechanisms to correct predictive bias in real time. Despite these simplifications, this study bridges the gap between probabilistic clinical prediction and operational ICU staffing.

Data and Code Availability

The MIMIC-IV dataset used in this study is available on PhysioNet [16]: https://physionet.org/content/mimiciv/3.1/. To facilitate reproducibility, the code is available at https://github.com/jiaya12/uncertainty-aware-icu-staffing.

References

1. Bates, D.W., Saria, S., Ohno-Machado, L., Shah, A., Escobar, G.: Big data in health care: using analytics to identify and manage high-risk and high-cost patients. Health Aff. **33**(7), 1123–1131 (2014)
2. Bertsimas, D., Kallus, N.: From predictive to prescriptive analytics. Manage. Sci. **66**(3), 1025–1044 (2020)
3. Burke, E.K., De Causmaecker, P., Vanden Berghe, G., Van Landeghem, H.: The state of the art of nurse rostering. J. Sched. **7**(6), 441–499 (2004)
4. Churpek, M.M., Yuen, T.C., Winslow, C., Meltzer, D.O., Kattan, M.W., Edelson, D.P.: Multicenter comparison of machine learning methods and conventional regression for predicting clinical deterioration on the wards. Crit. Care Med. **44**(2), 368–374 (2016)
5. Davis, J., Goadrich, M.: The relationship between precision-recall and ROC curves. In: Proceedings of the 23rd International Conference on Machine Learning, pp. 233–240 (2006)
6. De Pater, I., Reijns, A., Mitici, M.: Alarm-based predictive maintenance scheduling for aircraft engines with imperfect remaining useful life prognostics. Reliability Eng. Syst. Saf. **221**, 108341 (2022)
7. Defraeye, M., Van Nieuwenhuyse, I.: Staffing and scheduling under nonstationary demand for service: a literature review. Omega **58**, 4–25 (2016)
8. Elmachtoub, A.N., Grigas, P.: Smart 'predict, then optimize'. Manage. Sci. **68**(1), 9–26 (2022)
9. Ernst, A.T., Jiang, H., Krishnamoorthy, M., Sier, D.: Staff scheduling and rostering: a review of applications, methods and models. Eur. J. Oper. Res. **153**(1), 3–27 (2004)
10. Fawcett, T.: An introduction to ROC analysis. Pattern Recogn. Lett. **27**(8), 861–874 (2006)
11. Finlayson, S.G., et al.: The clinician and dataset shift in artificial intelligence. N. Engl. J. Med. **385**, 283–286 (2021)
12. Green, L.V., Kolesar, P.J., Whitt, W.: Coping with time-varying demand when setting staffing requirements. Prod. Oper. Manag. **16**(1), 13–39 (2007)
13. van der Haar, J.F., Drent, C., Boute, R.N.: Predict-and-optimize machine learning for feature-based maintenance optimization (2024). SSRN: https://ssrn.com/abstract=5225643
14. Harutyunyan, H., Khachatrian, H., Kale, D.C., et al.: Multitask learning and benchmarking with clinical time series data. Sci. Data **6**(1), 96 (2019)
15. Huang, Y., Yang, Z., Rahmani, A.M.: MIMIC-Sepsis: a curated benchmark for modeling and learning from sepsis trajectories in the ICU. In: Proc. IEEE-EMBS International Conference on Biomedical and Health Informatics (2025)
16. Johnson, A.E.W., Bulgarelli, L., Shen, L., et al.: MIMIC-IV, a freely accessible electronic health record dataset. Sci. Data **10**(1), 1–14 (2023)
17. Kim, S., Mehrotra, S.: A two-stage stochastic integer programming approach to integrated staffing. Oper. Res. **63**(6), 1431–1451 (2015)
18. Kotary, J., Fioretto, F., Van Hentenryck, P., Wilder, B.: End-to-end constrained optimization learning: a survey. In: Proceedings of the Thirtieth International Joint Conference on Artificial Intelligence, pp. 4475–4482 (2021)
19. Moor, M., Bennet, N., Plecko, D., et al.: Predicting sepsis using deep learning across international sites. eClinical Med. **24**, 100428 (2020)

20. Nemati, S., Holder, A., Razmi, F., Stanley, M.D., Clifford, G.D., Buchman, T.G.: An interpretable machine learning model for accurate prediction of sepsis in the ICU. Crit. Care Med. **46**(4), 547–553 (2018)
21. Rajkomar, A., Oren, E., Chen, K., et al.: Scalable and accurate deep learning with electronic health records. npj Digital Med. **1**(1), 18 (2018)
22. Royal College of Physicians: National Early Warning Score (NEWS): Standardising the assessment of acute-illness severity in the NHS. Royal College of Physicians London (2012)
23. Saville, C., Griffiths, P., Ball, J., Monks, J.: How many nurses do we need? a review and discussion of operational research techniques applied to nurse staffing. Int. J. Nurs. Stud. **97**, 7–13 (2019)
24. Sendak, M.P., et al.: Presenting machine learning model information to clinical end users with model facts labels. npj Digital Med. **3**, 41 (2020)
25. Shah, S., Wang, K., Wilder, B., Perrault, A., Tambe, M.: Decision-focused learning without decision-making: learning locally optimized decision losses. Adv. Neural. Inf. Process. Syst. **35**, 1320–1332 (2022)
26. Shickel, B., Tighe, P.J., Bihorac, A., Rashidi, P.: Deep EHR: a survey of recent advances in deep learning techniques for electronic health record (EHR) analysis. IEEE J. Biomed. Health Inform. **22**(5), 1589–1604 (2017)
27. Subbe, C.P., Kruger, M., Rutherford, P., Gemmel, L.: Validation of a modified early warning score in medical admissions. QJM: Int. J. Med. **94**(10), 521–526 (2001)
28. Wiens, J., et al.: Do no harm: a roadmap for responsible machine learning for health care. Nat. Med. **25**(9), 1337–1340 (2019)
29. Wu, E., Wu, K., Daneshjou, R., Ouyang, D., Ho, D.E., Zou, J.: How medical AI devices are evaluated: limitations and recommendations from an analysis of FDA approvals. Nat. Med. **27**(4), 582–584 (2021)

Heterogeneity-Aware Dynamic Pricing for On-Demand Service via Graph-Fused Multi-agent Reinforcement Learning

Hai Wang[1,2], Xiaolei Zhou[1,2](✉), Xinyao Xu[1,2], and Kun Ding[1,2]

[1] The Sixty-third Research Institute, National University of Defense Technology, Nanjing, China
{haiwang,zhouxiaolei,xuxinyao24,dingkun18}@nudt.edu.cn

[2] National Key Laboratory of Big Data and Decision, Changsha, China

Abstract. Dynamic pricing plays a central role in on-demand service platforms by balancing supply and demand, improving resource utilization, and enhancing operational revenue. However, large-scale service networks exhibit heterogeneous agent capabilities, spatially coupled demand, and rapidly evolving market conditions, making effective pricing a challenging sequential decision problem. Existing approaches often rely on simplified optimization models or homogeneous learning policies, which struggle to capture agent-specific behavior and spatial interactions in real-world service systems. In this paper, we propose **GFMRL**, a Graph-Fused Multi-Agent Reinforcement Learning framework for heterogeneity-aware dynamic pricing in on-demand service platforms. We model the service network as a graph-structured multi-agent system and enable scalable coordination through centralized training with decentralized execution. Specifically, a graph attention module captures spatial dependencies among agents, while a heterogeneity-aware policy generator learns personalized pricing strategies from agent-specific operational states. To reduce the dimensionality of large-scale joint state-action spaces, we further introduce a graph fusion module that compresses multi-agent representations into a compact global representation. A transformer-based centralized critic is then used to model system-level dependencies and improve credit assignment during policy learning. Experiments conducted in a trace-driven environment calibrated from large-scale operational logs of a logistics platform show that GFMRL consistently outperforms representative optimization-based and MARL-based baselines in revenue, fulfillment, and service satisfaction.

Keywords: Heterogeneity-Aware Dynamic Pricing · On-Demand Service · Multi-Agent Reinforcement Learning

1 Introduction

Dynamic pricing has become a core operational mechanism in on-demand service platforms, where service providers must continuously balance supply, demand,

M. Ceci et al. (Eds.): ECML PKDD 2026, LNAI 16948, pp. 306–323, 2027.
https://doi.org/10.1007/978-3-032-37679-4_18

and service quality under highly dynamic market conditions. In logistics, ride-hailing, and other spatially distributed service systems, the price offered for a request directly influences whether service agents are willing to accept tasks, how quickly requests are fulfilled, and how effectively resources are allocated across regions. Unlike static pricing, dynamic pricing must respond to stochastic request arrivals, heterogeneous agent capacities, and rapidly changing local market conditions in real time. These challenges are particularly pronounced in large-scale service networks, where pricing decisions made by one agent may affect neighboring agents through competition for overlapping requests and shared demand pools. As a result, dynamic pricing in on-demand platforms is not merely an isolated per-request decision problem, but a large-scale sequential coordination problem that requires jointly modeling agent heterogeneity, spatial interaction, and long-term system performance.

Current dynamic pricing research falls into two categories. Traditional optimization methods like dynamic programming [11,23], genetic algorithms [21], and game theory [4,32] offer solid theoretical foundations but often rely on unrealistic assumptions and struggle with real-world complexities [18,37]. Reinforcement Learning (RL) methods [1,11,13,30] are gaining attention for their adaptability, as they allow an agent to learn an optimal pricing strategy by interacting with the environment. However, existing approaches often assume homogeneous agent behavior, model only local or loosely coupled interactions, and struggle to scale when the joint state-action space becomes large.

This work views large-scale dynamic pricing in on-demand services as a heterogeneity-aware, graph-structured sequential decision problem. Pricing decisions are interdependent, shaped by agent heterogeneity (e.g., location, capacity, and task history), spatial competition for overlapping requests, and system-wide supply–demand dynamics. These factors necessitate joint modeling of personalized agent behavior, structured local interactions, and global coordination. Key challenges include: (1) agent heterogeneity, which precludes a one-size-fits-all policy; (2) spatial coupling, where nearby agents' pricing choices mutually affect task acceptance; (3) scalability, as the joint action space explodes with agent count, overwhelming conventional multi-agent reinforcement learning; and (4) the need to capture long-range dependencies, such as cascading shortages or demand surges, to optimize long-term system performance.

To address these challenges, we propose **Graph-Fused Multi-Agent Reinforcement Learning (GFMRL)**, a scalable MARL framework for heterogeneity-aware dynamic pricing in on-demand service platforms. GFMRL follows the paradigm of centralized training with decentralized execution. At the agent level, we design a heterogeneity-aware policy generator that leverages recurrent representations to encode each agent's temporal operational state and produce customized pricing actions. To model inter-agent dependencies, we construct a dynamic interaction graph and employ a graph attention mechanism to aggregate spatially relevant neighbor information. To address the curse of dimensionality in large-scale MARL, we further introduce a graph fusion module that compresses high-dimensional multi-agent observations into a compact yet informative global representation. On top of this representation, we design a transformer-based centralized critic to capture long-range dependencies and improve global credit assignment during policy learning. By integrating graph-based local interaction modeling with global representation learning, GFMRL enables coordinated and scalable pricing decisions while maintaining efficient decentralized execution at inference time.

Our contributions are summarized as follows.

- We formulate dynamic pricing in on-demand service systems as a heterogeneity-aware and graph-structured cooperative MARL problem, emphasizing that effective pricing requires jointly modeling agent-specific operating conditions, spatial interdependence, and system-level supply-demand coordination.
- We propose GFMRL, a scalable framework that integrates heterogeneity-aware recurrent policy generation, graph-based interaction modeling, graph-fused state compression, and a transformer-based centralized critic within a unified centralized-training-decentralized-execution architecture.
- We conduct experiments in a trace-driven environment built from large-scale operational logs collected from two city markets of a logistics platform. The results demonstrate consistent improvements over representative baselines, while ablation studies verify the contribution of the heterogeneity encoder, graph interaction module, graph fusion module, and transformer critic.

2 Problem Formulation

We consider an on-demand service platform with a set of service agents $\mathcal{N} = 1, \ldots, n$ and a stream of geographically distributed customer requests. At each decision step t, the platform observes a set of incoming requests $\mathcal{Q}_t$. Each request $q \in \mathcal{Q}_t$ is associated with a location l_q, a base service price p_q^{base}, a workload requirement $w_{t,i,q}$ if served by agent i, and a service deadline. Each agent i has a location c_t^i, a current workload w_t^i, a maximum service capacity W_i, and a feasible request set $\mathcal{Q}_t^i \subseteq \mathcal{Q}_t$.

We formulate dynamic pricing as a cooperative multi-agent Markov decision process $\langle \mathcal{N}, \mathcal{S}, \mathcal{O}, \mathcal{A}, \mathcal{P}, r, \gamma \rangle$. The global state $s_t \in \mathcal{S}$ contains the platform-level operating status, including agent locations, workloads, capacities, and current requests. Each agent observes a local observation $\mathbf{o}_t^i = \{\mathbf{c}_t^i, w_t^i, W_i, \mathcal{Q}_t^i, \mathcal{N}_t^i\}$, where $\mathcal{N}_t^i$ denotes the neighboring agents that may compete or cooperate with agent i through overlapping feasible requests. For each feasible agent-request pair (i, q), the policy outputs a pricing multiplier $a_{t,i,q} \in [0, \lambda]$, and the final incentive price is computed as $p_{t,i,q} = a_{t,i,q} \cdot p_q^{base}$.

When a compact action representation is used, a_t^i denotes the vector of pricing multipliers over all requests in $\mathcal{Q}_t^i$.

The reward at time step t combines normalized revenue, customer satisfaction, and fulfillment success:

$$r_t = \sum_{q \in \mathcal{Q}_t} (\bar{v}_{t,q} + \alpha \bar{m}_{t,q} + \beta u_{t,q}) \tag{1}$$

where $\bar{v}_{t,q} \in [0, 1]$ is the normalized revenue obtained from request q, $\bar{m}_{t,q} \in [0, 1]$ is the normalized customer satisfaction score, and $u_{t,q} \in 0, 1$ indicates whether request q is successfully fulfilled within the operational constraints. The coefficients α and β balance satisfaction and fulfillment relative to revenue.

The objective is to learn a joint policy $\pi = \{\pi_1, \ldots, \pi_n\}$ that maximizes the expected discounted cumulative reward:

$$\begin{aligned} &\max_{\pi} \; \mathbb{E}_{\pi} \left[\sum_{t=0}^{T} \gamma^t r_t \right] \\ &\text{s.t.} \quad \sum_{q \in \mathcal{Q}t} x_{t,i,q} w_{t,i,q} \leq W_i, \quad \forall i \in \mathcal{N}. \end{aligned} \tag{2}$$

where $x_{t,i,q} \in 0, 1$ indicates whether request q is assigned to agent i. This formulation captures the sequential nature of pricing decisions, the heterogeneity of service agents, and the spatial coupling among agents that share overlapping request pools.

3 Methodology

3.1 System Overview

We propose a novel framework named **Graph-Fused Multi-Agent Reinforcement Learning (GFMRL)** to address dynamic pricing in large-scale on-demand service systems. Dynamic pricing in spatial service platforms involves complex interactions among heterogeneous service agents. Pricing decisions made by one agent can affect the behavior of nearby agents through competition for requests and shared service demand. At the same time, large-scale systems introduce significant challenges in coordination and scalability.

GFMRL addresses these challenges through three key design principles. First, we introduce a heterogeneity-aware policy generation mechanism that allows agents with different workloads, locations, and service capacities to learn customized pricing strategies. Second, we model inter-agent dependencies using a graph attention network, enabling agents to adapt their decisions based on spatially relevant neighbors. Third, we design a graph-fused global representation that compresses the high-dimensional joint state-action space and feeds it into a transformer-based centralized critic, allowing the system to capture long-range dependencies across the service network (Fig. 1).

3.2 Heterogeneity-Aware Agent Representation

In on-demand service platforms, service agents exhibit substantial heterogeneity in their operational states, including location, workload, and service history.

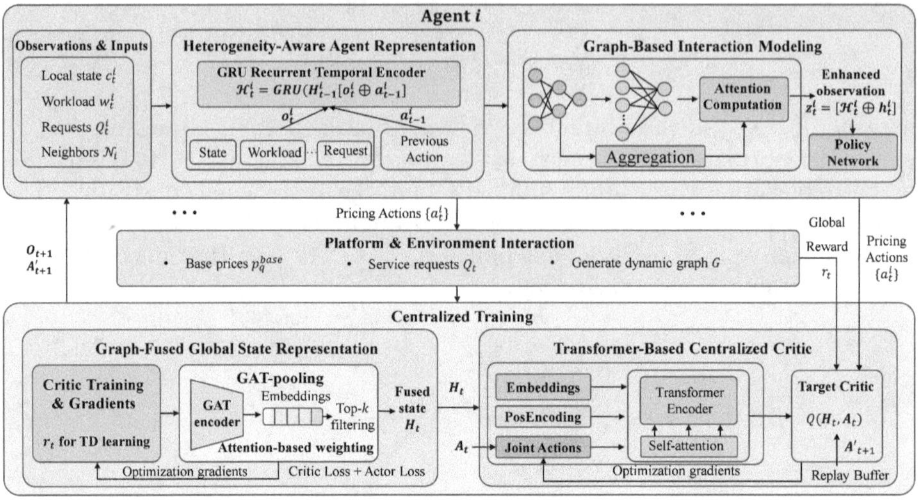

Fig. 1. Overview of the proposed *GFMRL* framework.

These differences lead to heterogeneous pricing behaviors and require individualized decision policies. Service agents differ significantly in their operational conditions, making it difficult for a single shared policy to capture diverse pricing preferences across agents.

To capture agent-specific temporal operating patterns, we maintain a recurrent hidden representation for each agent. For agent i, the hidden state $\mathbf{H}_t^i$ summarizes its historical observations and previous pricing decisions. At time step t, the recurrent state is updated by

$$\mathbf{H}_t^i = \text{GRU}\left(\mathbf{H}_{t-1}^i, \left[\mathbf{o}_t^i \oplus a_{t-1}^i\right]\right) \tag{3}$$

where $\mathbf{o}_t^i$ is the current local observation, a_{t-1}^i is the previous pricing multiplier, and $\oplus$ denotes vector concatenation. This recurrent representation enables the policy network to capture temporal dependencies such as workload accumulation, local demand fluctuation, and historical pricing responses.

3.3 Graph-Based Interaction Modeling

Service agents operating in spatially overlapping regions interact through competition and cooperation for service requests. Such interactions are inherently structured by geographic proximity and workload distribution. In spatially distributed service systems, pricing decisions of one agent may influence nearby agents competing for the same requests, creating complex spatial dependencies that must be explicitly modeled.

To model spatial dependencies among agents, we represent the service network at time step t as a dynamic agent interaction graph $G_t = (\mathcal{N}, \mathcal{E}_t)$. Each node corresponds to a service agent. An edge is created between agents i and

j when they share at least one reachable request, or equivalently when their service coverage overlaps around current demand:

$$\delta_t^{ij} = \begin{cases} 1, & \exists q \in \mathcal{Q}_t \text{ s.t. } d(\mathbf{c}_t^i, l_q) \leq \epsilon \text{ and } d(\mathbf{c}_t^j, l_q) \leq \epsilon \\ 0, & \text{otherwise} \end{cases} \tag{4}$$

Here $d(\cdot, \cdot)$ is the geographical distance function and ϵ denotes the service radius. This graph construction explicitly captures short-term spatial competition and cooperation caused by overlapping request pools. Request attributes are not treated as separate graph nodes; instead, they are included in each agent's local observation $\mathbf{o}_t^i$.

To capture heterogeneous interaction strength, we employ a graph attention mechanism. Let $\mathbf{g}_t^{ij} = f(\delta_t^{ij})$ denote the edge feature embedding. The attention logit between agents i and j is computed as

$$\ell_t^{ij} = \mathbf{v}^\top \tanh\left(\mathbf{W}_1\mathbf{H}_t^i + \mathbf{W}_2\mathbf{H}_t^j + \mathbf{W}_3\mathbf{g}_t^{ij}\right) \tag{5}$$

and the normalized attention weight is

$$\rho_t^{ij} = \frac{\exp(\ell_t^{ij})}{\sum_{k\in\mathcal{N}_t^i\cup i}\exp(\ell_t^{ik})} \tag{6}$$

The spatial interaction representation of agent i is then obtained by aggregating information from its graph neighbors:

$$\mathbf{h}_t^i = \sigma\left(\mathbf{W}_h \sum_{j\in\mathcal{N}_t^i\cup i} \rho_t^{ij}\left[\mathbf{H}_t^j \oplus \mathbf{g}_t^{ij}\right]\right) \tag{7}$$

Finally, the enhanced representation of agent i is defined as $\mathbf{z}_t^i = \left[\mathbf{H}_t^i \oplus \mathbf{h}_t^i\right]$ and the pricing action is generated by a shared policy network:

$$a_t^i = \lambda \cdot \sigma\left(\mathbf{W}_a\mathbf{z}_t^i + \mathbf{b}_a\right) \tag{8}$$

This design allows agents with different operating states to share policy parameters while still producing personalized pricing decisions conditioned on both their own temporal state and spatial interaction context.

3.4 Graph-Fused Global State Representation

In large-scale multi-agent systems, directly concatenating all agent observations leads to high-dimensional global states and poor scalability. Moreover, simple concatenation ignores the graph structure among agents. To address this issue, we introduce a graph fusion module that compresses agent-level representations into a compact global representation while preserving influential interaction patterns.

Let $\mathbf{Z}_t = [\mathbf{z}_t^1; \mathbf{z}_t^2; \ldots; \mathbf{z}_t^n] \in \mathbb{R}^{n \times d_z}$ denote the matrix of enhanced agent representations. We first apply a graph encoder to obtain structurally enriched embeddings:

$$\mathbf{X}_t = \mathrm{GAT}_{pool}(\mathbf{Z}_t, G_t), \quad \mathbf{X}_t \in \mathbb{R}^{n \times d_x} \tag{9}$$

A learnable projection vector $\mathbf{m} \in \mathbb{R}^{d_x}$ assigns an importance score to each agent: $\mathbf{y}_t = \mathbf{X}_t \mathbf{m}$

We then select the top-k most influential agents according to their projection scores:

$$(\mathcal{I}_t, \mathbf{y}_t^k) = \mathrm{TopK}(\mathbf{y}_t, k), \quad \mathbf{X}_t^k = \mathbf{X}_t[\mathcal{I}_t] \tag{10}$$

The selected embeddings are weighted by normalized importance scores:

$$\widetilde{\mathbf{X}}_t = \mathbf{X}_t^k \odot \mathrm{softmax}(\mathbf{y}_t^k) \tag{11}$$

where $\odot$ denotes element-wise multiplication with broadcasting. The compact global representation is computed by combining sum pooling and max pooling:

$$\bar{\mathbf{H}}_t = \left[\sum_{i \in \mathcal{I}_t} \widetilde{\mathbf{x}}_t^i \oplus \max_{i \in \mathcal{I}_t} \widetilde{\mathbf{x}}_t^i \right] \tag{12}$$

This graph-fused representation reduces the dimensionality of the joint state while preserving the most influential local interaction structures. Compared with direct concatenation, the proposed fusion module provides a more scalable representation for centralized critic learning.

3.5 Transformer-Based Centralized Critic

While graph attention captures local spatial dependencies, dynamic pricing may also involve system-level dependencies across distant regions. For example, a demand surge in one area may attract service agents from neighboring areas and cause cascading supply imbalances. To model such long-range dependencies, we use a transformer-based centralized critic during training.

Let $\mathbf{A}_t = [a_t^1, a_t^2, \ldots, a_t^n]$ denote the joint pricing action of all agents, and let $\bar{\mathbf{H}}_t$ denote the graph-fused global representation. To construct the critic input, we build a state-action token for each agent by combining its enhanced representation, its pricing action, and the graph-fused global context:

$$\mathbf{e}_t^i = \phi_e \left(\mathbf{z}_t^i \oplus \phi_a(a_t^i) \oplus \phi_g(\bar{\mathbf{H}}_t) \right) + \mathbf{p}_i \tag{13}$$

where $\phi_a(\cdot)$, $\phi_g(\cdot)$, and $\phi_e(\cdot)$ are learnable projection functions, $\mathbf{p}_i$ is the positional or agent-index embedding, and $\oplus$ denotes vector concatenation. The complete critic input sequence is $\mathbf{E}_t = [\mathbf{e}_t^1; \mathbf{e}_t^2; \ldots; \mathbf{e}_t^n]$

The centralized action-value function is estimated by applying self-attention over the multi-agent state-action sequence:

$$Q_\psi(\bar{\mathbf{H}}_t, \mathbf{Z}_t, \mathbf{A}_t) = \mathbf{w}_Q^\top \text{Pool}\left(\text{Transformer}_\psi(\mathbf{E}_t)\right) + b_Q \tag{14}$$

where $\mathbf{Z}_t = [\mathbf{z}_t^1; \ldots; \mathbf{z}_t^n]$, Pool$(\cdot)$ denotes sequence-level pooling over transformer outputs, and ψ denotes the critic parameters.

The critic is trained by temporal-difference learning. The next-step target action is generated by the target actors:

$$\mathbf{A}'_{t+1} = [\mu_{\theta'_1}(\mathbf{z}_{t+1}^1), \mu_{\theta'_2}(\mathbf{z}_{t+1}^2), \ldots, \mu_{\theta'_n}(\mathbf{z}_{t+1}^n)] \tag{15}$$

The TD target is computed as

$$y_t = \text{sg}\left[r_t + \gamma(1 - d_t) Q_{\psi'}(\bar{\mathbf{H}}_{t+1}, \mathbf{Z}_{t+1}, \mathbf{A}'_{t+1})\right] \tag{16}$$

where $Q_{\psi'}$ is the target critic, $d_t \in \{0, 1\}$ is the terminal indicator, and sg$[\cdot]$ denotes the stop-gradient operation. The critic loss is

$$\mathcal{L}(\psi) = \mathbb{E}\left[\left(Q_\psi(\bar{\mathbf{H}}_t, \mathbf{Z}_t, \mathbf{A}_t) - y_t\right)^2\right] \tag{17}$$

The actor is optimized by deterministic policy gradient. For agent i, the policy gradient is

$$\nabla_{\theta_i} J \approx \mathbb{E}\left[\nabla_{\theta_i} \mu_{\theta_i}(\mathbf{z}_t^i) \nabla_{a_t^i} Q_\psi(\bar{\mathbf{H}}_t, \mathbf{Z}_t, \mathbf{A}_t)\Big|_{a_t^i = \mu_{\theta_i}(\mathbf{z}_t^i)}\right] \tag{18}$$

Equivalently, the joint actor objective can be written as

$$\nabla_\theta J \approx \mathbb{E}\left[\sum_{i=1}^{n} \nabla_{\theta_i} \mu_{\theta_i}(\mathbf{z}_t^i) \nabla_{a_t^i} Q_\psi(\bar{\mathbf{H}}_t, \mathbf{Z}_t, \mathbf{A}_t)\right] \tag{19}$$

The centralized critic is used only during training. During execution, each agent generates its pricing action using its local observation, recurrent state, and graph-based neighbor information. Therefore, the proposed method remains consistent with the centralized-training-decentralized-execution paradigm.

4 Experiments

4.1 Data Description

We evaluate GFMRL using a trace-driven environment calibrated from operational logs of a large on-demand logistics platform. The logs cover two city markets in China, Beijing and Chengdu, which represent different urban density and demand patterns. The dataset contains 20 service hubs, 294 service agents, 1,020,466 delivery tasks, and 91,157 on-demand requests. The raw records include task tracking logs, agent trajectories, request attributes, base prices, deadlines, and agent behavior records.

The historical logs are not used to train pricing policies by supervised imitation. Instead, they are used to calibrate the environment dynamics, including empirical request arrival patterns, spatial demand distribution, workload requirements, service deadlines, initial agent states, and capacity constraints. During training and evaluation, each pricing policy interacts with the same calibrated environment and replaces the historical pricing decisions with its own actions. The environment then updates request assignment, workload, fulfillment status, satisfaction, and revenue according to the state-action-reward interface defined in Sect. 2.

Due to commercial and privacy constraints, the raw operational logs cannot be publicly released. Therefore, the released implementation provides a lightweight synthetic generator with the same observation space, action space, graph construction rule, reward definition, and training pipeline. The synthetic generator is intended for implementation verification and reproducibility of the algorithmic pipeline, while the numerical results reported in this paper are obtained from the proprietary trace-driven environment calibrated from real platform logs.

4.2 Experimental Setup

Implementation Details. We implement GFMRL and all ablation variants using PyTorch 2.0 with Python 3.10. For each city market, the logs are split chronologically into training, validation, and test partitions with a ratio of 70%/10%/20%. The validation split is used for hyperparameter selection, and the test split is used only for final reporting. All methods are trained and evaluated under the same environment dynamics, action space, reward function, and capacity constraints. Unless otherwise specified, we report the mean and standard deviation over five independent random seeds.

The Adam optimizer is used with a learning rate of 3×10^{-4}, a batch size of 64, and an experience replay buffer of size 5×10^4. The discount factor γ is set to 0.99, and each episode contains 50 decision steps. The reward coefficients are fixed as $\alpha = 0.6$ and $\beta = 0.4$ for all methods. The graph interaction module adopts a two-layer GATv2 encoder with four attention heads and hidden dimension 128. The heterogeneity-aware policy generator uses a one-layer GRU with hidden dimension 128. The centralized critic employs a two-layer Transformer encoder with four attention heads, embedding dimension 128, and feed-forward dimension 256. During online execution, the centralized critic and replay buffer are not required; each agent only uses the learned actor with local observation and graph-based neighbor information.

Baselines. We compare GFMRL with representative baselines from different methodological categories. SDP [23] is an optimization-based stochastic dynamic programming method, and EA [21] is a search-based evolutionary algorithm. These two methods represent non-RL pricing strategies. For RL and MARL baselines, MADDPG [22] is a centralized-training-decentralized-execution actor-critic method for continuous multi-agent control; ATOC [15] models attentional communication among agents; HAMA [27] introduces hierarchical graph attention for multi-agent coordination; and MAGC [35] is a graph-based multi-agent reinforcement learning method for dynamic pricing. All baselines are adapted to the same observation space, action range, reward definition, and capacity constraints for fair comparison. Since public benchmarks for on-demand logistics pricing are limited, our comparison aims to cover representative optimization-based, communication-based, graph-based, and MARL-based pricing strategies rather than exhaustively covering all possible pricing methods.

Metrics. To comprehensively evaluate our model, we adopt four key metrics commonly used in on-demand service evaluation:

- **Average Service Revenue (ASR)** measures the average normalized revenue per arrived request. Unfulfilled requests contribute zero revenue.
- **Customer Satisfaction Rate (CSR)** measures the average normalized satisfaction score over all requests. The score is computed from response timeliness and service-quality-related factors and is scaled to $[0, 1]$.
- **Fulfillment Success Rate (FSR)** is the ratio of successfully fulfilled requests to all arrived requests.
- **Fulfillment Timeliness Rate (FTR)** measures the proportion of requests completed within their specified service time windows.

4.3 Experimental Results

Overall Performance. Table 1 and Table 2 report the overall performance of *GFMRL* compared with several baseline methods.

(1) MARL-based approaches consistently outperform traditional optimization methods such as SDP and EA. This result indicates that modeling dynamic pricing as a sequential decision-making problem with cooperative agents leads to better system-level outcomes. By optimizing long-term rewards rather than myopic objectives, MARL methods enable agents to coordinate pricing strategies over time, resulting in improved operational efficiency and service quality.

Table 1. Overall performance on **Beijing**.

Methods	Beijing City			
	ASR	CSR	FSR	FTR
SDP	0.781 ± 0.024	0.960 ± 0.015	0.901 ± 0.018	0.863 ± 0.017
EA	0.783 ± 0.028	0.956 ± 0.021	0.903 ± 0.020	0.859 ± 0.018
MADDPG	0.785 ± 0.019	0.957 ± 0.022	0.906 ± 0.023	0.876 ± 0.022
ATOC	0.791 ± 0.025	0.961 ± 0.016	0.911 ± 0.013	0.889 ± 0.010
HAMA	0.813 ± 0.017	0.964 ± 0.011	0.914 ± 0.012	0.898 ± 0.010
MAGC	0.831 ± 0.016	0.978 ± 0.015	0.932 ± 0.006	0.903 ± 0.007
GFMRL	**0.879 ± 0.012**	**0.994 ± 0.005**	**0.961 ± 0.007**	**0.953 ± 0.010**

Table 2. Overall performance on **Chengdu**.

Methods	Chengdu City			
	ASR	CSR	FSR	FTR
SDP	0.790 ± 0.020	0.958 ± 0.013	0.905 ± 0.011	0.865 ± 0.015
EA	0.786 ± 0.024	0.963 ± 0.012	0.907 ± 0.015	0.848 ± 0.019
MADDPG	0.786 ± 0.020	0.966 ± 0.007	0.912 ± 0.013	0.883 ± 0.016
ATOC	0.790 ± 0.016	0.958 ± 0.015	0.909 ± 0.017	0.888 ± 0.014
HAMA	0.811 ± 0.007	0.961 ± 0.011	0.917 ± 0.014	0.898 ± 0.015
MAGC	0.832 ± 0.008	0.974 ± 0.009	0.928 ± 0.009	0.901 ± 0.011
GFMRL	**0.880 ± 0.009**	**0.995 ± 0.011**	**0.957 ± 0.006**	**0.949 ± 0.007**

(2) *GFMRL* achieves the best performance across all evaluation metrics. Compared with MAGC, the strongest baseline in Table 1 and Table 2, GFMRL improves the average ASR, CSR, FSR, and FTR across the two city markets by approximately 5.77%, 1.90%, 3.12%, and 5.43%, respectively. These improvements indicate that the proposed framework can simultaneously enhance revenue-oriented and service-quality-oriented objectives. In particular, the gains in ASR and FTR suggest that the learned pricing policies encourage more timely task acceptance and completion, while the improvements in CSR and FSR reflect better alignment between service supply and customer demand.

(3) *GFMRL* demonstrates consistent performance improvements on both Beijing and Chengdu. Since both city markets are collected from the same logistics platform, these results should be interpreted as within-platform validation across different urban demand patterns rather than full cross-platform generalization. Nevertheless, the stable improvements suggest that modeling agent heterogeneity and spatial interactions is beneficial under different city-level operating conditions.

(4) Compared with MAGC, the strongest MARL baseline, *GFMRL* achieves consistently higher performance across all metrics. This advantage can be attributed to the integrated design of the proposed framework. By combining heterogeneity-aware policy learning, graph-based interaction modeling, and scalable global state representation, *GFMRL* is able to capture both local agent interactions and global system dynamics, leading to more effective and coordinated pricing decisions.

Ablation Study. To evaluate the contribution of each component in GFMRL, we conduct a series of ablation experiments. We compare the full GFMRL framework with four degraded variants: **w/o Heterogeneity Modeling**: removing the GRU-based agent representation and using a shared policy network. **w/o Graph Interaction**: replacing the graph attention module with a simple MLP encoder. **w/o Graph Fusion**: removing the graph pooling mechanism and

Table 3. Ablation study

Method	ASR	CSR	FSR	FTR
GFMRL	**0.879**	**0.994**	**0.961**	**0.953**
w/o Heterogeneity Modeling	0.821	0.952	0.923	0.897
w/o Graph Interaction	0.742	0.878	0.861	0.825
w/o Graph Fusion	0.827	0.961	0.927	0.901
w/o Transformer Critic	0.833	0.982	0.927	0.911

directly concatenating agent observations. **w/o Transformer Critic**: replacing the transformer critic with a standard MLP-based critic.

We conduct ablation experiments to analyze the contribution of each key component in *GFMRL*. Table 3 reports the performance of different variants. Several observations can be made. First, removing the heterogeneity-aware policy generator (**w/o Heterogeneity Modeling**) leads to a noticeable performance degradation across all metrics. This result highlights the importance of modeling agent-specific operational states, as service agents exhibit diverse workloads, locations, and service capacities. A shared policy fails to capture such diversity, resulting in less effective pricing decisions. Second, eliminating the graph interaction module (**w/o Graph Interaction**) significantly reduces system performance. Without explicitly modeling spatial dependencies among agents, the model cannot effectively account for competition and cooperation among nearby agents, leading to suboptimal pricing coordination in spatially coupled service environments. Third, removing the graph fusion module (**w/o Graph Fusion**) results in reduced performance and less stable learning. This finding indicates that directly concatenating multi-agent observations fails to provide an effective global representation in large-scale environments, while the proposed graph fusion mechanism helps capture critical interaction structures while mitigating the curse of dimensionality. Finally, replacing the transformer-based critic with a standard MLP critic (**w/o Transformer Critic**) also leads to performance degradation. This suggests that the transformer architecture improves global credit assignment by capturing long-range dependencies among agents and system-level dynamics that are difficult to model using conventional critics.

Impact of Factors. To further understand the behavior of different pricing strategies under varying operational conditions, we analyze the impact of two key factors: the time of day and the number of available service agents.

Impact of Time of Day. Figures 2 and 3 present the performance of different methods across different time periods of the day. *GFMRL* consistently outperforms competing baselines, especially during high-demand periods. In these periods, service requests arrive more frequently and competition among agents becomes more intense, making pricing decisions more dependent on spatial interactions and real-time system dynamics. By combining graph-based interaction

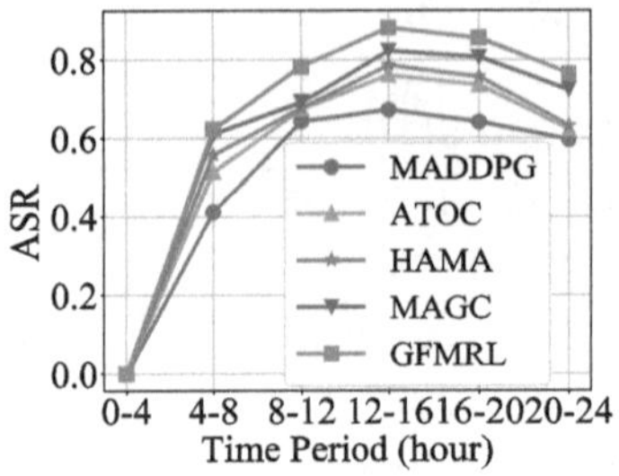

Fig. 2. ASR across different time periods

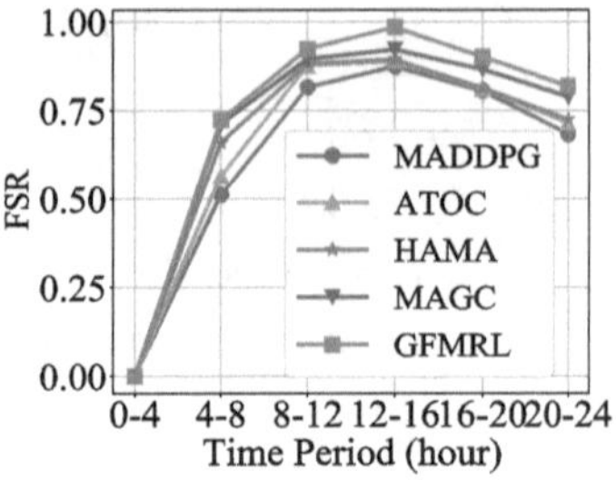

Fig. 3. FSR cross different time period

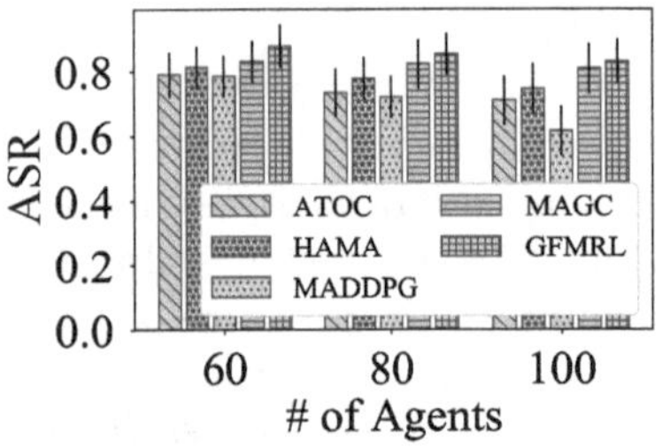

Fig. 4. The ASR with Different Number of Agents

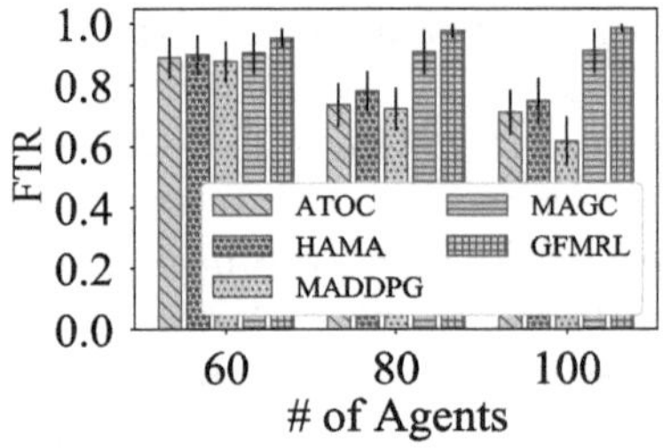

Fig. 5. The FTR with Different Number of Agents

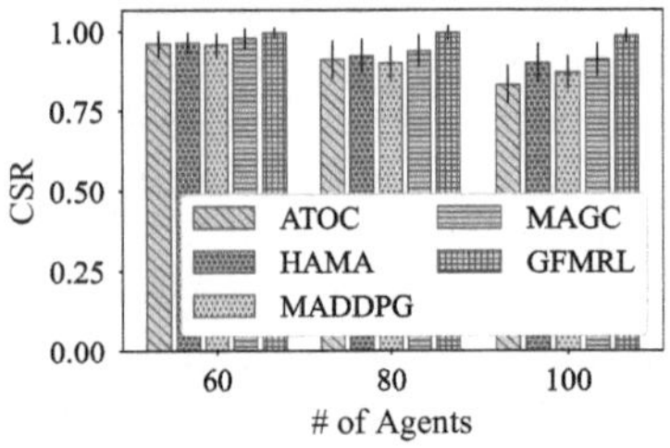

Fig. 6. The CSR with Different Number of Agents

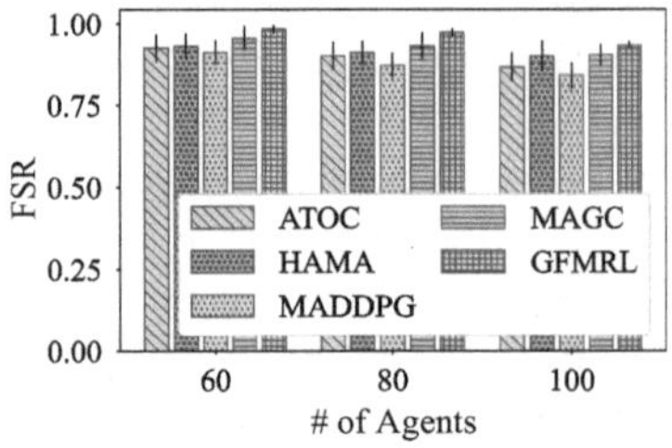

Fig. 7. The FSR with Different Number of Agents

modeling with heterogeneity-aware policy learning, *GFMRL* achieves higher ASR and FSR across time periods, indicating that it can adapt pricing decisions to dynamic demand conditions more effectively than the baselines.

Impact of the Number of Agents. Figures 4, 5, 6, and 7 illustrate the performance of *GFMRL* and baseline methods as the number of agents increases from 60 to 100. Overall, *GFMRL* maintains stable performance across different agent scales, indicating strong scalability in large multi-agent environments. As the number of agents increases, per-agent revenue gradually decreases while the customer satisfaction rate increases. This phenomenon reflects typical supply–

demand dynamics in service platforms: a larger agent pool improves service availability and reduces customer waiting time, but also intensifies competition among agents for available requests. Despite this increased competition, *GFMRL* continues to outperform baseline methods, suggesting that the proposed graph-based interaction modeling and global state representation help agents coordinate pricing decisions effectively even in larger systems.

4.4 Practical Implications and Limitations

The experimental results provide several practical insights for on-demand service pricing. First, heterogeneous agent states should be explicitly considered in pricing decisions. Agents with different workloads, capacities, and local demand conditions may require different pricing incentives, and a homogeneous pricing policy can lead to inefficient allocation. Second, spatial competition induced by overlapping service coverage is important. Agents that can serve the same request pool should not be priced independently, since their decisions jointly affect fulfillment and timeliness. Third, global training signals can improve decentralized online pricing. *GFMRL* uses a centralized critic only during training, while online execution relies on the learned actor and local graph-based information, which makes the framework compatible with practical platform deployment.

The current study also has several limitations. First, the real-data evaluation is based on one logistics platform and two city markets, which supports within-platform validation but does not fully establish cross-platform generalizability. Second, the current interaction graph is constructed from short-term request-overlap relationships and may not fully capture long-term strategic repositioning, driver incentives, or delayed behavioral responses. Third, *GFMRL* integrates recurrent encoding, graph attention, graph pooling, and a transformer critic, which increases engineering complexity compared with simpler pricing rules. Finally, the framework is empirically validated but does not provide formal convergence or optimality guarantees. Future work will investigate cross-platform validation, richer graph construction with long-term mobility and incentive signals, and more deployment-oriented cost analysis.

5 Related Work

Dynamic pricing has been extensively studied in logistics, transportation, and service platforms [2,3,5,8,12,16,28,38]. Existing approaches can be broadly categorized into optimization-based methods and RL-based methods.

5.1 Dynamic Pricing Approaches

Optimization-based Methods. Traditional dynamic pricing methods formulate the problem as a constrained optimization task [9,18,37]. A wide range of analytical techniques have been proposed, including linear programming [9], Lyapunov optimization [18], stochastic or dynamic programming [11,23], genetic algorithms [21], queuing theory [37], and game-theoretic models [4,32]. These approaches typically rely on explicit mathematical models of demand, supply, or market equilibrium. However, accurately modeling real-world on-demand service environments is challenging due to stochastic demand patterns, spatial heterogeneity, and dynamic agent behavior. As a result, optimization-based methods often suffer from limited adaptability and high computational complexity, making it difficult to deploy them in large-scale real-time systems.

RL-Based Methods. To address the limitations of model-based approaches, RL has been widely adopted for dynamic pricing in stochastic environments [6,7,24,29]. These methods learn pricing policies through interactions with the environment and can adapt to changing market conditions. RL-based pricing strategies have been applied to various domains, including EV charging revenue optimization [11,24,29], social welfare improvement [1,26], and profit maximization for cloud services [10]. More recently, MARL approaches have been explored to manage multiple service stations or distributed resources [19,33], and policy-gradient algorithms have been used for large-scale pricing and resource allocation problems [17]. Despite these advances, existing RL-based approaches often struggle with scalability in large networks due to the rapidly increasing state-action space. Moreover, many studies assume homogeneous agents or overlook the complex spatial interactions among service providers.

5.2 Multi-agent Reinforcement Learning

Multi-agent reinforcement learning (MARL) extends single-agent RL to interactive settings, facing challenges like non-stationarity and credit assignment [34]. A prevalent paradigm—decentralized execution with centralized training [25], enables coordination via global information during training while using local observations at execution, with success in traffic control [31], ride-hailing [20], and EV recommendations [36]. However, many MARL methods employ shared policies or coarse agent aggregation, failing to capture structured dependencies in large-scale systems. Recent efforts integrate graph neural networks into MARL, modeling agents as nodes and using message passing or attention to encode spatial interactions [14], thereby enhancing coordination. Yet these approaches typically focus on local neighborhoods and fall short in handling large-scale dynamic pricing challenges, such as heterogeneous agent behaviors, high-dimensional global states, and long-range system dependencies.

6 Conclusion

In this paper, we studied dynamic pricing in large-scale on-demand service platforms, where heterogeneous service agents, spatially distributed demand, and rapidly changing market conditions make pricing a complex multi-agent decision problem. We proposed *GFMRL*, a graph-fused multi-agent reinforcement learning framework that combines personalized policy learning, graph-based interaction modeling, and compact global representation learning. Experiments in a trace-driven environment calibrated from operational logistics data show that *GFMRL* improves key operational metrics compared with representative optimization-based and MARL-based baselines. These results indicate the importance of jointly modeling agent heterogeneity, spatial competition, and global market dynamics for coordinated pricing. At the same time, the current study is based on data from a single platform and two city markets. Broader cross-platform validation, richer graph construction with long-term relocation incentives, and further analysis of deployment cost remain important directions for future work.

Acknowledgments. This work was supported by the National Natural Science Foundation of China (grant numbers 62502532, 72471236) and the Innovation Research Foundation of the National University of Defense Technology (grant number ZK25-99).

Disclosure of Interests. The authors have no competing interests to declare that are relevant to the content of this article.

References

1. Abdalrahman, A., Zhuang, W.: Dynamic pricing for differentiated pev charging services using deep reinforcement learning. IEEE Trans. Intell. Transp. Syst. **23**(2), 1415–1427 (2020)
2. Abdulaal, A., Polat, A., Narayan, H., Zeng, W., Yi, Y.: Dynamic pricing for multi-retailer delivery platforms with additive deep learning and evolutionary optimization. In: Proceedings of the 30th ACM SIGKDD Conference on Knowledge Discovery and Data Mining, pp. 4741–4751 (2024)
3. Ai, R., Simchi-Levi, D., Zhu, F.: Dynamic service fee pricing under strategic behavior: actions as instruments and phase transition. Adv. Neural. Inf. Process. Syst. **37**, 53525–53570 (2024)
4. Aujla, G.S., Kumar, N., Singh, M., Zomaya, A.Y.: Energy trading with dynamic pricing for electric vehicles in a smart city environment. J. Parallel Distributed Comput. **127**, 169–183 (2019)
5. Bae, S., Kulcsár, B., Gros, S.: Personalized dynamic pricing policy for electric vehicles: Reinforcement learning approach. Transp. Res. Part C: Emerg. Technol. **161**, 104540 (2024)
6. Brero, G., Eden, A., Gerstgrasser, M., Parkes, D., Rheingans-Yoo, D.: Reinforcement learning of sequential price mechanisms. In: Proceedings of the AAAI Conference on Artificial Intelligence, vol. 35, pp. 5219–5227 (2021)
7. Cai, Q., Filos-Ratsikas, A., Tang, P., Zhang, Y.: Reinforcement mechanism design for e-commerce. In: Proceedings of the 2018 World Wide Web Conference, pp. 1339–1348 (2018)
8. Chen, L., Shang, S., Yao, B., Li, J.: Pay your trip for traffic congestion: Dynamic pricing in traffic-aware road networks. In: Proceedings of the AAAI Conference on Artificial Intelligence, vol. 34, pp. 582–589 (2020)
9. Chen, Q., Wang, F., Hodge, B.M., Zhang, J., Li, Z., Shafie-Khah, M., Catalão, J.P.: Dynamic price vector formation model-based automatic demand response strategy for pv-assisted ev charging stations. IEEE Trans. Smart Grid **8**(6), 2903–2915 (2017)

10. Du, B., Wu, C., Huang, Z.: Learning resource allocation and pricing for cloud profit maximization. In: Proceedings of the AAAI conference on artificial intelligence, vol. 33, pp. 7570–7577 (2019)
11. Fang, C., Lu, H., Hong, Y., Liu, S., Chang, J.: Dynamic pricing for electric vehicle extreme fast charging. IEEE Trans. Intell. Transp. Syst. **22**(1), 531–541 (2020)
12. He, S., Shin, K.G.: Spatio-temporal adaptive pricing for balancing mobility-on-demand networks. ACM Trans. Intell. Syst. Technol. (TIST) **10**(4), 1–28 (2019)
13. Huang, J.: Deep reinforcement learning-based trajectory pricing on ride-hailing platforms. ACM Trans. Intell. Syst. Technol. (TIST) **13**(3), 1–19 (2022)
14. Jiang, J., Dun, C., Huang, T., Lu, Z.: Graph convolutional reinforcement learning, (2018). arXiv preprint arXiv:1810.09202
15. Jiang, J., Lu, Z.: Learning attentional communication for multi-agent cooperation. In: Advances in neural information processing systems, p. 31 (2018)
16. Jo, S., Lee, G.M., Moon, I.: Airline dynamic pricing with patient customers using deep exploration-based reinforcement learning. Eng. Appl. Artif. Intell. **133**, 108073 (2024)
17. Kavoosi, A., Tavakkoli-Moghaddam, R., Sajedi, H., Tajik, N., Tafakkori, K.: Dynamic pricing and inventory control of perishable products by a deep reinforcement learning algorithm. Expert Syst. Appl. **291**, 128570 (2025)
18. Kim, Y., Kwak, J., Chong, S.: Dynamic pricing, scheduling, and energy management for profit maximization in phev charging stations. IEEE Trans. Veh. Technol. **66**(2), 1011–1026 (2016)
19. Lee, S., Choi, D.H.: Dynamic pricing and energy management for profit maximization in multiple smart electric vehicle charging stations: A privacy-preserving deep reinforcement learning approach. Appl. Energy **304**, 117754 (2021)
20. Li, Y., Zheng, Y., Yang, Q.: Efficient and effective express via contextual cooperative reinforcement learning. In: Proceedings of the 25th ACM SIGKDD International Conference on Knowledge Discovery & Data Mining, pp. 510–519 (2019)
21. Limmer, S., Rodemann, T.: Peak load reduction through dynamic pricing for electric vehicle charging. Int. J. Electr. Power Energy Syst. **113**, 117–128 (2019)
22. Lowe, R., Wu, Y.I., Tamar, A., Harb, J., Pieter Abbeel, O., Mordatch, I.: Multi-agent actor-critic for mixed cooperative-competitive environments. Advances in neural information processing systems, p. 30 (2017)
23. Luo, C., Huang, Y.F., Gupta, V.: Stochastic dynamic pricing for ev charging stations with renewable integration and energy storage. IEEE Trans. Smart Grid **9**(2), 1494–1505 (2017)
24. Mrkos, J., Komenda, A., Jakob, M.: Revenue maximization for electric vehicle charging service providers using sequential dynamic pricing. In: AAMAS, pp. 832–840 (2018)
25. Niu, Y., Paleja, R.R., Gombolay, M.C.: Multi-agent graph-attention communication and teaming. AAMAS, pp. 964–973 (2021)
26. Qian, T., Shao, C., Li, X., Wang, X., Shahidehpour, M.: Enhanced coordinated operations of electric power and transportation networks via ev charging services. IEEE Trans. Smart Grid **11**(4), 3019–3030 (2020)
27. Ryu, H., Shin, H., Park, J.: Multi-agent actor-critic with hierarchical graph attention network. In: Proceedings of the AAAI Conference on Artificial Intelligence, vol. 34, pp. 7236–7243 (2020)
28. Streviniotis, E., Georgara, A., Bistaffa, F., Chalkiadakis, G.: Fairplay: a multi-sided fair dynamic pricing policy for hotels. In: Proceedings of the AAAI Conference on Artificial Intelligence, vol. 38, pp. 22368–22376 (2024)

29. Wang, S., Bi, S., Zhang, Y.A.: Reinforcement learning for real-time pricing and scheduling control in ev charging stations. IEEE Trans. Industr. Inf. **17**(2), 849–859 (2019)
30. Wang, Y., Tong, Y., Long, C., Xu, P., Xu, K., Lv, W.: Adaptive dynamic bipartite graph matching: A reinforcement learning approach. In: 2019 IEEE 35th International Conference on Data Engineering (ICDE), pp. 1478–1489. IEEE (2019)
31. Wei, H., et al.: Colight: learning network-level cooperation for traffic signal control. In: Proceedings of the 28th ACM International Conference on Information and Knowledge Management, pp. 1913–1922 (2019)
32. Xiong, Y., Gan, J., An, B., Miao, C., Soh, Y.C.: Optimal pricing for efficient electric vehicle charging station management. In: AAMAS, pp. 749–757 (2016)
33. Yan, Z., Xu, Y.: A multi-agent deep reinforcement learning method for cooperative load frequency control of a multi-area power system. IEEE Trans. Power Syst. **35**(6), 4599–4608 (2020)
34. Zhang, K., Yang, Z., Başar, T.: Multi-agent reinforcement learning: a selective overview of theories and algorithms. In: Handbook of Reinforcement Learning and Control, pp. 321–384 (2021)
35. Zhang, W., Liu, H., Han, J., Ge, Y., Xiong, H.: Multi-agent graph convolutional reinforcement learning for dynamic electric vehicle charging pricing. In: Proceedings of the 28th ACM SIGKDD Conference on Knowledge Discovery and Data Mining, pp. 2471–2481 (2022)
36. Zhang, W., et al.: Intelligent electric vehicle charging recommendation based on multi-agent reinforcement learning. In: Proceedings of the Web Conference 2021, pp. 1856–1867 (2021)
37. Zhang, Y., You, P., Cai, L.: Optimal charging scheduling by pricing for ev charging station with dual charging modes. IEEE Trans. Intell. Transp. Syst. **20**(9), 3386–3396 (2018)
38. Zhou, X., Cai, Y., Meng, Q., Ji, Y.: A user behavior and reinforcement learning based dynamic pricing method for idle connection time reduction at charging stations. Transp. Res. Part A: Policy Practice **192**, 104358 (2025)

Navigating Demand Uncertainty in Container Shipping: Deep Reinforcement Learning for Enabling Adaptive and Feasible Master Stowage Planning

Jaike van Twiller[1(✉)], Yossiri Adulyasak[2,3], Erick Delage[2,3,4], Djordje Grbic[1], and Rune Møller Jensen[1]

[1] IT University of Copenhagen, Copenhagen, Denmark
jaiv@itu.dk
[2] HEC Montréal, Montreal, Qc, Canada
[3] GERAD, Montreal, Qc, Canada
[4] Mila - Quebec AI Institute, Montreal, Qc, Canada

Abstract. Reinforcement learning (RL) has successfully solved various deterministic and stochastic planning problems. However, conventional RL struggles with complex real-world constraints, particularly when feasibility is explicit and depends on the current state or trajectory. In this work, we address stochastic sequential decision-making with state-dependent constraints through a real-world case study of the master stowage planning problem in container shipping, which aims to optimize revenue and costs under demand uncertainty and operational constraints. We propose a deep RL framework with an encoder-decoder model that integrates problem instance, solution, and uncertainty information to guide planning. We introduce differentiable projection layers that enforce convex polyhedral constraints, while Jacobian corrections offset the projections to yield unbiased policy gradient estimates. Experiments show that our model efficiently finds adaptive, feasible solutions that generalize across distribution shifts and scale to longer planning horizons, outperforming state-of-the-art baselines in constrained RL and stochastic programming. As such, our policies enable adaptive, uncertainty-aware planning that can support resilient and sustainable supply chains.

Keywords: Deep reinforcement learning for combinatorial optimization · Stochastic sequential decision-making · Constrained Markov decision processes · Maritime logistics · Container stowage planning

1 Introduction

In recent years, reinforcement learning (RL) has performed well on planning benchmarks such as vehicle routing and scheduling [4,17,22,23,27]. Yet these

M. Ceci et al. (Eds.): ECML PKDD 2026, LNAI 16948, pp. 324–341, 2027.
https://doi.org/10.1007/978-3-032-37679-4_19

benchmarks are often deterministic with implicit feasibility, whereas real-world decision problems are stochastic, sequential, and deal with state/trajectory-dependent hard constraints. In this setting, traditional stochastic programs based on explicit scenario trees can become computationally expensive [30], while many constrained-RL methods enforce approximate feasibility [43]. Instead, exact per-step projection onto state-dependent polyhedra can be used but often exceeds operational time budgets [1,21], motivating fast feasibility mechanisms for longer-horizon planning under uncertainty.

We study this challenge in container shipping, which transports 45% of global goods ($8.1 trillion/year) [38] and emits >200 million tons of CO_2 per year [25], yet is central to decarbonization due to low emissions per ton-mile [14]. Container shipping involves several constrained sequential decision problems with inherent uncertainty, e.g., berth allocation [26], pre-marshalling [18], quay crane scheduling [16], and container vessel stowage planning [39]. The latter can decompose into two challenging subproblems: the upstream master planning problem (MPP) assigns cargo to clusters of slots, and the downstream slot planning problem (SPP) allocates containers to individual slots [28]. As uncertainty drives frequent demand updates, fast re-planning is needed to assess the downstream feasibility of MPP decisions and support resilient, sustainable supply chains.

We propose a deep reinforcement learning (DRL) framework to generate feasible, high-profit solutions for the MPP under demand uncertainty. We formulate the problem as an action-constrained MDP and learn a planning policy that conditions on instance features, the current solution state, and demand realizations. The policy uses a projected encoder–decoder model, with feasibility enforced by fast differentiable projections onto state-dependent convex polyhedral constraint sets. Because actions are projected during training, we apply a Jacobian-based log-probability correction to obtain unbiased policy-gradient estimates.

Our main contributions are:

- **MPP environment:** A novel MDP formulation for MPP under demand uncertainty with state-dependent coupled constraints, integrating stochastic revenue management and stowage decisions. The benchmark is released as open-source to support reproducible evaluation and mitigate data scarcity.[1]
- **Fast feasibility projection:** We propose a differentiable projection layer that minimizes violations of state-dependent coupled convex polyhedral constraints, enabling feasible policy learning with tight computational budgets.
- **Adaptive planning under uncertainty:** Our model outperforms stochastic programs and constrained-RL baselines by efficiently generating feasible, high-profit plans that show robustness under distribution shift and scale to longer voyages. Ablation studies also isolate the impact of key components.

2 Domain Preliminaries

We present some domain preliminaries to provide context. For a comprehensive review, we refer to [19].

[1] https://github.com/OptimalPursuit/navigating_uncertainty_in_mpp.

Liner shipping companies operate vessels on fixed-schedule, closed-loop voyages, much like a maritime bus service. These journeys, often exceeding ten ports, typically originate in supply-surplus regions (e.g., Asia) and finish in high-demand areas (e.g., Europe). A voyage can be described as a directed path graph $G_P = (P, E_P)$, where $P = \{1, 2, \ldots, N_P\}$ are the nodes representing ports, and $E_P = \{(i, j) \in P^2 \mid j = i + 1\}$ are the edges representing legs between ports. We define sub-voyages by the set $P_{\text{start}}^{\text{end}} = \{p \in P \mid \text{start} \leq p \leq \text{end}\}$. Containers have a port of load (*pol*) and a port of discharge (*pod*), named transports or origin-destination pairs. A transport $tr = (pol, pod)$ is defined with $pol \in P_1^{N_P\text{-}1}$ and $pod \in P_2^{N_P}$. The set of all possible transports is $TR = \{(i, j) \in P^2 \mid i < j\}$.

A standard container unit is the twenty-foot equivalent unit (TEU). Container cargo can be categorized as follows: lengths (20 ft or 1 TEU, 40 ft or 2 TEU), weight classes (light, medium, heavy), and customer contracts (long-term, spot market) to determine cargo revenue (*rev*). Long-term contracts offer lower but stable revenue and high volumes, taking priority over spot market contracts, which provide higher yet volatile revenue in lower volumes. The lack of no-show fees creates uncertainty in container demand, although this becomes more predictable closer to the arrival date. This necessitates dynamic cargo allocation to vessels during the voyage. Containers are often grouped into cargo classes by characteristics, such as $K = \{20ft, 40ft\} \times \{Light, Medium, Heavy\} \times \{Spot, Long\}$.

Figure 1 shows the cellular layout of vessels with standard coordinates of *(bay, row, tier)*. It is divided into bays (02-38) ranging from the front (e.g., bay 02) to the rear (e.g., bay 38), also named from fore to aft. Bays are defined by an ordered set $B = \{1, 2, \ldots, N_B\}$, ranging from fore to aft with N_B being the last bay. Each bay contains stacks of cells, whereas cells contain two slots that can hold two 20-foot containers or one 40-foot container. Bays are horizontally separated by hatch covers into above and below deck sections, introducing the set of decks $D = \{d^{above}, d^{below}\}$. Note that hatch covers introduce complexity, as below-deck cargo can only be discharged if the above-deck cargo is cleared.

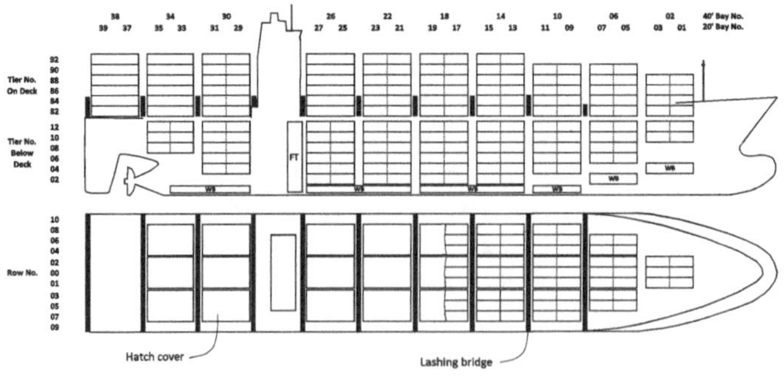

Fig. 1. The side and top view of a container vessel.

Vessel utilization $u_p \in \mathbb{Z}_{\geq 0}^{|B|\times|D|\times|K|\times|TR|}$ represents the number of containers at departure from port p across bays B, decks D, cargo types K, and transports TR. The number of containers loaded at port p are defined by $u_p^+ \in \mathbb{Z}_{\geq 0}^{|B|\times|D|\times|K|\times|TR|}$, whereas the number of containers discharged at port p are denoted by $u_p^- \in \mathbb{Z}_{\geq 0}^{|B|\times|D|\times|K|\times|TR|}$. The utilization at port p is defined as $u_p = u_{p-1} + u_p^+ - u_p^- \; \forall p \in P$, where u_0 is the vessel's arrival condition at the first port. We also define the vessel's pre-loading utilization $u_p' = u_{p-1} - u_p^-$.

The MPP creates a capacity management plan for each general location (bay, deck) to maximize revenue and minimize costs, while the subsequent SPP assigns containers to specific slots. In multi-port voyages, each decision affects future feasibility and optimality. Due to frequent re-planning, runtimes over 10 min are found impractical [28]. Key efficiency objectives include minimizing overstowage (an NP-hard problem [37]) and crane makespan. Overstowage occurs when containers block access to those below that need to discharge, resulting in unnecessary moves. Minimizing makespan reduces port stay duration and associated costs. Furthermore, vessels must satisfy safety constraints for seaworthiness, particularly their weight distribution. The longitudinal (lcg) and vertical center of gravity (vcg) must remain within bounds for utilization u_p, where $\otimes$ denotes the outer product and $\odot$ the element-wise Hadamard product. All operands are vectorized before the product (w is broadcast to match u_p), so $\mathbf{1}^\top(\cdot)$ sums over all entries. Hence, we get the following bounds for lcg and vcg:

$$\underline{lcg} \leq \frac{\mathbf{1}^\top(lm \odot u_p)}{\mathbf{1}^\top(w \odot u_p)} \leq \overline{lcg}, \qquad \forall p \in P \tag{1}$$

$$\underline{vcg} \leq \frac{\mathbf{1}^\top(vm \odot u_p)}{\mathbf{1}^\top(w \odot u_p)} \leq \overline{vcg}, \qquad \forall p \in P \tag{2}$$

where $lm = ld \otimes w$ and $vm = vd \otimes w$ are longitudinal and vertical moments, with $w \in \mathbb{R}_{>0}^{|K|\times|TR|}$ being container weights, and $ld, vd \in \mathbb{R}^{|B|\times|D|}$ denoting the respective longitudinal and vertical distances from the center of gravity.

The problem's scale and complexity, combined with data scarcity and a practical runtime limit of 10 min, make most models focus on constraint subsets for tractability. This highlights the need for efficient solution methods.

3 Related Work

Container stowage planning has been addressed via exact methods [32], heuristics [9], and hybrid frameworks [6]. Our recent survey notes that scalable methods for representative stowage planning and the MPP remain open [39]. Much of the literature further focuses on deterministic, cost-minimizing variants, while practice often requires profit maximization under uncertain demand. We target this gap by optimizing the MPP under demand uncertainty.

Uncertainty in optimization is classically handled by stochastic programming [30], which represents uncertainty via a scenario tree of size $\mathcal{O}(b^T)$ with branching factor b and stages T. This quickly becomes impractical for multi-stage decisions. Common mitigations include scenario reduction [33], decomposition (Benders/Lagrangian) [31], and progressive hedging for non-anticipativity [8]. Approximate approaches can also improve tractability: stochastic dual dynamic programs rely on known distributions [36], while sample average approximation uses Monte Carlo samples to solve deterministic surrogates [10].

Sequential stochastic decisions are often modeled as MDPs and solved with RL, avoiding explicit scenario-tree enumeration but shifting complexity to sampling and function approximation [30]. Enforcing constraints throughout learning is also challenging. Constrained MDP methods use penalties [43], primal–dual updates [12], or soft barriers [42], but may yield weak feasibility guarantees. Action masks and safety shields [2] can break differentiability, hinder learning when few actions are feasible, and require solving complex feasibility subproblems.

Another line of work addresses (state-dependent) action constraints in ML and DRL. Implicit optimization layers and constrained policy improvement operators [1,24,29] can ensure feasibility but typically solve and differentiate through constrained optimization at each online decision, which can be costly. Alternatives include projection mechanisms and feasible parameterizations [5,13,34], and recent benchmarks highlight tradeoffs among feasibility, stability, and computational overhead in action-constrained DRL [21]. For stochastic policies, feasible projection alters the induced action density, which biases policy-gradient updates. Several projection-based RL methods ignore this effect [13,34]. In contrast to costly approaches, we propose a fast differentiable feasibility operator for state-dependent convex polyhedral constraints with a Jacobian-based log-probability correction, allowing feasible and efficient gradient-based training.

4 Markov Decision Processes

We formulate the MPP as an MDP with action constraints. Intuitively, the MDP tracks what is loaded and needed at each port (state), chooses how to load (action), updates the vessel and demand per port (transition), and measures profit after every decision (reward). To improve learning efficiency, we decompose the MDP into a sequence of simpler decisions, thereby reducing the action space. We provide supporting details on the MDP and its decomposition in Appendix A.

4.1 Markov Decision Process

Let $\mathcal{M} = (S, X, \mathcal{T}, \mathcal{R}, P_1^{N_P\text{-}1}, \gamma)$ define an episodic discounted MDP, where S is a set of states, X is a set of actions, $\mathcal{T} : S \times X \to \Delta(S)$ is the transition function with $\Delta(S)$ being a distribution over set S, $\mathcal{R} : S \times X \times P_1^{N_P\text{-}1} \to \mathbb{R}$ is the reward function, $P_1^{N_P\text{-}1}$ is the finite horizon of load ports with final port N_P-1, and $\gamma \in (0, 1)$ is the discount factor.

The state $s_p = (u_p, q_p, \zeta)$ includes vessel utilization $u_p \in \mathbb{R}^{n_u}_{\geq 0}$, realized demand $q_p \in \mathbb{R}^{n_q}_{\geq 0}$, and instance parameters ζ. The initial state $s_0 = (u_0, q_0, \zeta)$ has an empty vessel $u_0 = \mathbf{0}^{n_u}$, realized demand q_0 of first port, and a generated problem instance ζ. Note that $n_u = |B| \times |D| \times |K| \times |TR|$, $n_c = |B| \times |D|$, and $n_q = |K| \times |TR|$ are the shapes of utilization, location, and demand, respectively.

At each port p, an action $x_p \in \mathbb{R}^{n_u}_{\geq 0}$ specifies how many containers of each group to load at each vessel position. To ensure safety and efficiency, actions must satisfy a set of linear but coupled constraints defined by the polyhedron $PH(s_p) = \left\{x_p \in \mathbb{R}^{n_u}_{\geq 0} : A(s_p)x_p \leq b(s_p)\right\}$, where $A(s_p) \in \mathbb{R}^{m_u \times n_u}$ is the constraint matrix and $b(s_p) \in \mathbb{R}^{m_u}$ is the vector of bounds, with m_u constraints.

The constraints below are expressed in action x_p and pre-loading utilization u'_p, i.e., the utilization after discharging cargo. We use real-valued actions, as downstream planning (e.g., SPP) discretizes the plans [28]. Constraint (3) limits x_p by demand q_p, while Constraint (4) limits x_p by the available TEU capacity, with TEU vector $teu \in \{1,2\}^{n_q}_{>0}$, and TEU capacity $c \in \mathbb{Z}^{n_c}_{>0}$. Here, $\mathbf{1}_{n_c}$ contracts the (B, D) axes to leave n_q, and teu contracts the (K, TR) axes to leave n_c. Constraints (5)–(6) enforce lcg limits, while Constraints (7)–(8) impose similar bounds on vcg. These stability bounds are derived from Constraints (1) and (2).

$$\mathbf{1}_{n_c} x_p \leq q_p \tag{3}$$
$$x_p teu \leq c - u'_p teu \tag{4}$$
$$-\mathbf{1}^\top((lm - \underline{lcgw}) \odot x_p) \leq -\mathbf{1}^\top((\underline{lcgw} - lm) \odot u'_p) \tag{5}$$
$$\mathbf{1}^\top((lm - \overline{lcgw}) \odot x_p) \leq \mathbf{1}^\top((\overline{lcgw} - lm) \odot u'_p) \tag{6}$$
$$-\mathbf{1}^\top((vm - \underline{vcgw}) \odot x_p) \leq -\mathbf{1}^\top((\underline{vcgw} - vm) \odot u'_p) \tag{7}$$
$$\mathbf{1}^\top((vm - \overline{vcgw}) \odot x_p) \leq \mathbf{1}^\top((\overline{vcgw} - vm) \odot u'_p) \tag{8}$$

A stochastic transition function $\mathcal{T}(s_{p+1} \mid s_p, x_p)$ updates a state to port $p+1$:

- Upon port arrival, the true demand q_{p+1} is revealed, while future port demand remains unknown.
- Cargo is unloaded: $u_{p+1} = u_p \odot (1 - \mathbf{e}^-_p)$, with $\mathbf{e}^-_p$ marking discharge cargo.
- New cargo is loaded: $u_{p+1} = u_{p+1} + x_p$, where x_p should satisfy $PH(s_p)$.

Equation (9) defines a reward function that computes profit as revenue minus costs for any state s, action x, and port p. Revenue is computed per transport–cargo class as the elementwise minimum between loaded containers and realized demand: $rev^\top \min(x^\top \mathbf{1}_{n_c}, q)$, where $rev \in \mathbb{R}^{n_q}_{>0}$ is the vector of per-class revenues, $x^\top \mathbf{1}_{n_c} \in \mathbb{R}^{n_q}_{\geq 0}$ aggregates loaded containers over locations (B, D), and the min is taken elementwise so that containers exceeding demand q earn no revenue. Costs are determined using two state-dependent auxiliary variables: hatch overstows $ho(s,p) \in \mathbb{R}^{|B|}_{\geq 0}$ and excess crane moves $cm(s,p) \in \mathbb{R}^{|B|-1}_{\geq 0}$. Coefficients weight both components $ct^{ho} \in \mathbb{R}_{>0}$ and $ct^{cm} \in \mathbb{R}_{>0}$, respectively.

$$\mathcal{R}(s,x,p) = rev^\top \min(x^\top \mathbf{1}_{n_c}, q) - ct^{ho}\mathbf{1}^\top ho(s,p) - ct^{cm}\mathbf{1}^\top cm(s,p) \tag{9}$$

4.2 Decomposed Markov Decision Process

The MDP has an action space of size $|X| \propto |B| \cdot |D| \cdot |K| \cdot |P|$, where each action x_p determines how cargo types and transport options are placed on the vessel per port. However, this action space is large, which can hinder learning efficiency [20]. To address this, we decompose the MDP into granular, sequential steps based on an index (i, j, k) $\forall (i, j) \in TR, k \in K$. Figure 2 illustrates the decomposed MDP for a single port. Instead of placing all transport and cargo types simultaneously, we take a decomposed action for each transport (p, j) and cargo type k at port p, then departing to a new port. This reduces the action space to $|X| = |B| \cdot |D|$, while unfolding transports and cargo types over an extended time horizon $t \in H = \{0, 1, \ldots, T_{seq}\}$ with $T_{seq} = |K| \cdot |TR| - 1$.

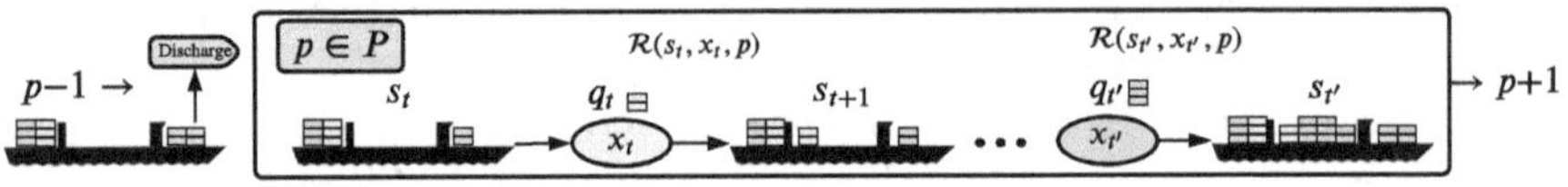

Fig. 2. Illustration of the decomposed MDP for MPP. At port p, the vessel discharges cargo, observes realized demand q_t, then sequentially loads container type–POD pairs before sailing to the next port p+1. Colors indicate PODs.

The state $s_t = (u_t, q_t, \zeta)$ depends on time step t, where $u_t \in \mathbb{R}^{n_u}_{\geq 0}$ is vessel utilization, and $q_t \in \mathbb{R}^{n_q}_{\geq 0}$ is realized demand. The instance ζ remains unchanged. Given the time t, however, we can extract relevant parameters from ζ, such as $(pol_t, pod_t, k_t, rev^{(pol_t, pod_t, k_t)})$. Action $x_t \in \mathbb{R}^{n_c}_{\geq 0}$ assigns real number of containers to utilization u_t for step t. Each action is subject to $PH(s_t) = \{x_t \in \mathbb{R}^{n_c}_{\geq 0} : A(s_t)x_t \leq b(s_t)\}$. Here, $A(s_t) \in \mathbb{R}^{m_c \times n_c}$ is the constraint matrix, $b(s_t) \in \mathbb{R}^{m_c}$ is the bound vector, and m_c is the number of constraints. Constraints (3)–(8) are re-indexed for the decomposed steps by replacing (x_p, s_p) with (x_t, s_t), which collapses x_t onto the (B, D) axes alone. The inequalities define the same polyhedron, but are instantiated at step t based on s_t, yielding $PH(s_t)$. At each time t, the transition includes loading, where x_t is added to u_t. Discharges and demand realizations occur when arriving at new ports $t \in T_{\text{new port}}$. The revenue at step t is computed as $rev(pol_t, pod_t, k_t) \min(\mathbf{1}^\top x_t, q_t^{(pol_t, pod_t, k_t)})$. Costs, however, require all discharge and loading operations at port p to be finalized, as they depend on the vessel utilization u_t before departure, aggregated at the final step $t \in T_{\text{leave port}}$. The hatch-overstow and crane-move costs depend on the full vessel utilization at departure ($t \in T_{\text{leave port}}$), so they are defined at port granularity rather than per step. Decomposing them into per-step signals would require approximations. We therefore evaluate the cost signal once per port p, which yields structurally sparse costs.

5 Proposed Architecture

Figure 3 shows our projected encoder–decoder model, which embeds instance, context, and dynamic data to parameterize the multivariate Gaussian policy $\pi_\theta(\cdot \mid s_t) = \mathcal{N}\left(\mu_\theta(s_t), \text{diag}(\sigma^2_\theta(s_t))\right)$. A sampled action vector $x_t \sim \pi_\theta(\cdot \mid s_t)$ is projected by layer $\mathcal{P}$ to ensure feasibility, and the adjusted action is applied in the decomposed MDP. We train the projected policy using actor–critic RL, with the critic evaluating actions along the trajectory.

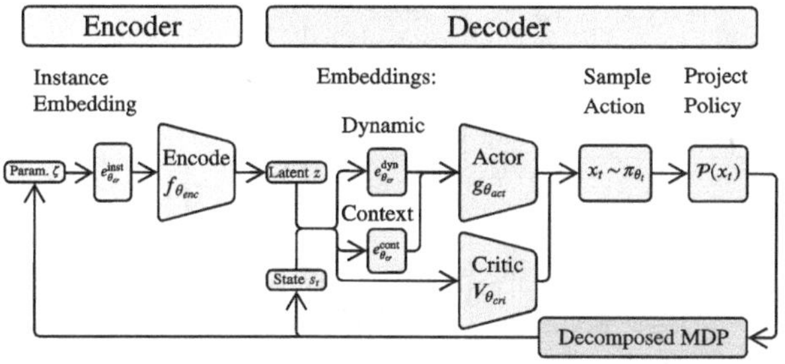

Fig. 3. DRL architecture with feasibility projection for actor-critic methods.

5.1 Encoder-Decoder Model

Our model, inspired by [22], is illustrated in Fig. 4. The instance embedding $e^{\text{inst}}(\zeta)$, parameterized by θ_{in}, maps problem instance ζ to a feature representation used by the encoder to condition policies on instances. Sinusoidal positional encoding is then applied to inform the model of element order in sequences [40]. An attention encoder $f(e^{\text{inst}}(\zeta))$ parameterized by θ_{enc} maps embedding $e^{\text{inst}}(\zeta)$ to latent variable z using multi-head attention (MHA) with keys (K), queries (Q) and values (V) to identify relevant features dynamically and handle variable input size [40]. Then, we use a feed-forward network (FFN) with ReLU activation, layer normalization, residual connections, and dropout. The context embedding $e^{\text{cont}}(u_t, z)$, parameterized by θ_{co}, extracts features from the current solution u_t and the latent variable z. This embedding provides the MHA query, helping the attention mechanism focus on relevant information, with the solution context at time t, enabling the policy to make informed decisions on the current state. The dynamic embedding $e^{\text{dyn}}(q_t, z)$, parameterized by θ_{dn}, extracts features from demand q_t across all time steps in the horizon H, capturing temporal patterns over the episode. By combining actual demand with latent information, attention selects (key) and retrieves (values) demand-relevant context over time, improving anticipation of future conditions and long-term decisions.

Following [22], the actor decoder $g(e^{\text{cont}}(u_t, z), e^{\text{dyn}}(q_t, z))$ is an attention model (AM) parameterized by θ_{act}. The MHA layer uses context embedding as queries and dynamic embedding as keys and values encoding demand across the horizon, with a forward-looking mask on steps $\{t, t+1, \dots, T_{seq}\}$ to link present context with future trends. An FFN extracts features, a pointer mechanism selects relevant future steps [41], and softplus activation then outputs positive parameters $(\mu_\theta(s_t), \sigma_\theta(s_t))$. Our critic model $V(s_t, z)$, parameterized by θ_{cri},

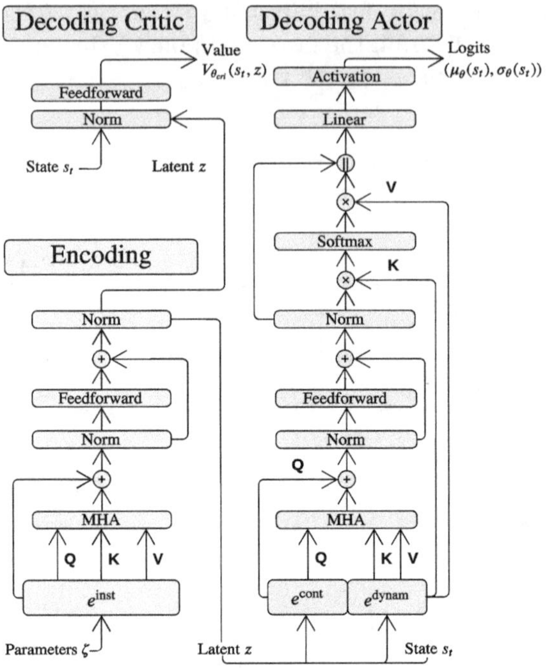

Fig. 4. Layers of the encoder and the actor-critic decoder.

estimates the value of state s_t and latent variable z through an FFN outputting $V_{\theta_{cri}}(s_t, z) \in \mathbb{R}$. The actor logits parameterize a multivariate Gaussian policy $\pi_\theta(\cdot \mid s_t) = \mathcal{N}(\mu_\theta(s_t), \text{diag}(\sigma_\theta^2(s_t)))$, from which a raw action vector is sampled as $x_t \sim \pi_\theta(\cdot \mid s_t)$ and then used to construct solutions.

5.2 Feasibility Regularization in Actor-Critic Methods

Actor-critic methods such as proximal policy optimization (PPO) [35] and soft actor critic (SAC) [15] are widely used in unconstrained problems where feasibility is enforced implicitly through the environment dynamics. A common approach for handling constraints without environment enforcement is to augment the actor loss with a soft penalty term [43]. This actor loss is defined as:

$$\mathcal{L}(\theta) = \mathcal{L}_{\text{actor}}(\theta) + \mathcal{L}_{\text{feas}}(\theta) \tag{10}$$

$$\mathcal{L}_{\text{feas}}(\theta) = \mathbb{E}_t \left[\lambda_f^\top \left(A(s_t)x_\theta(s_t) - b(s_t)\right)_+\right] \tag{11}$$

where $(\cdot)_+$ denotes the ReLU function applied elementwise, penalizing only constraint violations. The vector $\lambda_f \in \mathbb{R}^m_{>0}$ weights the regularization terms for the m constraints. For algorithms that do not propagate gradients through the action, such as PPO, $x_\theta(s_t)$ is replaced by the policy mean $\mu_\theta(s_t)$. Tuning

λ_f is difficult under coupled constraints and even more so in dynamic, state-dependent feasible regions $PH(s_t)$, where the reward–feasibility trade-off varies over time [13]. Primal–dual methods learn the policy and λ_f jointly, but can still struggle to enforce hard constraints. Both methods are mainly useful as constrained RL baselines.

Algorithm 1. Unbiased violation projection (UVP) layer

Require: $x \in \mathbb{R}^n_{\geq 0}$, parameters (A, b, η_v, δ_v), iterations

Initialize $x' \leftarrow x$
Define $\mathcal{V}(x) \leftarrow (Ax - b)_+$
for $i = 1$ **to** iterations **do**
  Set $x \leftarrow x'$
  Update $x' \leftarrow x - \eta_v A^\top \mathcal{V}(x)$
  if $|\mathbf{1}^\top \mathcal{V}(x') - \mathbf{1}^\top \mathcal{V}(x)| \leq \delta_v$ **then**
    break
  end if
end for
return x'

5.3 Feasibility Projection Layers

Rather than penalizing violations after they occur, we ensure feasibility by mapping each sampled action onto the feasible region before it is used in the MDP or the policy update. To avoid feasibility-loss augmentation, we insert a differentiable feasibility map $\mathcal{P}$ that transforms sampled actions $x_t \sim \pi_\theta(\cdot \mid s_t)$ into constraint-satisfying actions before they enter the decomposed MDP or the policy update. For the state-dependent convex polyhedron $PH(s_t)$, we execute $x'_t = \mathcal{P}(x_t) \in PH(s_t)$. Because $\mathcal{P}$ changes the action distribution, the policy gradient would be biased unless this transformation is accounted for. We therefore apply a change-of-variables log-probability correction using the map's Jacobian [7], valid wherever $\mathcal{P}$ is locally invertible, which holds almost everywhere as $\mathcal{P}$ is piecewise-linear. This keeps the gradient estimates unbiased (a.e.), hence the name UVP. Unlike implicit differentiable convex optimization layers with intractable Jacobians and biased, costly gradients [1], our feasibility maps admit explicit Jacobians, making the correction efficient.

Algorithm 1 implements the unbiased violation projection (UVP) by iteratively reducing constraint violation with respect to $PH(s_t)$. Starting from a raw action x, UVP computes the violation $\mathcal{V}(x) = (Ax - b)_+$ and updates $x \leftarrow x - \eta_v A^\top \mathcal{V}(x)$ to reduce the total violation. The update corresponds to gradient descent on the squared violation $\|(Ax - b)_+\|_2^2$. Repeating this update for a fixed number of steps (training) or until violation improvement is below a threshold (inference) yields a (near-)feasible action while remaining differentiable almost everywhere, enabling end-to-end learning with the Jacobian log-probability adjustment. Since this objective is $2\|A\|_2^2$-smooth and can be steep when A has large singular values, we normalize the step size as $\eta_v = \tilde{\eta}_v / \|A\|_2^2$ to ensure stable iterations. Technical details on the Jacobian correction and UVP convergence are provided in Appendix B.

6 Experimental Results

We compare methods across demand distributions on objective value (Obj.) and training and test times in seconds (Time). An ablation study assesses the contribution of individual components, while managerial insights analyze information value, computational cost, adapting to uncertainty, and scaling to larger instances. DRL used an NVIDIA RTX A6000 GPU, while CPLEX used an AMD EPYC 7742 48-core CPU. Hyperparameters are consistent across DRL models.

6.1 Experimental Setup

Training instances are based on 4-port voyages and a 1,000 TEU vessel. These synthetic instances are sampled from Gaussian distributions $\mathcal{N}(\mu^{(i,j,k)}, \sigma^{(i,j,k)})$ for all $(i, j) \in TR$ and $k \in K$, where means $\mu^{(i,j,k)}$ are uniformly randomized and the standard deviations follow $\sigma^{(i,j,k)} = CV\mu^{(i,j,k)}$ with coefficient of variation CV. While instances are synthetic, the distributional parameters follow established instance generators from prior work [3,11], ensuring a realistic transport mix and high capacity utilization. Generalization instances use continuous uniform samples $\mathcal{U}(lb^{(i,j,k)}, ub^{(i,j,k)})$ for all $(i, j) \in TR$ and $k \in K$, where (lb, ub) are selected to match the spread of the training distribution, isolating effects of distributional shift. Details are found in Appendix C.

Guided by a taxonomy of action-constrained DRL [21] and loss-augmented RL [12,43], we include one representative baseline from each major family. Our end-to-end RL baselines are penalty loss (Pen-DRL), a primal–dual approach (Lag-DRL), an implicit convex optimization layer (CP) [1], Frank–Wolfe policy improvement [24], and α-map projection [34]. For baselines that may output infeasible actions, we include an inference-time recovery layer (R) that projects actions exactly onto $PH(s_t)$ via CP. We use on-policy PPO [35] and off-policy SAC [15] to show that trends are agnostic to DRL algorithms. As non-learning baselines, we include multi-stage stochastic programs on explicit scenario trees with non-anticipativity (SP-NA; no foresight) and with perfect information (SP-PI; full-foresight upper bound). We exclude methods that optimize alternative uncertainty objectives (e.g., robust/deterministic methods) and feasibility mechanisms that are non-differentiable or enforce subsets of the constraints, as these are not compatible with gradient-based action-constrained RL. Appendix D and Appendix E provide implementation details of the SP and RL, respectively.

6.2 Policy Evaluation

Table 1 reports the performance of methods that consistently produce feasible solutions. Our AM-P with UVP+R achieves the best average performance, with variability comparable to the AM-P baselines (CP, FW, α). Its objective value is significantly higher than loss-augmented DRL and SP-NA, while matching the training and inference time of loss-augmented DRL. In contrast, SP-NA has an average runtime of 23 min, while SP-PI is slower at 100 min. Among AM-P models, UVP achieves objectives similar to CP and FW, while α performs slightly worse. The AM-P baselines also require much higher training cost than UVP, whereas the inference cost is small for each AM-P. These trends are consistent across test and generalization instances, and across off-policy (SAC) and on-policy (PPO) settings. Overall, AM-P with UVP+R achieves the best trade-off across baselines, delivering high-quality solutions for the MPP under demand uncertainty at substantially lower training cost.

Table 1. Our AM-P vs. baselines, with **best trade-off**, methods significantly worse than UVP+R are marked with † (paired two-sided Wilcoxon signed-rank test, Holm-adjusted $p < 0.001$), and expected upper bound is marked with *.

Methods			Train	Testing ($N = 30$)		Generalization ($N = 30$)	
Model	Alg.	Proj.	Time (s)	Obj. ($)	Time (s)	Obj. ($)	Time (s)
AM-P	**SAC**	**UVP+R**	1,857	1,494.4±90.7	4.8±0.3	1,509.5±108.8	4.8±0.3
AM-P	SAC	CP	70,181	1,493.9±89.9	3.1±0.2	1,508.9±109.5	3.3±0.3
AM-P	SAC	FW	83,948	1,488.8±92.5	11.5±0.4	1,509.7±106.8	11.5±0.3
AM-P	SAC	α	40,883	1,476.9±88.0	1.3±0.1	1,494.2±107.8	1.3±0.0
AM†	Pen-SAC	R	1,528	1,307.1±96.3	1.8±0.3	1,323.9±80.6	1.8±0.3
AM†	Lag-SAC	R	865	1,000.2±80.2	1.3±0.0	995.6±65.6	1.3±0.0
AM-P	**PPO**	**UVP+R**	1,346	1,490.7±91.4	5.4±0.5	1,509.5±107.5	5.9±0.7
AM-P	PPO	CP	85,285	1,480.7±89.4	5.9±0.6	1,497.0±107.8	5.9±0.6
AM-P	PPO	FW	97,060	1,485.5±91.8	5.6±0.7	1,505.5±107.5	5.7±0.5
AM-P	PPO	α	74,583	1,431.7±96.3	1.3±0.1	1,461.4±92.4	1.3±0.1
AM†	Pen-PPO	R	957	1,070.9±80.8	1.3±0.1	1,066.6±64.2	1.3±0.0
AM†	Lag-PPO	R	1,041	979.5±74.5	1.3±0.0	975.2±58.8	1.3±0.0
SP-NA†	CPLEX	-	-	1,036.0±153.1	1,334.5±13.8	1,108.2±150.3	1,364.4±23.8
SP-PI*	CPLEX	-	-	1,689.7±121.7	5,232.3±124.6	1,705.7±114.0	6,642.8±453.4

Figure 5 presents an ablation study isolating the contribution of key components; Figs. 5(b) and 5(c) contain overlapping lines with similar values.

In Fig. 5(a), high-quality solutions lie in the top-left corner. Compared to UVP, feasibility recovery (+R) and a larger budget of 150 iterations (UVP*) both reduce violations, though UVP* requires tuning the iteration budget. Even so, UVP, UVP+R, and UVP* reach similar profits despite residual training violations, with small violation norms of about 0.07, 0.004, and 0.003, respectively. Replacing projection with loss-augmentation (Pen, Lag) degrades the objective and feasibility. Removing projections (e.g., ~~UVP~~) shows that AM-P relies on them to find high-quality solutions.

Figure 5(b) plots the average training objective with 95% confidence intervals for SAC and PPO over five random seeds. With Jacobian correction (JC), training is more stable; without it (NC), runs often experience policy collapse. The Jacobian adjustment is irrelevant for PPO as the change-of-variable term is an additive correction, $\log|\det J(a, s)|$, independent of θ. Since PPO uses the likelihood ratio $\log \pi_\theta(a \mid s) - \log \pi_{\theta_{\text{old}}}(a \mid s)$, this term cancels when applied consistently, leaving the updates unchanged. Overall, PPO training remains stable.

Despite the sparse per-port cost signal, both PPO and SAC with JC converge stably over multiple seeds, indicating the signal is sufficient for the critic to learn effective policies under structurally sparse costs.

Figures 5(c) and 5(d) show the effect of UVP iterations without feasibility recovery. Beyond 100–150 iterations, SAC and PPO with normalized η_v show diminishing returns and higher compute costs. Compared with static $\tilde{\eta}_v$, normalized η_v avoids parameter tuning and reaches high-profit, low-violation solutions faster and more reliably.

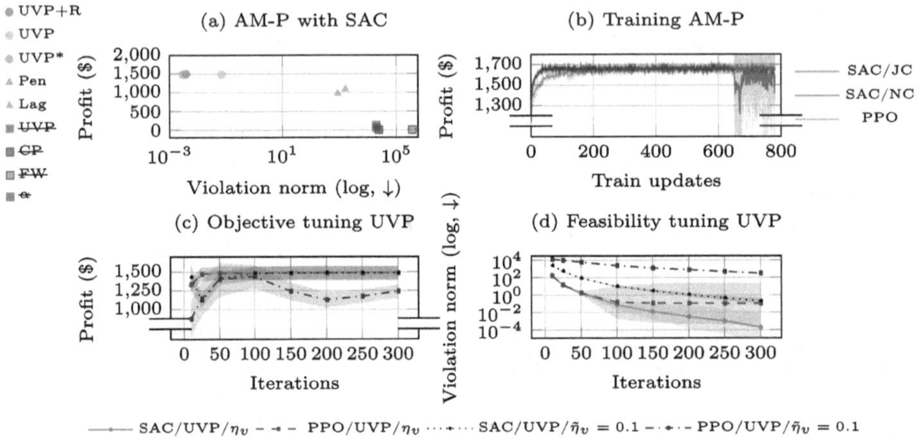

Fig. 5. Ablation results on (a) projection, (b) training, (c,d) tuning UVP.

6.3 Managerial Insights

Figure 6 performs sensitivity analyses on SP scenario size, demand uncertainty, and voyage length, reporting averages and standard deviations with $N = 30$.

Figure 6(a) reports profits of SP-NA, SP-PI, and our AM-P policies. SP-PI drops non-anticipativity to gain full foresight. DRL is non-anticipative: it observes the realized demand per port and uses the same demand model as SP-NA. The PI–NA gap approximates the value of perfect information in our scenario tree, whereas the DRL–NA gap reflects the benefit of a learned policy under the same information structure. As the number of scenarios increases, SP-NA and SP-PI better approximate the uncertainty, and their profits converge. At 80 scenarios, SP-PI yields a 60–65% improvement over SP-NA, whereas DRL improves by 45–50% over SP-NA, showing that learning can enhance solution quality over SP-NA while leaving a gap to the perfect-information upper bound.

Figure 6(b) shows the average computational cost. SP-NA's time grows substantially with the scenarios, reaching 23 min per instance at 80 scenarios. Whereas SP-PI scales even more poorly, rising to 88 minutes per instance. Using

SAC and PPO, we train AM-P with UVP within 25-30 minutes. Inference, however, is near-instant for all DRL methods. When amortizing training time over $N = 30$, SAC and PPO cost 45–60 s per solution. Hence, DRL is efficient and meets the practical limit of 10 minutes.

Figure 6(c) shows how policies adapt as demand variability measured by the coefficient of variation (CV) changes across unseen instances. Our samples are clamped at 0 to ensure non-negativity, which can skew demand distributions at higher CVs. As variability and uncertainty increase, SAC and PPO policies exhibit stable, feasible performance and slightly increase profit by exploiting the demand skewness, demonstrating their adaptability to shifting distributions.

Figure 6(d) shows that policies trained in $|P| = 4$ can scale to longer voyages $|P| \in \{6, 8, 10\}$, and hence policies perform a zero-shot transfer without retraining. However, the policy's share of the maximum revenue declines as $|P|$ grows, alongside an increase in per-step average capacity utilization from 55% to 80%. This suggests that tighter capacity leaves less flexibility to load demand. Inference costs grow linearly with the problem size, while solutions remain feasible. Note that scaling to larger vessels currently requires retraining.

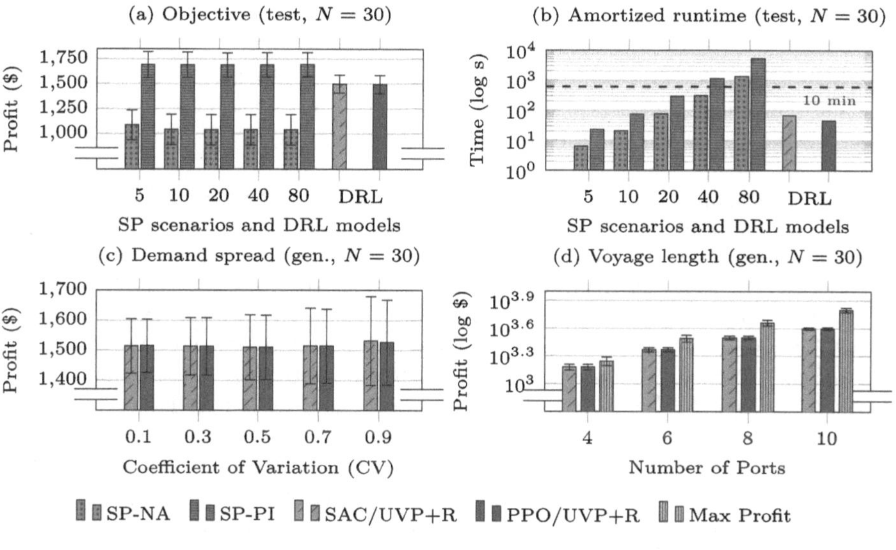

Fig. 6. Sensitivity analyses: (a) objective and (b) runtime per SP scenario and DRL model, (c) generalization across CV levels, and (d) across voyage lengths.

6.4 Industrial Realism and Scope

Large-scale stowage datasets are hard to obtain as demand, contractual, and planning data are proprietary and fragmented across systems. We therefore use expert-informed generators with realistic operational parameters and high capacity utilization to stress the interaction between uncertainty and constraints. This supports reproducible evaluation in realistic conditions, but does not fully capture industrial dynamics, non-convex constraints, or downstream coordination. We thus view the results as evidence of deployment potential, while industrial deployment will require representative generators at scale or large-scale datasets.

7 Conclusion and Future Directions

We presented a DRL approach for the MPP under demand uncertainty, modeling the problem as a stochastic MDP with hard state-dependent constraints. Our encoder–decoder attention policy with differentiable feasibility projections enables the learning of feasible policies under limited compute budgets. The resulting policies provide fast, feasible decision support for the MPP within practical runtime limits, while remaining robust under distribution shift and scaling to longer voyages. More broadly, we show that differentiable feasibility mechanisms can make DRL viable for realistic constrained planning. Future work should address efficient non-convex projections, validation on representative industrial-scale instances, and integration with related planning tasks.

Acknowledgments. This work is partially sponsored by the IT University of Copenhagen and the Danish Maritime Fund under research grant 2025-039 and grant 2023-047 for the Maritime Hub at the IT University of Copenhagen.

Ethical Statement. Human oversight is critical in container shipping decision-support tools for fairness, accountability, and transparency. While models enhance decision-making and provide optimized, feasible plans, human judgment remains essential, especially in safety-critical situations like vessel stability and dangerous cargo. Optimizing solely for revenue might inadvertently bias cargo prioritization, impacting customers and voyages. Safeguards such as challengeable outputs and continuous auditing help mitigate automation bias and build trust in these systems. Efficient vessel utilization also reduces fuel consumption and greenhouse gas emissions.

Generative AI Statement. During the preparation of this manuscript, the authors used generative AI tools to assist with language editing and to support code development. All content was subsequently reviewed and verified by the authors, who take full responsibility for the final result.

References

1. Agrawal, A., Amos, B., Barratt, S., Boyd, S.: Differentiable Convex Optimization Layers. In: Advances in Neural Information Processing Systems (2019). https://doi.org/10.5555/3454287.3455145
2. Alshiekh, M., Bloem, R., Ehlers, R., Könighofer, B., Niekum, S., Topcu, U.: Safe Reinforcement Learning via Shielding. In: Proceedings of the AAAI Conference on Artificial Intelligence, vol. 32 (2018). https://doi.org/10.1609/aaai.v32i1.11797

3. Avriel, M., Penn, M., Shpirer, N., Witteboon, S.: Stowage planning for container ships to reduce the number of shifts. Ann. Oper. Res. **76**(1–4), 55–71 (1998). https://doi.org/10.1023/A:1018956823693
4. Bengio, Y., Lodi, A., Prouvost, A.: Machine learning for combinatorial optimization: A methodological tour d'horizon. Eur. J. Oper. Res. **290**(2), 405–421 (2021). https://doi.org/10.1016/j.ejor.2020.07.063
5. Bhatia, A., Varakantham, P., Kumar, A.: Resource constrained deep reinforcement learning. In: International Conference on Automated Planning and Scheduling, pp. 610–620. AAAI Press (2019)
6. Bilican, M.S., Evren, R., Karatas, M.: A Mathematical Model and Two-Stage Heuristic for the Container Stowage Planning Problem with Stability Parameters. IEEE Access 8, (2020). https://doi.org/10.1109/ACCESS.2020.3003557
7. Bishop, C.M.: Pattern recognition and machine learning. Information science and statistics, Springer, New York (2006)
8. Boland, N., Christiansen, J., Dandurand, B., Eberhard, A., Linderoth, J., Luedtke, J., Oliveira, F.: Combining progressive hedging with a frank-wolfe method to compute Lagrangian dual bounds in stochastic mixed-integer programming. SIAM J. Optim. **28**(2), 1312–1336 (2018). https://doi.org/10.1137/16M1076290
9. Chang, Y., Hamedi, M., Haghani, A.: Solving integrated problem of stowage planning with crane split by an improved genetic algorithm based on novel encoding mode. Meas. Control (2022). https://doi.org/10.1177/00202940221097981
10. Chen, R., Luedtke, J.: On sample average approximation for two-stage stochastic programs without relatively complete recourse. Math. Program. **196**(1-2), 719–754 (2022). https://doi.org/10.1007/s10107-021-01753-9
11. Ding, D., Chou, M.C.: Stowage Planning for Container Ships: A Heuristic Algorithm to Reduce the Number of Shifts. European J. Oper. Res. (2015). https://doi.org/10.1016/j.ejor.2015.03.044, http://linkinghub.elsevier.com/retrieve/pii/S0377221715002660
12. Ding, D., Zhang, K., Basar, T., Jovanovic, M.: Natural Policy Gradient Primal-Dual Method for Constrained Markov Decision Processes. In: Advances in Neural Information Processing Systems, vol. 33, pp. 8378–8390 (2020)
13. Donti, P.L., Rolnick, D., Kolter, J.Z.: DC3: A learning method for optimization with hard constraints. In: Proceedings of the 9th International Conference on Learning Representations (2021). https://doi.org/10.48550/arXiv.2104.12225
14. European Commission: reducing Emissions from the Shipping Sector (2023), https://climate.ec.europa.eu/eu-action/transport/reducing-emissions-shipping-sector
15. Haarnoja, T., Zhou, A., Abbeel, P., Levine, S.: Soft Actor-Critic: off-Policy Maximum Entropy Deep Reinforcement Learning with a Stochastic Actor. In: Proceedings of the 35th International Conference on Machine Learning (2018). https://doi.org/10.48550/arXiv.1801.01290
16. Herup, M.O., Thiesgaard, G.C.W., Van Twiller, J., Jensen, R.M.: A Linear Time Algorithm for Optimal Quay Crane Scheduling. In: Computational Logistics, pp. 60–73, Barcelona, Spain (2022). https://doi.org/10.1007/978-3-031-16579-5
17. Hottung, A., Kwon, Y.D., Tierney, K.: Efficient Active Search for Combinatorial Optimization Problems. In: Proceedings of the International Conference on Learning Representations(2022)
18. Hottung, A., Tanaka, S., Tierney, K.: Deep learning assisted heuristic tree search for the container pre-marshalling problem. Comput. Oper. Res. **113**, 104781 (2020). https://doi.org/10.1016/j.cor.2019.104781

19. Jensen, R.M., Pacino, D., Ajspur, M.L., Vesterdal, C.: Container Vessel Stowage Planning, Weilbach (2018)
20. Kanervisto, A., Scheller, C., Hautamäki, V.: Action Space Shaping in Deep Reinforcement Learning. In: 2020 IEEE Conference on Games (CoG) (2020), https://api.semanticscholar.org/CorpusID:214775114
21. Kasaura, K., Miura, S., Kozuno, T., Yonetani, R., Hoshino, K., Hosoe, Y.: Benchmarking actor-critic deep reinforcement learning algorithms for robotics control with action constraints. IEEE Robot. Autom. Lett. **8**(8), 4449–4456 (2023). https://doi.org/10.1109/LRA.2023.3284378
22. Kool, W., van Hoof, H., Welling, M.: Attention, Learn to Solve Routing Problems! In: Proceedings of the International Conference on Learning Representations (2019) https://openreview.net/forum?id=ByxBFsRqYm
23. Kwon, Y.D., Choo, J., Kim, B., Yoon, I., Gwon, Y., Min, S.: POMO: Policy Optimization with Multiple Optima for Reinforcement Learning. In: Proceedings of the 34th Conference on Neural Information Processing Systems (2020)
24. Lin, J.L., Hung, W., Yang, S.H., Hsieh, P.C., Liu, X.: Escaping from zero gradient: revisiting action-constrained reinforcement learning via Frank-Wolfe policy optimization. Uncertainty in artificial intelligence **161**, 397–407 (2021)
25. Lloyd's List: shipping emissions rise 4.9% in 2021 (2022) https://lloydslist.com/LL1139627/Shipping-emissions-rise-49-in-2021
26. Martin-Iradi, B., Pacino, D., Ropke, S.: The multiport berth allocation problem with speed optimization: exact methods and a cooperative game analysis. Transp. Sci. **56**(4), 972–999 (2022). https://doi.org/10.1287/trsc.2021.1112
27. Mazyavkina, N., Sviridov, S., Ivanov, S., Burnaev, E.: Reinforcement learning for combinatorial optimization: a survey. Comput. Oper. Res. **134**, 105400–105400 (2021). https://doi.org/10.1016/j.cor.2021.105400
28. Pacino, D., Delgado, A., Jensen, R.M., Bebbington, T.: Fast Generation of Near-Optimal Plans for Eco-Efficient Stowage of Large Container Vessels. In: Böse, J.W., Hu, H., Jahn, C., Shi, X., Stahlbock, R., Voß, S. (eds.) ICCL 2011. LNCS, vol. 6971, pp. 286–301. Springer, Heidelberg (2011). https://doi.org/10.1007/978-3-642-24264-9_22
29. Pham, T.H., Magistris, G.D., Tachibana, R.: OptLayer - practical constrained optimization for deep reinforcement learning in the real world. In: International Conference on Robotics and Automation, pp. 6236–6243. IEEE (2018). https://doi.org/10.1109/ICRA.2018.8460547
30. Powell, W.B.: Reinforcement Learning and Stochastic Optimization: a Unified Framework for Sequential Decisions, vol. 22, Wiley (2022). 1st edn
31. Rahmaniani, R., Crainic, T.G., Gendreau, M., Rei, W.: The Benders decomposition algorithm: a literature review. Eur. J. Oper. Res. **259**(3), 801–817 (2017). https://doi.org/10.1016/j.ejor.2016.12.005
32. Roberti, R., Pacino, D.: A decomposition method for finding optimal container stowage plans. Transp. Sci. **52**(6), 1444–1462 (2018). https://doi.org/10.1287/trsc.2017.0795
33. Römisch, W.: Scenario Reduction Techniques in Stochastic Programming. In: Watanabe, O., Zeugmann, T. (eds.) SAGA 2009. LNCS, vol. 5792, pp. 1–14. Springer, Heidelberg (2009). https://doi.org/10.1007/978-3-642-04944-6_1
34. Sanket, S., Sinha, A., Varakantham, P., Perrault, A., Tambe, M.: Solving online threat screening games using constrained action space reinforcement learning. In: AAAI Conference on Artificial Intelligence, pp. 2226–2235. AAAI Press (2020). https://doi.org/10.1609/AAAI.V34I02.5599

35. Schulman, J., Wolski, F., Dhariwal, P., Radford, A., Klimov, O.: Proximal Policy Optimization Algorithms (2017). https://doi.org/10.48550/arXiv.1707.06347
36. Shapiro, A.: Analysis of stochastic dual dynamic programming method. Eur. J. Oper. Res. **209**(1), 63–72 (2011). https://doi.org/10.1016/j.ejor.2010.08.007
37. Tierney, K., Pacino, D., Jensen, R.M.: On the complexity of container stowage planning problems. Discret. Appl. Math. **169**, 225–230 (2014). https://doi.org/10.1016/j.dam.2014.01.005
38. United Nations: review of Maritime Transport. In: Conference on Trade and Development (2021) https://unctad.org/publication/review-maritime-transport-2021
39. Van Twiller, J., Sivertsen, A., Pacino, D., Jensen, R.M.: Literature survey on the container stowage planning problem. Eur. J. Oper. Res. **317**(3), 841–857 (2024). https://doi.org/10.1016/j.ejor.2023.12.018
40. Vaswani, A., et al.: Attention is All you Need. In: Advances in Neural Information Processing Systems, vol. 30, Curran Associates, Inc (2017)
41. Vinyals, O., Fortunato, M., Jaitly, N.: Pointer Networks. In: Advances in Neural Information Processing Systems. vol. 28. Curran Associates, Inc. (2015)
42. Wang, Y., et al.: Enforcing Hard Constraints with Soft Barriers: safe Reinforcement Learning in Unknown Stochastic Environments. In: Proceedings of the 40th International Conference on Machine Learning (2023). https://doi.org/10.5555/3618408.3619930
43. Zhang, L., et al.: Penalized Proximal Policy Optimization for Safe Reinforcement Learning. In: Proceedings of the Thirty-First International Joint Conference on Artificial Intelligence. pp. 3744–3750 (2022). https://doi.org/10.24963/ijcai.2022/520

OPTIMUS: Optimal Offline Bidding Strategy for Manual Targeting Advertising Campaigns

Abhirup Mondal(✉), Akhil Kandregula, Sanjay Agrawal, and Vivek Sembium

Amazon, Bengaluru, India
{mabhirup,kandakhi,sanjagr,viveksem}@amazon.com

Abstract. Real-time bidding (RTB) in sponsored search advertising has been extensively studied, yet a critical gap remains: how should advertisers set optimal bids in Manual Targeting (MT) campaigns where bids must be specified upfront without real-time adjustment? Unlike Automated Targeting campaigns that dynamically modify bids based on auction context, MT campaigns, which account for nearly 30% of advertisers on major e-commerce platforms, require advertisers to commit to fixed keyword-level bids offline. We present **OPTIMUS**, a novel algorithm for optimal offline bid recommendation in MT campaigns. We formulate the problem as constrained optimization over sales maximization subject to budget constraints, and prove that at optimality, the marginal return on ad spend must be equalized across all targeting clauses. This insight yields an efficient Lagrangian-based algorithm that leverages bid landscape forecasting, click-through rate, and conversion rate models trained on historical auction logs. We establish theoretical guarantees for optimality and demonstrate that OPTIMUS scales to millions of campaigns. Extensive experiments on a major e-commerce advertising platform show that OPTIMUS achieves **2–6% improvements in sales, units sold, and click volume over production baselines** in online A/B tests, while also improving end-user experience through higher CTR and CVR by preferentially bidding on more relevant query-product pairs.

Keywords: Real-time bidding · Bid optimization · Display advertising · Manual targeting · Constrained optimization

1 Introduction

Online advertising has fundamentally transformed how businesses reach consumers and how users discover products and services on the web [5,11,13]. Sponsored search [9], where paid advertisements appear alongside organic search results, has emerged as a cornerstone of this ecosystem. For e-commerce platforms, sponsored search serves a dual purpose: it generates substantial advertising revenue while enabling sellers to increase the visibility of their products to potential buyers. The mechanism underlying sponsored search is Real-Time

M. Ceci et al. (Eds.): ECML PKDD 2026, LNAI 16948, pp. 342–357, 2027.
https://doi.org/10.1007/978-3-032-37679-4_20

Bidding (RTB) [22], where advertisers compete in auctions for ad placements each time a user submits a search query. The winning ads are displayed to the user, and advertisers are typically charged when their ad is clicked (pay-per-click). The bid an advertiser places directly influences both their probability of winning the auction and the cost they incur, making bid optimization a critical challenge.

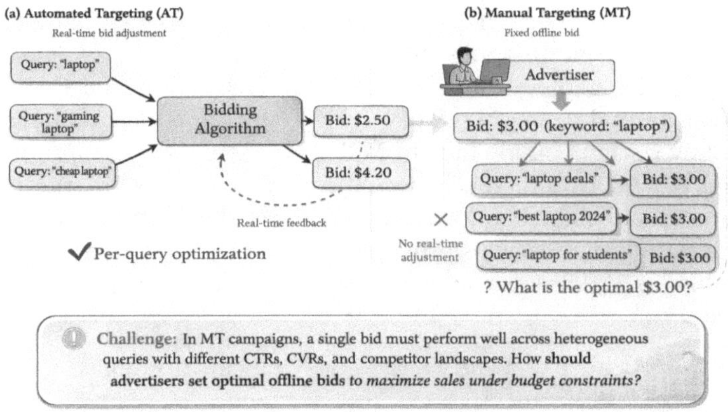

Fig. 1. Comparison of bidding mechanisms in online advertising. In Automated Targeting (AT), the platform dynamically adjusts bids per impression based on real-time signals. In Manual Targeting (MT), advertisers specify a single offline bid per keyword, used uniformly across all matched queries, creating a challenging offline optimization problem.

Advertising campaigns on major platforms can be broadly classified into two categories based on how bids are determined. In ***Automated Targeting (AT)*** campaigns, the advertising platform dynamically adjusts bids in real-time based on contextual signals such as user demographics, device type, time of day, and predicted conversion likelihood. In contrast, ***Manual Targeting (MT)*** campaigns require advertisers to specify their bids upfront at the keyword level, without the ability to modify them based on real-time auction context. Figure 1 illustrates this fundamental distinction: while AT campaigns benefit from per-query optimization with real-time feedback, MT campaigns must use a single fixed bid across all queries matching a keyword, creating a challenging offline optimization problem.

Despite the growing sophistication of automated bidding systems, MT campaigns remain prevalent. On major e-commerce advertising platforms, nearly 30% of advertisers use MT campaigns, often because they prefer direct control over their bidding strategy or operate in domains where automated systems lack sufficient historical data. For these advertisers, the question of how to set optimal offline bids (bids that maximize their key performance indicators such as sales, Return on Ad Spend, or click volume) is of paramount importance.

While the literature on online bid optimization in RTB is extensive [8,18,19], the problem of setting optimal *offline* bids for MT campaigns has received surprisingly little attention. The seminal work of Zhang et al. [22] established that in second-price auctions, the optimal bid for each impression should be proportional to its expected value. However, this result assumes the ability to set different bids for each impression opportunity, a capability that MT campaigns fundamentally lack. In MT campaigns, a single bid must be specified for each targeting clause (product-keyword-match type tuple), and this same bid is used across all queries that match that keyword. This constraint renders existing online bidding strategies inapplicable.

To address this gap, we propose **OPTIMUS** (Optimal Offline Bidding Strategy for Manual Targeting Advertising Campaigns), a novel algorithm for recommending optimal offline bids in MT campaigns. Our key insight is that at the optimal bid allocation, the marginal return on ad spend (the incremental sales generated per incremental dollar of advertising cost) must be equalized across all targeting clauses. This principle, derived from Lagrangian optimization theory, enables us to develop an efficient algorithm that finds the globally optimal bid configuration.

Contributions. This paper makes the following contributions:

1. **Problem Formulation.** We formally define the offline bid optimization problem for MT campaigns and establish its distinction from online bid optimization (Sect. 3.4). We prove that sales maximization subject to budget constraints and ROAS maximization subject to minimum sales constraints are equivalent formulations (Sect. 3).
2. **Optimal Algorithm.** We derive OPTIMUS , a theoretically optimal algorithm for offline bid recommendation based on equalizing marginal returns across targeting clauses (Sect. 4). The algorithm leverages bid landscape forecasting, click-through rate (CTR), and conversion rate (CVR) models trained on historical auction logs, and scales efficiently to millions of campaigns.
3. **Empirical Validation.** We demonstrate the efficacy of OPTIMUS through extensive experiments on a major e-commerce advertising platform (Sect. 5). In online A/B tests, OPTIMUS achieves 2–6% improvements in sales, units sold, and click volume over production baselines. Offline experiments on auction logs show consistent outperformance against value-based and relevance-based bidding strategies.

2 Related Work

Optimal Bidding in RTB. Zhang et al. [22] established that in second-price auctions, the optimal bid for an impression with expected value u_i is $b_i^* = u_i/\lambda$, where λ enforces budget constraints. This foundational result assumes advertisers can set *per-impression bids*, a capability unavailable in Manual Targeting campaigns, where a single bid must apply uniformly across all matched queries. This constraint motivates our work.

Dynamic Bidding Strategies. Dynamic approaches adapt bids in real-time using control-theoretic methods [20] or, more recently, Reinforcement Learning [2,8,18, 23]. RL-based methods model bidding as an MDP where states encode auction characteristics, actions adjust bids, and rewards reflect advertiser KPIs. While powerful, these methods require real-time inference, which is unavailable in MT campaigns where bids are fixed at campaign creation. OPTIMUS addresses the complementary problem of setting optimal *static* bids.

Bid Landscape Forecasting. Predicting competitor bid distributions is essential for bid optimization. Approaches range from parametric models (Gaussian, Log-Normal, Gamma distributions) [3,4,15,22] to non-parametric deep learning methods like Deep Landscape Forecasting [14]. OPTIMUS is model-agnostic; we use a classification-based approach [12] that estimates the CDF of competitor bids for efficient win probability and CPC computation.

Response Prediction. CTR and CVR prediction has evolved from logistic regression and Factorization Machines [10,16] to deep learning approaches. DeepFM [7] combines factorization machines with neural networks for strong industrial performance. OPTIMUS uses DeepFM-based models with temperature calibration to ensure well-calibrated probability estimates for aggregate optimization.

Positioning. To our knowledge, OPTIMUS is the first to address optimal *offline* bid setting for Manual Targeting campaigns. Unlike online methods that optimize per-impression bids, our key insight is that optimal offline bids must *equalize marginal returns* across targeting clauses, a different optimality condition derived from Lagrangian optimization applied to historical auction logs.

3 Problem Formulation

We formalize the offline bid optimization problem for Manual Targeting (MT) campaigns. We first establish notation and the problem setup, then present the optimization objectives and prove key structural properties that enable our solution.

3.1 Notation and Setup

Consider an MT advertising campaign $\mathcal{M}$ consisting of m *targeting clauses* $\mathcal{T} = \{t_1, t_2, \ldots, t_m\}$. Each targeting clause t_i is a tuple (A_i, k_i, τ_i) comprising a product A_i with price V_i, a keyword k_i, and a match type $\tau_i \in \{\text{exact}, \text{phrase}, \text{broad}\}$. The advertiser assigns a bid $b_i \in \mathbb{R}_{>0}$ to each targeting clause. Table 1 summarizes our notation.

When a user submits query q, the advertising platform matches it to targeting clauses based on keyword relevance and match type. Let $\mathcal{Q}_i = \{q_1^{(i)}, q_2^{(i)}, \ldots, q_{n_i}^{(i)}\}$ denote the set of historical queries matched to targeting clause t_i, with $n = \sum_{i=1}^{m} n_i$ total impression opportunities.

Table 1. Summary of notation.

Symbol	Description
$\mathcal{T} = \{t_1, \ldots, t_m\}$	Set of m targeting clauses
$t_i = (A_i, k_i, \tau_i)$	Product, keyword, match type for clause i
V_i	Price of product A_i
b_i	Offline bid for targeting clause t_i
$\mathcal{Q}_i$	Set of queries matched to clause t_i
$\text{ctr}(q, A_i)$	Click-through rate for query q, product A_i
$\text{cvr}(q, A_i)$	Conversion rate (given click)
$w(q, b_i)$	Auction win probability at bid b_i
$\text{cpc}(q, b_i)$	Expected cost-per-click at bid b_i
B	Campaign budget constraint

For each matched query, the campaign participates in a real-time auction. We assume a second-price auction mechanism [17], where the winner pays the second-highest bid. Let Z_q denote the random variable representing the maximum competitor bid for query q. The auction win probability and expected cost-per-click are:

$$w(q, b) = \Pr[Z_q < b] = \int_0^b p_q(z)\, dz \tag{1}$$

$$\text{cpc}(q, b) = \mathbb{E}[Z_q \mid Z_q < b] = \frac{\int_0^b z \cdot p_q(z)\, dz}{\int_0^b p_q(z)\, dz} \tag{2}$$

where $p_q(z)$ is the probability density of competitor bids for query q.

3.2 Expected Sales and Cost

For a query $q \in \mathcal{Q}_i$ matched to targeting clause t_i, a sale occurs through the following sequence: (1) the ad wins the auction with probability $w(q, b_i)$; (2) the user clicks the ad with probability $\text{ctr}(q, A_i)$; (3) the user purchases with probability $\text{cvr}(q, A_i)$, generating revenue V_i. The advertiser incurs cost $\text{cpc}(q, b_i)$ upon click.

The expected sales and cost for a single query-clause match are:

$$\mathbb{E}[S(q, t_i)] = w(q, b_i) \cdot \text{ctr}(q, A_i) \cdot \text{cvr}(q, A_i) \cdot V_i \tag{3}$$

$$\mathbb{E}[C(q, t_i)] = w(q, b_i) \cdot \text{ctr}(q, A_i) \cdot \text{cpc}(q, b_i) \tag{4}$$

Aggregating over all queries and targeting clauses, the total expected sales and cost for campaign $\mathcal{M}$ are:

$$\mathbb{E}[S(\mathbf{b})] = \sum_{i=1}^{m} \sum_{q \in \mathcal{Q}_i} w(q, b_i) \cdot \text{ctr}(q, A_i) \cdot \text{cvr}(q, A_i) \cdot V_i \tag{5}$$

$$\mathbb{E}[C(\mathbf{b})] = \sum_{i=1}^{m} \sum_{q \in \mathcal{Q}_i} w(q, b_i) \cdot \text{ctr}(q, A_i) \cdot \text{cpc}(q, b_i) \tag{6}$$

where $\mathbf{b} = (b_1, b_2, \ldots, b_m)$ is the vector of bids.

3.3 Optimization Objectives

Advertisers typically seek to maximize sales subject to a budget constraint, or maximize return on ad spend (ROAS) subject to minimum sales requirements. We formalize both objectives.

Sales Maximization. Given budget $B > 0$:

$$\max_{\mathbf{b} \in \mathbb{R}^m_{>0}} \mathbb{E}[S(\mathbf{b})] \quad \text{subject to} \quad \mathbb{E}[C(\mathbf{b})] \leq B \tag{7}$$

ROAS Maximization. Given budget $B > 0$ and minimum sales target $S_{\min} > 0$:

$$\max_{\mathbf{b} \in \mathbb{R}^m_{>0}} \frac{\mathbb{E}[S(\mathbf{b})]}{\mathbb{E}[C(\mathbf{b})]} \quad \text{subject to} \quad \mathbb{E}[C(\mathbf{b})] \leq B,\ \mathbb{E}[S(\mathbf{b})] \geq S_{\min} \tag{8}$$

We now establish that these two formulations are equivalent under appropriate parameter choices. We suppress the expectations for brevity of notations.

Lemma 1 (Diminishing Returns). *The marginal return on cost is positive and decreasing:* $\frac{dS}{dC} > 0$ *and* $\frac{d^2S}{dC^2} < 0$.

Proof. Using the chain rule, $\frac{dS}{dC} = \frac{\partial S/\partial b}{\partial C/\partial b}$. From Eqs. (1)–(2) and the fundamental theorem of calculus:

$$\frac{\partial w}{\partial b} = p_q(b), \qquad \frac{\partial (w \cdot \text{cpc})}{\partial b} = b \cdot p_q(b)$$

Thus $\frac{\partial S}{\partial b} \propto \text{ctr} \cdot \text{cvr} \cdot V \cdot p_q(b)$ and $\frac{\partial C}{\partial b} \propto \text{ctr} \cdot b \cdot p_q(b)$, yielding:

$$\frac{dS}{dC} \propto \frac{\text{cvr} \cdot V}{b} > 0$$

Since $\frac{dS}{dC}$ decreases in b and C is monotonically increasing in b, we have $\frac{d^2S}{dC^2} < 0$.

Theorem 1 (Equivalence of Objectives). *Let* $(\mathbf{b}_1^*, S_1^*, C_1^*)$ *be the optimal solution to* (7) *and* $(\mathbf{b}_2^*, S_2^*, C_2^*)$ *be the optimal solution to* (8). *If* $S_{\min} = S_1^*$, *then* $\mathbf{b}_1^* = \mathbf{b}_2^*$, $S_1^* = S_2^*$, *and* $C_1^* = C_2^* = B$.

Proof. Since S is increasing in C (Lemma 1), the budget constraint in (7) is tight at optimality: $C_1^* = B$.

For (8), diminishing returns implies S/C is decreasing in C. Thus, ROAS is maximized at the minimum feasible cost, which occurs when $S = S_{\text{min}}$. Setting $S_{\text{min}} = S_1^*$ yields $S_2^* = S_1^*$. Since S is monotonic in C, equal sales implies equal costs: $C_2^* = C_1^* = B$.

This equivalence allows us to focus on the sales maximization formulation (7) without loss of generality.

3.4 Distinction from Online Bid Optimization

The offline bid optimization problem differs fundamentally from online RTB optimization. In online settings, Zhang et al. [22] showed that the optimal bid for impression j with expected value $u_j = \text{ctr}_j \cdot \text{cvr}_j \cdot V_j$ is:

$$b_j^* = \frac{u_j}{\lambda} \tag{9}$$

where λ is a Lagrange multiplier enforcing the budget constraint.

This result requires setting *different bids for each impression*. In MT campaigns, we face a stricter constraint: a single bid b_i must be used for *all* queries $q \in \mathcal{Q}_i$ matched to targeting clause t_i. The queries in $\mathcal{Q}_i$ are heterogeneous: they have different CTRs, CVRs, and competitor bid distributions, yet must share a common bid.

This constraint fundamentally changes the optimization landscape. Rather than optimizing per-impression bids, we must find bids that perform well *in aggregate* across the query distribution for each targeting clause. In Sect. 4, we derive the optimality conditions for this setting and present an efficient algorithm.

4 Optimization Algorithm

We now derive an efficient algorithm for solving the offline bid optimization problem (7). Our approach is grounded in Lagrangian duality theory [1] and exploits the separable structure of the objective function. Figure 2 provides an overview of the complete OPTIMUS framework.

4.1 Key Insight: Marginal Return Equalization

By Theorem 1, we focus on the sales maximization formulation. Let $S_i(b_i)$ and $C_i(b_i)$ denote the expected sales and cost for targeting clause t_i as functions of bid b_i. The optimization problem can be written compactly as:

$$\max_{\mathbf{b} \in \mathbb{R}_{>0}^m} \sum_{i=1}^{m} S_i(b_i) \quad \text{subject to} \quad \sum_{i=1}^{m} C_i(b_i) \leq B \tag{10}$$

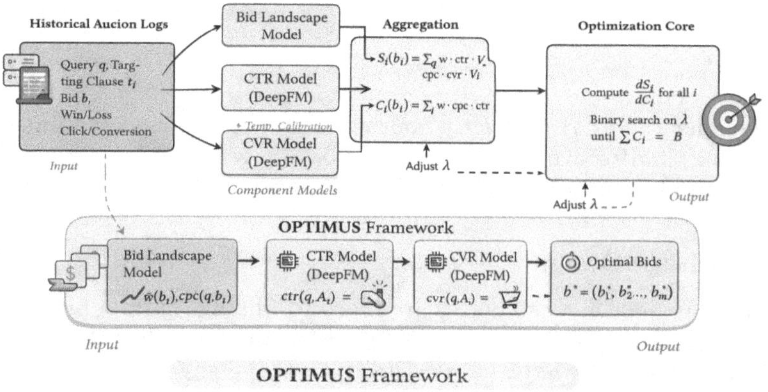

Fig. 2. OPTIMUS pipeline: auction logs feed bid landscape, CTR, and CVR models to compute sales/cost curves per targeting clause. Binary search over λ equalizes marginal returns and satisfies the budget constraint.

The key insight underlying OPTIMUS is that *at optimality, the marginal return on ad spend must be equalized across all targeting clauses.* Intuitively, if one targeting clause offers a higher marginal return than another, we could improve total sales by reallocating budget from the lower-return clause to the higher-return one. For instance, if $\frac{dS_1}{dC_1} = 2$ and $\frac{dS_2}{dC_2} = 3$, shifting \$1 from t_1 to t_2 gains \$1 in sales at zero net cost change, so the original allocation cannot be optimal.

This intuition is formalized in the following theorem.

Theorem 2 (Optimality Conditions). *The optimization problem* (10) *admits a unique solution* $\mathbf{b}^* = (b_1^*, \ldots, b_m^*)$ *satisfying:*

1. ***Equal Marginal Returns:*** *There exists* $\lambda^* > 0$ *such that for all* $i \in \{1, \ldots, m\}$*:*

$$\left.\frac{dS_i}{dC_i}\right|_{b_i = b_i^*} = \lambda^* \tag{11}$$

2. ***Budget Exhaustion:*** *The budget constraint is tight:* $\sum_{i=1}^{m} C_i(b_i^*) = B$.

Proof. Since both S_i and C_i are strictly increasing in b_i (higher bids win more auctions), we can apply the Implicit Function Theorem to express S_i as a function of C_i. The optimization becomes:

$$\max_{C_1,\ldots,C_m} \sum_{i=1}^{m} S_i(C_i) \quad \text{s.t.} \quad \sum_{i=1}^{m} C_i \leq B \tag{12}$$

The Lagrangian is $\mathcal{L} = \sum_{i=1}^{m} S_i(C_i) - \lambda(\sum_{i=1}^{m} C_i - B)$, where $\lambda \geq 0$ is the Lagrange multiplier. The first-order optimality conditions (KKT conditions) require:

$$\frac{\partial \mathcal{L}}{\partial C_i} = \frac{dS_i}{dC_i} - \lambda = 0 \quad \Rightarrow \quad \frac{dS_i}{dC_i} = \lambda \quad \forall i \tag{13}$$

By Lemma 1, $S_i(C_i)$ is strictly concave, ensuring uniqueness. Since $\frac{dS_i}{dC_i} > 0$ (positive marginal returns), we have $\lambda^* > 0$, implying the budget constraint is active by complementary slackness.

4.2 Algorithm Design

Theorem 2 provides a constructive approach to finding optimal bids. The equal marginal return condition (11) implies that for any candidate λ, we can determine the corresponding bid $b_i(\lambda)$ for each targeting clause by solving $\frac{dS_i}{dC_i}\big|_{b_i} = \lambda$. The budget exhaustion condition then determines the correct value of λ^* (Fig. 3).

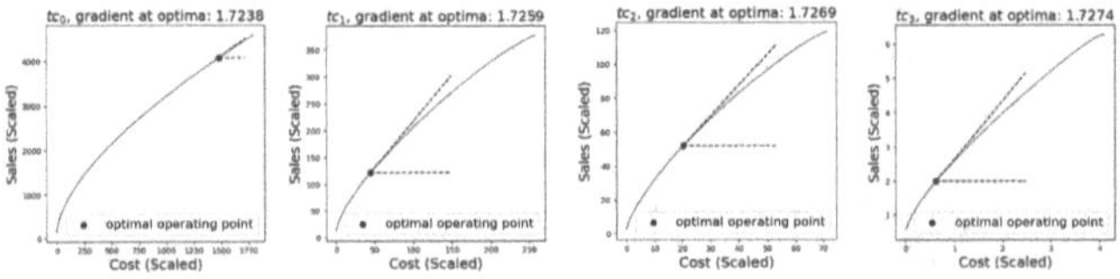

Fig. 3. Illustration of the optimality condition for a campaign with four targeting clauses $\{t_0, t_1, t_2, t_3\}$. Each curve shows the sales-cost relationship $S_i(C_i)$ for one clause. At the optimum (marked points), all marginal returns $\frac{dS_i}{dC_i}$ are equal to λ^*, and the total cost equals the budget B.

The algorithm proceeds in two phases:

Phase 1: Precomputation. For each targeting clause t_i, we discretize the bid space $[b_{\min}, b_{\max}]$ into L values and compute the corresponding (S_i, C_i) pairs using the CTR, CVR, and bid landscape models. We then compute the marginal return $g_i^{(l)} = \frac{S_i^{(l)} - S_i^{(l-1)}}{C_i^{(l)} - C_i^{(l-1)}}$ for each bid level.

Phase 2: Binary Search over λ. By Lemma 1, the marginal return $\frac{dS_i}{dC_i}$ is monotonically decreasing in b_i. This monotonicity enables binary search: for a given λ, we find the bid $b_i(\lambda)$ where the marginal return equals λ, compute the total cost $C(\lambda) = \sum_i C_i(b_i(\lambda))$, and adjust λ accordingly until $C(\lambda) = B$.

Algorithm 4 presents the complete procedure.

4.3 Complexity Analysis

Let n denote the total number of historical impressions across all targeting clauses, m the number of targeting clauses, and L the bid discretization granularity.

Algorithm 1: OPTIMUS : Optimal Offline Bid Optimization
Input: Targeting clauses $\{t_1, \ldots, t_m\}$, budget B, bid range $[b_{\min}, b_{\max}]$, tolerance ϵ
Output: Optimal bids $\mathbf{b}^* = (b_1^*, \ldots, b_m^*)$
// Phase 1: Precomputation
for $i = 1$ to m **do**
  Discretize bids: $\mathcal{B}_i = \{b_{\min}, b_{\min} + \delta, \ldots, b_{\max}\}$
  for each $b \in \mathcal{B}_i$ **do**
    Compute $S_i(b)$ and $C_i(b)$ using Eqs. (5)–(6)
  Compute marginal returns $g_i(b) = \frac{\Delta S_i}{\Delta C_i}$ for each bid level
// Phase 2: Binary Search over λ
Initialize $\lambda_{\text{lo}} \leftarrow 0$, $\lambda_{\text{hi}} \leftarrow \max_i g_i(b_{\min})$
while $\lambda_{\text{hi}} - \lambda_{\text{lo}} > \epsilon$ **do**
  $\lambda \leftarrow (\lambda_{\text{lo}} + \lambda_{\text{hi}})/2$
  for $i = 1$ to m **do**
    $b_i(\lambda) \leftarrow \arg\min_{b \in \mathcal{B}_i} |g_i(b) - \lambda|$
  $C_{\text{total}} \leftarrow \sum_{i=1}^{m} C_i(b_i(\lambda))$
  if $C_{\text{total}} < B$ **then** $\lambda_{\text{hi}} \leftarrow \lambda$
  else $\lambda_{\text{lo}} \leftarrow \lambda$
return $\mathbf{b}^* = (b_1(\lambda), \ldots, b_m(\lambda))$

Fig. 4. The OPTIMUS algorithm for optimal offline bid optimization.

Precomputation (Phase 1): Computing (S_i, C_i) for each bid level requires evaluating CTR, CVR, and bid landscape models over all queries in $\mathcal{Q}_i$. This takes $O(n \cdot L)$ time across all clauses.

Binary Search (Phase 2): Each iteration requires $O(m \cdot \log L)$ time to find bids matching the target λ (using binary search within each clause). With $O(\log(1/\epsilon))$ iterations for convergence, the total is $O(m \cdot \log L \cdot \log(1/\epsilon))$.

Overall: The dominant cost is precomputation, yielding $O(n \cdot L)$ complexity. Since L is typically small (a few hundred bid levels), OPTIMUS scales linearly with the number of impressions and can efficiently handle campaigns with millions of historical queries.

4.4 Component Models

Algorithm 4 requires three predictive models trained on historical auction logs. Importantly, OPTIMUS is *model-agnostic*: any improvements in these component models directly translate to better bid recommendations.

The *bid landscape model* estimates the CDF of competitor bids $P_q(b) = \Pr[Z_q < b]$ using a classification-based approach [12], enabling computation of win probability $w(q, b) = P_q(b)$ and expected CPC via integration by parts. For *CTR and CVR prediction*, we employ DeepFM [7], a factorization-machine based neural network that captures both low-order and high-order feature interactions from query, product, and contextual features. Both models are calibrated using temperature scaling [6] to ensure well-calibrated probability estimates for aggregate optimization.

5 Experiments

We evaluate OPTIMUS through both offline counterfactual analysis on historical auction logs and online A/B experiments on live traffic. This dual evaluation strategy validates both the theoretical soundness of our approach and its practical effectiveness in production environments.

5.1 Experimental Setup

Dataset Description. We collected historical auction logs from a major e-commerce advertising platform over a 7-day period. Table 2 summarizes the dataset characteristics.

Table 2. Dataset statistics for offline evaluation.

Attribute	Value
Total ad requests	~4 billion
Time period	7 days
Training set	Days 1–4
Test set	Days 5–7
Campaigns evaluated	10,000+
Avg. targeting clauses per campaign	50–200

Each auction log record contains query information (user search query and timestamp), auction participants (all competing ads and their submitted bids, including non-winners), model predictions (pre-computed CTR and CVR estimates for each query-ad pair), and outcome labels (click and conversion indicators for winning impressions). The exhaustive recording of all participant bids (not just winners) enables counterfactual evaluation: given any bid value b, we can determine whether the ad would have won and at what cost.

Evaluation Metrics. We measure performance using Sales (total attributed sales value in millions), Units (number of units sold in thousands), Clicks (total clicks received in millions), Impressions (total ad impressions served), and CTR/CVR (click-through and conversion rates). For A/B experiments, we report percentage improvement of Treatment over Control. Statistical significance is assessed using two-sample t-tests with $p < 0.01$ threshold.

Baseline Methods. Since limited prior work addresses offline bid optimization for MT campaigns, we developed two competitive baselines:

Value-Based Bidding (VBB) [22]: Extends real-time bidding theory to the offline setting. The optimal per-impression bid is u_i/λ where $u_i = \text{ctr}(q, A_i) \cdot \text{cvr}(q, A_i) \cdot V_i$. Since MT requires a single bid per targeting clause, we average across matched queries:

$$b_i = \frac{1}{|\mathcal{Q}_i|} \sum_{q \in \mathcal{Q}_i} \frac{u_q}{\lambda} \tag{14}$$

The Lagrange multiplier λ is tuned via line search to satisfy the budget constraint.

Relevance-Based Bidding (RBB) [21]: Assigns higher bids to targeting clauses with stronger query-product relevance:

$$b_i = \frac{1}{|\mathcal{Q}_i|} \sum_{q \in \mathcal{Q}_i} \frac{\text{rel}(q, A_i)}{\lambda} \tag{15}$$

where $\text{rel}(q, A_i)$ is a learned relevance score. The multiplier λ is determined via cross-validation.

The key distinction is that VBB and RBB use *averaged* signals to set bids, while OPTIMUS optimizes based on *marginal returns*, a fundamentally different criterion derived from our theoretical analysis.

5.2 Offline Evaluation

Counterfactual Simulation. Using the logged auction data, we simulate campaign performance under different bidding strategies. For each targeting clause bid b_i, we replay all historical auctions to compute win rate (fraction of auctions won), expected cost (sum of CPCs for won auctions), and expected sales (attributed conversions × product values). This counterfactual approach answers: "What would have happened if we had bid b instead of the observed bid?"

Results. Table 3 presents the offline evaluation results.

Table 3. Offline performance comparison (Sales in \$M, Units in K, Clicks in M).

Method	Sales	Units	Clicks
OPTIMUS	**6.81**	**59.7**	**0.391**
VBB	6.23	56.1	0.359
RBB	6.18	55.2	0.349
OPTIMUS vs VBB	+9.3%	+6.4%	+8.9%
OPTIMUS vs RBB	+10.2%	+8.2%	+12.0%

OPTIMUS achieves 9–10% higher sales than both baselines while operating under identical budget constraints. The improvement stems from the marginal return equalization principle: OPTIMUS reallocates budget from low-efficiency targeting clauses to high-efficiency ones, whereas VBB and RBB distribute budget based on average (not marginal) value signals.

5.3 Online A/B Experiments

Experimental Design. We conducted four A/B experiments on live traffic: MT campaigns were randomly assigned to Treatment (OPTIMUS) or Control (expert-set bids), with the objective of maximizing sales subject to advertiser-specified budget. Experiments ran for 2–4 weeks each. Campaign segments $\mathcal{E}^1, \mathcal{E}^2$ represent mature campaigns (tenure >30 days), while $\mathcal{E}^3, \mathcal{E}^4$ represent new campaigns (tenure <30 days).

Results. Table 4 summarizes the A/B experiment results.

Table 4. Online A/B results: % improvement of OPTIMUS over Control ($p < 0.01$ for all).

Exp.	Sales	Units	Impr.	Clicks
$\mathcal{E}^1$	+2.85	+2.48	+2.37	+2.10
$\mathcal{E}^2$	+3.21	+3.28	+1.26	+1.20
$\mathcal{E}^3$	+6.24	+5.89	+3.79	+2.74
$\mathcal{E}^4$	+1.97	+1.38	+2.83	+3.79
Average	**+3.57**	**+3.26**	**+2.56**	**+2.46**

Key observations: OPTIMUS consistently outperforms expert-set bids across all experiments and metrics. Larger gains on newer campaigns ($\mathcal{E}^3$: +6.24% sales) suggest OPTIMUS is particularly effective when historical performance data is limited. All improvements are statistically significant ($p < 0.01$).

5.4 Analysis and Insights

Bid Reallocation Behavior. Figure 5 visualizes how OPTIMUS modifies bids relative to initial values. Each point represents a targeting clause; the x-axis shows the marginal cost-to-sales ratio dC/dS at the initial bid.

The pattern confirms our theoretical prediction: OPTIMUS increases bids for targeting clauses with low marginal cost (high efficiency) and decreases bids for those with high marginal cost (low efficiency), driving toward the equilibrium where all marginal returns are equalized.

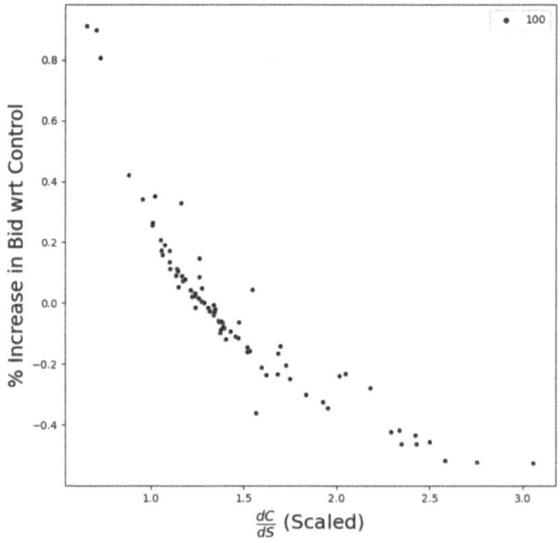

Fig. 5. Bid adjustments by OPTIMUS . Targeting clauses with high dC/dS (inefficient) have bids reduced; those with low dC/dS (efficient) have bids increased.

Impact on User Experience. An unexpected benefit of OPTIMUS is improved CTR and CVR in live traffic. By bidding higher on targeting clauses with strong query-product relevance (which correlates with high CVR), OPTIMUS preferentially wins auctions for highly relevant ads. This creates a virtuous cycle: better ad relevance → higher CTR/CVR → improved user experience.

Computational Efficiency. In production, OPTIMUS processes campaigns with 50–200 targeting clauses and millions of historical impressions. The two-phase algorithm (Sect. 4.2) enables efficient optimization: Phase 1 (precomputation) is parallelizable across targeting clauses, while Phase 2 (binary search) converges in $O(\log(1/\epsilon))$ iterations. End-to-end bid optimization completes in under 10 s per campaign on commodity hardware.

6 Conclusion

We introduced OPTIMUS , the first algorithm for optimal *offline* bid recommendation in Manual Targeting (MT) campaigns, a setting that governs nearly 30% of advertisers yet has been largely overlooked by the real-time bidding literature. Our central result is a characterization of optimality: at the optimal allocation, the marginal return on ad spend is equalized across all targeting clauses. This condition yields a provably optimal two-phase algorithm that runs in $O(n \cdot r + m \log(1/\epsilon))$ time and scales to millions of campaigns. Across offline auction-log experiments and online A/B tests on a major e-commerce platform, OPTIMUS delivers 9–10% offline and 2–6% online ($p < 0.01$) gains in sales over production baselines, while raising CTR and CVR by shifting spend toward more relevant query–product pairs, an outcome that benefits advertisers and users alike.

Two assumptions bound these results: stationary market conditions and the use of point estimates from the component bid-landscape, CTR, and CVR models. Relaxing them motivates our future work on robust optimization under model uncertainty and adaptation to non-stationary environments. We also see promising directions in modeling cross-targeting-clause dependencies and extending the framework to multi-objective settings beyond sales maximization.

Disclosure of Interests. The authors have no competing interests to declare that are relevant to the content of this article.

References

1. Boyd, S., Vandenberghe, L.: Convex Optimization. Cambridge University Press, Cambridge (2004)
2. Cai, H., Ret al.: Real-time bidding by reinforcement learning in display advertising. In: Proceedings of the Tenth ACM International Conference on Web Search and Data Mining. WSDM '17, New York, NY, USA, pp. 661–670. Association for Computing Machinery (2017). https://doi.org/10.1145/3018661.3018702
3. Chapelle, O.: Offline evaluation of response prediction in online advertising auctions. In: Proceedings of the 24th International Conference on World Wide Web. WWW '15 Companion, New York, NY, USA, pp 919–922. Association for Computing Machinery (2015). https://doi.org/10.1145/2740908.2742566
4. Cui, Y., Zhang, R., Li, W., Mao, J.: Bid landscape forecasting in online ad exchange marketplace. In: Proceedings of the 17th ACM SIGKDD International Conference on Knowledge Discovery and Data Mining. KDD '11, New York, NY, USA, pp. 265–273. Association for Computing Machinery (2011). https://doi.org/10.1145/2020408.2020454
5. Goldfarb, A., Greenstein, S.M., Tucker, C.E.: Economic Analysis of the Digital Economy. University of Chicago Press (2015). https://doi.org/10.7208/chicago/9780226206981.001.0001, https://www.nber.org/books-and-chapters/economic-analysis-digital-economy
6. Guo, C., Pleiss, G., Sun, Y., Weinberger, K.Q.: On calibration of modern neural networks. CoRR abs/1706.04599 (2017). http://arxiv.org/abs/1706.04599
7. Guo, H., Tang, R., Ye, Y., Li, Z., He, X.: DeepFM: a factorization-machine based neural network for CTR prediction. CoRR abs/1703.04247 (2017). http://arxiv.org/abs/1703.04247
8. He, Y., et al.: A unified solution to constrained bidding in online display advertising. In: Proceedings of the 27th ACM SIGKDD Conference on Knowledge Discovery & Data Mining. KDD '21, pp. 2993–3001, New York, NY, USA. Association for Computing Machinery (2021). https://doi.org/10.1145/3447548.3467199
9. Jansen, J., Mullen, T.: Sponsored search: an overview of the concept, history, and technology. IJEB **6**, 114–131 (2008). https://doi.org/10.1504/IJEB.2008.018068
10. Juan, Y., Lefortier, D., Chapelle, O.: Field-aware factorization machines in a real-world online advertising system. In: Proceedings of the 26th International Conference on World Wide Web Companion. WWW '17 Companion, Republic and Canton of Geneva, CHE, pp. 680–688. International World Wide Web Conferences Steering Committee (2017). https://doi.org/10.1145/3041021.3054185

11. Lewis, R., Rao, J.M., Reiley, D.H.: Measuring the Effects of Advertising: The Digital Frontier, pp. 191–218. In: [5] (2015). https://doi.org/10.7208/chicago/9780226206981.003.0007, http://www.nber.org/chapters/c12991
12. Li, X., Zhang, M.M., Wang, Z., Tong, Y.: Arbitrary distribution modeling with censorship in real-time bidding advertising. In: Proceedings of the 28th ACM SIGKDD Conference on Knowledge Discovery and Data Mining. KDD '22, New York, NY, USA, pp. 3250–3258. Association for Computing Machinery (2022). https://doi.org/10.1145/3534678.3539048
13. Liu-Thompkins, Y.: A decade of online advertising research: what we learned and what we need to know. J. Advertising **48**(1), 1–13 (2019). https://doi.org/10.1080/00913367.2018.1556138
14. Ren, K., Qin, J., Zheng, L., Yang, Z., Zhang, W., Yu, Y.: Deep landscape forecasting for real-time bidding advertising. CoRR abs/1905.03028 (2019). http://arxiv.org/abs/1905.03028
15. Ren, K., Zhang, W., Chang, K., Rong, Y., Yu, Y., Wang, J.: Bidding machine: learning to bid for directly optimizing profits in display advertising. IEEE Trans. Knowl. Data Eng. **30**(4), 645–659 (2018). https://doi.org/10.1109/TKDE.2017.2775228
16. Rendle, S.: Factorization machines with LibFM. ACM Trans. Intell. Syst. Technol. **3**(3) (2012). https://doi.org/10.1145/2168752.2168771
17. Roughgarden, T.: Algorithmic game theory. Commun. ACM **53**(7), 78–86 (2010). https://doi.org/10.1145/1785414.1785439
18. Wang, H., et al.: Roi-constrained bidding via curriculum-guided bayesian reinforcement learning. In: Proceedings of the 28th ACM SIGKDD Conference on Knowledge Discovery and Data Mining. KDD '22, New York, NY, USA, pp. 4021–4031. Association for Computing Machinery (2022). https://doi.org/10.1145/3534678.3539211
19. Wu, D., et al.: Budget constrained bidding by model-free reinforcement learning in display advertising. In: Proceedings of the 27th ACM International Conference on Information and Knowledge Management. ACM (2018). https://doi.org/10.1145/3269206.3271748
20. Yang, X., et al.: Bid optimization by multivariable control in display advertising. In: Proceedings of the 25th ACM SIGKDD International Conference on Knowledge Discovery & Data Mining. KDD '19, New York, NY, USA, pp. 1966–1974. Association for Computing Machinery (2019). https://doi.org/10.1145/3292500.3330681
21. Yao, S., Tan, J., Chen, X., Yang, K., Xiao, R., Deng, H., Wan, X.: Learning a product relevance model from click-through data in e-commerce. In: Proceedings of the Web Conference 2021. WWW '21, ACM (2021). https://doi.org/10.1145/3442381.3450129
22. Zhang, W., Yuan, S., Wang, J.: Optimal real-time bidding for display advertising. In: Proceedings of the 20th ACM SIGKDD International Conference on Knowledge Discovery and Data Mining. KDD '14, New York, NY, USA, pp. 1077–1086. Association for Computing Machinery (2014). https://doi.org/10.1145/2623330.2623633
23. Zhao, J., Qiu, G., Guan, Z., Zhao, W., He, X.: Deep reinforcement learning for sponsored search real-time bidding. In: Proceedings of the 24th ACM SIGKDD International Conference on Knowledge Discovery & Data Mining. KDD '18, New York, NY, USA, pp. 1021–1030. Association for Computing Machinery (2018). https://doi.org/10.1145/3219819.3219918

Explainability, Robustness and Responsible AI

Exposing the Illusion of Fairness: Auditing Vulnerabilities to Distributional Manipulation Attacks

Valentin Lafargue[1,2,3,4(✉)], Adriana Laurindo Monteiro[5], Emmanuelle Claeys[4,6], Laurent Risser[1,3], and Jean-Michel Loubes[2,3]

[1] Institut de Mathématiques de Toulouse (IMT), Toulouse, France
valentin.lafargue@math.univ-toulouse.fr
[2] Institut national de recherche en sciences et technologies du numérique (INRIA), Bordeaux, France
[3] Artificial and Natural Intelligence Toulouse Institute 2 (ANITI 2), Toulouse, France
[4] Institut de Recherche en Informatique de Toulouse (IRIT), Toulouse, France
[5] Rio de Janeiro, Brazil
[6] CNRS IRL CROSSING, Adelaide, Australia

Abstract. The rapid deployment of AI systems in high-stakes domains, including those classified as high-risk under the The EU AI Act (Regulation (EU) 2024/1689), has intensified the need for reliable compliance auditing. For binary classifiers, regulatory risk assessment often relies on global fairness metrics such as the Disparate Impact ratio, widely used to evaluate potential discrimination. In typical auditing settings, the auditee provides a subset of its dataset to an auditor, while a supervisory authority may verify whether this subset is representative of the full underlying distribution. In this work, we investigate to what extent a malicious auditee can construct a fairness-compliant yet representative-looking sample from a non-compliant original distribution, thereby creating an illusion of fairness. We formalize this problem as a constrained distributional projection task and introduce mathematically grounded manipulation strategies based on entropic and optimal transport projections. These constructions characterize the minimal distributional shift required to satisfy fairness constraints. To counter such attacks, we formalize representativeness through distributional distance based statistical tests and systematically evaluate their ability to detect manipulated samples. Our analysis highlights the conditions under which fairness manipulation can remain statistically undetected and provides practical guidelines for strengthening supervisory verification. We validate our theoretical findings through experiments on standard tabular datasets for bias detection. Code is publicly available at https://github.com/ValentinLafargue/Inspection.

Keywords: Auditing · Vulnerabilities · Distributional Manipulation · Attacks · Fairness evaluation · Optimization

A. L. Monteiro—Independent Researcher.

M. Ceci et al. (Eds.): ECML PKDD 2026, LNAI 16948, pp. 361–379, 2027.
https://doi.org/10.1007/978-3-032-37679-4_21

1 Introduction

Fairness auditing has emerged as a critical practice to ensure that machine learning models comply with ethical and legal standards by not exhibiting discriminatory bias [4,6,30,36]. High-profile investigative audits, such as the ProPublica analysis of the COMPAS recidivism risk tool, have exposed significant biases against certain demographic groups [2]. These findings underscored the societal harms of unverified AI systems and prompted calls for regular fairness audits by independent parties [32].

In response, regulators have begun instituting fairness compliance requirements. The Regulation (EU) 2024/1689 establishes strict requirements on high-risk AI systems. Under Article 9, providers must implement a comprehensive risk management system that identifies, analyzes, and evaluates risks related to the system's intended use and ensure that any residual risk is reduced to an acceptable level before deployment.

Auditing an algorithm is a long multidimensional process that aims to verify a long list of properties in order to establish regulatory compliance. In this paper, we focus on a specific part of this long pipeline process: evaluating whether the AI system may induce discriminatory outcomes with respect to regulator-designated sensitive attributes. We refer to this objective as fairness compliance. In the United States, such assessments are commonly operationalized through disparate impact analysis, which evaluates indirect discrimination in algorithms to a legally protected group [15]. One practical strategy to operationalize such obligations is outcome-based evaluation. In the US, this is commonly implemented through disparate impact analysis in EEOC guidelines [26], and supported by case law (e.g., Griggs v. Duke Power Co., 401 U.S. 424 (1971)). In this case, the US Supreme Court ruled illegal a hiring process if it results in disparate impact; even if the hiring decision is not calculated based on the protected attribute.

The auditee chooses a sample of the dataset on which the fairness measure is estimated. Hence, ensuring the good faith of the auditee is critical, as exemplified by the Volkswagen emissions scandal [22], in which vehicles were engineered to detect auditing conditions and deceive regulators by temporarily producing compliant behavior. Similar concerns arise in machine learning, where inconsistencies in model behavior during auditing have been documented, such as in the case of Meta's models discussed in [7].

In this work, our objective is to support auditors by identifying potential strategies that audited entities might use to circumvent fairness audits and by providing tools to detect such attempts. Building on the notion of *manipulation-proof* introduced in [39], we show how a dataset that initially violates a fairness criterion, such as Disparate Impact, can be minimally altered to appear compliant, with limited distributional shift as measured by the KullbackâĂŞLeibler (KL) divergence or the Wasserstein distance. By systematically analyzing these plausible manipulations, we aim to raise awareness of audit vulnerabilities and to equip oversight bodies with methods to detect suspicious modifications, thereby strengthening the reliability and robustness of fairness auditing processes.

Our contributions are the following:

- We present a mathematical analysis of data manipulation aimed at artificially improving fairness. Our framework considers distributional shifts of the evaluation sample designed to satisfy fairness constraints while remaining statistically indistinguishable from the original distribution. We study two approaches: entropic projections and optimal-transport projections.
- We provide a testing methodology to assess whether, and to what extent, a sample from the projected distribution can artificially increase the Disparate Impact, thereby faking fairness, while remaining undetected by distribution-based statistical tests.

2 Problem Statement

Our auditing framework involves three entities:

1. **Auditee.** The product owner holds the full dataset and trained predictor f (binary classifier, $\widehat{Y} \in \{0, 1\}$). For regulatory or sovereignty reasons, only a subset of the data is disclosed to the auditor. The auditee is liable (i) if the model is not fairness-compliant and (ii) if the submitted subset does not enable the auditor to evaluate the fairness of the system.
2. **Auditor.** The auditor is an external entity in charge of computing prescribed fairness metrics and determining whether the system satisfies the relevant compliance criteria. The auditor's evaluation is conducted solely on the basis of the information disclosed by the auditee. In particular, using the empirical distribution of the submitted sample, it estimates a fairness metric. In most of the paper we consider the example where the prescribed metric is the Disparate Impact Ratio.
3. **Supervisory authority.** A higher-level oversight body, such as a regulator acting as a market surveillance authority, for instance the ACPR for banking regulations, or a court-appointed expert intervening in juridical cases or regulatory verification. It may intervene in regulatory reviews or judicial proceedings. In particular it has access to the full dataset, and can (i) compute fairness metric on full data and (ii) determine subset representativeness. It is responsible for ensuring that the audit was conducted correctly and in accordance with applicable requirements.

In this paper we consider a use case where the auditee has developed a model which has fairness issues. It tries to hide the problem by picking a subsample while optimizing the fairness metric that will be computed by the auditor. Yet, from the supervisory authority, submitting a non-representative sample constitute a deceptive attempt by the auditee to obstruct or distort the assessment.

2.1 Auditor Fairness Evaluation

One of the most desired fairness properties is the statistical parity, which ensures that the decision of the algorithm does not depend on the sensitive attribute. We note S the protected attribute, also called sensitive attribute in the machine learning literature. In this paper, the protected attribute will always be binary $S \in \{0,1\}$, this is standard to observe treatment disparity for gender, disability or ethnicity (one-versus-all paradigm); continuous variable such as income or age are transformed to binary using a threshold value as separator (i.e., above or below 40 years old). The auditor will apply a fairness metric, the Disparate Impact (DI) ratio, to evaluate the statistical parity of the subset provided by the audited entity; defined for a model $\widehat{Y} = f(X)$ and data following distribution $\mathbb{P}$ by

$$DI(f, \mathbb{P}, S) := \frac{\min(\mathbb{P}(\widehat{Y} = 1 \mid S = 0), \mathbb{P}(\widehat{Y} = 1 \mid S = 1)}{\max(\mathbb{P}(\widehat{Y} = 1 \mid S = 0), \mathbb{P}(\widehat{Y} = 1 \mid S = 1)}. \quad (1)$$

This quantity is equal to 1 when no probabilistic relationship exists between the outcome of the model and the sensitive variable, which implies a strict independence in the case where $f(X)$ is a two-class classification model. Hence, several norms or regulations impose that a model should have its disparate impact ratio greater than a given level t, often set to $t = 0.8$ [15,26,37]. While this work focuses on the DI ratio, our methods and results stands for other common global fairness metric, see in the Appendix, Sec. A.

2.2 Supervisory Verification

Let $(E, \mathcal{B}(E))$ be a measurable space. Denote by $\mathcal{P}(E)$ and $\mathcal{M}(E)$, respectively the space of probability measures on E and the space of finite measures in E. Let $Q_n = \frac{1}{n}\sum_{i=1}^{n} \delta_{Z_i}$ be the empirical underlying distribution of the auditee where Z_i is an i.i.d. sample of a random variable with value in E, δ_{Z_i} is the Dirac measure associated; and let $\widehat{Q}_m$ be the empirical distribution from the auditee sample $\mathcal{D}_m$ (with $m \leqslant n$). The supervisory goal is the verification that $\widehat{Q}_m$ is representative of Q_n. Consider a distance d in E, for $\widehat{Q}_m$ to be representative of Q_n, it needs to be close to Q_n: $d(\widehat{Q}_m, Q_n)$ needs to be small.

2.3 Malicious Auditee Optimization Problem

We propose a methodology that simulates how stakeholders could try to evade an audit on the Disparate Impact ratio, without any liability. The auditee aims to construct a distribution optimally close to the distribution of the original data, while ensuring that the fairness measure is above a threshold, as required by the regulations. In reality, the construction of a falsely compliant dataset is modeled as finding the solution to the optimization problem:

$$\text{argmin}_{P \in \mathcal{P}(E), DI(f,P,S) \geqslant t} d(P, Q_n). \quad (2)$$

Concerning which distance d to minimize, the malicious auditee will choose depending on the supervisory authority verification strategy.

Remark 1. The auditee is responsible to provide a representative subset on which the auditor will compute the fairness measure. The compliance result will be determined on this subset, which should be chosen to convey the general properties of the data of the auditee.

3 Related Work

Fairness auditing has increasingly been shown to be vulnerable to manipulation, commonly referred to as *fairwashing* [1]. A key vulnerability stems from the fact that global fairness metrics, such as Disparate Impact or Demographic Parity, are estimated on a test sample and therefore depend on the audited data distribution. Exploiting this dependence, Fukuchi et al. introduced stealthily biased sampling, showing how curated samples can appear fair while remaining close to the original biased distribution [16]. Proxy based attacks further demonstrate that interpretable surrogate models can be presented as evidence of fairness while masking discriminatory behavior [1]. Other works have studied decision manipulation during audits [28], empirical inconsistencies between audited and deployed behavior [32], and theoretical limits of detecting such manipulation [34].

Several fair washing strategies are closely related to classical bias mitigation techniques. Pre-processing approaches modify the data distribution to satisfy fairness constraints, including data massaging [27], feature repair [15], convex probabilistic transformations [8], and maximum entropy formulations [9]. Optimal transport methods have been proposed to reweigh or shift distributions while minimizing divergence [17]. Post processing techniques instead modify model outputs to enforce parity constraints, for example through linear programming adjustments [19] or Wasserstein barycentric projections [24]. Although originally designed for mitigation, these techniques can also be repurposed to simulate strategic manipulation.

From the auditing perspective, recent work emphasizes the importance of access models and statistical testing. Discussions on AI auditing argue that, at minimum, black box query access is required for meaningful oversight and highlight the parallels between auditing and hypothesis testing, including burden of proof and error trade offs [10]. Statistical inference methods have been proposed to provide confidence bounds for fairness metrics using bootstrap guarantees [11], and to adapt fairness testing to small or intersectional groups via size adaptive procedures. Complementary work studies black box audits for detecting group distribution shifts between training and deployment data using model queries [25], emphasizing that white box access is often unrealistic in practice.

In summary, fairness auditing is undergoing an arms race between auditees' capacity to fake compliance and auditors' ability to detect manipulation. Our work differs from prior fair washing studies by providing an explicit distributional projection formulation of audit evasion using entropic and optimal transport constructions, and by systematically analyzing the detectability of such manipulations through distribution based statistical tests. This positions fairness auditing as a constrained statistical inference problem, bridging distributional robustness, optimal transport, and hypothesis testing.

4 Fairwashing Detection by the Supervisory Authority: Statistical Tests Based on Distributional Distances

We outline below potential strategies a supervisory authority could adopt to assess whether the auditee provided a sample drawn from the original data distribution to the compliance evaluation. We note Q_t the distribution created by the auditee using Q_n, with $DI(f, Q_t, S) \geqslant t$. The non-malicious auditee always chooses $Q_t = Q_n$. Note that this distribution is never shared nor observable, even by the supervisory authority. The auditee presents a sample $\mathcal{D}_m \sim Q_t^{\otimes m}$, we denote by $\widehat{Q}_m$ the empirical distribution induced by $\mathcal{D}_m$ and let $t' := DI(f, \widehat{Q}_m, S)$.

To verify the authenticity of this sample, the authority must be granted access to the full dataset upon request. This access enables the authority to reconstruct the ground-truth distribution Q_n and determine whether the submitted data $\mathcal{D}_m$ arises from fairwashing manipulation Q_t or follows the initial distribution Q_n. To assess representativeness, the authority must rely on statistical testing. Two main categories of tests are available.

The first includes hypothesis tests that evaluate, at a chosen confidence level, whether the empirical distribution $\widehat{Q}_m$ induced by the submitted sample is statistically similar to Q_n. In their study, [16] apply a KolmogorovâĂŞSmirnov (KS) test for one-dimensional data ($X \in \mathbb{R}^1$), and a test based on the Wasserstein distance for higher-dimensional settings ($X \in \mathbb{R}^k$, with $k > 1$). In our framework, we apply both the KS test and the Wasserstein test on the conditional distribution $\widehat{Y} \mid S$.

The second approach evaluates whether the sample $\mathcal{D}_m$ could plausibly result from a random draw from the original distribution Q_n, by measuring a divergence or distance metric d. Let $Q_m^{(1)}, \cdots, Q_m^{(B)}$ denote empirical distributions obtained from independent samples of size m drawn from Q_n. The idea is to test whether the observed distance value $d(\widehat{Q}_m, Q_n)$ lies within the acceptance region induced by the $(1-\alpha)$-quantiles of the reference distribution. The confidence interval is estimated from the empirical distribution of

$$d(Q_m^{(b)}, Q_n), \quad b = 1, \cdots, B. \tag{3}$$

For the distance metric d, we considered several options, including the Maximum Mean Discrepancy (MMD) [18], the Wasserstein distance, and the KullbackâĂŞLeibler divergence. For the statistical tests we introduce based on distributional distances (all but KS), the detection threshold is based on the sample size provided by the auditee, making the results more robust to type I and II errors. All hypothesis tests reported in this paper use a 95% confidence level.

Remark 2. **Application to non-tabular data.** The statistical tests (and later the methods we develop) are originally meant to handle tabular data. However they are applicable directly on images or text flattened as vectors. Yet, using the Wasserstein distance, based on the L^2 distance between individuals, might not be the best way to capture semantic similarity between images or token distributions. A way to circumvent this issue is to represent the images in another space, where the regular distances would have semantic meanings. The construction of such a space has already seen numerous works using PCA projections or latent spaces of AE, VAE or CNN classifiers. We present such results on the CelebA dataset [29] in Section C of the Appendix.

5 Malicious Auditee Strategy: Optimized Fairwashing Methods

In the following, we will consider two distances: in Sect. 5.1, one is related to the similarity for probabilistic inference (KL information), while in Sect. 5.2, the other distance captures geometric information between distances (Monge-Kantorovitch a.k.a. Wasserstein distance). Consequently, fairwashing amounts to modifying the initial distribution of the data by providing a fake but plausible distribution Q_t in order to achieve that $DI(f, Q_t, S) = t$ or $DI(f, Q_t, S) \geqslant t$.

Developing such methods is unavoidable: only by simulating what a malicious auditee could do, can we study this scenario in order to raise regulators' awareness, and evaluate which detection strategies are effective.

5.1 Using Entropic Projection to Fake Fairness

We first present the main tool we are going to use to mimic how an auditee can build a fair-washed sample. To formalize the ideas presented in Sect. 2.3, we present a theorem on how to construct a distribution minimizing the KL divergence w.r.t to the true observation while satisfying a constraint on its mean, similar to a global fairness measure.

The KL information is $D_{\mathrm{KL}}(P \| Q) = \int_E \log \frac{\mathrm{d}P}{\mathrm{d}Q} \, \mathrm{d}P$, if $P \ll Q$ and $\log \frac{\mathrm{d}P}{\mathrm{d}Q} \in L^1(P)$, and $+\infty$ otherwise. For any resulting dimension $k \geqslant 1$, let $\Phi : Z = (X, S, \widehat{Y}, Y) \in E \mapsto \Phi(X, S, \widehat{Y}, Y) \in \mathbb{R}^k$ be a measurable function representing the magnitude of the stress deformation on the whole input. Note that our results are stated for a generic function Φ of all variables $Z = (X, S, \widehat{Y}, Y)$. This includes the case of functions depending only on X, (X, Y) or $(X, \widehat{Y})$. We set for two vectors $x, y \in \mathbb{R}^k$ the scalar product as $\langle x, y \rangle = x^\top y$. The problem can be stated as follows: given the distribution Q_n, our aim is to construct a distribution close to Q_n while satisfying a prescribed moment constraint, namely that the expectation of the chosen function Φ under the distribution equals a given value $t \in \mathbb{R}^k$. More precisely, a new distribution Q_t satisfying the constraint $\int_E \Phi(z) \, \mathrm{d}Q_t(z) = t$ and being the closest possible to the initial empirical distribution Q_n in the sense of KL divergence, i.e. with $D_{\mathrm{KL}}(Q_t \| Q_n)$ as small as possible. The following theorem, whose proof can be found in [3], characterizes the distribution solution Q_t.

Theorem 1 (Entropic Projection under constraint). *Let $t \in \mathbb{R}^k$ and $\Phi : E \to \mathbb{R}^k$ be measurable. Assume that t can be written as a convex combination of $\Phi(X_1, S_1, \widehat{Y}_1, Y_1), \ldots, \Phi(X_n, S_n, \widehat{Y}_n, Y_n)$, with positive weights. Assume also that the empirical covariance matrix of $\Phi(X, S, \hat{Y}, Y)$ is invertible.*

Let $\mathcal{D}_{\Phi,t}$ be the set of all probability measures P on E such that $\int_E \Phi(x)\,\mathrm{d}P(x) = t$. Then,

$$Q_t := \operatorname{arginf}_{P\in\mathcal{D}_{\Phi,t}} D_{\mathrm{KL}}(P\|Q_n) \tag{4}$$

exists and is unique. It can also be computed as

$$Q_t = \frac{1}{n}\sum_{i=1}^{n} \lambda_i^{(t)} \delta_{X_i,S_i,\widehat{Y}_i,Y_i} \tag{5}$$

with, for $i \in \{1,\ldots,n\}$, $\lambda_i^{(t)} = \exp\left(\langle\xi(t), \Phi(X_i,S_i,\widehat{Y}_i,Y_i)\rangle - \log Z(\xi(t))\right)$, where for a vector $\xi \in \mathbb{R}^k$, let $Z(\xi) := \frac{1}{n}\sum_{i=1}^{n} e^{\langle\Phi(X_i,S_i,\widehat{Y}_i,Y_i),\xi\rangle}$; and $\xi(t)$ is the unique minimizer of the strictly convex function $H(\xi) := \log Z(\xi) - \langle\xi,t\rangle$.

This theorem directly allows to fake statistical parity using entropic projection. Let t_{init} be such that $DI(f,Q_n,S) = t_{\text{init}}$. It enables to optimally (for the KL divergence) construct a distribution Q_t such that $DI(f,Q_n,S) = t_{\text{new}} \geqslant t_{\text{init}}$ for a given t_{new}. The fairness improvement can be defined as $\Delta_{DI} := DI(f,Q_t,S) - DI(f,Q_n,S)$. Note that $DI(f,Q_n,S) = \frac{\lambda_0/n_0}{\lambda_1/n_1}$ where for $i \in \{0,1\}$, $n_s = |\{i=1,\ldots,n|S_i = s\}|$ and $\lambda_s = |\{i=1,\ldots,n|\widehat{Y}_i = 1 \wedge S_i = s\}|$. Note also that $\lambda_0 = \sum_{i=1}^{n}\widehat{Y}_i(1-S_i)$ and $\lambda_1 = \sum_{i=1}^{n}\widehat{Y}_i S_i$. Hence modifying the DI can be achieved applying Theorem 1 for $Z = (S,\widehat{Y})$ and selecting the function

$$\Phi(s,f(x)) = \begin{pmatrix}(1-s)f(x)\\ sf(x)\\ s\\ 1-s\end{pmatrix} \text{ and } t = \begin{pmatrix}\lambda_0+\delta_0\\ \lambda_1-\delta_1\\ n_1\\ n_0\end{pmatrix}. \tag{6}$$

Our purpose is to improve the perceived fairness of the model. Accordingly, we only consider increasing the numerator $+\delta_0 \geqslant 0$ and decreasing the denominator $-\delta_1 \leqslant 0$. Because $DI_{\text{init}} \leqslant DI_{\text{new}} \leqslant 1$, the new distribution will always be at least as fair as the original one.

Proposition 1 (KL-fair washing method). *Finding a solution Q_t such that $D_{\mathrm{KL}}(Q_t\|Q_n)$ is minimum and $DI(f,Q_t,S) = DI(f,Q_n,S) + \Delta_{DI}$ is achieved by finding the solution to (4) with Φ defined as in (6) and with the two possible choices of parameters:*

- *Balanced case: set $\delta_0 = \delta_1$ and $\delta_1 = \dfrac{\lambda_1}{1+\frac{n_1}{n_0\Delta_{DI}}(1+\frac{\lambda_0}{\lambda_1})}$*
- *Proportional case: set $\dfrac{\delta_0}{n_0} = \dfrac{\delta_1}{n_1}$ and $\delta_1 = \dfrac{\lambda_1}{1+\frac{1}{\Delta_{DI}}(1+\frac{n_1\lambda_0}{n_0\lambda_1})}$*

Remark 3 The balanced case corresponds to modifying the individuals from both classes equally, while the proportional one adjusts the amount of modification in proportion to the classes sizes. We refer respectively in the Experimental section to the two methods as `Entropic_balanced` and `Entropic_proportional`.

5.2 Fairwashing Using Optimal Transport

Monge Kantorovich (MK) Projection. For two distributions P and Q_n over $E \subset \mathbb{R}^d$ a compact subset, endowed with the norm $\|.\|$, recall that their 2 Monge-Kantorovich, a.k.a. Wasserstein distance, is defined as:

$$W_2^2(P, Q_n) = \min_{\pi \in \Pi(P,Q_n)} \int_{x \in E, y \in E} \| x - y \|^2 \, d\pi(x, y), \tag{7}$$

where $\Pi(P, Q_n)$ denotes the set of distributions on $E \times E$ with marginals P and Q_n. We will write $T_\sharp Q = Q \circ T^{-1}$ to denote the push-forward of a measure by the transport map. As in Sect. 5.1, consider for a given $k \geqslant 1$, a continuous function $\Phi \colon E \longrightarrow \mathbb{R}^k$ representing the constraints. For fixed $t \in \mathbb{R}^k$, the set $\mathcal{D}_{\Phi,t} = \{P \in \mathcal{M}(E) \mid \int_E \Phi(x) dP(x) = t\}$ is closed for the weak convergence and convex, since it is linear in P. The function $P \mapsto W_2^2(P, Q_n)$ is convex as it is the supremum of linear functionals by Kantorovich duality [33], therefore the following projection problem $\operatorname{arginf}_{P \in \mathcal{D}_{\Phi,t}} W_2^2(P, Q_n)$ is well-defined.

Theorem 2. *Consider* $Q_n = \frac{1}{n} \sum_{i=1}^n \delta_{Z_i}$. *Then* Q_t *is a solution to*

$$\operatorname{arginf}_{P \in \mathcal{D}_{\Phi,t}} W_2^2(P, Q_n) \tag{8}$$

if, and only if, it is defined as $Q_t = T_{\lambda^\star} \sharp Q_n = \dfrac{1}{n} \sum_{i=1}^n \delta_{T_{\lambda^\star}(Z_i)}$, *where* T_λ *is defined as*

$$T_\lambda(Z_i) \in \arg\min_{x \in E} \|x - Z_i\|^2 - \langle \lambda, \Phi(x) \rangle \tag{9}$$

and $\lambda^\star$ *satisfies* $t = \frac{1}{n} \sum_{i=n}^n \Phi(T_{\lambda^\star}(Z_i))$.

Remark 4. The previous result stated for the empirical distribution is valid for any distribution Q. The constraint can be modified to include the condition $\mathcal{D}_{\Phi,t} = \{P \in \mathcal{M}(E) \mid \int_E \Phi(x) dP(x) \geqslant t\}$. This is detailed in Proposition 2 in the Appendix.

Following the framework of the previous section, for a fixed λ, we set $\Phi(x, s, f(x), y) = f(x)$. Then the constraint on the Disparate Impact $DI(f, Q, S) \geqslant t$, can be reformulated with double inequality given S.

Following Theorem 2, we compute for all $Z_i = x$, the solution $T_\lambda(x)$ of the minimization problem w.r.t x:

$$\mathcal{L}(x, \lambda) = \|Z_i - x\|_2^2 + \langle \lambda, t - f(x) \rangle. \tag{10}$$

This minimization does not have a closed form in general, but it can be achieved using a gradient descent using a learning step of η and computing $x^k = x^{k-1} - \eta \frac{\partial \mathcal{L}}{\partial z}(x^k)$ with $\frac{\partial \mathcal{L}}{\partial x} = 2(z - x) - \langle \lambda, \nabla_x f(x) \rangle$. We provide further implementation information in the Appendix, Sec. K.3.

Contrary to the entropic projection which is only a different sampling of the original individuals, this method creates new individuals. Yet it may create some out of bounds individuals by violation of some restriction of types (discrete variable staying discrete, i.e., age = 1.002) or of bounds (age = −1). Thereby, we created a variant of this method that constrains the covariates of new individuals: we transport, variable per variable, each covariate toward the nearest (for the L_2 norm) achieved value in the dataset; we call this variant the 1D-transport variant.

To summarize, we have introduced four methods: (1) `Grad_balanced`, and (2) `Grad_proportional`, which differ based on the gradient constraints satisfying $\delta_0 = \delta_1$ or $\frac{\delta_0}{n_0} = \frac{\delta_1}{n_1}$; and (3) `Grad_balanced_1D-transport`, and (4) `Grad_proportional_1D-transport`, which apply the corresponding 1D-transport variant of each method.

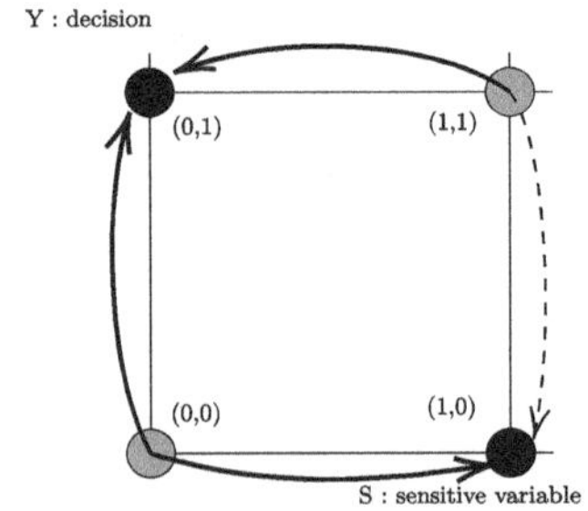

Fig. 1. Admissible modifications of $\tau : 0,1^2 \mapsto 0,1^2$ that increase Disparate Impact using the `Replace` method.

Algorithm 1. `Replace`$(S,\widehat{Y})$ algorithm

$Z^j = (Z_1, \cdots, Z_n), Z_i = (S_i, \widehat{Y}_i), t \in]0,1[$
$\tau_i := (\tau, j)$ such as $\tau \in \mathcal{A}, i \in 1, \cdots, n$
while $\mathrm{DI}(Z^j) < t$ **do**
  $\tau_{i_0} \in \operatorname{argmax}\ \mathrm{DI}(\tau_{i_0}(Z^j)) - \mathrm{DI}(Z^j)$
with $\tau_{i_0}(Z^j) := (Z_i, \cdots, \tau(Z_{i_0}), \cdots, Z_n)$
  $Z^j \leftarrow Z^{j+1} = \tau_{i_0}(Z^j)$
end while
return Z^j

Faking Statistical Parity Using Sensitive Attributes Replacement. In the previous subsection, we assumed that the auditor could compute $f(X)$ from any observation X. Hereafter, we assume that it does not have access to the model f and only requests the outcome of the algorithm $\widehat{Y}$, without computing it.

In this setting, faking fairness can be achieved by manipulating only the outcomes and sensitive attributes associated with each individual. Let $Z_i = (S_i, \widehat{Y}_i)$ and $Q_n = \frac{1}{n}\sum_{i=1}^{n} \delta_{S_i,\widehat{Y}_i}$. In this context, a solution to the optimization problem can be achieved as follows. First, note that $\widehat{Y} \in \{0,1\}$ and $S \in \{0,1\}$, thus we only have 4 possible values for the points. Each individual with characteristic $Z_i \in \{0,1\}^2$ can be modified to the individual $\tau(Z_i) = (\tau_S(S_i), \tau_{\widehat{Y}}(\widehat{Y}_i)) \in \{0,1\}^2$. Not all solutions improve the disparate impact and we can therefore restrict ourselves to a set of admissible changes $\tau \in \mathcal{A}$ as pointed in Fig. 1, see Section K.2 in the Appendix. We approximate the exact solution by an iterative method starting from $Z = (Z_1, \cdots, Z_n)$ and testing every possible modification $Z^j = (Z_1, \cdots, Z_n)$ maximizing the DI at each step j. The method based on this algorithm is denoted by `Replace`$(S,\widehat{Y})$ in our experiments (see Algorithm 1).

Faking Statistical Parity Using Constrained Matching. In the previous case, only the labels are transported while the observations X_i are not taken into account. A natural variant consists in combining previous minimization scheme and adding a discrete displacement on the variables X. Namely, we define a matching algorithm using $Z = (X, S, \widehat{Y})$ and $\tau(Z_i) = Z_k$, with $k \in \{1, \cdots, n\}$. We use the same procedure as Algorithm 1awith the newly defined τ, but at each iteration j of the while loop, we maximize for every candidate τ_{i_0}:

$$\frac{\mathrm{DI}(\tau_{i_0}(Z^j)) - \mathrm{DI}((Z^j))}{\|\tau_{i_0}(Z^j) - Z^j\|} \tag{11}$$

In our experiments, we refer to the method based on this algorithm as $M_{W(X,S,\widehat{Y})}$.

Remark 5. This algorithm transports individuals towards others ($\tau(Z_i) = Z_k$), therefore, contrary to its counterpart, it can be used in any type of audit (with or without access to the model).

Table 1. Dataset presentation, protected variable (S) associated, and original Disparate Impact (DI)

	Adult	INC	TRA	MOB	BAF	EMP	PUC
S chosen	Sex	Sex	Sex	Age	Age	Disability	Disability
DI	0.30	0.67	0.69	0.45	0.35	0.30	0.32

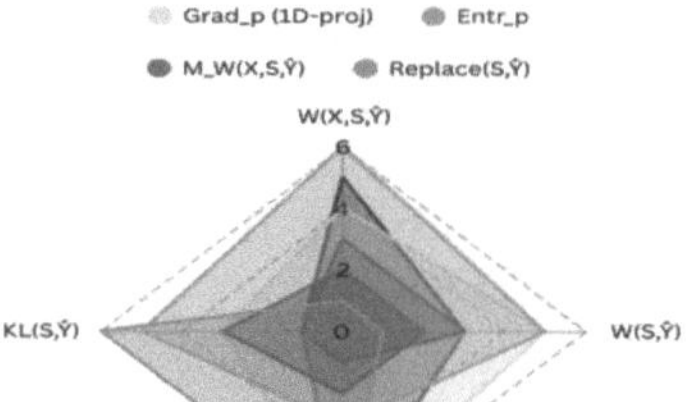

Fig. 2. Radar graph ranking D_{KL} and W similarity results depending on the fairwashing method (lower is better). The visualization highlights why $M_{W(X,S,\widehat{Y})}$, considering X or not on the similarity provides the most balanced overall performance. Entr_b and Entr_p are respectively for `Entropic_balanced` and `Entropic_proportional`.

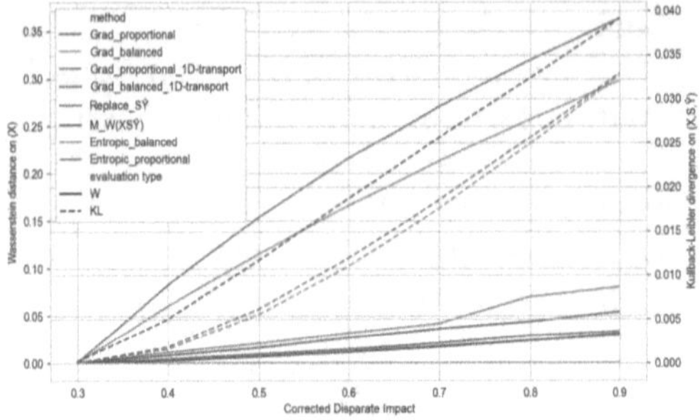

Fig. 3. Line plot illustrating the trade-off between fairness correction and distribution shift (on X for the Wasserstein distance and $(X, S, \widehat{Y})$ for the D_{KL}) with the Adult dataset. KL divergence and Wasserstein distance, between the fully modified and the original datasets are reported for each method. Methods with infinite D_{KL} are omitted.

6 Experimental Settings

Datasets. We use 7 benchmarking datasets: Adult Census Income dataset where Y is whether an individual's income is above 50k (Adult) [5]. We also use 5 benchmark datasets [14] which records information about the USA's population, including income (INC), mobility (MOB), employment (EMP), travel time to work (TRA) and public system coverage (PUC). We also include the Bank Account Fraud generated dataset (BAF) [23]. We refer to Table 1 for the sensitive variable and the original Disparate Impact (DI) of each dataset. In our experiments, a part of the dataset was used to learn the outcome decision, we selected 5k individual of the test set for Adult, and 20k individuals of the test set for the other datasets.

Neural Network Predictions. For every dataset classification task, we trained an MLP. As we are working only with tabular data, we provide a $\widehat{Y}$ with a multilayer perceptron (MLP) neural network f ending with a sigmoid activation function ($f(x) \in [0, 1]$). Accuracy performance was not the main goal in this study, see in the Appendix Sec. D. For that reason, the model's architecture and the training protocol are classical: 80% of the dataset size was used as training set (including validation set) and the remainaing 20% for the test set. We set the starting learning rate at 0.001 using the AdamW Schedule-free optimizer [12]. All configurations for each dataset are available in our GitHub repository. The models have been uploaded to Hugging Face, and the original and manipulated distributions are available at Hugging Face Datasets.

7 Results

Fairness Cost: Distribution Shift per Method. Figure 2 illustrates the comparative performance of each method across different distance metrics (D_{KL}, W). Specifically, D_{KL} and W quantify the magnitude of the distributional shift, either marginally or conditional on the input features X, and thus assess each method's detectability by statistical tests. We also provide complementary results on simulated data and the computation time and memory cost of each method in the Appendix (see Sec I). The smallest surface area in the radar chart is archived by $M_{W(X,S,\widehat{Y})}$, hence, given the results, this method appears to be the most suitable method for someone seeking to disguise their dataset, as it significantly improves the DI while preserving a distribution close to the original data.

Table 2. Results of the 7 tests independently; for each unbiasing method (DI = 0.8) and datasets. Sampling is stopped as soon as one sample do not reject the $\mathcal{H}_0$ hypothesis, or after 30 tries if none do. The symbol – means the method was undetected by the tests for both sampling sizes of 10% and 20% ($\mathcal{H}_0$ not rejected), ○ means that only the 20% sampling size was undetected ($\mathcal{H}_0$ not rejected for 20% and rejected for 10%); and ◎ means that the method was detected at both 10% and 20% sample sizes ($\mathcal{H}_0$ rejected). Positional and color coding indicate which test each result corresponds to, in the following order and color scheme: $D_{\mathrm{KL}}(X, S, \widehat{Y})$, $D_{\mathrm{KL}}(S, \widehat{Y})$, $W(X, S, \widehat{Y})$, $W(S, \widehat{Y})$, K-S($\widehat{Y}$), MMD($X, S, \widehat{Y}$), MMD($S, \widehat{Y}$). `Grad_proportional` (Grad_p) and `Grad_balanced` (Grad_b) have been merged with their 1D counterpart due to identical test results. Entropic_b and Entropic_p are respectively for `Entropic_balanced` and `Entropic_proportional`.

	Methods					
Dataset	Grad_p(1D-t)	Grad_b(1D-t)	Rep $(S, \widehat{Y})$	$M_{W(X,S,\widehat{Y})}$	Entropic_b	Entropic_p
ADULT	◎ ◎ – ◎ ◎ – ◎	◎ ◎ – ◎ ◎ – ◎	◎ ◎ – ◎ ◎ – ◎	○ ◎ – ◎ ◎ ○ ◎	– ◎ – ◎ ◎ – ◎	– ◎ – ◎ ◎ – ◎
EMP	◎ ◎ ◎ ◎ ◎ ◎ ◎	◎ ◎ ○ ◎ ◎ ○ ◎	◎ ◎ – ◎ ◎ – ◎	◎ ◎ – ◎ ◎ ○ ◎	○ ◎ ◎ ◎ ◎ ○ ◎	○ ◎ ◎ ◎ ◎ – ◎
INC	◎ – – – – – –	◎ – – – – – –	◎ – – – – – –	– – – – – – –	– – – – – – –	– – – – – – –
MOB	◎ ◎ ◎ ◎ ◎ ◎ ◎	◎ ◎ – ◎ ◎ – ◎	◎ ◎ – ◎ ◎ – ◎	◎ ◎ – ◎ ◎ ○ ◎	○ ◎ ○ ◎ ◎ ○ ◎	○ ◎ ◎ ◎ ◎ ◎ ◎
PUC	◎ ◎ ◎ ◎ ◎ ◎ ◎	◎ ◎ ○ ◎ ◎ ○ ◎	◎ ◎ ○ ◎ ◎ ○ ◎	◎ ◎ ○ ◎ ◎ ◎ ◎	○ ◎ ◎ ◎ ◎ ○ ◎	○ ◎ ◎ ◎ ◎ ◎ ◎
TRA	◎ – – – – – –	◎ – – – – – –	◎ ○ – – – – –	– – – – – – –	– – – – – – –	– – – – – – –
BAF	◎ ○ – – – – –	◎ ○ – – – – –	◎ – – – – – –	– – – – – – –	– – – – – – –	– ○ – – – – –

Fraud Detection Through Distributional Shifts. Using statistical tests, is it possible to detect a fraud attempt based on the provided sample $\mathcal{D}_m$ and the original dataset Q_n? For each optimized fairwashing method presented in Sect. 5, we obtain a modified distribution Q_t for every dataset. For each method-dataset combination, we draw multiple samples $\mathcal{D}_m$ such that $DI(f, \widehat{Q}_m, S) \geqslant 0.8$, where $\widehat{Q}_m$ denotes the empirical distribution induced by the sample. More precisely, we repeatedly sample from each Q_t and apply the seven statistical tests described in Sect. 4. For every combination of fairwashing method, dataset, and statistical test, we record whether the null hypothesis $\mathcal{H}_0$ is rejected, thereby assessing whether the original and sampled distributions can be considered equivalent. Table 2 reports the results obtained from samples drawn from the modified distributions for each dataset. The sample sizes considered are 10% and 20% of the original dataset (i.e., $m = \frac{n}{10}$ and $m = \frac{n}{5}$, respectively). Rejection of the null hypothesis $\mathcal{H}_0$ indicates that the fairwashing strategy employed by a malicious auditee would be detected by the supervisory authority. Consequently, a malicious auditee would seek to construct a fair yet detection-free sample by repeatedly drawing samples from Q_t. Additional details regarding the probability of passing the statistical tests are provided in Section N.1 of the Appendix.

Methods modifying individual characteristics (`Grad` methods) are easily detected (rejection of $\mathcal{H}_0$) regardless of the sampling size. The fairwashing done by the $M_{W(X,S,\widehat{Y})}$ and Entropic-based methods is undetected for the INC, TRA and BAF datasets. For the TRA and INC datasets, the DIs of the original data were close to that of the modified data (see Table 3), implying that the required modifications were smaller than the others, and therefore the fairwashing was more difficult to detect. For the BAF dataset, because $\mathbb{E}(Y) \approx 0.01$, only limited individual modifications were needed. The results on the BAF dataset shows that the original Disparate Impact value is not the only criteria to consider when evaluating fairwashing detection difficulty. We provide complementary information in the Appendix about the simulation setup in Sec I, which confirms the superior trade-off achieved by $M_{W(X,S,\widehat{Y})}$ and we report the computational costs of the different methods in Section K.4 in the Appendix.

Trade-Off: DI Improvement vs Distribution Shift. Figure 3 illustrates the trade-off between fairness correction and distribution shift on the Adult datasets by the Wasserstein distance and KL divergence between the full original and modified distributions. `Replace` $(S, \widehat{Y})$, $M_{W(X,S,\widehat{Y})}$ and `Grad` variant methods preserve the structure of the input space and are better alternatives to the entropic projection method. We recall that since `Replace` only modifies S and $\widehat{Y}$, it naturally leads to null difference between distributions on X. Note that the relative ordering of methods presented on the Adult dataset remains largely consistent across datasets.

Fairest Undetected Sample. Given the results reported in Table 2, which show that achieving $DI(f, \widehat{Q}_m, S) \geqslant 0.8$ while evading detection is generally not possible in multiple datasets, we investigate the maximum fairness improvement that a malicious auditee could achieve without being detected by the supervisory authority. This analysis follows the fairness-detectability trade-off discussed previously. Note that such an optimization would only be possible if the malicious auditee were aware of the statistical tests employed by the supervisory authority, which constitutes a reasonable legal assumption.

Table 3 reports the highest Disparate Impact (DI) values achieved by samples that were not rejected by any of the seven statistical tests. For each modified distribution Q_t, we generate 100 random samples comprising either 10% or 20% of the original dataset size. We then progressively decrease the target fairness level t in increments of 0.05. More precisely, the procedure starts from $Q_{t=1}$. If at least one undetected sample $\mathcal{D}_m$ satisfying $DI(\mathcal{D}_m) \geqslant t$ is found, we retain the sample with the highest observed DI value, denoted t'. Otherwise, the procedure is repeated with a lower target fairness level, setting $t \leftarrow t - 0.05$. The process continues until $t - 0.05 < DI(Q_n)$. The samples drawn from the four `Grad` method variants and the `Replace` method failed to increase DI without

Table 3. Highest undetected achievable Disparate Impact for each dataset, sample size (Size) and fairwashing method. The symbol – indicates that some methods couldn't reach a DI improvement. To emphasize the best method to use in order to deceive the auditor, we put the DI achieved in bold when one or two overperformed the others.

Dataset	Original	Size (%)	Grad_p	Grad_b	Grad_p 1D	Grad_b 1D	Rep $(S, \widehat{Y})$	Entr_b	Entr_p	$M_{W(X,S,\widehat{Y})}$
ADULT	0.30	10	0.47	0.43	0.49	0.44	0.50	**0.54**	0.52	**0.54**
		20	0.39	0.40	0.38	0.39	0.41	**0.42**	0.41	**0.42**
EMP	0.30	10	–	–	–	–	–	0.36	0.36	**0.37**
		20	–	–	–	–	–	0.34	**0.36**	0.35
INC	0.67	10	0.75	–	–	–	0.88	0.94	**0.95**	0.93
		20	–	–	–	–	0.83	0.83	**0.84**	**0.84**
MOB	0.45	10	0.53	0.51	–	0.50	**0.53**	0.52	–	0.52
		20	–	–	–	0.48	0.50	0.50	–	0.50
PUC	0.32	10	–	–	–	–	–	0.33	**0.35**	**0.35**
		20	–	–	–	–	–	–	–	–
TRA	0.69	10	0.72	0.79	0.77	0.73	0.80	0.83	0.84	**0.85**
		20	–	–	–	–	0.77	0.79	0.79	**0.80**
BAF	0.35	10	–	–	–	–	–	1	1	1
		20	–	–	–	–	–	0.77	**0.80**	0.79

detection on three common datasets (EMP, PUC, and BAF). This outcome is primarily due to the consistent rejection of these samples by the D_{KL}-based tests (100% rejection rate). These results emphasize the importance of combining multiple statistical tests: methods optimized with respect to the Wasserstein distance are effectively detected by tests based on the D_{KL} divergence. This observation highlights the advantage of the `Entropic` methods and the matching approach $M_{W(X,S,\widehat{Y})}$, which avoid scenarios where $D_{\mathrm{KL}}(Q_t \| Q_n) = +\infty$ and therefore exhibit greater robustness. Overall, $M_{W(X,S,\widehat{Y})}$ consistently achieves the strongest performance.

The results reported in Table 3 also underscore the influence of sample size. For example, on the PUC dataset, undetected fairwashing was possible when using samples comprising 10% of the original dataset, but not when using 20% samples. This finding suggests that, as the sample size increases relative to the original dataset, it becomes increasingly difficult to improve DI without being detected. We further investigate this phenomenon in Fig. 7 of Appendix J.

8 Concluding Guidelines

Our results highlight a key limitation of fairness auditing: global fairness metrics can be manipulated if the evaluation distribution is controlled. We showed both theoretically and empirically that samples can be constructed to appear representative while satisfying fairness constraints, even when the full dataset violates them. Consequently, if the auditee controls the audit sample, fairness compliance may be artificially created. Representativeness must therefore be treated as a primary objective of the audit process. Auditors should avoid letting the auditee freely select the audit subset and, whenever possible, retain the ability to access the full dataset or request additional samples to estimate the reference distribution.

We propose a practical strategy for assessing representativeness based on combining statistical tests that capture complementary properties of distributions. While this significantly reduces the room for manipulation, our experiments show that carefully designed transformations can still remain statistically undetectable, especially if the auditee is aware of the supervisory authority detection protocol. In practice, the most effective lever to limit manipulation is the audit sample size. Larger samples substantially reduce the space of undetectable distributional shifts. We therefore recommend requiring sufficiently large samples, combining multiple representativeness tests. We hope this work contributes to the development of more robust auditing frameworks and provides practical guidance for regulators and practitioners seeking to ensure that fairness claims remain meaningful under adversarial incentives.

Ethical Considerations

This work studies how malicious actors could manipulate audit datasets to appear compliant with fairness metrics such as Disparate Impact. Our objective is to expose these vulnerabilities in order to strengthen auditing procedures and regulatory oversight. By analyzing both manipulation strategies and statistical detection methods, we aim to support the development of more robust fairness auditing frameworks.

Reproducibility Statement

Our experiments on both our simulated dataset and publicly available datasets [5,14,23,29], together with all code required to reproduce the results reported in this paper using fixed random seeds and archived intermediate results, are available through our GitHub repository, Hugging Face model repository, and Hugging Face dataset repository.

Our GitHub repository is organized as follows:

- **Data**: datasets (primarily CSV files).
- **Pre-processing**: Jupyter notebooks.
- **Src**: Python functions implementing our fairwashing methods.
- **Project**: network training and inference, fairness evaluation, fairwashing, and fraud detection using statistical tests.
- **Results**: final and intermediate results (CSV, NPY, and JSON files).

Because GitHub imposes file size limits, we host the datasets on Google Drive and Hugging Face. The appendix is available at this link.

Funding Information. This paper has been partially funded by the Agence Nationale de la Recherche under grants ANR-23-CE23-0029 Regul-IA. The authors also acknowledge the support of the AI Cluster ANITI (ANR-23-IACL-0002).

Disclosure of Interests. The authors have no competing interests to declare that are relevant to the content of this article.

References

1. Aivodji, U., Arai, H., Fortineau, O., Gambs, S., Hara, S., Tapp, A.: Fairwashing: the risk of rationalization. In: Proceedings of the 36th International Conference on Machine Learning. Proceedings of Machine Learning Research, vol. 97, pp. 161–170. PMLR (2019)
2. Angwin, J., Larson, J., Mattu, S., Kirchner, L.: Machine bias-there's software used across the country to predict future criminals. and it's biased against blacks. ProPublica (2016)
3. Bachoc, F., Gamboa, F., Halford, M., Loubes, J.M., Risser, L.: Explaining machine learning models using entropic variable projection. Inf. Inference J. IMA **12**(3), 1686–1715 (2023)
4. Barocas, S., Hardt, M., Narayanan, A.: Fairness and Machine Learning: Limitations and Opportunities. MIT Press (2023)
5. Becker, B., Kohavi, R.: Adult[Dataset]. UCI Machine Learning Repository (1996)
6. Besse, P., del Barrio, E., Gordaliza, P., Loubes, J.M., Risser, L.: A survey of bias in machine learning through the prism of statistical parity. Am. Stat. **76**(2), 188–198 (2022)
7. Bourrée, J.G., et al.: Robust ML auditing using prior knowledge. In: ICML Workshop on Technical AI Governance (TAIG) (2025)
8. Calmon, F., Wei, D., Vinzamuri, B., Natesan Ramamurthy, K., Varshney, K.R.: Optimized pre-processing for discrimination prevention. In: Advances in Neural Information Processing Systems, vol. 30, Curran Associates, Inc. (2017)
9. Celis, L.E., Keswani, V., Yildiz, O., Vishnoi, N.K.: Data preprocessing to mitigate bias: a maximum entropy based approach. In: International Conference on Machine Learning, ICML (2020)
10. Cen, S.H., Alur, R.: From transparency to accountability and back: a discussion of access and evidence in AI auditing. In: Proceedings of the 4th ACM Conference on Equity and Access in Algorithms, Mechanisms, and Optimization. EAAMO '24, New York, NY, USA. Association for Computing Machinery (2024). https://doi.org/10.1145/3689904.3694711
11. Cherian, J.J., Candès, E.J.: Statistical inference for fairness auditing. J. Mach. Learn. Res. **25**(149), 1–49 (2024)
12. Defazio, A., Yang, X.A., Khaled, A., Mishchenko, K., Mehta, H., Cutkosky, A.: The road less scheduled. In: The Thirty-eighth Annual Conference on Neural Information Processing Systems, p. 2024 (2024)
13. Devlin, J., Chang, M.W., Lee, K., Toutanova, K.: BERT: pre-training of deep bidirectional transformers for language understanding. In: Proceedings of the 2019 Conference of the North American Chapter of the Association for Computational Linguistics: Human Language Technologies, Volume 1 (Long and Short Papers), Minneapolis, pp. 4171–4186. Association for Computational Linguistics (2019)
14. Ding, F., Hardt, M., Miller, J., Schmidt, L.: Retiring adult: new datasets for fair machine learning. In: Proceedings of the 35th International Conference on Neural Information Processing Systems. NIPS '21, Red Hook, USA. Curran Associates Inc. (2021)
15. Feldman, M., Friedler, S.A., Moeller, J., Scheidegger, C., Venkatasubramanian, S.: Certifying and removing disparate impact. In: Proceedings of the 21th ACM SIGKDD International Conference on Knowledge Discovery and Data Mining. KDD '15, New York, USA, pp. 259–268. Association for Computing Machinery (2015)

16. Fukuchi, K., Hara, S., Maehara, T.: Faking fairness via stealthily biased sampling. In: Proceedings of the AAAI Conference on Artificial Intelligence, vol. 34, pp. 412–419 (2020)
17. Gordaliza, P., Barrio, E.D., Fabrice, G., Loubes, J.M.: Obtaining fairness using optimal transport theory. In: Proceedings of the 36th International Conference on Machine Learning. Proceedings of Machine Learning Research, vol. 97, pp. 2357–2365. PMLR (2019)
18. Gretton, A., Borgwardt, K.M., Rasch, M.J., Schölkopf, B., Smola, A.: A kernel two-sample test. J. Mach. Learn. Res. **13**(25), 723–773 (2012)
19. Hardt, M., Price, E., Srebro, N.: Equality of opportunity in supervised learning. In: Advances in Neural Information Processing Systems (2016)
20. He, K., Zhang, X., Ren, S., Sun, J.: Deep residual learning for image recognition. In: Proceedings of the IEEE Conference on Computer Vision and Pattern Recognition (CVPR) (2016)
21. Heusel, M., Ramsauer, H., Unterthiner, T., Nessler, B., Hochreiter, S.: GANs trained by a two time-scale update rule converge to a local Nash equilibrium. In: Advances in Neural Information Processing Systems, vol. 30, Curran Associates, Inc (2017)
22. Jacobs, D., Kalbers, L.P.: Volkswagen emissions scandal (2019). https://www.cpajournal.com/2019/07/22/9187/
23. Jesus, S., et al.: Turning the tables: biased, imbalanced, dynamic tabular datasets for ml evaluation. In: Advances in Neural Information Processing Systems (2022)
24. Jiang, R., Pacchiano, A., Stepleton, T., Jiang, H., Chiappa, S.: Wasserstein fair classification. In: Proceedings of The 35th Uncertainty in Artificial Intelligence Conference. Proceedings of Machine Learning Research, vol. 115, pp. 862–872. PMLR (2020)
25. Juarez, M., Yeom, S., Fredrikson, M.: Black-box audits for group distribution shifts (2022). https://arxiv.org/abs/2209.03620
26. of Justice, D., Commission, E.E.O., of Labor including the OFCCP, D., Commission, C.S.: Uniform guidelines on employee selection procedures (1978). https://www.uniformguidelines.com/uniform-guidelines.html
27. Kamiran, F., Calders, T.: Classifying without discriminating. In: 2nd International Conference on Computer, Control and Communication, pp. 1–6 (2009)
28. Merrer, L., Pons, E., Trédan, R., G.: Algorithmic audits of algorithms, and the law. AI and Ethics, 1–21 (2023)
29. Liu, Z., Luo, P., Wang, X., Tang, X.: Deep learning face attributes in the wild. In: Proceedings of the 2015 IEEE International Conference on Computer Vision (ICCV). ICCV '15, USA, pp. 3730–3738. IEEE Computer Society (2015)
30. Oneto, L., Chiappa, S.: Fairness in machine learning. In: Recent Trends in Learning From Data: Tutorials from the INNS Big Data and Deep Learning Conference (INNSBDDL2019, pp. 155–196 (2020)
31. Peypouquet, J.: Convex Optimization in Normed Spaces, Theory, Methods and Examples. SpringerBriefs in Optimization, 1st edn. Springer, Cham (2015)
32. Raji, I.D., et al.: Closing the AI accountability gap: defining an end-to-end framework for internal algorithmic auditing. In: Proceedings of the 2020 Conference on Fairness, Accountability, and Transparency. FAT* '20, New York, NY, USA, pp. 33–44. Association for Computing Machinery (2020)
33. Santambrogio, F.: Gradient flows. In: Optimal Transport for Applied Mathematicians. PNDETA, vol. 87, pp. 285–323. Springer, Cham (2015). https://doi.org/10.1007/978-3-319-20828-2_8

34. Shahin Shamsabadi, A., et al.: Washing the unwashableâĂŕ: on the (IM)possibility of fairwashing detection. In: Advances in Neural Information Processing Systems, vol. 35, pp. 14170–14182. Curran Associates, Inc (2022)
35. Szegedy, C., Vanhoucke, V., Ioffe, S., Shlens, J., Wojna, Z.: Rethinking the inception architecture for computer vision. In: Proceedings of the IEEE Conference on Computer Vision and Pattern Recognition (CVPR) (2016)
36. Wang, X., Zhang, Y., Zhu, R.: A brief review on algorithmic fairness. Manage. Syst. Eng. **1**(1), 7 (2022)
37. Wright, L., et al.: Null compliance: nyc local law 144 and the challenges of algorithm accountability. In: Proceedings of the 2024 ACM Conference on Fairness, Accountability, and Transparency. FAccT '24, New York, NY, USA, pp. 1701–1713. Association for Computing Machinery (2024)
38. Yamamoto, Y., Hara, S.: Fast stealthily biased sampling using sliced Wasserstein distance. In: Proceedings of the 16th Asian Conference on Machine Learning. Proceedings of Machine Learning Research, vol. 260, pp. 873–888. PMLR (2025)
39. Yan, T., Zhang, C.: Active fairness auditing. In: Proceedings of the 39th International Conference on Machine Learning. Proceedings of Machine Learning Research, vol. 162, pp. 24929–24962. PMLR (2022)

Measuring What Matters: A Unified Evaluation Framework for GNN Explainability

Francesco Paolo Nerini[1(✉)], Mirko Zaffaroni[2], Paolo Baracco[3], Gabriele Ciravegna[4], and Alan Perotti[2]

[1] Sapienza University of Rome, Rome, Italy
nerini@diag.uniroma1.it
[2] Intesa Sanpaolo AI Research, Turin, Italy
{mirko.zaffaroni,alan.perotti}@intesasanpaolo.com
[3] Anti Financial Crime Digital Hub, Turin, Italy
paolo.baracco@intesasanpaolo.com
[4] Intesa Sanpaolo Innovation Center, Turin, Italy
gabriele.ciravegna@intesasanpaolo.com

Abstract. Graph eXplainable AI (G-XAI) is increasingly important for making Graph Neural Networks interpretable and accountable. While a growing number of explainers are available, choosing the right method and assessing the trustworthiness of its outputs remains unclear. Consistent evaluation practices and actionable guidance are still missing, hindering practical adoption. In this paper, we introduce a unified, quantitative benchmarking framework for G-XAI that requires no ground-truth assumptions. We formalize tabular explainability metrics for graph data, evaluating topological structure and node features as independent components. Our large-scale benchmarking study identifies explainers that consistently lie on the Pareto front across metric pairs and tasks, establishing robustly non-dominated solutions - while confirming that no single explainer achieves universal superiority. We distill our findings into actionable G-XAI usability guidelines to support Machine Learning practitioners in evaluating and deploying trustworthy GNN-based pipelines.

Keywords: Graph Machine Learning · Explainable Artificial Intelligence · Explanation Evaluation

1 Introduction

Graph Neural Networks (GNNs) have emerged as a powerful paradigm for modeling relational data, achieving state-of-the-art performance across domains such as financial transaction monitoring, social network analysis, and biological interaction networks [1,2]. However, their inherently recursive message-passing mechanisms render internal decision processes opaque. With legal frameworks such as the EU AI Act increasingly mandating transparency for high-risk AI systems,

M. Ceci et al. (Eds.): ECML PKDD 2026, LNAI 16948, pp. 380–398, 2027.
https://doi.org/10.1007/978-3-032-37679-4_22

this "black-box" nature represents a critical barrier to deployment in regulated environments: one cannot deploy what one cannot explain.

To address this tension, the field of Graph eXplainable AI (G-XAI) has introduced numerous post-hoc techniques that augment GNN predictions with interpretable information, typically by highlighting the most relevant nodes, edges, or features [3–5]. Yet this proliferation of explainers has created a new challenge: the problem is no longer a lack of solutions, but how to navigate them: there is no consensus on what constitutes a "good" graph explanation, leaving ML practitioners without objective, quantitative guidance for selecting the right tool for a given pipeline. Moreover, while the literature heavily favors node and graph classification for attribution-based methods, real-world applications routinely involve link classification and regression tasks as well.

Recent evaluation efforts have either focused on tabular or image data [6], or relied on synthetic graph datasets with artificially injected ground-truth motifs [7–9]. However, in real scenarios the model may have internalized patterns that diverge from human-defined labels, and we argue that it is the model's behavior, not the oracle, that explanations must faithfully reflect. Furthermore, a production-ready G-XAI framework must also focus on the pragmatic properties of explanation generation time, algorithmic reproducibility and human comprehensibility. This work is guided by the following Research Questions:

RQ1 How can core explanation properties be rigorously operationalized for graph-structured data, accounting for both topological and feature-level attributions, without relying on synthetic ground-truth motifs?

RQ2 How do state-of-the-art graph explainers compare across different GraphML tasks, and what trade-offs emerge between core explanation properties?

RQ3 Can benchmarking results transfer to operational guidelines to guide practitioners in explainer selection?

To answer these questions, we introduce a unified, quantitative framework for benchmarking G-XAI methods across the full spectrum of GraphML tasks. Our main contributions are: (i) **a quantitative, ground-truth-free evaluation framework for graphs**, where we adapt and extend three tabular metrics - *Stability*, *Pertinence*, and *Effective Compactness*, in addition to *Time* - to graph-structured explanations, independently evaluating both edge-based and feature-based attributions to capture the dual nature of graph explanations; (ii) **an exhaustive, multi-task benchmarking study**, in which we evaluate 8 strictly vetted explainers across 10 GraphML tasks and multiple GNN architectures, generating $\sim$2M explanations and revealing critical insights such as the generally high stability but severely lacking pertinence of various widely adopted methods; and (iii) **operational guidelines** where we provide empirically derived criteria for metric acceptability to assist practitioners in explainer selection, alongside a structural approach to translating complex graph attributions into natural language for regulatory compliance.

2 Related Work

Graph Machine Learning (Graph ML) utilizes GNNs to process non-Euclidean relational data via message-passing mechanisms [10]. Formally, a graph is defined as $G = (V, E)$, and its inputs are characterized by their dual nature: a feature matrix $X \in \mathbb{R}^{n \times m}$ representing the attributes of $n = |V|$ nodes with m features, and an adjacency matrix $A \in \{0, 1\}^{n \times n}$ capturing the topological structure. A GNN learns a mapping from this joint input space to a target prediction y, effectively modeling the function $(X, A) \to y$. The foundational formulation of GNNs was initially introduced to extend neural network models to process cyclic, directed, and undirected graph structures directly [11]. Standard modern architectures include Graph Convolutional Networks (GCNs) [12], Graph Attention Networks (GATs) [13], GraphSAGE [2], Graph Isomorphism Networks (GINs) [14] and Spatial GCNs [15]. Recent advancements integrate self-supervised pre-training to establish Graph Foundation Models (GFMs) [16].

These architectures are deployed across various levels of granularity, typically categorized into node-level, edge-level, and graph-level tasks. At the node level, the primary objective is *node classification*, where the model predicts the target label y_v of a specific node $v \in V$ based on its feature vector x_v and the broader structural context provided by the adjacency matrix A. At the link level, edge-classification models aim to infer the existence of an unobserved connection between a pair of nodes u and v, a fundamental task for recommendation systems and knowledge graph completion. Finally, *graph classification* operates at the macroscopic level, predicting a global property y_G for the entire graph. This requires the application of a readout or pooling function to aggregate localized node embeddings into a comprehensive global representation. All three tasks have their regression counterpart when the target y is continuous.

G-XAI considers explainers that identify the topological substructures, nodes, and features determining GNN predictions [10]. These methods are categorized into post-hoc and self-interpretable models that generate factual or counterfactual explanations. Post-hoc factual methods are primarily driven by attribution or perturbation mechanisms, often adapting general deep learning techniques to the graph domain. Gradient-based techniques leverage the model internal gradients to assign importance scores; these include fundamental approaches such as Saliency maps [17], Input $\times$ Gradient [18], and Integrated Gradients [19], which aggregate gradients along a path from a baseline to the input. Advanced back-propagation variants like Guided Backpropagation [20] and Deconvolution [21] highlight influential features by suppressing negative gradients, while Layer-wise Relevance Propagation (LRP) [22] has been specifically reformulated for graphs as GNN-LRP [23] to decompose the final prediction score into relevance contributions that flow through the message-passing layers. In contrast, perturbation-based algorithms identify influential subgraphs by observing changes in the output when the input structure is masked. GNNExplainer [3] learns a soft mask over the adjacency matrix and the node features to identify an influential subgraph, while PGExplainer [24] extends this through a parameterized approach to produce global explanations. GraphMask [25] introduces a differentiable gating mechanism to selectively erase unnecessary edges during the message-passing process and revealing which path are actually essential for the model's prediction. Other structural methods include GraphSHAP [26], which adapts Shapley values to graph neighborhoods, and SubgraphX [5], which uses Monte Carlo tree search to identify high-value subgraphs under a Shapley-based objective. Counterfactual explainers such as CF-GNNExplainer [27] and CLEAR [28] characterize model reasoning by identifying minimal topological perturbations that alter the prediction. Conversely, self-interpretable models constrain representations during training to produce inherently interpretable latent spaces, offering explanations via prototypes [29] or high-level concepts [30].

G-XAI Evaluation requires standardized metrics and frameworks. Key metrics include Fidelity, Sparsity, Stability, Graph Explanation Accuracy (GEA), Graph Explanation Faithfulness (GEF), and Graph Explanation Fairness (GECF) [8]. Benchmarking frameworks systematize these evaluations but differ markedly in scope and assumptions. GraphXAI uses the ShapeGGen generator to synthesize graphs with planted ground-truth explanations [8], while BAGEL's plausibility and correctness metrics likewise require reference rationales [7]; both presuppose a known ground truth. GraphFramEx instead evaluates post-hoc methods on real-world graphs via a fidelity-based Characterization Score [31], and GnnX-Bench studies the stability and architectural sensitivity of perturbation-based explainers [32]. More specialized efforts target molecular datasets (B-XAIC [33]) and medical reasoning models (CURE-Bench [34]). Our framework differs along three axes. First, it is *ground-truth-free*: instead of scoring agreement with a planted rationale (as in GraphXAI and BAGEL), our metrics measure an explanation's consistency with the model's own behaviour, applying even to proprietary data with no reference explanation. Second, it spans a broader *task spectrum*: prior benchmarks target classification, mostly at the node level, whereas we also cover regression and edge-level tasks, scoring feature and edge attributions jointly. Third, it targets *production constraints*: we select explainers by software license and dual-attribution support, scale to ~2M explanations via statistical early stopping, and distill the results into operational thresholds—aspects often absent from existing frameworks.

3 Metrics for G-XAI Evaluation

In this section, we describe our G-XAI evaluation framework. We define metrics to cover both node features and graph structure, and introduce optimizations to make them computationally tractable at industrial scale. Following the approach in [6], we identify four main qualities an explanation should possess for industrial applications: (i) algorithmic reproducibility and quasi-determinism; (ii) low cognitive load for a human; (iii) adherence to the model's inner mechanism; (iv) low execution time to produce the explanation. The four quality dimensions we consider follow [6], but each operationalises a long-established explanation-quality property rather than a new one. Effective Compactness is adapted from

Algorithm 1: Stability

```
Input  : target t, graph G, model M, Explainer ℰ, task_type, EarlyStop
Output: feat_stability, edge_stability
ℒ_feat, ℒ_edge ← [], [] ;                                        // Empty lists
i ← 0;
while ¬(EarlyStop(i, ℒ_feat) ∧ EarlyStop(i, ℒ_edge)) do
    (f_j, s_j) ← ℰ(t, G, M)   ∀ j ∈ {1, 2} ;                      // Two attribution passes
    ℒ_feat.Append(StabilityPairFeat(f_1, f_2, t, M, task_type, G)) ;   // Alg. 2
    ℒ_edge.Append(StabilityPairEdge(s_1, s_2, t, M, task_type, G)) ;   // Alg. 3
    i ← i + 1;
return Average(ℒ_feat), Average(ℒ_edge);
```

the tabular metric of [6]; Stability reuses its same-input formulation of the classic consistency/robustness criterion; Pertinence is a faithfulness measure; and Time is a standard efficiency measure. Our contribution is to adapt these properties to the dual nature of graph data - scoring edge and feature attributions independently - and to keep them ground-truth-free. Each quality dimension is evaluated through a dedicated metric, described subsequently. Every metric has two implementations depending on whether it operates on the node feature attribution matrix $f \in \mathbb{R}^{n \times m}$ (with n the number of nodes, and m the number of features) or the edge attribution $s \in \mathbb{R}^{|E|}$, with slight variations adopted per task. Execution time is measured directly during explanation generation. Time is a standard efficiency measure: the wall-clock runtime required to produce the explanation. Pseudocode is provided for each metric.

Stability captures how deterministic an explainer is: given the same datapoint and model, does the explainer produce consistent explanations? We adapt this same-input formulation of Stability from the tabular benchmark of [6]. It parallels Graph Explanation Stability [8] and, unlike input-perturbation robustness, serves to isolate the non-deterministic explainers that must be invoked several times. We measure this by generating multiple pairs of explanations for the same input, computing their similarity, and averaging across pairs - as formalised in Algorithm 1. Let $G = (V, E)$ represent a graph, M a model, and t an explanation target. We generate N independent pairs of explanations for the input (t, G, M). We denote the sequence of explanation pairs as $((f_1^{(k)}, s_1^{(k)}), (f_2^{(k)}, s_2^{(k)}))_{k=1}^{N}$, with f the feature attribution matrix and s the edge attribution vector.

In edge attributions (Algorithm 2), for a pair s_1 and s_2, we restrict the vectors to E_{rel} (the edges in the computational graph of t), and apply the L2 normalization as $\hat{s}_i = \frac{s_i[E_{rel}]}{\|s_i[E_{rel}]\|_2}$ for $i \in \{1, 2\}$. For each pair we compute $\rho_{edge}(s_1, s_2) = 1 - \frac{\|\hat{s}_1 - \hat{s}_2\|_2}{2}$, and the overall stability is the average of these pairwise similarities:

$$\text{Stability}_{edge}(\mathcal{E}, t, M, G) = \frac{1}{N} \sum_{k=1}^{N} \rho_{edge}(s_1^{(k)}, s_2^{(k)})$$

For feature attributions (Algorithm 3), we partition each f_i into $f_{A,i}$, which comprises the attributions of the target t, and $f_{B,i}$, which encompasses all

Algorithm 2: StabilityPairEdge

Input : s_1, s_2, target t, model M, task_type, graph G
Output: edge_stability_pair

if *task_type* == *"node"* **then**
  $E_{rel} \leftarrow$ GetEdgesInCompGraph(t, M, G);
else if *task_type* == *"link"* **then**
  $(n_1, n_2) \leftarrow t$;
  $E_{rel} \leftarrow$ GetEdgesInCompGraph$(n_1, M, G) \cup$ GetEdgesInCompGraph(n_2, M, G);
$a_i \leftarrow s_i[E_{rel}]/\|s_i[E_{rel}]\|_2 \quad \forall i \in \{1, 2\}$; // Filter & Norm.
return $1 - \|a_1 - a_2\|_2/2$;

Algorithm 3: StabilityPairFeature

Input : f_1, f_2, target t, model M, task_type, graph G
Output: feat_stability_pair

if *task_type* == *"node"* **then**
  $V_{neigh} \leftarrow$ GetNodesInCompGraph(t, M, G);
  $f_{A,i} \leftarrow f_i[t] \quad \forall i \in \{1, 2\}$;
else if *task_type* == *"link"* **then**
  $(v_1, v_2) \leftarrow t$;
  $V_{neigh} \leftarrow$ GetNodesInCompGraph$(v_1, M, G) \cup$ GetNodesInCompGraph(v_2, M, G);
  $f_{A,i} \leftarrow f_i[v_1] \oplus f_i[v_2] \quad \forall i \in \{1, 2\}$;
$f_{B,i} \leftarrow$ Flatten$(f_i[V_{neigh}]) \quad \forall i \in \{1, 2\}$;
$f_{X,i} \leftarrow f_{X,i}/\|f_{X,i}\|_2 \quad \forall X \in \{A, B\},\ i \in \{1, 2\}$; // L2 Norm.
$d_X \leftarrow \|v_{X,1} - v_{X,2}\|_2/2 \quad \forall X \in \{A, B\}$;
return $1 - (d_A + d_B)/2$;

remaining nodes within the computational graph. Both components are normalized (L2 element-wise norm) into $\hat{f}_{A,i}$ and $\hat{f}_{B,i}$, and we then compute d_A and d_B as: $d_X = \frac{\|\hat{f}_{X,1} - \hat{f}_{X,2}\|_2}{2}$ for $X \in \{A, B\}$. For each pair we then define: $\rho_{feat}(f_1, f_2) = 1 - \frac{d_A + d_B}{2}$, and we compute their average to obtain:

$$\text{Stability}_{feat}(\mathcal{E}, t, M, G) = \frac{1}{N} \sum_{k=1}^{N} \rho_{feat}(f_1^{(k)}, f_2^{(k)})$$

Effective Compactness (EC) captures the amount of information in the explanation required to impact the black-box model significantly. EC is adapted from [6] and operationalises the classic conciseness/Sparsity property [31]; it is conceptually related to the Effective Complexity of Nguyen and Martinez [35], but defined here in counterfactual terms, as the number of modifications needed to flip the prediction. However, in graphs, an explanation can easily involve thousands of different node-feature pairs and edges: since EC is mostly relevant for human interactions with the model, excessively large values of the metric can be considered equivalent. For a target t with computational graph G_{target} and prediction as $\hat{y} = M(t, G_{target})$, EC computes the number of iterative modifications, bounded by a maximum of 100, needed to change $\hat{y}$ (i.e., the class is modified, or the regression output surpasses a threshold).

On edge attributions (Algorithm 4), we first sort the edges in the computational graph E_{rel} by descending attribution score, obtaining the sequence I_{sorted}. Let $G^{(i)}_{mod}$ represent the graph obtained after removing the first i edges of I_{sorted}

Algorithm 4: ECEdge

Input : Edge attribution s, target t, graph G, model M
Output: edge_ec

```
E_rel ← GetEdgesInCompGraph(t, M, G);
I_sorted ← ArgSort(s[E_rel]) ;                    // Sort edges by attribution
G_target ← GetSubgraph(G, t, M);
G_mod ← G_target;
i ← 0;
while M(t, G_mod) = M(t, G_target) ∧ i < min(100, |E_rel|) do
    G_mod ← RemoveEdge(I_sorted[i], G_mod);
    i ← i + 1;
return i;
```

from G_{target}. The edge EC is the smallest number of removals required to alter the original prediction, bounded by the maximum allowed iterations and the total size of E_{rel}:

$$\mathrm{EC}_{edge}(s,t,M,G) = \min\left(\{i \geq 1 \mid M(t, G_{mod}^{(i)}) \neq \hat{y}\} \cup \{100, |E_{rel}|\}\right)$$

For feature EC (Algorithm 5), modifications are performed via substitutions from reference graphs. We identify a set of reference computational graphs $\mathcal{G}_{ref}$ from medoid targets t_{ref} whose baseline predictions $\hat{y}'$ differ from $\hat{y}$. In a regression task, we select medoids from the sets of nodes or edges that fall one standard deviation above and below the target prediction, while in a classification task we extract one medoid for class. Let V_{neigh} be the nodes in G_{target} different from t. We split f in the target (f_{target}) and neighbor (f_{neighs}) attribution vectors. For a node t we have $f_{target} = f[t] \in \mathbb{R}^m$; for edge targets $t = (v_1, v_2)$, we define it by concatenation: $f_{target} = f[v_1] \oplus f[v_2] \in \mathbb{R}^{2m}$. We obtain f_{neighs} by performing a max pooling across nodes in V_{neigh}. We then construct a priority vector by concatenation ($f_C = f_{target} \oplus f_{neighs}$) and compute I_{sorted}, the indices which sort f_C in descending order. For each reference target t_{ref} and corresponding G_{ref}, we establish a random mapping ϕ from V_{neigh} to the nodes in the neighborhood of t_{ref}. Then, we perform iterative substitutions according to I_{sorted}. When the i-th element of I_{sorted} corresponds to a target feature, it is replaced with the corresponding value from t_{ref}. If instead it corresponds to a neighbor feature, the substitution is applied across all nodes in V_{neigh} using the mapping ϕ. If $G_{mod}^{(i)}(G_{ref})$ denote the modified graph after i substitutions using G_{ref}, we define $k(G_{ref}) = \min\left(\{i \geq 1 \mid M(t, G_{mod}^{(i)}(G_{ref})) \neq \hat{y}\} \cup \{100, |f_C|\}\right)$. The feature EC is defined as the minimum across all G_{ref}:

$$\mathrm{EC}_{feat}(f,t,M,G) = \min_{G_{ref} \in \mathcal{G}_{ref}} k(G_{ref})$$

Pertinence addresses the adherence of the explanation to the actual model. Pertinence is a faithfulness measure in the family of Fidelity and Graph Explanation Faithfulness (GEF) [8]. It adapts the rank-based idea of the Rank Quality Index of [6] and, like GraphFramEx [31], is ground-truth-free, but it additionally scores

Algorithm 5: ECFeature

```
Input  : Attribution matrix f, target t, graph G, model M, # features N_f
Output: feature_ec
V_neigh ← GetNodesInCompGraph(t, M, G);
f_C ← f[t] ⊕ Max(f[V_neigh], dim = 1) ;                    // f[v_1]⊕f[v_2] for links
I_sorted ← ArgSort(f_C);
𝒢_ref ← GetRefGraphs(G);
G_target ← GetSubgraph(G, t, M);
feature_ec ← 100;
foreach (t_ref, G_ref) ∈ 𝒢_ref s.t. M(t_ref, G_ref) ≠ M(t, G_target) do
    φ ← CreateNodeMapping(G_target, G_ref);
    G_mod ← G_target;
    i ← 0;
    while M(t, G_mod) = M(t, G_target) ∧ i < min(100, |f|) do
        if I_sorted[i] < |f| − N_f then
            G_mod ← SetTargetFeat(I_sorted[i], G_mod, G_ref, φ);
        else
            G_mod ← SetNeighsFeats(I_sorted[i] mod N_f, G_mod, G_ref, φ);
        i ← i + 1;
    feature_ec ← min(feature_ec, i);
return feature_ec;
```

the attribution ordering against random baselines. A highly-pertinent explanation should impact the black-box model more than any randomly-generated one, while a low-pertinence one is indistinguishable from (or worse than) random baselines. We use the iterative modification procedures established for EC. Let K be the EC score (EC_{edge} or EC_{feat}). We define a deletion curve $C(k)$ as the model's output after k successive modifications ($1 \leq k \leq K$). We define C_{del} as the deletion curve constructed according to the explanation ranking I_{sorted}, while $\mathcal{C}_{rand} = \{C^{(j)}_{rand}\}_{j=1}^{N}$ is a set of N random curves, generated by applying modifications according to a random permutation of I_{sorted}. The pertinence score relative to a single $C^{(j)}_{rand}$ is the proportion of points where C_{del} degrades the output *strictly faster*: $p(C_{del}, C_{rand}) = \frac{1}{K}\sum_{k=1}^{K} \mathbb{I}(C_{del}(k) < C_{rand}(k))$.

For edge attributions (Algorithm 6), the modifications are sequential edge removals from G_{target}. The edge pertinence is the average of $p(C_{del}, C_{rand})$:

$$\mathrm{Pertinence}_{edge}(s, t, M, G) = \frac{1}{N}\sum_{j=1}^{N} p(C_{del}, C^{(j)}_{rand})$$

For feature attributions (Algorithm 7), modifications consist of feature substitutions. We construct a deletion curve $C_{del}(G_{ref})$ and a set of random curves $\mathcal{C}_{rand}(G_{ref})$ for each reference graph $G_{ref} \in \mathcal{G}_{ref}$. The feature pertinence is the average success ratio across all random permutations and reference graphs:

$$\mathrm{Pertinence}_{feat}(f, t, M, G) = \frac{1}{|\mathcal{G}_{ref}|N}\sum_{G_{ref}\in\mathcal{G}_{ref}}\sum_{j=1}^{N} p(C_{del}(G_{ref}), C^{(j)}_{rand}(G_{ref}))$$

Computational Optimisation. While our metrics do not introduce computational overhead beyond the explainer itself, repeated runs for stability and

Algorithm 6: PertinenceEdge

```
Input  : Edge attribution s, edge_ec, target t, graph G, model M
Output: edge_pertinence
E_rel ← GetEdgesInCompGraph(t, M, G);
I_sorted ← ArgSort(s[E_rel]);
C_del ← CreateEdgeDelCurve(I_sorted, edge_ec, t, G, M) ;          // Deletion curve
L_pert ← [];
i ← 0;
while ¬EarlyStop(i, L_pert) do
    C_rand ← CreateEdgeDelCurve(RandPerm(I_sorted), edge_ec, t, G, M);
    L_pert.Append(CompareCurves(C_del, C_rand));
    i ← i + 1;
return Average(L_pert);
```

Algorithm 7: PertinenceFeature

```
Input  : Attribution matrix f, feat_ec, target t, graph G, model M
Output: feature_pertinence
V_neigh ← GetNodesInCompGraph(t, M, G);
I_sorted ← ArgSort(f[t] ⊕ Max(f[V_neigh], dim=1));
𝒢_ref ← GetRefGraph(G, task_type);
L_pert ← [];
foreach (t_ref, G_ref) ∈ 𝒢_ref s.t. M(t_ref, G_ref) ≠ M(t, G_target) do
    C_del ← CreateFeatDelCurve(I_sorted, feat_ec, t, G_ref, G, M);
    L_curr ← [];
    i ← 0;
    while ¬EarlyStop(i, L_curr) do
        C_rand ← CreateFeatDelCurve(RandPerm(I_sorted), feat_ec, t, G_ref, G, M);
        L_curr.Append(CompareCurves(C_del, C_rand));
        i ← i + 1;
    L_pert.Append(Average(L_curr));
return Average(L_pert);
```

pertinence estimation can be costly in time-sensitive pipelines. To mitigate this, we implement an early stopping strategy that monitors the convergence of the observed distribution across runs, terminating evaluation once the estimate has stabilized - reducing wall-clock time without sacrificing accuracy.

Let $\mathcal{M} = \{m_1, m_2, \ldots, m_i\}$ be the set of stability/pertinence values collected after i independent trials. For $i \geq 30$, we model the confidence interval of the mean $\mu_{\mathcal{M}}$ using the standard error $SE = \sigma_{\mathcal{M}}/\sqrt{i}$, where $\sigma_{\mathcal{M}}$ represents the empirical standard deviation. We define two convergence tests based on a 95% confidence level:

1. **Mean Convergence:** Given a threshold τ, we perform a one-tailed z-test where the process terminates if $z = \frac{|\mu_{\mathcal{M}} - \tau|}{SE} > 1.645$.
2. **Precision Tolerance:** To ensure the stability of the estimate, we stop if the standard error falls within a predefined tolerance ϵ: $z = \frac{\epsilon}{SE} > 1.96$, corresponding to a two-tailed test.

In all experiments we set $\tau = 0.5$ (the random-baseline expectation for Pertinence) and $\epsilon = 0.05$. We begin checking convergence after $i = 30$ trials and cap at $N = 100$. In our benchmarking, this approach reduced the required iterations from a fixed $N = 100$ to an average of 35–40, yielding a significant reduction in wall-clock time with minimal impact on estimation variance. The metrics differ in evaluation cost. Stability re-invokes the explainer N times, so its cost scales with the explainer's runtime (negligible for gradient methods, high for GNNExplainer and GraphMask). Effective Compactness is cheap, requiring a single deletion sequence of at most 100 model inferences, whereas Pertinence is the most expensive: it repeats that sequence over N random baselines, at a cost on the order of N times Effective Compactness. The early-stopping scheme above targets precisely the repeated estimation in Stability and Pertinence.

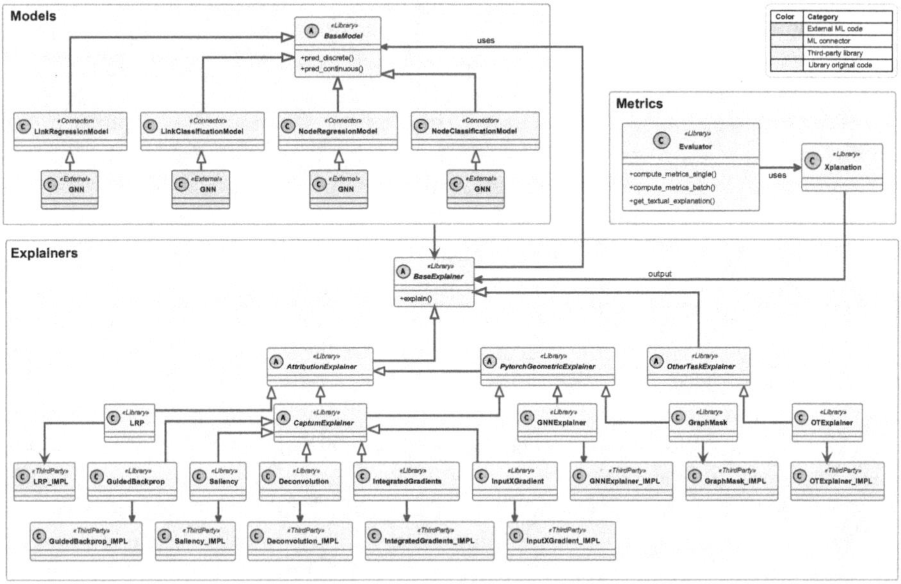

Fig. 1. Architectural overview of the proposed XAI framework, illustrating the decoupling between core evaluation logic (green), ML model connectors (orange), and the explainer suite (purple models and blue explainers). (Color figure online)

4 G-XAI Library

The proposed framework is implemented as a modular Python library designed to make GNN explanation quality measurable within existing ML pipelines with minimal integration overhead. The library is proprietary and cannot be released as open source due to company copyright restrictions. To support reproducibility and follow-up research within these constraints, the authors can be contacted for access to selected snippets of code. Figure 1 illustrates the overall architecture, which is built upon the PyTorch Geometric module and follows an object-oriented design to ensure modularity and extensibility.

Core Abstractions. The library's design is centered around four fundamental abstraction layers:

- `BaseModel`: An abstract wrapper that standardizes the interface for diverse GNN tasks. It handles the dual nature of graph inputs (feature matrix $X \in \mathbb{R}^{n\times f}$ and adjacency matrix $A \in \{0,1\}^{n\times n}$) and provides uniform methods for both discrete (`pred_discrete`) and continuous (`pred_continuous`) outputs.
- `BaseExplainer`: A high-level interface for explanation generation. We provide specialized subclasses for *Attribution Methods* (e.g., Integrated Gradients, LRP), while the architecture is designed to accommodate additional explainer families via the `OtherTaskExplainer` extension point.
- `Xplanation`: A container class that encapsulates generated attribution matrices alongside metadata regarding the target node/link and the explainer's hyperparameters. It also stores computed metrics to avoid redundant recomputations.
- `Evaluator`: The orchestration layer responsible for metric computation. It facilitates batch processing of metrics and integrates a Natural Language eXplanation (NLX) module to translate technical importance scores into human-intelligible summaries.

Integration and Performance. The library implements custom model wrappers for *Node* and *Link* tasks across both classification and regression settings. For link-level tasks, the library automatically handles the generation of computational subgraphs for the target edge (u, v), ensuring that the explanation captures the relational context of both endpoints. This is a non-trivial requirement in link prediction tasks where neither node alone determines the prediction. The library supports hardware acceleration (CUDA) and provides automated utilities for mapping neighborhood-level feature attributions back to a target-centric representation, making the output immediately interpretable within standard ML workflows.

Natural Language Explanations. To bridge the gap between technical attributions and regulatory compliance, the library includes a Natural Language eXplanation (NLX) module via the `Evaluator.get_textual_explanation()` method. Given an `Xplanation` object, the module: (i) ranks the top-k influential features and edges by attribution magnitude; (ii) maps indices to human-readable names using a user-provided dictionary; and (iii) composes them into natural language via customizable templates. For instance, in a loan approval task, the module might output: *"The application was denied primarily due to a high Debt-to-Income Ratio (importance: 0.73). While Credit History was positive, the Debt level exceeded thresholds. The model also considered connections to 3 accounts with prior defaults."* This approach ensures explanations remain faithful to the attributions while meeting EU AI Act transparency requirements. Templates support multi-lingual outputs and domain-specific terminology. We stress that the NLX module is a utility of the library for producing human-readable summaries; it is neither a benchmarked component nor part of the quantitative evaluation in Sect. 5.

5 Experiments

For each task-dataset combination, we explain 100 target predictions (on either nodes or edges, according to the task), with the same targets across different models and explainers. We measure Pertinence, Effective Compactness, and Stability, alongside the time required by each explainer. We finally average the metrics across explanations, models, and datasets.

Datasets and Models. We selected five graph datasets for classification and regression, using each on both node-level and edge-level tasks - thus creating 10 GraphML tasks. For classification tasks we utilized Cora [36], GitHub [37], and BAShapes [3]. To address the scarcity of regression benchmarks, we curated a modified version of MovieLens [38] and generated a second fully synthetic dataset. For each dataset and task, we use two-layer GCNs and GAT. We provide additional details on both datasets and models in the Appendix.

Explainers. We initially identified many graph post-hoc explainers for our benchmark. However, in order to use them across different tasks and settings, we filtered them for their ability to handle both node and edge features, to explain classification and regression tasks on nodes and edges, and to output both feature and edge attributions. Due to the industrial application of our framework, we additionally had to exclude explainers without an explicit open-source software license. Many state-of-the-art graph explainers were excluded by these criteria, such as PGExplainer [24], SubgraphX [5], GNN-LRP [23], GraphLIME [4], Degree [39] and Clear [28]. We ended in eight explainers for our benchmark: Saliency [17], Input×Gradient [18], Integrated Gradients [19], Guided Backpropagation [20], Deconvolution [21], Layer-wise Relevance Propagation (LRP) [22], GNNExplainer [3], and GraphMask [25]. They fall into two categories: gradient-based (e.g. Saliency) or attribution-redistribution approaches (e.g. LRP), both of which compute importance by backpropagating signals from the output to the input, and perturbation-based masking approaches (e.g. GNNExplainer), that optimize "soft masks" to isolate the most influential subgraphs and features.

5.1 Results

We compare explainers across the four main tasks we considered. We average the metrics across explanation targets, datasets, and models, providing a robust empirical benchmark of the explainers' performances for each task. We report these results in Table 1. Input×Gradient and IntegratedGradients emerge as the top-performing explainers in effective compactness. In contrast, GraphMask consistently ranks as the least in the metric. The 100-iteration cap reflects a comprehensibility limit rather than a mere computational bound: an explanation that requires altering more than 100 elements to change the prediction is already beyond what a human can meaningfully inspect. Within this range, Effective Compactness rewards the virtuous explainers that reach the decision boundary by acting on the fewest elements.

Table 1. Benchmark results across models, datasets and tasks (best in bold).

Task	Explainer	Feature Pertinence	Edge Pertinence	Feature Eff. Comp.	Edge Eff. Comp.	Feature Stability	Edge Stability	Execution Time
Node Class.	Deconv	0.58 ± 0.25	0.84 ± 0.10	67.9 ± 22.2	39.6 ± 24.7	**1.00 ± 0.00**	**1.00 ± 0.00**	**0.01 ± ± 0.00**
Node Class.	GNNExp	0.90 ± 0.10	0.54 ± 0.12	32.2 ± 12.8	42.8 ± 23.0	0.97 ± 0.01	0.96 ± 0.03	0.87 ± 0.10
Node Class.	GraphMask	0.52 ± 0.16	0.43 ± 0.04	82.6 ± 18.3	61.4 ± 28.1	0.96 ± 0.00	0.86 ± 0.08	3.36 ± 2.82
Node Class.	GuidedBP	0.61 ± 0.25	0.84 ± 0.10	66.8 ± 21.6	39.6 ± 24.4	**1.00 ± 0.00**	**1.00 ± 0.00**	**0.01 ± 0.00**
Node Class.	Input×Grad	**0.94 ± 0.06**	0.86 ± 0.08	**25.1 ± 10.9**	38.4 ± 23.3	**1.00 ± 0.00**	**1.00 ± 0.00**	**0.01 ± 0.00**
Node Class.	IntGrad	**0.94 ± 0.06**	**0.87 ± 0.08**	25.5 ± 11.2	**37.0 ± 22.3**	**1.00 ± 0.00**	**1.00 ± 0.00**	0.32 ± 0.09
Node Class.	LRP	0.87 ± 0.09	0.75 ± 0.05	35.9 ± 9.5	43.1 ± 28.6	**1.00 ± 0.00**	**1.00 ± 0.00**	**0.01 ± 0.00**
Node Class.	Saliency	0.61 ± 0.25	0.68 ± 0.06	50.3 ± 26.6	42.1 ± 27.5	**1.00 ± 0.00**	**1.00 ± 0.00**	**0.01 ± 0.00**
Node Reg.	Deconv	0.63 ± 0.09	**1.00 ± 0.00**	21.9 ± 36.6	**24.5 ± 32.5**	**1.00 ± 0.00**	**1.00 ± 0.00**	**0.02 ± 0.01**
Node Reg.	GNNExp	0.67 ± 0.16	0.48 ± 0.12	30.9 ± 43.0	40.7 ± 38.5	0.96 ± 0.00	0.98 ± 0.00	2.44 ± 0.73
Node Reg.	GraphMask	0.53 ± 0.05	0.48 ± 0.03	34.7 ± 56.1	56.3 ± 37.8	0.97 ± 0.00	0.88 ± 0.14	7.89 ± 5.61
Node Reg.	GuidedBP	0.63 ± 0.09	**1.00 ± 0.00**	21.9 ± 36.6	**24.5 ± 32.5**	**1.00 ± 0.00**	**1.00 ± 0.00**	0.03 ± 0.01
Node Reg.	Input×Grad	**0.90 ± 0.07**	**1.00 ± 0.00**	**7.0 ± 9.9**	**24.5 ± 32.5**	**1.00 ± 0.00**	**1.00 ± 0.00**	**0.02 ± 0.01**
Node Reg.	IntGrad	**0.90 ± 0.07**	**1.00 ± 0.00**	7.3 ± 11.0	24.9 ± 33.2	**1.00 ± 0.00**	**1.00 ± 0.00**	0.93 ± 0.34
Node Reg.	LRP	0.75 ± 0.17	0.74 ± 0.25	20.5 ± 20.7	37.0 ± 30.1	**1.00 ± 0.00**	**1.00 ± 0.00**	**0.02 ± 0.02**
Node Reg.	Saliency	0.57 ± 0.13	0.57 ± 0.20	21.8 ± 36.0	32.6 ± 26.9	**1.00 ± 0.00**	**1.00 ± 0.00**	0.03 ± 0.01
Edge Class.	Deconv	0.56 ± 0.25	0.81 ± 0.25	86.9 ± 14.9	50.7 ± 14.9	**1.00 ± 0.00**	**1.00 ± 0.00**	**0.02 ± 0.01**
Edge Class.	GNNExp	0.76 ± 0.26	0.54 ± 0.21	44.7 ± 19.3	63.3 ± 18.6	0.97 ± 0.00	0.96 ± 0.02	1.75 ± 0.86
Edge Class.	GraphMask	0.31 ± 0.24	0.31 ± 0.21	90.8 ± 5.2	82.9 ± 13.7	0.96 ± 0.00	0.80 ± 0.15	12.43 ± 18.19
Edge Class.	GuidedBP	0.58 ± 0.26	0.81 ± 0.24	82.8 ± 17.9	51.3 ± 14.4	**1.00 ± 0.00**	**1.00 ± 0.00**	**0.02 ± 0.01**
Edge Class.	Input×Grad	**0.87 ± 0.20**	0.83 ± 0.25	28.7 ± 21.0	50.9 ± 15.0	**1.00 ± 0.00**	**1.00 ± 0.00**	**0.02 ± 0.01**
Edge Class.	IntGrad	**0.87 ± 0.20**	**0.84 ± 0.25**	**27.7 ± 21.8**	**48.7 ± 15.0**	**1.00 ± 0.00**	**1.00 ± 0.00**	0.73 ± 0.34
Edge Class.	LRP	0.60 ± 0.25	0.58 ± 0.18	73.4 ± 18.5	63.9 ± 12.6	**1.00 ± 0.00**	**1.00 ± 0.00**	0.03 ± 0.01
Edge Class.	Saliency	0.51 ± 0.24	0.63 ± 0.21	82.5 ± 24.3	55.4 ± 12.8	**1.00 ± 0.00**	**1.00 ± 0.00**	**0.02 ± 0.01**
Edge Reg.	Deconv	0.57 ± 0.07	0.97 ± 0.05	49.0 ± 53.8	**49.0 ± 52.1**	**1.00 ± 0.00**	**1.00 ± 0.00**	**0.03 ± 0.00**
Edge Reg.	GNNExp	0.60 ± 0.13	0.60 ± 0.22	51.2 ± 55.2	74.6 ± 35.9	0.96 ± 0.01	0.99 ± 0.01	2.74 ± 0.44
Edge Reg.	GraphMask	0.61 ± 0.14	0.38 ± 0.19	51.3 ± 68.8	78.1 ± 31.0	0.97 ± 0.00	0.89 ± 0.09	7.44 ± 1.32
Edge Reg.	GuidedBP	0.57 ± 0.07	0.97 ± 0.05	49.0 ± 53.8	**49.0 ± 52.1**	**1.00 ± 0.00**	**1.00 ± 0.00**	**0.03 ± 0.00**
Edge Reg.	Input×Grad	**0.78 ± 0.15**	0.97 ± 0.05	**47.9 ± 52.7**	**49.0 ± 52.1**	**1.00 ± 0.00**	**1.00 ± 0.00**	**0.03 ± 0.00**
Edge Reg.	IntGrad	0.77 ± 0.15	**0.98 ± 0.03**	**47.9 ± 52.7**	49.1 ± 52.2	**1.00 ± 0.00**	**1.00 ± 0.00**	1.32 ± 0.02
Edge Reg.	LRP	0.55 ± 0.10	0.68 ± 0.17	49.3 ± 52.3	56.3 ± 39.1	**1.00 ± 0.00**	**1.00 ± 0.00**	**0.03 ± 0.01**
Edge Reg.	Saliency	0.56 ± 0.06	0.59 ± 0.29	48.9 ± 53.7	51.0 ± 38.5	**1.00 ± 0.00**	**1.00 ± 0.00**	**0.03 ± 0.00**

The high performance of gradient methods in explanation fidelity/faithfulness to the model is also consistent with the G-XAI literature [8,9,31,33,40]. Since pertinence evaluates how faithfully an explanation reflects model decisions, gradient methods benefit from direct access to internal weights, allowing for a fine-grained behavior analysis. In contrast, graph-based explainers like GNNExplainer and GraphMask do not have access to the internal model, and have to rely on random perturbations, introducing noise in the explanations.

A subset of methods scores pertinence below the 0.5 random baseline. This is not necessarily evidence of an attribution worse than random: coincident points of the explanation and random deletion curves are counted as failures, so tasks with few features (or many relevant ones) produce frequent ties that depress pertinence below 0.5. A distinct, task-level effect arises when opposing classes are characterized by a multimodal distribution: the medoid reference targets then may poorly represent the target's nearest alternative and feature perturbations may lead to unstable prediction flips, letting random orderings degrade the output almost as fast as the attribution (we detail these cases in the Appendix). Computation variants that explicitly consider this phenomenon and remove this sub-baseline regime are left to future work.

Notably, however, several methods exhibit specialized performance: GNNExplainer (in classification tasks) and LRP (in node tasks) excel at feature-level

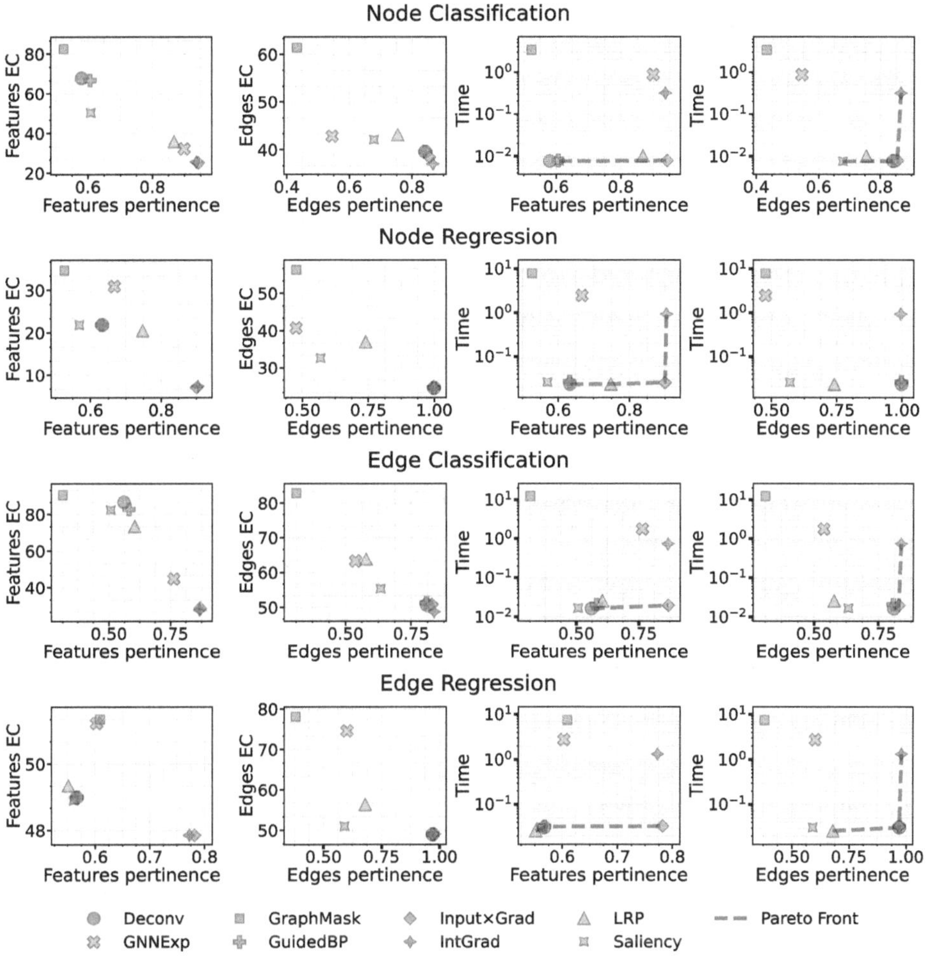

Fig. 2. Pareto plots comparing the explainers across pairs of metrics. In all cases, the bottom-right region of the plot corresponds to more desirable trade-offs.

explanations, while Deconvolution and GuidedBackProp always perform better on edge attributions. In terms of stability, all explainers, with the exceptions of GNNExplainer and GraphMask, yield constant results due to their non-stochastic algorithms. A Stability of 1.00 means the explainer is fully deterministic, so a single invocation already yields a reproducible attribution. The metric's main practical value is thus to isolate the non-deterministic explainers (here GNNExplainer and GraphMask), which must be invoked several times before their attributions can be considered reliable. Execution times, finally, vary drastically across the methods. Gradient-based methods are extremely efficient, typically requiring less than 0.01 s, as they only need one model call. However, Integrated Gradients, GNNExplainer and GraphMask are significantly slower, lagging by two to four orders of magnitude, as they all require several model calls to generate an explanation.

The Pareto plots in Fig. 2 reveal no significant trade-off between pertinence and effective compactness: Input×Gradient and Integrated Gradients function as dominant solutions across both metrics. This finding is consistent across most tasks, except for edge regression, where most methods show comparable performance regarding feature effective compactness. In this case, the feature pertinence provides a more nuanced evaluation, showing that Integrated Gradients and Input×Gradient still perform significantly better than the random baseline (which, for the way we defined the metric, corresponds to 0.5). We excluded stability due to its consistency across different explainers. When comparing execution time against feature and edge pertinence, instead, other gradient-based methods (LRP and Saliency) appear on the Pareto front due to their speed, with Input×Gradient offering the best balance: it provides a substantial boost in pertinence for both edges and features with only a negligible increase in latency. Conversely, the marginal performance gains often offered by Integrated Gradients do not seem to justify an execution time that is two orders of magnitude higher. When considering edge pertinence, however, Deconvolution and Guided Backpropagation are almost on par with Input×Gradient. Finally, we observe that edges serve as the primary information source for models in regression tasks. However, this effect, alongside the limited variability in feature effective compactness in edge regression, may derive from the specific synthetic datasets used and might not generalize to other contexts.

5.2 Operational Guidelines

From our benchmarking results, we distill a set of practical guidelines for explainer selection and quality assessment, detailed in the Appendix. Amongst the most relevant components are empirically grounded quality thresholds, transferability considerations, and explainer recommendations.

Quality Thresholds. Based on our benchmarking results, we derive empirically grounded thresholds for Stability, Pertinence, and EC across all four Graph ML tasks, alongside transferability considerations and explainer recommendations. Stability thresholds transfer reliably across datasets, while Pertinence and Effective Compactness should be revalidated on proprietary data - particularly Edge EC, which varies with node degree. Full guidelines, including deployment workflows and tabular summaries, are provided in the Appendix.

Transferability Notes. Stability transfers reliably from benchmarks to new datasets, as it primarily depends on the explainer's algorithm. Pertinence and Effective Compactness are indicative but should be revalidated on proprietary data - particularly Edge EC, which varies with node degree. We recommend a minimum sample of 50–100 instances for initial assessment and 200+ for production validation.

Explainer Recommendation. For most graph tasks, **Input×Gradient** offers the best trade-off: near-optimal pertinence and compactness with execution times under 0.03 s. Integrated Gradients provides marginal gains at 100× higher latency, justified only when time is unconstrained. GraphMask consistently underperforms and should be avoided.

6 Conclusion

In this paper, we introduced an empirical evaluation framework for GNN post-hoc explanations designed for seamless application across diverse real-world datasets, models, and tasks. By implementing these metrics within a dedicated library, we enabled the integration and testing of ML models alongside a wide selection of explainers. Our benchmarking across both node and link tasks revealed that Input×Gradient (a relatively simple, deterministic, gradient-based technique) outperforms or matches the performance of more complex or graph-specific explainers. Our findings cross-validate results in the G-XAI benchmark literature and demonstrate a clear relationship between current fidelity metrics and our proposed Pertinence and Effective Compactness metrics.

The scope of our benchmark was constrained by our selection criteria: each explainer had to handle node and edge tasks under both classification and regression, and to produce feature and edge attributions simultaneously (dual-attribution). We further stress that our metrics deliberately measure consistency with the model's own behaviour rather than correctness with respect to real-world phenomena: in line with the true-to-the-model paradigm, it is the model, not an external oracle, that explanations must faithfully reflect. Validating explanations against domain knowledge is a complementary, human-centred direction that we leave to future work. While necessary for a uniform comparison across tasks, these criteria introduce a selection bias, since several graph-native explainers do not meet them and thus fall outside our comparison. Nevertheless, our modular methodology provides a robust foundation for the future integration of new techniques and tasks. Subsequent research will expand this framework to include emerging graph explainability approaches, such as counterfactuals, while leveraging the insights from this benchmark to develop more flexible and effective graph explainers.

GenAI Disclosure. The authors disclose the use of generative AI for proofreading and to improve the grammatical clarity of this manuscript.

References

1. Zonghan, W., Pan, S., Chen, F., Long, G., Zhang, C., Philip, S.Y.: A comprehensive survey on graph neural networks. IEEE Trans. Neural Networks Learn. Syst. **32**(1), 4–24 (2020)
2. Hamilton, W., Ying, Z., Leskovec, J.: Inductive representation learning on large graphs. In: Advances in Neural Information Processing Systems (NeurIPS), vol. 30 (2017)

3. Ying, Z., Bourgeois, D., You, J., Zitnik, M., Leskovec, J.: Gnnexplainer: generating explanations for graph neural networks. In: Advances in Neural Information Processing Systems, vol. 32 (2019)
4. Huang, Q., Yamada, M., Tian, Y., Singh, D., Chang, Y.: Graphlime: local interpretable model explanations for graph neural networks. IEEE Trans. Knowl. Data Eng. **35**(7), 6968–6972 (2022)
5. Yuan, H., Yu, H., Wang, J., Li, K., Ji, S.: On explainability of graph neural networks via subgraph explorations. In: International Conference on Machine Learning (ICML), pp. 12241–12252. PMLR (2021)
6. Perotti, A., Borile, C., Miola, A., Nerini, F.P., Baracco, P., Panisson, A.: Explainability, quantified: benchmarking XAI techniques. In: Longo, L., Lapuschkin, S., Seifert, C. (eds.) xAI 2024. CCIS, vol. 2153, pp. 421–444. Springer, Cham (2024). https://doi.org/10.1007/978-3-031-63787-2_22
7. Rathee, M., Funke, T., Anand, A., Khosla, M.: Bagel: a benchmark for assessing graph neural network explanations. In: Thirty-sixth Conference on Neural Information Processing Systems Datasets and Benchmarks Track (2022)
8. Agarwal, C., Queen, O., Chugh, H., Zitnik, M.: Evaluating explainability for graph neural networks. Sci. Data **10**(1), 144 (2023)
9. Monti, C., Bajardi, P., Bonchi, F., Panisson, A., Perotti, A.: A true-to-the-model axiomatic benchmark for graph-based explainers. Trans. Mach. Learn. Res. 2024 (2024)
10. Nandan, M., Mitra, S., De, D.: GraphXAI: a survey of graph neural networks (GNNs) for explainable AI (XAI). Neural Comput. Appl. **37**(17), 10949–11000 (2025)
11. Scarselli, F., Gori, M., Tsoi, A.C., Hagenbuchner, M., Monfardini, G.: The graph neural network model. IEEE Trans. Neural Networks **20**(1), 61–80 (2008)
12. Thomas, N., Kipf, M., Welling: Semi-supervised classification with graph convolutional networks. In: International Conference on Learning Representations (2017)
13. Veličković, P., Cucurull, G., Casanova, A., Romero, A., Liò, P., Bengio, Y.: Graph attention networks. In: International Conference on Learning Representations (2018)
14. Xu, K., Hu, W., Leskovec, J., Jegelka, S.: How powerful are graph neural networks? In: International Conference on Learning Representations (2018)
15. Danel, T., et al.: Spatial graph convolutional networks. In: Yang, H., Pasupa, K., Leung, A.C.-S., Kwok, J.T., Chan, J.H., King, I. (eds.) ICONIP 2020. CCIS, vol. 1333, pp. 668–675. Springer, Cham (2020). https://doi.org/10.1007/978-3-030-63823-8_76
16. Zhao, Z., Yixin, S., Li, Y., Zou, Y., Li, R., Zhang, R.: A survey on self-supervised graph foundation models: knowledge-based perspective. IEEE Trans. Knowl. Data Eng. (2025)
17. Simonyan, K., Vedaldi, A., Zisserman, A.: Deep inside convolutional networks: visualising image classification models and saliency maps. arXiv preprint arXiv:1312.6034 (2013)
18. Shrikumar, A., Greenside, P., Kundaje, A.: Learning important features through propagating activation differences. In: International Conference on Machine Learning, pp. 3145–3153. PMlR (2017)
19. Sundararajan, M., Taly, A., Yan, Q.: Axiomatic attribution for deep networks. In: International Conference on Machine Learning. PMLR (2017)
20. Springenberg, J., Dosovitskiy, A., Brox, T., Riedmiller, M.: Striving for simplicity: the all convolutional net. In: ICLR (Workshop Track) (2015)

21. Zeiler, M.D., Fergus, R.: Visualizing and understanding convolutional networks. In: Fleet, D., Pajdla, T., Schiele, B., Tuytelaars, T. (eds.) ECCV 2014. LNCS, vol. 8689, pp. 818–833. Springer, Cham (2014). https://doi.org/10.1007/978-3-319-10590-1_53
22. Bach, S., Binder, A., Montavon, G., Klauschen, F., Müller, K.-R., Samek, W.: On pixel-wise explanations for non-linear classifier decisions by layer-wise relevance propagation. PLoS ONE **10**(7), e0130140 (2015)
23. Schnake, T., et al.: Higher-order explanations of graph neural networks via relevant walks. IEEE Trans. Pattern Anal. Mach. Intell. **44**(11), 7581–7596 (2021)
24. Luo, D., et al.: Parameterized explainer for graph neural network. Adv. Neural. Inf. Process. Syst. **33**, 19620–19631 (2020)
25. Schlichtkrull, M.S., Cao, N.D., Titov, I.: Interpreting graph neural networks for NLP with differentiable edge masking. In: International Conference on Learning Representations (2021)
26. Perotti, A., Bajardi, P., Bonchi, F., Panisson, A.: Explaining identity-aware graph classifiers through the language of motifs. In: 2023 International Joint Conference on Neural Networks (IJCNN), pp. 1–8 (2023)
27. Lucic, A., Maartje A Ter, Hoeve, G., Tolomei, M., De Rijke, F., Silvestri: CF-gnnexplainer: counterfactual explanations for graph neural networks. In: International Conference on Artificial Intelligence and Statistics. PMLR (2022)
28. Ma, J., Guo, R., Mishra, S., Zhang, A., Li, J.: Clear: generative counterfactual explanations on graphs. Adv. Neural. Inf. Process. Syst. **35**, 25895–25907 (2022)
29. Zhang, Z., Liu, Q., Wang, H., Chengqiang, L., Lee, C.: ProtGNN: towards self-explaining graph neural networks. In: Proceedings of the AAAI Conference on Artificial Intelligence, vol. 36, pp. 9127–9135 (2022)
30. Azzolin, S., Longa, A., Barbiero, P., Lio, P., Passerini, A.: Global explainability of GNNs via logic combination of learned concepts. In: The Eleventh International Conference on Learning Representations (2023)
31. Amara, K., et al.: GraphFrameX: towards systematic evaluation of explainability methods for graph neural networks. In: Learning on Graphs Conference, pp. 44–1. PMLR (2022)
32. Kosan, M., et al.: GNNX-BENCH: unravelling the utility of perturbation-based GNN explainers through in-depth benchmarking. In: The Twelfth International Conference on Learning Representations (2024)
33. Proszewska, M., Danel, T., Rymarczyk, D.: B-xaic dataset: benchmarking explainable AI for graph neural networks using chemical data. arXiv preprint arXiv:2505.22252 (2025)
34. Gao, S., et al.: Cure-bench (2025). https://kaggle.com/competitions/cure-bench. 2025 Neural Information Processing Conference (Neurips 2025) Competition
35. Nguyen, A., Martínez, M.R.: On quantitative aspects of model interpretability (2020)
36. Yang, Z., Cohen, W., Salakhudinov, R.: Revisiting semi-supervised learning with graph embeddings. In: International Conference on Machine Learning, pp. 40–48. PMLR (2016)
37. Rozemberczki, B., Allen, C., Sarkar, R.: Multi-scale attributed node embedding. J. Complex Networks **9**(2), cnab014 (2021)
38. Harper, F.M., Konstan, J.A.: The Movielens datasets: history and context. ACM Trans. Interact. Intell. Syst. (TIIS) **5**(4), 1–19 (2015)

39. Feng, Q., Liu, N., Yang, F., Tang, R., Du, M., Hu, X.: Degree: decomposition based explanation for graph neural networks. In: 10th International Conference on Learning Representations, ICLR 2022 (2022)
40. Nerini, F.P., Bonchi, F., Panisson, A.: A true-to-the-model benchmark for edge-level attributions of GNN explainers. In: Ribeiro, R.P., et al. (eds.) ECML PKDD 2025. LNCS, vol. 16016, pp. 78–93. Springer, Cham (2025). https://doi.org/10.1007/978-3-032-06078-5_5

The Reliability Gap in Benchmark Auditing: Distribution Shift and Scale as Failure Modes of Contamination Detection

Wojciech Zarzecki[1,2(✉)], Jan Dubiński[1,2], and Sebastian Cygert[1,3]

[1] NASK National Research Institute, Warsaw, Poland
wojciechzarzecki5@gmail.com
[2] Warsaw University of Technology, Warsaw, Poland
[3] Gdańsk University of Technology, Gdańsk, Poland

Abstract. Benchmark contamination, where evaluation examples appear in a model's training data, threatens the validity of LLM assessment. Statistical tools for detecting training-data membership exist, but have been validated almost exclusively in controlled academic regimes: large, homogeneous pre-training corpora and transparent, single-stage training pipelines. Whether these methods remain reliable in realistic auditing scenarios remains unclear. We identify two under-studied failure modes: distribution shift, which arises when suspect and validation sets violate the IID assumption, and scale constraints, which arise because benchmarks are orders of magnitude smaller than pre-training corpora. We systematically evaluate three leading paradigms: LLM Dataset Inference, Post-Hoc Dataset Inference, and CoDeC across 25 models from multiple families (including Pythia, OLMo 2, and specialised cultural and medical LLMs) and scales (up to 27B). We then further extend our analysis to frontier industry models. Across 335 evaluations, only 201 yield correct outcomes. LLM Dataset Inference results in false positives under distribution shift, Post-Hoc Dataset Inference is underpowered at benchmark scale, and CoDeC provides only coarse provenance signals that are insufficient to verify individual benchmark splits. Our results reveal a systematic reliability gap between controlled validation and practical benchmark auditing, and show that statistical detection cannot yet replace transparent data provenance. We open-source our benchmark for further research.

Keywords: benchmark contamination · dataset inference · LLM evaluation · distribution shift · training data auditing

W. Zarzecki—This work was conducted mostly while the author was at NASK National Research Institute.

M. Ceci et al. (Eds.): ECML PKDD 2026, LNAI 16948, pp. 399–417, 2027.
https://doi.org/10.1007/978-3-032-37679-4_23

1 Introduction

In the era of rapidly scaling large language models, both model size and training data volume have increased by orders of magnitude. This scaling has unlocked new capabilities in reasoning, mathematics, and multi-domain knowledge, pushing performance on many public benchmarks to saturation. At the same time, benchmark contamination has emerged as a serious threat to the validity of LLM evaluation.

When benchmark splits leak into scraped or aggregated corpora, benchmark performance may reflect prior exposure rather than genuine generalization. As models saturate widely used benchmarks, distinguishing between reasoning capability and memorization has become a central challenge of modern LLM assessment.

Existing literature addresses this issue by developing principled statistical tools for detecting training data, including *LLM Dataset Inference* [23], *Post-Hoc Dataset Inference* [31], and direct contamination measures such as *CoDeC* [30]. However, these methods are primarily validated in restricted academic settings, for example using the Pythia [3] suite trained on The Pile [12], where full data transparency and strict distributional assumptions hold. Academic model suites typically rely on relatively simple, single-stage pre-training on large, homogeneous corpora, which simplifies contamination analysis.

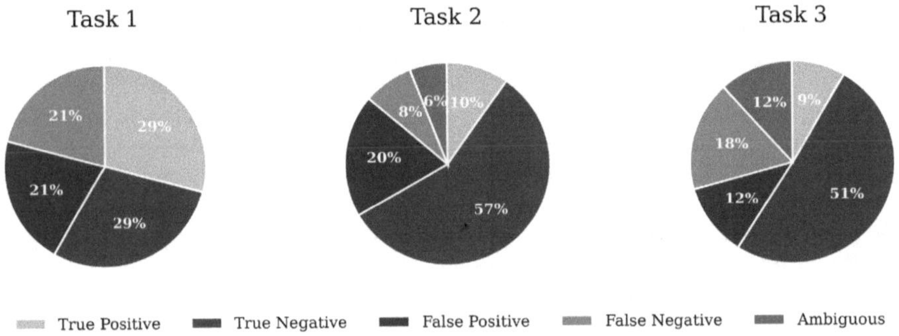

Fig. 1. Summary of our evaluation of methods for detecting whether a model was trained on a benchmark, across three tasks: Task 1 evaluates vulnerability to limited reference data (Table 1); Task 2 evaluates split-level benchmark exposure on instruction-tuned OLMo 2 (Table 2); and Task 3 evaluates specialised post-training datasets, for medical QA and Polish-language LLMs (Tables 3 and 4). The counts aggregate detection outcomes from these tables. Overall, only 201 out of 335 (60%) of the detection challenges are solved, suggesting that current approaches are not yet reliable for certifying benchmark integrity.

It remains unclear whether these methods remain reliable in more realistic settings. In practice, benchmark auditing concerns evaluation sets that are orders of magnitude smaller than pre-training corpora, and models that undergo multiple post-training stages, including instruction tuning on curated mixtures. To study this beyond academic model suites, our evaluation includes 21 openly available instruction-tuned models with sizes reaching 27B parameters (plus 4 pre-trained-only models, for 25 in total). Therefore, in this work, we investigate whether existing detection mechanisms function effectively *in the wild.* We define this setting through two constraints: (1) the target of detection is a benchmark rather than a massive pre-training corpus, and (2) the audited models are instruction-tuned variants that have undergone multi-stage post-training.

Our main contributions are as follows. **First in-the-wild evaluation of benchmark auditing.** We provide the first systematic evaluation of three state-of-the-art detection paradigms, *LLM Dataset Inference*, *Post-Hoc Dataset Inference*, and *CoDeC*, beyond controlled academic corpora and in realistic benchmark auditing scenarios for which we open-source our code[1].

Throughout our extensive evaluation, we find that:

1. **Current auditing methods are not yet reliable enough to consistently verify benchmark exposure.** As summarized in Fig. 1, correct detection outcomes are matched by many failures across our evaluations.
2. **At limited dataset scale, only LLM DI works, but only under favorable conditions.** When the investigated dataset is as small as a typical benchmark, LLM DI can still detect training exposure if it has access to a genuinely unseen and approximately IID reference set. Post-Hoc DI does not have enough data to build a reliable synthetic reference set, and CoDeC assigns similar scores to closely matched train and test splits (Sect. 5.1).
3. **None of the methods can reliably tell which split of a benchmark was used for training.** In split-level auditing, LLM DI can mistake distribution differences for training exposure, Post-Hoc DI remains unstable, and CoDeC does not clearly separate seen and unseen splits from the same benchmark (Sect. 5.2 and 5.5).
4. **For specialised post-training datasets and industry models, we find that the signals become less stable and harder to interpret.** For domain-specific post-training datasets, detection performance degrades. For industry models, the methods can detect differences at the level of model families. (Sect. 5.3 and 5.4).

These findings suggest several practical recommendations. LLM DI is only usable when a genuinely unseen and approximately IID validation set is available. Post-Hoc DI appears less suitable for standard benchmark-sized datasets unless the quality of the synthetic held-out data can be independently assessed. CoDeC is best interpreted as a comparative contamination indicator rather than a certification tool. Our results suggest that transparent data provenance remains the most reliable basis for benchmark-integrity claims, with statistical auditing serving as complementary evidence.

[1] https://anonymous.4open.science/r/reliability-gap-benchmark-auditing/.

2 Related Work

Membership and Dataset Inference. Membership inference attacks (MIAs) study whether a particular record was part of a model's training set, typically by exploiting systematic differences in model behavior on seen versus unseen examples [28]. For large models, including LLMs, single-example MIAs can be noisy [11,23], motivating *dataset inference* methods that aggregate weak per-sample signals over a suspect set and compare them to an unseen reference set [10,20,23]. A key practical challenge for these tests is obtaining a reference or validation set that is truly unseen and sufficiently IID with the suspect set; violations of this assumption can lead to confounded detections.

Benchmark Contamination. Benchmark contamination refers to the overlap between a benchmark dataset and a model's training data [4]. This overlap may occur when benchmark train or test splits are directly included in pre-training corpora, or when near-duplicate or highly overlapping variants are present in large scraped mixtures [22]. In such cases, benchmark performance may reflect prior exposure rather than generalization to unseen data. As benchmarks are repeatedly reused and increasingly incorporated into post-training mixtures, contamination becomes both more likely and more difficult to detect [2].

In parallel to documenting contamination risk, recent efforts have focused on developing methods for detecting it. Retrieval-based and behavioral auditing approaches test whether benchmark items can be recovered from candidate corpora or elicited from the model itself [8,13]. More recently, performance-based methods have framed contamination detection as a statistical problem, asking whether unusually strong benchmark results are better explained by prior exposure than by genuine generalization [7]. Another recent direction is in-context contamination detection: CoDeC [30] measures how adding examples from the same dataset changes model confidence, using these shifts to produce an interpretable dataset-level contamination score. The method requires only gray-box access to token probabilities and assumes no prior knowledge of the training corpus, making it particularly attractive for practical benchmark auditing.

3 Methods

In our experiments, we use the following methods: Post-Hoc Dataset Inference, LLM Dataset Inference, and CoDeC, which are described in this section.

LLM Dataset Inference. This method [23] builds on membership inference attacks, but shifts the unit of analysis from *individual samples* to *datasets.* For LLMs, a single-sample MIA is often too noisy to be reliably useful: many sequences are "easy" (low loss) even if they were never seen during training, and the membership signal for any particular example becomes faint as models scale.

Dataset inference addresses this by *aggregating weak membership signals across many samples* and testing whether, in aggregate, a *suspect set* looks more train-like than an *unseen validation set.* Concretely, one computes a collection of MIA-derived scores (e.g., loss or perplexity-based and related features) for samples from both sets, learns a simple aggregation of these features, and then performs a statistical test, typically a one-sided t-test, on held-out samples to decide whether the suspect set exhibits systematically stronger membership evidence than the validation set.

The output of dataset inference is a **p-value**. Under the null hypothesis H_0 that the model was not trained on the suspect set, the observed separation between suspect and validation should be explainable by chance. A small p-value (e.g., $p < 0.1$ as in [23]) is interpreted as evidence against H_0, that is, as a detection of training on the suspect dataset. Importantly, this p-value is only meaningful under a key assumption: the validation set must be unseen during training and IID with the suspect set. If the two sets differ in distribution, for example a benchmark train split versus its test split, the test can become confounded and may yield false positives.

Post-Hoc Dataset Inference. Post-hoc DI is designed to relax the practical requirement of LLM dataset inference for an unseen, IID validation set. Instead of requiring a naturally occurring validation set, post-hoc DI constructs a synthetic validation set that is intended to be distribution-matched to the suspect data. The procedure has two stages.

(1) Held-out data generation. Starting from a corpus of documents for a given dataset, the method segments documents into short snippets and splits them into two disjoint pools. A small generator model is trained with a causal language modeling objective on one pool. The second pool is converted into prefix–suffix pairs; the generator is then used to produce artificial suffixes conditioned on the prefixes. The resulting dataset contains real suffixes, which form the suspect set, and synthetic suffixes, which serve as the validation set. Both sets share surface-level distributional properties, but only the suspect set could contain memorized training data from the audited model.

(2) Post-hoc calibration. The method trains two classifiers to distinguish suspect versus synthetic validation examples: (i) a text-only classifier c_{text}, and (ii) a combined classifier c_{comb} that augments text with MIA-derived features such as loss statistics. The central statistical question is whether the MIA features provide additional separability beyond what is already achievable from text alone. Concretely, one computes per-example classification scores and performs a one-sided t-test to determine whether the combined classifier improves separation relative to the text-only baseline. The output is a **p-value** under the null hypothesis H_0 that MIA features do not add meaningful signal once text is accounted for. A small p-value, for example $p < 0.1$, is interpreted as evidence that the audited model was trained on the suspect distribution.

Context-Based Contamination Signals. Complementary to likelihood- and classifier-based auditing, CoDeC (Contamination Detection via Context) detects dataset-level contamination by measuring how same-dataset in-context examples affect next-token likelihood [30]. In-context learning often improves predictions on unseen data, but can become unhelpful or harmful when memorization is triggered. This yields an interpretable contamination score defined as the fraction of samples for which in-context examples reduce model confidence.

The key observation is that in-context learning is typically helpful when the model has not internalized the target distribution. Adding a few examples provides dataset-specific cues such as format or vocabulary and improves next-token likelihood. In contrast, if the model has already been trained on the dataset or a close variant, in-context examples provide little new information.

Operationally, for each sample x from a dataset $\mathcal{D}$, CoDeC compares the model's average log-likelihood on x in two settings: (i) a baseline setting where the model predicts x directly, and (ii) an in-context setting where x is preceded by a small number of other samples from $\mathcal{D}$. The per-sample score is the log-likelihood difference $\Delta(x)$, defined as in-context minus baseline. The dataset **contamination score** is the fraction of samples for which $\Delta(x) < 0$. Higher values indicate that in-context learning is frequently unhelpful or harmful, which is consistent with stronger contamination.

4 Experimental Setup

In this section, we describe the experimental setup used to evaluate contamination-detection methods across multiple model families, datasets, and auditing scenarios. We create a publicly available codebase which adapts each method to shared interface for benchmarking and detail the method configurations, audited models and benchmarks, and the notation used to interpret detection outcomes in the experiments that follow.

4.1 Detection Methods Configuration.

LLM DI: This method mirrors the MIA metrics, statistical test, outlier handling, and normalization strategy of Post-Hoc DI. Datasets are evenly split: set A computes metrics and trains a linear classifier using 250 samples per side, while set B evaluates the final t-test using at least 1 000 texts, the maximum number of texts per split evaluated by authors of methods [23].

Post-Hoc DI: We follow the original method as closely as possible in our benchmark-auditing setting. We subsample 2 000 texts per set and clip outliers symmetrically at 2.5% per tail. A `Meta-Llama-3.1-8B` model fine-tuned with LoRA generates 128-token suffixes for paraphrasing. Calibration relies on a GPT-2 baseline text classifier, while combined features are evaluated using a linear classifier trained for 1 000 epochs with Adam. MIA metrics are z-score normalized prior to training. We utilize perplexity, k-min-probs (k=0.05), reversed k-max-probs (k=0.05), and zlib ratio as our MIA metrics. We apply a one-sided independent samples t-test with a significance threshold of $p < 0.1$,[2] taking the mean over 3 independent runs.

[2] increased from $p < 0.05$ due to high p-values for members (where an ideal method should have very low p-values for members) and consistency with LLM DI.

CoDeC: The contamination score is calculated as a binary per-sample classification, assigning a value of 1 if confidence drops when context is added. To avoid prompt artifacts, log-probabilities are averaged from the 10th token onward, we strictly utilize 1 randomly sampled context example—following the official description of CoDeC pipeline [30].

4.2 Audited Models and Datasets.

Open Model Suites: Fully open model suites enable rigorous contamination studies by allowing inspection of training data to support ground-truth membership claims. We evaluate the **Pythia suite**, known for its tight coupling with **The Pile** reference corpus. We also audit **OLMo 2**, which details its broad knowledge pre-training [24], rigorous post-training (incorporating datasets like *UltraFeedback* [6], *tulu3 sft math* [21], *Competition Math* [15], and *GSM8K* [5]), and extensive evaluation phases.

Evaluation Benchmarks: For the open-model experiments, we evaluate benchmark exposure on OLMo 2 using high-impact evaluation sets frequently audited for leakage as their train splits are widely available and exert strong optimization pressure. Representative benchmarks include **GSM8K** [5] (grade-school math word problems), **MATH** and **Competition Math** [15] (multi-step competition mathematics), **DROP** [9] (discrete reasoning over paragraphs), and **MMLU** [14] (multi-domain knowledge evaluation).

PLLuM: A family of Polish language LLMs [19], which undergoes supervised fine-tuning using automatic and manual datasets, followed by preference-based alignment. We audit the Llama-PLLuM-8B, PLLuM-12B, and non-commercial PLLuM-12B-nc variants.

Medical LLMs: We evaluate domain-specialised models fine-tuned on public medical QA benchmarks. Tested benchmarks include MedQA-USMLE [16], MedMCQA [25], PubMedQA [17], and MedExpQA [1]. Audited models include variants of MedGemma [27] (4B, 27B), Meditron3 [26] (8B, 9B), Meerkat [18] (7B, 8B), and Neeto-1.0-8B [29].

4.3 Notation for Detection Outcomes

Throughout the tables in this section, we report detection outcomes using colored symbols to indicate correctness at a glance:

- + (green +): *true positive*; the method correctly identifies that the model was trained on the given data.
- − (green −): *true negative*; the method correctly determines that the model was not trained on the given data.
- + (red +): *false positive*; the method incorrectly indicates that the model was trained on the data when it was not.

- – (red –): *false negative*; the method fails to detect that the model was in fact trained on the data.

The detection decision (+ vs. –) is derived differently for each method. For *LLM Dataset Inference*, a detection (+) is declared when the one-sided t-test p-value falls below 0.1, following the threshold used in [23]. For *CoDeC*, a detection (+) is declared when the contamination score is higher than 0.8 indicating strong contamination, no detection (–) when contamination score is below 0.6, and inconclusive (?) when the score is between 0.6 and 0.8, as suggested in the original work [30]. Tables with numerical values instead of symbols can be found in the supplementary material.

5 Experiments

We first test whether current contamination detection methods remain effective when only benchmark-scale reference sets are available for inspection, rather than full pre-training corpora (Sect. 5.1). We then examine whether these methods can distinguish between seen and unseen splits within the same benchmark (Sect. 5.2). Next, we evaluate the most effective approaches on specialised post-training datasets (Sect. 5.3). Finally, we apply a comparative analysis on industry models (Sect. 5.4) and analyze the failure modes underlying these results (Sect. 5.5).

5.1 Task 1: Auditing with Limited Reference Data

A fundamental challenge in applying current detection methods "in the wild" is the vast disparity in data scale: while pre-training corpora typically encompass gigabytes of text, specific evaluation benchmarks often consist of only a few megabytes. To rigorously evaluate detection performance under these constrained conditions, we simulate the data scarcity characteristic of benchmark auditing. We find that Post-Hoc DI becomes ineffective when trained on only a few thousand examples, while CoDeC cannot distinguish split-level membership when train and test distributions are too similar. Only LLM DI, which requires access to an IID validation set, remains reliable at benchmark scale.

Task Setup. Instead of utilizing the full corpus, we restrict the reference data to $n = 2,000$ documents per dataset subsampled from various subsets of The Pile. We then evaluate the detection methods across multiple Pythia model sizes, effectively mimicking a scenario where the auditor has access to only a fraction of the data distribution, comparable to the size of a standard evaluation benchmark, rather than the massive datasets used in prior academic validations.

Findings. As shown in Table 1, LLM Dataset Inference correctly distinguishes train from test splits across all model sizes, confirming that our implementation reproduces prior academic findings under controlled conditions. Post-Hoc Dataset Inference, however, does not reject the null hypothesis of non-membership in most cases. At benchmark scale, the generator trained on only

Table 1. Detection of training on train and test splits of the Pile (Limited Data). We reorganize the results into a grid to highlight consistency across diverse subsets. Symbols: + = correctly detected as trained on, − = correctly detected as *not* trained on, + = false positive, − = false negative, ? = uncertain signal.

	Pile CC		Pile Europarl		Corr./Tot.
	Train	Test	Train	Test	
Pythia sizes	0.4B/1.4B/2.8B/6.9B	0.4B/1.4B/2.8B/6.9B	0.4B/1.4B/2.8B/6.9B	0.4B/1.4B/2.8B/6.9B	
LLM DI	−/−/−/−	−/−/−/−	+/+/+/+	−/−/−/−	12/16
Post-Hoc DI	−/−/−/−	−/−/−/−	−/−/−/−	−/−/−/−	8/16
CoDeC	+/+/+/+	+/+/+/+	+/+/+/+	+/+/+/+	8/16

	Pile Hacker News		Pile Stack Exchange		Corr./Tot.
	Train	Test	Train	Test	
Pythia sizes	0.4B/1.4B/2.8B/6.9B	0.4B/1.4B/2.8B/6.9B	0.4B/1.4B/2.8B/6.9B	0.4B/1.4B/2.8B/6.9B	
LLM DI	+/+/+/+	−/−/−/−	+/+/+/+	−/−/−/−	16/16
Post-Hoc DI	−/−/−/−	+/+/+/+	−/−/−/−	−/−/−/−	4/16
CoDeC	+/+/+/+	+/+/+/+	+/+/+/+	+/+/+/+	8/16

2,000 samples per subset is too weak to produce realistic synthetic validation data, leading to uninformative calibration statistics. This interpretation is supported by an analysis of a full-scale held-out generation setting at Sect. 5.5. CoDeC assigns high contamination scores to both splits when distributions are similar. As a result, high scores may reflect exposure to either the train split alone or both splits, indicating sensitivity to distributional overlap rather than precise membership.

5.2 Task 2: Detecting Split-Level Benchmark Exposure

In this task, we move from controlled Pythia/Pile simulations to realistic benchmark auditing on instruction-tuned OLMo 2, and assess if current methods can distinguish between seen and unseen splits within the same benchmark. We find that none of the methods can robustly distinguish seen from unseen splits once the setting shifts from corpus-level datasets to split-level benchmark exposure.

Task Setup. We utilize OLMo 2, whose post-training mixture explicitly includes the training split of GSM8K, while their test splits are reserved for evaluation. As controls for entirely unseen benchmark data, we include MMLU and DROP: although OLMo 2 is evaluated on these benchmarks, it was not trained on their training splits. Our objective is to verify if detection mechanisms can correctly flag the train splits of GSM8K and Competition Math as contaminated, while refraining from flagging their test splits or the entirely held-out benchmarks (MMLU and DROP).

Findings. The results in Table 2 reveal clear failure modes for each method. LLM Dataset Inference produces false positives on DROP and MMLU even though OLMo 2 was not trained on their train splits. One possible explanation

Table 2. Detection of training on train and test splits for OLMo 2. Symbols: + = correctly detected as trained on, − = correctly detected as *not* trained on, + = falsely detected as trained on (false positive), − = missed detection (false negative), ? = uncertain signal. Test set of GSM8K was not large enough to run Post-Hoc DI.

	GSM8K		MMLU		DROP		Corr./Tot.
	Train	Test	Train	Test	Train	Test	
OLMo 2 version	1B / 7B / 13B		1B / 7B / 13B		1B / 7B / 13B		
LLM DI	+/ +/ +	−/ −/ −	+/ +/ +	−/ −/ −	+/ +/ +	−/ −/ −	12/18
Post-Hoc DI	−/ −/ +	n/a / n/a / n/a	−/ −/ −	−/ −/ −	−/ −/ −	−/ −/ −	13/18
CoDeC	+/ −/ −	+/ +/ ?	−/ ?/ −	−/ −/ −	+/ −/ −	+/ ?/ −	9/18

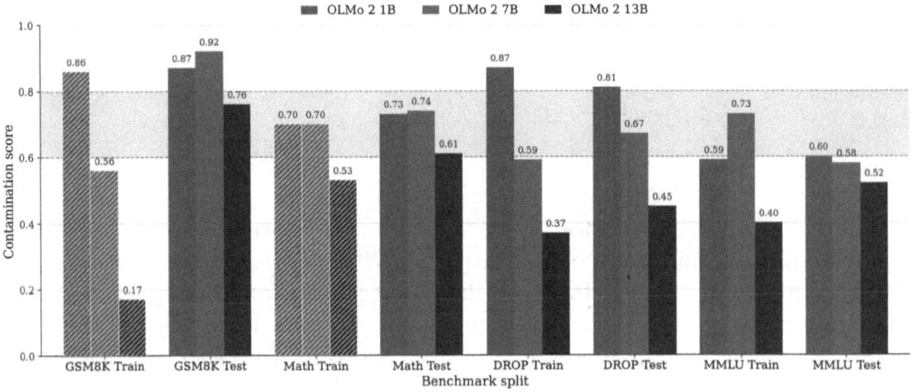

Fig. 2. CoDeC scores for Task 2. CoDeC contamination scores for benchmarks. Hatched bars indicate that this split was used as training split. We can observe trend between model sizes, however training splits do not have higher scores.

is that, although train and test splits of the same benchmark appear to be natural IID proxies, they can still differ in difficulty, style, or construction. In such cases, LLM DI can be driven by split-level distribution differences rather than by training exposure. Post-Hoc Dataset Inference again fails to cleanly separate train and test splits. As in Task 1, synthetic validation data introduces artifacts that dominate the statistical test. CoDeC assigns elevated contamination scores to GSM8K, consistent with its known post-training exposure; however, DROP and MMLU receive only slightly lower scores, so the signal does not provide clear evidence of split-level membership. Instead, the scores decrease with model size, a trend that Fig. 2 reinforces by extending the same pattern to a further member benchmark, Competition Math.

5.3 Task 3: Auditing Specialised Post-Training Datasets

In this task, we examine whether contamination detection transfers from controlled benchmark settings to specialised post-training domains, specifically medical LLMs and mid-resource language models. We find that detection performance is highly inconsistent across these settings and deteriorates substantially when the available benchmark splits are small.

Task Setup. We apply LLM DI and CoDeC, the two methods that remained most effective in earlier experiments and were also the most practical to apply, to two downstream settings. For medical question answering, we evaluate MedGemma [27], Meditron3 [26], Meerkat [18], and Neeto-1.0 [29] on the train and test splits of MedQA-USMLE [16] and MedMCQA [25]. For Polish culture-aware language models, we evaluate the PLLuM-12B and Llama-PLLuM-8B families on train/test (or train/validation) splits from Automatic SFT, Manual SFT, and Alignment datasets. Because some held-out splits are very small, we subsample the larger split to match the smaller one, yielding evaluation sets of approximately 1,600 examples for Automatic SFT and 1,150 for Manual SFT. This setting tests whether contamination signals remain informative on small, domain-specific post-training datasets.

Table 3. Detection of training on train and test splits for medical LLMs. Symbols: + = correctly detected as trained on, − = correctly detected as *not* trained on, + = falsely detected as trained on (false positive), − = missed detection (false negative), ? = uncertain signal.

		MedQA-USMLE		**MedMCQA**		**Corr./Tot.**
		Train	Test	Train	Test	
medgemma 4B / 27B	LLM DI	−/ −	−/ −	−/ +	−/ −	5/8
	CoDeC	−/ −	−/ −	−/ −	−/ −	4/8
Meditron3 8B / 9B	LLM DI	−/ −	−/ −	+/ +	−/ −	6/8
	CoDeC	?/ −	?/ −	−/ −	−/ −	3/8
meerkat 7B / 8B	LLM DI	−/ −	−/ −	+/ −	−/ −	5/8
	CoDeC	?/ ?	?/ ?	−/ −	−/ −	2/8
Neeto-1.0 8B	LLM DI	−	−	−	−	2/4
	CoDeC	−	−	−	−	2/4

Findings. The results in Tables 3 and 4 show that detection performance degrades substantially in downstream settings. For medical QA, LLM DI detects training on the MedMCQA train split for most models, though it misses it for medgemma-4B, meerkat-8B, and Neeto-1.0, and it consistently fails on MedQA-USMLE, missing the train split for every model. Held-out test splits are uniformly identified as non-members. CoDeC is less stable: it correctly identifies some train splits, but its behavior varies across models and does not consistently separate seen from unseen data.

Table 4. Detection of training on SFT and alignment data for PLLuM models. Symbols: + = correctly detected as trained on, − = correctly detected as *not* trained on, + = falsely detected as trained on (false positive), − = missed detection (false negative), ? = uncertain signal. base* = updated base checkpoint (250801).

		Automatic SFT		Manual SFT		Alignment		Corr./Tot.
		Train	Val	Train	Val	Train	Test	
PLLuM-12B base	*base / base* / nc-base*							
	LLM DI	−/−/−	−/−/−	−/−/−	−/−/−	+/+/+	−/−/−	15/18
	CoDeC	+/−/−	+/−/−	?/−/−	?/−/−	−/−/−	−/−/−	14/18
PLLuM-12B SFT	*chat / inst. / nc-chat / nc-inst.*							
	LLM DI	+/−/−/−	−/−/−/−	−/−/−/−	−/−/−/−	+/+/+/+	−/−/−/−	15/24
	CoDeC	+/+/+/?	+/+/?/−	?/?/?/−	?/?/+/?	?/−/+/−	?/−/+/−	9/24
Llama-PLLuM 8B base	*base / base**							
	LLM DI	−/−	−/−	−/−	−/−	+/+	−/−	10/12
	CoDeC	+/−	+/−	?/?	+/−	−/−	−/−	7/12
Llama-PLLuM 8B SFT	*chat / inst.*							
	LLM DI	−/−	−/−	−/−	−/−	+/+	−/−	7/12
	CoDeC	+/+	+/+	+/?	+/+	+/−	+/?	5/12

For PLLuM, both methods are further limited by the small size of the evaluation splits. LLM DI often misses training on Automatic and Manual SFT, yielding repeated false negatives on train splits, while also producing false positives on Alignment. CoDeC shows partial success for the PLLuM-12B family, but performs substantially worse for Llama-PLLuM-8B and again tends to assign elevated scores to both train and held-out splits from the same dataset.

5.4 Task 4: Comparative Auditing of Industry Models

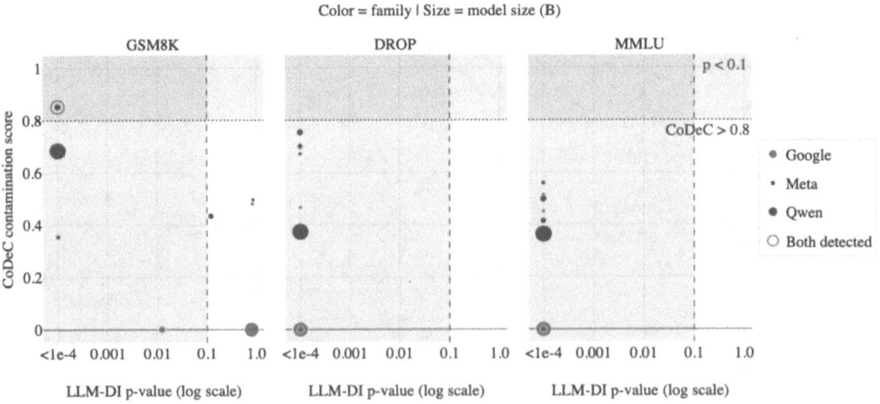

Fig. 3. Application of CoDeC and LLM Dataset Inference to industry models. We try to detect training on train splits of frontier benchmarks.

In this task, we extend the analysis to closed or partially disclosed industry models. We ask whether LLM DI and CoDeC provide consistent signals of prior exposure to benchmark data for frontier evaluations. We find that the signals are suggestive rather than definitive: most model families are flagged on at least some benchmarks, while Google's Gemma-3 family stands out as the only series not flagged by LLM DI on GSM8K and having consistently lower CoDeC scores.

Task Setup. We evaluate LLM Dataset Inference and CoDeC on several industry model families—Google: Gemma 3 (1B, 4B, 12B); Alibaba: Qwen 3 (1.7B, 4B, 14B); Meta: Llama 3.2 (1B, 3B)—using public benchmarks: GSM8K, MMLU, and DROP. Because training data for these models is not fully disclosed, ground-truth membership is unavailable. Our goal is therefore comparative: to assess whether contamination signals differ systematically across model families.

Findings. As shown in Fig. 3, most model families receive elevated CoDeC scores across benchmarks, and LLM DI frequently flags benchmark training. Gemma-3 is the main exception: it consistently shows lower CoDeC scores, and on GSM8K it is the only family not flagged by LLM DI on the train split. Based on this evidence, we infer that the Gemma-3 series was not likely trained on the GSM8K training set.

5.5 Diagnosis of Failure

The methods evaluated in previous tasks do not yield consistent outcomes. As shown in Fig. 1, the number of successful detections is comparable to the number of failures; overall, just over 60% of the outcomes are correct. To understand these results, we examine the assumptions and failure modes of each method.

LLM Dataset Inference. LLM DI critically depends on the availability of a validation set that is both unseen and truly IID with the suspect dataset. This explains the contrast between Tasks 1 and later Tasks: LLM DI works in the controlled setting of Task 1. However, benchmark splits used in the later Tasks may break the IID assumption. These splits may differ in difficulty or construction, leading to the test capturing such differences rather than training exposure.

Post-Hoc Dataset Inference. On benchmark-sized subsets, Post-Hoc DI is dominated by the mismatch between real and synthetic held-out text rather than by memorization signal. As shown in Table 5, the text-only classifier is already highly discriminative, indicating strong separability between real and synthetic suffixes even without MIA features. In a well-calibrated Post-Hoc DI setup, MIA features should provide an additional discriminative signal beyond the text-only baseline. Here, however, adding MIA features yields only marginal improvements. For example, Common Crawl (410M) increases from 0.880 to 0.899, and Europarl (Train) slightly decreases from 0.895 to 0.890. This shows that the classification task is driven primarily by real-versus-synthetic distribution shift, not by training membership signal.

Calibration test p-values in Table 6 are correspondingly inconsistent. For Common Crawl (410M), train yields $p = 0.583$ while validation yields $p = 0.396$, both above the rejection threshold. Europarl produces $p \approx 1.000$ across splits

Table 5. Calibration-stage classifier AUCs, benchmark-scale subsampling. *Base* uses text only; *Comb* adds MIA features. Uniformly high Base AUCs (> 0.78) mean the real-vs-synthetic distribution shift alone is discriminative and MIA features barely help—the regime in which Post-Hoc DI fails. Cf. full-scale Table 7.

	Pythia 410M		Pythia 1.4B		Pythia 2.8B		Pythia 6.9B	
Dataset (Split)	*Base*	*Comb*	*Base*	*Comb*	*Base*	*Comb*	*Base*	*Comb*
CC (Train)	0.880	0.899	0.880	0.901	0.880	0.902	0.880	0.901
CC (Val)	0.882	0.899	0.882	0.900	0.882	0.902	0.882	0.900
Europarl (Train)	0.895	0.890	0.895	0.893	0.895	0.894	0.895	0.895
Europarl (Val)	0.887	0.890	0.887	0.891	0.887	0.893	0.887	0.893
Hacker News (Train)	0.899	0.911	0.899	0.912	0.899	0.915	0.899	0.914
Hacker News (Val)	0.899	0.928	0.899	0.929	0.899	0.929	0.899	0.930
Stack Exchange (Train)	0.788	0.804	0.788	0.803	0.788	0.805	0.788	0.803
Stack Exchange (Val)	0.832	0.844	0.832	0.844	0.832	0.845	0.832	0.844

Table 6. Calibration-test *p*-values, benchmark-scale subsampling (n = 2,000). Symbols: + = correctly trained on ($p < 0.1$), − = correctly *not* trained on, + = false positive, − = false negative. The test fails to reject the null for nearly every train split (12/32 correct), the failure mode caused by the distribution shift in Table 5. Cf. full-scale Table 8.

	Pythia 410M		Pythia 1.4B		Pythia 2.8B		Pythia 6.9B		Corr./Tot.
Dataset	Train	Val	Train	Val	Train	Val	Train	Val	
Pile CC	0.583 −	0.396 −	0.444 −	0.281 −	0.402 −	0.258 −	0.385 −	0.236 −	4/8
Europarl	1.000 −	1.000 −	1.000 −	0.999 −	1.000 −	0.999 −	1.000 −	0.999 −	4/8
Hacker News	0.450 −	0.049 +	0.441 −	0.007 +	0.315 −	0.006 +	0.388 −	0.009 +	0/8
Stack Exch.	0.709 −	0.821 −	0.707 −	0.811 −	0.700 −	0.755 −	0.747 −	0.788 −	4/8

and model sizes. Hacker News (Val) produces extremely small values such as $p = 0.007$ for 1.4B despite being a non-member split.

To test it is this failure intrinsic to Post-Hoc DI, or just a symptom of limited data at benchmark scale, we re-run the calibration stage on the authors' released held-out sets, whose generator is trained on nearly the full Pile subsets. Text-only AUCs collapse to around 55% (Table 7, e.g. Common Crawl Base: 0.548), so the distribution shift that dominated the benchmark-scale setting (Table 5) largely vanishes. With the artifact gone, the calibration test recovers, rising from 12/32 to 23/32 correct *p*-values (Table 8 vs. Table 6). Post-Hoc DI is underpowered at benchmark scale, working only with enough data to train a well-matched synthetic generator.

CoDeC. CoDeC exhibits a different limitation than the DI-based methods: it preserves broad provenance differences, but lacks the resolution needed for split-level

Table 7. Calibration-stage classifier AUCs, full-scale held-out generation (authors' released sets, generator trained on nearly the full subset). *Base* uses text only; *Comb* adds MIA features. Base AUCs fall to around 55% (e.g. Common Crawl Base: 0.548): real and synthetic suffixes become nearly indistinguishable and the distribution-shift artifact of Table 5 largely vanishes.

	Pythia 410M		Pythia 1.4B		Pythia 2.8B		Pythia 6.9B	
Dataset (Split)	*Base*	*Comb*	*Base*	*Comb*	*Base*	*Comb*	*Base*	*Comb*
CC (Train)	0.548	0.557	0.548	0.556	0.548	0.564	0.548	0.567
CC (Val)	0.506	0.513	0.506	0.515	0.506	0.517	0.506	0.523
Europarl (Train)	0.509	0.532	0.509	0.555	0.509	0.567	0.509	0.575
Europarl (Val)	0.514	0.516	0.514	0.523	0.514	0.526	0.514	0.533
Hacker News (Train)	0.525	0.567	0.525	0.578	0.525	0.585	0.525	0.591
Hacker News (Val)	0.570	0.569	0.570	0.571	0.570	0.578	0.570	0.577
Stack Exchange (Train)	0.540	0.554	0.540	0.562	0.540	0.567	0.540	0.574
Stack Exchange (Val)	0.518	0.523	0.518	0.533	0.518	0.534	0.518	0.538

Table 8. Calibration-test p-values (Diff), full-scale held-out generation (same subsets as Table 7). Symbols as in Table 6. With the distribution-shift artifact removed, the test aligns far better with ground truth than at benchmark scale (Table 6): 23/32 vs. 12/32 correct, with Hacker News and Europarl train splits now flagged on larger models, though Common Crawl and Stack Exchange remain undetected.

	Pythia 410M				Pythia 1.4B				Pythia 2.8B				Pythia 6.9B				Corr./Tot.
Dataset	Train		Val		Train		Val		Train		Val		Train		Val		
Pile CC	0.775	−	0.728	−	0.829	−	0.647	−	0.580	−	0.717	−	0.582	−	0.547	−	4/8
Europarl	0.184	−	0.882	−	0.000	+	0.675	−	0.000	+	0.696	−	0.000	+	0.350	−	7/8
Hacker News	0.002	+	0.744	−	0.007	+	0.958	−	0.000	+	0.774	−	0.002	+	0.876	−	8/8
Stack Exch.	0.598	−	0.830	−	0.254	−	0.435	−	0.216	−	0.377	−	0.116	−	0.247	−	4/8

auditing. In Fig. 4, contamination scores for known pre-training corpora are substantially higher than for evaluation-only benchmarks, reproducing prior findings. However, train and test splits within the same dataset yield only marginal differences, indicating difficulty distinguishing near-IID conditions.

In instruction-tuned models (Fig. 5), aggregation by dataset provenance reveals a coarse ordering: pre-training sources receive the highest scores, post-training datasets are intermediate, and evaluation-only benchmarks are lowest. At the level of individual datasets and model sizes, however, the scores remain variable and overlapping. CoDeC is therefore best interpreted as a coarse contamination indicator rather than a precise split-level detector. Used comparatively—many models on one dataset, flagging outliers—it still offers a useful relative signal of likely contamination.

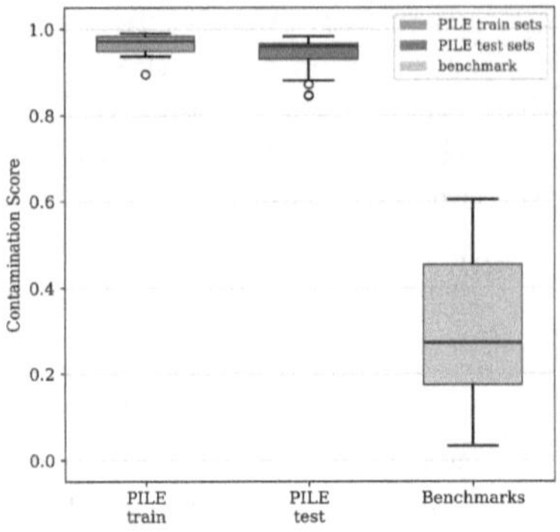

Fig. 4. CoDeC contamination scores on Pythia. Evaluation-only benchmarks score lower than pre-training corpora (reproducing prior work), but train and test splits of the same corpus score nearly identically.

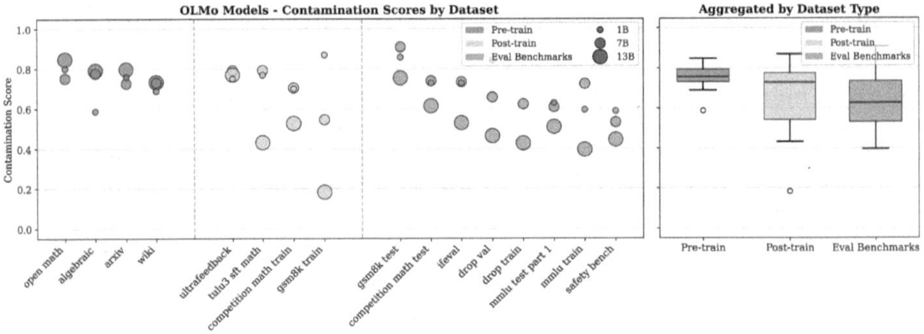

Fig. 5. CoDeC scores for OLMo 2 (instruction-tuned) grouped by data provenance. Pre-training sources receive the highest contamination scores, post-training datasets used during instruction tuning are intermediate, and evaluation-only benchmarks score lowest. This coarse ordering is consistent with known data membership, but the overlap between adjacent groups limits the method's utility for certifying individual benchmark integrity.

6 Limitation and Future Work

Our study has several limitations that also point to future work. Our results come from configurations run under a shared interface with default hyperparameters rather than exhaustive per-task tuning, which might otherwise improve the effectiveness of the evaluated methods. Our open-weight audit reaches 27B parameters and centres on math, QA, and knowledge benchmarks in English, with additional Polish (PLLuM) and medical models; larger open models, other languages and modalities, and free-form generation benchmarks are not covered, and behaviour may differ at frontier scale. For closed industry models we lack verified membership, so that evidence is comparative across model families rather than definitive. Finally, we characterise *when* and *why* current methods fail in the wild, but do not propose a new detector that overcomes these failures. Quantifying how much distribution shift or how little data each method can tolerate, and designing auditing tools robust to both, remains open.

7 Conclusions

In this work, we examined the reliability of contamination detection methods by moving from the controlled settings of prior literature to the realistic, "in-the-wild" regime of modern instruction-tuned models. We stress-tested three leading detection paradigms against the complexities of post-training mixtures and opaque data provenance. Our findings reveal that the transition from academic validation to practical auditing is fraught with challenges:

- **The I.I.D. assumption is a critical vulnerability.** We found that *LLM Dataset Inference* [23] is highly sensitive to distribution shifts. While effective when a perfect I.I.D. validation set exists, it yields significant false positives when using standard benchmark test splits as validation proxies (as seen with DROP and MMLU). This makes it dangerous to use as a sole arbiter for leaderboard integrity without verifying distributional alignment.
- **Benchmark-scale datasets are too small for generative methods.** While *Post-Hoc Dataset Inference* [31] theoretically removes the need for natural validation data, we showed it is impractical for standard benchmarks. Unlike massive pre-training corpora, benchmarks like GSM8K lack the text volume required to effectively train the required generators.
- **Detection granularity is limited.** *CoDeC* [30] provides a valuable coarse-grained signal—effectively separating pre-training sources from held-out tasks in aggregate. However, its high variance at the individual dataset train level (Fig. 5) limits its utility for certifying specific benchmark results.

We conclude that there is currently no "silver bullet" for detecting contamination in the wild. Consequently, statistical auditing cannot yet fully replace **transparent data provenance**.

Acknowledgments. This research was supported by the Polish National Science Centre (NCN) within grants no. 2025/57/N/ST6/04025. We gratefully acknowledge Polish high-performance computing infrastructure PLGrid, HPC Center: ACK Cyfronet AGH, for providing computer facilities and support within computational grant no. PLG/2024/017781 and PLG/2025/018634.

Disclosure of Interests. The authors have no competing interests to declare that are relevant to the content of this article.

References

1. Alonso, I., Oronoz, M., Agerri, R.: Medexpqa: multilingual benchmarking of large language models for medical question answering. ArXiv abs/2404.05590 (2024)
2. Balloccu, S., Schmidtová, P., Lango, M., Dušek, O.: Leak, cheat, repeat: data contamination and evaluation malpractices in closed-source LLMs. ArXiv abs/2402.03927 (2024)
3. Biderman, S., Schoelkopf, H., Anthony, Q., Bradley, H., O'Brien, K., et al.: Pythia: a suite for analyzing large language models across training and scaling. ArXiv abs/2304.01373 (2023)
4. Brown, T.B., Mann, B., Ryder, N., Subbiah, M., Kaplan, J.: Language models are few-shot learners. ArXiv abs/2005.14165 (2020)
5. Cobbe, K., Kosaraju, V., Bavarian, M., Chen, M., Jun, H.: Training verifiers to solve math word problems. ArXiv abs/2110.14168 (2021)
6. Cui, G., Yuan, L., Ding, N., Yao, G., Zhu, W.: Ultrafeedback: boosting language models with high-quality feedback. ArXiv abs/2310.01377 (2023)
7. Dekoninck, J., Müller, M.N., Vechev, M.: Constat: performance-based contamination detection in large language models. ArXiv abs/2405.16281 (2024)
8. Deng, C., Zhao, Y., Tang, X.: Investigating data contamination in modern benchmarks for large language models. ArXiv abs/2311.09783 (2024)
9. Dua, D., Wang, Y., Dasigi, P., Stanovsky, G., Singh, S.: DROP: a reading comprehension benchmark requiring discrete reasoning over paragraphs. ArXiv abs/1903.00161 (2019)
10. Dubiński, J., Kowalczuk, A., Boenisch, F., Dziedzic, A.: CDI: copyrighted data identification in diffusion models. In: Proceedings of the Computer Vision and Pattern Recognition Conference, pp. 18674–18684 (2025)
11. Dubiński, J., Kowalczuk, A., Pawlak, S., Rokita, P., Trzciński, T., Morawiecki, P.: Towards more realistic membership inference attacks on large diffusion models. In: Proceedings of the IEEE/CVF Winter Conference on Applications of Computer Vision, pp. 4860–4869 (2024)
12. Gao, L., Biderman, S., Black, S., Golding, L., Hoppe, T.: The pile: an 800gb dataset of diverse text for language modeling. ArXiv abs/2101.00027 (2020)
13. Golchin, S., Surdeanu, M.: Time travel in LLMs: tracing data contamination in large language models. ArXiv abs/2308.08493 (2024)
14. Hendrycks, D., Burns, C., Basart, S., Zou, A., Mazeika, M., et al.: Measuring massive multitask language understanding. ArXiv abs/2009.03300 (2021)
15. Hendrycks, D., Burns, C., Kadavath, S., Arora, A.: Measuring mathematical problem solving with the MATH dataset. ArXiv. abs/2103.03874 (2021)
16. Jin, D., Pan, E., Oufattole, N., Weng, W.H., Fang, H., et al.: What disease does this patient have? a large-scale open domain question answering dataset from medical exams. ArXiv abs/2009.13081 (2020)
17. Jin, Q., Dhingra, B., Liu, Z., Cohen, W., Lu, X.: PubMedQA: a dataset for biomedical research question answering. In: Proceedings of the 2019 Conference on Empirical Methods in Natural Language Processing and the 9th International Joint Conference on Natural Language Processing (EMNLP-IJCNLP) (2019)
18. Kim, H., Hwang, H., Lee, J., Park, S., Kim, D., et al.: Small language models learn enhanced reasoning skills from medical textbooks. ArXiv abs/2404.00376 (2024)
19. Kocoń, J., Piasecki, M., Janz, A., Ferdinan, T., Łukasz, R.: Pllum: a family of polish large language models. ArXiv abs/2511.03823 (2025)

20. Kowalczuk, A., Dubiński, J., Boenisch, F., Dziedzic, A.: Privacy attacks on image autoregressive models. arXiv preprint arXiv:2502.02514 (2025)
21. Lambert, N., Morrison, J.D., Pyatkin, V., Huang, S.: Tülu 3: pushing frontiers in open language model post-training. ArXiv abs/2411.15124 (2024)
22. Lee, K., Ippolito, D., Nystrom, A., Zhang, C., Eck, D.: Deduplicating training data makes language models better. ArXiv abs/2107.06499 (2022)
23. Maini, P., Jia, H., Papernot, N., Dziedzic, A.: LLM dataset inference: did you train on my dataset? ArXiv abs/2406.06443 (2024)
24. OLMo, T., Walsh, P., Soldaini, L., Groeneveld, D., Lo, K., et al.: Olmo 2: Furious. ArXiv abs/2501.00656 (2025)
25. Pal, A., Umapathi, L.K., Sankarasubbu, M.: Medmcqa: a large-scale multi-subject multi-choice dataset for medical domain question answering. ArXiv abs/2203.14371 (2022)
26. Sallinen, A., Solergibert, A.J., Zhang, M., Boyé, G.B.: Llama-3-meditron: an open-weight suite of medical LLMs based on llama-3.1. In: Workshop on Large Language Models and Generative AI for Health at AAAI 2025 (2025)
27. Sellergren, A., Kazemzadeh, S., Jaroensri, T., Kiraly, A., Traverse, M.: Medgemma technical report. ArXiv abs/2507.05201 (2025)
28. Shokri, R., Stronati, M., Song, C., Shmatikov, V.: Membership inference attacks against machine learning models. ArXiv abs/1610.05820 (2017). https://doi.org/10.1109/SP.2017.41
29. Verma, S.: Neeto: a specialized medical LLM for neet-pg/ukmle/usmle preparation (2025). https://huggingface.co/S4nfs/Neeto-1.0-8b
30. Zawalski, M., Boubdir, M., Bałazy, K., Nushi, B., Ribalta, P.: Detecting data contamination in LLMs via in-context learning. ArXiv abs/2510.27055 (2025)
31. Zhao, B., Maini, P., Boenisch, F., Dziedzic, A.: Unlocking post-hoc dataset inference with synthetic data. ArXiv abs/2506.15271 (2025)

Toward Green Clustering AutoML: A Benchmark of Performance–Energy Trade-offs and Meta-learning Insights

Erick Fiestas and Radwa ElShawi(✉)

Institute of Computer Science, University of Tartu, Tartu, Estonia
{erick.fiestas,radwa.elshawi}@ut.ee

Abstract. Automated Machine Learning for clustering has progressed rapidly, yet its performance–energy trade-offs remain underexplored. We present the first benchmark that jointly evaluates clustering quality, stage-wise energy consumption, and scalability in clustering-focused AutoML systems across 119 datasets, covering AutoML4Clust, AutoCluster, cSmartML, and ML2DAC. Energy usage is measured using software-based profiling for all frameworks, with hardware-level power metering used to validate estimates and assess system-level behavior. Our results reveal substantial variation not only in overall energy efficiency but also across initialization, search, and ensemble stages, highlighting distinct sources of energy overhead within each AutoML system. ML2DAC and AutoML4Clust achieve the most favorable quality–energy trade-offs, while AutoCluster and cSmartML show consistently higher consumption and unstable time-budget adherence. We further analyze how dataset characteristics and cluster geometry influence performance and energy outcomes. To support energy-aware deployment, we estimate large-scale CO_2 emissions and monetary cost, and introduce a meta-learning model that predicts energy usage and clustering quality to recommend efficient configurations. Overall, the benchmark offers actionable insights for greener AutoML workflows.

1 Introduction

Clustering enables the discovery of latent data structures with minimal manual intervention, while automated machine learning (AutoML) broadens access by automating model configuration and selection [18]. A key drawback of such systems is their computationally intensive search and resulting energy consumption. To address these concerns, Tornede et al. introduced *Green AutoML* as a paradigm for improving the sustainability of AutoML [21]. Motivated by this, we investigate how energy is consumed across clustering AutoML systems and identify design choices that influence efficiency. Tornede et al. [16] distinguish three stages of the AutoML process where energy is consumed—development, execution, and inference—which we follow for clustering: *development* (system-level configuration, including search-space and design decisions and the preparation of possible meta-knowledge used by the framework), *execution* (search

M. Ceci et al. (Eds.): ECML PKDD 2026, LNAI 16948, pp. 418–434, 2027.
https://doi.org/10.1007/978-3-032-37679-4_24

initialization—comprising warm-starting when supported—; search, that evaluates clustering configurations through repeated algorithm runs; and a possible consensus/ensemble construction stage), and *cluster assignment* (grouping data points into clusters utilizing the best algorithm configuration) [21]. Execution is typically the most demanding in clustering due to large search spaces, repeated clustering runs with cluster validity indices (CVIs), and warm-start/meta-learning overheads; consensus or ensemble methods further increase cluster assignment cost through additional aggregation and validation [5,8,15]. Several clustering-specific AutoML frameworks—AutoML4Clust [24], AutoCluster [15], cSmartML [5], and ML2DAC [23]—report quality gains, yet their performance–energy behavior, scalability, and sensitivity to data and design choices remain insufficiently characterized. To address this gap, we present a performance- and energy-aware benchmark that standardises evaluation and provides insights for greener clustering AutoML. Our contributions are as follows:

- A unified benchmark evaluating AutoML4Clust, AutoCluster, cSmartML, and ML2DAC on 119 datasets, reporting clustering quality Adjusted Rand Index and energy consumption during execution and cluster assignment.
- Energy measurement using software-based profiling for all frameworks, with selective hardware validation on representative systems to assess measurement accuracy and cross-platform behaviour.
- Analysis of stage-wise energy usage (initialization, search, ensemble) and overall performance–energy behavior across dataset characteristics, cluster geometry, scalability, and time-budget adherence.
- Estimation of large-scale energy usage, CO_2 emissions, and monetary cost, alongside a meta-learning model predicting energy and ARI for Pareto-efficient configuration recommendations.
- To support reproducibility, we provide a code repository containing all benchmarking scripts and experimental pipelines.[1]

2 Related Work

AutoML has primarily focused on supervised learning tasks such as classification and regression, where the Combined Algorithm Selection and Hyperparameter Optimization (CASH) problem [12] has served as a foundational formulation. Systems like Auto-sklearn [9] and TPOT [17] have demonstrated strong performance by automating model selection and tuning across diverse datasets and domains, benefiting from extensive research on search strategies, meta-learning, and pipeline optimization. In contrast, unsupervised learning—especially clustering—has received comparatively less attention in the AutoML community, despite its central role in exploratory data analysis and scientific discovery [18]. Recent efforts have begun to address this gap by developing clustering-specific AutoML frameworks [1,5,24]. However, these systems

[1] https://github.com/DataSystemsGroupUT/GreenAutoML-Evaluating-Energy-Efficiency-of-Automated-Clustering-Frameworks.

are primarily focused on improving clustering quality, leaving their computational and environmental costs underexplored. As the demand for sustainable AI grows [22,27], it becomes critical to evaluate AutoML frameworks not only in terms of performance but also in terms of energy efficiency—particularly in unsupervised settings where search spaces are large and validation is inherently more complex.

Table 1. Design decisions and architectural choices of clustering AutoML frameworks. BO: Bayesian Optimization, RS: Random Search, HB: Hyper-Band, BOHB: BO with HB, EA: Evolutionary Algorithm.

Framework	Search Space	Init. strategy	Search	Ensemble
AutoCluster	10 algorithms	Warmstarting	BO	Majority voting
AutoML4Clust	4 algo.	Random	RS, BO/HB/BOHB	-
cSmartML	8 algo.	Warmstarting	EA	-
ML2DAC	10 algo.	Warmstarting	BO	-

Benchmarking efforts in supervised AutoML are relatively well-established. AMLB [10] provides a large-scale, reproducible benchmark that evaluates nine AutoML frameworks across 71 classification and 33 regression tasks, analyzing performance, inference time, and failure rates. Zöller and Huber [28] complement this with a combined survey and empirical evaluation of six frameworks on 73 classification datasets, offering a detailed taxonomy of AutoML methods and their applicability across domains. Additionally, AutoMLBench [4] presents a comprehensive experimental evaluation of supervised AutoML frameworks, comparing their predictive performance, robustness, and runtime behavior in diverse datasets. However, these efforts remain largely confined to supervised learning. In contrast, benchmarking efforts in clustering-focused AutoML remain relatively limited. The study by Silva et al. [19] provides a comparative evaluation of clustering AutoML frameworks against multiple datasets, focusing on clustering quality and robustness. However, the benchmark primarily emphasizes cluster validity metrics and does not systematically evaluate the computational or environmental costs associated with AutoML execution. Our work complements and extends this line of research by introducing the first energy-aware benchmark for clustering AutoML frameworks. By incorporating both software-based and hardware-based energy profiling, we offer a holistic evaluation of clustering performance and sustainability, addressing a critical gap in the current AutoML literature.

3 Energy Efficiency Implications of AutoML Design Decisions

Table 1 outlines how various clustering AutoML frameworks implement key steps in the AutoML process. In the following, we discuss the impact of different design choices on energy consumption.

Search Space significantly impacts computational overhead and energy consumption. Frameworks with a broader search space, such as AutoCluster and ML2DAC (both supporting 9 algorithms), offer greater flexibility but require more extensive evaluations, increasing energy demands. Their inclusion of density-based and affinity propagation models further adds to computational complexity due to iterative distance calculations and neighborhood-based operations. cSmartML, with 8 supported algorithms, prioritizes hierarchical models while incorporating some density-based and graph-theoretic methods, leading to additional computational load. In contrast, AutoML4Clust, with the smallest search space (4 algorithms), focuses on partitioning-based clustering and Gaussian Mixture Models, reducing computational overhead. While broader search spaces improve adaptability, they also raise energy consumption, particularly when complex clustering techniques are involved.

Initialization Strategy plays a crucial role in energy efficiency by determining how clustering algorithms are selected at the beginning of the search process. Random initialization, as used in AutoML4Clust, explores the search space without prior knowledge, potentially leading to inefficient early evaluations and unnecessary computations. In contrast, AutoCluster, ML2DAC, and cSmartML employ warm-starting strategies through meta-learning, leveraging prior knowledge to make informed initial selections, thus improving efficiency. Although warm-starting requires additional computational effort during the development phase to build and maintain meta-knowledge, it ultimately minimizes energy consumption during execution by avoiding ineffective clustering configurations.

Search Strategy explores the space of clustering configurations, including algorithm selection and hyperparameter tuning. Most frameworks adopt Bayesian Optimization (BO) [8] (e.g., AutoCluster, ML2DAC) or evolutionary algorithms (EA) (e.g., cSmartML) to efficiently explore this space. Others, such as AutoML4Clust, support random search (RS), BO, and BOHB/Hyperband (HB) [7,14]. A known challenge in AutoML for clustering is the risk of overfitting to internal clustering validation metrics [26], particularly when large and flexible search spaces are employed. One strategy to mitigate this issue is to reduce the size of the parameter space, as demonstrated by AutoML4Clust, which limits the number of candidate algorithms and hyperparameters.

Ensembling typically improves clustering robustness and reduces bias—but at the cost of increased computational overhead. AutoCluster employs a Multi-CVI Clustering Ensemble Construction strategy, where multiple clustering results are evaluated using different CVI's and combined into a consensus solution, enhancing generalization while mitigating individual model bias. In contrast, ML2DAC, cSmartML, and AutoML4Clust target single-model optimization.

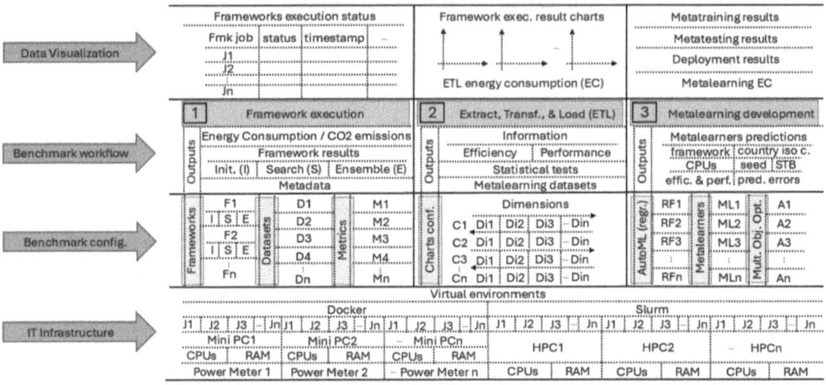

Fig. 1. Benchmarking design overview.

4 Benchmarking Design

Reference Frameworks: cSmartML uses meta-learning by extracting dataset meta-features, retrieving relevant past configurations from a meta-base, and tuning the recommended clustering algorithm via multi-objective optimization and an Evolutionary Algorithm [5]. **AutoML4Clust** explores a hierarchical space of clustering algorithms and hyperparameters using RS, BO, HB, and BOHB, optimizing the number of clusters according to a chosen internal validity measure [25]. **AutoCluster** leverages meta-learning with rich meta-features and constructs a multi-CVI ensemble for improved robustness [15]. **ML2DAC** uses an offline meta-knowledge repository to warm-start configurations, select suitable CVIs via a trained model, and refine solutions through Bayesian optimization [23]. Table 1 summarizes the design decisions of each framework.

Benchmarking Pipeline: The *execution phase* runs each framework under fixed computational budgets while recording performance and energy. As shown in Fig. 1, the pipeline consists of three stages: (i) *Initialization*, which loads the search space and applies warm-starting when supported; (ii) *Search*, which evaluates and optimizes clustering configurations; and (iii) *Ensemble*, where frameworks that support consensus construct ensemble solutions and all frameworks produce final cluster assignments. Following [16], each framework assigns clusters to 66% of the dataset during search and to the remaining 34% during the final assignment stage. The *ETL phase* aggregates raw logs, normalizes outputs, and computes stage-wise energy, CO_2 estimates, and Adjusted Rand Index

(ARI). In the *meta-learning phase*, FLAML-based regressors predict search-phase energy and cluster-assignment ARI across heterogeneous conditions (time budgets, seeds, CPU allocations, execution regions). Configuration recommendations are obtained by constructing a Pareto front via NSGA-II to balance energy efficiency and clustering quality. The benchmark is extensible, can support multiple frameworks, metrics, and visualization views, and currently includes 100 synthetic and 19 real-world datasets.

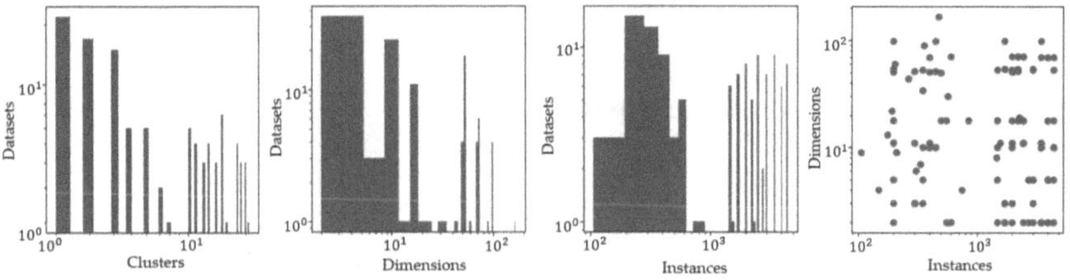

Fig. 2. Properties of 119 datasets considered for the benchmarking suite.

Infrastructure and Visualization: Experiments are executed in Docker containers on a miniPC or via SLURM on an HPC node to ensure consistent, controlled evaluation across heterogeneous hardware (Fig. 1). The miniPC (Lenovo M710q, 4-CPUs, 8GB, Intel i3-6100T, Debian 12) is connected to a Shelly Plug S power meter for hardware-level energy measurement, while the HPC system (dual AMD EPYC 7763, 128 CPUs, 16GB, RedHat 9.4) supports large-scale parallel execution. Visualization components summarize the outputs of each pipeline stage, including energy traces, ARI distributions, Pareto fronts, and total energy/CO_2/cost estimates, enabling interpretable comparisons across frameworks and environments.

Datasets: The benchmark comprises 119 datasets: 100 synthetic datasets generated from controlled clustering archetypes (varying dimensionality, number of clusters, sample size, imbalance, aspect ratios, and cluster geometry) and 19 real-world datasets from UCI with ground-truth labels. Figure 2 shows basic properties of the 119 clustering datasets, including the distributions of the number of clusters, dimensionality, and sample size, as well as the relationship between instances and dimensions for both synthetic and real-world data. Full generation details and per-dataset metadata are provided in the supplementary material and artifact repository.

Energy Measurement. Energy consumption is used as a platform-independent proxy for environmental impact, since CO_2 emissions depend on region-specific electricity mixes [21]. We record energy usage through both

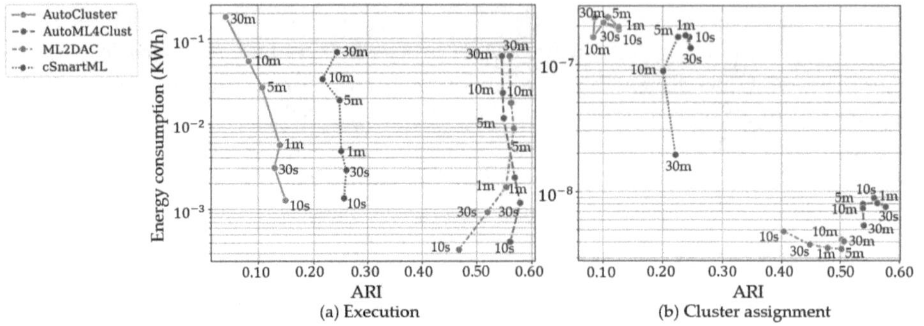

Fig. 3. Impact of search time and ARI on energy consumption during execution and cluster assignment.

software-based estimation (CodeCarbon, using Intel RAPL counters for CPU and DRAM [13]) and hardware-level measurement via Shelly Plug S power meters, which capture whole-system consumption at 1 Hz with 0.1 W resolution. Hardware meters provide system-level ground truth including components not monitored by RAPL (e.g., storage and I/O), ensuring accurate and reproducible end-to-end energy accounting.

5 Results

5.1 Single-Core Execution and Clustered Instances Energy Consumption

To evaluate the energy efficiency of AutoML systems, we follow standard benchmarking practices by setting fixed search time limits (10 s, 30 s, 1 min, 5 min, 10 min, and 30 min) as proxies for expected model performance [11]. In certain cases, the actual search duration differs from the allocated time budget, as shown in Table 3. The full setup required 7 days of computation to run 5 times each experiment. We measure energy consumption during both the AutoML execution (Fig. 3a) and cluster assignment (Fig. 3b) phases, and analyze its relationship to clustering performance using ARI. Energy usage (in kWh) is recorded during framework execution, and for cluster assignment, we report per-instance energy consumption. Each line represents a framework, with individual points corresponding to search times (10 s, 30 s, 1 min, 5 min, 10 min, and 30 min). These points jointly illustrate the trade-offs between runtime, ARI, and energy consumption across stages.

In execution (Fig. 3a), AutoCluster exhibits the highest energy consumption and the lowest ARI across all time budgets. cSmartML also shows consistently elevated energy use and low ARI. At smaller budgets, AutoML4Clust achieves strong ARI but is later surpassed by ML2DAC at larger budgets while consistently consuming less energy across all search times. Overall, ML2DAC provides the best balance, reaching the highest ARI while keeping energy consumption

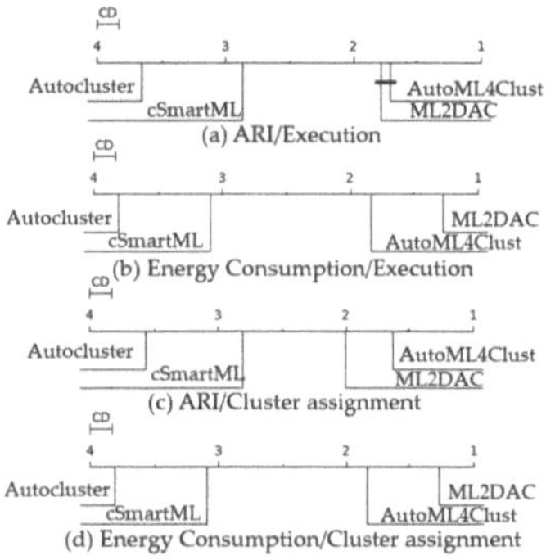

Fig. 4. CD plot for ARI and energy consumption during AutoML framework execution and cluster assignment.

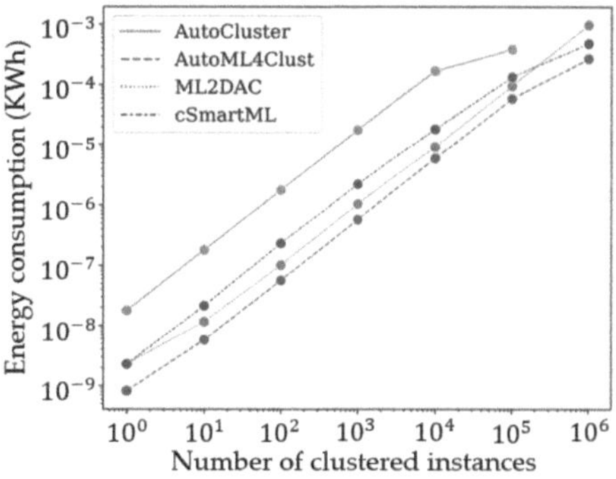

Fig. 5. Comparing AutoML systems with respect to energy consumption for different scales of clustered instances.

low, whereas AutoCluster and cSmartML remain clearly inferior in both accuracy and efficiency. For cluster assignment (Fig. 3b), AutoCluster again shows the highest energy consumption and the lowest ARI. AutoML4Clust consistently achieves the highest ARI with moderate energy usage, while ML2DAC offers competitive ARI with minimal energy cost. cSmartML maintains low ARI with consistently high energy consumption—second only to AutoCluster.

Figure 4 shows the Critical Distance (CD) diagrams [2] for ARI and energy consumption. We applied the Friedman test ($p < 0.05$) with Nemenyi post-hoc comparisons. For ARI in execution (Fig. 4a), AutoML4Clust and ML2DAC form the top group with no significant differences between them and both significantly better than AutoCluster and cSmartML. For execution energy (Fig. 4b), ML2DAC is the most efficient, followed by AutoML4Clust, with AutoCluster and cSmartML consuming substantially more; all pairwise differences are significant. For ARI in assignment (Fig. 4c), AutoML4Clust ranks highest, followed by ML2DAC, cSmartML, and AutoCluster, with all pairwise differences significant. For assignment energy (Fig. 4d), ML2DAC is the most efficient, then AutoML4Clust, cSmartML, and AutoCluster, again with all pairwise differences significant. Overall, AutoML4Clust and ML2DAC offer the best accuracy–energy trade-off, particularly in execution, whereas AutoCluster and cSmartML are consistently inferior in both metrics.

Figure 5 presents the total energy consumption of various frameworks as the number of clustered instances increases, accounting for cluster assignment, averaged over all time budgets. This combined analysis is essential, as Fig. 3 revealed variations in energy consumption between AutoML frameworks when execution and cluster assignment were examined separately. On average, AutoML4Clust achieves the lowest energy consumption, with ML2DAC and cSmartML following at comparable levels. In contrast, AutoCluster exhibits markedly higher energy consumption. These findings indicate that AutoML4Clust is better suited for large-scale energy-efficient clustering, whereas AutoCluster exhibits limited scalability due to its elevated energy consumption.

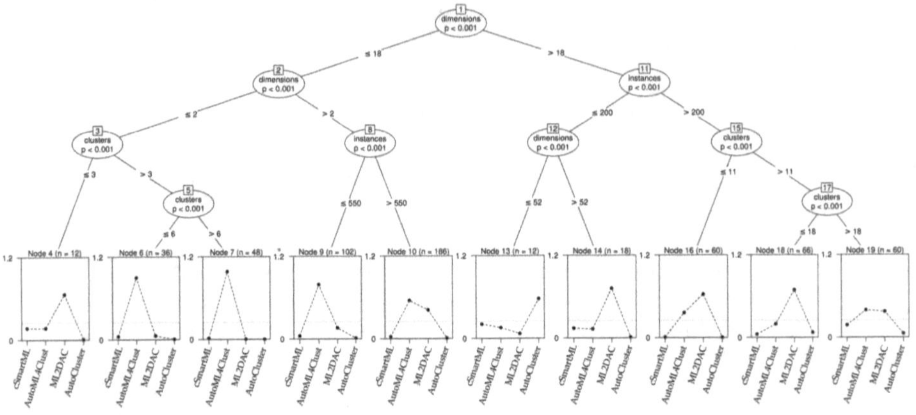

Fig. 6. Bradley-Terry tree of depth 5 for paired comparisons between the AutoML frameworks' cluster assignment results. The n value denotes the number of observations in the leaf node.

Fig. 7. Energy consumption versus clustering performance (ARI) of AutoML frameworks across varying cluster shapes.

5.2 Impact of Data Complexity on Performance and Energy Efficiency

To analyze how dataset characteristics influence the relative performance and energy efficiency of AutoML clustering frameworks, we employ Bradley–Terry (BT) trees [2]. BT trees extend the Bradley–Terry paired comparison model through model-based recursive partitioning [20], enabling hierarchical decomposition of framework rankings conditioned on dataset properties such as dimensionality, number of clusters, and sample size. The algorithm operates as follows: at each node, a BT model is fitted to paired comparisons of frameworks across datasets. A statistical test of parameter instability determines whether any dataset characteristic significantly affects the model parameters. If instability is detected, the tree splits on the characteristic with the strongest effect (lowest p-value), and the process recurses until no significant instability remains or stopping criteria are met. Each leaf node thus represents a subset of datasets with similar complexity, and the associated probabilities indicate the likelihood of each framework being preferred under those conditions. The BT trees were constructed using the mean aggregation of results across all six search time budgets (10 s, 30 s, 1min, 5min, 10min, and 30min), providing a comprehensive view of framework behavior under varying computational constraints.

Clustering Performance (ARI). Figure 6 shows the BT tree for ARI (depth 5). In low-dimensional tasks ($\leq$ 18), rankings are governed mainly by cluster multiplicity: very small k favors `ML2DAC`, while richer cluster structure shifts preference toward `AutoML4Clust`. Specifically within this regime, when dimensionality is low ($\leq$ 18) *and* exceeds two features, `AutoML4Clust` is generally the top-ranked framework. For high-dimensional datasets (> 18 features), the combination of sample size and cluster count becomes decisive. Smaller high-dimensional ($\leq$ 52 features) tasks retain competitiveness for `AutoCluster` unless dimensionality becomes very high, in which case `ML2DAC` takes the lead. In larger high-dimensional datasets, a moderate number of clusters still favors `ML2DAC`, but very large k consistently benefits `AutoML4Clust`.

5.3 Impact of Cluster Shapes on Performance and Energy Efficiency

Figure 7 analyzes how different cluster shapes (well-separated, overlapping, center-based, and density-based) influence the trade-off between clustering performance (ARI) and energy consumption for both the AutoML execution phase (Fig. 7a) and the cluster assignment phase (Fig. 7b).

Execution Phase. Across cluster shapes, `ML2DAC` and `AutoML4Clust` exhibit the lowest energy consumption, whereas `cSmartML` is consistently highest (most pronounced for centre-based and overlapping shapes), with `AutoCluster` typically intermediate. Regarding clustering quality (ARI), `AutoML4Clust` achieves the best scores on well-separated and centre-based data, while `ML2DAC` attains the highest ARI on density-based and overlapping data; `AutoCluster` and `cSmartML` generally underperform.

Cluster Assignment Phase. Energy consumption is lowest for `ML2DAC`, followed closely by `AutoML4Clust`; `cSmartML` remains intermediate, and `AutoCluster` is the most energy-demanding across shapes. In terms of ARI, `AutoML4Clust` remains superior on well-separated, density-based and centre-based clusters, whereas `ML2DAC` yields the highest ARI on overlapping data; `AutoCluster` exhibits the lowest clustering quality.

5.4 Impact of Parallelism on cSmartML

Among the evaluated frameworks, only `cSmartML` supports parallel execution. As shown in Fig. 8, the ARI–energy relationships show that short search budgets yield the most favourable trade-offs: the highest overall ARI is attained with 1 core at 30 s, though at slightly higher energy than multi-core runs at the same budget. Increasing the budget beyond 30 s does not systematically improve accuracy; instead, ARI generally declines for most core counts, with the 4-core setting exhibiting the sharpest degradation at 1–5 min. The 8-core configuration shows a distinct exception: while its ARI typically decreases with the budget, it achieves the best ARI among all cores at the 1 min budget. Energy consumption increases monotonically with the budget for all configurations and is lowest at 10 s across cores. Overall, these trends indicate that parallelism in `cSmartML` primarily enhances energy efficiency at short budgets; longer runs increase energy expenditure without delivering consistent accuracy gains.

5.5 Estimating Energy, CO_2 Emissions, and Costs at Scale

Table 2. Cost of 1 trillion clustered instances across AutoML clustering frameworks.

AutoML	One trillion clustered instances		
	Energy (KWh)	$C0_2$ (Kg)	Costs (EUR)
AutoCluster	1.49e+04	6.22e+03	2.99e+03
	5.54e+02	2.31e+02	1.11e+02
	1.20e+03	5.01e+02	2.41e+02
	1.76e+03	7.34e+02	3.53e+02

To assess the energy impact of clustering at scale, we estimate the total energy consumption, CO_2 emissions, and monetary cost required to assign cluster labels to one trillion instances using each AutoML framework. This analysis is based on the best-performing configuration (i.e., highest ARI averaged across time budgets) reported in Fig. 3. Energy is measured in kWh, emissions are calculated using an emissions factor of 0.187 $kgCO_2e/kWh$ (based on the average electricity price in Europe [6]), and monetary cost assumes an average electricity price of 0.20 EUR/kWh in Europe [3]. Table 2 summarizes the projected impact. `AutoCluster` exhibits by far the largest energy requirement, with correspondingly high emissions and cost. In contrast, `AutoML4Clust` is markedly more efficient, requiring only a small fraction of the resources of `AutoCluster`, with proportional reductions in environmental and monetary impact. `ML2DAC` and `cSmartML` occupy an intermediate position, reflecting moderate energy use and sustainability footprints. These findings show the substantial practical advantages of selecting energy-efficient AutoML frameworks for large-scale clustering workloads.

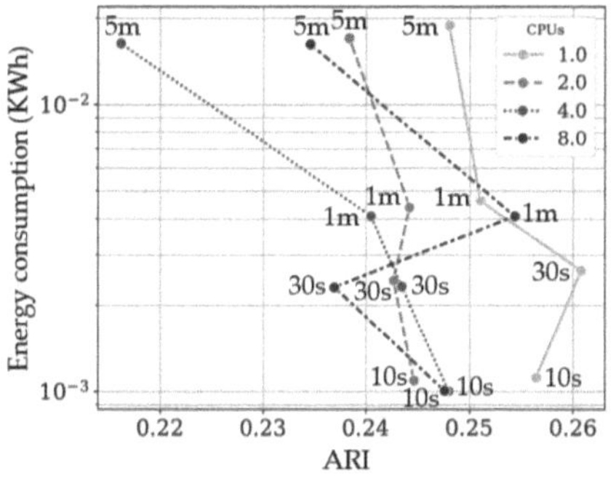

Fig. 8. ARI and CPU energy consumption during execution of cSmartML across CPU cores.

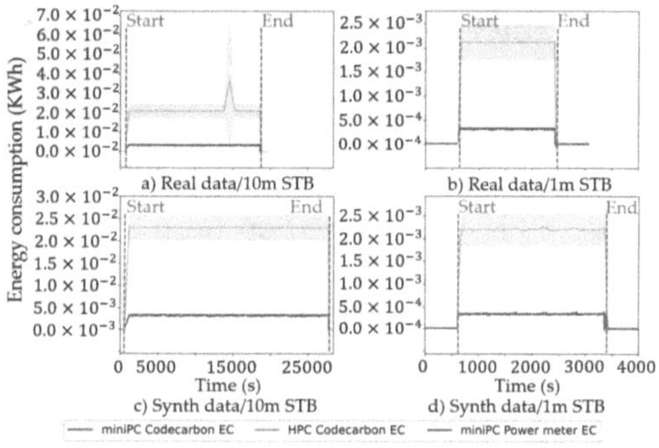

Fig. 9. Energy consumption comparison between Code carbon measurements of experiments on an HPC and a mini PC, and real values obtained using the power meter attached to the mini PC.

5.6 Trade-off Between Runtime and Energy Consumption

Table 3 presents the runtimes of various AutoML clustering frameworks under fixed search-time budgets. In general, longer runtimes result in higher energy consumption, but runtime alone is not a reliable proxy for energy efficiency, as frameworks utilize resources differently [21]. Consistent with previous AutoML benchmarks [11], we use search time as the common termination criterion. `ML2DAC` and `AutoML4Clust` adhere closely to the specified limits across all budgets, with minimal deviation and low variance; specially, `AutoML4Clust`. In contrast, `AutoCluster` systematically exceeds the allotted budgets—requiring nearly four times the intended duration at 10 s and exhibiting substantial overruns even at longer settings. `cSmartML` displays the most irregular behavior, characterized by prolonged runtimes and large variance across all budgets, with instability particularly evident in the lower-budget settings.

Table 3. Actual execution time for specified time budgets.

AutoML Framework	10 s	30 s	1 m	5 m	10 m	30 m
ML2DAC	10.54 ± 2.60	29.11 ± 8.06	57.01 ± 15.74	279.476 ± 79.05	557.77 ± 157.76	1672.84 ± 473.53
AutoML4Clust	11.11 ± 0.58	31.03 ± 0.48	61.01 ± 0.54	300.10 ± 0.57	616.29 ± 39.11	1805.39 ± 20.47
AutoCluster	36.81 ± 9.52	96.94 ± 12.81	186.13 ± 15.88	905.50 ± 55.69	1795.49 ± 148.51	$4661.84 \pm 1899.06.31$
cSmartML	35.31 ± 91.27	81.94 ± 103.46	144.98 ± 132.45	582.24 ± 436.09	1084.02 ± 841.02	1959.62 ± 329.31

5.7 Energy Consumption Profiles Across Frameworks and Computing Environments

Figure 9 shows the energy consumption over time during the execution phase for ML2DAC and AutoML4Clust under 1-min and 10-min search time budgets (STBs), measured on both a miniPC and an HPC node. These frameworks were selected for profiling due to their consistent adherence to time budgets (see Table 3) and favorable energy-performance trade-offs. Energy was recorded using CodeCarbon and an external power meter. On the miniPC, both measurement methods were used; on the HPC, only CodeCarbon was available. Figures 9a and 9b report results for real-world datasets under 10-min and 1-min STBs, respectively, while Figs. 9c and 9d show the same for synthetic datasets. The results show that the power meter and CodeCarbon traces on the miniPC are nearly identical across both real and synthetic datasets, confirming that CodeCarbon provides accurate estimates for CPU-bound workloads on this platform. In contrast, the HPC traces consistently show higher cumulative energy consumption than the miniPC for both frameworks and STBs, reflecting the higher baseline power draw and resource overhead of the HPC environment. A transient spike in Fig. 9a likely reflects an OS-level event on the HPC cluster node. Additionally, SLURM assigns different nodes for each run, introducing hardware variability that contributes to the increased variance observed in the shaded region.

To better understand how these energy patterns relate to computational behavior, Fig. 10 illustrates the relationship between CPU utilization and energy consumption for AutoML4Clust and ML2DAC across platforms (miniPC vs. HPC) and time budgets (1-min vs. 10-min). Despite HPC nodes exhibiting significantly higher average single-core CPU utilization—often exceeding 10$\times$ that of the miniPC—their total energy consumption remains in a comparable range, especially for 1-min executions. This indicates that high per-core utilization does not necessarily translate to proportionally higher energy draw, likely due to efficient power scaling and optimized thermal design in HPC infrastructure. For 10-min executions, however, energy consumption on the HPC increases noticeably, reflecting the sustained operation of high-performance components. In contrast, the miniPC shows relatively stable energy usage between short and long runs, suggesting better energy proportionality under extended workloads. These findings highlight the importance of considering hardware efficiency, workload duration, and utilization behavior—particularly single-core characteristics—when deploying AutoML pipelines under energy constraints.

Figure 11 summarizes (a) stage-wise energy consumption and (b) stage-wise execution time for each framework across Initialization, Search, and Ensemble. In both subfigures, AutoCluster exhibits the largest values across stages, reflecting the overhead of its multi-CVI consensus procedure. cSmartML also shows elevated energy and time profiles because its evolutionary search. AutoML4Clust is most efficient in Initialization (it does not warm-start), and for this framework energy and time are weakly coupled—its runtime variability is largely dataset-

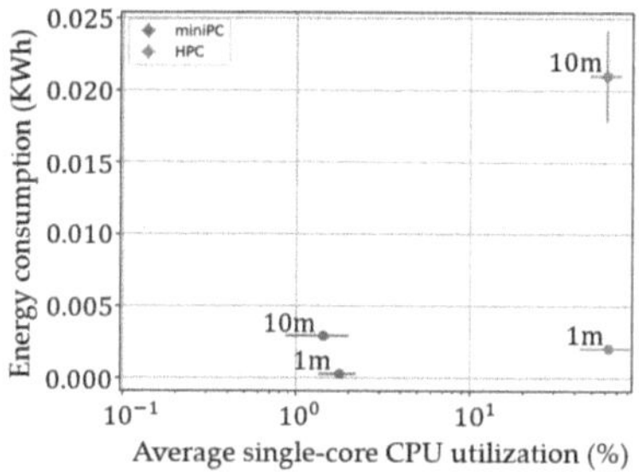

Fig. 10. CPU utilization versus energy consumption for MiniPC and HPC platforms under 1 and 10-min STBs.

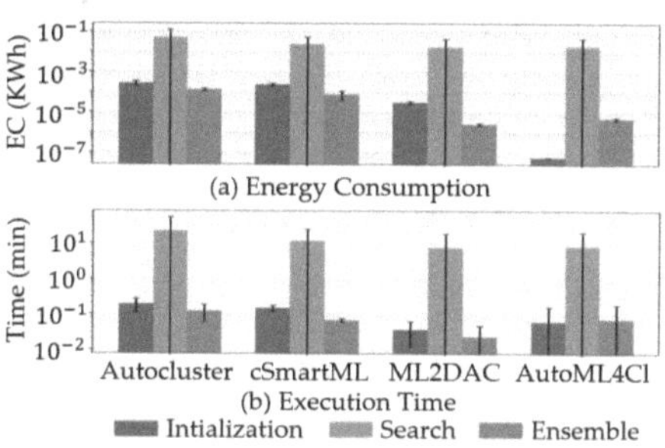

Fig. 11. Stage-wise energy and time by framework (Initialization, Search, Ensemble).

dependent. In the Ensemble stage, ML2DAC shows a more favorable profile, indicating a more efficient algorithm instantiation for cluster assignment.

5.8 Meta-learning for Energy-Aware Configuration Recommendation

We utilize the rich benchmark data collected in this study to learn fast predictors that recommend energy-efficient configurations while maintaining acceptable clustering quality. After ETL, we build a meta-dataset of 4,989 instances and use a 75/25 train/test split. The feature set includes execution-context variables (time budget, seed, CPU count, region code) and dataset descriptors (instances, dimensions). Following our earlier analysis, we retain `AutoML4Clust` and `ML2DAC` for meta-modeling.

We fit four FLAML regressors (30 s per target; RMSE objective) to predict phase energy—Initialization (IEC), Search (SEC), Ensemble (EEC)—and cluster-assignment ARI (CAARI). On the held-out split (Table 4), *SEC* is highly learnable ($R^2 \approx 0.999$), *CAARI* is moderately predictable ($R^2 \approx 0.65$), *IEC* shows partial fit ($R^2 \approx 0.48$), and *EEC* remains weak ($R^2 \approx 0.09$). These results motivate focusing recommendation on the SEC–CAARI trade-off, using SEC as the primary energy proxy.

At recommendation time, we predict {SEC, CAARI} for candidate configurations defined by new datasets (instances, dimensions) and the execution context (budget, CPUs), construct the SEC–CAARI Pareto set, and select the lowest-SEC non-dominated point. On five held-out synthetic datasets (Table 5), the selected configuration (`AutoML4Clust`, 10 s, 1 CPU) yields observed SEC tightly clustered around $4.08\text{–}4.17 \times 10^{-4}$ kWh with small relative error (FEEC err $\approx$ 0.14–0.17). CAARI spans 0.00–0.87 across tasks, indicating that energy-optimal choices do not guarantee high ARI on the hardest instances—consistent with the broader ARI distributions in Fig. 3b. Overall, the meta-recommender produces energy-efficient configurations while maintaining competitive clustering quality.

Table 4. Metatraining: FLAML regressors (30 seconds) predicting IEC, SEC, EEC, and CAARI; performance reported on a 75/25 split with following metrics RMSE, MAE, R^2.

Metalearner	RMSE	MAE	R^2	Model
IEC	$1.59e-05$	$4.89e-06$	$4.80e-01$	extra tree
SEC	$7.60e-04$	$2.16e-04$	$9.99e-01$	xgb limitdepth
EEC	$4.96e-06$	$2.85e-06$	$9.11e-02$	rf
CAARI	$2.37e-01$	$1.67e-01$	$6.53e-01$	xgboost

Table 5. Metatesting: five synthetic datasets; lowest-SEC choice from the SEC–CAARI Pareto front with observed SEC ($\times 10^{-4}$ kWh), CAARI, and relative SEC error (FEEC err).

Dataset	DDim	DClu	DIns	Seed	CAARI	SEC (e-04)	FEEC err
D1	5	20	264	45	0.02	4.12	0.15
D2	49	20	1407	13	0.77	4.21	0.17
D3	88	20	1001	13	0.62	4.12	0.15
D4	92	21	360	13	0.00	4.09	0.14
D5	3	17	1344	1	0.87	4.09	0.14

6 Conclusion

We presented an audited, energy-aware benchmark of prominent clustering AutoML frameworks. Across all analyses, `AutoML4Clust` and `ML2DAC` consistently offered the most favorable accuracy–energy trade-offs, whereas `AutoCluster` and `cSmartML` were substantially less efficient. Performance and energy patterns were strongly influenced by dataset characteristics and cluster geometry, and notable disparities in runtime reliability and large-scale energy cost were observed across frameworks. A meta-learning approach further enabled energy-aware configuration selection with low prediction error. Overall, the study provides clear evidence to guide the choice of clustering AutoML methods under energy constraints.

Acknowledgments. This is funded by the project *Increasing the knowledge intensity of Ida-Viru entrepreneurship* co-funded by the European Union.

References

1. Autoclust: a framework for automated clustering based on cluster validity indices. In: 2020 IEEE International Conference on Data Mining (ICDM), pp. 1140–1145. IEEE (2020). https://doi.org/10.1109/ICDM50108.2020.00153. https://ieeexplore.ieee.org/document/9338346
2. Demšar, J.: Statistical comparisons of classifiers over multiple data sets. J. Mach. Learn. Res. **7**(Jan), 1–30 (2006)
3. ec.europa.eu: Electricity price statistics (2023). https://ec.europa.eu/eurostat/statistics-explained/index.php?title=Electricity_price_statistics. Accessed: 30-Mar-2025
4. Eldeeb, H., Maher, M., Elshawi, R., Sakr, S.: Automlbench: a comprehensive experimental evaluation of automated machine learning frameworks. Expert Syst. Appl. **91**, 1–20 (2024). https://doi.org/10.1016/j.eswa.2023.122877

5. ElShawi, R., Lekunze, H., Sakr, S.: csmartml: a meta learning-based framework for automated selection and hyperparameter tuning for clustering. In: 2021 IEEE International Conference on Big Data (Big Data), pp. 1119–1126. IEEE (2021)
6. European Environment Agency: greenhouse gas emission intensity of electricity generation in Europe (2025). https://www.eea.europa.eu/en/analysis/indicators/greenhouse-gas-emission-intensity-of-1. Accessed: 05-Mar-2026
7. Falkner, S., Klein, A., Hutter, F.: Bohb: robust and efficient hyperparameter optimization at scale. In: International Conference on Machine Learning, pp. 1437–1446. PMLR (2018)
8. Feurer, M., Klein, A., Eggensperger, K., Springenberg, J., Blum, M., Hutter, F.: Efficient and robust automated machine learning. Adv. Neural Inf. Process. Syst. **28** (2015)
9. Feurer, M., Klein, A., Eggensperger, K., Springenberg, J., Blum, M., Hutter, F.: Efficient and robust automated machine learning. In: Advances in Neural Information Processing Systems, vol. 28 (2015)
10. Gijsbers, P., et al.: Amlb: an automl benchmark. J. Mach. Learn. Res. **25**(101), 1–65 (2024). http://jmlr.org/papers/v25/22-0493.html
11. Gijsbers, P., LeDell, E., Poirier, S., Thomas, J., Bischl, B., Vanschoren, J.: An open source automl benchmark. In: 6th ICML Workshop on Automated Machine Learning (2019)
12. Hutter, F., Kotthoff, L., Vanschoren, J.: Automated Machine Learning: Methods, Systems, Challenges. Challenges Mach. Learn. Springer (2019). https://doi.org/10.1007/978-3-030-05318-5. https://link.springer.com/book/10.1007/978-3-030-05318-5
13. Khan, K.N., Hirki, M., Niemi, T., Nurminen, J.K., Ou, Z.: Rapl in action: experiences in using RAPL for power measurements. ACM Trans. Model. Perform. Evaluation Comput. Syst. (TOMPECS) **3**(2), 1–26 (2018)
14. Li, L., Jamieson, K., DeSalvo, G., Rostamizadeh, A., Talwalkar, A.: Hyperband: a novel bandit-based approach to hyperparameter optimization. J. Mach. Learn. Res. **18**(185), 1–52 (2018)
15. Liu, Y., Li, S., Tian, W.: Autocluster: meta-learning based ensemble method for automated unsupervised clustering. In: Pacific-Asia Conference on Knowledge Discovery and Data Mining, pp. 246–258. Springer (2021)
16. Neutatz, F., Lindauer, M., Abedjan, Z.: How green is automl for tabular data? In: Simitsis, A., Kemme, B., Queralt, A., Romero, O., Jovanovic, P. (eds.) Proceedings 28th International Conference on Extending Database Technology, EDBT 2025, Barcelona, Spain, 25–28 March 2025, pp. 350–363. OpenProceedings.org (2025). https://doi.org/10.48786/EDBT.2025.28. https://doi.org/10.48786/edbt.2025.28
17. Olson, R.S., Bartley, N., Urbanowicz, R.J., Moore, J.H.: Evaluation of a tree-based pipeline optimization tool for automating data science. GECCO (2016)
18. Poulakis, Y., Doulkeridis, C., Kyriazis, D.: A survey on automl methods and systems for clustering. ACM Trans. Knowl. Discov. Data **18**(5), 1–30 (2024)
19. Silva, M.C.d., Licari, B., Tavares, G.M., Barbon Junior, S.: Benchmarking automl clustering frameworks. In: AutoML Conference (2024)
20. Strobl, C., Wickelmaier, F., Zeileis, A.: Accounting for individual differences in Bradley-terry models by means of recursive partitioning. J. Educ. Behavioral Statistics **36**(2), 135–153 (2011). https://doi.org/10.3102/1076998610375837
21. Tornede, T., Tornede, A., Hanselle, J., Mohr, F., Wever, M., Hüllermeier, E.: Towards green automated machine learning: status quo and future directions. J. Artif. Intell. Res. **77**, 427–457 (2023)

22. Tornede, T., Tornede, A., Hanselle, J., Mohr, F., Wever, M., Hüllermeier, E.: Towards green automated machine learning: status quo and future directions. J. Artif. Intell. Res. **77**, 427–457 (2023). https://doi.org/10.1613/jair.1.14340
23. Treder-Tschechlov, D., Fritz, M., Schwarz, H., Mitschang, B.: Ml2dac: Metalearning to democratize automl for clustering analysis. Proc. ACM Manage. Data (2023)
24. Tschechlov, D., Fritz, M., Schwarz, H.: Automl4clust: efficient automl for clustering analyses. In: EDBT (2021)
25. Tschechlov, D., Fritz, M., Schwarz, H.: Automl4clust: efficient automl for clustering analyses. In: Velegrakis, Y., Zeinalipour-Yazti, D., Chrysanthis, P.K., Guerra, F. (eds.) Proceedings of the 24th International Conference on Extending Database Technology, EDBT 2021, Nicosia, Cyprus, March 23 - 26, 2021, pp. 343–348. OpenProceedings.org (2021). https://doi.org/10.5441/002/EDBT.2021.32. https://doi.org/10.5441/002/edbt.2021.32
26. Ullmann, T., Hennig, C., Boulesteix, A.L.: Validation of cluster analysis results on validation data: a systematic framework. Wiley Interdisc. Rev. Data Min. Knowledge Discovery **12**(3), e1444 (2022)
27. Wu, C.J., et al.: Sustainable AI: environmental implications, challenges and opportunities. Proc. Mach. Learn. Syst. **4**, 795–813 (2022)
28. Zöller, M.A., Huber, M.F.: Benchmark and survey of automated machine learning frameworks. J. Artif. Intell. Res. **70**, 409–472 (2021). https://doi.org/10.1613/jair.1.12292

Understanding Latent Flow Models for Tabular Data Synthesis: Targets, Paths, and Sampling

Bahrul Ilmi Nasution(✉)

Department of Social Statistics, The University of Manchester, Manchester, UK
bahrul.nasution@manchester.ac.uk

Abstract. Synthetic tabular data enables microdata sharing in regulated domains, yet deploying continuous-time generative models requires balancing analytical utility, disclosure risk, and computational cost. Latent-space flow models are flexible, but theoretical equivalences across learning targets, probability paths, and sampling dynamics can translate into different behaviour under finite-step integration and explicit compute budgets. We present an empirical study of tabular latent flow models across seven datasets, evaluating velocity, score, noise, and posterior matching objectives under optimal transport (OT) and variance-preserving (VP) paths, ODE and SDE sampling, and varying integration budgets. Our contributions are threefold: (1) we show that different learning targets yield different utility-risk results, with velocity and posterior matching tending to yield higher utility, while score and noise matching tend to achieve lower disclosure risk; (2) we demonstrate that configuration and sampling choices shift performance, with midpoint often improving distributional fidelity and OT paths often tolerating earlier stopping than VP, enabling compute savings under fixed budgets or risk thresholds; and (3) we distil these findings into actionable defaults and practical configuration guidance to support pre-release model selection under disclosure risk and resource constraints. The code implementation and supplementary materials can be accessed in https://github.com/rulnasution/tabular-latent-flow/.

Keywords: Diffusion · flow matching · latent flow models · tabular data synthesis · sampling dynamics

1 Introduction

Data owners, such as National Statistics Offices (NSOs) and financial institutions, face a persistent dilemma: enabling external researchers and policymakers to analyse microdata without revealing individual information. Tabular data synthesis addresses this challenge by generating data that preserves statistical properties but has different records from the original data [13]. However, compared with images and text, tabular data poses distinct generative challenges. The

M. Ceci et al. (Eds.): ECML PKDD 2026, LNAI 16948, pp. 435–453, 2027.
https://doi.org/10.1007/978-3-032-37679-4_25

tabular generative model mixes continuous and categorical variables, exhibits complex dependencies, and requires understanding of the relationship between utility and disclosure risk [14,27]. Mastering these challenges is central for data synthesis in regulated domains.

Deep generative models have recently improved the quality of synthetic tabular data, with flow-based approaches, such as flow matching (FM), becoming increasingly prominent [8,18]. FM [2,12] is a continuous-time generative framework that learns a vector field transporting a simple base distribution to the data distribution through an ordinary differential equation, while supporting simulation-free training. Flow-based and diffusion-based models can also be trained in latent spaces, where the generative dynamics operate on continuous representations that are later decoded back to the data space using a variational autoencoder (VAE) [4,21]. For tabular data, recent latent-space generators adopt this strategy by training diffusion [27] or flow-matching models [18] on tabular latent representations. By mapping mixed-type tabular records into a continuous latent space, these approaches can simplify generative modelling and reduce the cost of operating directly on heterogeneous features, which has competitive performance in prior works [18,27].

Existing theory on diffusion and flow-based generative models shows that, under Gaussian probability paths, velocity, score, and noise matching are analytically connected [10,12]. Similarly, reverse-SDE samplers and probability-flow ODE samplers can share the same continuous-time marginal distributions [22]. Meanwhile, posterior matching, or variational flow matching (VFM), is also closely related to flow matching in continuous Gaussian settings, while introducing a variational training formulation and an associated stochastic sampling procedure [6,8]. However, these theoretical connections do not determine which configuration works best in finite-step latent tabular synthesis, where models are learned approximately, sampled under limited compute, and trained using different objectives. Thus, an empirical evaluation of learning targets, probability paths, sampling dynamics, and numerical solvers becomes essential in practice.

This work addresses these questions through a systematic empirical study of latent tabular flow models. In this study, latent tabular flow models refer to latent continuous-time generative models defined by a probability path and sampled through ODE or SDE dynamics. Flow, noise, score, and posterior matching denote different learning-target parameterisations within this shared setup, rather than separate model families. We evaluate representative target–path configurations across datasets and quantify utility, disclosure risk, and efficiency under controlled changes in learning target, probability path, sampling dynamics, solver family, integration endpoint, and integration steps. The goal is to provide practitioner-facing guidance on how to configure latent tabular flow models for different circumstances. Specifically, we study the following research questions:

- **Q1**: Does training with different learning targets (velocity, score, noise, and posterior matching) produce empirically equivalent results in tabular latent flow models, as suggested by theory?

- **Q2**: How does the choice of probability path (OT versus VP), affect utility and disclosure risk across learning targets?
- **Q3**: How do sampling dynamics and numerical solvers compare across trained tabular latent flow models in terms of data quality and disclosure risk?
- **Q4**: How does the integration endpoint affect the quality of the synthetic data for each target-path configuration?
- **Q5**: How do integration steps affect the synthetic data quality for each target-path configuration?

Together, these questions clarify how theoretical modeling choices translate into empirical behavior in tabular data synthesis, and they support informed configuration decisions under competing utility, disclosure risk, and computational constraints.

2 Related Work

Flow and Diffusion Models. Diffusion models learn reverse-time dynamics through SDEs and are strong baselines for high-quality generation [9,22,23]. Instead, FM learns a deterministic velocity field, with conditional FM enabling simulation-free training [12,15]. Both frameworks are based on probability path design, where OT (for FM) and VP (for diffusion) paths are common choices and ODE/SDE sampling can be closely related under Gaussian paths [2,10,12]. VFM further connects velocity learning to variational inference and score-based objectives [6,8]. Recent work also models latent distributions learnt by VAEs using diffusion or flow models, including in tabular settings [4,18,21,27].

Tabular Synthesis and Practical Design Choices. Tabular synthesis should handle mixed feature types, limited data, and also utility and risk. Diffusion-based approaches such as TabDDPM and latent diffusion variants (e.g., TabSyn) demonstrate strong utility and fidelity [11,17,25,27]. On the other hand, FM and VFM provide a more sampling-efficient alternative in both latent and data space on tabular benchmarks [8,18]. However, within a unified latent continuous-time setup, the practical impact of choosing learning targets, paths (OT vs. VP), deterministic versus stochastic sampling, and solver families remains less systematically studied. Our work addresses this by benchmarking these choices under controlled sampling budgets for tabular latent flow models.

3 Background

This section discusses the essentials for our study, covering flow model fundamentals and probability paths (Sect. 3.1), followed by a brief understanding of learning targets including velocity, score, noise, and posterior (Sect. 3.2).

3.1 Flow Model and Conditional Gaussian Paths

A flow model generates samples by *moving* a point over time from an initial distribution (usually a standard Gaussian) to the data distribution [2,12]. In common practice, we start from noise $x_0 \sim \mathcal{N}(0, I)$ and evolve it with a learnt time-dependent vector field v_t^θ to obtain data $x_1 \sim p_{data}$ based on ODE:

$$\frac{dx_t}{dt} = v_t^\theta(x_t), \quad t \in [0, 1]. \tag{1}$$

Intuitively, v_t^θ tells each point "where to move next" so that the evolving distribution matches the data distribution at $t = 1$. Training v_t^θ can use *conditional* flow [10], which constructs a conditional probability path anchored at an endpoint $x_1 \sim p_{\text{data}}$ [12]. The most convenient choice is a Gaussian conditional path:

$$x_t = \alpha_t x_1 + \sigma_t x_0, \quad x_0 \sim \mathcal{N}(0, I), \tag{2}$$

which implies $p_t(x_t \mid x_1) = \mathcal{N}(\alpha_t x_1, \sigma_t^2 I)$. The path is defined by interpolants (α_t, σ_t). There are two common interpolants, namely optimal transport (OT) which is defined as a straight path and variance-preserving diffusion (VP) path [12]. Both paths are defined as

$$\alpha_t^{\text{OT}} = t, \quad \sigma_t^{\text{OT}} = 1 - (1 - \sigma_{\min})t \tag{3}$$

$$\alpha_t^{\text{VP}} = \sqrt{\bar{\alpha}(1 - t)}, \quad \sigma_t^{\text{VP}} = \sqrt{1 - (\alpha_t^{\text{VP}})^2} \tag{4}$$

with $\bar{\alpha}(t) = \exp\Big(- \int_0^t \beta(s)\, ds\Big)$. The interpolants move the process from a noise-dominated state at $t = 0$ toward the data endpoint at $t = 1$. Generation reduces to solving ODE in (1) (or an SDE variant), so the main engineering questions are what the network should learn, which path to follow, and how the solver and compute budget affect quality.

3.2 Targets: Velocity, Score, Noise, and Posterior

Differentiating the Gaussian probability path in Eq. (2) with respect to time yields a tractable conditional velocity target [12]:

$$u_t(x_t \mid x_1) = \dot{\alpha}_t x_1 + \dot{\sigma}_t x_0. \tag{5}$$

Flow matching regresses the model velocity $v_t^\theta(x_t)$ to $u_t(x_t \mid x_1)$. Furthermore, the same Gaussian probability path also provides a closed-form conditional score,

$$\nabla_{x_t} \log p_t(x_t \mid x_1) = -\frac{x_t - \alpha_t x_1}{\sigma_t^2}, \tag{6}$$

which leads to score matching by regressing a predicted score $s_t^\theta(x_t)$ to this target [23]. Finally, DDPM-style noise prediction follows directly from Eq. (2) by regressing the predicted noise $\epsilon_t^\theta(x_t)$ with the initial noise, $x_0 = (x_t -$

$\alpha_t x_1)/\sigma_t$ [9,12]. These parameterisations are related under Gaussian paths, differing mainly by time-dependent scalings. In practice, they can behave differently under finite-step sampling and limited compute budgets, which motivates our empirical comparisons.

While FM, SM, and NM specify a direct regression target at time t, variational flow matching (VFM) [6,8] replaces direct target regression with posterior inference over the endpoint. Specifically, VFM learns a variational posterior $q_t^\theta(x_1 \mid x_t)$ and recovers the velocity by conditional expectation:

$$v_t^\theta(x_t) = \mathbb{E}_{q_t^\theta(x_1|x_t)}[u_t(x_t \mid x_1)] \,. \tag{7}$$

In the Gaussian distribution, $q_t^\theta(x_1 \mid x_t)$ is parameterised by a mean $\mu_t^\theta(x_t)$, which can be interpreted as predicting an endpoint. We show interface for deterministic (ODE) and stochastic (SDE) samplers in later sections.

4 Designing Flow Models on Latent Variables: Theory and Implementation

We study latent-space flow models for tabular synthesis by fixing the latent representation and varying a small set of design axes that affect utility, disclosure risk, and runtime. Given fixed model architecture, we vary five design axes that matter for configuration and evaluation:

- **Learning target:** what the network predicts during training (velocity, score, noise, or posterior mean).
- **Path:** OT versus VP, which determines the interpolants (α_t, σ_t).
- **Sampling dynamics:** deterministic ODE versus stochastic SDE.
- **Solver family:** Euler vs Midpoint.
- **Sampling budget:** integration endpoint and steps.

4.1 Training Pipeline

Let $z_1 \sim p_{\mathcal{Z}}$ denote the latent representation of a preprocessed real record x^{data}, obtained from a pretrained VAE encoder, $z_1 = \text{Enc}(x^{\text{data}})$. During training, we sample $z_0 \sim \mathcal{N}(0, I)$ and $t \sim \text{Uniform}(0,1)$, then construct the interpolated latent state

$$z_t = \alpha_t z_1 + \sigma_t z_0. \tag{8}$$

Let $\text{F}_t^\theta(z_t) = \text{NN}_\theta(z_t, t)$ denote the network output. All target parameterisations use this same latent interpolation, but differ in the training target and in how the velocity and score components required for sampling are recovered, as summarised in Table 1. The full training algorithm is provided in Appendix A.

4.2 Learning Targets

First, note two tractable conditional quantities under Eq. (8):

$$u_t(z_t \mid z_1) = \dot{\alpha}_t z_1 + \dot{\sigma}_t z_0, \tag{9}$$

$$\nabla_{z_t} \log p_t(z_t \mid z_1) = -\frac{z_t - \alpha_t z_1}{\sigma_t^2}. \tag{10}$$

We use these as targets for training FM and SM, respectively. In contrast, NM uses z_0 and VFM uses endpoint z_1 as a target. At sampling time, ODE solvers require a velocity field, while SDE solvers require both a velocity and a score. The mapping used for each variant is defined in Sect. 4.3 and listed in Table 1.

Table 1. Learning target for latent flow models. The table shows what the model predicts, the training loss, and how we obtain the components required by ODE and SDE sampling.

Flow model	Model output $\mathrm{F}_t^\theta(z_t)$	Training loss	$v_t^\theta(\tilde{z}_t)$	$t^\theta(\tilde{z}_t)$
FM	Velocity $v_t^\theta(z_t)$	$\mathbb{E}\lVert \mathrm{F}_t^\theta(z_t) - u_t(z_t \mid z_1)\rVert_2^2$	$\mathrm{F}_t^\theta(z_t)$	Equation (17)
SM	Scaled score $\mathrm{F}_t^\theta(z_t) = \sigma_t\, s_t^\theta(z_t)$	$\mathbb{E}\big[\sigma_t^2 \lVert \frac{\mathrm{F}_t^\theta(z_t)}{\sigma_t} + \frac{z_t - \alpha_t z_1}{\sigma_t^2} \rVert_2^2\big]$	Equation (14)	$\mathrm{F}_t^\theta(\tilde{z}_t)/\sigma_t$
NM	Noise $\epsilon_t^\theta(z_t)$	$\mathbb{E}\big[\lVert \mathrm{F}_t^\theta(z_t) - z_0 \rVert_2^2\big]$	Equation (14)	$-\mathrm{F}_t^\theta(\tilde{z}_t)/\sigma_t$
VFM	Posterior mean $\mu_t^\theta(z_t)$	$\mathbb{E}\big[\lambda(t) \lVert \mathrm{F}_t^\theta(z_t) - z_1 \rVert_2^2\big]$	Equation (15)	Equation (18)

4.3 Sampling and Parameterisation Mappings

We generate a latent sample by drawing $\tilde{z}_0 \sim \mathcal{N}(0, I)$ and simulating the ODE/SDE process to obtain latent samples $\tilde{z}_1$. Finally, latent samples generated by the flow model are passed through the fixed VAE decoder to reconstruct synthetic tabular records, followed by inverse preprocessing to obtain the original format of the records.

A Shared Identity Under Gaussian Paths. The following identity links velocity and score under Gaussian paths and provides a principled conversion between parameterisations.

Proposition 1 (Velocity–score equivalence; adapted from [10]). *Let* $z_t = \alpha_t z_1 + \sigma_t z_0$, $z_0 \sim \mathcal{N}(0, I)$ *define a Gaussian probability path. Then, for any* t *such that* $\alpha_t \neq 0$ *and* $\sigma_t > 0$*, the conditional velocity field* $u_t(z_t \mid z_1)$ *and the conditional score function* $\nabla_{z_t} \log p_t(z_t \mid z_1)$ *satisfy*

$$u_t(z_t \mid z_1) = \left(\sigma_t^2 \frac{\dot{\alpha}_t}{\alpha_t} - \dot{\sigma}_t \sigma_t\right) \nabla_{z_t} \log p_t(z_t \mid z_1) + \frac{\dot{\alpha}_t}{\alpha_t} z_t. \tag{11}$$

The proof is in Appendix B.1 of the supplementary material. However, this theoretical equivalence does not necessarily imply identical finite-step sampling behaviour. In practice, model approximation error, discretisation error, solver choice, time-step schedules, and limited compute budgets can lead to different empirical behaviour under finite-step sampling. Proposition 1 allows us to compare targets fairly under matched sampling definitions.

Deterministic Sampling (ODE). ODE sampling integrates

$$d\tilde{z}_t = v_t^\theta(\tilde{z}_t)\,dt, \quad \tilde{z}_0 \sim \mathcal{N}(0, I). \tag{12}$$

For FM, the velocity is predicted directly:

$$v_t^\theta(\tilde{z}_t) = \mathrm{F}_t^\theta(\tilde{z}_t). \tag{13}$$

For SM or NM, we first obtain a score $s_t^\theta(\tilde{z}_t)$ as in Table 1, then convert the score to velocity via Proposition 1:

$$v_t^\theta(\tilde{z}_t) = \left(\sigma_t^2\frac{\dot{\alpha}_t}{\alpha_t} - \dot{\sigma}_t\sigma_t\right)s_t^\theta(\tilde{z}_t) + \frac{\dot{\alpha}_t}{\alpha_t}\tilde{z}_t. \tag{14}$$

For VFM, the mean $\mu_t^\theta(\tilde{z}_t)$ yields the velocity of Eq. (7):

$$v_t^\theta(\tilde{z}_t) = \left(\dot{\alpha}_t - \frac{\dot{\sigma}_t}{\sigma_t}\alpha_t\right)\mu_t^\theta(\tilde{z}_t) + \frac{\dot{\sigma}_t}{\sigma_t}\tilde{z}_t. \tag{15}$$

Stochastic Sampling (SDE). SDE sampling integrates

$$d\tilde{z}_t = \left[v_t^\theta(\tilde{z}_t) + \tfrac{g_t^2}{2}s_t^\theta(\tilde{z}_t)\right]dt + g_t\,dW_t, \tag{16}$$

For SM and NM, s_t^θ is obtained directly from the model output as listed in Table 1. In contrast, FM recovers the score by inverting Eq. (11):

$$s_t^\theta(\tilde{z}_t) = \frac{\alpha_t v_t^\theta(\tilde{z}_t) - \dot{\alpha}_t\tilde{z}_t}{\sigma_t^2\dot{\alpha}_t - \alpha_t\dot{\sigma}_t\sigma_t}. \tag{17}$$

For VFM, the score can be calculated using Eq. (18).

$$s_t^\theta(\tilde{z}_t) = -\frac{\tilde{z}_t - \alpha_t\mu_t^\theta(\tilde{z}_t)}{\sigma_t^2}, \tag{18}$$

Algorithm 1 summarises the sampling process of latent flow models in general. In brief, sampling starts from Gaussian noise, integrates the learned latent dynamics using the selected ODE or SDE solver, and decodes the generated latent sample using the fixed VAE decoder.

Algorithm 1. Latent flow sample generation

Input: Trained latent flow model $NN(\cdot)$, discrete step interval Δ, trained decoder from VAE Dec(.), integrator (ODE or SDE), starting time t_{start}, end time t_{int}

$\tilde{z}_0 \sim \mathcal{N}(0, I)$.
$t = t_{\text{start}}$
while $t \leq t_{int}$ **do**
  $\mathrm{F}_t^\theta(\tilde{z}_t) = \mathrm{NN}(\tilde{z}_t, t)$
  Calculate $v_t^\theta(\tilde{z}_t)$ ▷ both ODE and SDE
  if SDE **then** Calculate $s_t^\theta(\tilde{z}_t)$ ▷ SDE only
  end if
  Update $\tilde{z}_{t+\Delta}$ using integrator.
  $t{+}{=}\Delta$
end while
$\tilde{x}^{\text{data}} = \mathrm{Dec}(\tilde{z}_{t_{int}})$ ▷ Decode using pretrained VAE decoder
return $\tilde{\mathcal{D}} = \mathrm{InverseTransform}(\tilde{x}^{\text{data}})$

5 Experimental Results

This section reports empirical findings, covering the experiment setup and evaluation (Sects. 5.1 and 5.2), a comparison of learning targets, paths, sampling dynamics, and solvers (Sect. 5.3), as well as integration time and step budget (Sects. 5.4 and 5.5).

5.1 Experimental Setup

We adopt the experimental framework from previous works [8,18] with adaptations specific to the objectives of this study. Tables 1 and 2 in Appendix C of the supplementary material summarise the implementation details.

Datasets. We evaluate seven tabular datasets that span census and machine learning benchmarks (Table 2). We use five public census datasets (UK, Canada, Fiji, Rwanda, Indonesia), which can be obtained from the IPUMS repository [16]. On the other hand, we also provide additional comparisons using UCI datasets commonly used in tabular generative model evaluations [8,11].

Network Architecture. We use the Transformer-based VAE encoder–decoder from TabSyn [27]. All flow models use an MLP with four hidden layers of widths [1024, 2048, 2048, 1024], with SiLU activations and no batch normalisation. We encode time using a 512-dimensional sinusoidal embedding [18].

Training Setup. We begin by preprocessing the data. We transform numerical variables using quantile transformer, and categorical variables using one-hot encoding. We then feed the preprocessed data to VAE. We follow β-VAE training setup from [27] who trained the VAE for 4000 epochs. Using the trained VAE encoder, we encode the data into its latent space representation. Subsequently, we used the flow models we discussed in Sect. 4 to learn the latent distribution. We used both OT and VP paths for all algorithms; therefore, there are *eight*

Table 2. Summary of datasets used in this study.

Dataset	Records	#Num.	#Cat.	Source
UK Census	104,267	1	14	IPUMS
Canada Census	32,149	4	21	IPUMS
Fiji Census	84,323	1	18	IPUMS
Rwanda Census	31,455	1	12	IPUMS
Indonesia Census	177,429	1	12	IPUMS
Adult	48,842	5	10	UCI Repo
Churn	10,000	4	7	UCI Repo

models to compare. For each model, we used the model with the lowest training loss in 10,000 epochs, consistent with previous tabular synthesis work [8,18,27]. This keeps the training budget consistent across latent flow variants.

Sampling and Integration. Unless stated otherwise, we sample with an ODE solver using Euler integration for 100 steps up to $t_{\text{int}} = 1$. For numerical stability, VP-based runs stop at $t_{\text{int}} = 1 - 10^{-5}$ to avoid the numerical issues when converting to a score near $t = 1$[1]. For OT sampling with NM and SM, we additionally clamp the start time to $t_{\text{start}} = 10^{-2}$ (see Appendix B.2 of the supplementary material for motivation). For SDE sampling and solver comparisons, we decouple the injected noise from the path variance to keep the diffusion term non-negligible. We use $g_t = \sigma_t^{\text{VP}}$ on the OT path and $g_t = \sigma_t^{\text{OT}}$ on the VP path.

External Comparison Baselines. To understand the position of the latent flow models in generative models, we also compared our representative configurations with standard tabular synthesisers from major model families, following common baseline choices in recent tabular generative modelling studies [17,26]. We compare against Bayesian Network [3], Tabular Variational Autoencoder (TVAE) and Robust TVAE (RTVAE) [1,26], Conditional Tabular Generative Adversarial Networks (CTGAN) [26], and Normalising Flows [5,20]. Using the `synthcity` implementations [20], we keep algorithm-specific hyperparameters at their default values and only adjust shared training-budget settings where supported. These include batch size, maximum number of iterations, and network architecture when the implementation exposes directly configurable architecture settings. Further, we also include TabDDPM and TabSyn as modern diffusion-based references, with results taken from [18] under the same evaluation protocol.

5.2 Evaluation Metrics

Following established practice in synthetic tabular data evaluation [7,14,24], we focus primarily on two dimensions: analytical utility and disclosure risk. Our

[1] This avoids division by σ_t when converting to a score near $t = 1$, primarily for SM, NM, and VFM.

evaluation is motivated by a practical pre-release setting in which a data owner may select a synthetic tabular data generator before sharing data for external analysis or research access. In this setting, synthetic data is useful only if it preserves statistical properties required for downstream analysis, but it should not introduce unnecessary disclosure risk.

Utility (Preservation of Statistical Properties): Utility value ranges from 0 (no preservation) to 1 (perfect preservation), computed as:

$$\mathrm{U} = \frac{1}{3}\left(\mathrm{ROC}_{\mathrm{univ}} + \mathrm{ROC}_{\mathrm{biv}} + \mathrm{CIO}\right), \tag{19}$$

where ROC measures frequency preservation (univariate and bivariate) and CIO measures statistical inference validity via confidence interval overlap.

Disclosure Risk: Disclosure risk ranges from 0 to 1 and measures the normalised increase in empirical attribution success above a baseline adversary who only uses the original-data equivalence class structure. We use Targeted Correct Attribute Probability (TCAP) to evaluate a record-linkage-style attribute disclosure scenario, where an adversary knows a set of key variables and attempts to infer sensitive attributes using the synthetic data. The reported value should therefore be interpreted as an empirical disclosure risk diagnostic rather than a general privacy risk measure or release-safety guarantee. For example, $R = 0.2$ does not mean that the dataset has a 20% absolute privacy risk. Instead, it means that, relative to the baseline attribution uncertainty, the synthetic data accounts for 20% of the remaining possible increase in empirical attribution success under the specified key and sensitive variables.

Additional Diagnostic Metrics: In addition to utility and risk, we also report Shape and Trend as complementary fidelity diagnostics that are widely used in synthetic data evaluation [8,17,19,27]. Shape measures column-wise distributional agreement between real and synthetic data, while Trend measures how well pairwise relationships between variables are preserved. These metrics complement utility and disclosure risk by capturing marginal and relational fidelity in the generated tabular data. We report these metrics as means over 20 independently generated synthetic datasets. Additional and detailed evaluations, including α-precision, β-recall, and Wasserstein distance, are reported in the appendix due to space constraints (Appendices D and E).

5.3 Configuration Study: Targets, Paths, Sampling Dynamics, and Solvers

The paired OT–VP plots in Fig. 1 and Table 3 summarise how latent tabular flow models behave under three practical design choices: the *learning target* (FM, SM, NM, VFM), the *path* (OT vs. VP), and the *sampling implementation* (ODE vs. SDE, and Euler vs. Midpoint)[2]. We report utility and disclosure risk as primary

[2] We used 100 integration steps. As a consequence, Euler and Euler–Maruyama use one model evaluation per step, while Midpoint uses two, so Midpoint has roughly twice the evaluation cost at the same step count.

decision metrics, and use shape and trend as secondary fidelity checks. Because aggregate metric values can be affected by dataset-specific scale and structure, we also report per-dataset, rank-based, and pareto front summaries in Appendix E.1 of the Supplementary Material.

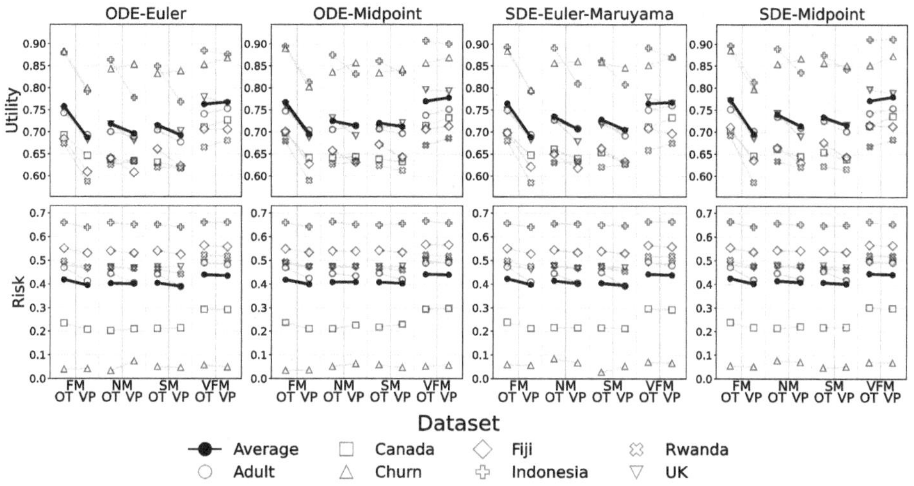

Fig. 1. Paired OT vs. VP comparisons across learning targets (FM, NM, SM, VFM) and integrators. Each line connects the same dataset under OT and VP. Each hollowed shape corresponds to the datasets while the black, solid line represents the **average** values across all datasets. Top: Utility, bottom: disclosure risk. On average, FM, NM, and SM tend to favour the OT path in utility, whereas VFM is more competitive across OT and VP. Midpoint and SDE sampling shift the utility-risk values, with effects that depend on the target and dataset.

Q1 (Targets). Across datasets and integrators, FM-OT and VFM form a high-utility group, while NM and SM can be characterised as a risk-conservative but utility-limited group. FM typically generates synthetic data with strong utility and moderate disclosure risk. In contrast, NM and SM tend to produce lower-utility synthetic data, but their post-hoc disclosure risk evaluation indicates lower risk levels. VFM achieves high utility across integrator settings, although its disclosure risk profile is generally higher than NM and SM. This makes VFM more attractive when utility is prioritised, provided that the resulting disclosure risk remains within an acceptable threshold.

Q2 (Paths: OT vs. VP). The comparison between interpolants or probability paths is target-dependent and mainly shows a consistent direction in the averaged paired comparisons. For FM, NM, and SM, switching from OT to VP generally decreases utility, but can also move the configuration toward a lower disclosure-risk regime, particularly for FM and SM. For VFM, VP tends to

Table 3. Aggregate Shape and Trend comparison addressing Q3 across learning targets, sampling dynamics, and numerical solvers. Values are averaged over 20 runs per dataset and then averaged across datasets. Lower values are better. Bold and underlined entries denote the best and second-best integrator setting for each target-path combination, respectively.

Evaluation	Algorithm	ODE-Euler	ODE-Midpoint	SDE-EM	SDE-Midpoint
Shape (%,↓)	FM-OT	1.2329	<u>1.1796</u>	1.1816	**1.1537**
	FM-VP	1.9641	**1.9260**	1.9595	<u>1.9346</u>
	NM-OT	1.6587	1.5818	<u>1.3962</u>	**1.3484**
	NM-VP	1.9462	<u>1.5993</u>	1.7573	**1.5845**
	SM-OT	1.6847	1.5709	<u>1.4109</u>	**1.3656**
	SM-VP	1.8760	<u>1.6242</u>	1.7145	**1.5958**
	VFM-OT	1.3813	<u>1.3792</u>	**1.3703**	1.3869
	VFM-VP	**1.2621**	1.2935	<u>1.2705</u>	1.2992
Trend (%,↓)	FM-OT	2.6514	<u>2.5246</u>	2.5604	**2.4821**
	FM-VP	3.8475	**3.7307**	3.8586	<u>3.7479</u>
	NM-OT	3.2847	3.1623	<u>2.9751</u>	**2.8352**
	NM-VP	3.5545	<u>3.0452</u>	3.3029	**3.0073**
	SM-OT	3.3477	3.1546	<u>2.9753</u>	**2.8713**
	SM-VP	3.5654	<u>3.0739</u>	3.3311	**3.0319**
	VFM-OT	<u>2.6307</u>	**2.5351**	2.6630	2.6504
	VFM-VP	2.4862	**2.4542**	2.4962	<u>2.4555</u>

increase average utility relative to OT, while disclosure-risk changes are smaller than the corresponding utility shifts. Practically, OT is a more reliable default for FM when utility is prioritised, and it can also benefit NM and SM when used with a practical start-time clamp. By contrast, VFM is comparatively less sensitive to the path, with VP often slightly better.

Q3 (Sampling Dynamics and Solver Choice). Table 3 shows that solver and sampling dynamics interact with the target–path choice. Midpoint integration often improves Shape and Trend errors over Euler at the same step count, although it requires roughly twice as many model evaluations. SDE-Midpoint is frequently the best or second-best setting, especially for NM and SM, but its advantage is not uniform: ODE sampling remains competitive for FM-VP and VFM. Figure 1 shows that utility and disclosure risk effects are more target- and dataset-dependent. Thus, stochastic sampling should be viewed as a calibration option rather than a universally better default, especially EM method.

5.4 Integration Endpoint

We vary the ODE integration endpoint $t_{\text{int}} \in [0.6, 1]$ to study the effect of early stopping during generation. Figure 2 reports averages across seven datasets as

t_{int} increases from truncated to near-complete integration. Across all methods, utility increases with t_{int}, accompanied by a simultaneous increase in disclosure risk. The path choice impacts truncation sensitivity. OT-based variants (FM-OT, VFM-OT) achieve high utility in the earlier stage ($t_{\text{int}} \approx 0.7-0.8$) but also accumulate risk faster. In contrast, VP-based variants (FM-VP, SM, NM, VFM-VP) are more sensitive to truncation, requiring nearly full integration ($t_{\text{int}} \approx 1.0$) to match the utility of OT paths. Among the methods, VFM (red lines) generally yields the highest utility envelope across the integration range, whereas SM and NM (orange/green dashed) lag slightly behind in the early stages. Dataset-specific results are reported in Appendix E.3 of the supplementary material.

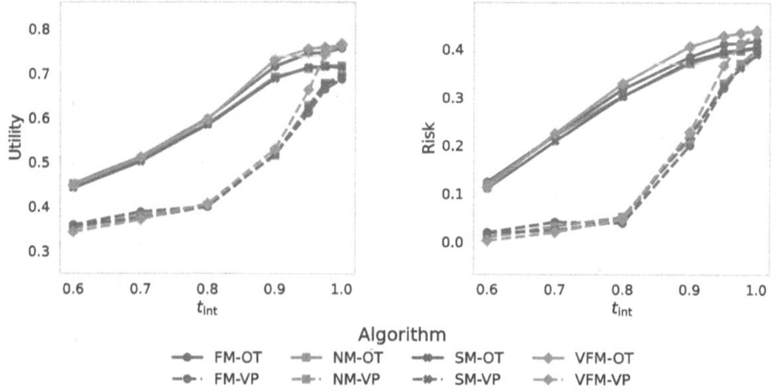

Fig. 2. Average performance across seven datasets on integration time $t_{\text{int}} \in [0.6, 1.0]$. The solid lines (OT) show consistently higher utility and risk at earlier stages compared to dashed lines (VP). The utility and risk increase monotonically as $t_{\text{int}} \to 1$.

5.5 Integration Steps

We study sampling budget by varying the number of discrete steps during numerical integration. Figure 3 reports average utility and disclosure risk across seven datasets for steps from 4 to 1024, with the vertical dashed line marking our default setting (100 steps). For interpretation, we group budgets into three regimes: **Phase I** (4–32 steps), **Phase II** (64–256 steps), and **Phase III** (512–1024 steps).

Across methods, utility increases sharply in Phase I and then shows diminishing returns, while disclosure risk rises more steadily as budget increases. Differences between configurations are most pronounced under tight budgets: OT-based settings reach higher utility with fewer evaluations, whereas VP-based settings typically require substantially larger budgets to approach similar utility. Beyond the default range, performance gaps narrow and marginal utility

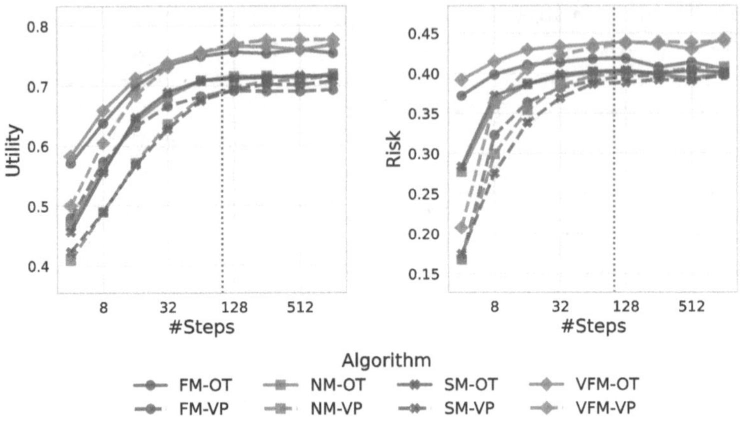

Fig. 3. Average performance across seven datasets for varying steps ($2^n, n \in [2, 10]$). The vertical line marks the baseline of 100 steps. OT paths (solid) achieve useful utility at lower budgets (< 32 steps) compared to VP paths (dashed). Performance for all methods tends to converge and plateau beyond 100 steps.

gains become small while risk continues to increase. Overall, these trends support 100 steps as a reasonable default, with higher budgets best reserved for utility-first settings where additional cost and a modest increase in risk are acceptable. Dataset-specific results are reported in Appendix E.4 of the supplementary material.

5.6 Comparison with Standard Tabular Synthesisers

To contextualise the internal configuration study, we compare representative latent flow configurations with standard tabular synthesisers. Based on the internal results, we select FM-OT as a balanced latent flow configuration and VFM-VP as a utility-first configuration. Both are evaluated with the default ODE-Euler sampler, so that the external comparison reflects model-level differences.

Table 4 contextualises the recommended latent flow configurations against standard tabular synthesisers. FM-OT and VFM-VP improve shape and trend errors over the non-diffusion baselines and achieve higher utility than the neural baselines, while remaining competitive with TabSyn. VFM-VP achieves the highest average utility and the lowest trend error, while FM-OT achieves the lowest shape error. The main trade-off is disclosure risk: lower-risk baselines such as RTVAE preserve less statistical structure. The comparison therefore supports viewing these methods as configuration based on overall performance.

6 Discussions

This section interprets the empirical results and derives practical guidance. Section 6.1 discusses the key findings across learning targets, probability paths, and sampling numerics, and Sect. 6.2 translates these findings into practical configuration guidance with actionable defaults for practitioners.

6.1 Discussion of Findings

The performance of latent tabular synthesis is governed by three interacting choices: the learning objective, the probability path, and the sampling numerics.

Targets Set the Utility–Risk Regime (Q1). FM and VFM occupy the higher-utility regime, while NM and SM are more conservative, trading lower utility for reduced disclosure risk. FM-OT emerges as a balanced choice. Meanwhile, VFM is more suitable when utility is prioritised within an acceptable risk threshold, but it generally has a less conservative disclosure risk profile than NM and SM.

Table 4. Comparison with standard tabular synthesisers. Results are averaged across seven datasets. TabDDPM and TabSyn results are taken from [18] under the same evaluation protocol. FM-OT and VFM-VP are representative latent flow configurations selected from the internal configuration study and evaluated with the default ODE-Euler sampler. Utility is higher-is-better, while disclosure risk, shape error, and trend error are lower-is-better.

Model	Utility ↑	Risk ↓	Shape ↓	Trend ↓
Bayesian Network	0.6275	0.3674	10.0305	17.0801
TVAE	0.5145	0.3392	11.4874	21.3613
RTVAE	0.4531	**0.0563**	18.4225	42.1489
CTGAN	0.5164	0.2484	14.8998	24.8076
Normalising Flow	0.5149	0.2472	13.7603	20.8416
TabDDPM [18]	0.5561	0.2620	17.0871	27.6257
TabSyn [18]	0.7670	0.4314	1.2429	2.6557
FM-OT	0.7582	0.4187	**1.2329**	2.6514
VFM-VP	**0.7679**	0.4352	1.2621	**2.4862**

Path Effects are Target-Dependent and Asymmetric (Q2). OT and VP are not interchangeable across targets. Switching to VP tends to reduce utility for FM, NM, and SM, while often moving FM and SM toward more conservative disclosure-risk positions. VFM behaves differently: VP often improves utility relative to OT at broadly comparable risk. OT is therefore a more reliable default for FM, NM, and SM, whereas VFM benefits more reliably from VP in utility-first settings.

Sampling numerics lead to different performance (Q3–Q5). The results for Q3–Q5 show that sampling configurations should be treated as calibration decisions rather than fixed implementation details. For Q3, SDE sampling effects are more target- and dataset-dependent. Midpoint can improve fidelity over Euler at roughly doubled evaluation cost, whereas Euler remains a sensible default under tighter compute budgets. For Q4, the integration endpoint t_{int} controls an explicit utility–risk relationship: later stopping generally increases utility but also raises disclosure risk, with OT paths reaching higher utility earlier than VP paths. For Q5, increasing the number of integration steps improves utility most strongly under small budgets, but the gains diminish beyond the mid-range while disclosure risk can continue to increase. Together, these results support a risk-constrained configuration strategy: choose the target and path first, then tune solver, dynamics, endpoint, and step budget to meet the intended utility, fidelity, risk, and compute budget.

6.2 Practical Configuration Guidance

Figure 4 summarises how the empirical findings can guide configuration choices before any domain-specific disclosure review. The workflow separates training-time design from sampling-time calibration. Based on our results, **FM-OT** is a balanced default, **VFM** is preferable when utility is prioritised, and **SM** or **NM** can be used for more conservative settings. For SM and NM under the OT path, one can avoid starting exactly at $t = 0$ by using a small start-time clamp.

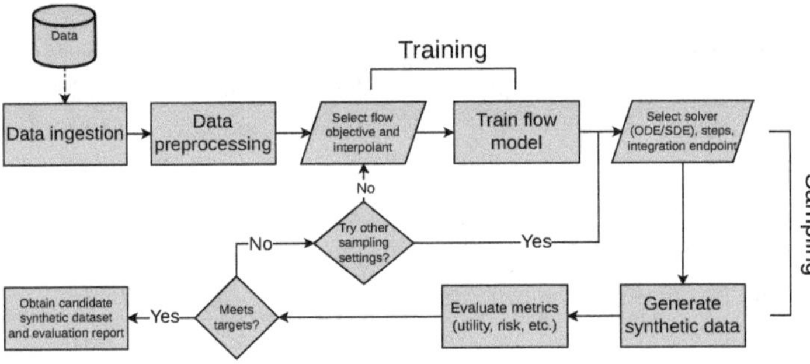

Fig. 4. Configuration workflow for latent flow tabular synthesis. A training-time design is selected first, then sampling settings such as ODE/SDE dynamics, solver, integration steps, and t_{int} are calibrated against pre-defined utility and disclosure risk constraints. The workflow produces a candidate synthetic dataset and evaluation report for subsequent domain-specific review.

After training, sampling choices changes the performance results under a fixed compute budget. Euler is the simplest default and uses one model evaluation per step, while Midpoint can improve fidelity at higher evaluation cost. SDE sampling often improves shape and trend errors in our aggregate results, but should be used only when the resulting disclosure risk remains acceptable. Integration steps and t_{int} provide additional controls over the utility and disclosure risk. In practice, users first impose a disclosure risk constraint, then select the most useful and faithful configuration within that constraint. Acceptable values of disclosure risk are therefore domain-dependent and should be treated as release-context constraints rather than universal safety thresholds.

7 Concluding Remarks

We presented a controlled empirical study of latent-space tabular flow models, showing that theoretically related learning targets and sampling dynamics can lead to different empirical behaviour under finite-step budgets. The utility–risk relationship is primarily governed by target and path choice: VFM-VP is a utility-first configuration, FM-OT provides a strong high-utility default with lower disclosure risk than VFM, and lower-risk regimes are generally obtained by accepting reduced utility, especially under VP-based or NM/SM configurations. Sampling choices then adjust the performance: SDE sampling, particularly Midpoint can improve fidelity at higher evaluation cost, and OT paths enable compute savings or risk-aware synthesis through early stopping. Although the effect is target- and dataset-dependent, these findings support pre-release configuration and evaluation of latent flow tabular synthesis under domain-specific utility, risk, and compute constraints.

While the study provides practical configuration guidance, we also acknowledge several limitations. First, we set the VAE architecture to isolate the impact of flow dynamics as fixed. Second, utility–risk trajectories are dataset-dependent, so practitioners should perform target-domain validation before any release decision. Third, we restrict the analysis to fixed-step numerical solvers. Future work should evaluate broader architectures, adaptive ODE/SDE integrators, additional tabular domains, and mixed-effect modelling on the evaluation for more comprehensive insights.

Acknowledgments. B.I. Nasution is supported by the Indonesia Endowment Fund for Education (LPDP) scholarship. B.I. Nasution thanks Mark Elliot and Richard Allmendinger for their supervision and valuable feedback on this work.

Disclosure of Interests. The author declares that there are no competing interests.

LLM Usage Statement. During the preparation of this manuscript, the author used large language models (LLMs) primarily for editing and improving the readability of the text. All analyses and claims are entirely the author's original work and responsibility.

References

1. Akrami, H., Joshi, A.A., Li, J., Aydöre, S., Leahy, R.M.: A robust variational autoencoder using beta divergence. Knowl.-Based Syst. **238**, 107886 (2022)
2. Albergo, M.S., Boffi, N.M., Vanden-Eijnden, E.: Stochastic interpolants: a unifying framework for flows and diffusions (2023)
3. Ankan, A., Textor, J.: pgmpy: a python toolkit for Bayesian networks. J. Mach. Learn. Res. **25**(1) (2024)
4. Dao, Q., Phung, H., Nguyen, B., Tran, A.: Flow matching in latent space (2023)

5. Durkan, C., Bekasov, A., Murray, I., Papamakarios, G.: Neural spline flows. In: Proceedings of the 33rd International Conference on Neural Information Processing Systems (2019)
6. Eijkelboom, F., Bartosh, G., Naesseth, C.A., Welling, M., van de Meent, J.W.: Variational flow matching for graph generation. In: The Thirty-Eighth Annual Conference on Neural Information Processing Systems (2024)
7. Elliot, M., Little, C., Allmendinger, R.: Do samples taken from a synthetic microdata population replicate the relationship between samples taken from an original population? In: 2023 Expert Meeting on Statistical Data Confidentiality, Conference of European Statisticians (2023)
8. Guzmán-Cordero, A., Eijkelboom, F., van de Meent, J.W.: Exponential family variational flow matching for tabular data generation. In: Forty-Second International Conference on Machine Learning (2025)
9. Ho, J., Jain, A., Abbeel, P.: Denoising diffusion probabilistic models. In: Proceedings of the 34th International Conference on Neural Information Processing Systems (2020)
10. Holderrieth, P., Erives, E.: An introduction to flow matching and diffusion models (2025)
11. Kotelnikov, A., Baranchuk, D., Rubachev, I., Babenko, A.: TabDDPM: modelling tabular data with diffusion models. In: Proceedings of the 40th International Conference on Machine Learning, vol. 202, pp. 17564–17579 (2023)
12. Lipman, Y., Chen, R.T.Q., Ben-Hamu, H., Nickel, M., Le, M.: Flow matching for generative modeling. In: The Eleventh International Conference on Learning Representations (2023)
13. Little, C., Allmendinger, R., Elliot, M.: Synthetic census microdata generation: a comparative study of synthesis methods examining the trade-off between disclosure risk and utility. J. Official Stat. **41**(1), 255–308 (2025)
14. Little, C., Elliot, M., Allmendinger, R.: Comparing the utility and disclosure risk of synthetic data with samples of microdata. In: Privacy in Statistical Databases: International Conference, pp. 234–249 (2022)
15. Liu, X., Gong, C., Liu, Q.: Flow straight and fast: learning to generate and transfer data with rectified flow (2022)
16. Minnesota Population Center: Integrated public use microdata series, international: Version 7.4 [dataset]. IPUMS. IPUMs Census Data, Minneapolis, MN (2023)
17. Mueller, M., Gruber, K., Fok, D.: Continuous diffusion for mixed-type tabular data. In: The Thirteenth International Conference on Learning Representations (2025)
18. Nasution, B.I., Eijkelboom, F., Elliot, M., Allmendinger, R., Naesseth, C.A.: Flow matching for tabular data synthesis. Trans. Mach. Learn. Res. (2026)
19. Patki, N., Wedge, R., Veeramachaneni, K.: The synthetic data vault. In: IEEE International Conference on Data Science and Advanced Analytics (DSAA), pp. 399–410 (2016)
20. Qian, Z., Davis, R., van der Schaar, M.: Synthcity: a benchmark framework for diverse use cases of tabular synthetic data. In: Proceedings of the 37th International Conference on Neural Information Processing Systems (2023)
21. Rombach, R., Blattmann, A., Lorenz, D., Esser, P., Ommer, B.: High-resolution image synthesis with latent diffusion models (2022)
22. Song, Y., Durkan, C., Murray, I., Ermon, S.: Maximum likelihood training of score-based diffusion models. In: Proceedings of the 35th International Conference on Neural Information Processing Systems (2021)

23. Song, Y., Ermon, S.: Generative modeling by estimating gradients of the data distribution. In: Proceedings of the 33rd International Conference on Neural Information Processing Systems (2019)
24. Taub, J., et al.: The synthetic data challenge. In: Joint UNECE/Eurostat Work Session on Statistical Data Confidentiality, October 29–31 2019, The Hague, the Netherlands (2019)
25. Villaizán-Vallelado, M., Salvatori, M., Segura, C., Arapakis, I.: Diffusion models for tabular data imputation and synthetic data generation. ACM Trans. Knowl. Discov. Data **19**(6) (2025)
26. Xu, L., Skoularidou, M., Cuesta-Infante, A., Veeramachaneni, K.: Modeling tabular data using conditional GAN. In: Advances in Neural Information Processing Systems, vol. 32 (2019)
27. Zhang, H., et al.: Mixed-type tabular data synthesis with score-based diffusion in latent space. In: The Twelfth International Conference on Learning Representations (2024)

Foundation Models and AI for Biology and Medicine

ADXpertNet: Deep Learning Approach for Capturing Local and Global Spatial Relationship Between FTIR Spectra and Component Data of Milk for Adulterant Detection

Anupama[1,2], Poonam Goyal[1(✉)], Yi-Ping Phoebe Chen[2], Aniruddha Desai[3], Shanmuga Sundar Dhanabalan[2], and Navneet Goyal[1]

[1] Birla Institute of Technology and Science, Pilani 333031, India
{p20210021,poonam,goel}@pilani.bits-pilani.ac.in

[2] La Trobe University, Bundoora, VIC 3083, Australia
{A.Anupama,Phoebe.Chen,S.Dhanabalan}@latrobe.edu.au

[3] Centre for Technology Infusion, La Trobe University, Bundoora, VIC 3083, Australia
A.Desai@latrobe.edu.au

Abstract. Milk is a vital source of essential nutrients and is widely consumed as part of a balanced diet. Its high demand has led to increasing instances of adulteration compromising quality and posing significant health risks. Although spectroscopy is widely used for quality assessment due to its accuracy, its effectiveness in adulteration detection remains limited. Spectral data often exhibit overlapping absorption bands and long-range wavelength dependencies, while component attributes such as fat, protein, etc. reflect the underlying chemical composition. Existing methods separately process either spectra or component data and thus do not exploit correlation between two modalities. To address this problem, we propose ADXpertNet, an automated unified framework that learns from both high-resolution spectral patterns and structured compositional features and then leverages their contextual relationships to enhance predictive performance. To simulate real-world instrumental variability, controlled noise is introduced into the spectral data, improving robustness by exposing the model to realistic signal fluctuations thereby enhancing generalization. Additionally, data augmentation techniques are used to increase sample diversity and class balance. Experimental results show that ADXpertNet outperforms existing benchmark and baseline models, achieving SOTA performance across both milk and other datasets. These findings highlight the effectiveness of integrating spectroscopic analysis with compositional data for milk adulteration detection, offering a promising advancement towards food safety and quality control systems.

Keywords: Adulterant Detection · Spectroscopy and Component data · Multimodal Data Fusion · Food Quality Assessment

M. Ceci et al. (Eds.): ECML PKDD 2026, LNAI 16948, pp. 457–474, 2027.
https://doi.org/10.1007/978-3-032-37679-4_26

1 Introduction

Milk and its products hold significant socioeconomic importance and are consumed by billions of people worldwide. It plays a key role in ensuring nutritional security, particularly in regions where access to high-nutrient food sources is limited. A United Nations agency, in collaboration with the Food and Agriculture Organization [8], projects global milk production to reach 1146 million tonnes by 2034, growing at a CAGR of 1.8%. Thus dairy industry contributes substantially to the global economy, supporting millions of livelihoods across the value chain. To meet high demand and increase the profit margin, milk is usually adulterated at different points of sale, compromising its quality and safety [2,15,24,25]. Common adulterants like sucrose, starch, ammonium sulphate, urea, and hydrogen peroxide are usually added to milk to increase its density, nitrogen content, or shelf life. These substances can cause severe health issues, including gastrointestinal problems, worsened diabetic conditions, and damage to organs such as the heart, liver, and kidneys [3,4,20,33].

Traditionally, wet chemical analysis or reference chemical methods such as gerber, gravimetric oven drying, colorimetry are used globally for identifying and quantifying milk components such as fat, protein, lactose, etc. in a milk sample. To ensure that milk is safe for consumption and has balanced milk constituents, it is essential to detect and other factors, viz., adulterant-free composition and other nutritional profiles, for a comprehensive quality assessment. Although wet methods are accurate and widely applicable, but they are often labor-intensive and not well suited for automation and scale. To address these limitations, dairy processors increasingly rely on data-driven approaches that utilize spectroscopy as an efficient and non-invasive analytical technique.

Fourier Transform Infrared (FTIR) spectroscopy [6] and Lactoscope [1] are commonly used in laboratories or dairy processors across countries to analyze milk composition and adulterant detection. Lactoscope use spectra and apply chemometrics techniques [13,17,21,29] such as principal component analysis (PCA) or partial least square regression (PLSR) to provide rapid analysis of milk components, supporting fair payment at the collection point. PCA and PLSR rely on linear dependencies and do not capture complex, nonlinear relationships in spectral data, potentially reducing the accuracy of prediction. Lactoscope generates component data that is typically stored in a structured format whereas a FTIR system generates spectral data for each sample, which can be represented as an image or a sequence for further processing. The plot of spectral intensities against wavenumbers does not follow a smooth or linear curve for each sample. Instead, the relationship between spectral intensity and wavenumber in milk spectra is complex and highly non-linear which is depicted by peaks, valleys, and irregular patterns. These pattern surface due to factors like chemical interactions, multiple compounds, or complex absorption behaviors in presence of adulterants. Existing methods usually explore spectra data for adulteration detection using ML or shallow neural network methods [7,22,26,31,40].

Component data captures the compositional properties of milk, which are relatively static and represent independent features that remain stable under

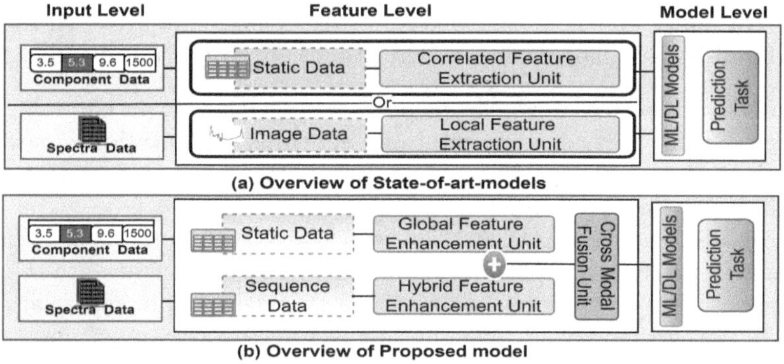

Fig. 1. (a) Approaches in previous work which process spectra data, represented as image and component data separately to train ML/DL model and focus only on correlated local features. (b) The proposed approach achieves the extraction of global relationship from milk component holding milk constituents and local and global enhanced representation from spectra data.

suitable environmental conditions. To model the implicit relationships in data, correlated features are typically extracted and used in ensemble learning models for compositional analysis. In contrast, spectra data consists of sequentially ordered features (wavenumbers) that exhibit dependencies and spatial relationships between adjacent values. Existing methods neither apply ML/DL techniques to exploit the interrelationship and combination of both spectra and component as complementary dimensions as shown in Fig. 1(a). Other predictive tasks such as shelf-life and freshness prediction etc., also require automated systems capable of capturing and processing compositional information and spectral data.

In this paper, we focus on the detection of adulterants to ensure the standard quality of milk, preserving its nutritional content and preventing harmful substances. For this, we develop a deep learning model that performs global feature learning on the component data [5,16,23] to extract a component-enhanced representation and treats spectra data as a sequential signal where both the order and spatial relationships are learned. A fusion mechanism [10,11,14,35,37] is then applied to model the contextual relationships between them. The fused representation is then passed for classification as illustrated in Fig. 1(b). We have introduced three dedicated modules for handling heterogeneous milk data sources. Firstly, a Global Feature Enhancement Unit (GFEU) to emphasize the most relevant milk component enhanced representation. Secondly, a Hybrid Feature Enhancement Unit (HFEU), to extract spatially localized patterns from FTIR spectral data and global feature representation of spectra data. Finally, a Cross-Modality Fusion Unit (CMFU), which integrates the outputs of both data through cross-attention to enable robust adulterant detection.

We validate the effectiveness of the proposed model on four publicly available datasets [18,22,30,34] from diverse domains, including VNIR soil spectra and milk spectra collected using multiple spectroscopic techniques such as FTIR, NIR, and mid-infrared spectroscopy. The salient contributions of our paper are:

- We provide empirical evidence demonstrating a strong latent relationship between FTIR spectral representations and milk compositional parameters through PCA-based correlation analysis, motivating the integration of both modalities for improved milk adulteration detection.
- We propose a model, ADXpertNet, which extracts both global and local enhanced representations from milk spectra and component data separately and fuses them to capture meaningful features and complex relationships between the two modalities. We offer a novel perspective on bridging the gap between the modalities by representing spectra data as sequential rather than image data.
- Our comprehensive experimentation on four publicly available datasets shows that ADXpertNet outperforms all benchmark models and baselines.

2 Related Work

Several studies apply ML/DL techniques for analyzing spectral and component data separately in the domain of milk quality assessment and adulteration detection. Early research efforts primarily focused on the use of compositional features alone to identify adulterants [12,22]. But, with advancements in spectroscopic techniques and the growing adoption of learning models, spectral data have increasingly been leveraged to analyse peak variation indicative of adulteration.

Machine Learning Approaches for Adulteration Detection: One of the non-invasive ways to estimate adulterants in milk is by using the FTIR spectra data. Chu et al. [6] have used 1060 spectral points for distinguishing the adulterant type and used 9 classification model and 13 regression models as linear and non-linear modeling algorithm such as support vector machine (SVM), multiLayer perceptron, partial least squares regression to predict the level of adulterant in milk. Colak et al. [7] developed SVM, kNN, Decision Tree, and ensemble bagged tree models using FTIR spectral data to detect adulteration when cow milk is mixed with buffalo milk. Yan et al. [36] employed an ensemble of ML models to analyze FTIR spectra for microplastics detection. Surkova et al. [32] utilize hyperspectral images of milk samples acquired using scanning confocal Raman microscopy and analyzed through multivariate methods for the quantification of milk compositional analysis. Frizzarin et al. [9] applied statistical ML techniques to predict cow milk quality traits using routinely collected spectral data. The study highlights the potential of ML to extract meaningful information from spectra for applications in the dairy industry. For performance improvement, researchers have preprocessed the spectra data using standard normal variable, and Savitzky-Golay filter [13,21,27,29], which may cause the model to lose important information for some tasks, and poor selection of parameters for these techniques can lead to over-smoothing of key spectral features.

Deep Learning Approaches for Adulteration Detection: With the advancement in data analytics and the reduction of the requirement of data preprocessing, Neto et al. [22] used a 1D CNN for both binary and multiclass classification to detect milk adulterants using spectra. The model captures localized spectral features such as peaks and valleys through convolutional filters. Rahul et al. [19] used 20% of the publicly available samples from [22] to construct hybrid DL models, where a two-layer 1D CNN extracted local features that were then processed by RNN, and combined with a softmax-based meta learner to train on edge devices and provide real-time milk quality analysis. Ribeiro et al. [26] work focus on the quantification of lactose in milk using FTIR spectral image to train the CNN model and filter the characteristics of the spectrum. CNNs are effective at detecting local patterns, they are well-suited for analyzing spectral data. Said et al. [27] employed a semi-supervised DL model using a miniaturized MEMS spectrometer for cow milk analysis, targeting fat measurement and water adulteration detection. The model integrates unlabeled and labeled data within a multi-task framework, using an autoencoder to enhance feature learning and improve generalization across diverse samples and instrument variations. Zhang et al. [38] introduce a temporal convolutional explorer to analyze and interpret the learning behavior of 1D CNNs in time series classification, particularly from the perspective of the frequency domain. The tool helps understand how 1D-CNNs capture temporal patterns in sequential data.

Initial investigations into ML approaches demonstrated computational efficiency but limited capacity to capture spatial dependencies within spectral data. In contrast, DL models, particularly CNNs, effectively learn localized spectral patterns for classifying milk adulteration. On the other hand, RNNs, which are designed for sequential data, are not effective for FTIR spectra. However, to date, no comprehensive studies are performed in the context of FTIR data that incorporates both spectral and compositional features. Also, the correlation between these features as shown in Fig. 2, is mostly neglected. Thus, we focus on both the inter and intra relationships between different sources of information. To the best of our knowledge, no previous work has investigated the building of a model on the composition of components and spectra data together for the detection of adulterants in milk.

3 Relationship Between Spectra Variability and Milk Compositional Features

To investigate the relationship between milk compositional parameters and FTIR spectra data, a pearson correlation analysis is conducted between 12 standardized compositional features and the first four principal components (PCA1PCA4) derived from the spectral domain (see Fig. 2). The results revealed that PCA2 exhibited the highest positive correlation with Solids, followed by strong associations with Lactose, Fat, and Freezing Point, indicating these components predominantly influence the variance captured by the principal component. PCA3 showed moderate correlations with Protein, Lactose, FrzPoint, SNF, and Casein, suggesting their partial contribution to the spectral variance.

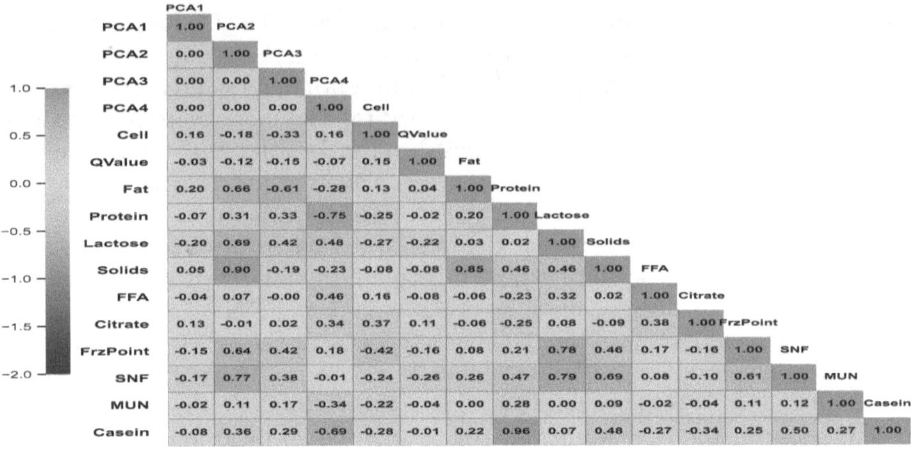

Fig. 2. A correlation heatmap illustrating the association between the first four principal components extracted from FTIR spectral data arranged in descending order of variance and the compositional features of milk. The heatmap highlights the extent to which spectral variability aligns with compositional attributes, providing insights into underlying biochemical relationships.

Further, notable inter-feature correlations were observed, particularly between Protein and Casein, as well as Fat and Solids, reflecting known biochemical dependencies. Apart from above, there can be a non-linear relationship, which may not be fully captured by Pearson correlation alone. These observations demonstrate that the correlation between the principal components of FTIR spectra data and compositional features indicates a strong latent relationship between two modalities, suggesting that spectral variations are closely linked to the underlying biochemical composition of milk.

4 Problem Definition

The objective of adulteration detection is to learn a complex function ψ that maps input space $X_1 \in \mathbb{R}^{d_1}$ and $X_2 \in \mathbb{R}^{d_2}$ to the target space Y_i, where d_1 and d_2 denote the dimentionality of respective inputs. Using various learning techniques, the model derives the target representation by leveraging both component-based and spectra-enhanced features. To facilitate this, the function ψ is decomposed into three components: f_1 and f_2, which capture global and local feature representations, respectively, and f_3, which performs the multimodal fusion. The final model learns a composite function $\psi : (f_1, f_2, f_3) \rightarrow Y_i$ that performs classification to determine whether milk contains an adulterant and, if present, predicts the specific type of adulterant by utilizing multimodal representations.

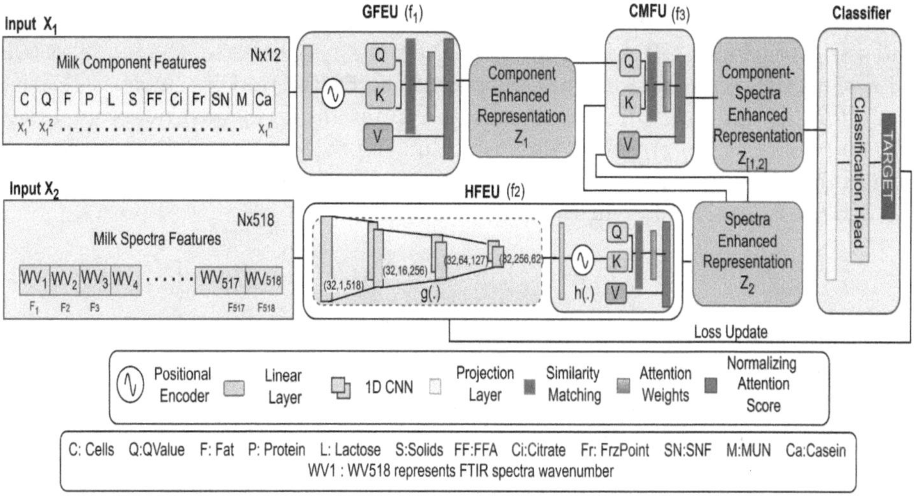

Fig. 3. ADXpertNet is a multimodal deep learning model that integrates component (X_1) and spectra (X_2) data for adulterant detection. Component features are enhanced using Global Feature Enhancement Unit, while spectral data are processed through a Hybrid Feature Enhancement Unit. The fused representations are passed via Cross-Modal Fusion Unit and then passed to the classifier to predict the adulterant class.

5 Methodology

We propose a classification model, ADXpertNet, which learns to differentiate milk adulteration types leveraging both component and spectral features. The high dimensionality of the spectral region necessitates effective feature extraction; therefore, an attention mechanisms is employed to learn feature importance. The attended representations from both modalities are then fused and passed through fully connected layers to predict the adulteration class. Given an input X_1 and X_2, the predicted class is obtained by feeding the input to the model and retrieving the output through a complex function ψ. In this case, $f_1 : X_1 \rightarrow Z_1 \in \mathbb{R}^{d_1}$ captures the global enhanced features from component data. And $f_2 : X_2 \rightarrow Z_2 \in \mathbb{R}^{d_2}$ that captures localized feature followed by attention which highlights relationship between spectra data and then $f_3 : Z_{[1,2]} \rightarrow Z \in \mathbb{R}^{[d_1,d_2]}$ used to extract the relationship between f_1 and f_2. Finally a classifier $Class : Z \rightarrow Y \in \mathbb{R}^{|C|}$ that assign projected features to their corresponding classes, where C denotes the set of classes. Figure 3 illustrates the proposed model which has three modules: Global Feature Enhancement Unit (GFEU); Hybrid Feature Enhancement Unit (HFEU); Cross-modal Fusion Unit (CMFU) and a classification head for downstream task.

Global Feature Enhancement Unit (GFEU): It leverages a self-attention mechanism to enhance feature representation to learn milk composition or nutrient profile and reduce reliance on redundant or irrelevant features. When multi-head self-attention (MHSA) is applied to the reference features, the model learns and assigns attention weights to the specific attributes that are most indicative of adulterant. This module transforms the input data X_1 into query (Q), key (K), and value (V) representations using linear projections to 64 dimensions to learn embedding and provide an expressive and context-aware representation. The MHSA is given below in Eq. 1

$$Z_1 = f_1(X_1) = \text{MHSA}(X_1) \tag{1}$$

where $\text{Attention}(Q, K, V) = \text{softmax}\left(\frac{QK^T}{\sqrt{d_k}}\right)V$. The outputs of all heads are concatenated and linearly projected to obtain the final representation Z_1. In the self-attention setting, the query, key, and value matrices are derived from the same input component features.

Hybrid Feature Enhancement Unit (HFEU): This unit enhances spectral representations by combining CNN-based local feature extraction with self-attention to capture local and highlight dependencies across wavenumbers. A three-layer 1D CNN encoder with 16, 64, and 256 filters (kernel sizes 8, 4, and 4) processes the input spectra, with each convolution layer followed by batch normalization, ReLU activation, and dropout (0.3) to extract local spectral patterns such as peaks and valleys. The extracted features are then passed to a multi-head self-attention layer (4 heads), where attention scores dynamically emphasize the most discriminative wavenumber regions associated with adulterants, such as specific IR absorption bands affected by substances like starch, peroxide, or bicarbonate. By modeling positional dependencies between spectral peaks, the mechanism captures subtle spectral variations across wavenumbers, producing an enhanced representation for subsequent classification layers. This is represented as :

$$Z_2 = f_2(X_2) = h(g(X_2)) \tag{2}$$

The hybrid spectral feature extractor applies two sequential transformations to the spectral input X_2 as defined in Eq. 2. First, an intermediate spectral representation $H = g(X_2)$ is obtained, which captures localized patterns from the spectra. This intermediate representation $g(\cdot)$ is then processed by a attention mechanism $h(\cdot)$ to capture broader relationships among the extracted spectral features, producing the final spectral representation Z_2.

Cross-Modality Fusion Unit (CMFU): To enhance the interaction between global and local spectral representations, a cross-attention mechanism is employed in CMFU on enhanced representation of X_1 and X_2 using Eq. 3. In this module, the component-spectra enhanced features are obtained where the query (Q) comes from one modality and the key (K) and value (V) come from another.

This enables the model to align and fuse complementary information, and allows the model to ask questions about one modality using the context of the other, e.g., "Which part of the spectra is most relevant for this set of component values?". It also helps in modeling interactions across modalities, especially in the case of adulterant detection, where some adulterants cause spectral changes that depend on concentration changes in specific components. Here it is used as:

$$Z_{[1,2]} = f_3(X_1, X_2) = \text{CrossAttention}(f_1(X_1), f_2(X_2)) \quad (3)$$

Classifier: The resulting fused representation $Z_{[1,2]}$, which captures both local and global interactions is concatenated. This combined vector is then passed through a fully connected network consisting of two dense layers. The first layer contains 128 neurons activated by ReLU, enabling the model to learn complex nonlinear relationships. The final output layer uses softmax activation and contains neurons corresponding to the classification task, either two for binary classification or six for multiclass adulterant detection. The model is capable of distinguishing among five adulterants, such as sucrose, starch, formaldehyde, peroxide, and bicarbonate, and classifying them effectively. To ensure that the predictor correctly classifies the classes from f_3, we used cross-entropy as our loss function L_f^y (defined in Eq. 4).

$$L_f^y = -[f_y log \hat{f}_y + (1 - f_y) log(1 - \hat{f}_y)] \quad (4)$$

where f_y and $\hat{f}_y$ are the true and predicted labels, respectively.

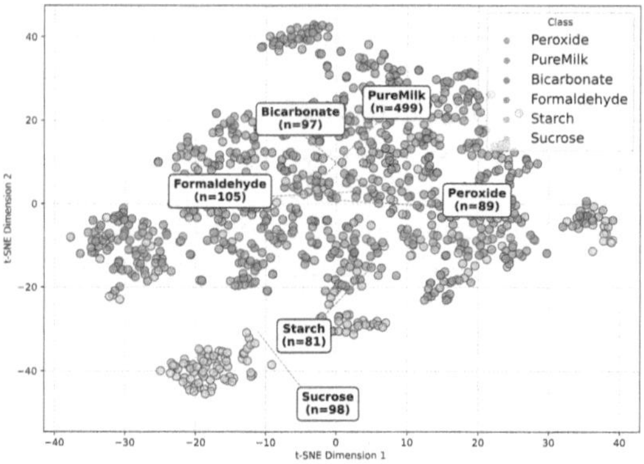

Fig. 4. FTIR milk dataset representing the class distribution of each adulterant, where pure milk samples are comparatively higher than the spiked samples

6 Experimental Setup and Baselines

Experimental Setup: All experiments with baselines and ADXpertNet are conducted on Intel® Core™ i7-6700 CPU @ 3.40 GHz × 8, 32 GB RAM desktop. The implementations is done using Pytorch 2.6.0 and Cuda 12.4 on Ubuntu 20.04. The computation of performance metrics are acquired using Scikit-learn library.

Dataset: We use an open-source milk FTIR dataset [22], which consists of 910 data points as presented in Fig. 4 with the distribution of raw milk and spiked samples. The first 12 columns of the dataset represent the milk constituents as component data. Each data point is considered as a row, and 518 spectral features from the 13th column of the dataset represent structured information about the milk in wavenumbers ranging from 3000 to 1000 per centimeter.

To demonstrate the robustness and generalization capability of the proposed model, experiments are also conducted on three other publicly available datasets [18,30,34] from different application domains. These datasets contain spectral as well as compositional or physicochemical information and are used to evaluate the model beyond the milk adulteration detection task (Refer to Appendix A of the supplementary material for dataset details. It is hosted on GitHub and Zenodo, and can be accessed through the links provided below).

Data Augmentation: In dairy applications, obtaining large numbers of adulterated milk samples is challenging, often leading to class imbalance. To address this, we apply SMOTE (Synthetic Minority Over-sampling Technique) to generate synthetic samples for underrepresented classes and balance the dataset. For each minority sample, SMOTE selects its five nearest neighbors and creates synthetic instances by interpolating between the sample and one of its neighbors. As illustrated in Fig. 4 using a two-dimensional t-SNE visualization of spectral features, SMOTE mitigates bias toward the majority class (PureMilk). After applying SMOTE, each class was balanced to 349 samples, resulting in a total of 2,094 training samples. Since the original training set contained 678 samples, 1,416 new synthetic samples were generated to balance the minority classes.

Noise Injection for Model Robustness: To improve model robustness and generalization, we apply two types of noise such as Gaussian noise and random spectral shift with peak broadening [28,39]. Gaussian noise sampled from a normal distribution with zero mean and a standard deviation of 0.01, is added to the spectra to simulate measurement noise commonly observed in spectroscopic instruments. This is applied with a different probability in the range of 0.25–0.60. To further account for wavelength misalignment and spectral variations, a random spectral shift was introduced by circularly shifting the spectra by ± 3 spectral points. After shifting, peak broadening is simulated using a moving average convolution kernel with a randomly selected size of 3 or 5. This transformation is also applied with a probability of 0.25, 0.5, and 0.60. Together, these noise injections introduce realistic spectral variations, enabling the model to learn noise-invariant and shift-tolerant representations, thereby improving robustness and generalization to unseen data.

Baseline Models: As our method is the first to integrate the learning of component and spectra data, there are no baselines available for direct comparison for fusion. Thus, we implement a range of baseline ML and DL models including Naive Bayes, Decision Tree, Logistic Regression, and Support Vector Machine (SVM) with both linear and RBF kernels. In addition, XGBoost is employed for gradient-boosting classification. The hyperparameters for all models were optimized using Bayesian optimization via the Optuna framework. We developed two additional models by integrating the CNN backbone with sequential units, namely LSTM and GRU, while keeping the convolutional architecture identical to the baseline CNN. To capture long-range dependencies in spectral data, two stacked LSTM layers were added after the CNN feature extractor, followed by dropout regularization; in the CNNGRU variant, the LSTM layers were replaced with GRU layers while keeping other hyperparameters unchanged. Compared with prior CNN designs in [19,22], our architecture adopts a different layer of convolutional structure and dense layers without pooling to enable richer hierarchical feature learning.

Training: We perform a two-step stratified split of the dataset into training set (70%), validation set (15%) and test set (15%). This ensures that the model is trained on sufficient data while still being evaluated on independent validation and test sets. During training, a cross-entropy loss function is minimized using an optimizer. The training loop iterates over 100 epochs, with a batch size of 32, performing forward propagation, computing loss, and updating weights through backpropagation. Model performance is evaluated on the validation set after each epoch tracking loss and accuracy. When the accuracy surpasses the previously recorded best accuracy, our model's parameters are saved to save the best-performing model and are retained for future use. For evaluation, classification performance is reported using overall accuracy and class-wise accuracy, while additional metrics such as F1-score, precision, and recall are provided (see Appendix B of supplementary material). For the regression task, performance is evaluated using the root mean square error (RMSE). All metrics are computed using macro-averaging methods to ensure fair interpretation of the model's classification across all adulterant types.

7 Results

Comparative Analysis for Binary Classification: In this set of experiments, we compare ADXpertNet with baselines and existing results for binary classification whether adulterant is present or not. The results presented in

Table 1. Performance comparison of AdXpertNet with six ML models and four CNN-based models including one state-of-the-art for binary class classification for FTIR dataset. The best results are shown in bold. NA - Not Available

Model Type	Accuracy	Class-wise Accuracy	
		Adulterated	UnAdulterated
ML Baseline Models on Composite Data			
Naive Bayes	65.34 ± 0.03	78.17 ± 0.05	53.20 ± 0.08
Decision Tree	87.40 ± 0.03	86.34 ± 0.04	88.40 ± 0.05
Logistic Regression	97.05 ± 0.01	96.90 ± 0.02	97.20 ± 0.01
SVM (Linear)	97.60 ± 0.01	98.03 ± 0.01	97.20 ± 0.02
SVM (RBF)	96.37 ± 0.01	97.61 ± 0.02	95.20 ± 0.02
XGBoost	95.68 ± 0.02	96.20 ± 0.03	95.20 ± 0.02
DL Baseline Models on Composite Data			
CNN	97.52 ± 0.01	97.87 ± 0.02	97.16 ± 0.01
CNN + LSTM	96.44 ± 0.01	97.39 ± 0.02	95.45 ± 0.01
CNN + GRU	96.65 ± 0.01	97.41 ± 0.02	95.87 ± 0.01
State of art Model trained only on spectra data			
Neto et al. [22]	97.94	NA	NA
ADXpertNet	**99.32** ± **0.01**	**100** ± **0.02**	**98.67** ± **0.01**

Table 1 demonstrate that ADXpertNet achieves the best overall performance, with an accuracy of 99.32%, outperforming all baseline ML and DL models across different performance metrics such as accuracy and class-wise accuracy. Unlike traditional ML models such as Naive Bayes, Decision Tree, Logistic Regression, SVM-RBF, and XGBoost, and DL baselines like CNN, our model consistently delivers superior performance across multiple runs. Among the traditional ML methods, the linear SVM achieved an accuracy of 97.6%, followed closely by logistic regression with 97.05% accuracy. Decision Tree and Naive Bayes performed comparatively lower with accuracies of 87.4% and 65.34%, respectively. Deep learning models demonstrated slightly higher predictive capability, with CNN achieving 97.52% accuracy, CNNGRU achieving 96.65%, and CNNLSTM achieving 96.44%. Furthermore, it surpasses previously reported state-of-the-art model by Neto et al. [22], establishing a new benchmark in adulterant detection with a lesser amount of data available in the public domain.

Comparative Analysis for Multiclass Classification: We also compare ADXpertNet with all baselines and existing models for multiclass classification where we treat each type of adulterant as class. The results in Table 2 establish the effectiveness of ADXpertNet, achieving the highest overall accuracy of 97.26% and demonstrating robust performance across all six adulterant classes. Naive Bayes exhibited a significant drop in accuracy to 28.7%, indi-

Table 2. Performance comparison of AdXpertNet with six ML models and five CNN-based models including two state-of-the-art for multiclass classification on FTIR dataset. The best results are shown in bold. NA - Not Available.

Model Type	Accuracy	Class-wise Accuracy					
		Peroxide	Formaldehyde	Bicarbonate	UnAdulterated	Starch	Sucrose
ML Baseline Models on Composite Data							
Naive Bayes	28.70 ± 0.03	46.92 ± 0.18	21.88 ± 0.18	49.33 ± 0.14	6.13 ± 0.03	77.50 ± 0.12	73.33 ± 0.11
Decision Tree	77.26 ± 0.03	56.92 ± 0.15	61.88 ± 0.10	80.67 ± 0.11	83.07 ± 0.04	66.67 ± 0.09	87.33 ± 0.06
Logistic Regression	92.47 ± 0.01	82.31 ± 0.13	94.37 ± 0.05	100.00 ± 0.00	93.87 ± 0.02	84.17 ± 0.11	91.33 ± 0.07
SVM (Linear)	95.21 ± 0.02	83.85 ± 0.10	96.88 ± 0.04	100.00 ± 0.00	96.27 ± 0.02	91.67 ± 0.08	96.00 ± 0.04
SVM (RBF)	86.10 ± 0.02	62.31 ± 0.11	75.62 ± 0.11	96.00 ± 0.04	93.07 ± 0.03	74.17 ± 0.10	82.67 ± 0.10
XGBoost	89.18 ± 0.02	63.85 ± 0.14	79.37 ± 0.09	92.67 ± 0.05	95.33 ± 0.03	86.67 ± 0.06	89.33 ± 0.06
DL Baseline Models on Composite Data							
CNN	95.21 ± 0.01	84.62 ± 0.07	87.50 ± 0.06	100.00 ± 0.04	98.67 ± 0.01	91.67 ± 0.05	93.33 ± 0.04
CNN + LSTM	95.89 ± 0.01	84.62 ± 0.08	87.50 ± 0.07	100.00 ± 0.01	98.67 ± 0.01	91.67 ± 0.04	100.00 ± 0.03
CNN + GRU	96.26 ± 0.01	92.31 ± 0.05	93.75 ± 0.07	100.00 ± 0.01	97.67 ± 0.01	91.67 ± 0.04	100.00 ± 0.04
State of art Models trained only on spectra data							
Neto et al. [22]	96.08	97.56	93.02	89.58	98.44	90.24	96.36
Rahul et al. [19]	96.68	98.77	97.75	95.15	94.20	96.15	98.09
ADXpertNet	**97.26 ± 0.02**	**84.62 ± 0.08**	**100.00 ± 0.09**	**100.00 ± 0.03**	**100.00 ± 0.02**	**91.67 ± 0.03**	**93.33 ± 0.05**

cating its limitation in handling complex multiclass spectral patterns. Decision Tree improved moderately with an accuracy of 77.26%, while SVM with a linear kernel maintained strong performance with 95.21% accuracy. Logistic regression and XGBoost achieved accuracies of 92.47% and 89.18%, respectively. Among the deep learning models, CNN achieved 95.21% accuracy, while CNNLSTM and CNNGRU achieved slightly higher accuracies of 95.89% and 96.26% respectively. It also outperforms existing state-of-the-art models, including Neto et al. [22] and Rahul et al. [19], setting a new standard for multiclass adulteration detection.

Table 3. Model performance under different noise injection probabilities for two noise types. A checkmark (✓) indicates the applied noise type.

Exp.	Probability	Gaussian	RandomShift	Accuracy	F1-score	Precision	Recall
1	0.00			97.26	96.24	97.15	95.82
2	0.25	✓		97.26	96.07	96.54	95.82
3	0.50	✓		97.26	95.73	95.73	95.82
4	0.60	✓		97.26	96.15	95.98	95.82
5	0.25		✓	95.89	93.85	94.22	93.67
6	0.50		✓	95.21	92.72	92.88	92.63
7	0.60		✓	96.58	94.30	95.26	93.62
8	0.25	✓	✓	96.58	94.07	95.15	93.65
9	0.50	✓	✓	95.89	93.08	94.23	92.33
10	0.60	✓	✓	96.58	94.37	93.72	95.61

Table 4. Performance on additional benchmark datasets are evaluated using RMSE for comparison of AdXpertNet for multiclass classification with State-of-art-models (SOTA). Lower values indicate better performance.

Dataset	SOTA	ADXpertNet
Trop. Soil VNIR [34]	27.32	**21.32**
Milk MIR [18]	1.57	**1.09**
Milk NIR [30]	0.18	**0.09**

Table 5. Ablation study of AdXpert-Net for multiclass classification: only on component data (GFEU), only on spectra data (HFEU) and on full dataset where CNN is removed from HFEU (HFEU-CNN)

Model Variant	Acc. (%)
GFEU	85.62
HFEU	95.21
HFEU-CNN	91.10

- **Performance analysis with noisy data:** We added Gaussian noise and random spectral shift in spectra with different probabilities separately and together as shown in Table 3 to test the performance of the model under noise for multiclass classification. It is clear from the table that the performance of the model is reasonably comparable to that of without noise showing model's generalization capabilities and robustness to noise.
- **Performance on other datasets:** We also evaluate the model on other publicly available datasets with a regression task to examine its applicability to other tasks such as prediction of clay content, color prediction (Chroma Meter CR400 value), fat prediction. The performance of our model and SOTA model, i.e., partial least squares regression, is presented in Table 4. The results demonstrate that ADXpertNet reduces the RMSE by 21.96%, 30.57% and 50% for Tropical Soil VNIR, Milk MIR and Milk NIR, respectively.
- **Ablation Study:** We conducted an ablation study on the multiclass adulteration detection task to assess the contribution of individual modalities and architectural components. The results are summarized in Table 5.

The effectiveness of the GFEU was first evaluated using only the compositional attributes. In this setting, the model achieved an accuracy of 85.62%, indicating that the compositional information provides useful discriminative cues for adulteration detection. However, a substantially higher accuracy of 95.21% was obtained when the HFEU was applied to the spectral data (only), highlighting the superior discriminative capability of spectral signatures. To further investigate the contribution of local feature learning within HFEU, we removed the 1D-CNN component while retaining the remaining architecture. This modification resulted in a noticeable decrease in accuracy of 4.11%. The performance degradation demonstrates that the 1D-CNN plays a critical role in capturing local spectral patterns and wavenumber dependencies, that are not fully represented by the attention mechanism.

Overall, the ablation results confirm that both modalities contribute complementary information for adulteration detection, while the HFEU serves as a key component for learning discriminative spectral features. In particular, the inclusion of the 1D-CNN significantly enhances the model's ability to capture fine-grained local spectral characteristics, leading to improved classification performance. These findings validate the design choice of ADXpertNet in effectively exploiting both global and local feature representations.

8 Conclusion

We propose ADXpertNet, a novel multimodal learning approach for the detection of adulterants in milk. Existing work does not exploit the relationship between different data sources. Our model leverages both component and spectra data, using feature learning techniques for enhanced feature representation. In addition, it integrates two different modalities, revealing insights into the relative relationship with the final classification decisions. Our result show that the model maintains comparable performance under different levels of noise, indicating strong robustness and good generalization capability within FTIR dataset. Various performance metrics such as macro average accuracy and individual class accuracy show that our model significantly outperforms all competitive models. Our approach outperforms the ML and DL baselines by at least 1.72% and 1.80% on composite data and the benchmark model by 1.38% for binary class classification. Our model also shows superior performance on state-of-the-art models by 1.18% and ML and DL baseline models by at least 2.05% and 1%, respectively. The standard deviation (maximum of 0.09) of our model also demonstrates that the proposed model exhibits consistent performance across multiple runs. This can be attributed to the proposed local and global feature learning and the effective fusion strategy of the model. To overcome data scarcity, we applied the SMOTE method for data augmentation on each class and increased the samples by almost two thousand to smoothly work with DL models. We plan to tackle multitask learning using both modalities, facilitating more robust adulteration detection on a larger variety of adulterations as future work.

Supplementary Materials. The source code, data and material are available at: https://github.com/AnupamaBITS/ADXpertNet and also available at https://doi.org/10.5281/zenodo.20593970.

Acknowledgment. This work is carried out in the Disruptive Technologies lab which is supported by the Department of Science and Technology (DST), Govt. of India in the form of FIST Level-1 grant to the Department of CSIS, BITS Pilani.

Disclosure of Interests. The authors have no competing interests to declare that are relevant to the content of this article.

References

1. Perkinelmer lactoscope 300 ft-ir dairy analyzer homepage (2026). https://www.perkinelmer.com/category/lactoscope-300-ft-ir-dairy-analyzer

2. Aqeel, M., Sohaib, A., Iqbal, M., Ullah, S.S.: Milk adulteration identification using hyperspectral imaging and machine learning. J. Dairy Sci. **108**(2), 1301–1314 (2025)
3. Azad, T., Ahmed, S.: Common milk adulteration and their detection techniques. Int. J. Food Contaminat. **3**(1), 22 (2016)
4. Ceniti, C., et al.: Recent advances in the determination of milk adulterants and contaminants by mid-infrared spectroscopy. Foods **12**(15), 2917 (2023)
5. Chen, Q., Zhang, Z., Chen, S., Wen, S., Ma, H., Xu, Z.: A self-attention based global feature enhancing network for semantic segmentation of large-scale urban street-level point clouds. Int. J. Appl. Earth Obs. Geoinf. **113**, 102974 (2022)
6. Chu, C., et al.: Rapid detection and quantification of melamine, urea, sucrose, water, and milk powder adulteration in pasteurized milk using fourier transform infrared (ftir) spectroscopy coupled with modern statistical machine learning algorithms. Heliyon **10**(12) (2024)
7. Colak, S., Uzunsoy, I., Narin, A., Duran, U.: Adulteration detection of cow milk in buffalo milk using fourier-transform infrared spectroscopy and artificial intelligence-based techniques. J. Food Compos. Anal. **140**, 107203 (2025)
8. Food, O.., of the United Nations, A.O.: Oecd/fao (2025), oecd-fao agricultural outlook2025–2034 (2025). https://www.oecd.org/content/dam/oecd/en/publications/reports/2025/07/oecd-fao-agricultural-outlook-2025-2034_3eb15914/601276cd-en.pdf
9. Frizzarin, M., Gormley, I.C., Berry, D., Murphy, T.B., Casa, A., Lynch, A., McParland, S.: Predicting cow milk quality traits from routinely available milk spectra using statistical machine learning methods. J. Dairy Sci. **104**(7), 7438–7447 (2021)
10. Gao, W., Zhang, Y., Akoudad, Y., Chen, J.: Mssf-net: a multimodal spectral-spatial feature fusion network for hyperspectral unmixing. IEEE Trans. Geosci. Remote Sens. (2025)
11. Goyal, P., Kaur, A., Ram, A., Goyal, N.: Efficient representation learning of satellite image time series and their fusion for spatiotemporal applications. In: Proceedings of the AAAI Conference on Artificial Intelligence, vol. 38, pp. 8436–8444 (2024)
12. Hansen, L., Ferrão, M.F.: Identification of possible milk adulteration using physicochemical data and multivariate analysis. Food Anal. Methods **11**(7), 1994–2003 (2018)
13. Julmohammad, N., Tan, E.: Atr-ftir with chemometrics tools for classification and prediction of hydrogen peroxide in liquid milk. J. Food Compos. Anal. **140**, 107223 (2025)
14. Kaur, A., Goyal, P., Goyal, N.: Lsfusenet: dual-fusion of landsat-8 and sentinel-2 multispectral time series for permutation invariant applications. In: 2023 IEEE 10th International Conference on Data Science and Advanced Analytics (DSAA), pp. 1–10. IEEE (2023)
15. Khomane, V., Kamble, D., Lokhande, A., Patil, B., Lashkare, S., Kubade, K., Khobragade, S.: A comprehensive review on adulteration of milk. Int. J. Adv. Biochem. Res. **8**(4S), 316–324 (2024)
16. Lee, K.H., Chen, X., Hua, G., Hu, H., He, X.: Stacked cross attention for image-text matching. In: Proceedings of the European Conference on Computer Vision (ECCV), pp. 201–216 (2018)
17. Liang, Q., et al.: Detection of water adulteration levels in milk using near-infrared spectroscopy combined with chemometrics. J. Dairy Sci. **108**(7), 6852–6866 (2025)

18. McDermott, A., Visentin, G., McParland, S., Berry, D., Fenelon, M., De Marchi, M.: Effectiveness of mid-infrared spectroscopy to predict the color of bovine milk and the relationship between milk color and traditional milk quality traits. J. Dairy Sci. **99**(5), 3267–3273 (2016)
19. Mhapsekar, R.U., O'Shea, N., Davy, S., Abraham, L.: Hybrid blended deep learning approach for milk quality analysis. IEEE Trans. Emerg. Topics Comput. Intell. **8**(3), 2253–2268 (2024)
20. Musa, M.A., Yang, S.: Detection and quantification of cow milk adulteration using portable near-infrared spectroscopy combined with chemometrics. Afr. J. Agric. Res. **17**(2), 198–207 (2021)
21. do Nascimento Pereira, H.J., dos Santos Pereira, E.V., Ferreira, J.L.A., Ramalho, R.T.E., de Sousa Fernandes, D.D., Diniz, P.H.G.D.: A miniaturized nir-based approach for quantifying fat content and cow milk adulteration in goat milk. Spectrochimica Acta Part A: Molec. Biomolec. Spectrosc. **340**, 126341 (2025)
22. Neto, H.A., Tavares, W.L., Ribeiro, D.C., Alves, R.C., Fonseca, L.M., Campos, S.V.: On the utilization of deep and ensemble learning to detect milk adulteration. BioData Mining **12**(1), 13 (2019)
23. Pan, X., et al.: On the integration of self-attention and convolution. In: Proceedings of the IEEE/CVF Conference on Computer Vision and Pattern Recognition, pp. 815–825 (2022)
24. Patil, G., Wani, S., Bafna, P., Bagul, V., Kalaskar, M., Mutha, R.: Milk adulteration: from detection to health impact. Food Humanit **3**, 100339 (2024)
25. Rachah, A., et al.: Exploring dry-film ftir spectroscopy to characterize milk composition and subclinical ketosis throughout a cow's lactation. Foods **10**(9), 2033 (2021)
26. Ribeiro, D.C., et al.: Determination of the lactose content in low-lactose milk using fourier-transform infrared spectroscopy (ftir) and convolutional neural network. Heliyon **9**(1) (2023)
27. Said, M., Wahba, A., Khalil, D.: Semi-supervised deep learning framework for milk analysis using nir spectrometers. Chemom. Intell. Lab. Syst. **228**, 104619 (2022)
28. Sáiz-Abajo, M., Mevik, B.H., Segtnan, V., Næs, T.: Ensemble methods and data augmentation by noise addition applied to the analysis of spectroscopic data. Anal. Chim. Acta **533**(2), 147–159 (2005)
29. Saji, R., Ramani, A., Gandhi, K., Seth, R., Sharma, R.: Application of ftir spectroscopy in dairy products: a systematic review. Food Human. **2**, 100239 (2024)
30. Sikiru, Y., Aernouts, B., Erkinbaev, C.: Conditional generation of near-infrared spectra using a transformer-based gan for spectral data augmentation in milk composition. Food Control 112042 (2026)
31. Sowmya, N., Ponnusamy, V.: Development of spectroscopic sensor system for an iot application of adulteration identification on milk using machine learning. IEEE Access **9**, 53979–53995 (2021)
32. Surkova, A., Bogomolov, A.: Analysis of milk microstructure using raman hyperspectral imaging. Molecules **28**(6), 2770 (2023)
33. Hebling e Tavares, J.P., da Silva Medeiros, M.L., Barbin, D.F.: Near-infrared techniques for fraud detection in dairy products: a review. J. Food Sci. **87**(5), 1943–1960 (2022)
34. Tavares, T.R., et al.: Multi-sensor approach for tropical soil fertility analysis: comparison of individual and combined performance of vnir, xrf, and libs spectroscopies. Agronomy **11**(6), 1028 (2021)

35. Wei, X., Zhang, T., Li, Y., Zhang, Y., Wu, F.: Multi-modality cross attention network for image and sentence matching. In: Proceedings of the IEEE/CVF Conference on Computer Vision and Pattern Recognition, pp. 10941–10950 (2020)
36. Yan, X., Cao, Z., Murphy, A., Qiao, Y.: An ensemble machine learning method for microplastics identification with ftir spectrum. J. Environ. Chem. Eng. **10**(4), 108130 (2022)
37. Zhang, J., et al.: Multimodal data imputation and fusion for trustworthy fault diagnosis of mechanical systems. Eng. Appl. Artif. Intell. **150**, 110663 (2025)
38. Zhang, J., Feng, L., He, Y., Wu, Y., Dong, Y.: Temporal convolutional explorer helps understand 1d-cnn's learning behavior in time series classification from frequency domain. In: Proceedings of the 32nd ACM International Conference on Information and Knowledge Management, pp. 3351–3360 (2023)
39. Zhang, X., et al.: Application of spectral small-sample data combined with a method of spectral data augmentation fusion (sda-fusion) in cancer diagnosis. Chemom. Intell. Lab. Syst. **231**, 104681 (2022)
40. Zheng, J., Zhou, H., Liu, X., Lyu, Y., Yang, Z., Ge, Z.: Subspace deep learning of independent component regression model for ensemble spectroscopic calibration. IEEE Sens. J., (2025)

Are Tabular Foundation Models Robust to Realistic Query Distribution Shifts in Microbiome Data?

Giulia Perciballi[1(✉)], Ahmad Fall[1], Federica Granese[2], Jean-Daniel Zucker[1,3], and Edi Prifti[1,3]

[1] IRD, Sorbonne Université, Unité de Modélisation Mathématique et Informatique des Systèmes Complexes (UMMISCO), Paris, France
{giulia.perciballi,ahmad.fall,jean-daniel.zucker,edi.prifti}@ird.fr
[2] Inria, CNRS, I3S, Université Côte d'Azur, Valbonne, France
federica.granese@inria.fr
[3] INSERM, Nutrition et Obésités; Approches Systémiques, NutriOmique, AP-HP, Hôpital Pitié-Salpêtrière, Paris, France

Abstract. Tabular foundation models (TFMs) achieve strong performance on microbiome abundance data, yet their robustness under realistic distribution shift remains poorly characterized. We introduce a benchmark that evaluates the robustness of TFMs to biologically inspired perturbations across six gut microbiome datasets spanning four disease contexts. In this in-context learning setting, models receive unperturbed support sets as context and are evaluated on perturbed query samples. To isolate robustness beyond "shortcut" features, we preserve the most discriminative taxa and apply three controlled perturbation strategies: (i) removal of high-abundance (uninformative) taxa, (ii) sparsification via increased zero-inflation, and (iii) zero-imputation via spurious non-zero injections. Our results show that protecting discriminative features is insufficient to guarantee stability under support-query shift: across datasets, all perturbations degrade models' performances, with zero-imputation consistently the most harmful, indicating that corrupting global feature structure can break generalization even when key taxa are retained. Sparsification disproportionately affects TFMs relative to a classical random-forest baseline, suggesting greater sensitivity to zero-inflationtype shifts. We provide the code publicly available at https://github.com/UMMISCO/metagenomics-fm/.

Keywords: tabular foundation models · robustness · metagenomics · zero-inflation · distribution shift · query-time perturbations

1 Introduction

The human microbiome, meaning the collection of microorganisms residing in and on the human body, plays a key role in influencing, directly or indirectly, a broad range of physiological processes in both health and disease.

M. Ceci et al. (Eds.): ECML PKDD 2026, LNAI 16948, pp. 475–493, 2027.
https://doi.org/10.1007/978-3-032-37679-4_27

Consequently, microbiome datasets have become an important testing ground for machine learning methods in biomedical applications. Microbiome studies characterize microbial communities by profiling the relative abundance of taxa across samples, producing matrices in which rows correspond to samples and columns to taxa (i.e., features). Compared to standard tabular data, microbiome data exhibit two distinctive structural properties: *compositionality*, since features represent relative abundances that sum to a constant, and pronounced *zero-inflation*, as many taxa are unobserved in a given sample due to biological absence or limited sequencing depth [2]. In addition, substantial variability arises across cohorts due to differences in populations, sequencing protocols, and preprocessing pipelines.

Particularly, in this work, we focus on the gut microbiome, which has been associated with a wide range of systemic diseases, including type 2 diabetes, obesity, inflammatory bowel disease, and liver cirrhosis, and it is known to be particularly diverse compared to other body sites, and its composition varies considerably among healthy individuals [21]. These sources of variability make such datasets a challenging setting for machine learning models, particularly when models trained or conditioned on one cohort are applied to samples drawn from different populations or experimental conditions [2].

Tabular foundation models (TFMs) have emerged as a powerful alternative to classical machine learning approaches in low-data regimes, such as those encountered in microbiome data. These models leverage in-context learning (ICL): at inference time, a labeled support set is provided as context, and predictions are generated in a single forward pass without parameter updates. Because ICL relies on similarity between support and query examples rather than parameter updates, its effectiveness may be particularly sensitive to distributional mismatch between the contextual examples and the query sample. Despite their strong performance on standard tabular benchmarks [8], it is unclear if they are well-suited to the compositional and sparse structure of microbiome data. To investigate this issue, we provide the following contributions:

1. We present an evaluation protocol tailored to TFMs based on *query distribution shift*, in which the support set remains unperturbed while perturbations are applied only to query samples. This design isolates the robustness of in-context learning under supportquery mismatch (cf. Sect. 3.2).
2. We develop three biologically inspired perturbation algorithms to modify key structural properties of microbiome abundance data, namely compositionality and zero-inflation, while preserving informative features. This design isolates model robustness to distributional shifts without removing the underlying predictive signal (cf. Sect. 3.1).
3. Through extensive experiments on six gut microbiome datasets and six state-of-the-art TFMs, we analyze how different forms of distributional perturbations affect tabular foundation models compared to classical baselines, revealing distinct robustness patterns across perturbation types (cf. Sect. 5).

1.1 Related Works

Traditional machine learning models such as XGBoost [3], Random Forests [1] and multi-layer perceptrons have long dominated tabular data classification, but they require task-specific training and rely heavily on hyperparameters and encoded inductive biases. To better capture the complex patterns in tabular data, recent approaches have reframed tabular prediction as a table completion problem, where missing entries are predicted from observed ones. From this perspective, TabPFN [10] was introduced as the first foundation model for tabular data, leveraging ICL to classify new examples directly from prompts without gradient-based fine-tuning. Building on TabPFN, several models have extended this paradigm to larger datasets and higher-dimensional feature spaces. TabICL [20] uses a factorized transformer with column-wise and row-wise attention to scale ICL efficiently. TabDPT [14] combines retrieval-augmented transformers with Flash Attention to handle real-world tabular datasets without dataset-specific tuning. ContextTab [22] incorporates semantic embeddings of column names to leverage feature meanings in large-scale tables. These models demonstrate how the table-completion framing enables transformer-based foundation models to generalize across diverse tabular tasks while avoiding per-task retraining. Several extensions have been built on this idea. TabPFN-Wide [12] and TabFLEX [24] apply ICL to wider and more complex tables, while newer versions of TabICL and TabPFN (Sect. 4.1) further improve efficiency and feature coverage through factorized transformer architectures and optimized prompts. Among domain-specific applications, the authors in [18] have, instead of modifying the architecture of TabPFN, adapted the prior of PFN models to generate metagenomic-like synthetic data.

2 Preliminaries

2.1 Microbiome Abundance Data

Microbiome abundance data is represented as a matrix (a taxonomic abundance table) $\mathbf{X} \in \mathbb{R}^{n \times d}$, where rows represent samples, columns represent taxa (i.e., the features from a machine learning perspective), and each entry $\mathbf{X}_{ij}$ denotes the abundance of taxon j in sample i. This data type exhibits two structural properties that distinguish it from generic tabular data [2]:

1. **Compositionality**. In taxonomic abundance tables, the individual components of a sample sum to a constant, and consequently, the features lie on a simplex, which means increasing the abundance of one taxon necessarily decreases the relative contribution of others. Formally, $\mathbf{X}$ is a compositional set if and only if $\forall i \in \{1, \dots, n\}$ the vector row $\mathbf{x}_i$ of $\mathbf{X}$ is in the simplex

$$\mathcal{C}^d = \left\{ \mathbf{x}_i \in \mathbb{R}^d \ : \ \forall j, x_{ij} > 0; \sum_{j=1}^{d} x_{ij} = \kappa \right\},$$

where $\kappa > 0$ is a constant, generally 1.

2. **Sparsity**. Taxonomic abundance tables have a high percentage of zero values, implying right-skewed distributions with considerable point mass at zero (*zero-inflation*). Notably, zeros should be treated with caution, as they may result either from the biological heterogeneity of microbial communities, in which many organisms are detected in only a few samples, or from technical limitations that prevent the detection of some low-abundance taxa.

The two above properties directly motivate the algorithms in Sect. 3.1. Compositionality implies that locally perturbing one component, i.e., a taxon, directly impacts all other components of the sample, motivating our Algorithm 1) and Algorithm 3). The zero-inflation structure makes models sensitive to perturbations that alter the zero/non-zero pattern of the samples, motivating our Algorithm 2).

2.2 Tabular Foundation Models

TFMs are a new class of neural networks tailored for tabular data. Their outstanding performance stems from performing predictions via *ICL*: at inference time, a labeled *support set* $\mathcal{S}$ is provided as context, and the model produces predictions for unseen *query samples* $\mathcal{Q}$ in a single forward pass, without any parameter updates. TFMs are based on the Prior-Data Fitted Networks (PFNs) framework [16], in which a transformer is pre-trained on synthetic datasets sampled from a prior over tasks. This process meta-learns an approximation to Bayesian posterior predictive inference, allowing the model to generalize to new tasks at test time, provided the target distribution is consistent with the pretraining prior.

TFMs have shown strong performance across a wide range of use cases. However, their robustness on microbiome abundance data remains poorly understood. While a previous work [18] explored adapting the prior distribution of TabPFN [10] to this data type, it did not systematically analyze the failure modes of TFMs in this domain. Furthermore, that work preceded the recent proliferation of TFMs, and more capable models are now available. This motivates our systematic robustness evaluation of TFMs on microbiome data.

2.3 TFM Pretraining

The pretraining regime fundamentally shapes TFMs' behavior at inference time. TabPFN and TabICL are both pretrained on synthetic datasets sampled from a structured prior over tasks, and consequently carry no implicit prior over real feature distributions. However, TabICL introduces a column-wise Set Transformer that is explicitly distribution-aware with respect to the support set. ConTextTab and TabDPT, on the contrary, utilize large-scale pretraining on real-world data, T4 [6] and OpenML [23] datasets, respectively. As a result, they develop priors over realistic data distributions.

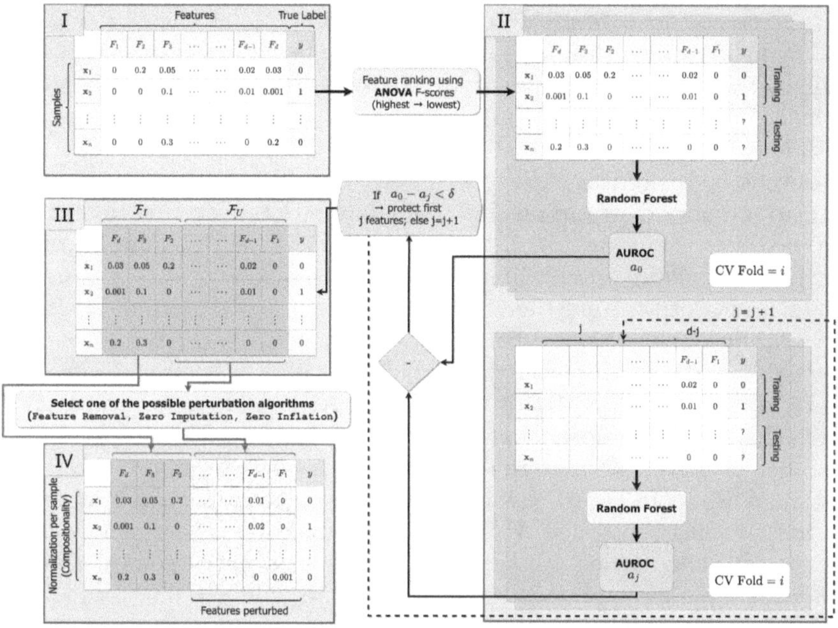

Fig. 1. Perturbation pipeline – Starting from the raw taxonomic abundance matrix $\mathbf{X}$, informative features $\mathcal{F}_I$ are identified via ANOVA F-test and Random Forest and protected from perturbation. One of three perturbation algorithms is then applied exclusively to the uninformative features $\mathcal{F}_U$. The perturbed matrix $\mathbf{X}'$ is finally reconstructed by concatenating $\mathcal{F}'_U$ with the original $\mathcal{F}_I$, followed by row-wise renormalization to preserve the compositional constraint.

3 Method

This section describes the proposed framework to assess the robustness of TFMs on microbiome abundance data. We first introduce our biologically inspired perturbation strategies, and then we describe the evaluation protocol. Additional details on the experimental parameters are provided in Sect. 4.1.

3.1 Perturbation Pipeline

The goal of the perturbation pipeline (cf. Fig. 1) is to design a framework introducing controlled distribution shifts targeting the two structural properties of microbiome data: compositionality and sparsity (i.e., zero-inflation). In what follows, we will call $\mathbf{X}'$ the taxonomic abundance matrix after perturbations. Notably, in our algorithms, we require that $\mathbf{X}'$ remains compositional. We relegate in Section A.2 (of supplementary materials) the pseudocode of the proposed perturbation algorithms. We provide the mean abundance distributions of individual features across increasing perturbation levels, stratified by class in Fig. 5 (of supplementary materials).

***Informative* vs. *uninformative* feature selection.** To avoid trivial failure modes, we first distinguish *informative* from *uninformative* features. Specifically, we define a feature as *informative* if it contributes significantly to the predictive performance of a model on the task of interest. We note that features deemed important by a machine learning model may not coincide with those considered relevant by a domain expert. However, since our goal is to assess model robustness to query distribution shift, we adopt a data-driven notion of feature importance. Perturbing highly discriminative taxa would trivially degrade performance and therefore provide limited insight into robustness under distribution shift. Our perturbations are therefore applied exclusively to uninformative features, isolating robustness beyond reliance on shortcuts.

Let $\mathbf{y} \in \mathcal{Y}^n$ denote the vector of target labels for the task of interest. We first rank features by importance via one-way ANOVA F-tests, which provides a model-agnostic ordering without requiring a secondary learner. To determine the number of truly informative features in a dataset, we apply the following procedure. A Random Forest classifier is trained on the full dataset under cross-validation, yielding a baseline AUROC a_0. We then iteratively remove the top-ranked feature and recompute the AUROC a_j after each removal step j. As long as $a_{j-1} - a_j < \delta$ (i.e., the drop is below threshold $\delta = 0.03$), the removed feature is considered informative. The process stops at the first step $j^\star$ where the drop exceeds δ, and we define $\mathcal{F}_I = \{1, \ldots, j^\star\}$ as the set of informative features and $\mathcal{F}_U = \{j^\star + 1, \ldots, d\}$ as the uninformative ones. Indeed, microbiome abundance data are known for their high heterogeneity across datasets [2]. Fixing the number of informative features a priori (e.g., always retaining the top-5 ranked features) would introduce evaluation bias: performance differences across datasets could then reflect the arbitrary choice of cutoff rather than true differences in model robustness (cf. Figure 6 of supplementary materials). By keeping $\mathcal{F}_I$ fixed, perturbations target only uninformative features, ensuring that performance differences reflect the model's sensitivity to distributional shift rather than loss of essential signal.

Perturbations Algorithms. Given the set $\mathcal{F}_U$ and the taxonomic abundance matrix $\mathbf{X}$, we consider the following perturbation strategies.

Feature Removal *(Algorithm 1.)* It evaluates model robustness to changes in feature availability, a common reason of variability in microbiome data, where differences in sequencing protocols can result in certain taxa being observed in some samples but absent in others [5]. We remove the k uninformative features with the highest mean abundance across samples. This creates a challenging scenario because, although uninformative for classification, high-abundance taxa contribute substantially to the data's compositional structure. The renormalization of the rows after removal of such taxa systematically inflates the relative abundances of the remaining ones, shifting their marginal distributions and altering the global compositional structure. This perturbation strategy most directly stresses the compositional structure of microbiome data.

Zero Inflation *(Algorithm 2.)* It directly targets the zero-inflation structure of microbiome data, simulating the variability in sparsity patterns that arises from technical differences in how microbiome samples are processed and sequenced. Given a target sparsity level $\rho^\star$, we compute the number of zeros k to introduce into $\mathcal{F}_U$ as $k = \min\{\rho^\star - \rho, \phi_U\}$, where ρ is the current number of zeros, ϕ_U is the number of non-zero entries available in $\mathcal{F}_U$. We then apply power transformation

$$\tilde{x}_{ij} = (x_{ij})^{1+\gamma} \cdot \mathbb{1}\left[(x_{ij})^{1+\gamma} \geq \tau \right], \qquad j \in \mathcal{F}_U, \tag{1}$$

where $\gamma > 0$ controls the degree of shrinkage and $\tau = 10^{-6}$ is a fixed detection threshold. Equation (1) preferentially suppresses low-abundance taxa while preserving the relative ordering among dominant features. To reach the target zero count k, we exploit the fact that larger values of γ produce more aggressive shrinkage and therefore more zeros. We search for the γ that minimizes $|\rho'_U - k|$ via binary search, where ρ'_U counts the newly introduced zeros at each iteration. The best iterate is retained if exact convergence is not achieved within T iterations. After transformation, rows are renormalized to restore compositionality, inflating the relative abundances of the remaining taxa and altering the global compositional structure. This perturbation, therefore, jointly tests robustness to increased zero-inflation and to compositional redistribution.

Zero Imputation *(Algorithm 3.)* It directly targets the zero-inflation structure of microbiome data, but in the opposite direction to `Zero Inflation`: rather than introducing new zeros, it fills existing ones. Given a target sparsity level $\rho^\star$, we compute $k = \rho - \rho^\star$, where ρ is the current number of zeros, as the number of zeros to fill, capped at $|\mathcal{Z}|$, the number of zero entries available in $\mathcal{F}_U$. We randomly select k positions from $\mathcal{Z}$ and replace each zero entry (i, j) with a value drawn uniformly from $\mathcal{V}_j$, the set of observed non-zero values of feature j across all samples. This ensures that filled values are not synthetic noise but plausible abundance levels already observed in the dataset for that taxon. If feature j has no observed non-zero values, a fallback feature is selected uniformly at random from $\mathcal{F}_U$. After filling, rows are renormalized to restore compositionality. As with the previous algorithms, this renormalization alters the global compositional structure beyond the mere injection of non-zero values, jointly analyzing robustness to reduced zero-inflation and to compositional redistribution.

3.2 Evaluation Pipeline

Query Distribution Shift. We evaluate TFMs under a setting we name *query distribution shift*: the support set $\mathcal{S}$ is always drawn from the original unperturbed data while the query set $\mathcal{Q}$ is replaced by its perturbed counterpart $\mathcal{Q}'$ obtained via the algorithms we define in Sect. 3.1. The distribution shift is therefore defined with respect to the support, and its magnitude is controlled by the parameter of the perturbations (e.g., k, $\rho^\star$, τ).

This setting differs from two related notions: adversarial attacks [7] and out-of-distribution (OOD) generalization [9]. In adversarial settings, perturbations are typically optimized to maximize model error under norm constraints and need not correspond to biologically meaningful transformations of the data. In contrast, OOD generalization studies scenarios where the test distribution differs from the distribution used to train the model. In our ICL setting, however, there is no task-specific training phase: the model receives $\mathcal{S}$ as context at inference time and must generalize to $\mathcal{Q}'$ in a single forward pass. As a result, the distribution shift arises between the support and query sets rather than between training and test distributions.

Why Perturbing only the Query. Each perturbation family is designed to approximate a distinct source of support-query mismatch that may arise in clinical microbiome datasets. `Feature Removal` captures scenarios in which features that are observed in the reference cohort are absent in the new samples, for instance, due to differences in sequencing depth, measurement procedures, or preprocessing pipelines. `Zero Inflation` models an increase in zero-inflation at query time, reflecting settings where query samples contain fewer observable taxa or where the measurement process produces sparser observations. `Zero Imputation` represents the opposite situation, where features absent in the support set become observable in the query, which may occur when models are applied across cohorts with higher measurement sensitivity or processed with different protocols. In all three cases, the informative features $\mathcal{F}_I$ are preserved, ensuring that the discriminative signal underlying the task remains available, and that performance differences can be attributed to the distributional mismatch rather than to the removal of task-relevant information.

4 Experiments

The proposed framework comprises 6 datasets $\times$ 6 models $\times$ 3 perturbation families $\times$ 15 perturbation levels $\times$ 5 CV folds = 8,100 evaluations in total.

4.1 Experimental Setting

Datasets. We consider publicly curated metagenomic datasets from ExperimentHub [17], which includes six cohorts with data at six taxonomic levels. We focused on the species-level taxa (microbial species relative abundance) across five cohorts: Cirrhosis (discovery: 178 samples, 83/95 control/case, 520 features; validation: 54 samples, 31/23, 394 features), Inflammatory Bowel Disease (IBD; 110 samples, 85/25, 443 features), Obesity (253 samples, 89/164, 465 features), Type 2 Diabetes in Chinese patients (T2D; 344 samples, 174/170, 572 features), and Type 2 Diabetes in European women (WT2D; 96 samples, 43/53, 381 features).

For each cohort, the task is binary classification. No preprocessing was applied to any dataset.

Perturbation Pipeline Parameter Setting. We described the selection process for informative and uninformative features in Sect. 3.1. Specifically, we perform 5-fold stratified cross-validation and set the δ threshold to $a_0 - a_j < \delta = 0.03$, meaning the AUROC degrades by at most 3 percentage points. This threshold represents a reasoned balance: a 5% degradation would suggest that a substantial biological signal has been removed, while a more stringent threshold would protect very few features, providing insufficient sensitivity to perturbations. Additional discussion is provided in Section C.1 (of supplementary materials).

Perturbation Algorithms Parameter Setting. We described the perturbation algorithms in Sect. 3.1. In particular because of the heterogeneity of microbiome datasets, we set the perturbation parameters in a data-dependent manner, anchored to the original sparsity ρ and the number of taxa d of each dataset.

Algorithm 1: the number of removed features k ranges over a grid of 10 evenly spaced values between 1 to $d/2$.

Algorithm 2: the target sparsity is varied over a grid of 5 evenly spaced values between the original sparsity ρ and 0.99 (we increase the number of zeros). The binary search runs for at most $T = 50$ iterations with $\gamma_{\min} = 0$, $\gamma_{\max} = 10$, and detection threshold $\tau = 10^{-6}$. The upper bound $\gamma_{\max} = 10$ ensures sufficient shrinkage coverage: for any relative abundance $x < 10^{-6/11} \approx 0.285$, we have $x^{11} < \tau = 10^{-6}$, so the entry is set to zero. Since microbiome abundance data are compositional and our datasets contain hundreds of taxa, the vast majority of non-zero values fall below this threshold in practice. Moreover, when the number of available non-zero entries in $\mathcal{F}_U$ is insufficient to reach the target, i.e. $\phi_U < \rho^\star - \rho$, the algorithm clips k to ϕ_U, and the resulting sparsity will be lower than $\rho^\star$. In our experiments, this situation does not arise, as all datasets contain sufficiently many non-zero entries in $\mathcal{F}_U$ relative to the perturbation targets. Finally, the algorithm terminates early once $|\rho'_U - k| \leq 1$, i.e., when the number of newly introduced zeros differs from the target by at most one entry. This condition is met well before T iterations in all our experiments, confirming that $T = 50$ acts as a reasonable upper bound on the number of iterations.

Algorithm 3: the target sparsity is varied over a grid of 5 evenly spaced values between 0.01 and ρ (we reduce the number of zeros).

TFMs. We evaluate four TFMs together with two classical machine-learning baselines: Random Forest (RF) [1] and XGBoost [3], both configured with 100 estimators, as detailed in Sect. 3.2. All methods are assessed using 5-fold stratified cross-validation to ensure that class proportions are preserved across folds. As for the TFMs, we consider the following models introduced in Sect. 1.1. TabPFN [8,10,11] (`v6.3.2`) is run with its default settings, including the 3-model ensemble and no gradient computation. TabICL [19,20] (`v2.0.1`) is also used with default parameters, with 32 estimators for ensemble predictions. TabDPT [14] (`v1.1.12`) is included as well with 8 estimators as default; this model supports up to 100 features, applying PCA-based reduction when needed. ContextTab [22] (`v1.0.1`) is used with a `context_size` of 2048 and a `bagging_factor` of 1.

5 Results

We assess model robustness using the algorithms in Sect. 3.1, which simulate distribution shifts commonly faced when deploying microbiome classifiers across cohorts, sequencing platforms, or clinical sites. Figure 2a summarizes the mean AUROC degradation across all datasets and perturbations, and Fig. 2a characterizes the tradeoff between baseline discriminative performance and robustness. Baseline AUROC values are reported in Table 2 (of supplementary materials). Throughout this section, all significance tests use the DeLong test [4] at $\alpha = 0.05$, and we denote by n_{sig} the number of model–dataset–perturbation-level combinations reaching significance. Additional results in Section C.3 (of supplementary materials).

`Feature Removal` Removing the most abundant (uninformative) features has a generally mild effect on AUROC (Fig. 2a, green bars), which is expected given the high taxonomic redundancy of microbiome profiles. The most significant results fall under IBD, where all models degrade monotonically with the number of removed features k. This suggests that the discriminative signal in IBD is spread across many taxa rather than carried by a few dominant species. *TabDPT* shows the steepest drop on IBD (−13 pp), followed by *RF* and *TabPFN*. Only *ContextTab* and *TabPFN* on Cirrhosis 2 show sensitivity to feature removal.

Interestingly, removal can also *help*. Both tree-based models improve on WT2D, with mean gains of +7.4 pp (*RF*) and +5.9 pp (*XGBoost*) across perturbation levels, reaching up to +11.0 pp and +11.6 pp, respectively, at individual levels ($p < 0.05$). This is consistent with overfitting to noisy high-abundance features that the perturbation eliminates. For *XGBoost*, this is the only significant result under feature removal across all datasets, suggesting that split-based feature selection already provides implicit regularisation. *TabDPT* shows a similar trend on datasets with more features than its fixed input capacity (d_{feat}), where removing features reduces the need to compress the input and may preserve more signal, though the gains do not reach significance. These patterns are also visible at the individual prediction level. The flip rate (Fig. 3, solid lines) rises steeply for IBD, reaching ~55% of predictions changed at maximum perturbation, whereas Cirrhosis 1 stays below 15% for all models, confirming the stability of its discriminative signal. This contrast may also be partly amplified by class balance: IBD's pronounced imbalance (85/25) implies as few as ~5 minority-class samples per test fold under 5-fold stratified CV, whereas Cirrhosis 1 is nearly balanced (83/95), yielding comparatively more stable per-fold estimates (Table 2 of supplementary materials). Overall, with respect to `Feature Removal`, the results suggest that robustness is primarily determined by the structure of the discriminative signal in each dataset rather than by model architecture.

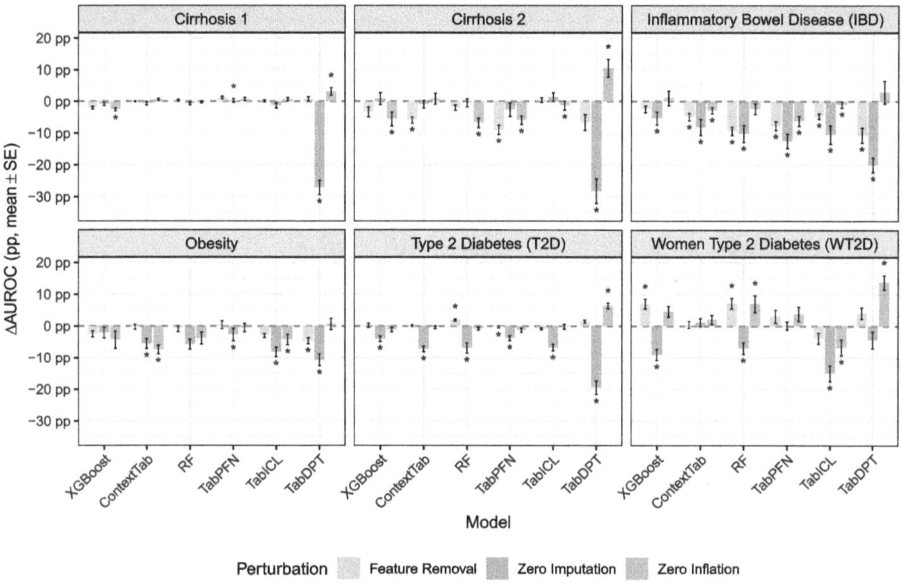

(a) **AUROC degradation under perturbation** – Mean change in AUROC (percentage points) relative to baseline for each model across datasets, grouped by perturbation. Error bars show ±1 standard error across cross-validation folds and perturbation levels. Asterisks denote model–dataset–perturbation combinations where at least one perturbation level had a statistically significant AUROC change *(DeLong test, $p < 0.05$).*

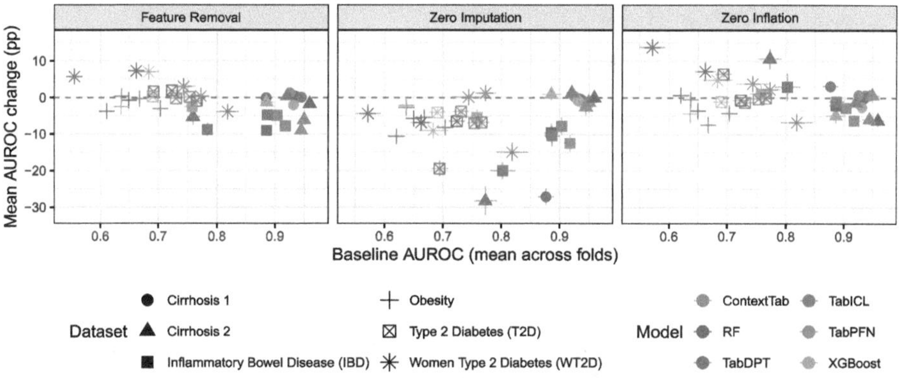

(b) **Robustness–accuracy tradeoff** – Relationship between baseline AUROC and mean AUROC change under perturbation for each model–dataset combination. Each point represents one model on one dataset. Error bars show ±1 standard error on both axes. Points near the dashed line *($y = 0$)* are robust, points in the upper-right quadrant combine high baseline accuracy with minimal degradation.

Fig. 2. Model robustness under compositional perturbations. (a) AUROC degradation by model and perturbation type. (b) Baseline accuracy versus robustness tradeoff per perturbation type.

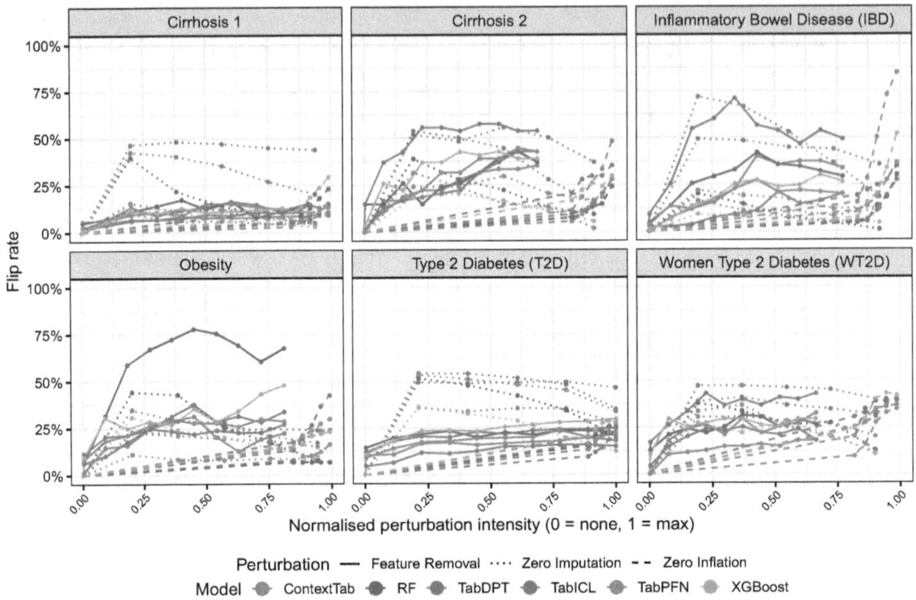

Fig. 3. Prediction flip rate under perturbation – Fraction of test samples whose predicted class changes relative to baseline as a function of normalised perturbation intensity *(0 = unperturbed, 1 = maximum perturbation)*. A higher flip rate indicates greater decision instability the model would assign a different classification to the same patient depending on data quality.

`Zero Imputation` While feature removal affects models moderately, zero imputation is far more damaging as it fills structural zeros with realistic non-zero values. No model improves under any condition; all significant results are degradations. Figure 2b (*center panel*) shows the widest vertical spread of the three perturbation types, reflecting large differences in how models respond.

TabDPT stands out with 23 significant degradations, losing up to −31.6 pp on Cirrhosis 1 and −32.1 pp on Cirrhosis 2. In the scatter plot, its points lie well below those of all other models, regardless of baseline AUROC. *TabDPT* operates as an in-context learner: at inference time, it conditions its predictions on a set of training examples (the context) passed alongside the test sample. The transformer's attention mechanism implicitly retrieves the most relevant context examples to inform its output. Because *TabDPT* was pre-trained on data with many structural zeros, this retrieval works best when test inputs are similarly sparse. Zero imputation fills those zeros with realistic non-zero values, making the test input look fundamentally different from the context examples the model relies on. The attention mechanism can no longer match the test sample to relevant training patterns, resulting in large performance drops.

TabICL is the next most affected ($n_{\text{sig}} = 16$). Its column-wise Set Transformer estimates the distribution of each feature across samples and uses these per-feature summaries to build row-level representations. As more zeros are replaced with imputed values, the observed feature distributions shift further from the true ones, and *TabICL*'s representations become increasingly unreliable, which explains why its degradation grows monotonically with the fraction of imputed values. *ContextTab* ($n_{\text{sig}} = 12$) degrades mainly on IBD, Obesity, and T2D, while *RF*, *TabPFN*, and *XGBoost* are affected more selectively.

From the dataset side, T2D is the most vulnerable cohort ($n_{\text{sig}} = 25$, all six models degrade significantly), followed by IBD ($n_{\text{sig}} = 17$). Cirrhosis 1, by contrast, yields only 6 significant degradations, all from *TabDPT*, and sits in the upper-right quadrant of the scatter plot. Its high density of informative features likely buffers against the introduction of spurious non-zero values.

Figure 3 (dotted lines) confirms how severe this perturbation is at the sample level: *TabDPT* exceeds 50% on Cirrhosis 2, and even *XGBoost*, the most stable model overall, reaches 15–25% on IBD and T2D. This shows that zero imputation affects not only aggregate metrics but also individual patient-level decisions.

This perturbation targets a central ambiguity of metagenomic data: zeros may denote true biological absence or technical dropout driven by sequencing depth or protocol differences [13]. Our results, however, indicate that the observed degradation can be primarily attributable to model-side weaknesses rather than to this biological ambiguity: RF and XGBoost remain substantially more robust under zero imputation (Fig. 2as), while TabDPT, TabICL, and ContextTab lose up to 30+ AUROC points. This asymmetry points to an architecture-specific reliance on the distributional structure of $\mathcal{F}_U$ - for instance, attention-based retrieval or per-feature distribution estimation, as the primary driver of the observed fragility - though ruling out alternative explanations entirely would require additional analyses motivated by the limitations of Zero Imputation discussed in (Sect. 7).

`Zero Inflation` This perturbation increases sparsity by replacing non-zero abundance values with zeros. *TabDPT* is the only model to improve significantly ($n_{\text{sig}} = 11$): up to +19.7 pp on WT2D, +13.6 pp on Cirrhosis 2, and +8.8 pp on T2D, while all other models degrade moderately. In the scatter plot, *TabDPT* points are the only ones consistently above the zero line, confirming that increasing sparsity moves the input towards the sparse patterns of its training input, improving retrieval quality.

Conversely, the models that were relatively resilient to zero imputation now degrade. *ContextTab* loses up to −12.1 pp on Obesity ($n_{\text{sig}} = 4$) and −11.0 pp on IBD, while *TabICL* drops up to −9.9 pp on Obesity ($n_{\text{sig}} = 3$), −11.2 pp on Cirrhosis 2, and −10.0 pp on WT2D. Despite differing architectures, both models share a key property: they have learned realistic abundance distributions during pre-training. *TabICL* does so through its column-wise Set Transformer, which builds feature-distribution-aware embeddings, *ContextTab* relies on column-name embeddings that couple feature identity with abundance patterns. Zero inflation destroys precisely these learned distributions by replacing informative values with zeros. *TabPFN*, despite sharing a dual-attention architecture with *ContextTab*, is comparatively resilient – trained exclusively on synthetic data, it carries no prior on real feature distributions. Tree-based models degrade modestly and only on specific datasets. Cirrhosis 1, as under feature removal, shows no significant degradation for any model.

Flip rates (Fig. 3, dashed lines) vary strongly across datasets. IBD reaches ∼85% for *ContextTab* at maximum perturbation, while T2D and Obesity remain below 30% for most models, likely reflecting differences in the fraction of biologically meaningful non-zero entries. This perturbation, therefore, shows a genuine fragility: models are sensitive to changes in abundance values that should carry negligible discriminative weight.

Cross-Model Shift Concordance. The results above do not reveal whether models fail on the same samples. To answer this question, we compute pairwise Spearman correlations of per-sample prediction shifts across all perturbation levels and datasets (Fig. 4). The results indicate a clear stratification. ICL-based foundation model pairs (*ContextTab–TabICL*, *ContextTab–TabPFN*, *TabICL–TabPFN*) and the *ContextTab–RF* pair show the highest concordance (median $\rho \approx 0.6$–0.85) across all three perturbation types: when one model shifts its prediction on a sample, the other shifts in the same direction. These models share failure modes at the instance level. All pairs involving *TabDPT* cluster at the bottom, with median correlations near zero and sometimes negative under zero inflation. This means *TabDPT* fails on different samples and often in the opposite direction compared to other models. Despite its fragility under zero imputation, this complementarity makes it a valuable candidate for ensemble strategies. Importantly, this concordance structure is stable across perturbations: pairs that are concordant under feature removal remain concordant under zero imputation and zero inflation. This suggests that the similarity of failure patterns reflects shared architectural priors, in particular the ICL paradigm, rather than properties of the perturbation. In practice, the ensembling potential of a model pair can therefore be assessed from a single perturbation type.

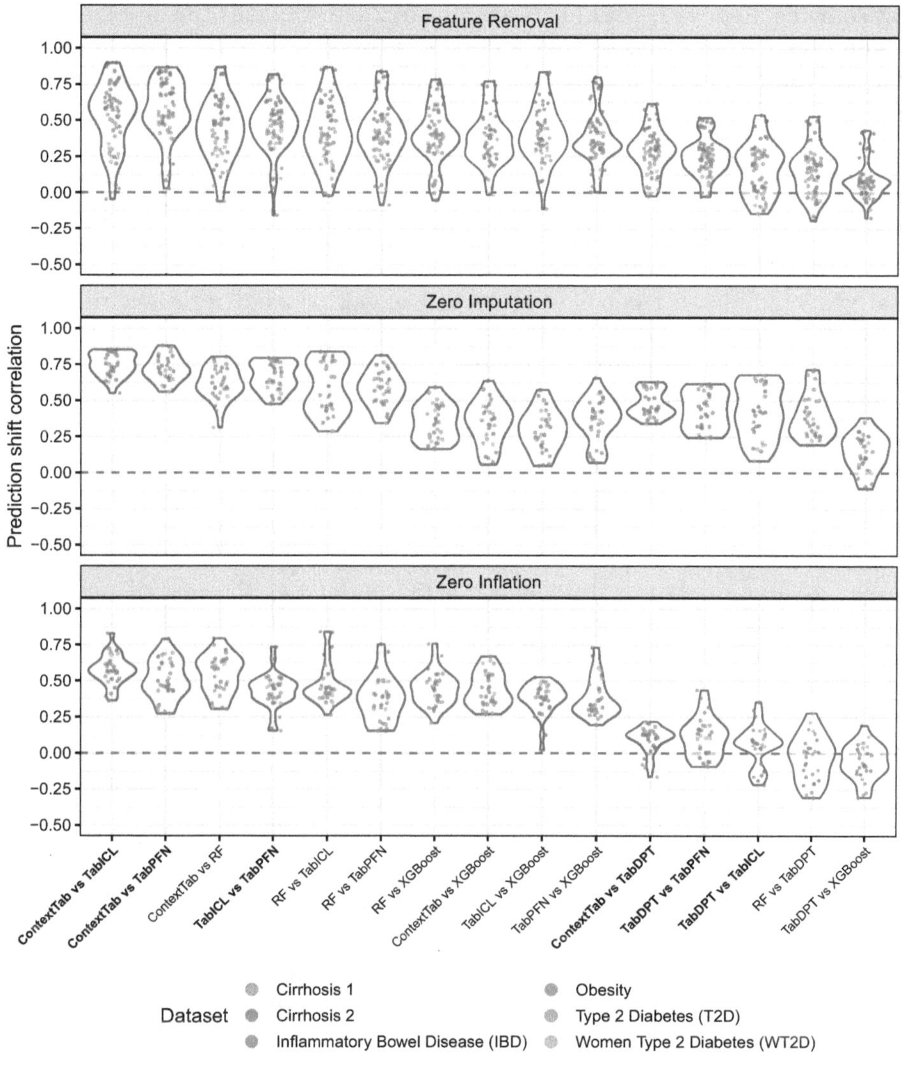

Fig. 4. Pairwise prediction shift concordance – Distribution of Spearman correlations between per-sample prediction shifts across all model pairs, faceted by perturbation type. Each point represents a dataset at a given perturbation level. High positive correlations indicate that both models are affected in the same direction on the same samples *(shared vulnerabilities)*, low or negative correlations indicate complementary failure modes, favorable for ensembling.

6 Conclusions

We proposed a framework to evaluate TFMs on microbiome data under realistic query distribution shifts. Using three biologically motivated perturbation strategies: `Feature Removal`, `Zero Inflation` and `Zero Imputation`, applied across six gut microbiome datasets and six models, we characterized how structural properties unique to microbiome data challenge in-context learners in ways that standard benchmarks do not reveal.

We report three main findings. First, **no model is robust across all perturbation types**: every model degrades significantly under at least one condition, and the pattern of vulnerabilities differs across architectures. `Zero Imputation` is consistently the most harmful perturbation, causing widespread degradation across all models and datasets, whereas `Feature Removal` has comparatively mild, dataset-dependent effects. Second, **protecting discriminative features is insufficient to guarantee stability**: even when informative taxa are fully preserved, corrupting the global compositional and sparsity structure of query samples degrades in-context learning, indicating that TFMs rely on global feature structure beyond the discriminative signal itself. Third, **there is a tradeoff between semantic richness and distributional robustness**. Models that have learned realistic abundance distributions during pre-training – such as *TabICL* and *ContextTab* – achieve stronger baseline performance but are disproportionately sensitive to zero inflation type shifts. Conversely, *TabPFN* exhibits greater robustness to sparsity perturbations at the cost of richer representational capacity. *TabDPT* occupies a complementary niche: severely vulnerable to zero imputation yet uniquely benefiting from increased sparsity, with failure modes largely uncorrelated with other models.

From a practical standpoint, dataset properties matter as much as model choice. Models on the Cirrhosis 1 dataset remain robust under all perturbations, unlike in T2D and IBD, suggesting that the density and redundancy of informative features contribute to robustness. When sparsity patterns or cohort composition may differ between training and deployment, as is common in multi-site microbiome studies, simpler models or architecturally diverse ensembles may offer better reliability than any single TFM. Our findings also raise questions about interpretability and clinical relevance, as model-based feature importance may not reflect biological function. Taxa considered uninformative by our criterion may still be clinically meaningful, while model-relied features may capture cohort artefacts rather than true biological signal.

7 Future Work

Improving Robustness. Our findings motivate several directions for future work. The most immediate is to move from characterizing fragility to mitigating it. Fine-tuning TFMs on metagenomic cohorts would align their priors with the compositional, zero-inflated structure that synthetic pretraining does not capture, while data augmentation exposing models to support-query sparsity mismatch during training, together with post-hoc calibration, offers complementary routes toward greater stability under distribution shift.

Data Representation. We evaluated models on raw relative abundances, leaving compositional transforms such as the centered log-ratio (CLR) and its robust variants unexplored [15]. Whether such transforms help or hinder TFM representations remains an open question: these models apply their own internal normalization, which an external log-ratio transform might disrupt rather than complement.

Perturbation Refinement. Zero Imputation fills structural zeros by sampling from each feature's empirical non-zero distribution. However, technical false zeros (taxa present but undetected owing to limited sequencing depth) are more plausibly located just above the detection limit; restricting sampling to the lower tail of each feature's distribution would therefore yield a more biologically faithful densification and constitutes a natural refinement of Algorithm 3.

Feature Selection Criterion. The partition into protected and perturbed features relies on ANOVA F-tests and a Random Forest wrapper, which may not capture the non-linear dependencies that foundation models exploit. A model-agnostic attribution method such as SHAP, or controlled experiments with a known ground-truth signal, would help clarify whether the measured degradation reflects genuine robustness gaps or artifacts of the importance criterion. Such analyses would also help bridge the gap between data-driven importance and biological relevance, since taxa deemed uninformative by our criterion may nonetheless be clinically meaningful.

Benchmark Extension and Biological Validation. The benchmark could also be extended with larger context sizes, alternative support-query compositions, and a broader model pool—though the Pasolli cohorts, spanning four disease contexts and six datasets of varying size, class balance, and sparsity structure, already provide a representative testbed for the biological variability of interest. Targeted biological validation—for instance, datasets with experimentally verified absent taxa—would further strengthen the cross-model evidence reported in Sect. 5 and help establish whether the sparsity patterns that TFMs rely on reflect genuine biological signal or cohort-specific artifacts.

Acknowledgment. This work was supported by a grant from the French Agence Nationale de la Recherche (ANR) for the DeepIntegrOmics project (number ANR-21-CE45-0030). This work was granted access to the HPC resources of IDRIS (Institut du dveloppement et des ressources en informatique scientifique) under the allocations 2023-AD011014580, 2024-AD011014580R1 and 2024-AD011015723R1 made by GENCI (Grand quipement National de Calcul Intensif).

References

1. Breiman, L.: Random forests. Mach. Learn. **45**(1), 5–32 (2001)
2. Busato, S., et al.: Compositionality, sparsity, spurious heterogeneity, and other data-driven challenges for machine learning algorithms within plant microbiome studies. Curr. Opin. Plant Biol. **71**, 102326 (2023)
3. Chen, T., Guestrin, C.: XGBoost: a scalable tree boosting system. In: Proceedings of the 22nd ACM SIGKDD international Conference on Knowledge Discovery and Data Mining, pp. 785–794 (2016)
4. DeLong, E.R., DeLong, D.M., Clarke-Pearson, D.L.: Comparing the areas under two or more correlated receiver operating characteristic curves: a nonparametric approach. Biometrics 837–845 (1988)
5. Forry, S.P., et al.: Variability and bias in microbiome metagenomic sequencing: an interlaboratory study comparing experimental protocols. Sci. Rep. **14**(1), 9785 (2024)
6. Gardner, J., Perdomo, J.C., Schmidt, L.: Large scale transfer learning for tabular data via language modeling. Adv. Neural. Inf. Process. Syst. **37**, 45155–45205 (2024)
7. Goodfellow, I.J., Shlens, J., Szegedy, C.: Explaining and harnessing adversarial examples. arXiv preprint arXiv:1412.6572 (2014)
8. Grinsztajn, L., et al.: TabPFN-2.5: advancing the state of the art in tabular foundation models. arXiv preprint arXiv:2511.08667 (2025)
9. Hendrycks, D., Gimpel, K.: A baseline for detecting misclassified and out-of-distribution examples in neural networks. arXiv preprint arXiv:1610.02136 (2016)
10. Hollmann, N., Müller, S., Eggensperger, K., Hutter, F.: TabPFN: a transformer that solves small tabular classification problems in a second. arXiv preprint arXiv:2207.01848 (2022)
11. Hollmann, N., et al.: Accurate predictions on small data with a tabular foundation model. Nature **637**(8045), 319–326 (2025)
12. Kolberg, C., Eggensperger, K., Pfeifer, N.: TabPFN-Wide: continued pre-training for extreme feature counts. arXiv preprint arXiv:2510.06162 (2025)
13. Kumar, B., Lorusso, E., Fosso, B., Pesole, G.: A comprehensive overview of microbiome data in the light of machine learning applications: categorization, accessibility, and future directions. Front. Microbiol. **15**, 1343572 (2024)
14. Ma, J., et al.: TabDPT: scaling tabular foundation models on real data. arXiv preprint arXiv:2410.18164 (2024)
15. Martino, C., Morton, J.T., Marotz, C.A., Thompson, L.R., Tripathi, A., Knight, R., Zengler, K.: A novel sparse compositional technique reveals microbial perturbations. MSystems **4**(1), 10–1128 (2019)
16. Müller, S., Hollmann, N., Arango, S.P., Grabocka, J., Hutter, F.: Transformers can do bayesian inference. arXiv preprint arXiv:2112.10510 (2021)
17. Pasolli, E., Schiffer, L., Manghi, P., Renson, A., Obenchain, V., Truong, D.T., Beghini, F., Malik, F., Ramos, M., Dowd, J.B., et al.: Accessible, curated metagenomic data through experimenthub. Nat. Methods **14**(11), 1023–1024 (2017)
18. Perciballi, G., Granese, F., Fall, A., Zehraoui, F., Prifti, E., Zucker, J.D.: Adapting tabPFN for zero-inflated metagenomic data. In: NeurIPS 2024 Third Table Representation Learning Workshop (2024)
19. Qu, J., HolzmÃžller, D., Varoquaux, G., Morvan, M.L.: TabICL: a tabular foundation model for in-context learning on large data. arXiv preprint arXiv:2502.05564 (2025)

20. Qu, J., Holzmüller, D., Varoquaux, G., Morvan, M.L.: TabICLV2: a better, faster, scalable, and open tabular foundation model. arXiv preprint arXiv:2602.11139 (2026)
21. Shreiner, A.B., Kao, J.Y., Young, V.B.: The gut microbiome in health and in disease. Curr. Opin. Gastroenterol. **31**(1), 69–75 (2015)
22. Spinaci, M., Polewczyk, M., Schambach, M., Thelin, S.: ConTextTab: a semantics-aware tabular in-context learner. arXiv preprint arXiv:2506.10707 (2025)
23. Vanschoren, J., Van Rijn, J.N., Bischl, B., Torgo, L.: Openml: networked science in machine learning. ACM SIGKDD Explor. Newsl. **15**(2), 49–60 (2014)
24. Zeng, Y., Dinh, T., Kang, W., Mueller, A.C.: TabFlex: scaling tabular learning to millions with linear attention. arXiv preprint arXiv:2506.05584 (2025)

Benchmarking Geometric Deep Learning for Hippocampal Shape Analysis

Ariel Iporre-Rivas[1,2,3](✉), Nico Scherf[1,2,3], Gerik Scheuermann[1,3], and Christofer Meinecke[1,3]

[1] Leipzig University, Augustuspl. 10, 04109 Leipzig, Germany
nscherf@cbs.mpg.de
[2] Max Planck Institute for Human Cognitive and Brain Sciences, Stephanstraße 1a, 04103 Leipzig, Germany
[3] Center for Scalable Data Analytics and Artificial Intelligence ScaDS.AI, Dresden/Leipzig - Humboldtstrasse 25, 04105 Leipzig, Germany
rivas@cbs.mpg.de

Abstract. Quantitative morphometry, including shape analysis, is widely used in neuroscience to study the geometry of brain structures, where anatomical differences can be subtle and difficult to detect through routine visual inspection of brain scans. For the hippocampus in particular, localized shape variations have been shown to reflect pathological pathways associated with established disease biomarkers, making hippocampal anatomy a relevant testbed for learning biologically meaningful geometric representations. Methodologically, geometric deep learning enables learning representations directly from manifolds and meshes, facilitating the construction of shape descriptors that support end-to-end learning and incorporate geometric inductive biases. However, despite this potential, the application of geometric deep learning to neuroanatomical data remains inconsistently explored in the literature. Moreover, objective comparison is challenging given the sensitivity to methodological choices such as cohort selection and preprocessing pipelines. As a result, there is a lack of systematic evaluations of geometric deep learning methods that also examine associations between learned representations and biological biomarkers. Normative modeling provides a framework that can be applied to quantitative responses while accounting for data heterogeneity, enabling subject-level inference. In this paper, we conduct a comparative study of geometric deep learning models for hippocampal shape analysis. We evaluate their performance in shape retrieval, shape classification, and metric learning tasks. Finally, using normative modeling, we investigate how coordinates in the learned shape space relate to established biomarkers, including β-amyloid burden, cognitive scores, and genetic phenotypes.

Keywords: Geometric Deep Learning · Shape Analysis · Hippocampus

M. Ceci et al. (Eds.): ECML PKDD 2026, LNAI 16948, pp. 494–511, 2027.
https://doi.org/10.1007/978-3-032-37679-4_28

1 Introduction

Brain atrophy is a well-established biomarker for Alzheimer's disease (AD). In particular, the hippocampus is one of the first affected regions, with morphological changes appearing before symptom onset. Recent work has demonstrated the applicability of CNNs for the analysis of anatomical changes associated with AD [14,39]. However, CNNs present important limitations for this task: spatial convolutions on images or volumes produce an oversimplified representation of hippocampal shape, and CNN-based models have been shown to struggle with capturing geometrically meaningful shape features without relying on precomputed shape descriptors or auxiliary biological markers [23,38]. Shape analysis can instead obtain descriptions directly from meshes through purely geometrical calculations, capturing intrinsic geometric properties invariant to isometric deformations [41]. Geometric deep learning has demonstrated state-of-the-art performance on shape representation tasks across widely used benchmarks, including ModelNet40 [53], FAUST [4], and ShapeNet [7]. Nonetheless, its application to hippocampal shape analysis remains understudied. Furthermore, existing studies have assessed clinical relevance primarily through group-level comparisons such as classification accuracy, which is insufficient to confirm whether learned representations capture biologically meaningful variation [42,51].

In this study, we conduct an extended set of evaluations of shape analysis of the hippocampus across a broad range of geometric deep learning approaches. The evaluated methods encompass the most commonly employed geometric deep learning paradigms: multi-view, point-cloud, and mesh-based convolutional neural networks. Furthermore, we extend the benchmark by investigating normative modeling on the shape space as an approach for assessing the clinical relevance of the compared methods. Specifically, we estimate a normative distribution from the healthy control population and derive individual outlier scores, which are then associated with identifiable Alzheimer biomarkers such as cognitive, β-amyloid, and genetic phenotype expressions by linear regressions. This benchmark provides the research community with a standardized evaluation and identification of strengths and weaknesses of existing geometric deep learning methods previously unexplored for hippocampus shape analysis.

In summary, our contributions are: i) A comparative study of different geometric deep learning models for shape retrieval, classification, and metric learning. ii) An assessment of the relevance of the shape space in comparison to established biomarkers such as β-amyloid levels, cognitive tests, and genetic phenotypes, using a normative modeling approach. The code is available in https://github.com/aiporre/gdl-bsa

2 Related Work

Geometric Deep Learning in Shape Analysis. Recent advances extend the idea of convolutional neural networks to handle data on non-Euclidean domains such as graphs, point-clouds, and manifolds [6]. In the field of shape analysis, these methods have already shown promising results across diverse application domains, including neuroscience [13,19], molecular science [1,2], and medical imaging [3,46]. However, despite the theoretical advances in architectures such as manifold convolutions and graph neural networks, their systematic evaluation in domain-specific tasks remains limited. Most existing studies primarily report performance on benchmark datasets with object classes that have distinct characteristics, making the problem substantially simpler than biological or medical shape analysis, where inter-class boundaries are far less pronounced. Hippocampal shape datasets present far more nuanced sources of variation, arising from individual anatomy, age-related changes, and pathological processes such as Alzheimer's disease (AD). These subtle yet critical differences make hippocampal shape analysis significantly more challenging [17,33]. This gap underscores the need for a more comprehensive framework that characterizes hippocampal shape variation across populations, which is essential for advancing our understanding of disease progression [43].

Hippocampus Shape Analysis. Shape analysis of the hippocampus opens an exceptionally informative window into the brain's function, organization, and disease. Hippocampus shape is central in the diagnosis of AD, as changes in shape precede symptom onset by many years [10,44].

Closely related to our study, [43] presents a study on the representation of the hippocampus using volumes, meshes, and point-clouds. The study considers two tasks: classification (differential diagnosis) and Healthy Controls (HC) to AD progression (prognosis), with particular emphasis on time-to-progression analysis and a rigorous cross-validation strategy. In [12], morphological features are extracted directly from hippocampal surfaces, and in [11], anatomical features are mapped onto the unfolded surface of the hippocampus, demonstrating that the underlying data representation does not lie on regular grids. This motivates the use of geometric deep learning methods, which are better suited to this structure than standard CNNs. In [28], a graph convolutional network (GCN) is applied in which nodes correspond to shape features, and edges are defined by functional distances, achieving state-of-the-art classification accuracy of 84% on the Alzheimer's Disease Neuroimaging Initiative (ADNI) dataset.

Normative Modeling and Biomarker Association Strategies. Normative modeling, or normative analysis, is used to study changes in AD biomarkers in longitudinal datasets, where Gaussian distributions are estimated from biological measurements of healthy controls [50,51]. Subsequent studies have used normative analysis to model neuroanatomical features, for example, reconstruction errors or differences from autoencoders [35,54], as well as multimodal or voxel-wise morphometry [32,48], showing associations with clinical assessments and disease stages. Nevertheless, these approaches rely predominantly on scalar summaries or voxel-wise measures rather than the shape itself. The study of correlations with biomarkers and shape descriptors derived from data-driven models remains unexplored.

3 Method

We aim to evaluate the performance of geometric deep learning (GDL) algorithms in a metric learning setting. We train each GDL model to map an input $\boldsymbol{u}_i \in \mathcal{X}$ from meshes, point-clouds, 3D masks, or multi-view sets to a shape embedding $\boldsymbol{v}_i \in \mathbb{R}^d$, defined as $\boldsymbol{v}_i = \Psi(\boldsymbol{u}_i)$. The models are optimized with metric learning losses acting on distances $d(\boldsymbol{v}_i, \boldsymbol{v}_j) \in \mathbb{R}$, such that samples with similar labels cluster together in the embedding space, while samples with different labels are pushed farther apart. An overview of the pipeline is shown in Fig. 1. In effect, we investigate whether GDL methods can effectively encode shape information into embedding vectors and whether these shape embeddings capture biologically relevant information. To this end, we consider the following evaluation tasks:

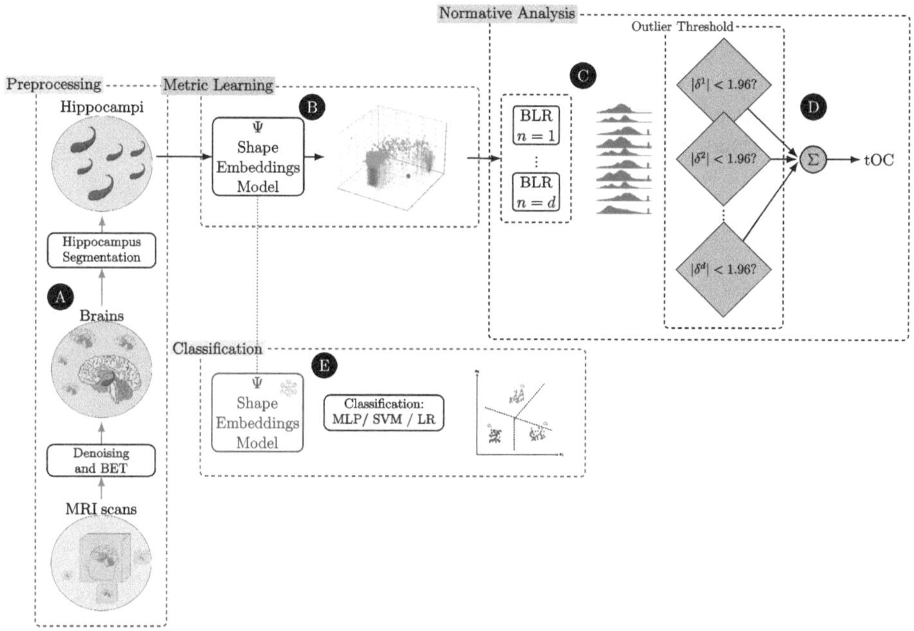

Fig. 1. Our evaluation pipeline. Each model Ψ is trained and evaluated on hippocampal data. (A) Every hippocampal sample is processed from an MRI scan. (B) The sample is transformed by the trained Ψ model into embeddings. (C) Normative models are built for each embedding dimension to compute z-scores. (D) The total outlier count (tOC) represents the number of dimensions where the sample is an outlier. (E) A classification model is trained on the frozen shape embeddings model.

1. Metric learning evaluation: train the models with a metric learning loss using diagnosis labels from the ADNI dataset.

2. Transfer learning classification: evaluate the quality of the learned embeddings in a downstream classification task.
3. Biomarker linear regression: evaluate the embeddings as biomarkers for group differences across diagnosis labels, and for regression analyses with cognitive scores, AD risk-related gene expression, and β-amyloid burden.

To quantify embedding quality, we evaluate retrieval, clustering, and downstream separability in the learned feature space. For retrieval, we report Precision@k for $k \in \{1, 4, 10\}$ to characterize local neighborhood quality. In addition, to understand the global embedding quality, we calculate the R-Precision (RP) and mean Average Precision at R ($mAP@R$), where RP summarizes the proportion of relevant samples in the query with respect to the top-R, and $mAP@R$ rewards how early in the query the relevant queries appear [31].

Finally, as a secondary analysis, we trained simple classifiers on the learned embeddings to evaluate their diagnostic separability. The embeddings were evaluated with progressively increasing complexity: Logistic Regression, Support Vector Machine (SVM), and Multilayer Perceptron (MLP) classifiers. This analysis serves as a measure of embedding quality, indicating whether diagnostically relevant information is linearly separable or requires modeling through more complex nonlinear relationships.

Datasets. For training metric learning models, we use 1854 subjects from the ADNI dataset[1] across multiple time points, using the conversion and quality-control tools provided in [40]. After preprocessing, the dataset contains 17324 hippocampal meshes, including both left and right hippocampi; however, we used only the left hippocampus. For normative modeling, we evaluate the trained models on external datasets, including 481 samples from the Australian Imaging, Biomarker & Lifestyle Flagship Study of Ageing (AIBL), 1390 samples from the Human Connectome Project Aging (HCP-Aging), and 581 samples from the IXI brain development dataset.

The dataset is stratified into five partitions, where each partition contains approximately 3500 samples and 370 subjects. Because multiple time points exist per subject, stratification is performed at the subject level to avoid data leakage; each stratification is referred to as a partition. One partition, corresponding to 20% of the data, is reserved for hyperparameter optimization (HPO). The remaining four partitions are randomly rearranged into five training setups, each consisting of one training partition, one validation partition, and two partitions for testing. This corresponds to 25% training data, 25% validation data, and 50% testing data. The preprocessing pipeline first performs skull stripping using the FSL BET tool with robust brain estimation enabled and the fractional intensity threshold reduced to 0.3 [47]. The hippocampi are then segmented using a pretrained U-Net model [20]. Registration is applied using rotational alignment only, as implemented in the hippocampus segmentation framework [20]. Finally,

[1] The ADNI dataset comes from a project launched in 2003 as a public-private partnership, led by Principal Investigator Michael W. Weiner, MD, to study the progression of Alzheimer's disease. For more information, see https://doi.org/andi.loni.usc.edu.

surface meshes are extracted using the marching cubes algorithm and resampled to 3000 vertices.

Shape Analysis Algorithms. The selection of models aims to cover representative paradigms in geometric deep learning and baseline models. The models considered in this study fall into five categories:

Meshes. Mesh-based models process signals directly on the surface by exploiting the triangular connectivity of the mesh. Convolutional kernels are defined in local neighborhoods and adapted to the intrinsic geometry of the manifold. We evaluate four representative architectures. *Mixture Model Network* (MoNet) defines learnable weighting functions modeled as Gaussian kernels in local pseudo-coordinates [29]. *Geodesic CNN* (GCNN) constructs geodesic patch operators and applies rotated kernels to approximate rotational equivariance [27]. *SplineCNN* introduces continuous B-spline kernels on manifolds, enabling efficient and flexible convolution operations [15]. Finally, *SpiralNet++* aggregates features of neighboring vertices ordered along a spiral sequence around each node, providing an efficient alternative to conventional mesh convolutions [18].

Point-Clouds. Point-cloud models represent geometry as sets of 3D coordinates without explicit connectivity. While flexible, processing unordered point sets can be computationally challenging. Deep learning approaches have significantly improved efficiency and performance in this domain. We include *PointNet* and *PointNet++* [8,36], which respectively learn global point features and hierarchical local representations. Additionally, we evaluate the *Point Transformer* [55], a more recent architecture that leverages attention mechanisms to model local geometric relationships.

Multi-view. Multi-view models represent 3D objects through collections of 2D renderings, enabling the use of well-established CNN architectures while capturing relationships between views. These models often achieve competitive performance by combining image-based learning with geometric information. We adopt the baseline *MV-CNN* architecture [49].

CNNs. We also apply a standard 3D CNN directly to a binary volumetric mask of the hippocampus, following the architecture described in [43].

Others. Finally, we include three special cases. The Spherical CNN (S2CNN) performs convolution on spherical signals using spherical harmonics. The graph convolutional network (GCN) is also a spectral approach, but based on the Laplacian of the input graph [21]. Finally, we evaluate the same GCN with higher architectural complexity: GCN-DenseNet uses skip connections to better preserve the signal in deeper layers [52,56].

Training Protocol. We first determine the architectural configuration of each model through hyperparameter optimization (HPO). The rationale for using HPO is that there is no established model architecture in the literature for hippocampal shape datasets. We use HPO to reduce bias in model architecture selection. The search space focuses on core architectural capacity controls, namely:

the number of backbone layers, dropout, batch normalization, the dimensionality of the first fully connected layer, and global pooling methods (average, max, covariance matrix, and combinations thereof). We adopt an asynchronous multi-fidelity Successive Halving Algorithm (SHA) [24] to improve computational efficiency.

We identified two limitations of the HPO procedure. First, as the search is conducted on a single reserved partition, the selected configuration may be slightly biased toward that split. Second, early stopping and pruning can discard configurations that converge more slowly when early validation signals are noisy. To mitigate these limitations while keeping the search computationally feasible, SHA is run over successive rungs of 180, 90, and 45 trials on 85% of the data, advancing only the top 20 configurations at each stage. The final configuration is then selected from these promoted candidates via cross-validation on the full reserved partition.

After this selection step, all models are trained from scratch for 200 epochs using a metric learning loss with semi-hard triplet mining, a fixed margin of 0.31, a batch size of 32, a learning rate of 1×10^{-5}, a weight decay of 5×10^{-3}, and a weighted Adam optimizer. For the base comparative experiments, the metric learning objective is the SoftTriple loss [37], hereafter referred to as *soft-loss*. For the classification transfer experiments, a classification head is appended to the frozen metric learning backbone. The normative analysis likewise operates on the same frozen metric learning representations.

The input features vary by model family. Mesh-based, point-cloud, and GCN-based models use raw vertex coordinates, encouraging the networks to learn geometric representations directly rather than relying on handcrafted or precomputed shape descriptors. For 3DMask-CNN and multi-view models, the inputs are derived from the 3D masks: CNN-Mask operates on raw voxel grids, whereas the multi-view model uses rendered images generated with Phong shading [34]. For S2CNN, we follow the original input formulation [9].

Ablation Study Design. In the literature, there are a variety of training configurations for these models. To ensure a consistent comparison, we conducted an ablation study on selected design choices, framed around three specific research questions:

Q1 (MNI vs. Subject Space): Montreal Neurological Institute (MNI) space provides standardization of the whole brain through linear and non-linear registration to a brain template, which represents the average of 152 individual brain scans. This is useful when comparing populations, as it reduces inter-subject variability. However, retaining individual variability may be important for some analyses, and there is a concern that MNI processing could remove this information. This trade-off is investigated in this study.

Q2 (Two-Label Classification): In hippocampal studies, classification tasks typically fall into two main types. The first is the prediction of conversion from mild cognitive impairment (MCI) to Alzheimer's disease (AD), where subjects initially diagnosed with MCI may progress to AD; the goal is to predict the probability of this transition. The second involves direct classification between AD and healthy controls (HC), which focuses on distinguishing AD subjects from cognitively normal individuals.

Q3 (Loss Function Selection): We consider three loss functions from metric learning: soft-loss [37], triplet loss [45], and Proxy-NCA [30]. Triplet loss defines sharp boundaries by directly comparing individual samples, whereas Proxy-NCA constructs probability-based boundaries around a finite set of proxy points. soft-loss lies between these two approaches, combining aspects of both: it incorporates sample-to-sample distances while also referencing pseudo-fixed points.

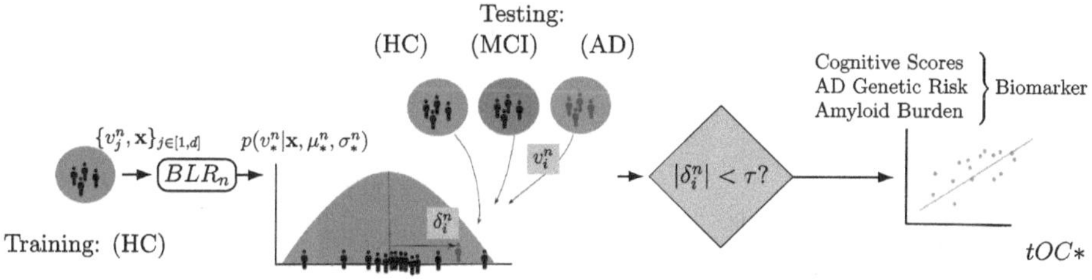

Fig. 2. Normative analysis pipeline. BLR models fitted per embedding dimension $n \in [1, d]$ estimate covariate-conditioned distributions; subject deviations are expressed as z-scores (δ_i^n) and aggregated into an outlier count (tOC_*), which is then regressed against clinical biomarkers.

Normative Modeling. A straightforward approach to assess the relevance of shape features with respect to biological markers would be to fit a regression model to group averages. However, biological measurements such as hippocampal morphometry vary substantially with age, sex, and imaging site, meaning that the underlying distribution shifts across individuals depending on these confounding factors. Consequently, a group-level model treats subjects as equivalent despite these differences. For example, an older subject near the group average volume may, in fact, have a remarkably large hippocampus for their age group, a meaningful deviation that is entirely invisible at the group level. In general, group-average models can obscure meaningful individual variability, and observed differences may reflect population heterogeneity rather than targeted biological effects [42].

Normative modeling provides a statistical framework for quantifying subject-level deviations from an expected biological distribution while accounting for known sources of variability, such as age, sex, and data acquisition site. The reference distribution is built from healthy controls across these covariate variables. Analogous to growth charts in pediatric medicine, where a child's height is only meaningful when compared within a reference sample of the same age and sex [26], normative models express each individual measurements as deviations from what is expected given their specific group characteristics.

As illustrated in Fig. 2, we apply normative modeling to each embedding dimension by fitting a Bayesian Linear Regression (BLR) model that estimates a likelihood distribution conditioned on the covariates $\boldsymbol{x}_i$ (age, sex, and site), with design features $\phi(\boldsymbol{x}) \in \mathbb{R}^K$ capturing non-linear relations [16]. The predicted response is $v_i^n \in \mathbb{R}$ for the n-th embedding dimension of the i-th subject. In this formulation, the shape descriptors are the output of the frozen shape embedding model $\boldsymbol{v} = \psi(\boldsymbol{u}) \in \mathbb{R}^d$, where $\boldsymbol{u}$ represents the neuroanatomical input.

The learned parameters on the n-th dimension $w^n \sim \mathcal{N}(0, \lambda I)$ are used to define a Gaussian predictive distribution for computing z-scores of new samples. For a subject with new covariates $\boldsymbol{x}_*$ and new shape embeddings $\boldsymbol{v}_*$, the n-th embedding dimension is given by $p(v_*^n|\boldsymbol{x}_*, w^n) = \mathcal{N}\left(v_* \mid \mu_*^n, \sigma_*^n\right)$,

where μ_*^n and σ_*^n denote the mean and standard deviation of the predictive distribution for v_*^n. The z-score δ^n is defined as

$$\delta^n = \frac{v^n - \mu_*^n}{\sigma_*^n}, \tag{1}$$

The outlier count tOC_* is computed by counting all z-scores across the d dimensions of $\boldsymbol{v}$. The outlier is considered if the deviation falls outside outside the 95% reference interval i.e. the range of $|\delta| < \tau$ with $\tau = 1.96$. For all shape descriptor coordinates:

$$\mathrm{tOC}_*(\tau) = \sum_{n=1}^{d} \mathbb{1}\left[|\delta^n| > \tau\right]. \tag{2}$$

Finally, tOC_* is used as a predictor in linear regressions for different biomarker responses $y_{\mathrm{biomarker}}$ associated with the neurological conditions as:

$$y_{\mathrm{biomarker}} = \beta_0 + \beta_1 \mathrm{tOC}_*(\tau). \tag{3}$$

Regression quality was assessed using Explained Variance (EXPV), Root Mean Squared Error (RMSE), Spearman's Rank Correlation Coefficient (Rho), Mean Standardized Log Loss (MSLL), and the Shapiro-Wilk statistic (ShapiroW).

4 Shape Embeddings Experiments

We compute the average and standard deviation of retrieval metrics using the soft-loss. The results summarized in Table 1 show that *Point Transformer* and *MoNet* provide the strongest local neighborhood structure, achieving the highest values for P@1, P@4, and P@10. In contrast, differences in mAP@R and R-Precision are comparatively small across methods, with S2CNN obtaining the best overall scores for these metrics. This pattern suggests that the main differences between models arise in the quality of the nearest neighbors rather than in the broader recovery of relevant samples within the top-R ranking. Overall, transformer-based and anisotropic convolutional models appear particularly effective for highly local diagnosis-aware shape retrieval, whereas spherical representations yield the most balanced performance across the full relevant set.

The relatively larger spread observed in P@k compared with the narrower range of mAP@R and R-Precision further indicates that improvements across architectures are concentrated within the first few retrieved neighbors. In other words, some models learn embeddings that provide stronger local compactness, while global class separation across the embedding space remains relatively similar across methods.

Table 1. Retrieval metrics soft-loss (SoftTriplet loss, mean ± std %). In bold back for **first** and bold blue for **second** best values.

Method	P@1	P@4	P@10	mAP@R	RP
GCNN	48.87±0.85	46.54±1.10	45.38±1.17	20.46±1.54	42.07±1.23
MoNet	**63.37±1.42**	**54.66±0.86**	**49.91±0.92**	21.09±1.61	42.66±1.47
Spiral++	44.53±0.95	43.41±1.04	43.37±1.07	20.61±1.56	42.54±1.34
SplineCNN	52.88±0.97	49.32±0.70	47.20±1.03	21.20±1.59	42.86±1.36
GCN	50.52±0.69	47.45±1.06	46.01±1.11	20.59±1.58	42.08±1.37
GCN-DenseNet	47.08±1.56	45.91±1.19	45.14±1.37	21.07±1.77	42.95±1.44
PointNet	43.06±1.97	43.22±1.36	43.03±1.30	20.53±1.55	42.59±1.42
PointNet++	53.56±1.47	48.97±1.19	46.92±1.06	21.33±1.38	43.56±1.12
PointTrans	**63.09±1.52**	**54.48±1.15**	**50.26±1.04**	21.56±1.57	43.21±1.31
MVCNN	44.20±1.38	43.60±0.36	43.56±0.50	20.68±0.42	42.84±0.44
3DMask-CNN	46.53±1.40	45.84±1.25	45.30±1.17	**21.57±1.66**	**43.71±1.39**
S2CNN	56.09±0.92	51.17±0.54	48.48±0.68	**21.75±1.46**	**43.72±1.21**

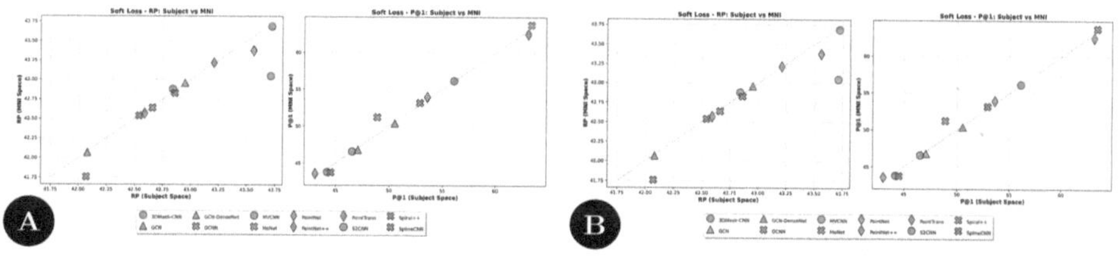

Fig. 3. Evaluation of models trained with SoftTriplet loss (soft-loss) in MNI versus subject space. Performance is measured using P@1 (A) and RP (B).

MNI and subject space show very similar performance as shown in Fig. 3. This similarity is observed both in the local clustering metric (P@1) and the global metric (RP). Some models slightly favor MNI space in terms of RP, while others show better local performance in subject space. This suggests that local embeddings may benefit from remaining in subject space, whereas global variability may be better captured after normalization to MNI space. However, these differences are minimal overall, and the spatial normalization does not play a major role in the performance of most models. Notably, MNI becomes relevant for some types of models that rely on global structures, such as spherical CNN or 3DMask-CNN, while mesh-based models perform consistently well regardless of the space.

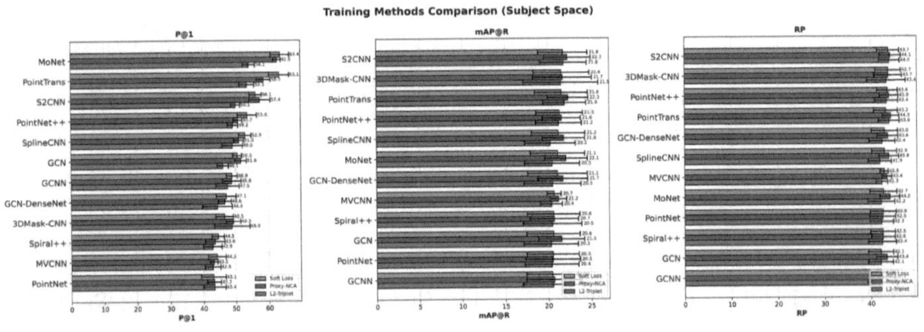

Fig. 4. Performance comparison of models trained with soft-loss, Proxy-NCA, and triplet loss. Results are reported using P@1, mAP@R and RP.

Figure 4 compares different metric learning losses. Overall, the ranking of models is broadly consistent with the main experiment using soft loss. For local geometry, as measured by P@1, MoNet and Point Transformer achieve the strongest performance, indicating better preservation of local shape relationships in the embedding space. In contrast, in the global retrieval setting, the ranking changes slightly, with Spherical CNNs moving from third to first position, and this pattern remains stable across the three evaluated losses. For local geometry, we observe that consistently, soft-loss and Proxy-NCA perform better than triplet loss, whereas in the global setting, there is no clear winner. The gap between the mAP@R and RP indicates that relevant samples are often retrieved within the top-R set, but their internal ranking remains suboptimal.

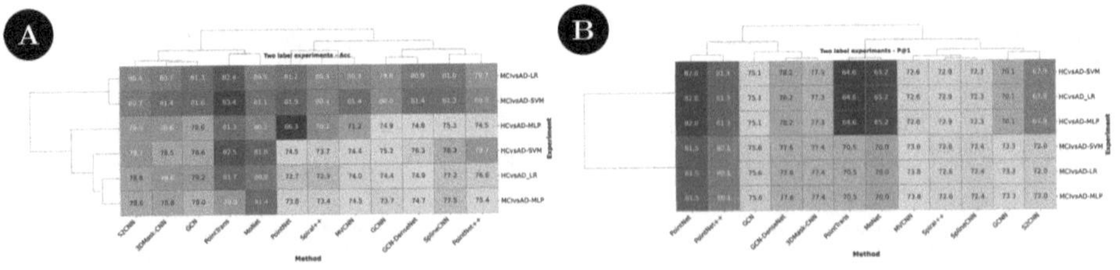

Fig. 5. (A) Classification accuracy for SVM, Logistic Regression (LR), and Multi-Layer Perceptron (MLP). (B): Precision@1.

In Fig. 5, we contrast downstream classification methods with first neighbor retrieval precisions from shape embeddings. Overall, the classification results lie within the range of commonly reported values for geometric deep learning methods in the literature. Nevertheless, our goal is not to optimize the classifier for state-of-the-art performance, but rather to use downstream classifiers to investigate the geometry of the shape embedding space.

In particular, we observe that the MCI vs. AD task forms two high-performing clusters for logistic regression and SVMs. This suggests that the latent shape representations have relatively low complexity and may be close to linearly separable. Initially, we expected MCI to behave as a noisy transitional label between HC and AD. Instead, the results suggest that models capable of capturing more global shape feature relations are better suited for this learning task, further indicating that the distinction between MCI and AD is better reflected on a global metric level.

The AD vs. HC task appears to be easier from the perspective of local retrieval metrics. In this setting, point-cloud models are among the strongest in preserving local geometry, but this does not necessarily translate into superior classification performance. Together, the results suggest that good local neighbor structure in the embedding space is not sufficient to obtain class separability. Local and global properties may consequently support different aspects of shape representation.

5 Toward Biomarker Associations

The biomarker relevance analysis is performed using the embeddings generated by *MoNet*, due to the stability observed in the previous experiments. The embeddings are trained using two partitions: one for model optimization and another for model selection (see Fig. 2). Two additional partitions are then used for testing and for the biomarker relevance analysis. Normative modelling typically requires at least 1000 samples to obtain moderately reliable results [5]. Therefore, we complemented our dataset with approximately 2452 additional samples from the publicly available HCP-Aging, AIBL, and IXI datasets. The normative model is trained using 80% of all HC samples. The remaining 20% are combined with samples from MCI, AD, and other smaller diagnostic subcategories for evaluation. It is important to note that not all samples contain the complete set of biological measurements, and some datasets exhibit different distributions in age, sex, and acquisition site. The analysis pipeline is implemented using *PCNtoolkit* [42].

Several embedding dimensions obtained high values of prediction quality (EXPV, MSLL, Shapiro; see Table 2a), suggesting that the normative model successfully captures dominant axes of variation within the embedding space. This aligns with typical results in normative analyses, where certain cortical regions tend to respond better as biomarkers; in this case, the informative features correspond to specific embedding dimensions.

The regression statistics shown in Table 2b indicate modest but statistically significant associations, with values broadly comparable to those reported in the literature. For example, [25] reports small negative slopes with low but significant values for β-amyloid burden. Likewise, the cognitive score MMSE shows a strong negative correlation, consistent with findings reported in [22], where the normative model is trained using embeddings derived from a Variational Autoencoder. In Fig. 6, the relations follow diagnostic meaningful directions: cognitive scores and CSF β-amyloid decrease as tOC increases, whereas AD-risk genotype increasing with the tOC.

In Table 2c, the group-wise analysis of tOC reveals a significant effect of diagnosis, confirmed by the ANOVA results ($F = 10.57$, $p < 0.001$) with a medium overall effect size ($\eta^2 = 0.069$). This indicates that the total outlier count is not randomly distributed across diagnostic groups but instead follows a meaningful clinical trend. In the post-hoc analysis, the clearest difference appears between cognitively normal controls and AD subjects, with a medium effect size ($d = -0.549$). Although the extended dataset was not used to train the shape-embedding model and the sample size remains limited, the effect-size analysis reveals statistically significant differences between diagnostic groups, particularly between AD and HC, supporting the potential of shape embeddings for biomarker discrimination. Additionally, future work should include a sensitivity analysis on the choice of confidence interval used to compute tOC, which was not performed in the present study. To further support the robustness of the findings, additional statistical analyses are reported in the appendix.

Table 2. Normative modeling evaluation:

(a) Normative modeling evaluation metrics per embedding dimension (MoNet, Fold-1).

$\boldsymbol{v}$.	EXPV	RMSE	Rho	MSLL	ShapiroW
v^0	0.64	0.93	0.65	1.22	0.80
v^1	0.49	1.15	0.63	0.89	0.78
v^2	0.95	0.34	0.72	2.18	0.87
v^3	0.19	1.53	0.41	0.64	0.94
v^4	0.15	1.66	0.38	0.32	0.89
v^5	0.90	0.49	0.74	2.01	0.95
v^6	0.70	0.87	0.71	1.87	0.67
v^7	0.61	0.94	0.66	0.89	0.89
v^8	0.91	0.44	0.75	2.04	0.97
v^9	0.14	1.48	0.30	0.51	0.97

(b) Biomarker association statistics.

Biomarker	slope	p-value	r
MMSE	-0.1520	p<0.001	-0.1104
APOE-4	0.0078	p<0.001	0.0223
CSF-β-amyloid	-0.0005	p<0.001	-0.018

(c) Pairwise effect sizes for tOC.

	Cohen's d:	effect
HC-AD	-0.5490	medium
AD-MCI	-0.4672	small
HC-MCI	-0.0934	negligible

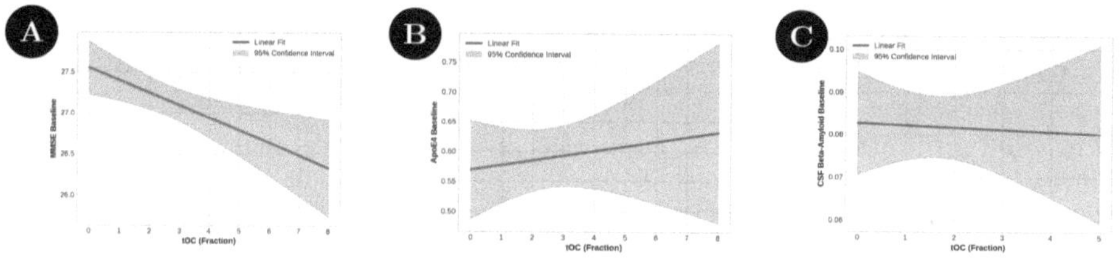

Fig. 6. Linear regression for $tOC(\tau = 1.96)$ or $CI - 95\%$ vs diagnosis biomarkers: (A) Mini-Mental State Examination (MMSE), (B) APOE4. Genotyping test for variants of the APOE-alleles, or AD-risk gene (C) CSF β-amyloid. Proteins measured in the cerebrospinal fluid that are associated with AD risk.

6 Conclusions

In this work, we propose a unified benchmark for investigating shape features in a biomedical dataset. This framework enables consistent comparison across retrieval, transfer learning, and normative modeling tasks aimed at studying biomarker-related responses.

Using this framework, we analyze various questions related to implementing geometric deep learning methods to learn hippocampal shape representations. In particular, we investigate discrepancies and nuances in the design of shape analysis models within a well-structured pipeline. Specifically, we conduct a comprehensive study of five types of geometric deep learning models, including mesh-based, spherical, point-cloud, and multi-view approaches, and compare their performance against a 3DMask-CNN baseline.

The study expands beyond retrieval and classification performance by including biomarker relevance as an additional validation of the learned shape representations. The biomarker relevance analysis measures the ability of the shape embeddings to capture continuous biological variation associated with disease progression. This distinction is particularly important in biomedical applications, beyond hippocampal analysis, as most biological processes often evolve gradually rather than following discrete class boundaries.

Regarding the biological relevance of the shape embeddings, the learned shape space shows a consistent association with biomarker-related responses. Normative modeling allows us to obtain subject-level deviations while accounting for demographic and acquisition-related factors. This allows us to quantify individual deviations from the expected hippocampal morphology and relate them to biomarkers.

Although the sample size is limited and the analysis would benefit from controlling for additional covariates, these results provide preliminary evidence that shape embeddings capture biologically meaningful patterns. The proposed methodology is not restricted to hippocampal datasets and can be applied to other biomedical datasets with non-Euclidean representations, such as meshes or point-clouds. Future work could expand this analysis to other brain structures, although the hippocampus remains particularly relevant for the study of aging and Alzheimer's disease.

Acknowledgements. A.I.R. was supported by the Landesstipendium awarded by the Free State of Saxony. The authors acknowledge the financial support by the Federal Ministry of Education and Research of Germany and by Sächsische Staatsministerium für Wissenschaft, Kultur und Tourismus in the programme Center of Excellence for AI-research "Center for Scalable Data Analytics and Artificial Intelligence Dresden/Leipzig", project identification number: SCADS24B.

Data collection and sharing for ADNI are funded by the National Institute on Aging, NIH Grant U19AG024904. The grantee organization is the Northern California Institute for Research and Education. ADNI has also received support from the National Institute of Biomedical Imaging and Bioengineering, the Canadian Institutes of Health Research, nonprofit organizations, and private-sector partners through the Foundation for the NIH.

Disclosure of Interests. The authors have no competing interests to declare that are relevant to the content of this article.

References

1. Atz, K., Grisoni, F., Schneider, G.: Geometric deep learning on molecular representations. Nat. Mach. Intell. **3**(12), 1023–1032 (2021)
2. Bai, Q., Xu, T., Huang, J., Perez-Sanchez, H.: Geometric deep learning methods and applications in 3D structure-based drug design. Drug Discovery Today **29**(7), 104024 (2024)
3. Besson, P., Parrish, T., Katsaggelos, A.K., Bandt, S.K.: Geometric deep learning on brain shape predicts sex and age. Comput. Med. Imaging Graph. **91**, 101939 (2021)
4. Bogo, F., Romero, J., Loper, M., Black, M.J.: FAUST: dataset and evaluation for 3D mesh registration. In: Proceedings IEEE Conference on Computer Vision and Pattern Recognition (CVPR), IEEE, Piscataway, NJ, USA (2014)
5. Bozek, J., Griffanti, L., Lau, S., Jenkinson, M.: Normative models for neuroimaging markers: impact of model selection, sample size and evaluation criteria. Neuroimage **268**, 119864 (2023)
6. Bronstein, M.M., Bruna, J., LeCun, Y., Szlam, A., Vandergheynst, P.: Geometric deep learning: going beyond Euclidean data. IEEE Signal Process. Mag. **34**(4), 18–42 (2017). https://doi.org/10.1109/MSP.2017.2693418
7. Chang, A.X., et al.: ShapeNet: an information-rich 3D model repository (2015). arXiv preprint arXiv:1512.03012
8. Charles, R.Q., Su, H., Kaichun, M., Guibas, L.J.: PointNet: deep learning on point sets for 3D classification and segmentation. In: 2017 IEEE Conference on Computer Vision and Pattern Recognition (CVPR), pp. 77–85. iSSN: 1063-6919 (2017)
9. Cohen, T.S., Geiger, M., Köhler, J., Welling, M.: 6th International Conference on Learning Representations ICLR, vol. 1, pp. 1–15 (2018). Spherical CNNs
10. Csernansky, J.G.: Preclinical detection of Alzheimer's disease: hippocampal shape and volume predict dementia onset in the elderly. Neuroimage **25**(3), 783–792 (2005)

11. DeKraker, J., et al.: Automated hippocampal unfolding for morphometry and subfield segmentation with hippunfold. elife **11**, e77945 (2022)
12. Diers, K., Baumeister, H., Jessen, F., Düzel, E., Berron, D., Reuter, M.: An automated, geometry-based method for hippocampal shape and thickness analysis. Neuroimage **276**, 120182 (2023). https://doi.org/10.1016/j.neuroimage.2023.120182
13. Dunn, T.W., et al.: Geometric deep learning enables 3D kinematic profiling across species and environments. Nat. Methods **18**(5), 564–573 (2021)
14. El-Assy, A., Amer, H.M., Ibrahim, H., Mohamed, M.: A novel CNN architecture for accurate early detection and classification of Alzheimer's disease using MRI data. Sci. Rep. **14**(1), 3463 (2024)
15. Fey, M., Lenssen, J.E., Weichert, F., Müller, H.: SplineCNN: fast geometric deep learning with continuous b-spline kernels. In: Proceedings of the IEEE Conference on Computer Vision and Pattern Recognition, pp. 869–877 (2018)
16. Fraza, C.J., Dinga, R., Beckmann, C.F., Marquand, A.F.: Warped Bayesian linear regression for normative modelling of big data. Neuroimage **245**, 118715 (2021)
17. Gerardin, E., et al.: Multidimensional classification of hippocampal shape features discriminates Alzheimer's disease and mild cognitive impairment from normal aging. Neuroimage **47**(4), 1476–1486 (2009)
18. Gong, S., Chen, L., Bronstein, M., Zafeiriou, S.: SpiralNet++: a fast and highly efficient mesh convolution operator. In: 2019 IEEE/CVF International Conference on Computer Vision Workshop (ICCVW), pp. 4141–4148. iSSN: 2473-9944 (2019)
19. Gosztolai, A., Peach, R.L., Arnaudon, A., Barahona, M., Vandergheynst, P.: MARBLE: interpretable representations of neural population dynamics using geometric deep learning. Nat. Methods **22**(3), 612–620 (2025). https://doi.org/10.1038/s41592-024-02582-2
20. Hazarika, R.A., Maji, A.K., Syiem, R., Sur, S.N., Kandar, D.: Hippocampus segmentation using U-Net convolutional network from brain magnetic resonance imaging (MRI). J. Digit. Imaging **35**(4), 893–909 (2022)
21. Kipf, T.N., Welling, M.: Semi-supervised classification with graph convolutional networks. In: 5th International Conference on Learning Representations, ICLR 2017, Toulon, France, April 24-26, 2017, Conference Track Proceedings. OpenReview.net (2017)
22. Kumar, S., et al.: Analyzing heterogeneity in Alzheimer disease using multimodal normative modeling on imaging-based ATN biomarkers. Alzheimer's & Dementia **21**(4), e70143 (2025)
23. Li, A., Li, F., Elahifasaee, F., Liu, M., Zhang, L., Initiative, A.D.N.: Hippocampal shape and asymmetry analysis by cascaded convolutional neural networks for Alzheimer's disease diagnosis. Brain Imaging Behav. **15**(5), 2330–2339 (2021)
24. Li, L., Jamieson, K., DeSalvo, G., Rostamizadeh, A., Talwalkar, A.: Hyperband: a novel bandit-based approach to hyperparameter optimization. J. Mach. Learn. Res. **18**(185), 1–52 (2018)
25. Loreto, F., et al.: Alzheimer's disease heterogeneity revealed by neuroanatomical normative modeling. Alzheimer's Dement. Diagn. Assess. Dis. Monit. **16**(1), e12559 (2024)
26. Marquand, A.F., Rezek, I., Buitelaar, J., Beckmann, C.F.: Understanding heterogeneity in clinical cohorts using normative models: beyond case-control studies. Biol. Psychiat. **80**(7), 552–561 (2016)
27. Masci, J., Boscaini, D., Bronstein, M., Vandergheynst, P.: Geodesic convolutional neural networks on Riemannian manifolds. Proceedings of the IEEE International Conference on Computer Vision Workshops, pp. 37–45 (2015)

28. Mayer, J., Baum, D., Ambellan, F., von Tycowicz, C., Initiative, A.D.N.: Shape-based disease grading via functional maps and graph convolutional networks with application to Alzheimer's disease. BMC Med. Imaging **24**(1), 342 (2024)
29. Monti, F., Boscaini, D., Masci, J.: Geometric deep learning on graphs and manifolds using mixture model CNNs. Proceedings of the IEEE Conference on Computer Vision and Pattern Recognition, pp. 5115–5124(2017)
30. Movshovitz-Attias, Y., Toshev, A., Leung, T.K., Ioffe, S., Singh, S.: No Fuss Distance Metric Learning Using Proxies. In: 2017 IEEE International Conference on Computer Vision (ICCV), pp. 360–368. IEEE, Venice (2017)
31. Musgrave, K., Belongie, S., Lim, S.N.: A metric learning reality check. In: Vedaldi, A., Bischof, H., Brox, T., Frahm, J.M. (eds.) Computer Vision – ECCV 2020. Lecture Notes in Computer Science, vol. 12370, pp. 681–699. Springer International Publishing, Cham (2020)
32. Palma, M., Tavakoli, S., Brettschneider, J., Staicu, A.M., Nichols, T.E., Initiative, f.t.A.D.N.: Smooth normative brain mapping of three-dimensional morphometry imaging data using skew-normal regression. Human Brain Mapping **46**(4), e70185 (2025)
33. Patenaude, B., Smith, S.M., Kennedy, D.N., Jenkinson, M.: A Bayesian model of shape and appearance for subcortical brain segmentation. Neuroimage **56**(3), 907–922 (2011)
34. Phong, B.T.: Illumination for computer generated pictures. Commun. ACM **18**(6), 311–317 (1975)
35. Pinaya, W.H., et al.: Using normative modelling to detect disease progression in mild cognitive impairment and Alzheimer's disease in a cross-sectional multi-cohort study. Sci. Reports **11**(1), 15746 (2021)
36. Qi, C.R., Yi, L., Su, H., Guibas, L.: PointNet++: deep hierarchical feature learning on point sets in a metric space. In: Guyon, I., et al. (eds.) Advances in Neural Information Processing Systems, vol. 30. Curran Associates, Inc. (2017)
37. Qian, Q., et al.: SoftTriple loss: deep metric learning without triplet sampling. In: 2019 IEEE/CVF International Conference on Computer Vision (ICCV), pp. 6449–6457. IEEE, Seoul, Korea (South) (2019)
38. Rabbi, J., Kiechle, J., Beaulieu, C., Ray, N., Cobzas, D.: Disentangling Hippocampal Shape Variations: a Study of Neurological Disorders Using Mesh Variational Autoencoder with Contrastive Learning. Machine Learning for Biomedical Imaging **2**(November 2024 issue), 2268–2293 (2024). https://doi.org/10.59275/j.melba.2024-267f
39. Ramani, R., Ganesh, S.S., Rao, S.P.V.S., Aggarwal, N.: Integrated multi-modal 3D-CNN and RNN approach with transfer learning for early detection of Alzheimer's disease. Iranian J. Sci. Technol., Trans. Electr. Eng. **49**(1), 383–407 (2025). https://doi.org/10.1007/s40998-024-00769-z
40. Routier, A., et al.: Clinica: an Open-Source Software Platform for Reproducible Clinical Neuroscience Studies. Front. Neuroinform. **15** (2021), publisher: Frontiers
41. Rustamov, R.M.: Laplace-beltrami eigenfunctions for deformation invariant shape representation. In: Proceedings of the Fifth Eurographics Symposium on Geometry Processing, pp. 225–233. SGP '07, Eurographics Association, Goslar, DEU (2007)
42. Rutherford, S., et al.: The normative modeling framework for computational psychiatry. Nature Protocols **17**(7), 1711–1734 (2022), publisher: Nature Publishing Group
43. Sarasua, I., Pölsterl, S., Wachinger, C.: Hippocampal representations for deep learning on Alzheimer's disease. Scientific Reports 12(1), 8619 (2022). https://doi.org/10.1038/s41598-022-12533-6 publisher: Nature Publishing Group

44. Scher, A., et al.: Hippocampal shape analysis in Alzheimer's disease: a population-based study. Neuroimage **36**(1), 8–18 (2007)
45. Schroff, F., Kalenichenko, D., Philbin, J.: FaceNet: a unified embedding for face recognition and clustering. In: 2015 IEEE Conference on Computer Vision and Pattern Recognition (CVPR), pp. 815–823. iSSN: 1063-6919 (2015)
46. Sinzinger, F., Astaraki, M., Smedby, O., Moreno, R.: Spherical convolutional neural networks for survival rate prediction in cancer patients. Front. Oncol. 12, (2022). publisher: Frontiers
47. Smith, S.M.: Fast robust automated brain extraction. Hum. Brain Mapp. **17**(3), 143–155 (2002). https://doi.org/10.1002/hbm.10062
48. Song, S., Bai, Z., Wang, G., Xu, Y., Cheng, M., Chen, H.: Multi-modal heterogeneous encoder-decoder for Alzheimer's disease anomaly detection. In: Proceedings of the 2024 5th International Conference on Intelligent Medicine and Health, pp. 40–47. ICIMH '24, Association for Computing Machinery, New York, NY, USA (2025)
49. Su, H., Maji, S., Kalogerakis, E., Learned-Miller, E.: Multi-view convolutional neural networks for 3D shape recognition. In: 2015 IEEE International Conference on Computer Vision (ICCV), pp. 945–953. IEEE, Santiago, Chile (2015)
50. Verdi, S., et al.: Revealing Individual Neuroanatomical Heterogeneity in Alzheimer Disease Using Neuroanatomical Normative Modeling. Neurology **100**(24) (2023). https://doi.org/10.1212/WNL.0000000000207298 number: 24
51. Verdi, S., et al.: Personalizing progressive changes to brain structure in Alzheimer's disease using normative modeling. Alzheimer's & Dementia **20**(10), 6998–7012 (2024)
52. Wang, Q., Li, Y., Zheng, C., Xu, R.: DenseCNN: a densely connected CNN model for Alzheimer's disease classification based on Hippocampus MRI data. AMIA Ann. Symp. Proc. **2020**, 1277–1286 (2021)
53. Wu, Z., et al.: 3D ShapeNets: a deep representation for volumetric shapes. In: Proceedings of the IEEE Conference on Computer Vision and Pattern Recognition, pp. 1912–1920 (2015)
54. Zabihi, M., et al.: Nonlinear latent representations of high-dimensional task-fMRI data: unveiling cognitive and behavioral insights in heterogeneous spatial maps. PLoS ONE **19**(8), e0308329 (2024)
55. Zhao, H., Jiang, L., Jia, J., Torr, P., Koltun, V.: Point transformer. In: 2021 IEEE/CVF International Conference on Computer Vision (ICCV), pp. 16239–16248. iSSN: 2380-7504 (2021)
56. Zhu, Y., Newsam, S.: DenseNet for dense flow. In: 2017 IEEE International Conference on Image Processing (ICIP), pp. 790–794. iSSN: 2381-8549 (2017)

GENATATORs: ab Initio Gene Annotation With DNA Language Models

Aleksei Shmelev[1,6](✉), Artem Shadskiy[1,3], Yuri Kuratov[1,2], Mikhail Burtsev[4], Olga Kardymon[7], and Veniamin Fishman[1,3,5]

[1] AXXX, Moscow, Russia
minja.fishman@gmail.com
[2] Moscow Independent Research Institute of Artificial Intelligence, Moscow, Russia
[3] Sirius University, Sochi, Russia
[4] London Institute for Mathematical Sciences, London, UK
[5] Institute of Cytology and Genetics, Novosibirsk, Russia
[6] HSE University, Moscow, Russia
avshmelev@hse.ru
[7] Quantori, Belgrade, Serbia

Abstract. Inference of gene structure and location from genome sequences - known as *de novo* gene annotation - is a fundamental task in biological research. However, sequence grammar encoding gene structure is complex and poorly understood, often requiring costly transcriptomic data for accurate gene annotation. In this work, we benchmark current solutions and develop new methods of gene annotation. We show that pretrained DNA language model (DNA LM) embeddings do not capture the features necessary for precise gene segmentation, and that task-specific fine-tuning remains essential. We comprehensively evaluate the impact of model architecture, training strategy, receptive field size, dataset composition, and data augmentations on gene segmentation performance. We revisit standard evaluation protocols, showing that commonly used per-token and per-sequence metrics fail to capture the challenges of real-world gene annotation. We introduce and theoretically justify new biologically grounded metrics, along with benchmarking datasets that better capture annotation quality. We show that fine-tuned DNA LMs outperform existing annotation tools, generalizing across species separated by hundreds of millions of years from those seen during training, and providing segmentation of previously intractable non-coding transcripts and untranslated regions of protein-coding genes. Our results thus provide a foundation for new biological applications centered on accurate gene annotation.

Keywords: DNA language models · genome annotation · ab initio · long sequence processing · recurrent models · state space models · computational genomics

A. Shmelev and A. Shadskiy—Contributed equally.

M. Ceci et al. (Eds.): ECML PKDD 2026, LNAI 16948, pp. 512–529, 2027.
https://doi.org/10.1007/978-3-032-37679-4_29

1 Introduction

The rapid development of DNA sequencing technologies, such as third-generation sequencing and Hi-C, has led to an exponential growth in the availability of genome assemblies across the tree of life. This genomic data is invaluable for fundamental research, biotechnology, and biomedicine, but raw DNA sequences alone are insufficient for most applications. To interpret these data, genomes must be annotated, enabling the identification of functional elements. Gene annotation is the most important here, since it identifies genes and reveals their structural elements, which are critical for almost all downstream applications.

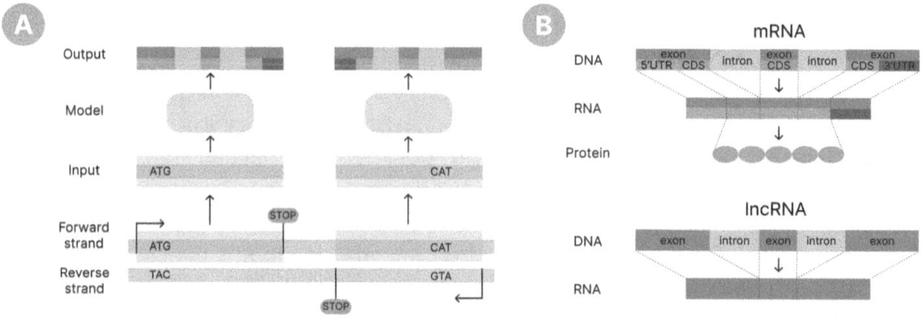

Fig. 1. Gene structure and segmentation problem. Panel A shows transcript types in the dataset, where the model predicts all five classes but only intron and exon labels are relevant for lncRNAs, while all five are meaningful for mRNAs. Panel B illustrates that the model always receives DNA sequence from the forward strand (light green box) during training, yet these sequences may correspond to genes located on either strand. (Color figure online)

A gene is a continuous subsequence of genomic DNA that serves as the template for transcription, the process by which RNA molecules are synthesized from DNA. Genes are directional, and their direction is defined collinear with the direction of RNA synthesis. Therefore, genes can appear in forward or reverse orientation relative to the reference genome (Fig. 1A). In the genomes, approximately half of the annotated genes are in the forward orientation and half in the reverse.

The two largest gene classes are messenger RNAs (mRNAs) and long non-coding RNAs (lncRNAs). In the human genome, approximately 40.5% of genes are annotated as mRNAs and 35.2 % as lncRNAs, which is why this paper focuses only on these two classes. mRNAs encode proteins, and their sequence is segmented into exons and introns, with exons containing coding sequence (CDS) and untranslated regions (UTRs) at the 5′ and 3′ ends (Fig. 1B). Translation of the CDS provides the amino acid sequence of proteins, each amino acid encoded by three CDS letters (codon). Thus, even a single nucleotide shift in an exon boundary can change all downstream codons. By contrast, lncRNAs lack CDS and do not produce proteins, but instead regulate diverse biological processes, including chromatin remodeling, immune response, viral defense, and cancer progression [15,20]. Untranslated regions of mRNAs are biologically important as well. Although they are not translated into proteins, UTRs influence transcript stability, translation efficiency, and localization [4]. They may encode short functional peptides, and mutations in UTRs can be linked to human diseases [7]. Thus, a complete view of gene structure requires accurate recovery not only of coding exons (CDS parts) but also of UTRs and non-coding genes.

Annotating lncRNAs and UTRs is a qualitatively different task compared to annotating mRNA CDS. Protein-coding gene fragments can often be recognized from conserved protein-coding fragments, while lncRNAs and mRNA gene UTRs lack such signals, evolve more rapidly, and are often expressed only in specific tissues, which makes their detection particularly challenging without additional evidence such as RNA-seq. Learning the sequence rules that govern transcription and protein synthesis should, in principle, enable the prediction of gene structure directly from DNA sequence. Methods that attempt this are known as *ab initio* gene predictors, yet in practice they underperform approaches that incorporate evidence beyond the genome sequence [18]. Common sources of such evidence include gene annotations from closely related species and RNA-sequencing data from the target species [17]. However, these resources are not consistently available across organisms or conditions, which sustains the demand for robust *ab initio* gene annotation methods that deliver high-quality results from sequence alone.

In this work, we address these gaps by applying DNA language models to gene segmentation and developing `GENATATORs`, a family of fine-tuned models specifically designed for *ab initio* annotation. Using biologically inspired metrics, justified by theoretical analysis and empirical validation, we demonstrate that pretrained DNA language model embeddings are insufficient for precise segmentation, making task-specific fine-tuning necessary. We then investigate how architecture, input context length, species diversity in training data, and augmentation strategies affect performance. Finally, we benchmark `GENATATORs` against existing methods and evaluate generalization on human and other species, showing that our models achieve state-of-the-art performance in gene segmentation due to the capacity to uncover previously untrackable lncRNAs and UTRs of mRNA, while maintaining comparable accuracy to the best existing tools on segmentation restricted to mRNA CDS.

2 Related Work

Early *ab initio* approaches relied on probabilistic models such as `AUGUSTUS` [21], which is based on HMMs that hardcode biological rules of gene grammar. These models capture statistical patterns of protein-coding genes, including the presence of a start codon to initiate CDS, a stop codon to terminate it, the absence of in-frame stops within the CDS, and canonical dinucleotides at splice junctions. Such models are effective for identifying protein-coding genes but fail to capture UTRs and lncRNAs [18]. To address these gaps, deep learning methods have been introduced to learn gene segmentation rules from DNA sequences. Both `Helixer` and `Tiberius` combined CNNs with HMMs for gene annotation, with `Tiberius` achieving state-of-the-art accuracy on protein-coding gene annotation [9,10]. Although effective, these models remain constrained. `Tiberius` focuses on protein-coding genes and is not capable of retrieving UTRs or lncRNAs, and its CNN backbone is restricted to relatively short contexts (up to 10Kb) despite many human genes exceeding 30 Kb and spanning over 1 Mb.

Large DNA LMs have emerged as versatile backbones for genomic predictions [3,5,8,13,19,23]. Based on transformer or SSM architectures, they can be pretrained on large genomic datasets. DNA LMs have matched or surpassed classical approaches across tasks such as splice-site prediction, promoter identification, and polyA signal detection. `SegmentNT` [6], a fine-tuned `Nucleotide Transformer` DNA LM [5] with a U-Net head, is a nucleotide-resolution classifier that outputs probabilities for each gene element directly from DNA sequence. Authors of `SegmentNT` also introduced variants of this model pretrained on expression data—`SegmentBorzoi` and `SegmentEnformer`. `NTv3` [2] further scales context length to the megabase range. However, as we demonstrate below, classification performance on individual gene elements does not reliably reflect the accuracy of full gene reconstruction. Consequently, the utility of these models for real-world biological applications remains unclear.

Recently, `AlphaGenome` has been introduced as a foundation model of the genome that predicts multiple modalities from sequence, including RNA-seq, chromatin accessibility, and splicing-related outputs [1]. In the splicing domain, it performs nucleotide-level classification of donor and acceptor sites, prediction of splice-site usage, and quantitative splice-junction prediction. While not being a gene annotation system, such splicing predictions of the model are directly relevant to exonintron boundary detection and therefore to transcript assembly.

Alongside these methods, several benchmarks have been proposed to assess gene annotation-related tasks. GUE [23] includes splice-site prediction. However, it assigns a single label to 400 bp input sequences, which makes it biologically irrelevant: gene annotation requires single-nucleotide precision in the detection of boundaries between gene elements. BEND [14] instead operates at the nucleotide level, but it uses short input sequences, relies on metrics that are not biologically rigorous, and does not evaluate critical elements such as UTRs or lncRNA genes. A detailed comparison between benchmarks developed in this work, BEND, and GUE is provided in Appendix A.

Building on these observations, it is clear that systematic evaluations of modern DNA LMs for full gene segmentation are still missing. In particular, SSMs have not been comprehensively benchmarked, and among transformer-based models, only a single context-extension method [16] has been applied to process genes longer than the default receptive field. A unified benchmark is therefore needed to clarify how modern DNA LMs perform on gene segmentation, especially for lncRNAs and UTRs that remain inaccessible to most existing tools.

3 Formal Definition of the Problem and Metrics

We formalize gene segmentation as a multiclass nucleotide level classification task. The objective is to learn a function f that maps an input representation $\boldsymbol{X} \in \mathbb{R}^{N_l \times H}$ to an output label matrix $\boldsymbol{L} \in \mathbb{R}^{N_l \times 5}$, where H is the token embedding dimension, N_l is the input length in nucleotides, and 5 is the number of target classes which are exon, intron, coding sequence (CDS), $5'$ untranslated region (5-UTR), and $3'$ untranslated region (3-UTR).

3.1 Segmentation Scoring

Interval-Level Scoring. Segmentation performance can be assessed using conventional classification metrics such as precision, recall, f1-score, and PR-AUC computed per class at the nucleotide level. However, these metrics evaluate classification independently for each nucleotide and therefore may not capture biological dependencies between predictions. For instance, a misclassification of a single nucleotide within a megabase long gene has a negligible impact on the overall metric, while the same error can alter the interpretation of all downstream sequence, since shifting a protein coding exon boundary by one nucleotide modifies all downstream trinucleotide blocks and yields a different amino acid sequence, a frame shift effect known in molecular biology.

To address this limitation, we use *interval level* segmentation scoring inspired by prior work [18]. In this approach, a target interval is a continuous sequence of nucleotides with identical ground truth class labels. A predicted interval is counted as a true positive only when it has complete reciprocal overlap with a ground truth interval, which means that the predicted and true intervals coincide.

Formally, let the ground truth class label sequence be $L = (l_1, l_2, \ldots, l_{N_l})$. An interval $I_m = [i, j]$ is assigned to class K when $l_k = K$ for all $k \in [i, j]$. For each class K, let $\mathcal{I}^K_{\text{pred}}$ be the set of predicted intervals and let $\mathcal{I}^K_{\text{true}}$ be the set of ground truth intervals. We compute the following quantities. True positives are the number of predicted intervals that exactly match a ground truth interval. False positives are the number of predicted intervals without an exact match in $\mathcal{I}^K_{\text{true}}$. False negatives are the number of ground truth intervals that are not recovered in $\mathcal{I}^K_{\text{pred}}$.

The final interval level f1-score for class K is

$$\mathrm{F1}^{K}_{\mathrm{interval}} = \frac{2\,\mathrm{TP}}{2\,\mathrm{TP} + \mathrm{FP} + \mathrm{FN}}. \tag{1}$$

This metric penalizes biologically important segmentation errors and provides a realistic assessment of model performance.

Gene-Level Scoring. We also extend interval level scoring to evaluate the overall accuracy of gene structure prediction (defined as *gene level* metric). In gene level scoring, a gene is counted as a true positive only when all of its intervals are reconstructed correctly. Reference annotations may include multiple valid transcript structures for the same gene, known as transcription *isoforms*, which define different segmentations. To account for this ambiguity, we use a gene level rule that accepts a prediction as correct when the predicted interval set exactly matches the interval set of any annotated isoform of the target gene.

Gene-Level Scoring for CDS-only Models. Many HMM-based models, including `Tiberius` and `AUGUSTUS`, rely on hard-coded parameters tailored to coding sequence identification, which makes them unable to detect exons that include untranslated regions. Therefore, for protein coding transcripts we report two gene level metrics, one where the complete exon structure is reconstructed (exon-mRNA) and one where only the coding sequence part is reconstructed (CDS-mRNA). For non-coding transcripts such as lncRNA, which have no CDS annotation, we compute gene level metrics using exon intervals only. To obtain an overall gene level score we sum the number of correctly predicted lncRNA genes by exon matching and the maximum of exon mRNA and CDS mRNA counts for protein coding genes, which allows a fair comparison across models

$$\mathrm{Score}_{\mathrm{gene}} = \mathrm{TP}_{\text{exon-lncRNA}} + \max\Big(\mathrm{TP}_{\text{exon-mRNA}}, \mathrm{TP}_{\text{CDS-mRNA}}\Big). \tag{2}$$

In Appendix B.1, we present a theoretical analysis that derives how the sensitivity of conventional PR-AUC and interval level metrics scales with boundary errors, justifying the need for the latter. This is followed by empirical evidence in Appendix B.2, where we demonstrate that relying on PR-AUC can lead to incorrect model rankings.

4 Experiments

Input Data. The training dataset consists of genes from all human chromosomes except 8, 20, and 21, which were held out for validation during training. When specified, we also included genes from all chromosomes of 39 additional mammalian species. All models were evaluated on human chromosome 20 from the T2T human assembly, since the human genome provides the most accurate annotation among all available species. This chromosome is part of the held-out set for several widely used models, including SegmentNT, Tiberius, and Helixer, enabling an unbiased comparison. For genes with multiple annotated isoforms, we selected a single isoform per gene with the longest cumulative length of exons. A detailed description of dataset preparation is provided in Appendix C.

Models. We evaluated models representing different families of DNA LM architectures. From the SSM family, we included Evo2-1B [3] and Caduceus (with PH and PS modifications) [19]. For Transformer-based models, we selected GENA-LM equipped with Recurrent Memory Transformer (RMT), capable of processing sequences comparable in length to complete genes [11]. DNABERT-2, DNABERT-S, and similar architectures were not included due to the limited receptive fields. Additionally, we incorporated previously developed gene segmentation models based on the Nucleotide Transformer DNA LM: (SegmentNT and SegmentNT_multispecies), as well as models pretrained on gene expression data (SegmentEnformer and SegmentBorzoi), as well as classical models (HMM-based AUGUSTUS and the CNN&HMM hybrid Tiberius and Helixer), in the final benchmarks. Besides, we evaluated the recently released NTv3 and AlphaGenome models. However, we did not evaluate embeddings, re-optimize dataset preparation or training procedures for these models, as such studies have been reported previously [6,9]. We refer to the Appendix D Table A7 for the summary of all models benchmarked in this study.

For models operating at single-nucleotide resolution (Evo2 and Caduceus), we appended a linear projection layer of shape $(H, 5)$ to map the model outputs to the five target classes. For non-single-nucleotide resolution models (Nucleotide Transformer, GENA-LM), token embeddings were upsampled by repeating each token representation to match its corresponding nucleotide span and further processed using a U-Net architecture as proposed in [6].

All models were trained using cross-entropy loss, and the best-performing checkpoint was selected based on exon-level f1-score on the validation set. Further details on model architectures and training protocols are provided in Appendix C.

4.1 Training on Embeddings

DNA language models are expected to capture essential genomic features during pretraining. To evaluate whether gene-structure information can be extracted directly from frozen representations, we conducted experiments where the DNA LM weights were fixed and only a shallow classifier was trained. Specifically, we used a linear projection layer for models operating at nucleotide resolution (Evo2, Caduceus) and a U-Net decoder for the token-based GENA-LM (bytepairencoded inputs).

As shown in Appendix E, Table A8, none of the models produced embeddings containing sufficient information for accurate gene segmentation. The slightly higher performance of GENA-LM is likely attributable to the U-Net decoder, which, unlike the linear layer used in Evo2 and Caduceus, can aggregate local contextual signals.

To understand why pretrained models fail at segmentation, we analyzed final-layer hidden states on ten randomly selected human genes (six mRNA and four lncRNA) using `Caduceus` and `GENA-LM`. For `GENA-LM`, which uses BPE tokens, we expanded each token embedding uniformly across its nucleotide span to obtain one vector per base for both models. PCA projections of the `Caduceus` embeddings revealed four distinct clusters corresponding to nucleotide identity (A, C, G, T), rather than gene structure (Appendix F, Figure A2). `GENA-LM` embeddings formed diffuse clusters that also did not align with gene elements (Appendix F, Figure A1). This contrasts sharply with embeddings obtained after fine-tuning on the gene segmentation task described in Sect. 4.2, which show clear separation of gene elements (Appendix F, Figure A2). Quantitatively, fine-tuning increased the homogeneity of k-means (k=5) clusters with respect to exon, intron, CDS, 5′UTR, and 3′UTR labels from 0.003 to 0.583 for `Caduceus` and from 0.0 to 0.497 for `GENA-LM`.

These probing experiments should be interpreted in the context of our evaluation setup. In contrast to the BEND [14] benchmark, where authors employ task-specific trainable heads on top of frozen representations, our goal here is to assess what current pretrained encoders capture without relying on complex decoders. To keep the probing strictly aligned with this goal, we use only minimal heads (a linear layer for `Evo2` and `Caduceus`, and a shallow U-Net for `GENA-LM` to enable nucleotide resolution), which reveals the information present in the embeddings themselves rather than what can be recovered by a powerful decoder.

Together, these results indicate that pretraining alone is insufficient to encode the features required for precise gene segmentation and that task-specific fine-tuning remains essential for achieving high segmentation accuracy.

4.2 Fine-Tuning of DNA Language Models

We next conducted a series of fine-tuning experiments, where both the DNA LM parameters and the classification head were trainable. These experiments were designed to systematically investigate how model architecture and the biological information available during training influence gene segmentation performance.

As a baseline, we considered models trained on human genomic sequences with a model context length of 4,096 bp. Building on this setup, we explored the effect of extending the model context to 32 Kb, which provided a broader genomic window. We also examined whether expanding the training data to include genes from 39 additional mammalian species improved performance by leveraging evolutionary conservation, and we tested the impact of restricting the training set to protein-coding transcripts while excluding lncRNAs, so that the models were exposed only to sequences with well-defined coding structures. We additionally evaluated the effect of incorporating an auxiliary loss applied to intermediate model layers. Finally, in a complementary experiment, we evaluated training on multiple isoforms per gene vs using single representative isoform per gene in the baseline. In all experiments, we focused on `Caduceus PS` and `Caduceus PH` as representative SSMs, while `GENA-LM` served as the representative

Transformer-based model, and we did not include `Evo-1` and larger versions of `Evo-2`, since their size exceeded our available resources for running multiple fine-tuning experiments.

Table 1. Gene-level performance metrics for dataset and model modifications: absolute number of correctly reconstructed genes (abs) and differences (diff) compared to baseline (presented in the first column). The gene type (all+) means that all isoforms of all genes were included in the dataset.

Chunk length (N_l), bp			4096	4096	**32000**	4096	4096	4096	4096	4096	4096	4096
Gene type			all	all+	all	**mRNA**	all	all	all	all	all	all
Species			human	human	human	human	**39 mammals**	human	human	human	human	human
Test-time augmentation			no	no	no	no	no	no	**RC**	**splice-site filter**	**CDS heuristics**	**RC & splice-site filter & CDS heuristics**
Auxiliary loss			no	no	no	no	no	**yes**	no	no	no	no
Model/dataset	**Gene type**	**Class**	**abs**	**diff**	**diff**	**diff**	**diff**	**diff**	**diff**	**diff**	**diff**	**diff**
GENA base	mRNA	exon	40	-14	35	8	18	3	12	14	0	31
		CDS	4	-4	8	5	3	-3	2	1	56	88
	lncRNA	exon	18	-7	9	-7	2	-2	1	4	0	10
	all RNA	exon	58	-21	44	1	20	-1	13	18	0	41
Caduceus PH	mRNA	exon	60	-9	63	-3	37	45	44	15	0	72
		CDS	1	-1	1	13	66	8	4	3	110	184
	lncRNA	exon	6	2	24	-2	7	21	3	0	0	7
	all RNA	exon	66	-7	87	-5	44	66	47	15	0	79
Caduceus PS	mRNA	exon	84	-13	51	24	43	10	52	28	0	86
		CDS	17	2	-11	28	91	-9	15	11	138	196
	lncRNA	exon	3	2	19	4	8	14	5	1	0	6
	all RNA	exon	87	-11	70	28	51	24	57	29	0	92

Our results (Table 1) indicate that increasing the input sequence length yields the most substantial improvement in segmentation performance, with approximately 1.6–2× gains across models. Incorporating multiple species into the training set improved performance by approximately 1.2–1.5×. Excluding lncRNAs from the training data resulted in improved CDS detection for both `Caduceus` models. However, this came at the expense of reduced lncRNA segmentation performance, although the decrease was not as pronounced. This observation suggests that the sequence grammar underlying non-coding transcripts can, to a large extent, be learned from protein-coding sequences. In contrast to CDS detection, we did not observe consistent improvements in exon segmentation for protein-coding genes when excluding lncRNA. Specifically, `GENA-LM` and `Caduceus PS` achieved a modest improvement of approximately 10%, whereas `Caduceus PH` exhibited a similar decrease in performance. Overall, we concluded that transcript filtering does not substantially improve training performance. We also found that using multiple isoforms per gene slightly reduced accuracy, confirming that the single-isoform strategy remains preferable.

Motivated by the auxiliary classifiers introduced in the Inception vision model, which use intermediate losses to improve optimization [22], we in particular evaluated the use of an auxiliary loss from the middle of the model. Concretely, for `Caduceus` we attached an independent linear projection head to the embeddings from layer 8 (`Caduceus` model has 16 layers), whereas for `GENA-LM` we attached an independent U-Net decoder to layer 6 (`GENA-LM base` total depth is 12 layers). During training, the losses from the intermediate and final heads were averaged to obtain the final training objective. As shown in Table 1, this modification substantially improved gene-level performance for `Caduceus`, with the strongest gains for Caduceus PH and consistent improvements for Caduceus PS, but it did not improve GENA-LM overall. This difference is likely related to the segmented nature of the Recurrent Memory Transformer architecture [11]. In RMT the model has access only to the current segment and the memory carried over from preceding segments, but not to future tokens. As a result, auxiliary losses applied to earlier layers are less effective because those layers are required to make predictions before the model has traversed the full input sequence and accumulated the necessary long-range context. Based on this result, we used auxiliary loss in all final Caduceus experiments, but not in GENA-LM.

To investigate the biological features underlying model errors, we analyzed the precision and recall of exon detection, stratifying exon-intron boundary errors based on their flanking dinucleotide sequences (Appendix G, Figure A3). Although the frequency of predicted boundaries at each dinucleotide generally reflects the true distribution, we identified samples where dinucleotides flanking predicted boundaries never occur at boundary positions in the actual data. Explicitly excluding exons flanked by these "illegal" dinucleotides, designated as a "splice site filter" improves the performance of all models (Table 1).

As noted in the Introduction (Fig. 1A), genes occur in both orientations relative to the reference genome, and for this reason, we apply a test-time reverse-complement (RC) augmentation in which each sequence is processed in its reference and RC orientations using average of the predictions as final output. As shown in Table 1, this approach yields substantial improvements in performance for all models. Notably, Caduceus PS, whose architecture explicitly enforces RC equivariance in the DNA input representation, still benefits significantly from test-time RC augmentation and achieves a $\approx 1.5\times$ improvement in performance. This effect arises because sequences are segmented into fixed-size chunks and opposite orientations induce different chunkings, so averaging behaves like an ensembling. Furthermore, RC augmentation provides greater performance gains than applying a splice-site filter for both Caduceus models. To the best of our knowledge, this is the first study applying reverse-complement augmentation in the context of the gene segmentation task.

We additionally applied a CDS heuristic as a post-processing step for protein-coding transcripts. It concatenates the predicted exons, translates them in all reading frames, selects the longest resulting protein consistent with valid start and stop codons, and maps it back onto the predicted exons (Appendix I, Figure A4). As shown in Table 1, this substantially improves CDS reconstruction for mRNA transcripts, while not affecting lncRNA predictions.

Finally, we compared performance across model architectures. Consistent with previous benchmarks [19], Caduceus PS outperformed Caduceus PH in all experimental settings. The Transformer-based GENA-LM exhibited superior performance in lncRNA detection, whereas the SSM Caduceus detected a substantially higher number of protein-coding genes and achieved markedly better CDS segmentation compared to GENA-LM. We hypothesized that nucleotide counting is required to identify triplet-organized CDS. Whereas GENA-LM utilizes variable-length BPE tokens, making the counting task challenging, Caduceus employs single-nucleotide tokenization, which may explain improved performance for the CDS class. In contrast, GENA-LM consistently outperformed Caduceus in lncRNA segmentation, a task that is more challenging than mRNA for both models, and this advantage aligns with model capacity, since GENA base has approximately 120M parameters compared to 16M in Caduceus. When we trained the same base setup but with the larger 360M parameter GENA-LM, lncRNA segmentation performance improved by 25%, further highlighting the benefits of model scaling for this task (Appendix J, Table A12).

4.3 Scaling

To further improve model performance, we scaled and combined the features identified as most impactful for gene segmentation. Specifically, we increased the input sequence length to 250 Kb, utilized data from 39 mammalian species, and included all gene types in the training set. For the Transformer-based architecture, we employed a larger instance of GENA-LM with an increased number of parameters (GENA large), while for the SSM we used the Caduceus PS variant, which consistently demonstrated performance superior to Caduceus PH in our benchmarks.

At test time, we applied splice-site filtering, reverse-complement (RC) augmentation, and the CDS heuristic described earlier. We refer to the resulting models as GENATATORs, a DNA language model-based family of gene annotators.

After scaling, the Caduceus PS model achieved the best overall gene-level performance (Fig. 2), outperforming GENA large and all other evaluated methods. In this final configuration, Caduceus PS was trained with auxiliary loss, longer context, and multispecies data, and this combination yielded best overall result. Contrary to our earlier observations in smaller-scale experiments, the scaled Caduceus PS model no longer shows a trade-off relative to GENA large, but instead achieves higher scores across all evaluated transcript categories, including CDS mRNA, exon mRNA, and lncRNA. GENA large remains the second-best model overall, whereas Tiberius retains competitive performance only on CDS-level protein-coding reconstruction and falls far behind on the full gene-level benchmark, which also evaluates exon-level mRNA reconstruction, including UTRs and lncRNA annotation.

4.4 Benchmarking GENATATOR Against Other Gene-Annotation Tools

We evaluated the performance of the GENATATOR models in comparison with several state-of-the-art gene annotation tools, including the HMM-based AUGUSTUS [21], the CNN+HMM model Tiberius [9] and Helixer [10], the DNA LM-based SegmentNT (with variants trained on human-only and multispecies data) [6], and transformer-based models pretrained on gene expression, namely SegmentEnformer and SegmentBorzoi [6]. We also included the recently developed AlphaGenome [1] and NTv3 [2].

We first compared models using the conventional PR-AUC metric (Appendix J, Table A13). According to this evaluation, GENATATORs outperform SegmentNT, SegmentBorzoi, and SegmentEnformer, with an improvement of about 10% between the best-performing GENATATOR and the best-performing SegmentNT.

We then assessed performance using the gene-level metrics described above, reporting results as the total number of correctly segmented genes across all evaluated categories, namely CDS mRNA, exon mRNA including UTRs, and lncRNA (Fig. 2, with detailed metrics and model usage provided in Appendix I). Under this scoring scheme, GENATATORs identify substantially more genes than previously developed alternatives. In total, across these categories, GENATATORs show more than a threefold increase in the number of correctly segmented genes compared to Tiberius and AlphaGenome, and the gap to other models is even larger. Visual inspection of predicted gene structures reveals that lower-performing models such as SegmentNT frequently extend exon boundaries by several nucleotides, which in the case of mRNA leads to reading-frame shifts and consequently to biologically invalid truncated peptides. This observation underscores the importance of gene-level evaluation metrics for capturing biologically meaningful segmentation accuracy.

We attribute the improved performance of GENATATORs to a combination of training optimizations, including the use of multispecies data, extended input context lengths, and data augmentation strategies. As shown in Table 1, a basic training configuration with human-only data, a 4,096 bp input length, and no augmentations, or isolated modifications of this setup, produces results that are comparable to or worse than those achieved by SegmentNT.

GENATATORs also significantly outperform AUGUSTUS in the total number of correctly segmented genes. Stratifying performance by transcript type reveals that the Caduceus-based GENATATOR outperforms all other evaluated models, establishing a new state-of-the-art result in the total number of correctly segmented genes. In contrast, Tiberius outperforms the GENA-based GENATATOR in the number of correctly segmented protein-coding genes. However, Tiberius was developed primarily for protein-coding gene annotation and does not support broad annotation of lncRNA genes and UTRs within mRNA genes. This narrower annotation scope limits its overall gene annotation performance and leads to a lower total number of correctly segmented genes compared to GENATATOR.

The common metric for assessing the completeness of genome annotation is BUSCO [12]. To compute BUSCO, the predicted exon-intron structure of a gene is used to generate an amino acid sequence, which is then compared to a set of proteins that are specific to a particular taxonomy group. The results of BUSCO are presented as a number of proteins that were identified from a selected dataset. These proteins are divided into two categories: Complete and Fragmented, where fragmented proteins have some segments missing.

Using the mammalia-specific BUSCO dataset, GENATATORs recovered a comparable number of BUSCO orthologs to Tiberius, but with a larger fraction of fragmented genes. Caduceus identified 252 orthologs (222 complete and 30 fragmented), while GENA identified 251 orthologs (224 complete and 27 fragmented).

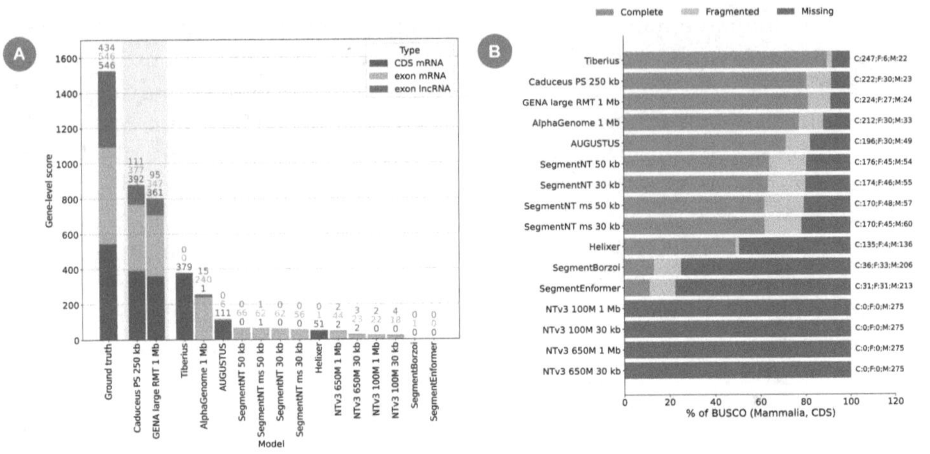

Fig. 2. Comparison of gene segmentation performance across different annotation models. A. Gene-level metrics, GENATATORs are highlighted in green. Exon mRNA type also ensures correct UTRs prediction compared to CDS mRNA type. B. Mammalian BUSCO metrics.

In comparison, Tiberius identified 253 orthologs, including the highest number of complete BUSCOs (247) and only 6 fragmented genes. The three leading models, GENATATORs and Tiberius, were followed by AlphaGenome, which recovered 212 complete and 30 fragmented genes.

These results are consistent with the design of the BUSCO benchmark. BUSCO evaluates only a conserved subset of protein-coding transcripts. On chromosome 20, the RefSeq annotation contains 3,146 mRNA transcripts, whereas only 1,310 are represented in BUSCO. Accordingly, the advantage of GENATATORs is more evident in our transcript-level reconstruction metrics than in BUSCO, while Tiberius appears biased toward more conserved isoforms.

Other models, including SegmentNT, SegmentBorzoi, SegmentEnformer and NTv3 showed substantially lower BUSCO recovery rates, consistent with their lower gene level segmentation performance. These results further reinforce the conclusion that conventional classification metrics such as PR-AUC are poor proxies for evaluating the biological utility of the models.

We next investigated whether segmentation errors made by different tools are shared or model-specific. Shared errors would suggest the presence of genes with structural features that are out-of-distribution relative to the training data, while model-specific errors would indicate that each tool fails on a unique subset of genes. To explore this, we analyzed the overlap of correctly segmented genes among the three top-performing models: the two GENATATOR variants and Tiberius. As shown in Fig. 3, there is a substantial intersection of correctly segmented genes across all models, supporting the hypothesis that certain genes present a challenge to all tools. At the same time, each model also segments a distinct subset of genes not correctly annotated by the others. In compar-

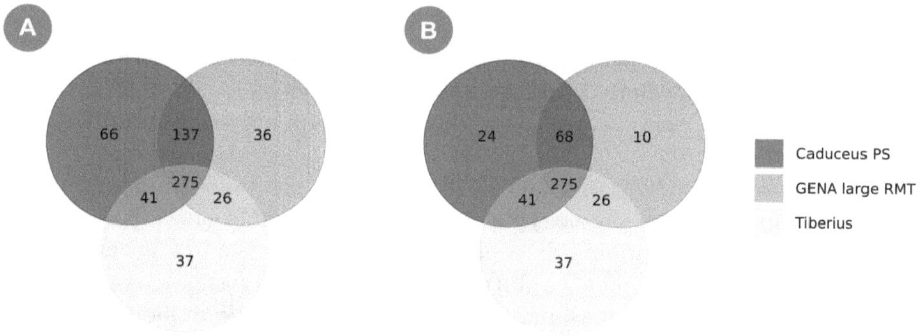

Fig. 3. Each model provides unique set of annotated genes, yet large portion of errors are shared accross models. Overlap of correctly segmented genes shown for protein-coding and lncRNA genes together (A), and for protein-coding genes only (B).

isons between `GENATATORs` and `Tiberius`, the unique gene set recovered by `GENATATORs` is largely composed of lncRNAs, which `Tiberius` is not designed to annotate. Meanwhile, the unique gene set recovered by `Tiberius` is likely enriched in conserved genes, which may explain the higher number of complete BUSCO genes recovered by this model (Fig. 2B). These findings suggest that model ensembling is currently the most effective strategy for maximizing gene annotation coverage across both coding and non-coding transcripts.

Overall, our results position `GENATATORs` as state-of-the-art models for gene annotation, with particular strength in the detection of non-coding genes and UTRs. The computational resource requirements of our models are described in Appendix H.

4.5 `GENATATORs` generalize across unseen species at large evolutionary distances

Table 2. Gene-level performance of different models on evolutionarily distant species. `Tiberius` (specialized) column denotes the use of model weights pretrained on the phylogenetic group corresponding to the target organism (Eudicotyledons for *A. thalian* and Fungi for *S. cerevisiae*).

Species	Chromosome	Gene type	Class	Ground Truth	Caduceus PS	GENA large	Tiberius	Tiberius (specialized)	AUGUSTUS
A. thaliana	NC_003075.7	mRNA	EXON	4180	**1355**	1330	0	0	298
			CDS		1462	1476	594	1127	**2286**
		lncRNA	EXON	513	**310**	307	0	0	22
		all RNA	EXON	4693	**1665**	1637	0	0	320
S. cerevisiae	NC_001136.10	mRNA	EXON	766	**733**	697	0	0	0
			CDS		**725**	689	0	0	358
		lncRNA	EXON	NA	NA	NA	NA	NA	NA
		all RNA	EXON	766	**733**	697	0	0	0

A key application of *ab initio* gene predictors is the annotation of genomes from previously unannotated species. To evaluate the cross-species generalization of our models, we first evaluated performance using gene-level metric on two evolutionarily remote species representing different kingdoms of life: the flowering plant *Arabidopsis thaliana* (GCF_000001735.4) and the budding yeast *Saccharomyces cerevisiae* (GCF_000146045.2) (Table 2). At the nucleotide level, there is effectively no sequence homology between their genes and those of mammalian species included in the training dataset, and thus the models had never encountered any comparable sequences during training. Despite this extreme divergence, the models retained reasonable accuracy. For *A. thaliana*, both Caduceus PS and GENA large showed strong cross-species generalization, with Caduceus PS achieving the best exon-level reconstruction overall and substantially outperforming Tiberius, including its specialized version, as well as AUGUSTUS. In CDS reconstruction for *A. thaliana*, however, AUGUSTUS achieved the best result, whereas both versions of Tiberius remained well below Caduceus PS and GENA large. For *S. cerevisiae*, whose compact genome lacks spliceosomal introns, Caduceus PS again achieved the best performance and outperformed all baselines, whereas Tiberius and its specialized version failed to recover any genes. NA entries in the lncRNA row of Table 2 indicate the absence of annotated lncRNAs in the reference genome.

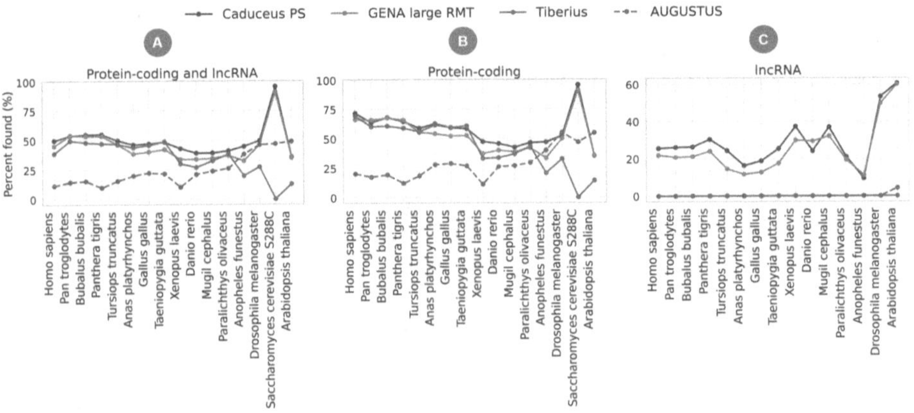

Fig. 4. GENATATORs generalize to previously unseen species. Performance of the models in human and 13 other species for all (A), protein-coding (B), and lncRNA (C) genes. *S. cerevisiae* was excluded from panel (C) because it lacks lncRNA genes. See Appendix J Tables A16 for more information on metrics.

Same results were obtained when we excluded all genes with detectable protein-level similarity to mammals, to ensure that models can not find homology even after internally translating DNA to amino acid code. Under this stringent setting, GENATATORs reconstructed more than twice as many genes as AUGUSTUS, despite the latter being run with a species-specific profile (Appendix K). Thus, although not tuned for plants or fungi, the models were able to produce useful first-pass annotations in such genomes, providing strong evidence that their capabilities extend beyond mere memorization of homologous patterns.

In addition to this extreme test, we benchmarked the models across a spectrum of animal species, ranging from primates closely related to humans to distant lineages such as insects (Fig. 4). The ranking of methods remained largely consistent across species. DNA language models outperformed classical annotation tools, with `Caduceus PS` achieving the best overall performance and `GENA large` usually ranking second. In contrast, `Tiberius` and `AUGUSTUS` performed substantially worse on evolutionarily distant organisms. For protein-coding genes, segmentation accuracy decreased with evolutionary distance from human, whereas lncRNA detection was lower in mammals but higher in several distant taxa. In most species, `Caduceus PS` matched or exceeded `GENA large`.

Conclusions

In this work, we comprehensively evaluated the utility of DNA LMs for the gene segmentation task. We show, both theoretically and empirically, that interval level metrics better reflect biological relevance than conventional token level classifiers and introduce dedicated benchmark to score gene segmentation models.

We demonstrated that embeddings from pretrained DNA LMs do not contain sufficient information for accurate gene segmentation. However, by identifying optimal training regimes, datasets, augmentations, and output filters, we enabled efficient fine-tuning and inference of gene structure. We further showed that scaling DNA LMs under these conditions substantially improves performance, leading to state-of-the-art results.

We found that sensitivity to different functional gene elements, such as CDS and UTRs, varies across DNA LM architectures. Nonetheless, all evaluated DNA LMs were capable of detecting lncRNA genes, which remain inaccessible to current state-of-the-art tools such as `Tiberius`.

Furthermore, `GENATATORs`, our fine-tuned DNA LM-based models, generalize effectively to unseen species across large evolutionary distances. These results highlight the potential of DNA LMs to serve as powerful tools for *de novo* genome annotation in a wide range of biological and evolutionary studies.

Limitations. While `GENATATORs` demonstrate strong performance in benchmarking studies, their accuracy remains far from perfect. Currently, only approximately 30–40% of all human genes can be correctly segmented by any of the models evaluated in this study.

Another limitation lies in gene discovery. Although gene segmentation is a critical component of genome annotation, complete annotation also requires accurate identification of gene boundaries, including non-coding untranslated regions (UTRs), which remains challenging for all evaluated tools.

Finally, the poor results observed in our embedding-only training experiments highlight a fundamental limitation of current DNA language models: they do not capture gene structure during the pretraining phase. This underscores the need for architectural or training paradigm improvements in future DNA LM development.

Acknowledgment. Support from the Basic Research Program of HSE University is gratefully acknowledged (HSE-BR-2025–020).

Code availability. HuggingFace versions of the datasets and models, in PyTorch, can be found via HuggingFace at https://huggingface.co/collections/AIRI-Institute/genatator. The gene-segmentation benchmark is available via HuggingFace at https://huggingface.co/spaces/AIRI-Institute/genatator-ab-initio-segmentation-leaderboard.

References

1. Avsec, Ž., et al.: AlphaGenome: advancing regulatory variant effect prediction with a unified DNA sequence model. bioRxiv pp. 2025–06 (2025)
2. Boshar, S., et al.: A foundational model for joint sequence-function multi-species modeling at scale for long-range genomic prediction. bioRxiv pp. 2025–12 (2025)
3. Brixi, G., et al.: Genome modeling and design across all domains of life with Evo 2. BioRxiv pp. 2025–02 (2025)
4. Castillo-Hair, S., et al.: Optimizing 5'UTRS for mRNA-delivered gene editing using deep learning. Nat. Commun. **15**(1), 5284 (2024)
5. Dalla-Torre, H., et al.: Nucleotide transformer: building and evaluating robust foundation models for human genomics. Nat. Methods 1–11 (2024)
6. De Almeida, B.P., et al.: Annotating the genome at single-nucleotide resolution with DNA foundation models. Nat. Methods, 1–15 (2025)
7. Filatova, A., et al.: Annotation of uORFs in the OMIM genes allows to reveal pathogenic variants in 5' UTRs. Nucleic Acids Res. **51**(3), 1229–1244 (2023)
8. Fishman, V., et al.: GENA-LM: a family of open-source foundational DNA language models for long sequences. Nucleic Acids Res. **53**(2), gkae1310 (2025)
9. Gabriel, L., Becker, F., Hoff, K.J., Stanke, M.: Tiberius: end-to-end deep learning with an hmm for gene prediction. Bioinformatics **40**(12), btae685 (2024)
10. Holst, F., et al.: Helixer: ab initio prediction of primary eukaryotic gene models combining deep learning and a hidden markov model. Nat. Methods 1–8 (2025)
11. Kuratov, Y., Shmelev, A., Fishman, V., Kardymon, O., Burtsev, M.: Recurrent memory augmentation of GENA-LM improves performance on long DNA sequence tasks. In: ICLR 2024 Workshop on Machine Learning for Genomics Explorations (2024). https://openreview.net/forum?id=K671lCX90x
12. Manni, M., Berkeley, M.R., Seppey, M., Zdobnov, E.M.: BUSCO: assessing genomic data quality and beyond. Current Protocols **1**(12), e323 (2021)
13. Marchal, I.: Evo learns biological complexity from the molecular to genome scale. Nat. Biotech. **42**(12), 1793–1793 (2024)
14. Marin, F.I., et al.: BEND: benchmarking DNA language models on biologically meaningful tasks. arXiv preprint arXiv:2311.12570 (2023)
15. Mattick, J.S., et al.: Long non-coding RNAs: definitions, functions, challenges and recommendations. Nat. Rev. Mol. Cell Biol. **24**(6), 430–447 (2023)

16. Peng, B., Quesnelle, J., Fan, H., Shippole, E.: YaRN: efficient context window extension of large language models. arXiv preprint arXiv:2309.00071 (2023)
17. Raghavan, V., Kraft, L., Mesny, F., Rigerte, L.: A simple guide to de novo transcriptome assembly and annotation. Briefings Bioinform. **23**(2), bbab563 (2022)
18. Scalzitti, N., Jeannin-Girardon, A., Collet, P., Poch, O., Thompson, J.D.: A benchmark study of ab initio gene prediction methods in diverse eukaryotic organisms. BMC Genomics **21**, 1–20 (2020)
19. Schiff, Y., Kao, C.H., Gokaslan, A., Dao, T., Gu, A., Kuleshov, V.: Caduceus: Bi-directional equivariant long-range DNA sequence modeling (2024). https://arxiv.org/abs/2403.03234
20. Sharma, S., Houfani, A.A., Foster, L.J.: Pivotal functions and impact of long con-coding RNAs on cellular processes and genome integrity. J. Biomed. Sci. **31**(1), 52 (2024)
21. Stanke, M., Steinkamp, R., Waack, S., Morgenstern, B.: AUGUSTUS: a web server for gene finding in eukaryotes. Nucleic Acids Res. **32**(suppl_2), W309–W312 (2004)
22. Szegedy, C., et al.: Going deeper with convolutions. In: Proceedings of the IEEE Conference on Computer Vision and Pattern Recognition, pp. 1–9 (2015)
23. Zhou, Z., Ji, Y., Li, W., Dutta, P., Davuluri, R., Liu, H.: DNABERT-2: efficient foundation model and benchmark for multi-species genome. arXiv preprint arXiv:2306.15006 (2023)

KARL: Knowledge-Attentive Representation Learning for Wearable Hand Gesture Recognition in Motor-Impaired Individuals

Riyad Bin Rafiq(✉), Weishi Shi, and Mark V. Albert

University of North Texas, Denton, USA
riyadbinrafiq@my.unt.edu, {weishi.shi,mark.albert}@unt.edu

Abstract. Hand gestures provide a flexible and spontaneous means of communication for people. Current hand gesture recognition approaches depend on predefined gestures and require many training examples to build an accurate classification model. This poses significant challenges for the motor-impaired population, as collecting training examples is extremely difficult and expensive. Moreover, due to the health condition, the severity of impairment, and motion pattern, the impaired individuals' data is highly variable and noisy. These characteristics introduce instability and complexity into the learning process, making it more difficult for this population to achieve reliable gesture recognition. To address this, we introduce Knowledge-Attentive Representation Learning (KARL) in a replay-based Few-Shot Continual Learning (FSCL) framework that can learn gesture classes incrementally using a few training examples per class. KARL leverages attention mechanisms to effectively learn a representation with limited training data by utilizing preserved gesture prior knowledge. This allows motor-impaired individuals to effectively use wearable devices, facilitating the learning and application of their unique movement styles in human-computer interaction and social communication. Ours code is available at this link.

Keywords: Attention · Continual Learning · Motor Impairment · Wearable Hand Gesture

1 Introduction

Hand gestures offer an important means of communication for individuals with speech or motor impairments. They also provide a convenient interaction alternative for the general population in scenarios where traditional input methods are limited or impractical, such as in libraries, underwater operations, or emergency rescue settings. These dual roles motivate the development of effective hand gesture recognition systems. To support this goal, researchers have explored a wide range of approaches, including the use of images and videos [35], electromyography (EMG) [21], and wearable sensors [33]. The increasing popularity

M. Ceci et al. (Eds.): ECML PKDD 2026, LNAI 16948, pp. 530–546, 2027.
https://doi.org/10.1007/978-3-032-37679-4_30

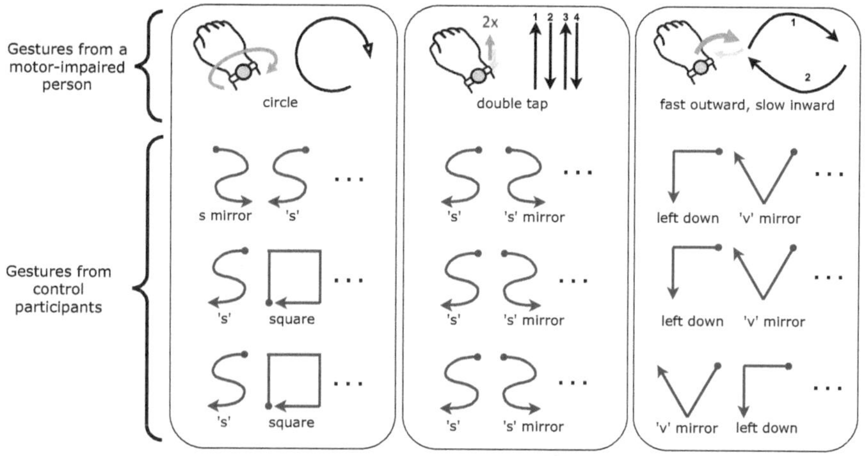

Fig. 1. Illustration of how our model leverages control-participant gestures to generalize limited motor-impaired gestures during training. In this example, the model is trained on three gestures, each with three examples. Each large panel shows one impaired gesture (left: gesture depiction, right: its 2D motion trajectory). For each gesture, we plot the top-2 control gestures that receive the highest attention weights for three different training examples. Although control participants never perform the impaired gesture directly, the model automatically selects control gestures whose motion patterns partially approximate the impaired shape or its irregularities (e.g., the combination of an 's' and 'square' approximates a noisy circle). These control gestures compensate for the scarcity of impaired data and provide richer structural and noise patterns, enabling the model to better capture the impaired gestures variability.

of wearable gesture technology unlocks exciting possibilities across diverse fields, such as entertainment, smart home control, clinical applications, and communication [17,23]. Unfortunately, the gestures of motor-impaired individuals cannot be utilized with wearables in the same way as they are for the general population since these devices are primarily designed for typical users [27]. For typical users, these systems assume a certain level of motor ability and consistent gesture execution. As motor-impaired individuals may not have these abilities, the systems face significant challenges in recognition and interaction. Additionally, the severity of motor impairment creates individual differences and distinct motion styles [34]. As a result, a large underrepresented population is excluded from benefiting from this technology, which is limiting the broader social impact of gesture-based interaction systems.

An intuitive solution to overcoming the challenges in gesture recognition for motor-impaired individuals would be to collect a large-scale labeled dataset from the motor-impaired population to build a robust gesture classification model. However, extensive data collection is impractical and burdensome for motor-impaired individuals due to the nature of their health conditions and the severity of their impairments [32]. Transfer learning can play an important role in solving this. In transfer learning, a model is initially trained in a source domain and then adapted to a target domain using knowledge from the previously learned task [22]. However, the performance degrades during fine-tuning when limited [11] and out-of-distribution [9] training examples are observed in the target domain. To mitigate this issue, few-shot learning can be employed to utilize limited training examples effectively [4], reducing the burden on users while enabling the model to capture the necessary pattern. Few-shot learning can specifically address the problem of high variability in gesture examples from motor-impaired individuals, which fine-tuning alone cannot resolve. Individuals lacking fine motor skills may struggle to perform pre-defined gestures and often require custom, flexible gestures due to greater memorability, enhanced interaction efficiency, and better accessibility [1,18]. Consequently, not all gesture classes may be available initially, and new, unseen classes may need to be added incrementally. This is where continual learning comes into play, allowing the model to learn a series of disjoint classes incrementally [19]. These challenges highlight the need for a systematic approach that combines elements of transfer learning, few-shot learning, and continual learning.

The challenge is straightforward in our setting: we have sufficient gesture examples from individuals without motor impairments (referred to as control participants). However, only a few training examples of various gestures can be collected from individuals with motor impairments when needed. This raises an important research question: *how can we effectively leverage the labeled training examples from control participants to train a custom gesture model using only a few labeled examples for a motor-impaired individual in a continual learning setting?* As a solution, we introduce a method called Knowledge-Attentive Representation Learning (KARL) which leverages three latent representation spaces: the *preserved*, *temporary*, and *learned* spaces. The *preserved latent representation* works as gesture prior knowledge. The *temporary* and the *learned* maintain an intra-gesture divergence using available gesture classes. They collectively aid the fine-tuning approach in navigating toward a diversified and robust feature representation space. Figure 1 illustrates how each target gesture leverages relevant patterns learned from the control participants gestures. Therefore, our framework can help motor-impaired people take full advantage of wearable devices and assist them in the interaction between humans and computers. Our contributions are as follows:

- We investigate wearable hand gesture recognition from the motor-impaired population. Moreover, we propose KARL in a replay-based few-shot continual learning setting that can construct a diverse representation space utilizing the attention mechanism referred to as the knowledge-attention module.
- We use two public gesture datasets to evaluate KARL. It shows better performance compared to other methods.

2 Related Work

Wearable Hand Gesture Recognition. Researchers and practitioners have made significant contributions to wearable hand gesture recognition in terms of algorithms and applications [5]. Early work relied on hand-crafted statistical features, such as mean, median, variance, maximum, and minimum, derived from three-axis acceleration data [10]. Deep learning approaches, including Convolutional Neural Networks (CNN) and Recurrent Neural Networks (RNN), have demonstrated satisfactory performance by automatically extracting features from training data examples [6,23]. However, these methods sometimes fail to consider inter-feature information and are constrained by sequential processing. The community has turned to a new state-of-art-approach: Transformer to address these limitations. The key attribute of the Transformer is the attention mechanism that can capture the spatio-temporal context of long-range dependencies in time-series signals. Originally showing great performance in natural language processing [31] and vision tasks [3], currently, Transformers are also excelling in wearable gesture recognition [29].

Learning Methods and Motor-Impaired People. To minimize the burden on users, the wearable approach should utilize a limited number of data examples. Early trajectory-based approaches, including Hidden Markov Models (HMM) [15] and Dynamic Time Warping (DTW) [12] show promising results using few examples. However, these are applied to a known set of gestures. Practitioners have developed frameworks that allow for the learning of new custom gestures using only a few training examples [2,16]. This advancement enhances the flexibility and applicability of various use cases. This context introduces concepts such as few-shot learning and continual learning, which together aim to enable a deep neural network to incrementally learn new classes with a minimal number of training examples while retaining knowledge of previously learned classes [30]. For instance, a hand gesture customization framework has been introduced by [33] that learns custom hand gestures incrementally using limited training examples. Wearable sensor data is also utilized for few-shot hand gesture recognition using a self-supervised and fine-tuning approach [8]. These works only focus on the control participants' data. Furthermore, these methods are ineffective for motor-impaired users as their provided samples are highly variable and noisy. In the literature, some research explored the interactions with smartwatches for individuals with upper-body motor impairments but these works only consider touch gestures [7,14]. Multiple wearable sensors have been used to implement gesture recognition for post-stroke participants within a few-shot learning framework [26]. Only the LEE framework considered a small number of labeled training examples on motion gestures from motor-impaired participants within a continual learning setting [24]. The primary difference between existing research and our work is that we leverage a pre-trained self-attention model and introduce a knowledge-attention module to fine-tune the classification model using a limited number of out-of-distribution training examples.

3 Problem Statement

Setting Description. A domain is defined as a joint probability distribution $\mathbb{P}_{\mathbf{x},y}$ on $\mathcal{X} \times \mathcal{Y}$, where $\mathcal{X}$ represents the instance space and $\mathcal{Y}$ represents the label space following the standard definition from [20]. We have two datasets: the source dataset, denoted as $\mathcal{D}^s = \{(x_i, y_i)\}_{i=1}^{n_s}$, which consists of independent and identically distributed (i.i.d) samples from the distribution P^s, and the target dataset, denoted as $\mathcal{D}^t = \{(x_i, y_i)\}_{i=1}^{n_t}$, which consists of i.i.d samples from the distribution P^t. In our protocol, n_s is the number of source dataset examples, while n_t is the number of target dataset examples. The relationship $n_t << n_s$ shows that target examples are much fewer than source examples. The source represents data from control individuals, while the target represents data from motor-impaired individuals. Each gesture example, $x \in \mathbb{R}^{L\times3}$ denotes a signal of length L with three-axis acceleration data recorded from wearable sensors at each timestamp. Although the two domains share the same feature space ($\mathcal{X}^s = \mathcal{X}^t$), they have different label spaces ($\mathcal{Y}^s \neq \mathcal{Y}^t$). Moreover, their probability distributions are different i.e. $P^s(x_i, y_i) \neq P^t(x_i, y_i)$. The data distribution for $\mathcal{D}^t$ is more challenging to learn than $\mathcal{D}^s$ because of high-level noise and variation in spatio-temporal context in the feature space. Consequently, it is difficult for any statistical model to capture the pattern with limited examples.

Objective. Following the standard continual learning paradigm, $\mathcal{D}^t$ contains mutually disjoint classes, $\mathcal{C}^i$, where any two classes are $\mathcal{C}^i \cap \mathcal{C}^j = \varnothing$. Since new classes become available over time, ensuring that the model does not forget them while learning new ones, a memory buffer ($\mathcal{M}$) can be used. A memory buffer ($\mathcal{M}$) is a mechanism that stores training examples from previously learned classes to prevent forgetting when incorporating new classes. Therefore, our objective is to build a pre-trained model on the source dataset $f : \mathcal{X}^s \rightarrow \mathcal{Y}^s$ that can be fine-tuned with a limited number of training examples to acquire knowledge of the classes present in the target domain.

4 Method

4.1 Pre-trained Self-attention Model

Pre-trained models provide a robust and generalizable feature extractor rather than training from scratch [36]. This feature extractor possesses a generalizable representation space that helps address our challenges, such as a limited number of examples and noisy data in the target domain. Therefore, we pre-train a self-attention model using data from the source domain. We adopt the self-attention architecture from [13], retaining three components: positional encoding, self-attention blocks, and global temporal attention for our problem. The positional encoding helps the model understand the temporal order of the data by adding sine and cosine values to the sequence. The self-attention blocks adjust the feature value of each time step by considering its similarity to all other time steps,

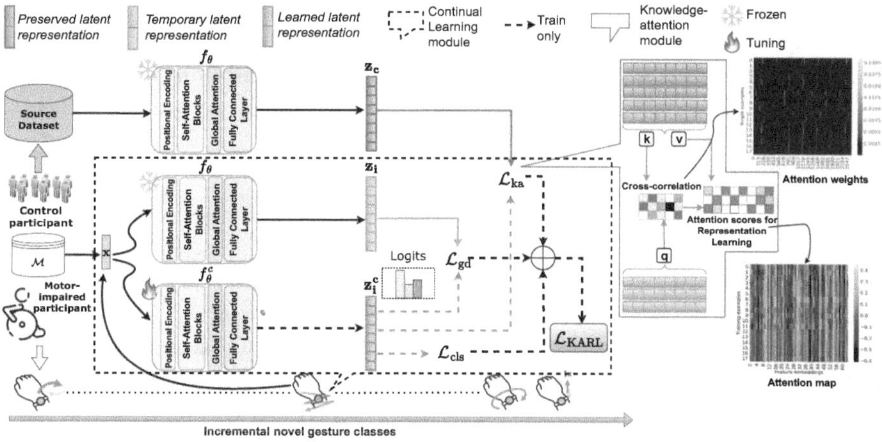

Fig. 2. The complete framework while learning a new gesture class. The *preserved latent representation*, $\mathbf{z_c}$ from the control population, is conserved as gesture prior knowledge. Two additional representations including *temporary latent representation*, $\mathbf{z_i}$ and *learned latent representation*, $\mathbf{z_i^c}$ maintain intra-gesture divergence. $\mathcal{M}$ denotes a memory buffer that stores training examples from old classes and makes them available while training on a new class. The knowledge-attention module demonstrates how the *learned latent representation* draws on relevant and necessary information from the gesture prior knowledge.

and the global temporal attention layer refines the representation for final classification. We remove the sensor modality attention, as it is designed for scenarios involving multiple sensors, which is unnecessary in our single-sensor context.

4.2 Overall Framework

The proposed framework in Fig. 2 highlights continual learning and knowledge-attention module. Our approach integrates elements of transfer learning and few-shot continual learning. We consider three multipurpose latent representations: *preserved*, *temporary*, and *learned* in this framework. The *preserved latent representation* from the control population is preserved by utilizing the feature extractor (deep encoder) of our pre-trained self-attention model and this representation serves as gesture prior knowledge, aiding the model in learning new out-of-distribution gesture examples incrementally and mitigating overfitting. Additionally, two identical feature extractors generate two latent representations (*temporary* and *learned*) using available gesture classes from motor-impaired subjects, with one being updated during training. Consequently, the acquired latent representation demonstrates a robust capability in classifying highly variable data during inference. The total loss, $\mathcal{L}_{\text{KARL}}$ in weighted summation is as follows:

$$\mathcal{L}_{\text{KARL}} = \alpha\mathcal{L}_{\text{ka}} + \beta\mathcal{L}_{\text{gd}} + \gamma\mathcal{L}_{\text{cls}} \tag{1}$$

where $\mathcal{L}_{\text{ka}}$ is a knowledge-attentive loss between the *preserved latent representation* and the *learned latent representation*, $\mathcal{L}_{\text{gd}}$ is the loss between the *learned latent representation* and the *temporary latent representation* and $\mathcal{L}_{\text{cls}}$ represents the classification loss. α, β and γ are not learnable parameters; they are manually set trade-off hyper-parameters where $\alpha + \beta + \gamma = 1$ and α, β, $\gamma > 0$. More discussion on α, β and γ will be found in appendix. The following sections describe each component of the total loss.

Knowledge-Attentive Representation. The *learned latent representation* diversifies and expands the feature space utilizing the *preserved latent representation* and works as a cross-attention mechanism. In our scenario, the cross-attention mechanism determines relative weights for each input example representation by considering its similarity to all preserved representations from the source domain. Consequently, the *learned latent representation* holds a transformed feature space with relevant and enriched information from the gesture prior knowledge even though only a few training examples per class are provided. For this, we employ the feature extractor, f_θ (deep encoder), from the pre-trained self-attention model to construct a *preserved latent representation*, $\mathbf{z_c} = f_\theta(\mathcal{X}^s)$ where $\mathcal{X}^s$ is the feature space from the source domain, which consists of control participants. This *preserved latent representation* serves as prior knowledge because it captures general patterns from the large and diverse source domain data that are likely to be relevant in the target domain. The model can effectively guide learning in the target domain with limited examples by extracting these common patterns. This extraction process is data-driven, ensuring that the identified patterns are reliable and useful for the target domain, following the principles of Bayesian inference. The input to our model is represented as $\mathbf{x}$. In our continual learning module, two additional identical deep encoders, f_θ and f_θ^c generate a *temporary latent representation*, $\mathbf{z_i}= f_\theta(\mathbf{x})$ and a *learned latent representation*, $\mathbf{z_i^c}= f_\theta^c(\mathbf{x})$ respectively. We compute the cross-attention function using the following equation:

$$\mathrm{f_{ca}}(\mathbf{q}, \mathbf{k}, \mathbf{v}') = \mathrm{softmax}(\frac{\mathbf{q} \cdot \mathbf{k}^T}{\sqrt{d_k}})\mathbf{v}' \quad (2)$$

where

$$\mathbf{v}' = \frac{\mathbf{v} - \min(\mathbf{v})}{\max(\mathbf{v}) - \min(\mathbf{v})} \quad (3)$$

The terms $(\mathbf{q}, \mathbf{k}, \mathbf{v}')$ are known as query, key, and value. In our context, the query is the *learned latent representation* vector while the key and the value both represent the *preserved latent representation* vector. We normalize the value vector as the magnitude of the value affects the computation. In this context, the query can be seen as the transformed vector from input data that is then compared to the key vector of every other data example from the source domain using the dot product. The dot product result is then scaled by $\sqrt{d_k}$ to prevent overly large outcomes and normalized using the softmax function to produce the attention weights. These weights are subsequently used to obtain a weighted representation of the value vectors for each data example. In Eq. 2, f_{ca} could have been implemented using simpler one-to-one similarity measures like cosine similarity. However, the chosen attention mechanism considers long-distance relationships between inputs, which allows for a more comprehensive integration of relevant information from the *preserved latent representation*. This approach not only captures immediate similarities but also leverages the broader context, making it particularly suitable for scenarios where subtle and distributed patterns are crucial. The entire process is implemented through matrix multiplication, as described in Eq. 2. In our module, it is essential to utilize similar and relevant information from our prior knowledge in the maximum way to minimize the loss:

$$\mathcal{L}_{\mathrm{ka}}(f_\theta^c; \mathbf{x}, \mathbf{z_c}) = 1 - \mathrm{f}_{\mathrm{ca}}(f_\theta^c(\mathbf{x}), \mathbf{z_c}) \quad (4)$$

Intra-Gesture Divergence. In the initial training phase, the *learned latent representation* and the *temporary latent representation* are identical. During training, the *learned latent representation* seeks to maximize the distance from the corresponding *temporary latent representation*, a process referred to as intra-gesture divergence. This is because the *temporary latent representation*, at the beginning, serves as a naive or suboptimal representation of the gesture features. By promoting dissimilarity between the two through self-repulsion, the model is guided to learn richer, more discriminative, and robust features. To maximize the dissimilarity between $\mathbf{z_i}$ and $\mathbf{z_i^c}$, the loss can be defined as follows:

$$\mathcal{L}_{\mathrm{gd}}(f_\theta, f_\theta^c; \mathbf{x}) = \mathcal{S}_c(f_\theta(\mathbf{x}), f_\theta^c(\mathbf{x})) \quad (5)$$

where $\mathcal{S}_c$ represents the cosine similarity given by:

$$\mathcal{S}_c(\mathbf{z_i}, \mathbf{z_i^c}) = \frac{\mathbf{z_i}^T \cdot \mathbf{z_i^c}}{||\mathbf{z_i}||||\mathbf{z_i^c}||} \quad (6)$$

Learning Goal. The goal of the model is to recognize gesture categories, which involve converting input sensor signals into gesture classes. Consequently, class labels are used in the final classification layer to guide the *learned latent representation* throughout training. For this classification task, we employ the standard cross-entropy loss function:

$$\mathcal{L}_{\mathrm{cls}}(f_\theta^c; \mathcal{X}^t, \mathcal{Y}^t) = -\mathbb{E}_{(\mathbf{x},y)\in\mathcal{X}^t\times\mathcal{Y}^t} \sum_{c=1}^{C} y \log \delta_c(f_\theta^c(\mathbf{x})) \quad (7)$$

where C and y represent the number of classes and true class labels, respectively. The $\delta_c(f_\theta^c(\mathbf{x}))$ function provides the predicted probability where δ_c is the softmax function.

5 Experimental Settings

5.1 Dataset

Source Dataset. The SmartWatch Gesture Dataset [2] was collected using arm gestures to interact with mobile applications. Eight participants provided 20 distinct gestures, each performed 20 times. During data collection, the users wore a first-generation Sony smartwatch with a built-in 3-axis accelerometer on their right wrist. The dataset contains 3200 sequences, each representing acceleration data.

Target Dataset. The Motion Gesture Dataset [32] was collected to comprehend the gesture articulation of upper-body motor-impaired people. To our knowledge, this is the only dataset that has been made available for research purposes. A group of 12 individuals (six males and six females) with upper-body motor impairments, aged 27 to 65 years, performed six different motion gestures for the study. The six gestures are: 'hand tap', 'double tap', 'circle', 'shake', 'fast outward slow inward', and 'slow outward fast inward'. The participants had a diverse range of disabilities, including spinal cord injury (3), multiple sclerosis (2), Parkinson's disease (2), spastic quadriplegia (2), spina bifida (1), Friedreichs ataxia (1), phocomelia (1). During data collection, the participants used a Samsung Gear Fit 2 smartwatch to perform eight repetitions for each gesture.

5.2 Compared Methods

Our method combines transfer learning, few-shot learning, and continual learning. Therefore, we compare our approach with alternative methods from each of these learning domains. Vanilla-Ft is a naive fine-tuning approach implemented utilizing the pre-trained self-attention model. MAML [4] facilitates a deep learning model to learn a class using a few examples. Prototypical Networks [28] learns a metric space where classification is achieved by calculating distances to the prototype representations of each class. We adapt the methods to account for the limited training examples available from the target domain. iCaRL [25] has shown promising results in solving many continual learning tasks. LEE [24] uniquely utilizes a latent embedding extracted from a source dataset to learn target classes incrementally using a few labeled examples.

6 Results

6.1 Overall Performance

Training data are limited in the motor-impaired population, so we use only a few examples to evaluate KARL. In our study, we focus on continual learning adaptation tailored to each user, which is why the results are presented on a

Table 1. Test accuracies and F1 score (mean) for a motor-impaired individual with spinal cord injury in a few-shot continual learning setting. The accuracy and score reflect the total performance across all encountered gesture classes, trained with one, three, and five training examples per class. The highest accuracy and F1 score are highlighted in bold. More results across different impairments are provided in the appendix.

Number of gestures	2		3		4		5		6	
Metrics	Acc	F1	Acc	F1	Acc	F1	Acc	F1	Acc	F1
1 example per class										
Vanilla-Ft	0.65	0.63	0.63	0.58	0.46	0.43	0.40	0.35	0.34	0.26
MAML-Ft [4]	0.48	0.40	0.38	0.30	0.25	0.19	0.22	0.14	0.21	0.15
Prototypical Network-Ft [28]	0.67	0.61	0.59	0.51	0.45	0.36	0.32	0.23	0.26	0.18
iCaRL [25]	**0.77**	**0.76**	-	-	0.50	0.45	-	-	0.39	0.34
LEE [24]	0.66	0.59	0.69	0.63	0.56	0.50	0.52	0.45	0.42	0.35
KARL (Ours)	0.66	0.65	**0.78**	**0.75**	**0.64**	**0.61**	**0.62**	**0.56**	**0.52**	**0.47**
3 examples per class										
Vanilla-Ft	0.75	0.73	0.72	0.67	0.50	0.45	0.46	0.40	0.39	0.33
MAML-Ft [4]	0.58	0.51	0.40	0.32	0.28	0.20	0.22	0.15	0.21	0.16
Prototypical Network-Ft [28]	0.76	0.72	0.62	0.54	0.48	0.40	0.34	0.23	0.30	0.20
iCaRL [25]	**0.84**	**0.83**	-	-	0.45	0.28	-	-	0.35	0.24
LEE [24]	0.78	0.75	0.75	0.70	**0.65**	**0.60**	0.59	0.53	0.47	0.40
KARL (Ours)	0.77	0.75	**0.79**	**0.77**	0.62	0.58	**0.63**	**0.58**	**0.58**	**0.52**
5 examples per class										
Vanilla-Ft	0.77	0.76	0.71	0.67	0.53	0.47	0.49	0.45	0.42	0.37
MAML-Ft [4]	0.56	0.50	0.45	0.36	0.28	0.20	0.24	0.17	0.19	0.12
Prototypical Network-Ft [28]	0.78	0.75	0.66	0.58	0.53	0.46	0.37	0.28	0.33	0.22
iCaRL [25]	**0.82**	**0.80**	-	-	0.46	0.31	-	-	0.24	0.14
LEE [24]	0.81	0.79	0.81	0.79	**0.67**	0.61	0.64	0.60	0.53	0.48
KARL (Ours)	0.80	0.79	**0.82**	**0.79**	0.65	**0.63**	**0.64**	**0.62**	**0.59**	**0.56**

per-user basis. Table 1 represents the accuracy of the classification of gestures and the F1 score for an individual with spinal cord injury when classes are incrementally trained. Compared to existing methods, KARL shows its advantages. However, as more training examples are provided, KARL outperforms LEE. Although iCaRL performs better at two initial gestures, its performance deteriorates significantly for incrementally added classes. For instance, iCaRL achieves 84% accuracy with three training examples, but it drops to 35% (a 49% decline) when four additional gestures are introduced. We observe an improvement in accuracy as more training examples are stored in the memory buffer. From Table 1, we observe that KARL achieves 78%, 62%, and 52.0% accuracy using only one training example for three, five, and six gestures, respectively. This improves to 79% (a 1.0% improvement), 63% (a 1.0% improvement), and

58% (a 6.0% improvement) accuracy with three training examples. KARL effectively leverages relevant gesture knowledge, even when only a few examples are available. Additionally, our learning mechanism enables the model to gain valuable insights into identifying important and useful gesture patterns based on the provided examples.

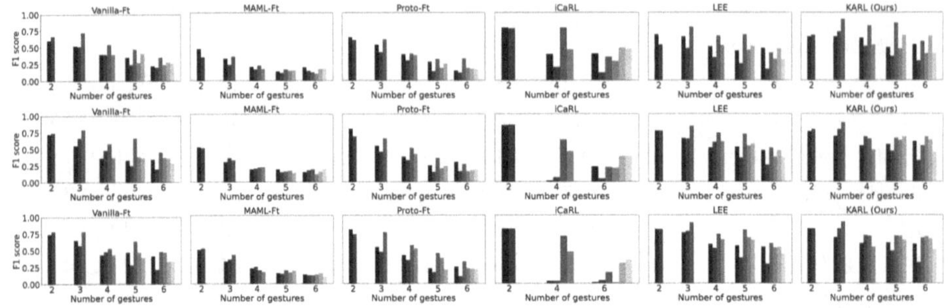

Fig. 3. Class-wise F1 score (mean) when gesture classes are incrementally added and trained using one (top row), three (middle row) and five examples (bottom row) for an individual with spinal cord injury.

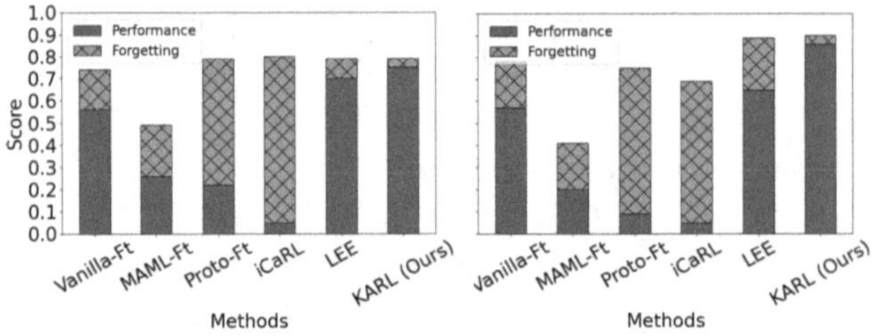

Fig. 4. Performance-*forgetting* scaled score for *Gesture 1* (left) and *Gesture 3* (right) for a motor-impaired participant with spinal cord injury after training on six gestures using five examples each.

6.2 Class-Wise Performance

In a continual learning setting, retaining strong performance on previously learned gesture classes is essential while training the model to recognize new classes. Figure 3 illustrates the F1 scores achieved by adding gesture classes incrementally using one, three, and five training examples per class. KARL consistently achieves a higher macro F1 score than other approaches, maintaining stable performance across new and old classes. In contrast, iCaRL effectively learns new gestures but tends to forget previously learned classes when additional new classes are introduced. MAML struggles to learn new classes. LEE demonstrates comparable performance to KARL but does not match KARLs ability to maintain accuracy in older classes. For example, when the sixth gesture is introduced in the setup, *Gesture 1* has an F1 score of 0.57, which is 7% higher than the second-best result from LEE. Figure 4 shows the performance-*forgetting* scores for *Gesture 1* and *Gesture 3* after training on six gestures. Prototypical Network-Ft and iCaRL exhibit more forgetting for these gestures than other methods. Although LEE offers a competitive *forgetting* score compared to KARL, KARL demonstrates 12.2% less forgetting for *Gesture 1* and 25.5% less forgetting for *Gesture 3* than LEE.

Table 2. Ablation study for a participant with spinal cord injury, test accuracies (mean) are provided with different combinations of components.

Components		Number of gestures														
		1 example per class					*3 examples per class*					*5 examples per class*				
$\mathcal{L}_{ka}$	$\mathcal{L}_{gd}$	2	3	4	5	6	2	3	4	5	6	2	3	4	5	6
✓	✓	0.66	**0.78**	**0.64**	0.62	**0.52**	**0.77**	0.79	0.62	0.63	**0.58**	**0.80**	**0.82**	0.65	0.64	**0.59**
✗	✓	**0.70**	0.76	0.62	**0.63**	0.52	0.77	**0.81**	0.59	**0.64**	0.58	0.79	0.80	0.65	0.63	0.58
✓	✗	0.64	0.76	0.62	0.60	0.52	0.76	0.81	**0.64**	0.63	0.56	0.79	0.79	**0.67**	**0.65**	0.57
✗	✗	0.65	0.63	0.46	0.40	0.34	0.75	0.72	0.50	0.46	0.39	0.77	0.71	0.53	0.49	0.42

6.3 Ablation Study

We conduct an ablation study to assess the effectiveness of different components of the total loss. We remove each component at a time and evaluate the performance. According to Table 2, our ablation study demonstrates the critical contributions of both components, $\mathcal{L}_{ka}$ and $\mathcal{L}_{gd}$ to the overall performance of our framework. When both components are included, the model achieves the highest accuracy in most cases. Interestingly, when either is individually removed, the model still maintains reasonably good performance, indicating that each component independently provides significant value. However, removing both components leads to a substantial drop in accuracy, underscoring their combined importance. These results suggest that both $\mathcal{L}_{ka}$ and $\mathcal{L}_{gd}$ work independently and interactively to enhance model performance, with their joint presence being crucial for achieving optimal results.

6.4 Knowledge-Attention Module Interpretation

Influence of Source Gestures. Figure 5 presents the t-SNE visualization of target and source gesture examples (Fig. 1) during a training phase in the two-dimensional representation space. The dots represent gesture examples from the

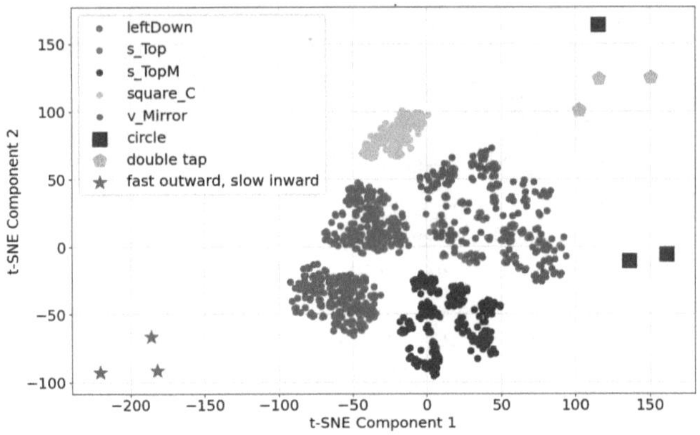

Fig. 5. A t-SNE plot showing target gesture examples (colored shapes: square, pentagon, star) and the corresponding source gesture examples (dots) in the lower-dimensional representation space. This visualization illustrates which source gestures influence each target gesture during training.

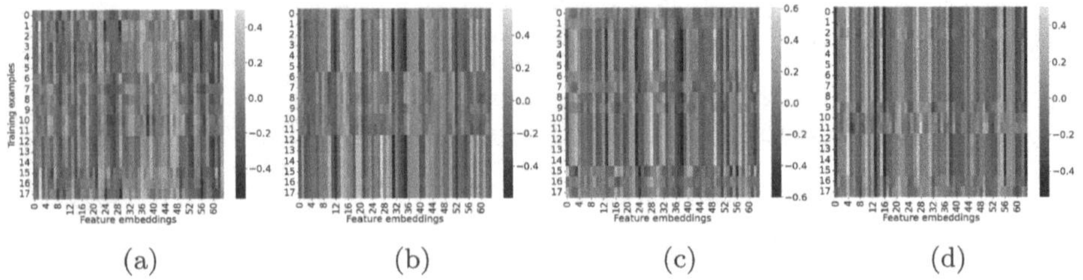

Fig. 6. Attention scores on different feature embeddings using three examples per class for training six gestures. The attention maps are visualized for four individuals with (a) No impairment, (b) Spinal cord injury, (c) Multiple sclerosis, and (d) Parkinson's disease.

control participants (source gestures), while the distinct colored shapes indicate the corresponding target gestures from a motor-impaired individual. We observe that each target gesture is influenced by relevant source gestures, reflecting the models ability to leverage prior knowledge. For instance, the target gesture 'fast outward, slow inward' draws patterns from 'v_Mirror' and 'leftDown', which are neighboring gestures to the target gesture. These source gestures' motion patterns partially approximate the impaired gesture or its irregularities. This demonstrates how examples from control participants gestures guide the learning of target gestures, allowing the model to generalize effectively under limited training data conditions.

Feature Embeddings Attention. Figure 6 illustrates the distributed attention scores across various feature embeddings, demonstrating how the method adjusts attention based on different participants, utilizing prior knowledge of gestures. The x-axis represents 64 feature embeddings, while the y-axis represents the training examples from the target domain. Attention varies across different embeddings for individuals with and without motor impairments. As mentioned earlier, various types of motor impairments result in individual variations and unique movement styles, leading to differences in attention on features among motor-impaired individuals within the same gesture class (Fig. 6b, 6c and 6d). We can interpret Fig. 6 from the perspective of the models ability to "learn meaningful features". The attention pattern appears quite random for individuals without impairments (Fig. 6a), with no clear pattern being learned. However, the attention maps for the three other types of motor impairments exhibit distinct and obvious patterns that are dependent on the type of impairment. This is particularly satisfying because it shows that the model, even in an unsupervised setting (where it does not know the type of impairment associated with each gesture), has learned gesture features that are dependent on the impairment type. This is highly beneficial for the learner when accurately classifying gestures, as the model can infer, for example, that a user has Parkinsons disease based on the input and subsequently penalize the samples variance (caused by the individuals uncontrolled hand shaking) to recognize the gesture better.

7 Conclusion and Future Work

Hand gestures are a natural and versatile means of communication. However, existing wearable hand gesture solutions are primarily designed for the general population and struggle to accurately capture the highly variable and inconsistent data from motor-impaired individuals. In real-world scenarios, motor-impaired individuals often find it challenging to perform predefined gestures, and many useful applications require the acquisition of new gestures. To address this, we introduce Knowledge-Attentive Representation Learning (KARL) in a few-shot continual learning framework to incrementally learn new gesture classes using only a limited number of training examples. The experimental results demonstrate that our method outperforms existing baselines in accuracy and reduced forgetting. KARL can potentially transform those individuals' lives by enhancing interactions and easing caregiver burden. In the future, we plan to integrate our method with a smartwatch to conduct testing with an extended number of fine-grained and complex gestures from motor-impaired individuals. This integration will allow us to evaluate the usability and accuracy of our approach in daily life scenarios, providing insights into how well the method supports users needs.

Supplementary material. Available at this link.

Acknowledgment. Research reported in this publication was supported by the Eunice Kennedy Shriver National Institute of Child Health & Human Development of the National Institutes of Health under Award Number P2CHD101899.

References

1. Anthony, L., Kim, Y., Findlater, L.: Analyzing user-generated youtube videos to understand touchscreen use by people with motor impairments. In: Proceedings of the SIGCHI Conference on Human Factors in Computing Systems, pp. 1223–1232 (2013)
2. Costante, G., Porzi, L., Lanz, O., Valigi, P., Ricci, E.: Personalizing a smartwatch-based gesture interface with transfer learning. In: 22nd European Signal Processing Conference (EUSIPCO), pp. 2530–2534. IEEE (2014)
3. Dosovitskiy, A., et al.: An image is worth 16×16 words: transformers for image recognition at scale. arXiv preprint arXiv:2010.11929 (2020)
4. Finn, C., Abbeel, P., Levine, S.: Model-agnostic meta-learning for fast adaptation of deep networks. In: International Conference on Machine Learning, pp. 1126–1135. PMLR (2017)
5. Gong, J., et al.: WrisText: one-handed text entry on smartwatch using wrist gestures. In: Proceedings of the 2018 CHI Conference on Human Factors in Computing Systems, pp. 1–14 (2018)
6. Khodabandelou, G., Jung, P.G., Amirat, Y., Mohammed, S.: Attention-based gated recurrent unit for gesture recognition. IEEE Trans. Autom. Sci. Eng. **18**(2), 495–507 (2020)
7. Kim, J.E., Bessho, M., Sakamura, K.: Towards a smartwatch application to assist students with disabilities in an IoT-enabled campus. In: IEEE 1st Global Conference on Life Sciences and Technologies (LifeTech), pp. 243–246. IEEE (2019)
8. Kimura, N.: Self-supervised approach for few-shot hand gesture recognition. In: Adjunct Proceedings of the 35th Annual ACM Symposium on User Interface Software and Technology, pp. 1–4 (2022)
9. Kumar, A., Raghunathan, A., Jones, R., Ma, T., Liang, P.: Fine-tuning can distort pretrained features and underperform out-of-distribution. arXiv preprint arXiv:2202.10054 (2022)
10. Laput, G., Xiao, R., Harrison, C.: ViBand: high-fidelity bio-acoustic sensing using commodity smartwatch accelerometers. In: Proceedings of the 29th Annual Symposium on User Interface Software and Technology, pp. 321–333 (2016)
11. Li, Z., Thaker, K., He, D.: Siakey: A method for improving few-shot learning with clinical domain information. In: 2023 IEEE EMBS International Conference on Biomedical and Health Informatics (BHI), pp. 1–4. IEEE (2023)
12. Liu, J., Zhong, L., Wickramasuriya, J., Vasudevan, V.: uWave: accelerometer-based personalized gesture recognition and its applications. Pervasive Mob. Comput. **5**(6), 657–675 (2009)
13. Mahmud, S., et al.: Human activity recognition from wearable sensor data using self-attention. In: ECAI 2020, pp. 1332–1339. IOS Press (2020)
14. Malu, M., Chundury, P., Findlater, L.: Exploring accessible smartwatch interactions for people with upper body motor impairments. In: Proceedings of the 2018 CHI Conference on Human Factors in Computing Systems, pp. 1–12 (2018)
15. Mckenna, S.J., Morrison, K.: A comparison of skin history and trajectory-based representation schemes for the recognition of user-specified gestures. Pattern Recogn. **37**(5), 999–1009 (2004)
16. Mezari, A., Maglogiannis, I.: An easily customized gesture recognizer for assisted living using commodity mobile devices. J. Healthc. Eng. **2018**(1), 3180652 (2018)

17. Oubre, B., Lee, S.I.: Estimating post-stroke upper-limb impairment from four activities of daily living using a single wrist-worn inertial sensor. In: 2022 IEEE-EMBS International Conference on Biomedical and Health Informatics (BHI), pp. 01–04. IEEE (2022)
18. Ouyang, T., Li, Y.: Bootstrapping personal gesture shortcuts with the wisdom of the crowd and handwriting recognition. In: Proceedings of the SIGCHI Conference on Human Factors in Computing Systems, pp. 2895–2904 (2012)
19. Parisi, G.I., Kemker, R., Part, J.L., Kanan, C., Wermter, S.: Continual lifelong learning with neural networks: a review. Neural Netw. **113**, 54–71 (2019)
20. Qian, H., Pan, S.J., Miao, C.: Latent independent excitation for generalizable sensor-based cross-person activity recognition. In: Proceedings of the AAAI Conference on Artificial Intelligence, vol. 35, pp. 11921–11929 (2021)
21. Quivira, F., Koike-Akino, T., Wang, Y., Erdogmus, D.: Translating sEMG signals to continuous hand poses using recurrent neural networks. In: 2018 IEEE EMBS International Conference on Biomedical & Health Informatics (BHI), pp. 166–169. IEEE (2018)
22. Rafiq, R.B., Albert, M.V.: Transfer Learning: leveraging trained models on novel tasks. In: Bridging Human Intelligence and Artificial Intelligence, pp. 65–74. Springer (2022)
23. Rafiq, R.B., Karim, S.A., Albert, M.V.: An LSTM-based gesture-to-speech recognition system. In: 2023 IEEE 11th International Conference on Healthcare Informatics (ICHI), pp. 430–438. IEEE (2023)
24. Rafiq, R.B., Shi, W., Albert, M.V.: Wearable sensor-based few-shot continual learning on hand gestures for motor-impaired individuals via latent embedding exploitation. arXiv preprint arXiv:2405.08969 (2024)
25. Rebuffi, S.A., Kolesnikov, A., Sperl, G., Lampert, C.H.: iCaRL: incremental classifier and representation learning. In: Proceedings of the IEEE conference on Computer Vision and Pattern Recognition, pp. 2001–2010 (2017)
26. Sarwat, H., Alkhashab, A., Song, X., Jiang, S., Jia, J., Shull, P.B.: Post-stroke hand gesture recognition via one-shot transfer learning using prototypical networks. J. Neuroeng. Rehabil. **21**(1), 100 (2024)
27. Siean, A.I., Vatavu, R.D.: Wearable interactions for users with motor impairments: systematic review, inventory, and research implications. In: Proceedings of the 23rd International ACM SIGACCESS Conference on Computers and Accessibility, pp. 1–15 (2021)
28. Snell, J., Swersky, K., Zemel, R.: Prototypical networks for few-shot learning. Adv. Neural Inf. Proces. Syst. **30** (2017)
29. Tang, Y., Pan, M., Li, H., Cao, X.: A convolutional-transformer based approach for dynamic gesture recognition of data gloves. IEEE Trans. Instrum. Meas. (2024)
30. Tao, X., Hong, X., Chang, X., Dong, S., Wei, X., Gong, Y.: Few-shot class-incremental learning. In: Proceedings of the IEEE/CVF Conference on Computer Vision and Pattern Recognition, pp. 12183–12192 (2020)
31. Vaswani, A., et al.: Attention is all you need. Adv. Neural Inf. Proces. Syst. **30** (2017)
32. Vatavu, R.D., Ungurean, O.C.: Understanding gesture input articulation with upper-body wearables for users with upper-body motor impairments. In: Proceedings of the 2022 CHI Conference on Human Factors in Computing Systems, pp. 1–16 (2022)
33. Xu, X., et al.: Enabling hand gesture customization on wrist-worn devices. In: Proceedings of the 2022 CHI Conference on Human Factors in Computing Systems, pp. 1–19 (2022)

34. Yamagami, M., Portnova-Fahreeva, A.A., Kong, J., Wobbrock, J.O., Mankoff, J.: How do people with limited movement personalize upper-body gestures? considerations for the design of personalized and accessible gesture interfaces. In: Proceedings of the 25th International ACM SIGACCESS Conference on Computers and Accessibility, pp. 1–15 (2023)
35. Zhou, B., Li, Y., Wan, J.: Regional attention with architecture-rebuilt 3D network for RGB-D gesture recognition. In: Proceedings of the AAAI Conference on Artificial Intelligence, vol. 35, pp. 3563–3571 (2021)
36. Zhou, D.W., Sun, H.L., Ning, J., Ye, H.J., Zhan, D.C.: Continual learning with pre-trained models: a survey. arXiv preprint arXiv:2401.16386 (2024)

Knowledge-Driven XRD Phase Identification via Multi-view Retrieval and Explanation

Doaa Mohamed(✉) and Markus Stricker

Materials Informatics and Data Science Group, Interdisciplinary Centre for Advanced Materials Simulation (ICAMS), Ruhr University Bochum, Bochum, Germany
{doaa.mohamed,markus.stricker}@ruhr-uni-bochum.de

Abstract. X-ray diffraction (XRD) is a key experimental technique for determining the phase composition and structure of crystalline materials. However, interpreting XRD patterns is inherently challenging, particularly in high-throughput materials discovery, where many novel materials may need to be characterized and no reference patterns are available for comparison. Consequently, machine learning is increasingly used to accelerate and automate the analysis process while reducing errors associated with human interpretation. We propose a multi-decision framework for XRD phase analysis that integrates representation learning, similarity-based retrieval, and explainable decision support within a unified reference database. A convolutional autoencoder learns compact latent representations of XRD patterns that preserve structural similarity while remaining robust to variations arising from experimental noise and measurement conditions. By integrating multiple decision pathways within a shared latent space, the framework moves beyond single-label prediction toward ranked and interpretable phase analysis that mirrors expert practice based on reference matching and peak inspection. During inference, complementary decision mechanisms are applied, including latent-space classification and retrieval, explanation-guided similarity using Integrated Gradients, and composition-based similarity search. These mechanisms generate ranked candidate phase lists that are aggregated into a final prediction with an associated confidence score. Experiments on synthetic datasets demonstrate strong predictive performance, achieving 98.85 % accuracy for crystal system classification and 95.82 % accuracy for space group prediction on the test set, while maintaining robustness under realistic perturbations. The framework supports reliable, analyst-friendly identification of crystal phases and structures in high-throughput and exploratory materials discovery settings.

Keywords: Autoencoder · Crystal structure · X-ray diffraction · Integrated Gradients

M. Ceci et al. (Eds.): ECML PKDD 2026, LNAI 16948, pp. 547–564, 2027.
https://doi.org/10.1007/978-3-032-37679-4_31

1 Introduction

High-throughput materials discovery generates large volumes of characterization data that enable the extraction of physical properties and structure-property relationships; however, it requires detailed analyses that are traditionally conducted by human experts [13,16]. A prominent example is the vast amount of characterization data produced by X-ray diffraction (XRD), which is a powerful technique for characterizing crystallographic structures, grain size, and molecular structures [12]. In an XRD experiment, an X-ray beam interacts with a crystalline sample, producing a diffraction pattern that records scattered intensity as a function of the diffraction angle 2θ. The characteristic peaks in this diffractogram encode information about the crystal structure and phase composition of the material. Experimental XRD patterns are typically analyzed by comparing peak descriptors such as positions, intensities, and full widths at half maximum (FWHM) with reference databases such as the Crystallography Open Database (COD) [7] and the Inorganic Crystal Structure Database (ICSD) [3]. Early attempts to automate this process relied on peak indexing [1] and full-profile matching algorithms [6]. However, these approaches often show limited accuracy because experimental spectra may deviate from ideal references due to defects, disorder, impurities, or missing reference patterns for novel materials. More recently, deep learning methods have emerged as powerful alternatives that learn directly from diffraction data and improve robustness to experimental variability [11,12,15,20]. Despite their strong performance, most deep learning approaches for XRD analysis remain purely discriminative classifiers that produce single-label predictions, providing limited interpretability and struggling with generalization across synthetic and experimental domains, particularly for structurally ambiguous or previously unseen compounds, which remains an important limitation in the context of materials discovery [9,10].

Such requirements naturally motivate representation-learning approaches, in which models learn compact latent embeddings that capture the essential structural information contained in diffraction patterns. Variational autoencoders (VAEs) have shown promise for XRD analysis by organizing diffraction patterns into low-dimensional latent spaces where structurally similar patterns cluster naturally [2]. These latent representations enable visualization, clustering, and novelty detection through reconstruction error or latent distance metrics. Beyond visualization and clustering, latent representations also provide a natural foundation for similarity-based retrieval, allowing query patterns to be compared directly against structurally related reference examples. Interpretability is essential for diffraction analysis because reliable predictions require physically meaningful explanations. We therefore integrate explainability with similarity-based reasoning to align model decisions with expert-driven peak interpretation workflows. In addition to interpretability, effective XRD phase identification benefits from flexible decision strategies that combine both parametric and nonparametric reasoning. In this context, parametric models refer to classifiers with learned parameters, such as neural networks, that map diffraction patterns to phase labels through a fixed set of trained weights. These models are efficient and perform well when query patterns closely match the training distribution. In contrast, non-parametric approaches rely on similarity-based comparison with stored reference examples rather than a fixed parametric mapping. Methods such as nearest-neighbor retrieval in latent representation space allow query patterns to be matched against known reference cases, which can provide more robust behavior in the presence of experimental variability or structural ambiguity [4,18].

Furthermore, diffraction data alone may not always be sufficient to uniquely identify a phase. Chemical composition provides complementary information that constrains the set of physically plausible structures and can therefore support or refine diffraction-based inference. Recent advances in representation learning enable chemical compositions to be encoded into continuous embedding spaces for similarity-based retrieval [14,17,21]. In contrast, our framework performs decision-level fusion over multiple complementary evidence sources, enabling ranked and interpretable crystallographic inference. These developments have opened new opportunities for incorporating compositional evidence into materials informatics workflows, including phase identification and materials discovery.

In this work, we introduce a unified framework for XRD phase analysis that integrates representation learning, similarity-based retrieval, chemical composition information, and explainable decision support to enable phase identification together with the prediction of key crystallographic descriptors, including crystal system and space group. An overview of the proposed framework is shown in Fig. 1. In crystallography, identifying the crystal system and space group is a fundamental step in determining the atomic arrangement of a material. The crystal system provides a coarse description of lattice symmetry, while the space group specifies the full symmetry of the structure, making these labels essential descriptors for characterizing and comparing crystalline phases from diffraction data. A convolutional autoencoder is trained to learn a compact latent representation of augmented experimental and simulated XRD patterns that preserves structural similarity while accounting for variations arising from experimental noise and measurement conditions. After training, the encoder is frozen and used to embed both reference and query patterns into a shared latent space. A latent reference library is constructed by embedding diffraction patterns generated from crystallographic information files under realistic instrumental, background, and sample-related variations, enabling similarity-based reasoning and interpretable comparison between measured and reference patterns. For a new diffraction measurement, phase identification is formulated as a multi-decision inference process rather than a single classification step. The query pattern is first encoded using the trained encoder to obtain its latent embedding. Cosine similarity between the normalized query embedding and the latent reference library enables retrieval of structurally similar candidate phases. In parallel, the classifier provides a prediction over the crystal systems and space groups. Peak-level explanations are computed using Integrated Gradients (IG) to identify influential diffraction regions and support explanation-guided peak matching. When available, chemi-

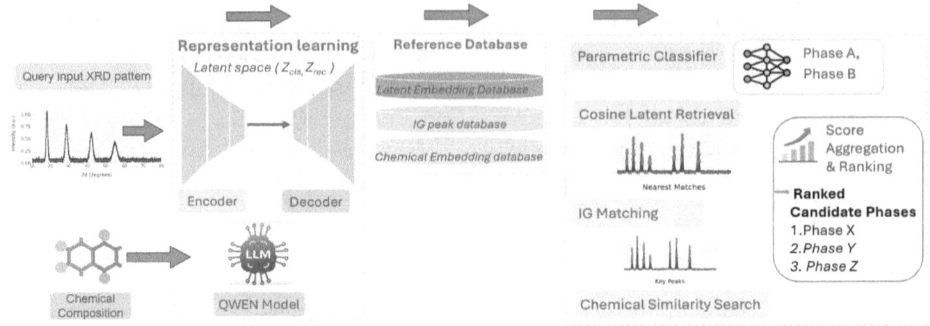

Fig. 1. Overview of the HyPhID framework for XRD phase identification. A query diffraction pattern is embedded using a convolutional autoencoder. Predictions combine classifier output, latent-space retrieval, Integrated Gradients (IG) similarity, and composition-based retrieval. The aggregated evidence produces ranked crystallographic predictions.

cal composition similarity is also incorporated. The ranked candidates and confidence scores from all components are aggregated to produce the final phase and crystallographic symmetry predictions. While the retrieval and classifier primarily contribute to predictive performance, the IG-based module mainly supports interpretability and case-based reasoning. We refer to this aggregated multi-decision inference strategy as Hybrid Physics-Informed Decision (HyPhID) inference, which produces ranked and interpretable crystallographic predictions. The main contributions of this work are: (i) a unified multi-view framework combining representation learning, retrieval, and explainable reasoning for XRD phase identification; (ii) an adaptive cosine-retrieval strategy enabling non-parametric, ranked label inference; (iii) an explanation-guided retrieval mechanism using Integrated Gradients attribution fingerprints; (iv) integration of chemical composition embeddings as complementary structural evidence.

2 Synthetic XRD Dataset Generation

To train and evaluate the proposed model under controlled and physically meaningful conditions, a large synthetic X-ray diffraction (XRD) dataset is constructed from crystallographic information files (CIFs) obtained from the Materials Project (MP) [8] and the Crystallography Open Database (COD). In total, 68,958 crystal structures are collected (58,418 from MP and 10,540 from COD). The COD database primarily contains experimentally determined crystal structures, whereas the MP mainly provides density-functional-theory (DFT) relaxed structures, resulting in a dataset that combines both experimentally derived and computationally generated structures. Each CIF is treated as a distinct crystal-structure prototype from which multiple diffraction patterns are generated to emulate realistic experimental variability. For crystallographic symmetry prediction, two datasets are constructed. For space-group prediction, approximately 2000 CIF structures are sampled per space group from 22 representative space groups selected from the 230 crystallographic space groups to maintain a balanced dataset with sufficient training samples. For crystal-system prediction, approximately 7000 CIF structures are sampled for each of the seven crystal systems (triclinic, monoclinic, orthorhombic, tetragonal, trigonal, hexagonal, and cubic). For each CIF, 15 additional diffraction patterns are generated using physically motivated data augmentation. Diffraction patterns are simulated over a fixed angular range and discretized onto a uniform intensity grid. Experimental variability is simulated through physically-motivated augmentations such as peak broadening, preferred orientation, background contributions, intensity scaling, and small peak shifts, simulating realistic instrumental and sample-related conditions while preserving the underlying crystallographic phase label. Because a single composition can form multiple crystal structures (polymorphism), diffraction patterns reflect crystallographic symmetry rather than composition alone. The use of physically-motivated augmentation is particularly important for bridging the gap between simulated and experimental diffraction patterns. In practice, experimental measurements are influenced by instrumental resolution, preferred orientation, sample preparation, strain effects, and background noise. These factors can substantially alter peak intensities and peak shapes without changing the underlying crystal symmetry. By incorporating such perturbations during data generation, the model is encouraged to learn robust structural representations rather than memorizing idealized diffraction signatures.

3 Model Architecture and Training

We employ a physics-informed convolutional autoencoder augmented with an auxiliary classifier for XRD phase analysis. The model jointly supports phase classification, similarity-based retrieval, and structured representation learning under realistic experimental variability. The physics-informed aspect arises from incorporating domain-specific constraints during training, including peak-aware reconstruction weighting and smoothness regularization that encourage physically plausible diffraction signals. A shared convolutional encoder extracts compact features that are disentangled into a reconstruction latent representation and a discriminative classification latent representation. The reconstruction branch enables faithful signal reconstruction, while the classification branch supports supervised learning and contrastive structuring of the latent space.

3.1 Architecture

The encoder consists of residual one-dimensional convolutional blocks with progressive downsampling. Early layers employ large convolutional kernels to capture broad peak envelopes and background variations, whereas deeper layers focus on fine diffraction features. Each residual block includes batch normalization, GELU activation, and an optional channel-attention mechanism that enhances informative feature channels. Residual skip connections improve optimization stability and preserve weak but structurally meaningful reflections. Given an input diffraction pattern $x \in \mathbb{R}^L$, the encoder produces a feature tensor that is flattened and mapped into two latent vectors:

$$z_{\text{rec}} \in \mathbb{R}^{d_{\text{rec}}}, \qquad z_{\text{cls}} \in \mathbb{R}^{d_{\text{cls}}}.$$

Layer normalization is applied independently to both latent spaces. The reconstruction latent z_{rec} encodes information required for accurate signal reconstruction, including background and noise characteristics. A fully connected expansion layer followed by a convolutional decoder with progressive upsampling reconstructs the input signal:

$$\hat{x} \in \mathbb{R}^L.$$

The classification latent z_{cls} captures discriminative structural features relevant for phase prediction and similarity learning. Predictions are obtained by passing z_{cls} through a lightweight residual multilayer perceptron with dropout regularization. During training, an optional projection head is applied to z_{cls} to enable contrastive learning and improve latent space organization.

3.2 Training Objectives

The model is trained end-to-end using a multi-objective loss that balances reconstruction fidelity, classification accuracy, smoothness regularization, and latent space structuring. Signal reconstruction is optimized using a peak-aware loss that assigns greater importance to diffraction peak regions:

$$\mathcal{L}_{\text{rec}} = \text{MSE}_{\text{weighted}}(x, \hat{x}) + \lambda_1 \|x - \hat{x}\|_1. \tag{1}$$

Peak regions are identified using an intensity threshold relative to the maximum peak height, ensuring preservation of weak but structurally meaningful reflections. To encourage physically plausible smooth reconstructions, a gradient sparsity penalty is introduced:

$$\mathcal{L}_{\text{smooth}} = \|\nabla \hat{x}\|_1, \tag{2}$$

where $\nabla \hat{x}$ denotes the discrete first derivative of the reconstructed signal. Phase prediction is optimized using cross-entropy loss:

$$\mathcal{L}_{\text{cls}} = -\sum_k y_k \log p_k. \tag{3}$$

To explicitly structure the discriminative latent space, supervised contrastive learning is applied to projected embeddings:

$$\mathcal{L}_{\text{sup}} = -\frac{1}{N} \sum_i \frac{1}{|P(i)|} \sum_{p \in P(i)} \log \frac{\exp(z_i \cdot z_p / \tau)}{\sum_{a \neq i} \exp(z_i \cdot z_a / \tau)}, \tag{4}$$

where $P(i)$ denotes samples sharing the same phase label as sample i, and τ is a temperature parameter. This objective encourages samples belonging to the same phase to cluster in latent space, improving similarity-based retrieval and robustness to structural ambiguity. The overall loss function is defined as

$$\mathcal{L} = \lambda_{\text{rec}}\mathcal{L}_{\text{rec}} + \lambda_{\text{cls}}\mathcal{L}_{\text{cls}} + \lambda_{\text{smooth}}\mathcal{L}_{\text{smooth}} + \lambda_{\text{sup}}\mathcal{L}_{\text{sup}}. \tag{5}$$

The weighting coefficients λ_{rec}, λ_{cls}, λ_{smooth}, and λ_{sup} correspond to the reconstruction loss, classification loss, smoothness regularization term, and supervised contrastive loss, respectively. The weights are selected empirically using validation experiments to balance reconstruction and classification performance.

4 Integrated Gradients Database for Explainable Case-Based Prediction

Reliable XRD phase identification requires interpretability aligned with physics-based reasoning. We therefore integrate Integrated Gradients (IG) explanations into a retrieval-based prediction framework. For a diffraction pattern $x \in \mathbb{R}^L$ and model $F(x)$, IG assigns feature importance as

$$\phi_i(x) = (x_i - x_i') \int_0^1 \frac{\partial F(x' + \alpha(x - x'))}{\partial x_i}\, d\alpha, \tag{6}$$

where x' is a zero-intensity baseline and the integral is approximated numerically. For each training sample, we compute $\boldsymbol{\phi} = \text{IG}(x, y_{\text{true}})$ using the ground-truth class as attribution target. All attribution vectors are stored together with their labels and dataset indices. To enable efficient similarity search, attributions are mean-centered and ℓ_2-normalized:

$$\tilde{\boldsymbol{\phi}} = \frac{\boldsymbol{\phi} - \text{mean}(\boldsymbol{\phi})}{\|\boldsymbol{\phi} - \text{mean}(\boldsymbol{\phi})\|_2}. \tag{7}$$

During inference, IG explanations are computed for a query pattern when additional interpretability is required (e.g., high uncertainty or model-retrieval disagreement). Explanation similarity is measured via cosine similarity,

$$S_{\text{IG}}(q, i) = \tilde{\boldsymbol{\phi}}(x_q)^\top \tilde{\boldsymbol{\phi}}(x_i), \tag{8}$$

and the top-k neighbors contribute class evidence through similarity-weighted voting:

$$V_c = \sum_{i \in \mathcal{N}_k} \max(0, S_{\text{IG}}(q, i))\, \mathbf{1}[y_i = c]. \tag{9}$$

Class probabilities are obtained via temperature-scaled softmax,

$$P_c = \frac{\exp(V_c/\tau)}{\sum_j \exp(V_j/\tau)}. \tag{10}$$

This procedure yields an explanation-driven prediction based on similarity of attribution patterns, enabling case-based reasoning in attribution space.

Algorithm 1: Adaptive Cosine Retrieval with Decisive-k Selection

Input: Query sample x_q; encoder f; latent database $\mathcal{D}_{\text{train}}$; candidate sizes $\mathcal{K}$; similarity threshold τ_s; temperature T; top-n size n
Output: Predicted label $\hat{y}$ and top-n candidates
Compute latent $\mathbf{z}_q = f(x_q)$ and normalize all latents;
Compute cosine similarities s_i and sort in descending order;
Initialize best prediction $\leftarrow$ None;
foreach $k \in \mathcal{K}$ **do**
  Select top-k neighbors $\mathcal{N}_k$;
  Compute average similarity $\bar{s}_k = \frac{1}{k}\sum_{i\in\mathcal{N}_k} s_i$;
  if $\bar{s}_k < \tau_s$ **then**
    break
  Aggregate class scores $S_c(k) = \sum_{i\in\mathcal{N}_k,\, y_i=c} \tilde{s}_i$;
  Compute probabilities $p_c(k) = \text{softmax}(S_c(k)/T)$;
  Update best result if $\max_c p_c(k)$ increases;
Return label with highest probability and top-n candidates;

5 Adaptive Cosine Retrieval for Latent-Space Classification

We perform non-parametric classification directly in the latent space of a trained autoencoder. After training, the encoder is frozen and used as a deterministic feature extractor. All training samples are embedded once to form a latent reference database $\mathcal{D}_{\text{train}} = \{(\mathbf{z}_i, y_i)\}_{i=1}^{N}$. Given a query sample x_q, its latent representation $\mathbf{z}_q = f(x_q)$ is ℓ_2-normalized together with all stored latents. Classification is then performed via cosine-similarity retrieval. Instead of using a fixed number of neighbors, we evaluate multiple neighborhood sizes and adaptively select the most informative one: the neighborhood that yields the most decisive prediction, measured by the highest top-1 class probability. For each candidate neighborhood size, class evidence is accumulated by summing similarity contributions of neighbors belonging to the same class. Negative similarities may optionally be ignored to prevent contradictory evidence. The aggregated class scores are converted into probabilities using a temperature-scaled softmax, where the temperature parameter T controls the sharpness of the probability distribution (lower values produce sharper class probabilities). The neighborhood size producing the most decisive prediction (highest top-1 probability) is selected, and the corresponding label is returned together with the top-n candidate classes for interpretability. Algorithm 1 summarizes the retrieval procedure. In the pseudocode, "$\leftarrow$" denotes variable assignment, and "None" indicates that no prediction has been selected yet.

6 Embedding-Based Chemical Retrieval

We investigate whether learned embeddings of chemical compositions capture meaningful chemical similarity. Given a query composition, the goal is to retrieve chemically similar compositions from a reference database based on similarity in the learned embedding space. Since each composition corresponds to a material with a known crystal structure (defined by its crystal system and space group), composition-based retrieval can provide complementary structural evidence for phase identification. Chemical composition embeddings are generated using the Qwen2.5-1.5B-Instruct model [19]. To study different representation granularities, we compare two learned encoding strategies with a physically motivated baseline based on Magpie descriptors. In the element-level encoder, a composition is represented as a weighted sum of element embeddings scaled by their stoichiometric fractions. The composition-level encoder embeds the full chemical formula as a textual sequence using the Qwen model. Embeddings are extracted from the final transformer layer and mean-pooled, yielding fixed-dimensional vectors ($d = 2048$). As a physically motivated baseline, we use Magpie descriptors [17], which capture statistical properties of constituent elements (e.g., atomic number and electronegativity). Features are imputed, standardized, and represented as 145-dimensional vectors. All formulas are converted to a canonical representation and ℓ_2-normalized prior to similarity computation. Nearest neighbors are retrieved using cosine similarity between normalized representations. For each query composition, the top-k most similar training compositions are selected. Retrieval performance is evaluated using *chemical accuracy@k*, defined as the fraction of retrieved compositions sharing at least half of their constituent elements with the query. We additionally report *retrieval overlap@k*, which quantifies agreement between the element-level and composition-level encoders. Both metrics are applied consistently across learned embeddings and the Magpie baseline.

7 Results and Discussion

This section evaluates the proposed framework from three complementary perspectives. First, we analyze model decision behavior using Integrated Gradients to assess whether the learned representations rely on physically meaningful diffraction features. Second, we evaluate the effectiveness of composition-based retrieval using learned chemical embeddings. Finally, we report classification performance for crystal system and space group prediction and discuss how the different inference components contribute to the final decision.

7.1 Integrated Gradients Analysis of Model Decisions

To explain the classification behavior, we analyze model decisions using Integrated Gradients (IG). IG attributions are aggregated across correctly classified samples to construct *class-level attribution fingerprints*. For each diffraction pattern, absolute IG values are computed along the 2θ domain and averaged within each class to produce normalized importance profiles indicating influential diffraction regions. Relationships between crystallographic classes are quantified by computing cosine distances between attribution fingerprints and

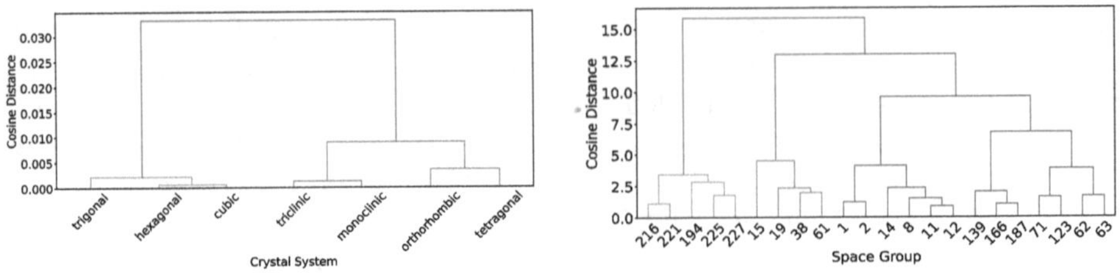

(a) Hierarchical clustering of crystal systems based on cosine distances between normalized attribution fingerprints.

(b) Hierarchical clustering of space groups based on cosine distances between normalized Integrated Gradients attribution fingerprints.

Fig. 2. Hierarchical clustering of crystallographic classes derived from cosine distances between normalized Integrated Gradients attribution fingerprints: (a) crystal systems and (b) space groups.

applying hierarchical clustering. The resulting dendrograms (Fig. 2) show space-group clustering on the left and crystal-system clustering on the right. The clusters follow crystallographic similarity rather than training labels, suggesting that explanation patterns capture underlying structural relationships. Higher-symmetry systems tend to group together due to reliance on dominant diffraction peaks, whereas lower-symmetry systems form broader clusters reflecting more distributed diffraction signatures. Overall, IG analysis indicates that model predictions rely on physically meaningful diffraction features and provides interpretable evidence linking learned representations with crystallographic structure. The observed attribution patterns are consistent with crystallographic expectations, where a limited number of characteristic reflections often carry substantial information about lattice symmetry. This suggests that the model is learning physically meaningful decision rules rather than relying on dataset-specific artifacts. Furthermore, the attribution fingerprints provide an alternative representation of diffraction patterns that can be compared independently from the latent representations learned by the autoencoder. This motivates the use of attribution-based retrieval as an additional source of evidence during inference.

7.2 Results of Embedding-Based Chemical Retrieval

We evaluate compositional retrieval using the metrics defined in Sect. 6. Table 1 compares element-level and composition-level Qwen embeddings. Element-level embeddings achieve higher chemical accuracy@5 and substantially lower variance, indicating more stable retrieval of chemically similar compositions. The low retrieval overlap and weak embedding correlation further suggest that the two encoders capture different notions of chemical similarity. We find the element-level encoder outperforms the composition-level encoder, so we compare the element-level encoder with the conventional Magpie descriptors [17] and report the results in Table 2. Element-level Qwen embeddings outperform Magpie fea-

Table 1. Chemical retrieval performance of Qwen embeddings ($k = 5$).

Metric	Element-level	Composition-level
Chemical accuracy@5 (mean)	0.985	0.887
Chemical accuracy@5 (std)	0.093	0.227
Retrieval overlap@5	0.167	
Embedding space correlation	0.241	

Table 2. Retrieval performance of Magpie vs. Qwen embeddings ($k = 5$).

Embedding method	Chemical accuracy@5 (mean)	Std
Magpie descriptors	0.843	0.244
Qwen (element-level)	**0.982**	0.093

tures in both accuracy and stability, demonstrating the advantage of learned representations over hand-engineered descriptors. Figure 3 visualizes the chemical embedding spaces using t-SNE, including Qwen element-level embeddings, Qwen composition-level embeddings, and Magpie descriptor representations. Element-level embeddings form compact clusters consistent with element-based similarity, whereas composition-level embeddings exhibit a more diffuse organization. To enable joint visualization, Magpie and Qwen embeddings are first aligned by composition, meaning that identical compositions are matched across the different representations. Each representation is then independently projected to a lower-dimensional space using principal component analysis (PCA) to reduce dimensionality while preserving the variance structure of each representation. The PCA-reduced representations are then concatenated and embedded using t-SNE, allowing both learned and hand-crafted representations to be visualized within a shared map. The resulting visualization reveals clearly distinct structural layouts between Magpie descriptors and the learned Qwen embeddings. Similar differences between learned and descriptor-based chemical representations have been discussed in recent work on embedding spaces and linear mixing behavior [22]. Based on the quantitative retrieval results in Table 2, we adopt element-level Qwen embeddings as the compositional retrieval module in our phase identification framework. During inference, a query composition retrieves the top-k chemically similar references using cosine similarity, and the associated crystallographic metadata (crystal system and space group) is used as complementary structural evidence to support diffraction-based prediction.

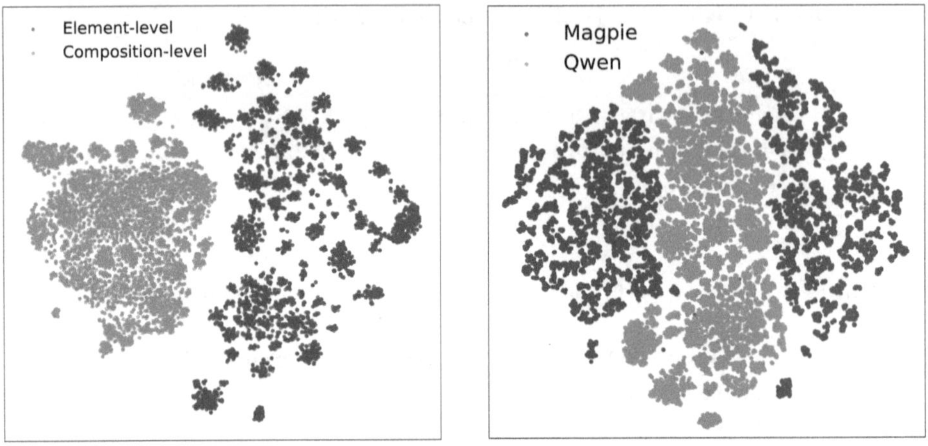

(a) Qwen element-level vs composition-level embeddings.

(b) Magpie descriptors vs Qwen element-level embeddings after alignment.

Fig. 3. t-SNE visualization of chemical embedding spaces. (a) Element-level vs. composition-level Qwen embeddings. (b) Magpie descriptors compared with Qwen element-level embeddings after alignment to a shared representation space.

7.3 Classification Performance

We evaluate our framework on two tasks: crystal system classification and space group classification, using a 10% randomly selected holdout set for both tasks. To avoid data leakage, the split is performed at the CIF level, ensuring that all augmented diffraction patterns derived from the same structure remain within the same partition. The model achieves 98.85% accuracy for crystal system prediction. Space group prediction is more challenging due to the finer structural distinctions among the 22 symmetry classes; nevertheless, the framework achieves 95.82% accuracy on the same holdout set. Both tasks are evaluated using the same encoder architecture and training procedure. The only difference between the two models is the final classification layer, which is adjusted to predict either the 7 crystal systems or the 22 space groups. To further assess robustness, we evaluate the framework on an external dataset of 50 CIF structures from the experimental RRUFF database [5]. These compositions are unseen during training and internal testing. For each CIF, 15 augmented diffraction patterns are generated, resulting in 750 evaluation samples. Unlike the COD/MP training dataset, which includes both experimentally derived and DFT-relaxed structures, the RRUFF dataset contains experimentally reported, non-relaxed structures, making it a more challenging test scenario. As expected, performance on this external dataset is lower than on the internal holdout set due to the domain shift between simulated and experimentally measured diffraction patterns. On the internal holdout set, HyPhID achieves 98.85% accuracy for crystal system prediction and 95.82% accuracy for space group prediction, while on the experimental RRUFF dataset the accuracy decreases to 81.07% and 56.13%, respectively. The substantial performance gap between the internal and external evaluations highlights the challenge of generalization in diffraction analysis. While synthetic datasets enable large-scale supervised training, experimentally measured diffraction patterns often exhibit sources of variability that are difficult to model completely. These include instrumental effects, preferred orientation, peak broadening, background artifacts, and sample impurities. As a result, performance on external datasets provides a more realistic estimate of practical applicability. The larger performance reduction observed for space-group prediction is expected because space groups represent much finer crystallographic distinctions than crystal systems. Many space groups share similar peak positions and differ only through subtle intensity variations or weak reflections that may be difficult to distinguish in noisy experimental measurements. In comparison, Vecsei et al. [15] reported 85% crystal-system accuracy and 76% space-group accuracy on simulated data, with performance dropping to 56% and 42% on the experimental RRUFF dataset. Table 3 summarizes the performance of the individual decision components together with the final HyPhID inference results on the RRUFF dataset. Interestingly, latent retrieval slightly outperforms the standalone classifier on the RRUFF dataset for both crystal-system and space-group prediction. This observation suggests that similarity-based reasoning is less sensitive to domain shift than purely parametric classification. Rather than extrapolating from learned decision boundaries, retrieval directly compares a query pattern against structurally related examples, allowing physically similar reference structures to contribute to the final decision. In contrast, the IG and composition modules exhibit lower standalone accuracies. This behavior is expected because these components are not designed to function as independent classifiers. Instead, they provide complementary evidence that can support or refine predictions produced by the classifier and retrieval modules. The final HyPhID prediction benefits from aggregating these diverse sources of information. In this evaluation, we report the predictions of all HyPhID decision modules on the external test set, since the multi-decision inference strategy improves robustness by combining complementary reasoning sources. Because the retrieval-based modules are based on similarity to reference patterns, their standalone accuracies may vary compared to the classifier performance observed on the synthetic holdout set. The final HyPhID prediction aggregates normalized scores from all decision components. Let $p_{\text{model}}(c)$, $p_{\text{retrieval}}(c)$, $p_{\text{IG}}(c)$, and $p_{\text{comp}}(c)$ denote the class probabilities produced by the classifier, latent retrieval, IG-based similarity, and composition retrieval modules, respectively. The final class score is computed as

$$S(c) = w_1 p_{\text{model}}(c) + w_2 p_{\text{retrieval}}(c) + w_3 p_{\text{IG}}(c) + w_4 p_{\text{comp}}(c), s$$

where the weights satisfy $w_1 + w_2 + w_3 + w_4 = 1$. The weights are selected empirically using validation test sets, and the final prediction is obtained as $\arg\max_c S(c)$. Latent-space retrieval often produces reliable predictions and can correctly classify samples even when the classifier fails, highlighting the value

Table 3. Accuracy of individual decision components and the final HyPhID inference for crystal system (CS) and space group (SG) classification.

Method	CS Acc. (%)	SG Acc. (%)
Classifier Model	76.13%	50.80%
Latent Retrieval	78.13%	56.67%
IG Similarity	52.93%	16.80%
Composition	32.00%	22.00%
HyPhID (Final)	**81.07%**	**56.13%**

of similarity-based reasoning. The IG module mainly supports interpretability, while composition-based retrieval provides complementary structural evidence despite polymorphism effects. Overall, HyPhID improves crystal system prediction by combining complementary evidence sources. To analyze robustness under distribution shift, we examine the most distant RRUFF samples in latent space. Figure 4(a) visualizes the distribution of training samples, internal test samples, and external RRUFF structures in the learned latent representation, where the most distant samples are marked with red crosses. An example inference case for one of these distant samples is illustrated in Fig. 4(b), showing the reconstructed diffraction pattern and IG attribution maps highlighting the most influential peaks. Finally, Fig. 5 presents a detailed inference output example summarizing the predictions produced by the classifier, latent retrieval, IG-based similarity, and composition-based reasoning, together with the top-k candidate classes returned by each component. This example illustrates disagreement between inference components. While the correct space group is SG 225, the retrieval module favors SG 166. However, the correct class (SG 225) still appears among the top retrieved candidates. Importantly, our framework is trained in a composition-agnostic manner and does not require explicit composition-specific supervision during training. This contrasts with approaches such as [13], which incorporate composition constraints or probabilistic modeling of phase mixtures. Instead, HyPhID enables flexible inference by combining multiple evidence sources and returning a ranked list of plausible crystallographic classes, which can assist users in narrowing the search space for possible structures even when the top-1 prediction is uncertain.

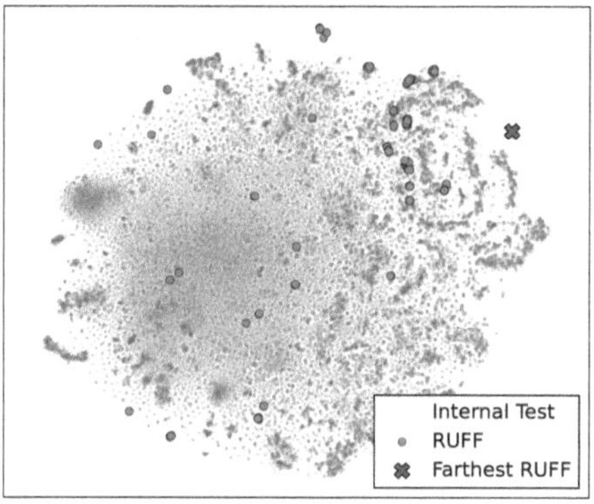

(a) Latent-space visualization of training samples, internal test samples, and external RRUFF samples. Red crosses indicate the most distant samples used for robustness evaluation.

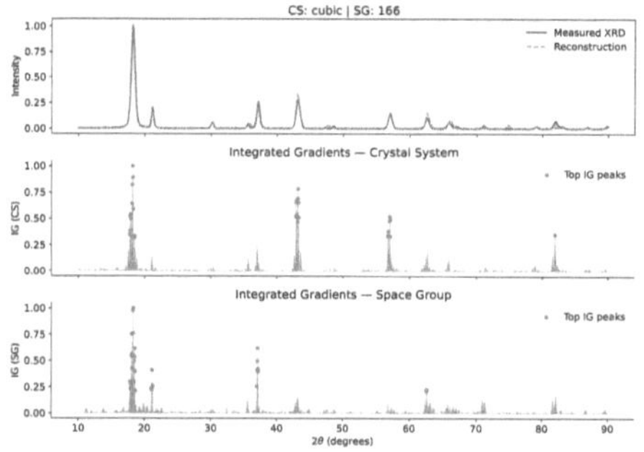

(b) Representative prediction example showing the measured XRD pattern, reconstruction, and Integrated Gradients (IG) attribution maps for crystal system and space group prediction.

Fig. 4. Latent-space visualization and example HyPhID inference. (a) Distribution of training, internal test, and external RRUFF samples. (b) Example prediction showing the measured pattern, reconstruction, and IG-based peak attribution.

8 Conclusion

We present an explainable and retrieval-enhanced framework for automated phase identification from X-ray diffraction (XRD) data that combines representation learning, similarity-based retrieval, and interpretable decision support. A convolutional autoencoder learns a discriminative latent representation of diffraction patterns through joint reconstruction and classification objectives. Building on this representation, we introduce an adaptive cosine-retrieval strategy that performs non-parametric inference through class-wise similarity aggregation, enabling robust prediction beyond purely parametric classifiers. To improve transparency and scientific validity, we incorporate Integrated Gradients into a peak-level explanation database and develop explanation-guided retrieval, allowing predictions to be supported by explicit diffraction evidence aligned with expert reasoning. In addition, compositional retrieval using large language model embeddings provides chemically-grounded prior information that complements diffractogram-based inference. Evaluation on experimentally measured XRD patterns demonstrates strong performance for both crystal system and space group prediction while yielding interpretable decision mechanisms consistent with crystallographic principles. Although our work focuses on 22 space groups, the framework can be extended to all 230 crystallographic space groups if sufficient data are available. Overall, our framework bridges data-driven learning with domain-aware reasoning, enabling reliable and interpretable materials characterization. Future work will focus on predicting previously unseen compounds, incorporating uncertainty-aware retrieval, mixed-phase signals, and integration with

Representative inference output **True:** CS=cubic, SG=225

Crystal System (CS)

Final: cubic
Model: cubic (0.995)
Retrieval: trigonal (1.000)
IG: triclinic (1.00000)
Composition: orthorhombic

Space Group (SG)

Final: 166
Model: 1 (0.52860)
Retrieval: 166 (1.00000)
IG: 1 (1.00000)
Composition: 62

Additional signals

Reconstruction error: 3.78×10^{-4}

Top-k candidates (probability / similarity)

Crystal System (CS)

IG

#	Class	Sim.
1	triclinic	1.000
2	monoclinic	0.001
3	orthorhombic	0.001

Retrieval

#	Class	Sim.
1	trigonal	1.000
2	cubic	0.001

Composition

#	Class	Prob.
1	tetragonal	0.400
2	orthorhombic	0.400
3	trigonal	0.200

Space Group (SG)

IG

#	SG	Sim.
1	1	1.000
2	14	0.000
3	38	0.000

Retrieval

#	SG	Sim.
1	166	1.000
2	8	0.030
3	225	0.020

Composition

#	SG	Prob.
1	71	0.500
2	62	0.500
3	63	0.000

Fig. 5. Representative inference example showing disagreement between inference sources. The model predicts the correct crystal system (cubic), while retrieval and IG signals suggest alternative symmetries. For space-group prediction, retrieval selects SG 166 although the ground truth is SG 225.

materials knowledge graphs for autonomous discovery workflows. In addition, we aim to extend the framework into a publicly accessible reference platform that enables automated and explainable phase retrieval, allowing researchers to upload diffraction patterns and obtain ranked predictions supported by physically interpretable evidence.

The implementation accompanying this study, which specifies all architectural design choices, training hyperparameters, data augmentation procedures, and inference settings, is available at: https://github.com/lab-mids/xrd_classification

Acknowledgements. All authors gratefully acknowledge funding by the Deutsche Forschungsgemeinschaft (DFG, German Research Foundation) for CRC1625 A05, INF, project number 506711657.

References

1. Altomare, A., et al.: Advances in powder diffraction pattern indexing: N-treor09. J. Appl. Crystallogr. **42**(5), 768–775 (2009)
2. Banko, L., Maffettone, P.M.: Deep learning for visualization and novelty detection in large X-ray diffraction datasets. npj Comput. Mater. **7**(1), pp. 104 (2021)
3. Belsky, A., Hellenbrandt, M., Karen, V.L., Luksch, P.: New developments in the inorganic crystal structure database (ICSD). Acta Crystallogr. B **58**(3), 364–369 (2002)
4. Cover, T.M., Hart, P.E.: Nearest neighbor pattern classification. IEEE Trans. Inf. Theory **13**(1), 21–27 (1967)
5. Downs, R.T.: The RRUFF project: an integrated study of the chemistry, crystallography, raman and infrared spectroscopy of minerals. In: Program and Abstracts of the 19th General Meeting of the International Mineralogical Association in, pp. 2006, Kobe, Japan (2006)
6. Gilmore, C.J., Barr, G., Paisley, J.: High-throughput powder diffraction. i. a new approach to qualitative and quantitative powder diffraction pattern analysis using full pattern profiles. J. Appl. Crystallogr. **37**(2), 231–242 (2004)
7. Grazulis, S., et al.: Crystallography open database (cod): an open-access collection of crystal structures. Nucleic Acids Res. **40**(D1), D420–D427 (2012)
8. Jain, A., Ong, S.P., Hautier, G., et al.: The materials project: A materials genome approach to accelerating materials innovation. APL Mater. **1**(1), 011002 (2013)
9. Lee, B.D., Lee, J.W., Ahn, J., Kim, S., Park, W.B., Sohn, K.S.: A deep learning approach to powder X-ray diffraction pattern analysis: addressing generalizability and perturbation issues simultaneously. Adv. Intelli. Syst. **5**(9), 2300140 (2023)
10. Leeman, J., et al.: Challenges in high-throughput inorganic materials prediction and autonomous synthesis. PRX Energy **3**(1), 011002 (2024)
11. Maffettone, P.M., Banko, L., Cui, P., Lysogorskiy, Y., Little, M.A., Olds, D., Ludwig, A., Cooper, A.I.: Crystallography companion agent for high-throughput materials discovery. Nature Comput. Sci. **1**(4), 290–297 (2021)
12. Oviedo, F., Ren, Z., Sun, S.: Fast and interpretable classification of small x-ray diffraction datasets using data augmentation and deep neural networks. npj Comput. Mater. **5**(1), pp. 60 (2019)
13. Szymanski, N.J., Bartel, C.J., Zeng, Y., Tu, Q., Ceder, G.: Probabilistic deep learning approach to automate the interpretation of multi-phase diffraction spectra. Chem. Mater. **33**(11), 4204–4215 (2021)
14. Tshitoyan, V., Dagdelen, J., Weston, L., et al.: Unsupervised word embeddings capture latent knowledge from materials science literature. Nature **571**, 95–98 (2019)

15. Vecsei, P.M., Choo, K., Chang, J., Neupert, T.: Neural network based classification of crystal symmetries from X-ray diffraction patterns. Phys. Rev. B **99**(24), 245120 (2019)
16. Wang, H., et al.: Rapid identification of X-ray diffraction spectra based on very limited data by interpretable convolutional neural networks. arXiv preprint arXiv:1912.07750 (2019)
17. Ward, L., Agrawal, A., Choudhary, A., Wolverton, C.: A general-purpose machine learning framework for predicting properties of inorganic materials. npj Comput. Mater. **2**, 16028 (2016)
18. Wu, Z., Xiong, Y., Yu, S.X., Lin, D.: Unsupervised feature learning via non-parametric instance discrimination. In: Proceedings of the IEEE Conference on Computer Vision and Pattern Recognition (CVPR), pp. 3733–3742 (2018)
19. Yang, A., et al.: Qwen2. 5-math technical report: Toward mathematical expert model via self-improvement. arXiv preprint arXiv:2409.12122 (2024)
20. Zaloga, A.N., Stanovov, V.V., et al.: Crystal symmetry classification from powder X-ray diffraction patterns using a convolutional neural network. Mater. Today Commun. **25**, 101662 (2020)
21. Zhang, L., Stricker, M.: MatNexus: a comprehensive text mining and analysis suite for materials discovery. Softwarex, vol. 26, pp. 101654 (2024)
22. Zhang, L., Stricker, M.: Electrocatalyst discovery through text mining and multi-objective optimization. arXiv preprint arXiv:2502.20860 (2025)

MultiSigBERT: Beyond Survival Analysis Through Multimodal and Sequential Modeling in Oncology

Paul Minchella[1(✉)], Stéphane Chrétien[1], Guillaume Metzler[1], Loic Verlingue[2], and Rémi Vaucher[3]

[1] Université Lumiére Lyon 2, 69500 Bron, France
{paul.minchella,stephane.chretien,guillaume.metzler}@univ-lyon2.fr
[2] Léon Bérard Center, 69008 Lyon, France
loic.verlingue@lyon.unicancer.fr
[3] EPITA, 69007 Lyon, France
remi.vaucher@epita.fr

Abstract. Machine learning has become an essential component of modern healthcare, where the integration of heterogeneous data sources offers unprecedented opportunities to improve clinical decision-making. Electronic Health Records (EHR) contain complementary information – including narrative clinical reports, numerical measurements, and structured variables – yet most survival models remain limited to a single modality or fail to exploit the temporal nature of patient trajectories. We propose MultiSigBERT, a unified framework for multimodal sequential survival modeling in oncology based on path signature representations. Here, narrative medical reports (free-text) are converted into sentence embeddings by extracting and averaging contextual word embeddings. These representations are then compressed via modality-specific PCA and concatenated with structured covariates to form joint temporal trajectories which are then encoded using the Signature transform, a tool from Rough Paths theory that efficiently captures higher-order temporal interactions across modalities without supervision needed. The computed Signature features are finally incorporated as high dimensional features into a LASSO-regularized Cox model to estimate individualized risk scores. The performance of our novel MultiSigBERT pipeline is illustrated on the analysis of a real-world oncology cohort from the Léon Bérard Center, comprising over 120,000 medical reports and structured records from more than 2,500 patients. The model achieves a concordance index of 0.743 (sd 0.029). on an independent test set, demonstrating the benefit of jointly modeling multimodal temporal dynamics together with patient-level geometric structure for survival prediction.

Keywords: Multimodal · NLP · Signature Transform · Survival Analysis · Oncology

M. Ceci et al. (Eds.): ECML PKDD 2026, LNAI 16948, pp. 565–582, 2027.
https://doi.org/10.1007/978-3-032-37679-4_32

1 Introduction

1.1 Background and Challenges

Survival analysis aims to model the time until an event of interest occurs, such as death, recurrence, or disease progression. In oncology, accurate survival prediction is essential for treatment selection, clinical trial inclusion, and follow-up planning.

Modern electronic health records (EHRs) contain heterogeneous and complementary information, including structured clinical variables, laboratory measurements, molecular data, and narrative medical reports. This diversity offers strong potential to improve survival modeling. However, integrating these data sources remains challenging. Most classical survival models rely on static baseline covariates and ignore the longitudinal nature of patient follow-up. Even recent machine learning approaches often struggle with irregular, asynchronous, and time-dependent clinical data.

In addition, many existing methods are unimodal, focusing either on structured variables or unstructured text. Such approaches fail to capture the interactions between modalities that shape patient trajectories and influence prognosis.

To address these limitations, we introduce MultiSigBERT, a multimodal and sequential survival framework designed to integrate heterogeneous clinical data while modeling temporal dynamics in a principled and interpretable manner. By combining embedding representations, rough path signatures, graph-based clustering, and sparse survival modeling, this model provides a unified approach for analyzing real-world multimodal oncology data.

1.2 Related Works

Survival analysis is a fundamental task in clinical research, aiming to estimate the time to an event such as death or relapse. The Cox Proportional Hazards model [7] remains the classical reference due to its interpretability and solid theoretical basis. Regularized extensions, notably LASSO penalization [21], have enabled its application to high-dimensional settings. More recently, neural-network-based survival models have been proposed to capture non-linear effects and complex feature interactions. DeepSurv [14] adapted the Cox partial likelihood to deep architectures for personalized prediction from structured static data. To model longitudinal dynamics, Dynamic-DeepHit [16] introduced recurrent networks with temporal attention. DySurv [18] further incorporated conditional variational autoencoders to integrate time-dependent EHR features.

From a mathematical perspective, rough path theory has recently emerged as a principled framework for encoding temporal data. CoxSig [3] introduced signature transforms into survival modeling, demonstrating strong empirical performance together with theoretical guarantees such as universality and invariance to time reparameterization.

The authors of SigBERT [20] introduced a framework combining a domain-specific language model with rough path signature features for temporal survival analysis in oncology. Applied to narrative reports from the Léon Bérard Center, SigBERT achieved a concordance index of 0.75 (sd 0.014) and a time-dependent AUC of 0.80 (sd 0.029), demonstrating that properly encoded clinical text can substantially improve survival risk estimation.

However, SigBERT focuses exclusively on narrative medical reports and does not explicitly address the integration of additional clinical modalities. More broadly, the principled combination of heterogeneous clinical data sources remains a major challenge in survival modeling. A summary of the related methods is provided in the first table of the Supplementary Material.

1.3 Our Contributions

Building upon SigBERT [20], which focused on narrative medical reports, we extend this approach to a multimodal setting. Moreover, the original framework was not formulated within a landmark prediction design, which may allow temporal information leakage when constructing temporal features.

To address these limitations, we introduce , a multimodal survival modeling framework designed to integrate heterogeneous clinical data in oncology. The proposed approach jointly leverages unstructured clinical text, structured numerical variables, and their longitudinal evolution within a unified temporal representation. More precisely, this work makes three main contributions.

First, we introduce a multimodal temporal encoding framework that combines textual embeddings and structured clinical variables into synchronized trajectories prior to signature transformation. Narrative reports are first encoded into sentence embeddings using OncoBERT [22]. Structured numerical variables are processed separately and aligned with the same temporal axis, thanks to linear interpolation. The two modalities are then concatenated at each time point to form multimodal vectors, which are subsequently encoded using the signature transform, enabling the model to capture higher-order temporal dependencies and cross-modal interactions in a mathematically principled way.

Second, we propose a robust landmark-based survival modeling pipeline that prevents temporal information leakage by restricting feature construction to observations available before the prediction time, thereby enabling well-defined dynamic risk prediction from longitudinal clinical data.

Finally, we provide an efficient and interpretable survival modeling framework combining signature features with sparse Cox regression. This design enables scalable analysis of large clinical cohorts while maintaining interpretability of the predictive factors. In addition, we conduct a systematic empirical comparison of modality-specific contributions by evaluating text-only fully multimodal configurations, thereby quantifying the added value of multimodal fusion for survival prediction.

To our knowledge, is the first survival framework that jointly combines multimodal temporal encoding of textual and structured numerical data with sparse survival modeling within a coherent and computationally efficient pipeline. The complete implementation is available in the associated GitHub repository at https://github.com/MINCHELLA-Paul/MultiSigBERT. The main notebook `multisigbert_study.ipynb` contains additional experimental results, and all descriptive statistics figures are provided in `results/descriptive_statistics`.

2 Method

2.1 Global Overview

The proposed MultiSigBERT framework integrates heterogeneous clinical data into a unified temporal representation for survival modeling. The dataset consists of longitudinal patient-level records combining narrative medical reports, structured time-dependent clinical variables, and right-censored survival outcomes. Formally, for each patient i, we observe a sequence of clinical time points

$$\left\{t_1^{(i)}, \ldots, t_{N_i}^{(i)}\right\},$$

at which textual reports and structured covariates are recorded. Each report is encoded as a sentence embedding, yielding a time-indexed representation of the patient's clinical trajectory. In addition, we observe structured longitudinal variables measured at irregular time points and aligned with the same temporal axis.

The survival outcome is defined by a pair (T_i, D_i), where $T_i \geq 0$ denotes the observed time-to-event or censoring, and $D_i \in \{0, 1\}$ is the event indicator, with $D_i = 1$ if the event (e.g., death) is observed and $D_i = 0$ if the observation is right-censored. The objective is to learn a mapping from the patient-specific temporal representation to a risk function compatible with the Cox proportional hazards framework.

For each patient, clinical notes are observed at successive timestamps, forming an ordered sequence of unstructured text that reflects disease progression, treatment response, and medical decisions over time. In our cohort, these documents consist mainly of consultation reports (68%) and hospitalization reports (27%), offering a rich temporal source of prognostic information. In parallel, structured variables such as *Weight*, *Karnofsky Index*, *Blood Pressure*, and *Pulse Rate* are recorded at irregular timepoints. These quantitative measures provide complementary information about the patient's physiological state. All modalities are preprocessed and temporally aligned to construct coherent multimodal trajectories. Detailed descriptive statistics are reported in the notebook `descriptive_statistics.ipynb` provided in the associated GitHub repository.

To prevent information leakage and define a consistent prediction task, we adopt a landmark design. For a fixed landmark time $\mathbf{L}$, only data observed within the backward window $[\mathbf{L} - \mathbf{w}, \mathbf{L}]$ are used to construct the patient representation, and survival is predicted beyond $\mathbf{L}$. This framework preserves temporal causality and ensures that signature coefficients are computed on finite, well-ordered trajectories without incorporating future information.

Each modality is first embedded in a dedicated vector space, optionally compressed, and concatenated across time. The resulting multimodal sequences are encoded using the signature transform, producing fixed-dimensional representations that capture higher-order temporal interactions. Moreover, the signature transform is particularly well suited to handle irregularly sampled time points and heterogeneous data modalities, both of which constitute major challenges in real-world machine learning settings.

Finally, these signature-derived features are used to fit a LASSO-regularized Cox model, producing individualized risk scores while ensuring sparsity, strong predictive performance, and computational efficiency.

An overview of the complete pipeline – from embedding extraction and temporal encoding to geometric clustering and survival estimation – is illustrated in Fig. 1.

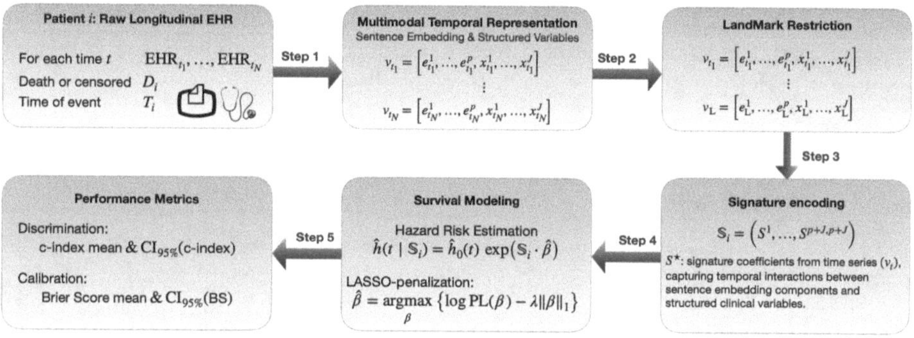

Fig. 1. Overview of the MultiSigBERT pipeline. ***Step 1: Multimodal representation.*** Narrative clinical reports are converted into sentence embeddings and combined with structured variables observed at times $t_1, \ldots, t_N$ to form multimodal vectors v_t. ***Step 2: Landmark restriction.*** Only observations within the window $[\mathbf{L} - \mathbf{w}, \mathbf{L}]$ are retained to avoid temporal information leakage. ***Step 3: Signature encoding.*** The truncated sequence $(v_t)_t$ is encoded via the path signature transform, producing a fixed-dimensional representation $\mathbb{S}_i$ capturing temporal interactions across modalities. ***Step 4: Survival modeling.*** A LASSO-regularized Cox model is fitted on the signature features to estimate individualized risk scores. ***Step 5: Evaluation.*** Performance is assessed using the C-index and the Brier score.

2.2 Multimodal Embedding Extraction

Clinical datasets combine structured numerical variables with unstructured data such as free-text reports. To integrate these heterogeneous modalities into a unified survival framework, each input must first be transformed into a numerical vector representation.

Let's first consider narrative medical reports. These longitudinal documents capture the patient's clinical follow-up, including consultation reports, hospitalization summaries, and medical observations recorded over time. We encode them using OncoBERT [22], a CamemBERT-based [19] language model fine-tuned on oncology notes from the Léon Bérard Center. This domain-specific fine-tuning improves the semantic representation of oncology terminology and clinical context. Let $\mathscr{R}_i(t)$ denote the raw clinical report associated with patient i at time t. The OncoBERT encoder Φ_{OncoBERT} maps this report into a sequence of contextualized token embeddings:

$$\left(e_w\right)_{w \in \mathscr{R}_i(t)} = \Phi_{\text{OncoBERT}}(\mathscr{R}_i(t)),$$

where $e_w \in \mathbb{R}^p$ denotes the contextualized embedding associated with token w, with $p = 768$. A fixed-dimensional sentence representation $v_i(t) \in \mathbb{R}^p$ is then obtained from these contextualized token embeddings using the Smooth Inverse Frequency (SIF) pooling strategy [2]. Specifically,

$$v_i(t) = \frac{1}{|\mathscr{R}_i(t)|} \sum_{w \in \mathscr{R}_i(t)} \frac{a}{\mathrm{f}(w) + a} e_w,$$

where $\mathrm{f}(w)$ denotes the frequency of word w, $|\mathscr{R}_i(t)|$ denotes the number of tokens in the report, and a is a smoothing parameter, typically set to $a = 10^{-3}$.

The resulting vector $v_i(t)$ constitutes the sentence embedding associated with patient i at time t and serves as the elementary observation in the subsequent longitudinal trajectory. We adopt Smooth Inverse Frequency (SIF) embeddings rather than the standard CLS token representation. Empirically, SIF consistently outperformed CLS in our retrospective experiments, yielding higher C-index values (0.74 vs. 0.70) and lower Brier scores. This gain can be attributed to the re-weighting and averaging mechanism of SIF, which mitigates the influence of frequent or uninformative tokens and produces more stable sentence representations. In addition, SIF naturally accommodates long clinical documents by aggregating token embeddings beyond the 512-token limitation of BERT models. For a detailed methodological and empirical discussion, we refer the reader to [20]. A patient with N_i reports is thus represented by the time-indexed sequence of sentence embeddings

$$\left(v_i(t_1), \ldots, v_i(t_{N_i})\right), \qquad v_i(t_j) \in \mathbb{R}^p,$$

which can equivalently be viewed as an element of $\mathbb{R}^{N_i \times p}$.

Since the signature transform scales exponentially with the input dimension, dimensionality reduction is required. We apply Principal Component Analysis (PCA) on the training embeddings and retain the first r principal components, yielding a projection matrix $R_{\text{comp}} \in \mathbb{R}^{r \times p}$. Each sentence embedding is then compressed according to

$$\widetilde{v}_i(t) = R_{\text{comp}} \cdot v_i(t) \in \mathbb{R}^r.$$

The resulting trajectory $(\widetilde{v}_i(t_1), \ldots, \widetilde{v}_i(t_{N_i}))$ is subsequently used for temporal encoding through the signature transform. The dimension r is selected empirically to balance predictive performance and computational cost. In our experiments, performance stabilized from $r = 25$, which we then adopt in the sequel.

2.3 Integration of Structured Clinical Variables

Beyond text, patients are characterized by longitudinal structured variables being *Weight*, *Karnofsky Index*, *Blood Pressure*, and *Pulse* (meaning that the number of structured clinical covariates is given by $K = 4$). These measurements form irregular time series that reflect physiological evolution. To integrate them with textual embeddings, we construct synchronized multimodal trajectories. For each structured variable x^k, $k = 1, \ldots, K$, observations are first sorted chronologically; missing internal values are then linearly interpolated, boundary values are propagated forward or backward when necessary, and all variables are finally standardized to zero mean and unit variance. At each timestamp t, the compressed textual representation of patient i is given by $\widetilde{v}_i(t) \in \mathbb{R}^r$, while the structured measurements are represented by

$$x_i(t) = \left(x_i^1(t), \ldots, x_i^K(t)\right) \in \mathbb{R}^K.$$

In our setting, a patient i will be represented by the synchronized multimodal trajectory

$$X_i : [0, T_i] \longrightarrow \mathbb{R}^q,$$

whose coordinates define a collection of q one-dimensional paths evolving over time. The ambient dimension q is obtained by concatenating the compressed embedding representation of size r, the K structured clinical variables, and the temporal coordinate required to preserve the chronological ordering of observations, yielding $q = r + K + 1$. The multimodal observation at time t is defined by concatenation:

$$X_i(t) = \left(t, \widetilde{v}_i(t), x_i^1(t), \ldots, x_i^K(t)\right) \in \mathbb{R}^q,$$

where the first coordinate corresponds to the temporal component, $\widetilde{v}_i(t) \in \mathbb{R}^r$ denotes the compressed textual representation extracted from the clinical report, and $x_i^k(t)$ denotes the value of the k-th structured clinical variable at time t. Given the observation times $0 \leq t_1 < \cdots < t_{N_i} \leq T_i$, the trajectory of patient i can be represented equivalently as the matrix

$$X_i = \left(X_i(t_1), \ldots, X_i(t_{N_i})\right)^\top \in \mathbb{R}^{N_i \times q}, \tag{1}$$

whose rows correspond to successive multimodal observations and whose columns correspond to the different coordinates of the trajectory. This representation jointly encodes the semantic evolution extracted from clinical narratives and the temporal evolution of structured physiological measurements over the N_i available observation times.

In the next section, the signature transform is applied to the trajectory X_i in order to extract higher-order temporal features describing the patient's longitudinal evolution.

2.4 Signature Feature Extraction

The signature of a path [5], later adapted to rough path theory by Lyons [17], provides a systematic way of encoding sequential data through collections of iterated integrals. To ensure uniqueness of the signature representation, a monotone coordinate is typically appended to the path, most commonly the time component. Writing $X_i(t) = \big(X_i^1(t), \ldots, X_i^q(t)\big)$, the iterated-integral signature coordinate associated with the multi-index $(j_1, \ldots, j_\ell) \in \{1, \ldots, q\}^\ell$ is defined by

$$S(X_i)_{0,t}^{(j_1,\ldots,j_\ell)} = \int_{0<t_1<\cdots<t_\ell<t} \mathrm{d}X_i^{j_1}(t_1)\cdots \mathrm{d}X_i^{j_\ell}(t_\ell).$$

The collection of these features is organized in tensor form which uniquely encodes the path and is defined as:

$$S^\ell(v) = \left(S(v)_{0,T}^{(j_1,\ldots,j_\ell)}\right)_{(j_1,\ldots,j_\ell)\in\{1,\ldots,q\}^\ell} \in (\mathbb{R}^q)^{\otimes \ell}.$$

Thus, the truncated signature up to order L naturally belongs to the truncated tensor algebra $\mathcal{T}^{\leq L}(\mathbb{R}^q) = \bigoplus_{\ell=0}^{L} (\mathbb{R}^q)^{\otimes \ell}$ of order L over $\mathbb{R}^q$:

$$S^{\leq L}(v) := \big(S^\ell(v)\big)_{\ell=0}^{L} \in \mathcal{T}^{\leq L}(\mathbb{R}^p).$$

In the remainder of this work, we explicitly denote the truncated-signature operator of order L by

$$\mathrm{Sig}^{(L)}(X_i) := S^{\leq L}(X_i),$$

denoting the collection of all iterated-integral coordinates of the multimodal trajectory X_i up to level L.

In addition to encoding temporal dynamics, this approach handles sequences of varying lengths and is invariant to translation and temporal reparameterization (see [6]), making it well-suited for patients with different study entry points and durations. Finally, for a given patient i, the collection of signature covariates extracted from the multimodal trajectory X_i, truncated at order $m = 2$, is denoted by $\mathbb{S}_i = \mathrm{Sig}^{(2)}(X_i)$. More explicitly, the truncated signature can be written as

$$\mathbb{S}_i = \left(1, S^{(1)}, \ldots, S^{(q)}, S^{(1,1)}, \ldots, S^{(q,q)}\right)_i.$$

Each patient trajectory, initially represented as a time series, is therefore summarized by a fixed-dimensional vector of signature coefficients $\mathbb{S}_i$ encoding its temporal dynamics. These signature covariates provide a structured representation of longitudinal evolution in a Euclidean space. This representation avoids the direct manipulation of irregular time series and enables the use of standard machine learning models for downstream tasks while preserving temporal consistency.

2.5 Survival Analysis Modeling

The Cox proportional hazards model [7] remains the gold standard in survival analysis, notably because it naturally accounts for right-censored observations, i.e., patients for whom the event of interest T (such as death or relapse) has not yet occurred during the observation period. In this work, we therefore adopt the Cox model to illustrate the impact of combining textual data with clinical variables. All censored patients still contribute to the likelihood estimation, helping to reduce bias and improve the robustness of predictions. The goal is to estimate the probability of a patient surviving beyond time t, noted as $\mathcal{S}(t \mid \mathbb{S}) := \mathbb{P}(T \geq t \mid \mathbb{S})$ when knowing their covariates $\mathbb{S}$. This estimation relies on the key concept of instantaneous hazard rate h, which quantifies the infinitesimal probability of the event occurring at t and is related to survival through the following equation:

$$\mathcal{S}(t \mid \mathbb{S}) = \exp\left(-\int^{t} h(s \mid \mathbb{S})\,\mathrm{d}s\right).$$

David R. Cox proposed the generalized linear model:

$$h(t \mid \mathbb{S}) \;=\; h_0(t) \cdot \exp\left(\mathbb{S} \cdot \boldsymbol{\beta}\right),$$

where $\boldsymbol{\beta} \in \mathbb{R}^Q$ is the vector of parameters to be estimated, and h_0 is the baseline hazard, common to all patients, as estimated by [4]. We define $\eta := \mathbb{S} \cdot \boldsymbol{\beta}$, referred to as the risk score. Estimating $\boldsymbol{\beta}$ involves managing a substantial number of covariates. As mentioned earlier, this is due to the signature transform, which generates a high-dimensional feature space: for q input channels and a truncation level L, the number of resulting signature coefficients scales as $O(q^L)$. Even after dimensionality reduction, the resulting covariate space remains large. To reduce the risk of overfitting and improve model stability, we apply the LASSO (*Least Absolute Shrinkage and Selection Operator*) regularization to the Cox model, as originally introduced by Robert Tibshirani in [21]:

$$\widehat{\boldsymbol{\beta}} \in \underset{\boldsymbol{\beta}}{\operatorname{argmax}} \; \log \mathrm{PL}(\boldsymbol{\beta}) - \lambda \|\boldsymbol{\beta}\|_1, \tag{2}$$

where $\mathrm{PL}(\boldsymbol{\beta})$ is the partial likelihood defined and fully detailed in [8], and $\lambda > 0$ denotes the regularization parameter. $\|\boldsymbol{\beta}\|_1$ is the ℓ_1-norm of the parameters $\boldsymbol{\beta}$. The impact of LASSO regularization is twofold: it shrinks some coefficients towards zero, effectively removing less relevant covariates, and it selects only the most important predictors for survival, enhancing model stability.

Beyond its statistical advantages, this sparsity pattern provides structural insight: only a limited subset of signature coordinates appears to carry prognostic information. In other words, although the signature transform embeds patient trajectories into a high-dimensional feature space, the effective predictive signal lies along a small number of directions. This suggests that progression patterns may have a low intrinsic dimensionality within the signature representation, highlighting the importance of both regularization and structured feature extraction in our framework. Moreover, by enforcing sparsity, the LASSO-regularized Cox model significantly reduces the number of active covariates, leading to faster computational performance. This suggests that the model achieves a favorable balance between overfitting and underfitting, leveraging a compact and efficient representation of the risk factors while maintaining strong predictive power.

To put this idea into practice, model parameters are obtained by maximizing the penalized objective function in (2), whose explicit, form when log applied, is given by:

$$\mathcal{L}(\boldsymbol{\beta}) = \sum_{i:\delta_i=1} \left[\mathbb{S}_i\boldsymbol{\beta} - \log \sum_{j\in\mathcal{R}_i} \exp\left(\mathbb{S}_j\boldsymbol{\beta}\right) \right] - \lambda \sum_{k=1}^{Q} |\beta_k|.$$

Here, $\delta_i \equiv \mathbb{1}_{\{D_i=1\}} \in \{0,1\}$ indicates whether the event (e.g., death) has been observed for patient i, with associated study duration T_i. The set $\mathcal{R}_i$ denotes the risk set, i.e., the individuals still at risk at time T_i, formally defined as $\mathcal{R}_i = \{j : T_j \geq T_i\}$.

Finally, the estimated risk score under LASSO regularization is obtained simply as the dot product

$$\widehat{\eta} = \mathbb{S} \cdot \widehat{\boldsymbol{\beta}}.$$

Each patient characterized by a sequence of clinical reports and associated sequential covariates is assigned an individualized risk score $\widehat{\eta}$ that summarizes the temporal evolution of their clinical trajectory. Overall, this pipeline provides a straightforward framework to integrate heterogeneous EHR modalities into a unified representation suitable for survival analysis.

To ensure a well-defined prediction task and avoid temporal information leakage, it is however necessary to construct these representations using only information available up to a given prediction time. In the next section, we therefore introduce a landmark design that restricts the computation of signature coefficients to observations occurring before a fixed time point, ensuring that the model is trained exclusively on past information.

2.6 Landmark Modeling for Dynamic Survival Prediction

Landmarking provides a principled framework for dynamic survival prediction by conditioning on a fixed prediction time $\mathbf{L}$ [1,12]. Rather than using the entire longitudinal process, including information recorded after the prediction time, the analysis is restricted to the landmark risk set

$$\mathcal{R}_{\mathbf{L}} = \{i : E_i \geq \mathbf{L}\}, \tag{3}$$

where $E_i = \min(T_i, C_i)$ denotes the observed survival time, obtained from the true event time T_i and censoring time C_i. Consequently, only patients who remain under observation at time $\mathbf{L}$ contribute to the landmark analysis. For each patient $i \in \mathcal{R}_{\mathbf{L}}$, survival is re-indexed relative to the landmark:

$$R_i = E_i - \mathbf{L} \geq 0.$$

The corresponding landmark event indicator is defined by $\delta_i(\mathbf{L}) = \delta_i \, \mathbb{1}_{\{E_i > \mathbf{L}\}}$ where $\delta_i = \mathbb{1}_{\{T_i \leq C_i\}}$ still denotes the usual event indicator. This formulation ensures that both the outcome and the covariates are defined relative to the same prediction time $\mathbf{L}$, thereby preventing temporal leakage and guaranteeing that predictions are conditional on survival up to the landmark. An illustration of the landmark principle is provided in Fig. 2.

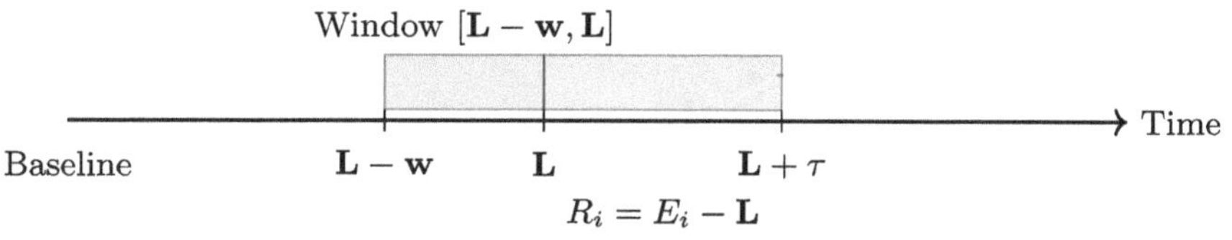

Fig. 2. Landmark design: features are constructed from the backward window $[\mathbf{L}-\mathbf{w}, \mathbf{L}]$ and survival is re-indexed by $R_i = E_i - \mathbf{L}$. The prediction task is to estimate the conditional survival probability $\mathbb{P}(T_i > \mathbf{L}+\tau \mid \mathbb{X}_i(\mathbf{L}))$, using only information observed before the landmark time.

Let's apply this setup to our context. For a fixed landmark time $\mathbf{L}$, feature extraction is restricted to the backward window $[\mathbf{L} - \mathbf{w}, \mathbf{L}]$, thereby ensuring that only information available prior to the prediction time is used. Denoting by $X_i(\mathbf{L})$ the restriction of the trajectory X_i (defined in 1) to this interval, the landmark-specific signature representation is defined as

$$\mathbb{S}_i(\mathbf{L}) = \mathrm{Sig}^{(2)}(X_i(\mathbf{L}))\,.$$

To account for patients with limited clinical history prior to the landmark, we introduce the binary indicator

$$\zeta_i(\mathbf{L}) = \mathbb{1}_{\{\mathbf{L} - t_i^{\mathrm{diag}} < \mathbf{w}\}},$$

where t_i^{diag} denotes the diagnosis time (or, equivalently, the first available clinical observation). This indicator identifies patients whose available history before $\mathbf{L}$ is shorter than the landmark window. This indicator is particularly relevant in landmark modeling, as some patients may have entered the study less than $\mathbf{w}$ time units before the landmark and therefore lack a complete history over the window $[\mathbf{L} - \mathbf{w}, \mathbf{L}]$. The final landmark covariate vector is obtained by concatenation:

$$\mathbb{X}_i(\mathbf{L}) = [\mathbb{S}_i(\mathbf{L}),\ \zeta_i(\mathbf{L})]^\top \in \mathbb{R}^{Q+1}.$$

The resulting landmark dataset consists of triplets $\Big(\mathbb{X}_i(\mathbf{L}),\ \delta_i(\mathbf{L}),\ R_i\Big)$, for each $i \in \mathcal{R}_{\mathbf{L}}$, which are used to estimate conditional survival beyond the landmark time. More precisely, the prediction task consists of estimating

$$\mathbb{P}\Big(T_i > \mathbf{L} + \tau \,\Big|\, \mathbb{X}_i(\mathbf{L})\Big),$$

that is, the probability that patient i survives an additional horizon τ beyond the landmark time, given all information available up to $\mathbf{L}$.

This framework is particularly well suited to longitudinal clinical data and signature-based representations. By construction, it ensures temporal coherence, prevents information leakage, accommodates irregular follow-up patterns, and allows patients with heterogeneous observation histories to be compared at a common prediction time.

3 Experiments

3.1 Cohort

This study complies with the General Data Protection Regulation (GDPR) and falls within the scope of scientific research conducted in the legitimate interest of cancer research, in accordance with Articles 6.1.f and 9.2.j of Regulation (EU) No. 2016/679. This project has been officially registered under the MR004 declaration (V3.2, 23/08/2021) at the Léon Bérard Center, ensuring compliance with legal and ethical standards for processing health data. The data have been carefully anonymized and can only be used within the framework of this study. No patient were opposed to this study. To ensure the reliability of our data, we selected a study cohort consisting of patients hospitalized – at least once – at the Léon Bérard Center from 2000 to 2024, with comprehensive follow-up throughout their medical care to ensure data completeness and accuracy.

All results reported in this section are obtained under a landmark design with landmark time $\mathbf{L} = 36$ months and backward window size $\mathbf{w} = 12$ months. In other words, we consider patients who remain at risk three years after their initial diagnosis or first hospitalization, and construct covariates using information collected during the one-year period preceding the landmark.

The dataset consists of longitudinal medical reports collected from a comprehensive oncology cohort. It includes 2,527 patients and a total of 124,049 clinical reports, with an average of 49 reports per patient, reflecting dense longitudinal follow-up. Among these patients, 1,629 experienced the event of interest and 898 were right-censored.

The cohort covers a wide spectrum of cancer types. The most represented diagnoses are breast cancer (782 patients, 31.0%), and to name a few more, gynecological cancers (232, 9.2%), intestinal cancers (227, 9.0%), prostate cancer (201, 8.0%), and lung cancer (96, 3.8%). Additional cases include other oncological subtypes, ensuring heterogeneity in disease trajectories and survival patterns. The longitudinal structure of the data makes it particularly suitable for landmark modeling. At each landmark time $\mathbf{L}$, only patients still at risk are considered, and covariates are constructed from the backward window $[\mathbf{L} - \mathbf{w}, \mathbf{L}]$, ensuring temporal coherence and preventing information leakage. Descriptive statistics and additional cohort characteristics (cancer types, number of reports per patient, study duration, diagnosis dates, and Kaplan–Meier curves) are available in the associated GitHub repository (https://github.com/MINCHELLA-Paul/MultiSigBERT/tree/main/results/descriptive_statistics).

3.2 Hyperparameter Search

Our experimental setup is designed to ensure reproducibility, robustness, and realistic evaluation in a complex real-world clinical context. The NLP model used in this study OncoBERT is previously fine-tuned on oncology-specific clinical notes. It is used as is throughout the experiments, without further task-specific adaptation, in order to reflect realistic deployment scenarios. The survival model was trained on a cohort of 1,264 patients (9,696 reports) and evaluated on a separate test set of 1,263 patients (9,752 reports), using a structured and stratified train-test split to preserve temporal and distributional consistency. To calibrate the model, we conducted a grid search for the LASSO regularization parameter λ within the range $[0.01, 16]$, using a fixed step size of 0.01. We selected the value that maximized the cross-validation concordance index (C-index) averaged over five independent validation folds, within the training dataset.

At this step, the longitudinal data were transformed using the signature method, effectively eliminating any temporal constraints that could arise when subdividing the dataset for cross-validation. The selection criterion aimed to maximize the C-index through five-fold cross-validation. Specifically, for each candidate value of λ, the model was trained on a partition of the training cohort and evaluated on held-out subsets – within the training set –, maintaining equal proportions across folds.

The optimal value was then chosen as the one yielding the highest mean C-index, promoting robust generalization and avoiding overfitting. This tuning process was crucial for balancing model sparsity and predictive accuracy (Table 1).

Table 1. Optimal regularization LASSO-parameter λ selected by validation for each modeling scenario. Performance is reported as the mean C-index on the validation sets with its standard deviation (higher is better) and the Integrated Brier Score at 3 years (IBS@3y, lower is better).

Scenario	λ	C-index Val. ↑	IBS@3y ↓
Reports Only	5.15	0.747 (sd 0.027)	0.1280 (sd 0.004)
Reports & Structured Variables	4.60	0.743 (sd 0.025)	0.1280 (sd 0.004)

3.3 Performance Metrics

Model validation is performed using repeated random splitting: the test set is divided into ten disjoint subsets, and evaluation is repeated independently on each split. Reported values correspond to the mean and standard deviation across splits.

We first assess discrimination using the concordance index (C-index) [11], computed on the landmark cohort $\mathcal{R}_L$ from (3). The C-index measures the proportion of correctly ordered comparable pairs. If patient j experiences the event before patient i, a well-specified model should assign a higher risk score $\widehat{\eta}_j > \widehat{\eta}_i$. Using the landmark outcomes $(R_i, \delta_i(\mathbf{L}))$, it can be written as

$$\text{C-index} = \frac{\sum_{i,j \in \mathcal{R}_\mathbf{L}} \mathbb{1}_{\{R_j < R_i\}} \mathbb{1}_{\{\widehat{\eta}_j > \widehat{\eta}_i\}} \delta_j(\mathbf{L})}{\sum_{i,j \in \mathcal{R}_\mathbf{L}} \mathbb{1}_{\{R_j < R_i\}} \delta_j(\mathbf{L})}.$$

A value of 1 indicates perfect ranking, whereas 0.5 corresponds to random performance.

While discrimination remains important, calibration has become equally critical in modern survival modeling. A model may rank patients correctly while providing inaccurate survival probabilities. To assess calibration, we use the Brier Score (BS), which measures the squared difference between the predicted landmark survival probability $\widehat{\mathcal{S}}(t \mid \mathbb{X}_i(\mathbf{L}))$ and the observed landmark outcome. To account for right censoring, we employ inverse probability of censoring weighting (IPCW) [10]:

$$\text{BS}(t) = \frac{1}{|\mathcal{R}_\mathbf{L}|} \sum_{i \in \mathcal{R}_\mathbf{L}} \Bigg[\mathbb{1}_{\{R_i \leq t,\ \delta_i(\mathbf{L})=1\}} \frac{\widehat{\mathcal{S}}(t \mid \mathbb{X}_i(\mathbf{L}))^2}{\widehat{G}(R_i)} + \mathbb{1}_{\{R_i > t\}} \frac{\left(1 - \widehat{\mathcal{S}}(t \mid \mathbb{X}_i(\mathbf{L}))\right)^2}{\widehat{G}(t)} \Bigg]. \quad (4)$$

where $\widehat{G}$ denotes the Kaplan–Meier estimator [13] of the censoring distribution. In the landmark setting, the Brier Score evaluates the accuracy of predicted residual survival probabilities beyond the landmark time $\mathbf{L}$.

The Brier Score directly quantifies the accuracy of predicted survival probabilities. This property is crucial in clinical applications, where predicted survival probabilities may influence treatment decisions, patient stratification, and follow-up strategies. A value substantially below the naive reference value of 0.25 – corresponding to a constant prediction of 0.5 for all individuals – indicates good calibration. Finally, to summarize predictive accuracy over a given time interval rather than at a single time point, we use the Integrated Brier Score (IBS) that provides a global calibration measure by integrating (4) over a time interval $[\tau_1, \tau_2]$. In practice, it can be evaluated up to a fixed horizon, for example 3 years, by setting $\tau_1 = 0$ and $\tau_2 = 3\text{y}$.

3.4 Experimental Results

All results obtained under the landmark design ($\mathbf{L} = 36$, $\mathbf{w} = 12$) are summarized in Table 2. The models adapted to this architecture include DeepSurv [14], CoxTime [15], and the time-varying Cox model implemented via CoxTimeVaryingFitter [9], denoted CTVF. CoxTime and CTVF are trained and applied directly on the longitudinal time-series representation via Equation (2.3), whereas DeepSurv operates on the fixed-length feature representation obtained after computing the signature coefficients. We consider two experimental configurations: (i) *Reports Only*, relying exclusively on signature features extracted from textual embeddings (therefore, corresponding to the initial model SigBERT [20]); and (ii) *Reports + Sequential Structured Data*, where interpolated longitudinal clinical variables are concatenated with textual embeddings prior to the signature transformation.

Overall, as shown in Table 2, MultiSigBERT achieves strong predictive performance under the landmark design. In the *Reports Only* configuration, it reaches a mean test C-index of **0.741** (sd 0.027), substantially outperforming several classical survival baselines such as CoxTime (0.646) and CTVF (0.619). It also clearly improves upon neural survival models based on aggregated representations, such as DeepSurv, which attains a mean C-index of 0.600. In terms of calibration, MultiSigBERT yields a relatively low prediction error with an $\text{IBS}_{@3y}$ of **0.128** (sd 0.006), indicating accurate survival probability estimates across the evaluation horizon.

Table 2. Test-set performance under the landmark design (Train = 1,263 patients; Test = 1,264 patients). Values are reported as mean with 95% Jackknife confidence intervals in brackets. RO: Reports Only; RS: Reports + Sequential Structured Data. ↑ indicates that higher values are better; ↓ indicates that lower values are better.

Model	C-index ↑ (Test)	IBS ↓ (Test)
MultiSigBERT (RO)	**0.741 [0.724, 0.758]**	0.1282 [0.1243, 0.1322]
DeepSurv (RO)	0.600 [0.583, 0.614]	0.1512 [0.1406, 0.1619]
CoxTime (RO)	0.646 [0.638, 0.654]	**0.091 [0.081, 0.101]**
CTVF (RO)	0.619 [0.594, 0.645]	0.207 [0.185, 0.229]
MultiSigBERT (RS)	**0.743 [0.725, 0.761]**	0.1339 [0.1293, 0.1385]
DeepSurv (RS)	0.650 [0.620, 0.676]	0.1490 [0.1386, 0.1593]
CoxTime (RS)	0.651 [0.640, 0.661]	**0.091 [0.081, 0.101]**
CTVF (RS)	0.618 [0.594, 0.645]	0.209 [0.185, 0.229]

When sequential structured covariates are incorporated, MultiSigBERT maintains essentially the same level of predictive performance. The mean test C-index slightly increases to **0.743** (sd 0.029), while the calibration error becomes $\text{IBS}_{@3y} = 0.134$ (sd 0.007). These results suggest that adding structured variables provides only marginal gains in discrimination while slightly degrading calibration.

Compared with neural survival baselines such as DeepSurv, MultiSigBERT offers a substantially better overall trade-off between discrimination and calibration. Even when structured variables are included, DeepSurv reaches a mean C-index of only 0.650, remaining clearly below the performance achieved by MultiSigBERT. Although CoxTime achieves the lowest $\text{IBS}_{@3y}$ (around 0.091), its discrimination remains substantially lower (C-index ≈ 0.65), which limits its usefulness for clinical risk stratification where reliable patient ranking is essential.

From a clinical perspective, this trade-off is particularly important. Effective decision support requires models that can both correctly rank patients by risk and provide reasonably calibrated survival probabilities. In this respect, MultiSigBERT provides a robust compromise: it achieves substantially higher discrimination than traditional Cox-based approaches while maintaining stable and interpretable survival predictions.

Finally, the limited improvement observed when incorporating sequential structured variables suggests that a large part of the prognostic signal carried by routinely collected structured measurements is already implicitly captured in longitudinal clinical narratives. Since these variables must be interpolated over the backward window $[\mathbf{L} - \mathbf{w}, \mathbf{L}]$ due to their irregular recording times, this interpolation introduces smoothing assumptions and may propagate measurement noise. Consequently, the multimodal configuration provides only limited additional predictive value in this setting.

4 Conclusion

We introduced MultiSigBERT, a multimodal survival modeling framework that integrates longitudinal clinical narratives and structured variables within a unified temporal representation. The proposed pipeline combines domain-specific language embeddings concatenated with sequential structured variables, dimensionality reduction, path signature encoding, and sparse Cox regression, yielding a computationally efficient and interpretable approach for survival prediction.

Experiments on a large real-world oncology cohort show that MultiSigBERT achieves strong predictive performance under a landmark design, with a C-index around 0.743 (sd 0.029) and stable calibration. Importantly, the landmark framework ensures a well-defined dynamic prediction task and prevents temporal information leakage by restricting feature construction to observations available prior to the prediction time, therefore providing a robust and reproducible pipeline for longitudinal survival modeling.

The proposed architecture naturally supports multimodal integration. By embedding heterogeneous clinical data into synchronized trajectories prior to signature encoding, the model captures temporal interactions across modalities in a principled geometric representation. In addition, the aggregation strategy enables the use of an arbitrary number of clinical reports per patient while preserving temporal ordering. The entire pipeline remains computationally lightweight and can be trained on standard CPU hardware, offering a favorable trade-off between predictive performance, interpretability, and computational cost.

Some limitations should nevertheless be acknowledged. The structured variables considered in this study remain limited, and their irregular sampling requires interpolation within the landmark window. Future work will investigate additional static covariates, such as tumor type, sex, or age at diagnosis, which can be straightforwardly incorporated into the proposed framework.

Overall, MultiSigBERT provides a robust and scalable framework for multimodal survival analysis from longitudinal clinical data. A key contribution of this work lies in the use of path signatures as a unified representation of heterogeneous temporal modalities. Signature transforms encode temporal dependencies and higher-order interactions into a fixed-dimensional vector while naturally handling irregularly sampled trajectories, making them particularly suitable for real-world clinical data. Our results also suggest that classical sparse survival models remain highly competitive when combined with expressive temporal representations. The combination of landmarking, signature-based feature extraction, and Cox–LASSO regularization achieved a favorable trade-off between predictive performance, interpretability, computational efficiency, and robustness. Future work will explore richer multimodal representations and external validation on independent oncology cohorts.

Disclosure of Interests. The authors declare no potential conflicts of interest.

References

1. Anderson, J., Cain, K., Gelber, R.: Analysis of survival by tumor response. J. Clin. Oncol. **1**(11), 710–719 (1983). https://doi.org/10.1200/JCO.1983.1.11.710
2. Arora, S., Liang, Y., Ma, T.: A simple but tough-to-beat baseline for sentence embeddings. In: International Conference on Learning Representations (ICLR) (2017). published as a conference paper at ICLR
3. Bleistein, L., Nguyen, V.T., Fermanian, A., Guilloux, A.: Dynamical survival analysis with controlled latent states. arXiv:2401.17077 (2024) [stat.ML]. https://arxiv.org/abs/2401.17077
4. Breslow, N.E.: Contribution to the discussion of the paper by. In: Cox, D.R. (ed.) J. Roy. Stat. Soc.: Ser. B (Methodol.), pp. 216–217 (1972)
5. Chen, K.T.: Iterated integrals and exponential homomorphisms. Proc. Lond. Math. Soc. **3**(4), 502–512 (1954)
6. Chevyrev, I., Kormilitzin, A.: A primer on the signature method in machine learning. arXiv:1603.03788 (2025) [stat.ML]. https://arxiv.org/abs/1603.03788
7. Cox, D.R.: Regression models and life-tables. J. Roy. Stat. Soc.: Ser. B (Methodol.) **34**(2), 187–202 (1972). https://doi.org/10.1111/j.2517-6161.1972.tb00899.x
8. Cox, D.R.: Partial likelihood. Biometrika **62**(2), 269–276 (1975). https://doi.org/10.1093/biomet/62.2.269
9. Davidson-Pilon, C.: lifelines: Survival analysis in Python. J. Open Source Softw. **4**(40), 1317 (2019). https://doi.org/10.21105/joss.01317
10. Graf, E., Schmoor, C., Sauerbrei, W., Schumacher, M.: Assessment and comparison of prognostic classification schemes for survival data. Stat. Med. **18**(17–18), 2529–2545 (1999)
11. Harrell, F.E., Califf, R.M., Pryor, D.B., Lee, K.L., Rosati, R.A.: Evaluating the yield of medical tests. J. Am. Med. Assoc. **247**(18), 2543–2546 (1982)
12. an Houwelingen, H.C., Putter, H.: Dynamic predicting by landmarking as an alternative for multi-state modeling. Lifetime Data Anal. **14**(4), 447–463 (2008). https://doi.org/10.1007/s10985-008-9099-8
13. Kaplan, E.L., Meier, P.: Nonparametric estimation from incomplete observations. J. Am. Stat. Assoc. **53**(282), 457–481 (1958). https://doi.org/10.2307/2281868

14. Katzman, J.L., Shaham, U., Cloninger, A., Bates, J., Jiang, T., Kluger, Y.: DeepSurv: personalized treatment recommender system using a Cox proportional hazards deep neural network. BMC Med. search Methodol. **18**(1) (2018). https://doi.org/10.1186/s12874-018-0482-1
15. Kvamme, H., Borgan, Ø., Scheel, I.: Time-to-event prediction with neural networks and Cox regression. J. Mach. Learn. Res. **20**(116), 1–30 (2019). http://jmlr.org/papers/v20/18-424.html
16. Lee, C., Yoon, J., van der Schaar, M.: Dynamic-DeepHit: a deep learning approach for dynamic survival analysis with competing risks based on longitudinal data. IEEE Trans. Biomed. Eng. (2019). https://par.nsf.gov/servlets/purl/10099761
17. Lyons, T.J.: Differential equations driven by rough signals. Revista Matemática Iberoamericana **14**(2), 215–310 (1998)
18. Mesinovic, M., Watkinson, P., Zhu, T.: DySurv: dynamic deep learning model for survival analysis with conditional variational inference. arXiv:2310.18681 (2024) cs.LG
19. Martin, L., Muller, B., Ortiz Suárez, P.J., Dupont, Y., Romary, L., de la Clergerie, É., Seddah, D., Sagot, B.: CamemBERT: a tasty French language model. In: Proceedings of the 58th Annual Meeting of the Association for Computational Linguistics. Association for Computational Linguistics (2020). https://doi.org/10.18653/v1/2020.acl-main.645
20. Minchella, P., Verlingue, L., Chrétien, S., Vaucher, R., Metzler, G.: Sigbert: combining narrative medical reports and rough path signature theory for survival prediction in oncology. In: Machine Learning and Knowledge Discovery in Databases. Applied Data Science Track. ECML PKDD 2025. Lecture Notes in Computer Science, vol. part IX. Springer (2025)
21. Tibshirani, R.: The lasso method for variable selection in the cox model. Stat. Med. **16**(4), 385–395 (1997). https://doi.org/10.1002/(SICI)1097-0258(19970228)16:4<385::AID-SIM380>3.0.CO;2-3
22. Vienne, R., Filori, Q., Susplugas, V., Crochet, H., Verlingue, L.: Abstract 3475: prediction of nausea or vomiting, and fatigue or malaise in cancer care. Can. Res. **84**, 3475–3475 (2024). https://doi.org/10.1158/1538-7445.AM2024-3475

PRISM-CTG: A Foundation Model for Cardiotocography Analysis with Multi-view SSL

Sheng Wong[1(✉)], Beth Albert[1], Lin Li[2], Hao Fei[2], Ravi Shankar[1], Imane Ben M'Barek[3], Manu Vatish[1], and Gabriel Davis Jones[1]

[1] Nuffield Department of Women's & Reproductive Health, University of Oxford, Oxford, UK
sheng.wong@wrh.ox.ac.uk

[2] OATML, Department of Computer Science, University of Oxford, Oxford, UK

[3] Université Paris Cité, Paris, France

Abstract. Supervised deep learning models for automated cardiotocograph (CTG) analysis are typically constrained by narrowly curated labelled datasets and limited patient cohorts, leaving substantial volumes of physiologically informative clinical recordings untapped. To address this limitation, we propose Physiology-aware Representation Learning via Integrated Self-supervision and Metadata for CTG (PRISM-CTG), a clinically grounded self-supervised foundation model (FM) for CTG that leverages large-scale unlabelled recordings to learn transferable domain-level representations. PRISM-CTG is pretrained using a multi-view self-supervised framework that jointly optimises 3 complementary pretext objectives: random-projected guided masked signal reconstruction, clinical variable prediction, and feature classification. Each objective is associated with a dedicated task-specific token, enabling specialised representation learning, while controlled cross-attention facilitates information exchange across clinical context. By reframing patient metadata and domain knowledge, which are often underutilised in conventional training as prediction targets, PRISM-CTG transforms readily available clinical information into additional supervisory targets that guide clinically meaningful representation learning. Extensive experiments across 7 downstream CTG tasks in both antepartum and intrapartum domains demonstrated that PRISM-CTG consistently outperforms in-domain and self-supervised baselines. Notably, PRISM-CTG demonstrated strong generalisation under external validation on 2 datasets, while achieving comparable performance to studies trained on substantially larger, privately labelled datasets. To our knowledge, this is the first study to introduce large-scale FM for CTG that learns domain-level representations. Our code and data are available at https://github.com/sfwon17/Prism-CTG.

Keywords: CTG Analysis · Self-supervised Learning · Foundation Model

M. Ceci et al. (Eds.): ECML PKDD 2026, LNAI 16948, pp. 583–600, 2027.
https://doi.org/10.1007/978-3-032-37679-4_33

1 Introduction

Cardiotocography (CTG) provides indirect measures of fetal brain activity. It comprises simultaneous time-series recordings of fetal heart rate (FHR) and uterine activity (UA), and remains the primary clinical tool for continuous, non-invasive fetal health assessment during pregnancy and labour [17]. Despite its widespread adoption, interpreting CTGs is both time-consuming and inherently subjective, requiring constant attention over prolonged monitoring periods [15]. This creates diagnostic uncertainty and could potentially lead to delayed or suboptimal decision-making. In response, deep learning (DL) models have been proposed for automated CTG analysis to assist clinicians in CTG interpretation. However, the performance of these models remains constrained by limited patient cohorts and narrowly curated datasets designed for predefined tasks [19,20,30,43].

These supervised DL models rely on large quantities of high-quality, clearly defined labels to learn task-specific predictions, with labels typically derived from neonatal outcomes or clinical criteria. In real-world settings, however, many CTG recordings do not align cleanly into these label categories due to several factors, including early recordings that do not reflect final neonatal status, borderline or ambiguous cases, or recordings with significant dropout [10,19]. Consequently, a large volume of physiologically informative CTGs is excluded from the training pipeline despite containing meaningful physiological patterns, as illustrated in Fig. 1. This results in models that are trained on highly selective subsets of CTG recordings, leading to task-specific representations that lack robustness even within their respective predefined tasks (see supplementary material S1).

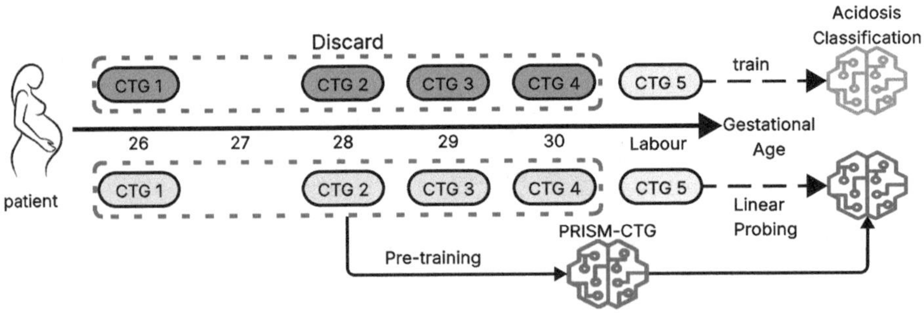

Fig. 1. Overview of a major limitation in conventional supervised CTG training. Supervised models typically select temporally aligned recordings for a single predefined task, discarding CTGs acquired earlier in the gestational period (top). In contrast, PRISM-CTG leverages CTGs from the full gestational period during pretraining to learn general representations that are transferable across multiple downstream tasks.

Pretraining via self-supervised learning (SSL) [1,13] offers an alternative for learning meaningful representation from unlabelled data and has demonstrated strong performance in the physiological signals domain, enabling the development of foundation models (FMs) that are capable of multiple downstream tasks in their respective domain [5,12,28,39]. However, SSL-based FMs have not been investigated in the domain of CTGs. Additionally, existing SSL approaches adopted by these FMs predominantly rely on single signal pretext objectives, which, while effective at capturing low-level signal characteristics, largely overlook available clinical context. In practice, clinical context, including patient metadata and domain-engineered features, is often ignored or discarded, despite encoding clinically meaningful physiological and contextual information [3,10,17]. Although individually insufficient for diagnosis, this information reflects expert knowledge routinely used in clinical interpretation and can provide valuable inductive bias during SSL [3,10,17].

To this end, this work presents **PRISM-CTG**, a FM for CTG analysis that learns clinically grounded, transferable CTG representations. PRISM-CTG is pretrained on over 250,000 h of CTGs collected across 3 decades using a multiview SSL framework that leverages 3 complementary supervisory signals: random-projected guided masked signal reconstruction (Best-RQ-MAE) to learn general CTG patterns, patient metadata prediction, and prediction of domain-engineered features. By reframing otherwise discarded clinical information as free supervisory targets, PRISM-CTG integrates signal-level and patient-level context through dedicated task-specific tokens with controlled cross-attention. This design mirrors clinical CTG interpretation, where signal inputs are evaluated alongside patient context, enabling the model to learn context-aware representations that are robust and transferable across downstream tasks. In summary, the main contributions of this study are **the first CTG FM** pretrained to learn transferable domain-level representations by integrating morphology-guided reconstruction with clinically informed supervision. **Multi-view objective with task-specific representation specialisation** through isolated task tokens and controlled cross-attention that integrates signal-level, patient-level, and feature-level supervision during pretraining. PRISM-CTG is **transferable** across antepartum and intrapartum domains, achieving an average Area Under the Curve (AUC) improvement of 4.93% to 19.31% over supervised models. PRISM-CTG also demonstrated strong **cross-institution generalisation**, achieving average improvements of 2.76% and 8.62% in AUC on two external datasets, despite minimal intrapartum data during pretraining.

2 Related Work

2.1 CTG Analysis

Recent advances in automated CTG analysis have largely been driven by supervised learning approaches [6,19,22,30,32,43]. These models are typically trained explicitly on single clinical objectives such as fetal acidemia detection or abnormality classification, relying on very small volumes of CTG recordings. In an attempt to address label scarcity, some studies have explored supervised pretraining strategies to improve on the task performance [6,19,22] (See supplementary material S2 for more details). Although these methods improve optimisation stability and task-specific performance, they were not aimed to learn general CTG representations, only task-specific representations. More recently, a small number of works in the field of CTG analysis have incorporated SSL techniques [21,34,38]. However, these approaches are still typically embedded within a task-specific pipeline, where the focus was not on large-scale pretraining. In summary, previous work has largely focused on task-specific optimisation with pretraining, instead of learning transferable, general representations. PRISM-CTG addresses this gap through large-scale SSL, learning a robust general representation that is transferable to multiple downstream tasks.

2.2 Foundation Models for Physiological Time-Series

Self-supervised pretraining for physiological time series is well established. They are often adapted from other vision or time-series domains to build domain-specific FMs [2,5,12,16,25,28,33,35,39,42]. Trained on large in-domain physiological data, these FMs have demonstrated transferability across multiple downstream tasks. However, these domain-specific approaches, along with general-purpose time-series SSL methods, do not transfer well to CTG analysis. Many rely on assumptions that do not hold for CTG signals. For example, some studies rely on inter-channel or cross-signal representation alignment, an approach well suited to multimodal physiological settings where signals are recorded synchronously and reflect shared underlying neural or cardiac activities [26,33]. Other FMs utilised signal transformations to derive domain-informative representations during pretraining, including spectral and frequency-domain representations, to guide representation learning [5,12,39]. In contrast, CTG comprises two physiologically distinct signals. FHR is a non-periodic signal reflecting autonomic regulation of the fetus, while UA originates from the maternal uterine contractions that exhibits periodicity and temporal frequency that varies with the stage of pregnancy. As such, we argue that these methods are not well-suited to learning robust representations from CTG signals.

2.3 Pretraining with Auxiliary Information

Traditionally, SSL relies solely on the target modality during pretraining. Some FMs in this domain extend beyond signal-only SSL by incorporating auxiliary inputs or targets such as textual reports or engineered features to guide representation learning. Several domain-specific FMs employ cross-modal alignment strategies with paired signal and text data to learn semantically transferable embeddings [24,35,42]. Other approaches adopt predictive pretraining paradigms that use auxiliary signals or engineered features supervision signals to guide representation learning [9,25,31], relying on strong domain knowledge as pretraining objectives, resulting in representations that reflect in-domain physiological or clinical-features characteristics. Motivated by these methods, we incorporated patients' metadata and engineered features directly into the pretraining objectives to guide representation learning within a predictive paradigm, without relying on additional signal modalities.

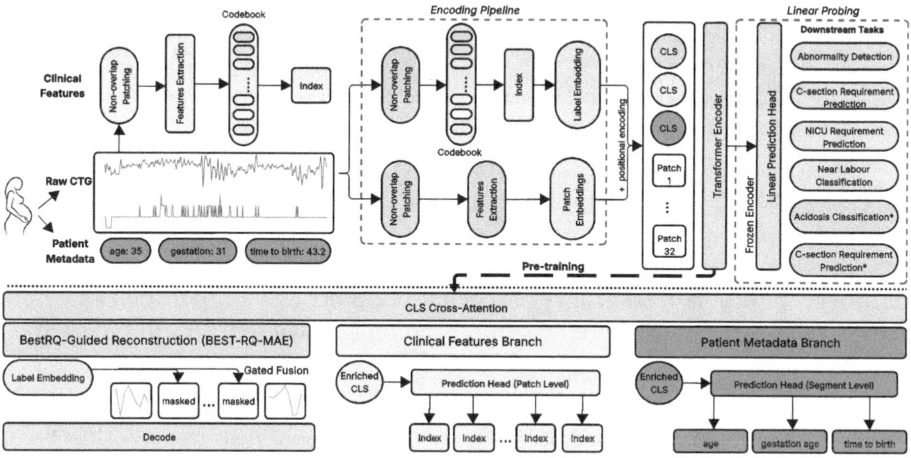

Fig. 2. PRISM-CTG architecture. The model is pretrained with 3 pretext objectives and evaluated via linear probing by freezing the encoder and training a task-specific linear head on 6 downstream tasks (four antepartum, two intrapartum).

3 Methods

In this section, we describe the overall architecture of PRISM-CTG, specifically highlighting the modules that are unique from standard SSL. We use the terms task token and classification `CLS` token interchangeably. A CTG recording is represented as a multivariate time series $\mathbf{X} \in \mathbb{R}^{L \times C}$, where $C = 2$ (FHR and UA) and L is timepoints. The model jointly optimises 3 complementary pretext objectives: (i) Best-RQ-MAE, (ii) patient metadata prediction, and (iii) domain feature label classification. We assign 3 task-specific tokens, where they independently aggregate information from the input during encoding via an isolation attention mask. This enforces objective-specific specialisation from shared patch tokens. After encoding, we apply dedicated `CLS` cross-attention blocks, allowing controlled information exchange only after each task token has formed its own summary. Notably, in our proposed Best-RQ-MAE module, a parallel frozen random-projection tokeniser assigns discrete pseudo-labels to raw patches, and the resulting label embeddings are injected into both encoder and decoder to provide morphology-aware, signal-level guidance during reconstruction. In the decoder, label embeddings are fused with patch representations through a learned gate, and patch tokens are further conditioned on task-specific CLS summaries via patch-to-CLS cross-attention. The 3 objectives are jointly optimised with learned uncertainty-based weighting to balance heterogeneous scaling losses. Figure 2 provides an overview of our proposed PRISM-CTG architecture. (see supplementary material S3 for the full configurations and details).

3.1 Encoding Pipeline

Given a CTG recording $\mathbf{X} \in \mathbb{R}^{L \times C}$ ($C = 2$: FHR and UA), PRISM-CTG builds patch tokens through two parallel streams: a learned CNN patch embedding and a frozen random-projection label embedding.

CNN Backbone and Patch Embedding. The CNN backbone, which consists of multiple residual convolutional blocks, extracts local features from the raw CTG signal without temporal downsampling. The resulting feature maps are partitioned into non-overlapping patches using a strided 1D convolution. Each patch is then linearly projected to an embedding dimension D, producing $\mathbf{h}_i$.

Signal Tokenisation and Label Embedding. In parallel with patch embedding, we adopt a frozen random-projection quantizer, inspired by BEST-RQ to assign each patch a discrete pseudo-label [7]. Specifically, non-overlapping patches are first projected into a fixed latent space using a random projection and matched to the nearest neighbour in a frozen codebook, producing discrete indices that act as pseudo-labels. They are then mapped into D-dimensional embedding vectors via a learnable embedding table, forming label embeddings, $\mathbf{e}_{\ell_i}$. Importantly, the novelty does not lie in the quantisation itself, but in how the pseudo-labels are integrated into the pretraining framework. By grouping patches with similar characteristics, these embedding labels projected from pseudo-labels provide signal-level structural guidance during representation learning.

Patch Fusion. For each patch position i, the encoder input token is formed by element-wise addition of $3D$-dimensional components: $\mathbf{z}_i = \mathbf{h}_i + \mathbf{e}_{\ell_i} + \mathbf{p}_i^{\text{pos}}$ where $\mathbf{h}_i$ is the CNN-derived patch embedding, $\mathbf{e}_{\ell_i}$ is the label embedding and $\mathbf{p}_i^{\text{pos}}$ represents positional encoding. Together, the components serve as the input representation for Transformer encoding.

3.2 Clinical-Aware Transformer Encoding

Conventionally, transformers employ a single `CLS` token to capture global information for downstream tasks. To enable clinical-aware representation learning, we instead prepend 3 learnable task tokens to the patch-token sequence: $\texttt{CLS}_r$ (BestRQ-MAE), $\texttt{CLS}_v$ (patient metadata prediction), and $\texttt{CLS}_f$ (feature classification). We explain the architecture design choice below.

CLS Isolation Attention Mask. Rather than allowing all tokens to attend freely, we enforce an isolation constraint through attention masking. Each `CLS` token attends only to itself and to all patch tokens. This forces each `CLS` token to independently aggregate information from the patches, developing a specialised summary controlled by its respective task objective. After encoding, the output is partitioned into the three enriched `CLS` tokens and the remaining patch embeddings, defined as $\hat{\mathbf{H}} \in \mathbb{R}^{N \times D}$.

Task-Wise Cross-Attention. After Transformer encoding with the isolation mask, each CLS token contains task-specific summaries. We then introduce cross-attention to enable controlled information exchange between CLS tokens, where for each task token, we compute $\mathbf{cls}'_{task} = \mathrm{CrossAttn}(\mathbf{cls}_{task}, [\mathbf{cls}_r; \mathbf{cls}_v; \mathbf{cls}_f])$, and $task \in \{r, v, f\}$. From a clinical perspective, CTG interpretation is inherently multi-factorial: signal characteristics, patient context, and clinical features inform one another. For example, the interpretation of a CTG may depend on the baseline and gestational age. The cross-attention component reflects this controlled interaction by enabling each objective to adaptively integrate relevant clinical information while preserving task-specific structure.

3.3 Multi-task Pretext Objectives

The model is jointly trained on 3 complementary pretext objectives that operate at different levels of granularity, each utilising a dedicated enriched CLS token. Best-RQ-MAE encourages the learning of long-range temporal dependencies and signal characteristics, patient metadata prediction provides global recording-level supervision grounded in patient context, and feature classification enforces local patch-level representations that align with domain knowledge.

Best-RQ-MAE. For the reconstruction objective, we adopt an MAE-style pretraining strategy in which masked patches are reconstructed from visible patches using a lightweight decoder. The key design change lies in introducing morphology-aware conditioning within the decoder through label embeddings derived from the frozen signal tokeniser. Since the tokeniser groups patches with similar signal morphology or patterns, the resulting label embeddings capture the general structure of a CTG signal, providing structured guidance during reconstruction. We compute a gating vector $\mathbf{g}_i = \sigma(W_g[\mathbf{x}_i; \mathbf{e}_{\ell_i}])$ and fuse the signal guidance as $\tilde{\mathbf{x}}_i = \mathbf{x}_i + \mathbf{g}_i \odot \mathbf{e}_{\ell_i}$, where $\mathbf{x}i$ denotes the restored representation at position i, and $\mathbf{e}\ell_i$ is the corresponding label embedding computed from the *full unmasked* signal. In addition, we inject clinical aware information, CLS, through cross-attention. Specifically, each restored decoder representation queries the enriched reconstruction token $\mathbf{cls}'_r$, enabling incorporation of clinically informed global context before final reconstruction. The reconstructed raw patches are then supervised using masked-patch mean squared error (MSE).

The rationale behind this design is to maintain a lightweight decoder while compensating with structured guidance, avoiding the problem identified by [41] where a shallow decoder forces the encoder to sacrifice capacity for low-level reconstruction at the expense of semantic understanding. While deeper decoders can improve reconstruction ability, they introduce additional computational overhead [41]. Instead, we provide the decoder with 'morphological hints' derived from the frozen Best-RQ tokeniser, together with additional clinical information from the CLS, allowing the lightweight decoder to reconstruct effectively without requiring additional depth.

Patient Metadata Prediction. Clinical interpretation of CTG is context-dependent, where similar morphology patterns may carry different clinical meanings under different patient conditions. To encode the clinical information as global context into the learned representation, we use the enriched token $\mathbf{cls}'_v$ with a lightweight head that predicts d_v continuous patient metadata. This objective is trained as regression with MSE. This task encourages the model to learn recording-level, clinically contextual representations rather than relying solely on morphological patterns. In this study, the 3 patient metadata used are gestational age, time to birth, and maternal age. (See supplementary materials S3.2.)

Engineered Features Classification. Clinical interpretation of CTG signals relies on established domain-relevant features such as baseline FHR and short-term variability, which reflect underlying autonomic regulation of the fetus and are central to deciding neonatal status. As such, these features can serve as supervisory targets to guide representation learning toward clinically relevant signal characteristics. To align learned patch representations with domain knowledge used in clinical CTG assessment, we introduce a patch-level feature prediction objective. For each visible raw patch, we extract 17 handcrafted clinically relevant features. They are then converted into discrete pseudo-labels using a second frozen random-projection quantiser (BEST-RQ), independent of the signal tokeniser. This approach reduces a high-dimensional continuous target to a single classification objective, trained with cross-entropy loss. Similarly, we utilise the enriched $\mathbf{cls}'_f$ with a lightweight classification head to predict the feature pseudo-labels. (See supplementary materials S3.3.)

3.4 Linear Probing

For downstream tasks, we use linear probing to assess the performance and transferability of the pretrained representations. The encoder is frozen, and a linear classification head, mapped to the number of classes, is trained. In this study, we selected all three `CLS` tokens and concatenate them for downstream classification.

4 Experiments and Results

4.1 Data

Preprocessing. CTG recordings were segmented into 20-min windows for model training. The signals were downsampled from 4 Hz to 1 Hz, consistent with existing studies [19,22]. Training segments with more than 50% missing data were discarded during pretraining, while downstream evaluation datasets were retained without additional filtering to better reflect real-world clinical settings. (See supplementary material S4.1)

Pretraining Data. We curated our pretraining data from two complementary sources covering both antepartum and intrapartum periods. The primary pretraining data is drawn from the Oxford Maternity (OXMAT) database, comprising of around 94% antepartum CTG recordings along with the corresponding patient's information, collected between 1990 and 2024 from 5 healthcare institutions in the Oxfordshire region [18]. We additionally incorporated the publicly available unannotated intrapartum SPAM CTG dataset [11], consisting of 300 intrapartum recordings. The final pretraining dataset comprises 51,336 pregnancies and approximately 753,352 segments. This amounts to over 250,000 h of training data. (See supplementary material S4.2)

Downstream Datasets. For antepartum tasks, we curated CTG recordings recorded between 2024–2025 from the same healthcare institutions (OXMAT-2025), which do not overlap temporally with the OXMAT database. To evaluate performance beyond both the antepartum setting and our training institutions, we utilise the publicly available CTU-UHB (Czech Republic) [8] and the soon-to-be-released APHP-CTG (France) intrapartum dataset, comprising 552 and 450 patients with intrapartum CTG recordings, respectively. Both datasets originate from external institutions, providing a rigorous evaluation of cross-site transferability and generalisability. Notably, CTU-UHB is widely used for benchmarking intrapartum fetal acidosis classification, enabling us to compare PRISM-CTG with existing studies trained with private datasets. (See supplementary material S4.2)

4.2 Models Comparisons

Baselines Models. We compare PRISM-CTG with domain-specific CTG architectures: NeuroFetalNet [32], PatchCTG [19], CTGNet [6], Multiscale-LSTM [30], DWT-CNNBiLSTM [20], TGLCN [43], and general-purpose models: ResNet [14], TimesNet [37], and TimeMixer [36]. The selected domain-specific models represent recent and high-performing antepartum and intrapartum architectures. The general-purpose models include a widely used CNN baseline, ResNet, and two state-of-the-art time-series models, TimesNet and TimeMixer. All supervised models are trained from scratch on each downstream task and are therefore task-specific. Additionally, we select SSL methods representative of the major pretraining frameworks adopted in physiological FMs: BEST-RQ [7], VQ-MTM [12], CLIP-style [29], DINO [4], MAE [13], Pixio [41], JEPA [1], and NEPA [40]. All SSL baselines follow the same pretraining protocol as PRISM-CTG. (see supplementary material S5 for additional details)

Downstream Tasks and Evaluation. To comprehensively evaluate model performance, we selected 7 downstream tasks that are among the most widely studied and clinically significant in fetal monitoring research for both antepartum and intrapartum settings: (T1) abnormal classification, (T2) caesarean delivery prediction, (T3) intensive care admission prediction, (T4) delivery proximity classification, fetal acidosis classification on (T5) CTU-UHB and (T6) APHP, and (T7) caesarean delivery classification. T1 to T4 are antepartum tasks, while the remaining are intrapartum tasks. The downstream dataset was split into an 80/20 traintest ratio with no patient overlap between the training and test sets, and results were averaged over 5 runs. We follow other studies and use AUC as the primary evaluation metric, with standard deviation (SD) reported in supplementary material S6 Table 4 and 5.

Ablation Analysis. To evaluate the contribution of each architectural module and design choice in PRISM-CTG, we conducted multiple ablations. Specifically, we investigate the effect of: (a) Convolution layers (b) Signal Tokenisation and Label Embedding (c) patient metadata prediction and features classification (Multiview), (d) BEST-RQ-MAE, (e) Frequency representation as input, and (f) Uncertainty Weighting.

4.3 Results and Discussions

In this study, we present PRISM-CTG, a CTG FM pretrained with a multiview SSL framework. PRISM-CTG achieves the best average AUC of 0.808, consistently outperforming all baselines on 6 of 7 tasks, as shown in Table 1, indicating transferability across both antepartum and intrapartum settings. No other SSL methods achieved performance comparable to PRISM-CTG, with the strongest SSL baseline, MAE at 0.773, followed by the supervised NeuroFetalNet model at 0.771. Notably, PRISM-CTG achieves the largest performance gains on T7 and T4 against the best supervised models (5.32% and 5.10% improvement), both caesarean delivery classification tasks, suggesting that our pretraining strategy is particularly effective for modelling signal characteristics relevant to delivery method prediction and for identifying high-risk cases. Additionally, CLIP-1, which incorporates clinical context through alignment-based training, performed worse than single-signal pretext objectives, suggesting that alignment-based pretraining with clinical information may not be optimal for CTG representation learning. To provide a more comprehensive and clinically relevant evaluation beyond task-specific performance, we further examine PRISM-CTG under limited training data, on external cohorts to test generalisation, and across varying levels of signal dropout.

Effect of Training Size. To simulate clinical settings where labelled CTGs are limited or computational resources are constrained, we evaluate PRISM-CTG under varying training data regimes. As shown in Fig. 3(Left), PRISM-CTG maintains strong performance compared with the top baseline models across all data regimes. PRISM-CTG trained with 75% of labelled data achieves an AUC of 0.765, which is comparable to or exceeds the performance of the top 3 supervised models trained on the full dataset: NeuroFetalNet (0.771), TimeMixer (0.749), and ResNet (0.746). Under the extremely low-data setting (10% training data), the advantage of pretraining becomes clear. PRISM-CTG outperforms the

Table 1. Comparison of AUC performance across antepartum and intrapartum CTG tasks. The best AUC for each task is shown in **bold**, and the second-highest is underlined.

Model	Pre-training	Antepartum				Intrapartum			Average
		T1	T2	T3	T4	T5	T6	T7	
• **Supervised Learning**									
ResNet	✗	0.664	0.684	0.670	0.772	0.819	0.802	0.808	0.746
TimesNet	✗	0.536	0.607	0.622	0.708	0.703	0.761	0.807	0.678
TimeMixer	✗	0.640	0.668	0.663	0.768	0.829	<u>0.810</u>	0.865	0.749
CTGNet	✗	0.629	0.631	0.628	0.711	0.781	0.768	0.849	0.714
PatchCTG	✗	0.659	0.610	0.649	0.628	0.767	0.774	0.782	0.696
NeuroFetalNet	✗	0.670	0.720	0.713	0.784	0.857	0.796	0.856	0.771
MS-LSTM	✗	0.646	0.663	0.575	0.647	0.742	0.659	0.813	0.678
TGLCN	✗	0.720	0.671	0.651	0.621	0.819	**0.813**	0.834	0.733
CNN-BiLSTM	✗	0.700	0.660	0.620	0.664	0.852	0.769	0.814	0.726
• **Self-Supervised Learning**									
BestRQ	✓	0.533	0.646	0.635	0.675	0.738	0.657	0.780	0.666
VQMTM	✓	0.656	0.592	0.604	0.670	0.720	0.740	0.761	0.678
CLIP-1	✓	0.630	0.653	0.665	0.785	0.844	0.719	0.814	0.730
CLIP-2	✓	0.625	0.703	0.690	0.731	0.802	0.786	0.873	0.744
Dino	✓	0.659	0.726	0.728	0.795	0.733	0.679	0.827	0.735
MAE	✓	0.648	<u>0.729</u>	<u>0.731</u>	0.797	0.850	0.768	0.890	<u>0.773</u>
Pixio	✓	0.665	0.716	0.694	0.772	0.820	0.769	<u>0.904</u>	0.763
NEPA	✓	0.626	0.621	0.620	0.704	0.725	0.734	0.731	0.680
JEPA	✓	<u>0.731</u>	0.726	0.715	<u>0.802</u>	<u>0.873</u>	0.685	0.820	0.765
PRISM-CTG	✓	**0.743**	**0.731**	**0.753**	**0.824**	**0.883**	0.806	**0.911**	**0.808**

best supervised baseline, ResNet, with an average improvement of 16.41%, and the strongest supervised model trained on the full dataset, NeuroFetalNet, at 20.18%, with even larger gains observed for specific tasks, such as T7 (+30.14%) under extremely low-data settings. By pretraining on a large volume of CTG recordings to learn a general representation, PRISM-CTG requires fewer data to achieve competitive performance, while the best supervised models remain heavily reliant on larger training data, failing in settings when labelled data are limited.

Ablation Analysis. As seen in Fig. 3(Right), removing the proposed BEST-RQ-MAE module, one of the pretext objectives leads to the largest degradation, reducing average performance by 7.169%, indicating that BEST-RQ-MAE provides guidance essential for learning a more robust CTG representation. Removing the clinical (multiview) pretext objectives leads to a performance reduction

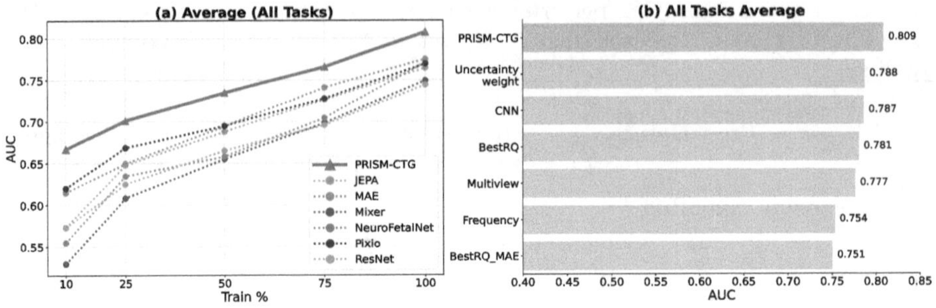

Fig. 3. (Left) Average performance across all tasks under different data regimes with the top performing SSL and supervised models. (Right) Ablation study of PRISM-CTG showing average AUC for the full model and its variants.

of 3.95%, suggesting that clinical context helps the model encode global information that guides better representation learning, thereby improving downstream task performance. Additionally, removing label embeddings (BestRQ) resulted in a 3.46% drop in performance, indicating that signal-level guidance improves representation learning. Finally, we replace the time-domain CTG input with a frequency-domain representation to investigate whether frequency transformations, commonly used in physiological FMs benefit representation learning. However, this results in a 6.80% decrease in performance, indicating that frequency-domain representations did not provide additional benefit for CTG representation learning. To provide a more comprehensive evaluation beyond task-specific performance, we further assess PRISM-CTG under limited-data settings, external validation, and varying levels of signal dropout.

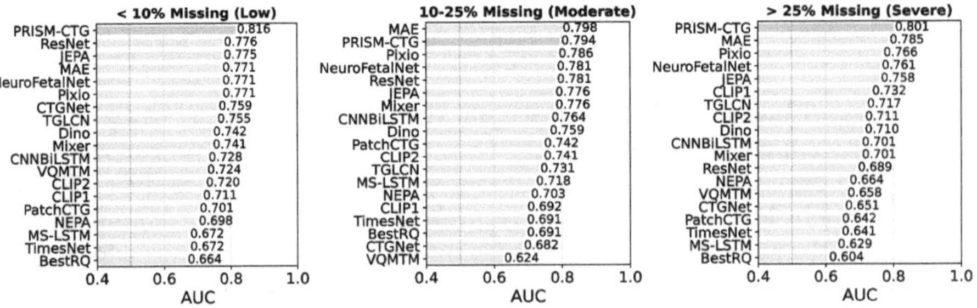

Fig. 4. Average performance grouped by proportion of signal dropout.

Impact of Missing Data. CTG segments are inherently noisy, with signal dropout being one of the most common artefacts, often caused by maternal or

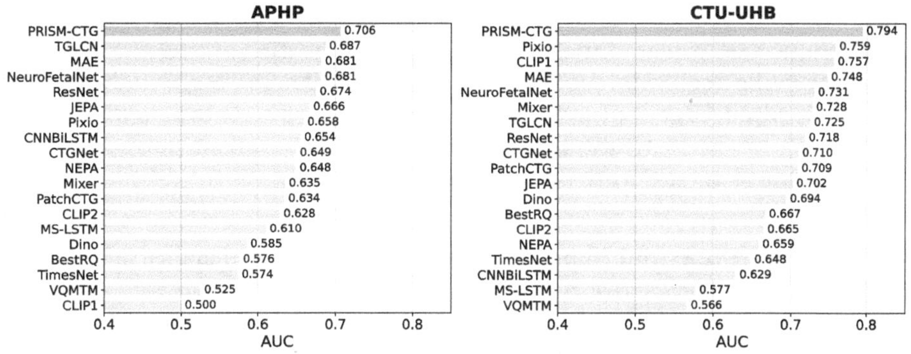

Fig. 5. Average performance on external validation on APHP and CTU-UHB.

fetal movement. To investigate the impact of missingness, we separately evaluate CTG segments grouped according to their proportion of missing data. As seen in Fig. 4, We observe that models pretrained via SSL, including PRISM-CTG, demonstrated robustness to signal dropout. In particular, PRISM-CTG and MAE maintain relatively stable performance across increasing levels of signal dropout, while supervised models such as ResNet and TimeMixer experience performance degradation when signal dropout exceeds 25%. Another interesting finding is that pixel-reconstruction-based SSL methods, including PRISM-CTG, MAE, and Pixio, perform better than all other baselines under moderate to severe signal dropout, suggesting that reconstruction objectives may preserve useful information when portions of the input are missing. These findings indicate that large-scale SSL pretraining on diverse, real-world CTG recordings improves robustness to signal dropout, resulting in more stable downstream performance under clinically realistic conditions.

External Validation. To demonstrate generalisability, we conducted external validation on the acidosis classification task. Specifically, models were trained on CTU-UHB (T5) and evaluated on APHP-CTG (T6), and vice versa. This cross-dataset evaluation reflects realistic deployment, in which models trained at one institution must generalise to data collected at a different location. As shown in Fig. 5, PRISM-CTG remains the best performing model in both tasks and outperforms the best supervised baselines by 2.76% on APHP-CTG and 8.62% on CTU-UHB. Notably, intrapartum recordings constitute less than 6% of the total pretraining data, yet PRISM-CTG maintains superior cross-database performance. We further compared PRISM-CTG with previously published studies trained on large private intrapartum cohorts [22,23,27]. While our model achieves a lower AUC than some of the highest reported results (AUC = 0.82), those studies were trained on substantially larger datasets, often exceeding 35,000 patients. In contrast, we evaluated our pretrained encoder using linear probing on a cohort of 450 patients (see supplementary material Table 7).

Despite the smaller training cohort, performance remains within the range of models trained on private intrapartum cohorts, indicating strong external generalisation while requiring substantially less data. These results indicate that the pretrained encoder captures generalisable CTG representations that transfer effectively across institutions, even when the target domain (intrapartum) is minimally represented during pretraining.

Benefits and Potential Applications. PRISM-CTG demonstrates strong generalist performance across a wide range of tasks in CTG analysis. This capability suggests PRISM-CTG has the potential to be integrated and adapted as a unified clinical decision-support system throughout the pregnancy cycle, from antepartum to intrapartum care without requiring large task-specific labelled datasets, assisting clinicians by providing objective and consistent assessments that complement existing tools and help reduce the subjectivity inherent in manual CTG interpretation. This includes supporting clinicians in identifying the risk of caesarean delivery or potential adverse neonatal outcomes, with the potential to improve safety, reduce morbidity and mortality, and ease clinical burden. Such a framework would also benefit clinical researchers exploring DL for CTG analysis who may lack the computational resources or the volume of training data typically needed to achieve competitive performance, as the pretrained model can be adapted to a target task with minimal additional training. Most importantly, it can be shaped to address a wide range of tasks in the field as required, offering a flexible foundation for future clinical and research applications. Finally, its ability to generalise across multiple external institutions shows that PRISM-CTG could be deployed at new sites with different patient populations and acquisition practices while maintaining performance, allowing smaller institutions to benefit from a robust, ready-to-use algorithm that would otherwise be difficult to develop.

Limitations. Although evaluated on the largest available CTG datasets across multiple tasks, the overall data scale remains modest compared to other physiological domains due to limited public availability. Moreover, intrapartum recordings constitute only a small portion of the pretraining data, which may constrain labour-specific representation learning despite strong generalisation. However, the generalisation to intrapartum tasks (T5–T7) may be explained by the shared representation space between antepartum and intrapartum CTG, where large-scale pretraining yields general, domain-level representations rather than antepartum-specific ones, further reinforced by antepartum recordings closest to labour onset already containing intrapartum-like physiological patterns (see supplementary material S7). A further limitation is that the pretraining of PRISM-CTG incorporates patient metadata, which may not be uniformly available across all datasets and could limit applicability, although such metadata are typically recorded in institutional datasets given their clinical importance.

5 Conclusion

PRISM-CTG demonstrates that large-scale self-supervised pretraining can be effectively applied to CTG to learn transferable and generalisable in-domain representations. By incorporating patient metadata and engineered features as supervisory signals, the model learns clinically grounded representations that extend beyond purely morphological patterns. The results show consistent improvements over task-specific supervised models, stronger robustness to missing data, and improved cross-institutional generalisation. Collectively, our findings indicate that future work in automated CTG analysis should be driven by large-scale, clinically informed self-supervised pretraining as the primary training strategy, instead of continued reliance on narrow task-specific supervised optimisation.

Acknowledgments. This research was supported by the UKRI Medical Research Council (MR/X029689/1)

Disclosure of Interests. The authors have no competing interests to declare.

References

1. Assran, M., et al.: Self-supervised learning from images with a joint-embedding predictive architecture. In: Proceedings of the IEEE/CVF Conference on Computer Vision and Pattern Recognition, pp. 15619–15629 (2023)
2. Avramidis, K., et al.: Scaling representation learning from ubiquitous ECG with state-space models. IEEE J. Biomed. Health Inform. **28**(10), 5877–5889 (2024)
3. Ben M'Barek, I., Jauvion, G., Ceccaldi, P.F.: Computerized cardiotocography analysis during labor-a state-of-the-art review. Acta Obstet. Gynecol. Scand. **102**(2), 130–137 (2023)
4. Caron, M., et al.: Emerging properties in self-supervised vision transformers. In: Proceedings of the IEEE/CVF International Conference on Computer Vision, pp. 9650–9660 (2021)
5. Chen, Y., et al.: EEGFormer: towards transferable and interpretable large-scale EEG foundation model. arXiv preprint arXiv:2401.10278 (2024)
6. Chiou, N., et al.: Development and evaluation of deep learning models for cardiotocography interpretation. npj Women's Health **3**(1), 21 (2025)
7. Chiu, C.C., Qin, J., Zhang, Y., Yu, J., Wu, Y.: Self-supervised learning with random-projection quantizer for speech recognition. In: International Conference on Machine Learning, pp. 3915–3924. PMLR (2022)
8. Chudáček, V., et al.: Open access intrapartum CTG database. BMC Pregnancy Childbirth **14**(1), 16 (2014)
9. Coppola, E., et al.: Hubert-ECG as a self-supervised foundation model for broad and scalable cardiac applications. medRxiv, 2024–11 (2024)
10. Davis Jones, G., Cooke, W.R., Vatish, M.: Identifying high-risk pre-term pregnancies using the fetal heart rate and machine learning. Bioengineering **13**(2), 203 (2026)

11. Georgieva, A., et al.: Computer-based intrapartum fetal monitoring and beyond: a review of the 2nd workshop on signal processing and monitoring in labor (October 2017, Oxford, UK). Acta Obstet. Gynecol. Scand. **98**(9), 1207–1217 (2019)
12. Gui, H., Li, X., Chen, X.: Vector quantization pretraining for EEG time series with random projection and phase alignment. In: International Conference on Machine Learning, pp. 16731–16750. PMLR (2024)
13. He, K., Chen, X., Xie, S., Li, Y., Dollár, P., Girshick, R.: Masked autoencoders are scalable vision learners. In: Proceedings of the IEEE/CVF Conference on Computer Vision and Pattern Recognition, pp. 16000–16009 (2022)
14. He, K., Zhang, X., Ren, S., Sun, J.: Deep residual learning for image recognition. In: Proceedings of the IEEE Conference on Computer Vision and Pattern Recognition, pp. 770–778 (2016)
15. Hernandez Engelhart, C., Gundro Brurberg, K., Aanstad, K.J., Pay, A.S.D., Kaasen, A., Blix, E., Vanbelle, S.: Reliability and agreement in intrapartum fetal heart rate monitoring interpretation: a systematic review. Acta Obstet. Gynecol. Scand. **102**(8), 970–985 (2023)
16. Jiang, W.B., Zhao, L.M., Lu, B.L.: Large brain model for learning generic representations with tremendous EEG data in BCI. arXiv preprint arXiv:2405.18765 (2024)
17. Jones, G.D., Cooke, W.R., Vatish, M., Redman, C.W.: Computerized analysis of antepartum cardiotocography: a review. Maternal-Fetal Med. **4**(02), 130–140 (2022)
18. Khan, M.J., Duta, I., Albert, B., Cooke, W., Vatish, M., Jones, G.D.: The OxMat dataset: a multimodal resource for the development of ai-driven technologies in maternal and newborn child health. arXiv preprint arXiv:2404.08024 (2024)
19. Khan, M.J., Vatish, M., Davis Jones, G.: PatchCTG: a patch cardiotocography transformer for antepartum fetal health monitoring. Sensors **25**(9), 2650 (2025)
20. Liu, M., Lu, Y., Long, S., Bai, J., Lian, W.: An attention-based CNN-BiLSTM hybrid neural network enhanced with features of discrete wavelet transformation for fetal acidosis classification. Exp. Syst. Appl. **186**, 115714 (2021)
21. Mai, P., Feng, J., Li, L., Chen, Q., Liu, G., Wei, H.: CTGGAN: a modified generative adversarial network for imbalanced CTG signal classification during labor. In: 2024 IEEE International Conference on Bioinformatics and Biomedicine (BIBM), pp. 5001–5008. IEEE (2024)
22. M'Barek, I.B., et al.: DeepCTG® 2.0: development and validation of a deep learning model to detect neonatal acidemia from cardiotocography during labor. Comput. Biol. Med. **184**, 109448 (2025)
23. McCoy, J.A., Levine, L.D., Wan, G., Chivers, C., Teel, J., La Cava, W.G.: Intrapartum electronic fetal heart rate monitoring to predict acidemia at birth with the use of deep learning. Am. J. Obstet. Gynecol. **232**(1), 116-e1 (2025)
24. Nguyen, H.D., Pham, T.T., Le, N., Nguyen, V.: TolerantECG: a foundation model for imperfect electrocardiogram. In: Proceedings of the 33rd ACM International Conference on Multimedia, pp. 8097–8105 (2025)
25. Nie, G., et al.: A zero-burden sleep foundation model built on cardiorespiratory signals from 800,000+ hours of multi-ethnic sleep recordings. medRxiv, 2025-09 (2025)
26. Nie, G., et al.: AnyPPG: an ECG-guided ppg foundation model trained on over 100,000 hours of recordings for holistic health profiling. arXiv preprint arXiv:2511.01747 (2025)

27. Petrozziello, A., Redman, C.W., Papageorghiou, A.T., Jordanov, I., Georgieva, A.: Multimodal convolutional neural networks to detect fetal compromise during labor and delivery. IEEE Access **7**, 112026–112036 (2019)
28. Pillai, A., Spathis, D., Kawsar, F., Malekzadeh, M.: PaPaGei: open foundation models for optical physiological signals. arXiv preprint arXiv:2410.20542 (2024)
29. Radford, A., et al.: Learning transferable visual models from natural language supervision. In: International Conference on Machine Learning, pp. 8748–8763. PMLR (2021)
30. Rao, L., Lu, J., Wu, H.R., Zhao, S., Lu, B.C., Li, H.: Automatic classification of fetal heart rate based on a multi-scale LSTM network. Front. Physiol. **15**, 1398735 (2024)
31. Shu, Y., Charlton, P.H., Kawsar, F., Hernesniemi, J., Malekzadeh, M.: CLEF: clinically-guided contrastive learning for electrocardiogram foundation models. arXiv preprint arXiv:2512.02180 (2025)
32. Sun, B., Zhao, J., Miao, X., Wu, Y., Fang, M.: NeuroFetalNet: advancing remote electronic fetal monitoring with a new dataset and comparative analysis of FHR and UCP impact. In: 2024 IEEE International Conference on Digital Health (ICDH), pp. 181–188. IEEE (2024)
33. Thapa, R., et al.: SleepFM: multi-modal representation learning for sleep across brain activity, ECG and respiratory signals. arXiv preprint arXiv:2405.17766 (2024)
34. de Vries, I.R., Huijben, I.A.M., Kok, R.D., van Sloun, R.J.G., Vullings, R.: Contrastive predictive coding for anomaly detection of fetal health from the cardiotocogram. In: 2022 IEEE International Conference on Acoustics, Speech and Signal Processing (ICASSP), ICASSP 2022, pp. 3473–3477 (2022). https://doi.org/10.1109/ICASSP43922.2022.9747178
35. Wang, F., Xu, J., Yu, L.: From token to rhythm: a multi-scale approach for ECG-language pretraining. arXiv preprint arXiv:2506.21803 (2025)
36. Wang, S., et al.: TimeMixer: decomposable multiscale mixing for time series forecasting. arXiv preprint arXiv:2405.14616 (2024)
37. Wu, H., Hu, T., Liu, Y., Zhou, H., Wang, J., Long, M.: TimesNet: temporal 2D-variation modeling for general time series analysis. arXiv preprint arXiv:2210.02186 (2022)
38. Wu, J., Wang, H., Yang, Z., Wu, J.: MCTG: a multimodal self-supervised contrastive learning framework based on CTG. In: Proceedings of the 7th ACM International Conference on Multimedia in Asia, pp. 1–7 (2025)
39. Xiong, W., Lin, J., Li, J., Li, J., Jiang, C.: ALFEE: adaptive large foundation model for EEG representation. arXiv preprint arXiv:2505.06291 (2025)
40. Xu, S., et al.: Next-embedding prediction makes strong vision learners. arXiv preprint arXiv:2512.16922 (2025)
41. Yang, L., et al.: In pursuit of pixel supervision for visual pre-training. arXiv preprint arXiv:2512.15715 (2025)

42. Yu, H., Guo, P., Sano, A.: ECG semantic integrator (ESI): a foundation ECG model pretrained with LLM-enhanced cardiological text. arXiv preprint arXiv:2405.19366 (2024)
43. Zhou, Z., Zhao, Z., Zhang, X., Zhang, X., Jiao, P., Ye, X.: Identifying fetal status with fetal heart rate: deep learning approach based on long convolution. Comput. Biol. Med. **159**, 106970 (2023)

PathogenKG: Cross-Species Drug Repurposing via Heterogeneous Knowledge Graph Link Prediction

Giovanni Maria De Filippis(✉), Antonio Maria Rinaldi, and Cristian Tommasino

Department of Electrical Engineering and Information Technology, University of Naples Federico II, Via Claudio 21, Naples, Italy
giovannimaria.defilippis@unina.it

Abstract. Antimicrobial resistance is a critical global health challenge, yet systematic computational frameworks for discovering drug–target interactions (DTIs) across diverse bacterial species remain lacking. Existing knowledge graph (KG)-based drug repurposing systems are centered on human disease biology and do not model pathogen-specific proteomes or cross-species molecular relationships. We present PathogenKG, a heterogeneous KG embedding framework for cross-species antimicrobial drug repurposing. It integrates protein–protein interaction networks from 31 bacterial pathogens, orthology relationships, functional annotations, and validated drug–target associations into a unified graph of over 3 million triples, enabling drug–target evidence to propagate between phylogenetically related organisms. To handle the extreme class imbalance inherent in this setting—only 302 known DTI edges among millions of triples—we design a training pipeline combining focal loss, type-constrained negative sampling, and targeted oversampling, validated on an established biomedical KG benchmark. We compared heterogeneous GNN encoders and evaluated the framework through a compound-centric repurposing protocol that ranks all pathogen proteins as candidate targets. Domain-expert analysis of top-ranked predictions in nine case study compounds confirms that the model recovers known interactions and generates mechanistically grounded cross-species hypotheses, with 22.2% of the top-20 predictions rated biologically plausible. PathogenKG is the first multi-pathogen KG framework specifically designed for cross-species antimicrobial drug repurposing via link prediction.

Keywords: Drug Repurposing · Knowledge Graph Embedding · Link Prediction · Heterogeneous Graph Neural Networks · Pathogen Proteomics

1 Introduction

Antimicrobial resistance (AMR) is among the most urgent global health challenges. The Global Burden of Disease AMR Collaborators estimated that bacterial AMR directly caused 1.14 million deaths in 2021 and was associated

M. Ceci et al. (Eds.): ECML PKDD 2026, LNAI 16948, pp. 601–618, 2027.
https://doi.org/10.1007/978-3-032-37679-4_34

with 4.71 million more, with projections reaching 1.91 million annual deaths by 2050 [6]. Traditional drug development is too slow and costly to keep up with resistance evolution [18], making drug repurposing (finding new uses for existing compounds with safety profile) an attractive complementary strategy [4]. However, while repurposing has been explored against individual pathogens [14], there is no systematic computational framework to predict drug–target interactions (DTIs) across multiple bacterial species simultaneously.

Knowledge graphs (KGs) offer a natural formalism for this task. Systems such as Hetionet [7] and DRKG [8] have demonstrated effective compound prioritisation through graph-based link prediction [17]. However, these frameworks are centered on human disease biology and do not represent pathogen proteomes, intra-pathogen molecular networks, or the cross-species orthology that would allow drug–target evidence to propagate between related organisms.

We present PathogenKG, a heterogeneous KG embedding framework that fills this gap. The graph integrates protein–protein interaction (PPI) networks from STRING [22] for 31 bacterial pathogens, COG orthology [23], Gene Ontology annotations [1], and validated compound–protein associations from DrugBank [25] into a unified graph of over 3 million triples. A central challenge is extreme class imbalance: only 302 TARGET edges exist among the full edge set. We address this with a training pipeline combining focal loss [11], type-constrained filtered negative sampling, and controlled oversampling, validated on the DRKG benchmark before application to PathogenKG. We compared heterogeneous Graph Neural Network (GNN) encoders (R-GCN [19], CompGCN [24]) with a DistMult decoder [27] through Bayesian hyperparameter optimisation. A compound-centric evaluation protocol ranks all pathogen proteins as candidate targets for each drug, and biological plausibility analysis of top predictions confirms recovery of known interactions and generation of mechanistically grounded cross-species hypotheses.

Our main contributions are:

1. **PathogenKG dataset:** the first multi-pathogen KG integrating PPI, orthology, functional annotation, and drug–target data for 31 organisms, designed for cross-species drug repurposing.
2. **Training pipeline for extreme class imbalance:** a complete pipeline validated on an established biomedical KG benchmark (DRKG).
3. **Drug repurposing evaluation protocol:** compound-centric ranking against the full pathogen proteome with per-compound and pooled retrieval metrics.
4. **Biological plausibility validation:** domain-expert analysis demonstrating recovery of known interactions and generation of novel cross-species hypotheses.

2 Related Work

Over the past decade, knowledge graphs have become a central tool for computational drug repurposing [17]. Hetionet [7] was among the first large-scale efforts, integrating 29 public biomedical sources into a heterogeneous network that enabled systematic identification of drug–disease associations through meta-path reasoning. DRKG [8] substantially expanded this paradigm by merging Hetionet with DrugBank, GNBR, STRING, and other resources into approximately 97,000 entities and 5.8 million triples, and was specifically designed for drug repurposing via knowledge graph embedding methods. Domain-specific KGs have further demonstrated the value of the approach within focused therapeutic areas: GP-KG [5] applied CompGCN to a genotypic-phenotypic graph of over 61,000 entities to infer drug–disease interactions, while ADInt [26] built a 162,000-node Alzheimer's-centred graph and reported competitive link prediction results with both R-GCN and CompGCN.

A common thread across all these works is their focus on human disease biology: entities, relations, and evaluation protocols are organised around human genes, human diseases, and compound–disease or compound–gene interactions. None of them represents pathogen proteomes, intra-pathogen molecular networks, or the cross-species orthology that would enable drug–target evidence to transfer between related organisms. Table 1 summarises how PathogenKG differs from these resources along the dimensions most relevant to antimicrobial repurposing.

Among the learning methods applied to biomedical KGs, GNN-based encoders are particularly relevant to our setting because they explicitly propagate information along the graph structure, rather than learning static entity embeddings in isolation. R-GCN [19] handles multi-relational graphs by associating each relation with a dedicated weight matrix, regularised through basis decomposition to control parameter growth. CompGCN [24] extends this idea by jointly embedding entities and relations through learnable composition operators—subtraction or circular correlation—achieving competitive or superior results on standard benchmarks. In the biomedical domain, the REx framework [16] evaluated CompGCN on Hetionet for the compound–treats–disease task, reporting MRR of 0.292 and Hits@10 of 0.543; these figures serve as reference points for our own results in Sect. 4. We adopt both R-GCN and CompGCN as candidate encoders, paired with a DistMult [27] bilinear decoder, a combination that balances expressiveness with computational tractability given the scale of PathogenKG (over 3 million edges, 13 relation types) and the need for extensive hyperparameter search.

Drug–target interaction (DTI) prediction encompasses a broad methodological landscape, from molecular docking to deep learning on compound–protein pairs [18]. Graph-based DTI methods have gained prominence, but they typically frame the problem as pairwise classification without leveraging the broader biological context—PPIs, orthology, functional annotations—that a knowledge graph can provide. In the antimicrobial domain, repurposing efforts have relied predominantly on experimental high-throughput screening or single-pathogen computational pipelines [4], each targeting one organism at a time without exploiting the evolutionary relationships between pathogen protein families that could enable knowledge transfer across species.

The biological basis for such transfer is well established: orthologous proteins identified through COG [23] frequently conserve ligand-binding sites and catalytic residues, while Gene Ontology annotations [1] allow functional comparison even when sequence divergence is substantial. PathogenKG leverages these principles by encoding intra-species PPIs from STRING [22], cross-species COG orthology, GO functional annotations, and validated compound–protein edges from DrugBank [25] into a single heterogeneous graph. Three features set it apart from the human-centred frameworks above. First, it is built around pathogen proteomes from 31 species rather than human disease biology. Second, COG orthology and GO annotation edges act as cross-species bridges that let the model transfer drug–target evidence between phylogenetically related organisms, a capability absent from those resources. Third, it pairs this resource with a training pipeline designed for the extreme class imbalance of the setting (302 `TARGET` edges among over 3 million), validated on the DRKG benchmark before application.

Table 1. PathogenKG compared with existing biomedical KGs for drug repurposing.

KG	Entities	Triplets	Pathogen PPI	Cross-species
Hetionet [7]	47K	2.2M	No	No
DRKG [8]	97K	5.8M	No	No
GP-KG [5]	61K	1.2M	No	No
ADInt [26]	162K	1.0M	No	No
PathogenKG	**143K**	**3.0M**	**Yes (31 spp.)**	**Yes (COG+GO)**

3 Methods

The PathogenKG framework consists of four stages, illustrated in Fig. 1: (i) construction of a multi-relational knowledge graph from heterogeneous biological databases; (ii) training of heterogeneous GNN encoders for link prediction on the TARGET relation; (iii) compound-centric drug repurposing evaluation against the full pathogen proteome; and (iv) biological plausibility analysis of top-ranked predictions. This section details stages (i) and (ii); the evaluation protocol and the biological case study are presented in Sects. 4 and 5, respectively.

3.1 Dataset Construction

Design Rationale and Graph Schema. PathogenKG was designed following the multi-relational schema established by DRKG [8], but with a fundamentally different scope: whereas DRKG centers on human genes, diseases, and compound–disease treatment associations, PathogenKG places pathogen proteins at the

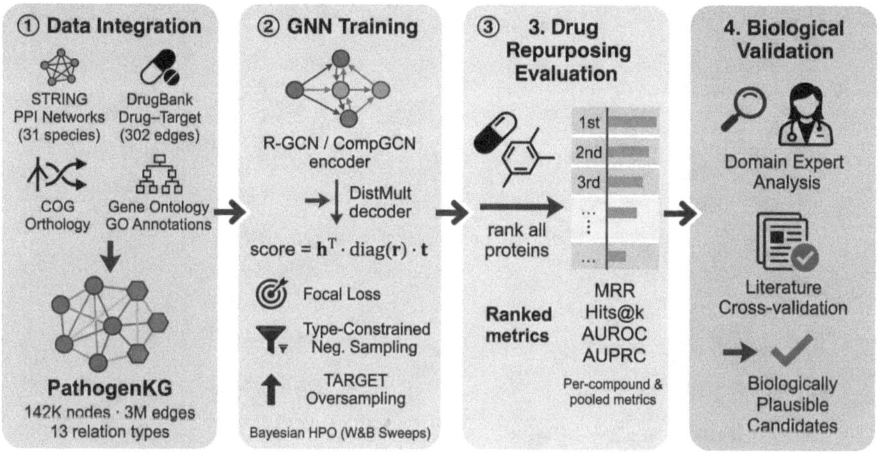

Fig. 1. Overview of the PathogenKG framework. Heterogeneous biological data are integrated into a multi-relational knowledge graph (Sect. 3.1). A GNN encoder–decoder architecture is trained for link prediction on the TARGET relation (Sect. 3.2). The trained model ranks all pathogen proteins for each compound (Sect. 5), and top predictions are assessed for biological plausibility (Sect. 5).

core of the graph. The goal is to encode sufficient biological context around pathogen protein targets—through intra-species molecular interactions, cross-species orthology, and functional annotations—so that a link prediction model can transfer drug–target evidence across phylogenetically related organisms.

The graph contains two entity types: **ExtGene** (pathogen proteins, identified by UniProt accession) and **Compound** (drug molecules, identified by PubChem CID). Entities are connected through 13 relation types organised into four functional classes, as shown in Table 2: protein–protein interactions (PPI), orthology relationships, Gene Ontology annotations, and drug–target associations, as shown in Fig. 2.

Data Sources and Integration. PathogenKG integrates data from four primary sources.

Protein–protein interactions were obtained from the STRING database [22] for 31 bacterial pathogen species classified as "core" organisms in STRING, selected for having curated PPI networks and relevance to human health (13 established human pathogens and 18 opportunistic pathogens; see Table 3). We retained interactions above the medium confidence threshold (combined score $\geq$ 400). PPI edges are mapped to eight relation types reflecting the nature of the interaction: `ASSOCIATION`, `GENE_BIND`, `ACTIVATION`, `REACTION`, `CATALYSIS`, `PTMOD` (post-translational modification), `INHIBITION`, and `EXPRESSION`.

Orthology relationships were derived from the COG (Clusters of Orthologous Groups) database [23], which assigns proteins to families of evolutionary-

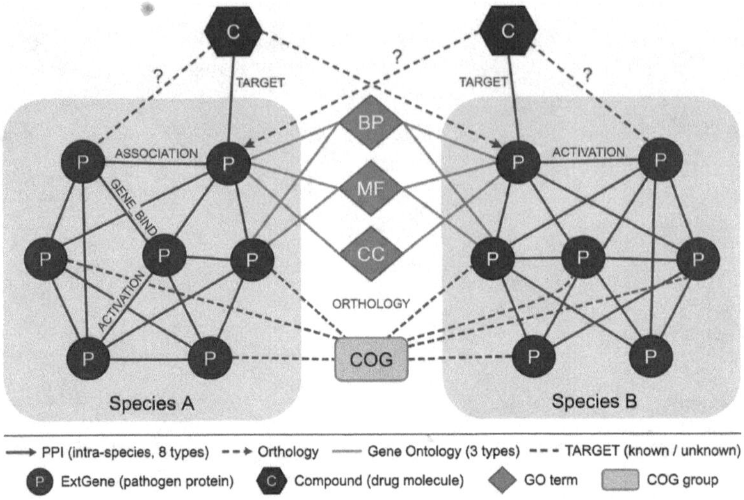

Fig. 2. Schema of PathogenKG. ExtGene nodes represent pathogen proteins from 31 species; Compound nodes represent drug molecules. Relation types are grouped into four functional classes: protein–protein interactions (blue), COG orthology (green), Gene Ontology annotations (orange), and drug–target associations (red). (Color figure online)

related sequences across prokaryotic genomes. Each `ORTHOLOGY` edge connects a pathogen protein to its COG group, providing a cross-species bridge: two proteins from different pathogens that belong to the same COG family are implicitly linked, allowing the GNN message-passing mechanism to propagate information—including drug–target signals—between species.

Gene Ontology annotations [1] provide standardised functional descriptors across three sub-ontologies: Biological Process (BP), Molecular Function (MF), and Cellular Component (CC). GO terms are represented as additional nodes, and each ExtGene–GO edge is typed by the corresponding sub-ontology. These edges enrich the embedding of each protein with functional context that is comparable across species, even when sequence similarity is limited.

Drug–target associations (`TARGET` edges) were extracted from DrugBank [25], linking Compound entities to their experimentally validated protein targets within the pathogen PPI networks. These edges constitute the prediction target: the model is trained to score unseen (Compound, `TARGET`, ExtGene) triples, and the evaluation protocol ranks all pathogen proteins as potential targets for each compound.

Entity Resolution and Quality Control. Integration relies on stable cross-database identifiers rather than name matching: proteins are keyed on UniProt accessions and compounds on PubChem CIDs, so nodes are deduplicated by construction, while COG groups and GO terms provide standardised controlled vocabularies that align across sources exactly. STRING interactions are kept only above the medium-confidence threshold defined above, and a DrugBank `TARGET` edge is retained only when its protein endpoint already exists in the pathogen PPI networks, discarding associations that dangle outside the graph. Missing annotations are left as absent edges rather than imputed: proteins lacking COG or GO terms simply carry fewer functional edges.

Graph Statistics and Class Imbalance. The resulting PathogenKG graph comprises 3,047,256 triples distributed across 13 relation types. Table 2 reports the full edge distribution. Gene Ontology annotations dominate the graph, accounting for 91.8% of all edges (BP: 53.2%, MF: 26.0%, CC: 12.7%), followed by PPI edges (5.1%) and orthology edges (3.1%). The TARGET relation contributes only 302 edges—representing 0.010% of the total—involving 229 unique compounds and 157 unique protein targets across 31 pathogen species.

This extreme class imbalance is the defining challenge of the PathogenKG prediction task. The ratio between the most frequent relation (BiologicalProcess, 1,619,727 edges) and the TARGET relation is approximately 5,400:1. The model must learn to distinguish genuine drug–target interactions from a vast background of non-TARGET edges, using only a few hundred positive examples for training. The largest connected component covers 98.5% of nodes, ensuring that the GNN message-passing mechanism can reach nearly all entities.

Table 2. Edge distribution in PathogenKG by relation type, grouped into four functional classes.

Class	Relation type	Edges	%
Gene Ontology	BiologicalProcess	1,619,727	53.15
	MolecularFunction	791,371	25.97
	CellularComponent	386,668	12.69
PPI (STRING)	ASSOCIATION	120,029	3.94
	GENE_BIND	29,725	0.98
	ACTIVATION	2,815	0.09
	REACTION	994	0.03
	CATALYSIS	151	<0.01
	PTMOD	150	<0.01
	INHIBITION	10	<0.01
	EXPRESSION	3	<0.01
Orthology	ORTHOLOGY	95,311	3.13
Drug–Target	TARGET	302	0.010
Total		**3,047,256**	**100.0**

Table 3. Pathogen species included in PathogenKG (31 core organisms from STRING). *Targets* indicates the number of unique protein targets of known drugs from DrugBank.

Species	Targets	Pathogen status
Bacillus subtilis str. 168	66	Opportunistic
Salmonella enterica sv. Typhimurium	33	Established
Helicobacter pylori 26695	10	Established
Pseudomonas fluorescens	9	Opportunistic
Streptococcus pyogenes	3	Established
Listeria monocytogenes EGD-e	3	Established
Pseudomonas putida KT2440	3	Opportunistic
Wolinella succinogenes	3	Opportunistic
Alcaligenes faecalis	3	Opportunistic
Burkholderia cepacia	2	Established
Enterococcus faecium	2	Established
Shewanella oneidensis MR-1	2	Opportunistic
Lysinibacillus sphaericus	2	Opportunistic
19 additional species	1 each	7 Est.12 Opp.

3.2 Heterogeneous Graph Neural Networks

Problem Formulation. We formulate drug–target prediction as a link prediction task on the TARGET relation in the PathogenKG heterogeneous graph. Let $\mathcal{G} = (\mathcal{V}, \mathcal{E}, \mathcal{R})$ denote the knowledge graph, where $\mathcal{V}$ is the set of entities, $\mathcal{E} \subseteq \mathcal{V} \times \mathcal{R} \times \mathcal{V}$ is the set of observed triples, and $\mathcal{R}$ is the set of relation types. The objective is to learn a scoring function $f(h, r, t) \in \mathbb{R}$ such that observed drug–target interactions receive higher scores than unobserved ones. At inference time, for each compound h, we rank all ExtGene entities by their score $f(h, \texttt{TARGET}, t)$ and evaluate against held-out ground truth.

Encoder–Decoder Architecture. We evaluate two heterogeneous GNN encoders that produce entity embeddings via multi-layer message passing over the full multi-relational graph. Both architectures initialise entity embeddings through learnable lookup tables $\mathbf{E} \in \mathbb{R}^{|\mathcal{V}| \times d}$.

R-GCN [19] handles the multi-relational structure by associating each relation with a dedicated weight matrix. To control the parameter growth that would result from maintaining separate matrices for all 13 relation types, R-GCN employs basis decomposition: each relation matrix is expressed as a linear combination of a small number of shared basis matrices with learnable per-relation coefficients. Neighbours are normalised by their in-degree within each relation type.

CompGCN [24] takes a different approach by jointly embedding entities and relations through composition operators. At each layer, messages from incoming, outgoing, and self-loop edges are aggregated separately using direction-specific weight matrices. Before aggregation, each neighbour's embedding is combined with its relation embedding via a composition function—either element-wise subtraction or circular correlation, selected via hyperparameter search. This joint entity–relation embedding is particularly suited to our setting, where the model must learn to distinguish the sparse TARGET signal from 12 other relation types spanning five orders of magnitude in frequency.

Both encoders are paired with a *DistMult* [27] decoder, a bilinear scoring function that computes $f(h,r,t) = \sum_k \mathbf{h}_h[k] \cdot \mathbf{r}_r[k] \cdot \mathbf{h}_t[k]$, where $\mathbf{h}_h$, $\mathbf{r}_r$, and $\mathbf{h}_t$ are the learned entity and relation embeddings. DistMult assumes symmetric relations, which is a reasonable simplification for the TARGET relation (if drug h targets protein t, the reverse association is equally meaningful for repurposing purposes). The final prediction probability is obtained via a sigmoid: $p = \sigma(f(h,r,t))$.

Data Splitting. The 302 `TARGET` edges are partitioned at the edge level into training, validation, and test sets (203/28/71 edges, from nominal 0.2 test and 0.1 validation fractions). The split is stratified by target protein: proteins with a single `TARGET` edge are always assigned to training, while proteins with multiple edges contribute to validation and test, so that every test protein is also seen during training at least once. The split is fixed by a dedicated seed and held constant across the 12 runs of each architecture, which differ only in model initialisation. We do not cluster the split by chemical scaffold or protein-sequence similarity; similarity-driven leakage between near-duplicate compounds or homologous proteins is therefore not controlled for, a limitation we return to in Sect. 6.

Training Pipeline. Three design choices address the extreme class imbalance described in Sect. 3.1. We replace standard binary cross-entropy with a focal loss [11] that down-weights well-classified examples and focuses learning on hard cases. The total loss combines a mean focal loss over positive examples, an adversarially weighted focal loss over negatives, and L_2 regularisation:

$$\mathcal{L} = \underbrace{\frac{1}{|P|} \sum_{i \in P} \alpha (1-p_i)^{\gamma} \log p_i}_{\text{positive focal loss}} + \underbrace{\sum_{j \in N} w_j \, \alpha \, (1-p_j)^{\gamma} \log(1-p_j)}_{\text{weighted negative focal loss}} + \lambda \, \mathcal{L}_{\text{reg}} \quad (1)$$

where $\alpha = 0.25$ and $\gamma = 3.0$ are the focal loss parameters, and the adversarial weights $w_j = \exp(\alpha_{\text{adv}} \cdot p_j) / \sum_{k \in N} \exp(\alpha_{\text{adv}} \cdot p_k)$ with $\alpha_{\text{adv}} = 2.0$ concentrate the gradient on the hardest negatives—those that the model currently scores close to positives.

For each positive TARGET triple (h, r, t), we generate negatives by corrupting the head with a random Compound entity or the tail with a random ExtGene entity, respecting the type constraints of the TARGET relation. All known true triples (from train, validation, and test splits) are filtered out, preventing the sampler from creating false negatives. This procedure yields biologically plausible negatives: a randomly substituted compound–protein pair that does not appear in DrugBank.

Since the graph contains over 3 million edges but only 302 TARGET triples, we oversample TARGET edges ($5\times$ repetition) in the training set and undersample non-TARGET edges (retaining 50%) to rebalance the learning signal without discarding structural context entirely. These factors were fixed *a priori* as a pragmatic trade-off rather than tuned, retaining enough background edges for message passing while raising the effective weight of the few hundred positives.

Training uses AdamW [15] with an exponential learning rate scheduler and gradient clipping. Early stopping monitors validation loss with configurable patience. The evaluation metrics, hyperparameter optimisation strategy, and pipeline validation are described in Sect. 4.

4 Experimental Results

This section first defines the evaluation metrics and describes the hyperparameter optimisation strategy and pipeline validation on an external benchmark, then presents the architecture comparison and the performance of the final model on PathogenKG.

Evaluation Metrics. Models are assessed on held-out TARGET triples using both classification and ranking metrics. *Classification*: the Area Under the ROC curve (AUROC) and the Area Under the Precision–Recall curve (AUPRC) measure the model's ability to distinguish true from false drug–target pairs, with AUPRC being particularly informative under class imbalance. *Ranking*: for each positive test triple (h, r, t), the tail entity t is ranked among all type-valid candidates (i.e., all ExtGene entities), with known true triples filtered out. We report Mean Reciprocal Rank (MRR) and Hits@k for $k \in \{1, 3, 10\}$. Importantly, we use **type-constrained** filtered evaluation: when ranking tail candidates for a TARGET triple, only ExtGene entities are considered, and when ranking heads, only Compound entities. This ensures that ranking difficulty reflects a biologically meaningful comparison rather than an artificially easy one that includes entity types that could never participate in a TARGET relation.

Hyperparameter Optimisation. We conduct Bayesian hyperparameter search using Weights & Biases sweeps [2], optimising a composite validation metric:

$$\mathcal{M} = 0.2 \cdot \text{AUROC} + 0.4 \cdot \text{AUPRC} + 0.4 \cdot \text{MRR} \tag{2}$$

The weights prioritise ranking quality, which is the operative objective in link-prediction–based drug repurposing. MRR and AUPRC, the metrics that capture how well true targets are ranked under class imbalance, together account for 80% of $\mathcal{M}$, whereas the purely classification-oriented AUROC, least informative under extreme imbalance, is down-weighted to 0.2. The weights are a fixed model-selection criterion for the sweep, not a tuned hyperparameter. The search space covers architectural parameters (1–2 convolutional layers, hidden dimensions in $\{64, 128, 200\}$, number of bases in $\{10, 15, 20\}$, composition operator in $\{\text{sub}, \text{corr}\}$) and training hyperparameters (learning rate in

$[10^{-4}, 3\times10^{-3}]$, dropout in $[0.2, 0.5]$, weight decay in $[10^{-3}, 5\times10^{-2}]$, scheduler decay γ in $[0.99, 0.999]$, gradient clipping norm in $[0.5, 2.0]$, L_2 regularisation in $[10^{-4}, 10^{-2}]$).

Pipeline Validation on DRKG. Before applying the pipeline to PathogenKG, we validated it on the DRKG benchmark [8], training the same architecture (CompGCN + DistMult) on the TREATMENT relation (drug–disease prediction), using the best configuration identified by the Bayesian sweep. On 11,211 held-out TREATMENT triples, the pipeline achieved test AUROC 0.708 and AUPRC 0.701, confirming that the training procedure, negative sampling strategy, and evaluation protocol produce results consistent with published benchmarks for drug repurposing on established biomedical KGs. This validation step ensures that performance differences observed on PathogenKG reflect the intrinsic difficulty of the dataset (smaller TARGET set, pathogen-specific graph structure) rather than implementation artifacts.

Architecture Comparison: R-GCN vs. CompGCN. Both architectures were optimised independently through the Bayesian hyperparameter search described above, then evaluated over 12 runs with different random seeds to assess stability. Table 4 reports the mean and standard deviation across these runs.

Table 4. R-GCN vs. CompGCN on PathogenKG TARGET link prediction (12 runs, filtered evaluation). No difference is statistically significant (Welch t-test, $p > 0.05$ for all metrics).

Metric	CompGCN	R-GCN
AUROC	$\mathbf{0.510 \pm 0.050}$	0.490 ± 0.021
AUPRC	$\mathbf{0.516 \pm 0.042}$	0.500 ± 0.019
MRR	0.031 ± 0.015	$\mathbf{0.034 \pm 0.012}$
Hits@1	0.006 ± 0.011	$\mathbf{0.009 \pm 0.012}$
Hits@3	0.015 ± 0.019	$\mathbf{0.021 \pm 0.013}$
Hits@10	0.050 ± 0.033	$\mathbf{0.058 \pm 0.018}$
Composite $\mathcal{M}$	$\mathbf{0.321 \pm 0.030}$	0.311 ± 0.011

The two architectures perform comparably, with no statistically significant differences (lowest $p = 0.24$, for AUROC). This is expected given the limited statistical power afforded by ~70 test triples. R-GCN achieves slightly higher ranking metrics (MRR, Hits@k), while CompGCN leads on classification metrics and on the composite $\mathcal{M}$.

We select **CompGCN** as the final architecture for three reasons. First, it achieves the higher composite $\mathcal{M}$ on the best run (0.376 vs. 0.328), the criterion the Bayesian sweep was explicitly optimising, and obtains the highest individual AUROC (0.598) and AUPRC (0.588) among all 24 runs, whereas R-GCN's mean AUROC falls below 0.5, indicating near-random binary discrimination. Second,

CompGCN exhibits more stable training dynamics: its validation loss converges smoothly across runs, whereas R-GCN displays oscillatory behaviour with several instances of non-convergence. Third, CompGCN is the established reference for drug repurposing on heterogeneous biomedical KGs, outperforming R-GCN by 2.2× in MRR on Hetionet [16] and achieving the best GNN-based results on GP-KG [5].

Final Model Performance. The best CompGCN configuration uses two convolutional layers with hidden dimension 200, circular correlation as composition operator, 15 basis matrices, dropout 0.3, learning rate 10^{-3}, and weight decay 5×10^{-2}. On the held-out test set this model achieves AUROC 0.598, AUPRC 0.588, MRR 0.052, and Hits@10 0.106. These are the figures of the single best-selected run; the corresponding mean±s.d. over the 12 runs on the same test set are reported in Table 4 (e.g., AUROC 0.510±0.050), the gap reflecting run-to-run variance with ∼70 test triples. These values are modest compared to the DRKG pipeline test performance (AUROC 0.708, AUPRC 0.701), but the two settings differ dramatically in supervised signal: DRKG provides 51,681 TREATMENT triples for training versus only ∼210 TARGET triples in PathogenKG. The practical value of the framework therefore lies in the quality of ranked candidate lists for individual compounds, which we assess next.

5 Case Study: Biological Plausibility Analysis

Compound-Centric Ranking Protocol. The standard link prediction metrics (Sect. 4) average over all test triples and do not directly address the practical repurposing question: *given a specific compound, which pathogen proteins are the most promising novel targets?* We therefore adopt a compound-centric evaluation protocol. For each compound h, the trained model scores every ExtGene entity t in PathogenKG via $p = \sigma(f(h, \texttt{TARGET}, t))$, producing a ranked list over the entire pathogen proteome (over 142,000 proteins across 31 species). Known positive targets from the training and validation splits are excluded (filtered setting), so that only genuinely novel predictions appear at the top. Unlike standard KGE evaluation, the ranking pool here encompasses all pathogen proteins, not only those involved in known TARGET edges, and the goal is to produce an actionable shortlist for biological assessment rather than aggregate ranking statistics.

Plausibility Assessment. We applied this protocol to nine compounds with diverse mechanisms of action. For each compound, the best CompGCN model ranked all pathogen proteins, and a domain expert assessed the top 20 predictions against the published literature, assigning one of three plausibility tiers: **High** (direct mechanistic or experimental support), **Moderate** (indirect but defensible biological connection), or *Low* (no clear link identified). This tiered scheme follows the evaluation strategy of recent KG-based repurposing studies [5,16], adapted to the cross-species setting. Complete per-compound tables with annotations are provided in the Supplementary Material (Tables S1–S9).

Summary of Findings. Table 5 summarises the assessment across all nine compounds. Every compound yielded at least one **High**-plausibility prediction within its top 20, and all nine produced multiple predictions rated **Moderate** or above. In total, 16 out of 180 predictions (8.9%) were rated **High** and a further 24 (13.3%) **Moderate**, yielding 40 biologically supported candidates (22.2%) from a ranking pool of over 142,000 proteins per compound. Given that the model receives no compound structure or sequence information, relying entirely on graph topology, this hit rate is notable.

The detailed per-compound analyses, including literature references and mechanistic reasoning for each High and Moderate prediction, are discussed in Sect. 6 and reported in full in the Supplementary Material.

6 Discussion

PathogenKG represents, to our knowledge, the first knowledge graph framework that explicitly integrates pathogen proteomes, intra-species molecular networks, and cross-species orthology to support drug repurposing via link prediction across multiple bacterial pathogens simultaneously. Existing KG-based repurposing systems, including DRKG [8], Hetionet [7], and GP-KG [5], are centered on human disease–drug–gene associations and do not model pathogen-specific biology. Our framework fills this gap by placing pathogen proteins at the core of the graph and encoding sufficient biological context, PPI topology from STRING, COG orthology, and Gene Ontology annotations, to enable the propagation of drug–target evidence between phylogenetically related organisms through the GNN message-passing mechanism. The architectural choice of CompGCN with composition operators is well suited to this setting: by jointly embedding entities and relations, the model can learn relation-specific transformations that distinguish the sparse TARGET signal from the dominant GO and PPI background (a frequency ratio of approximately 5,400:1). The training pipeline, combining focal loss, type-constrained filtered negative sampling, and controlled oversampling, was validated on the DRKG benchmark (test AUROC 0.708, AUPRC 0.701 on 11,211 held-out TREATMENT triples), confirming that the observed performance on PathogenKG reflects the intrinsic difficulty of the dataset rather than implementation artifacts.

The biological plausibility analysis of nine case study compounds provides the most direct evidence of the framework's practical utility. Across 180 top-20 predictions, a domain expert rated 16 (8.9%) as **High** plausibility and a further 24 (13.3%) as **Moderate**, yielding 40 biologically supported candidates (22.2%) from a ranking pool exceeding 142,000 proteins per compound (Table 5). Several predictions illustrate the model's capacity to capture mechanistically grounded associations. For **Merimepodib**, an IMPDH inhibitor developed as an antiviral, the model identified purine nucleoside phosphorylase DeoD from *H. pylori* at rank 4, an organism that lacks de novo purine synthesis and relies on the salvage pathway where DeoD is essential [10]. This cross-indication leap from

Table 5. Biological plausibility of the top-20 predicted targets per compound. Each prediction was rated by a domain expert based on literature evidence.

Compound	Primary mechanism	High	Mod.	Low	H+M
Ciprofloxacin	DNA gyrase/topo. IV	2	3	15	5
Triclosan	Enoyl-ACP reductase	2	2	16	4
Acetohydroxamic acid	Urease (Ni^{2+} chelation)	2	3	15	5
Berberine	FtsZ/DNA intercalation	3	3	14	6
Sulfapyridine	Dihydropteroate synthase	1	4	15	5
Imipenem	Penicillin-binding proteins	1	3	16	4
Merimepodib	IMPDH	1	2	17	3
Virginiamycin M1	50S ribosomal subunit	2	3	15	5
Ecabet	Anti-adhesion/urease	2	1	17	3
Total (180)		**16**	**24**	**140**	**40**

antiviral to antibacterial along a functionally adjacent metabolic step exemplifies the value of pathway-level signal propagation through the KG. For **Virginiamycin M1**, a streptogramin targeting the 50S ribosomal peptidyl-transferase center, two rRNA methyltransferases (RsmB in *S. oneidensis* and RsmC in *C. amalonaticus*) appeared at ranks 8 and 9. Enzymatic rRNA methylation is a characterised resistance mechanism against ribosome-targeting antibiotics; for streptogramin A, the canonical example is Cfr, which methylates A2503 of the 23S peptidyl-transferase center [13]. Although RsmB and RsmC modify the 16S rRNA, their recovery still points to a biologically meaningful association with the rRNA-modification machinery rather than a spurious topological correlation. For **Berberine**, the nucleoid-associated protein lmo2703 of *L. monocytogenes* (rank 13) matches berberine's known DNA-intercalating mechanism, and anti-*Listeria* activity has been independently documented [9]. **Ecabet**'s top-ranked prediction, a Zn-dependent metallo-β-lactamase-fold hydrolase in *C. butyricum*, is consistent with its metal-chelating pharmacophore, and the identification of a second zinc metalloenzyme at rank 8 reinforces this pattern [3]. Notably, for **Ciprofloxacin**, a Toprim domain-containing protein in *E. faecium* (rank 5) was identified, Toprim domains are shared between DNA gyrase and primase, representing a direct mechanistic match for fluoroquinolone activity. Because the filtered setting hides only targets already present in PathogenKG, a top-ranked pair can be novel with respect to the graph yet correspond to a mechanism documented elsewhere; this is precisely the cross-species transfer we seek, in which a known drug class is re-proposed against a pathogen for which no edge existed. High-plausibility predictions are therefore best read as literature-consistent, KG-novel cross-species hypotheses. Complete per-compound prediction tables with expert annotations are reported in the Supplementary Material (Tables S1–S9).

Several limitations should be acknowledged, though each is partially mitigated by design choices or contextual factors. First, the limited number of TAR-

GET edges (302 out of over 3 million triples) constrains the training signal and the statistical power of the evaluation. With approximately 70 test triples, ranking metrics carry non-negligible variance, and the non-significant differences between R-GCN and CompGCN (Table 4) reflect this regime. However, data scarcity is a well-recognised challenge in biomedical KG embedding, even in established benchmarks such as Hetionet, the *treats* relation has only 82 test triples, and recent work has shown that pretraining on large multi-relational KGs can partially compensate for sparse supervision in downstream tasks. Our pipeline's validation on DRKG (Sect. 4) confirms that the approach produces reliable results when more labelled data are available, and the biological plausibility analysis provides complementary, qualitative evidence of model utility. Relatedly, while the filtered ranking setting prevents leakage through known edges, the split is not clustered by chemical scaffold or protein-sequence similarity, so some test performance may stem from near-duplicate compounds or homologous proteins shared with training; scaffold- or sequence-aware splitting is a natural refinement for future evaluations. Second, 77.8% of top-20 predictions received a *Low* plausibility rating. This proportion should be interpreted with caution: a substantial share of predicted targets are unannotated proteins for which no functional characterisation exists in current databases, a pervasive issue across prokaryotic proteomes, where the functionally characterised fraction remains remarkably small even in well-studied model organisms. For these proteins, *Low* reflects the absence of evidence rather than evidence of absence, and future functional annotation efforts may reclassify some of these predictions. Third, PathogenKG currently relies entirely on graph topology without incorporating compound structural features (e.g., molecular fingerprints) or protein sequence representations. While this limits the model's ability to discriminate chemically distinct compounds that occupy similar graph neighbourhoods, it also means that the observed biological plausibility of predictions emerges solely from relational patterns in the KG, a finding that underscores the informativeness of the integrated biological context. Fourth, PPI data completeness in STRING varies across species [22], potentially favouring well-studied organisms such as *B. subtilis* and *S. enterica*. STRING partially mitigates this through its interolog transfer pipeline, which propagates interaction evidence from model organisms to less-studied species via orthology [22], and our inclusion of COG and GO edges provides additional cross-species connectivity that reduces the isolation of data-poor organisms.

These limitations are counterbalanced by several distinctive strengths. Unlike molecular property prediction approaches such as those employed in the discovery of halicin [21], which predict whole-cell antibacterial activity without identifying molecular targets, PathogenKG produces target-level predictions across multiple species, providing mechanistic hypotheses that can guide experimental validation. The framework is inherently extensible: adding new pathogen organisms requires only their PPI networks and COG/GO annotations, with no retraining of the data integration pipeline. From an applied perspective, PathogenKG is designed to prioritise candidates for experimental screening in the context of antimicrobial resistance [6]: the ranked lists produced by the compound-centric evaluation protocol (Sect. 5) directly support the selection of drug–target pairs for biochemical or microbiological assays, reducing the search space from hundreds of thousands of possible interactions to a manageable shortlist.

7 Conclusion

We presented PathogenKG, a multi-pathogen heterogeneous knowledge graph that links pathogen proteomes across species through orthology and functional-annotation edges, together with a link-prediction pipeline and compound-centric ranking protocol designed for the extreme class imbalance of drug–target discovery. The framework offers both a reusable resource and a methodology for cross-species antimicrobial drug repurposing, yielding literature-consistent, KG-novel hypotheses to prioritise candidate drug–target pairs for experimental validation.

Looking ahead, the most immediate improvement would be the incorporation of compound molecular features and protein sequence embeddings (e.g., from ESM-2 [12]) as node-level inputs, which would allow the model to exploit chemical and sequence similarity beyond what graph topology alone provides. On the training side, the focal loss could be replaced by objectives tailored to extreme imbalance, such as the weighted focal differentiable MCC loss [20]. Expanding the KG with additional pathogen species and relation types, such as gene expression data, resistance gene annotations, or host–pathogen interactions, would further enrich the biological context available for cross-species transfer; beyond link prediction, the resulting resource also lends itself to complementary uses such as graph-based exploration, similarity clustering, and KG question answering. Finally, integration with large language model-based explanation modules, as explored in recent KG-based repurposing systems [17], could improve the interpretability and trustworthiness of predictions for downstream users in drug discovery pipelines.

Data Availability. The source code is provided as Supplementary Material. The dataset and full pipeline are available on GitHub (https://github.com/johndef64/PathogenKG) and HuggingFace (https://huggingface.co/datasets/johndef64/PathogenKG).

Disclosure of Interests. The authors declare that they have no competing interests.

References

1. Ashburner, M., et al.: Gene ontology: tool for the unification of biology. Nat. Genet. **25**(1), 25–29 (2000). https://doi.org/10.1038/75556
2. Biewald, L.: Experiment tracking with weights and biases (2020). https://www.wandb.com/

3. Crowder, M.W., Spencer, J., Vila, A.J.: Metallo-β-lactamases: novel weaponry for antibiotic resistance in bacteria. Acc. Chem. Res. **39**(10), 721–728 (2006). https://doi.org/10.1021/ar0400241
4. Farha, M.A., Brown, E.D.: Drug repurposing for antimicrobial discovery. Nat. Microbiol. **4**(4), 565–577 (2019). https://doi.org/10.1038/s41564-019-0357-1
5. Gao, Z., Ding, P., Xu, R.: KG-predict: a knowledge graph computational framework for drug repurposing. J. Biomed. Inform. **132**, 104133 (2022). https://doi.org/10.1016/j.jbi.2022.104133
6. GBD 2021 Antimicrobial Resistance Collaborators: Global burden of bacterial antimicrobial resistance 1990–2021: a systematic analysis with forecasts to 2050. Lancet **404**(10459), 1199–1226 (2024). https://doi.org/10.1016/S0140-6736(24)01867-1
7. Himmelstein, D.S., et al.: Systematic integration of biomedical knowledge prioritizes drugs for repurposing. eLife **6**, e26726 (2017). https://doi.org/10.7554/eLife.26726
8. Ioannidis, V.N., et al.: DRKG - drug repurposing knowledge graph for covid-19 (2020)
9. Kim, J.W., Mistry, B., Shin, H.S., Kang, S.S.: Anti-biofilm activity of N-Mannich bases of berberine linking piperazine against Listeria monocytogenes. Food Control **121**, 107668 (2021). https://doi.org/10.1016/j.foodcont.2020.107668
10. Liechti, G., Goldberg, J.B.: Helicobacter pylori relies primarily on the purine salvage pathway for purine nucleotide biosynthesis. J. Bacteriol. **194**(4), 839–854 (2012). https://doi.org/10.1128/JB.05757-11
11. Lin, T.Y., Goyal, P., Girshick, R., He, K., Dollár, P.: Focal loss for dense object detection. In: Proceedings of the IEEE International Conference on Computer Vision (ICCV), pp. 2980–2988 (2017). https://doi.org/10.1109/ICCV.2017.324
12. Lin, Z., et al.: Evolutionary-scale prediction of atomic-level protein structure with a language model. Science **379**(6637), 1123–1130 (2023). https://doi.org/10.1126/science.ade2574
13. Long, K.S., Poehlsgaard, J., Kehrenberg, C., Schwarz, S., Vester, B.: The Cfr rRNA methyltransferase confers resistance to phenicols, lincosamides, oxazolidinones, pleuromutilins, and streptogramin A antibiotics. Antimicrob. Agents Chemother. **50**(7), 2500–2505 (2006). https://doi.org/10.1128/AAC.00131-06
14. Lorente-Torres, B., et al.: Innovative strategies in drug repurposing to tackle intracellular bacterial pathogens. Antibiotics **13**(9), 834 (2024). https://doi.org/10.3390/antibiotics13090834
15. Loshchilov, I., Hutter, F.: Decoupled weight decay regularization. In: Proceedings of the 7th International Conference on Learning Representations (ICLR) (2019). https://openreview.net/forum?id=Bkg6RiCqY7
16. Nunes, S., Badreddine, S., Pesquita, C.: Rewarding explainability in drug repurposing with knowledge graphs. In: Proceedings of the Thirty-Fourth International Joint Conference on Artificial Intelligence (IJCAI-25), pp. 4624–4632 (2025). https://doi.org/10.24963/ijcai.2025/515
17. Perdomo-Quinteiro, P., Belmonte-Hernández, A.: Knowledge graphs for drug repurposing: a review of databases and methods. Brief. Bioinform. **25**(6), bbae461 (2024). https://doi.org/10.1093/bib/bbae461
18. Pushpakom, S., et al.: Drug repurposing: progress, challenges and recommendations. Nat. Rev. Drug Discov. **18**(1), 41–58 (2019). https://doi.org/10.1038/nrd.2018.168

19. Schlichtkrull, M., Kipf, T.N., Bloem, P., van den Berg, R., Titov, I., Welling, M.: Modeling relational data with graph convolutional networks. In: The Semantic Web (ESWC 2018). Lecture Notes in Computer Science, vol. 10843, pp. 593–607. Springer (2018). https://doi.org/10.1007/978-3-319-93417-4_38
20. Seber, P.: Predicting O-GlcNAcylation sites in mammalian proteins with transformers and RNNs trained with a new loss function (2024). https://doi.org/10.48550/arXiv.2402.17131, https://arxiv.org/abs/2402.17131
21. Stokes, J.M., et al.: A Deep Learning Approach to Antibiotic Discovery. Cell **180**(4), 688–702.e13 (2020). https://doi.org/10.1016/j.cell.2020.01.021
22. Szklarczyk, D., et al.: The STRING database in 2023: protein-protein association networks and functional enrichment analyses for any sequenced genome of interest. Nucleic Acids Res. **51**(D1), D99–D106 (2023). https://doi.org/10.1093/nar/gkac1000
23. Tatusov, R.L., Galperin, M.Y., Natale, D.A., Koonin, E.V.: The COG database: a tool for genome-scale analysis of protein functions and evolution. Nucleic Acids Res. **28**(1), 33–36 (2000). https://doi.org/10.1093/nar/28.1.33
24. Vashishth, S., Sanyal, S., Nitin, V., Talukdar, P.: Composition-based multi-relational graph convolutional networks (2020). https://doi.org/10.48550/arXiv.1911.03082, http://arxiv.org/abs/1911.03082
25. Wishart, D.S., et al.: DrugBank 5.0: a major update to the DrugBank database for 2018. Nucleic Acids Res. **46**(D1), D1074–D1082 (2018). https://doi.org/10.1093/nar/gkx1037
26. Xiao, Y., et al.: Repurposing non-pharmacological interventions for Alzheimer's disease through link prediction on biomedical literature. Sci. Rep. **14**(1), 8693 (2024). https://doi.org/10.1038/s41598-024-58604-8
27. Yang, B., Yih, W.t., He, X., Gao, J., Deng, L.: Embedding entities and relations for learning and inference in knowledge bases. In: Proceedings of the 3rd International Conference on Learning Representations (ICLR) (2015). https://arxiv.org/abs/1412.6575

Rethinking Cell Counting with Self-supervision: Application to Avian Blood Analysis

Dimitris Ntantakas[1(✉)], Dimitris Dimitriadis[1], Constantina N. Tsokana[2], Labrini V. Athanasiou[3], and Grigorios Tsoumakas[1]

[1] School of Informatics, Aristotle University, 54124 Thessaloniki, Greece
{dntantak,dndimitri,greg}@csd.auth.gr
[2] School of Veterinary Medicine, Aristotle University, 54124 Thessaloniki, Greece
ctsokana@vet.auth.gr
[3] Faculty of Veterinary Medicine, University of Thessaly, 43100 Karditsa, Greece
lathan@vet.uth.gr

Abstract. Avian hematology involves the identification, differentiation, and quantification of blood cells to evaluate health status, disease progression, and treatment response. However, automated analysis is challenging because avian blood cells have unique morphological characteristics compared to mammalian cells. Traditional automated approaches, such as object detection, require extensive labeled data and significant manual effort, limiting scalability and applicability. We introduce a novel three-stage framework that leverages self-supervised learning to reduce reliance on annotated datasets while maintaining high classification accuracy. In the first stage, we employ Cellpose, a model specialized in cellular segmentation, to accurately localize and isolate individual cells from smear images. In the second stage, the segmented cell regions are used to train a Bootstrap Your Own Latent (BYOL) model, to learn robust feature embeddings without labeled data. Finally, a lightweight supervised classifier is applied to these embeddings for final cell type assignment. The results show that our approach substantially outperforms the baselines for classes with a small number of instances, achieving improvements of 9–10%, while maintaining comparable or slightly better performance (by 1–3%) on more common cell types. These findings underscore the effectiveness of combining domain-specific segmentation with self-supervised representation learning, offering a scalable, data-efficient, and accurate solution for automated avian hematology analysis.

Keywords: Avian hematology · Blood cell classification · Self-supervised learning · Bootstrap Your Own Latent (BYOL) · Cellpose segmentation · Representation learning · Automated microscopy analysis

M. Ceci et al. (Eds.): ECML PKDD 2026, LNAI 16948, pp. 619–635, 2027.
https://doi.org/10.1007/978-3-032-37679-4_35

1 Introduction

Hematological testing is an important component of health assessment in all animal patients, including avian species. Historically, blood from galliform birds, mainly chickens and turkeys, was the first to be evaluated [41]. However, the introduction of exotic species into veterinary medicine and clinical care led to more extensive research and clinical applications involving these species [4]. Currently, most avian hematology data originate from psittacines and raptors, which are the species most frequently presented to veterinary clinics equipped with diagnostic laboratories [39]. In contrast, poultry farms are often located far from diagnostic laboratories, and there is also limited availability of automated hematology analyzers validated for chicken blood [14].

The identification and quantification of white blood cell (WBC) subpopulations has significant value in avian diagnostics and research. Microscopic examination of blood smears can reveal inflammation and/or infection as well as stress based on characteristic quantitative and qualitative changes in leukocyte subpopulations [6,22]. This is particularly relevant for evaluating the cellular immune responses of birds to pathogens and for assessing vaccination efficacy [21].

However, microscopic examination of blood smears is widely considered an imperfect gold standard for hematologic testing because of its inherent limitations. Its accuracy depends heavily on the observer's expertise and on the quality of slide preparation and staining. In addition, it is labor-intensive and prone to errors [9,27,33]. The evaluation of blood cell populations in chickens is even more challenging because avian hematology differs significantly from that of domestic mammals. Characteristics such as nucleated erythrocytes, heterophils with variable granule staining that may be confused with eosinophils, and small lymphocytes that resemble thrombocytes complicate interpretation for veterinarians who are more familiar with the blood smears of common domestic mammals [15].

Deep learning can help us address some of these challenges. However, while convolutional neural networks (CNNs) have revolutionized human hematology [16,42], avian applications are hindered by a scarcity of large-scale, annotated datasets compared to human benchmarks [1,10,34]. To bypass this "annotation bottleneck", we propose a three-stage framework for avian blood cell analysis that employs self-supervised learning (SSL) in order to learn morphological features from unlabeled data (Fig. 1).

Our framework utilizes Cellpose [38] for instance segmentation, Bootstrap Your Own Latent (BYOL) [12] for self-supervised feature extraction, and a lightweight downstream classifier. Our approach outperforms YOLO-based detectors in localization and classification, particularly for rare WBC subclasses and boundary-case morphologies. Our contributions include:

- A publicly available dataset of 4,600 high-resolution avian blood cell images with expert annotations in a subset of them[1].
- An SSL-based pipeline that achieves superior F1 scores ($\geq$0.90) in low-data regimes compared to traditional object detection.

[1] https://doi.org/10.5281/zenodo.20703287.

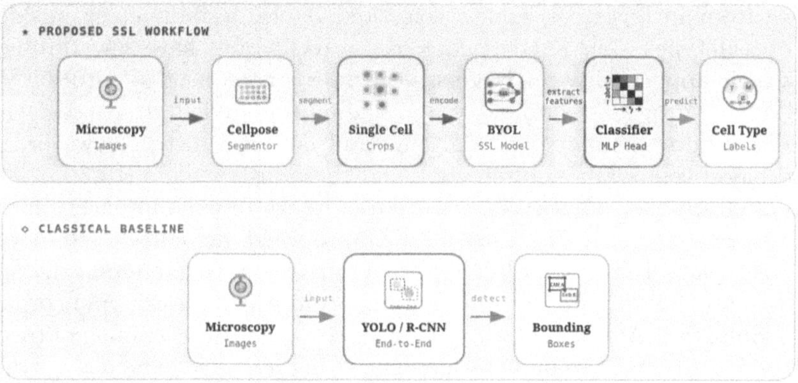

Fig. 1. Illustration of the proposed self-supervised workflow versus traditional object detection.

– Open-source code to facilitate reproducible research in computational avian hematology[2].

The rest of this paper is organized as follows: Sect. 2 reviews related work. Sections 3, 4 detail our dataset and methodology. Sections 5, 6 and 7 present our experimental setup, results and qualitative analysis. Section 8 discusses the potential deployment of the method and its transferability to related microscopy tasks. Finally, Sect. 9 concludes this work and discusses future research directions.

2 Related Work

Earlier methods for counting avian blood cells primarily relied on the hemocytometer, a glass chamber that allows trained personnel to manually enumerate cells under a microscope [7]. While providing basic concentration estimates, this approach is complicated by the presence of nucleated erythrocytes and thrombocytes. To improve leukocyte differentiation, various staining and dilution techniques, such as the Natt and Herrick and the Phloxine B methods, have been developed [7,28,30]. Comparative studies of these methods have highlighted their respective strengths and limitations. For instance, the Natt and Herrick method offers a direct total WBC count but requires careful identification of individual cells, which can be challenging due to nucleated erythrocytes and thrombocytes [7]. In contrast, the Unopette method is easier to perform and relies on differential counts from stained blood smears, though it provides only an indirect estimate of total leukocytes. Such methodological variations directly influence both the accuracy and practicality of manual counts.

Despite their widespread use, manual hemocytometer-based methods are inherently labor-intensive and prone to observer variability [13]. Counting errors

[2] https://github.com/JimNtantakas/Self-Supervised-cell-counting.

can arise from inconsistent square selection, operator fatigue, or misidentification of cell types [30]. Furthermore, these techniques have low throughput, limiting their applicability for large-scale studies or frequent monitoring [5]. To address these limitations, automated and semi-automated alternatives have been explored, including hematology analyzers and flow cytometry; however, nucleated red blood cells (RBCs) often confound these instruments [13,30].

Recent efforts have focused on systematic, image-based approaches for avian blood cell counting. Meechart et al. [26] proposed an automated detection method using adaptive thresholding in smear images, which dynamically adjusts for contrast and lighting variations to segment cells despite overlapping or uneven staining. Similarly, Autaiem et al. [2] introduced a multi-stage image-processing pipeline to improve RBCs enumeration, employing iterative refinement strategies to enhance cell boundaries. While these methods improve segmentation relative to simple thresholding, their accuracy remains insufficient for real-world applications, as morphological constraints often fail to resolve complex cell overlaps or distinguish between RBCs and WBCs consistently.

Deep learning models, particularly CNNs, have become state-of-the-art in many computer vision tasks, yet only a few have been applied to avian blood cell analysis. Govind et al. [11] developed a hybrid framework for whole slide images that combines handcrafted algorithms for erythrocyte detection with a GoogLeNet model for species classification. Kittichai et al. [18] applied YOLOv3 for detecting chicken erythrocytes in thin blood smears, followed by CNN architectures to classify the developmental stages of avian malaria parasites. More recently, Vogelbacher et al. [40] proposed a deep learning-based framework for directly identifying and counting avian blood cells in whole slide images. Their approach integrates a tile-selection model to locate suitable regions and an instance segmentation model for individual cell detection and classification. While achieving high accuracy for common cell types, performance was limited for rare leukocytes due to their low representation in training data.

Collectively, these studies demonstrate significant progress toward automated avian hematology but also highlight persistent challenges, including overlapping cells, rare cell types, and the limited availability of large annotated datasets. These limitations motivate the development of more robust, data-efficient approaches, such as self-supervised learning frameworks, to achieve scalable and accurate blood cell analysis.

3 Dataset

The dataset consists of 4,600 high-resolution avian blood smear images, covering five blood cell types: RBCs, thrombocytes, lymphocytes, heterophils, and monocytes. Image resolutions range from 1280 × 720 to 3264 × 1840 pixels. In addition, the images exhibit substantial variability in cell density. Some smears contain sparsely distributed cells with minimal overlap, whereas others show densely packed cells with frequent overlaps and partially visible cells. Despite standardized preparation protocols, variations in illumination and staining intensity introduce additional visual inconsistencies across the dataset. These factors collectively make automated detection and classification of avian blood cells a challenging task. Representative examples of these blood smear images are shown in Fig. 2.

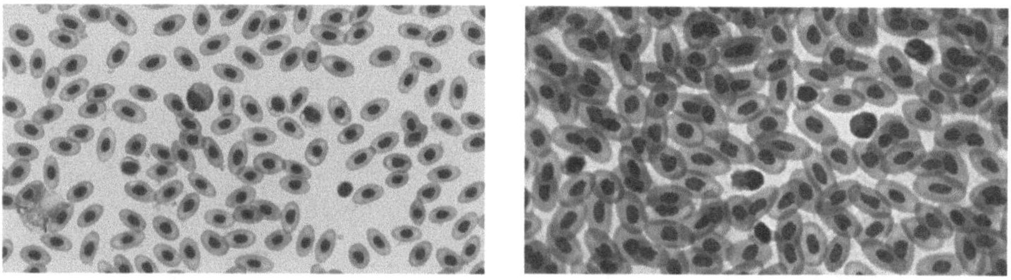

Fig. 2. Representative examples of avian blood smear images from the dataset.

To support both segmentation-based and detection-based approaches, two types of annotations were created for the dataset: pixel-wise segmentation masks and bounding box annotations. The segmentation masks enable precise localization of individual cells and are used for training the segmentation model employed in our pipeline. The bounding box annotations constitute the ground truth labels for object detection, where each annotated object is assigned to one of the five predefined cell types. All annotations were created using the CVAT[3] annotation platform. Figure 3 illustrates examples of bounding box and segmentation annotations applied to the blood smear images.

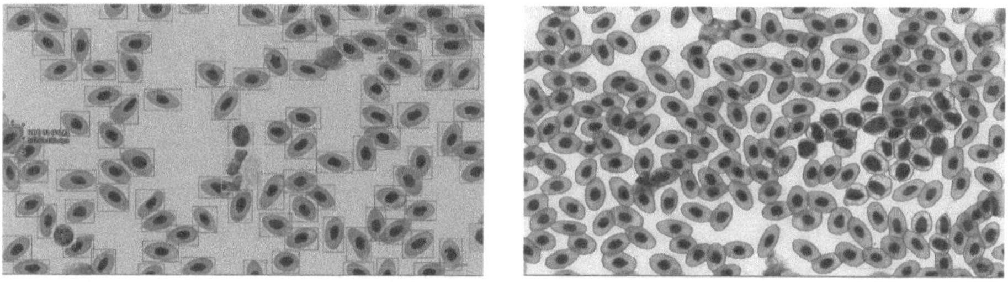

Fig. 3. Illustration of the annotations in our dataset. The left image shows bounding box annotations around cells, while the right image shows precise pixel-wise segmentation annotations.

Manual annotation being time-consuming, only a subset of images was labeled. Specifically, 1,000 images were randomly selected: 500 were annotated with both segmentation masks and bounding boxes, while the other 500 were annotated with bounding boxes only. The remaining 3,600 images are unlabeled

[3] https://www.cvat.ai/.

and were used for self-supervised representation learning. Table 1 summarizes the dataset splits.

Table 1. Dataset composition and usage in the proposed pipeline.

Dataset Split	# Images	Annotation Type	Usage
Training Set	500	Masks, Boxes	Cellpose/YOLO/Classifier training
Unlabeled Set	3,600	None	BYOL training
Test Set	500	Boxes	Evaluation
Total	4,600	Mixed	Entire study

Cell type distribution is also imbalanced. Table 2 shows the number of images with cells of each class, along with the total number of cells of each class in the 500-image test set. It is very clear that RBCs are dominant, appearing in every image and more than a 100 times per image on average. WBCs such as lymphocytes and monocytes appear in 20% to 46% of images, but only once or twice per image on average. This class imbalance further complicates the task of avian blood cell classification and counting.

Table 2. Number of images and cells per red blood cell category in the test set.

Class	Images	Cells
RBC	500	60,456
Heterophils	285	471
Monocytes	101	119
Lymphocytes	231	345
Thrombocytes	459	2,165
Total	500	63,556

4 Proposed Method

The core idea of our approach is to operate at the level of individual cells rather than analyzing the entire image, as is commonly done in traditional object detection frameworks. This allows us to utilize the cropped cells from the unlabeled images for self-supervised learning of vector representations of cells. The pipeline consists of the following three stages: cell localization, representation learning, and cell classification. An overview of the pipeline is illustrated in the upper part of Fig. 1.

4.1 Cell Localization

The first stage employs the cell segmentation model Cellpose-SAM [29], the latest version of Cellpose [38], in order to isolate individual cells via pixel-level segmentation masks. Unlike bounding-box detectors, Cellpose accurately delineates overlapping cells and preserves fine-grained morphological boundaries (Fig. 4). We fine-tuned Cellpose-SAM on the training set using mask annotations. After fine-tuning, the model was applied to the unlabeled dataset to generate single-cell crops. These isolated instances serve as input to the subsequent self-supervised representation learning stage.

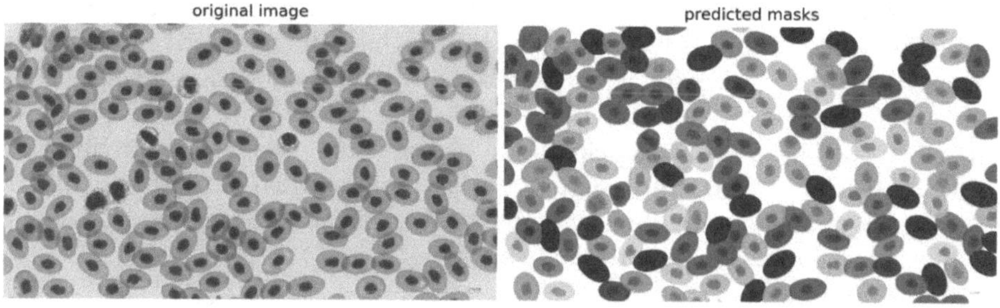

Fig. 4. Example of Cellpose generated cell masks. There is no class assignment; colors are assigned from a small pallet, such that no two touching cells share the same color.

4.2 Representation Learning

After constructing a dataset of individual cell images, we employ an SSL framework to learn meaningful visual representations without relying on manual labels. Self-supervised learning allows the model to capture morphological patterns present in the data by solving a pretext task that encourages consistency between different transformed views of the same image.

In particular, we adopt the BYOL [12] framework to learn cell representations. During training, two different views of the same cell are generated via multiple types of augmentation, including random resizing, flips, color jitter, Gaussian blur, and grayscale conversion. The two views are processed by an online (student) and a target (teacher) network. The parameters of the target network are an exponential moving average of the parameters of the online network. The target/teacher network provides the regression targets to train the online/student network. The online network is this way optimized to produce similar embeddings for the two views using the negative cosine similarity loss. This learning objective encourages the model to encode morphological characteristics such as cell shape, texture, and structural patterns while remaining robust to variations in illumination, staining, and imaging conditions. Figure 5 illustrates the process of representation learning using the BYOL framework.

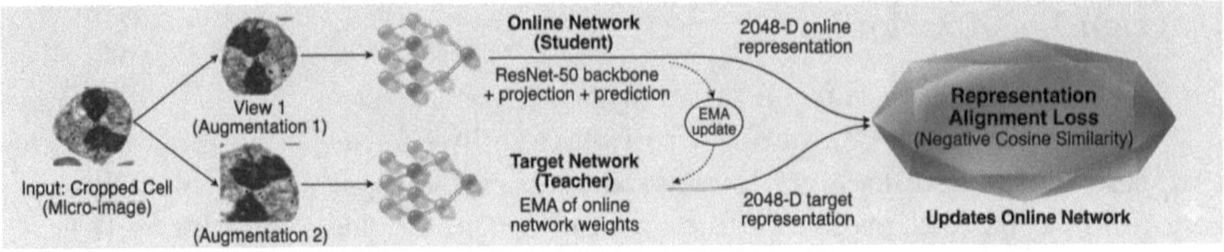

Fig. 5. BYOL-based self-supervised representation learning of individual cells.

4.3 Cell Classification

The final stage of the pipeline utilizes the learned representations for the downstream task of cell-type classification. Although the self-supervised model learns informative feature embeddings, it does not directly predict class labels.

To perform classification, a lightweight feedforward network (a linear layer) is attached to the fine-tuned backbone of the previous stage. This architecture is optimized using the training dataset with the individual cells obtained from the annotation masks, enabling the model to map the learned embeddings of the previous stage to specific avian blood cell types (Fig. 6).

Fig. 6. Overview of the pipeline. Downstream cell-type classification training using a lightweight feedforward network.

5 Experimental Setup

This section describes the experimental setup used to evaluate the proposed approach. We first present implementation details for each stage of our pipeline. Then, we present the configurations of the two competitor YOLO object detection models. For computational efficiency, all images were resized to (640×640) pixels prior to model training. This resizing altered the original aspect ratio to produce square images; no padding or cropping was applied.

5.1 Proposed Method

At the cell localization stage, we fine-tune Cellpose-SAM for 50 epochs with a learning rate of 10^{-4}, weight decay of 10^{-4}, and a batch size of 4.

At the representation learning stage, we use a ResNet-50 [20] backbone (ImageNet-1k [8] initialization), as preliminary tests showed it outperformed

EfficientNet [19] in latent space separability. While ConvNeXt and ConvNeXt-V2 [43] represent stronger modern alternatives, they were not considered because they incur substantially higher computational costs and training complexity. ResNet-50 on the other hand, remains the standard backbone for self-supervised representation learning, facilitating comparison with prior BYOL studies [3,23,32].

We used the negative cosine similarity loss and an exponential moving average (EMA) update for the target network with momentum ranging from 0.996 to 1.0. Training follows a two-stage strategy to address the extreme class imbalance of RBCs:

1. Initially, BYOL is trained on all Cellpose-extracted crops from the unlabeled set, resized to 128×128 pixels, for 500 epochs.
2. Subsequently, we cluster the obtained embeddings, and assuming that the largest cluster contains RBCs, we randomly sampled 5% of this cluster. This leads to a more balanced training set and allows to learn adequate representations for all classes. The model was then retrained from scratch on this filtered dataset for 1000 epochs.

At the final classification stage, we employed a cosine annealing scheduler and differential learning rates: 10^{-4} for the backbone and 10^{-3} for the classifier head. Training followed a two-stage approach:

1. For 5 initial epochs only the classification head was trained using Adam with a learning rate of 10^{-3}, while the backbone was frozen.
2. Subsequently, the entire network was trained for 20 epochs using SGD with momentum 0.9 and weight decay 10^{-4}.

5.2 Object Detection Methods

To evaluate our framework against state-of-the-art object detection methods, we selected the medium-scale variants of two recent YOLO architectures: YOLO11m [17] and YOLO26m [36]. These models offer an optimal balance between representational capacity and generalization for our specific dataset size. Both were initialized with COCO-pretrained weights to leverage transfer learning.

The two models were fine-tuned using the *ultralytics* framework [37] for a maximum of 200 epochs with a batch size of 16. We employed the "auto" optimizer configuration, which defaulted to AdamW (learning rate: 0.000833, momentum: 0.9). To prevent overfitting, early stopping was implemented with a patience of 50 epochs based on the validation mean Average Precision (mAP). The final evaluation was performed using the best-performing checkpoint from each run.

6 Results

In this section, we first present the results of cell localization. Following this, we evaluate the classification performance, where detected cells are categorized into the five distinct cell types.

6.1 Localization

We report the F1 score calculated at an Intersection over Union (IoU) of 0.5. As illustrated in Fig. 7, Cellpose consistently outperforms the more recent YOLO architectures in the localization task, maintaining a remarkably stable performance profile even under extreme low-data regimes. While Cellpose achieves a high baseline F1 score of 0.983 with only 20 images, the YOLO models exhibit significant volatility at small sample sizes; specifically, YOLO26m experiences a performance degradation to 0.764 with 50 images before recovering. Although the performance of both YOLO11m and YOLO26m improves as the training set expands, eventually plateauing at an F1 score of approximately 0.933, Cellpose maintains a superior trajectory throughout the experiment, reaching a peak of 0.993. This consistent margin of approximately 6% at the highest data levels, coupled with the immediate convergence at minimal sample sizes, demonstrates that Cellpose significantly surpasses the YOLO variants in both raw localization precision and algorithmic data efficiency. This performance advantage motivates its adoption as the primary instance segmentation component in our framework.

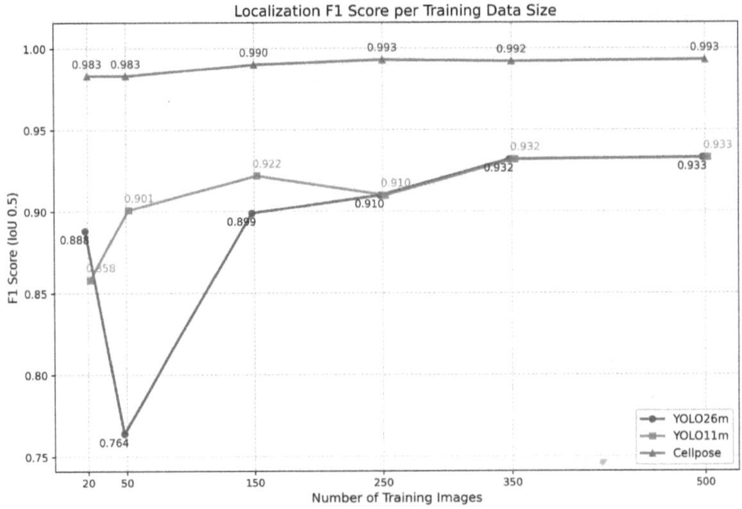

Fig. 7. Comparison of localization performance between Cellpose and the two different versions of YOLO.

6.2 Classification

Table 3 shows that all three approaches achieve near-perfect performance on RBC detection, reflecting the abundance and morphological consistency of this class. The most pronounced differences emerge for the less represented white blood cell populations, where the YOLO-based detectors exhibit greater variability across precision and recall. In contrast, the proposed framework maintains consistently high recall while preserving competitive precision, resulting in more stable performance across all leukocyte subtypes. This trend is further confirmed by the Matthews Correlation Coefficient (MCC), where the proposed method consistently achieves the highest scores across all cell classes, resulting in the best average MCC (0.90) compared with YOLO26m (0.78) and YOLO11m (0.79). This highlights its more reliable overall performance, particularly under class imbalance.

This behavior highlights the advantage of the proposed decoupled pipeline. Rather than jointly optimizing localization and classification, Cellpose first isolates individual cells independently of their semantic class, allowing the BYOL encoder to learn morphology-driven representations from accurately segmented instances. Consequently, the downstream classifier operates on compact cell-centered embeddings instead of full-image features, improving discrimination of morphologically similar and underrepresented cell types. These findings suggest that separating localization from representation learning is particularly beneficial in highly imbalanced blood smear datasets, where rare leukocyte populations are easily overshadowed by the predominance of erythrocytes.

Table 3. Performance comparison of YOLO11m (Y11m), YOLO26m (Y26m) and our approach in terms of precision, recall, F1 and Matthews Correlation Coefficient (MCC) measure per cell class.

Class	Images	Cells	Precision			Recall			F1			MCC		
			Y26m	Y11m	Our	Y26m	Y11m	Our	Y26m	Y11m	Our	Y26m	Y11m	Our
RBC	500	60456	0.97	0.99	0.99	0.99	0.99	1.00	0.98	0.99	0.99	0.74	0.83	0.90
Heterophils	285	471	0.80	0.88	0.85	0.82	0.78	0.96	0.81	0.83	0.90	0.80	0.83	0.90
Monocytes	101	119	0.90	0.71	0.90	0.75	0.92	0.95	0.82	0.80	0.92	0.77	0.73	0.90
Lymphocytes	231	345	0.78	0.82	0.84	0.83	0.76	0.96	0.81	0.79	0.90	0.73	0.72	0.88
Thrombocytes	459	2165	0.86	0.92	0.88	0.94	0.89	0.99	0.90	0.90	0.93	0.88	0.86	0.94
		Avg.	0.86	0.86	0.89	0.87	0.87	0.97	0.86	0.86	0.93	0.78	0.79	0.90

7 Qualitative Analysis

As discussed in the previous section, models from the YOLO family tend to struggle with rare cell types, particularly when visual patterns are ambiguous or when training samples are limited. Figure 8 illustrates such a case. Both YOLO and the proposed approach identify heterophils in the central region of the image; however, the quality of the detections differs substantially. YOLO produces several bounding boxes classified as heterophils, many of which correspond to false positives (red boxes), while simultaneously exhibiting false negatives by missing

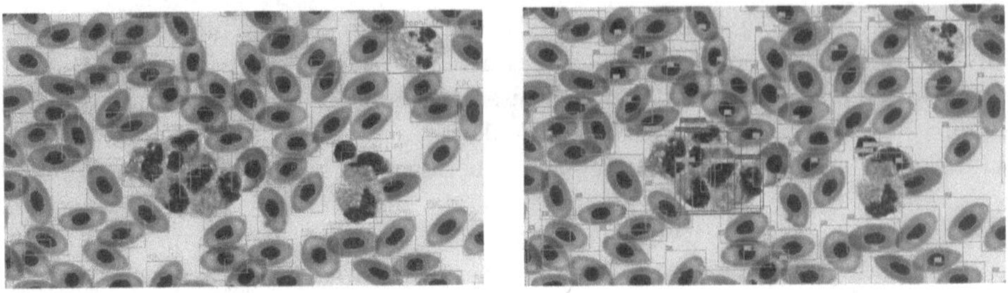

(a) Proposed approach (b) YOLO detection

Fig. 8. Detection of heterophils in a challenging image. The proposed approach produces fewer false positives and avoids ambiguous detections near the image boundaries compared to YOLO. Green boxes indicate TP, red boxes indicate FP and orange boxes indicate FN (example 1). (Color figure online)

several true heterophil instances (blue boxes). The green boxes correspond to correct, true positive predictions.

Similar behavior can be observed in Fig. 9. In this example, YOLO confuses thrombocytes and lymphocytes, incorrectly labeling a thrombocyte as a lymphocyte, while failing to detect the actual lymphocyte present in the image. Additionally, several RBC detections appear along the image borders where only partial cell structures are visible. At the same time, a partial cell that exhibits RBC morphological characteristics at the bottom is not detected.

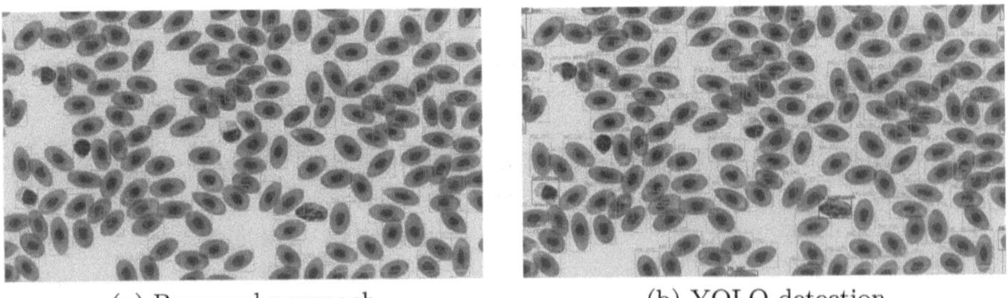

(a) Proposed approach (b) YOLO detection

Fig. 9. Misclassification between thrombocyte and lymphocyte by YOLO. The proposed approach demonstrates improved robustness and more reliable identification based on morphological details. Green boxes indicate TP, red boxes indicate FP and blue boxes indicate FN (example 2). (Color figure online)

The detection of partial cells near the image boundaries is a recurring issue for YOLO that is also evident in 8. YOLO frequently assigns RBC labels to truncated structures appearing at the edges of the image, even when only a small fragment of the cell is visible and its identity cannot be reliably determined. These detections increase the number of spurious predictions and reduce the overall reliability of the model. In contrast, the proposed approach produces fewer spurious detections and demonstrates improved consistency in identifying cell types, particularly in visually challenging regions. These observations suggest that our method places greater emphasis on fine morphological details, allowing it to better handle ambiguous cases, rare classes, and partially visible cells.

7.1 Latent Space Visualization and Clustering of Cell Morphology

UMAP [25] projection of the 2048-dimensional latent space learned with BYOL in two dimensions confirms that the ResNet backbone encodes complex morphological features without manual labels. HDBSCAN [24] successfully identified distinct clusters (Fig. 10) that align with genuine phenotypic similarities. The labels for each cluster were obtained by manual visual examination of a small representative sample of the cells of the cluster by an expert veterinary scientist.

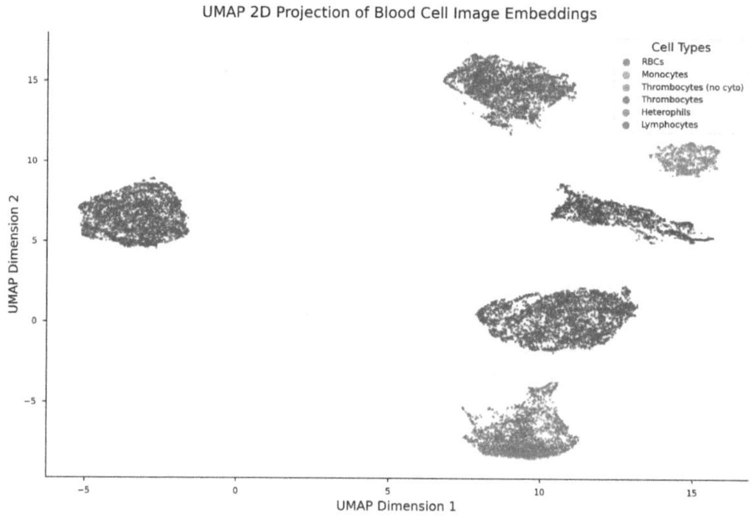

Fig. 10. UMAP projection of the representation space learned with BYOL. Clusters obtained by applying HDBSCAN reveal phenotypic structure.

Crucially, the model distinguished between thrombocyte sub-populations based on the presence (red) or absence (green) of cytoplasm. This finding is significant as it demonstrates that the self-supervised embeddings capture fine-grained biological nuances–not just broad categories-proving the framework's high sensitivity to clinically relevant cellular structures.

8 Deployment and Future Extensions

While the proposed framework demonstrates strong performance as a benchmark for avian hematology analysis, its translation to routine laboratory deployment and extension to related microscopy applications requires careful consideration of system integration, computational efficiency, and domain adaptation.

For deployment in resource-constrained environments, the pipeline can be further optimized through model compression strategies such as quantization [35] or knowledge distillation into lightweight architectures like MobileNetV3 [31]. In addition, practical adoption in laboratory workflows may be facilitated through integration with established bioimage analysis platforms, such as ImageJ/Fiji[4] or Napari[5], via plugin-based interfaces and modular APIs that enable seamless execution of segmentation and downstream analytical components.

Furthermore, the modular nature of the self-supervised representation learning framework supports transferability across related species and microscopy tasks. The fine-tuned encoder can be reused as a general-purpose feature extractor and adapted via lightweight fine-tuning to other vertebrate hematology domains, including reptilian, amphibian, and piscine blood analysis, which share structurally similar nucleated cell morphologies. Moreover, the learned embedding space may be extended to downstream diagnostic applications, such as intracellular parasite detection (e.g., avian malaria), by replacing the classification head and fine-tuning on limited annotated datasets, thereby reducing the dependency on large-scale manual annotations.

9 Conclusions and Future Work

In this study, we proposed a cell-level analysis pipeline for avian blood smear images that combines precise segmentation, self-supervised representation learning, and downstream cell-type classification. By operating at the level of individual cells, our approach effectively captures fine-grained morphological features that are often lost in conventional object detection frameworks. Experimental results demonstrate that the proposed method consistently surpasses traditional object detection models in both detection accuracy and classification performance, particularly for underrepresented cell types such as lymphocytes and monocytes.

Beyond improved accuracy, our framework offers additional advantages, including robustness to variations in staining, illumination, and cell density, as well as reduced reliance on large amounts of labeled data thanks to the self-supervised learning component. These properties make it a practical and scalable solution for automated avian hematology analysis.

Looking forward, several avenues could further enhance the proposed approach. First, extending the pipeline to multi-species datasets could validate its generalizability across different avian taxa. Second, integrating advanced augmentation strategies or contrastive learning techniques may further strengthen the robustness of the learned representations. Third, leveraging temporal or sequential blood smear data could enable dynamic monitoring of hematological changes over time. Finally, combining the cell-level analysis with interpretable

[4] https://imagej.net/.
[5] https://napari.org/.

visualization techniques could assist experts in understanding model decisions, fostering trust and adoption in real-world clinical and ecological settings.

Acknowledgments. The authors have no acknowledgments.

Disclosure of Interests. The authors declare no competing interests.

Generative AI Disclosure. The authors used the AI tools ChatGPT (OpenAI), Gemini (Google), Claude (Anthropic) solely to improve language, grammar, and readability of the text. No content, ideas, or scientific knowledge was generated or added by the AI. The authors take full responsibility for the accuracy, originality, and integrity of the submitted manuscript.

References

1. Acevedo, A., Merino, A., Alférez, S., Molina, Á., Boldú, L., Rodellar, J.: A dataset of microscopic peripheral blood cell images for development of automatic recognition systems. Data Brief **30**, 105474 (2020)
2. Autaiem, T., Auethavekiat, S., Sa-ing, V., Nakgoi, K., Prasertsincharoen, N., Arreesnsom, P.: A novel iterative method for automatic avian red blood cell counting. In: 2019 12th Biomedical Engineering International Conference (BMEiCON), pp. 1–5. IEEE (2019)
3. Buktash, A., Görür, A.K.: Self-supervised learning with byol for non-alcoholic fatty liver disease diagnosis using ultrasound imaging. Signal Image Video Process. **19**(15), 1–10 (2025)
4. Capitelli, R., Crosta, L.: Overview of psittacine blood analysis and comparative retrospective study of clinical diagnosis, hematology and blood chemistry in selected psittacine species. Vet. Clin.: Exotic Anim. Pract. **16**(1), 71–120 (2013)
5. Centofanti, C., Lozzi, D., Cococcetta, C., Marotta, A.: An efficient edge-based system for nucleated oval-shaped red blood cell counting. IEEE Access **12**, 195629–195641 (2024)
6. Cotter, P.F.: An examination of the utility of heterophil-lymphocyte ratios in assessing stress of caged hens. Poult. Sci. **94**(3), 512–517 (2015)
7. Dein, F.J., Wilson, A., Fischer, D., Langenberg, P.: Avian leucocyte counting using the hemocytometer. J. Zoo Wildl. Med. **25**(3), 432–437 (1994)
8. Deng, J., Dong, W., Socher, R., Li, L.J., Li, K., Fei-Fei, L.: ImageNet: a large-scale hierarchical image database. In: 2009 IEEE Conference on Computer Vision and Pattern Recognition (CVPR), pp. 248–255. IEEE (2009). https://doi.org/10.1109/CVPR.2009.5206848
9. Flatland, B., Freeman, K.P., Vap, L.M., Harr, K.E.: ASVCP guidelines: quality assurance for point-of-care testing in veterinary medicine. Vet. Clin. Pathol. **42**(4), 405–423 (2013)
10. Gan, L., Li, X., Wang, X.: A curated and re-annotated peripheral blood cell dataset integrating four public resources. Sci. Data **12**(1), 1694 (2025)
11. Govind, D., Lutnick, B., Tomaszewski, J.E., Sarder, P.: Automated erythrocyte detection and classification from whole slide images. J. Med. Imaging **5**(2), 027501 (2018)

12. Grill, J.B., et al.: Bootstrap your own latent: a new approach to self-supervised learning. Adv. Neural. Inf. Process. Syst. **33**, 21271–21284 (2020)
13. Im, O., Kim, S.R., Na, K.J., Min, K.D., Jeong, D.H.: Reference intervals for hematology and biochemistry in juvenile eastern spot-billed ducks (Anas zonorhyncha) and validation of an automated hematology analyzer for avian blood analysis. PLoS ONE **20**(10), e0334942 (2025)
14. Jones, M.P.: Avian hematology. Vet. Clin. North Am. Exot. Anim. Pract. **18**(1), 51–61 (2015). https://doi.org/10.1016/j.cvex.2014.09.012. pMID: 25421026
15. Jones, M.P.: Avian hematology. Clin. Lab. Med. **35**(3), 649–659 (2015). https://doi.org/10.1016/j.cll.2015.05.013. pMID: 26297411
16. Khan, S., Sajjad, M., Hussain, T., Ullah, A., Imran, A.S.: A review on traditional machine learning and deep learning models for WBCs classification in blood smear images. IEEE Access **9**, 10657–10673 (2020)
17. Khanam, R., Hussain, M.: YOLOv11: an overview of the key architectural enhancements. arXiv preprint arXiv:2410.17725 (2024)
18. Kittichai, V., et al.: Classification for avian malaria parasite Plasmodium gallinaceum blood stages by using deep convolutional neural networks. Sci. Rep. **11**(1), 16919 (2021)
19. Koonce, B.: EfficientNet. In: Convolutional neural networks with swift for Tensorflow: image recognition and dataset categorization, pp. 109–123. Springer (2021)
20. Koonce, B.: Resnet 50. In: Convolutional Neural Networks with Swift for Tensorflow: Image Recognition and Dataset Categorization, pp. 63–72. Springer (2021)
21. Koutsianos, D., et al.: Evaluation of hematological variables in layer pullets after vaccination and challenge with E. coli. Comp. Clin. Pathol. **30**(2), 113–118 (2021)
22. Latimer, K.S., Tang, K.N., Goodwin, M.A., Steffens, W.L., Brown, J.: Leukocyte changes associated with acute inflammation in chickens. Avian Dis. **32**(4), 760–772 (1988)
23. Li, G., Togo, R., Ogawa, T., Haseyama, M.: Tribyol: Triplet byol for self-supervised representation learning. In: ICASSP 2022-2022 IEEE International Conference on Acoustics, Speech and Signal Processing (ICASSP), pp. 3458–3462. IEEE (2022)
24. McInnes, L., Healy, J., Astels, S.: hdbscan: Hierarchical density based clustering. J. Open Sour. Softw. **2**(11), 205 (2017). https://doi.org/10.21105/joss.00205
25. McInnes, L., Healy, J., Melville, J.: UMAP: Uniform manifold approximation and projection for dimension reduction. arXiv preprint arXiv:1802.03426 (2018)
26. Meechart, K., Auethavekiat, S., Saing, V.: An automatic detection for avian blood cell based on adaptive thresholding algorithm. In: 2019 12th Biomedical Engineering International Conference (BMEiCON), pp. 1–4. IEEE (2019)
27. Nabity, M.B., Harr, K.E., Camus, M.S., Flatland, B., Vap, L.M.: ASVCP guidelines: allowable total error hematology. Vet. Clin. Pathol. **47**(1), 9–21 (2018)
28. Natt, M.P., Herrick, C.A.: A new blood diluent for counting the erythrocytes and leucocytes of the chicken. Poult. Sci. **31**(4), 735–738 (1952)
29. Pachitariu, M., Rariden, M., Stringer, C.: Cellpose-SAM: superhuman generalization for cellular segmentation. bioRxiv (2025). https://doi.org/10.1101/2025.04.28.651001
30. Prud'homme, Y., et al.: Comparison of 3 leukogram determination methods in avian species: Phloxine B stain, blood smear, and an automated analyzer. J. Avian Med. Surg. **39**(2), 88–95 (2025)
31. Qian, S., Ning, C., Hu, Y.: MobileNetv3 for image classification. In: 2021 IEEE 2nd International Conference on Big Data, Artificial Intelligence and Internet of Things Engineering (ICBAIE), pp. 490–497. IEEE (2021)

32. Richemond, P.H., et al.: Byol works even without batch statistics. arXiv preprint arXiv:2010.10241 (2020)
33. Riond, B., Weissenbacher, S., Hofmann-Lehmann, R., Lutz, H.: Performance evaluation of the Sysmex pocH-100iV Diff hematology analyzer for analysis of canine, feline, equine, and bovine blood. Vet. Clin. Pathol. **40**(4), 484–495 (2011)
34. Roboflow: BCCD Dataset (Blood Cell Count and Detection) (2022). https://universe.roboflow.com/joseph-nelson/bccd. Accessed 6 Feb 2026
35. Rokh, B., Azarpeyvand, A., Khanteymoori, A.: A comprehensive survey on model quantization for deep neural networks in image classification. ACM Trans. Intell. Syst. Technol. **14**(6), 1–50 (2023)
36. Sapkota, R., Cheppally, R.H., Sharda, A., Karkee, M.: YOLO26: key architectural enhancements and performance benchmarking for real-time object detection. arXiv preprint arXiv:2509.25164 (2025)
37. Sapkota, R., Karkee, M.: Ultralytics yolo evolution: an overview of YOLO26, YOLO11, YOLOv8 and YOLOv5 object detectors for computer vision and pattern recognition. arXiv preprint arXiv:2510.09653 (2025). https://doi.org/10.48550/arXiv.2510.09653
38. Stringer, C., Wang, T., Michaelos, M., Pachitariu, M.: Cellpose: a generalist algorithm for cellular segmentation. Nat. Methods **18**(1), 100–106 (2021)
39. Vaz, F.F., Locatelli-Dittrich, R., Beltrame, O.C., Sipinski, E.A.B., Abbud, M.C., Sezerban, R.M.: Hematologic and biochemical reference intervals of free-living red-tailed Amazon parrot (Amazona brasiliensis) nestlings on Rasa Island, Paraná, Brazil. Vet. Clin. Pathol. **45**(4), 615–622 (2016)
40. Vogelbacher, M., et al.: Identifying and counting avian blood cells in whole slide images via deep learning. Birds **5**(1), 48–66 (2024). https://doi.org/10.3390/birds5010004
41. Wakenell, P.S.: Hematology of chickens and turkeys. Schalm's Vet. Hematol. **1**(1), 958–967 (2010)
42. Wang, J.: Deep learning in hematology: from molecules to patients. Clin. Hematol. Int. **6**(4), 19 (2024)
43. Woo, S., et al.: ConvNext v2: co-designing and scaling convnets with masked autoencoders. In: Proceedings of the IEEE/CVF Conference on Computer Vision and Pattern Recognition, pp. 16133–16142 (2023)

Self-supervised Rotation-Invariant Representations for Unsupervised Motif Discovery in Molecular Dynamics

Vsevolod Morozov[1,2](✉), Emilie Devijver[1], Charlotte Laclau[3], Paul Krzakala[3], and Noel Jakse[2]

[1] Université Grenoble Alpes, CNRS, Grenoble INP, LIG, Grenoble, France
{vsevolod.morozov,emilie.devijver}@univ-grenoble-alpes.fr
[2] Université Grenoble Alpes, CNRS, Grenoble INP, SIMaP, Grenoble, France
noel.jakse@grenoble-inp.fr
[3] LTCI, Télécom Paris, Institut Polytechnique de Paris, Palaiseau, France
{charlotte.laclau,paul.krzakala}@telecom-paris.fr

Abstract. Identifying local structures in 3D point clouds remains challenging for unsupervised methods, particularly in scientific settings such as molecular dynamics simulations of crystallization, where meaningful motifs correspond to subtle geometric arrangements of atoms. While recent advances in point-cloud representation learning focus primarily on object-level shape understanding, they are less suited to capturing fine-grained local geometric patterns under rotational symmetry. We propose a self-supervised framework for learning rotation-aware representations of atomic neighborhoods and clustering them into local structural motifs. Our method combines a rotation-equivariant encoder with a VICReg objective and a spatially consistent view construction that encourages smooth representations across overlapping neighborhoods. On both synthetic benchmarks and large-scale molecular dynamics simulations, the learned embeddings organize local environments into coherent and interpretable clusters that reveal spatially structured transitions between disordered and ordered atomic configurations. These results demonstrate the potential of self-supervised geometric learning for uncovering physically meaningful structure in large scientific point clouds.

Keywords: Point clouds · Self-supervised learning · Atomic structure

1 Introduction

Understanding local geometric structure in 3D point clouds is central to many problems, including fine-grained part segmentation [18], scene analysis [24], and atomic structure identification [21]. While recent advances have addressed object-level recognition, semantic segmentation, or shape reconstruction, the fully unsupervised discovery of multiple local structural motifs within a single point cloud remains largely unexplored [3,4,12]. This gap is particularly striking in atomic-scale and discrete-particle simulations, where the combinatorial

M. Ceci et al. (Eds.): ECML PKDD 2026, LNAI 16948, pp. 636–652, 2027.
https://doi.org/10.1007/978-3-032-37679-4_36

diversity of local atomic structures and the complexity of atomic neighborhoods challenge traditional approaches. Automatically identifying these motifs is crucial for exploring structure-property relationships in systems like high-entropy alloys or metallic glasses, where traditional descriptors fail.

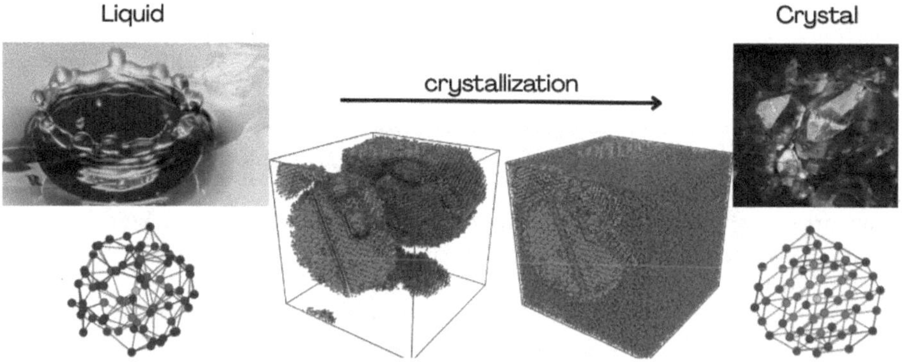

Fig. 1. Homogeneous crystal nucleation in aluminium: early stages of the phase transition from liquid to crystalline states. (Left) Typical local atomic structure of the liquid, characterized by disordered atomic arrangements. (Middle) The snapshots illustrate the emergence of nuclei formed by perfect and defective crystalline local structural motifs during the homogeneous nucleation process. The structural identification captures well-defined crystalline nuclei within the liquid (red atoms), including their defects, orientations, and morphologies. (Right) Local structure in a perfect crystalline arrangement. This transition highlights the complexity of the phenomenon, motivating the need for robust unsupervised geometric analysis in molecular dynamics.

The challenge goes beyond mere identification: in molecular dynamics simulations, classifying the structure of the complete simulation box is not sufficient for capturing phase transformations, *e.g.* crystal nucleation. The objective is rather to cluster local atomic environments into motifs ranging from perfectly ordered, crystal-like configurations to disordered, liquid-like arrangements (see Fig. 1), with the latter largely unknown *a priori*. In this way, subtle changes in local structures in transient configurations can be monitored, revealing critical information about the mechanisms that drive phase transformations such as nucleation or glass formation. Capturing these nuances thus demands representations that not only respect geometric symmetries (e.g., SO(3) equivariance) but also vary smoothly with local deformations, a requirement that existing methods struggle to meet in an unsupervised setting.

Learning such representations raises two main challenges. First, atomic neighborhoods are defined up to arbitrary global rotations, so representations must handle SO(3) symmetry appropriately. Standard invariant pipelines, by construction, discard orientation information early in the processing chain, potentially erasing geometrically meaningful information that is critical for distinguishing subtle structural variants. By contrast, equivariant architectures preserve structured features that transform predictably under rotation. Although this simplification may suffice for tasks such as object classification, it is not enough to analyze local atomic environments, where relative orientation often encodes physically relevant information. Enforcing equivariance aligns with the data's symmetry and preserves meaningful directional information during training. Here, a rotation-equivariant Vector Neurons (VN) encoder is used to capture these nuances, deriving invariant embeddings from its equivariant features for clustering to retain structure. Second, the problem is intrinsically local but also highly overlapping and spatially continuous: each atom's neighborhood yields a dense collection of sub-clouds sharing many points. Since crystallization develops spatially, nearby neighborhoods correspond to gradually evolving local structures, and their embeddings should reflect this continuity. Most self-supervised frameworks treat these neighborhoods as independent samples, ignoring their spatial relationships and the gradual evolution of local structures, despite the fact that, in reality, nearby atoms often belong to the same evolving structural motif. This oversight produces embeddings that are either overly rigid (failing to capture smooth evolution) or unstable (collapsing to degenerate solutions). To address this, we adapt a self-supervised strategy from VICReg to an equivariant framework, processing two spatial sub-samplings of each neighborhood through a shared equivariant encoder. Invariant embeddings, derived from these features, are clustered with K-Means without introducing any clustering-specific objective. The result is a latent space where local atomic environments form spatially smooth clusters, faithfully reflecting physical continuity.

The resulting pipeline provides a fully learned, unsupervised alternative to the hand-crafted, descriptor-based pipelines traditionally used for motif discovery in atomistic point clouds [2,3,14,22]. For example, in simulations of aluminium crystallization, our embeddings reveal a smooth transition from liquid-like to FCC-like environments, with intermediate states corresponding to pre-nucleation clusters that are invisible to traditional descriptors (see Sect. 5). This continuity is critical for understanding mechanisms like homogeneous nucleation or polymorphic phase competition. Our main contributions are: (i) formulating local motif discovery in atomistic point clouds as a fully unsupervised representation learning problem under global SO(3) symmetry with overlapping neighborhoods; (ii) combining a rotation-equivariant VN encoder [7] with a spatially-aware view sampling strategy within the VICReg framework [1], yielding stable invariant embeddings that are both discriminative and spatially smooth without relying on clustering-specific losses; (iii) demonstrating that simple K-Means clustering of the learned embeddings captures ordered, disordered, and intermediate local structures and reveals spatial transition patterns during crystallization; (iv) introducing a synthetic polycrystal benchmark dataset to evaluate local geometric sensitivity in label-scarce settings.

2 Related Work

Our work lies at the intersection of self-supervised learning for 3D point clouds, SO(3)-equivariant representation learning, and unsupervised analysis of local atomic environments.

Self-supervised Learning for 3D Point Clouds. Self-supervised learning (SSL) has become a standard paradigm for learning representations without manual annotations. In computer vision, contrastive methods such as SimCLR [6] learn invariances by maximizing agreement between augmented views, while non-contrastive objectives such as Barlow Twins [30] and VICReg [1] combine view consistency with redundancy reduction and variance preservation. For 3D point clouds, PointContrast [28] applies contrastive pre-training to large-scale 3D scenes, while Point-BERT [29], Point-MAE [16], PointM2AE [32], and PointGPT [5] adapt masked modeling or autoregressive pre-training to point sets. More recently, rotation-robust variants such as RI-MAE [23] incorporate rotational invariance into self-supervised point cloud learning. These approaches primarily focus on object-level representation learning for supervised tasks. In contrast, our goal is to directly organize local neighborhoods into clusterable embeddings.

SO(3)-Equivariant Architectures for Geometric Learning. Rotational symmetry is central to 3D learning, inspiring extensive work on equivariant neural networks. Tensor Field Networks [25], SE(3)-Transformers [9], and related architectures enforce consistent feature transformation under rigid motions. Vector Neurons (VN) [7] offer a lightweight, practical alternative for point clouds by using 3D vector features. Equivariance has also been paired with self-supervision, as in ConDor [20], which learns canonical poses for shapes. While effective when a stable reference frame exists, these methods can struggle with highly symmetric or locally isotropic neighborhoods, common in atomistic data.

Local Representation Learning in Atomistic Systems. In atomistic simulations, local structure has traditionally been characterized using hand-crafted descriptors such as Steinhardt bond-order parameters [22], averaged bond-order parameters [14], and SOAP-like representations [2]. While highly successful for materials analysis, these descriptors require a priori choices about which geometric features to encode. However, more recent work explores the unsupervised discovery of local atomic environments directly from simulation data. Existing approaches combine structural descriptors with clustering or manifold learning techniques to identify representative local environments and defects [3,4,12,19,31]. Other work investigates large-scale pre-training of geometric graph networks to learn transferable atomistic representations, primarily for transfer or zero-shot analysis rather than clustering of local motifs [17].

Position of Our Work. These works highlight the promise of unsupervised atomistic representation learning, but most existing pipelines still rely on fixed descriptors, either hand-crafted structural descriptors, topological summaries, or features inherited from atomistic potentials, followed by clustering or manifold analysis. In contrast, our approach learns the representation directly from raw local coordinates using self-supervision while explicitly respecting global SO(3) symmetry through an equivariant encoder. Furthermore, unlike most prior SSL methods for point clouds, our setting involves dense collections of strongly overlapping neighborhoods extracted from the same atomic configuration. Nearby samples should therefore remain geometrically and spatially consistent in the latent space. This combination of equivariant self-supervision, overlapping local neighborhoods, and clustering-oriented representation learning defines the regime we target in this work.

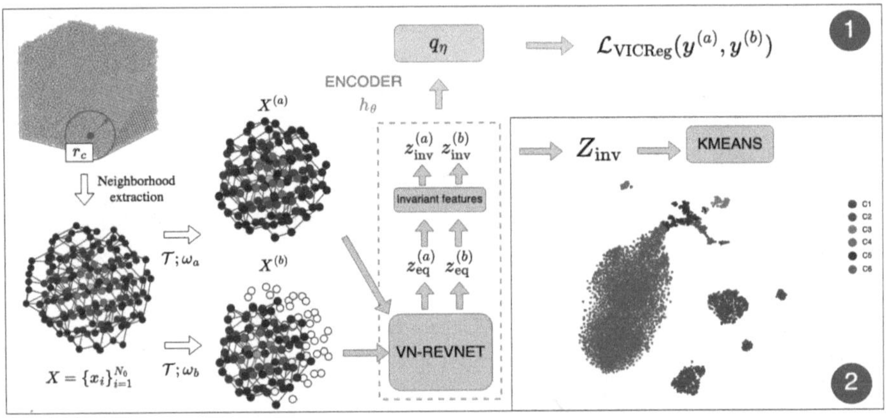

Fig. 2. Overview of the self-supervised learning pipeline for motif discovery in molecular dynamics. (1) Self-supervised training: A neighborhood X of N_0 atoms is extracted from the simulation box and augmented into two views, $X^{(a)}$ and $X^{(b)}$, using transformations $\mathcal{T}$. The VN-RevNet encoder processes these views to produce equivariant z_{eq} and invariant z_{inv} embeddings. The VICReg loss $\mathcal{L}_{\text{VICReg}}$ is applied to the projected embeddings $y^{(a)}$ and $y^{(b)}$ to learn robust representations. (2) Clustering: The invariant embeddings Z_{inv} are clustered using K-Means, revealing distinct structural motifs in the data. The resulting clusters are visualized using t-SNE, demonstrating the method's ability to capture local geometric patterns without supervision.

3 Proposed Method

We present a self-supervised framework for learning rotation-invariant representations of atomic neighborhoods. An equivariant encoder produces invariant embeddings trained with VICReg on augmented views, after which clustering reveals local motifs. Figure 2 illustrates the overall pipeline.

3.1 Problem Statement and Neighborhood Construction

Setup. Given an atomic configuration represented as a point cloud, we aim to discover recurring local geometric motifs without supervision. Rather than operating on entire configurations, our approach focuses on local atomic neighborhoods, which capture the structural environments around individual atoms.

Formally, let $X = \{x_i \in \mathbb{R}^3\}_{i=1}^{N_0}$ denote a local neighborhood extracted from a configuration. Our goal is to learn two complementary representations: (i) a rotation-equivariant latent z_{eq} that transforms predictably under rotations, and (ii) a rotation-invariant embedding z_{inv} suitable for clustering.

We therefore learn an encoder h_θ, parameterized by θ

$$(z_{\text{inv}}, z_{\text{eq}}) = h_\theta(X), \quad \text{s.t.} \quad z_{\text{eq}}(RX) = R\, z_{\text{eq}}(X), \quad z_{\text{inv}}(RX) = z_{\text{inv}}(X)$$

for any rotation $R \in \mathrm{SO}(3)$. Enforcing equivariance in z_{eq} acts as a geometric inductive bias that preserves directional information during representation learning [26], rather than collapsing it prematurely into rotation-invariant scalars. The invariant embedding z_{inv} is subsequently derived from z_{eq} through invariant operations described in Sect. 3.2.

Atomic Neighborhood Construction. For each atom, we collect all atoms within a cutoff radius r_c. If more than N_0 atoms fall within this radius, we retain the N_0 closest ones. This defines a point cloud $X = \{x_i \in \mathbb{R}^3\}_{i=1}^{N_0}$. Each neighborhood is centered on its central atom, and coordinates are normalized by r_c, keeping magnitudes typically below one. This procedure yields a dense set of overlapping neighborhoods across the configuration.

3.2 Equivariant Encoder and Invariant Embeddings

To capture the geometric structure of atomic neighborhoods while respecting rotational symmetry, we employ a rotation-equivariant neural encoder based on Vector Neurons (VN) [7]. VN networks represent intermediate features as 3D vectors and ensure that these features transform consistently under rotations of the input. Given a neighborhood X, the encoder produces a set of equivariant vector features $z_{\text{eq}} = f_\theta(X)$, where each feature channel corresponds to a vector in $\mathbb{R}^3$. Depending on the backbone configuration, these features can be either global, $z_{\text{eq}} \in \mathbb{R}^{B \times C \times 3}$, or per-point, $z_{\text{eq}} \in \mathbb{R}^{B \times N_{\text{model}} \times C \times 3}$, where B denotes the batch size, C the number of feature channels, and N_{model} the number of points provided to the encoder for each neighborhood.

Invariant Feature Construction. To obtain rotation-invariant descriptors suitable for clustering, we derive an invariant embedding from the equivariant features. Let $z_{\text{eq}} = (v_1, \ldots, v_C)$ with $v_i \in \mathbb{R}^3$ denote the vector channels produced by the equivariant encoder. We construct scalar invariants from these vectors using rotation-invariant operations. First, we compute channel-wise norms $n(v_i) = \|v_i\|_2$, which are unchanged under global rotations. Optionally, additional geometric information can be captured through pairwise dot products $d(v_i, v_j) = \langle v_i, v_j \rangle$. The resulting scalars are concatenated into a feature vector

$$g = [\, n(v_1), \ldots, n(v_C),\ d(v_{i_1}, v_{j_1}), \ldots],$$

which is then normalized to produce the invariant embedding $z_{\text{inv}} = \mathrm{Norm}(g)$.

3.3 Self-supervised Training

The encoder is trained in a self-supervised manner using the VICReg objective [1]. Given an input neighborhood X, we generate two views

$$X^{(a)} = \mathcal{T}(X; \omega_a), \qquad X^{(b)} = \mathcal{T}(X; \omega_b),$$

where $\mathcal{T}$ denotes a stochastic view generator and ω_a, ω_b are independent random draws. The two views are processed by a shared encoder h_θ to obtain invariant embeddings, i.e., $z_{\text{inv}}^{(a)} = h_\theta(X^{(a)})$ and $z_{\text{inv}}^{(b)} = h_\theta(X^{(b)})$. During training, the embeddings are further mapped by a projection head q_η, such that $y^{(a)} = q_\eta(z_{\text{inv}}^{(a)})$ and $y^{(b)} = q_\eta(z_{\text{inv}}^{(b)})$.

The VICReg objective combines three complementary terms that enforce view consistency, prevent dimensional collapse, and reduce redundancy across feature dimensions:

$$\mathcal{L}_{\text{VICReg}} = \lambda_{\text{inv}}\mathcal{L}_{\text{inv}} + \lambda_{\text{var}}\mathcal{L}_{\text{var}} + \lambda_{\text{cov}}\mathcal{L}_{\text{cov}}.$$

$\mathcal{L}_{\text{inv}}$ encourages agreement between embeddings of the two views, while $\mathcal{L}_{\text{var}}$ and $\mathcal{L}_{\text{cov}}$ ensure sufficient feature variance across the batch and reduce correlations between embedding dimensions.

View Construction. The view operator $\mathcal{T}$ generates views of a neighborhood through spatial resampling. Starting from a neighborhood centered on an atom c, we randomly choose to keep the original center or to shift the center to one of its neighboring atoms. Let c' denote the selected center. The new neighborhood is then defined by selecting the N_{model} atoms closest to c':

$$X' = \text{TopK}_{N_{\text{model}}}\left(\|x_i - c'\|\right), \quad x_i \in X.$$

In practice, we first sample N_{sample} points from the N_0 points of the neighborhood and then retain the N_{model} closest points after the potential center shift. For the main experiments, we use $N_{\text{sample}} = 128$ and $N_{\text{model}} = 80$. This neighbor-centered resampling produces pairs of views corresponding to slightly shifted local environments. Since neighboring atoms share many nearby points, the resulting views strongly overlap while exhibiting small geometric variations. As a consequence, nearby neighborhoods tend to produce nearby embeddings, promoting spatial smoothness in the learned representation.

In addition to center-shift resampling, we optionally apply small geometric perturbations (e.g., coordinate jitter or random point removal) that increase view diversity while preserving the identity of the local atomic motif.

3.4 Clustering Protocol

Clustering has been widely studied and many approaches have been developed for a variety of circumstances. We focus on the standard clustering algorithm K-Means, but other clustering algorithms can be used. For a fixed number of clusters k, the k-means algorithm takes a set of vectors as input, in our case the normalized invariant embeddings z_{inv}, and clusters them into k distinct groups based on a geometric criterion. This jointly learns a centroid matrix C and the cluster assignments $(c_n)_{n=1,\dots,N}$ of each local structure:

$$\min_{C} \frac{1}{N} \sum_{n=1}^{N} \min_{c_n \in \{0,1\}^k} \|z_{\text{inv}}^{(n)} - Cc_n\|_2^2 \text{ such that } c_n^T \mathbf{1}_k = 1.$$

When labels are available, we report ACC, NMI, and ARI on the resulting assignments; when no ground truth is available, we interpret the clusters as homogeneous groups.

4 Experiments on the Synthetic Polycrystal Benchmark

We compare our method to state-of-the-art methods on a novel synthetic polycrystal benchmark. The code and configuration files required to reproduce the benchmark dataset are included in the paper's linked code repository.

4.1 Synthetic Polycrystal Benchmark

Quantitative evaluation of motif discovery in molecular dynamics (MD) is hindered by the lack of ground-truth labels and the need to capture rotation-invariant local geometric cues, a task for which standard self-supervised learning (SSL) methods are ill-suited. Unlike object-level benchmarks, where classes differ by coarse topology, MD data consists of metrically similar point clouds distinguished solely by angular correlations in neighbor shells. To address this gap, we introduce a controlled polycrystal benchmark that isolates three key challenges:

(i) *Known ground-truth motifs*: a cubic simulation box is tessellated into $G = 16$ Voronoi grains, each randomly assigned one of four phases (three ordered, BCC/FCC/HCP, and one disordered, amorphous). All phases share a nearest-neighbor distance of 2.49 Å and iron-like densities.
(ii) *Decoupling motif identity from orientation*: crystalline grains are created by tiling unit cells with random rotations $R \sim \text{SO}(3)$, while the amorphous phase is refined to match realistic short-range order (coordination ≈ 11).
(iii) *Realistic disorder*: to replicate ambiguous neighborhoods near grain boundaries, we introduce thermal displacements (Debye model at $T = 325$ K, calibrated to iron); localized rotation bubbles (rigid micro-rotations of $\approx 12°$ in spheres of radius 7 Å); point vacancies (0.8% dropout + relaxation) and density bubbles (local atom depletion/concentration).

We sample local neighborhoods as point clouds using a grid with spacing $\Delta = 2r_{\text{cut}}(1 - K_{\text{overlap}})$, centering each neighborhood on an atom and normalizing coordinates by r_{cut}. After excluding centers near the box boundary to avoid edge artifacts, we retain the $N_0 = 128$ nearest atoms per center. Neighborhoods

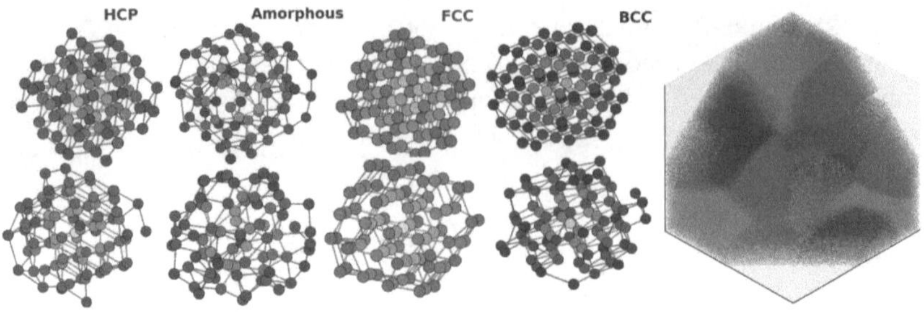

Fig. 3. Synthetic polycrystal benchmark. (Left) Representative 80-point local environments for the four classes: FCC (face-centered cubic), BCC (body-centered cubic), HCP (hexagonal close-packed), and amorphous, shown in distinct colors. For each class, the upper example is the pure structure and the lower example is a deformed version. (Right) Synthetic polycrystal simulation box colored by class (diagonal cut through the full box). (Color figure online)

are further filtered to include only those with atoms from a single grain, yielding a clean 4-class benchmark (BCC/FCC/HCP/amorphous) focused on motif identity.

With 50,653 neighborhoods, this benchmark reveals the limitations of existing SSL methods that rely on global pose cues, and it establishes a rigorous framework to evaluate local geometric sensitivity in label-scarce MD. It is illustrated in Fig. 3.

4.2 Implementation Details

We use a VN-RevNet encoder [15] to extract equivariant features from local neighborhoods. Invariant embeddings are obtained by taking the norms of the equivariant vector channels, producing representations of dimension $L = 240$. During self-supervised training, each sample generates two augmented views, including volume-preserving strain, occlusion, coordinate jitter, and neighbor-centered re-centering on one of the $k = 6$ nearest atoms. Each view contains $N_{\text{model}} = 80$ points. The model is trained with VICReg [1]. At inference time, the projector is discarded and clustering is performed on frozen invariant embeddings z_{inv} using K-Means with `K-Means++` initialization.

We compare against classical descriptors used as fixed representations and clustered by K-Means, namely Steinhardt, CNA, and SOAP. We also compare against self-supervised point-cloud baselines including PointGPT [5], Point-M2AE [32], PointContrast [28], and RI-MAE [23]. All learned baselines are reimplemented in a shared PyTorch Lightning training and evaluation pipeline and trained on the balanced synthetic polycrystalline benchmark using the same data split, normalization, model-selection criterion, and SO(3) robustness protocol. We retain the best run for each method after a targeted tuning pass. Because self-supervised pretraining losses are not directly comparable across methods, we report only clustering-quality metrics. Full baseline architecture, training, and tuning details are provided in the supplementary material.

Code Availability. The code for our method and experiments is available at https://github.com/maloq/md-motif-ssl.

Table 1. Unsupervised classification on the synthetic polycrystal benchmark. Clustering quality of classical physically motivated baselines, self-supervised point-cloud baselines, and our rotation-invariant embeddings. Clustering is performed with K-Means ($K = 4$) and Hungarian matching for ACC. Reported results correspond to means ±std computed on 5 runs. Canonical: default dataset orientation. SO(3)-randomized: each test shape is rotated by a random $R \sim SO(3)$.

	Canonical			SO(3)-randomized		
Method	ACC	NMI	ARI	ACC	NMI	ARI
Steinhardt (Q_ℓ)	0.89±.005	0.69±.009	0.73±.011	0.89±.005	0.69±.009	0.73±.010
CNA	0.68±.006	0.50±.008	0.43±.008	0.68±.006	0.50±.008	0.43±.008
SOAP	0.92±.004	0.77±.009	0.79±.007	0.92±.004	0.77±.009	0.79±.007
PointGPT [5]	0.35±.04	0.10±.04	0.09±.03	0.28±.04	0.08±.03	0.05±.02
Point-M2AE [32]	0.46±.03	0.25±.04	0.18±.03	0.47±.04	0.23±.04	0.17±.03
PointContrast [28]	0.85±.02	0.71±.06	0.69±.06	0.85±.02	0.71±.06	0.70±.06
RI-MAE [23]	0.80±.03	0.58±.05	0.34±.05	0.80±.03	0.58±.05	0.34±.05
Ours	**0.95±.03**	**0.84±.08**	**0.88±.08**	**0.95±.04**	**0.84±.09**	**0.88±.08**

4.3 Results on the Synthetic Polycrystal Benchmark

Table 1 reports clustering results on the synthetic polycrystal benchmark. Our method outperforms all baselines by a clear margin across all metrics (ACC/NMI/ARI), indicating that the representation learned by our approach is meaningful for the clustering task. While only RI-MAE is explicitly rotation-invariant, several other methods perform similarly in the canonical and SO(3)-randomized settings because training-time rotation augmentation already provides some robustness. However, an equivariant design is preferable in our context.

4.4 Ablation Study on the Synthetic Polycrystal Benchmark

We now present the ablation study over the encoder, the proposed views, the number of sampled points, the invariant embedding dimension, and the self-supervised loss.

Encoder. For the encoder, we compare VN-RevNet with competitive architectures, including PointNet [18] and DGCNN [27], along with their VN variants

Table 2. Encoder ablation on the synthetic polycrystal dataset. All encoders are trained with the same self-supervised protocol and evaluated by clustering frozen invariant embeddings with $K = 4$. Reported results correspond to means ±std computed on 5 runs.

Encoder	Canonical			SO(3)-randomized		
	ACC	NMI	ARI	ACC	NMI	ARI
PointNet	0.51±0.07	0.29±0.07	0.23±0.09	0.43±0.02	0.22±0.02	0.17±0.02
VN-PointNet	0.78±0.10	0.73±0.07	0.73±0.09	0.77±0.10	0.70±0.10	0.69±0.13
DGCNN	0.86±0.06	0.70±0.08	0.70±0.16	0.62±0.06	0.55±0.05	0.49±0.09
VN-DGCNN	0.93±0.02	0.79±0.04	0.81±0.05	0.92±0.02	0.79±0.04	0.81±0.04
VN-RevNet	**0.95±0.03**	**0.84±0.08**	**0.88±0.08**	**0.95±0.04**	**0.84±0.08**	**0.88±0.08**

(VN-PointNet and VN-DGCNN). The results are summarized in Table 2. As expected, PointNet and DGCNN are rotation-variant when operating directly on coordinates, leading to a clear performance drop under SO(3)-randomized evaluation. DGCNN remains competitive in the canonical setting thanks to EdgeConv capturing local geometric patterns, but without explicit rotation constraints, it does not generalize across arbitrary global rotations. Overall, VN architectures provide the most robust representations across both canonical and randomized poses, with VN-RevNet being the most effective.

Views. We study the role of view construction with a leave-one-out ablation (Fig. 4a). Removing the neighbor view causes the largest performance drop, highlighting its importance for learning consistent representations across overlapping neighborhoods. In contrast, removing strain or jitter has a more moderate effect.

Evolution with Respect to the Number of Points. We study how performance varies with the number of model input points N_{model}, ranging from 24 to 160. To preserve the neighborhood structure, we keep the ratio N_{model}/N_0 fixed at 0.625, scaling N_0 accordingly (Fig. 4b). Very small values of N_{model} provide insufficient geometric information, while performance improves steadily beyond $N_{\text{model}} = 80$. We therefore select $N_{\text{model}} = 80$ as a trade-off between performance and spatial resolution (Fig. 3).

The invariant dimension controls the number of scalar features extracted from the equivariant representation. Performance improves substantially from $L = 64$ to $L = 240$, after which it saturates or slightly decreases, suggesting that $L = 240$ offers a favorable trade-off between expressivity and redundancy. We also compare three self-supervised redundancy-reduction objectives. W-MSE performs substantially worse in our setting. This suggests that batch whitening may be too restrictive for dense collections of overlapping atomic neighborhoods, where correlated feature dimensions can still be useful for capturing local geometric motifs. Barlow Twins and VICReg produce more clusterable representations, with VICReg giving the best overall performance and being less sensitive to hyperparameter tuning in our experiments.

Experiment	ACC	NMI	ARI
Baseline (all active)	0.95±0.03	0.84±0.08	0.88±0.08
Neighbor both views	0.94±0.03	0.84±0.08	0.86±0.04
No neighbor view	0.90±0.04	0.82±0.06	0.81±0.06
No jitter	0.92±0.02	0.83±0.05	0.84±0.04
No strain	0.93±0.02	0.83±0.05	0.84±0.05

(a)

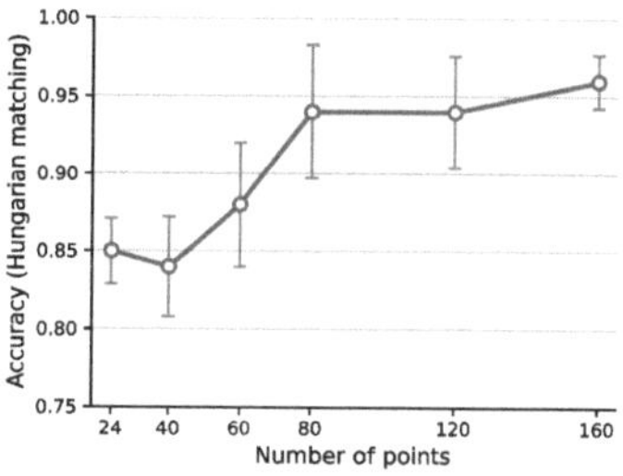

(b)

Fig. 4. Ablation of view construction and neighborhood size. (a) Leave-one-out ablation of the VICReg view augmentations (mean ±std computed on 5 runs). (b) Clustering accuracy as a function of the number of sampled points N_{model} used in the views.

5 Real Molecular Dynamics Experiments

Experimental Setup. Our method is applied to the homogeneous nucleation pathway of aluminium studied in a recent work [3], generated by large-scale molecular dynamics simulations with LAMMPS using an embedded atom model (EAM) potential. The simulation contains 10^6 atoms in a fully periodic box. A liquid configuration above the melting point is rapidly quenched below the melting point in the undercooled regime, and homogeneous nucleation is then

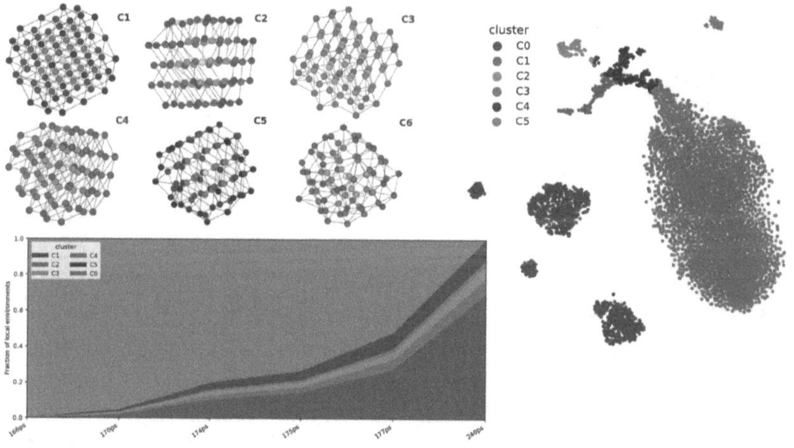

Fig. 5. Latent-space organization and temporal evolution of the discovered clusters during crystallization on the real MD dataset. *Top left*: representative neighborhoods for the six discovered clusters, selected as samples nearest to the cluster centers in the learned embedding space. *Right*: t-SNE projection of the invariant embeddings z_{inv}, colored by K-Means cluster assignment. *Bottom left*: fraction of neighborhoods assigned to each cluster over time.

Table 3. Ablation of invariant embedding dimension and self-supervised objective. All variants are evaluated on the synthetic polycrystal benchmark by K-Means clustering of frozen invariant embeddings with $K = 4$.

Variant	ACC	NMI	ARI
Invariant embedding dimension L			
64	0.81	0.55	0.57
160	0.91	0.80	0.76
240	**0.95**	**0.84**	**0.88**
320	0.94	0.83	0.84
728	0.93	0.82	0.84
Self-supervised objective			
W-MSE [8]	0.71	0.40	0.39
Barlow Twins [30]	0.90	0.80	0.81
VICReg [1]	**0.95**	**0.84**	**0.88**

monitored at $T = 650$ K near the nose of the time-temperature-transformation curve [3, 11]. The selected simulation output consists solely of atomic coordinates at six time points: 166, 170, 174, 175, 177, and 240 ps, spanning the transition from a supercooled liquid to a fully crystallized polycrystal. Additional details are provided in the supplementary material.

Local neighborhoods are extracted with cutoff radius $r_{\text{cut}} = 7.2$ Å using grid-based sampling with overlap parameter $K_{\text{overlap}} = 0.1$. Central atoms are chosen near the nodes of a cubic grid with spacing $\Delta = 2r_{\text{cut}}(1 - K_{\text{overlap}})$. For each selected center, atoms within r_{cut} are collected and truncated to $N_0 = 128$ points; during training, each view further subsamples $N_{\text{model}} = 80$ points. Across the six snapshots, this procedure yields 1,738,803 local neighborhoods. Thus, the real-MD experiment evaluates the method in a large-scale unlabeled regime where local structures are sampled densely across liquid, interfacial, defective, and crystalline regions.

Latent Space and Unsupervised Clustering. Clustering of the real MD neighborhoods is performed with K-Means using $K = 6$ to obtain a sufficient diversity of local structures involved in the formation of crystalline nuclei. The K-Means model is fitted on local structures sampled from all six simulation boxes mentioned above, reflecting the expectation that the trajectory contains not only liquid-like and crystal-like environments but also intermediate structures associated with nucleation fronts and defects. Importantly, clustering is performed purely in the learned embedding space, without relying on handcrafted structural descriptors such as bond-order parameters [22], common neighbor analysis (CNA) [10], or polyhedral template matching (PTM) [13].

Figure 5 presents a t-SNE projection of the invariant embeddings, with representative neighborhoods near cluster centers. The latent space clearly separates disordered, ordered, and intermediate motifs into distinct groups. While we do not enforce direct alignment with the clusters in [3], we use it as a physical reference. That study shows that aluminium crystallization follows a one-step pathway: embryos form in low-five-fold-symmetry liquid regions, growing with FCC ordering and often featuring patchy morphology and stacking faults.

Interpretation of the Discovered Clusters. Cluster C_6 corresponds to the most disordered, liquid-like environment and dominates the early snapshots. At the opposite end, cluster C_1 contains the most ordered crystalline neighborhoods and becomes the dominant motif in the final state. The remaining clusters C_2–C_5 occupy intermediate positions both in latent space and in the simulation box and can be interpreted as partially ordered, defective, or interfacial structures.

Among these intermediate motifs, C_5 appears early during nucleation and forms extended shells around the growing crystalline regions before remaining in the final polycrystal. This behavior is consistent with a near-crystalline interfacial motif, i.e. a distorted close-packed environment surrounding the ordered crystal core during growth and later persisting at grain boundaries. The weakly populated clusters C_2–C_4 are located on crystal surfaces, internal defective regions, and boundary-like structures; following the reference analysis of [4], they are plausibly associated with defective close-packed motifs, including stacking-fault-rich or otherwise distorted crystalline environments. We keep this interpretation deliberately cautious, since the clusters are discovered without supervision and are not constrained to match a predefined structural taxonomy.

This interpretation is supported by the temporal evolution of the cluster populations shown in Fig. 5. At 166 ps, the system is almost entirely assigned to C_6, confirming that the initial configuration is dominated by liquid-like neighborhoods. As crystallization proceeds, the fraction of C_6 decreases monotonically while the population of C_1 grows steadily. By the final frame at 240 ps, C_1 accounts for roughly 70% of the neighborhoods, whereas C_6 has nearly disappeared. The intermediate clusters remain individually subdominant but together represent a substantial fraction of the system during nucleation and growth, and persist in the final polycrystal. This behavior is consistent with clusters encoding interfaces, stacking-faulted regions, and grain-boundary environments rather than bulk liquid or bulk crystal.

Spatial Evolution During Crystallization. The spatial distribution of the clusters is shown in Fig. 6. Early frames are dominated by the liquid-like background (C_6). As crystallization begins, compact regions of ordered and partially ordered environments emerge within this background, corresponding to crystalline nuclei and their surrounding transition layers. These regions grow, impinge, and progressively fill the simulation box. The second row removes the dominant liquid-like background and highlights only the ordered and intermediate clusters, which makes the nucleation-and-growth process clearer. Early frames show compact precrystalline islands dominated by C_5, while a crystalline core (C_1) develops inside these regions as growth proceeds. At later times,

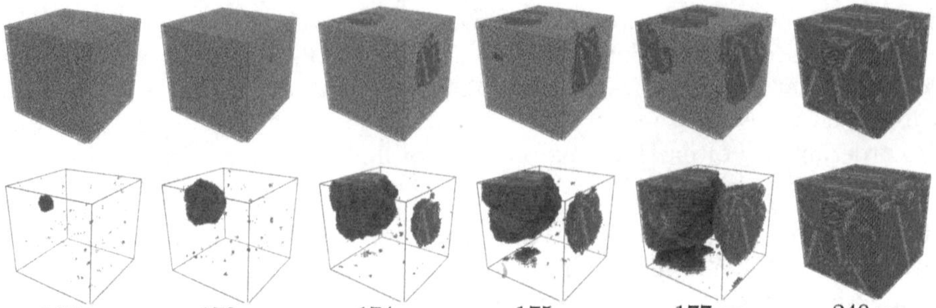

Fig. 6. Spatial evolution of the identified clusters during homogeneous nucleation. Columns correspond to successive simulation times from 166 ps to 240 ps. *Top row*: full simulation box colored by cluster assignment. The early frames are dominated by the liquid-like cluster C_6, while ordered and intermediate clusters progressively nucleate and expand. *Bottom row*: the same snapshots with the liquid-like cluster removed, highlighting the emergence, growth, and impingement of ordered and interfacial motifs. The final configuration is a polycrystal composed of large ordered domains enriched in C_1, separated by boundary regions where intermediate clusters, especially C_5, remain prominent.

ordered domains expand and eventually impinge, producing a final polycrystal in which C_1 occupies grain interiors and the intermediate clusters are enriched at liquid–nucleus interfaces during growth and at grain boundaries in the final polycrystal (see the interpretation of clusters above). This spatial organization is consistent with the physical picture reported for the same aluminium trajectory in [3], where nucleation proceeds through direct FCC ordering followed by growth of patchy nuclei containing stacking faults and interfacial distortions. Notably, this interpretation emerges without temporal supervision or handcrafted descriptors: neighborhoods are embedded independently from their geometry, yet the resulting clusters organize into spatially coherent motifs that evolve smoothly during crystallization. Based on this proof of concept, a refinement of the structural description of the liquid to account for its heterogeneity is planned in a subsequent work.

6 Conclusion

We presented a self-supervised method for clustering local atomic environments in 3D point clouds. By combining a rotation-equivariant encoder, invariant embeddings derived from equivariant features, and a VICReg objective on overlapping neighborhoods, the method learns symmetry-aware representations that remain directly clusterable. On a synthetic polycrystal benchmark, the learned embeddings outperform recent self-supervised point-cloud baselines as well as classical structural descriptors for unsupervised motif discovery. Applied to molecular dynamics simulations of aluminium crystallization, the method recovers spatially coherent clusters corresponding to liquid-like, ordered, and intermediate environments and reveals their evolution during nucleation and growth without labels or handcrafted order parameters. Finally, to assess generalization beyond the evaluation benchmark, we also perform a real-to-synthetic transfer experiment in which the encoder is pretrained on real MD trajectories and evaluated directly on the synthetic polycrystal dataset. Full details and results are provided in the supplementary material.

These results illustrate the potential of self-supervised geometric learning for large scientific point clouds, where local structure is subtle and difficult to capture with fixed descriptors. Future work will extend the approach to multi-species systems, incorporate temporal information during training, and further connect learned motifs with physical observables.

References

1. Bardes, A., Ponce, J., LeCun, Y.: VICReg: Variance-invariance-covariance regularization for self-supervised learning. In: International Conference on Learning Representations (2022). https://openreview.net/forum?id=xm6YD62D1Ub
2. Bartók, A.P., Kondor, R., Csányi, G.: On representing chemical environments. Phys. Rev. B **87**(18), 184115 (2013)
3. Becker, S., Devijver, E., Molinier, R., et al.: Unsupervised topological learning approach of crystal nucleation. Sci. Rep. **12**, 3195 (2022)
4. Becker, S., Devijver, E., Molinier, R., Jakse, N.: Unsupervised topological learning for identification of atomic structures. Phys. Rev. E **105**(4), 045304 (2022)
5. Chen, G., et al.: Pointgpt: Auto-regressively generative pre-training from point clouds. In: Oh, A., Naumann, T., Globerson, A., Saenko, K., Hardt, M., Levine, S. (eds.) Advances in Neural Information Processing Systems. vol. 36, pp. 29667–29679. Curran Associates, Inc. (2023)
6. Chen, T., Kornblith, S., Norouzi, M., Hinton, G.: A simple framework for contrastive learning of visual representations. In: ICML (2020)
7. Deng, C.: Vector neurons: A general framework for so(3)-equivariant networks. In: ICCV (2021)
8. Ermolov, A., Siarohin, A., Sangineto, E., Sebe, N.: Whitening for self-supervised representation learning. In: Proceedings of the IEEE/CVF International Conference on Computer Vision (ICCV) (2021)
9. Fuchs, F.B., Worrall, D.E., Fischer, V., Welling, M.: Se(3)-transformers: 3d roto-translation equivariant attention networks. In: Advances in Neural Information Processing Systems (NeurIPS) (2020)
10. Honeycutt, J.D., Andersen, H.C.: Molecular dynamics study of melting and freezing of small lennard-jones clusters. J. Phys. Chem. **91**, 4950–4963 (1987)
11. Jakse, N., et al.: Machine learning interatomic potentials for aluminium: application to solidification phenomena. J. Phys.: Condens. Matter **35**(3), 035402 (2023)
12. Kývala, L., de Hijes, P.M., Dellago, C.: Unsupervised identification of crystal defects from atomistic potential descriptors. npj Comput. Mater. **11**, 50 (2025)
13. Larsen, P.M., Schmidt, S., Schiøtz, J.: Robust structural identification via polyhedral template matching. Modell. Simul. Mater. Sci. Eng. **24**, 055007 (2016)
14. Lechner, W., Dellago, C.: Accurate determination of crystal structures based on averaged local bond order parameters. J. Chem. Phys. **129**(11), 114707 (2008)

15. Ni, Z., Steinbach, E.: Revnet: A rotational equivariant vector neuron network for 3d point cloud analysis (2026)
16. Pang, Y., Wang, W., Tay, F.E.: Masked autoencoders for point cloud self-supervised learning. In: ECCV (2022)
17. Pengmei, Z., Shen, Z., Wang, Z., Collins, M., Rangwala, H.: Pushing the limits of all-atom geometric graph neural networks: Pre-training, scaling, and zero-shot transfer. In: ICLR (2025)
18. Qi, C.R., Su, H., Mo, K., Guibas, L.J.: Pointnet: Deep learning on point sets for 3d classification and segmentation. In: CVPR (2017)
19. Roncoroni, F., Sanz-Matias, A., Sundararaman, S., Prendergast, D.: Unsupervised learning of representative local atomic arrangements in molecular dynamics data. Phys. Chem. Chem. Phys. **25**, 13741–13754 (2023)
20. Sajnani, R., Poulenard, A., Aigerman, N., Lipman, Y.: Condor: Self-supervised canonicalization of 3d pose for partial shapes. In: Proceedings of the IEEE/CVF Conference on Computer Vision and Pattern Recognition (CVPR) (2022)
21. Schütt, K.T., Kindermans, P.J., Sauceda, H.E., Chmiela, S., Tkatchenko, A., Müller, K.R.: Schnet: A continuous-filter convolutional neural network for modeling quantum interactions. In: Advances in Neural Information Processing Systems, vol. 30, pp. 992–1002 (2017)
22. Steinhardt, P.J., Nelson, D.R., Ronchetti, M.: Bond-orientational order in liquids and glasses. Phys. Rev. B **28**(2), 784–805 (1983)
23. Su, K., et al.: Ri-mae: Rotation-invariant masked autoencoders for self-supervised point cloud representation learning. In: AAAI Conference on Artificial Intelligence (2024)
24. Thomas, H.: Kpconv: Flexible and deformable convolution for point clouds. In: Proceedings of the IEEE/CVF International Conference on Computer Vision, pp. 6411–6420 (2019)
25. Thomas, N., et al.: Tensor field networks: Rotation- and translation-equivariant neural networks for 3d point clouds. In: Advances in Neural Information Processing Systems (NeurIPS) (2018)
26. Wang, Y., Hu, K., Gupta, S., Ye, Z., Wang, Y., Jegelka, S.: Understanding the role of equivariance in self-supervised learning. In: Proceedings of the 38th International Conference on Neural Information Processing Systems. NIPS '24, Curran Associates Inc., Red Hook, NY, USA (2024)
27. Wang, Y., Sun, Y., Liu, Z., Sarma, S.E., Bronstein, M.M., Solomon, J.M.: Dynamic graph cnn for learning on point clouds. ACM Trans. Graph. **38**(5) (2019)
28. Xie, S.: Pointcontrast: Unsupervised pre-training for 3d point cloud understanding. In: ECCV (2020)
29. Yu, X.: Point-bert: Pre-training 3d point cloud transformers with masked point modeling. In: CVPR (2022)
30. Zbontar, J.: Barlow twins: Self-supervised learning via redundancy reduction. In: ICML (2021)
31. Zeni, C., et al.: Data-driven simulation and characterisation of gold nanoparticle melting. Nat. Commun. **12**(1), 6056 (2021)
32. Zhang, R., et al.: Point-m2ae: multi-scale masked autoencoders for hierarchical point cloud pre-training. In: Proceedings of NeurIPS, Curran Associates Inc, Red Hook, NY, USA (2022)

TANGraph: Hierarchical Heterogeneous Graph Neural Network for Predicting RNA Torsion Angles

Eleni Giovanoudi(✉) and Dimitrios Rafailidis

University of Thessaly, Volos, Greece
{egiovanoudi,draf}@uth.gr

Abstract. The biological functionality of RNA is fundamentally governed by its three-dimensional (3D) conformation, which is determined by its torsion and pseudo-torsion angles. Despite continuous advancements in RNA 3D structure prediction, existing methods still struggle with stereochemical inconsistencies. Moreover, current computational approaches specifically designed for RNA torsion angle prediction ignore the spatial proximity imposed by secondary structure information and treat individual torsion angles as independent targets, oversimplifying their physical interdependencies. To address these limitations, we propose TANGraph, a novel RNA torsion angle prediction model based on a Hierarchical Heterogeneous Graph Neural Network. We represent RNA as a heterogeneous graph that jointly models the secondary structure and torsion angle structural topology. Through hierarchical graph neural networks operating at different levels of encoding, TANGraph learns a coherent multi-scale representation of the RNA structure. Experimental evaluation on benchmark datasets demonstrates that TANGraph achieves state-of-the-art torsion angle prediction accuracy, outperforming both 3D structure prediction and torsion angle prediction methods. Source code is publicly available at https://github.com/egiovanoudi/TANGraph.

Keywords: Hierarchical graph neural network · Heterogeneous graph neural network · RNA torsion angle · RNA secondary structure

1 Introduction

The RNA macromolecule plays a fundamental role in various biological processes. Its functionality is directly linked to its three-dimensional (3D) conformation, underscoring the importance of accurate structural characterization [32]. Central to the geometric complexity of RNA are its torsion angles. Unlike proteins, which are defined by only three backbone torsion angles, RNA flexibility is governed by a dynamic set of spatial parameters that allow it to adopt multiple conformations [14]. In particular, as illustrated in Fig. 1, each nucleotide in an RNA structure is described by six ribose-phosphate backbone torsion angles ($\alpha, \beta, \gamma, \delta, \epsilon, \zeta$) and one glycosidic angle (χ), which determines the orientation of

M. Ceci et al. (Eds.): ECML PKDD 2026, LNAI 16948, pp. 653–669, 2027.
https://doi.org/10.1007/978-3-032-37679-4_37

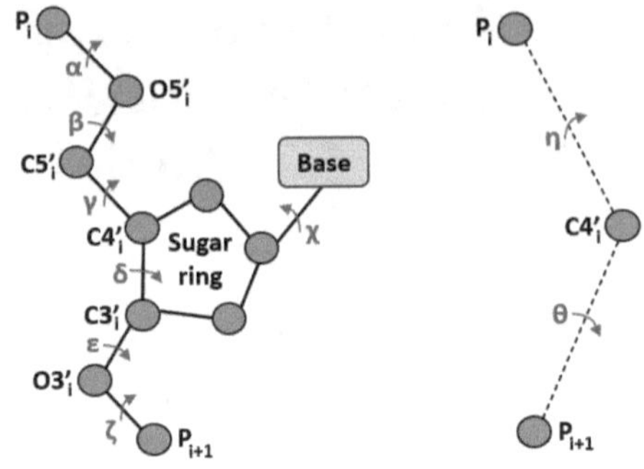

(a) (b)

Fig. 1. Illustration of the RNA (a) torsion and (b) pseudo-torsion angles.

the base relative to the sugar ring. RNA backbone representation can also be simplified using two pseudo-torsion angles (η and θ) [31]. Collectively, these angles determine RNA folding patterns and, consequently, its 3D shape, enabling RNA to perform diverse biological functions, including gene expression regulation, cellular localization, and catalysis [19,32]. Moreover, RNA torsion angles are used for quality assessment, evaluating and comparing predicted RNA 3D structures [21]. Their significance extends to Nuclear Magnetic Resonance (NMR) spectroscopy, where RNA torsion angles are used to interpret and refine NMR structures [25]. Although experimental methods facilitate RNA structure determination, they remain limited by high costs and time-intensive procedures.

Several computational methods have been developed for predicting RNA 3D structures from sequence, many of which incorporate RNA secondary structure information. The primary structure of RNA consists of a linear nucleotide sequence linked by phosphodiester bonds along the backbone. The secondary structure arises when complementary bases within the RNA strand form hydrogen bonds. These base-pairing interactions, between A-U and C-G pairs, as well as less stable G-U pairs, create various structural motifs [12]. Existing RNA 3D structure prediction methods are categorized into physics-based, knowledge-based, and deep learning-based approaches [3]. For instance, Li and Chen [16] propose a physics-based coarse-grained model that leverages RNA sequence and secondary structure information to perform molecular dynamics simulations. Li et al. [17] introduce a knowledge-based method that identifies motifs from a template database given an RNA sequence and its secondary structure. Wang et al. [33] develop a deep learning model that incorporates Multiple Sequence Alignment (MSA) and RNA secondary structure features. The final 3D structure is generated through energy minimization using 1D and 2D geometric constraints. Despite significant advancements in RNA 3D structure prediction, existing models exhibit stereochemical inconsistencies, including errors in torsion angle configurations [8,30].

To overcome the need for dedicated local conformational descriptors, methods specifically designed for RNA torsion angle prediction have been developed. The first study was conducted by Singh et al. [29], employing residual dilated Convolutional Neural Networks (CNNs) to predict torsion and pseudo-torsion angles from RNA sequences. Subsequently, Bernard et al. [4] incorporate a pre-trained DNA language model and adapt its neural weights for RNA torsion angle prediction. Moreover, Abir et al. [1] utilize RNA language model embeddings, combining inception networks with dilated CNNs and multi-head attention. Nevertheless, none of these methods take into account the RNA secondary structure information, which governs 3D spatial proximity. Additionally, these methods treat each torsion and pseudo-torsion angle as an independent regression target at the output layer, oversimplifying the angular interdependence [24]. Meanwhile, Graph Neural Networks (GNNs) have proven to be effective in modeling heterogeneous entities and diverse interactions between them [13,18,20]. Consequently, integrating GNNs into RNA torsion angle prediction represents a promising strategy for capturing the structural and conformational complexity of RNA.

To address the limitations of existing approaches, we propose the TANGraph model, making the following contributions:

- We introduce a novel Hierarchical Heterogeneous GNN architecture to improve RNA torsion and pseudo-torsion angle prediction. In particular, we design three hierarchical GNNs, that is the Nucleotide GNN, the Angle GNN, and the Bipartite GNN.
- We encode the RNA sequence at the nucleotide level, leveraging the RNA secondary structure information. In doing so, the Nucleotide GNN captures both local and long-range dependencies on the RNA backbone.
- We model RNA at the angle level, utilizing the angular structural topology. This approach enables the Angle GNN to learn interactions and interdependencies among individual torsion angles, providing deeper structural resolution.
- We design an intermediate bipartite level that connects each nucleotide to its corresponding angles, facilitating cross-level communication. Specifically, the Bipartite GNN performs bidirectional message-passing between the nucleotide- and angle-level representations, yielding a structurally coherent RNA encoding.

The rest of the paper is organized as follows, in Sect. 2 we formulate our problem and Sect. 3 details the proposed TANGraph model. Our experimental evaluation is presented in Sect. 4, and we conclude the study in Sect. 5.

2 Problem Formulation

Let l denote the RNA sequence length, that is the number of nucleotides, and $\mathcal{K} = \{\alpha, \beta, \gamma, \delta, \epsilon, \zeta, \chi, \eta, \theta\}$ represent the set of torsion and pseudo-torsion angle types per nucleotide. We model an RNA molecule as a hierarchical heterogeneous graph, defined as follows:

Nucleotide Graph. At the nucleotide level, the RNA molecule is modeled as a graph $\mathcal{G}_N = (\mathcal{V}_N, \mathcal{E}_N)$, with nodes corresponding to nucleotides and edges defined according to the RNA secondary structure. The feature matrix of the node set $\mathcal{V}_N = \{u_0, u_1, \dots, u_{l-1}\}$ is initialized with the sequence embedding $\mathbf{H}_S \in \mathbb{R}^{l \times h}$, where h denotes the hidden embedding dimension. The RNA secondary structure comprises two types of bonds: i) phosphodiester bonds between consecutive nucleotides and ii) hydrogen bonds between complementary bases. The edge set corresponding to phosphodiester bonds is defined as:

$$\mathcal{E}_{phos} = \{(u_i, u_{i+1}, w_{phos}) \mid 0 \leq i \leq l-2\} \tag{1}$$

where $w_{phos}(u_i, u_{i+1}) = 1$ is the edge weight, reflecting the deterministic presence of these bonds. To model hydrogen bonds, we employ the RNAplfold package [5], which, provided an RNA sequence, computes base-pairing probabilities based on thermodynamic principles. Instead of relying exclusively on the single minimum free energy structure, we consider an ensemble of probable secondary structures to account for the intrinsic uncertainty and dynamic nature of RNA folding. A secondary structure X associated with sequence R is assigned a probability $p(X|R) = \frac{1}{Z} e^{-\lambda E(X,R)}$, following the Boltzmann distribution, where Z is the partition function and $E(X, R)$ is the free energy of sequence R under structure X [23,34]. Considering all possible secondary structures within a thermodynamic equilibrium, nucleotides i and j have a base-pairing probability $p([i,j]|R) = \sum_{[i,j] \in X} p(X|R)$. Thus, the hydrogen-bond edge set includes all pairs with a non-zero probability of interaction:

$$\mathcal{E}_{hyd} = \{(u_i, u_j, w_{hyd}) \mid p([i,j]|R) > 0\} \tag{2}$$

where $w_{hyd}(u_i, u_j) = p([i,j]|R)$ represents the likelihood of base pairing between the two nucleotides. The complete edge set of the nucleotide graph is:

$$\mathcal{E}_N = \mathcal{E}_{phos} \cup \mathcal{E}_{hyd} \tag{3}$$

resulting in a probabilistically weighted structural representation of the RNA.

Angle Graph. At the angle level, the RNA molecule is represented as a graph $\mathcal{G}_A = (\mathcal{V}_A, \mathcal{E}_A)$, where nodes correspond to the torsion and pseudo-torsion angles of each nucleotide, and edges are defined based on the angular structural topology while preserving the RNA secondary structure. The feature matrix of the node set $\mathcal{V}_A = \{v_0, v_1, \dots, v_{|\mathcal{K}|l-1}\}$ is initialized with the angle embedding $\mathbf{H}_A \in \mathbb{R}^{|\mathcal{K}|l \times h}$. The topology of the angle graph is constructed from three types of connectivity: i) internal nucleotide structure, ii) sequential connectivity between adjacent nucleotides, and iii) spatial nucleotide interactions induced by base pairing. The edge set $\mathcal{E}_{intra}$ encodes the fixed internal topology among the $|\mathcal{K}|$ angles within each nucleotide, with unit edge weights. To model the continuous physical and virtual polymer backbones, specific angle nodes of adjacent nucleotides are connected. In particular, the ζ angle connects to the α angle of the next nucleotide, and the θ angle connects to the η angle of the subsequent nucleotide:

$$\mathcal{E}_{seq} = \{(v_i^{k_1}, v_{i+1}^{k_2}, w_{seq}) \mid 0 \leq i \leq l-2 \ \wedge \ (k_1, k_2) \in \{(\zeta, \alpha), (\theta, \eta)\}\} \tag{4}$$

where $w_{seq}(v_i^{k_1}, v_{i+1}^{k_2}) = 1$. To incorporate hydrogen-bonding interactions, the base pairing edges from the nucleotide graph are mapped to specific angle nodes. Provided the hydrogen-bond edge set $\mathcal{E}_{hyd}$, the interactions are routed between the χ angles of paired nucleotides:

$$\mathcal{E}_{spatial} = \{(v_i^k, v_j^k, w_{spatial}) \mid (u_i, u_j, w_{hyd}) \in \mathcal{E}_{hyd} \ \wedge \ k \in \{\chi\}\} \tag{5}$$

where $w_{spatial}(v_i^k, v_j^k) = w_{hyd}(u_i, u_j)$. The complete edge set of the angle graph is:

$$\mathcal{E}_A = \mathcal{E}_{intra} \cup \mathcal{E}_{seq} \cup \mathcal{E}_{spatial} \tag{6}$$

mirroring the multi-scale physics of the RNA molecule.

Bipartite Graph. The flow of information between the two graph levels is facilitated through a bipartite graph $\mathcal{G}_B = (\mathcal{V}_B, \mathcal{E}_B)$, connecting each nucleotide to its corresponding angles. The node set is defined as the disjoint union of the nucleotide and angle node sets:

$$\mathcal{V}_B = \mathcal{V}_N \sqcup \mathcal{V}_A \tag{7}$$

The edge set establishes a directed mapping from every nucleotide node to its $|\mathcal{K}|$ associated angle nodes:

$$\mathcal{E}_B = \{(u_i, v_i^k, \mathbf{e}_i^k) \mid 0 \leq i \leq l-1 \ \wedge \ k \in \mathcal{K}\} \tag{8}$$

where $\mathbf{e}_i^k \in \{0,1\}^9$ is the edge feature vector, computed as the one-hot encoding of the target angle type k, distinguishing between the different nucleotide-angle connections.

3 The Proposed TANGraph Model

The TANGraph model is designed to predict the torsion and pseudo-torsion angles of each nucleotide in an RNA molecule based on its sequence. The architecture comprises a heterogeneous GNN operating across three hierarchical graph levels: i) the nucleotide level encoding the RNA sequence, ii) the angle level representing torsion and pseudo-torsion angles within each nucleotide, and iii) the intermediate level facilitating communication between nucleotides and their associated angles. A schematic overview of the TANGraph architecture is provided in Fig. 2.

The input to the model is a sequence feature matrix $\mathbf{S}$ for each RNA molecule. Firstly, a CNN encodes $\mathbf{S}$ into the sequence embedding $\mathbf{H}_S \in \mathbb{R}^{l \times h}$, which is subsequently used to initialize a heterogeneous GNN consisting of f iterative

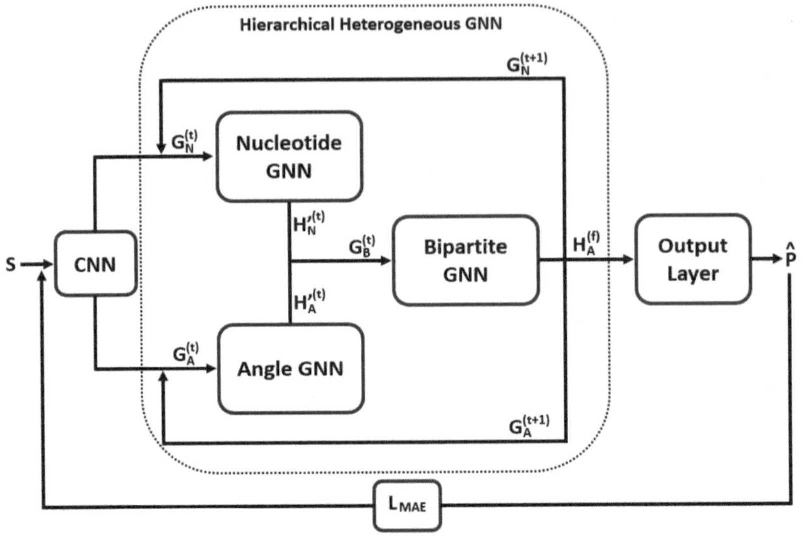

Fig. 2. Overview of the proposed TANGraph model.

message-passing steps. Specifically, $\mathbf{H}_S$ is used to construct two initial graph representations, that is the nucleotide graph $\mathcal{G}_N^{(0)} = (\mathcal{V}_N^{(0)}, \mathcal{E}_N)$, derived from the RNA secondary structure, and the angle graph $\mathcal{G}_A^{(0)} = (\mathcal{V}_A^{(0)}, \mathcal{E}_A)$, defined according to the torsion and pseudo-torsion angle topology (Fig. 1). At each iteration t, the graphs $\mathcal{G}_N^{(t)}$ and $\mathcal{G}_A^{(t)}$ are encoded separately at their respective levels via the Nucleotide GNN and the Angle GNN, producing updated node embeddings $\mathbf{H}_N'^{(t)} \in \mathbb{R}^{l \times h}$ and $\mathbf{H}_A'^{(t)} \in \mathbb{R}^{|\mathcal{K}|l \times h}$, accordingly. Communication between the two graph levels is achieved through a bipartite graph $\mathcal{G}_B^{(t)} = (\mathcal{V}_B^{(t)}, \mathcal{E}_B^{(t)})$, where the node set $\mathcal{V}_B^{(t)}$ comprises the nucleotide and angle embeddings $\mathbf{H}_N'^{(t)}$ and $\mathbf{H}_A'^{(t)}$, while the edge set $\mathcal{E}_B$ connects each nucleotide node in $\mathcal{G}_N^{(t)}$ to its corresponding $|\mathcal{K}|$ angle nodes in $\mathcal{G}_A^{(t)}$. This interaction yields updated graph representations $\mathcal{G}_N^{(t+1)}$ and $\mathcal{G}_A^{(t+1)}$ with refined embeddings $\mathbf{H}_N^{(t+1)} \in \mathbb{R}^{l \times h}$ and $\mathbf{H}_A^{(t+1)} \in \mathbb{R}^{|\mathcal{K}|l \times h}$, accordingly, which are propagated to the next iteration of the heterogeneous GNN. After f iterations, the final angle embeddings $\mathbf{H}_A^{(f)}$ are passed to the output layer, consisting of $|\mathcal{K}|$ Feed-forward Neural Networks (FNNs), one for each angle type. The model generates the predicted angles $\hat{\mathbf{P}} \in \mathbb{R}^{l \times |\mathcal{K}|}$, with values constrained to the range $[-180, 180]$ for each nucleotide. During the training process, TANGraph minimizes the error between the predicted $\hat{\mathbf{P}}$ and ground truth $\mathbf{P}$ angles using the $\mathcal{L}_{MAE}$ loss.

3.1 Nucleotide GNN

The TANGraph model takes as input an RNA sequence feature matrix $\mathbf{S} = (\mathbf{s}_0, \mathbf{s}_1, \ldots, \mathbf{s}_{l-1})$, where each $\mathbf{s}_i$ denotes a nucleotide embedding obtained from the pretrained RNA language model RiNALMo [26]. The sequence $\mathbf{S}$ is processed by a two-layer CNN with batch normalization and the non-linear activation function LeakyReLU, producing the refined sequence embedding $\mathbf{H}_S \in \mathbb{R}^{l \times h}$:

$$\mathbf{H}_S = \mathrm{CNN}(\mathbf{S}) \tag{9}$$

According to Eq. (9) the pretrained embeddings are enriched with local sequential context via convolutional operations.

The embedding $\mathbf{H}_S$ is subsequently processed by the Hierarchical Heterogeneous GNN, which performs f iterative message-passing steps. As shown in Fig. 2, at the nucleotide level, during iteration t, the graph $\mathcal{G}_N^{(t)} = (\mathcal{V}_N^{(t)}, \mathcal{E}_N)$ is passed to the Nucleotide GNN, denoted as GNN_N. The network consists of an auto-regressive moving average graph convolutional (ARMAConv) layer [6] followed by LeakyReLU activation, yielding the nucleotide embedding $\mathbf{H}_N'^{(t)} \in \mathbb{R}^{l \times h}$:

$$\mathbf{H}_N'^{(t)} = \mathrm{GNN}_N(\mathcal{G}_N^{(t)}) = \sigma(\mathbf{D}_N^{-\frac{1}{2}} \mathbf{A}_N \mathbf{D}_N^{-\frac{1}{2}} \mathbf{H}_N^{(t)} \mathbf{W}_{1,N} + \mathbf{H}_N^{(t)} \mathbf{W}_{2,N}) \tag{10}$$

Here, $\mathbf{H}_N^{(0)} = \mathbf{H}_S$, $\mathbf{A}_N \in \mathbb{R}^{l \times l}$ is the weighted nucleotide adjacency matrix constructed from $\mathcal{E}_N$, $\mathbf{D}_N$ is the corresponding degree matrix, $\mathbf{W}_{1,N}, \mathbf{W}_{2,N} \in \mathbb{R}^{h \times h}$ are trainable parameters, and $\sigma(\cdot)$ represents LeakyReLU. This design enables the Nucleotide GNN to model structural dependencies induced by potential RNA secondary structures. As formulated in Eq. (10), nucleotide embeddings are updated by aggregating messages from phosphodiester and hydrogen-bond interactions, capturing both local and long-range dependencies.

3.2 Angle GNN

At the angle level, the initial node representation of the graph $\mathcal{G}_A = (\mathcal{V}_A, \mathcal{E}_A)$ is provided by the angle embedding $\mathbf{H}_A \in \mathbb{R}^{|\mathcal{K}|l \times h}$. This embedding is constructed by projecting the nucleotide-level sequence embedding $\mathbf{H}_S$ into the angle space and augmenting it with a learnable, angle-type-specific embedding $\mathbf{M} \in \mathbb{R}^{|\mathcal{K}| \times h}$. This formulation preserves the global context of each angle node, that is the nucleotide to which it belongs, while distinguishing between different angle types within the same nucleotide. As depicted in Fig. 2, in parallel with the Nucleotide GNN, at each iteration t, the graph $\mathcal{G}_A^{(t)}$ is passed to the Angle GNN, denoted as GNN_A. The network utilizes an ARMAConv layer with LeakyReLU activation, resulting in the updated angle embedding $\mathbf{H}_A'^{(t)} \in \mathbb{R}^{|\mathcal{K}|l \times h}$:

$$\mathbf{H}_A'^{(t)} = \mathrm{GNN}_A(\mathcal{G}_A^{(t)}) = \sigma(\mathbf{D}_A^{-\frac{1}{2}} \mathbf{A}_A \mathbf{D}_A^{-\frac{1}{2}} \mathbf{H}_A^{(t)} \mathbf{W}_{1,A} + \mathbf{H}_A^{(t)} \mathbf{W}_{2,A}) \tag{11}$$

where $\mathbf{H}_A^{(0)} = \mathbf{H}_A$, $\mathbf{A}_A \in \mathbb{R}^{|\mathcal{K}|l \times |\mathcal{K}|l}$ is the weighted angle adjacency matrix, $\mathbf{D}_A$ is the corresponding degree matrix, $\mathbf{W}_{1,A}, \mathbf{W}_{2,A} \in \mathbb{R}^{h \times h}$ are trainable parameters, and $\sigma(\cdot)$ denotes LeakyReLU. This way, the RNA is encoded at a deeper structural resolution, facilitating the propagation of torsional information across the continuous polymer backbone and the long-range spatial base-pairing interactions via Eq. (11).

3.3 Bipartite GNN

Once the Nucleotide and Angle GNNs have independently processed their respective graph levels, cross-level communication is performed through the bipartite graph $\mathcal{G}_B = (\mathcal{V}_B, \mathcal{E}_B)$. At iteration t, the nucleotide and angle embeddings $\mathbf{H}_N'^{(t)}$ and $\mathbf{H}_A'^{(t)}$ are passed to the Bipartite GNN, as shown in Fig. 2. Here, two message-passing steps take place across $\mathcal{G}_B$, from nucleotides to angles and from angles back to nucleotides, using two different generalized graph convolution (GENConv) layers [15]. Firstly, information flows from nucleotide nodes to angle nodes through a residual connection, yielding the angle embedding for the next iteration $t+1$, denoted as $\mathbf{H}_A^{(t+1)} \in \mathbb{R}^{|\mathcal{K}|l \times h}$:

$$\mathbf{H}_A^{(t+1)} = \mathbf{H}_A'^{(t)} + \mathrm{GENConv}_A\big((\mathbf{H}_N'^{(t)}, \mathbf{H}_A'^{(t)}), \mathcal{E}_B\big) \tag{12}$$

The $\mathrm{GENConv}_A$ layer is computed as:

$$\mathrm{GENConv}_A(\cdot) = \mathrm{MLP}_A\Big(\mathbf{H}_A'^{(t)} + \mathrm{AGG}_A\big(\sigma(\mathbf{H}_N'^{(t)} + \mathbf{E}_B\mathbf{W}_A)\big)\Big) \tag{13}$$

where $\mathrm{MLP}_A(\cdot)$ is a Multi-Layer Perceptron, $\mathrm{AGG}_A(\cdot)$ denotes softmax aggregation, $\sigma(\cdot)$ is the ReLU activation function, $\mathbf{E}_B \in \mathbb{R}^{|\mathcal{K}|l \times |\mathcal{K}|}$ is the bipartite edge feature matrix, and $\mathbf{W}_A \in \mathbb{R}^{|\mathcal{K}| \times h}$ is a trainable parameter. Subsequently, the updated angle representations are propagated back to the nucleotide nodes via a similar residual connection. Operating over the reversed bipartite edge set $\mathcal{E}_B^{re}$, this step produces the nucleotide embedding for iteration $t+1$, denoted as $\mathbf{H}_N^{(t+1)} \in \mathbb{R}^{l \times h}$:

$$\mathbf{H}_N^{(t+1)} = \mathbf{H}_N'^{(t)} + \mathrm{GENConv}_N\big((\mathbf{H}_A^{(t+1)}, \mathbf{H}_N'^{(t)}), \mathcal{E}_B^{re}\big) \tag{14}$$

where

$$\mathrm{GENConv}_N(\cdot) = \mathrm{MLP}_N\Big(\mathbf{H}_N'^{(t)} + \mathrm{AGG}_N\big(\sigma(\mathbf{H}_A^{(t+1)} + \mathbf{E}_B\mathbf{W}_N)\big)\Big) \tag{15}$$

Here, $\mathrm{MLP}_N(\cdot)$ is a Multi-Layer Perceptron, $\mathrm{AGG}_N(\cdot)$ represents softmax aggregation, and $\mathbf{W}_N \in \mathbb{R}^{|\mathcal{K}| \times h}$ is a trainable parameter. According to Eq. (12) each torsion and pseudo-torsion angle is updated based on the global topological state of the RNA molecule encoded at the nucleotide level. Conversely, nucleotides are informed by the local torsional geometry of their associated angles via Eq. (14). Overall, this bidirectional message-passing mechanism establishes a hierarchical information exchange, resulting in a structurally coherent RNA encoding.

After f iterations of the Hierarchical Heterogeneous GNN, the final angle embedding $\mathbf{H}_A^{(f)}$ is forwarded to the output layer, consisting of $|\mathcal{K}|$ parallel FNNs, one for each angle type. Each FNN comprises two linear layers followed by LeakyReLU and Tanh activations, respectively. For every angle node, the model predicts two values, mapped to the sine and cosine range $[-1, 1]$. These trigonometric pairs are converted into the final angle predictions $\hat{\mathbf{P}} \in \mathbb{R}^{l \times |\mathcal{K}|}$ via the arctangent function, ranging from $-180°$ to $180°$.

3.4 Model Optimization

To train the TANGraph model, we optimize a periodic Mean Absolute Error (MAE) loss function between the ground truth $\mathbf{P}$ and predicted $\hat{\mathbf{P}}$ angles, considering the circular periodicity of angular data:

$$\mathcal{L}_{MAE} = \frac{1}{|\mathcal{K}|l} \sum_{i=0}^{l-1} \sum_{k \in \mathcal{K}} \Delta(\mathbf{P}_{i,k}, \hat{\mathbf{P}}_{i,k}) \tag{16}$$

where $\Delta(\mathbf{P}_{i,k}, \hat{\mathbf{P}}_{i,k}) = \min(|\mathbf{P}_{i,k} - \hat{\mathbf{P}}_{i,k}|, 360° - |\mathbf{P}_{i,k} - \hat{\mathbf{P}}_{i,k}|)$.

Optimization. Our proposed TANGraph model is implemented in PyTorch. During training, we employ a subgraph sampling strategy to handle large RNA molecules efficiently. Specifically, we select a contiguous sequence window up to a predefined maximum nucleotide length and construct the corresponding node-induced heterogeneous subgraph. In each epoch, the model learns a low-dimensional representation of the RNA sequence by minimizing the prediction error defined in Eq. (16). Optimization is achieved via backpropagation using the AdamW optimizer and the ReduceLROnPlateau learning rate scheduler.

4 Experiments

4.1 Datasets

Based on prior studies [1,4,29], we evaluate the examined models using independent RNA datasets for training, validation, and testing.

Training Set. All available RNA structures with resolution < 3.5Å were retrieved from the Protein Data Bank, excluding any targets present in the validation and test sets. The remaining structures were split into individual chain sequences using Biopython [9]. To prevent data leakage, CD-HIT-EST [11] was applied to remove training samples sharing ≥ 80% sequence similarity with sequences in the validation and test sets. In addition, internal redundancy within the training set was minimized by clustering the remaining sequences at a 100% identity threshold, ensuring each training sample represents a unique RNA sequence. To further achieve a rigorous evaluation, we employed BLAST-N [2] with an e-value cut-off of 10. Any training sequence producing a hit against validation or test sequences was excluded from the dataset. The final training set comprises 772 RNA chains. Notably, although the number of available RNA structures is limited, torsion angle prediction is formulated as a nucleotide-level task. Consequently, training is performed over 176,862 nucleotide samples.

Validation & Test Sets. For validation, we utilized the benchmark validation set from [29], consisting of 30 RNA sequences. Model evaluation is conducted on two independent benchmark test sets. The first set, denoted as T1, was created in [29] and contains 63 RNA sequences. The second test set, denoted as T2, was introduced in [4], combining two established datasets, namely RNA-Puzzles [22] and CASP-RNA [10]. This merged set includes 39 sequences.

To obtain ground truth torsion and pseudo-torsion angles, all datasets were created using the Barnaba software [7] to calculate native angular values from the RNA structures.

4.2 Evaluation Protocol

Following the evaluation protocol of relevant studies [1,4,29], we assess model performance in RNA torsion angle prediction using the following evaluation metrics:

- *Mean Circular Quantities (MCQ)* between the ground truth $\mathbf{P}_k$ and predicted $\hat{\mathbf{P}}_k$ values for a specific angle type $k \in \mathcal{K}$ [35]:

$$\mathrm{MCQ}(\mathbf{P}_k, \hat{\mathbf{P}}_k) = \arctan\left(\frac{\sum_{i=0}^{l-1} \sin \Delta(\mathbf{P}_{i,k}, \hat{\mathbf{P}}_{i,k})}{\sum_{i=0}^{l-1} \cos \Delta(\mathbf{P}_{i,k}, \hat{\mathbf{P}}_{i,k})}\right) \tag{17}$$

- *Mean Absolute Error (MAE)* between the ground truth $\mathbf{P}_k$ and predicted $\hat{\mathbf{P}}_k$ values for a specific angle type $k \in \mathcal{K}$:

$$\mathrm{MAE}(\mathbf{P}_k, \hat{\mathbf{P}}_k) = \frac{1}{l}\sum_{i=0}^{l-1} \Delta(\mathbf{P}_{i,k}, \hat{\mathbf{P}}_{i,k}) \tag{18}$$

4.3 Compared Methods

We evaluate the performance of the proposed TANGraph model against two categories of baselines: methods that predict i) RNA 3D structures and ii) RNA torsion angles. For the 3D structure prediction approaches, torsion and pseudo-torsion angles are extracted from the predicted 3D coordinates using the Barnaba software.

RNA 3D structure prediction methods:

- **trRosettaRNA**[1] employs a transformer network that predicts 1D and 2D geometries from MSA and RNA secondary structure representations, respectively. These geometries are subsequently used as restraints during energy minimization [33].
- **RNAJP**[2] is a physics-based, coarse-grained model that performs molecular dynamics simulations utilizing RNA sequence and secondary structure information [16].
- **Vfold-Pipeline**[3] is a knowledge-based method that integrates RNA sequences and secondary structures with a 3D template database of various motifs [17].

[1] https://zenodo.org/records/10616895.
[2] https://rna.physics.missouri.edu/RNAJP.
[3] https://rna.physics.missouri.edu/vfoldPipeline.

RNA torsion angle prediction methods:

- **SPOT-RNA-1D**[4] utilizes RNA sequences and residual dilated CNNs [29].
- **RNA-TorsionBERT**[5] adapts the neural weights of the pretrained DNA language model DNABERT [4].
- **DeepRNA-Twist**[6] encodes RNA sequences using the RNA language model RiNALMo. The method integrates transformer encoders, inception blocks, dilated convolutions, and multi-head attention mechanisms [1].
- **TANGraph-N** is a variant of the proposed model that operates solely on the nucleotide graph, omitting the Angle and Bipartite GNNs.
- **TANGraph-A** is a variant of the proposed model that encodes exclusively the angle graph, disregarding the Nucleotide and Bipartite GNNs.
- **TANGraph-C** is a variant of the proposed model without the bipartite graph, replacing the Bipartite GNN with a fusion mechanism. The nucleotide and angle embeddings are concatenated and projected through a linear layer.
- **TANGraph** is the proposed model.

The deep learning models are retrained from scratch on our training set. Their parameters are determined based on performance on the validation set, and we report the best results in our experiments. For the proposed TANGraph method, the learning rate is set to 1e-3 with a batch size of 32 and a sequence window up to 400 nucleotides. Early stopping is employed to prevent overfitting. The parameter analysis of TANGraph is further investigated in Sect. 4.5.

4.4 Performance Evaluation

In Tables 1 and 2, we present the experimental results of the examined models on the T1 and T2 benchmark test sets, respectively, reporting MCQ and MAE for each angle type as well as overall performance. The results indicate that the proposed TANGraph model and its variants outperform the baseline methods across both metrics and datasets. In particular, the 3D structure prediction approaches, that is trRosettaRNA, RNAJP, and Vfold-Pipeline, yield the highest prediction errors in terms of both MCQ and MAE. This observation is consistent with the stereochemical inconsistencies inherent to coordinate-based prediction methods. Consequently, when torsion angles are derived from predicted 3D coordinates, local structural deviations translate into amplified angle-level inaccuracies. The RNA torsion angle prediction methods, namely SPOT-RNA-1D, RNA-TorsionBERT, and DeepRNA-Twist, outperform the 3D structure predictors. However, by ignoring the RNA secondary structure and torsion angular topology, they fail to fully capture the conformational dependencies governing the RNA structure. Regarding the variants, TANGraph-N, TANGraph-A, and TANGraph-C surpass the baselines, underscoring the contributions of the Nucleotide and Angle GNNs. Nevertheless, TANGraph-N and TANGraph-A

[4] https://github.com/jaswindersingh2/SPOT-RNA-1D.
[5] https://github.com/EvryRNA/RNA-TorsionBERT.
[6] https://github.com/abrarrahmanabir/DeepRNA-Twist.

Table 1. Performance comparison of the examined models in terms of MCQ and MAE on the T1 dataset. Bold values indicate the best method.

Metrics	Methods	α	β	γ	δ	ϵ	ζ	χ	η	θ	Overall
MCQ	trRosettaRNA	39.7611	26.6020	33.1921	15.8280	23.7805	27.0136	26.5690	20.3421	22.6815	25.0171
	RNAJP	35.0068	25.5282	23.6002	12.9632	26.4028	28.2248	14.9962	22.4279	25.8008	23.3678
	Vfold-Pipeline	35.0706	22.0773	22.9005	12.8866	25.8400	26.9871	18.2985	22.1268	25.2583	22.9827
	SPOT-RNA-1D	32.2309	19.7946	26.4025	13.9479	17.0510	20.1651	15.8986	20.5800	23.1163	20.2945
	RNA-TorsionBERT	31.5464	19.0977	26.4723	11.9578	16.9979	20.1861	14.8531	16.2021	20.9504	19.3417
	DeepRNA-Twist	30.9362	19.0848	26.3131	12.6578	17.4987	19.3468	14.6339	16.2153	21.0340	19.2813
	TANGraph-N	28.5497	18.6749	21.4311	9.5203	15.7743	18.3552	12.8085	15.6543	19.1491	17.2953
	TANGraph-A	27.3118	18.6168	21.7435	9.1948	15.7643	18.3679	12.6289	15.2921	18.8901	17.0669
	TANGraph-C	26.6359	18.5546	21.2999	9.2046	15.6143	18.2712	12.6329	14.3271	18.6457	16.8271
	TANGraph	**26.1663**	**18.4183**	**20.8947**	**8.8919**	**15.5637**	**17.9156**	**12.4030**	**14.0384**	**18.5378**	**16.5871**
MAE	trRosettaRNA	50.6199	26.7045	45.2868	16.1747	25.0553	34.3406	35.6212	24.8769	26.9021	31.0902
	RNAJP	46.1922	25.2772	32.6938	14.3009	25.7427	33.2990	18.9983	26.8323	27.6539	27.3722
	Vfold-Pipeline	45.4229	23.6824	30.1241	14.4967	30.4308	35.7980	22.6013	29.3355	31.2876	29.1965
	SPOT-RNA-1D	41.9348	20.0291	32.1218	14.8005	19.1426	28.2807	18.3597	27.0406	27.6695	25.5114
	RNA-TorsionBERT	42.1071	22.0698	32.8890	13.7007	18.2166	28.0360	16.3253	24.1814	26.3546	24.8557
	DeepRNA-Twist	42.0195	20.1801	32.5571	13.6984	19.6478	28.1062	17.0451	24.0227	26.3066	24.8227
	TANGraph-N	40.3805	19.6726	29.5432	10.9500	18.0905	27.1731	15.3649	23.0819	24.4316	23.1642
	TANGraph-A	39.0921	19.6674	29.5813	10.5843	17.9250	26.5007	15.1761	21.7711	23.9020	22.6088
	TANGraph-C	38.3680	19.6885	29.3831	10.5979	17.8585	26.3572	15.1765	20.5631	23.7507	22.3972
	TANGraph	**37.8874**	**19.5610**	**29.1579**	**10.2968**	**17.8130**	**26.0913**	**14.9025**	**20.2175**	**23.4905**	**22.1401**

underperform compared to TANGraph-C and the proposed TANGraph model, highlighting the importance of jointly modeling nucleotide- and angle-level representations. Furthermore, TANGraph-C performs worse than TANGraph, demonstrating the contribution of cross-level communication facilitated by the Bipartite GNN. Overall, TANGraph achieves the best performance with average relative improvements of 12.53% and 9.22% in terms of MCQ and MAE, accordingly, compared to the second-best method DeepRNA-Twist. Through hierarchical heterogeneous modeling of RNA, TANGraph learns structurally coherent angle representations, thereby producing the most accurate torsion and pseudo-torsion angle predictions.

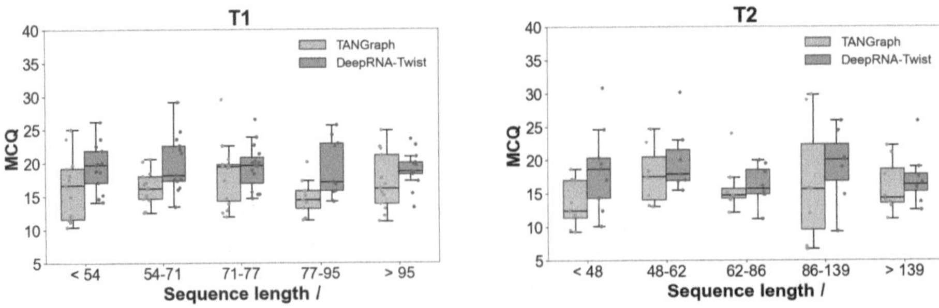

Fig. 3. MCQ performance comparison of TANGraph and DeepRNA-Twist with respect to the RNA sequence length on the T1 and T2 datasets.

Table 2. Performance comparison of the examined models in terms of MCQ and MAE on the T2 dataset. Bold values indicate the best method.

Metrics	Methods	α	β	γ	δ	ϵ	ζ	χ	η	θ	Overall
MCQ	trRosettaRNA	48.5674	25.4620	47.8326	16.3429	22.3182	29.9654	26.8919	20.3983	23.5139	27.7866
	RNAJP	44.0533	27.9646	34.4664	14.2462	26.0047	31.9942	18.9631	20.0005	21.0883	26.5313
	Vfold-Pipeline	44.0338	24.1432	33.7247	14.8964	25.1998	29.8940	18.8968	22.3879	28.1122	25.8581
	SPOT-RNA-1D	29.5477	16.6472	25.5465	15.8400	18.2129	19.6245	15.7138	21.4771	22.0074	20.1111
	RNA-TorsionBERT	29.8414	17.7732	24.5417	9.4992	15.5321	19.0296	12.1613	13.6066	18.5580	17.4671
	DeepRNA-Twist	25.2750	16.0008	23.0273	12.8936	17.9301	18.1445	12.1397	13.2916	18.3374	17.0779
	TANGraph-N	25.1470	15.6228	21.3005	8.0212	14.3573	16.9991	11.3351	13.4370	17.8806	15.6050
	TANGraph-A	26.0413	15.6265	21.5226	7.8234	14.3521	17.1976	10.8859	13.4936	18.1524	15.6342
	TANGraph-C	24.9623	15.5636	21.2930	8.1077	14.4355	16.5212	11.0891	13.0202	17.8534	15.4651
	TANGraph	**24.7937**	**15.5412**	**21.0390**	**7.7095**	**14.2453**	**16.2305**	**10.6890**	**12.7137**	**17.3393**	**15.1860**
MAE	trRosettaRNA	56.3282	27.4321	54.5974	17.1705	25.0125	37.4000	36.1036	24.1457	28.3580	34.0842
	RNAJP	54.8472	28.3839	45.7377	16.0013	25.0583	37.7476	18.9866	25.9685	27.1951	31.1029
	Vfold-Pipeline	53.9699	25.6299	42.1942	16.0256	29.3188	38.7582	22.9990	29.8145	35.0701	32.6057
	SPOT-RNA-1D	39.7905	17.7108	31.8941	16.1188	19.4581	27.0004	18.2071	25.8767	26.4270	24.7011
	RNA-TorsionBERT	37.2923	19.5100	30.5621	13.5974	16.8759	26.5670	14.6676	20.1156	25.3316	22.6595
	DeepRNA-Twist	37.0945	17.0886	29.9149	13.3431	19.1798	25.6170	14.9411	18.7485	23.2514	22.0661
	TANGraph-N	37.0478	16.8395	29.6248	8.8416	15.9265	24.0663	14.1153	18.7905	22.4130	20.8005
	TANGraph-A	37.6107	16.8031	29.7381	8.7209	15.9052	24.8915	13.6685	18.4513	22.6580	20.8605
	TANGraph-C	36.8005	16.6822	29.5548	8.9190	15.8777	24.4027	13.8086	17.8940	22.3832	20.6880
	TANGraph	**36.4902**	**16.6378**	**29.3831**	**8.5128**	**15.7142**	**23.8168**	**13.4487**	**17.5531**	**21.8886**	**20.3799**

To further investigate model performance, we group the test RNA samples according to the sequence length distribution in each test set. Figure 3 showcases the overall MCQ across the $|\mathcal{K}|$ angle types for the proposed TANGraph model and DeepRNA-Twist based on the RNA sequence length on the T1 and T2 sets. TANGraph outperforms DeepRNA-Twist across all length ranges on both datasets. Furthermore, the predictive accuracy of TANGraph remains stable across different sequence lengths, demonstrating the model's ability to generalize to diverse RNA molecules.

4.5 Parameter Tuning

The most critical parameters in our model are the hidden embedding dimension h and the number of iterative message-passing steps f in the Hierarchical Heterogeneous GNN. In Fig. 4a, we study the effect of the hidden embedding dimension h on the overall MCQ across the $|\mathcal{K}|$ angle types, varying $h \in \{32, 64, 128, 256, 512\}$. We observe that the best performance is achieved with $h = 128$, as lower values lead to insufficient representational capacity, while higher values introduce overfitting, limiting the model's ability to generalize and effectively capture the complex RNA conformation. Figure 4b demonstrates the impact of the number of iterative message-passing steps f on the performance of TANGraph in terms of overall MCQ, when varying $f \in [1, 5]$ by a step of 1. Aiming for an architecture that allows individual angles to be informed by both local torsional geometry and global structural topology of RNA, while avoiding oversmoothing effects caused by repeated message aggregations, we fix f to 2.

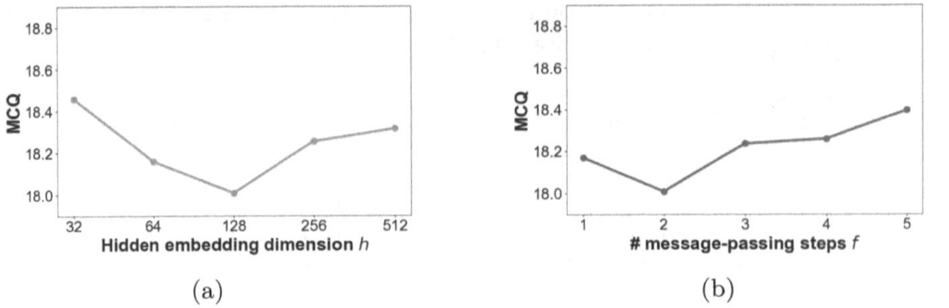

Fig. 4. Impact of (a) the hidden embedding dimension h and (b) the number of iterative message-passing steps f on TANGraph.

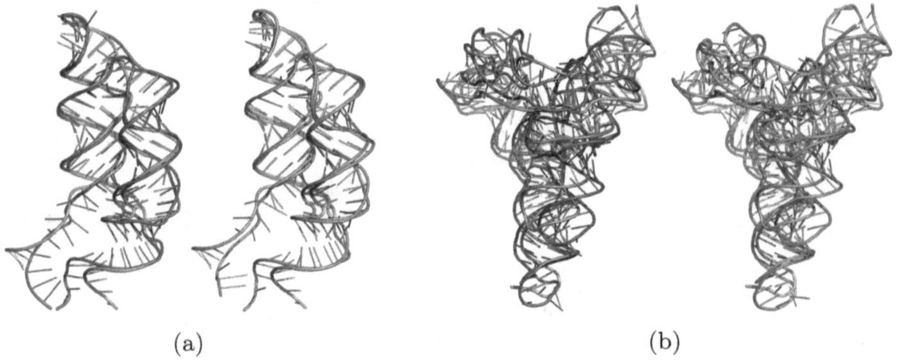

Fig. 5. Superposition of RNA structures (a) 3SUH and (b) 4P9R predicted by the trRosettaRNA baseline (red) and the TANGraph-restrained trRosettaRNA variant (blue), compared with the ground truth structures (gray). (Color figure online)

4.6 Case Study: Guiding RNA 3D Structure Prediction with TANGraph

To assess whether TANGraph can contribute to RNA 3D structure prediction, we modify the trRosettaRNA folding process to integrate the torsion angles predicted by our model as restraints during the energy minimization procedure. Using the 3SUH and 4P9R RNAs from the T1 and T2 test sets, respectively, we generate 3D structures utilizing the original trRosettaRNA baseline and the TANGraph-restrained variant. In Fig. 5, the resulting structures are superimposed with the native ground truth conformations using PyMOL [28]. While the global folds predicted by the baseline trRosettaRNA model approximate the native structures, incorporating TANGraph's torsion angles refines the predicted conformations toward their native states. In particular, for 3SUH, trRosettaRNA yields a Root Mean Square Deviation (RMSD) of 2.0792 Å and an overall MCQ of 27.0418°, whereas the TANGraph-restrained variant reduces the RMSD to 1.8011 Å and the overall MCQ to 21.6784°. Likewise, for 4P9R, the TANGraph restraints improve the RMSD from 7.6707 Å to 7.0362 Å and the overall MCQ from 31.4959° to 26.8364°. These results confirm that TANGraph effectively guides the RNA folding process by correcting local stereochemical inconsistencies while preserving the global structural topology.

5 Conclusion

In this work, we presented a Hierarchical Heterogeneous GNN-based approach for RNA torsion angle prediction. In the proposed TANGraph model, we formulate the RNA molecule as a heterogeneous graph, where nodes correspond to nucleotides and torsion angles, incorporating RNA secondary structure information and angular structural topology. Through three hierarchical GNNs, TANGraph captures multi-scale structural dependencies within the RNA. Evaluation against 3D structure prediction and torsion angle prediction methods demonstrates the robustness and superior predictive accuracy of our model, with average relative improvements of 12.53% and 9.22% in terms of overall MCQ and MAE, respectively, when compared with the second-best competing method. Moreover, a case study showcases the contribution of TANGraph to RNA 3D structure prediction. Given the limited number of experimentally solved RNA structures, a promising future direction is the integration of physics-informed neural networks, introducing biophysical constraints into the torsion angle prediction process [27].

Disclosure of Interests. The authors have no competing interests to declare that are relevant to the content of this article.

References

1. Abir, A.R., Tahmid, M.T., Rayan, R.I., Rahman, M.S.: DeepRNA-twist: language-model-guided RNA torsion angle prediction with attention-inception network. Brief. Bioinf. **26**(3), bbaf199 (2025)
2. Altschul, S.F., Gish, W., Miller, W., Myers, E.W., Lipman, D.J.: Basic local alignment search tool. J. Mol. Biol. **215**(3), 403–410 (1990)
3. Bernard, C., Postic, G., Ghannay, S., Tahi, F.: State-of-the-RNArt: benchmarking current methods for RNA 3D structure prediction. NAR Genomics Bioinf. **6**(2), lqae048 (2024)
4. Bernard, C., Postic, G., Ghannay, S., Tahi, F.: RNA-TorsionBERT: leveraging language models for RNA 3D torsion angles prediction. Bioinformatics **41**(1), btaf004 (2025)
5. Bernhart, S.H., Hofacker, I.L., Stadler, P.F.: Local RNA base pairing probabilities in large sequences. Bioinformatics **22**(5), 614–615 (2006)
6. Bianchi, F.M., Grattarola, D., Livi, L., Alippi, C.: Graph neural networks with convolutional arma filters. IEEE Trans. Pattern Anal. Mach. Intell. **44**(7), 3496–3507 (2021)
7. Bottaro, S., Bussi, G., Pinamonti, G., Reißer, S., Boomsma, W., Lindorff-Larsen, K.: Barnaba: software for analysis of nucleic acid structures and trajectories. RNA **25**(2), 219–231 (2019)

8. Carrascoza, F., Antczak, M., Miao, Z., Westhof, E., Szachniuk, M.: Evaluation of the stereochemical quality of predicted RNA 3D models in the RNA-Puzzles submissions. RNA **28**(2), 250–262 (2022)
9. Cock, P.J., et al.: Biopython: freely available Python tools for computational molecular biology and bioinformatics. Bioinformatics **25**(11), 1422 (2009)
10. Das, R., et al.: Assessment of three-dimensional RNA structure prediction in CASP15. Proteins: Struct. Funct. Bioinf. **91**(12), 1747–1770 (2023)
11. Fu, L., Niu, B., Zhu, Z., Wu, S., Li, W.: CD-HIT: accelerated for clustering the next-generation sequencing data. Bioinformatics **28**(23), 3150–3152 (2012)
12. Higgs, P.G.: RNA secondary structure: physical and computational aspects. Q. Rev. Biophys. **33**(3), 199–253 (2000)
13. Jing, Y., Zhang, D., Li, L.: H2GnnDTI: hierarchical heterogeneous graph neural networks for drug–target interaction prediction. Bioinformatics **41**(4), btaf117 (2025)
14. Keating, K.S., Humphris, E.L., Pyle, A.M.: A new way to see RNA. Q. Rev. Biophys. **44**(4), 433–466 (2011)
15. Li, G., Xiong, C., Thabet, A., Ghanem, B.: Deepergcn: All you need to train deeper gcns, (2020). arXiv preprint arXiv:2006.07739
16. Li, J., Chen, S.J.: RNAJP: enhanced RNA 3D structure predictions with non-canonical interactions and global topology sampling. Nucleic Acids Res. **51**(7), 3341–3356 (2023)
17. Li, J., Zhang, S., Zhang, D., Chen, S.J.: Vfold-Pipeline: a web server for RNA 3D structure prediction from sequences. Bioinformatics **38**(16), 4042–4043 (2022)
18. Liang, S., et al.: HMCDA: a novel method based on the heterogeneous graph neural network and metapath for circRNA-disease associations prediction. BMC Bioinf. **24**(1), 335 (2023)
19. Lilley, D.M.: The origins of RNA catalysis in ribozymes. Trends Biochem. Sci. **28**(9), 495–501 (2003)
20. Ma, Y., Zhang, H., Jin, C., Kang, C.: Predicting lncRNA-protein interactions with bipartite graph embedding and deep graph neural networks. Front. Genet. **14**, 1136672 (2023)
21. Mackowiak, M., Adamczyk, B., Szachniuk, M., Zok, T.: RNAtango: Analysing and comparing RNA 3D structures via torsional angles. PLoS Comput. Biol. **20**(10), e1012500 (2024)
22. Magnus, M., et al.: RNA-Puzzles toolkit: a computational resource of RNA 3D structure benchmark datasets, structure manipulation, and evaluation tools. Nucleic Acids Res. **48**(2), 576–588 (2020)
23. McCaskill, J.S.: The equilibrium partition function and base pair binding probabilities for RNA secondary structure. Biopol. Original Res. Biomol. **29**(6-7), 1105–1119 (1990)
24. Murray, L.J., Arendall, W.B., III., Richardson, D.C., Richardson, J.S.: RNA backbone is rotameric. Proc. Natl. Acad. Sci. **100**(24), 13904–13909 (2003)
25. Nozinovic, S., Fürtig, B., Jonker, H.R., Richter, C., Schwalbe, H.: High-resolution NMR structure of an RNA model system: the 14-mer cUUCGg tetraloop hairpin RNA. Nucleic Acids Res. **38**(2), 683–694 (2010)
26. Penić, R.J., Vlašić, T., Huber, R.G., Wan, Y., Šikić, M.: Rinalmo: General-purpose rna language models can generalize well on structure prediction tasks. Nat. Commun. **16**(1), 5671 (2025)
27. Raissi, M., Perdikaris, P., Karniadakis, G.E.: Physics-informed neural networks: A deep learning framework for solving forward and inverse problems involving nonlinear partial differential equations. J. Comput. Phys. **378**, 686–707 (2019)

28. Schrodinger, L.: The PyMOL molecular graphics system. Version **1**, 8 (2015)
29. Singh, J., Paliwal, K., Singh, J., Zhou, Y.: RNA backbone torsion and pseudotorsion angle prediction using dilated convolutional neural networks. J. Chem. Inf. Model. **61**(6), 2610–2622 (2021)
30. Stasiewicz, J., Mukherjee, S., Nithin, C., Bujnicki, J.M.: QRNAS: software tool for refinement of nucleic acid structures. BMC Struct. Biol. **19**(1), 5 (2019)
31. Wadley, L.M., Keating, K.S., Duarte, C.M., Pyle, A.M.: Evaluating and learning from RNA pseudotorsional space: quantitative validation of a reduced representation for RNA structure. J. Mol. Biol. **372**(4), 942–957 (2007)
32. Wan, Y., Kertesz, M., Spitale, R.C., Segal, E., Chang, H.Y.: Understanding the transcriptome through RNA structure. Nat. Rev. Genet. **12**(9), 641–655 (2011)
33. Wang, W., et al.: trRosettaRNA: automated prediction of RNA 3D structure with transformer network. Nat. Commun. **14**(1), 7266 (2023)
34. Yan, Z., Hamilton, W.L., Blanchette, M.: Graph neural representational learning of RNA secondary structures for predicting RNA-protein interactions. Bioinformatics **36**(Supplement_1), i276–i284 (2020)
35. Zok, T., Popenda, M., Szachniuk, M.: MCQ4Structures to compute similarity of molecule structures. CEJOR **22**(3), 457–473 (2014)

Zero-To-Hero: Knowledge-Guided Unsupervised Active Learning for EEG-Based Detection of Interictal Epileptiform Discharges

Shen Liang[1], Cihang Yu[2], Qitong Wang[3(✉)], Delphine Roussel[4], Stephen Whitmarsh[5], Katia Lehongre[5], Alexandra Levchenko[6], Vincent Navarro[5], and Themis Palpanas[1]

[1] LIPADE, Université Paris Cité, Paris, France
shen.liang@u-pariscite.fr, themis@mi.parisdescartes.fr
[2] ENSEA, Cergy, France
cihang.yu@ensea.fr
[3] School of Engineering and Applied Sciences, Harvard University, Cambridge, USA
qitong@seas.harvard.edu
[4] Centre Institut de l'Audition, Institut Pasteur, Paris, France
delphine.roussel@pasteur.fr
[5] Sorbonne Université, Institut du Cerveau (ICM), Inserm, CNRS, APHP, Pitié-Salpêtrière Hospital, Paris, France
{stephen.whitmarsh,katia.lehongre,vincent.navarro}@icm-institute.org
[6] Isep, LISITE, Issy-les-Moulineux, France
alexandra.levchenko@isep.fr

Abstract. In electroencephalography (EEG) data, fast, high-amplitude transients called Interictal Epileptiform Discharges (IEDs) are highly valuable for epilepsy diagnosis and clinical research. Despite advances in deep learning-based IED detection, studies on reducing manual labeling of training data remain limited, particularly in selecting the most informative examples to label, a challenge largely due to data imbalance and heterogeneity. In this work, we propose Zero-to-Hero (Z2H), an Unsupervised Active Learning (UAL) pipeline that starts from a *completely unlabeled* EEG dataset to select high-quality labeled data with a limited manual labeling budget. With a knowledge-guided initialization module, an actively enhanced positive-unlabeled transduction module, and a knowledge-guided data filtering module, Z2H can achieve an optimal trade-off between data heterogeneity, balance, and label correctness. The data selected by Z2H can be used to both train a small IED detection model from scratch and fine-tune a pre-trained EEG Foundation Model (FM). Z2H can outperform multiple baselines and enable real-time user interaction. When paired with an FM, Z2H can reduce manual labeling by 95% while yielding similar or better IED detection accuracy.

Keywords: Interictal Epileptiform Discharge (IED) · electroencephalography (EEG) · Unsupervised Active Learning (UAL) · domain knowledge

M. Ceci et al. (Eds.): ECML PKDD 2026, LNAI 16948, pp. 670–688, 2027.
https://doi.org/10.1007/978-3-032-37679-4_38

1 Introduction

Epilepsy, the second most burdensome neurological disorder, is characterized by recurrent seizures. For some drug-resistant patients with focal epilepsy, surgery targeting the epileptogenic zone might be an option. As part of the clinical evaluation, recordings from implanted electroencephalography (EEG) electrodes are used to identify the seizure onset zone [12]. Such recordings might include Interictal Epileptiform Discharges (IEDs) (Fig. 1a), which are fast, high-amplitude EEG transients, typically followed by slow waves [5,31]. IEDs are valuable for epilepsy diagnosis and clinical research [26]. However, manual detection of IEDs within EEG recordings lasting days to weeks remains time-intensive.

To date, numerous deep learning models have been proposed for IED detection, mostly formulating IED detection as two-class (IED/non-IED) classification [7,8,21,24,29]. Most of these models are fully supervised [21,24,29], trained on fixed training sets that can be highly costly to manually label. Some reduce human effort by semi-supervision [7,24] or data augmentation [7,8], yet an important question remains unanswered: *Given an unlabeled EEG training set, which examples to select for manual labeling to minimize human effort while retaining high IED detection accuracy?*

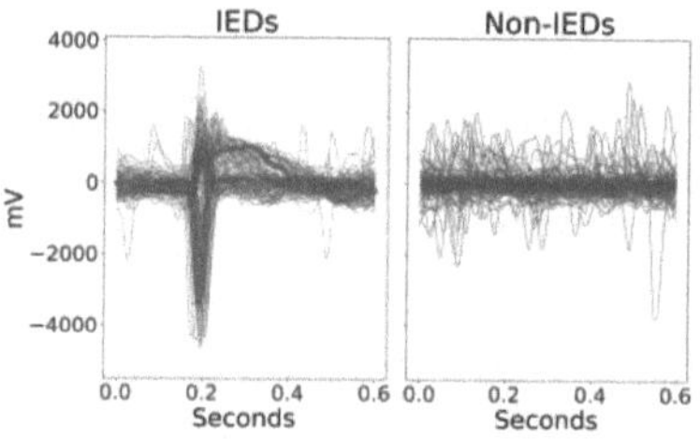

Fig. 1. Butterfly plots of 100 IEDs (with one shown in red) and 100 non-IEDs. Here we only plotted a single channel, while our method is adapted to *multi-channel* EEG. (Color figure online)

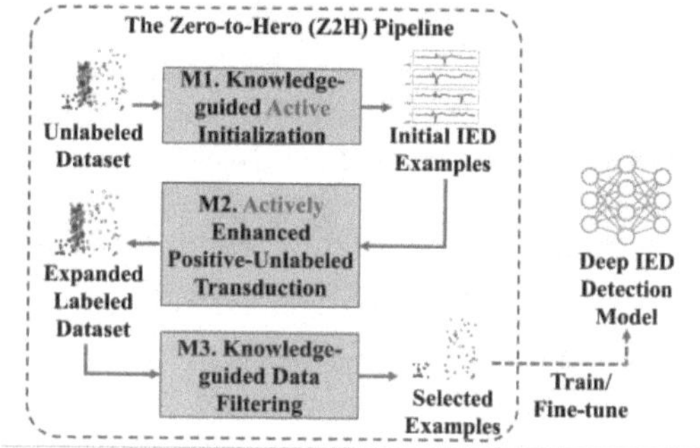

Fig. 2. A summary of the Z2H pipeline, with three modules M1-M3.

This question translates to **Unsupervised Active Learning (UAL)**, a type of Active Learning (AL) that aims to select a limited number (known as the AL *budget*) of candidate examples for manual labeling, starting from an *unlabeled* dataset. Existing UAL methods [10,14–17,20,27] typically favor examples that best reconstruct all or part of the dataset in a latent space. These methods have limited capacity to address two challenges within IED detection. First, IEDs are rare events, leading to significant **data imbalance** [29]. Second, both IEDs and non-IEDs exhibit **data heterogeneity**: On the one hand, despite their relatively well-defined morphologies [5], as shown in Fig. 1 *left)*, IEDs can entail a degree of diversity even for a single subject. On the other hand, as shown in Fig. 1 *right)*, the non-IED class is not well-defined and has a variance far greater than that of the IEDs. Notably, while some existing UAL methods [15,27] address data heterogeneity and imbalance with K-means in the latent space to preserve local clusters, as shown in Fig. 1 *right)*, the heterogeneity of the non-IEDs is characterized by highly random patterns, not by defined clusters. Thus, K-means (and other clustering methods) often have limited effectiveness, and we need to *increase the selected data size* to fully represent the non-IED space. However, existing UAL methods only produce training sets that are purely manually labeled and disregard any data that could be labeled automatically via semi-supervision. Thus, their selected data size is limited to the AL budget, which is often small. While these methods can be fused with a separate semi-supervised learner to expand the data size in a posterior manner, the lack of *built-in* semi-supervision can still limit their effectiveness.

In this work, we propose **Zero-to-Hero** (**Z2H**, Fig. 2), a UAL pipeline that starts from an EEG dataset with *zero* labeled examples and selects a set of labeled data to train/fine-tune an accurate IED detection model (hence *Zero-to-Hero*). Z2H includes three modules: 1) A knowledge-guided active initialization module (M1) that is *intentionally* biased to the IED class to address data imbalance; 2) A heterogeneity-aware active Positive-Unlabeled (PU) [18,30] transduction module (M2) that labels more data both *manually* and *automatically*, thereby expanding the labeled data size beyond the AL budget; 3) A knowledge-guided data filtering module (M3) that removes likely mislabeled data while enhancing data balance, yielding a high-quality set of labeled examples.

In summary, our contributions in this work are as follows:

- We propose Z2H, which is, to the best of our knowledge, the first UAL method tailored for IED detection, adopting a knowledge-guided, active-PU approach to achieve an optimal trade-off between data balance, heterogeneity, and label correctness. Z2H is *model-agnostic*, and the selected data can be used to build any *user-defined* IED detection model, including both training a small model from scratch and fine-tuning a pre-trained EEG Foundation Model (FM).
- Experimentally, Z2H can outperform multiple existing UAL methods while enabling real-time user interaction. When paired with an FM, it can reduce human labeling by 95% with little to no decay in IED detection accuracy.

2 The Proposed Method

2.1 M1: Knowledge-Guided Active Initialization

In Module M1 of Z2H, starting with an unlabeled dataset, we use AL to query the user for the labels of some initial seed examples. To handle data imbalance, we aim to *query examples likely to be IEDs first* to create an *intentional* bias to the IED class, using two pieces of domain knowledge:

1) IEDs are usually of high amplitude [5] compared to background activity, and likely have higher **Peak-to-Peak (P2P) amplitudes** (the difference between the highest and lowest points), as shown in Fig. 3a.
2) Despite a degree of heterogeneity, IED morphology is generally well-defined by a sharp spike, followed by a slow wave [5]. This suggests that the IED space is likely more compact than the non-IED space which entails more randomness. Consequently, the **Nearest Neighbor (NN) distance** of an IED, i.e., its distance (here we use z-normalized Euclidean Distance) to its nearest neighbor, is not likely to be large, as shown in Fig. 3b.

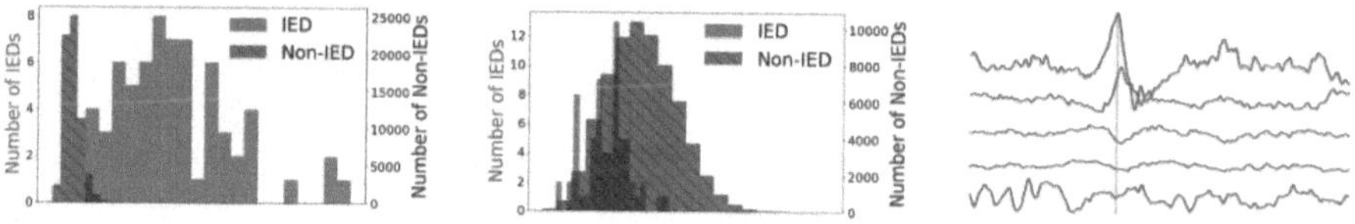

(a) Histogram of Peak-to-Peak (P2P) amplitude

(b) Histogram of Nearest Neighbor (NN) distance

(c) An IED event (IED spike indicated by grey line)

Fig. 3. Rationale behind the Amp_{Dist} sampling strategy. (a)(b) Histograms of P2P amplitudes and NN distances of single-channel EEG signals from a mouse. IEDs tend to have higher amplitudes and lower NN distances. (c) An IED in a multi-channel EEG snippet. Its spike is present in only part of all channels.

With this knowledge, we propose a *single-channel* $\boldsymbol{Amp_{Dist}}$ **sampling strategy**: *For a single-channel EEG dataset, query the examples in P2P amplitude descending order, but skip those with NN distances larger than some threshold* δ.

Here, we use P2P amplitudes to decide the primary query order, relegating NN distances to data filtering, as P2P amplitudes are more discriminative than NN distances. As shown in Fig. 3a and b, the histograms of P2P amplitudes are more separated between IEDs and non-IEDs than NN distances, as IEDs vary more in morphology than in amplitude.

Next, we extend Amp_{Dist} to *multi-channel* EEG as follows.

Step 1: *For a multi-channel EEG dataset with* n *examples, denoting the P2P amplitude of the* j*-th channel of the* i*-th example as* $a_{i,j}$*, let the mean-normalized P2P amplitude of the* j*-th channel of the* i*-th example be* $\tilde{a}_{i,j} = na_{i,j} / \sum_{i'=0}^{n-1} a_{i',j}$. *We define the normalized P2P amplitude of the* j*-th channel as* $\max_{i'} \tilde{a}_{i',j}$. *Rank all channels in normalized P2P amplitude-descending order.*

Step 2: In the aforementioned order, go through each channel in a round-robin manner; for each channel, query ‘-channel Amp_{Dist} before moving on to the next channel, until an IED is queried in a certain "target channel". Afterward, disregard all other channels and continue applying the single-channel Amp_{Dist} on the target channel.

Here, we opt for a single target channel rather than all channels, as IED spikes can often be present in only certain channels (Fig. 3c). In Step 1, we mean-normalize the P2P amplitudes to account for differing baseline amplitudes across channels. Then, for each channel, we use the amplitude of the example with the highest amplitude in that channel to represent the channel's amplitude, as such an example is most likely to be an IED. However, the channel ranking obtained this way can be interfered with by high-amplitude noise. Thus, we use the round-robin approach in Step 2 to robustify the choice of the target channel.

Efficiency-wise, in interactive AL, we mainly focus on *user interaction response time* [19], i.e., the delay between two consecutive user queries. For Amp_{Dist}, by pre-computing and pre-sorting the amplitudes and distances, we can minimize response time by using simple lookups to find the next example to query.

2.2 M2: Actively Enhanced Positive-Unlabeled (PU) Transduction

From M1, we could get a set PL of manually labeled positive (i.e., IED) examples and a set NL of negative (i.e., non-IED) ones. We denote the set of all remaining unlabeled examples as U. In M2, we label (part of) U examples with both *manual labeling* and *automatic inference* to expand the labeled data size beyond the AL budget, thus handling data heterogeneity, especially the highly random non-IEDs. To do so, we draw on *Positive Unlabeled (PU)* [18] transduction, a type of one-class semi-supervision that jointly uses PL and U to label U. We favor this one-class approach over using both PL and NL, for M1 created an intentional bias to the IEDs. Thus, NL cannot accurately represent the negative space.

Concretely, we use the one-class **Self-Training 1-Nearest-Neighbor (ST-1NN)** [30] algorithm (Fig. 4) for PU transduction, with two phases:
ST-1NN Phase 1: *Initialize an ordered set R with PL examples; iteratively find the U example with the smallest NN distance to R (measured by z-normalized Euclidean distance over all channels in our case) and move it from U to R. Examples moved into R earlier are considered more likely to be positive.*
ST-1NN Phase 2: *Decide the decision boundary with a* **stopping criterion** [9, 30] *splitting R into two: the first positive and the second negative.*

While simple, ST-1NN is generally suitable for use cases such as IED detection, where the positive class is relatively compact, while the negative class is highly diverse and without well-defined clusters. However, ST-1NN alone often yields sub-optimal results. In particular, besides a diverse negative class, IED detection also involves a heterogeneous positive class. Despite relatively well-defined morphologies, IEDs can exhibit a degree of diversity even within a single patient. ST-1NN largely disregards this diversity, as in Phase 2, it draws on a **Positive/Negative Conglomeration (PNC)** assumption: *in the ordered set R, the positive and negative examples conglomerate at the beginning and the end, with a single boundary between the two defined by the stopping criterion.* This often fails to hold. For instance, in Fig. 4b, with heterogeneous initial PL examples 0, 1, 2, the neighborhoods around positive examples 6 and 7 are different, with 7 closer to negative examples 8 and 9 than 6 is to positive example 11. As

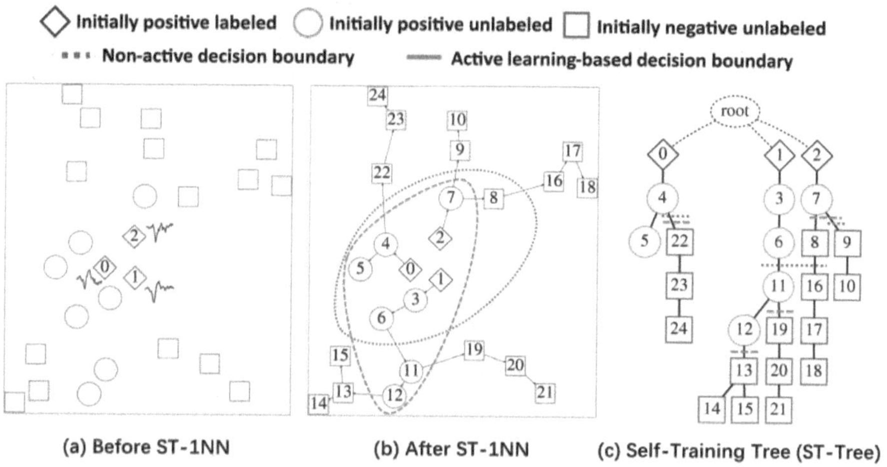

Fig. 4. An illustration of ST-1NN. (a)(b) are the states before and after ST-1NN. Numbers in the nodes are in the order in which they were moved to the ordered set R. The edges link them to their NNs in R when they were moved. Drawing on the ST-Tree in (c), our AL-based approach can yield a better decision boundary.

a result, 11 (whose NN in U was 6 when 11 was moved from U to R) and 12 were moved to R after negative examples 8 (whose NN was 7), 9 and 10

In response, we draw on the *Self-Training Tree (ST-Tree)* [19] (Fig. 4c), where each example is a node with an edge between it and its NN in R when it was moved from U to R. ST-Tree naturally encodes data heterogeneity, as examples in different *branches* (paths from an initial PL example to a leaf node) tend to diverge in morphology. Thus, while the PNC assumption is too rigid, the following **Branch-wise PNC (BPNC)** assumption is far more realistic: *each branch has 1) all positive nodes, or 2) positive and negative nodes conglomerated at the beginning and the end, separated by a branch-wise decision boundary.* For instance, in Fig. 4c, the branch 0– 4– 5 is all positive, while 0– 4– 22– 23– 24 has a clear branch-wise boundary between 4 and 22. Note that a branch cannot be all negative, as it must start with a PL example.

Based on BPNC, we propose a novel AL-based branch-wise inference method to replace the non-AL-based stopping criterion in ST-1NN Phase 2. As shown in Alg. 1, we actively infer the labels of U examples in as many branches as possible (we will discuss the ordering of the branches later), finding an individualized decision boundary for each branch. For a given branch, we first query from the user the ground truth label of its leaf node, which can be one of 2 cases.

Case 1: The leaf is positive (line 4 of Alg. 1). By BPNC, this branch is most likely all positive.

E.g.: For the branch 0– 4– 5 *in Fig.* 4c, *with* 5 *actively queried as positive,* 4 *is automatically inferred as positive.*

Algorithm 1: Active Branch-wise Inference

Input : initial unlabeled examples U, an ST-Tree *tree* from ST-1NN Phase 1
Output: inferred positive and negative examples *infP* and *infN*

1 $infP, infN = [], []$;
2 **while** *AL budget remains* **do**
3     $branch$ = nextBranch($tree$); $label$ = activeQuery($branch.leaf$);
4   **if** *isPositive(label)* **then** $infP$.add($branch$);
5   **else**
6         $firstN, lastP$ = activeBinarySearchBranchwiseBoundary($branch$);
7         $infP$.add($branch.first : lastP$); $infN$.add($tree$.subTree($firstN$));
8     $tree$.trim($infP, infN$);

Case 2: The leaf is negative (line 5-line 7). By BPNC, we find the branch-wise boundary via an *active binary search*. Concretely, for each node checked, we query the ground truth labels of it and its parent: if both are positive, then we are in the positive space and need to check the examples after this node; if both are negative, we check those before it. The search ends when we have found a negative node *firstN* whose parent *lastP* is positive, with the branch-wise boundary in between.

E.g., in the branch 1– 3– 6– 11– 12– 13– 14 we observe that the leaf node 14 is negative. Following binary search, we query 11 and its parent 6 (which are at the midpoint of the branch) and find both to be positive. This indicates that the decision boundary is after 11. Again, following binary search, we then query 13 and its parent 12, and find that 13 is negative and 12 is positive. Thus, we determine 13 as *firstN* and 12 as *lastP*, with the branch-wise boundary between them. All unlabeled examples before 13 are inferred as positive (i.e., 3). Also, by BPNC, all unlabeled examples in the sub-tree rooted at *firstN* (i.e., 15) are inferred as negative.

Having checked the current branch, in line 8, we trim part of the sub-tree rooted at its initial *PL* example, removing all nodes in it with both themselves and all their descendants already labeled (queried or inferred). For instance, having labeled 1– 3– 6– 11– 12– 13– 14 (and 15), we can remove 12, 13, 14, 15, but keep 1, 3, 6, 11 as they have unlabeled descendants 19, 20, 21.

As for the order in which the branches are queried, we aim to maximize the number of examples inferred per query. Concretely, by finding *firstN* in one branch $\mathcal{B}$, we can potentially trim the entire sub-tree $\mathcal{T}$ rooted at its initial *PL* example. We denote the number of U nodes in $\mathcal{T}$ as u. Also, we need $O(lg(l))$ queries to find *firstN*, l being the number of examples yet to be labeled in $\mathcal{B}$. We score $\mathcal{B}$ by its estimated number of examples inferred per query, i.e. $u/lg(l)$. The branch with the highest score is queried next.

Note that in [19], we proposed a similar AL-based post-processing method for ST-1NN. However, that method can only select one or several non-AL-based ST-1NN configurations from a set of candidates, whereas in M2 of Z2H, we can surpass the non-AL-based alternatives. Critically, [19] relies on the ensemble of non-AL-based candidates to determine the decision boundary, while in M2, the branch-wise boundaries are independent of any non-AL-based stopping criteria. As we will show in Sect. 3.2, compared to these non-AL-based stopping criteria, our AL-based branch-wise method can significantly enhance the automatic inference accuracy of ST-1NN. Efficiency-wise, our method has a worst-case user interaction response time of $O(|U|)$, where $|U|$ is the number of U examples before ST-1NN. See [1] for a proof of this complexity. As will be shown in Sect. 3.2, the delays are usually negligible.

2.3 M3: Knowledge-Guided Data Filtering

M2 expanded the labeled data beyond the AL budget, and our AL-based decision boundary greatly enhanced inference quality. Still, some misinferred data may remain. To filter them, in M3, we again draw on the domain knowledge that IEDs tend to have high amplitudes, and *filter all examples inferred as IEDs/non-IEDs but with P2P amplitudes (in the target channel found in M1) below/above some threshold* γ. The remaining labeled data is used to train/fine-tune a user-defined deep IED detection model (called the **core model**).

While simple, M3 is effective for three reasons: 1) Rooted in domain knowledge, it can further enhance **label correctness**. 2) It can still preserve a large number of automatically inferred examples in M2, retaining the ability to break the **data size** limit imposed by the AL budget. 3) Besides duly filtering misinferred examples, M3 can filter some correctly inferred examples, which may seem undesirable, but can actually improve data quality. This is because M3 typically filters a higher proportion of (correctly inferred) non-IEDs than IEDs, enhancing the **data balance** of the resulting dataset. Specifically, we have the following theorem:

Theorem 1. *Suppose that IEDs account for $x\%$ of all examples in the dataset, where $x < 50$. Assume that the distributions of correctly inferred IEDs and non-IEDs are the same as those of all IEDs and non-IEDs. Let A_P and A_N denote the P2P amplitudes of a randomly chosen IED and a randomly chosen non-IED. Define $F_P(a) = P(A_P < a)$ and $F_N(a) = P(A_N < a)$ as the proportions of IEDs and non-IEDs whose P2P amplitudes are lower than some threshold a. Assume that A_P first-order stochastically dominates A_N, namely, $\forall a, F_P(a) \leq F_N(a)$. Assume further that the relevant distributions are continuous and that the mixture distribution of all P2P amplitudes is strictly increasing in the relevant range. Let a_t be a threshold satisfying $F_P(a_t) + F_N(a_t) = 1$. Suppose that the M3 filtering threshold γ is set to the y-th percentile of the P2P amplitudes of all examples. Let r_P and r_N be the proportions of correctly inferred IEDs and non-IEDs that are filtered by M3 among all correctly inferred IEDs and non-IEDs, respectively. Then,*

$$F_P(a_t) \leq 0.5 \tag{1}$$

and

$$r_N > r_P \iff y < (100 - x) - (100 - 2x)F_P(a_t). \tag{2}$$

From Theorem 1, we have the following lemma.

Lemma 1. ***Lemma 2.*** *Under the same assumptions as in Theorem 1, if* $x \ll 50$ *and* $F_P(a_t) \ll 0.5$*, then* $r_N > r_P$ *holds for most choices of* y *below* $100 - x$*, except when* y *is very close to* $100 - x$*.*

See [1] for the proofs of Theorem 1 and Lemma 1, which indicate that if the IEDs generally have greater P2P amplitudes than non-IEDs, with good separation between the distributions of the two, and that the proportion of IEDs in the dataset is very small, then γ can usually be set to a very wide range of values to improve data balance among the correctly inferred examples. As we will show in Sect. 3.1, it is an optimal trade-off between label correctness, data size and data balance that enables Z2H to yield high-quality labeled data.

Table 1. Data statistics. $|P|$ and $|N|$ are the numbers of IEDs and non-IEDs. Unless an *inter*-subject setting is explicitly stated, all experiments were done *independently* for each subject, without referencing data from other subjects.

Dataset	Sampling Rate (Hz)	Length (seconds)	Number of Channels	Train (initially unlabeled)			Test		
				|P|	|N|	|P|/|N|	|P|	|N|	|P|/|N|
H1	512	1.5	5	1782	93788	0.019	357	18758	0.019
H2				2769	95981	0.029	554	19197	0.029
H3				10178	84477	0.120	2036	16896	0.121
H4				3043	93137	0.033	609	18628	0.033
H5				5526	90297	0.061	1105	18060	0.061
H6				2561	87229	0.029	512	17446	0.029
H7				8089	72915	0.111	1618	14583	0.111
H8				2208	90339	0.024	442	18068	0.024
MO1		0.09		2639	56048	0.047	528	11210	0.047
MO2				394	56666	0.007	79	11334	0.007
MO3			4	66	66110	0.001	14	13222	0.001

3 Experimental Evaluation

We evaluate Z2H using data from two groups of real-world datasets: 1) **H1–H8:** 24-h EEG data from 8 human patients. All intracranial EEG procedures for the requisition of these data were performed according to clinical practice and the epilepsy features of the patients [13]. Patients gave written informed consent (Project C11-16 conducted by INSERM and approved by the local ethics committee, CPP Paris VI). 2) **MO1–MO3:** 1-h EEG data from 3 mice, for which experimental procedures were conducted in compliance with the European Committee Council Directive (2010/63/EU) and received approval from the French Ministry for Research and the local Ethical Committee. Following the practice of [29], we bandpass-filtered (1–50 Hz) and downsampled (from 4,096 to 512 Hz) the data before using sliding windows (1.5 s for humans, 0.09 s for mice) to segment the continuous recordings into individual examples, which are split into training and test sets at 5 : 1. Table 1 summarizes the data statistics. See [1] for detailed data acquisition and preprocessing protocols.

Z2H can be fused with any user-defined core model for IED detection. Here we consider the following two groups of core models: 1) *AiED* [21], *iEDeal* [29], which are small models trained from scratch with data selected by Z2H. 2) *EEGPT* [28], *Neuro-GPT* [4], which are pre-trained EEG Foundation Models (FMs) using Z2H for fine-tuning data selection. See [1] for their detailed hyper-parameter settings.

We ran our experiments with an Intel Xeon Platinum 8468 CPU, an NVIDIA H100 GPU and 512 GB RAM on the Jean Zay supercomputer. All code is Python. Next, we will first compare Z2H with rival UAL methods, and its ablations, in both *intra-* and *inter-subject* settings. We then explore the effects of parameter settings and design choices in each module, as well as user-interaction efficiency. All our source code and the mouse data MO1-MO3 are available at [1].

3.1 Comparison with Baselines and Ablation

We compare Z2H with the following baseline and ablation methods.

- **Fully-Supervised (FS):** manually label *all* available data. Intuitively, this is an *upper bound* of any UAL method, but it can be outperformed sometimes.
- **Random:** a random sampling strategy, averaged over 10 seeds.
- **ALSL-U** [16], **ALLG** [20], **ALMS** [14], **DUAL-S3P** [15]: UAL methods.
- **Z2H-Only-M1, Z2H-M1-M2:** Z2H ablations. Z2H-Only-M1 only selects examples manually labeled in M1; Z2H-M1-M2 omits data filtering in M3.

We set the total AL budget to $5\%, 10\%, \ldots, 30\%$ of all training examples. Z2H has 3 parameters: 1) allocation of AL budget between M1 and M2 (M3 does not have an AL component), for which we use a 7 : 3 ratio; 2) the NN distance threshold δ in M1, which we set to the 50-percentile (median) of all NN distances; 3) the amplitude threshold γ in M3, which we also set to the 50-percentile. These parameters are shared by Z2H-Only-M1 and Z2H-M1-M2, except that for Z2H-Only-M1, we reallocate the AL budget intended for M2 to M1 for a fair comparison. See [1] for the parameter settings of the other methods.

We compare the methods above by pairing them with the core deep models mentioned earlier and evaluate them by their online IED detection F1-scores on test sets. Due to page limits, we cannot present all raw results here. Instead, we draw on the Critical Difference (CD) diagram [6] to compare their statistical differences (Fig. 5). Specifically, we compare the methods across all combinations of core models, human/mouse subjects, and total AL budget, using the Friedman test and the Wilcoxon signed-rank test [3,19]. In each CD diagram, methods to the right rank higher on average. Should several methods show no statistically significant difference, they would be grouped into the same clique (not present in our results). Besides the CD diagrams, we focus on the case with the smallest

Table 2. F1-scores of core models on the test sets with a total AL budget of 5% of all data, using Z2H, its ablations, and rival methods for training/fine-tuning data selection. Best results except for *Fully Supervised (FS)* are shown in **bold**; second bests are underlined. "–" indicates failed training or invalid fields.

Method	H1	H2	H3	H4	H5	H6	H7	H8	MO1	MO2	MO3	Avg. F1	Avg. Rank
Core Model: AiED													
FS	0.66	0.59	0.83	0.70	0.87	0.81	0.90	0.75	0.92	0.96	–	0.80	–
Random	0.51	–	0.72	0.45	0.79	0.55	0.82	0.60	0.86	–	–	0.66	5.62
ALSL-U	0.55	–	0.73	–	0.75	0.56	0.47	–	0.84	–	–	0.65	6.00
ALLG	0.54	–	**0.74**	0.49	0.78	0.58	0.83	0.62	0.86	0.87	–	0.70	4.11
ALMS	0.56	–	0.72	0.49	0.80	0.51	0.82	0.61	**0.87**	–	–	0.67	4.25
DUAL-S3P	0.57	0.16	0.67	0.49	0.80	0.48	0.79	0.67	0.86	0.89	–	0.64	4.50
Z2H-Only-M1	0.60	0.25	**0.74**	0.53	0.80	0.64	0.83	0.70	0.81	0.91	–	0.68	2.70
Z2H-M1-M2	**0.63**	0.39	0.63	0.58	0.68	0.65	0.72	0.70	0.72	0.89	–	0.66	4.30
Z2H (ours)	0.58	**0.43**	**0.74**	**0.66**	**0.82**	**0.77**	**0.86**	**0.73**	**0.87**	**0.94**	**0.78**	**0.74**	**1.18**
Core Model: iEDeal													
FS	0.84	0.75	0.93	0.87	0.94	0.93	0.96	0.88	0.91	0.79	0.60	0.85	–
Random	0.56	0.39	0.75	0.58	0.78	0.61	0.84	0.71	0.87	0.59	0.47	0.65	4.64
ALSL-U	0.55	0.22	0.75	0.46	**0.80**	0.63	0.84	0.71	0.86	0.76	–	0.66	4.70
ALLG	0.55	0.39	0.74	0.53	**0.80**	0.59	0.84	0.69	0.86	0.47	–	0.65	5.20
ALMS	0.54	0.39	0.75	0.58	0.79	0.59	0.85	0.71	0.80	0.43	0.58	0.64	5.00
DUAL-S3P	0.58	0.40	0.71	0.53	0.79	0.57	0.82	0.73	**0.88**	0.76	0.65	0.67	4.55
Z2H-Only-M1	0.63	0.43	0.77	0.62	**0.80**	0.65	0.84	0.75	0.87	0.81	**0.67**	0.71	**2.27**
Z2H-M1-M2	**0.71**	**0.58**	0.68	**0.73**	0.74	**0.82**	0.78	0.79	0.71	0.82	0.50	0.71	4.09
Z2H (ours)	0.61	0.37	**0.86**	0.60	0.79	0.70	**0.90**	**0.84**	**0.88**	**0.83**	0.61	**0.73**	2.45
Core Model: EEGPT (Foundation Model)													
FS	0.84	0.60	0.90	0.84	0.93	0.86	0.95	0.89	0.91	0.86	0.73	0.85	–
Random	0.77	0.59	0.87	0.82	0.90	0.76	0.93	0.87	0.89	0.82	0.13	0.76	4.55
ALSL-U	0.79	0.60	**0.88**	0.78	**0.91**	0.76	**0.94**	**0.88**	0.89	0.80	0.35	0.78	3.82
ALLG	0.77	0.58	0.87	0.80	0.90	0.79	0.93	0.86	**0.90**	0.82	–	0.82	4.40
ALMS	0.81	0.58	0.87	0.82	**0.91**	0.77	0.93	0.86	0.89	0.85	0.64	0.81	3.27
DUAL-S3P	0.79	0.62	0.87	0.81	0.90	0.77	0.93	0.85	0.89	0.83	0.80	0.82	3.82
Z2H-Only-M1	0.36	0.66	**0.88**	**0.84**	**0.91**	0.81	0.93	0.87	**0.90**	0.83	0.78	0.80	2.55
Z2H-M1-M2	0.81	0.43	0.68	0.76	0.77	0.70	0.78	0.79	0.62	0.83	0.60	0.71	6.73
Z2H (ours)	**0.82**	**0.70**	0.87	**0.84**	**0.91**	**0.83**	**0.94**	**0.88**	0.88	**0.88**	**0.83**	**0.85**	**1.73**
Core Model: Neuro-GPT (Foundation Model)													
FS	0.87	0.71	0.92	0.87	0.94	0.93	0.95	0.89	0.86	0.94	0.25	0.83	–
Random	0.82	0.65	**0.90**	0.82	0.91	0.89	0.93	0.84	0.76	0.57	0.02	0.74	4.00
ALSL-U	0.83	0.65	0.89	0.79	0.90	0.89	0.92	0.83	0.76	0.37	0.08	0.72	5.09
ALLG	0.82	0.66	**0.90**	0.81	0.91	0.88	0.92	0.83	0.76	0.52	–	0.80	4.40
ALMS	0.84	0.65	**0.90**	0.84	0.91	0.88	0.93	0.87	0.59	0.34	0.35	0.74	3.82
DUAL-S3P	0.81	0.69	0.89	0.83	**0.92**	0.88	0.93	0.87	0.69	0.67	0.26	0.77	3.73
Z2H-Only-M1	0.80	0.64	0.89	**0.85**	0.90	**0.93**	**0.94**	0.86	0.58	0.76	0.36	0.77	4.09
Z2H-M1-M2	**0.86**	0.60	0.70	0.75	0.67	0.82	0.79	0.86	0.64	**0.91**	0.13	0.70	5.91
Z2H (ours)	0.85	**0.71**	0.89	**0.85**	**0.92**	**0.93**	**0.94**	**0.88**	**0.81**	0.87	**0.55**	**0.84**	**1.45**

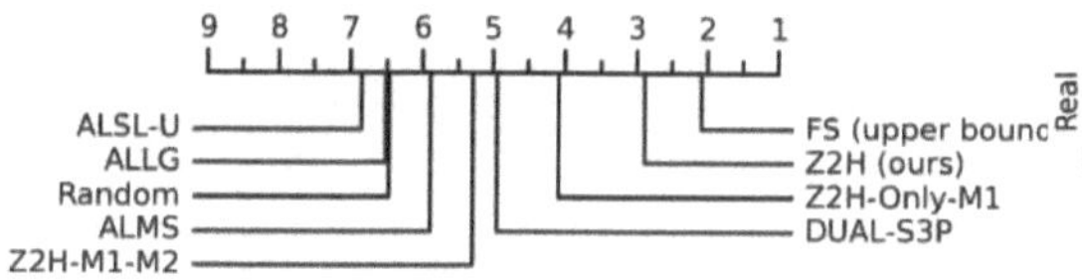

Fig. 5. CD diagram of Z2H, its ablations and rival UAL methods. Methods to the right are better. *FS* denotes fully supervised training with all available data manually labeled and is an intuitive *upper bound* for UAL methods.

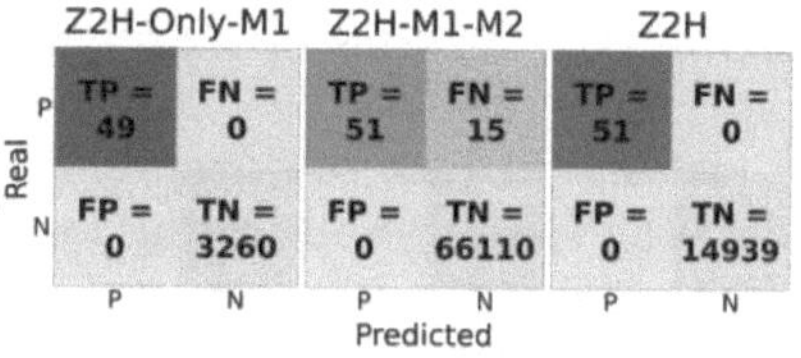

Fig. 6. Confusion matrices of the selected training data on MO3 (not to be confused with the online IED detection results on the test set in Fig. 5 and Table 2).

total AL budget, just 5% of all examples, as this reduces human labor the most (by 95%). The raw F1-scores in this case are shown in Table 2.

As shown in Fig. 5, except Z2H and its ablations, the best rival UAL method is DUAL-S3P, likely because it explicitly addresses data heterogeneity and imbalance with K-Means. However, it is still limited in its capacity to handle the high level of randomness in the non-IED space. By contrast, Z2H significantly outperforms all other non-FS rivals, as is corroborated by the raw results in Table 2. Specifically, Z2H generally performs better when paired with pre-trained FMs (especially EEGPT) than with models trained from scratch, highlighting the superiority of FMs. Also, the FMs with Z2H often have results very close to FS with just 5% of manual labeling, and in certain cases (e.g., MO3), it greatly outperforms FS, thanks to the power of Z2H to select the most informative examples. Among the Z2H ablations, Z2H-Only-M1 generally outperforms Z2H-M1-M2, which seems to suggest that M2 has a negative effect. However, we now explore *why* Z2H performs well and how M2 has a positive impact on it.

Specifically, we examine MO3, the most imbalanced subject with an extreme positive-to-negative ratio of 0.001. We show the confusion matrices of the selected training data by all variants of Z2H in Fig. 6. Here, Z2H-Only-M1 has the best data balance, yet its performance is limited by the labeled data size, which is restricted to the AL budget. This prevents Z2H-Only-M1 from adequately capturing the heterogeneity of the negative space. On the other hand, Z2H-M1-M2 greatly expands the data size, but is affected by misinferred data and poor data balance. By contrast, Z2H, as we claimed in Sect. 2.3, has the best trade-off between data size, data balance, and label correctness. This highlights the contribution of M2, which enables Z2H to exceed the AL budget limit and achieve far greater data size, thus better handling data heterogeneity.

The reader may have noticed that with iEDeal as the core model, Z2H has weaker results than when paired with the other core models, while Z2H-M1-M2 is stronger than usual, outperforming Z2H in multiple cases. This is likely because iEDeal is tailored to imbalanced data, with a loss function that simulates the F-score as well as a negative sampling strategy. Thus, the gains of Z2H over

Z2H-M1-M2 in terms of data balance are not as pronounced for iEDeal as for other core models.

[***Inter*-subject results**] So far, we have focused on an *intra*-subject setting where the training and testing were done on the same subject. We now examine an *inter*-subject setting where the training and testing are on different subjects, offering greater real-world utility. Here, we apply a leave-one-out strategy for the human data, training the core model on all humans except one and using the latter for testing. Due to limited GPU hours, we only consider the total AL budget setting of 5% of all data, and use EEGPT (which generally performed best in the *intra*-subject setting in Table 2) as the core model. As shown in Table 3, where Hi' means the subject Hi is used for testing, Z2H again has the best overall results. However, its advantage has been diminished. It is likely that we need to incorporate Z2H with some domain adaptation/generalization technique to fully unleash its potential in the inter-subject setting where the data distributions of the training and testing data can be drastically different, which we will address in our future work.

Table 3. F1-scores of EEGPT in an *inter*-subject setting, with a total AL budget of 5% of all data, using Z2H, its ablations and rivals for fine-tuning data selection.

Method	H1$'$	H2$'$	H3$'$	H4$'$	H5$'$	H6$'$	H7$'$	H8$'$	Avg. F1	Avg. Rank
FS	0.59	0.30	0.85	0.82	0.85	0.57	0.74	0.84	0.70	–
Random	0.64	0.30	<u>0.85</u>	<u>0.80</u>	<u>0.80</u>	0.49	0.70	0.83	0.68	<u>3.38</u>
ALSL-U	<u>0.67</u>	0.28	0.84	**0.81**	0.75	0.35	0.68	0.84	0.65	4.50
ALLG	0.66	0.24	<u>0.85</u>	<u>0.80</u>	0.70	**0.52**	0.69	0.83	0.66	3.88
ALMS	0.54	0.32	**0.86**	<u>0.80</u>	<u>0.80</u>	0.47	0.66	0.82	0.66	4.00
DUAL-S3P	0.59	0.34	**0.86**	<u>0.80</u>	0.74	<u>0.50</u>	<u>0.74</u>	0.82	0.67	3.50
Z2H-Only-M1	0.66	<u>0.37</u>	<u>0.85</u>	0.78	<u>0.80</u>	0.41	**0.88**	0.78	<u>0.69</u>	3.88
Z2H-M1-M2	0.52	0.11	0.82	0.58	0.65	0.12	0.21	<u>0.85</u>	0.48	7.25
Z2H (ours)	**0.72**	**0.41**	<u>0.85</u>	0.78	**0.82**	0.46	0.66	**0.86**	**0.70**	**3.00**

3.2 Parameter Analysis and Further Experiments

We now examine the effects of parameter settings and the design of each module, before looking into the efficiency of user interaction.

[**Module M1**] We examine the effect of the NN distance threshold δ in our $\boldsymbol{Amp_{Dist}}$ strategy in M1, as well as some rival methods. For δ, we consider the $10, 20, \ldots, 90$-percentiles on all NN distances. For the rivals of Amp_{Dist}, besides the UAL methods used in Sect. 3.1, we consider 3 knowledge-guided variants of Amp_{Dist}: ***Dist*** which follows an NN distance ascending order with no consideration of amplitude, ***Amp*** which follows a P2P distance descending order with no NN distance-based skipping, and $\boldsymbol{Dist_{Amp}}$ which follows an NN distance ascending order while skipping examples with P2P amplitudes *below* some threshold, for which we also choose from $10, 20, \ldots, 90$-percentiles and only report the best result among them for fairness to this rival method.

Recall that in M1, we aim to query likely IED examples first. Thus, for the evaluation metric, we use the *precision at k (p@k)*, i.e. the proportion of IEDs among the first k examples queried. The results are shown in Fig. 7 where we focus on $k = 100$. As shown in Fig. 7 *left)*, when δ is between 40 and 60-percentiles, the $p@100$ value is generally high for most datasets, thus justifying our choice of the 50-percentile in Sect. 3.1. Note that the trend on H2 differs from the other subjects, where the 50-percentile yields a relatively low $p@100$, likely due to unusually high noise on H2. In fact, the scores on H2 are generally lower than those on the others.

In Fig. 7 *right)*, among the four knowledge-guide methods, $Dist$ and $Dist_{Amp}$ are generally outperformed by &and Amp_{Dist}, justifying our choice to use the P2P amplitudes (rather than the NN distances) to decide the primary query order. &and Amp_{Dist} also outperform the non-knowledge-guided methods, with Amp_{Dist} edging out &thanks to the incorporation of NN distances.

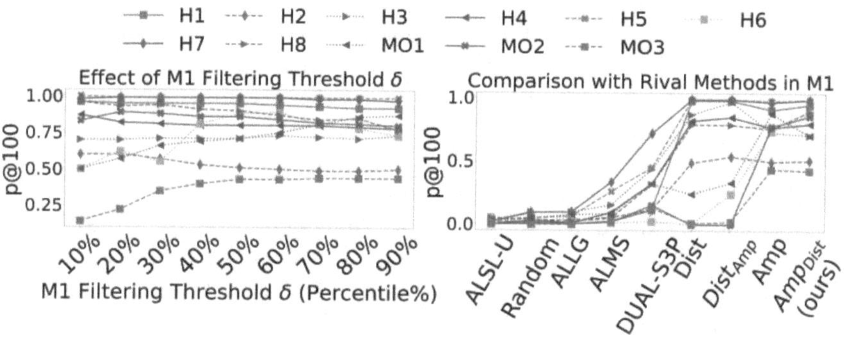

Fig. 7. Precision at 100 ($p@100$) in Module M1. *left)* The effect of the NN distance threshold δ on our Amp_{Dist} sampling strategy. *right)* Comparison between Amp_{Dist} (with δ being 50-percentile) and its rivals. The methods on the x-axis are placed from left to right in ascending order of their average $p@100$.

[Module M2] We now examine the AL budget allocation between M1 and M2, and compare our method with rival methods in terms of translation F1-score, i.e., the F1-score of the automatic inference of U examples in M2. For budget allocation, we consider $M1 : M2 = 1 : 9, 2 : 8, \ldots, 10 : 0$ (note that $0 : 10$ is not feasible). When the budget is not enough to find the decision boundaries for all ST-Tree branches, we use the non-AL-based stopping criterion GBTRM [9] to decide the labels of U examples on those branches, as GBTRM tends to outperform other stopping criteria empirically. For rival methods, we consider **ST-1NN**, **TC-ST-1NN**, **RoSAS** [32], **FeaWAD** [34] and **DeepSAD** [23], which are semi-supervised learners. ST-1NN equates M2 with no AL-based

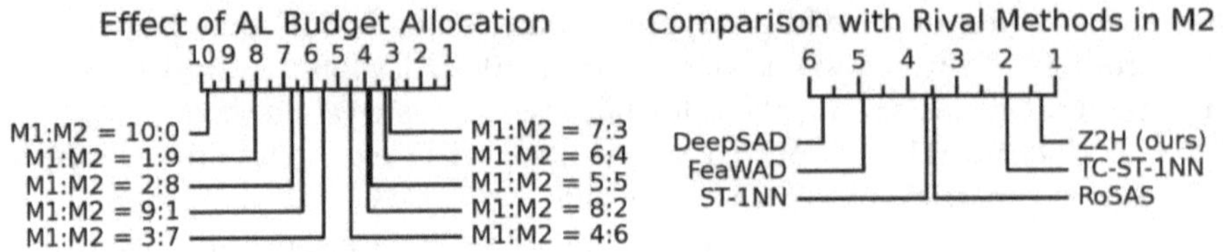

Fig. 8. CD diagrams of transduction F1-scores in M2. Methods to the right are better. *left)* Effect of AL budget allocation between M1 and M2. *right)* Comparison between Z2H ($M1 : M2 = 7 : 3$) with rival methods.

enhancement, using GBTRM as the stopping criterion; TC-ST-1NN is the two-class variant of ST-1NN that uses both the PL and NL sets obtained in M1; the others are deep learners. Since these methods cannot benefit from AL in M2, we set $M1 : M2 = 10 : 0$ for them to fully exploit the total AL budget and ensure fairness. See [1] for detailed settings of rival methods.

The results are shown in Fig. 8, which are CD diagrams for all combinations of the total AL budget ($5\%, 10\%, \ldots, 30\%$) and the subject. Figure 8 *left)* shows $M1 : M2 = 7 : 3$ as the best budget allocation, justifying our use of it in Sect. 3.1. Figure 8 *right)* shows that ST-1NN is beaten by TC-ST-1NN, which seems to contradict our choice of this one-class solution over the two-class one. However, this is mainly due to the limited power of ST-1NN's non-AL-based stopping criterion to handle data heterogeneity. With our AL-based decision boundary, Z2H significantly outperforms all rival methods, including TC-ST-1NN.

[**Module M3**] We now examine the P2P amplitude threshold γ in M3, for which we consider the $10, 20, \ldots, 90$-percentiles. Again limited by GPU hours, we only consider the F1-score of EEGPT with a total AL budget of 5% of all data. As shown in Fig. 9, Z2H is generally insensitive to γ, with the 50-percentile generally yielding good results, which justifies our choice of it in Sect. 3.1.

[**Efficiency**] We examine the user interaction response time in M1 and M2 (M3 does not entail user interaction), i.e., the delays between user queries, averaged over 50 runs. As shown in Fig. 10, on average, M1 has smaller delays than M2, as the former requires only simple lookups (which empirically take constant time in most cases) while the latter takes $O(|U|)$ time. The delays in M2 exhibit large variance because the actions to take between two queries vary. In general, the delay will be longer if the current query is the last query made on an ST-Tree branch, as we need to find the next branch to query. In most cases, the delays in both M1 and M2 are negligible, enabling real-time interaction.

4 Related Work

[**IED Detection**] To date, various machine learning methods have been proposed for IED detection. While early works drew on shallow learners with pre-defined features [2,25], recent ones mainly adopt deep models such as CNN [7,21,24,29], LSTM [8], and Transformer [22]. Some works have explored

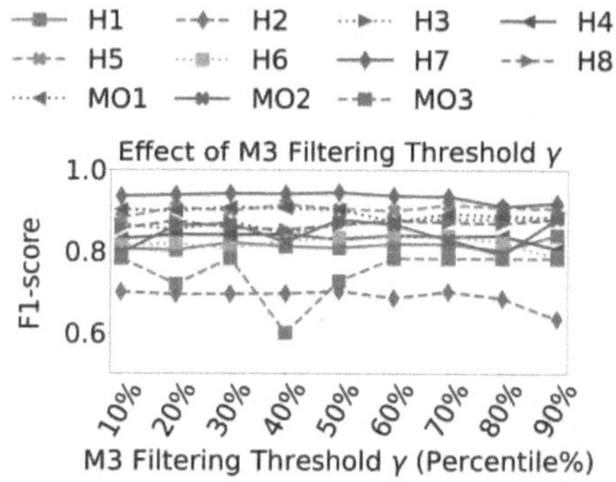

Fig. 9. F1-scores of EEGPT with Z2H under varying settings of the M3 filtering threshold γ, with a total AL budget of 5% of all data.

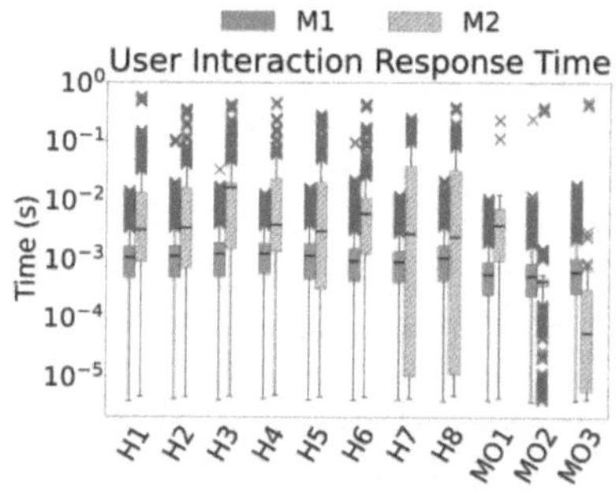

Fig. 10. User interaction response times in M1 and M2. Time axis on a log scale. ×" indicates outliers. These response times are mostly negligible in real-time interactions.

reducing manual labeling via semi-supervision [7] and data augmentation [7,8], yet they can still require large numbers of pre-existing manual labels, entailing no AL elements. Regarding data imbalance, in [29], we proposed a novel loss function to optimize the F-score, coupled with a negative sampling strategy. However, that method relied on a fully labeled training set, without looking into training data selection. In the broader EEG community, several Transformer-based foundation models [4,11,28,33] have been proposed, which can also be fine-tuned for IED detection. Our Z2H can drastically reduce (by 95% in Table 2) the amount of manual labeling required to train or fine-tune the aforementioned models.

[UAL] With no prior labeled data, existing UAL methods rank the candidate examples by their power to reconstruct the data [10,14–17,20,27] or reduce uncertainty [27] in a latent space. To address data heterogeneity, some methods [10,17] account for data locality by reconstructing examples using those close to them as much as possible. ALLG [20] conducts UAL on learned graphs derived from nearest neighbor information, which helps better capture local characteristics. ALSL-U [16] transforms the data into a low-rank representation to better preserve the underlying subspaces. Some recent works [15,27] more explicitly handle data imbalance and heterogeneity using K-means in the latent space to preserve local clusters. However, such methods can be limited in their ability to handle highly random patterns that do not form well-defined clusters (such as non-IEDs), and are constrained by the AL budget regarding the selected data size, while our Z2H can effectively address these issues.

5 Conclusions

In this work, we proposed Z2H, a model-agnostic, knowledge-guided UAL pipeline for training/fine-tuning data selection for a user-defined deep IED detection model. By effectively handling data imbalance and heterogeneity, Z2H can reduce manual labeling by 95% while yielding similar or better results when paired with a pre-trained EEG foundation model [4,28].

Z2H may offer a promising avenue for improving the neurological examination of EEG data by drastically reducing the time and effort required to annotate the data visually, particularly for long, continuous recordings. Moreover, Z2H has shown promising results on both human and mouse subjects that have varying data acquisition parameters and electrode configurations. This can facilitate scientific inferences from diverse datasets, potentially significantly accelerating clinical decision-making and research. For future work, we plan to further develop Z2H for more diverse cohorts, recording setups, and clinical contexts. We will also further improve the robustness of Z2H against high-amplitude noise and artifacts, as well as its performance in *inter*-subject settings, in conjunction with domain adaptation/generalization techniques.

Acknowledgments. This work is supported by EU Horizon projects AI4Europe (101070000), TwinODIS (101160009), ARMADA (101168951), DataGEMS (101188416) and RECITALS (101168490), and by $Y\Pi AI\Theta A$ & NextGenerationEU project HARSH ($Y\Pi 3TA - 0560901$) that is carried out within the framework of the National Recovery and Resilience Plan "Greece 2.0" with funding from the European Union NextGenerationEU, and was provided with HPC and storage resources by GENCI at IDRIS thanks to the grant 2025-A0191012641 on the supercomputer Jean Zay's H100 partition. Part of this work was performed at the Paris Brain Institute Electrophysiology Core Facility (RRID:SCR_026412), the Data Analysis Core Facility (RRID:SCR_026138), and the CENIR neuroimaging Core Facility. This work was done while Cihang Yu was a master's intern at LIPADE and while Qitong Wang was with LIPADE.

References

1. Source code, mouse datasets and additional experimental results. https://github.com/sliang11/Z2H
2. Abdi-Sargezeh, B., Valentin, A., Alarcon, G., Sanei, S.: Incorporating uncertainty in data labeling into automatic detection of interictal epileptiform discharges from concurrent scalp-EEG via multi-way analysis. Int. J. Neural Syst. **31**(08) (2021)
3. Bagnall, A., Lines, J., Bostrom, A., Large, J., Keogh, E.: The great time series classification bake off: a review and experimental evaluation of recent algorithmic advances. Data Min. Knowl. Discov. **31**(3), 606–660 (2017)
4. Cui, W., et al.: Neuro-GPT: towards a foundation model for EEG. In: ISBI (2024)
5. de Curtis, M., Avanzini, G.: Interictal spikes in focal epileptogenesis. Prog. Neurobiol. **63**(5) (2001)
6. Demšar, J.: Statistical comparisons of classifiers over multiple data sets. J. Mach. Learn. Res. **7**, 1–30 (2006)
7. Fürbass, F., Kural, M.A., Gritsch, G., Hartmann, M., Kluge, T., Beniczky, S.: An artificial intelligence-based EEG algorithm for detection of epileptiform EEG discharges: validation against the diagnostic gold standard. Clin. Neurophysiol. **131**(6) (2020)

8. Geng, D., Alkhachroum, A., Bicchi, M.A.M., Jagid, J.R., Cajigas, I., Chen, Z.S.: Deep learning for robust detection of interictal epileptiform discharges. J. Neural Eng. **18**(5) (2021)
9. González, M., Bergmeir, C., Triguero, I., Rodríguez, Y., Benítez, J.: On the stopping criteria for k-nearest neighbor in positive unlabeled time series classification problems. Inf. Sci. **328** (2016)
10. Hu, Y., Zhang, D., Jin, Z., Cai, D., He, X.: Active learning via neighborhood reconstruction. In: IJCAI (2013)
11. Jiang, W., Wang, Y., Lu, B.l., Li, D.: NeuroLM: a universal multi-task foundation model for bridging the gap between language and EEG signals. In: ICLR 2025
12. Jobst, B.C., et al.: Intracranial EEG in the 21st century. Epilepsy Curr. **20**(4) (2020)
13. Lehongre, K., et al.: Long-term deep intracerebral microelectrode recordings in patients with drug-resistant epilepsy: proposed guidelines based on 10-year experience. NeuroImage 119116 (2022)
14. Li, C., Li, R., Yuan, Y., Wang, G., Xu, D.: Deep unsupervised active learning via matrix sketching. TIP **30**, 9280–9293 (2021)
15. Li, C., Ma, H., Yuan, Y., Wang, G., Xu, D.: Structure guided deep neural network for unsupervised active learning. TIP **31**, 2767–2781 (2022)
16. Li, C., Mao, K., Liang, L., Ren, D., Zhang, W., Yuan, Y., Wang, G.: Unsupervised active learning via subspace learning. In: AAAI 2021
17. Li, C., Wang, X., Dong, W., Yan, J., Liu, Q., Zha, H.: Joint active learning with feature selection via cur matrix decomposition. TPAMI **41**(6), 1382–1396 (2018)
18. Li, X.L., Liu, B.: Learning from positive and unlabeled examples with different data distributions. In: ECML (2005)
19. Liang, S., Zhang, Y., Ma, J.: Active model selection for positive unlabeled time series classification. In: ICDE (2020)
20. Ma, H., Li, C., Shi, X., Yuan, Y., Wang, G.: Deep unsupervised active learning on graphs. TNNLS **35**(2), 2894–2900 (2022)
21. Quon, R.J., et al.: AiED: artificial intelligence for the detection of intracranial interictal epileptiform discharges. Clin. Neurophysiol. (2022)
22. Rao, W., et al.: Automatic multi-label classification of interictal epileptiform discharges (ied) detection based on scalp EEG and transformer. In: ICIC 2024 (2024)
23. Ruff, L., et al.: Deep semi-supervised anomaly detection. In: ICLR 2019 (2019)
24. de Sousa, A.M.A., van Putten, M.J., van den Berg, S., Haeri, M.A.: Detection of interictal epileptiform discharges with semi-supervised deep learning. Biomed. Signal Process. Control **88**, 105610 (2024)
25. Spyrou, L., Martín-Lopez, D., Valentín, A., Alarcón, G., Sanei, S.: Detection of intracranial signatures of interictal epileptiform discharges from concurrent scalp EEG. Int. J. Neural Syst. **26**(04) (2016)
26. Staley, K.J., Dudek, F.E.: Interictal spikes and epileptogenesis. Epilepsy Curr. **6**(6) (2006)
27. Wan, C., Jin, F., Qiao, Z., Zhang, W., Yuan, Y.: Unsupervised active learning with loss prediction. Neural Comput. Appl. **35**(5), 3587–3595 (2023)
28. Wang, G., Liu, W., He, Y., Xu, C., Ma, L., Li, H.: EEGPT: pretrained transformer for universal and reliable representation of EEG signals. NeurIPS **37** (2024)
29. Wang, Q., Whitmarsh, S., Navarro, V., Palpanas, T.: iedeal: a deep learning framework for detecting highly imbalanced interictal epileptiform discharges. VLDB **16**(3) (2022)
30. Wei, L., Keogh, E.: Semi-supervised time series classification. In: KDD (2006)

31. Whitmarsh, S., et al.: Sleep increases firing rate modulation during interictal epileptiform discharges in mesial temporal structures. Brain Commun. **8**(3) (2026)
32. Xu, H., Wang, Y., Pang, G., Jian, S., Liu, N., Wang, Y.: RoSAS: deep semi-supervised anomaly detection with contamination-resilient continuous supervision. Inf. Process. Manag. **60**(5) (2023)
33. Zhou, X., et al.: Brain foundation models: a survey on advancements in neural signal processing and brain discovery. IEEE Signal Process. Mag. **42**(5), 22–35 (2025)
34. Zhou, Y., Song, X., Zhang, Y., Liu, F., Zhu, C., Liu, L.: Feature encoding with autoencoders for weakly supervised anomaly detection. TNNLS **33**(6) (2021)

Graph Learning and Structured Representation Learning

CoDAC-SVF: Robust Multimodal Structural Variant Filtering via Collaborative Denoising and Adaptive Constraints

Chunxiao Lai[1], Haohao Zhang[1], Di Deng[1], Jing Peng[1(✉)], and Xiaohui Yuan[1,2,3]

[1] School of Computer Science and Artificial Intelligence, Wuhan University of Technology, Wuhan 430070, China
{laichunxiao,haohaozhang,316273,pengjing}@whut.edu.cn, yuanxh@gooalgene.com
[2] Yazhouwan National Laboratory, Sanya 572024, Hainan, China
[3] Engineering Research Centre of Chinese Ministry of Education for Edible and Medicinal Fungi, Jilin Agricultural University, Changchun 130118, China

Abstract. Structural variant (SV) filtering in long-read sequencing is fundamentally challenged by high false-positive rates inherent in single-modality methods. Integrating structural cues with genomic sequence content offers promising insights, yet conventional fusion strategies often suffer from cross-modal noise resonance. This is primarily due to the heterogeneous noise distributions across these modalities, where alignment artifacts in the structural modality contrast sharply with sequencing errors in the nucleotide modality. In this paper, we propose CoDAC-SVF, a novel Confidence-Driven Collaborative Denoising framework with Adaptive Constraint-Aware Learning for robust multimodal SV filtering. CoDAC-SVF treats multimodal fusion as an active, asymmetric error-correction process. By dynamically quantifying local feature reliability through Genomic Prior Knowledge (GPK), the Confidence-Driven Collaborative Denoising (CDCD) module utilizes high-confidence modal anchors to suppress stochastic noise and prevent error propagation. Furthermore, we introduce Multi-granularity Adaptive-awareness Constraints (MAC) to inject domain-specific biological priors into the representation learning objective. This design ensures that the joint embeddings remain both logically coherent and biologically plausible under pervasive data uncertainty. Evaluated on multiple real-world long-read datasets, CoDAC-SVF significantly outperforms state-of-the-art methods in both precision and robustness. Our work provides a principled paradigm for reliable multimodal knowledge discovery in genomic regions plagued by complex noise patterns. The code is available at https://github.com/sokolo05/CoDAC-SVF.

Keywords: Multimodal Fusion · Adaptive Learning · Genomic Prior Knowledge · Structural Variation Filtering

M. Ceci et al. (Eds.): ECML PKDD 2026, LNAI 16948, pp. 691–707, 2027.
https://doi.org/10.1007/978-3-032-37679-4_39

1 Introduction

Structural variants (SVs) are closely associated with hereditary diseases [8], tumorigenesis [29], and drug responses [23], making their reliable interpretation paramount for clinical diagnosis and therapeutic decision-making [4]. Within the genomic analysis pipeline, SV filtering serves as a critical trust bridge between raw high-throughput long-read sequencing data and dependable downstream clinical applications [21]. While deep learning-based SV detection [13] has made significant strides, most existing methodologies rely predominantly on alignment-derived structural features [1]. This reliance creates a single-modality bottleneck that overlooks the rich, text-like sequence signals inherent in the nucleotide modality. Consequently, these models are particularly error-prone in complex genomic regions [17] where alignment artifacts are prevalent.

We observe that nucleotide base sequences provide intrinsic and fine-grained cues [15,18] that can serve as complementary evidence to cross-verify structural anomalies. Crucially, the noise mechanisms in these two sources are fundamentally different. Structural noise arises from alignment-induced artifacts [17], whereas sequence-level noise stems from technology-induced sequencing errors [14]. Treating these as a single information source allows modality-specific noise to propagate and amplify, leading to heterogeneous reliability across different genomic regions.

Recent advances in multimodal learning [7,12,16] have explored uncertainty modeling and noise-aware fusion, which lay a foundation for robustness. However, existing methods remain inadequate for long-read SV filtering due to severe local noise heterogeneity and the lack of effective integration of domain-specific biological priors. To bridge this gap, we propose CoDAC-SVF, a Confidence-Driven Collaborative Denoising framework with Adaptive Constraint-Aware Learning.

CoDAC-SVF transitions from traditional single-modality analysis to a robust dual-modality paradigm. Guided by Genomic Prior Knowledge (GPK), such as GC content and mapping quality, the framework introduces coordinated innovations across three critical dimensions. At the encoding stage, CoDAC-SVF employs parameter-isolated dual-branch encoders (f_{str} and f_{seq}) to separately model heterogeneous CIGAR-based structural features and sequence modalities, effectively isolating modality-specific noise at the source. Building upon these isolated features, the Confidence-Driven Collaborative Denoising (CDCD) module dynamically estimates local feature reliability to perform asymmetric cross-modal correction. By utilizing high-confidence modal regions as anchors to refine their low-confidence counterparts, the framework actively suppresses stochastic noise and prevents error propagation. To further ground the learning process, Multi-granularity Adaptive-awareness Constraints (MAC) inject domain-specific biological priors into the optimization objective. Through a unified loss function incorporating classification, awareness-modulated contrastive, and cross-modal consistency terms, MAC ensures that the joint embedding is both highly discriminative and biologically plausible. The contributions of our work are summarized in the following three aspects:

- **Transition from Single to Dual-Modality Paradigm.** We redefine SV filtering by introducing raw nucleotide sequences as a distinct modality to complement CIGAR-based structural features. By employing parameter-isolated encoders (M_{cigar} and M_{bases}), CoDAC-SVF captures fine-grained genomic cues while isolating modality-specific noise at the source, effectively breaking the information bottleneck of existing single-modality filters.
- **Confidence-Driven Collaborative Denoising (CDCD).** We propose a novel fusion mechanism that explicitly quantifies local feature reliability. Through an asymmetric calibration strategy, the framework utilizes high-confidence modal anchors to actively suppress stochastic noise in paired modalities. This approach prevents cross-modal noise resonance and significantly enhances model robustness in complex genomic regions.
- **Multi-granularity Adaptive-awareness Constraints (MAC).** We bridge the gap between deep learning and genomic heuristics by embedding Genomic Prior Knowledge (GPK) into a unified optimization framework. The MAC module employs adaptively weighted constraints to dynamically calibrate the trade-off between logical consistency and biological plausibility, ensuring that learned representations remain strictly grounded in biological reality.

2 Related Work

2.1 Structural Variant Detection and Filtering

Deep learning for SV analysis primarily targets two distinct stages: detection (calling) [10,11,24] and post-call filtering. SV detection methods, such as the Transformer-based SVHunter [6] and the dual-attention network DASV [25], focus on precisely identifying variant regions from raw alignments. In contrast, SV filtering acts as a critical "trust bridge" designed to eliminate false positives from these initial calls. Dedicated filters remain sparse, with CSV-Filter [26] being a representative baseline. However, both detectors and existing filters predominantly rely on alignment-derived structural features, creating a single-modality bottleneck. They often fail in complex genomic regions where alignment artifacts are prevalent, as they overlook the rich sequence-level semantics. CoDAC-SVF reformulates SV filtering by introducing an independent sequence modality to cross-verify structural anomalies, suppressing false-positive propagation through multimodal collaborative reasoning.

2.2 Multimodal Fusion and Denoising

Conventional fusion strategies, such as simple feature concatenation or late fusion, typically assume uniform modality reliability across the input space [28, 30]. However, this assumption is fundamentally flawed in long-read SV analysis, where structural noise (originating from alignment artifacts) and sequence noise (technology-induced sequencing errors) exhibit distinct, stochastically independent patterns. While recent advances in uncertainty-guided fusion [2,3] and cross-modal self-refining [19] offer general frameworks for handling noise, they remain largely domain-agnostic and fail to account for the fine-grained, position-specific reliability inherent in genomic coordinates. In biological data, the signal-to-noise ratio fluctuates drastically based on local genomic contexts, such as GC-rich regions or tandem repeats. CoDAC-SVF diverges from these global fusion approaches by introducing Confidence-Driven Collaborative Denoising ($CDCD$). By leveraging Genomic Prior Knowledge (GPK) as a dynamic reliability estimator, Confidence-Driven implements an asymmetric calibration strategy where high-confidence modal "anchors" are utilized to actively suppress and refine noisy counterparts in the paired modality, preventing cross-modal noise resonance.

2.3 Constraint-Aware Optimization for Multimodal Learning

Robust multimodal optimization often seeks to align disparate feature spaces through uncertainty-aware gating [5] or hierarchical consistency regularization [20,27]. Despite their effectiveness in general CV or NLP tasks, these objectives remain largely passive toward the inherent biological contradictions found in noisy sequencing data, particularly the mismatch between distorted CIGAR strings and raw nucleotide signals. To address this, CoDAC-SVF introduces Multi-granularity Knowledge-Aware Constraints (MAC), which transform discrete genomic heuristics into continuous learning objectives. By integrating an awareness-modulated contrastive loss with cross-modal consistency terms, the framework ensures that the joint representation is not only mathematically discriminative but also strictly grounded in biological plausibility. This dual-constraint approach ensures that the learned embeddings maintain logical agreement between structural topology and sequence content, providing the high-fidelity "trust bridge" required for sensitive clinical applications.

3 Methods

3.1 Problem Definition

We formulate genomic structural variant (SV) filtering as a multi-class classification task on noisy, heterogeneous multimodal data. For a candidate SV site, the input is defined as a dual-modal tuple:

$$(\mathbf{x}_{str}, \mathbf{x}_{seq}), \quad \mathbf{x}_{str} \in \mathcal{X}_{str}, \ \mathbf{x}_{seq} \in \mathcal{X}_{seq}, \tag{1}$$

where $\mathbf{x}_{str}$ represents the *structural modality* derived from CIGAR alignments, and $\mathbf{x}_{seq}$ represents the *sequence modality* comprising flanking nucleotides. The objective is to learn a robust mapping:

$$f : (\mathcal{X}_{str} \times \mathcal{X}_{seq} \mid \mathcal{G}) \rightarrow \mathcal{Y}, \quad \mathcal{Y} = \{0, 1, 2\}, \tag{2}$$

where $\mathcal{G}$ denotes the Genomic Prior Knowledge (GPK). The label space $\mathcal{Y} = \{0, 1, 2\}$ categorizes candidates as False Positive (0, MATCH), denoting spurious variants identified by upstream SV callers that are actually mapping artifacts; Deletion (1, DEL), representing a true SV where the nucleotide sequence confirms a missing segment relative to the reference; or Insertion (2, INS), representing a true SV where the sequence modality verifies the presence of extra incorporated nucleotides. This classification enables CoDAC-SVF to differentiate between algorithmic misalignments and biologically grounded variants, effectively refining raw caller outputs through multimodal cross-verification.

To address heterogeneous noise, the *knowledge-conditioned mapping* f is designed with three strategic goals: (1) isolating structural and sequence features through parameter-isolated encoders to prevent early noise entanglement; (2) suppressing modality-specific noise via dynamic reliability estimates during fusion; and (3) integrating $\mathcal{G}$ as differentiable constraints to enforce biological consistency. This formulation underpins the CoDAC-SVF framework, enabling collaborative denoising and constraint-aware fusion for robust SV filtering.

3.2 Architectural Overview

To realize the knowledge-conditioned mapping f^*, CoDAC-SVF progressively processes and refines multimodal representations through an end-to-end pipeline consisting of five sequential stages, as illustrated in Fig. 1. The process begins with **Data Preparation**, which consolidates heterogeneous raw genomic inputs into structural and sequence modalities. Subsequently, the **Dual-Stream Feature Encoding** stage extracts parameter-isolated feature embeddings $\mathbf{H}_{str}$ and $\mathbf{H}_{seq}$ to isolate modality-specific noise at the source. To actively mitigate cross-modal noise resonance, the **Confidence-Driven Collaborative Denoising (CDCD)** stage introduces Genomic Prior Knowledge (GPK) to quantify local feature reliability, generating modality-specific confidence maps $\mathbf{C}_{str}$ and $\mathbf{C}_{seq}$. These maps then guide the **Confidence-Weighted Cross-Attention (CWCA)** stage, which performs asymmetric cross-modal calibration using high-confidence anchors to yield a purified joint representation $\mathbf{H}_{fusion}$. Finally, during the **Classification & Filtering** stage, the Multi-granularity Adaptive-awareness Constraints (MAC) module regularizes the joint embedding distribution to enforce biological consistency, ultimately outputting a robust, high-fidelity filter decision.

3.3 Dual-Stream Feature Encoding

To capture heterogeneous genomic signals, CoDAC-SVF extracts spanning reads and their flanking regions for each candidate SV site, transforming them into two distinct modalities. The structural modality $\mathcal{X}_{str}$ is generated via a CIGAR-to-RGB mapping $M_{str}(\cdot)$, while the sequence modality $\mathcal{X}_{seq}$ is constructed via nucleotide-to-image mapping $M_{seq}(\cdot)$. To prevent early-stage noise entanglement, we employ parameter-isolated encoders to project these inputs into distinct high-dimensional embeddings $\mathbf{H}_{str}$ and $\mathbf{H}_{seq}$:

$$\mathbf{H}_{str} = f_{str}(\mathcal{X}_{str}; \theta_{str}), \quad \mathbf{H}_{seq} = f_{seq}(\mathcal{X}_{seq}; \theta_{seq}) \tag{3}$$

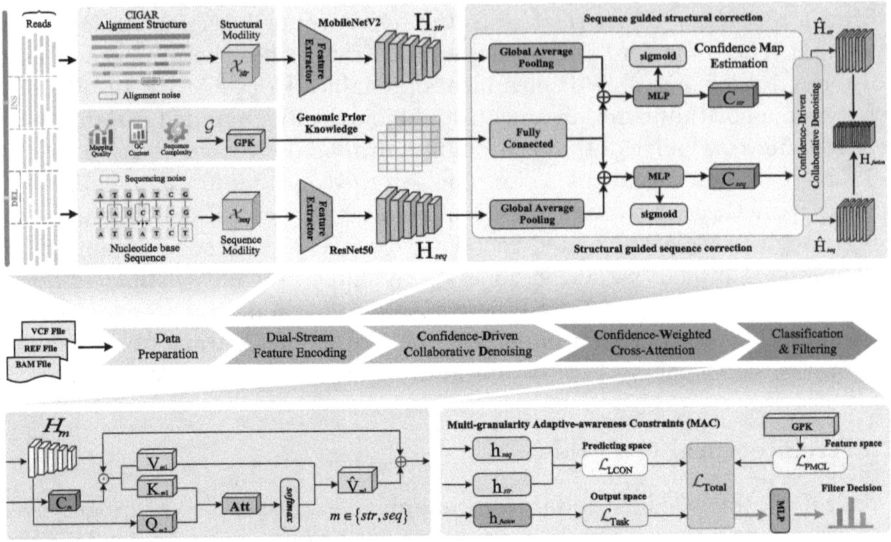

Fig. 1. The overall architecture of CoDAC-SVF for multimodal SV filtering.

where f_{str} and f_{seq} denote the MobileNetV2 [22] and ResNet50 [9] backbones, respectively. Specifically, MobileNetV2 is utilized to capture topological structural patterns within CIGAR strings, whereas ResNet50 extracts fine-grained semantic features from raw nucleotide sequences. Both encoders leverage ImageNet pre-trained weights and task-specific fine-tuning to adapt to modality-specific noise distributions. By isolating the parameters $\theta_{str} \neq \theta_{seq}$, the framework ensures that sequencing-level errors in the sequence modality do not contaminate the structural representations during the initial feature extraction phase.

3.4 Confidence-Driven Collaborative Denoising (CDCD)

The CDCD module illustrated in Fig. 1 mitigates cross-modal noise resonance by leveraging Genomic Prior Knowledge (GPK) to perform active feature rectification. This module comprises two synergistic components: **Confidence Map Estimation (CME)** for reliability quantification and **Confidence-Weighted Cross-Attention (CWCA)** for asymmetric feature calibration.

Confidence Map Estimation (CME): To quantify feature reliability under heterogeneous noise conditions, the CME component embedded within the CDCD pipeline projects explicit biological heuristics into a latent prior space and interacts them with modality-specific global statistics. Formally, the raw GPK vector $\mathcal{G} = [q_{map}, c_{gc}, x_{comp}, ...]^\top$ quantitatively aggregates **Mapping Quality, GC Content**, and **Sequence Complexity** extracted from the reference genome and alignment records. This vector is encoded through a Fully Connected (FC) layer to provide domain-specific grounding. For each individual modality $m \in \{str, seq\}$, the joint GPK encoding and global feature extraction are formulated as follows:

$$\mathbf{g} = \text{ReLU}(\mathbf{W}_g\mathcal{G} + \mathbf{b}_g) \tag{4}$$

$$\mathbf{z}_m = \text{GAP}(\mathbf{H}_m) \tag{5}$$

The modality-aware confidence score $C_m \in [0, 1]$ is then computed by fusing the prior and latent cues:

$$C_m = \sigma\left(\mathbf{W}_2 \cdot \text{ReLU}(\mathbf{W}_1[\mathbf{z}_m \oplus \mathbf{g}] + \mathbf{b}_1) + \mathbf{b}_2\right) \tag{6}$$

where $\mathbf{H}_m \in \mathbb{R}^{C\times H\times W}$ denotes the initial embedding, GAP$(\cdot)$ is global average pooling, and $\oplus$ represents feature concatenation. The estimated C_m serves as a reliability anchor to modulate subsequent information flow.

3.5 Confidence-Weighted Cross-Attention (CWCA):

The CWCA mechanism integrated into the fusion pipeline utilizes the calculated confidence map $\mathbf{C}_m$ to achieve active cross-modal feature rectification. Unlike standard cross-attention paradigms, this approach employs the modality-specific confidence score to dynamically gate the source fields, thereby ensuring that only features from high-confidence genomic regions participate in the subsequent cross-modal retrieval. As illustrated in the structural-guided sequence correction and sequence-guided structural correction blocks of Fig. 1, high-confidence modal regions serve as anchors to guide information flow. Taking the structural-guided sequence correction as a formal example, the Query ($\mathbf{Q}_{str}$), Key ($\mathbf{K}_{seq}$), and Value ($\mathbf{V}_{seq}$) vectors are defined as follows:

$$\mathbf{Q}_{str} = \mathbf{H}_{str}\mathbf{W}_Q, \quad \mathbf{K}_{seq} = (\mathbf{H}_{seq} \odot C_{seq})\mathbf{W}_K, \quad \mathbf{V}_{seq} = (\mathbf{H}_{seq} \odot C_{seq})\mathbf{W}_V \tag{7}$$

where $\odot$ denotes the Hadamard product with spatial broadcasting. The rectified sequence feature $\hat{\mathbf{H}}_{seq}$ is then derived through a confidence-modulated attention mechanism:

$$\text{Attn}(\mathbf{H}_{str}, \mathbf{H}_{seq}) = \text{Softmax}\left(\frac{\mathbf{Q}_{str}\mathbf{K}_{seq}^{\top}}{\sqrt{d_k}}\right)\mathbf{V}_{seq} \tag{8}$$

$$\hat{\mathbf{H}}_{seq} = \text{LN}(\mathbf{H}_{seq} + \text{Attn}(\mathbf{H}_{str}, \mathbf{H}_{seq})) \tag{9}$$

where LN$(\cdot)$ is Layer Normalization and d_k is the scaling factor. By suppressing unreliable regions in $\mathbf{K}$ and $\mathbf{V}$, the mechanism allows $\mathbf{Q}_{str}$ to retrieve salient cues from stable sequence regions. A symmetric operation yields the purified structural feature $\hat{\mathbf{H}}_{str}$.

Joint Representation Generation: The final joint embedding $\mathbf{H}_{fusion}$ is generated by fusing the purified dual-modality features through a Feed-Forward Network (FFN):

$$\mathbf{H}_{cat} = [\hat{\mathbf{H}}_{str} \oplus \hat{\mathbf{H}}_{seq}] \tag{10}$$

$$\mathbf{H}_{fusion} = \mathrm{LN}(\mathbf{H}_{cat}\mathbf{W}_F + \mathbf{b}_F) \tag{11}$$

This strategy compresses complementary cross-modal information into a compact latent space, providing a robust foundation for the Multi-granularity Adaptive-awareness Constraints (MAC) module.

3.6 Multi-Granularity Adaptive-Awareness Constraints (MAC)

The MAC module integrated into the optimization stage transforms the explicit GPK into differentiable constraints structurally distributed across three distinct granularities: the feature space, the predicting space, and the output space, as illustrated in Fig. 1. This hierarchical supervision regularizes the learning process to ensure that the generated joint embeddings remain both highly discriminative and biologically consistent with genomic topology. Under this multi-granularity optimization paradigm, the total objective function is defined as a dynamic weighted sum of the primary and auxiliary losses:

$$\mathcal{L}_{total} = \mathcal{L}_{task} + \alpha(t)\mathcal{L}_{PMCL} + \beta(t)\mathcal{L}_{LCON} \tag{12}$$

where t denotes the current training epoch. To facilitate a stable transition from feature exploration to logic optimization, $\alpha(t)$ and $\beta(t)$ are formulated as time-dependent adaptive functions that gradually increase from initial values to their respective optimal states. The primary task loss $\mathcal{L}_{task}$ is the Cross-Entropy loss applied to the final classification head based on $\mathbf{H}_{fusion}$:

$$\mathcal{L}_{task} = -\frac{1}{N}\sum_{i=1}^{N}\sum_{c=1}^{C} y_{i,c}\log(\hat{y}_{i,c}) \tag{13}$$

where y and $\hat{y}$ denote the ground truth and predicted probability for C SV types, respectively.

Prior-Modulated Contrastive Loss (PMCL): Within the feature space, the PMCL component regularizes the joint embedding distribution by injecting domain semantics derived from the GPK, as illustrated in the optimization pipeline of Fig. 1. To effectively leverage these prior biological heuristics, we define a prior-awareness kernel K_{ij} to modulate the similarity weights of sample pairs:

$$K_{ij} = \exp\left(-\gamma \cdot \|\mathcal{G}_i - \mathcal{G}_j\|_2^2\right) \tag{14}$$

where $\mathcal{G}$ denotes the GPK vector, and $\|\cdot\|_2^2$ represents the squared L_2 norm. Let $s_{ij} = (\mathbf{H}_{f,i} \cdot \mathbf{H}_{f,j})/\tau$ represent the cosine similarity in the fusion space scaled by temperature τ. The PMCL is formulated as:

$$\mathcal{L}_{PMCL} = -\frac{1}{N}\sum_{i=1}^{N} \log \frac{\sum_{j\in\Omega(i)} K_{ij} e^{s_{ij}}}{\sum_{k\neq i} K_{ik} e^{s_{ik}}} \tag{15}$$

where $\Omega(i)$ denotes the set of positive pairs. By prioritizing pairs with high GPK correlation via K_{ij}, PMCL ensures the joint feature distribution consistently reflects underlying biological relationships.

Logic Consistency Constraint (LCON): To ensure decision consistency in the predicting space, we minimize the divergence between the probability distributions p_{str} and p_{seq} generated from the rectified features $\hat{\mathbf{H}}_{str}$ and $\hat{\mathbf{H}}_{seq}$ via auxiliary heads, as shown in Fig. 1. For the i-th sample, the constraint is defined using the Jensen-Shannon Divergence (JSD), calculated via the Kullback-Leibler (KL) divergence as:

$$M^{(i)} = \frac{1}{2}\left(p_{str}^{(i)} + p_{seq}^{(i)}\right) \tag{16}$$

$$\mathcal{L}_{LCON} = \frac{1}{2N}\sum_{i=1}^{N}\left(D_{KL}(p_{str}^{(i)} \parallel M^{(i)}) + D_{KL}(p_{seq}^{(i)} \parallel M^{(i)})\right) \tag{17}$$

where $D_{KL}(P \parallel Q) = \sum P \log(P/Q)$. By enforcing a unified decision logic across modalities, $\mathcal{L}_{LCON}$ enhances the robustness of fusion representations. Notably, these auxiliary classifiers are utilized exclusively during training to maintain inference efficiency.

4 Experiment

4.1 Experimental Settings

Benchmark Datasets: We evaluate CoDAC-SVF using the Genome In a Bottle (GIAB) HG002 benchmark [31] aligned to the hs37d5 reference genome. True positive events, including Insertions (INS) and Deletions (DEL), are curated from the GIAB high-confidence SV callset. To construct a balanced benchmark, we generate *MATCH* samples from non-overlapping genomic regions that exhibit no SV evidence, ensuring their length and read-depth distributions are consistent with the positive instances. The framework is cross-validated on both PacBio CLR and Oxford Nanopore Technologies (ONT) platforms to assess its cross-platform robustness.

Data Partitioning: To prevent data leakage and ensure event-level independence, we adopt a chromosome-aware stratified split: 70% of the events from autosomes (Chr1–22) are utilized for training and validation, while the remaining 30% constitute the independent test set. We strictly verify that no overlapping genomic coordinates exist between the training and testing partitions, ensuring the model's ability to generalize to unseen genomic regions.

Baselines and Metrics: We compare CoDAC-SVF against three state-of-the-art SV callers [10,11,24] and the latest filtering baseline, CSV-Filter [26]. Model performance is quantitatively assessed using Precision, Recall, and F1-score.

Implementation Details. Experiments are conducted via PyTorch on Ubuntu 22.04 using four NVIDIA RTX 4070 Ti GPUs with Distributed Data Parallel (DDP). Input images are resized to 224×224 pixels; backbones (MobileNetV2 and ResNet50) utilize ImageNet pre-trained weights for initialization. We employ the AdamW optimizer (weight decay 10^{-2}) with a total batch size of 128. The learning rate follows a cosine annealing schedule, decaying from 1.0×10^{-4} to 1.0×10^{-6}. To refine the optimization trajectory, we implement an adaptive schedule where $\alpha(t)$ and $\beta(t)$ increase monotonically toward their optimal values as functions of epoch t. Training is capped at 30 epochs with an early stopping patience of 5 epochs. At inference, auxiliary heads are deactivated to ensure computational efficiency.

4.2 Performance Across Platforms and Species

To evaluate the efficacy and cross-species generalization of CoDAC-SVF, we conduct a unified benchmarking against the single-modal SOTA baseline, CSV-Filter. As summarized in Table 1, CoDAC-SVF consistently achieves the highest F1-scores across all callers and platforms, demonstrating superior robustness in noisy long-read scenarios.

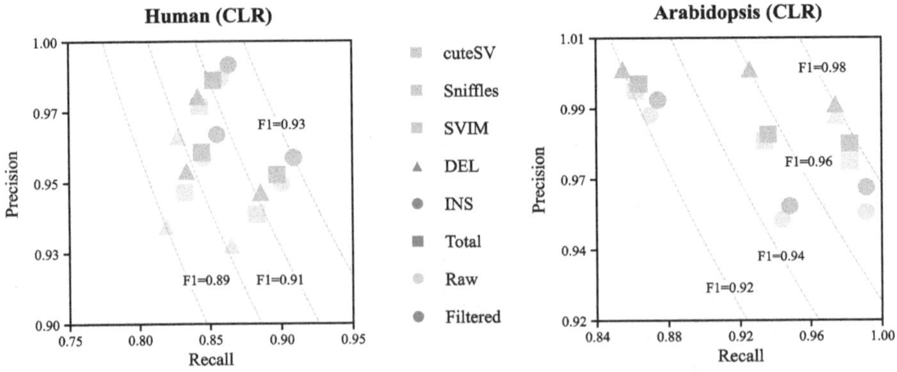

Fig. 2. Precision-Recall performance across species under CLR sequencing. Results for cuteSV, Sniffles, and SVIM are shown for *Human* (left) and *Arabidopsis* (right) at 30× coverage.

Notably, CoDAC-SVF excels in false-positive suppression where single-modal methods often falter. For the Sniffles caller on the PacBio CLR platform, while CSV-Filter suffers from a precision drop compared to the No-Filter baseline

Table 1. Comparison with SOTA methods on PacBio CLR and ONT data. Max values per caller are in bold.

Platform	Caller cuteSV [11]	Model	PRE	REC	F1
CLR	svim [10]	No-Filter	0.8955	0.9186	0.9069
		CSV-Filter [26]	0.8958	**0.9303**	0.9127
		Ours	**0.9026**	0.9259	**0.9141**
	Sniffles [24]	No-Filter	0.9552	0.8536	0.9015
		CSV-Filter [26]	0.9494	**0.8604**	0.9027
		Ours	**0.9571**	0.8552	**0.9033**
	cuteSV [11]	No-Filter	0.7176	0.9321	0.8109
		CSV-Filter [26]	0.7057	**0.9472**	0.8088
		Ours	**0.7235**	0.9379	**0.8169**
ONT	svim [10]	No-Filter	0.8752	0.9564	0.9140
		CSV-Filter [26]	0.8795	**0.9696**	0.9224
		Ours	**0.8861**	0.9695	**0.9259**
	Sniffles [24]	No-Filter	0.9004	0.9071	0.9037
		CSV-Filter [26]	0.9023	**0.9162**	0.9092
		Ours	**0.9085**	0.9125	**0.9105**
		No-Filter	0.8965	0.9491	0.9221
		CSV-Filter [26]	0.9024	0.9513	0.9262
		Ours	**0.9064**	**0.9601**	**0.9325**

(0.7176 to 0.7057), CoDAC-SVF effectively reverses this trend, elevating precision to 0.7235. This advantage is further validated across species with distinct genomic complexities. The multi-species benchmarks, CoDAC-SVF consistently shifts the precision-recall curves of all baseline callers toward the upper-right quadrant.

Specifically, As illustrated in Fig. 2, on the CLR platform at 30× coverage , CoDAC-SVF achieves a robust F1-score of 0.94 in the complex human genome, while in the model plant *A. thaliana*, the peak F1-score reaches 0.98. Even in resource-constrained 5× ultra-low coverage scenarios, our MAC-calibrated filtering maintains a substantial lead by effectively bridging the gap left by sparse physical evidence. These results underscore the universal capability of CoDAC-SVF to discern true biological variants by collaboratively modeling alignment-derived structural features and raw nucleotide sequence content, consistent with the cross-modal denoising paradigm proposed in our framework.

4.3 Ablation Studies

To further validate the effectiveness of different components in our method, we conducted a series of ablation experiments.

Ablation Study on Different Modalities. To evaluate the effectiveness of dual-modal modeling, we perform a modality-level ablation by comparing Sequence-only, Structural-only, and Dual-modalities configurations.

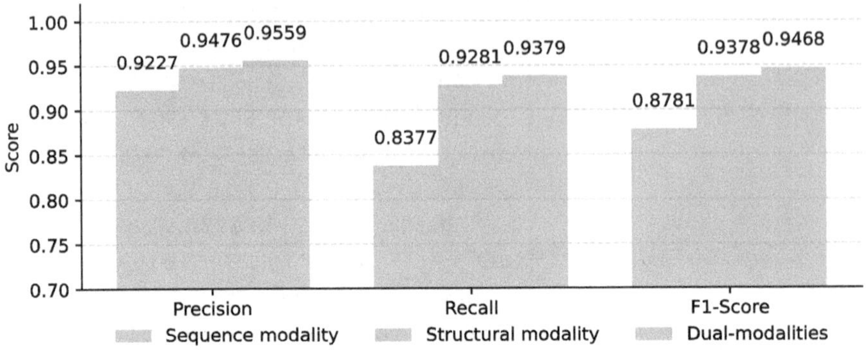

Fig. 3. Ablation study on different modalities.

As illustrated in Fig. 3, the Dual-modalities setting consistently achieves the best performance across all metrics. Specifically, it improves precision from 0.9227 to 0.9559 and F1-score from 0.8781 to 0.9468 compared to the sequence-only model, with similar gains over the structural-only variant. These results indicate that single-modal information is insufficient to capture complex SV characterization, whereas dual-modalities modeling provides a more robust and discriminative representation for effective SV filtering under noisy conditions.

Ablation Study of CDCD. To further verify the performance gains arise from confidence-aware denoising rather than dual-modality modeling alone, we conduct a targeted ablation study under a fixed dual-modality setting by progressively introducing cross-modal interaction and confidence guidance.

Table 2. Ablation study on the CDCD module under the dual-modality setting.

Fusion	CM[a]	CDCD	PRE	REC	F1
Concatenation	×	×	0.9412	0.9290	0.9350
Cross-Attention	✓	×	0.9498	0.9335	0.9415
Ours	✓	✓	**0.9559**	**0.9379**	**0.9468**

[a]Cross Modality.

As shown in Table 2, simple Concatenation yields the lowest F1-score (0.9350), as it fails to capture explicit cross-modal interactions. While standard Cross-Attention improves the F1-score to 0.9415, the gains are limited by the unchecked propagation of modality-specific noise.In contrast, our CDCD module, which integrates CME and CWCA, achieves a peak Precision of 0.9559 and F1-score of 0.9468. These results validate the efficacy of confidence-aware denoising in mitigating cross-modal noise resonance and enabling robust feature correction under heterogeneous noise conditions.

Table 3. Ablation study on MAC under the dual-modality setting.

Variant	L_{task}	PMCL	LCON	PRE	REC	F1
CE	✓	×	×	0.9512	0.9320	0.9415
+ PMCL	✓	✓	×	0.9543	0.9354	0.9448
+ LCON	✓	×	✓	0.9526	0.9361	0.9441
Ours	✓	✓	✓	**0.9559**	**0.9379**	**0.9468**

Ablation Study of MAC. We evaluate the contribution of each component in the MAC under a fixed dual-modality setting. Starting from the cross-entropy baseline, we progressively introduce PMCL and LCON. As shown in Table 3, both constraints consistently improve performance.

Introducing PMCL increases the F1-score from 0.9415 to 0.9448, indicating that prototype-level multi-granularity contrastive learning enhances representation discriminability. LCON also yields a noticeable gain by enforcing cross-modal decision consistency. Combining both constraints achieves the best performance with an F1-score of 0.9468, demonstrating that MAC effectively regularizes multimodal representations at complementary levels.

4.4 Qualitative Feature Space Analysis

To evaluate the capability of CoDAC-SVF framework in suppressing heterogeneous noise, enhancing intra-class compactness, and maintaining biological logic consistency within complex genomic environments, we perform a qualitative assessment via t-SNE visualization.

As illustrated in Fig. 4, ours method yields more compact clusters with well-defined boundaries compared to baselines, demonstrating its efficacy in rectifying low-confidence features. Notably, the MATCH samples (purple) significantly reduces false-positive "drifts" into variant clusters, highlighting the superiority of confidence-driven denoising. Furthermore, the distinct separation between DEL (red) and INS (blue) clusters, confirms that CoDAC-SVF effectively captures the structural and text-like features of genome while maintaining biological logic consistency.

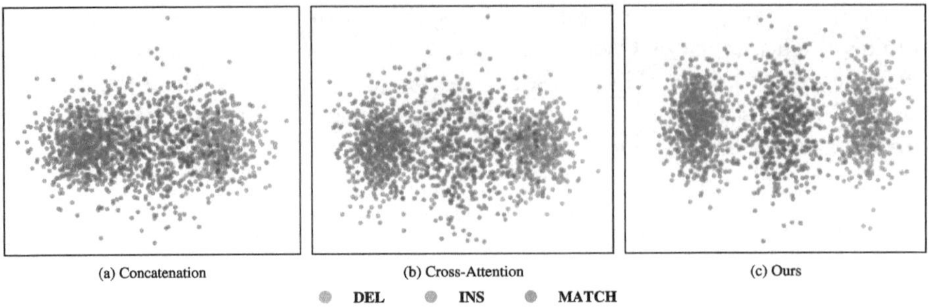

Fig. 4. Qualitative feature space analysis via t-SNE across different fusion strategies. (Color figure online)

4.5 Evolutionary Dynamics of Adaptive Constraints

To further examine the optimization trajectory, we visualize the adaptive weighting schedule of $\alpha(t)$ and $\beta(t)$ during the end-to-end training process Fig. 5. The evolution reveals a distinct two-stage paradigm: *Modality Alignment* followed by *Logic Refinement.*

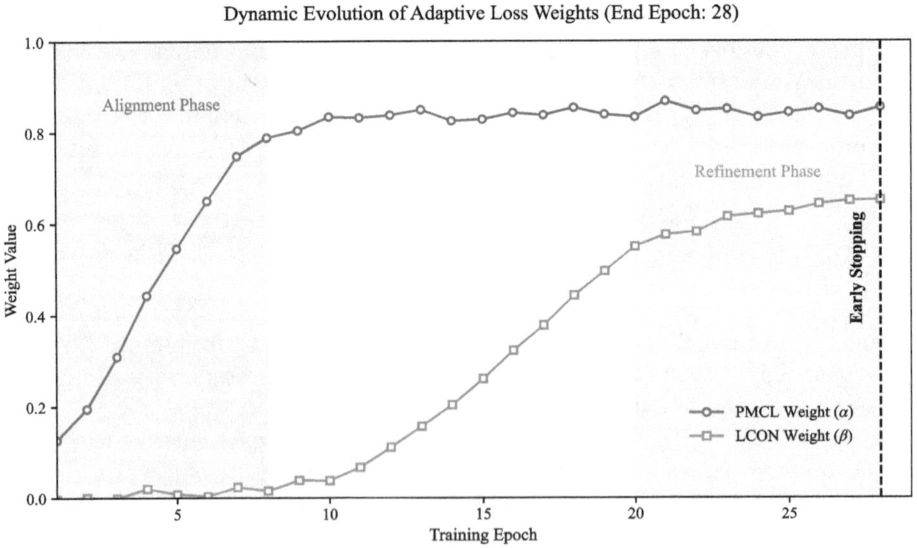

Fig. 5. Dynamic evolution of adaptive loss weights α and β during the training process.

In the initial stage (Epoch 1–8), the rapid ascent of $\alpha(t)$ to approximately 0.85 indicates that the framework prioritizes establishing a coherent multimodal latent space via GPK-guided contrastive learning. Conversely, the consistency weight $\beta(t)$ is initially suppressed to prevent premature convergence on unrefined representations. In the subsequent stage (Epoch 9–28), $\beta(t)$ gradually increases and plateaus at 0.65, shifting the optimization focus toward enforcing structural-functional consistency. This progressive transition ensures that joint embeddings are both discriminative and biologically grounded. The stabilization of both parameters prior to early stopping (Epoch 28) confirms that our adaptive schedule effectively identifies the equilibrium points necessary for robust SV filtering.

5 Discussion and Outlook

The empirical success of CoDAC-SVF marks a transition from passive classification to knowledge-driven multimodal reasoning in SV filtering. While traditional methods are often misled by alignment artifacts in repetitive or low-complexity regions—where CIGAR-based cues suffer from information bottlenecks—CoDAC-SVF overcomes these constraints by treating nucleotide sequences as an independent, semantic modality. Our results confirm that the synergy between alignment-derived structural topology and raw sequence content enables cross-modal verification, effectively suppressing technology-induced noise that single-modal features cannot resolve.

The core innovation of CoDAC-SVF lies in the collaborative denoising through CDCD and the biological grounding provided by MAC. These mechanisms ensure that the joint representation remains consistent with the underlying "genomic grammar" by enforcing physical and topological alignment. While CoDAC-SVF currently utilizes task-specific encoders to achieve state-of-the-art precision, the rapid evolution of **Genomic Foundation Models (GFMs)** presents a transformative opportunity for future research. Integrating pre-trained GFMs as a sequence backbone could provide CoDAC-SVF with deeper evolutionary insights and long-range genomic dependencies. Such a transition toward *foundation-model-augmented filtering* would further enhance the robustness of SV analysis.

6 Conclusion

In this study, we propose a novel multimodal framework, CoDAC-SVF, that transcends single-modality limitations in structural variant (SV) filtering through synergistic denoising and fusion. By coupling alignment-derived structural cues with nucleotide sequence semantics, CoDAC-SVF effectively mitigates technology-induced noise. The Confidence-Driven Collaborative Denoising (CDCD) module facilitates robust feature rectification via prior-guided attention, while the Multi-granularity Adaptive-awareness Constraints (MAC) ensure biological grounding by embedding domain priors across latent spaces. Extensive evaluations on GIAB benchmarks demonstrate that CoDAC-SVF achieves state-of-the-art performance across both PacBio and ONT platforms. These findings underscore the pivotal role of genomic prior knowledge in robust multimodal learning. Future work will focus on architectural compression and domain-adaptive strategies to facilitate high-throughput clinical deployment.

Acknowledgments. This work was supported by the National Key Research and Development Program of China (Grant No. 2022YFD1200600).

References

1. Chaisson, M.J.P., et al.: Tradeoffs in alignment and assembly-based methods for structural variant detection with long-read sequencing data. Nat. Commun. **15**(1), 1–17 (2024)
2. Chen, L., Wang, J., Mortlock, T., Khargonekar, P., Al Faruque, M.A.: Hyperdimensional uncertainty quantification for multimodal uncertainty fusion in autonomous vehicles perception. In: Proceedings of the Computer Vision and Pattern Recognition Conference, pp. 22306–22316 (2025)
3. Chen, Z., Hu, W., He, G., Deng, Z., Zhang, Z., Hong, R.: Unveiling uncertainty: a deep dive into calibration and performance of multimodal large language models. In: Proceedings of the 31st International Conference on Computational Linguistics, pp. 3095–3109 (2025)
4. Collins, R.L., Talkowski, M.E.: Diversity and consequences of structural variation in the human genome. Nat. Rev. Genet. 1–20 (2025)
5. Dong, C., et al.: Ace-protonet: adaptive covariance eigen-gate and uncertainty-aware prototype learning for coronary artery segmentation. Med. Image Anal. 104040 (2026)
6. Gao, R., et al.: Svhunter: long-read-based structural variation detection through the transformer model. Brief. Bioinf. **26**(3), bbaf203 (2025)
7. Gao, Z., Jiang, X., Xu, X., Shen, F., Li, Y., Shen, H.T.: Embracing unimodal aleatoric uncertainty for robust multimodal fusion. In: Proceedings of the IEEE/CVF Conference on Computer Vision and Pattern Recognition, pp. 26876–26885 (2024)
8. Gillani, R., et al.: Rare germline structural variants increase risk for pediatric solid tumors. Science **387**(6729), eadq0071 (2025)
9. He, K., Zhang, X., Ren, S., Sun, J.: Deep residual learning for image recognition. In: Proceedings of the IEEE Conference on Computer Vision and Pattern Recognition, pp. 770–778 (2016)
10. Heller, D., Vingron, M.: Svim: structural variant identification using mapped long reads. Bioinformatics **35**(17), 2907–2915 (2019)
11. Jiang, T., et al.: Long-read-based human genomic structural variation detection with cutesv. Genome Biol. **21**(1), 189 (2020)
12. Jung, M.C., Zhao, H., Dipnall, J., Du, L.: Beyond unimodal: generalising neural processes for multimodal uncertainty estimation. Adv. Neural. Inf. Process. Syst. **36**, 42191–42216 (2023)
13. Junjun, R., Zhengqian, Z., Ying, W., Jialiang, W., Yongzhuang, L.: A comprehensive review of deep learning-based variant calling methods. Brief. Funct. Genomics **23**(4), 303–313 (2024)
14. Kim, J., et al.: False gene and chromosome losses in genome assemblies caused by gc content variation and repeats. Genome Biol. **23**(1), 204 (2022)
15. Lam, H.Y., et al.: Nucleotide-resolution analysis of structural variants using breakseq and a breakpoint library. Nat. Biotechnol. **28**(1), 47–55 (2010)
16. Liang, Z., Hu, Y., Yang, F., Liu, X.: Enhancing continual semantic segmentation via uncertainty and class balance re-weighting. IEEE Trans. Image Process. **34**, 3689–3702 (2025)

17. Morishita, S., Ichikawa, K., Myers, E.W.: Finding long tandem repeats in long noisy reads. Bioinformatics **37**(5), 612–621 (2021)
18. Poplin, R., et al.: A universal snp and small-indel variant caller using deep neural networks. Nat. Biotechnol. **36**(10), 983–987 (2018)
19. Qin, Y., Sun, Y., Peng, D., Zhou, J.T., Peng, X., Hu, P.: Cross-modal active complementary learning with self-refining correspondence. Adv. Neural. Inf. Process. Syst. **36**, 24829–24840 (2023)
20. Qu, Z., et al.: Multi-modal disease prediction with hierarchical self-supervised learning. IEEE J. Biomed. Health Inf. (2025)
21. Samarasinghe, S.R., Gaedigk, A., Swen, J.J., Guchelaar, H.J., Nagaraj, S.H.: Long-read sequencing enhances pharmacogenomic profiling by resolving complex haplotypes, novel star alleles, and structural variants. Clin. Pharmacol. Therapeut. **119**(2), 536–545 (2026)
22. Sandler, M., Howard, A., Zhu, M., Zhmoginov, A., Chen, L.C.: Mobilenetv 2: inverted residuals and linear bottlenecks. In: Proceedings of the IEEE Conference on Computer Vision and Pattern Recognition, pp. 4510–4520 (2018)
23. Shah, S.N.A., Aalam, J., Parveen, R.: Deep learning approaches to enhance lung cancer diagnosis using next generation sequencing: state of the art. Arch. Comput. Methods Eng. **33**(2), 2175–2203 (2026)
24. Smolka, M., et al.: Detection of mosaic and population-level structural variants with sniffles2. Nat. Biotechnol. **42**(10), 1571–1580 (2024)
25. Wang, H., Li, C., Yu, X., Gao, J.: Deletion variants calling in third-generation sequencing data based on a dual-attention mechanism. Brief. Bioinf. **25**(4) (2024)
26. Xia, Z., et al.: Csv-filter: a deep learning-based comprehensive structural variant filtering method for both short and long reads. Bioinformatics **40**(9), btae539 (2024)
27. Xu, Q., Wang, P., Li, Y., Qian, T., Wang, X.: Hsacnet: hierarchical scale-aware consistency regularized semi-supervised change detection. In: 2025 IEEE International Conference on Multimedia and Expo (ICME), pp. 1–6. IEEE (2025)
28. Yuan, Y., Li, Z., Zhao, B.: A survey of multimodal learning: methods, applications, and future. ACM Comput. Surv. **57**(7), 1–34 (2025)
29. Zeng, T., et al.: Multisite long-read sequencing reveals the early contributions of somatic structural variations to hbv-related hepatocellular carcinoma tumorigenesis. Genome Res. **35**(4), 671 (2025)
30. Zhao, F., Zhang, C., Geng, B.: Deep multimodal data fusion. ACM Comput. Surv. **56**(9), 1–36 (2024)
31. Zook, J.M., Hansen, N.F., Olson, N.D., et al.: A robust benchmark for detection of germline large deletions and insertions. Nat. Biotechnol. **38**(11), 1347–1355 (2020)

Pairwise Likelihood Ranking for Imbalanced Sequence Classification

Srijan Sood[1](✉), Maxime Kawawa-Beaudan[1], Tucker Balch[2], and Manuela Veloso[1]

[1] J.P. Morgan AI Research, New York, NY, USA
{srijan.sood,maxime.kawawa-beaudan}@jpmorgan.com, mmv@cs.cmu.edu
[2] Emory University, Atlanta, GA, USA
tucker.balch@emory.edu

Abstract. Sequence classification under extreme class imbalance degrades discriminative models, particularly in average precision. We show that pairwise likelihood comparisons between class-specific generative ensembles yield a composite score equivalent to a Mann-Whitney U statistic, making it rank-based, length-invariant, and threshold-free. We instantiate this framework as HMM-*e*: hundreds of Hidden Markov Models per class, each trained on a random 1% data subset, are compared pairwise to classify new sequences. Because the score depends on rank orderings rather than raw likelihoods, it is robust to the calibration failures that degrade discriminative models under extreme class imbalance. The ensemble likelihood vectors additionally serve as features for downstream classifiers (SVM, neural network), bridging generative sequence modeling with discriminative decision-making. On three of four genomics benchmarks at 50:1 imbalance, HMM-*e* with downstream classifiers outperforms CNN and LSTM baselines, achieving 98.4 AUC-ROC and 74.5 Average Precision where CNN baselines fall to 94.9 and 37.5 respectively. On the GLOBEM behavioral dataset, HMM-*e* matches deep-learning accuracy at 7× lower training cost and three orders of magnitude fewer parameters. These results demonstrate that rank-based aggregation of generative ensembles provides a principled, efficient path to imbalance-robust sequence classification that does not depend on the specific choice of base learner.

Keywords: Sequence classification · Class imbalance · Hidden Markov models · Ensemble methods · Rank statistics

S. Sood and M. Kawawa-Beaudan—Contributed equally.

Supplementary Information The online version contains supplementary material available at https://doi.org/10.1007/978-3-032-37679-4_40.

M. Ceci et al. (Eds.): ECML PKDD 2026, LNAI 16948, pp. 708–725, 2027.
https://doi.org/10.1007/978-3-032-37679-4_40

1 Introduction

Many real-world sequence classification tasks – from detecting fraudulent transactions [25] and system intrusions [13] to diagnosing disease from genomic data [10] – suffer from extreme class imbalance, where positive examples are orders of magnitude rarer than negative ones [11]. Deep learning models (RNNs, LSTMs, Transformers) excel on balanced data but degrade under extreme imbalance despite rebalancing techniques [16,29].

Hidden Markov Models (HMMs) [23] are attractive base learners for ensembles: Baum-Welch converges on small data subsets, the forward algorithm provides calibrated log-likelihoods, and random subsampling generates natural diversity, enabling hundreds of models per class at modest cost. However, a single HMM still inherits the class skew of its training data. By training class-specific ensembles on random subsets, each model sees only its own class, sidestepping the imbalance entirely. We propose HMM-e, an ensemble approach that trains class-specific groups of HMMs on random data subsets and aggregates their likelihoods via pairwise matchups. We demonstrate this approach on established genome classification benchmarks and a longitudinal human behavior classification task.

Our contributions are as follows:

1. **Pairwise likelihood ranking.** We introduce a scoring framework that classifies sequences via pairwise likelihood matchups between class-specific generative ensembles (Eq. 4). Under exchangeability, this composite score is a Mann-Whitney U statistic, making it rank-based, length-invariant, and invariant to monotone likelihood transformations – properties that are non-trivial because raw likelihoods vary with sequence length and model convergence. We instantiate this as HMM-e, using HMMs whose sample efficiency enables ensembles of hundreds of models per class (Algorithm 1).
2. **Ensemble likelihoods as discriminative features.** The per-model likelihood vectors (Eq. 5) transform variable-length sequences into fixed-dimensional representations where each component measures similarity to a learned behavioral archetype. Downstream classifiers (SVM, neural network) trained on these vectors achieve strong performance under extreme imbalance (Table 2), and the decoupled design allows the generative ensemble to be trained once and paired with any classifier.
3. **Imbalance robustness at low cost.** On three of four genomics benchmarks at 50:1 imbalance, HMM-e with downstream classifiers outperforms CNN and LSTM baselines, achieving 98.4 AUC-ROC and 74.5 Average Precision where CNN baselines fall to 94.9 and 37.5 respectively (Table 2). On the GLOBEM behavioral dataset, HMM-e matches the best deep-learning baseline at 7× lower training cost and three orders of magnitude fewer parameters (17,500 vs. 13.7M; Table 3).

2 Background and Related Work

Sequence classification – categorizing sequential data into predefined classes – spans domains from speech recognition to bioinformatics [31].

Sequential data may be categorical or continuous, single-feature or multi-feature; we demonstrate results on both: single-feature, categorical data in Table 2, and multi-feature, continuous data in Table 3. In this paper we focus on the binary classification setting; anomaly detection is a special case when one class represents normal behavior.

2.1 Imbalanced Sequence Classification

Many real-world problems involve the detection of rare events like system intrusions [13] and credit card fraud [25]. These anomaly detection problems are made difficult by class imbalance, or the scarcity of examples for the behavior of interest. One-class approaches model only nominal behavior and flag deviations; our two-class approach models both classes, enabling detection of specific anomaly types rather than any deviation from normal.

2.2 HMM-Based Sequence Modeling

Hidden Markov Models (HMMs) are statistical models for sequential data with a long history in NLP, finance, and bioinformatics [4,23]. An HMM models an observation sequence $\mathcal{O} = \{o_1, \ldots, o_T\}$ as emissions from a latent Markov chain over hidden states $\{a_1, \ldots, a_T\}$. Observations can be categorical or continuous (Gaussian HMMs). An HMM with n states and a vocabulary of m possible emissions is parameterized by an initial state distribution π, an $n \times n$ transition matrix A, and an $n \times m$ emission distribution B, collectively $\lambda = (A, B, \pi)$. HMMs make two fundamental assumptions: (1) the *Markov property* – a state depends only on its predecessor,

$$p(A_{t+1} = a_{t+1} \mid a_t, \ldots, a_1) = p(A_{t+1} = a_{t+1} \mid a_t) \tag{1}$$

and (2) *emission independence* – an observation depends only on the current state,

$$p(O_t = o_t \mid a_t, o_{t-1}, a_{t-1}, \ldots, o_1, a_1) = p(O_t = o_t \mid a_t) \tag{2}$$

The forward-backward algorithm computes $p(\mathcal{O} \mid \lambda)$ and the Baum-Welch algorithm learns λ to maximize it [23].

Despite the success of deep-learning approaches like transformers [27], HMMs remain applicable to time series analysis [17] and anomaly detection [1]. HMM ensembles have been used for time series segmentation [24], network intrusion detection [22], behavioral sequence modeling [14], and speech recognition [21]. We extend these works with formal analysis (Proposition 1), downstream classifiers, and comprehensive evaluation across domains and imbalance levels.

3 Pairwise Generative Ensembles

A natural baseline trains one HMM per class and classifies by maximum likelihood (Eq. 3). However, a single HMM inherits the class skew of its training data and cannot capture behavioral diversity within a class.

$$c(\mathcal{O}) = \mathbb{1}\{p(\mathcal{O} \mid \lambda^{+}) > p(\mathcal{O} \mid \lambda^{-})\} \tag{3}$$

Comparing raw likelihoods across varying-length sequences is also problematic – likelihood scales with sequence length due to sequential probability multiplication [4]. We address both limitations with HMM-*e* (Fig. 1), which uses generative base learners in a discriminative manner: class-specific ensembles are compared pairwise, yielding a rank-based score that decouples discriminative power from generative model calibration. Following Ng and Jordan [20] – generative classifiers converge with fewer samples but have higher asymptotic error – HMM-*e* exploits generative sample efficiency, training hundreds of HMMs from extreme subsamples, while mitigating asymptotic error through discriminative aggregation.

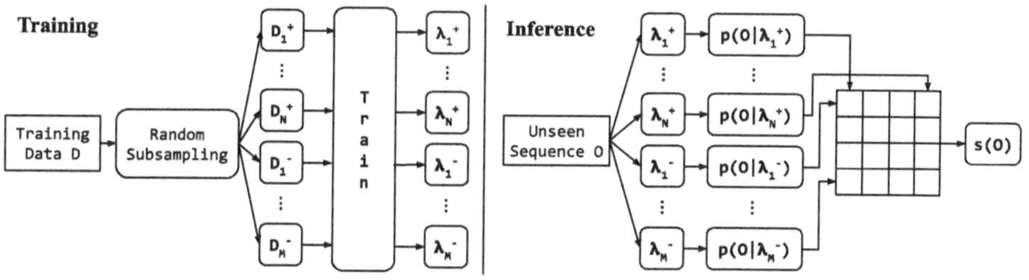

Fig. 1. Flow diagram of the HMM-*e* training and inference pipeline, as detailed in Sect. 3. Class-specific HMM ensembles are trained on random data subsets; at inference, pairwise likelihood matchups yield the composite score *s*.

3.1 Ensemble Training via Subsampling

Ensemble frameworks address both limitations by training multiple models on random data subsets [9], promoting diversity and mitigating class skew [15]. We adopt HMMs because they produce calibrated likelihoods via the forward algorithm, train cheaply enough for hundreds of models per class, and generate natural diversity from extreme subsampling – properties that neural base learners lack at this scale (see Sect. 5). Because the composite score (Eq. 4) operates on ranks rather than raw likelihoods, the scoring mechanism does not depend on HMMs specifically; probabilistic models such as GMMs or variational autoencoders could serve as alternative base learners.

Let D be the training dataset, consisting of positive class data D^+ and negative class data D^-. First, we train N models $\{\lambda_1^+, ..., \lambda_N^+\}$ on the positive class and M models $\{\lambda_1^-, ..., \lambda_M^-\}$ on the negative class. Each model is trained on a randomly selected subset of samples from the training data, obtained through a random subsampling process with a sampling rate of $r\%$: $D_i^+ \sim \text{RandomSubsample}(D^+, r)$, $D_j^- \sim \text{RandomSubsample}(D^-, r)$. Each model sees $r\%$ of the training data in its relevant class. We select these parameters (N, M, r) to promote diversity among models (see Sect. 3.1). For any given training sequence, the probability of not appearing in any model's subset is $(1-r)^N$; at $r = 1\%$ and $N = 250$, this is ~8%, so most training data is seen by at least one model. For more on hyperparameter selection and sensitivity, see Sect. 4.1, Sect. 5.3, and the supplementary material.

Diversity. Diversity among base learners is a prerequisite for effective ensembling: without it, models become redundant, effectively reducing ensemble size (Fig. 2). We measure diversity via pairwise HMM distance $D(\lambda_i, \lambda_j)$ from [1] – a sum of Hellinger distances between emission distributions of states matched using linear sum assignment, weighted by the stationary distribution.

Ensemble size N and subset factor r jointly control diversity – small N limits behavioral coverage, while large r produces redundant models (see Sect. 5.3). Varying the number of HMM states across models (e.g., $n \in [3, 4, 5]$) further improves diversity, yielding ~3% AUC-ROC gains.

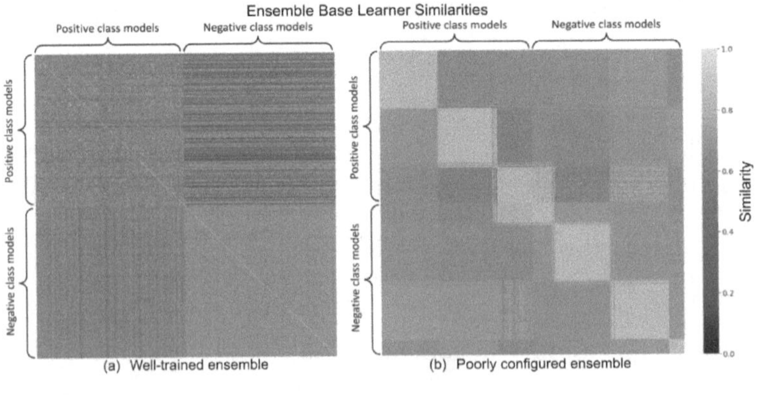

Fig. 2. Pairwise inter-HMM similarities for a 250-model ensemble on *demo_human_or_worm*. Left: properly configured (unique initializations, 25 iterations). Right: degenerate (shared initializations, 5 iterations). Without sufficient diversity the ensemble learns redundant models, effectively reducing ensemble size.

3.2 Pairwise Likelihood Ranking

For a previously unseen observation sequence $\mathcal{O}$, we compute the likelihood scores under all models: $\{p(\mathcal{O} \mid \lambda_1^+), ..., p(\mathcal{O} \mid \lambda_N^+)\}$ and $\{p(\mathcal{O} \mid \lambda_1^-), ..., p(\mathcal{O} \mid \lambda_M^-)\}$. We then compute the composite score:

$$s(\mathcal{O}) = \frac{1}{N \times M} \sum_{i=1}^{N} \sum_{j=1}^{M} \mathbb{1}\{p(\mathcal{O} \mid \lambda_i^+) > p(\mathcal{O} \mid \lambda_j^-)\} \tag{4}$$

where $\mathbb{1}\{P\}$ equals 1 when P is true and 0 otherwise. The composite score $s(\mathcal{O}) \in [0, 1]$ measures the proportion of matchups won by positive-class models.

Mann-Whitney Interpretation. The composite score has the form of a two-sample U-statistic with kernel $h(x, y) = \mathbb{1}\{x > y\}$ [12,19,30], estimating $P(X^+ > X^-)$ – the probability that a random positive-class model assigns higher likelihood than a random negative-class model.

Proposition 1. *If base learner scores within each class are exchangeable, then* $s(\mathcal{O}) \xrightarrow{p} P(X^+ > X^-)$ *as* $N, M \to \infty$*, where* X^+ *and* X^- *are drawn from the positive- and negative-class model score distributions respectively.*

Proof (Proof sketch). Under exchangeability, $s(\mathcal{O})$ is a two-sample U-statistic whose variance vanishes as $N, M \to \infty$ [12], so $s(\mathcal{O}) \xrightarrow{p} \mathbb{E}[h(X^+, X^-)] = P(X^+ > X^-)$. Strict exchangeability requires i.i.d. scores; in practice, training subsets share data, introducing weak dependence. At r=1% and N=250, expected pairwise overlap is ~0.01% of class data, so scores are approximately exchangeable. We treat this as a structural analogy motivating the rank-based design; Fig. 5 shows empirical performance under varying N.

Because $P(X^+ > X^-)$ equals the AUC of the model-score distributions [5], the composite score is a nonparametric rank statistic that depends only on pairwise orderings, not score magnitudes. As the ensembles grow, the score concentrates: the two-sample U-statistic has variance of order $1/N + 1/M$ [12], giving a stable estimate at N=M=250.

Invariance Properties. Because the composite score counts pairwise wins, it is invariant to monotone transformations of the likelihoods – a direct consequence of the rank-based U-statistic structure. Since each indicator evaluates the *same* sequence under both class models, sequence length scales both log-likelihoods in the same direction, preserving their ordering and hence the indicator value. This makes the score approximately length-invariant, assuming per-step divergences between class models remain stable across sequence lengths.

Classification. We classify sequences by thresholding the composite score (Algorithm 1, inference step 3). AUC-ROC and AP, our primary evaluation metrics, are threshold-independent; s_{thresh} is relevant only for operational deployment.

A sample distribution of composite scores over a corpus of held-out sequences, colored by class, is shown in Fig. 3. The classes are well-separated, and an effective classifier can be produced by thresholding, e.g., $s(\mathcal{O}) \approx 0.75$.

3.3 Ensemble Likelihoods as Features

The intermediate likelihood vectors contain richer information than the scalar score – each component $p(\mathcal{O}_i|\lambda_j)$ measures how similar a sequence is to the data subset underlying model λ_j. For each sequence $\mathcal{O}_i$, we construct the feature vector

$$f_i = \left[p(\mathcal{O}_i|\lambda_1^+), \ldots, p(\mathcal{O}_i|\lambda_N^+), p(\mathcal{O}_i|\lambda_1^-), \ldots, p(\mathcal{O}_i|\lambda_M^-)\right] \tag{5}$$

We L2-normalize f_i before training classifiers on $\{f_1, ..., f_S\}$, making the representation scale-invariant to sequence length (Sect. 3). L2 normalization preserves angular relationships between likelihood vectors and is scale-invariant, unlike min-max which is sensitive to outlier likelihoods.

Figure 4 shows UMAP projections of these features, in which the two classes form well-separated clusters, indicating that the likelihood vectors carry strong class-discriminative structure. We train two types of classifiers in this framework: support vector machines (**HMM-*e* + SVM**) and neural networks (**HMM-*e* + NN**).

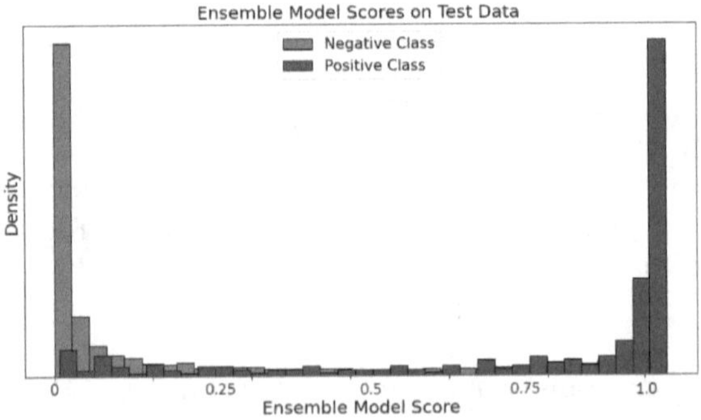

Fig. 3. The distribution of composite scores for test data in *demo_coding_vs_intergenomic_seqs*, using a 250-model ensemble in an imbalanced data setting with class ratio 50:1. We observe good class separation even with data imbalance.

Algorithm 1. Ensemble Training and Inference

Require: Training data D, number of positive models N, number of negative models M, subset factor r

Training Phase

Randomly sample subsets from D: $\{D_1^+, D_2^+, \ldots, D_N^+\}$ and $\{D_1^-, D_2^-, \ldots, D_M^-\}$ such that each subset contains $r\%$ of the relevant class data.
for $i = 1$ to N **do**
  $\lambda_i^+ \leftarrow \text{train\_model}(D_i^+)$
end for
for $j = 1$ to M **do**
  $\lambda_j^- \leftarrow \text{train\_model}(D_j^-)$
end for

Inference Phase

Require: Corpus of sequences $C = \{\mathcal{O}_1, ..., \mathcal{O}_S\}$
Initialize an empty list of composite scores $\mathcal{S}$
for each sequence $\mathcal{O}_i \in C$ **do**
  Compute likelihood scores $\{p(\mathcal{O}_i \mid \lambda_1^+), \ldots, p(\mathcal{O}_i \mid \lambda_N^+)\}$ and $\{p(\mathcal{O}_i \mid \lambda_1^-), \ldots, p(\mathcal{O}_i \mid \lambda_M^-)\}$
  Compute composite score $s(\mathcal{O}_i)$ and append to $\mathcal{S}$
end for
Determine threshold s_{thresh} based on scores in $\mathcal{S}$
for each sequence $\mathcal{O}_i \in C$ **do**
  Class $c(\mathcal{O}_i) = \mathbb{1}\{s(\mathcal{O}_i) \geq s_{\text{thresh}}\}$
end for

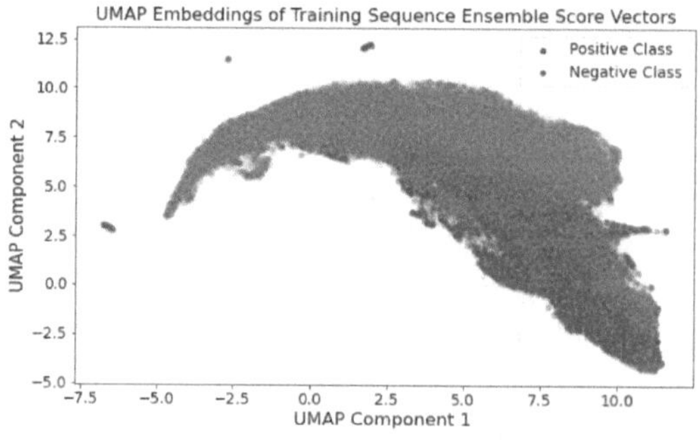

Fig. 4. UMAP embeddings of training data using the likelihood vectors from HMM-e with 250 sub-models per class. The two classes form clearly separated clusters, indicating strong class-discriminative structure in the feature space.

4 Experiments

Our experiments address three questions: (i) does pairwise-ranking aggregation make HMM-e robust to extreme class imbalance relative to discriminative baselines? (ii) do the ensemble likelihood vectors serve as effective features for downstream classifiers? and (iii) how does HMM-e's accuracy-cost trade-off compare to deep learning? We evaluate on two benchmarks: 1) an open-source genomics benchmark [10] that consists of eight datasets for different classification problems, all with a single discrete feature, and 2) GLOBEM, a longitudinal human behavior modeling dataset [33], with multiple continuous features. Our benchmarks span both data types: single-feature categorical sequences (genomics, Table 2) and multi-feature continuous time series (GLOBEM, Table 3).

4.1 Genomics Benchmark

Data. The genomics benchmark [10] contains sequences of nucleotide tokens (A, T, C, G, N) from human, mouse, and roundworm genomes, labeled by function (promoter, enhancer, or chromatin region). We evaluate on four datasets (Table 1).

HMM-Based Methods

HMMs and HMM-e. For the genomics experiments we use a hyperparameter grid search on the toy dataset *demo_human_or_worm* over ensemble sizes of [10, 50, 100, 250, 500, 1000], subsample sizes r of [0.1%, 1%, 10%], and numbers of HMM states [3, 4, 5, 6, 7]. Based on these results we adopt $N = M = 250$, a sampling rate of 1%, and 5 HMM states. Performance is sensitive to hyperparameter choice; see Sect. 5.3 and the supplementary material.

HMM-e + SVM. We train the downstream SVM using a radial basis function kernel, exploring an effective and simple model class in non-deep learning contexts.

HMM-e + NN. The architecture is similar to the baseline models in terms of number of layers and hidden dimensions; the classifier consists of three hidden fully connected layers with dimensions 512, 256, and 128, each followed by batch normalization, ReLU activation, and dropout. The model is trained using binary cross-entropy loss, with the Adam optimizer and a learning rate scheduler. To address data imbalance, we apply weighted sampling during training.

Table 1. Number of total samples and median sequence length for all experimental datasets. For additional details regarding data sources and tasks, see the supplementary material.

Dataset	Num. Samples	Med. Length
human_nontata_promoters	36,131	251
human_enhancers_ensembl	154,842	269
demo_human_or_worm	100,000	200
demo_coding_vs_intergenomic	100,000	200
GLOBEM	11,849	28

4.2 GLOBEM Dataset

Data. The GLOBEM longitudinal human behavior study features over 3,700 attributes from 497 participants across four years (2018–2021). The dataset includes survey, smartphone, and wearable data, with a focus on depression detection (the task we consider). Data includes mood assessments, step counts, location variability, and sleep metrics. We utilize the data standardization platform for reproducibility provided by the authors [32].

Feature Selection. While GLOBEM includes thousands of features, we select just four evaluated daily: smartphone moving/static time ratio, total screen time (minutes), total sleep time (minutes), and total steps. We train Gaussian HMMs on these continuous features. We use the raw feature for the current day rather than the 14-day history used by most deep-learning baselines, which we find boosts performance by ~3% for HMM-e. Preprocessing details (sequence construction, imputation, filtering) are in the supplementary material.

HMMs and HMM-*e*. For GLOBEM, we use the same ensemble size and sampling rate as in Sect. 4.1, but use 3 states in all of the ensemble models, based on hyperparameter grid search on a small subset of the training data.

Table 2. Performance comparison across four genomics datasets under balanced (1:1) and imbalanced (50:1) conditions. Metrics: AUC-ROC (AUC) and Average Precision (AP), scaled to 0–100 for readability. Bold indicates best per row. HMM-e +SVM and HMM-e +NN generally outperform baselines, particularly under extreme imbalance (50:1). CNN-e and LSTM-e omitted (near-random under subsampling; full results in the supplementary material). Single run; GLOBEM results (Table 3) include standard deviations.

Dataset		CNN		LSTM		HMM		HMM-e					
								base		*+SVM*		*+NN*	
		AUC	AP	AUC	AP	AUC	AP	AUC	AP	AUC	AP	AUC	AP
demo_human_or_worm	1:1	95.3	95.0	98.3	98.4	55.7	55.6	83.9	84.6	**99.2**	**99.1**	98.5	98.5
	50:1	94.9	37.5	94.8	53.9	61.4	14.0	87.2	27.5	96.8	73.2	**98.4**	**74.5**
human_nontata_promoters	1:1	**89.5**	**91.0**	84.0	88.4	76.8	66.1	82.0	73.2	**89.5**	84.0	88.0	86.2
	50:1	81.0	**13.4**	82.9	11.5	71.4	4.1	85.3	9.2	84.5	11.4	**90.5**	11.8
human_enhancers_ensembl	1:1	86.4	84.3	86.6	86.9	62.9	57.8	69.4	69.9	85.0	84.3	**87.4**	**87.3**
	50:1	**80.7**	14.6	77.6	11.0	57.5	2.4	68.2	6.4	76.0	**15.5**	80.5	15.2
demo_coding_vs_intergenomic	1:1	94.4	93.7	90.2	89.8	76.3	68.8	85.1	84.3	95.5	95.0	**96.7**	**96.6**
	50:1	88.2	32.6	88.4	23.1	74.6	4.9	87.9	24.3	85.0	46.0	**95.1**	**52.1**

4.3 Baselines

Neural networks trained by gradient-based optimization tend to favor the majority class under imbalance, leading to biased predictions [29]. Several mitigation techniques exist – weighted loss functions, data augmentation, advanced sampling, and hyperparameter tuning – but leveraging extremely imbalanced datasets with neural networks remains a persistent challenge [16]. We compare against CNN and LSTM baselines using weighted sampling rather than SMOTE [3] (inapplicable to variable-length discrete sequences), focal loss [18], or class-balanced loss [6]. Weighted sampling isolates the classification architecture from the rebalancing strategy. Focal loss and class-balanced loss are orthogonal techniques that could be applied to both neural baselines *and* HMM-e's downstream classifiers; evaluating these combinations is future work.

Genomics

CNN. We evaluate against the baseline CNN from [10]. The model comprises an embedding layer, a sequence of 1-D convolutional layers with ReLU activations, batch normalization, and max-pooling.

LSTM. We implement an LSTM model for binary sequence classification, using a single LSTM layer with a hidden dimension of 64. Both the LSTM and CNN models are trained with the Adam optimizer using binary cross-entropy loss.

To address data imbalance during training, we employ weighted sampling for both the CNN and LSTM. Each sample in the training set is assigned a weight inversely proportional to its class frequency, giving higher weights to underrepresented classes.

CNN and LSTM Ensembles. We also compare against ensembles of neural networks (CNN-e and LSTM-e), using random subsampling and majority vote, with 250 models and 1% subsampling rate for consistency with HMM-e. Majority vote is the standard aggregation for discriminative ensembles; pairwise ranking is specific to the generative setting, where each model produces a continuous likelihood rather than a class label.

Transformers. We omit Transformer baselines: with vocabulary size 5, sequence lengths 200–2,000, and as few as ∼360 positive samples at 50:1, our setting is well below the regime where attention outperforms simpler inductive biases [27].

GLOBEM. For GLOBEM, we compare against benchmark baselines: Canzian et al. [2] (SVM-based), Wahle et al. [28] (Random Forest, 450 trees on our four features), and the top-performing deep-learning model *Reorder* [33] (CNN-based).

4.4 Evaluation

Accuracy is misleading under class imbalance – a classifier can attain 99.9% accuracy by labeling every sample as normal. We report two threshold-independent metrics: **AUC-ROC**, the area under the receiver operating characteristic curve, and **Average Precision (AP)**, the weighted average of precisions at each recall threshold [7,26].

All genomics datasets are split by the benchmark authors into train and test sets. For GLOBEM, we use the "all-but-one" validation scheme [32] – training on three years and testing on the fourth. We artificially create imbalance by randomly subsampling the positive class; these subsets are fixed across all HMM approaches, and fixed separately across all deep-learning approaches. In practice, s_{thresh} is selected to maximize AUC-ROC on a held-out validation set; for GLOBEM, the threshold is tuned within each fold of the leave-one-year-out protocol.

Reproducibility. All datasets are publicly available – the genomics benchmarks through the Genomic Benchmarks suite [10] and GLOBEM through its standardized data platform [32]. The main text states our core configuration (N=M=250, 1% subsampling, five HMM states for genomics and three for GLOBEM, with downstream classifier settings in Sect. 4.1); the supplementary material provides the full hyperparameter grid, the hardware and software stack, and complete pseudocode for every component.

Table 3. AUC-ROC and Average Precision (0–100 scale) on GLOBEM. Bold indicates best per row. Our adopted SVM is as in [2], Random Forest as in [28], CNN as in [33]. HMM-*e* achieves the best performance under extreme imbalance (50:1) while remaining competitive at 1:1, and trains in 152 s versus Reorder's 1,073 s (7× speedup). Results are mean ± std over four leave-one-year-out folds.

		Canzian [2]		Wahle [28]		Reorder [33]		HMM		HMM-*e*	
		AUC	*AP*	*AUC*	*AP*	*AUC*	*AP*	*AUC*	*AP*	*AUC*	*AP*
Performance	1:1	49.9 ± 2.9	47.0 ± 3.2	53.6 ± 2.1	48.2 ± 2.8	**55.9 ± 3.2**	**51.6 ± 5.6**	51.8 ± 1.9	47.2 ± 2.8	54.6 ± 1.8	49.8 ± 3.7
	50:1	50.0 ± 4.6	46.8 ± 3.8	48.7 ± 1.3	44.5 ± 3.9	51.9 ± 3.2	47.6 ± 4.3	51.7 ± 0.9	46.7 ± 3.3	**52.1 ± 1.9**	**47.9 ± 3.1**
Training Time (s)		39.17 ± 7.89		143.80 ± 5.85		1072.76 ± 6.64		25.54 ± 2.13		151.81 ± 9.26	

5 Results and Discussion

5.1 Genomics

Table 2 presents a detailed performance evaluation of the various sequence classification approaches across the 4 genomics datasets in balanced (1:1) and imbalanced (50:1) class settings, reporting two metrics: AUC-ROC and AP.

Singleton vs. Ensemble. We find that our ensemble approach consistently outperforms the singleton HMM approach, yielding large gains in both AUC and AP. For example, on the *demo_human_or_worm* dataset, moving from a singleton HMM to an ensemble improves AUC from 55.7 to 83.9 and AP from 55.6 to 84.6. This trend continues under class imbalance: in the 50:1 class ratio setting, the singleton HMM achieves 61.4 AUC and 14.0 AP, while HMM-*e* achieves 87.2 AUC and 27.5 AP.

Comparison to Baselines. While the baseline CNN and LSTM classifiers perform adequately on the balanced datasets, their efficacy diminishes with high class imbalance despite implementing weighted sampling approaches to remedy this. The HMM-e + SVM and HMM-e + NN models consistently outperform other methods, particularly in the imbalanced data scenario (50:1). In the few instances where CNN or LSTM outperform HMM-e + SVM or HMM-e + NN at 1:1, AUC-ROC gaps are negligible but AP gaps can be larger – e.g., on human_nontata_promoters at 1:1, the CNN achieves 91.0 AP versus HMM-e + SVM's 84.0, while AUC-ROC is tied at 89.5. In balanced settings where labeled data is abundant, the advantage of HMM-e diminishes, confirming its primary value in the imbalanced regime.

Neural network ensembles (CNN-e, LSTM-e) perform substantially worse than HMM-e under imbalance (see the supplementary material). At 1% subsampling, individual CNN and LSTM models receive too few samples to learn meaningful representations, producing near-random likelihoods that degrade the pairwise scoring mechanism. This confirms that our approach requires base learners capable of learning from extreme subsamples – a property HMMs satisfy naturally via the Baum-Welch algorithm, which converges with few hundred sequences, while neural networks require orders of magnitude more data per model.

On `human_enhancers_ensembl` (154K samples), the CNN retains a slight advantage at 50:1 (80.7 vs 80.5 AUC-ROC); at this scale, even the minority class provides ~3,000 samples, enough for weighted sampling to remain effective.

While CNN and LSTM are end-to-end discriminative models, HMM-e combines generative base learner advantages (sample efficiency, fast training) with discriminative aggregation (pairwise ranking, length invariance). A three-seed uncertainty study on *demo_coding_vs_intergenomic* (Table 4) shows that HMM-e +NN and the base ensemble are the most stable methods, with HMM-e +NN's run-to-run variance well below both CNN and LSTM; the full analysis is in the supplementary material.

Table 4. Three-seed AUC-ROC and Average Precision (mean ± std dev) on *demo_coding_vs_intergenomic*. HMM-e +NN and the base ensemble are the most stable methods; HMM-e +NN's run-to-run variance is well below the CNN and LSTM baselines. Full tables (with standard error) are in the supplementary material.

	AUC-ROC		AP	
Method	1:1	50:1	1:1	50:1
CNN	93.92 ± 0.22	88.16 ± 0.46	92.48 ± 0.48	30.35 ± 2.69
LSTM	91.99 ± 1.28	88.30 ± 2.67	91.54 ± 1.48	23.36 ± 7.76
HMM	76.62 ± 0.22	77.21 ± 1.43	69.75 ± 0.43	5.03 ± 0.50
HMM-e	85.38 ± 0.05	87.91 ± 0.28	84.40 ± 0.23	25.21 ± 1.33
HMM-e + SVM	95.24 ± 0.18	86.08 ± 1.67	94.70 ± 0.22	44.61 ± 2.10
HMM-e + NN	96.72 ± 0.01	94.71 ± 0.17	96.66 ± 0.02	52.03 ± 0.50

To assess significance, we follow Demšar [8] and compare methods across the eight genomics conditions (four datasets × two imbalance levels). A Friedman test rejects the null of equal performance for both AUC-ROC ($\chi^2(5)=27.8$, $p<0.001$) and AP ($\chi^2(5)=30.6$, $p<0.001$). By a Nemenyi post-hoc test, HMM-e +NN holds the best mean rank, significantly above the singleton HMM and the base HMM-e variant; a Wilcoxon signed-rank test further confirms that ensembling improves over the singleton HMM across all eight conditions ($p=0.008$). HMM-e +NN's advantage over the CNN is favorable but not significant at this sample size ($p=0.055$ for AUC-ROC) – with only four datasets, no test confined to a single imbalance level can reach $p<0.05$ – so we ground HMM-e's case in its consistent rank advantage, lower seed variance, and 7× lower training cost. The supplementary material reports the full Friedman, Nemenyi, and pairwise tests.

5.2 GLOBEM

On the longitudinal human behavior dataset (Table 3), absolute performance across all methods remains modest (AUC 50–56), consistent with the inherently challenging nature of depression detection from passive sensing [33]. In this regime, HMM-e using just four features outperforms traditional ML baselines and matches deep-learning performance at a fraction of the cost. Using singleton HMMs, we beat Canzian et al. [2] (which uses up to 17 features) by 1.9 AUC and 0.2 AP; using HMM-e, this gap widens to 4.7 AUC and 2.8 AP. Compared to Wahle et al. [28], HMM-e improves AUC by 1.0 and AP by 1.6 points. HMM-e performs comparably to the deep-learning approach *Reorder*, falling 1.3 AUC and 1.8 AP short at 1:1 balance.

Critically, HMM-e is more robust to imbalance: from 1:1 to 50:1, HMM-e drops just 2.5 AUC and 1.9 AP, versus 4.0 AUC and 4.0 AP for Reorder, and 4.9 AUC and 3.7 AP for the random forest. At 50:1, HMM-e surpasses Reorder by 0.2 AUC and 0.3 AP, inverting the ranking observed at 1:1. Reorder's CNN relies on weighted sampling to handle class skew; as the minority class shrinks, the effective training signal degrades despite reweighting. HMM-e is inherently robust: each base learner trains on a small random subset of one class regardless of the global ratio, so the ensemble structure absorbs the imbalance rather than the individual models. The natural GLOBEM class ratio is approximately 1.19:1; the 50:1 setting is created by artificial subsampling to stress-test imbalance robustness.

Because GLOBEM provides only four leave-one-year-out folds, with inter-method gaps comparable to their across-fold standard deviations (Table 3), we treat these accuracy differences – including the imbalance-robustness gap – as indicative rather than statistically significant; HMM-e's decisive advantage on this dataset is instead its efficiency.

The training-time advantage is substantial: HMM-e trains in 152 s versus Reorder's 1,073 s – a 7× speedup (Table 3). This efficiency stems from the HMM's closed-form parameter updates (Baum-Welch), which require no gradient computation or backpropagation. The lightweight model also enables rapid iteration over hyperparameter configurations.

5.3 Ensemble Hyperparameter Sensitivity

Figure 5 summarizes an ablation on *demo_human_or_worm* over ensemble sizes, imbalance levels, and subsample rates: larger ensembles outperform smaller ones, though gains plateau beyond 100 models.

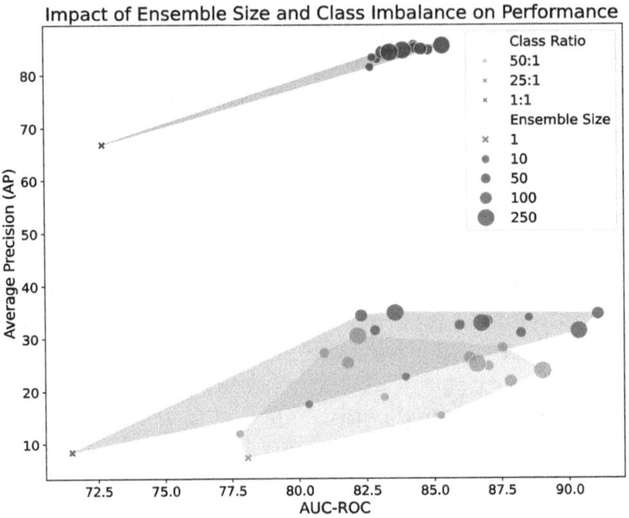

Fig. 5. Ablation on *demo_human_or_worm* over imbalance levels (1:1, 25:1, 50:1), ensemble sizes (1–250), and subsample rates (0.1–10%); multiple points per (size, ratio) are different rates r. Larger ensembles outperform smaller ones, plateauing beyond ~100 models. AUC-ROC rises with imbalance (base-rate effect) while AP decays.

5.4 Computational Efficiency

Each base learner with n states and f features learns $n + n^2 + nf$ parameters; across $N + M$ models, HMM-e uses 17,500 total parameters for genomics (vs. 13.7M for the CNN ensemble) and 12,000 for GLOBEM (vs. *Reorder*'s 10,099). On our hardware (detailed in the supplementary material), HMM-e trains GLOBEM in 152 s versus *Reorder*'s 1,073 s – a 7× speedup from Baum-Welch's closed-form updates requiring no gradient computation.

6 Conclusion

We introduced HMM-e, an ensemble method for sequence classification that trains class-specific groups of HMMs on random data subsets and aggregates their likelihoods via pairwise matchups. The resulting composite score (Eq. 4) – structurally a Mann-Whitney U statistic – provides rank-based, length-invariant sequence comparison, and ensemble likelihoods serve as effective features for downstream classifiers. Generative base learners, when aggregated discriminatively via pairwise ranking, can match or exceed end-to-end discriminative models under severe imbalance. On three of four genomics benchmarks at 50:1 imbalance, HMM-e with downstream classifiers outperforms CNN and LSTM baselines; on the fourth, the CNN retains a slight edge at larger dataset scale. On the GLOBEM behavioral dataset, where all methods achieve modest absolute performance, HMM-e matches the best deep-learning baseline at $7\times$ lower training cost. HMMs are well-suited base learners because Baum-Welch converges from extreme subsamples; because Eq. 4 operates on ranks, the scoring mechanism may extend to other probabilistic base learners.

Limitations. The Markov assumption limits modeling of long-range dependencies. Genomics results use a single primary seed, with a three-seed study on one dataset (in the supplementary material) confirming low variance; GLOBEM includes standard deviations across leave-one-year-out folds. Training time scales linearly with ensemble size, and we have not explored pruning redundant base learners. We evaluate the composite score only with HMMs; testing with alternative base learners (GMMs, variational autoencoders), mixed-type sequences, and higher-dimensional multivariate inputs beyond the four GLOBEM features remains future work. All experiments use CPU only (see the supplementary material); at inference, $O(N \times M)$ comparisons may bottleneck latency-sensitive deployment. Promising extensions include ensemble pruning, synthetic data augmentation via HMMs' generative properties, and multi-class classification.

Ethics Statement. The GLOBEM dataset uses anonymized, consented data collected under IRB approval as documented by the platform authors [32]. Depression detection from passive sensing carries risks of misdiagnosis; our method is intended for research and is not suitable for clinical deployment without further validation. All genomics datasets are publicly available benchmarks with no personally identifiable information. LLM tools were used for proofreading.

Disclaimer. This paper was prepared for informational purposes by the Artificial Intelligence Research group of JPMorgan Chase & Co. and its affiliates ("JP Morgan") and is not a product of the Research Department of JP Morgan. JP Morgan makes no representation and warranty whatsoever and disclaims all liability, for the completeness, accuracy or reliability of the information contained herein. This document is not intended as investment research or investment advice, or a recommendation, offer or solicitation for the purchase or sale of any security, financial instrument, financial product or service, or to be used in any way for evaluating the merits of participating in any transaction, and shall not constitute a solicitation under any jurisdiction or to any person, if such solicitation under such jurisdiction or to such person would be unlawful.

References

1. Azzalini, D., Castellini, A., Luperto, M., Farinelli, A., Amigoni, F.: Hmms for anomaly detection in autonomous robots. In: Proceedings of the 19th International Conference on Autonomous Agents and MultiAgent Systems, AAMAS 2020, pp. 105–113. International Foundation for Autonomous Agents and Multiagent Systems, Richland, SC (2020)
2. Canzian, L., Musolesi, M.: Trajectories of depression: unobtrusive monitoring of depressive states by means of smartphone mobility traces analysis. In: Proceedings of the 2015 ACM International Joint Conference on Pervasive and Ubiquitous Computing, UbiComp 2015, pp. 1293–1304. Association for Computing Machinery, New York, USA (2015). https://doi.org/10.1145/2750858.2805845
3. Chawla, N.V., Bowyer, K.W., Hall, L.O., Kegelmeyer, W.P.: SMOTE: synthetic minority over-sampling technique. J. Artifi. Intell. Res. **16**, 321–357 (2002)
4. Choo, K.H., Tong, J.C., Zhang, L.: Recent applications of hidden markov models in computational biology. Genomics, Proteomics Bioinform. **2**(2), 84–96 (2004). https://doi.org/10.1016/S1672-0229(04)02014-5
5. Cortes, C., Mohri, M.: AUC optimization vs. error rate minimization. In: Advances in Neural Information Processing Systems, vol. 16 (2004)
6. Cui, Y., Jia, M., Lin, T.Y., Song, Y., Belongie, S.: Class-balanced loss based on effective number of samples. In: Proceedings of the IEEE/CVF Conference on Computer Vision and Pattern Recognition, pp. 9268–9277 (2019)
7. Davis, J., Goadrich, M.: The relationship between precision-recall and roc curves. In: Proceedings of the 23rd International Conference on Machine Learning, pp. 233–240 (2006)
8. Demšar, J.: Statistical comparisons of classifiers over multiple data sets. J. Mach. Learn. Res. **7**, 1–30 (2006)
9. Dietterich, T.G.: Ensemble methods in machine learning. In: International workshop on multiple classifier systems, pp. 1–15. Springer (2000). https://doi.org/10.1007/3-540-45014-9_1 ¡error l="307" c="Invalid command: paragraph not started." /¿
10. Gresova, K., Martinek, V., Cechak, D., Simecek, P., Alexiou, P.: Genomic benchmarks: a collection of datasets for genomic sequence classification. BMC Genomic Data **24**, 25 (2023). https://doi.org/10.1186/s12863-023-01123-8
11. He, H., Garcia, E.A.: Learning from imbalanced data. IEEE Trans. Knowl. Data Eng. **21**(9), 1263–1284 (2009). https://doi.org/10.1109/TKDE.2008.239
12. Hoeffding, W.: A class of statistics with asymptotically normal distribution. Ann. Math. Stat. **19**(3), 293–325 (1948)
13. Jyothsna, V., Rama Prasad, V.V., Munivara Prasad, K.: A review of anomaly based intrusion detection systems. Inter. J. Comput. Appli. **28**(7), 26–35 (2011)
14. Kawawa-Beaudan, M., Sood, S., Palande, S., Mani, G., Balch, T., Veloso, M.: Behavioral sequence modeling with ensemble learning. In: NeurIPS 2024 Workshop on Behavioral Machine Learning (2024)
15. Kuncheva, L.I.: Combining pattern classifiers: methods and algorithms. John Wiley & Sons (2014)
16. Li, M., Zhang, X., Thrampoulidis, C., Chen, J., Oymak, S.: Autobalance: Optimized loss functions for imbalanced data. In: Advances in Neural Information Processing Systems, vol. 34, pp. 3292–3305 (2021)
17. Lin, T., Wang, M., Yang, M., Yang, X.: A hidden markov ensemble algorithm design for time series analysis. Sensors **22**(8) (2022). https://doi.org/10.3390/s22082950

18. Lin, T.Y., Goyal, P., Girshick, R., He, K., Dollár, P.: Focal loss for dense object detection. In: Proceedings of the IEEE International Conference on Computer Vision, pp. 2980–2988 (2017)
19. Mann, H.B., Whitney, D.R.: On a test of whether one of two random variables is stochastically larger than the other. Ann. Math. Stat. **18**(1), 50–60 (1947)
20. Ng, A.Y., Jordan, M.I.: On discriminative vs. generative classifiers: a comparison of logistic regression and naive Bayes. In: Advances in Neural Information Processing Systems, vol. 14 (2002)
21. Park, M., Warnow, T.: Hmmerge: an ensemble method for multiple sequence alignment. Bioinformatics Advances **3**(1) (2023). https://doi.org/10.1093/bioadv/vbad052
22. Peshave, A., Ganesan, A., Oates, T.: Predicting network threat events using hmm ensembles. In: Advanced Data Mining and Applications, pp. 229–240. Springer International Publishing, Cham (2022). https://doi.org/10.1007/978-3-030-95405-5_17
23. Rabiner, L., Juang, B.: An introduction to hidden markov models. IEEE ASSP Mag. **3**(1), 4–16 (1986). https://doi.org/10.1109/MASSP.1986.1165342
24. Rezek, I., Roberts, S.: Ensemble hidden markov models with extended observation densities for biosignal analysis. In: Probabilistic modeling in bioinformatics and medical informatics, pp. 419–450. Springer (2005). https://doi.org/10.1007/1-84628-119-9_14
25. Robinson, W.N., Aria, A.: Sequential fraud detection for prepaid cards using hidden markov model divergence. Expert Syst. Appl. **91**, 235–251 (2018). https://doi.org/10.1016/j.eswa.2017.08.043
26. Saito, T., Rehmsmeier, M.: The precision-recall plot is more informative than the roc plot when evaluating binary classifiers on imbalanced datasets. PLoS ONE **10**(3), e0118432 (2015)
27. Vaswani, A., et al.: Attention is all you need. In: Advances in Neural Information Processing Systems, vol. 30 (2017)
28. Wahle, F., Kowatsch, T., Fleisch, E., Rufer, M., Weidt, S.: Mobile sensing and support for people with depression: a pilot trial in the wild. JMIR Mhealth Uhealth **4**(3), e111 (2016). https://doi.org/10.2196/mhealth.5960
29. Wang, S., Liu, W., Wu, J., Cao, L., Meng, Q., Kennedy, P.J.: Training deep neural networks on imbalanced data sets. In: 2016 International Joint Conference on Neural Networks (IJCNN), pp. 4368–4374 (2016)
30. Wilcoxon, F.: Individual comparisons by ranking methods. Biometrics Bull. **1**(6), 80–83 (1945)
31. Xing, Z., Pei, J., Keogh, E.: A brief survey on sequence classification. ACM SIGKDD Explorations Newsl. **12**(1), 40–48 (2010)
32. Xu, X., et al.: Globem: cross-dataset generalization of longitudinal human behavior modeling. Proc. ACM Interact. Mob. Wearable Ubiquitous Technol. **6**(4) (2023). https://doi.org/10.1145/3569485
33. Xu, X., et al.: GLOBEM dataset: multi-year datasets for longitudinal human behavior modeling generalization. In: Advances in Neural Information Processing Systems, vol. 35, pp. 24655–24692 (2022)

Author Index

M. Ceci et al. (Eds.): ECML PKDD 2026, LNAI 16948, pp. 727–729, 2027.
https://doi.org/10.1007/978-3-032-37679-4

FSC
www.fsc.org
MIX
Papier | Fördert
gute Waldnutzung
FSC® C083411

Kolibri 360 GmbH
Ferdinand-Jühlke-Straße 7
99095 Erfurt, Deutschland
produktsicherheit@kolibri360.de